The University of Chicago School Mathematics Project

Algebra
Second Edition
Teacher's Edition
Part 1, Chapters 1-6

About the Cover The art on the cover was generated by a computer. The planes, grid, and intersecting lines suggest the integrated approach of *UCSMP Algebra*. This course uses geometry and statistics as a setting for work with linear expressions and sentences, and much work is done with graphing.

Authors

John W. McConnell   Susan Brown

Zalman Usiskin   Sharon L. Senk   Ted Widerski   Scott Anderson

Susan Eddins   Cathy Hynes Feldman   James Flanders   Margaret Hackworth

Daniel Hirschhorn   Lydia Polonsky   Leroy Sachs   Ernest Woodward

ScottForesman

A Division of HarperCollins*Publishers*

Editorial Offices: Glenview, Illinois
Regional Offices: Sunnyvale, California • Tucker, Georgia
Glenview, Illinois • Oakland, New Jersey • Dallas, Texas

ACKNOWLEDGMENTS

Authors

John W. McConnell
Instructional Supervisor of Mathematics,
Glenbrook South High School, Glenview, IL

Susan Brown
Mathematics Department Chair, York High
School, Elmhurst, IL

Zalman Usiskin
Professor of Education, The University of Chicago

Sharon L. Senk
Associate Professor of Mathematics, Michigan
State University, East Lansing, MI (Second
Edition only)

Ted Widerski
Mathematics Teacher, Waterloo High School,
Waterloo, WI (Second Edition only)

Scott Anderson
UCSMP (Second Edition only)

Susan Eddins
Mathematics Teacher, Illinois Mathematics and
Science Academy, Aurora, IL (First Edition only)

Cathy Hynes Feldman
Mathematics Teacher, The University of Chicago
Laboratory Schools (First Edition only)

James Flanders
UCSMP (First Edition only)

Margaret Hackworth
Mathematics Supervisor, Pinellas County Schools,
Largo, FL (First Edition only)

Daniel Hirschhorn
UCSMP (First Edition only)

Lydia Polonsky
UCSMP (First Edition only)

Leroy Sachs
Mathematics Teacher (retired), Clayton High School,
Clayton, MO (First Edition only)

Ernest Woodward
Professor of Mathematics, Austin Peay State
University, Clarksville, TN (First Edition only)

Design Development

Curtis Design

UCSMP Production and Evaluation

Series Editors: Zalman Usiskin, Sharon L. Senk
Directors of First Edition Studies: Sandra
  Mathison (director); Assistants to the Directors:
  Penelope Flores, Catherine Sarther
Directors of Second Edition Studies:
  Gurcharn Kaeley, Geraldine Macsai
Technical Coordinator: Susan Chang
Second Edition Teacher's Edition Editor:
  David Witonsky
Second Edition Consultants: Amy Hackenberg,
  Mary Lappan
First Edition Managing Editor: Natalie Jakucyn

We wish to acknowledge the generous support of the
Amoco Foundation and the Carnegie Corporation
of New York in helping to make it possible for the
First Edition of these materials to be developed,
tested, and distributed, and the continuing support
of the Amoco Foundation for the Second Edition.

We wish to thank the many editors, production
personnel, and design personnel at ScottForesman
for their magnificent assistance.

Multicultural Reviewers for ScottForesman

Winifred Deavens
St. Louis Public Schools, St. Louis, MO

Seree Weroha
Kansas City Public Schools, Kansas City, KS

Efraín Meléndez
Dakota School, Los Angeles, CA

Linda Skinner
Educator, Edmond, OK

Contents
of Teacher's Edition

The complete Table of Contents for the Student Edition begins on page *vi*.

Your UCSMP Professional Sourcebook is found at the back of this book, starting on page T20.

UCSMP Algebra

SECOND EDITION

"Students enrolled in UCSMP are better mathematical thinkers
and problem solvers. Our teachers of UCSMP see the direct correlation
of the thought processes (reading, computation, writing, justification)
necessary to meet the goals set by the NCTM Standards."

Sandra Caparell
Accokeek, Maryland

The University of Chicago School Mathematics Project

It works

Carefully developed by a prestigious team of authors in full accordance with the goals of the NCTM Standards, UCSMP has been refined through field testing and feedback from users. Millions of successful students and an ever-growing network of enthusiastic teachers have proven that UCSMP is a program that works.

Why it works as today's curriculum

UCSMP's flexible six-year curriculum emphasizes connections within mathematics and to other disciplines, develops concepts through real-world applications, implements the latest technology, and encourages independent learning.

How it works for today's students

Clear and inviting, *UCSMP Algebra* offers continual opportunities for problem solving, practice and review, and end-of-chapter mastery. Attention to individual needs and a broad approach to assessment help you offer success to all students.

The following section provides an overview of *UCSMP Algebra*. For more detailed information, see the Professional Sourcebook at the back of this book (page T20).

WHAT'S NEW in the Second Edition

In the Student Edition:
- Appealing, student-friendly layout
- Reading Organizers to outline each lesson
- In-class and In-lesson Activities
- Student Projects in every chapter
- Spreadsheet use
- Graphics calculator instruction

In the Teacher's Edition:
- Warm-up ideas for introducing each lesson
- Enhanced integration and connections
- Optional activities to reinforce and extend topics
- Frequent suggestions for adapting to individual needs
- Ideas for Setting Up the Next Lesson

PLUS—

In the support package:
- Two forms of Lesson Masters for extra practice
- An enhanced Assessment Sourcebook
- Study Skills Handbook
- Videodisc with multimedia CD-ROM

UCSMP — It works

Program development

The UCSMP Secondary Component Materials have been developed with extensive input from classroom teachers and a special advisory board. The project has been funded by several major corporations which recognize the need for exciting new materials for mathematics education.

An innovative approach

UCSMP is the first full mathematics curriculum to implement the NCTM Standards by teaching concepts *through* their applications, emphasizing the reading and writing of mathematics, providing a wide variety of meaningful problem-solving opportunities, and incorporating the latest technology.

"I have found the comments to be positive from both students and parents. Students feel UCSMP makes math come alive. Parents comment they wish they had a text like this when they learned math."

Faye Ruopp
Sudbury, Massachusetts

Proven success

The UCSMP materials have been carefully refined through years of field testing and feedback from users of the First Edition. Teachers throughout the country have discovered that UCSMP is the way to offer success to the greatest number of students.

The **best** book to help students learn algebra has gotten even better!

Results of the Second Edition Evaluation

Group		Mean Scores of Students in Matched Pairs				
	N	Pretest IAAT	Posttest HSST	Posttest Algebra	Posttest PS&U, A	Posttest PS&U, B
UCSMP 2nd Edition	234	49	18.29	22.77	4.96	7.63
UCSMP 1st Edition	245	48	17.83	21.79	5.27	7.23
UCSMP 2nd Edition	75	46	18.03	**18.72**	**5.53**	**6.57**
Other texts (non-UCSMP)	62	45	16.94	**14.05**	**3.08**	**3.15**

For more details, see the Professional Sourcebook at the back of Part 1 of the Teacher's Edition.

Mean scores in boldface for "UCSMP 2nd Edition" are significantly higher than the corresponding scores for non-UCSMP students using "other texts."

These results confirm conclusions from the First Edition studies, namely that *UCSMP Algebra* students maintain competence on traditional standardized tests while outperforming non-UCSMP students in tests of problem solving and understanding, and tests of the wide range of content found in the UCSMP texts. They also show that students using the Second Edition perform as well as those using the First Edition in all areas.

"This year's Michigan Educational Assessment Program test scores changed drastically from previous years. With UCSMP, more students can succeed."

Susan Kearney
Allendale, Michigan

Why it works as today's curriculum

Grades	Top 10% of 5th graders	50th-90th percentile of 6th graders	30th-70th percentile of 7th graders	15th-50th percentile of 8th graders
6	Transition Mathematics			
7	Algebra	Transition Mathematics		
8	Geometry	Algebra	Transition Mathematics	
9	Advanced Algebra	Geometry	Algebra	Transition Mathematics
10	Functions, Statistics, and Trigonometry	Advanced Algebra	Geometry	Algebra
11	Precalculus and Discrete Mathematics	Functions, Statistics, and Trigonometry	Advanced Algebra	Geometry
12	Calculus (Not part of UCSMP)	Precalculus and Discrete Mathematics	Functions, Statistics, and Trigonometry	Advanced Algebra

A flexible curriculum

UCSMP provides a complete program for students in middle school and high school. It spreads the usual secondary mathematics content over six years, allowing students to both broaden and deepen their understanding of each topic.

"Students realize the importance of mathematics. It is a result of all the real-world application problems in UCSMP."

Craig Fliestra
Hudsonville, Michigan

Real-world applications

By constantly answering the question, "When are we ever going to have to use this?," *UCSMP Algebra* develops lessons more meaningfully and motivates students to learn. *See pages 91, 141, 267, and 573 for further examples.*

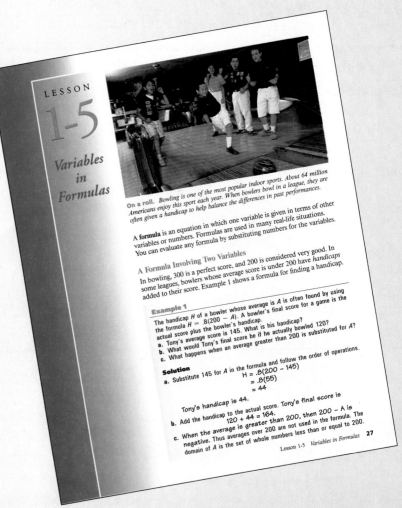

LESSON

1-5

Variables in Formulas

On a roll. Bowling is one of the most popular indoor sports. About 64 million Americans enjoy this sport each year. When bowlers bowl in a league, they are often given a handicap to help balance the differences in past performances.

A **formula** is an equation in which one variable is given in terms of other variables or numbers. Formulas are used in many real-life situations. You can evaluate any formula by substituting numbers for the variables.

A Formula Involving Two Variables

In bowling, 300 is a perfect score, and 200 is considered very good. In some leagues, bowlers whose average score is under 200 have *handicaps* added to their score. Example 1 shows a formula for finding a handicap.

Example 1

The handicap H of a bowler whose average is A is often found by using the formula $H = .8(200 - A)$. A bowler's final score for a game is the actual score plus the bowler's handicap.
a. Tony's average score is 145. What is his handicap?
b. What would Tony's final score be if he actually bowled 120?
c. What happens when an average greater than 200 is substituted for A?

Solution
a. Substitute 145 for A in the formula and follow the order of operations.
$$H = .8(200 - 145)$$
$$= .8(55)$$
$$= 44$$
Tony's handicap is 44.
b. Add the handicap to the actual score. Tony's final score is
$$120 + 44 = 164.$$
c. When the average is greater than 200, then $200 - A$ is negative. Thus averages over 200 are not used in the formula. The domain of A is the set of whole numbers less than or equal to 200.

Lesson 1-5 *Variables in Formulas* **27**

Integration and connections

UCSMP Algebra thoroughly integrates and makes connections to other areas of mathematics, to other disciplines, and to the real world. Students see how each mathematical idea fits into a larger context.
See pages 58, 155–156, 372, and 387 for further examples.

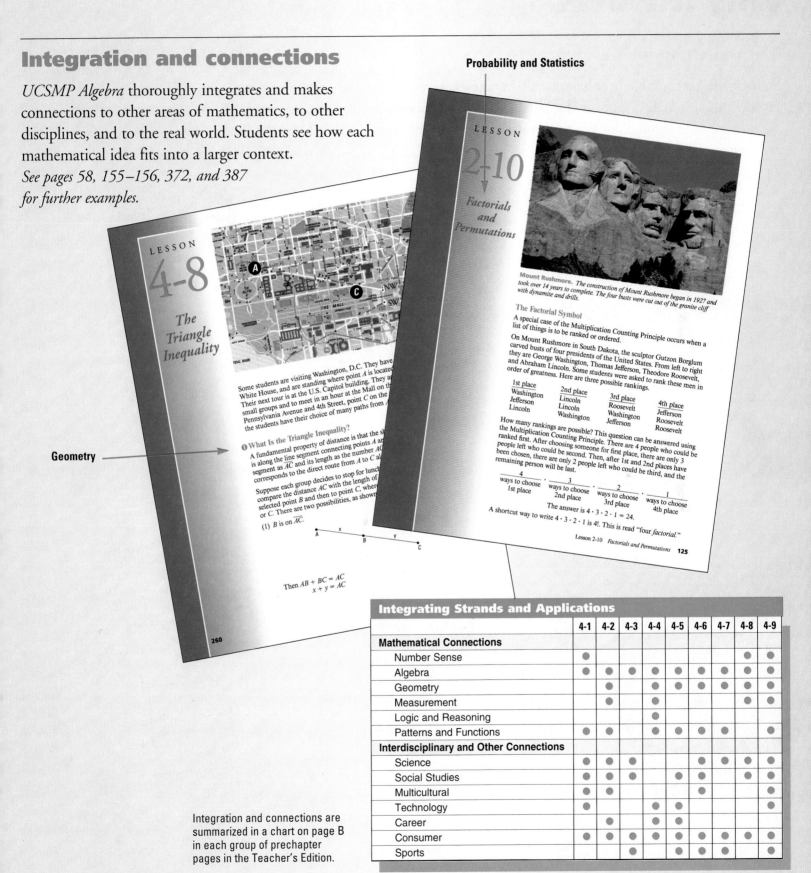

Geometry

Probability and Statistics

LESSON 4-8

The Triangle Inequality

Some students are visiting Washington, D.C. They have ... White House, and are standing where point A is located ... Their next tour is at the U.S. Capitol building. They a ... small groups and to meet in an hour at the Mall on th ... Pennsylvania Avenue and 4th Street, point C on the ... the students have their choice of many paths from A ...

❶ **What Is the Triangle Inequality?**
A fundamental property of distance is that the sh ... is along the line segment connecting points A an ... segment as $\overline{AC}$ and its length as the number AC ... corresponds to the direct route from A to C al ...

Suppose each group decides to stop for lunch ... compare the distance AC with the length of ... selected point B and then to point C, wher ... or C. There are two possibilities, as shown ...

(1) B is on $\overline{AC}$.

Then $AB + BC = AC$
$x + y = AC$

260

LESSON 2-10

Factorials and Permutations

Mount Rushmore. *The construction of Mount Rushmore began in 1927 and took over 14 years to complete. The four busts were cut out of the granite cliff with dynamite and drills.*

The Factorial Symbol
A special case of the Multiplication Counting Principle occurs when a list of things is to be ranked or ordered.

On Mount Rushmore in South Dakota, the sculptor Gutzon Borglum carved busts of four presidents of the United States. From left to right they are George Washington, Thomas Jefferson, Theodore Roosevelt, and Abraham Lincoln. Some students were asked to rank these men in order of greatness. Here are three possible rankings.

1st place	2nd place	3rd place	4th place
Washington	Lincoln	Roosevelt	Jefferson
Jefferson	Lincoln	Washington	Roosevelt
Lincoln	Washington	Jefferson	Roosevelt

How many rankings are possible? This question can be answered using the Multiplication Counting Principle. There are 4 people who could be ranked first. After choosing someone for first place, there are only 3 people left who could be second. Then, after 1st and 2nd places have been chosen, there are only 2 people left who could be third, and the remaining person will be last.

4	·	3	·	2	·	1
ways to choose 1st place		ways to choose 2nd place		ways to choose 3rd place		ways to choose 4th place

The answer is $4 \cdot 3 \cdot 2 \cdot 1 = 24$.

A shortcut way to write $4 \cdot 3 \cdot 2 \cdot 1$ is 4!. This is read "four *factorial.*"

Lesson 2-10 *Factorials and Permutations* **125**

Integrating Strands and Applications

	4-1	4-2	4-3	4-4	4-5	4-6	4-7	4-8	4-9
Mathematical Connections									
Number Sense	●							●	●
Algebra	●	●	●	●	●	●	●	●	●
Geometry			●	●		●	●	●	●
Measurement			●		●			●	●
Logic and Reasoning					●				
Patterns and Functions	●	●		●	●	●	●		●
Interdisciplinary and Other Connections									
Science		●	●	●			●	●	●
Social Studies		●	●	●		●	●		●
Multicultural		●	●				●		●
Technology		●			●	●			●
Career			●	●	●				
Consumer		●	●	●		●	●	●	●
Sports			●			●	●	●	●

Integration and connections are summarized in a chart on page B in each group of prechapter pages in the Teacher's Edition.

Sample from Chapter 4

Why it works

Technology

State-of-the-art technology enhances mathematical understanding and strengthens problem-solving skills. Applications using calculators, graphics calculators, and computers are incorporated throughout the text. A new videodisc with multimedia CD-ROM makes learning more interactive and engaging. *See pages 270, 292–293, 312–313, and 498–499 for further examples.*

LESSON 4-4
Spreadsheets

Then and now. *This house was custom-built in Chic $31,500. This is equivalent to a cost of over $300,000 t*

Construction Statement

	Tota Cont
	340.00	3
	15.30	1
Excavating		
Work Order #1	4385.00	4
Foundation	10.00	
Brickwork		
Work Order #1		
Ornamental Iron		
Structural Iron	6560.00	
Metal Windows & Damper	375.00	
Carpenter		
Work Order #1	195.00	
Insulation	25.00	
Roofing	1220.00	
Work Order #1	245.00	
Heating	(53.0	
Work Order #1		
Credit Order #1		

❶ What Is a Spreadsheet?

Shown above is a copy of part of a home to the family that was havi *spreadsheet*. In many situations, were used for records like these, storage and then spread out for got their name.

Notice that some numbers ar numbers in the spreadsheet. used to be quite difficult. If would need to be changed a were using computers for t

232

LESSON 5-5
Using an Automatic Grapher

Graph it your way. *This student is displaying the same graph on both the computer screen and the graphics calculator. Both tools allow you to display multiple graphs at one time and find points of intersection using a zoom feature.*

What Is an Automatic Grapher?

Graphs of equations are so helpful in solving problems that there are now several makes of calculators that will automatically display part of a graph. Also, there are programs for every personal computer that will display graphs. Because computer screens are larger than calculator screens, they can show a greater part of a graph, but graphing calculators are less expensive and easier to carry around.

Graphing calculators and computer graphing programs work in much the same way. As such we call them **automatic graphers** and do not distinguish between them. Of course, no grapher is completely automatic. For each you must learn particular keys to press. Here we discuss some of the general features of automatic graphers.

Instructions

The part of the coordinate grid that is shown is called a **window**. The screen below displays a window in which

$$-2 \leq x \leq 12$$
$$\text{and } -3 \leq y \leq 7.$$

310

"Students can now do problems that typical math classes would not be able to do before."

Ronald Conty
Claridge, Pennsylvania

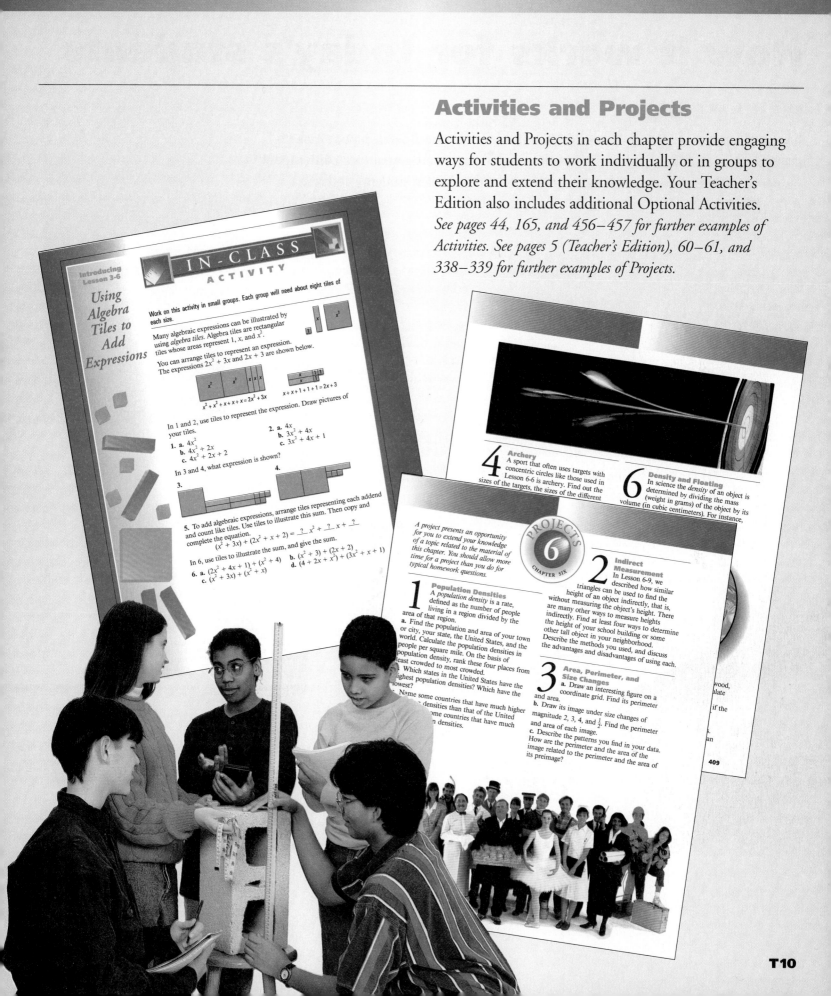

Activities and Projects

Activities and Projects in each chapter provide engaging ways for students to work individually or in groups to explore and extend their knowledge. Your Teacher's Edition also includes additional Optional Activities. *See pages 44, 165, and 456–457 for further examples of Activities. See pages 5 (Teacher's Edition), 60–61, and 338–339 for further examples of Projects.*

IN-CLASS ACTIVITY

Introducing Lesson 3-6

Using Algebra Tiles to Add Expressions

Work on this activity in small groups. Each group will need about eight tiles of each size.

Many algebraic expressions can be illustrated by using *algebra tiles*. Algebra tiles are rectangular tiles whose areas represent 1, x, and x^2.

You can arrange tiles to represent an expression. The expressions $2x^2 + 3x$ and $2x + 3$ are shown below.

$$x^2 + x^2 + x + x + x = 2x^2 + 3x$$

$$x + x + 1 + 1 + 1 = 2x + 3$$

In 1 and 2, use tiles to represent the expression. Draw pictures of your tiles.

1. a. $4x^2$
   b. $4x^2 + 2x$
   c. $4x^2 + 2x + 2$

2. a. $4x$
   b. $3x^2 + 4x$
   c. $3x^2 + 4x + 1$

In 3 and 4, what expression is shown?

3.

4.

5. To add algebraic expressions, arrange tiles representing each addend and count like tiles. Use tiles to illustrate this sum. Then copy and complete the equation.
$$(x^2 + 3x) + (2x^2 + x + 2) = \underline{?}\ x^2 + \underline{?}\ x + \underline{?}$$

In 6, use tiles to illustrate the sum, and give the sum.

6. a. $(2x^2 + 4x + 1) + (x^2 + 4)$
   b. $(x^2 + 3) + (2x + 2)$
   c. $(x^2 + 3x) + (x^2 + x)$
   d. $(4 + 2x + x^2) + (3x^2 + x + 1)$

---

4 Archery
A sport that often uses targets with concentric circles like those used in Lesson 6-6 is archery. Find out the sizes of the targets, the sizes of the different

6 Density and Floating
In science the *density* of an object is determined by dividing the mass (weight in grams) of the object by its volume (in cubic centimeters). For instance,

A project presents an opportunity for you to extend your knowledge of a topic related to the material of this chapter. You should allow more time for a project than you do for typical homework questions.

PROJECTS 6 CHAPTER SIX

1 Population Densities
A *population density* is a rate, defined as the number of people living in a region divided by the area of that region.
a. Find the population and area of your town or city, your state, the United States, and the world. Calculate the population densities in people per square mile. On the basis of population density, rank these four places from least crowded to most crowded.
b. Which states in the United States have the highest population densities? Which have the lowest?
c. Name some countries that have much higher densities than that of the United some countries that have much n densities.

2 Indirect Measurement
In Lesson 6-9, we described how similar triangles can be used to find the height of an object indirectly, that is, without measuring the object's height. There are many other ways to measure heights indirectly. Find at least four ways to determine the height of your school building or some other tall object in your neighborhood. Describe the methods you used, and discuss the advantages and disadvantages of using each.

3 Area, Perimeter, and Size Changes
a. Draw an interesting figure on a coordinate grid. Find its perimeter and area.
b. Draw its image under size changes of magnitude 2, 3, 4, and $\frac{1}{2}$. Find the perimeter and area of each image.
c. Describe the patterns you find in your data. How are the perimeter and the area of the image related to the perimeter and the area of its preimage?

409

How it works for today's students

Inviting design

The text's appealing and functional format and unique lesson development make concepts easy to follow and comprehend. Colorful pages and a wealth of contemporary visuals — including greatly enhanced graphs — help stimulate students' interest throughout the course.

"We are very happy with UCSMP. I love teaching from UCSMP Algebra."

Betty Kantrowitz
Newton, Massachusetts

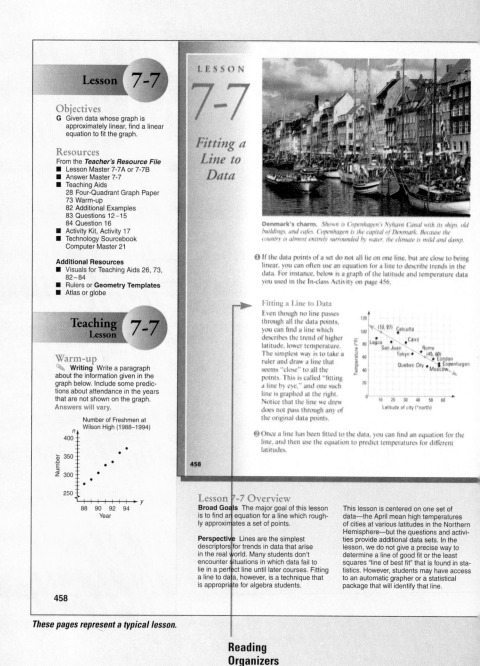

Lesson 7-7

Objectives
G Given data whose graph is approximately linear, find a linear equation to fit the graph.

Resources
From the *Teacher's Resource File*
■ Lesson Master 7-7A or 7-7B
■ Answer Master 7-7
■ Teaching Aids
   28 Four-Quadrant Graph Paper
   73 Warm-up
   82 Additional Examples
   83 Questions 12–15
   84 Question 16
■ Activity Kit, Activity 17
■ Technology Sourcebook
   Computer Master 21

Additional Resources
■ Visuals for Teaching Aids 26, 73, 82–84
■ Rulers or **Geometry Templates**
■ Atlas or globe

Teaching Lesson 7-7

Warm-up
✎ **Writing** Write a paragraph about the information given in the graph below. Include some predictions about attendance in the years that are not shown on the graph. Answers will vary.

Number of Freshmen at
Wilson High (1988–1994)

Number / Year

458

LESSON 7-7

Fitting a Line to Data

Denmark's charm. *Shown is Copenhagen's Nyhavn Canal with its ships, old buildings, and cafes. Copenhagen is the capital of Denmark. Because the country is almost entirely surrounded by water, the climate is mild and damp.*

❶ If the data points of a set do not all lie on one line, but are close to being linear, you can often use an equation for a line to describe trends in the data. For instance, below is a graph of the latitude and temperature data you used in the In-class Activity on page 456.

Fitting a Line to Data
Even though no line passes through all the data points, you can find a line which describes the trend of higher latitude, lower temperature. The simplest way is to take a ruler and draw a line that seems "close" to all the points. This is called "fitting a line by eye," and one such line is graphed at the right. Notice that the line we drew does not pass through any of the original data points.

❷ Once a line has been fitted to the data, you can find an equation for the line, and then use the equation to predict temperatures for different latitudes.

458

Lesson 7-7 Overview

Broad Goals The major goal of this lesson is to find an equation for a line which roughly approximates a set of points.

Perspective Lines are the simplest descriptors for trends in data that arise in the real world. Many students don't encounter situations in which data fail to lie in a perfect line until later courses. Fitting a line to data, however, is a technique that is appropriate for algebra students.

This lesson is centered on one set of data—the April mean high temperatures of cities at various latitudes in the Northern Hemisphere—but the questions and activities provide additional data sets. In the lesson, we do not give a precise way to determine a line of good fit or the least squares "line of best fit" that is found in statistics. However, students may have access to an automatic grapher or a statistical package that will identify that line.

These pages represent a typical lesson.

Reading Organizers

Communication

Instead of spending valuable time explaining the textbook, you can devote more time each day to exploring additional examples and applications. Students learn to read and understand mathematics on their own, and to express this understanding both orally and in writing. Reading Organizers in each lesson help direct students' attention to key ideas in the reading.

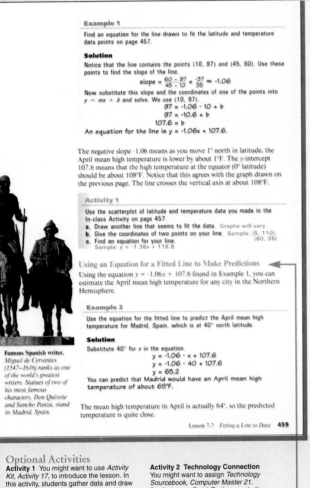

Example 1

Find an equation for the line drawn to fit the latitude and temperature data points on page 457.

Solution

Notice that the line contains the points (10, 97) and (45, 60). Use these points to find the slope of the line.

$$\text{slope} = \frac{60 - 97}{45 - 10} = \frac{-37}{35} \approx -1.06$$

Now substitute this slope and the coordinates of one of the points into $y = mx + b$ and solve. We use (10, 97).

$$97 = -1.06 \cdot 10 + b$$
$$97 = -10.6 + b$$
$$107.6 = b$$

An equation for the line is $y = -1.06x + 107.6$.

The negative slope -1.06 means as you move 1° north in latitude, the April mean high temperature is lower by about 1°F. The y-intercept 107.6 means that the high temperature at the equator (0° latitude) should be about 108°F. Notice that this agrees with the graph drawn on the previous page. The line crosses the vertical axis at about 108°F.

Activity 1

Use the scatterplot of latitude and temperature data you made in the In-class Activity on page 457.
a. Draw another line that seems to fit the data. Graphs will vary.
b. Give the coordinates of two points on your line. Sample: (5, 110); (60, 35)
c. Find an equation for your line. Sample: $y = -1.36x + 116.8$

Using an Equation for a Fitted Line to Make Predictions

Using the equation $y = -1.06x + 107.6$ found in Example 1, you can estimate the April mean high temperature for any city in the Northern Hemisphere.

Example 2

Use the equation for the fitted line to predict the April mean high temperature for Madrid, Spain, which is at 40° north latitude.

Solution

Substitute 40° for x in the equation.
$$y = -1.06 \cdot x + 107.6$$
$$y = -1.06 \cdot 40 + 107.6$$
$$y = 65.2$$

You can predict that Madrid would have an April mean high temperature of about 65°F.

The mean high temperature in April is actually 64°, so the predicted temperature is quite close.

Lesson 7-7 *Fitting a Line to Data* **459**

Famous Spanish writer.
Miguel de Cervantes (1547–1616) ranks as one of the world's greatest writers. Statues of two of his most famous characters, Don Quixote and Sancho Panza, stand in Madrid, Spain.

Notes on Reading

① You might want to have a globe or world map for students to examine. Have them locate the cities that are mentioned in the lesson.

Point out that there are no new mathematical techniques in this lesson—merely the application of the idea from the previous lesson to situations in which there are more than two points that do not lie on the same line.

② Students will naturally wonder how to determine if a line is a line of good fit. Because we are using the line to predict values, the critical idea in how well the line fits the point is the vertical distance from the point to the line. A line of good fit should have about as many points above it as below it, and the distances from the points to the line should balance. (In statistics, the line for which the sum of the squares of the vertical distances from the points to the line is minimized is defined as having the "best fit.")

Multicultural Connection All or part of Cervante's *Don Quixote* has been translated into more than 60 languages. Due to the widespread representation of Don Quixote and Sancho Panza in art, drama, and film, Cervante's figures are probably familiar to more people than any other fictitious characters in world literature.

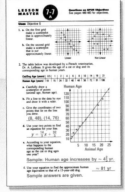

459

Reading Organizers

Optional Activities

Activity 1 You might want to use *Activity Kit, Activity 17,* to introduce the lesson. In this activity, students gather data and draw graphs. Their graphs should show points clustering in such a way that a line can be drawn to "fit" the data.

Activity 2 Technology Connection You might want to assign *Technology Sourcebook, Computer Master 21.* Students use *GraphExplorer* or similar software to plot data. Students then graph lines through pairs of data points and choose the line they think best fits the data.

> *"Students are happy with the course and like the style of learning. Teachers of UCSMP, as facilitators, can do more directing and probing within mathematics."*

Ted ter Haar
Jenison, Michigan

How it works

Problem solving

Students learn to use mathematics effectively through problem-solving experiences that include use of higher-order thinking skills in daily assignments, a wide variety of problem types in the questions, and open-ended problems. *See pages 47, 188, 268, and 303 for further examples.*

Additional Examples
These examples are also given on **Teaching Aid 82.**
1. The table shows the amount of gold that was mined in the world for the years 1984 to 1992.

Gold Production: 1984–1992 (millions of troy ounces)	
1984: 46.9	1989: 65.3
1985: 49.3	1990: 68.6
1986: 51.5	1991: 69.1
1987: 51.5	1992: 72.2
1988: 60.3	

a. Draw a scatterplot. Sample graph is shown below.
b. Use a ruler to fit a line to the data. One line is shown on the graph.
c. Write an equation for the line. An equation for the line through (88, 60) and (91, 69) is $y = 3x - 204$.

Gold Production

Troy ounces (millions) vs Year (84 86 88 90 92)

Located in the National Palace of Mexico City are the Diego Rivera murals. This one shows Hidalgo, Morelos, and Juárez—men who made important political contributions.

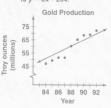

Shown is an outdoor marketplace in Calcutta, India. The city lies along the east bank of the Hooghly river and serves as India's chief port for trade with Southeast Asia.

460

Activity 2

Use the equation you found in Activity 1 to predict the mean high temperature in April for Madrid. By how much does your prediction differ from the actual value? Sample: $y = -1.36(40) + 116.8 = 62.4$. The prediction was off by 1.6°F.

Sometimes the fitted line does not predict temperature accurately. For instance, for a city at a latitude of 19° north, the line predicts a temperature of 87°. Both Bombay, India, and Mexico City are at this latitude. For Bombay the predicted temperature is accurate. But in Mexico City, the actual April mean temperature is 78°. The prediction is too high because Mexico City is at an altitude of about one mile, and temperatures at high altitudes are lower than those at sea level.

Being able to fit a line to data allows you to obtain a general formula from a few cases. This is such an important skill that some computer software and graphing calculators will find the line that *best fits* data. If you have access to such technology, you might want to enter these latitude and temperature data.

QUESTIONS

Covering the Reading

1. What does the latitude of a place on Earth signify? the distance a place is from the equator
2. What is the latitude of the equator? 0°
3. Which city is farther north, Calcutta or Cairo? Cairo
4. What does it mean to "fit a line by eye" to a scatterplot? Draw a line that seems closest to all of the points in the graph.
5. Once a line is fitted, what is a good first step toward getting an equation for the line? Estimate the coordinates of two points on the line.
6. a. Use the graph of the fitted line in this lesson to predict the mean high temperature in April in a city at 25° north latitude. about 81°F
   b. Use the equation in Example 1 to predict this temperature. 81.1°F
   c. Use the equation you found in Activity 1 to predict this temperature.
   d. What is true about your answers to parts a, b, and c? c) Answers will vary. Sample: 82.8°F; d) They are all close to 82°F
7. Refer to Activity 2. By how much does your prediction differ from the actual mean high temperature in Madrid? Answers may vary. Sample: My prediction differed from the actual mean temperature by 1.6°F.
8. a. Acapulco, Mexico, is at 17° north latitude. Use the equation in Example 1 to estimate its average April high temperature. ≈ 90°F
   b. The actual mean high temperature in April for Acapulco is 87°F. Give a reason why the answer in part a is closer to the actual value for Acapulco than the prediction was for Mexico City. Sample: Acapulco is at sea level.
9. a. What is the latitude of the North Pole? 90° North
   b. What is the predicted mean high temperature in April at the North Pole? ≈ 12.2°F

460

Applying the Mathematics

16a, b)
Temperature F°

Degrees north latitude
c) Sample: (6, 74); (30, 47)
d) $y = -1.125x + 80.75$
e) be about 1° colder.

10. If a city in the Northern Hemisphere has a mean high temperature in April of about 80°, at what latitude would you expect it to be? Explain how you got your answer. 26° north; by substituting 80 in the equation in Example 1, you get x = 26.
11. Below are the latitudes and April mean high temperatures for two cities in the Southern Hemisphere.
    Rio de Janeiro, Brazil (23° south, 69°F)
    Cape Town, South Africa (34° south, 58°F)
    Could you predict temperatures for cities south of the equator by using negative values of x in the equation in Example 1? No Explain your reasoning. Negative values of x would result in values of y that are always greater than 107.6°F.

In 12–15, tell whether fitting a line to the data points would be appropriate.

12. No   13. Yes   14. Yes   15. No

16. Use the following data.

City	North Latitude	January Mean Low Temperature (°F)
Lagos, Nigeria	6	74
San Juan, Puerto Rico	18	67
Calcutta, India	23	55
Cairo, Egypt	30	47
Tokyo, Japan	35	29
Rome, Italy	42	39
Quebec City, Canada	47	2
London, England	52	35
Copenhagen, Denmark	56	29
Moscow, Russia	56	9

See left for a, b, c, d.
a. Carefully draw a scatterplot showing a point for each city.
b. Fit a line to the data by eye and draw the line with a ruler.
c. Estimate the coordinates of two points on the line you drew.
d. Find an equation for the line through the points in part c.
e. Complete the following sentence: "As you go one degree north, the January mean low temperature tends to __?__."
f. What does the equation predict for a January mean low temperature at the equator? about 81°F; g) about -21°F
g. Predict the January mean low temperature for the North Pole.
h. Use your equation to predict the January mean low temperature for Acapulco, which is at 17° north latitude. (Note: the actual mean low is 70°F.) about 62°F

Lesson 7-7 *Fitting a Line to Data*

Adapting to Individual Needs
Challenge Geography Connection
Have students look up the meanings of the *prime meridian of longitude* and the *International Date Line* and explain how they are related to international time zones. [Students' answers might include: The prime meridian is an imaginary north-south line that passes through both the North and South poles and Greenwich, England. Longitude is measured 180° both east and west of the prime meridian. In 1884, worldwide time zones were established with the Greenwich meridian as the starting point. The zones are theoretically 15° longitude wide. The Greenwich meridian is in the middle of the first zone. Twelve zones are to the east of Greenwich, and twelve zones are to the west. The 12th zones east and west are each a half zone wide and are separated by the International Date Line. The time east of the Date Line is one day earlier than the time to the west of the line.]

Adapting to Individual Needs
Extra Help
Some students are frustrated by problems that do not have one correct answer. When trying to draw a line to fit data, they might attempt to connect all of the data points, forgetting that they have to find a straight line. Emphasize that the goal is to find a line that describes *trends* in the data and that the line may or may not pass through any of the actual data points. Help students to think of examples of data where trends might be important. One example would be the growth rates in children; another would be the winning times in certain Olympic events over a period of many years. Point out that some data will not suggest a linear trend, such as annual snowfall in a particular city.

460

Practice and review

Continual opportunities for practice and review throughout *UCSMP Algebra* help students strengthen conceptual understanding and ensure optimum performance.
See pages 173, 251–252, 343–346, and 347 for further examples.

See pages 172, 391, and 618 for further examples.

Student diversity

UCSMP materials have been carefully designed to accommodate the full range of today's diverse student population. Your Teacher's Edition is full of ideas for addressing the needs of each student.
See pages 172, 391, and 618 for further examples.

How it works

Progress checks for students

A Progress Self-Test at the end of each chapter helps students determine how well they've assimilated chapter concepts. Various types of problems, keyed to chapter objectives, provide ideal preparation for chapter tests and teach study skills.

PROGRESS SELF-TEST

Take this test as you would take a test in class. You will need graph paper and a calculator. Then check your work with the solutions in the Selected Answers section in the back of the book.

1. **a.** Evaluate $\frac{4^{12}}{4^6}$, and explain how you got your answer.

   b. Check your answer using another method.

2. Evaluate $\frac{5 \cdot 10^{20}}{5 \cdot 10^{16}}$.

3. Write $(8)^{-5}$ as a fraction without negative exponents.

In 4–7, simplify.

4. $b^7 \cdot b^{11}$

5. $(5y^4)^3$

6. $\frac{3z^6}{12z^4}$

7. $(y^{10})^4$

8. Rewrite $\left(\frac{3}{x}\right)^2 \cdot \left(\frac{x}{3}\right)^4$ as a single fraction.

9. Simplify and rewrite $\frac{48a^3b^7}{12a^4b}$ without fractions.

10. If $q = 11$, what is the value of $6q^0$?

11. Find a counterexample to the pattern $3x^2 = (3x)^2$.

12. Name the general property that justifies $2^{10} \cdot 2^3 = 2^{13}$.

13. Felipe invests $6500 in an account with an annual yield of 5%. Without any withdrawals or additional deposits, how much will be in the account after 5 years?

14. Darlene invests $1900 for three years at an annual yield of 5.8%. At the end of the three years, how much interest will she earn? Show your work.

In 15 and 16, use this information. The population of a city has been growing exponentially at 3% a year. The city currently has a population of 135,000. Assume this growth rate continues.

15. What will the population be five years from now?

16. What was the population 2 years ago?

17. For each of the following equations, tell whether or not it can describe exponential growth or decay.

   a. $y = \left(\frac{1}{3}\right)^x$

   b. $y = 27 + 14x$

   c. $y = \frac{1}{3}x$

   d. $y = 27 \cdot 14^x$

18. Graph $y = 3^x$ for $x = -2, -1, 0,$ [...]

19. A duplicating machine enlarges [...] 30%. If that enlarger is used 3 ti[...] many times as large as the origi[...] will the final picture be?

20. Recall that the volume V of a sp[...] radius r is $V = \frac{4}{3}\pi r^3$. The radiu[...] sun (roughly a sphere of gas) is [...] $6.96 \cdot 10^6$ km. Estimate the vol[...] of the sun.

The chart below keys the **Progress Self-Test** questions to the objectives in the **Chapter Review** on pages 543–545. This will enable you to locate those **Chapter Review** questions that correspond to questions missed on the **Progress Self-Test**. The lesson where the material is covered is also indicated on the chart.

Question	1	2	3	4	5	6	7	8	9	10
Objective	A	A	A	B	C	B	B	C	B	A
Lesson	8-7	8-7	8-6	8-5	8-8	8-7	8-5	8-8	8-7	8-2
Question	11	12	13	14	15	16	17	18	19	20
Objective	D	E	F	F	G	G	I	I	H	H
Lesson	8-9	8-5	8-1	8-1	8-2	8-6	8-4	8-6	8-3	8-8

A chart for each Progress-Self Test (at the back of the Student Edition) keys test questions to chapter objectives.

542

"I believe that my students are questioning the legitimacy of their answers more now than before."

Laurie Paladichuk
Miles City, Montana

End-of-chapter mastery

Comprehensive chapter reviews based on SPUR objectives — Skills, Properties, Uses, and Representations — ensure a multidimensional understanding of key concepts.

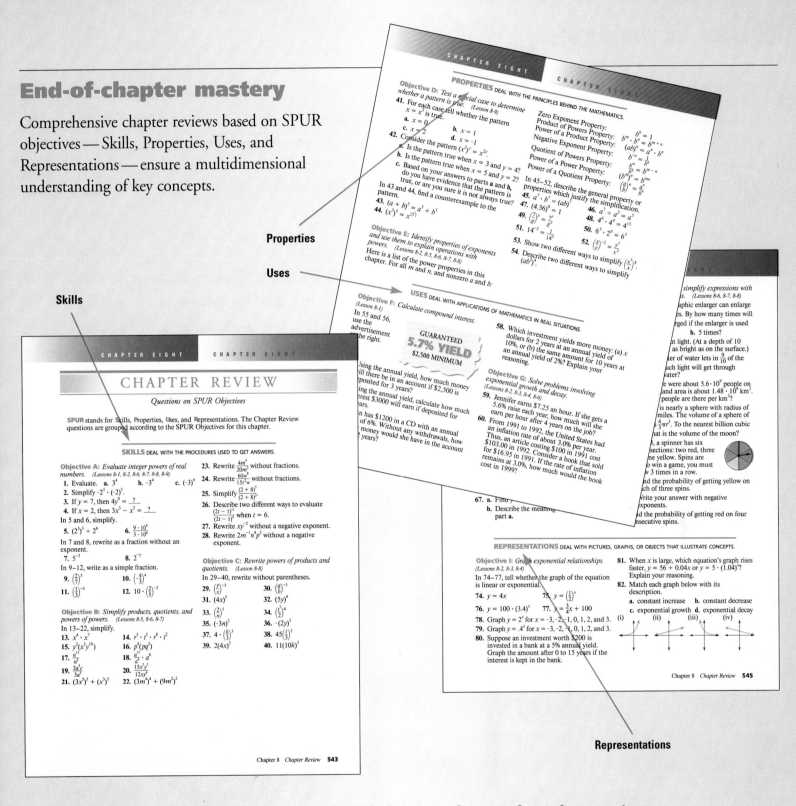

Properties

Uses

Skills

Representations

How it works

Multiple forms of assessment

Your *Assessment Sourcebook* includes quizzes, test forms A and B, performance tests C and D, and a cumulative test for each chapter, and comprehensive tests after Chapters 3, 6, 9, and 13. Plus, Quiz and Test Writer software enables you to adapt existing tests or create your own in various forms. Your *Assessment Sourcebook* also includes abundant resources for portfolio, problem-solving, cooperative-group, and self assessment.

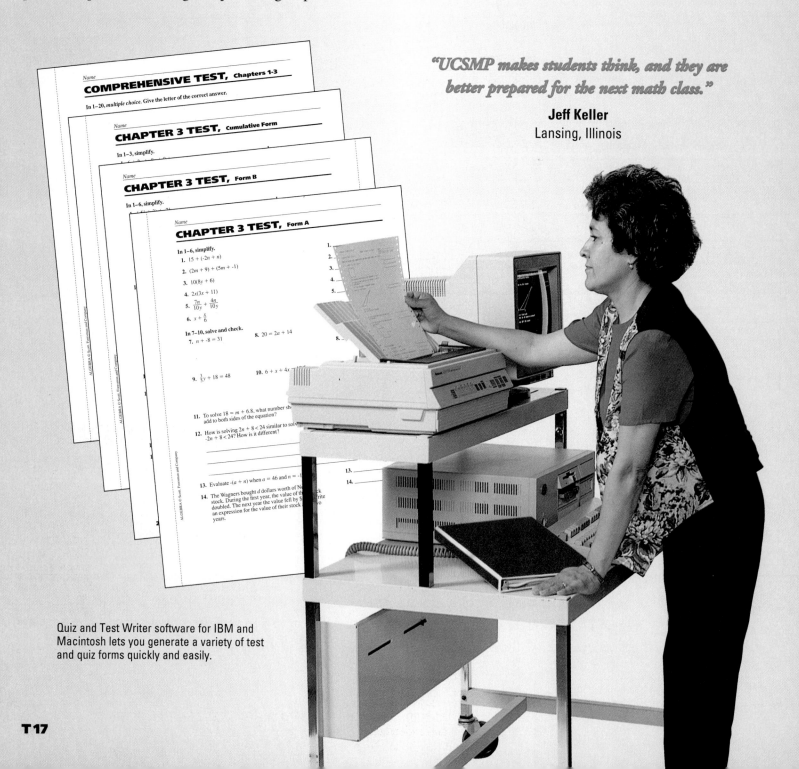

"UCSMP makes students think, and they are better prepared for the next math class."

Jeff Keller
Lansing, Illinois

Quiz and Test Writer software for IBM and Macintosh lets you generate a variety of test and quiz forms quickly and easily.

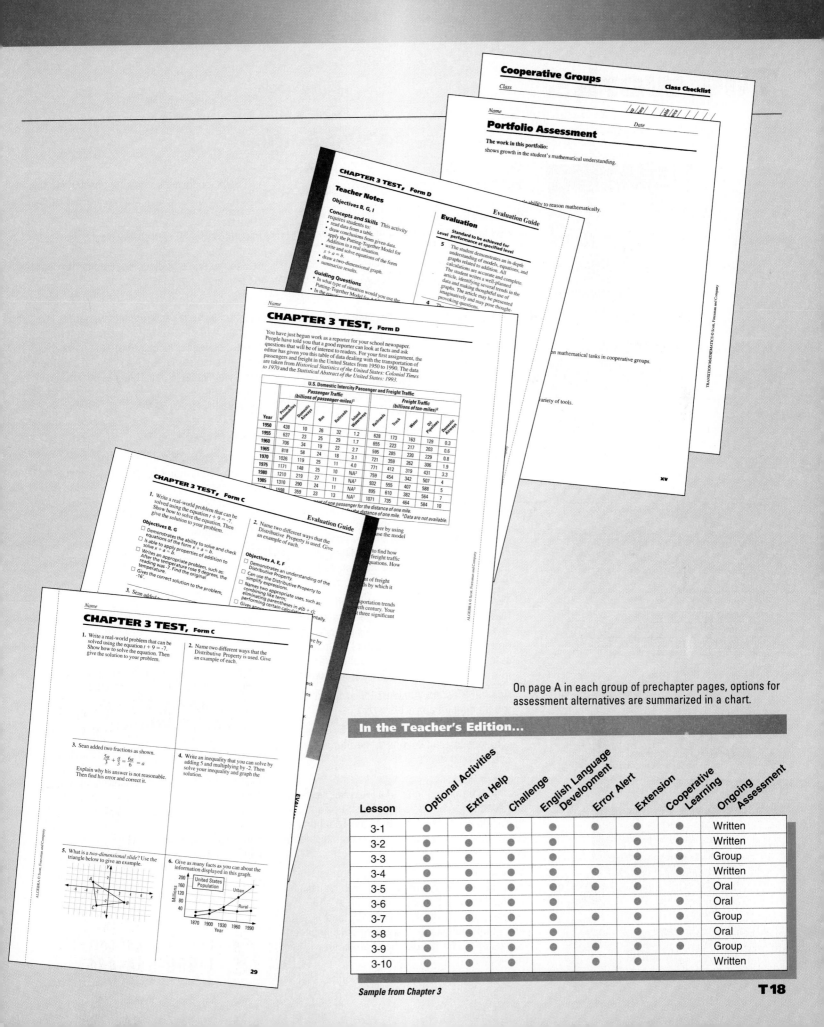

On page A in each group of prechapter pages, options for assessment alternatives are summarized in a chart.

In the Teacher's Edition...

Lesson	Optional Activities	Extra Help	Challenge	English Language Development	Error Alert	Extension	Cooperative Learning	Ongoing Assessment
3-1	●	●	●	●	●	●	●	Written
3-2	●	●	●	●	●	●	●	Written
3-3	●	●	●	●	●	●	●	Group
3-4	●	●	●	●	●	●	●	Written
3-5	●	●	●	●	●	●	●	Oral
3-6	●	●	●	●	●	●	●	Oral
3-7	●	●	●	●	●	●	●	Group
3-8	●	●	●	●	●	●	●	Oral
3-9	●	●	●	●	●	●	●	Group
3-10	●	●	●	●	●	●	●	Written

The works

Components of *UCSMP Algebra, Second Edition*

Student Edition
0-673-45765-6. With calculator: 0-673-45824-5.

Teacher's Resource File
Contains a Teacher's Edition, hundreds of blackline masters and a Solution Manual correlated to the Student Edition. Booklets are also available separately. 0-673-45854-7.

☐ **Teacher's Edition** (in two parts).
0-673-45768-0.

✗ ☐ **Lesson Masters A.** Single-page blackline masters correlated to each lesson in the Student Edition—ideal for extra practice.
0-673-45770-2.

✗ ☐ **Lesson Masters B.** Two pages of practice for each lesson, for students who need extra help. 0-673-45769-9.

☐ **Teaching Aid Masters.** All Warm-ups and many Additional Examples from the Teacher's Edition margin notes, tables, graphs, drawings, visual organizers, and more. 0-673-45771-0.

✗ ☒ **Assessment Sourcebook.** Quizzes, standard tests, performance assessment, and cumulative tests for each chapter, plus comprehensive tests and guidelines for portfolio, problem-solving, cooperative-group, and self assessment. 0-673-45772-9.

✓ ☐ **Technology Sourcebook.** Ideas for teacher-directed computer demonstrations and blackline-master activities for use with both calculators and computers. Helps students explore and extend concepts through the latest technologies. 0-673-45774-5.

✗ ☐ **Answer Masters.** Answers for all questions in the Student Edition. 0-673-45773-7.

☒ **Solution Manual.** Complete step-by-step solutions to all questions in the Student Edition. 0-673-45775-3.

Visual Aids
Overhead transparencies of all Answer Masters and Teaching Aids, including Warm-ups and many Additional Examples from the Teacher's Edition margin notes, to enhance your classroom presentations. 0-673-45778-8.

Activity Kit
Includes an Activity Sourcebook with blackline-master activities that enhance interest and understanding, encourage curiosity, and strengthen mathematical thinking. Also includes manipulatives for the overhead projector.
0-673-45784-2.

Study Skills Handbook
A UCSMP exclusive containing tips and models to help students develop study skills. 0-673-45823-7.

Geometry Template (package of 25)
Unique to UCSMP, this sturdy plastic tool is a combination compass and protractor and includes rulers, a grid, various geometric figures, and a center finder. 0-673-45825-3.

TI-30 Calculator
Designed by Texas Instruments with the assistance of the UCSMP team, this is the simplest scientific calculator on the market today. Available with the purchase of a Student Text. Also available in a caddy of ten and in an overhead version.
With Student Text: 0-673-45824-5.
Caddy of ten: 0-673-33990-4.
Overhead Version: 0-673-45406-1.

Explorer Series Software
Includes a Reference Guide and blackline-master activities.
☐ **GraphExplorer**
IBM: 0-673-44304-3; Macintosh: 0-673-44305-1.
☐ **GeoExplorer**
IBM: 0-673-45332-4; Macintosh: 0-673-44272-1;
Apple: 0-673-45331-6.
☐ **StatExplorer**
IBM: 0-673-44302-7; Macintosh: 0-673-44303-5.

Quiz and Test Writer software
(IBM and Macintosh)
Create a wealth of custom quizzes and tests quickly and easily, with a minimum of computer expertise. Includes extra challenge problems.
IBM: 0-673-45856-3; Macintosh: 0-673-45857-1.

Wide World of Mathematics Videotape, Videodisc, CD-ROM (IBM, Macintosh)
Interactive activities in a motivating newscast format demonstrate how math concepts are used in the real world. Activities introduce lessons in the Student Edition and can be used for demonstrations or in a laboratory setting.
Algebra Videotape Package: 0-673-37501-3.
Algebra Videodisc Package: 0-673-36500-5.
CD-ROM Macintosh: Available soon
CD-ROM IBM: Available soon

 **ScottForesman**
A Division of HarperCollinsPublishers

> ☎ **TO ORDER, JUST CALL**
> **1-800-554-4411**

UCSMP

ScottForesman

The University of Chicago School Mathematics Project

Algebra

Second Edition

About the Cover The art on the cover was generated by a computer. The planes, grid, and intersecting lines suggest the integrated approach of *UCSMP Algebra*. This course uses geometry and statistics as a setting for work with linear expressions and sentences, and much work is done with graphing.

Authors

John W. McConnell   Susan Brown

Zalman Usiskin   Sharon L. Senk   Ted Widerski   Scott Anderson

Susan Eddins   Cathy Hynes Feldman   James Flanders   Margaret Hackworth

Daniel Hirschhorn   Lydia Polonsky   Leroy Sachs   Ernest Woodward

ScottForesman

A Division of HarperCollins*Publishers*

Editorial Offices: Glenview, Illinois
Regional Offices: Sunnyvale, California • Tucker, Georgia
Glenview, Illinois • Oakland, New Jersey • Dallas, Texas

ACKNOWLEDGMENTS

Authors

John W. McConnell
Instructional Supervisor of Mathematics,
Glenbrook South High School, Glenview, IL

Susan Brown
Mathematics Department Chair, York High
School, Elmhurst, IL

Zalman Usiskin
Professor of Education, The University of Chicago

Sharon L. Senk
Associate Professor of Mathematics, Michigan
State University, East Lansing, MI (Second
Edition only)

Ted Widerski
Mathematics Teacher, Waterloo High School,
Waterloo, WI (Second Edition only)

Scott Anderson
UCSMP (Second Edition only)

Susan Eddins
Mathematics Teacher, Illinois Mathematics and
Science Academy, Aurora, IL (First Edition only)

Cathy Hynes Feldman
Mathematics Teacher, The University of Chicago
Laboratory Schools (First Edition only)

James Flanders
UCSMP (First Edition only)

Margaret Hackworth
Mathematics Supervisor, Pinellas County Schools,
Largo, FL (First Edition only)

Daniel Hirschhorn
UCSMP (First Edition only)

Lydia Polonsky
UCSMP (First Edition only)

Leroy Sachs
Mathematics Teacher (retired), Clayton High School,
Clayton, MO (First Edition only)

Ernest Woodward
Professor of Mathematics, Austin Peay State
University, Clarksville, TN (First Edition only)

Design Development

Curtis Design

UCSMP Production and Evaluation

Series Editors: Zalman Usiskin, Sharon L. Senk
Directors of First Edition Studies: Sandra
  Mathison (director); Assistants to the Directors:
  Penelope Flores, Catherine Sarther
Directors of Second Edition Studies:
  Gurcharn Kaeley, Geraldine Macsai
Technical Coordinator: Susan Chang
Second Edition Teacher's Edition Editor:
  David Witonsky
Second Edition Consultants: Amy Hackenberg,
  Mary Lappan
First Edition Managing Editor: Natalie Jakucyn

We wish to acknowledge the generous support of the
Amoco Foundation and the Carnegie Corporation
of New York in helping to make it possible for the
First Edition of these materials to be developed,
tested, and distributed, and the continuing support
of the Amoco Foundation for the Second Edition.

We wish to thank the many editors, production
personnel, and design personnel at ScottForesman
for their magnificent assistance.

Multicultural Reviewers for ScottForesman

Winifred Deavens
St. Louis Public Schools, St. Louis, MO
Seree Weroha
Kansas City Public Schools, Kansas City, KS
Efraín Meléndez
Dakota School, Los Angeles, CA
Linda Skinner
Educator, Edmond, OK

It is impossible to thank everyone who has helped create and test this book. We wish particularly to thank Carol Siegel, who coordinated the use of the test materials in schools; Tina Klawinski and Lynn Libby of our editorial staff; Sara Benson, Anil Gurnarney, Dae S. Lee, Jee Yoon Lee, and Sara Zimmerman of our technical staff; and Eileen Fernandez, Rochelle Gutiérrez, Suzanne Levin, Nancy Miller, and Gerald Pillsbury of our evaluation staff.

A first draft of *Algebra* was written and piloted during the 1985–86 school year. After a major revision, a field trial edition was tested in 1986–87 at these schools:

Clearwater High School
Clearwater, Florida

Aptakisic Junior High School
Buffalo Grove, Illinois

Washington High School
Von Steuben Metropolitan Science Center
Disney Magnet School
Austin Academy
Chicago, Illinois

Morton East High School
Cicero, Illinois

O'Neill Middle School
Downers Grove, Illinois

Glenbrook South High School
Glenview, Illinois

Elk Grove High School
Elk Grove Village, Illinois

McClure Junior High School
Western Springs, Illinois

Hubble Middle School
Wheaton, Illinois

Parkway West Middle School
Chesterfield, Missouri

Northeast High School
Clarksville, Tennessee

A second revision underwent a comprehensive nationwide test in 1987–88. The following schools participated in those studies:

Rancho San Joaquin Middle School
Lakeside Middle School
Irvine High School
Irvine, California

Mendocino High School
Mendocino, California

Lincoln Junior High School
Lesher Junior High School
Blevins Junior High School
Fort Collins, Colorado

Bacon Academy
Colchester, Connecticut

Rogers Park Junior High School
Danbury, Connecticut

Hyde Park Career Academy
Bogan High School
Chicago, Illinois

Morton East High School
Cicero, Illinois

John H. Springman School
Glenview, Illinois

Carl Sandburg Junior High School
Winston Park Junior High School
Palatine, Illinois

Fruitport High School
Fruitport, Michigan

Taylor Middle School
Van Buren Middle School
Albuquerque, New Mexico

Crest Hills Middle School
Shroder Paideia Middle School
Walnut Hills High School
Cincinnati, Ohio

Easley Junior High School
Easley, South Carolina

R.C. Edwards Junior High School
Central, South Carolina

Liberty Middle School
Liberty, South Carolina

Glen Hills Middle School
Glendale, Wisconsin

Robinson Middle School
Maple Dale Middle School
Fox Point, Wisconsin

Since the ScottForesman publication of the First Edition of *Algebra* in 1990, thousands of teachers and schools have used the materials and have made additional suggestions for improvements. The materials were again revised, and the following teachers and schools participated in field studies in 1992–1993:

Dallas Russell
D.W. Griffith Jr. High School
Los Angeles, California

Michael Mueller
Mendota High School
Mendota, Illinois

Pat Carlson
Fruitport High School
Fruitport, Michigan

Sally Jackman
Hanks High School
El Paso, Texas

Claire V. Giambalvo
Chaffey High School
Ontario, California

Sally Cadagin
Grant Middle School
Springfield, Illinois

Jerry Johnson
Sauk Rapids-Rice Schools
Sauk Rapids, Minnesota

Bonnie L. Buehler
John H. Springman School
Glenview, Illinois

Marilyn Morse
Eagleview Middle School
Colorado Springs, Colorado

Brian Anderson
Central Junior High School
Lawrence, Kansas

Michael R. Casey
Lake Oswego Sr. High School
Lake Oswego, Oregon

Sidney Caldwell
Safety Harbor Middle School
Safety Harbor, Florida

Melanie Kellum
Old Rochester High School
Mattapoisett, Massachusetts

Stephen Mazurek
Springfield High School
Springfield, Pennsylvania

We wish also to acknowledge the contribution of the text *Algebra Through Applications with Probability and Statistics,* by Zalman Usiskin (NCTM, 1979), developed with funds from the National Science Foundation, to some of the conceptualizations and problems used in this book.

THE UNIVERSITY OF CHICAGO SCHOOL MATHEMATICS PROJECT

The University of Chicago School Mathematics Project (UCSMP) is a long-term project designed to improve school mathematics in grades K–12. UCSMP began in 1983 with a 6-year grant from the Amoco Foundation. Additional funding has come from the National Science Foundation, the Ford Motor Company, the Carnegie Corporation of New York, the General Electric Foundation, GTE, Citicorp/Citibank, and the Exxon Education Foundation.

UCSMP is centered in the Departments of Education and Mathematics of the University of Chicago. The project has translated dozens of mathematics textbooks from other countries, held three international conferences, developed curricular materials for elementary and secondary schools, formulated models of teacher training and retraining, conducted a large number of large and small conferences, engaged in evaluations of many of its activities, and through its royalties has supported a wide variety of research projects in mathematics education at the University. UCSMP currently has the following components and directors:

Resources	Izaak Wirszup, Professor Emeritus of Mathematics
Elementary Materials	Max Bell, Professor of Education
Elementary Teacher Development	Sheila Sconiers, Research Associate in Education
Secondary	Sharon L. Senk, Associate Professor of Mathematics, Michigan State University Zalman Usiskin, Professor of Education
Evaluation Consultant	Larry Hedges, Professor of Education

From 1983 to 1987, the director of UCSMP was Paul Sally, Professor of Mathematics. Since 1987, the director has been Zalman Usiskin.

Algebra

The text *Algebra* has been developed by the Secondary Component of the project, and constitutes the core of the second year in a six-year mathematics curriculum devised by that component. The names of the six texts around which these years are built are:

Transition Mathematics
Algebra
Geometry
Advanced Algebra
Functions, Statistics, and Trigonometry
Precalculus and Discrete Mathematics

The content and questions of this book integrate geometry, probability, and statistics together with algebra. Pure and applied mathematics are also integrated throughout. It is for these reasons that the book is deemed to be a part of an integrated series. However, algebra is the trunk from which the various branches of mathematics studied in this book emanate. It is for this reason that we call this book simply *Algebra*.

The first edition of *Algebra* introduced many features that have been retained in this edition. There is **wider scope,** including significant amounts of geometry and statistics, and some combinatorics and probability. These topics are not isolated as separate units of study or enrichment. They are employed to motivate, justify, extend, and otherwise enhance important concepts of algebra. The geometry is particularly important because many students have in the past finished algebra without the content prerequisites for success in geometry. A **real-world orientation** has guided both the selection of content and the approaches allowed the student in working out exercises and problems. This is because being able to do mathematics is of little use to an individual unless he or she can apply that content. We require **reading mathematics,** because students must read to understand mathematics in later courses and must learn to read technical matter in the world at large. The use of **up-to-date technology** is integrated throughout, with *scientific calculators* assumed and *graphics calculators* strongly recommended.

Four dimensions of understanding are emphasized to maximize performance: skill in carrying out various algorithms; developing and using mathematics properties and relationships; applying mathematics in realistic situations; and representing or picturing mathematical concepts. We call this the SPUR approach: **S**kills, **P**roperties, **U**ses, **R**epresentations.

The **book organization** is designed to maximize the acquisition of both skills and concepts. Ideas introduced in a lesson are reinforced through Review questions in the immediately succeeding lessons. This daily review feature allows students several nights to learn and practice important concepts and skills. Then, at the end of each chapter, a carefully focused Progress Self-Test and a Chapter Review, each keyed to objectives in all the dimensions of understanding, are used to solidify performance of skills and concepts from the chapter so that they may be applied later with confidence. Finally, to increase retention, important ideas are reviewed in later chapters.

Since the ScottForesman publication of the first edition of *Algebra* in 1990, the entire UCSMP secondary series has been completed and published. Thousands of teachers and schools have used the first edition and some have made suggestions for improvements. There have been advances in technology and in thinking about how students learn. We have attempted to utilize these ideas in the development of the second edition.

Those familiar with the first edition will note a rather significant reorganization of the content in the second edition, a restructuring of the beginning of the course so that some ideas are introduced one or two months earlier than before. We were encouraged to do this because a high percentage of *Algebra* students enter this course with a better background than could have expected when we wrote the first edition. Many of these have benefited from *Transition Mathematics.*

There are many other changes. We have reorganized the material on square roots, absolute value, and quadratics somewhat. Technology that graphs functions, introduced in Chapter 12 in the first edition, is now introduced in Chapter 5 and applied thereafter.

There are also a number of features new to this edition, including the following: **Activities** have been incorporated into many of the lessons to help students develop concepts before or as they read. There are **projects** at the end of each chapter because in the real world much of the mathematics that is done requires a longer period of time than is customarily available to students in daily assignments. There are many more questions requiring **writing,** because writing helps students clarify their own thinking, and writing is an important aspect of communicating mathematical ideas to others. In the area of technology, **spreadsheets** are introduced early as a pattern-finding and a problem-solving tool.

Comments about these materials are welcomed. Please send them to: UCSMP, The University of Chicago, 5835 S. Kimbark, Chicago, IL 60637.

v

CONTENTS

CHAPTER 1   4

USES OF VARIABLES

CHAPTER 2   70

MULTIPLICATION IN ALGEBRA

vii

x

To the Student

GETTING STARTED

Welcome to Algebra.
We hope you enjoy this book; it was written for you.

Studying Mathematics

This book has several goals. It will introduce you to the language of algebra. It will help you prepare for geometry and other mathematics. It will help you learn about the many uses of algebra in the real world and deal with the mathematics around you.

A NOTHER GOAL OF this book is for you to continue to develop your study skills in mathematics. To accomplish this goal, you should take advantage of all the resources you have. The authors, who are experienced teachers, offer the following advice on studying algebra.

1 You can watch basketball hundreds of times on television. Still, to learn how to play basketball, you must actually dribble, shoot, and pass a ball. Mathematics is no different. You cannot learn much just by watching other people do it. You must participate. Some teachers have a slogan: *Mathematics is not a spectator sport.*

Mathematics is not a spectator sport.

2 You are expected to read each lesson, and it is vital for you to understand what you have read. Here are some ways to improve your reading comprehension.

Read slowly, paying attention to each word and symbol.

Look up the meaning of any word you do not understand.

Work examples yourself as you follow the steps in the text.

Reread sections that are unclear to you.

Discuss difficult ideas with a fellow student or your teacher.

Notes on Reading

The reading abilities of students who use UCSMP *Algebra* will differ from one another. You might begin by calling on students in turn to read a few sentences of this introduction aloud. This will give you some idea of the reading levels of students in your class. Alternatively, you could have students read this section on their own.

Discuss the equipment you expect students to bring to class. We recommend that both the ruler and protractor be transparent plastic. We also recommend graph paper with four or five lines to the inch.

Calculators Calculators are needed throughout this book, and their use should be allowed for all tests. Graphics calculators are encouraged, if available, but they are not required for this course.

Students need calculators starting with Lesson 1-4. This gives you time to assemble a classroom set or gives students time to obtain calculators. If you expect students to buy calculators, show them the kinds of calculators that are acceptable.

If students have never used scientific calculators, you might want to use Appendix A as a one-day lesson after Lesson 1-2. It is easier to explain how to use the calculator when all the students have the same model. However, many teachers think that students learn more if they can observe that different calculators operate differently. Advise your

(Notes on Reading continue on page 2.)

Overview

These pages contain three important bits of information about this book:
1. a list of the materials that are needed for the book;
2. a description of the active approach taken to learning, including participation, reading, writing, and problem solving;
3. a set of questions designed to familiarize students with the location of various features in the book.

If you have never taught from a UCSMP text, there are certain process features which you should note. First, students are expected to read. If they have never had to read in a mathematics course before, this may come as a surprise to them. You will have to make your expectations very clear. Notes for the individual lessons contain strategies to help you establish reading as a course requirement. Whether you use these ideas or develop your own, it is

important to focus on reading carefully for comprehension.

Reading mathematics differs from reading literature. Details are important, and many parts require more than one reading. Although some students may find reading uncomfortable at first, they almost always ease into it after the first few chapters, and

(Overview continues on page 2.)

students to bring the instructions for their calculators to class; otherwise they may flounder when trying to determine the role of a particular key. If your students are not familiar with scientific notation, which is used throughout this text, you should also plan a one-day lesson based on Appendix B. (You might teach both Appendices A and B in a single day.)

Reading Mathematics Encourage students to use the blue headline phrases that identify some of the key ideas taught in the lessons. Point out that these headlines can be used as reading organizers, helping students to organize their thoughts, preview the reading, and locate answers to questions about the lesson.

Also point out that, as students read, they should stop to examine any graphs and charts and to study all computations that might be in examples. Looking at pictures and photographs and reading captions are also considered part of the lesson. Point out that important terms are printed in boldface type throughout this book.

✎ **Writing** Writing is an important aspect of this course. When students are expected to give a response by writing a sentence or paragraph, a pencil logo (shown at the beginning of this paragraph) will appear in the Teacher's Edition notes.

Cooperative Learning Emphasize the cooperative nature of learning. Encourage students to discuss their mathematics assignments with each other in school or to call one another at home if they have difficulty understanding a problem or concept. You might want to check that each student in your class has the telephone number of at least two other students. Be sure to distinguish *cooperation* from *copying*.

3 Writing is a tool for communicating your solutions and thoughts to others. It can help you understand mathematics, too. So you will sometimes be asked to explain your solution to a problem, to justify an answer, or to write down information that can help you study. Writing good explanations takes practice. You can look at the solutions to the examples in each lesson as a guide for your own writing.

4 If you cannot answer a question immediately, don't give up! Read the lesson again. Read the question again. Look for examples. If you can, go away from the problem and return to it a little later. Ask questions and talk to others when you do not understand something.

Equipment Needed for This Book

You need to have some tools to do any mathematics. The most basic tools are paper, pencil, and erasers. For this book, you will also need the following equipment:

a ruler with both centimeter and inch markings,

a protractor,

graph paper,

and **a scientific calculator.**

The calculator should have the following keys:

x^y or y^x or $\wedge$ (powering),

$\sqrt{x}$ (square root), $x!$ (factorial),

$\pm$, $+/-$, or $(-)$ (for negative numbers),

π (pi), and $1/x$ (reciprocals).

Your calculator should also display very large or very small numbers in scientific notation.

Getting Acquainted with UCSMP *Algebra*

If you have never used a UCSMP book before, spend some time getting acquainted with this book. The questions that follow are designed to help you become familiar with *Algebra*.

We hope you join the hundreds of thousands of students who have enjoyed UCSMP *Algebra*. We wish you much success.

they become quite accustomed to reading by the end of the year. Students who have used *Transition Mathematics* should have already made this adjustment.

Second, even if you have taught from UCSMP materials before, you will notice an increased emphasis on writing. Student writing serves many purposes. For example, writing shows the students' work, and it enables you to more accurately respond to

them. If students write annotations, the writing shows you how they are thinking, which is just as valuable. Writing is also essential for communication; anyone who uses mathematics beyond the elementary level must be able to communicate those uses. And writing is a part of mathematics itself; a proof or other mathematical argument is as much a written demonstration as it is a conceptual argument. We hope that the emphasis on writing will result in students who are

not only better students of algebra, but also better students in their later mathematics courses. These students should be more able to communicate their understanding of mathematics to others.

QUESTIONS

Covering the Reading

1. What are the goals of *Algebra?* **See margin.**

2. List some materials you will need for your work in *Algebra.* **ruler, protractor, graph paper, and scientific calculator**

3. Explain the meaning of the statement, "Mathematics is not a spectator sport." **See margin.**

4. Of the five things listed that you can do to improve reading comprehension, list the three you think are most helpful. **Answers will vary.**

5. Where can you look for a model to help you write an explanation justifying your answer to a problem? **the solutions to the Examples**

Knowing Your Textbook

For 6–13, answer the questions by looking at the Table of Contents, the chapters, the appendices, or the index at the end of the book.

6. Refer to the Table of Contents beginning on page *vi*. What lesson would you read to learn about the factorial symbol? **Lesson 2–10**

7. The appendices contain information about topics you may need to review.   **3**
   a. How many appendices does *Algebra* have?
   b. What topics are reviewed? **scientific calculators, scientific notation, BASIC**

In 8 and 9, refer to Lesson 3-4.

8. What are the four categories of questions in Lesson 3-4? **Covering the Reading, Applying the Mathematics, Review, Exploration**

9. Suppose you just finished the questions in Lesson 3-4. On what page can you find answers to check your work? For which questions are answers given? **See margin.**

10. Refer to a Progress Self-Test at the end of a chapter. When you finish the test, what is recommended that you do? **See margin.**

11. What kinds of questions are in the Chapter Review at the end of each chapter? **Skills, Properties, Uses, Representations**

12. Use the index in the back of your book to find the pages where Mount Rushmore is mentioned. What are the page numbers? What is the title of that lesson? Which presidents are depicted on Mount Rushmore? **See margin.**

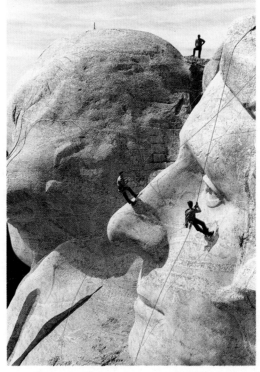

13. Each chapter is introduced with an application of a major idea from the chapter or a brief history of a mathematical concept presented in one of the lessons. Read the opener for Chapter 1. Who was François Viète, and what was his contribution to mathematics? **Viète, a French lawyer of the late 16th century, invented the use of letters to describe arithmetic patterns.**

In the Teacher's Edition, whenever there is a numbered red circle ❶ on a pupil page, the same numbered circle appears in the margin with a specific note corresponding to that section of the lesson. These circles do not appear in the Pupil Edition.

Notes on Questions

Discuss the questions in class. Alternatively, you might have the class go through only the questions in *Covering the Reading* (**Questions 1–5**), and then let students work on **Questions 6–13** on their own.

Cooperative Learning Another way to assign the questions is to divide the class into small groups. Have each group select a student to record answers. As each group goes through the questions, the recorder writes the answers on paper. You might want to walk around the room to monitor the groups and to keep them on task.

✎ **Question 3 Writing** Many questions in this book ask students to explain or justify their answers. Encourage students to use their own words, but stress that their answers should be clear both to themselves and to anyone else who might read them.

Additional Answers
1. The goals are to introduce the language of algebra; to prepare for geometry and other courses; and to teach about the uses of algebra in the real world.
3. You cannot learn mathematics just by watching other people do it. You must do mathematics to learn it.
9. page 842; in the back of the book; The answers to the odd-numbered questions in the sections Applying the Mathematics and the Review are given.
10. Check your work with the solutions in the back of the book. Make a list of the problems you got wrong. Then write down what you need to study most. Use what you write to help you study and review the chapter.
12. p. 125; *Factorials and Permutations;* Washington, Jefferson, Theodore Roosevelt, and Lincoln.

Setting Up Lesson 1-1

Homework If you have a short class period (15–30 minutes) tomorrow, or if your students have not studied from a UCSMP text before, you might assign the reading and **Questions 1–17** in Lesson 1-1.

If you have a full-length period and if most of your students have studied from a UCSMP text before, then assign the reading and all the questions in Lesson 1-1.

Error Alert Some students may feel that they can skip the *Chapter 1 Opener* on pages 4–5. Tell students that they should read all openers along with the first lessons of each chapter unless they are told otherwise.

Materials Students will need dictionaries for **Question 34** in Lesson 1-1.

Chapter 1 Planner

Adapting to Individual Needs

The student text is written for the vast majority of students. The chart at the right suggests two pacing plans to accommodate the needs of your students. Students in the Full Course should complete the entire text by the end of the year. Students in the Minimal Course will spend more time when there are quizzes and more time on the Chapter Review. Therefore, these students may not complete all of the chapters in the text.

Options are also presented to meet the needs of a variety of teaching and learning styles. For each lesson, the Teacher's Edition provides sections entitled: *Video* which describes video segments and related questions that can be used for motivation or extension; *Optional Activities* which suggests activities that employ materials, physical models, technology, and cooperative learning; and, *Adapting to Individual Needs* which regularly includes **Challenge** problems, **English Language Development** suggestions, and suggestions for providing **Extra Help.** The Teacher's Edition also frequently includes an **Error Alert,** an **Extension,** and an **Assessment** alternative. The options available in Chapter 1 are summarized in the chart below.

Chapter 1 Pacing Chart

Day	Full Course	Minimal Course
1	1-1	1-1
2	1-2	1-2
3	1-3	1-3
4	Quiz*; 1-4	Quiz*; begin 1-4.
5	1-5	Finish 1-4.
6	Appendix A**	1-5
7	Appendix B**	Appendix A**
8	1-6	Appendix B**
9	Quiz*; 1-7	1-6
10	1-8	Quiz*; begin 1-7.
11	1-9	Finish 1-7.
12	Self-Test	1-8
13	Review	1-9
14	Test*	Self-Test
15		Review
16		Test*

*in the Teacher's Resource File
**Optional

In the Teacher's Edition...

Lesson	Optional Activities	Extra Help	Challenge	English Language Development	Error Alert	Extension	Cooperative Learning	Ongoing Assessment
1-1	●	●	●	●	●	●	●	Group
1-2	●	●	●	●	●	●	●	Written
1-3	●	●	●	●	●	●	●	Oral
1-4	●		●	●		●		Oral/Written
1-5	●	●	●	●		●	●	Group
1-6	●	●	●	●		●		Oral
1-7	●	●	●	●	●	●	●	Written
1-8	●	●	●	●		●	●	Written
1-9	●	●	●	●		●	●	Group

In the Additional Resources...

Lesson	In the Teacher's Resource File								Video Segments
	Lesson Masters, A and B	Teaching Aids*	Activity Kit*	Answer Masters	Technology Sourcebook	Assessment Sourcebook	Visual Aids**	Technology	
1-1	1-1	1		1-1			1, AM		
1-2	1-2	1, 4, 5		1-2			1, 4, 5, AM		
1-3	1-3	1, 5, 6	1	1-3		Quiz	1, 5, 6, AM		
1-4	1-4	2		1-4			2, AM		
1-5	1-5	2		1-5	Comp 1		2, AM	Spreadsheet	
1-6	1-6	2, 7		1-6	Calc 1	Quiz	2, 7, AM		
1-7	1-7	3, 8	2	1-7			3, 8, AM		
In-class Activity		9		1-8			9, AM		
1-8	1-8	3, 10–12		1-8	Comp 2		3, 10–12, AM	GeoExplorer	
In-class Activity		12		1-9			12, AM		
1-9	1-9	3		1-9			3, AM		
End of chapter				Review		Tests			

*Teaching Aids are pictured on pages 4C and 4D. The activities in the Activity Kit are pictured on page 4C. Teaching Aid 9 which accompanies the In-class Activity preceding Lesson 1-8 is pictured with the lesson notes on page 44.

**Visual Aids provide transparencies for all Teaching Aids and all Answer Masters.

Also available is the Study Skills Handbook which includes study-skill tips related to reading, note-taking, and comprehension.

Integrating Strands and Applications

	1-1	1-2	1-3	1-4	1-5	1-6	1-7	1-8	1-9
Mathematical Connections									
Number Sense		●			●	●		●	
Algebra	●	●	●	●	●	●	●	●	●
Geometry						●	●	●	●
Measurement	●				●			●	
Logic and Reasoning		●	●			●			
Statistics/Data Analysis	●								
Patterns and Functions							●	●	●
Interdisciplinary and Other Connections									
Science	●	●		●	●	●		●	●
Social Studies		●			●		●	●	
Multicultural		●	●		●		●		●
Technology				●	●	●			
Career	●							●	●
Consumer			●		●	●	●	●	●
Sports	●		●		●				

Teaching and Assessing the Chapter Objectives

Chapter 1 Objectives (Organized into the SPUR categories—Skills, Properties, Uses, and Representations)	Lessons	Progress Self-Test Questions	Chapter Review Questions	Chapter Test, Forms A and B	Chapter Test, Forms	
					C	D
Skills						
A: Find solutions to open sentences using trial and error.	1-1	10, 11	1–6	18, 19	3	
B: Find unions and intersections.	1-3	7	7–10	16, 17	1	
C: Evaluate numerical and algebraic expressions.	1-4, 1-6	1–3, 5	11–18	2, 3	3	
D: Evaluate square roots with and without a calculator.	1-6	6, 14, 24	19–28	6–8	4	✓
Properties						
E: Read and interpret set language and notation.	1-2, 1-3	15	29–32	20, 22	1	
F: Use the Square of the Square Root Property.	1-6	4	33–36	9, 10	3	
G: Give instances or counterexamples of patterns.	1-7, 1-9	17	37–40	15	2	
H: Use variables to describe patterns in instances or tables.	1-7, 1-9	16, 18	41–46	21, 24	2	✓
Uses						
I: In real situations, choose a reasonable domain for a variable.	1-2	8, 9	47–50	5	5	
J: Evaluate formulas in real situations.	1-5	12, 13	51–54	4, 11		✓
K: Apply the Pythagorean Theorem to solve problems in real situations.	1-8	22, 23	55–58	23	4	✓
Representations						
L: Draw and interpret graphs of solution sets to inequalities.	1-2, 1-3	19–21	59–67	14	5	

Assessment Sourcebook
Quiz for Lessons 1-1 through 1-3
Quiz for Lessons 1-4 through 1-6
Chapter 1 Test, Forms A–D

Quiz and Test Writer
Multiple forms of chapter tests and quizzes; Challenges

Activity Kit

ACTIVITY 1

SETS AND VENN DIAGRAMS
Use with **Lesson 1-3.**

Materials: Number cards labeled 1 through 9
Group Size: Small groups

1. For each row in the table below, follow these steps.

Mix the cards, place them facedown, and draw five. Record the results under Draw 1. Replace the five cards facedown and mix. Draw five cards again and record the results in Draw 2. Record the numbers that were drawn **both** times in the third column. Then record all the numbers that were drawn **either** time in the last column. List each of the numbers only once.

	Draw 1	Draw 2	Numbers in Both Draws	Numbers in Either Draw
A				
B				
C				

Suppose the results for the Draw 1 is {1, 6, 7, 8, 9} and for Draw 2 is {2, 3, 4, 7, 9}. These results can be pictured in *Venn Diagrams*.

The numbers that were in both draws, 7 and 9, are in the *intersection* of the two sets of cards drawn. The numbers that were in either draw are in the *union* of the two sets of cards drawn.

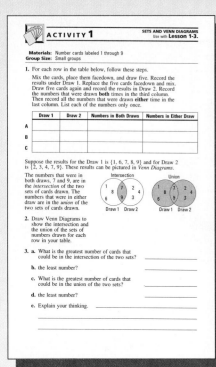

2. Draw Venn Diagrams to show the intersection and the union of the sets of numbers drawn for each row in your table.

3. a. What is the greatest number of cards that could be in the intersection of the two sets? _____

b. the least number? _____

c. What is the greatest number of cards that could be in the union of the two sets? _____

d. the least number? _____

e. Explain your thinking. _____

ACTIVITY 2

NUMBER PATTERNS
Use with **Lesson 1-7.**

Materials: Round markers or pennies
Group Size: Partners

1. Arrange some markers to match the diagrams. Nine is a square number. Eight is not.

a. Is 6 a square number? _____

b. Is 16 a square number? _____

c. Explain how you can use markers to demonstrate which numbers are square.

2. a.

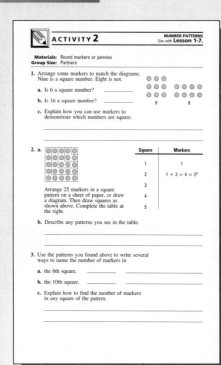

Square	Markers
1	1
2	$1 + 3 = 4 = 2^2$
3	
4	
5	

Arrange 25 markers in a square pattern on a sheet of paper, or draw a diagram. Then draw squares as shown above. Complete the table at the right.

b. Describe any patterns you see in the table.

3. Use the patterns you found above to write several ways to name the number of markers in

a. the 6th square. _____ _____

b. the 10th square. _____ _____

c. Explain how to find the number of markers in *any* square of the pattern.

▶ **ACTIVITY 2**   page 2

4. a.

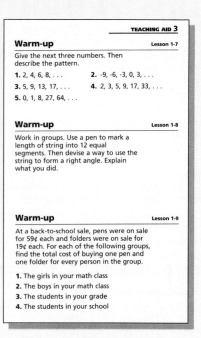

Square	Markers
1	1
2	$1 + 8 = 9 = 3^2$
3	
4	
5	

Arrange 25 markers again in a square pattern on a sheet of paper, or draw a diagram. Then draw squares as shown above. Complete the table at the right.

b. Describe any patterns you see in the table.

5. Use the patterns you found above to write several ways to name the number of markers in

a. the 6th square. _____ _____

b. the 8th square. _____ _____

c. Explain how to find the number of markers in *any* square of the pattern.

6. Predict the number of markers in each ring making up a square of 361 markers. Then check your prediction.

Teaching Aids

Warm-up
Lesson 1-1

For 1–4, fill in the blank to make the sentence true.

1. A mile is longer than a _____.

2. A triangle has _____ sides.

3. _____ plays basketball.

4. A _____ has four legs.

5. Make up a sentence with only one correct response.

Warm-up
Lesson 1-2

Describe each set of numbers. The three dots mean that the pattern continues.

1. {1, 3, 5, 7, 9, . . . }   **2.** {1, 3, 5, 7, 9}

3. {2, 3, 5, 7, 11, . . . }   **4.** {0, 1, 4, 9, 16, 25, . . . }

5. { . . ., -3, -2, -1, 0, 1, 2, 3, . . . }

Warm-up
Lesson 1-3

Let A = the set of people whose first and last names begin with a vowel and B = the set of people whose first or last name begins with a vowel.

1. Name at least one person in each set. If you cannot think of anyone, make up a name.

2. Which set do you think will have more members. Why?

Warm-up
Lesson 1-4

Put +, −, ×, or ÷ in the blanks below. You do not have to use every symbol, and you may not use any symbol more than once. Following the order of operations, what is the smallest number you can make?

8 ____ 1 ____ 6 ____ 4

Warm-up
Lesson 1-5

Write a formula that you remember learning at another time. Explain in writing what the formula is about and give an example of its use.

Warm-up
Lesson 1-6

1. Find the area of a square with sides 5 cm long.

2. Find the length of a side of a square whose area is 36 cm^2.

3. Find the area of a square with sides $\sqrt{11}$ cm long.

4. Find the length of a side of a square whose area is 7 cm^2.

Warm-up
Lesson 1-7

Give the next three numbers. Then describe the pattern.

1. 2, 4, 6, 8, . . .   **2.** -9, -6, -3, 0, 3, . . .

3. 5, 9, 13, 17, . . .   **4.** 2, 3, 5, 9, 17, 33, . . .

5. 0, 1, 8, 27, 64, . . .

Warm-up
Lesson 1-8

Work in groups. Use a pen to mark a length of string into 12 equal segments. Then devise a way to use the string to form a right angle. Explain what you did.

Warm-up
Lesson 1-9

At a back-to-school sale, pens were on sale for 59¢ each and folders were on sale for 19¢ each. For each of the following groups, find the total cost of buying one pen and one folder for every person in the group.

1. The girls in your math class

2. The boys in your math class

3. The students in your grade

4. The students in your school

Real Numbers

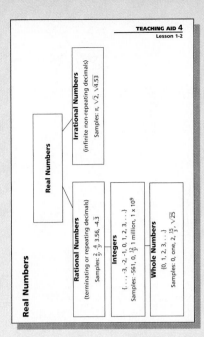

Number Lines

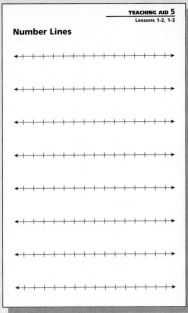

Number-Line Jeopardy

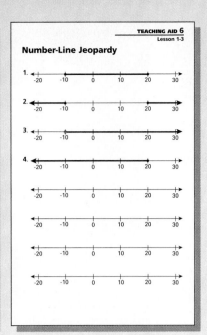

Squares and Square Roots

$\sqrt{n}$	n	n^2
1	1	1
1.414	2	4
1.732	3	9
2	4	16
2.236	5	25
2.449	6	36
2.646	7	49
2.828	8	64
3	9	81
3.162	10	100
	11	
	12	
	13	
	14	
	15	
	16	
	17	
	18	
	19	
	20	

Question 30

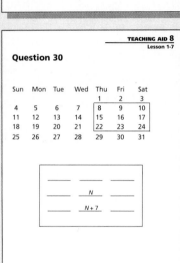

Question 26

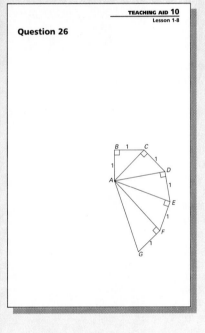

Additional Examples

1. What is the length of the hypotenuse of the right triangle shown at the right?

2. To get to school, Eddie travels 2.5 miles east and 1.5 miles north. If he could travel to school in a straight line, how far would he have to go?

3. Central Park in New York City is shaped like a rectangle. It is 0.8 kilometers wide and 4 kilometers long. About how far is it from the southeast corner of the park to the northwest corner?

Extension

Show that both squares have sides of length $a + b$. Then work in groups and show that $a^2 + b^2 = c^2$.

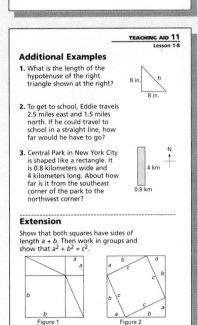

Figure 1   Figure 2

Centimeter Grid

Chapter Opener

Pacing

All the lessons in this book are designed to be covered in one day. At the end of the chapter, you should plan to spend 1 day to review the Progress Self-Test, 1 to 2 days for the Chapter Review, and 1 day for a test. You may wish to spend a day on projects, and a day may be needed for quizzes. Therefore, this chapter should take 12 to 14 days. If you assign the appendices, you should add 1 day for each appendix. We strongly advise that you not spend more than 14 days on this chapter (16 with appendices); there is ample opportunity to review ideas in later chapters.

Using pages 4–5

The chapter opener gives some history on how mathematicians came to use variables as abbreviations in formulas.

Multicultural Connection Over a thousand years ago, mathematicians from Chinese, Egyptian, Babylonian, Arab, and Greek cultures were able to solve problems that we think of today as algebra problems. Around 150 A.D., the Greek mathematician Diophantus used a letter to stand for an unknown number. But it was François Viète who first developed the process in which a letter could stand for any one of many numbers and could be operated on as if it were a number. He was the first to describe the solutions to quadratic equations in terms of the coefficients as we do today. Though Viète is relatively unknown in the United States, in some foreign textbooks he is appropriately called "the father of algebra."

CHAPTER 1

4

Chapter 1 Overview

"Algebra" is a mysterious word to many students. When doing work with equations in previous courses, they probably have been told that they were studying algebra. However, it is only when students appear in a class with the name "algebra" that they truly believe they have arrived in algebra.

This chapter introduces students to algebra by focusing on five uses of the most fundamental idea in all of algebra: that a symbol, called a *variable,* may stand for any one of a set of elements. Variables are used as

1. the language for translating some English expressions and sentences involving numbers.
2. abbreviations in formulas.
3. unknowns in open sentences.
4. the language for describing patterns.
5. identifiers of locations (often in computer or calculator registers) where numbers are stored.

It is not possible to cover any of these uses in depth in a single chapter. The ideas are presented here so that they may be utilized throughout the remainder of the book. The representation of variables in calculator and computer programs is first seen in Lesson 1-4. Students will need calculators beginning in Lesson 1-4. If students are required to have their own calculators, be sure they know what kinds are acceptable. See *To the Student: Getting Started* on

USES OF VARIABLES

About 3500 years ago, an Egyptian scribe, Ahmose, copied the following hieroglyphics from a source then about 200 years old. The hieroglyphics tell how to find the area of a rectangle with length 10 units and width 2 units.

Today's description in English can be shorter.
The area of a rectangle equals its length times its width.

The statement can be shortened more by using symbols for "equals" and "times."

$$\text{Area of a rectangle} = \text{length} \times \text{width}$$
$$= 10 \text{ units} \times 2 \text{ units}$$
$$= 20 \text{ square units}$$

The statement can be abbreviated even more by using *variables*.
$$A = \ell w$$

Today we call letters such as A, ℓ, and w variables because their values can vary. Beginning algebra is the study of variables like those found in formulas. For many people, formulas are clearer and easier to use than words. Formulas are one way in which algebra makes relationships between quantities easier to understand and use.

The first person to use letters to describe general arithmetic patterns as we do today was François Viète (Fran swah Vee yet), in 1591. He was also one of the greatest mathematicians of the 16th century. He believed that his invention was so powerful that with it "there is no problem that cannot be solved."

Viète was both right and wrong. Despite the power of algebra, there remain problems that algebra cannot solve.

In this chapter, you will see how variables appear in sentences, expressions, formulas, and tables.

5

Objectives

A Find solutions to open sentences using trial and error.

Resources

From the Teacher's Resource File
- Lesson Master 1-1A or 1-1B
- Answer Master 1-1
- Teaching Aid 1: Warm-up

Additional Resources
- Visual for Teaching Aid 1
- Dictionaries (Question 34)

Warm-up

You can use the *Warm-up*, or the *Additional Examples* on page 8, as questions for students to work on as you begin class.

As students arrive for class, write the following questions on the board, or use **Teaching Aid 1.**

For 1–4, fill in the blank to make the sentence true. **Answers will vary.**
1. A mile is longer than a ____.
2. A triangle has ____ sides.
3. ____ plays basketball.
4. A ____ has four legs.
5. Make up a sentence with only one correct response. **Sample: My full name is ____.**

Notes on Reading

Reading Mathematics To read well, students must read carefully and watch for important terms and symbols. You may want to go around

6

LESSON

1-1

Variables in Sentences

Electrifying facts. *Lightning travels at speeds up to 100,000 miles per second! A flash of lightning between a cloud and the ground could be 9 miles long.*

❶ What Is a Variable?

There is an old *rule of thumb* for estimating your distance from a flash of lightning. First, determine the number of seconds between the flash and the sound of thunder. Divide this number by 5. The result is the approximate distance in miles. For example, if you count 10 seconds between the flash and the sound of thunder, you are about $\frac{10}{5}$, or 2, miles from the lightning.

In the language of algebra, if s is the number of seconds between the flash and the thunder, then $\frac{s}{5}$ is your approximate distance (in miles) from the lightning. The letter s is a *variable*. A **variable** is a letter or other symbol that can be replaced by any number (or other object) from some set.

Variables may be capital or lower-case letters. In this situation the letter s was chosen because s is the first letter of "seconds." If m is your distance in miles from a flash of lightning, then in the language of algebra,

$$m = \frac{s}{5}.$$

The sentence "$m = \frac{s}{5}$" is read "m is equal to s divided by 5."

Types of Sentences Used in Algebra

A **sentence** in algebra is a grammatically correct set of numbers, variables, or operations that contains a verb.

The sentence $m = \frac{s}{5}$ uses the verb "is equal to," denoted by the symbol =. Any sentence using the verb = is called an **equation.** Symbols for other mathematical verbs are shown on the following page.

6

Lesson 1-1 Overview

Broad Goals Two content goals of this lesson are to review the use of variables in both equations and inequalities and to introduce vocabulary. Two process goals of the lesson are to introduce students to ideas which may be new to them, but which are not very difficult, and to engender the expectation of reading. If your students have not had *Transition Mathematics,* they may be surprised at this expectation.

Perspective Algebra is a language that helps us to describe numbers and the relationships between them. This lesson introduces two of the basic tools of algebra—variables and sentences.

We assume that students have studied simple equations and inequalities with variables before, but in case they have not, **Example 1** provides an illustration from arithmetic. At this point students are not

expected to know how to use algebra to solve sentences like those in **Example 2.** Do not try to teach solving equations here; instead, let students use trial and error. Learning to make smart guesses and learning from errors is important. Students are expected to enter this course with a working knowledge of operations with integers. **Examples 3 and 4** review the use of negative numbers as solutions to equations and inequalities.

A sentence with one of the verbs listed above is called an **inequality.** For instance, the sentence $\frac{1}{2} < \frac{5}{8}$ is an inequality.

In Example 1 and throughout this book we show what you might write using this special writing font.

Example 1

Write an inequality that compares $\frac{1}{3}$ and $\frac{3}{8}$.

② **Solution 1**

Convert $\frac{1}{3}$ and $\frac{3}{8}$ to equivalent fractions with a common denominator. The least common multiple of 3 and 8 is 24, so we use 24 as the denominator.

$$\frac{1}{3} = \frac{8}{24} \text{ and } \frac{3}{8} = \frac{9}{24}.$$
$$\text{Since } \frac{8}{24} < \frac{9}{24},$$
$$\frac{1}{3} < \frac{3}{8}.$$

Solution 2

A fraction indicates division. Perform the division to convert the fraction to a decimal.

$$\frac{1}{3} = 1 \div 3 = 0.\overline{3} \approx 0.333$$
$$\frac{3}{8} = 3 \div 8 = 0.375$$

In decimal form, $0.\overline{3}$ is seen to be smaller than 0.375.

$$\text{Since } 0.\overline{3} < 0.375,$$
$$\frac{1}{3} < \frac{3}{8}.$$

A correct answer using the "is greater than" sign is $\frac{3}{8} > \frac{1}{3}$.

Open Sentences and Solutions

A sentence with a variable is called an **open sentence.** The sentence $m = \frac{s}{5}$ is an open sentence with two variables. It is called "open" because its truth cannot be determined until the variables are replaced by values. The sentence $\frac{1}{3} < \frac{3}{8}$ is not an open sentence. There are no variables. A **solution** to an open sentence is a replacement for the variable that makes the statement true.

In later chapters you will learn methods for finding solutions to equations and inequalities. For now, you may have to solve equations and inequalities by using trial and error or what you know about numbers.

Lesson 1-1 *Variables in Sentences* **7**

Optional Activities

✎ **Writing** After students finish reading the lesson, have them **work in pairs.** Tell each student to write an open sentence and a corresponding problem in words for each symbol in the chart at the top of page 7 (≠, <, ≤, ≈, >, ≥). Have students exchange papers with their partners and give three solutions to each problem. Then suggest they discuss the solutions. Students could take notes during the discussion that they can keep with their problems and solutions.

---

the class and have students take turns reading aloud.

Note that there are often references in the reading to graphs, charts, or computations. Tell students to stop and examine these references. Point out that when terms in this book are in boldface, they are usually followed by a definition or description.

For more information on reading, see *General Teaching Suggestions: Reading* in the *Professional Sourcebook* which begins on page T20 in Part 1 of the Teacher's Edition.

❶ Health Connection Each year in the United States, about 100 people are killed by lightning, and many more are injured. Students might discuss safety measures they can take to avoid being struck by lightning. [Samples: take shelter; avoid touching metal; crouch down; stay away from water]

❷ Students should be able to explain where each line of the work comes from—sometimes from the previous line, sometimes from looking back to the question. Note that $a < b$ and $b > a$ are two ways of stating the same thing.

The script font that is introduced in **Example 1** is used to indicate what students might write.

---

❸ This equation is not one that we expect students to be able to solve at this point without giving them the choices 7, 8, and 9.

❹ Although we use multiplication of negative numbers in this example, this skill is not taught until Chapter 2. Note that 6 and –6 are the square roots of 36.

Additional Examples

These additional examples correspond to the examples in the Pupil Edition. You might want to use them when discussing the lesson.

1. Write an inequality that compares 0.41 and $\frac{5}{12}$.
   $\frac{5}{12} > 0.41$ or $0.41 < \frac{5}{12}$

2. Which of the numbers 7, 8, 9, or 10 is a solution to the open sentence $2 \cdot x + 42 > 7 \cdot x$? **7, 8**

3. Find all integer solutions to $x^3 = -8$. **–2**

4. Bob earns more than $25 a week.
   a. Write an open sentence describing the amounts e that Bob can earn in a week.
      $e > 25$ or $25 < e$
   b. List three possible solutions.
      Any amount greater than $25

8

---

❸ **Example 2**

Which of the numbers 7, 8, or 9 is a solution to the following open sentence?

$$3 \cdot x + 15 = 4 \cdot x + 6$$

(Recall that the dot means multiplication.)

Solution

Try 7. Does $3 \cdot 7 + 15 = 4 \cdot 7 + 6$? No, $36 \neq 34$.
Try 8. Does $3 \cdot 8 + 15 = 4 \cdot 8 + 6$? No, $39 \neq 38$.
Try 9. Does $3 \cdot 9 + 15 = 4 \cdot 9 + 6$? Yes, $42 = 42$.

So 9 is a solution.

❹ **Example 3**

Find all solutions to $p^2 = 36$.

Solution

Recall that p^2 means $p \cdot p$. Thus the equation above means $p \cdot p = 36$. To find p, ask yourself, "What number multiplied by itself equals 36?" You know that $6 \cdot 6 = 36$, so one solution is 6. Now, is any other number multiplied by itself equal to 36? Yes: $-6 \cdot -6 = 36$. So there are two solutions: 6 and -6. This may also be written:

$$p = 6 \text{ or } p = -6.$$

Example 4

Water will remain ice for all temperatures less than 0° Celsius.
a. Write an open sentence describing this situation.
b. Give three numbers that make the sentence true.

Solution

a. You may write: Let T be the Celsius temperature of the water. Then water is ice if $T < 0°$. ($0° > T$ would also be correct.)
b. The open sentence is $T < 0°$. Thus any number less than 0 is a solution. For instance,

$$-3°, -10°, \text{ and } -20° \text{ are three solutions.}$$

If at first you don't succeed. After three unsuccessful attempts in previous Olympic games, U.S. world champion speedskater Dan Jansen won an Olympic gold medal in 1994. He set a new world's record in the 1,000-meter race with a time of 1:12.43.

8

QUESTIONS

Covering the Reading

These questions are designed to check your understanding of the reading. If you cannot answer a question, you should go back to the reading for help in obtaining the answer.

1. You clocked the time between lightning and thunder as 8 seconds. About how far away was the lightning? **1.6 miles**

Adapting to Individual Needs

Extra Help

Have students extend tables like those at the right to show several more entries. Then illustrate how variables can be used to represent the numbers that change. For the first table, ask what number changes from row to row. [Number of feet] Then let f = the number of feet and write $f \cdot 12$ for the number of inches in f feet. When discussing the second table, let t = the number of objects and write $\frac{t}{12}$ for the number of dozen.

Feet	Inches	Objects	Dozen
1	$1 \cdot 12$	12	$\frac{12}{12}$
2	$2 \cdot 12$	24	$\frac{24}{12}$
3	$3 \cdot 12$	36	$\frac{36}{12}$
4	$4 \cdot 12$	48	$\frac{48}{12}$
f	$f \cdot 12$	t	$\frac{t}{12}$

2. What is a *variable?* a letter or other symbol that can be replaced by any number (or other object) from some set

In 3–6, identify each as a sentence, an open sentence, an equation, an inequality, or none of these. (More than one answer may apply.)

3) a sentence, an open sentence, an inequality

3. $5 \cdot x + 3 < 2$

4. $5 \cdot x + 3$ none of these

5) a sentence, an open sentence, an equation

5. $-5 = r$

6. $-5 \leq 0$ a sentence, an inequality

In 7 and 8, write a symbol for each phrase.

7. is approximately equal to $\approx$

8. is greater than $>$

In 9 and 10, two numbers are given.
a. Write an inequality to compare the two numbers.
b. Explain how you got your answer.   9b, 10b) See left.

9b) Sample: Change each to a fraction with a denominator of 56.
$\frac{5}{8} = \frac{35}{56}$ and $\frac{4}{7} = \frac{32}{56}$.
Since $\frac{35}{56} > \frac{32}{56}, \frac{5}{8} > \frac{4}{7}$.

9. $\frac{5}{8}, \frac{4}{7}$ a) $\frac{5}{8} > \frac{4}{7}$

10. $\frac{5}{6}, \frac{17}{20}$ a) $\frac{5}{6} < \frac{17}{20}$

10b) Sample: Change each to a decimal equivalent. $\frac{5}{6} \approx .833$ and $\frac{17}{20} = .850$. Since $.833 < .850$, then $\frac{5}{6} < \frac{17}{20}$.

11. *Multiple choice.* $z \geq 100$ means the same as which sentence?   (c)
(a) $z \leq 100$ (b) $100 \geq z$ (c) $100 \leq z$

12. Which of the numbers 5, 6, or 7 is a solution of $2 \cdot y + 3 = 4 \cdot y - 9$?
6

13. a. Which of the numbers 12, 72, or 142 is a solution to $x^2 = 144$?   12
b. Find the solution to $x^2 = 144$ that is not mentioned in part **a.**   -12

14. Find all solutions to $n^2 = 100$.   10 and -10

In 15 and 16, list three solutions to the sentence.

15. $p \geq 2$ Samples: 2, 3, and 10

16. $y < \frac{2}{3}$ Samples: -3, 0, and $\frac{1}{3}$

17. The temperature was above 10°F all day.
a. Write an open sentence to describe the situation.   t > 10°
b. List three solutions to the sentence in part **a.**
Samples: 11°, 15°, and 18°

If I had a hammer.
Home Improvement, *a popular television series, features actor Tim Allen as a carpenter who hosts his own television show, "Tool Time." At left is Bob Vila, who hosts his own home improvement show,* Home Again.

Applying the Mathematics

These questions extend your understanding of the content of the lesson. Study the examples and explanations if you cannot get an answer. For some questions, you can check your answers with those in the back of the book.

18. List all of the symbols $=, \neq, \approx, >, \geq, <,$ or $\leq$ that make a true statement when written in the blank.

$$8.999 \underline{\ \ ?\ \ } 9 \quad \neq, \approx, <, \leq$$

19. Order from smallest to largest: $\frac{7}{10}, \frac{2}{3}, \frac{3}{4}.$ $\frac{2}{3} < \frac{7}{10} < \frac{3}{4}$

20. Carpenters often measure lengths to the nearest fourth, eighth, or sixteenth of an inch.
a. A carpenter cut a piece of wood $15\frac{5}{16}''$ long. Write this measure in decimal form.   15.3125 in.
b. Will the piece of wood in part **a** fit in a space $15\frac{1}{4}''$ long? Why or why not?   No;   15.3125 > 15.25, so it will not fit.

Lesson 1-1   *Variables in Sentences*   **9**

▶ **LESSON MASTER 1-1B** *page 2*

In 13–15, let r = Ruth's math test score. Write a sentence in words for each algebraic sentence.   Samples are given.
13. $r \geq 84$ Ruth got at least 84 on the test.
14. $r \neq 84$ Ruth did not get 84 on the test.
15. $r < 100$ Ruth got less than 100 on the test.

16. Give a number that is a solution to the sentence in Question 15.   Sample: 91

17. Let A = the land area of Rhode Island in square miles. Write in inequality to describe the following statement:
The land area of Rhode Island is less than 2,000 square miles. $A < 2,000$

Skills Objective A: Find solutions to open sentences using trial and error.

18. Which of the numbers 3, 6, and 10 are solutions of $4 + n = 10$?   6
19. Which of the numbers 4, 5, and 8 are solutions of $9 - b = 4 \cdot b - 11$?   4
20. Which of the numbers 1, 4, and 7 are solutions of $2 \cdot m \geq 8$?   4, 7
21. Which of the numbers 8, 15, and 20 are solutions of $\frac{q}{4} < 8$?   8, 15

In 22 and 23, give three solutions to each open sentence.   Samples are given.
22. $u > 4.8$ 5   6   7.5
23. $v \leq 13.5$ 0   5.5   13.5

In 24 and 25, give both solutions to the equation.
24. $a^2 = 64$ $a = 8$ $a = -8$
25. $d^2 = 1$ $d = 1$ $d = -1$

26. Give an example of an inequality for which 6 is a solution.   Sample: $n > 4$

Adapting to Individual Needs

Challenge
Have students write an equation relating the two variables.

1. f = number of feet, i = number of inches
$[i = 12f$ or $f = \frac{i}{12}]$

2. x = number of meters, y = number of kilometers $[x = 1000y$ or $y = \frac{x}{1000}]$

3. f = number of feet, m = number of miles
$[f = 5280m$ or $m = \frac{f}{5280}]$

4. g = number of gallons, q = number of quarts $[q = 4g$ or $g = \frac{q}{4}]$

5. r = number of ounces, s = number of pounds $[r = 16s$ or $s = \frac{r}{16}]$

Notes on Questions

It is always appropriate to go over questions in class. As you do so, stop occasionally to ask students how many of them got a particular answer. If only a few correctly answered a particular question, be sure to discuss that question. To save time, encourage students to check their odd-numbered answers with those in the back of the book and to try to resolve difficulties they might have before coming to class.

Question 1 This brings out the need for flexibility in writing numbers. The answer that the lightning formula gives is $\frac{8}{5}$ seconds, but in this context $1\frac{3}{5}$ or 1.6 seconds conveys more information. Ultimately, students need to learn which forms of an answer are clear or easy to use and which are not.

✎ **Questions 9b, 10b Writing**
There is no one correct answer for either of these questions.

Questions 15–17 You may want to picture the students' solutions on a number line, thereby previewing a key idea of Lesson 1-2.

9

Notes on Questions

Question 21 Error Alert If students say that 8 is a solution, point out that 5 · 8 is not less than 40. However, 8 is an element of the solution set of 5 · $x \leq$ 40.

Question 29 Although a typical, closer approximation is found by using more 3s in the decimal expansion, even a number such as 0.3331 is closer to $\frac{1}{3}$ than 0.333 is.

Follow-up for Lesson 1-1

Practice

For more questions on SPUR Objectives, use **Lesson Master 1-1A** (shown on page 7) or **Lesson Master 1-1B** (shown on pages 8–9).

Assessment

Group Assessment Have each student write five algebraic sentences using five different "verbs." Then have students exchange papers, identify each sentence as an equation or an inequality, and tell whether or not the sentence is open. [Students recognize and understand inequality symbols and variables.]

Extension

Cooperative Learning Explain that the *density property* states that between any two rational numbers there is another rational number. Then have students **work in pairs** and generalize **Question 33** by giving a rule for finding a fraction between any two given fractions. [Possible response: write the fractions with a common denominator; then compare the numerators and write a fraction whose numerator is between the two numerators.]

---

21. Which of the values 2, 4, 8, and 16, are solutions to 5 · x < 40?
    2 and 4

22. *Multiple choice.* Let m = the number of miles per gallon your neighbor's car gets. Which of the following sentences means that your neighbor's car gets over 20 miles per gallon? **(b)**
    (a) 20 > m (b) 20 < m (c) $m \geq$ 20   (d) 20 $\leq m$

23. The following sentence contains two inequalities: Before 1990, households in the United States contained an average of more than 2.1 persons. **a) y < 1990**
    a. Use the variable y to write an inequality for "before 1990."
    b. Use the variable p to write "an average of more than 2.1 persons."
    p > 2.1

Review

Every lesson contains review questions to give you practice on ideas you have studied earlier.

In 24 and 25, what addition problem is pictured on the number line? *(Previous course)*

24.
    -2 + -3 = -5

25.
    -4 + 7 = 3

In 26–28, find the sum. *(Previous course)*

26. -7 + -5 **-12**   27. -11 + 7 **-4**   28. 8 + -20 + 17 **5**

29. In Example 1, the statement is made that $\frac{1}{3} \approx$ 0.333. Give a closer decimal approximation to $\frac{1}{3}$. *(Previous course)* **Sample: 0.3333**

Often it is quicker and more convenient to do problems in your head. Pressing calculator keys for simple problems is time consuming and may lead to careless mistakes. Do not use your calculator or work with paper and pencil on these problems. Just write an answer.

In 30–32, compute in your head. *(Previous course)*

30. 10 · 3.7 **37**   31. $1\frac{1}{2}$ · 2 **3**   32. 4 · $2.25 **$9.00**

Exploration

33a) Sample: $\frac{111}{200}$; $\frac{11}{20}$ = 0.55 and $\frac{14}{25}$ = 0.56, and .555 is between 0.55 and 0.56. 0.555 = $\frac{555}{1000}$ which can be rewritten as $\frac{111}{200}$.

c) infinitely many; Sample: You can always find the average of *any* two fractions. This gives you a fraction between the two.

These questions ask you to explore mathematics topics related to the chapter. Sometimes these questions require that you use dictionaries, encyclopedias, and other sources of information.

a) See left.

33. **a.** Find a fraction between $\frac{11}{20}$ and $\frac{14}{25}$. Describe the method you used.
    b. Find some other fractions between $\frac{11}{20}$ and $\frac{14}{25}$. **Samples: $\frac{221}{400}$, $\frac{223}{400}$**
    c. How many fractions are between $\frac{11}{20}$ and $\frac{14}{25}$? Explain your reasoning.

34. Explain the origin of the word *hieroglyphics*.
    From Greek, *Hier* means "sacred or holy"; *glyphen* means "to carve."

10

Adapting to Individual Needs

English Language Development
To help students remember the word *variable*, explain that *vary* means to change. Write the following sentence on the board: "_____ is sitting at my desk." Then demonstrate the term by having several students take turns sitting at your desk. For each instance, write the name of the person sitting at the desk in the sentence. Explain that only the names change; the names are the variables in the sentence.

Setting-Up Lesson 1-2

Homework Have students read and answer all the questions in Lesson 1-2. Or have them answer only the questions on *Covering the Reading* and then do the remainder of the questions in class. For more information on homework, see *General Teaching Suggestions: Homework* in the *Professional Sourcebook* which begins on page T20 of the Teacher's Edition.

Materials For **Question 36** in Lesson 1-2, students will probably need unabridged dictionaries.

*Sets and
Domains*

One for the records. *In 1992, Carol Moseley-Braun of Chicago, Illinois, became the first African-American woman to be elected to the United States Senate. She was sworn in by Vice President Dan Quayle in the presence of Senator George Mitchell.*

What Is a Set?

A **set** is a collection of objects called **elements** or **members.** Usually the elements are grouped for a purpose.

Name of set	Name of member
herd of dairy cattle	cow
team	player
committee	member
the U.S. Senate	senator
class	student
deck (of cards)	card

A set often has properties different from those of its members. For example, a team in baseball can win the World Series, but a player cannot. The Senate can pass legislation, but a senator cannot. A card might be a king, but a deck is not.

The standard symbols used for a set are braces { . . . }, with commas used to separate the elements. Sets are often named with letters. For instance, when Lulu, Mike, Nell, Oscar, Paula, and Quincy are the six members of a committee, you could call the committee *C* and write

$$C = \{\text{Lulu, Mike, Nell, Oscar, Paula, Quincy}\}.$$

The order of naming elements in a set makes no difference. {Oscar, Mike, Lulu, Nell, Paula, Quincy} is the same committee *C*. Two sets are **equal** if and only if they have the same elements.

Lesson 1-2 *Sets and Domains* **11**

Lesson 1-2

Objectives
E Read and interpret set language and notation.
I In real situations, choose a reasonable domain for a variable.
L Draw and interpret graphs of solution sets to inequalities.

Resources
From the **Teacher's Resource File**
■ Lesson Master 1-2A or 1-2B
■ Answer Master 1-2
■ Teaching Aids
  1 Warm-up
  4 Real Numbers
  5 Number Lines

Additional Resources
■ Visuals for Teaching Aids 1, 4, 5
■ Unabridged dictionaries (Question 36)

Teaching
Lesson 1-2

Warm-up
You can use the *Warm-up*, or the *Additional Examples* on page 13, as questions for students to work on as you begin class.

Discribe each set of numbers. The three dots mean that the pattern continues. **Sample answers are given.**
1. {1, 3, 5, 7, 9, . . . } **The set of odd whole numbers**
2. {1, 3, 5, 7, 9} **The set of odd whole numbers less than 10**
3. {0, 1, 4, 9, 16, 25, . . . } **The set of squares of whole numbers**
(Warm-up continues on page 12.)

Lesson 1-2 Overview

Broad Goals There are three broad goals in this lesson: (1) to review the graphing of inequalities and to differentiate between graphs that are discrete and those that are continuous; (2) to show that the domain of a variable makes a difference in the solution; (3) to review the names of commonly used number systems.

Perspective Many algebra textbooks have dropped the topic of sets. Why have we

chosen to include it, and why so early in this course? First, to understand the concept of variable, some notion of the possible values it may take is needed; sets provide a convenient language for describing these values. Second, we have found that the vocabulary of sets enhances our explanations and development of major ideas, such as those in probability and systems. Third, the formal notation of sets, particularly with intersection and union (to be discussed in

Lesson 1-3), provides contrast to the operations of addition and multiplication. We do not develop a formal algebra of sets in this book, but many of the properties of addition and multiplication, which may seem trite to students, usually have a less obvious counterpart in union and intersection.

4. {2, 3, 5, 7, 11, . . .} The set of prime numbers

5. { . . . –3, –2, –1, 0, 1, 2, 3, . . .} The set of integers

Notes on Reading

Students who have studied *Transition Mathematics* will be familiar with graphs of single inequalities. But those who have studied from other texts may not be familiar with them. Choosing a reasonable domain for a variable will likely be new for all students. Neither of these concepts is easy for beginning algebra students.

Teaching Aid 5, which contains number lines for graphing, can be used throughout this lesson.

❶ We do not denote these sets by letters, such as *W* for the set of whole numbers, because students might think that these letters are variables. Also, there is a very limited need for them in this course.

We do not use the term *subset* but you may find it helpful. We also do not mention the set of natural numbers; they are usually defined as {1, 2, 3, . . .}.

❷ We use the term *solution set* in this lesson, but we do not write solutions in set-builder notation {*x*: . . . }; at this time there is no need to be formal.

❸ You may want to point out that the sets of whole numbers and of integers are *discrete;* the set of real numbers is *continuous.* Also, while a discrete graph is made of individual dots, a continuous set can be graphed without lifting the pencil from the paper.

Frequently Used Sets of Numbers

The following sets are frequently used in arithmetic and algebra.

❶

Name of Set	Description	Examples of Elements
whole numbers	{0, 1, 2, 3, . . . }	five, $\frac{16}{2}$, 1995, 7 million
integers	{0, 1, –1, 2, –2, . . . }, the whole numbers and their opposites	$\frac{21}{3}$, –17.00, negative one thousand
real numbers	the set of all numbers that can be represented as terminating or non-terminating decimals	5, 0, π, –0.0042, $-3\frac{1}{3}$, $0.\overline{13}$, $\sqrt{2}$, one hundred thousand

Notice that all whole numbers are also integers, and all integers are also real numbers.

❷ **Domains of Variables**

All the values that *may* be meaningfully substituted for a variable make up the **domain** of the variable. The three sets mentioned above are often used as domains for variables. The **solution set** of an open sentence is the set of numbers from the domain that actually are solutions.

Solution sets for inequalities are often pictured on a number line. Notice how the domain can affect a solution set.

❸ **Example 1**

Graph all solutions to $x < 9$ when the domain of x is the indicated set.
a. whole numbers **b.** integers **c.** real numbers

Solution

a. The set of whole-number solutions is {0, 1, 2, 3, 4, 5, 6, 7, 8}. Draw a number line, label it with the variable x, and plot these points.

b. The solutions include those in part **a,** and all negative integers as well.

The larger arrow to the left of –2 means "and so on."

c. The solutions include all those in part **b,** and all other decimals less than 9. For instance, 7.3, 8.9, and 8.99 are also solutions. To show all solutions, draw a solid line through all points to the left of 9. Draw an open circle at 9 to indicate that 9 is not a solution.

12

Visual Organizer

Students might benefit from using this visual organizer to help them classify numbers. This chart is shown on **Teaching Aid 4.**

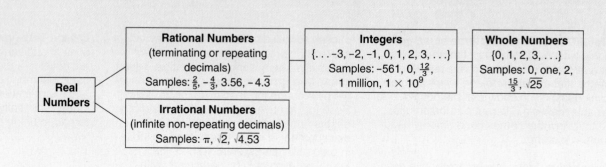

Choosing a Reasonable Domain

When solving real problems, you often must decide what domain makes sense for a situation.

Example 2

Let x = the number of people at a meeting.
a. Name a reasonable domain for x.
b. Assume there are more than 15 people at the meeting, and write an algebraic sentence using x.
c. Graph the solution set to part **b**.

Solution

a. Since x is a count of the number of people at the meeting, it does not make sense to have x be a fraction or a negative number. It *does* make sense for x to be any positive whole number or 0. **The domain for x is the set of whole numbers.**
b. $x > 15$
c. You must show all the whole numbers greater than 15. Each element in the solution set is marked with a dot on the number line. The dots are not connected because the numbers between these whole numbers are not in the domain of the variable.

In the next example, the variable can be any real number between two whole numbers. The graph is no longer a set of separate or *discrete* dots; it is connected.

Example 3

Let w = the weight of a meat roast.
a. Give a reasonable domain for w.
b. The roast weighs less than six pounds. Write this as an inequality using w.
c. Graph the solution set to part **b**.

Solution

a. The roast can weigh a fraction of a pound, but not a negative number. So, **The domain could be the set of positive real numbers.**
b. Here are two conditions: $w > 0$ (the weight must be positive), and $w < 6$. The two inequalities can be written as one: $0 < w < 6$. This is read "w is greater than 0 and less than 6."
c. You need to show all real numbers between 0 and 6, but not including 0 or 6. The graph is shown below.

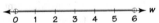

Lesson 1-2 *Sets and Domains* **13**

Preparing tomorrow's leaders. These students are participating in a mock legislative session held in the state senate chamber in Austin, Texas.

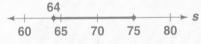
Optional Activities

Activity 1 After discussing **Example 3**, you might give students these formulas and have them describe a reasonable domain for each.
1. $P = 4s$, where P is the perimeter of a square with side s [The domain for s is the set of positive real numbers.]
2. $A = \frac{h}{t}$, where A is the batting average of a person with h hits in t times at bat [The domain for both h and t is the set of whole numbers.]
3. $C = \frac{5}{9}(F - 32)$, where C is degrees Celsius and F is degrees Fahrenheit [The domain for F is the set of real numbers.]
4. $V = e^3$, where V is the volume of a cube with edges of length e [The domain for e is the set of positive real numbers.]

13

Question 7 Error Alert Some
students will look at the number and
see it only as a real number. Remind
students that it is the number itself
that determines whether or not it is a
whole number, an integer, or a real
number. It is not how a number is
written. The Roman numeral III and
the Hindu-Arabic $\frac{6}{2}$ may not look like
integers, but they are.

Question 9 Zero poses problems of
classification for many students; it is
a whole number, an integer, and a
real number.

Multicultural Connection Many
ancient numeration systems were
incomplete because they lacked a
symbol for zero. The Mayas developed the concept of zero before
300 A.D. The Hindus also developed
the concept, but it was not until the
13th century that Hindu-Arabic
numerals were adopted, along with
zero, in Europe.

Question 10 Students who need a
review of scientific notation should
refer to Appendix B.

Intervals

The solution set in Example 3 is called an *interval*. An **interval** is a set of numbers between two numbers a and b, possibly including a, or b, or both a and b. The numbers a and b are called the **endpoints** of the interval. The interval $0 < w < 6$ is called an **open interval** because it does not include the endpoints. This is pictured on the graph by the open circles at 0 and 6. The interval $0 \le w \le 6$ is called a **closed interval** because its endpoints are included. An interval that includes one endpoint and not the other is neither open nor closed.

The table below shows four types of intervals. Notice how for each interval the inequality, graph, and verbal description describe the same set.

Interval	Inequality	Graph	Verbal Description
Open	$0 < w < 6$	(number line 0–6, open circles at 0 and 6) → w	all real numbers between 0 and 6
Closed	$0 \le w \le 6$	(number line 0–6, closed circles at 0 and 6) → w	all real numbers from 0 to 6
Neither open nor closed	$0 < w \le 6$	(number line 0–6, open circle at 0, closed at 6) → w	all positive real numbers less than or equal to 6
Neither open nor closed	$0 \le w < 6$	(number line 0–6, closed circle at 0, open at 6) → w	all non-negative real numbers less than 6

QUESTIONS

Covering the Reading

1. What are the objects in a set called? elements or members

In 2–4, a set and an element are given. Name another element in the set.

2. set: family; element: mother Samples: brother, father

3. set: {2, 11, -6}; element: 11 -6 or 2

4. set of real numbers; element: 2 Samples: $\sqrt{6}, \frac{3}{4}, -1.34$

5. Which of the following sets are equal? A and B
   $A = \{2, 0, -5\}$ $B = \{-5, 2, 0\}$ $C = \{-5, 2\}$

6a) no; b) yes; c) yes

7a) yes; b) yes; c) yes

8a) no; b) no; c) yes

9a) yes; b) yes; c) yes

10a) yes; b) yes; c) yes

11a) no; b) no; c) yes

In 6–11, a number is given. See left.
a. Is the number a whole number?
b. Is the number an integer?
c. Is the number a real number?

6. -10   7. $\frac{6}{2}$ 8. 0.5

9. 0   10. 3.6×10^9 11. 47.3928

14

Optional Activities

Activity 2 Geography Connection
Materials: Atlas or almanac

As an extension of **Question 24**, ask students to answer the same questions for
another country of their choosing. You might
have them identify the highest and lowest
elevations of each country on a world map.

Adapting to Individual Needs

Extra Help
Materials: **Teaching Aid 4**

Have each student write a fraction, a decimal, a negative number, and a number with
a radical symbol. Then have them **work in
groups** and classify each number using the
Visual Organizer on **Teaching Aid 4.**

In 12–14, graph the solutions to the sentence for each of the following domains: **a.** set of whole numbers; **b.** set of integers; **c.** set of real numbers. **See margin.**

12. $n < 3$ **13.** $n \geq 3$ **14.** $5 < x$

Multiple choice. In 15 and 16, which is the most reasonable domain for the variable?

(a) set of whole numbers (b) set of integers
(c) set of real numbers (d) set of positive real numbers

15. n = the number of performers at a piano recital (a)

16. t = the time in minutes to prepare a meal (d)

17. Let ℓ = the length of a sauropod. **See margin.**
  a. Give a reasonable domain for ℓ.
  b. Lengths of fully-grown sauropods (dinosaurs) ranged from about 23 m to 46 m. Write this fact as an algebraic sentence involving ℓ.
  c. Graph the solution set to part **b.**

In 18 and 19, a sentence and a domain are given.
a. Graph the solution set on a number line.
b. Tell whether the interval graphed is open, closed, or neither.

18. $2 < x < 9$, where x is a real number. **a)** [number line: 1 2 3 4 5 6 7 8 9 10, open circles at 2 and 9] **x**
b) open

19. $-7 < x \leq -3$, where x is a real number. **a)** [number line: -8 -7 -6 -5 -4 -3 -2, open at -7, closed at -3] **x**
b) neither

Applying the Mathematics

20. Let S be the solution set for the sentence $-8 < y < 8$. Graph S if y has the indicated domain. **See below.**
  a. the set of whole numbers **b.** the set of integers

21a) closed **b)** x is greater than or equal to zero and
In 21–23, an interval is graphed. less than or equal to ten. **c)** $0 \leq x \leq 10$
  a. Tell whether the interval is open, closed, or neither. **22a) open**
  b. Describe the set in words. **b)** y is greater
  c. Write an inequality to describe the interval. than negative
three and less
than four.

21. [number line: 0 to 10, closed dots at 0 and 10] **x** **c)** $-3 < y < 4$

22. [number line: -3, 0, 4, open circles at -3 and 4] **y** **23a) neither**
open nor closed
b) z is greater

23. [number line: -10, -4, 0, closed dot at -10, open circle at -4] **z** than or equal to
negative ten
and less than

24. Let E = the elevation of a place in the United States. negative four.
  a. Give a reasonable domain for E. **all real numbers** **c)** $-10 \leq z < -4$
  b. Elevations in the U.S. range from 86 meters below sea level (in Death Valley) to 6194 meters above sea level (at the top of Mt. McKinley). Write a sentence involving E. $-86 \leq E \leq 6194$
  c. Graph the solution set to part **b.** [number line: -86 to 6194] **E**

25. Using $\{3, 4, 6, 9\}$ as the domain for t, find the solution set of $5t + 2 > 23$. $\{6, 9\}$

20a) [number line: 0 1 2 3 4 5 6 7 8] **y** **b)** [number line: -8 -6 -4 -2 0 2 4 6 8] **y**

Lesson 1-2 *Sets and Domains* **15**

The super sauropods.
Called the "largest dinosaur ever found," sauropods were huge plant eaters during the late Jurrasic period, 152 million years ago. Shown above is archeologist, Jim Jensen, standing next to a reconstruction of a sauropod leg that is 6 meters tall.

15

Question 26 Science Connection
The boiling point of water is 100°C at sea level, but it is less than that at higher altitudes. Interested students might investigate the boiling point of water at other altitudes.

✎ **Question 37 Writing** With open-ended questions such as this one, it is usually productive to have students volunteer to read what they have written. Students may have some very interesting sets.

Follow-up for Lesson 1-2

Practice

For more questions on SPUR Objectives, use **Lesson Master 1-2A** (shown on page 13) or **Lesson Master 1-2B** (shown on pages 14–15).

Assessment

Written Communication Have students write a paragraph that explains how they can tell whether an interval is open, closed, or neither open nor closed. Then have them draw an example of an open interval, a closed interval, and an interval that is neither open nor closed. [Students can distinguish between open and closed intervals.]

Extension

Questions 21–23 are designed to help students make connections between symbolic, verbal, and graphic representations. You might ask students to describe real situations corresponding to each of these graphs. [Sample answers: **21.** The brochures cost $10 or less, and some of them are free. **22.** It was warmer than –3° today, but it was colder than 4°. **23.** During the week the river was always more than 4 feet below flood stage. At its lowest point, it was 10 feet below flood stage.]

Review

26. At sea level, water is steam at all temperatures greater than 100°C. Write an inequality describing this situation.   *(Lesson 1-1)* $t > 100$

27. Write a different inequality with the same meaning as $-15 < y$. *(Lesson 1-1)* $y > -15$

In 28 and 29, find all solutions.   *(Lesson 1-1)*

28. $x^2 = 16$ $x = 4$ or -4 　　　　29. $16^2 = x$ $x = 256$

30. Find the sum without using a calculator.   *(Previous course)*
    a. $-5 + -9$ -14 　　**b.** $-5 + 9$ 4 　　**c.** $5 + -9$ -4

In 31–34, evaluate each of the following without a calculator. *(Previous course)*

31. $3 \cdot -5$ -15 　　32. $4 \cdot -10$ -40 　　33. $5 \cdot -70$ -350 　　34. $-8 \cdot -25$ 200

35. For its grand opening, Harold's Electronics gave away pens to customers. The cost of the pens was $70.00 per day. What was the cost of pens for five days?   *(Previous course)* $350

Exploration

36. Collections of animals frequently are given special names. Match the group name with the correct animal as in "school of fish."

DENNIS THE MENACE

"THIS WEEK WE'RE STUDYING REAL DEEP STUFF, LIKE: A BUNCH OF SHEEP IS A FLOCK ... AND A FLOCK OF FLOWERS IS A BUNCH."

Group name	Animal
cloud gnats	ants
colony ants	bees
exaltation larks	crows
gaggle geese	fish
hive bees	foxes
leap leopards	geese
mob kangaroos	gnats
nest crows	kangaroos
pride lions	larks
school fish	leopards
skulk foxes	lions
watch nightingales	nightingales
yoke oxen	oxen

37. Name three sets outside of mathematics that are not mentioned in this lesson. For each, indicate what an element is usually called.
Samples: society, citizen; club, member; faculty, teacher

16

Adapting to Individual Needs

English Language Development
Suggest that students who are learning the English language get a set of index cards and start a file of new words. Suggest that they write each new word or phrase on a different card and include a definition in their own words and an illustration, if appropriate. For this lesson, you might explain the terms shown in bold: *set, equal sets, domain, solution set, open interval,* and *closed interval.*

Setting Up Lesson 1-3

Homework If students have read Lessons 1-1 and 1-2 aloud in class, you might want to have them read Lesson 1-3 to themselves. Then, in class, ask them to work with a partner on **Questions 1–8.**

Materials For Lesson 1-3, you might want students to have **Geometry Templates** for drawing Venn diagrams and colored pencils or pens for coloring the diagrams.

LESSON 1-3

Operations with Sets

Safety first! *Safety Village, in Clearwater, Florida, is a permanent miniature town. Children in primary grades take field trips there to learn safety skills. For example, children are taught how to walk safely as they cross an intersection.*

Intersection of Sets

A police report of an accident stated that "the car was in the intersection of Main and Oak Streets when it was struck by a truck." The intersection, the region where the streets overlap, is shaded in the map at the right. Since the car was in the intersection, it was in both Main Street and Oak Street.

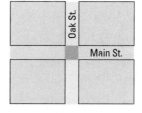

The term *intersection* has a similar meaning when used with sets.

Intersection of Sets

The **intersection** of sets A and B, written $A \cap B$, is the set of elements that are in both A and B.

Example 1

Let $A = \{1, 3, 5, 7, 9, 11\}$ and $B = \{1, 4, 7, 10\}$. Give the intersection of A and B.

Solution

The elements that are in both A and B are 1 and 7.

$A \cap B = \{1, 7\}$.

Lesson 1-3 *Operations with Sets* **17**

Objectives
B Find unions and intersections.
E Read and interpret set language and notation.
L Draw and interpret graphs of solution sets to inequalities.

Resources
From the **Teacher's Resource File**
■ Lesson Master 1-3A or 1-3B
■ Answer Master 1-3
■ Assessment Sourcebook: Quiz for Lessons 1-1 through 1-3
■ Teaching Aids
 1 Warm-up
 5 Number Lines
 6 Number-Line Jeopardy (Optional Activities)
■ Activity Kit, Activity 1

Additional Resources
■ Visuals for Teaching Aids 1, 5, 6
■ Geometry Templates (optional)
■ Colored pens or pencils (optional)

Teaching Lesson 1-3

Warm-up
The *Warm-up* or the *Additional Examples* can be given to students as you begin class.

Diagnostic Let A = the set of people whose first *and* last names begin with a vowel and B = the set of people whose first *or* last name begins with a vowel.
1. Name at least one person in each set. If you cannot think of anyone, make up a name.
 Responses will vary.

(*Warm-up continues on page 18.*)

Lesson 1-3 Overview

Broad Goals The operations of union and intersection are used to find solution sets which are represented on number lines and in Venn diagrams. The empty set is introduced.

Perspective Union and intersection of sets are usually not difficult for students. For union, we use the analogy of intersecting streets. Points in the *intersection* are on one street *and* the other. Points in the *union* are on one street *or* the other.

The symbols for union and intersection are easy for students to remember, since the union symbol looks like the letter U.

Note that the graph of $\{x: a \le x \le b\}$ on the number line is the intersection of $\{x: x \ge a\}$ and $\{x: x \le b\}$. Geometrically, the segment is the intersection of two rays. Similarly, an angle in geometry is the union of two rays with a common endpoint.

Optional Activities

Activity 1 You can use *Activity Kit, Activity 1,* to introduce this lesson. In the activity, students investigate union and intersection of sets illustrated with Venn diagrams.

2. Which set do you think will have more members. Why? Set *B* because all members of Set *A* are also members of Set *B*.

Notes on Reading

If you have had students read aloud in class for the past two lessons, we suggest that you have them read this lesson silently. Ask students to skim the first two pages of the lesson to find the names of the two operations with sets. Then ask them to silently read the sections on intersection of sets and union of sets. After they have read these sections, ask them to **work with a partner** to answer **Questions 1–8.** Students can check their answers to the odd-numbered questions with the answers in the back of the book. A brief class discussion can lead to a consensus among students on the answers to the even-numbered questions. You might ask students to describe in their own words, either orally or in writing, the meanings of intersection and union. Also ask them to make up some examples that illustrate these operations with sets.

When students draw Venn diagrams, they can either make their circles freehand or use the **Geometry Templates.** You may wish to use **Teaching Aid 5** when discussing **Examples 4–5** and the *Additional Examples.*

❶ Emphasize the main idea of intersection and union—that the intersection of sets consists of the elements in common and that the union of sets involves joining or putting sets together. To help students understand the meaning of union and intersection of sets, stress that ∪ and ∩ are symbols of operations just as + is the symbol for adding. When operating on sets, the answer is a set just as the sum of two numbers is a number.

Relations between sets can be illustrated by *Venn diagrams,* named after John Venn (1834–1923), an English mathematician who used these diagrams in his work. In a Venn diagram, each set is represented by a circle or other closed figure. In the Venn diagram below, the elements of set *A* from Example 1 are in the circle labeled *A.* The elements of set *B* are in the circle labeled *B.* Overlapping parts of figures represent the intersection of sets. $A \cap B$ is represented by the green overlap.

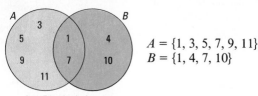

$A = \{1, 3, 5, 7, 9, 11\}$
$B = \{1, 4, 7, 10\}$

$A \cap B$ is shaded green.

Union of Sets

A second operation used with sets is *union.* The symbol for union looks like the letter U.

 Union of Sets
The **union** of sets *A* and *B,* written $A \cup B$, is the set of elements in either *A* or *B* (or in both).

Contrast the definition of union with that of intersection. The key word for intersection is "and"; the key word for union is "or." Notice that the union of two sets is not just the result of "putting them together." Elements are not repeated if they are in both sets.

Example 2

Let $A = \{1, 3, 5, 7, 9, 11\}$ and $B = \{1, 4, 7, 10\}$ as in Example 1.
a. Find $A \cup B$.
b. Make a Venn diagram of the two sets and shade the union.

Solution

a. The union is the set of elements in one set or the other or both.
$\{1, 3, 5, 7, 9, 11\} \cup \{1, 4, 7, 10\} = \{1, 3, 5, 7, 9, 11, 4, 10\}$.
Notice that the elements 1 and 7 are in both sets, but they are written only once in the union.

b.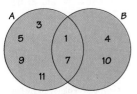

$A \cup B$ is shaded.

18

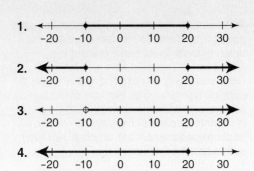

There is a set that has no elements in it. It is called the **empty set**, or **null set.** The symbol { } or the Danish letter ø can be used to refer to this set. The empty set might refer to many things, including,

the set of whole numbers between 11 and 12;
the set of U.S. presidents under 35 years of age;
the set of all living dinosaurs.

Example 3

Let E = the set of even integers and
O = the set of odd integers. Find $E \cap O$.

Solution

$E = \{\ldots, -6, -4, -2, 0, 2, 4, 6, \ldots\}$ and
$O = \{\ldots, -5, -3, -1, 1, 3, 5, \ldots\}$.
No integer is both odd and even.
❷ $E \cap O = \{\ \}$.

Graphs of Intersections and Unions

Parts of the number line can be described as the graph of the intersection or union of two sets.

Example 4

Graph the set of all numbers s such that $s > -2$ or $s \leq -10$.

❸ **Solution**

The word "or" in the above sentence indicates that you must find the union of the solution set to $s > -2$ and the solution set to $s \leq -10$. Draw the graph of $s > -2$.

Draw the graph of $s \leq -10$.

The union includes all points that satisfy either sentence or both sentences. It is:

❷ **Error Alert** The empty set is introduced in **Example 3.** Make sure students are aware that {ø} is not an acceptable symbol for the empty set.

❸ In **Examples 4 – 5,** we show three number lines because we think this helps beginning algebra students to organize their work. However, you will eventually want students to work on one number line. Students can use pencils of three different colors, one for each of the given inequalities and one for the answer.

Different colored pens are also effective when using an overhead projector. If you show the graph of $s > -2$ in red and the graph of $s \leq 5$ in blue, the intersection will be purple.

Additional Examples

For 1–2, let A = the set of whole numbers less than or equal to 10 and B = the set of positive even numbers less than or equal to 10.
1. **a.** Find $A \cap B$. {0, 2, 4, 6, 8, 10}
    b. Draw a Venn diagram of the sets and shade the intersection.

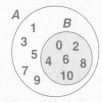

(Additional Examples continue on page 20.)

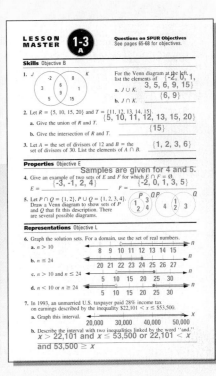

Adapting to Individual Needs

Extra Help
Write these sets on the board:
Household pets: P = {cat, dog, fish, canary}
Barnyard pets: B = {cat, dog, cow, horse, pig}

Ask if there are any animals in both sets, and if so, which ones? [Yes; cat, dog] Draw two intersecting circles on the board; label one P and the other B. Ask a student to shade and write "cat" and "dog" in the inter-

section of the circles. Explain that the shaded region shows the intersection of the sets. Now have students name the animals in set P that are not yet shown and write their names in the appropriate area. Similarly complete set B.

You might repeat the activity for two sets that have no members in common and for sets in which all the members of one set are members of the other set.

2. **a.** Find $A \cup B$. {0, 1, 2, 3, 4, 5, 6, 7, 8, 9, 10}
   b. Draw a Venn diagram to illustrate the sets and shade the union.

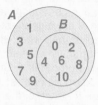

3. Give an example of two sets whose intersection is the empty set. **Sample: the set of multiples of 6 and the set of prime numbers**

For 4–5, graph the solution set. Use the set of real numbers as the domain.

4. Let M = the solution set for $x \geq -3$, and N = the solution set for $x \leq 5$.
   a. Graph $M \cap N$.

-4 -3 -2 -1 0 1 2 3 4 5 6

   b. Describe $M \cap N$ with a single inequality. $-3 \leq x \leq 5$

5. Graph the set of all numbers x where $x \geq -3$ or $x \leq 5$. **The graph is all points on the real number line.**

6. The label on a paint can says, "For best results, do not use if the temperature is above 90° or below 50°."
   a. Use an inequality to describe each interval in which you should not paint. $x < 50$ or $x > 90$

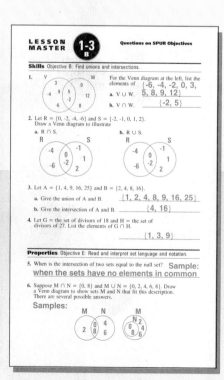

Example 5

A family wants to bake a casserole and muffins at the same time. The casserole recipe calls for an oven temperature of 325° to 375°. The muffins can bake at any temperature from 350° to 400°.
a. Describe each of the two intervals with an inequality.
b. Graph the intervals in part **a**, and describe their intersection with an inequality.
c. What temperature settings are right for both the casserole and muffins?

Solution

a. Let t be the oven temperature. Then for the casserole, $325 \leq t \leq 375$, and for the muffins, $350 \leq t \leq 400$.

b. First graph the solution to each inequality separately. It helps to line up the scales on the two number lines.

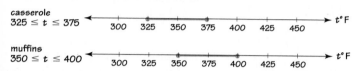

casserole
$325 \leq t \leq 375$
300 325 350 375 400 425 450 $t°F$

muffins
$350 \leq t \leq 400$
300 325 350 375 400 425 450 $t°F$

The intersection is that part of the number line where the two graphs overlap.

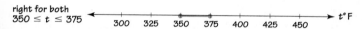

right for both
$350 \leq t \leq 375$
300 325 350 375 400 425 450 $t°F$

c. Temperature settings from 350° to 375° are right for both the casserole and muffins.

QUESTIONS

Covering the Reading

1. Define: *intersection* of two sets. **The intersection of sets A and B is the set of elements that are in both A and B.**
2. Define: *union* of two sets. **The union of sets A and B is the set of elements in either A or B or both.**
   In 3 and 4, let A = {2, 4, 6, 8, 10} and B = {3, 6, 9, 12, 15}.
3. Give the intersection of A and B. {6}
4. Find the union of A and B. {2, 3, 4, 6, 8, 9, 10, 12, 15}
   In 5 and 6, suppose R = {2, 5, 6, 11, 13} and S = {3, 4, 5, 6, 7}. Draw a Venn diagram to illustrate the set. **See left.**
5. $R \cap S$
6. $R \cup S$
7. **a.** What does ø represent? **null set or empty set**
   b. Give an example of a set equal to ø.
   Sample: whole numbers less than zero

5) R   2   3   S
   11   5
   13   6   4
        7

6) R   2   3   S
   11   5
   13   6   4
        7

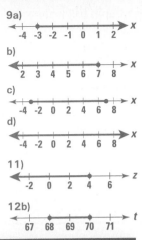

9a)

$\overset{\text{-4 -3 -2 -1 0 1 2}}{\xrightarrow{\hspace{3cm}}} x$

b)

$\overset{\text{2 3 4 5 6 7 8}}{\xleftrightarrow{\hspace{3cm}}} x$

c)

$\overset{\text{-4 -2 0 2 4 6 8}}{\xrightarrow{\hspace{3cm}}} x$

d)

$\overset{\text{-4 -2 0 2 4 6 8}}{\xleftrightarrow{\hspace{3cm}}} x$

11)

$\overset{\text{-2 0 2 4 6}}{\xleftrightarrow{\hspace{3cm}}} z$

12b)

$\overset{\text{67 68 69 70 71}}{\xleftrightarrow{\hspace{3cm}}} t$

A glimpse of Africa.
The National Museum of African Art in Washington, D.C., is the first museum in the U.S. devoted to the collection and exhibition of African art. As part of the Smithsonian Institution, admission is always free.

---

8. Suppose W = the set of whole numbers less than 5, and X = the set of whole numbers greater than 5 and less than 10. List the elements of each set.
- **a.** W {0, 1, 2, 3, 4}
- **b.** X {6, 7, 8, 9}
- **c.** $W \cup X$
  {0, 1, 2, 3, 4, 6, 7, 8, 9}
- **d.** $W \cap X$ { } or ø

9. Graph the solution sets. Use the set of real numbers for the domain.
- **a.** $x \geq -3$
- **b.** $x \leq 7$ See left.
- **c.** $x \geq -3$ and $x \leq 7$
- **d.** $x \geq -3$ or $x \leq 7$

10. Match the sentence at the left with its graph at the right.

- **a.** $y < -8$ or $y > 2$ I

  I $\xleftarrow{\hspace{1cm}\overset{\circ}{-8}\hspace{1cm}\overset{\circ}{2}\hspace{1cm}} y$

- **b.** $y < -8$ or $y < 2$ III

  II $\xleftarrow{\hspace{1cm}\overset{\circ}{-8}\hspace{1cm}\overset{\circ}{2}\hspace{1cm}} y$

- **c.** $y > -8$ and $y < 2$ II

  III $\xleftarrow{\hspace{1cm}\overset{}{-8}\hspace{1cm}\overset{\circ}{2}\hspace{1cm}} y$

11. Graph the set of all numbers z such that $z < -2$ or $z \leq 4$.
See left.

12. During the winter months, Mrs. King is comfortable with indoor temperatures of 68°F to 75°F. Mr. King is comfortable at temperatures of 65°F to 70°F. a) Mrs. King: $68 \leq t \leq 75$;   Mr. King: $65 \leq t \leq 70$
- **a.** Write each person's comfort zone as an inequality.
- **b.** Graph the temperatures that are comfortable for both Mr. and Mrs. King. See left.
- **c.** Write the set in part **b** as an inequality, and tell how it is related to the sets in part **a.** $68 \leq t \leq 70$;   It is the intersection of the sets in part a.

Applying the Mathematics

13. Let E = the set of odd numbers from 1 to 10.
Let F = the set of all multiples of 3 between 1 and 10.
Describe each set.
- **a.** $E \cap F$ {3, 9}
- **b.** $E \cup F$ {1, 3, 5, 6, 7, 9}

14. Let S = the solution set for $x^2 = 16$,
and T = the solution set for $x + 2 = 16$.
List the elements of each set.
- **a.** $S \cup T$ {-4, 4, 14}
- **b.** $S \cap T$ { } or ø

15. Graph the ages for which admission to a museum is free under the following rule: You will get in free if you are younger than 5 or a senior citizen (62 or older).

$\xleftarrow{\hspace{0.3cm}\overset{\circ}{\hspace{0.1cm}}\text{0 1 2 3 4 5}\hspace{0.8cm}\text{62 64}} a$

---

b. Graph the temperatures in which you should not paint. Then graph the recommended temperatures for painting, and describe them with an inequality.

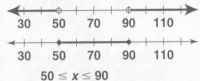

$\overset{\text{30 50 70 90 110}}{\xleftrightarrow{\hspace{4cm}}}$

$\overset{\text{30 50 70 90 110}}{\xleftrightarrow{\hspace{4cm}}}$

$50 \leq x \leq 90$

c. What temperatures are recommended for painting? Temperatures from 50° to 90°

Notes on Questions

You might want to let students use **Teaching Aid 5** for questions that require number-line graphs.

Questions 5–6 We tend to not draw graphs of solution sets that are finite. However, it is possible to graph these sets. You may want to do so and to show that both the Venn diagrams and number-line graphs represent the same sets.

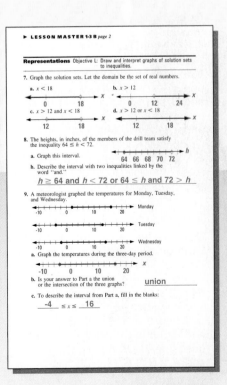

Adapting to Individual Needs

Challenge
Explain that if every member of set B is a member of set A, then B is called a *subset* of A. Point out that every set is a subset of itself and the empty set is a subset of every set. For example, if S = {a, b}, the subsets are {a}, {b}, {a, b}, and { }. Then have students answer the following questions.
1. Find all the possible subsets of set T if T = {a, b, c}. [{a, b, c}, {a, b}, {a, c}, {b, c}, {a}, {b}, {c}, { }]

2. Complete the table shown below.

Number of members in set	1	2	3	4
Number of subsets	[2]	[4]	[8]	[16]

3. Describe the pattern. [Sample: If a set has n members, there are 2^n subsets.]

Question 16 This is the first question involving operations with more than two sets. After introducing the use of parentheses in Lesson 1-4, students will have review questions involving both intersection and union.

Sports Connection Greg LeMond was the first American to win the *Tour de France,* a bicycle race that takes the contestants through 2,000 miles of French countryside. Interested students might investigate bicycle racing and give a short report to the class on how and why racers ride in packs, and how they use the wind to ride faster.

Questions 22–23 These questions are included for two reasons. First, they encourage students to look for patterns. Second, the patterns themselves justify the rules for multiplying integers, a skill we assume students have mastered before entering this course.

Follow-up for Lesson 1-3

Practice

For more questions on SPUR Objectives, use **Lesson Master 1-3A** (shown on page 19) or **Lesson Master 1-3B** (shown on pages 20–21).

Assessment

Quiz A quiz covering Lessons 1-1 through 1-3 is provided in the *Assessment Sourcebook.*

Oral Communication Have students describe two sets of people, *A* and *B,* so that the students would be members of *A* ∩ *B*. Then ask them to describe two sets, *C* and *D,* for which they would be members of *C* ∪ *D,* but not members of *C* ∩ *D*. [Students distinguish between union and intersection of sets.]

Extension

Cooperative Learning Have students **work in groups**. Tell each group to describe three sets and name them sets *A, B,* and *C*. Then have them draw a Venn diagram showing the sets. Have them describe *A* ∪ *B, A* ∪ *C, B* ∪ *C,* and *A* ∪ *B* ∪ *C*. Then have them describe *A* ∩ *B, A* ∩ *C, B* ∩ *C,* and *A* ∩ *B* ∩ *C*.

22

16. An outing club is planning a bicycle trip. The graphs below show the number of kilometers three people want to cycle per day.

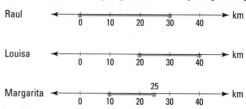

a. Draw a graph showing the distances that would be acceptable to all three. **See left.**
b. How is the graph in part **a** related to the graphs above?
The graph in part a shows the intersection of the three sets graphed above.

Review

17. Consider $Z < \frac{8}{3}$. Graph the solution set if Z has the given domain. *(Lesson 1-2)* **See left.**
   a. set of whole numbers   **b.** set of real numbers

18. Name an integer that
   a. is a whole number;   **b.** is not a whole number.
       Sample: 1   *(Lesson 1-2)*   Sample: -1

In 19–21, *true or false.* *(Lessons 1-1, 1-2)*

19. The number 13.23×10^5 is a whole number. **True**

20. $-0.125 < -0.1$ **True**

21. The number 7 is a solution to $7 \geq n$. **True**

In 22 and 23, fill in the blanks. Describe the patterns you see. *(Previous course)* **Patterns may vary.**

22.		**23.**	
$5 \cdot 3 = 15$		$-4 \cdot 3 = -12$	
$5 \cdot 2 = 10$		$-4 \cdot 2 = -8$	
$5 \cdot 1 = 5$		$-4 \cdot 1 = -4$	
$5 \cdot 0 = 0$		$-4 \cdot 0 = 0$	
$5 \cdot -1 = \underline{?}$	-5	$-4 \cdot -1 = \underline{?}$	4
$5 \cdot -2 = \underline{?}$	-10	$-4 \cdot -2 = \underline{?}$	8
$5 \cdot -3 = \underline{?}$	-15	$-4 \cdot -3 = \underline{?}$	12

Sample pattern $5 \cdot (-n) = -(5 \cdot n)$ Sample pattern $-4 \cdot (n) = -(4 \cdot n)$

Exploration

24. Is it possible to have sets *A* and *B* with *A* ∩ *B* having more elements than *A* ∪ *B*? Explain why or why not. **No; the intersection of sets A and B contains only those elements common to both sets, while the union of the sets contains all the elements in either set or both sets.**

Setting Up Lesson 1-4

Materials Beginning with Lesson 1-4, students will need to have calculators available. See *General Teaching Suggestions: Calculators* in the *Professional Sourcebook* which begins on page T20 in Part 1 of the Teacher's Edition for our calculator recommendations.

Previewing the Reading Tell students that they are expected to have calculators with them when they read the lesson and that

they should do the activities in the lesson before doing the questions.

Homework If you plan to give a quiz over Lessons 1-1 through 1-3 in the next class period, you may wish to assign only *Covering the Reading.*

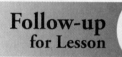

16a)

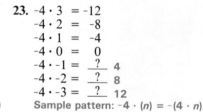

17a)

b)

LESSON 1-4

Variables in Expressions

Algebra uses the same symbols for numerical operations as arithmetic does, but with one exception. In algebra, multiplication is signified by either a raised dot or by putting two expressions next to each other with no symbol between. So "3 times x" is written either as $3 \cdot x$ or $3x$, and "5 times $(A + B)$" is written $5 \cdot (A + B)$ or $5(A + B)$.

Evaluating Expressions

Numerical expressions, like $6 + 3^2 - 1$, combine numbers only. An expression, such as $4 + 3x$, that includes one or more variables is called an **algebraic expression.** Expressions are not sentences because they do not contain verbs, such as equal or inequality signs. Finding the numerical value of an expression is called **evaluating** the expression. To evaluate an algebraic expression, you must have values to substitute for its variables. When evaluating any expression, you must do operations in the following order.

Order of Operations in Evaluating Expressions
1. Do operations within parentheses or other grouping symbols.
2. Within grouping symbols, or if there are no grouping symbols:
   a. Do all powers from left to right.
   b. Do all multiplications and divisions from left to right.
   c. Do all additions and subtractions from left to right.

Example 1

a. Evaluate $4 + 3x$ when $x = 9$.   **b.** Evaluate $4 + 3x$ when $x = -1$.

Solution

a. Let $x = 9$.   Then $4 + 3x = 4 + 3 \cdot 9$ Substitute 9 for x.
$\qquad\qquad\qquad\qquad\quad = 4 + 27$ Multiply first.
$\qquad\qquad\qquad\qquad\quad = 31$ Add.

b. Let $x = -1$.   Then $4 + 3x = 4 + 3 \cdot -1$ Substitute -1 for x.
$\qquad\qquad\qquad\qquad\quad = 4 + -3$
$\qquad\qquad\qquad\qquad\quad = 1$

Lesson 1-4

Objectives
C Evaluate numerical and algebraic expressions.

Resources
From the Teacher's Resource File
■ Lesson Master 1-4A or 1-4B
■ Answer Master 1-4
■ Teaching Aid 2: Warm-up

Additional Resources
■ Visual for Teaching Aid 2

Teaching 1-4
Lesson

Warm-up
You can use the *Warm-up*, or the *Additional Examples* on page 25, as questions for students to work on as you begin class.

Diagnostic Put $+$, $-$, $\times$, or $\div$ in the blanks below. You do not have to use every symbol, and you may not use any symbol more than once. Following the order of operations, what is the smallest number you can make?
$8 \_ 1 \_ 6 \_ 4$ $-16; 8 \div 1 - 6 \times 4$

Notes on Reading

Reading Mathematics Stress that students should analyze reading material that involves simplifying or evaluating expressions to see what is being done, why it is allowed, and what it achieves. When reading calculator key sequences, students should take out their calculators and press the indicated keys to verify what they have read. Whether students read this lesson on their own

---

Lesson 1-4 Overview

Broad Goals This lesson reviews the order of operations in algebraic expressions, which we assume students have seen in prior courses. The order of operations is the same in expressions written with paper and pencil, in most calculator key sequences, and in BASIC computer programs.

Perspective The need to have clear meanings for algebraic expressions is motivation

enough to have rules for order of operations. But the use of calculators and computers emphasizes this need because calculators and computers do not sort out the context or the particular preference of the user. For this reason, scientific calculator key sequences and expressions from BASIC computer programs are employed to illustrate and motivate the order of operations.

While the standard order of operations was originally a matter of choice, it is now part of the universal grammar of mathematics, and it is used throughout the world. Not all computer languages use the standard order of operations; however, the most widely used languages, such as FORTRAN, COBOL, Pascal, Logo, and BASIC, do use them.

or in class, encourage them to check the answers to **Examples 1–4** using their calculators. Some graphics calculators use the same symbol for powering, ⎡∧⎤, as is used in BASIC.

Make sure students understand that there is no priority between multiplication and division; they are done in the order they appear as you move from left to right. The same holds true for addition and subtraction.

The expressions in **Example 1** should be an easy review for students. Expressions like those in **Example 2** are often more difficult. In **part a,** the order of operations implies $7n^3$ means $7 \cdot n^3$. Because powers take precedence over multiplication, the exponent applies only to the n. In **part b,** the parentheses in $(7n)^3$ indicate that multiplication will be done before the powering.

❶ The placement of two symbols next to each other is called *juxtaposition*. This is the first example in this book in which juxtaposition is used to indicate multiplication. It is important that students realize that $3(4x - 5)$ means $3 \cdot (4x - 5)$. In denoting numbers in base 10, juxtaposition has a different meaning; that is, 32 does not mean 3 times 2.

You can count on them.
The first mechanical calculating device was the abacus. The first true mechanical calculator was an adding machine invented by Blaise Pascal in 1642. Today's advanced, scientific calculators perform many functions that are useful to people in all walks of life.

Example 2

a. If $n = 2$, find $7n^3$.   **b.** If $n = 2$, calculate $(7n)^3$.

Solution

a. Substitute 2 for n. There are no grouping symbols, so do the power before the multiplication.
$$7 \cdot 2^3 = 7 \cdot 8 = 56$$

b. Substitute 2 for n. Do the operation within the parentheses first.
$$(7 \cdot 2)^3 = 14^3 = 2744$$

Most scientific calculators use the same order of operations as algebra. Examples 1 and 2 could have been done with a calculator. Check Examples 1 and 2 using a calculator. (If you have never used a scientific calculator, see Appendix A.)

Example 1a: 4 ⎡+⎤ 3 ⎡×⎤ 9 ⎡=⎤ ⎡ 31 ⎤

Example 2a: 7 ⎡×⎤ 2 ⎡yˣ⎤ 3 ⎡=⎤ ⎡ 56 ⎤

Example 3

Evaluate $\frac{5(A + B)}{2}$, when $A = 3.4$ and $B = 7.2$.

Solution

Substitute 3.4 for A and 7.2 for B.

Then $\frac{5(A + B)}{2} = \frac{5(3.4 + 7.2)}{2}$ Work inside the parentheses.

$= \frac{5(10.6)}{2}$ The fraction bar is a grouping symbol, so work with the numerator and denominator separately. $5(10.6)$ means $5 \cdot 10.6$. Multiply.

$= \frac{53}{2}$

$= 26.5$

Computer programs and graphing calculators also use algebraic expressions, but the expressions must be in a language the computer understands. Most computer languages use the order of operations listed on page 23. In **BASIC** (Beginner's All-purpose Symbolic Instruction Code), + is used for addition, − for subtraction, * for multiplication, / for division, ^ for powering, and ( ) for grouping. Usually the symbol for *every* operation must be shown. So, in BASIC, $5(A + B)$ is written $5 * (A + B)$. The power 2^3 is written $2 \wedge 3$.

❶ **Example 4**

Write $3(4x - 5) + y$ in BASIC.

Solution

Use * for the multiplications and capital letters for the variables.
$$3 * (4 * X - 5) + Y$$

24

24

Optional Activities

Materials: Scientific and nonscientific calculators

Before discussing **Example 3,** you might have students evaluate expressions using calculators. Write "$4 + 3 \cdot 9$" on the board, and have students enter the numbers and operations in the order given on both scientific and nonscientific calculators. Discuss the two possible answers—31 and 63. Then ask students how they would enter each of

the following computations on a nonscientific calculator to get the correct answer.

1. $3 \times 5 + 4 \times 8$ [Sample: 3 ⎡×⎤ 5 ⎡=⎤ ⎡M+⎤ 4 ⎡×⎤ 8 ⎡=⎤ ⎡+⎤ ⎡MRC⎤ ⎡=⎤; display: 47]

2. $6 + 3^2$ [Sample: 3 ⎡×⎤ 3 ⎡+⎤ 6 ⎡=⎤; display: 15]

3. $\frac{4 \cdot 12}{2 + 4}$ [Sample: 2 ⎡+⎤ 4 ⎡=⎤ ⎡M+⎤ 4 ⎡×⎤ 12 ⎡=⎤ ⎡÷⎤ ⎡MRC⎤ ⎡=⎤; display: 8]

With most calculators and computer software, you must input fractions on one line. Then you must include grouping symbols. For instance, to evaluate $\frac{10 + 4}{2 + 5}$, you must enter $(10 + 4) / (2 + 5)$ to get the correct answer, 2. If you enter $10 + 4 / 2 + 5$, the machine will follow order of operations, do the division first, and get 17.

Example 5

What would you input in order to use a calculator or computer to evaluate $\left(\frac{x + 10.7}{y + 4}\right)^7$ when $x = 3.1$ and $y = 0.6$?

Solution

The computer expression is written $((X + 10.7) / (Y + 4)) \wedge 7$. Substitute for each variable and input

$$((3.1 + 10.7) / (0.6 + 4)) \wedge 7.$$

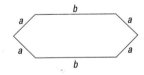

PCs. *In 1975, the world's first personal computer was introduced. PCs became popular around 1977 when smaller size and lower-cost models became available. Tomorrow's computers will undoubtedly be smaller, faster, and more powerful than today's models.*

QUESTIONS

Covering the Reading

In 1–3, identify each expression as numerical or algebraic.

1. $\frac{8(7) + 2}{12}$ numerical
2. $\frac{2x}{4 - 8}$ algebraic
3. $a^2 + b^2$ algebraic

In 4–9, evaluate.

4. $12 - 2 \cdot 4$ 4
5. $5^2 + 2^2$ 29
6. $(5 + 2)^2$ 49
7. $3(10 - 6)^3 + 15$ 207
8. $5 - \frac{4}{8}$ $4\frac{1}{2}$
9. $15 + \frac{9}{3} - 6$ 12

In 10–13, evaluate the expression for the given values of the variables.

10. $5m^2$ when $m = 3$ 45
11. $(5m)^2$ when $m = 3$ 225
12. $(-1 + r)^3$ when $r = 3$ 8
13. $\frac{a + 2b}{5}$ when $a = 11.6$ and $b = 9.2$ 6

14. **a.** Write a BASIC expression to evaluate $0.5H(A + H)$ when $H = 32$ and $A = 0.7$.   0.5 * 32 * (0.7 + 32)
    b. Evaluate the expression.   523.2

15. What would you input in order to use a computer to evaluate $\left(\frac{7x + y}{x - 6y}\right)^4$? $((7 * X + Y) / (X - 6 * Y)) \wedge 4$

Applying the Mathematics

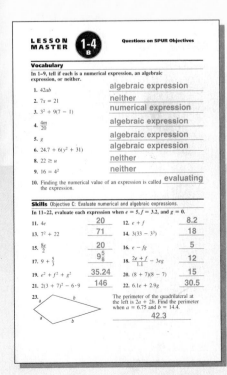

16. The perimeter of the hexagon at the left is $4a + 2b$. Find the perimeter when $a = 10$ mm and $b = 35$ mm.   110 mm

17. Evaluate $3x^2 - 9x + 6 - 3(x - 1)(x - 2)$ when $x = 10$.   0

18. Evaluate $6 + (5 - (4 + (3 - 2)))$.   6

Lesson 1-4   *Variables in Expressions*   **25**

Additional Examples

1. Evaluate $5y + 6$ when
   a. $y = 3$.   21
   b. $y = 0.2$.   7
2. Let $n = 3$. Evaluate
   a. $2n^4$.   162
   b. $(2n)^4$.   1296
3. Evaluate $\frac{4(A - B)}{5}$ when
   $A = 6.3$ and $B = 4.7$.   1.28
4. Write $pr^2 + 2prh$ in BASIC.
   P*R^2 + 2*P*R*H
5. **a.** Write a key sequence for your calculator or computer to evaluate $\left(\frac{13.5 + 5.7}{7.9 + 9.1}\right)^4$.
   Samples:
   ((13.5 + 5.7) ÷
   (7.9 + 9.1)) y^x 4
   =, $((13.5 + 5.7) / (7.9 + 9.1)) \wedge 4$
   b. Evaluate the expression in **part a.** ≈ 1.627

Notes on Questions

Questions 10–11 You might ask students if $5m^2$ is less than $(5m)^2$ for all values of m. [No; the expressions are equal when $m = 0$.]

Question 16 Ask students why the perimeter is $4a + 2b$. Note that $4a + 2b$ is short for $4 \cdot a + 2 \cdot b$ and that both multiplications are done before the addition.

Practice

For more questions on SPUR Objectives, use **Lesson Master 1-4A** (shown on page 24) or **Lesson Master 1-4B** (shown on pages 25–26).

Assessment

Oral/Written Communication Ask students to explain why it is necessary for everyone to use the same order of operations when evaluating expressions. Have each student write an example of an expression that has more than one value when the operations are performed in different orders. [Students recognize and use the rules for order of operations and can explain why these rules are necessary.]

Extension

Project Update If you have not had students look over the projects on pages 60–61, you might want to do so now. Project 2, *Order of Operations,* on page 60, relates to the content of this lesson. Students who chose to do this project can begin their letters.

Three generations of flight. *The Wright brothers' first airplane reached a maximum speed of 30 mph during its first flight in 1903. In 1928, a Boeing 80-A airplane began passenger service between Chicago and San Francisco. It cruised at 125 mph with a full load of 14 passengers. In 1970, the first jumbo jet, the Boeing 747 was introduced. With a full capacity of 490 passengers, it cruises at speeds over 625 mph.*

In 19 and 20, use this information. If you go somewhere at an average speed g, and come back at an average speed c, then your average speed for the trip is $\frac{2gc}{g + c}$.

19. Find the average speed for the trip if you bike somewhere averaging 12 mph but then bike back averaging 10 mph. ≈ **10.9 mph**

20. Find the average speed for the trip if a plane averages 800 kilometers per hour going from A to B with a tailwind, but only 700 kilometers per hour going from B to A due to a headwind. ≈ **747 km/h**

Review

21. Let P = the set of prime numbers and E = the set of even numbers. List all the elements of $P \cap E$. *(Lesson 1-3, Previous course)* {2}

22. Consider the interval $-4 \le y \le 6$. *(Lessons 1-2, 1-3)*
    a. Tell whether it is open, closed, or neither open nor closed. **closed**
    b. Describe the interval as the intersection of two other sets.
       The interval is the intersection of $-4 \le y$ and $y \le 6$.

23. A person makes more than $1800 a month. Let d be the amount made.
    a. What inequality describes this situation? *(Lesson 1-1)* $d > 1800$
    b. Graph the inequality. *(Lesson 1-2)*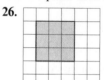
       1600   1800   2000

24. Compute in your head. *(Previous course)*
    a. $7 \cdot -8$ **-56**   b. $-7 \cdot 8$ **-56**   c. $-7 \cdot -8$ **56**

25. Molly has three and three-eighths yards of ribbon. If she uses half of it to make a bow, how much ribbon does she use? *(Previous course)* $1\frac{11}{16}$ yd

In 26 and 27, a square is shaded. **a.** Find the area of the square, using ☐ as one square unit. **b.** Explain how you got your answer. *(Previous course)*

26.
    a) 9 sq units
    b) Sample: three rows multiplied by three columns

27.
    a) 8 sq units
    b) 4 complete squares plus 8 half-squares equal 8.

Exploration

28. **a.** Evaluate these expressions:
    1 **1**
    $2 - 1$ **1**
    $3 - (2 - 1)$ **2**

    $4 - (3 - (2 - 1))$ **2**
    $5 - (4 - (3 - (2 - 1)))$ **3**
    $6 - (5 - (4 - (3 - (2 - 1))))$ **3**

    b. What patterns do you notice? The pattern of answers is 1, 1, 2, 2, 3, 3, 4, 4, 5, 5, ...
    c. What would you predict the value of
    $10 - (9 - (8 - (7 - (6 - (5 - (4 - (3 - (2 - 1)))))))))$ to be? **5**
    Why? Find its value. Was your prediction correct?
    It follows the pattern described in part b; yes.

26

Adapting to Individual Needs

English Language Development
You might have students read algebraic and numerical expressions aloud to help them relate parentheses with the phrase "the quantity" and powers of 2 and 3 with the phrases "squared" and "cubed." As students read, listen for the correct use of phrases such as "the sum of" and "the product of."

Setting Up Lesson 1-5

Materials If you use the *Assessment* on page 30, students will need the section of a newspaper that shows high and low Fahrenheit temperatures for various cities.

LESSON 1-5

Variables in Formulas

On a roll. *Bowling is one of the most popular indoor sports. About 64 million Americans enjoy this sport each year. When bowlers bowl in a league, they are often given a handicap to help balance the differences in past performances.*

A **formula** is an equation in which one variable is given in terms of other variables or numbers. Formulas are used in many real-life situations. You can evaluate any formula by substituting numbers for the variables.

A Formula Involving Two Variables

In bowling, 300 is a perfect score, and 200 is considered very good. In some leagues, bowlers whose average score is under 200 have *handicaps* added to their score. Example 1 shows a formula for finding a handicap.

Example 1

The handicap H of a bowler whose average is A is often found by using the formula $H = .8(200 - A)$. A bowler's final score for a game is the actual score plus the bowler's handicap.
a. Tony's average score is 145. What is his handicap?
b. What would Tony's final score be if he actually bowled 120?
c. What happens when an average greater than 200 is substituted for A?

Solution

a. Substitute 145 for A in the formula and follow the order of operations.
$$H = .8(200 - 145)$$
$$= .8(55)$$
$$= 44$$

Tony's handicap is 44.

b. Add the handicap to the actual score. Tony's final score is
$$120 + 44 = 164.$$

c. When the average is greater than 200, then 200 − A is negative. Thus averages over 200 are not used in the formula. The domain of A is the set of whole numbers less than or equal to 200.

Objectives
J Evaluate formulas in real situations.

Resources
From the *Teacher's Resource File*
- Lesson Master 1-5A or 1-5B
- Answer Master 1-5
- Teaching Aid 2: Warm-up
- Technology Sourcebook Computer Master 1

Additional Resources
- Visual for Teaching Aid 2
- Newspaper listing Fahrenheit temperatures for various cities (Assessment)

Teaching Lesson 1-5

Warm-up
The *Warm-up* or the *Additional Examples* can be given to students as you begin class.

✎ **Writing** Write a formula that you remember learning at another time. Explain in writing what the formula is about and give an example of its use. **Answers will vary.**

Notes on Reading
Multicultural Connection Bowling is one of the oldest sports. One form existed in Egypt as far back as 5200 B.C. Ancient Polynesians played a game that involved rolling balls at flat discs. The balls were rolled 60 feet, the length of a modern bowling alley. Bowling was also developed by American Indians.

Lesson 1-5 Overview

Broad Goals The rules for order of operations are applied in a wide variety of formulas in this lesson. The goals are twofold: to provide examples of the power of algebra and to reinforce the earlier work with algebraic expressions.

Perspective Formulas are one of the most commonly used mathematical tools of everyday life. The examples and questions show several realistic applications.

Calculators free us from being limited to problems with "nice," but artificial, numbers. With computers, huge numbers of values can be quickly calculated.

The formula in **Example 2** is quite complicated for this stage of the students' study of algebra, but the substitutions are not beyond students' abilities. Variables as unknowns in equations, as x in $50 = 4x$, have a mysterious quality that is not present

when variables are in formulas relating to familiar ideas. Thus, students can understand formulas involving expressions that are more complicated than any equations they might be able to solve.

A conscious effort is made throughout this book to discuss, introduce, and review ideas from geometry. You will notice several geometric formulas in this lesson.

1. If a car is traveling at r miles per hour and the brakes are applied, the car will take approximately d feet to stop, where $d = r + \frac{r^2}{20}$.
   a. What is the approximate braking distance for a car traveling 50 miles per hour? **175 feet**
   b. In one second, a car traveling 50 miles per hour will go about 73 feet. If a driver's reaction time (the time between realizing the brakes must be applied and applying them) is 0.5 second, about how many feet will a car going 50 mph travel before it stops? **About 212 feet**

2. Many high schools calculate students' grade-point averages on a scale in which an A is worth 4 points, a B is worth 3 points, a C is worth 2 points, a D is worth 1 point, and an F is worth 0 points. If a student gets As in m classes, Bs in n classes, Cs in r classes, Ds in s classes, and Fs in t classes, then the student's grade-point average g is:

$$g = \frac{4m + 3n + 2r + s}{m + n + r + s + t}.$$

Find the grade-point average of a student who got two As, one B, and three Cs. **2.83**

The equation $H = .8(200 - A)$ is called a *formula for H in terms of A*. We also say that *H depends on A*.

A Formula Involving Four Variables

Almost everyone has been in heavy traffic. Perhaps you have been in a traffic jam on your way to an amusement park, a sports event, or a concert. Have you ever wondered how many cars are on a given road? City planners and traffic safety engineers must be able to estimate the number of cars on roads to make decisions about road construction, speed limits, and safety improvements.

An estimate of the number of cars can be calculated using the formula below. Here N is the estimated maximum number of cars allowable on a road if the cars are traveling at safe distances from one another.

$$N = \frac{20Ld}{600 + s^2}$$

L = number of lanes of road
d = length of road (in feet)
s = average speed of the cars (in miles per hour)

This formula was derived by using principles from geometry and physics. In the formula, we say that N is given *in terms of L, d,* and *s*. We also say that N *depends on L, d,* and *s*. You can find N by substituting numbers for each of the other variables.

Example 2

Use the above formula to estimate the maximum number of cars there can safely be on a 1-mile stretch of a 2-lane highway, if the cars are traveling an average speed of 30 miles per hour.

Solution

Determine the value of each variable. Note that the length of the road is given in miles but the formula requires feet. Recall 5280 feet = 1 mile.

$$L = 2 \text{ lanes}$$
$$d = 1 \text{ mile} = 5280 \text{ feet}$$
$$s = 30 \text{ miles per hour}$$

Write the formula.

$$N = \frac{20Ld}{600 + s^2}$$

Replace the variables in the formula with their values.

$$N = \frac{20 \cdot 2 \cdot 5280}{600 + 30^2}$$

Evaluate this expression using the order of operations. A calculator can help. Here is a typical key sequence. Notice that you need parentheses to group the numbers in the denominator.

20 [×] 2 [×] 5280 [÷] [(] 600 [+] 30 [x²] [)] [=]

$$N = 140.8$$

There can be about 140 cars on the road.

Optional Activities

Technology Connection You might want to assign *Technology Sourcebook, Computer Master 1*. Students use a spreadsheet to find the maximum volume possible for a box formed by cutting squares from the corners of a sheet of paper and folding up the sides. Before assigning this master, show students how to enter text, numbers, and formulas on a spreadsheet.

Often formulas give values so large that a computer or calculator must display the result in scientific notation. For instance, the volume of Earth can be approximated using the formula $V = \frac{4}{3}\pi r^3$, with the radius $r \approx 8000$ miles. One calculator displays the result as 2.1447 12. Another displays 2.14466 E12. This stands for $2.14466 \cdot 10^{12}$, or 2,144,660,000,000. (To review scientific notation, see Appendix B.)

QUESTIONS

Covering the Reading

1. The opener for Chapter 1 on page 5 shows a formula known to Egyptians over 3500 years ago. What is this formula? $A = \ell w$

In 2–4, refer to Example 1.

2. Debra's bowling average is 120. What is her handicap? 64

3. *Multiple choice.* Which average does not entitle a bowler to a handicap?
   (a) 95   (b) 145   (c) 195   (d) 205   (d)

4. Substitute 200 for A in the handicap formula. Explain what you get.
   You get 0; the handicap of a 200 bowler is 0.

In 5–7, use the formula preceding Example 2, page 28.

5. In this formula, N is given in terms of which variables? L, d, and s

6. About how many cars can safely be on a 2-mile stretch of a 3-lane highway if the average speed of the cars is 50 mph? ≈ 204 cars

7. About how many cars can safely be on a 1.5-mile part of a 4-lane highway if the average speed of the cars is 20 mph? ≈ 633 cars

8. Use $V = \frac{4}{3}\pi r^3$ to estimate the volume of the planet Jupiter, whose radius is about 142,000 km. Write your answer in scientific notation. $\approx 1.20 \times 10^{16}$ km³

Applying the Mathematics

9. The circumference C of a circle with diameter d is given by the formula $C = \pi d$. To the nearest centimeter, what is the circumference of a circle with diameter 7.3 cm? 23 cm

In 10–12, note that some crickets, such as the Snowy Tree Cricket, chirp at a regular rate. You can estimate the Fahrenheit temperature T by counting the number of chirps C a cricket makes in one minute, and applying the formula
$$T = \tfrac{1}{4}C + 37.$$

10. What is a reasonable domain for C? whole numbers

11. A cricket chirps 200 times per minute. Estimate the temperature. 87°F

12. Estimate the temperature when a cricket chirps 150 times per minute. 74.5°F

Lesson 1-5   *Variables in Formulas*   **29**

Something worth chirping about. *In many countries, the presence of a cricket is a sign of good luck. In the Orient, crickets are caged for their songs and are kept as pets.*

Notes on Questions
Questions 10–12 If you are in a region where there are crickets, students can test the formula.

Multicultural Connection Children in Florence, Italy, have a cricket festival each spring; they catch the crickets and put them in tiny decorated cages. After parading with their crickets through a park along the Arno River, the children hang the cages outside their bedroom windows, hoping the crickets will sing. When the festival is over, the crickets are set free. Crickets are used in many different ways in eastern Asia. Some are fried and eaten and some are kept as pets because their songs are pleasant to hear.

(Notes on Questions continue on page 30.)

Follow-up for Lesson 1-5

Practice
For more questions on SPUR Objectives, use **Lesson Master 1-5A** (shown on page 28) or **Lesson Master 1-5B** (shown on pages 29–30).

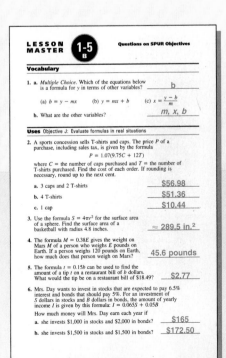

LESSON MASTER 1-5 B   Questions on SPUR Objectives

Vocabulary

1. a. *Multiple Choice.* Which of the equations below is a formula for y in terms of other variables?   b
   (a) $b = y - mx$ (b) $y = mx + b$ (c) $x = \frac{y - b}{m}$
   b. What are the other variables? m, x, b

Uses Objective J: Evaluate formulas in real situations

2. A sports concession sells T-shirts and caps. The price P of a purchase, including sales tax, is given by the formula
   $$P = 1.07(9.75C + 12T)$$
   where C = the number of caps purchased and T = the number of T-shirts purchased. Find the cost of each order. If rounding is necessary, round up to the next cent.
   a. 3 caps and 2 T-shirts $56.98
   b. 4 T-shirts $51.36
   c. 1 cap $10.44

3. Use the formula $S = 4\pi r^2$ for the surface area of a sphere. Find the surface area of a basketball with radius 4.8 inches. ≈ 289.5 in.²

4. The formula $M = 0.38E$ gives the weight on Mars M of a person who weighs E pounds on Earth. If a person weighs 120 pounds on Earth, how much does that person weigh on Mars?   45.6 pounds

5. The formula $t = 0.15b$ can be used to find the amount of a tip t on a restaurant bill of b dollars. What would the tip be on a restaurant bill of $18.49? $2.77

6. Mrs. Day wants to invest in stocks that are expected to pay 6.5% interest and bonds that should pay 5%. For an investment of S dollars in stocks and B dollars in bonds, the amount of yearly income I is given by this formula: $I = 0.065S + 0.05B$. How much money will Mrs. Day earn each year if
   a. she invests $1,000 in stocks and $2,000 in bonds? $165
   b. she invests $1,500 in stocks and $1,500 in bonds? $172.50

Adapting to Individual Needs

Extra Help
You might use familiar formulas, such as those below, to help students see what the variables represent.
1. $A = \ell w$ [The area of a rectangle (A) equals length (ℓ) times width (w).]
2. $P = 2\ell + 2w$ [The perimeter of a rectangle (P) equals 2 times the length (ℓ) plus 2 times the width (w).]
3. $C = \pi d$ [The circumference of a circle (C) equals pi (π) times the diameter (d).]

English Language Development
While students with limited English proficiency may understand the formulas, they may have difficulty identifying what each variable represents. Using colored chalk, write C in red and d in blue in the formula $C = \pi d$. Draw a circle labeling the two parts in the formula with their respective colors. Have students use colored pencils to copy the formula and color coding onto an index card. Repeat for other formulas.

Group Assessment

Materials: Newspaper with Fahrenheit temperatures for various cities

Have students **work in groups.** Tell each student to select the high and low Fahrenheit temperatures for one city. Then have them use the formula $C = \frac{5}{9}(F - 32)$ to convert the temperatures into degrees Celsius. Students should check one another's work. [Students demonstrate an ability to evaluate formulas.]

Extension

Cooperative Learning As an extension of *Additional Example 1,* have students **work in groups** and find the braking distance for cars traveling 10, 20, 30, and so on, up to 100 miles per hour. Then have them make a poster to display the information. [10 mph, 15 ft; 20 mph, 40 ft; 30 mph, 75 ft; 40 mph, 120 ft; 50 mph, 175 ft; 60 mph, 240 ft; 70 mph, 315 ft; 80 mph, 400 ft; 90 mph, 495 ft; 100 mph, 600 ft]

Project Update Project 4, *Formulas,* on page 60, relates to the content of this lesson.

Notes on Questions

Question 20 Students might be interested to know that in 1988, Hideaki Tomoyori, a 55-year-old man from Japan, recited from memory the first 40,000 digits of pi in 17 hours and 20 minutes.

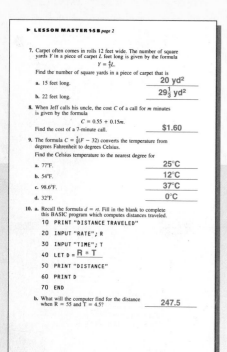

Taking a break from the books. *Albert Einstein, world-renowned physicist, was fond of classical music, played the violin, and enjoyed taking his bicycle out for a spin.*

► LESSON MASTER 1-5 B *page 2*

7. Carpet often comes in rolls 12 feet wide. The number of square yards Y in a piece of carpet L feet long is given by the formula
$$Y = \tfrac{4}{3}L.$$
Find the number of square yards in a piece of carpet that is
a. 15 feet long. ___20 yd²___
b. 22 feet long. ___$29\frac{1}{3}$ yd²___

8. When Jeff calls his uncle, the cost C of a call for m minutes is given by the formula
$$C = 0.55 + 0.15m.$$
Find the cost of a 7-minute call. ___$1.60___

9. The formula $C = \frac{5}{9}(F - 32)$ converts the temperature from degrees Fahrenheit to degrees Celsius.
Find the Celsius temperature to the nearest degree for
a. 77°F. ___25°C___
b. 54°F. ___12°C___
c. 98.6°F. ___37°C___
d. 32°F. ___0°C___

10. a. Recall the formula $d = rt$. Fill in the blank to complete this BASIC program which computes distances traveled.
```
10 PRINT "DISTANCE TRAVELED"
20 INPUT "RATE"; R
30 INPUT "TIME"; T
40 LET D = R * T
50 PRINT "DISTANCE"
60 PRINT D
70 END
```
b. What will the computer find for the distance when R = 55 and T = 4.5? ___247.5___

---

13. **a.** Fill in the blanks to complete this BASIC program which computes area and perimeter of rectangles.

```
10 PRINT "AREA AND PERIMETER OF A RECTANGLE"
20 INPUT "LENGTH"; L
30 INPUT "WIDTH"; W
40 LET A = _?_  L * W
50 LET P = _?_  2 * L + 2 * W
60 PRINT "AREA", "PERIMETER"
70 PRINT A, P
80 END
```

b. What will the computer find for the area and perimeter when L = 52.5 and W = 38? **area = 1995; perimeter = 181**

Review

14. Evaluate $77x - (29x + 2)$ when $x = 8$. *(Lesson 1-4)* **382**

15. Give the BASIC symbol for each operation. *(Lesson 1-4)*
 a. addition + **b.** division / **c.** multiplication * **d.** powering ^

16. Write $\left(\dfrac{3}{y + 2}\right)^{10}$ in the BASIC language. *(Lesson 1-4)* **(3/(Y + 2))^10**

17. The graph below is the union of the solution sets to what two inequalities? *(Lesson 1-3)* **$q < -36, q > 12$**

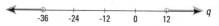

18. Graph all solutions to $4 < x \le 10$ when
 a. x is the length of a table (in feet);
 b. x is the number of sticks in a package of chewing gum. *(Lesson 1-2)*

19. Give an example of each. *(Lesson 1-2)*
 a. a whole number that is not positive **0**
 b. an integer that is not a whole number **Sample: -1**
 c. a real number that is not an integer **Sample: $\frac{1}{2}$**

20. Round π to the nearest hundred-thousandth. *(Previous course)* **3.14159**

21. A recipe for a cake that serves 12 people calls for $3\frac{1}{2}$ cups of flour. If you wish to halve the recipe to make the cake for 6 people, how much flour will you need? *(Previous course)* **$1\frac{3}{4}$ cups**

Exploration

22. One of the world's most famous formulas was discovered by Albert Einstein in 1905. It is $E = mc^2$. **a) energy, mass of an object, speed of**
 a. What do E, m, and c stand for? **light**
 b. What physical phenomenon does the formula describe?
 the relationship between the mass of an object and the energy it contains

30

Adapting to Individual Needs

Challenge Sports Connection

As an extension of **Example 1**, interested students might learn how to score a bowling game. Then give them the number of pins for 10 frames, such as those below, and have them score the game.

Frame	1	2	3	4	5	6	7	8	9	10
Ball 1	6	4	5	10	7	9	8	5	10	4
Ball 2	3	6	2	—	2	1	1	5	—	5

[9] [24] [31] [50] [59] [77] [86] [106] [125] [134]

"A wonderful square root. Let us hope it can be used for the good of mankind."

What Are Square Roots?

The term *square root* comes from the geometry of squares and their sides. Pictured below are squares with sides of lengths 4 and 4.5 units.

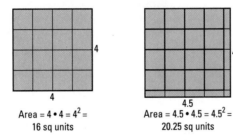

Area = 4 • 4 = 4^2 =
16 sq units

Area = 4.5 • 4.5 = 4.5^2 =
20.25 sq units

Because $16 = 4^2$, we say that 4 is a square root of 16. Similarly, 20.25 is the square of 4.5, so 4.5 is the square root of 20.25. In general, if $A = s^2$, then s is called a **square root** of A.

The symbol for square root, $\sqrt{}$, is called a radical sign. From the above, $\sqrt{16} = 4$ and $\sqrt{20.25} = 4.5$. Thus, if the area of a square is A, the length of a side is $\sqrt{A}$.

$\sqrt{A}$ Area = A

length of side = $\sqrt{A}$

Lesson **1-6**

Objectives

C Evaluate numerical and algebraic expressions.
D Evaluate square roots with and without a calculator.
F Use the Square of the Square Root Property.

Resources

From the *Teacher's Resource File*
- Lesson Master 1-6A or 1-6B
- Answer Master 1-6
- Assessment Sourcebook: Quiz for Lessons 1-4 through 1-6
- Teaching Aids
  2 Warm-up
  7 Squares and Square Roots (Question 11)
- Technology Sourcebook Calculator Master 1

Additional Resources
- Visuals for Teaching Aids 2, 7

Teaching
Lesson **1-6**

Warm-up

Diagnostic
1. Find the area of a square with sides 5 cm long. **25 cm²**
2. Find the length of a side of a square whose area is 36 cm². **6 cm**
3. Find the area of a square with sides $\sqrt{11}$ cm long. **11 cm²**
4. Find the length of a side of a square whose area is 7 cm². $\sqrt{7}$ **cm, or about 2.6 cm**

Lesson 1-6 Overview

Broad Goals Various aspects of the understanding of square roots are introduced in this lesson: (1) the skill of calculating them; (2) the property $\sqrt{n} \cdot \sqrt{n} = n$; (3) their use and representation involving the area and the side of a square. We strive for an intuitive approach rather than a mechanical one. Using calculators to give decimal approximations for roots helps students to develop a "feel" for them.

Perspective Square roots are introduced early in this book for three reasons. First, the idea of square root is a relatively difficult one for students. It takes time to develop a good understanding of the concept. Second, some evaluations with square roots force the issue of order of operations. Third, we wish to prepare students to use the Pythagorean Theorem, which is covered in Lesson 1-8.

It takes quite a bit of experience for students to fully understand that $\sqrt{17}$ is not a number that is close to 17, but one that is approximately 4. You will find questions throughout the rest of the chapter that ask students to find the whole number to which a given square root is closer; these questions should be done without a calculator.

Notes on Reading

❶ Stress that $\sqrt{a^2 + b^2}$ does not simplify to $a + b$. Here is the reason: In an expression like $\sqrt{a^2 + b^2}$, the radical sign is technically the $\sqrt{}$. The horizontal bar connected to the radical sign is a grouping symbol just like the horizontal bar in a fraction. The bar is called a *vinculum*, from the Latin word *vincula*, which means "to bind." In some places in the world, the expression would be written $\sqrt{(a^2 + b^2)}$. Because the bar next to a radical symbol acts as a grouping symbol, by the rules for order of operations, computations under the bar must be done before the root is taken.

Calculator Students must get a "feel" for the magnitude of square roots. The calculator is a valuable tool for this, particularly when a square root is embedded in an expression. Spend a few minutes discussing the key sequences for using a calculator to do **Example 2.**

Since students will be using their calculators to find square roots, you might point out that the square root key on many scientific calculators gives the square root of the value currently displayed. To illustrate this point, you might want to have students evaluate $\sqrt{144 + 25}$ with their calculators. On many scientific calculators, the key sequence

144 ⊕ 25 √x͏ ⊜ will give a

wrong answer of 149. However, ⦅

144 ⊕ 25 ⦆ √x͏ or 144 ⊕ 25

⊜ √x͏ will give the correct

answer. On a graphics calculator, the typical key sequence is √x͏ ⦅ 144

⊕ 25 ⦆, followed by pressing the enter key.

❷ $\sqrt{n} \cdot \sqrt{n}$ can be written as $(\sqrt{n})^2$, so $\sqrt{n} \cdot \sqrt{n} = n$. Although this property follows from the definition of square root, it is difficult for some students to understand. They are not accustomed to reasoning from symbols whose values they do not know. This property is used in **Example 4** in multiplying $4\sqrt{10} \cdot \sqrt{10}$. You might ask: What do we know about $\sqrt{10}$ from its definition? Look for the answer $(\sqrt{10})^2 = 10$. Use the answer to illustrate that $\sqrt{10} \cdot \sqrt{10} = 10$.

32

Example 1

The area of a square is 196 in². Give the length of a side:
a. using a radical symbol;
b. as a whole number or a decimal approximated to two decimal places.

Solution
a. Since the area is 196 in², *a side is* $\sqrt{196}$ *in.*
b. Use a calculator to evaluate $\sqrt{196}$.
    On some calculators a key sequence is 196 √x͏.
    On others you may use √ 196 EXE.
    On still others, you may need to use the 2nd function key:
    2nd √ 196 ENTER.
    You should see 14 on the display. *The length of a side is 14 in.*

Check
Does $14 \cdot 14 = 196$? $(14)^2 = 196$, so it checks.

Check how your calculator evaluates square roots by finding $\sqrt{196}$.

Like the fraction bar, the radical sign $\sqrt{}$ is a grouping symbol for any expression contained within it.

❶ ### Example 2

Evaluate $\sqrt{12^2 + 5^2}$.

Solution
Because the radical sign is a grouping symbol, begin by doing operations under the radical sign. First square 12 and 5; then add the result.

$$\sqrt{12^2 + 5^2} = \sqrt{144 + 25}$$
$$= \sqrt{169}$$
$$= 13$$

Square Roots That Are Not Whole Numbers

You are familiar with squares of whole numbers.
$$0^2 = 0 \quad 1^2 = 1 \quad 2^2 = 4 \quad 3^2 = 9 \quad 4^2 = 16 \text{ and so on.}$$

Squares of whole numbers are called **perfect squares.** Their square roots are whole numbers.
$$0 = \sqrt{0} \quad 1 = \sqrt{1} \quad 2 = \sqrt{4} \quad 3 = \sqrt{9} \quad 4 = \sqrt{16} \text{ and so on.}$$

You can get a rough estimate of a square root that is not a whole number by locating it between whole numbers. A good approximation can be found using a calculator.

Example 3

Estimate $\sqrt{2}$.

Solution 1
A rough estimate: Since $\sqrt{1} = 1$ and $\sqrt{4} = 2$, $\sqrt{2}$ is between 1 and 2.

Optional Activities

Activity 1
Materials: String, marbles, tape, stopwatch, meter stick

Before students do **Question 24**, you might want to have them **work in groups** to make a pendulum that is 85 cm long by taping a marble to one end of a string and taping the other end to the edge of a table. To start the pendulum, have students pull the marble to one side and then release it. When the swing becomes uniform, have them time how long it takes the pendulum to make 10 full swings. One full swing is a back-and-forth swing. Then have them estimate the time it takes to make one full swing.

Activity 2 Technology Connection
In *Technology Sourcebook, Calculator Master 1,* students explore patterns involving square roots and other roots.

Solution 2

A good approximation: Use a calculator.
An 8-digit display will show $\boxed{1.4142136}$.

The actual decimal for $\sqrt{2}$ is infinite and does not repeat. An estimate of $\sqrt{2}$ is the number 1.4142136.

Check

Multiply 1.4142136 by itself. One calculator shows that
$$1.4142136 \cdot 1.4142136 \approx 2.0000001.$$

When the value of a square root is not an integer, your teacher may expect two versions: (1) the exact value and (2) a decimal approximation rounded to the nearest hundredth or thousandth. For instance, the square root of 15 is exactly $\sqrt{15}$. Rounded to the nearest hundredth, $\sqrt{15}$ is 3.87.

The check to Example 3 is approximate because 1.4142136 is used to approximate $\sqrt{2}$. But $\sqrt{2} \cdot \sqrt{2} = 2$ exactly. In general, the following property is true.

② Square of the Square Root Property
For any nonnegative number n, $\quad \sqrt{n} \cdot \sqrt{n} = n$.

You can use this property to simplify or to evaluate expressions without using a calculator.

Example 4

Without using a calculator, multiply $4\sqrt{10} \cdot \sqrt{10}$.

Solution

Think of $4\sqrt{10}$ as being $4 \cdot \sqrt{10}$.
$$4\sqrt{10} \cdot \sqrt{10} = 4 \cdot \sqrt{10} \cdot \sqrt{10}$$

By the Square of the Square Root Property, $\sqrt{10} \cdot \sqrt{10} = 10$.

So
$$4\sqrt{10} \cdot \sqrt{10} = 4 \cdot 10$$
$$= 40$$

Check 1

Use your calculator. If you use the proper key sequence for $4\sqrt{10} \cdot \sqrt{10}$, you should see $\boxed{40}$. (You should check this.)

Check 2

Estimate $4\sqrt{10} \cdot \sqrt{10}$. $\sqrt{10}$ is a little more than 3, so $4\sqrt{10}$ is little more than 12. Multiply this by $\sqrt{10}$, which is a little more than 3, and the product of 40 seems reasonable.

Adapting to Individual Needs

Extra Help Calculator The following activity might help students develop number sense regarding square roots. Have them use a calculator and follow directions like these:
1. Enter 6. Square it. Take the square root. What happens? [$6^2 = 36$; $\sqrt{36} = 6$]
2. Enter 17. Square it. Take the square root. What happens? [$17^2 = 289$; $\sqrt{289} = 17$]

3. Enter 17. Take the square root. Square it. What happens? [$\sqrt{17} \approx 4.1231056$; $4.1231056^2 = 17$]

Now give students some square roots, such as $\sqrt{10}$, $\sqrt{37}$, $\sqrt{79}$, and $\sqrt{103}$. Have them estimate the square root and check their estimates on the calculator.
[$\sqrt{10}$; between 3 and 4; 3.162277
$\sqrt{37}$; between 6 and 7; 6.0827625

$\sqrt{79}$; between 8 and 9; 8.8881944
$\sqrt{103}$; between 10 and 11; 10.148892]

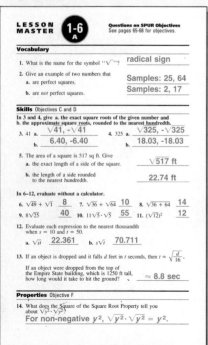

Squares and Square Roots in Equations

The equation $W^2 = 49$ has an obvious solution 7, because $7 \cdot 7 = 49$. However, $-7 \cdot -7 = 49$, so -7 is also a solution. Every positive number has *two* square roots, one positive and one negative. The radical sign symbolizes only the *positive* one. $\sqrt{49}$ means "the positive square root of 49," so $\sqrt{49} = 7$. The symbol for the *negative* square root of 49 is $-\sqrt{49}$. So, $-\sqrt{49} = -7$. The two square roots are opposites of each other.

When you solve equations such as $W^2 = 49$ or $97 = n^2$, you should assume that the domain of the variable contains positive and negative numbers and give all solutions, unless something from the situation limits the domain.

Example 5

Solve $97 = n^2$.

Solution

The exact solutions are n = $\sqrt{97}$ or n = $-\sqrt{97}$.
Rounded to the nearest hundredth, n ≈ 9.85 or n ≈ -9.85.

QUESTIONS

Covering the Reading

In 1 and 2, fill in the blanks.

1. Because $169 = 13 \cdot 13$, 13 is called a __?__ of 169.   square root

2. $72.25 = 8.5 \cdot 8.5$; so __?__ is a square root of __?__.   8.5; 72.25

3. The area of a square is 289 m². What is the length of a side?   17 m

4. If the area of a square is *A*, then the length of a side is __?__.   √A

In 5–7, compute in your head.

5. $\sqrt{100}$ 10

6. $-\sqrt{81}$ -9

7. $10\sqrt{81}$ 90

In 8–10, evaluate.

8. $\sqrt{3^2 + 4^2}$ 5

9. $\sqrt{3^2 \cdot 4^2}$ 12

10. $\sqrt{17^2 - 15^2}$ 8

11. **a.** At the right is a table of squares and square roots for the integers from 1 to 10. The approximations are rounded to the nearest thousandth. Copy the table and extend it to include all whole-number values of *n* through 20.
    b. Describe some patterns you observe in the table.

$\sqrt{n}$	n	n^2
1	1	1
1.414	2	4
1.732	3	9
2	4	16
2.236	5	25
2.449	6	36
2.646	7	49
2.828	8	64
3	9	81
3.162	10	100

11a)

$\sqrt{n}$	n	n^2
3.317	11	121
3.464	12	144
3.606	13	169
3.742	14	196
3.873	15	225
4	16	256
4.123	17	289
4.243	18	324
4.359	19	361
4.472	20	400

b) Sample: In the n^2 column, the units digits seem to follow a pattern of repeating 1, 4, 9, 6, 5, 6, 9, 4, 1, 0.

34

Adapting to Individual Needs

English Language Development
You might explain that the word *root* can refer to the origin, or primary source, of something. Thus we can think of the *root* of a square as the number used to produce the square. Explain that $\sqrt{121} = 11$ is read "the square root of 121 equals 11." It means $11^2 = 121$. Write other examples on the board and have students read them aloud.

12. a. Approximate $\sqrt{407}$ to the nearest hundredth using your calculator. **20.17**
  b. Check your answer. **20.17 · 20.17 = 406.8289 ≈ 407;   it checks.**

13. Evaluate without using a calculator.
  a. $(\sqrt{8})^2$ **8**   **b.** $\sqrt{8^2}$ **8**   **c.** $3\sqrt{8} \cdot \sqrt{8}$ **24**

14. Every positive number has __?__ square root(s). **two**

15. Name the two square roots of 16. **4, ⁻4**

In 16 and 17, an equation is given.
a. Describe each solution using the radical symbol.
b. Write each solution as a decimal rounded to the nearest hundredth.

16. $x^2 = 121$
  a) $x = \sqrt{121}$ or $x = -\sqrt{121}$
  b) $x = 11$ or $x = ⁻11$

17. $301 = b^2$ a) $b = \sqrt{301}$ or $b = -\sqrt{301}$
  b) $b = 17.35$ or $b = ⁻17.35$

Can pendulums swing by themselves? *Yes. The pendulum shown here is in the Museum of Science and Industry in Chicago, Illinois. Each evening, the pendulum's swing is stopped by securing it with a string. Each morning, a museum employee burns the string to allow the pendulum to swing freely.*

Applying the Mathematics

18. The area of the square at the left is 18 square units. (Count to check this.)
  a. Give the exact length of a side. $\sqrt{18}$
  b. Estimate the length of a side to the nearest hundredth. **4.24**

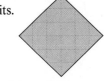

19. Tell how you can determine, without using a calculator, what two consecutive integers $\sqrt{32}$ is between.
  $\sqrt{25} = 5$ and $\sqrt{36} = 6$, so $5 < \sqrt{32} < 6$

20. Find the two solutions to $m^2 + 64 = 100$. *m* = 6 or *m* = ⁻6

21. For clarity, the product of a number y and the square root of x is usually written as $y\sqrt{x}$ instead of as $\sqrt{x} \cdot y$ or $\sqrt{xy}$. ($\sqrt{x} \cdot y$ can be mistaken for $\sqrt{xy}$.) When $x = 4$ and $y = 9$, evaluate.
  a. $y\sqrt{x}$ **18**   **b.** $\sqrt{xy}$ **6**   **c.** $x\sqrt{y}$ **12**

22. a. Use a calculator to evaluate $\sqrt{12.25}$. **3.5**
  b. Draw a square that has area 12.25 cm². **(Sides of square are 3.5 cm.)**
  c. Write a sentence or two to tell how parts **a** and **b** are related.
  See below.

23. If an object is dropped, it takes about $\sqrt{\dfrac{d}{16}}$ seconds to fall d feet. If an object is dropped from a 100-foot high building, about how long does it take the object to hit the ground? **2.5 seconds**

24. A *pendulum* is an object that is suspended from a fixed point and swings freely under the force of gravity. Scientists have established this formula for the time T it takes for one complete swing in terms of the length L of the pendulum and the acceleration due to gravity g:

$$T \approx 2\pi \sqrt{\dfrac{L}{g}}$$

A grandfather's clock has a pendulum of length 0.85 m. Use the formula to find T to the nearest hundredth, where $g \approx 9.8$ m/sec².
1.85 seconds

22c) The square root of a number is the length of a side of a square whose area is the number.

Practice

For more questions on SPUR Objectives, use **Lesson Master 1-6A** (shown on page 34) or **Lesson Master 1-6B** (shown on pages 35–36).

Assessment

Quiz A quiz covering Lessons 1-4 through 1-6 is provided in the *Assessment Sourcebook.*

Oral Communication Write the numbers 50, 7, 125, 234, and 0.5, one at a time, on the board. Without using calculators, ask students to name the two integers between which the positive square root of each number falls. [$\sqrt{50}$ is between 7 and 8; $\sqrt{7}$ is between 2 and 3; $\sqrt{125}$ is between 11 and 12; $\sqrt{234}$ is between 15 and 16; $\sqrt{0.5}$ is between 0 and 1.]

Extension

Science Connection Have students research the longest pendulum in the world, and use the formula in **Question 24** to predict the time it takes for this pendulum to make one full swing. [In 1994, a pendulum 27.4 meters long was installed in the Convention Center in Portland, Oregon; one full swing should take 10.5 seconds.]

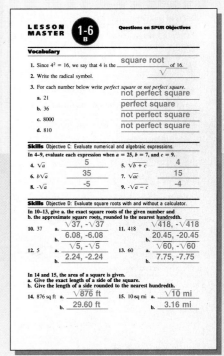

LESSON MASTER 1-6 B   Questions on SPUR Objectives

Vocabulary

1. Since $4^2 = 16$, we say that 4 is the __square root__ of 16.
2. Write the radical symbol. $\sqrt{}$
3. For each number below write *perfect square* or *not perfect square*.
  a. 21 — not perfect square
  b. 36 — perfect square
  c. 8000 — not perfect square
  d. 810 — not perfect square

Skills Objective C: Evaluate numerical and algebraic expressions.
In 4–9, evaluate each expression when $a = 25$, $b = 7$, and $c = 9$.
4. $\sqrt{a}$ — 5
5. $\sqrt{b+c}$ — 4
6. $b\sqrt{a}$ — 35
7. $\sqrt{ac}$ — 15
8. $-\sqrt{a}$ — -5
9. $-\sqrt{a-c}$ — -4

Skills Objective D: Evaluate square roots with and without a calculator.
In 10–13, give a. the exact square roots of the given number and b. the approximate square roots, rounded to the nearest hundredth.
10. 37 — a. $\sqrt{37}, -\sqrt{37}$ b. 6.08, -6.08
11. 418 — a. $\sqrt{418}, -\sqrt{418}$ b. 20.45, -20.45
12. 5 — a. $\sqrt{5}, -\sqrt{5}$ b. 2.24, -2.24
13. 60 — a. $\sqrt{60}, -\sqrt{60}$ b. 7.75, -7.75

In 14 and 15, the area of a square is given.
a. Give the exact length of a side of the square.
b. Give the length of a side rounded to the nearest hundredth.
14. 876 sq ft — a. $\sqrt{876}$ ft b. 29.60 ft
15. 10 sq mi — a. $\sqrt{10}$ mi b. 3.16 mi

Adapting to Individual Needs

Challenge
Refer students to **Exercise 35** on page 36. Then have them solve the following similar problem:

A person born in the twentieth century will be x years old in the year x^2. In what year was the person born? [The person will be 45 in the year 45^2, which is 2025. Therefore the person was born in 2025 – 45, or 1980.]

Project Update Project 3, *Estimating Square Roots*, on page 60, relates to the content of this lesson.

Notes on Questions

Question 33 The fractions have been chosen so that the computations can be checked by converting the fractions to decimals. You may need to remind students about this check.

Question 34 You may want to mention that although there is no real number whose square is -4, in later mathematics courses, students will study nonreal numbers that are square roots of negative numbers. Such numbers are called *imaginary numbers*.

29)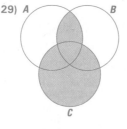

30c)

0 1 2 3 4 5 6 7

31c)
0 1 2 3 4 5 6 7 → w

34a) Samples:

4 [+/-] [√] or

[√] [(−)] 4 [ENTER]

Review

25. You invest $1000 in an account where interest is compounded yearly. The formula $A = 1000 + 1000r$ gives you the amount in the account after one year. Evaluate A when:
   a. r is 3%.   **b.** r is 4.5%.   *(Lesson 1-5, Previous course)*
       A = $1030   A = $1045

In 26–28, evaluate.   *(Lesson 1-4)*

26. $5^2 \cdot 5^3$ 3125   27. $57 - 3 \cdot 18$ 3   28. $(11 - 7)^3$ 64

29. Copy the Venn diagram below and shade in $(A \cap B) \cup C$.   *(Lesson 1-3)*
   See left.

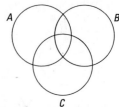

In 30 and 31, a situation and a variable are given.   *(Lesson 1-2)*
a. State a reasonable domain for the variable.
b. Rewrite the information as a sentence using the given variable.
c. Graph the solution set for the sentence. See left.

30. A house cat usually has no more than 6 kittens in a litter. Let n = the number of kittens in a typical litter. a) whole numbers; b) $1 \le n \le 6$

31. A typical adult female cat weighs at least 2 kg and no more than 6 kg. Let w = the weight in kg. a) positive real numbers;   b) $2 \le w \le 6$

32. Which of the numbers -4, 2, and 6 make the sentence $15 + n + -11 > 0$ true?   *(Lesson 1-1)* 2 and 6

33. *Skill sequence.* Compute.   *(Previous course)*
   a. $\frac{2}{3} + \frac{4}{3}$ 2   **b.** $\frac{2}{3} + \frac{4}{9}$ $\frac{10}{9}$ **c.** $\frac{2}{3} + \frac{4}{13}$ $\frac{38}{39}$

Exploration

34. Try to evaluate $\sqrt{-4}$ using your calculator.
   a. Write the key sequence you are using. See left.
   b. What does your calculator display? error
   c. Why does the calculator display what it does? In the domain of real numbers, a negative number has no square root.

35. Augustus De Morgan, an English mathematician who lived in the 19th century, once said, "I was x years old in the year x^2." In what year was he born? (Remember that you were born in the 20th century.) 1806

36

Celebrating *Kwanza.* *This African-American family celebrates* Kwanza, *a holiday centered around ideals such as unity and creativity. The bright colors and patterns in the family's clothes are based on traditional African dress.*

The formulas in Lesson 1-4 are sentences that describe numerical *patterns.* A **pattern** is a general idea for which there are many examples. An example of a pattern is called an **instance.** When values are substituted for the variables in a formula, an instance of the formula results. The formula $A = s^2$ tells how to calculate the area of a square with side of length s. If a square has sides 3 cm long, then $A = 3^2 = 9$ cm^2. This is an instance of the area formula.

Patterns Involving One Variable

A pattern may be described in several ways. Here is a pattern written in words.

Example 1

Consider the following pattern: If you double a number and then triple the answer, the result is the same as six times the original number.
a. Give three instances of this pattern. Tell if the pattern is true for each instance.
b. Use a variable to describe the pattern algebraically.

Solution

a. Choose three numbers, say 20, 1.5, and -4. For each number, write the sentence in symbols. Recall that "to double" means to multiply by 2, and "to triple" means to multiply by 3.

$(2 \cdot 20) \cdot 3 = 6 \cdot 20$ True, since $40 \cdot 3 = 120$
$(2 \cdot 1.5) \cdot 3 = 6 \cdot 1.5$ True, since $3 \cdot 3 = 9$
$(2 \cdot -4) \cdot 3 = 6 \cdot -4$ True, since $-8 \cdot 3 = -24$ ▶

Lesson 1-7 *Variables and Patterns* **37**

Lesson 1-7

Objectives
G Give instances or counterexamples of patterns.
H Use variables to describe patterns in instances.

Resources
From the Teacher's Resource File
- Lesson Master 1-7A or 1-7B
- Answer Master 1-7
- Teaching Aids
  3 Warm-up
  8 Question 30
- Activity Kit, Activity 2

Additional Resources
- Visuals for Teaching Aids 3, 8

Teaching
Lesson 1-7

Warm-up
Give the next three numbers. Then describe the pattern. **Sample answers are given.**
1. 2, 4, 6, 8, . . .
   10, 12, 14; add 2
2. -9, -6, -3, 0, 3, . . .
   6, 9, 12; add 3
3. 5, 9, 13, 17, . . .
   21, 25, 29; add 4
4. 2, 3, 5, 9, 17, 33, . . .
   65, 129, 257; multiply by 2, subtract 1
5. 0, 1, 8, 27, 64, . . .
   125, 216, 343; cube whole numbers

Notes on Reading
Reading Mathematics You may wish to have students read this lesson aloud in class. As they do so,

Lesson 1-7 Overview
Broad Goals Mathematics has been called "the science of patterns." In this characterization of mathematics, algebra is the language by which patterns are described. The goal of this lesson is to describe patterns for several given instances. And, since one needs to know when a description is incorrect, the idea of counterexample is a natural one.

Perspective This lesson is fundamental to the understanding of an important use of variables, namely to describe patterns. A student cannot possibly understand properties like $a + b = b + a$ unless he or she is able to determine the generalization from instances, or instances from the generalization.

Students who have studied UCSMP *Transition Mathematics* will have studied

these ideas in some detail, and they should find this lesson very easy. Only **Example 3** is a type that they have not seen before.

Of course, many patterns are properties of real numbers that have names; an example is the Commutative Property of Addition. However, these properties do not have to be discussed now. They will be studied in later chapters, at which time their names will be introduced.

stop at each pattern. Ask students to describe the pattern in their own words before they read the explanation in the text or examine the description with variables.

For students who have difficulty describing patterns, see *Extra Help* in *Adapting to Individual Needs*, on page 40.

Students should be able to respond to *any* letter used as a variable. However, the letters *a, b, c, d, m, n, x, y,* and *z* are used most often.

Social Studies Connection When discussing **Example 2,** you might share with students the following information about the growth of minority populations in the United States between 1980 and 1990.

African American	1990: 29.99 million 1980: 26.50 million Change: 13%
Native American	1990: 1.96 million 1980: 1.42 million Change: 38%
Hispanic	1990: 22.35 million 1980: 14.61 million Change: 53%
Asian or Pacific Islander	1990: 7.27 million 1980: 3.50 million Change: 108%

Additional Examples

1. Cubing a number is the same as using the number as a factor three times.
   a. Give three instances of this pattern. Is the pattern true for each instance? **Samples:**
   $2^3 = 2 \cdot 2 \cdot 2, 5^3 = 5 \cdot 5 \cdot 5.$
   $20^3 = 20 \cdot 20 \cdot 20$; yes, each instance is true.
   b. Use a variable to describe the pattern algebraically.
   $x^3 = x \cdot x \cdot x$

The mosaic art of St. Mark's. *The Basilica of St. Mark, in Venice, Italy is richly decorated with this artistic, mosaic tile floor. Notice the many squares and repeating geometric patterns in the tile's intricate design.*

38

> **b.** Notice what remains the same in the left column from instance to instance and what changes. Each instance has an equal sign; multiplication by 2, followed by multiplication by 3 on the left; and multiplication by 6 on the right. The things that stay the same in the instances are also the same in the pattern. Put blanks for the numbers that change.

$$(2 \cdot \underline{\quad}) \cdot 3 = 6 \cdot \underline{\quad}$$

What goes in the blanks? Each instance has a different number, but the numbers are the same for both blanks. Use a variable for this number that varies. We use *x*. The pattern is

$$(2 \cdot x) \cdot 3 = 6 \cdot x.$$

When you see a pattern in a number of instances, you may be able to describe that pattern with a formula, a sentence, or an algebraic expression.

Example 2

Throughout the 1980s, the African-American population of the United States increased by about 350,000 people per year. For example,
   it increased by about 350,000 people in 1 year;
   it increased by about 350,000 · 2 people in 2 years; and
   it increased by about 350,000 · 3 people in 3 years.

Describe this pattern, letting the variable *y* = the number of years.

Solution

Think of the first instance this way:

   The population increased by 350,000 · 1 people in 1 year.

Now all the instances look alike. The only things that change are the number of years and the number multiplied by 350,000. Write:

   The population increased by about 350,000 · ___ people in ___ years.

In each instance, the numbers in the blanks are the same, so *y* can represent both of them. Here is the pattern.

   The population increased by 350,000 · y people in y years.

Patterns Involving Two or More Variables

You can use more than one variable to describe a pattern. In Example 2, if we let *I* = the population increase in *y* years, we could describe the pattern with the formula $I = 350,000y$. Example 3 shows a pattern with several variables.

38

Optional Activities

Activity 1 After discussing the lesson, have students **work in groups** to solve this problem.

A school has 100 lockers and 100 students. All of the lockers are closed. As the students enter, the first student, S1, opens every locker. Then the second student, S2, begins with locker L2, and closes every other locker. S3 begins with L3 and changes every third locker—from open to closed or

from closed to open. S4 changes every fourth locker, S5 changes every fifth locker, and so on. After all students pass by the lockers, which of lockers 1 through 100 are open? [All locker numbers that are perfect squares: 1, 4, 9, 16, 15, 36, 49, 64, 81, 100]

To help students get started, have them make and extend a table until they see a pattern. Let O be an open locker and C be a closed one.

	L1	L2	L3	L4	L5	L6	L7	L8	L9
	C	C	C	C	C	C	C	C	C
S1	O	O	O	O	O	O	O	O	O
S2		C		C		C		C	
S3			C			O			C
S4				O				O	
S5					C				
S6						C			
S7							C		
S8								C	
S9									O

A putter's paradise.
Miniature golf, a fad of the late 1920s, has staged a major comeback in the 1990s. The boom is credited to the popularity of new larger-scale links. Some modern courses are built around adventure themes with waterfalls, mountains, and boat rides.

Example 3

A family consisting of two adults and three children under age 12 spent the following amounts on tickets while on vacation last month:

Activity	a = cost for 1 adult ($)	c = cost for 1 child ($)	T = total cost ($)
movie	6	3	$2 \cdot 6 + 3 \cdot 3$
ferryboat	10	4	$2 \cdot 10 + 3 \cdot 4$
miniature golf	4	2.50	$2 \cdot 4 + 3 \cdot 2.50$

Find a formula for T in terms of a and c.

Solution

Look at each expression in the *total cost* column. The instances are:

$$2 \cdot 6 + 3 \cdot 3$$
$$2 \cdot 10 + 3 \cdot 4$$
$$2 \cdot 4 + 3 \cdot 2.50$$

The pattern is $2 \cdot \underline{} + 3 \cdot \underline{}$,

where the first blank is the cost of an adult ticket, and the second is the cost of a child's ticket. So the total cost is $2 \cdot a + 3 \cdot c$.

The formula is $T = 2a + 3c$.

Example 4

Consider these true instances. Describe the pattern using variables.

$$6 + 1.2 = 6 \cdot 1.2$$
$$5 + 1\tfrac{1}{4} = 5 \cdot 1\tfrac{1}{4}$$
$$\tfrac{4}{3} + 4 = \tfrac{4}{3} \cdot 4$$
$$2 + 2 = 2 \cdot 2$$

Solution

First, describe the pattern in your own words. You may think of something like, "When you add two numbers you get the same result as multiplying them." Because two numbers vary, you need two variables. Choose two letters, perhaps a and b. Translate the pattern from words to variables.

$$a + b = a \cdot b$$

Notice that the fourth instance of the pattern has $a = 2$ and $b = 2$. It is possible for different variables to have the same value.

The description of the pattern in Example 4 is correct for the four instances given, but the pattern is not true in general. Writing the pattern with variables makes it easier to find instances where the rule does not work. If $a = 2$, and $b = 3$, the pattern would say

$$2 + 3 = 2 \cdot 3.$$

But $5 \neq 6$. This type of instance, which shows that a pattern is not always true, is called a **counterexample**. The instance in which $a = 2$ and $b = 3$ is a counterexample to the pattern $a + b = a \cdot b$.

Lesson 1-7 *Variables and Patterns* **39**

2. There are 43,560 square feet in an acre. There are $2 \cdot 43,560$ square feet in 2 acres. There are $3 \cdot 43,560$ square feet in 3 acres. Describe this pattern. Let n = the number of acres.
   There are $n \cdot 43,560$ square feet in n acres.

3. One salad costs $1.75, and one bottle of juice costs $1.25.
   a. Write the pattern for finding the total cost of s salads and b bottles of juice.
   $s \cdot \$1.75 + b \cdot \$1.25$
   b. Find a formula for T, the total cost of s salads and b bottles of juice. **$T = 1.75s + 1.25b$**

4. Consider these instances.
   $$4 \cdot 2 > \tfrac{4}{2}$$
   $$35 \cdot 7 > \tfrac{35}{7}$$
   $$0.15 \cdot 3 > \tfrac{0.15}{3}$$
   $$0.75 \cdot 8 > \tfrac{0.75}{8}$$
   a. Describe this pattern using variables. **$a \cdot b > \tfrac{a}{b}$**
   b. Is this pattern true for all numbers? If not, find a counter example. **No; sample counterexamples are $6 \cdot 1 \not> \tfrac{6}{1}$ and $0.75 \cdot 0.5 \not> \tfrac{0.75}{0.5}$.**

5. Find a counterexample to the statement: If n is divisible by 10, then $5n$ is divisible by 100.
   Sample: 30 (Any odd multiple of 10, such as 30, is a counterexample.)

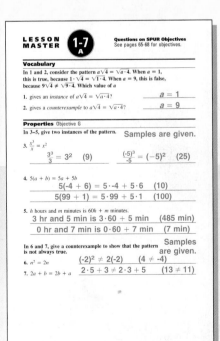
Activity 2 You can use *Activity Kit, Activity 2*, as an introduction or as a follow-up to the lesson. In the activity, students arrange markers in square arrays and observe several patterns.

In reviewing the questions, note that there can be many different correct descriptions of a pattern.

Question 4 An instance could either be 3 dogs have 4 · 3 legs, or 3 dogs have 12 legs. Point out that usually this information would be given as 12. Then a person would have to notice that 12 = 4 · 3 to see the pattern.

Question 6 If a student writes $(a + b) + c = d + e$, he or she has seen a pattern, but missed the commonality. The description $(a + b) + c = d + b$ is not what we prefer, but it is not totally incorrect. It is for this reason that we usually indicate how many variables to use in the description; the results are more uniform answers. In this case, using one variable gives $(3 + x) + 2 = 5 + x$. If students have studied the Commutative and Associative Properties of Addition (they will have if they have studied *Transition Mathematics*), then you can point out that this general pattern is true because of those properties.

Question 7 The general pattern itself is an instance of the Like Terms Form of the Distributive Property which is studied in Chapter 3.

Question 8 The general pattern is an instance of the Distributive Property.

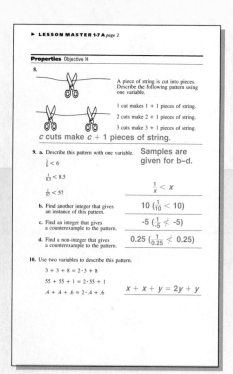

▶ **LESSON MASTER 1-7 A** *page 2*

Properties Objective H

8. A piece of string is cut into pieces. Describe the following pattern using one variable.

1 cut makes 1 + 1 pieces of string.

2 cuts make 2 + 1 pieces of string.

3 cuts make 3 + 1 pieces of string.

c cuts make $c + 1$ pieces of string.

9. a. Describe this pattern with one variable. Samples are given for b–d.

$\frac{1}{6} < 6$

$\frac{1}{8.5} < 8.5$

$\frac{1}{57} < 57$ $\frac{1}{x} < x$

b. Find another integer that gives an instance of this pattern. $10 \left(\frac{1}{10} < 10\right)$

c. Find an integer that gives a counterexample to the pattern. $-5 \left(\frac{1}{-5} \not< -5\right)$

d. Find a non-integer that gives a counterexample to the pattern. $0.25 \left(\frac{1}{0.25} \not< 0.25\right)$

10. Use two variables to describe this pattern.

$3 + 3 + 8 = 2 \cdot 3 + 8$

$55 + 55 + 1 = 2 \cdot 55 + 1$

$.4 + .4 + .6 = 2 \cdot .4 + .6$ $x + x + y = 2y + y$

Example 5

Find a counterexample to the following statement: If n is an integer, then $n + 1$ is an odd integer.

Solution

Try some values for n.

If $n = 2$, then $n + 1 = 3$, which is an odd integer. The statement is true. So 2 is not a counterexample. Try another value.

If $n = 3$, then $n + 1 = 4$, which is *not an odd integer*. So the pattern "If n is an integer, then $n + 1$ is an odd integer" is not true when $n = 3$. This means that 3 *is a counterexample.*

QUESTIONS

Covering the Reading

1a) Samples: $\frac{10 \cdot 7}{2} = 5 \cdot 7$ is true, since $\frac{70}{2} = 35$.

$\frac{10 \cdot -3}{2} = 5 \cdot -3$ is true, since $-\frac{30}{2} = -15$.

$\frac{10 \cdot 41.2}{2} = 5 \cdot 41.2$ is true, since $\frac{412}{2} = 206$.

2) Samples: $2 \cdot 1 = 2$; $-7 \cdot 1 = -7$

3) Samples: $5 \cdot 9 = 9 \cdot 5$; $7.2 \cdot 12.9 = 12.9 \cdot 7.2$

4) Samples: 3 dogs have 4 · 3 legs. 18 dogs have 4 · 18 legs.

1. The following sentence describes a pattern. "When a number is multiplied by ten and then divided by two, the result is five times the original number."
   a. Give three instances of the pattern. See left.
   b. Write an equation to describe the pattern. (Use n to stand for the number.) $\frac{10 \cdot n}{2} = 5 \cdot n$

In 2–4, give two instances of the pattern. See left.

2. $n \cdot 1 = n$ 3. $xy = yx$ 4. d dogs have $4d$ legs.

5. The population of Vacaville is decreasing by 250 people each month.
   a. At this rate, by how many people will the population decrease in 10 months? **2500 people**
   b. At this rate, by how many people will the population decrease in m months? **250m people**
   c. Does your answer to part **b** work when $m = 0$? Yes, because the population will not have decreased in 0 months.

In 6 and 7, describe the general pattern using one variable.

6. $(3 + 9) + 2 = 5 + 9$
   $(3 + 4) + 2 = 5 + 4$
   $(3 + 90) + 2 = 5 + 90$
   $(3 + n) + 2 = 5 + n$

7. $15 + 2 \cdot 15 = 3 \cdot 15$
   $\frac{1}{3} + 2 \cdot \frac{1}{3} = 3 \cdot \frac{1}{3}$
   $47.1 + 2 \cdot 47.1 = 3 \cdot 47.1$
   $n + 2 \cdot n = 3 \cdot n$

8. Use two variables to write a pattern that describes the following instances. $6 \cdot a + 6 \cdot b = 6 \cdot (a + b)$
   $$6 \cdot 3 + 6 \cdot 4 = 6 \cdot (3 + 4)$$
   $$6 \cdot 11 + 6 \cdot \frac{1}{3} = 6 \cdot (11 + \frac{1}{3})$$
   $$6 \cdot 7 + 6 \cdot 1000 = 6 \cdot (7 + 1000)$$

9. Refer to Example 3. How much would the family pay for tickets to a circus that cost $8 for each adult and $5 for each child? **$31**

10. What is a *counterexample*? It is an instance which shows that a pattern is not always true.

11. Refer to the pattern in Example 4. Give another counterexample. Sample: $a = 7$ and $b = 9$; $7 + 9 = 7 \cdot 9$ is not true because $16 \neq 63$.

40

Adapting to Individual Needs

Extra Help

If students have difficulty describing patterns, suggest that they look for the elements that stay the same in all instances. Then have them note the numbers that change from one instance to another. Finally, have students describe the pattern with variables, and check the description against the instances given. For example:

$\frac{3}{3} = 1$ $1\frac{1.5}{1.5} = 1$ $\frac{1}{2} \div \frac{1}{2} = 1$

The 1 is the same in each instance, so it will appear in the answer. The other numbers change from instance to instance, but the numerator and denominator are always the same within any one instance. They can be represented by a single variable, such as m. The pattern is $\frac{m}{m} = 1$.

12. Give a counterexample to show that the pattern
$$(a - 3) + b = a - (3 + b)$$
does not hold for all real numbers a and b.
Sample: $a = 10$ and $b = 2$; $(10 - 3) + 2 = 10 - (3 + 2)$ is not true because $7 + 2 \neq 10 - 5$.

Applying the Mathematics

13. Here are two instances of a pattern:
 2 heads of lettuce and 3 tomatoes cost $2 \cdot 89¢ + 3 \cdot 24¢$.
 5 heads of lettuce and 2 tomatoes cost $5 \cdot 89¢ + 2 \cdot 24¢$.
 a. Describe the pattern using variables. Let L = the number of heads of lettuce, and T = the number of tomatoes. See Left.
 b. Write another instance of this pattern. See left.
 c. If C = the total cost of lettuce and tomatoes, write a formula for C in terms of L and T. $C = .89L + .24T$

In 14–16, a pattern is given. **14–16) See left.**
 a. Give three instances of the pattern.
 b. Tell whether you think the pattern is true for all real numbers. Explain your reasoning.

14. $y + y + y = 3 \cdot y$ **15.** $10(x - y) = 10x - y$ **16.** $(a^2)a = a^3$

17. a. Describe this pattern using one variable. $n \cdot n > n$

$$2 \cdot 2 > 2$$
$$3 \cdot 3 > 3$$
$$4 \cdot 4 > 4$$
$$100 \cdot 100 > 100$$

b) Sample: $-8 \cdot -8 > -8$
c) Sample: $0 \cdot 0 = 0$
d) Sample: $\frac{1}{2} \cdot \frac{1}{2} < \frac{1}{2}$

 b. Find another integer that is an instance of the pattern.
 c. Find an integer that is a counterexample to the pattern.
 d. Find a non-integer that is a counterexample to the pattern.

18. A pizza is cut into pieces by making each cut go through the center.

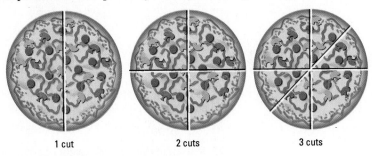

1 cut 2 cuts 3 cuts

 a. How many pieces are made with 4 cuts? 8 pieces
 b. Find a formula for the number of pieces p of pizza you get from c cuts. $p = 2c$
 c. What does your formula predict for the number of pieces from 12 cuts? 24 pieces

16a) Sample: $(4^2) 4 = 4^3$; true $64 = 64$ $(-5)^2 \cdot -5 = (-5)^3$; true $-125 = -125$
 $(0.1)^2 \cdot 0.1 = (0.1)^3$; true $.001 = .001$
 b) Yes; multiplying the square of a number by that number is the same as multiplying the number by itself three times.

Lesson 1-7 *Variables and Patterns* **41**

Vegetables grow in popularity—as well as in gardens. *Health concerns about fat and cholesterol levels in food have led many people to eat more vegetables. California is the leading state in the production of lettuce and tomatoes.*

13a) L heads of lettuce and T tomatoes cost $L \cdot 89¢ + T \cdot 24¢$.
b) Sample: 10 heads of lettuce and 4 tomatoes cost $10 \cdot 89¢ + 4 \cdot 24¢$.

14a) Sample:
$2 + 2 + 2 = 3 \cdot 2$; true $6 = 6$
$5 + 5 + 5 = 3 \cdot 5$: true $15 = 15$
$-7 + -7 + -7 = 3 \cdot -7$; true $-21 = -21$
b) Yes; adding a number to itself three times gives the same result as tripling the number.

15a) Sample:
$10(11 - 0) = 10 \cdot 11 - 0$; true $110 = 110$
$10(4 - 4) = 10 \cdot 4 - 4$; false $0 \neq 36$
$10(0 - 10) = 10 \cdot 0 - 10$; false $-100 \neq -10$
b) No; counterexamples can be found.

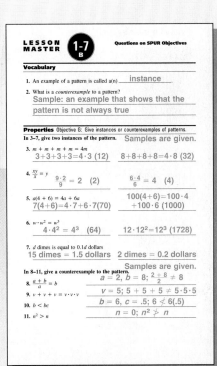

Adapting to Individual Needs

English Language Development
You might use the following example to help students understand the meaning of *counterexample*. Point to a clock and ask, "In which direction do the hands move?" [They move in the same order as the numbers on the face of the clock, or clockwise.] "Suppose that the clock has stopped at 3:15 and the actual time is 2:30. How might you move the hands to set the correct time?" [Move them in the opposite direction of clockwise,

or counterclockwise.] Point out that *counter* means *opposite*. Explain that if they are given several instances that are true, a counterexample is an instance that is false. Then you might give other examples of words with the same prefix, such as *counteract* (to act against) and *counterweight* (a weight that balances another weight).

Notes on Questions

Question 24 This question shows an instance of one of the proofs of the Pythagorean Theorem, which students study in the next lesson. To find the answer, students must be able to calculate the area of a right triangle.

Question 25 Error Alert Some students may forget to change the height from feet to inches and find that the person has a negative normal weight. Ask them if they think their answers are reasonable. Then suggest that they reread the sentence that introduces the question.

Question 30 Cooperative Learning This is a good question for group work. It is not hard, but the instances are unlike any others encountered in this lesson. Each 3-by-3 square is an instance, and they overlap. Students who understand this concept are well on the way to understanding the use of variables to describe patterns. **Teaching Aid 8** contains the calendar month for this question.

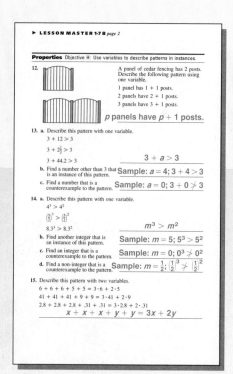

19a)

b) Sample: The first design has 3 pennies, the second design has $3 \cdot 2$ pennies, the third design has $3 \cdot 3$ pennies, and so on.

19. Below are four designs made with pennies.

a. Draw what you think the next design should be. a, b) See left.
b. Describe in words the patterns you see in these five designs.
c. If the designs continue to follow the same pattern, how many pennies will be needed to make the 20th design?
20 · 3 or 60 pennies

Review

In 20–22, evaluate without a calculator. *(Lesson 1-6)*

20. $\sqrt{49}$ 7   21. $\sqrt{400}$ 20   22. $\sqrt{401} \cdot \sqrt{401}$ 401

23. A bag of grass seed can cover an area of 3000 square feet. *(Lesson 1-6)*
    a. What is the side length of the largest square plot it can seed?
    b. Give the dimensions of a non-square plot it can seed. ≈ 54.7 ft
    Sample: 60 feet by 50 feet

24. Suppose each small square in the figure below has area 1 square unit. *(Lesson 1-6)*
    a. Find the area of *DFGH*. 25 square units
    b. What is the length of one side? 5 units

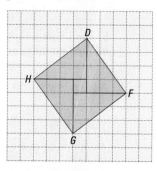

In 25 and 26, use this information. According to some medical charts, an adult's normal weight w (in pounds) can be estimated by the formula $w = \frac{11}{2} h - 220$ when his or her height h (in inches) is known. *(Lesson 1-5)*

25. Estimate the normal weight of a person who is 6 feet tall.
    176 pounds
26. a. According to this formula, what is the normal weight of a person who is 40 inches tall? 0 pounds
    b. Explain your answer to part **a** by relating it to a reasonable domain of the variable h. 40 inches is outside the domain of most adult heights, so the answer has no meaning.
27. Let $d = 3$. Find a value of n so that the following sentences are true.
    (Lessons 1-1, 1-5)

    a. $\frac{n}{d} > 1$ b. $\frac{n}{d} < 1$ c. $\frac{n}{d} = 1$
    Sample: 4   Sample: 2   3

Adapting to Individual Needs

Challenge
Have students find a counterexample to disprove the following statement:

The expression $n^2 + n + 11$ always yields a prime number when n is replaced by a positive whole number. [For $n = 10$, the expression equals 121, which is not a prime number. For $n = 0$ through 9, the expression yields 11, 13, 17, 23, 31, 41, 53, 67, 83, and 101, all of which are prime.]

28b) $V \cap W = \{15\}$ so
$T \cup (V \cap W) = \{10, 12,$
$14, 15, 16, 18, 20\}$.
$T \cup V = \{10, 12, 14, 15,$
$16, 18, 20\}$ so $(T \cup V) \cap$
$W = \{10, 15, 20\}$.
Thus $T \cup (V \cap W) \neq$
$(T \cup V) \cap W$.

28. Suppose $T = \{10, 12, 14, 16, 18, 20\}$, $V = \{12, 15, 18\}$ and
$W = \{5, 10, 15, 20\}$. *(Lesson 1-3)*
  a. Does $T \cup (V \cap W) = (T \cup V) \cap W$? No
  b. Explain how you got your answer. See left.

29. A machinist is making metal rods for lamps. The metal rods are to
be 1.25 inches in diameter with an allowable error of at most
0.005 inch. (The quantity 0.005 inch is called the *tolerance*.) Give
an interval for the possible diameters d of the rods. *(Lesson 1-2)*
$1.245 \le d \le 1.255$

Exploration

30. A monthly calendar
contains many
patterns.

a. Consider a 3 × 3 square such as the one drawn on the calendar.
Add the nine dates. What is the relationship between the sum
and the middle date? Try this again. Does it always seem to
work? The sum is 9 times the middle date. It seems to always work.
b. In a 3 × 3 square portion of the calendar, if the middle date is
expressed as N, then the date below it would be $N + 7$ because it
is 7 days later. Copy the chart below, and then fill in the other
blanks.

$N-8$	$N-7$	$N-6$
$N-1$	N	$N+1$
$N+6$	$N+7$	$N+8$

c. Show how your result from part **b** can be used to explain your
conclusion in part **a.** Adding the 9 expressions gives a sum of $9N$,
which explains why the result in part a is true.

Practice
For more questions on SPUR Objectives, use **Lesson Master 1-7A**
(shown on pages 39–40) or
Lesson Master 1-7B (shown on
pages 41–42).

Assessment
Written Communication Have students explain what a counterexample is and how it is used. Then have
them give an example of using a
counterexample. [Students recognize that a counterexample is used
to show that a pattern is not true for
all instances.]

Extension
✎ **Writing** This is an extension of
Question 30. Tell students to imagine that a friend has circled a 3-by-3
array on a calendar without allowing
them to see the array. The friend
tells them the first (smallest) number
in the array. Have students write a
paragraph explaining how they can
use this information to find the sum
of the numbers in the array without
adding them. [Sample: Add 8 to the
smallest number to get the middle
number. Then multiply that sum
by 9.]

Project Update Project 6, *Figurate
Numbers*, on page 61, relates to the
content of this lesson.

Setting Up Lesson 1-8
The In-class Activity on page 44 introduces
the Pythagorean Theorem which is studied
in Lesson 1-8.

Materials Students will need scissors,
tape, and **Teaching Aid 9** or tracing paper
for the In-class Activity. They will need string
and rulers or **Geometry Templates** for the
Warm-up in Lesson 1-8.

Resources

From the **Teacher's Resource File**
- Teaching Aid 9: Pythagorean Patterns
- Answer Master 1-8

Additional Resources
- Visual for Teaching Aid 9
- Tracing paper, scissors, and tape

This activity helps students to visually experience the Pythagorean Theorem. Have students **work in pairs.** Each pair will need tracing paper or **Teaching Aid 9,** scissors, and tape.

✎ **Writing** Have students write their pattern descriptions and ask some of them to share what they have written with the entire class. This discussion leads naturally into the discussion of the Pythagorean Theorem.

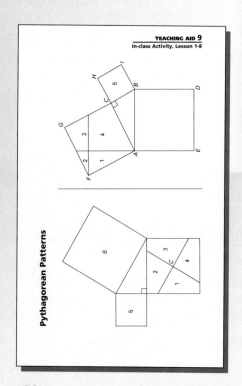

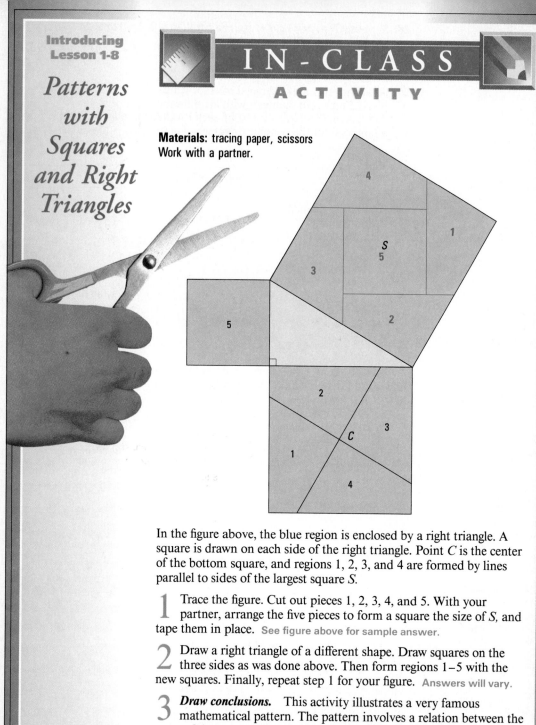

Introducing Lesson 1-8

IN·CLASS ACTIVITY

Patterns with Squares and Right Triangles

Materials: tracing paper, scissors
Work with a partner.

In the figure above, the blue region is enclosed by a right triangle. A square is drawn on each side of the right triangle. Point C is the center of the bottom square, and regions 1, 2, 3, and 4 are formed by lines parallel to sides of the largest square S.

1 Trace the figure. Cut out pieces 1, 2, 3, 4, and 5. With your partner, arrange the five pieces to form a square the size of S, and tape them in place. See figure above for sample answer.

2 Draw a right triangle of a different shape. Draw squares on the three sides as was done above. Then form regions 1–5 with the new squares. Finally, repeat step 1 for your figure. Answers will vary.

3 ***Draw conclusions.*** This activity illustrates a very famous mathematical pattern. The pattern involves a relation between the areas of the squares drawn on the three sides of a right triangle. Describe the pattern using words or variables. The sum of the areas of the two smaller squares is equal to the area of the largest square.

Optional Activities

Materials: **Teaching Aid 9**

Have students make the pattern shown at the right or use **Teaching Aid 9.** Point out that one dotted segment is an extension of side $\overline{EA}$ and the other segment is parallel to side $\overline{AB}$. Have students cover square *ABDE* using square *CHIB* and the four pieces in square *ACGF*. This pattern also demonstrates the Pythagorean Theorem.

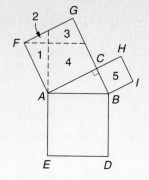

LESSON 1-8

The Pythagorean Theorem

Pythagoras the teacher. *Pythagoras was a Greek mathematician, philosopher, and teacher born around 580 B.C. The scene above, a detail from* School of Athens *by Raphael, depicts Pythagoras (forefront holding a book) surrounded by students.*

What Is the Pythagorean Theorem?

The In-class Activity on page 44 involves a very famous pattern known as the *Pythagorean Theorem*. To describe this pattern in words, we need some language about right triangles. Recall that in a right triangle, one of the angles must be 90°. In the figure below, the right angle is formed by the sides with lengths *a* and *b*. These sides are called the **legs** of the right triangle. The longest side of the triangle, the **hypotenuse,** is opposite the right angle. Here the hypotenuse has length *c*.

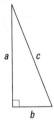

Look carefully at the figure in the In-class Activity. The purpose of the activity was for you to see that the squares built on the legs of a right triangle can be cut apart and reassembled to fill the square on the hypotenuse. You could do this because the sum of the areas of the two smaller squares equals the area of the largest square.

In some situations, this pattern can be verified by counting. Look carefully at the two instances at the top of the next page. Each shows a right triangle in the center with a square built on each side. Count to find the area of each square.

Lesson 1-8 *The Pythagorean Theorem* **45**

Resources
From the *Teacher's Resource File*
- Lesson Master 1-8A or 1-8B
- Answer Master 1-8
- Teaching Aids
  3 Warm-up
  10 Question 26
  11 Additional Examples and Extension
  12 Centimeter Grid (Extra Help)
- Technology Sourcebook
  Computer Master 2

Additional Resources
- Visuals for Teaching Aids 3, 10–12
- String, rulers or **Geometry Templates** (Warm-up)

Teaching
Lesson **1-8**

Warm-up
Activity
Materials: String, rulers or **Geometry Templates**

Work in groups. Use a pen to mark a length of string into 12 equal segments. Then devise a way to use the string to form a right angle. Explain what you did. **Sample: Use the string to form a 3-4-5 triangle. The right angle is between the 3- and 4-unit sides.**

Lesson 1-8 Overview

Broad Goals The goal of the lesson is to introduce the Pythagorean Theorem and to apply it in its simplest sense—as a formula by which one can calculate the length of the hypotenuse of a right triangle given the lengths of the two legs.

Perspective Many students will have seen the Pythagorean Theorem before. It is placed early in this course because of its

importance, because it gives opportunities for students to practice working with squares and square roots, and because there may be students who have not seen it before.

There are two forms in which the Pythagorean Theorem can be stated:
$c^2 = a^2 + b^2$ or $c = \sqrt{a^2 + b^2}$.

We do not give the second form, but you may wish to do so. If you do, stress that $\sqrt{a^2 + b^2}$ does not equal $a + b$.

❶ Whether students read this lesson at home or in class, ask them to explain how they found the areas in the figures labeled Instance 1 and Instance 2.

❷ After students read the statement of the Pythagorean Theorem and its geometric interpretation, ask them to find the lengths of $\overline{AB}$ in Instance 1 and of $\overline{DF}$ in Instance 2. [$\sqrt{18}$; 5]

History Connection You might mention that ancient mathematicians from Egypt, China, India, Sumer (now southern Iraq), and Babylonia made many discoveries about right triangles. The Egyptians and East Indians stretched rope knotted at equal intervals to form right triangles. The Chinese manuscript *Chou Pei Suan Ching*, written about 500 B.C., shows a proof of the Pythagorean Theorem. The Sumerian Babylonian cuneiform clay tables, written about 4,000 years ago, included the following problem: "A post of length 30 stands against a wall. The end has slipped down a distance of six. How far did the lower end move?" [18] Answering this problem involves finding the length of one leg of a right triangle in which the length of the other leg is 24 and the hypotenuse is 30.

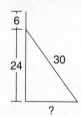

Instance 1   Instance 2

❶

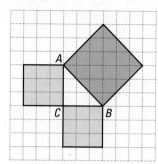 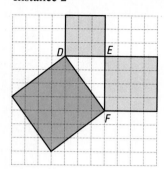

In Instance 1, you should find that the square built on leg $\overline{AC}$ has area 3^2, or 9. The square built on leg $\overline{BC}$ also has area 9. The area of the square on the hypotenuse $\overline{AB}$ of $\triangle ABC$ is 18. Notice that $9 + 9 = 18$.

In Instance 2, the area of the square on leg $\overline{DE}$ is $3^2 = 9$. The area of the square on leg $\overline{EF}$ is 4^2 or 16. The area of the square on the hypotenuse $\overline{DF}$ is 25. Notice that $9 + 16 = 25$.

If the legs of a right triangle have lengths a and b, and the hypotenuse has length c, then the areas of the squares built on the sides are a^2, b^2, and c^2.

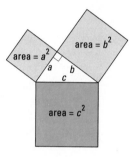

The pattern can be written as follows.

❷ **Pythagorean Theorem**
In a right triangle with legs of lengths a and b and hypotenuse of length c,
$$a^2 + b^2 = c^2.$$

Theorems are important properties that have been proved to be true. The Pythagorean Theorem is named after the Greek mathematician Pythagoras, who lived about 2,500 years ago. Pythagoras seems to have been the first to show that this pattern is true for every right triangle. It was applied even earlier by the Babylonians, and perhaps more than a thousand years before them by the architects of the pyramids in Egypt and the builders of Stonehenge in England. The Chinese also discovered this property independently. It is one of the most famous theorems in mathematics.

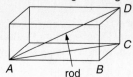

Using the Pythagorean Theorem to Find the Hypotenuse

The Pythagorean Theorem allows you to find the length of one side of a right triangle if you know the lengths of the other two sides. The following examples show how to find the length of the hypotenuse. In a later chapter you will learn to use the Pythagorean Theorem to find the length of a leg.

Example 1

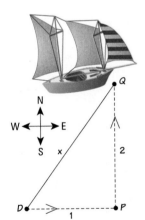

What is the length of the hypotenuse of the right triangle drawn on the left?

Solution

Substitute the lengths of the legs of the triangle for a and b in the Pythagorean Theorem. The hypotenuse is c.

In a right triangle, $a^2 + b^2 = c^2$.

Substituting,
$$15^2 + 20^2 = c^2$$
$$225 + 400 = c^2$$
$$625 = c^2.$$

This equation has two solutions, the positive and negative square roots of 625.

$$c = \sqrt{625} \text{ or } c = -\sqrt{625}$$

These square roots are integers.

$$c = 25 \text{ or } c = -25$$

However, the length of the hypotenuse cannot be negative, so use only the positive solution. **The hypotenuse is 25 cm.**

Example 2

A sailboat leaves its dock and travels 1 mi due east. Then it turns and sails 2 mi due north. At this point, how far is it from the dock?

Solution

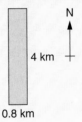

Draw a picture. Let $D =$ the position of the dock. Draw a path to represent 1 mi east; mark the turning point P. Mark a point Q 2 mi north of P. Form a right triangle with legs of length 1 and 2, by connecting Q to D. Find the length of the hypotenuse x. The domain of x is the set of positive real numbers. Use the picture on the left. According to the Pythagorean Theorem,

$$1^2 + 2^2 = x^2$$
$$1 + 4 = x^2$$
$$5 = x^2$$
$$x = \sqrt{5} \text{ or } x = -\sqrt{5}$$

We can discard $-\sqrt{5}$ because x must be positive.

The exact distance between the boat and the dock is $\sqrt{5}$ mi. This is approximately 2.2 mi.

Lesson 1-8 *The Pythagorean Theorem* **47**

Activity 3 Technology Connection You may wish to demonstrate how to use *Geo-Explorer* or similar software to draw and measure triangles. Then you could assign *Technology Sourcebook, Computer Master 2*. Students verify the Pythagorean Theorem, and show that there is not a similar theorem for obtuse and acute triangles.

Additional Examples

These examples are also given on **Teaching Aid 11.**

1. What is the length of the hypotenuse of the right triangle shown below?
   $\sqrt{128}$ in., or about 11.3 in.

2. To get to school, Eddie travels 2.5 miles east and 1.5 miles north. If he could travel to school in a straight line, how far would he have to go? $\sqrt{8.5}$ **miles, or about 2.9 miles**

3. Central Park in New York City is shaped like a rectangle. It is 0.8 kilometers wide and 4 kilometers long. About how far is it from the southeast corner of the park to the northwest corner?
   $\sqrt{16.64}$ km, or about 4.1 km

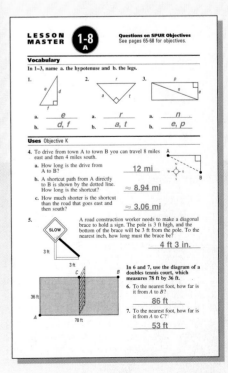

47

The Pythagorean Theorem is helpful when a right triangle can be identified in figures other than triangles.

Example 3

The figure below is a rectangle with sides of 2.5 cm and 6 cm. Find x, the length of the diagonal.

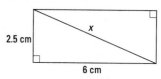

Solution

The diagonal forms two right triangles. Each has legs of length 2.5 cm and 6 cm. The diagonal of the rectangle is the hypotenuse of the right triangles. Use the Pythagorean Theorem to find x. Remember that x must be positive.

$$2.5^2 + 6^2 = x^2$$
$$6.25 + 36 = x^2$$
$$42.25 = x^2$$
$$\text{So} \qquad x = \sqrt{42.25}$$
$$= 6.5.$$

The diagonal is 6.5 cm long.

QUESTIONS

Covering the Reading

1. What is the longest side of a right triangle called? **hypotenuse**

2. Examine the right triangle shown at the right.
   a. Which sides are the legs? **j and n**
   b. Which side is the hypotenuse? **k**

3. $\triangle PQR$ is a right triangle with hypotenuse $\overline{PR}$. Describe the relation among the areas of squares I, II, and III. **area of square I + area of square II = area of square III**

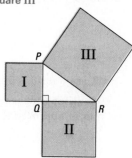

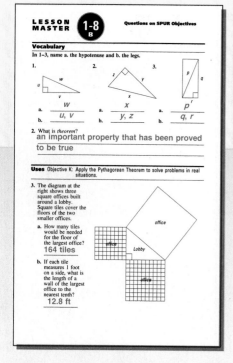
Adapting to Individual Needs

Extra Help

Materials: Grid paper or **Teaching Aid 12**, rulers or **Geometry Templates**

Have students who need more help with the Pythagorean Theorem **work with a partner**. Tell them to draw any right triangle on grid paper and to measure as accurately as possible the length of each side. Then have them square the measures. They should find that $a^2 + b^2 \approx c^2$. If the meas-

ures were exact, students would find that $a^2 + b^2 = c^2$. Now suggest that they draw any triangle that is not a right triangle and repeat the procedure. They should note that $a^2 + b^2 \neq c^2$ and conjecture that the Pythagorean Theorem applies only to right triangles.

4. State the Pythagorean Theorem. In a right triangle with legs of length a and b and hypotenuse of length c, $a^2 + b^2 = c^2$.
5. $\triangle ABC$ is a right triangle with $\angle B$ the right angle.
   a. What is the area of the square with side $\overline{AC}$? 34
   b. What is the length of $\overline{AC}$? $\sqrt{34} \approx 5.8$

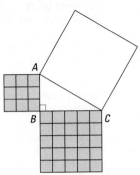

In 6–8, find the length of the hypotenuse. If the answer is not a whole number, find both its exact value and an approximation rounded to the nearest hundredth.

6.
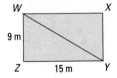
24
7
w 25

7.

17 a
8
15

8.
6 k $\sqrt{157} \approx 12.53$
11

9. A small plane travels 10 miles due west from an airport, then turns and flies due south for 15 miles. At this point how far is the plane from the airport? ≈ 18 miles

In 10 and 11, refer to rectangle $WXYZ$ below.

10. *True or false.* $\triangle WXY$ is a right triangle. Justify your answer.
    True, $\angle X$ is a right angle as are all angles in a rectangle.
11. If a rectangular garden has width 9 m and length 15 m, what is the length of the diagonal? $\sqrt{306} \approx 17.5$ m

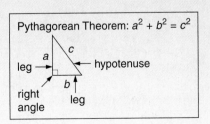
W X
9 m
Z 15 m Y

Lesson 1-8   *The Pythagorean Theorem*   **49**

Notes on Questions
Question 9 It might be helpful for some students to draw a picture of the plane's path.

Question 10 You might note that in any polygon which has a right angle *ABC* (where *A*, *B*, and *C* are consecutive vertices), the diagonal connecting *A* and *C* will form right triangle *ABC*.

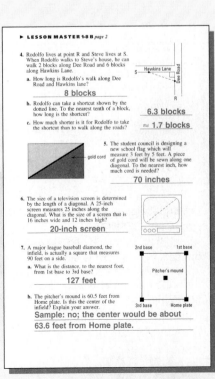

Adapting to Individual Needs
English Language Development
If students have difficulty remembering terms such as *hypotenuse* and *leg*, have them put the following information on an index card that they can use for reference. Suggest that students use colored pencils to label corresponding names and parts.

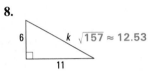

Pythagorean Theorem: $a^2 + b^2 = c^2$

leg → | a | c ← hypotenuse
right angle | b | leg

Question 12 Career Connection
You might talk with students about how a building developer, draftsperson, and carpenter might use the Pythagorean Theorem. [The developer, in initial sketches; the draftsperson, in scale drawings; and the carpenter, in squaring the various portions of the building and checking for right angles.]

Question 15 Students can get an answer that is nearly correct by using an approximation for $\sqrt{3}$. However, to get the exact answer, they must know how to square $\sqrt{3}$. Students should be able to do both calculations.

Question 26 Teaching Aid 10 contains this diagram.

12. A carpenter wants to make a garden gate with a cross brace for support. If the gate is to be 36 in. wide and 48 in. high, how long must the cross brace be? (Give your answer to the nearest inch.) 60 in.

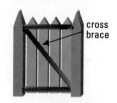
cross brace

13. Some pedestrians want to get from point *A* to point *B*. The two roads shown meet at right angles.
    a. If they follow the roads, how far will the pedestrians walk?
    b. Suppose that, instead of 6 km walking along the roads, they took the shortcut from *A* to *B*. Use the Pythagorean Theorem to find the length of the shortcut, rounded to the nearest tenth of a km. ≈ 4.5 km
    c. How much distance would they save by taking the shortcut? ≈ 1.5 km

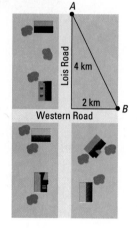
A
Lois Road
4 km
2 km
B
Western Road

14. The area of a square is 64 cm².
    a. Find the length of a side. 8 cm
    b. Use the Pythagorean Theorem to find the length of the diagonal. $\sqrt{128}$ cm ≈ 11.3 cm

15. A right triangle has legs of lengths 3 cm and $\sqrt{3}$ cm.
    a. How long is the hypotenuse? $\sqrt{12}$ ≈ 3.5 cm
    b. Draw a right triangle with the given dimensions and measure its hypotenuse. See students' drawings. The hypotenuse ≈ 3.5 cm.
    c. How close are your answers to parts **a** and **b**? Answers will vary. Sample: Both answers are close to 3.5 cm.

Review

16. a. Evaluate the expressions below.
    $\frac{2}{3} \cdot \frac{3}{2} = ?$ 1 $\frac{4}{5} \cdot \frac{5}{4} = ?$ 1 $\frac{9}{10} \cdot \frac{10}{9} = ?$ 1 $\frac{-3}{5} \cdot \frac{5}{-3} = ?$ 1
    b. Describe the pattern using the variables *a* and *b*. $\frac{a}{b} \cdot \frac{b}{a} = 1$
    c. Give another instance of your pattern. *(Lesson 1-7)*
    Sample: $\frac{-2}{-5} \cdot \frac{-5}{-2} = 1$

Adapting to Individual Needs

Challenge
A model of an 8-inch cube is hanging from the ceiling. A spider is sitting on the upper left corner of the cube. What is the shortest distance the spider would have to crawl to get to the diagonally opposite corner of the cube? [$\sqrt{320}$ in., or about 18 in.]

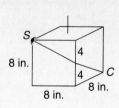
S
8 in.
4
4
C
8 in.
8 in.

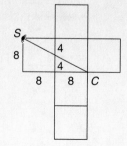
S
8
4
4
8   8   *C*

In 17 and 18, fill in the blank with =, <, or >. *(Lesson 1-6)*

17. $\sqrt{25} + \sqrt{4}$? $\sqrt{29}$ **>**

18. $(\sqrt{887})^2$? 887 **=**

19. In 1638, Galileo claimed that an object propelled into the air will reach a height that can be determined by a formula. If h is the height in meters, and the object is propelled from a height of 1 meter with a vertical velocity of 30 meters a second, then

$$h = -4.9t^2 + 30t + 1,$$

where t is the number of seconds that the object is in the air. Find the height of a batted ball 2 seconds after it is hit.   *(Lesson 1-5)*
41.4 meters

20. The domain for g is {-2, 0, 7}. For each element of the domain, evaluate $10g^2$.   *(Lessons 1-2, 1-4)* $10(-2)^2 = 40$; $10(0)^2 = 0$; $10(7)^2 = 490$

In 21–23, determine which is larger.   *(Lesson 1-1)*

21. $3\frac{1}{2}$ or 3.45 $3\frac{1}{2}$

22. $\frac{9}{4}$ or $\frac{9}{5}$ $\frac{9}{4}$

23. $\frac{4}{5}$ or $\frac{5}{6}$ $\frac{5}{6}$

24. Order from largest to smallest.   *(Previous course or Appendix B)*
$6.5 \cdot 10^{14}$, $7.2 \cdot 10^{15}$, $9.4 \cdot 10^{13}$ $7.2 \cdot 10^{15}$; $6.5 \cdot 10^{14}$; $9.4 \cdot 10^{13}$

25. Often 15% of a restaurant bill is left for a tip. If a bill is $29.88, then what would be a 15% tip? (Try to answer this question in your head by rounding $29.88 to the nearest dollar.)   *(Previous course)* ≈ $4.50

Exploration

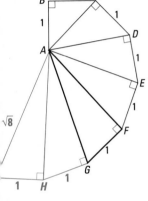

26. Six of the segments in the figure on the left have length one unit.
    a. Find the length of each of $\overline{AC}$, $\overline{AD}$, $\overline{AE}$, $\overline{AF}$, and $\overline{AG}$.
    b. Copy the drawing and add to it to make a segment whose length is $\sqrt{8}$.
    a) $AC = \sqrt{2}$; $AD = \sqrt{3}$; $AE = \sqrt{4}$ or 2; $AF = \sqrt{5}$; $AG = \sqrt{6}$

27. Use a sheet of graph paper to draw a square that has an area of 13 square units. (Hint: Find two perfect squares whose sum is 13.)
    See left.

28. Fill in the blank with =, <, >, ≤, or ≥ to make a true sentence for all non-negative real numbers.

$$\sqrt{x^2 + y^2}\ \underline{\ ?\ }\ x + y.\ \ \le$$

Is your sentence always true? How does this sentence relate to the Pythagorean Theorem and right triangles with legs of lengths x and y?
Yes. If x and y are both 0, then $\sqrt{x^2 + y^2} = x + y$. If x and y are greater than 0, then $\sqrt{x^2 + y^2} < x + y$ is true. This tells us that the length of the hypotenuse is always less than the sum of the lengths of the two legs.

27)
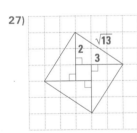

Practice
For more questions on SPUR Objectives, use **Lesson Master 1-8A** (shown on page 47) or **Lesson Master 1-8B** (shown on pages 48–49).

Assessment
Written Communication Have students draw a right triangle and identify the legs and the hypotenuse of the triangle. Then have them measure the length of each leg and use the Pythagorean Theorem to find the length of the hypotenuse. [Students demonstrate an understanding of the Pythagorean Theorem.]

Extension
Cooperative Learning Give students copies of the two squares below, or use **Teaching Aid 11**. Show that both squares have sides of length $a + b$. Then have students **work in groups** and show that $a^2 + b^2 = c^2$.

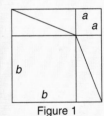
Figure 1

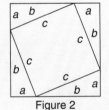
Figure 2

[The area of Figure 1 is the sum of the areas of two squares and two rectangles: $a^2 + b^2 + 2ab$. The area of Figure 2 is the sum of the areas of a square and four triangles: $c^2 + 4(\frac{1}{2}ab) = c^2 + 2ab$. Both figures have the same area, so $a^2 + b^2 + 2ab = c^2 + 2ab$, which simplifies to $a^2 + b^2 = c^2$.]

Project Update Project 1, *Interview with Pythagoras*, and Project 5, *Squares Surrounding Triangles*, on pages 60–61, relate to the content of this lesson.

Setting Up Lesson 1-9
Materials The In-class Activity requires each student to have about 40 tiles. Triangular and square blocks are needed for **Example 1** and **Question 12**. **Question 13** requires a newspaper.

Lesson 1-9 provides a rich opportunity for hands-on work with physical objects. You might want to model the patterns discussed in the lesson. Similarly, you might want to do **Questions 12 and 13** as a class project.

Resources

From the *Teacher's Resource File*
- Answer Master 1-9
- Teaching Aid 12: Centimeter Grid

Additional Resources
- Visual for Teaching Aid 12
- 40 square tiles or squares of paper for each group

This activity introduces Lesson 1-9. Have students **work in groups**. Give each group 40 square tiles, or have them draw the designs on grid paper. Encourage the groups who cannot find a formula for Step 5 to describe the patterns that they can see in words. If the groups come up with different formulas or sentences, have them share their responses with another group and decide which responses are correct.

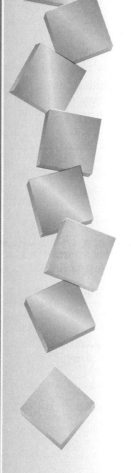

Introducing
Lesson 1-9

Variables and Tables

IN-CLASS
ACTIVITY

Materials: about 30 square tiles per group
Work in small groups.

In this chapter you have used many sentences and expressions. You may wonder where these sentences and expressions came from. In many cases, the answer is simple: Formulas, sentences, and expressions describe patterns that people have found. In this activity, you will make designs with square tiles and look for numerical patterns in the designs.

1 Arrange the tiles in the four designs shown below.

1st   2nd   3rd   5th   4th   6th

Use tiles to make the 5th and 6th designs. Draw these designs. See above.

2 Suppose the length of one side of a tile is 1. Then the perimeter of the first design is 4, and the perimeter of the second is 8. What is the perimeter of the third design? $p = 12$ in 3rd design.

perimeter = 4   perimeter = 8

3 Let n be the number of the design and p be its perimeter. For each design find p, then copy and complete the table at the right.

n	p
1	4
2	8
3	12
4	16
5	20
6	24

4 a. If you continued to make L-shaped designs like those in step 1, what would be the perimeter of the 10th design? $p = 40$

b. Explain how you got your answer. The perimeter is 4 times the number of the design.

5 *Draw conclusions.* Write a sentence or a formula that describes the relation between p and n. $p = 4n$

52

Optional Activities

Materials: Square tiles; grid paper or **Teaching Aid 12**

Tell students that a *pentomino* is formed when five congruent square tiles are joined at their edges. Explain that there are twelve ways to form pentominoes, and challenge students to find them. Suggest that they use grid paper to show their answers. Note that rotations of an arrangement are not counted as different pentominoes.

Examples of two squares joined at their edges

Examples of two squares not joined at their edges

After students find the arrangements, you might ask which of the pentomino patterns can be folded to make a box with no lid.
[Patterns 2, 3, 4, 6, 7, 9, 10, 12]

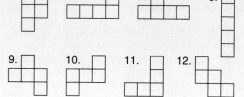

Art patterns in architecture. *Many homes in San Francisco, California, are two-story wooden buildings that share at least one wall with the house next door. Example 1 deals with patterns from rows of houses.*

When looking for patterns with variables, it sometimes helps to organize information in a table. For instance, suppose that some students are making designs from congruent triangular blocks. One student makes the following designs.

Each block design after the first is outlined by a trapezoid. How does the perimeter of the trapezoid change with the number of triangular blocks used?

Assume each side of the triangular block has length 1 unit. Add to determine the perimeter of each trapezoid.

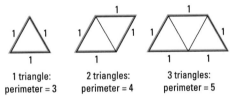

| 1 triangle: | 2 triangles: | 3 triangles: |
| perimeter = 3 | perimeter = 4 | perimeter = 5 |

Objectives
G Give instances or counterexamples of patterns.
H Use variables to describe patterns in tables.

Resources
From the *Teacher's Resource File*
- Lesson Master 1-9A or 1-9B
- Answer Master 1-9
- Teaching Aid 3: Warm-up

Additional Resources
- Visual for Teaching Aid 3
- Triangular and square blocks (Example 1 and Question 12)
- Newspaper (Question 13)

Teaching **1-9**
Lesson

Warm-up
At a back-to-school sale, pens were on sale for 59¢ each and folders were on sale for 19¢ each. For each of the following groups, find the total cost of buying one pen and one folder for every person in the group.

1. The girls in your math class
   .59*g* + .19*g*, where *g* is the number of girls
2. The boys in your math class
   .59*b* + .19*b* where *b* is the number of boys
3. The students in your grade
   .59*s* + .19*s*, where *s* is the number of students
4. The students in your school
   .59*s* + .19*s*, where *s* is the number of students

Lesson 1-9 Overview

Broad Goals The goal of this lesson is to use variables to describe patterns that are found in tables.

Perspective The problem-solving strategy "Make a Table" is a strategy that is familiar to most students. That strategy, which is often used to obtain answers to questions without using arithmetic, is elevated to an algebraic strategy here. This illustrates the power of algebra—once the table is described algebraically, any row (or column) can be completed without having to fill in the intervening rows (or columns). This strategy is used throughout UCSMP texts, and it should be thoroughly covered here.

In both this lesson and the next one, students must distinguish rows from columns. Outside of mathematics, anything in a line may be called a row. Within mathematics, rows are typically horizontal and columns are vertical; rows are read across and columns are read down.

The examples and questions in this lesson have simple formulas; virtually all of them are of one of these forms: $y = x + a$, $y = x - a$, $y = ax$, or $y = x^a$, or $y = a^x$. In later chapters, students will encounter more complicated forms.

Notes on Reading

Using Physical Models This lesson provides a rich opportunity for hands-on work with physical objects. The situations described in the reading and in **Question 12** can be modeled with plastic or wooden blocks, or from shapes cut from paper.

Each of the examples in the lesson takes about one-half of a page to describe, but they are not particularly difficult. The pattern discussed at the beginning of the lesson involves addition. **Example 1** is most easily described with multiplication, and **Examples 2 and 3** involve powers.

❶ If students have read this lesson on their own, the reading should be reviewed. Ask a student to explain how the formula $P = T + 2$ is found from the instances. Ask a different student to explain why b is equal to $3h$ in **Example 1**. Students may feel this example is quite easy, but **Question 12** poses a variant that is not as easy.

Career Connection When discussing **Example 1**, you might want to mention some of the many careers that are involved in the building of houses and housing communities: city planners, architects, general contractors, surveyors, heavy equipment operators, foundation builders, well drillers, carpenters, plumbers, masons, electricians, heating and cooling specialists, roofers, dry wall installers, painters, landscapers, and building inspectors. You might ask students to give one instance of using mathematics for each job.

---

❶

T	P
1	3
2	4
3	5
4	6
⋮	⋮
T	$T + 2$

In this situation, to find a formula relating the perimeter to the number of triangles, you need to see a relation between the numbers in *each row*. Ask, "What single rule relates 1 and 3? 2 and 4? 3 and 5? 4 and 6?"

In each case, the second number is 2 more than the first, so $P = T + 2$.

This formula is true for all whole numbers T, when $T \geq 1$. For instance, if $T = 1000$, then $P = 1000 + 2 = 1002$. When there are 1000 blocks placed in this design, the figure formed will have perimeter 1002.

Tables may be written horizontally or vertically. In Example 1, the numbers are written horizontally in a table.

Example 1

These designs show houses made from triangular and rectangular blocks.
a. How many blocks are needed to construct a row of 10 such houses?
b. Let h = the number of houses, and b = the number of blocks. Find a formula for b in terms of h.

Solution

a. Count the number of blocks needed to make 1, 2, 3, and 4 houses as shown above. Organize the data in a table.

h	1	2	3	4	⋯	10
b	3	6	9	12		?

Look for a pattern relating the values of h and b. Here the values of one variable are all in a row. So you must look down the columns to find pairs of variables. Notice that each value of b is 3 times the value of h. For 10 houses $3 \cdot 10 = 30$ blocks are needed.

b. $b = 3h$

Optional Activities

Using Physical Models
Materials: Square tiles

You might want to use this activity to introduce the lesson. Show students "trains" of 1, 2, and 3 tiles.

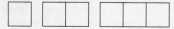

Let t = the number of tiles in a train and let p = the perimeter of the train. Then have students complete the following table.

t	1	2	3	4	5	6
p	[4]	[6]	[8]	[10]	[12]	[14]

Ask students to predict the value of p when t is 9 and to check their prediction by drawing a 9-tile train. [The perimeter of a 9-tile train is 20.] Finally, ask students which of the following equations describes the

relationship between t and p, and have them tell how they come to this conclusion.
a. $p = t + 2$ b. $p = t + 3$,
c. $p = 2t$ d. $p = 2t + 2$

[d. $p = 2t + 2$; sample explanation: the top and bottom of each tile plus the two ends of the train make up the perimeter.]

Check

a. Draw the design with 10 row houses. There are 30 blocks needed.
b. Check that the numbers in the table are instances of the formula. For example, is $h = 3$ and $b = 9$ an instance of $b = 3h$? Yes, $9 = 3 \cdot 3$.

You should be able to recognize when two variables are related by addition, subtraction, multiplication, division, powers, or square roots.

Example 2

Multiple choice. Which formula describes the numbers in the table?

x	2	3	4	5
y	4	9	16	25

(a) $y = x + 2$ (b) $y = 2x$ (c) $y = \sqrt{x}$ (d) $y = x^2$

Solution

Substitute numbers from the table for x and y. If each pair of x and y values gives a true sentence, then the formula describes the pattern. If you find a counterexample to the formula, the formula does not describe the numbers in the table. Formula (a) holds when $x = 2$ and $y = 4$ ($4 = 2 + 2$), but it does not hold for any other values. For instance, $9 \neq 3 + 2$. Similarly, formula (b) does not hold when $x = 3$ and $y = 9$ ($9 \neq 2 \cdot 3$). Formula (c) does not hold for any pairs of values in the table. For instance, $25 \neq \sqrt{5}$. Only formula (d) is true for all four values in the table.

$$4 = 2^2, \quad 9 = 3^2, \quad 16 = 4^2, \quad 25 = 5^2$$

So $y = x^2$.

Four generations.
Celebrating Thanksgiving are a boy, his two parents, his four grandparents, and one of his great-grandmothers.

Example 3

You have two biological parents. Each of your parents had two parents, and each of them had two parents. The table below looks back four generations. If you go back n generations, how many biological ancestors are in that generation?

Generation name	Number of generations back	Number of ancestors
parents	1	2
grandparents	2	4
great-grandparents	3	8
great-great-grandparents	4	16

Adapting to Individual Needs

Extra Help
Some students have trouble recognizing numerical patterns because they don't know what to look for. Encourage these students to start with the first three pairs of numbers in the table and to note any consistent differences, quotients, or powering. When students find such a pattern, they should check all given instances to see if the pattern is true. In **Example 3**, point out that the first two pairs might indicate the pattern $A = 2n$, but the third and fourth entries do not.

Stress that it is important for students to check enough instances so that they can be reasonably sure of the pattern.

---

② The formula in **Example 3** is more difficult than the others because there is a variable in the exponent. Students may not have seen a formula like this before.

Additional Examples

1. Refer to **Example 1** on page 54.
   a. How many rectangular blocks are needed to construct 10 houses? **20**
   b. Let h = the number of houses and r = the number of rectangular blocks. Find a formula for r in terms of h. **$r = 2h$**
2. *Multiple choice.* Which formula describes the numbers in the table? **c**

x	1	4	9	16
y	1	2	3	4

   (a) $y = x + 2$ (b) $y = 2x$
   (c) $y = \sqrt{x}$ (d) $y = x^2$
3. If a true-false test has only one question, two responses are possible: T or F. If the test has two questions, four responses are possible: TT, TF, FT, and FF. How many responses, P, are possible if there are q questions on the test? **$P = 2^q$**

56

► **Solution**

Look for patterns in the table. Notice that each number of ancestors is double the number in the previous generation. Each is also a power of 2. So rewrite the given numbers of ancestors as powers of 2.

Generation name	Number of generations back	Number of ancestors
parents	1	2^1
grandparents	2	2^2
great-grandparents	3	2^3
great-great-grandparents	4	2^4

Now read across the rows. Notice that in each row the generation number is the same as the exponent for the number of ancestors.

$$n \qquad\qquad 2^n$$

So, the pattern of the first four rows is that n generations back, a person has 2^n ancestors.

Let A be the number of ancestors n generations back. Then A = 2^n.

QUESTIONS

Covering the Reading

1. Refer to the opening example about the designs made from triangular blocks.
   a. Use the formula to find the perimeter of the polygon formed by placing 8 triangular blocks in a line. **10;**
   b. Draw a figure to justify your answer.

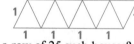

In 2 and 3, refer to Example 1.

2. How many blocks are needed to construct a row of 25 such houses?
   75 blocks

3. *True or false.* The formula $h = \frac{b}{3}$ describes the data in the table.
   True

In 4–6, *multiple choice.* Which formula describes the numbers in the table?
   (a) $y = x + 5$ (b) $y = 5x$ (c) $y = 5^x$ (d) $y = x^5$

4.

x	1	2	3	4	(b)
y	5	10	15	20	

5.

x	1	2	3	4	(c)
y	5	25	125	625	

6.

x	1	2	3	4	(a)
y	6	7	8	9	

56

Adapting to Individual Needs

English Language Development

Students with limited English proficiency might benefit from doing this lesson with an English-speaking partner. Encourage students to model the patterns using objects or drawings and to discuss the relationships that they discover.

In 7–10, refer to Example 3.

7. How many biological grandparents does every person have? 4

8. How many biological great-great-grandparents does a person have?
16

9. In the formula $A = 2^n$ for the number of biological ancestors, what do A and n stand for?
A is the number of ancestors; n is the number of generations back.

10. Explain why the formula $A = 2^n$ might not give the correct number of a person's ancestors 20 generations back.
Some of the ancestors share ancestors.

Applying the Mathematics

11. A small manufacturer makes windows with two rows of panes of glass. Below are four examples of their designs.

a. Complete the table below.

11b) The total number of panes in a design is equal to twice the number of panes in one row.

w = width of window	1	2	3	4	5
p = number of panes	2	4	6	8	10

b. Describe some patterns you find in the table in part **a.** See above.
c. Find a formula for p in terms of w. $p = 2w$

12. Below are the first three instances of a pattern made with triangular and square blocks.

12a)

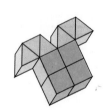 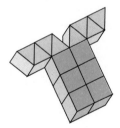

b) 30 blocks; 16 are triangular, and 14 are squares.
The number of square blocks is twice the number of instance. The number of triangular blocks is two more than the number of square blocks.

a. Draw the fourth instance. See left.
b. How many blocks will be needed to make the 7th instance of this pattern? How many will be triangular? How many will be square? Explain how you got your answers. See left.

Lesson 1-9 *Variables from Tables* **57**

Adapting to Individual Needs

Challenge
Show students the block designs at the right. Have them give the number of blocks in each design and find the next two numbers in the pattern. [4, 7, 10, 13, 16] Then have them write an equation showing the relationship between n and b if n = the number of the design and b = the number of blocks in the design. [$b = 3n + 1$]

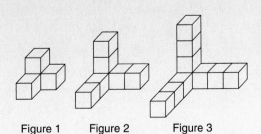

Figure 1   Figure 2   Figure 3

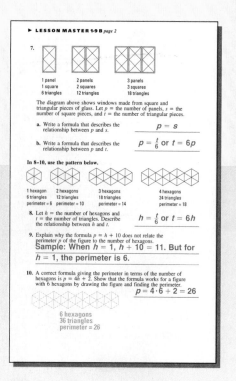

13. Take a sheet of newspaper. Call this a thickness of 1.
    a. Fold it in half and record the thickness of the folded paper. 2
    b. Fold it in half again (so you now have two folds) and record the thickness of the folded paper. 4
    c. Continue folding the paper in half and complete the table below.

n = number of folds	1	2	3	4
t = thickness of folded paper	2	4	8	16

    d. Find a formula for t in terms of n. $t = 2^n$
    e. How thick would the folded paper be if you could do 9 folds? 512

14. Refer to the table below. Find a formula relating x and y. $y = 3^x$

x	y
1	3
2	9
3	27
4	81

15. *Multiple choice.*   In the Chinese game of *wei ch'i* (way key), a player's pieces are captured and removed if they are surrounded by enemy pieces with no path to an empty point on the board. The drawing below shows situations in which black can capture the white pieces by placing a black piece on the marked point.

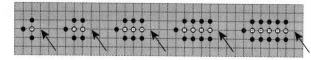

The number of black pieces required to capture each row of white pieces is shown in the table below. Which formula gives the number of black pieces, b, needed to capture a row of w white pieces? (b)

(a) $b = 2w + 1$
(b) $b = 2w + 2$
(c) $b = w + 3$
(d) $b = 3w$

w	b
1	4
2	6
3	8
4	10
5	12

Review

In 16 and 17, find the unknown length s.   *(Lesson 1-8)*

16.
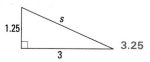

17.
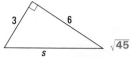

18. Refer to the figure at the left. Suppose the area of square I is 5 cm², and the area of square II is 20 cm². Find the length of each side. *(Lesson 1-8)*
    a. $\overline{AC}$ $\sqrt{5}$ cm
    b. $\overline{BC}$ $\sqrt{20}$ cm
    c. $\overline{AB}$ 5 cm

B — A — I — C
II

Out of this world. *The first U.S. astronaut to walk in space was Edward H. White II on June 3, 1965. White was firmly anchored to the Gemini 4 spacecraft by a 26-foot cord.*

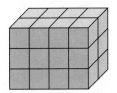

23c)
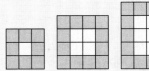

19. A museum charges a $5.00 entry fee for adults and a $1.50 fee for children.
   a. How much would it cost for 6 adults and 5 children? **$37.50**
   b. How much would it cost for a adults and c children? *(Lesson 1-7)*
   5.00a + 1.50c

20. A formula for the sum S of two fractions $\frac{a}{b}$ and $\frac{c}{d}$ is $S = \frac{ad + bc}{bd}$. *(Lesson 1-5, Previous course)*
   a. What values would a, b, c, and d be when finding the sum of $\frac{5}{8}$ and $\frac{3}{7}$? **$a = 5, b = 8, c = 3, d = 7$**
   b. Use the formula to compute the sum of $\frac{5}{8}$ and $\frac{3}{7}$. **$\frac{59}{56}$**
   c. Use the formula to compute the sum of $-\frac{2}{3}$ and $\frac{1}{2}$. **$-\frac{1}{6}$**

21. Suppose a person weighs w kg at sea level. Scientists have determined that the person's weight W at height h kilometers above the Earth is given by the formula $W = w\left(\frac{6400}{6400 + h}\right)^2$. An astronaut weighs 70 kg at sea level. How much does the astronaut weigh when traveling in space 16,000 km above Earth? *(Lesson 1-5)*
   ≈ 5.7 kilograms

22. *Multiple choice.* The graph pictures the solutions to which inequality? *(Lesson 1-2)* **(d)**

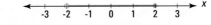

   (a) $-2 \le x \le 2$ (b) $-2 < x < 2$ (c) $-2 \le x < 2$ (d) $-2 < x \le 2$

23. **a.** What is the smallest whole number solution to $p > -7$? **0**
   b. What is the smallest integer solution to $p > -7$? **-6**
   c. Graph the solution set for $p > -7$, using the set of real numbers as domain. **See left.**
   d. Is there a smallest real number that solves $p > -7$? Why or why not? *(Lessons 1-1, 1-2)* **No. Between any two real numbers, there are always an infinite number of real numbers.**

24. One-inch cubes are stacked to form a rectangular solid as shown at left. *(Previous course)*
   a. How many cubes are used? **24 cubes**
   b. What is the volume of the rectangular solid? **24 in³**

Exploration

In 25 and 26, refer to Question 13.

25. Suppose you started with a very large sheet of paper, and could fold it 100 times.
   a. How many thicknesses of paper would you have? **$2^{100} \approx 1.268 \cdot 10^{30}$**
   b. Would this be thicker than your local telephone book? **Yes.** Justify your answer. **Even a "thick" phone book would only be 1000 or 2000 pages.**
   c. If you answered "yes" to part **b,** about how many phone books would you need to stack to equal the thickness of the paper in part **a?** **Sample: If a phone book has 1000 pages, it would take $1.268 \cdot 10^{27}$ phone books to equal the height of the folded paper.**

26. How many times can you fold a newspaper page? Explain how you arrived at your answer. **Answers will vary.**

Practice
For more questions on SPUR Objectives, use **Lesson Master 1-9A** (shown on pages 55–56) or **Lesson Master 1-9B** (shown on pages 57–58).

Assessment
Group Assessment Have students **work in groups.** Have each group write two formulas and make a table showing five solutions for each formula. Write the formulas and tables on the board in a random order. Then have students match each formula with a table. [Students demonstrate an understanding of how two variables are related in formulas and how solutions to the formulas can be displayed in a table to show a pattern.]

Extension
Show students the drawings below, and explain that the square tiles are arranged to show windows with 1-by-1, 2-by-2, and 3-by-3 openings.

1. Let s = the length of a side of an opening and t = the number of tiles in the frame. Make a table to show values of t when s is 1, 2, 3, 4, and 5.

s	1	2	3	4	5
t	8	12	16	20	24

2. Look for a pattern in the relationship between s and t. Predict the value of t when s is 7. How can you check your prediction? [32; Check by drawing a frame with a 7-by-7 window.]

3. Write a sentence or equation that describes the relationship between s and t. [$t = 4s + 4$ or $t = 4(s + 1)$]

Project Update Project 6, *Figurate Numbers,* on page 61, relates to the content of this lesson.

Chapter 1 Projects

Discuss Chapter 1 projects and what you expect students to do with them. For more information about how projects can be incorporated into the mathematics program, see *General Teaching Suggestions: Projects* in the *Professional Sourcebook* which begins on page T20 in Part 1 of the Teacher's Edition.

Chapter 1 projects relate to the content of the lessons as shown below. They can, however, be used at any time after the lessons have been taught. Suggestions for using a project are given in the lesson notes under *Project Update*.

Project	Lesson(s)
1	1-8
2	1-4
3	1-6
4	1-5
5	1-8
6	1-7, 1-9

1 Interview with Pythagoras
Recommend the use of mathematics history books as sources for information about Pythagoras. Encyclopedias provide succinct, limited information, so do not be surprised if several students turn in similar reports. Have students name their sources.

2 Order of Operations Some students may write their letters to students who have not worked with grouping symbols or exponents. Suggest that they explain how grouping symbols are used and include several examples that explain exponents.

3 Estimating Square Roots
Al-Karkhi's method estimates square roots by making equal divisions between square roots of consecutive perfect squares. For example, $\sqrt{27}$ is estimated as $\frac{2}{11}$ of the way between $\sqrt{25}$ and $\sqrt{36}$. Encourage students to look for patterns in the mixed-number answers. You might want to point out that the value of w is the square root of the nearest perfect square less than a. Also, for perfect squares, $a = w^2$, and the fractional part of Al-Karkhi's formula is equal to 0.

A project presents an opportunity for you to extend your knowledge of a topic related to the material in this chapter. You should allow more time for a project than you do for typical homework questions.

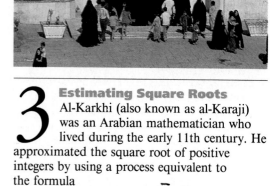

1 Interview with Pythagoras
Use a library to do some research on Pythagoras. Conduct an interview in which you, the interviewer, ask Pythagoras questions about his work. Write the interview as if it were to be printed in a magazine. Include responses you think Pythagoras might have given. You may want to perform your interview (with a partner) for your class.

2 Order of Operations
Write a letter to a student who has not yet taken algebra explaining the order of operations. Use examples to illustrate your explanation. You may want to give your letter to a younger student to read before you hand it in. If he or she has difficulty understanding your explanation, you may want to revise it before you give it to your teacher.

3 Estimating Square Roots
Al-Karkhi (also known as al-Karaji) was an Arabian mathematician who lived during the early 11th century. He approximated the square root of positive integers by using a process equivalent to the formula

$$\sqrt{a} = w + \frac{a + w^2}{2w + 1}.$$

The variable w stands for the whole number portion of the square root. Investigate al-Karkhi's method by making a table with different values for a from 1 to 50. Calculate $\sqrt{a}$ to the nearest thousandth using his method. Compare the results to what you obtain by finding $\sqrt{a}$ with a calculator. What conclusions can you make concerning al-Karkhi's method?

4 Formulas
Find ten formulas you have used that are not mentioned in this chapter. Make a poster or write a report to explain what the variables in the formulas represent and why you might want to use the formulas.

Possible responses

1. The following information is a sample of what students might include in their projects. Pythagoras was a Greek mathematician born about 572 B.C. He founded a community called the Pythagorean brotherhood. The community studied philosophy, science, and mathematics. Members were pledged to secrecy and became members for life. The Pythagoreans are credited with proving that the Pythagorean Theorem is true for any right triangle. They are also credited with discovering irrational numbers. The Pythagoreans assigned special meaning to numbers: even numbers were considered feminine and odd numbers were considered masculine. The number one was identified with reason, two with opinion, four with justice, five with marriage, seven with health, and eight with love and friendship.

2. Responses will vary.

5 Squares Surrounding Triangles

On a piece of grid paper, draw ten squares of different sizes. (Note: They don't *all* have to be different from one another.) Then carefully cut them out.

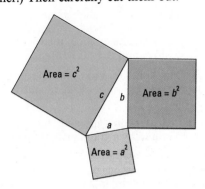

Area = c^2

c b Area = b^2

a

Area = a^2

a. (i) Lay three of the squares on the table to form a triangle, as shown above. Refer to the longest side as c and the shorter sides as a and b.

(ii) Add the areas of the two smaller squares, and write down the sum. Is the sum $(a^2 + b^2)$ equal to the area of the largest square (c^2)? If not, is the sum larger or smaller?

(iii) Use a protractor to measure the angle across from the longest side. Does it have the largest measure? Is it a right angle? If not, is it acute or obtuse?

b. Repeat this procedure for at least ten different triangles. Record your information in a table, and look for patterns in the data.

c. Write a brief report about what you have learned about triangles, their largest angles, and the lengths of their sides.

6 Figurate Numbers

Some numbers are called *figurate numbers* because they can be easily represented geometrically. Pictured below are the first four triangular numbers, the first four square numbers, and the first four pentagonal numbers.

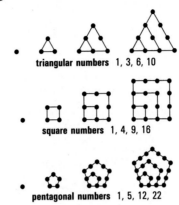

triangular numbers 1, 3, 6, 10

square numbers 1, 4, 9, 16

pentagonal numbers 1, 5, 12, 22

a. Draw a picture of the 5th triangular, 5th square, and 5th pentagonal numbers.

b. Based on the patterns in number of dots on the side of each figure, find the 10th triangular number, the 10th square number, and the 10th pentagonal number.

c. Make a poster or write a report about figurate numbers for your classroom.

4 Formulas

Students should be familiar with formulas for the perimeter, area, and volume of geometric shapes and will probably include several of these formulas in their lists. Encourage students to include a variety of formulas. They might include formulas used in sports statistics, science, probability, marketing, banking, government and so on.

5 Squares Surrounding Triangles

Students' tables should include the length of each side of a triangle, the sum of the areas of the two smaller squares, the area of the largest square, and the measure of the largest angle. Students may discover that not every combination of three squares results in a triangle.

6 Figurate Numbers

Some students may also find formulas for the nth triangular, square, and pentagonal numbers.

[nth triangular number: $\frac{n(n+1)}{2}$;

nth square number: n^2;

nth pentagonal number: $\frac{n(3n-1)}{2}$]

3. Number	Al-Karkhi's Estimate	Calculator Value	Number	Estimate	Calculator	Number	Estimate	Calculator
			12	3.429	3.464	24	4.889	4.899
1	1	1	13	3.571	3.606	25	5	5
2	1.333	1.414	14	3.714	3.742	26	5.091	5.099
3	1.667	1.732	15	3.857	3.873	27	5.182	5.196
4	2	2	16	4	4	28	5.273	5.292
5	2.200	2.236	17	4.111	4.123	29	5.364	5.385
6	2.400	2.449	18	4.222	4.243	30	5.455	5.477
7	2.600	2.64	19	4.333	4.359	31	5.545	5.568
8	2.800	2.828	20	4.444	4.472	32	5.636	5.657
9	3	3	21	4.556	4.583	33	5.727	5.745
10	3.143	3.162	22	4.667	4.690	34	5.818	5.831
11	3.286	3.317	23	4.778	4.796			

(Responses continue on page 62.)

SUMMARY

A variable is a letter or other symbol that can be replaced by (or represent) any element from a set, called its domain. Some common domains are the sets of whole numbers, integers, real numbers, and positive real numbers.

Two important operations with sets are union, denoted by the symbol $\cup$, and intersection, denoted by $\cap$. The union of two sets consists of all elements in the first set or the second set (or both). The intersection of two sets consists of those elements common to both sets.

Four uses of variables are described in this chapter. Variables are the language for translating some English expressions and sentences involving numbers into algebraic expressions and sentences. In algebraic expressions, the rules for order of operations are followed: work in parentheses or other grouping symbols first, then do powers, then do multiplications or divisions from left to right,

and then additions or subtractions from left to right. Scientific calculators and computer languages usually follow the same rules.

Variables may represent numbers or quantities in formulas like $A = lw$. Some formulas involve square roots of numbers. The positive square root of a positive number r is written $\sqrt{r}$.

Variables may stand for unknowns, as in the open sentence $x + 5 = 70$ or the inequality $3y - 2 > 8$.

The solutions to inequalities with one variable are often pictured by a graph on a number line.

Variables may be used to describe patterns. Among the most famous patterns is the Pythagorean Theorem: in a right triangle with legs a and b and hypotenuse c, $a^2 + b^2 = c^2$. General patterns can sometimes be found from studying specific instances or arranging information in tables.

VOCABULARY

Below are the most important terms and phrases for this chapter. You should be able to give a general description and a specific example of each.

Lesson 1-1
variable
sentence
equation, inequality
$=, \neq, <, \leq, \approx, >, \geq$
open sentence, solution

Lesson 1-2
set, element, { . . . }, equal sets
whole numbers, integers, real numbers
domain, solution set
interval, endpoints
open interval, closed interval
discrete

Lesson 1-3
intersection, $\cap$
union, $\cup$
Venn diagram
empty set, null set, ø, { }

Lesson 1-4
numerical expression
algebraic expression
evaluating an expression
order of operations

Lesson 1-5
formula
in terms of, depends on

Lesson 1-6
square root, $\sqrt{\ }$, radical sign
perfect squares
Square of the Square Root Property

Lesson 1-7
pattern, instance
counterexample

Lesson 1-8
leg, hypotenuse
Pythagorean Theorem

62

Additional responses, page 61

Number	Estimate	Calculator
35	5.909	5.916
36	6	6
37	6.077	6.083
38	6.154	6.164
39	6.231	6.245
40	6.308	6.325
41	6.385	6.403
42	6.462	6.481
43	6.538	6.557
44	6.615	6.633
45	6.692	6.708

Number	Estimate	Calculator
46	6.769	6.782
47	6.846	6.856
48	6.923	6.928
49	7	7
50	7.067	7.071

Sample conclusion: The estimates of square roots found by using Al-Karkhi's method are close to the actual values.

4. Sample formulas:
   a. To change from degrees Celsius, C, to degrees Fahrenheit, F:
   $F = 1.8C + 32$
   b. To find the circumference, C, or area, A, of a circle with radius r:
   $C = 2\pi r$ and $A = \pi r^2$
   c. To find the volume of cube with edge s: $V = s^3$
   d. To find simple interest I, with principal p, rate r, and time t: $I = prt$
   e. To find batting average, B, for h hits in t times at bat: $B = \frac{h}{t}$

PROGRESS SELF-TEST

Progress Self-Test

For the development of mathematical competence, feedback and correction, along with the opportunity to practice, are necessary. The Progress Self-Test provides the opportunity for feedback and correction; the Chapter Review provides additional opportunities and practice. We cannot overemphasize the importance of these end-of-chapter materials. It is at this point that the material "gels" for many students, allowing them to solidify skills and understanding. In general, student performance should be markedly improved after these pages.

Assign the Progress Self-Test as a one-night assignment. Worked-out *solutions* for all questions are in the Selected Answers section of the student book. Encourage students to take the Progress Self-Test honestly, grade themselves, and then be prepared to discuss the test in class.

Advise students to pay special attention to those Chapter Review questions (pages 65–68) which correspond to questions missed on the Progress Self-Test.

Take this test as you would take a test in class. You will need a ruler and calculator. Then check your work with the solutions in the Selected Answers section in the back of the book.

In 1–5, evaluate each expression.

1. $2(a + 3b)$, when $a = 3$ and $b = 5$ **36**

2. $5 \cdot 6^n$, when $n = 4$ **6480**

3. $\frac{p + t^2}{p - t}$, when $p = 5$ and $t = 2$ **3**

4. $(\sqrt{50})^2$ **50**

5. $10 * y \wedge 2 + 5$, when $y = 3$ **95**

6. Find the value of $3\sqrt{42}$ rounded to the nearest tenth. $\approx$ **19.4**

7. Let $M = \{2, 4, 6, 8, 10, 12, 14, 16\}$ and $N = \{3, 6, 9, 12, 15\}$. List the members of each set. **See below.**

   a. $M \cup N$ b. $M \cap N$

8. A road has a 25 mph speed limit. A person is driving at S mph and is speeding. Express the possible values of S with an inequality. $S >$ **25**

9. *Multiple choice.* t is the number of towels at a swimming pool. Which is the most appropriate domain for t? **(a)**
   (a) set of whole numbers
   (b) set of integers
   (c) set of real numbers

10. Which of the numbers 2, 5, and 8 make the open sentence $4y + 7 = 2y + 23$ true? **8**

11. Give three values for x that make $3x < 24$ true. **Samples: 6, 7, 7.9**

   7a) $\{2, 3, 4, 6, 8, 9, 10, 12, 14, 15, 16\}$
   b) $\{6, 12\}$

12. The formula $C = 23(n - 1) + 29$ gives the cost of first-class postage in 1993. In the formula, C is the cost in cents and n is the weight of the mail rounded up to the nearest ounce. What does it cost to mail a letter weighing 3.2 ounces? **98¢**

13. The area of a circle is given by the formula $A = \pi r^2$. To the nearest square meter, what is the area of a circle with radius 3 meters? (Use $\pi \approx 3.14159$.) $\approx$ **28 m²**

14. *True or false.* $\sqrt{100} + \sqrt{36} = \sqrt{136}$. **False** Explain your reasoning. **$10 + 6 = 16 \neq \sqrt{136}$**

15. Let $C =$ the set of original states in the U.S. How many elements does C have? **13**

16. One ticket costs $3.50. Four tickets cost **See** $3.50 \cdot 4$. Ten tickets cost $3.50 \cdot 10$. **below.** Describe the pattern using one variable.

17. Write three instances of the following pattern.
    $$\frac{a}{5} - \frac{b}{5} = \frac{a - b}{5}$$ **See below.**

18. Find a formula relating x and y in the table below. $y = 8x$

x	y
1	8
2	16
3	24
4	32

16) Sample: n tickets cost $3.50 \cdot n$.
17) Sample: $\frac{3}{5} - \frac{2}{5} = \frac{3 - 2}{5}$;
   $\frac{12}{5} - \frac{2}{5} = \frac{12 - 2}{5}, \frac{1.9}{5} - \frac{6.13}{5} = \frac{1.9 - 6.13}{5}$

5. a. Responses will vary.
   b. Responses will vary.
   c. The following information is a sample of what students might include: If $a^2 + b^2 > c^2$, the triangle is acute. If $a^2 + b^2 < c^2$, the triangle is obtuse with the obtuse angle opposite side c. If $a^2 + b^2 = c^2$, the triangle is a right triangle with the right angle opposite side c. The largest angle in the triangle is opposite the longest side.

6. a. Check students' drawings.
      5th triangular number: 15
      5th square number: 25
      5th pentagonal number: 35
   b. 10th triangular number: 55
      10th square number: 100
      10th pentagonal number: 145
   c. Responses will vary.

PROGRESS SELF-TEST

19. On a number line, graph the solution set for $n < 8$, where the domain is the set of whole numbers. 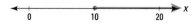 n

20. a. Write an inequality to describe the graph below. $x \geq 10$

b. Describe a real world situation that fits this graph. **Answers will vary.**

$\xrightarrow{\hspace{1cm}}$ x
0   10   20

21. Graph $x > 5$ or $x \leq -3$ on a number line using the set of real numbers as the domain. $\xleftarrow{\hspace{1cm}}$ x
-4 -3 -2 -1 0 1 2 3 4 5 6

22. Sir Gawain plans to use a ladder to get to the top of the wall of a castle. The wall is 45 ft tall and is protected by a moat that is 10 ft wide. How long must the ladder be? Round to the nearest tenth. ≈ 46.1 ft

45 ft

10 ft

23. An acre is 4840 yd^2, so a 40-acre field contains 193,600 yd^2. If a 40-acre field is in the shape of a square, how long is each side? **440 yd**

24. The "size" of a television screen is described by the length of its diagonal. What is the size of the TV screen below? **25 in.**

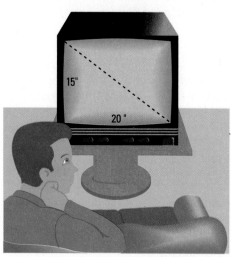

15"

20 "

After taking and correcting the Self-Test, you may want to make a list of the problems you got wrong. Then write down what you need to study most. If you can, try to explain your most frequent or common mistakes. Use what you write to help you study and review the chapter.

CHAPTER REVIEW

Questions on SPUR Objectives

SPUR stands for **S**kills, **P**roperties, **U**ses, and **R**epresentations. The Chapter Review questions are grouped according to the SPUR Objectives for this chapter.

SKILLS DEAL WITH THE PROCEDURES USED TO GET ANSWERS.

Objective A: *Find solutions to open sentences using trial and error.* *(Lesson 1-1)*

1. Which of the numbers 3, 4, or 5 is a solution to $2x + 13 = 3x + 9$? **4**

2. Using $\{1, 4, 7\}$ as a domain, give the solution set of $7x - 13 < 2x$. **{1}**

3. Find three values for x so that $-5 \le x \le -3$.

4. Give three values for y so that $2y \ge 150$. **Sample: 75, 75.5, 76**

In 5 and 6, find all solutions.

5. $x^2 = 9$ **3, -3**   6. $x^2 = 90$ $\sqrt{90}, -\sqrt{90}$

3) Sample: -5, -4.2, -3

Objective B: *Find unions and intersections.* *(Lesson 1-3)*

7. Let $A = \{11, 15, 19, 23, 25\}$, $B = \{10, 15, 20, 25, 30\}$. a) **{15, 25}**
   a. Find $A \cap B$.   b. Find $A \cup B$. **See below.**

8. Suppose $C = \{2, 8, 9\}$, $D = \{4, 8, 12\}$, and $E = \{6, 8, 9\}$.
   a. Find $(C \cup D) \cap E$. **{8, 9}**   b. Find $C \cup (D \cap E)$. **{2, 8, 9}**

9. Let W = the set of whole numbers and $X = \{-1, 0, 1, 2\}$. Describe each set.
   a. $W \cup X$ **See below.**   b. $W \cap X$ **{0, 1, 2}**

10. Let O = the set of odd whole numbers, and P = the set of prime numbers. List the five smallest numbers in each set.
    a. $O \cap P$ **3, 5, 7, 11, 13**   b. $O \cup P$ **1, 2, 3, 5, 7**

Objective C: *Evaluate numerical and algebraic expressions.* *(Lessons 1-4, 1-6)*

In 11–13, evaluate the expression.

11. a. $3 - \frac{2}{5} + 6$ **$8\frac{3}{5}$**   b. $(3 - 2)(5 + 6)$ **11**

12. $-35 + 5 \cdot 2$ **-25**   13. $(3 + 4 * 5) \wedge 2$ **529**

7b) {10, 11, 15, 19, 20, 23, 25, 30}
9a) {-1, 0, 1, 2, 3, . . . }

In 14–18, evaluate the expression for the given values of the variables.

14. $-2p$ when $p = 3.5$ **-7**

15. $4x^2$ when $x = 12$ **576**

16. $4(p - q)$ when $p = 13.8$ and $q = 5.4$ **33.6**

17. $5(M + N)$ when $M = \frac{2}{5}$ and $N = \frac{1}{5}$ **3**

18. $\left(\frac{n}{4}\right)^3$ when $n = 36$ **729**

Objective D: *Evaluate square roots with and without a calculator.* *(Lesson 1-6)*

19. $\sqrt{81}$ **9**   20. $-\sqrt{49}$ **-7**

21. $3\sqrt{100}$ **30**   22. $\sqrt{36} + \sqrt{64}$ **14**

23. *True or false.* $\sqrt{25} + \sqrt{4} = \sqrt{29}$. Explain your answer. **False; $5 + 2 \ne \sqrt{29}$**

24. Fill in the blank with one of $>$, $=$, or $<$. **=** $\sqrt{144} \cdot \sqrt{9}$ __?__ 36. Explain how you got your answer. **$12 \cdot 3 = 36$, so $\sqrt{144} \cdot \sqrt{9} = 36$**

25. $\sqrt{20}$ is between which two consecutive whole numbers? **4 and 5**

26. Find two consecutive whole numbers a and b such that $a < \sqrt{8} < b$. **2 and 3**

In 27 and 28, approximate the value to the nearest thousandth.

27. $\sqrt{199}$ **14.107**   28. $\sqrt{200^2 + 300^2}$ **360.555**

Chapter 1 Review

Resources

From the Teacher's Resource File
- Answer Master for Chapter 1 Review
- Assessment Sourcebook: Chapter 1 Test, Forms A–D

Additional Resources
- Quiz and Test Writer

The main objectives for the chapter are organized in the Chapter Review under the four types of understanding this book promotes—Skills, Properties, Uses, and Representations.

Skills include simple and complicated procedures for getting answers; at higher levels they include the study of algorithms.

Properties cover the mathematical justifications for procedures and other theories; at higher levels they include proofs.

Uses include real-world applications of the mathematics; at higher levels they include modeling.

Representations include graphs and diagrams; at higher levels they include the invention of new objects or metaphors to discuss the mathematics.

To the *lay person*, basic understanding of mathematics is usually found in Skills. The *mathematician* prefers to think of understanding in terms of Properties. The *engineer* often tests understanding by the ability to Use mathematics. The *psychologist* often views "true" understanding as being achieved through Representations or metaphors. The SPUR framework conveys the authors' views that all of these views have validity, and that together they contribute to the deep understanding of mathematics we want students to have.

Whereas end-of-chapter material may be considered optional in some texts, in *Algebra*, we have selected these objectives and questions with the expectation that they will be covered. Students should be able to answer these questions with about 85% accuracy after studying the chapter.

You may assign these questions over a single night to help students prepare for a test the next day, or you may assign the questions over a two-day period. If you work the questions over two days, then we recommend assigning the *evens* for homework the first night so that students get feedback in class the next day, then assigning the *odds* the night before the test, because answers are provided to the odd-numbered questions.

It is effective to ask students which questions they still do not understand and use the day or days as a total class discussion of the material which the class finds most difficult.

PROPERTIES DEAL WITH THE PRINCIPLES BEHIND THE MATHEMATICS.

Objective E: *Read and interpret set language and notation.* (*Lessons 1-2, 1-3*)

29. If S = the set of states in the United States, how many members does S have? **50**

30. Let B = the solution set to $-2 < n < 4$, where n is an integer. List the elements of B.

31. a. What does the symbol ø represent?
    b. Give an example of a set equal to ø.

32. *True or false.* The number -3 is an element of the set of whole numbers. **False**
    30) {-1, 0, 1, 2, 3}   31) See below.

Objective F: *Use the Square of a Square Root Property.* (*Lesson 1-6*)

In 33–35, evaluate without using a calculator.

33. $\sqrt{(7)}(\sqrt{7})$ **7** 34. $8(\sqrt{15}\cdot\sqrt{15})$ **120** 35. $(\sqrt{39})^2$ **39**

36. Find the area of a square with sides of length $\sqrt{6}$. **6**

Objective G: *Give instances or counterexamples of patterns.* (*Lessons 1-7, 1-9*)

In 37 and 38, a pattern is given. Write three instances of the pattern. **See below.**

37. $a + a = 2a$ 38. $8(x + y) = 8x + 8y$

39. A hardware store finds that the number of hammers h and the number of wrenches w that it sells are related by the formula $w = 4.5h$. Give two instances of this pattern. **See below.**

40. Hal simplified the following few fractions. He used the wrong method, but got the right answers!

$$\frac{16}{64} = \frac{1\cancel{6}}{\cancel{6}4} = \frac{1}{4} \qquad \frac{22}{22} = \frac{2\cancel{2}}{\cancel{2}2} = \frac{2}{2} = \frac{1}{1}$$

$$\frac{19}{95} = \frac{1\cancel{9}}{\cancel{9}5} = \frac{1}{5} \qquad \frac{49}{98} = \frac{4\cancel{9}}{\cancel{9}8} = \frac{4}{8} = \frac{1}{2}$$

Give a counterexample to show that Hal's method will not always work.
Sample: $\frac{17}{74} \neq \frac{1}{4}$

31a) empty or null set
b) Sample: the set of integers between -3 and -2
37) Sample: $2 + 2 = 2 \cdot 2$; $-3 + -3 = 2 \cdot -3$; $4.9 + 4.9 = 2 \cdot 4.9$
38) Sample: $8(7 + 9) = 8 \cdot 7 + 8 \cdot 9$; $8(-10 + 4) = 8 \cdot -10 + 8 \cdot 4$; $8(\frac{1}{2} + 2.1) = 8 \cdot \frac{1}{2} + 8 \cdot 2.1$
39) Sample: $9 = 4.5 \cdot 2$; $36 = 4.5 \cdot 8$
42) S shirts and J jeans cost $S \cdot 19 + J \cdot 27$ dollars.

Objective H: *Use variables to describe patterns in instances or tables.* (*Lessons 1-7, 1-9*)

In 41 and 42, three instances of a pattern are given. Use one or two variables to describe the pattern. **41) Sample: n sheep have $n \cdot 4$ legs.**

41. One sheep has $1 \cdot 4$ legs, 80 sheep have $80 \cdot 4$ legs, and six sheep have $6 \cdot 4$ legs.

42. Two shirts and three pair of jeans cost
    $2 \cdot \$19 + 3 \cdot \$27$.
    Four shirts and one pair of jeans cost
    $4 \cdot \$19 + 1 \cdot \$27$.
    Two shirts and five pair of jeans cost
    $2 \cdot \$19 + 5 \cdot \$27$. **See below.**

43. Since 1960 the population of Lincoln, Nebraska, has been increasing by about 2100 people per year. Assume that this rate continues indefinitely.
    a. How much will the population increase in a decade? **21,000 people**
    b. How much will the population increase in y years? **2100 y**

In 44 and 45, find a formula relating x and y.

44.

x	y
1	11
2	22
3	33
4	44

$y = 11 \cdot x$

45.

x	y
1	4
2	16
3	64
4	256

$y = 4^x$

46. The diagram below shows frames for photographs.
    a. Complete the table.
    b. Find a formula for t in terms of n. $t = n^2$

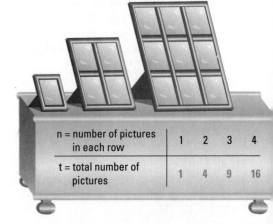

n = number of pictures in each row	1	2	3	4
t = total number of pictures	1	4	9	16

USES DEAL WITH APPLICATIONS OF MATHEMATICS IN REAL SITUATIONS.

Objective I: *In real situations, choose a reasonable domain for a variable.* *(Lesson 1-2)*

In 47–50, *multiple choice.* Choose a domain for the variable from these sets.

   (a) set of whole numbers
   (b) set of integers
   (c) set of positive real numbers
   (d) set of real numbers

47. *d,* the distance that a jogger runs in a day (c)

48. the weight *w* of a molecule (c)

49. *P,* the altitude of a point on the surface of Earth (d)

50. roast beef sandwiches for *n* people (a)

Objective J: *Evaluate formulas in real situations.* *(Lesson 1-5)*

51. The percent discount *p* on an item is given by the formula, $p = 100\left(1 - \frac{n}{g}\right)$, where *g* is the original price and *n* is the new price. Find the percent discount on a pair of jeans whose price is reduced from $20 to $15. **25%**

52. If a can of orange juice is *h* centimeters high and has a bottom radius of *r* centimeters, then the volume equals $\pi r^2 h$ cubic centimeters. What is the volume of a can 12 cm high with a radius of 6 cm? (Use $\pi \approx 3.14159$.) **≈ 1357.17cm³**

In 53 and 54, use this information. The cost *c* of carpeting a room is given by $c = p\left(\frac{\ell w}{9}\right)$, where *p* is the price of the carpeting per square yard and ℓ and *w* are the length and width of the room in feet.

53. Find the cost of carpeting a 12′ by 15′ room with carpeting that sells for $19.95 per square yard. **$399**

54. At $8.99 per square yard, what is the cost of carpeting an 8′ by 30′ deck? **$239.74**

Objective K: *Apply the Pythagorean Theorem to solve problems in real situations.* *(Lesson 1-8)*

55. Ben uses a guy wire to support a young tree. He attaches it to a point 6 ft up the tree trunk and stretches the wire to a stake 8 ft from the tree trunk. How long must the wire be? **10 ft**

6 ft

8 ft

56. Megan is flying a kite. The kite is 20 m from her along the ground and 10 m above her. How long is the string between Megan and the kite?

$\sqrt{500}$ m or ≈ 22.4 m

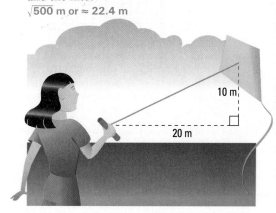

10 m

20 m

Chapter 1   *Chapter Review*   **67**

Assessment

57. A builder designing a house needs to consider the cost of the roof. How much longer is a rafter in Plan *B* than one in Plan *A*? ≈ **1.78 ft or about 2 ft**

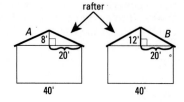

58. A rectangular field is 300 feet long and 100 feet wide. a) **316 ft**

  a. To the nearest foot, how far will you walk if you cut across the field diagonally?

  b. How much shorter is this than walking along the edges of the field? **84 ft**

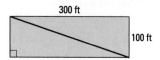

REPRESENTATIONS DEAL WITH PICTURES, GRAPHS, OR OBJECTS THAT ILLUSTRATE CONCEPTS.

Objective L: *Draw and interpret graphs of solution sets to inequalities.* *(Lessons 1-2, 1-3)*

59. Kim bought stamps for less than $25. On a number line, graph what she might have spent. **See margin.**

60. Consider the sign pictured below.

  a. Express the interval of the legal speeds as an inequality using *s* to represent speed.

  b. Graph all legal speeds.

  a) $45 \le s \le 65$ b) See margin.

61. Let *M* = the set of real numbers greater than -10, and *N* = the set of real numbers less than 6. Graph the set on a number line.

  a. $M \cap N$ **b.** $M \cup N$

62. If $x \ge 9$ or $x \le 4$, graph the possible values of *x* on a number line using as domain the set of real numbers. **61, 62) See margin.**

63. Graph the solution set to $y \ge 19$, if *y* has the given domain. **See margin.**

  a. set of real numbers   **b.** set of integers

In 64 and 65, *multiple choice.* Choose from the three graphs below.

(a)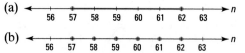

(b)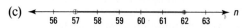

(c)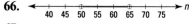

64. Which could be a graph of the solutions to $57 < n \le 62$ if *n* is a real number? (c)

65. Which represents the statement "There are from 57 to 62 students with green eyes in the school"? (b)

In 66 and 67, a graph is given.

  a. Write an inequality to describe the graph.

  b. Describe a real-world situation that fits this graph. 66a) $50 < n < 65$;   b) Answers will vary.

66.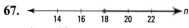

67.

  a) $n \ge 18$

  b) Sample: A U.S. citizen may vote when he or she is at least 18 years old.

Additional Answers

59.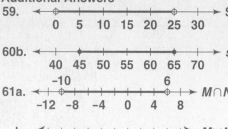

60b.
40 45 50 55 60 65 70 → *s*

61a.
-10   6
-12 -8 -4 0 4 8 → $M \cap N$

  b.
-12 -8 -4 0 4 8 → $M \cup N$

62.
3 4 5 6 7 8 9 10 11 → *x*

63a.
18 19 20 21 22 → *y*

  b.
18 19 20 21 22 → *y*

REFRESHER

Chapter 2, which discusses multiplication in algebra, assumes that you have mastered certain objectives in your previous mathematics courses. Use these questions to check your mastery.

1)15.087; 3)0.00666

A. Multiply any positive numbers or quantities.

1. $4.7 \cdot 3.21$

2. $0.04 \cdot 312$ 12.48

3. $666 \cdot 0.00001$

4. $.17 \cdot .02$ 0.0034

5. $\frac{2}{3} \cdot 30$ 20

6. $\frac{5}{2} \cdot 11$ $\frac{55}{2}$

7. $\frac{2}{9} \cdot \frac{3}{4}$ $\frac{1}{6}$

8. $\frac{1}{4} \cdot \frac{1}{3} \cdot \frac{1}{2}$ $\frac{1}{24}$

9. $1\frac{1}{4} \cdot 2\frac{1}{8}$ $2\frac{21}{32}$

10. $30\% \cdot 120$ 36

11. $3\% \cdot \$6000$ $180 **12.** $5.25\% \cdot 1500$ 78.75

B. Apply multiplication in rate-factor situations.

13. A school cafeteria sells 150 cartons of milk per day. How many cartons does it sell in a 180-day school year? 27,000 cartons

14. A sales clerk makes $6.50 an hour and works 37.5 hours a week. How much does the person earn per week? $243.75

15. The manufacturer claims that a new car gets 33.5 miles per gallon for highway driving. The gas tank holds 12 gallons. How far can the car travel on the highway on a full tank of gas? 402 miles

16. If a plane travels at 625 miles per hour for $2\frac{1}{2}$ hours, how far does it travel? 1562.5 miles

C. Multiply positive and negative integers.

17. $3 \cdot -2$ –6

18. $11 \cdot -11$ –121

19. $-6 \cdot 4$ –24

20. $-5 \cdot -5$ 25

21. $0 \cdot -1$ 0

22. $-14 \cdot 130$ –1820

23. $-60 \cdot -59$ 3540

24. $-3 \cdot -2 \cdot -1 \cdot -1$ 6

D. Solve equations of the form $ax = b$, when a and b are positive integers.

25. $3x = 12$ x = 4

26. $5y = 110$ y = 22

27. $10z = 5$ $z = \frac{1}{2}$

28. $1 = 9w$ $w = \frac{1}{9}$

29. $6 = 50a$ $a = \frac{3}{25}$

30. $b \cdot 21 = 14$ $b = \frac{2}{3}$

31. $8c = 4$ $c = \frac{1}{2}$

32. $7 = 2d$ $d = \frac{7}{2}$

E. Determine the area of a rectangle given its dimensions.

33. length 15″, width 12″ 180 in²

34. length 4.5 cm, width 3.2 cm 14.4 cm²

35. length 2 m, width 4 m 8 m²

36. length 100 ft, width 82 ft 8200 ft²

F. Determine the volume of a rectangular solid given its dimensions. 37-40) See below.

37. length 8 cm, width 4 cm, height 3 cm

38. length 12 in., width 9 in., height $1\frac{1}{2}$ in.

39. length $\frac{1}{2}$ ft, width $\frac{1}{2}$ ft, height $\frac{1}{2}$ ft

40. length 60 m, width 50 m, height 10 m

37) 96 cm³
38) 162 in³
39) $\frac{1}{8}$ ft³ or 0.125 ft³
40) 30,000 m³

Refresher

There are two ways you might use this Refresher. If you know that your students have a particularly weak background in multiplication as it relates to algebra, you may wish to assign this Refresher to better prepare them for Chapter 2. If you do not know what your students' backgrounds are, you can use these questions as both a diagnostic tool and as remediation.

Have students do the odd-numbered questions as part of the first assignment for the chapter and then have them check their answers with those given in the back of their books. If they missed more than a few questions, they should see you for help with the even-numbered questions.

Parts A, B, and C relate to the content of Lessons 2-3, 2-4, and 2-5, respectively. Part D covers the simplest equations of the form seen in Lesson 2-6. Parts E and F involve ideas that are reviewed in Lesson 2-1.

Setting Up Lesson 2-1

Homework We strongly recommend that you assign Lesson 2-1, both reading and some questions, for homework the evening of the test. It gives students work to do after they have completed the test and keeps the class moving.

Remind students that this assignment includes the *Chapter 2 Opener.*

Chapter 2 Pacing Chart

Day	Full Course	Minimal Course
1	2-1	2-1
2	2-2	2-2
3	2-3	2-3
4	Quiz*; 2-4	Quiz*; begin 2-4.
5	2-5	Finish 2-4.
6	2-6	2-5
7	2-7	2-6
8	Quiz*; 2-8	2-7
9	2-9	Quiz*; begin 2-8.
10	2-10	Finish 2-8.
11	Self-Test	2-9
12	Review	2-10
13	Test*	Self-Test
14		Review
15		Review
16		Test*

*in the Teacher's Resource File

Adapting to Individual Needs

The student text is written for the vast majority of students. The chart at the right suggests two pacing plans to accommodate the needs of your students. Students in the Full Course should complete the entire text by the end of the year. Students in the Minimal Course will spend more time when there are quizzes and more time on the Chapter Review. Therefore, these students may not complete all of the chapters in the text.

Options are also presented to meet the needs of a variety of teaching and learning styles. For each lesson, the Teacher's Edition provides sections entitled: *Video* which describes video segments and related questions that can be used for motivation or extension; *Optional Activities* which suggests activities that employ materials, physical models, technology, and cooperative learning; and, *Adapting to Individual Needs* which regularly includes **Challenge** problems, **English Language Development** suggestions, and suggestions for providing **Extra Help.** The Teacher's Edition also frequently includes an **Error Alert,** an **Extension,** and an **Assessment** alternative. The options available in Chapter 2 are summarized in the chart below.

In the Teacher's Edition...

Lesson	Optional Activities	Extra Help	Challenge	English Language Development	Error Alert	Extension	Cooperative Learning	Ongoing Assessment
2-1	•	•	•	•	•	•	•	Written
2-2	•	•	•	•		•	•	Oral
2-3	•	•		•	•	•	•	Group
2-4	•	•	•	•		•	•	Written
2-5	•	•	•	•		•		Written
2-6	•	•	•	•		•		Oral
2-7	•	•	•	•		•		Oral
2-8	•	•	•	•	•	•		Written
2-9	•	•	•	•		•	•	Written
2-10	•	•	•	•		•	•	Written

In the Additional Resources...

Lesson	Lesson Masters, A and B	Teaching Aids*	Activity Kit*	Answer Masters	Technology Sourcebook	Assessment Sourcebook	Visual Aids**	Technology	Video Segments
					In the Teacher's Resource File				
2-1	2-1	13, 16		2-1			13, 16, AM		
2-2	2-2	13		2-2			13, AM		
In-class Activity		17		2-3			17, AM		
2-3	2-3	13		2-3		Quiz	13, AM		
2-4	2-4	14, 18		2-4	Comp 3		14, 18, AM	Spreadsheet	
2-5	2-5	14		2-5			14, AM		
2-6	2-6	14, 19	3	2-6	Comp 4		14, 19, AM	Spreadsheet	
2-7	2-7	14		2-7		Quiz	14, AM		
2-8	2-8	5, 15		2-8			5, 15, AM		
2-9	2-9	15, 20	4	2-9	Comp 5		15, 20, AM		
2-10	2-10	15		2-10			15, AM		
End of chapter				Review		Tests			

*Teaching Aids are pictured on pages 70C and 70D. The activities in the Activity Kit are pictured on page 70C.

**Visual Aids provide transparencies for all Teaching Aids and all Answer Masters.

Also available is the Study Skills Handbook which includes study-skill tips related to reading, note-taking, and comprehension.

Integrating Strands and Applications

	2-1	2-2	2-3	2-4	2-5	2-6	2-7	2-8	2-9	2-10
Mathematical Connections										
Number Sense		●					●	●		
Algebra	●	●	●	●	●	●	●	●	●	●
Geometry	●	●	●		●	●		●	●	●
Measurement	●	●		●	●	●		●	●	●
Logic and Reasoning				●						
Probability									●	
Patterns and Functions					●		●	●	●	●
Discrete Mathematics	●					●		●	●	●
Interdisciplinary and Other Connections										
Art										●
Music								●		
Science	●			●	●	●				
Social Studies			●	●	●	●			●	●
Multicultural		●	●	●			●	●	●	
Technology		●			●		●			●
Career					●		●		●	
Consumer	●	●	●	●		●	●	●	●	●
Sports		●		●		●	●		●	●

Teaching and Assessing the Chapter Objectives

Chapter 2 Objectives (Organized into the SPUR categories—Skills, Properties, Uses, and Representations)	Lessons	Progress Self-Test Questions	Chapter Review Questions	Chapter Test, Forms A and B	Chapter Test, Forms	
					C	**D**
Skills						
A: Multiply and simplify algebraic fractions.	2-3	3–5	1–8	1–3	5	
B: Multiply positive and negative numbers.	2-5	2, 21, 22	9–18	4, 8	2	
C: Solve and check equations of the form $ax = b$.	2-6, 2-7	7, 8, 12	19–28	11, 12	6	
D: Solve and check inequalities of the form $ax < b$.	2-8	9–11	29–34	13, 14	6	✓
E: Evaluate expressions containing a factorial symbol.	2-10	1	35–41	5, 7	3	
Properties						
F: Identify and apply the following properties of multiplication. Commutative Property of Multiplication Associative Property of Multiplication Multiplicative identity Property of 1 Property of Reciprocals Multiplication Property of Zero Multiplication Property of Equality Multiplication Property of Inequality Multiplication Property of –1	2-1, 2-2, 2-5, 2-6, 2-7, 2-8	6, 13–15, 24	42–51	6, 9, 10, 16, 17	1	
Uses						
G: Apply the Area Model of Multiplication in real situations.	2-1, 2-8	19, 20, 25	52–57	22		✓
H: Apply the Rate Factor Model of Multiplication to real situations	2-4, 2-6, 2-8	16–18	58–66	18, 21	4	✓
I: Apply the Multiplication Counting Principle and Permutation Theorem.	2-9, 2-10	26–28	67–72	15, 19	3	
Representations						
J: Use rectangles, rectangular solids, or rectangular arrays to picture multiplication.	2-1, 2-3	23	73–80	20	5	

Assessment Sourcebook
Quiz for Lessons 2-1 through 2-3   Chapter 2 Test, Forms A–D
Quiz for Lessons 2-4 through 2-6   Chapter 2 Test, Cumulative Form

Quiz and Test Writer
Multiple forms of chapter tests
and quizzes; Challenges

Activity Kit

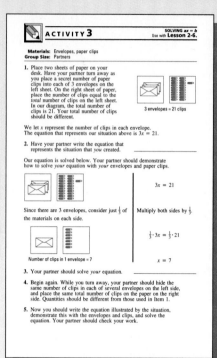

Materials: Envelopes, paper clips
Group Size: Partners

1. Place two sheets of paper on your desk. Have your partner turn away as you place a secret number of paper clips into each of 3 envelopes on the left sheet. On the right sheet of paper, place the number of clips equal to the *total* number of clips on the left sheet. In our diagram, the total number of clips is 21. Your total number of clips should be different.

3 envelopes = 21 clips

We let x represent the number of clips in each envelope. The equation that represents our situation above is $3x = 21$.

2. Have your partner write the equation that represents the situation that *you* created. _____

Our equation is solved below. Your partner should demonstrate how to solve *your* equation with *your* envelopes and paper clips.

	$3x = 21$
Since there are 3 envelopes, consider just $\frac{1}{3}$ of the materials on each side.	Multiply both sides by $\frac{1}{3}$.
	$\frac{1}{3} \cdot 3x = \frac{1}{3} \cdot 21$
Number of clips in 1 envelope = 7	$x = 7$

3. Your partner should solve *your* equation.

4. Begin again. While you turn away, your partner should hide the same number of clips in each of several envelopes on the left side, and place the same total number of clips on the paper on the right side. Quantities should be different from those used in Item 1.

5. Now you should write the equation illustrated by the situation, demonstrate this with the envelopes and clips, and solve the equation. Your partner should check your work.

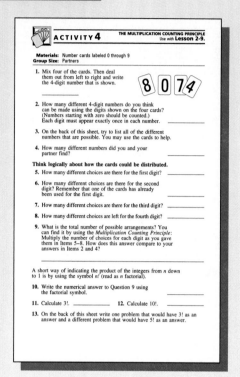

Materials: Number cards labeled 0 through 9
Group Size: Partners

1. Mix four of the cards. Then deal them out from left to right and write the 4-digit number that is shown.

8 0 7 4

2. How many different 4-digit numbers do you think can be made using the digits shown on the four cards? (Numbers starting with zero should be counted.) Each digit must appear exactly once in each number. _____

3. On the back of this sheet, try to list all of the different numbers that are possible. You may use the cards to help.

4. How many different numbers did you and your partner find? _____

Think logically about how the cards could be distributed.

5. How many different choices are there for the first digit? _____

6. How many different choices are there for the second digit? Remember that one of the cards has already been used for the first digit. _____

7. How many different choices are there for the third digit? _____

8. How many different choices are left for the fourth digit? _____

9. What is the total number of possible arrangements? You can find it by using the *Multiplication Counting Principle*: Multiply the number of choices for each digit as you gave them in Items 5–8. How does this answer compare to your answers in Items 2 and 4? _____

A short way of indicating the product of the integers from n down to 1 is by using the symbol $n!$ (read as n factorial).

10. Write the numerical answer to Question 9 using the factorial symbol. _____

11. Calculate 3!. _____   12. Calculate 10!. _____

13. On the back of this sheet write one problem that would have 3! as an answer and a different problem that would have 5! as an answer.

Teaching Aids

Teaching Aid 5, Number Lines, (shown on page 4D) can be used with **Lesson 2-8.**

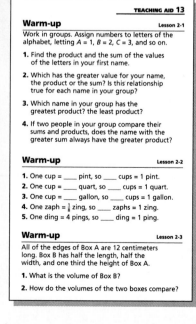

Warm-up Lesson 2-1
Work in groups. Assign numbers to letters of the alphabet, letting $A = 1$, $B = 2$, $C = 3$, and so on.

1. Find the product and the sum of the values of the letters in your first name.

2. Which has the greater value for your name, the product or the sum? Is this relationship true for each name in your group?

3. Which name in your group has the greatest product? the least product?

4. If two people in your group compare their sums and products, does the name with the greater sum always have the greater product?

Warm-up Lesson 2-2

1. One cup = ____ pint, so ____ cups = 1 pint.
2. One cup = ____ quart, so ____ cups = 1 quart.
3. One cup = ____ gallon, so ____ cups = 1 gallon.
4. One zaph = $\frac{1}{8}$ zing, so ____ zaphs = 1 zing.
5. One ding = 4 pings, so ____ ding = 1 ping.

Warm-up Lesson 2-3
All of the edges of Box A are 12 centimeters long. Box B has half the length, half the width, and one third the height of Box A.

1. What is the volume of Box B?

2. How do the volumes of the two boxes compare?

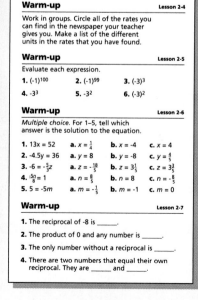

Warm-up Lesson 2-4
Work in groups. Circle all of the rates you can find in the newspaper your teacher gives you. Make a list of the different units in the rates that you have found.

Warm-up Lesson 2-5
Evaluate each expression.

1. $(-1)^{100}$ 2. $(-1)^{99}$ 3. $(-3)^3$
4. -3^3 5. -3^2 6. $(-3)^2$

Warm-up Lesson 2-6
Multiple choice. For 1–5, tell which answer is the solution to the equation.

1. $13x = 52$ **a.** $x = \frac{1}{4}$ **b.** $x = -4$ **c.** $x = 4$
2. $-4.5y = 36$ **a.** $y = 8$ **b.** $y = -8$ **c.** $y = \frac{4}{5}$
3. $-6 = -\frac{5}{3}z$ **a.** $z = -\frac{18}{5}$ **b.** $z = 3\frac{1}{5}$ **c.** $z = 3\frac{3}{5}$
4. $\frac{-5n}{8} = 1$ **a.** $n = \frac{8}{5}$ **b.** $n = 8$ **c.** $n = -\frac{8}{5}$
5. $5 = -5m$ **a.** $m = -\frac{1}{5}$ **b.** $m = -1$ **c.** $m = 0$

Warm-up Lesson 2-7

1. The reciprocal of -8 is _____.

2. The product of 0 and any number is _____.

3. The only number without a reciprocal is _____.

4. There are two numbers that equal their own reciprocal. They are _____ and _____.

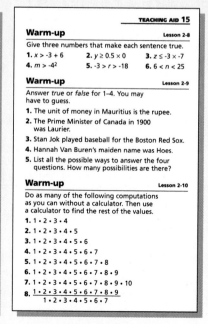

Warm-up Lesson 2-8
Give three numbers that make each sentence true.

1. $x > -3 + 6$ 2. $y \geq 0.5 \times 0$ 3. $z \leq -3 \times -7$
4. $m > -4^2$ 5. $-3 > r > -18$ 6. $6 < n < 25$

Warm-up Lesson 2-9
Answer *true* or *false* for 1–4. You may have to guess.

1. The unit of money in Mauritius is the rupee.
2. The Prime Minister of Canada in 1900 was Laurier.
3. Stan Jok played baseball for the Boston Red Sox.
4. Hannah Van Buren's maiden name was Hoes.
5. List all the possible ways to answer the four questions. How many possibilities are there?

Warm-up Lesson 2-10
Do as many of the following computations as you can without a calculator. Then use a calculator to find the rest of the values.

1. $1 \cdot 2 \cdot 3 \cdot 4$
2. $1 \cdot 2 \cdot 3 \cdot 4 \cdot 5$
3. $1 \cdot 2 \cdot 3 \cdot 4 \cdot 5 \cdot 6$
4. $1 \cdot 2 \cdot 3 \cdot 4 \cdot 5 \cdot 6 \cdot 7$
5. $1 \cdot 2 \cdot 3 \cdot 4 \cdot 5 \cdot 6 \cdot 7 \cdot 8$
6. $1 \cdot 2 \cdot 3 \cdot 4 \cdot 5 \cdot 6 \cdot 7 \cdot 8 \cdot 9$
7. $1 \cdot 2 \cdot 3 \cdot 4 \cdot 5 \cdot 6 \cdot 7 \cdot 8 \cdot 9 \cdot 10$
8. $\dfrac{1 \cdot 2 \cdot 3 \cdot 4 \cdot 5 \cdot 6 \cdot 7 \cdot 8 \cdot 9}{1 \cdot 2 \cdot 3 \cdot 4 \cdot 5 \cdot 6 \cdot 7}$

Additional Examples

1. Find the area of this figure. All of the angles are right angles. Explain how you found the area.

2. The Stuart Soup Company packs soup cans in cartons that are 40 cm wide, 48 cm long, and 20 cm tall. Find the volume of the carton.

3. If a box has dimensions $\ell = \frac{5}{2}$ in., $w = \frac{1}{2}$ in., and $h = 6$ in., find the volume using the formulas below.

   a. $V = \ell w h$ b. $V = Bh$

4. What is the area of this figure? All of the angles are right angles.

Dot Paper

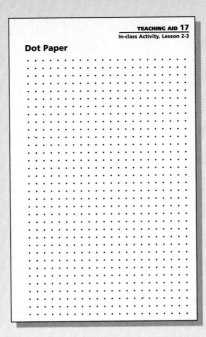

Additional Examples

1. It takes Felicia 25 minutes to walk one mile. At this rate, how long would it take her to walk 7 miles?

2. If a car travels 55 miles an hour, about how far will it travel in $3\frac{3}{4}$ hours?

3. If a car travels at 55 miles an hour, how far does it travel per second?

4. Refer to Example 4 on page 93. An average-sized person burns about 500 calories per hour swimming. If a person swims for a half hour, how much weight will he or she lose?

5. Suppose gasoline costs $1.20 a gallon. State the reciprocal rate and explain how it describes the same situation.

6. In 1962, Wilt Chamberlain set an NBA season scoring record, averaging 50.4 points per game. On the average, how many points did he score per minute? (There are 48 minutes in a basketball game.)

Balance-Scale Diagrams

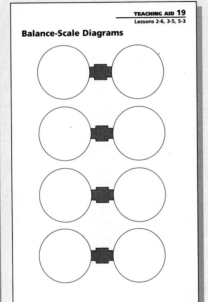

Additional Examples 2-5

2. A restaurant offers a special breakfast of eggs, meat, and juice. The eggs can be cooked in one of three different ways (scrambled, fried, poached); there are two choices for the meat (bacon, sausage) and three choices for the juice (orange, grapefruit, tomato). How many different breakfasts can be ordered?

3. While Kari was at summer camp, it was sunny for 7 days, and then it rained for 3 days. Each day Kari could do one special activity. On sunny days she had her choice of five different outside activities, and on rainy days she had her choice of two different inside activities. In how many ways could she choose her special activities?

4. a. A test has 10 true-false items and 15 multiple-choice items with 4 choices each. How many different answer sheets are possible?

   b. A test has T true-false items and M multiple-choice items with 4 choices each. How many different answer sheets are possible?

5. Suppose Mrs. Smith writes a chapter test that has 12 questions. It has four multiple-choice questions, each with r possible answers, three multiple-choice questions, each with p possible answers, and five true-false questions. How many ways are there to answer the questions?

Chapter Opener

Pacing

All of the lessons in this chapter are designed to be covered in one day. Lessons 2-1, 2-3, and 2-6 may take slightly longer, but they are followed by lessons that are shorter. At the end of the chapter, you should plan to spend 1 day to review the Progress Self-Test, 1 to 2 days for the Chapter Review, and 1 day for a test. You may wish to spend a day on projects, and perhaps a day is needed for quizzes. Therefore, this chapter should take 13 to 16 days. We strongly advise that you not spend more than 17 days on this chapter; there is ample opportunity to review the ideas in later chapters.

Using Pages 70–71

Literature Connection The formula on page 71 is from James Michener's novel *Space*, a fictionalized account of a forty-year period of American space exploration. It is remarkable that, despite its length, the only operation expressed in the formula is multiplication. Yet, in this regard, it is like the counting formulas that students will encounter toward the end of the chapter.

A formula similar to this one was developed by several research laboratories in preparation for testimony before a Congressional subcommittee; the subcommittee was looking into the probability of finding life elsewhere. This shows that Michener's formula and figures are not without some basis. Students will work with the formula again in **Question 1** on page 76 and in Project 1 on page 131.

70

Chapter 2 Overview

When students are learning to solve equations, one traditional sequence has been to proceed as one does in arithmetic. That is, begin with addition equations of the form $x + a = b$, followed by subtraction equations $x - a = b$, and then multiplication equations $ax = b$. In this book, we discuss multiplication equations first. There are two major reasons for this approach. First, it is difficult to find real-world situations that lead to equations of the form $a + x = b$ that can-

not be solved mentally. However, there are many situations that lend themselves to solving $ax = b$. Secondly, for students who have encountered equation-solving before—which we assume to be the predominant situation—solving $ax = b$ is more interesting and requires more practice than solving $a + x = b$.

In Chapter 3, solving equations of the form $a + x = b$ is treated as a special case of solving linear equations of the form $ax + b = c$.

Chapter 2 begins with applications of multiplication, proceeds to the solution of equations and inequalities involving multiplication, and concludes with additional applications of multiplication.

MULTIPLICATION IN ALGEBRA

Our galaxy, the Milky Way, looks somewhat like the Andromeda Galaxy pictured here. Ever since it was discovered that the other planets were bodies like Earth, rotating around the sun, people have wondered: Is there life on some other planet in our galaxy?

One formula for computing the number of planets N currently supporting intelligent life in our galaxy involves the product of seven numbers.

$$N = T \cdot P \cdot E \cdot L \cdot I \cdot C \cdot A$$

Of course you need to know what the letters in the formula represent. Here are their meanings and an estimated value for each from *Space,* a novel by James Michener.

T = *Total* number of stars in our galaxy = 400,000,000,000

P = fraction of stars with a *Planetary* system = $\frac{1}{4}$

E = fraction of planetary systems with a planet that has an *Ecology* able to sustain life = $\frac{1}{2}$

L = fraction of planets able to sustain life on which *Life* actually developed = $\frac{9}{10}$

I = fraction of planets with *Intelligent* life = $\frac{1}{10}$

C = fraction of planets with intelligent life that could *Communicate* outwardly = $\frac{1}{3}$

A = fraction of planets with communicating life which is *Alive* now = $\frac{1}{100,000,000}$

This yields a value of 15 for N, meaning that there may be 15 planets in our galaxy with intelligent life. However, no one knows the values of the variables in the formula exactly, and people disagree on them. Changing them can change the value of N by a great deal. For instance, if $P = \frac{1}{10}$ rather than $\frac{1}{4}$, then $N = 6$ instead of 15. This is only one of many situations involving multiplication you will see in this chapter.

Objectives

F Identify and apply the Commutative and Associative Properties of Multiplication.

G Apply the Area Model for Multiplication in real situations.

J Use rectangles, rectangular solids, or rectangular arrays to picture multiplication.

Resources

From the Teacher's Resource File

■ Lesson Master 2-1A or 2-1B
■ Answer Master 2-1
■ Teaching Aids
  13 Warm-up
  16 Additional Examples

Additional Resources

■ Visuals for Teaching Aids 13, 16

Teaching **2-1**
Lesson

Warm-up

Work in groups. Assign numbers to letters of the alphabet, letting A = 1, B = 2, C = 3, and so on.

Responses for 1–3 will vary.

1. Find the product and the sum of the values of the letters in your first name.

2. Which has the greater value for your name, the product or the sum? Is this relationship true for each name in your group?

3. Which name in your group has the greatest product? The least product?

4. If two people in your group compare their sums and products,

72

An early skyscraper. *The Pyramid of Kukulan is located in Chichen Itza, Mexico. Built by the Mayas before 800 A.D., the pyramid rises to a height of 24.1 m. What dimensions are needed to find the pyramid's base area and volume?*

Area of Rectangles and Rectangular Arrays

The operation of multiplication can be pictured using area. The area of any rectangle is the product of its two dimensions. The rectangles below are actual size.

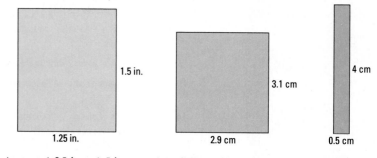

Area = 1.25 in. · 1.5 in.
= 1.875 square in.
= 1.875 in^2

A = 2.9 cm · 3.1 cm
= 8.99 square cm
= 8.99 cm^2

A = 0.5 cm · 4 cm
= 2 square cm
= 2 cm^2

The areas are in *square units* because the units are multiplied, as well as the numbers.

A **model** for an operation is a general pattern that includes many of the uses of the operation. The examples above are instances of the *Area Model for Multiplication.*

> **Area Model for Multiplication**
> The area A of a rectangle with length ℓ and width w is ℓw.

72

Lesson 2-1 Overview

Broad Goals The broad goal is to review a variety of concepts that are related to multiplication: the basic use of multiplication to obtain area and volume; the notions of square units and cubic units; the commutative and associative properties which guarantee that multiplications can be done in any order. All four SPUR dimensions are found in this lesson: the skills; the properties (commutativity and associativity); the

uses (actual areas and volumes); and the representations (rectangles and boxes).

Perspective The Area Model for Multiplication is based on the area of a rectangle. This gives a rationale for the Commutative Property of Multiplication. It is extended to the volume formula to justify the Associative Property of Multiplication. The area model is *continuous* in the sense that any measure could be used for lengths. This is in contrast

with the *discrete* version, which is applied to arrays. For arrays, the measures that are used must be whole numbers. The idea of a model of an operation is one that will be very familiar to students of *Transition Mathematics*. The Area Model and other models of operations, which are used in this book, describe the fundamental connections between the mathematical ideas and their uses in the real world.

Rectangle I below left has been rotated to give rectangle II. The two rectangles have the same dimensions. So they must have the same area. Thus the area formula could be written $A = w\ell$ as well as $A = \ell w$.

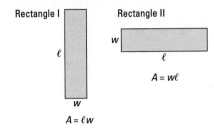

Rectangle I
ℓ
w
$A = \ell w$

Rectangle II
w
ℓ
$A = w\ell$

In this way, the area model pictures a general property named by François Servois (Fron swah Sayr vwah) in 1814. He used the French word *commutatif,* which means "switchable." The English name is "commutative."

Commutative Property of Multiplication
For any real numbers a and b, $ab = ba$.

In algebra and geometry, areas of many shapes can be found by working with rectangles.

Example 1

A driveway to a house has the shape shown at the right. All angles are right angles. Find the area of the driveway.

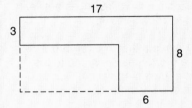

17 m
3 m
8 m
6 m

Solution

❶ There is no simple formula for an irregular shape like this. But the shape can be split into two rectangles. One way to split the figure is shown below. This splits the right side into lengths of 3 m and 5 m. Call the smaller areas A_1 and A_2. To find their areas, multiply the dimensions of the rectangles.

$A_1 = 3 \text{ m} \cdot 17 \text{ m} = 51 \text{ m}^2$
$A_2 = 5 \text{ m} \cdot 6 \text{ m} = 30 \text{ m}^2$

The total area is the sum of the areas of these parts.

Area of driveway = $A_1 + A_2$
$= 51 \text{ m}^2 + 30 \text{ m}^2$
$= 81 \text{ m}^2$

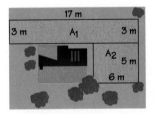

17 m
3 m
A_1
3 m
A_2
5 m
6 m

does the name with the greater sum always have the greater product? **Not always; for instance, JOHN has a product of 16,800 and a sum of 47, and WALT has a product of 5,520 but a sum of 56.**

Notes on Reading

We assume that students have studied perimeter and area of rectangles and volume of rectangular solids in previous courses. If, for some reason, students have never learned the formulas for the area of a rectangle or the volume of a rectangular solid, now is the time for these concepts to be learned. All students should know these formulas before they take a formal geometry course.

❶ Some problems involving decomposition of regions into rectangles can be solved by subtraction as well as addition. Here is a different way to do **Example 1.**

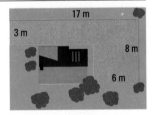

17
3
8
6

Area $= 17 \cdot 8 - 11 \cdot 5$
$= 136 - 55$
$= 81$

❷ This array provides another illustration of the Commutative Property of Multiplication. You might tell students to imagine that the stars in the array are members of a marching band and that they are in 8 columns of 6 marchers. However, if the marchers turn 90°, there would be 6 columns of 8 marchers. Either way, there are 48 marchers.

❸ Although formal development of the rules of exponents is in a later chapter, students will encounter x^n for small positive integer values of n in this chapter. Here they encounter $x^2 = x \cdot x$ and $x^3 = x \cdot x \cdot x$ as areas of squares and volumes of cubes with sides of length x.

❹ **Error Alert** Some students will have difficulty distinguishing between the commutative and associative properties. You might explain that the order of the numbers is kept in the associative property. In **Question 12,** students are asked to describe the similarities and differences between the two properties.

❺ Point out that in **Example 3** the basic properties are noted to the right of the computation. Discuss how these comments help justify the steps that are performed.

A set of objects that can be counted is a **discrete set.** The discrete form of a rectangle is a **rectangular array.** The stars at the left form a rectangular array with 5 rows and 9 columns, or a 5-by-9 array. The numbers 5 and 9 are the *dimensions* of the array. The total number of stars is 45, the product of the dimensions.

❷

The general pattern is the discrete form of the Area Model for Multiplication.

> **Area Model for Multiplication (discrete form)**
> The number of elements in a rectangular array with r rows and c columns is rc.

Volume of Rectangular Solids

The area model can be extended to three-dimensional figures. The **volume** of a **rectangular solid** is the product of its three dimensions.

$$\text{Volume} = \text{length} \cdot \text{width} \cdot \text{height}$$
$$V = \ell w h$$

Example 2

Find the volume of the rectangular solid pictured at the left.

$h = 4$ in.

$w = \frac{1}{2}$ in.

$\ell = \frac{3}{8}$ in.

Solution

Substitute the given dimensions for ℓ, w, and h in the volume formula.

$$V = \frac{3}{8} \text{ in.} \cdot \frac{1}{2} \text{ in.} \cdot 4 \text{ in.}$$

Recall that the product of fractions is the product of the numerators divided by the product of the denominators. So $\frac{3}{8} \cdot \frac{1}{2} = \frac{3}{16}$, and

$$V = \frac{3}{16} \text{ in}^2 \cdot 4 \text{ in.}$$
$$= \frac{12}{16} \text{ in}^3$$
$$= \frac{3}{4} \text{ in}^3$$

(Volume is measured in cubic units; in^3 means cubic inches.)

Check

Rewrite the dimensions as decimals.

$$\frac{3}{8} \cdot \frac{1}{2} \cdot 4 = 0.375 \cdot 0.5 \cdot 4$$
$$= 0.1875 \cdot 4$$
$$= 0.75$$

Because $\frac{3}{4} = 0.75$, the answer checks.

Adapting to Individual Needs

Extra Help
Some students might not understand the statement that both the commutative property and the associative property have to do with changing order. They probably learned earlier that the associative property involves grouping. Ask students why grouping symbols are used. Students might recall from Chapter 1, or from previous courses, that grouping symbols are used to indicate order of operations. Point out that changing the way numbers are grouped means that the order of operations is changed. So, the commutative property involves changing order of numbers, while the associative property involves changing order of operations.

❸ The area and volume models for multiplication date back to the time of the ancient Greeks. Pythagoras himself thought of multiplication this way and used area in the proof of his famous theorem. That is how the names "x squared" and "x cubed" became associated with x^2 and x^3.

In Example 2, we did not have to follow order of operations and multiply from left to right. You could first multiply $\frac{1}{2}$ in. by 4 in. This gives 2 in^2, and 2 in$^2 \cdot \frac{3}{8}$ in. $= \frac{3}{4}$ in^3. This illustrates that

$$(\ell \cdot w) \cdot h = \ell \cdot (w \cdot h).$$

Doing left multiplication first = Doing right multiplication first.

The general property, true for all numbers, is called the *Associative Property of Multiplication*. It was given its name in 1835 by the Irish mathematician Sir William Rowan Hamilton.

Associative Property of Multiplication
For any real numbers a, b, and c, $(ab)c = a(bc)$.

Enormous rectangular solids. *The 110-story, 1,350-foot-high World Trade Center, located along the Hudson River in New York City, is the world's largest office complex.*

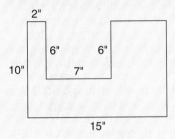

❹ Both the commutative and associative properties involve changing order. The commutative property says you can change the order of the *numbers* being multiplied. The associative property says you can change the order of the *multiplications* by *regrouping* the numbers. Together these properties let you multiply as many numbers as you please in any order. For instance, in the formula $N = TPELICA$ on page 71, you could multiply the 7 variables in any order, such as *PLICATE*.

In the volume formula $V = \ell wh$, since ℓw is the area of the base, the formula may be expressed as $V = Bh$, where B is the area of the base.

In the next example, the associative property is used to rearrange factors in a multiplication. This allows us to simplify the multiplication of expressions involving variables.

❺ **Example 3**

What is the volume of a box in which the height is $4xy$ and the area of the base is $5x^2$?

Solution

Volume = Bh

$$\begin{aligned}
V &= (5x^2)4xy \\
&= 4(5x^2)xy && \text{Commutative Property of Multiplication} \\
&= (4 \cdot 5)(x^2 \cdot x)y && \text{Associative Property of Multiplication} \\
&= 20x^3y && x^2 \cdot x = x^3
\end{aligned}$$

The volume of the box is $20x^3y$.

Lesson 2-1 *Areas, Arrays, and Volumes* **75**

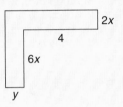
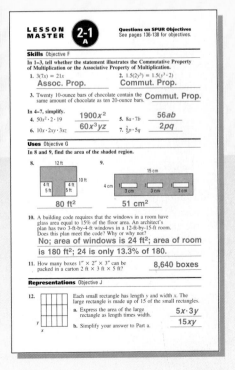

75

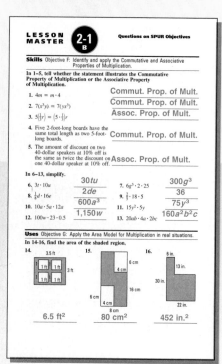

> **Check**

Pick values for x and y. See if the formula works for those values. We pick $x = 2$ and $y = 3$. Then $B = 5x^2 = 20$ and $h = 4xy = 24$, so the volume is 480. Now evaluate the answer $20x^3y$ with the same values of x and y.

$$20x^3y = 20 \cdot 2^3 \cdot 3 = 20 \cdot 8 \cdot 3 = 480, \text{ which checks.}$$

When units are not given, as in Example 3, you can assume they are the same—all inches, all centimeters, or all something else. Otherwise, make sure units are the same before multiplying.

QUESTIONS

Covering the Reading

1. A formula for computing the number of planets in our galaxy was discussed by a Congressional committee in 1975. Some astronomers from Green Bank, West Virginia, gave for their *low* estimate the following values of the variables: $T = 100,000,000,000$, $P = 0.4, E = 1, L = 1, I = 1, C = 0.1, A = \frac{1}{100,000,000}$. With these values, how many planets in our galaxy support intelligent life? **40**

2. State the Area Model for Multiplication.
   The area of a rectangle with length ℓ and width w is ℓw.

3. *Multiple choice.* If the length and width of a rectangle are measured in inches, in what unit is the area measured? **(b)**
   (a) inches   (b) square inches   (c) cubic inches

In 4 and 5, find the area of a rectangle with the given dimensions. Include units in your answer.

4. length 7.2 cm and width 4.3 cm **30.96 cm²**

5. length 8 in. and width y in. **8y in²**

6. Explain how to find the number of dots in the following rectangular array without counting them all. **Count the number of dots in one column. Then count the number of dots in one row. Multiply to find the total number of dots.**

7. In the figure at the right all angles are right angles. Find its area, and show how you found it. **188 mm²; Sample shown: 6 × 14 + 8 × 13**

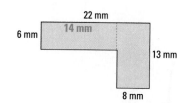

Sharper images in space. *The Hubble Space Telescope, launched by NASA in 1990, is a reflecting telescope built as an orbiting observatory. The Hubble telescope produces images about 10 times as sharp and observes objects 50 times as faint as any telescope on Earth. One goal of the telescope is to detect planets around stars other than our sun.*

Adapting to Individual Needs

Challenge
Calculator The number 64 is both a perfect square and a perfect cube, since $8^2 = 64$ and $4^3 = 64$. Have students use a calculator to find a 3-digit number and a 4-digit number with this same property. [$729 = 27^2$ and $729 = 9^3$; $4096 = 64^2$ and $4096 = 16^3$]

In 8–10, find the volume of the rectangular solid described. Be sure to include units where appropriate.

8. The dimensions are $\frac{1}{4}$ ft by $\frac{2}{3}$ ft by $\frac{1}{8}$ ft. $\frac{1}{48}$ ft^3

9. Its length is 3, width is $7x$, and height is y. **21xy cubic units**

10. The area of its base is $9p^2$ and its height is $12p$. **108p^3**

11. Which property guarantees that the two multiplication problems at right have the same answer? **Commutative Property of Multiplication**

$$\begin{array}{cc} 38.2 & 65 \\ \times\ 65 & \times\ 38.2 \end{array}$$

12. Describe the differences and similarities between the Commutative and Associative Properties of Multiplication. **See left.**

Applying the Mathematics

13. In each situation, tell whether "followed by" is a commutative operation.
    a. Putting on your socks followed by putting on your shoes **No**
    b. Putting cream in your coffee followed by putting sugar in your coffee **Yes**
    c. Writing on the blackboard followed by erasing the blackboard **No**
    d. Make up an example of your own. Tell whether it is commutative.
    Sample: Washing your hair followed by drying your hair; not commutative

In 14 and 15, use the associative and commutative properties to do the multiplication in your head.

14. $25 \cdot x \cdot 4 \cdot 341$ **34,100x**   15. $(2 \cdot 3x)(8x \cdot 5)$ **240x^2**

16. The O'Learys' garden is a rectangle 45 ft by 60 ft.
    a. What is the area of their garden? **2700 ft^2**
    b. If they put a fence around the garden, how long will the fence be? **210 ft**

17. Refer to the rectangle at the right.
    a. Write an expression for its area. **kn**
    b. Write an expression for its perimeter.
    k + k + n + n or 2k + 2n

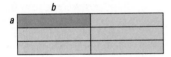

18. The largest rectangle below is made of six identical smaller ones, each with width a and length b.
    a. What is the width of the largest rectangle? **3a**
    b. What is the length of the largest rectangle? **2b**
    c. Express the area of the largest rectangle as width · length. **3a · 2b**
    d. Simplify your answer to part c. **6ab**

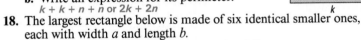

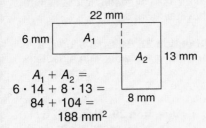

$$A_1 + A_2 = $$
$$6 \cdot 14 + 8 \cdot 13 = $$
$$84 + 104 = $$
$$188 \text{ mm}^2$$

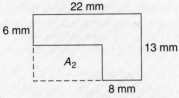

A_1 = area of large rectangle

$$A_1 - A_2 = 13 \cdot 22 - 7 \cdot 14$$
$$= 286 - 98$$
$$= 188 \text{ mm}^2$$

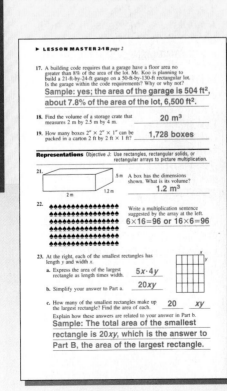

✎ **Question 23 Writing** You might ask volunteers to read what they have written.

Question 27 This question is a preview of the work with algebraic fractions that will be presented in Lesson 2-3.

✎ **Question 29 Writing** Point out that a number by itself is not a sufficient answer to this question. Some explanation regarding how the books fit into the box is needed as well.

Follow-up for Lesson **2-1**

Practice

For more questions on SPUR Objectives, use **Lesson Master 2-1A** (shown on page 75) or **Lesson Master 2-1B** (shown on pages 76–77).

Assessment

Written Communication Have students write paragraphs to their parents explaining how to use the formula for the volume of a rectangular solid to explain the Associative Property of Multiplication. [Explanations are clear and demonstrate an understanding of the property.]

Extension

Activity As an extension of Additional Example 1, have students **work in groups** and describe as many different ways as they can to find the area. In discussing responses, ask if anyone used subtraction to find the area. If so, have a student in that group explain what he or she did. If not, have students think about how subtraction can be used. [Sample answer: subtract the area of the 6×7 in² region from the 10×15 in² region.]

Project Update Projects 1, 2, 3, and 6, on pages 131–132, relate to the content of this lesson.

---

23) Sample: Area is the measure of the amount of 2-dimensional surface; volume is a measure of 3-dimensional space. The amount of space in a box is its volume; the size of one of its sides is an area.

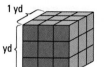
1 yd
1 yd

24b)

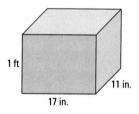

29a) The length and width of the book are about $10\frac{1}{4}$ in. and $8\frac{1}{16}$ in. So 2 books will fit in each layer. The book is about $1\frac{9}{16}$ in. thick, so 7 layers of 2 books each will fit.

1 ft
11 in.
17 in.

---

19. In the figure below, all angles are right angles. The unit is meters. Find the area. **576 m²**

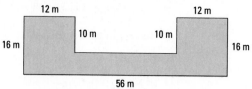

12 m   12 m
16 m   10 m   10 m   16 m
56 m

20. What is the volume of a rectangular solid in which the width is x cm, the length is $2x$ cm, and the height is $6x$ cm? **$12x^3$ cm³**

21. How many cubic inches are in a box 5 inches wide, 1 foot long, and 3 inches high? **180 in³**

22. One cubic yard is the volume of a cube with each edge of length 1 yard. How many cubic feet equal one cubic yard? **27 ft³**

23. In your own words, explain the difference between area and volume. Use an example or problem from this lesson to help illustrate your idea, or make up your own. **See left.**

Review

24. Carl runs more than three miles every morning.
  a. Write an inequality to describe how many miles he runs. **$c > 3$**
  b. Graph on a number line. *(Lesson 1-2)* **See left.**

In 25 and 26, let $L =$ the length of a segment. Write an expression for each of the following. *(Previous course)*

25. twice that length **$2L$**

26. one third that length **$\frac{1}{3}L$ or $\frac{L}{3}$**

27. Rewrite the fraction $\frac{36}{120}$ in lowest terms. *(Previous course)* **$\frac{3}{10}$**

28. There are 392 students in a school. Of these, $\frac{3}{8}$ play on an athletic team. How many students play on a team? *(Previous course)* **147 students**

Exploration

29. a. Measure the dimensions of this textbook. At most, how many texts could you fit inside the box at the left? Explain how you got your answer. **14 books; See left for explanation.**
  b. Give the dimensions of a box that could be used to pack 24 books. Explain how you would pack the books in the box. **Sample: $\ell = 38$ in., $w = 8.5$ in., $h = 10.5$ in. If you stand each book up on end, 24 books could fit in a box with these dimensions.**

***One** singular sensation! The musical,* A Chorus Line, *is the longest-running play in Broadway history. It ran for about 15 years for a total of 6,137 performances! The play's most popular song, "One," is a special number about a special number.*

The numbers 1 and 0 have special roles in multiplication.

Some Properties of the Number 1

Multiplying a number by the number 1 keeps the identity of that number. So 1 is called the **multiplicative identity.**

❶

> **Multiplicative Identity Property of 1**
> For any real number a, $a \cdot 1 = 1 \cdot a = a$.

If the length of a rectangle is x units and the width is 1 unit, the area is $x \cdot 1 = x$ square units.

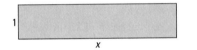

area = x square units

Because the number 1 is so important in multiplication, numbers whose product is 1 are also important. Such numbers are called *reciprocals* or *multiplicative inverses.* The **reciprocal** of a is the number that gives a product of 1 when multiplied by a. For instance, $4 \cdot \frac{1}{4} = 1$. So 4 and $\frac{1}{4}$ are reciprocals. Every number but 0 has a reciprocal.

> **Property of Reciprocals**
> Suppose $a \neq 0$. The reciprocal of a is $\frac{1}{a}$. That is, $a \cdot \frac{1}{a} = \frac{1}{a} \cdot a = 1$

Objectives
F Identify and apply the following properties of multiplication: Multiplicative Identity Property of 1; Property of Reciprocals; Multiplication Property of Zero.

Resources
From the *Teacher's Resource File*
■ Lesson Master 2-2A or 2-2B
■ Answer Master 2-2
■ Teaching Aid 13: Warm-up

Additional Resources
■ Visual for Teaching Aid 13

Teaching **2-2**
Lesson

Warm-up
Fill in the blanks.
1. One cup = _____ pint, so _____ cups = 1 pint. $\frac{1}{2}$; 2
2. One cup = _____ quart, so _____ cups = 1 quart. $\frac{1}{4}$; 4
3. One cup = _____ gallon, so _____ cups = 1 gallon. $\frac{1}{16}$, 16
4. One zaph = $\frac{1}{8}$ zing, so _____ zaphs = 1 zing. 8
5. One ding = 4 pings, so _____ ding = 1 ping. $\frac{1}{4}$

Notes on Reading
❶ Students have known the Multiplicative Identity Property of 1 since they began work with multiplication. But be sure to mention it, since it is applied in the next two lessons. It is

---

Lesson 2-2 Overview

Broad Goals This short lesson covers three ideas that are important in sentence solving: reciprocals; the properties of 1 and 0.

Perspective Most of this lesson is about reciprocals, and it is useful to distinguish the concept from the calculation. The Property of Reciprocals gives the two parts of the concept—the existence of reciprocals (two numbers whose product is one) and one

way of writing the reciprocal of a given number (the reciprocal of a is $\frac{1}{a}$). **Examples 1 and 2** show that we are not usually content to write the reciprocal of a number as 1 divided by that number. When the number given is written as a decimal, we usually want to write its reciprocal as a decimal. When the number given is written as a simple fraction, we usually want to write its reciprocal as a simple fraction.

Reciprocals of decimals are most easily found by using a calculator, so the reciprocal key on the calculator is introduced in this lesson. **Example 3** previews the Zero Product Property that is used to solve quadratics and other polynomials through factoring in later chapters. This property should be explained in simple terms at this time.

used as a justification for the Equal Fractions Property and as a means for converting from one unit to another.

❷ This paragraph will give you an opportunity to discuss when a calculator should be used and when it should not be used. In general, when a number or its reciprocal is an integer, or when the reciprocal is to be expressed as a fraction, use of the calculator is not appropriate. When the number is in decimal form, it is advantageous to use a calculator.

❸ This explanation of why the property of reciprocals applies only to nonzero numbers uses indirect reasoning. If you make sure your students understand indirect reasoning now, this exposure will pay off later when they study geometry.

In general, if the length of a rectangle is x units and its area is 1 square unit, its width is $\frac{1}{x}$ unit.

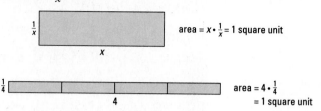

area $= x \cdot \frac{1}{x} = 1$ square unit

area $= 4 \cdot \frac{1}{4}$ = 1 square unit

The names of many metric measurement units are based on reciprocals. For instance, the prefix *centi-* means $\frac{1}{100}$. A centimeter is $\frac{1}{100}$ of a meter. So, 100 centimeters equals $100 \cdot \frac{1}{100}$ meter, or 1 meter.

❷ **Calculating Reciprocals**

Because the reciprocal of a is $\frac{1}{a}$, you can calculate the reciprocal of a number by dividing 1 by the number.

Every scientific and graphics calculator has a reciprocal key, usually `1/x` or `x⁻¹`. To find the reciprocal of the number n, key in: n `1/x`. On some calculators you may need to press `ENTER` to see the result. The answer will be displayed as a decimal.

Example 1

Give the reciprocal of 1.25.

Solution

The reciprocal of 1.25 is $\frac{1}{1.25}$. To find the decimal for $\frac{1}{1.25}$, you can divide 1 by 1.25. A calculator shows that $1 \div 1.25 = 0.8$. Or you can use the reciprocal key. Key in

1.25 `1/x` or 1.25 `x⁻¹` `ENTER`.

You will see `0.8`.
The reciprocal of 1.25 is 0.8.

You know that $0.8 = \frac{8}{10} = \frac{4}{5}$. So, $\frac{8}{10}$ and $\frac{4}{5}$ are other names for the reciprocal of 1.25. You also know that $1.25 = 1\frac{1}{4} = \frac{5}{4}$. So, the reciprocal of $\frac{5}{4}$ is $\frac{4}{5}$. This is an instance of the following property.

Reciprocal of a Fraction Property
Suppose $a \neq 0$ and $b \neq 0$. The reciprocal of $\frac{a}{b}$ is $\frac{b}{a}$.

Optional Activities

After students answer **Questions 12 and 13,** you might have them **work in groups.** Tell them to imagine that a box has a volume of 1 cubic unit and that none of the dimensions is 1 unit. Have them find sets of three numbers that might represent the dimensions of the box. Then ask volunteers to give their answers and to explain how they arrived at them. [Sample response: Select two numbers and multiply them. The reciprocal of that product is the third number.]

Example 2

Find the reciprocal of $\frac{8}{3}$.

Solution 1

Use the Reciprocal of a Fraction Property. The reciprocal of $\frac{8}{3}$ is $\frac{3}{8}$.

Solution 2

Use the Property of Reciprocals stated earlier. Divide 1 by $\frac{8}{3}$. On a calculator you must use parentheses. Key in

$$1 \;\boxed{\div}\; \boxed{(} \; 8 \; \boxed{\div} \; 3 \; \boxed{)} \; \boxed{=}.$$

You should see 0.375 on the display. The reciprocal of $\frac{8}{3}$ is 0.375. You may want to check the above on your calculator.

❸ Properties of the Number 0

The Property of Reciprocals, $a \cdot \frac{1}{a} = 1$, requires that $a \neq 0$ because 0 does not have a reciprocal. If $\frac{1}{0}$ existed, then it would have to be true that $0 \cdot \frac{1}{0} = 1$. But in fact, you know that 0 times any real number is 0. This property also has a name.

Multiplication Property of Zero
For any real number a, $a \cdot 0 = 0 \cdot a = 0$.

The Multiplication Property of Zero can save work in evaluating some otherwise complicated algebraic expressions.

Example 3

Evaluate $(w + 4.7)(2.6 - w)(w + 7.1)$ when $w = -4.7$.

Solution

Substituting gives

$$(-4.7 + 4.7)(2.6 - -4.7)(-4.7 + 7.1).$$

Because $-4.7 + 4.7 = 0$, the product is 0. There is no need to do the computation in the second or third set of parentheses.

QUESTIONS

Covering the Reading

1. The title of this lesson is "Special Numbers in Multiplication." Name the two special numbers that are discussed. 1, 0

Lesson 2-2 *Special Numbers in Multiplication* **81**

Additional Examples

1. Write the reciprocal of 0.3125 as a decimal. 3.2
2. Write the reciprocal of $5\frac{1}{4}$ as a simple fraction. $\frac{4}{21}$
3. Evaluate $(n - 3)(n + 7)(n - 18)$ for each value of n.
   a. $n = -3$ 504
   b. $n = -7$ 0

LESSON MASTER 2-2 A

Questions on SPUR Objectives
See pages 136-138 for objectives.

Properties Objective F

In 1–6, give the reciprocal.

1. $\frac{2}{3}$ $\frac{3}{2}$
2. $1\frac{2}{5}$ $\frac{5}{7}$
3. $\frac{-4}{p}$ $\frac{-p}{4}$
4. $\frac{1}{10}$ 10
5. -0.25 -4
6. $\frac{6}{a+b}$ $\frac{a+b}{6}$

7. Write a key sequence you could use to find the reciprocal of 1.333 on a calculator that has no reciprocal key.
   Sample: $1 \;\boxed{\div}\; 1.33 \;\boxed{=}$

8. *Multiple choice.* Which equation means that x and y are reciprocals? d
   (a) $\frac{x}{y} = 1$ (b) $1x = y$ (c) $x + y = 1$
   (d) $xy = 1$ (e) $\frac{x}{y} = \frac{y}{x}$

In 9–12, a. tell whether the two numbers are reciprocals, and b. briefly explain why or why not.
9. 5 and 0.2 a. yes b. $5 \cdot 0.2 = 1$
10. $-\frac{1}{3}$ and 3 a. no b. $-\frac{1}{3} \cdot 3 = -1$
11. -1 and -1 a. yes b. $-1 \cdot -1 = 1$
12. 100,000 and 0.000001 a. no b. $100{,}000 \cdot 0.000001 = 0.1$

In 13–16, a. simplify, and b. name the property you used.
13. $10(3x - 3x)$
    a. 0 b. Multiplication Property of Zero
14. $(a + b) \cdot \frac{1}{a+b}$
    a. 1 b. Property of Reciprocals
15. $\frac{4.7x^2}{4.7x^2} \cdot 5$
    a. 5 b. Multiplication Identity Property of 1
16. $(3t + 1)(2t - 2)(t + 3)(0)$
    a. 0 b. Multiplication Property of Zero

Adapting to Individual Needs

Extra Help

Some students tend to confuse the idea of *reciprocals* with that of *opposites*. When finding reciprocals, students should ask themselves, "If I multiply the two numbers, is the answer 1?" Also, remind students that a number and its opposite have different signs. Ask them if a number and its reciprocal could have different signs. [No; since the product of a number and its reciprocal is 1, the signs must be the same.]

English Language Development

Students who are learning English may have difficulty remembering the names of the properties. Have these students write the properties with some examples on index cards to use for review and quick reference.

✏️ **Question 5 Writing** Ask students what they wrote. The simplest correct reason is that the product of two reciprocals must be 1 and because of the Multiplication Property of Zero that cannot happen if one of the numbers is zero.

✏️ **Question 31 Writing** Note that pictures are helpful when writing about mathematics.

Question 32 This question shows that, if two fractions less than one represent the dimensions of a rectangle, their product represents a part of the area of a square unit.

Question 33 Multicultural Connection Write all the different words for "one" on the board. Point out how many of them seem to have the same origin.

Question 34 Trial and error can be used to solve this problem, but the number of trials can be decreased by considering the size of the factors. The values for a, b, and c are single digits. Neither a nor c can equal 0. Either ab or ca must be less than 100, because if both are greater than 100, the product will have at least 5 digits. The only powers that would be possible then would be powers of 1; the squares; and 2^3, 3^3, 4^3, 2^4, 3^4, 2^5, and 2^6. Since a is both a base and an exponent, it cannot equal 1. So a must be 2, 3, 4, 5, or 6.

14a) 1 square unit
b)

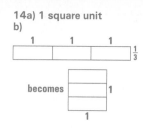

becomes

15) The prefix milli means $\frac{1}{1,000}$, so $1,000 \cdot \frac{1}{1,000}$ meter = 1 meter. This is an instance of the Property of Reciprocals.

What's your best time in the mile run? *In 1994, the men's world record for the mile run on an indoor track was 3:49.78. The men's world record for the mile run on an outdoor track in 1994 was 3:44.39.*

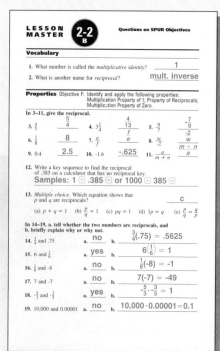

2. What number is the multiplicative identity? 1

3. Complete the following:
The numbers 18 and $\frac{1}{18}$ are reciprocals because their product is __?__. 1

4. What is another name for *reciprocal?* multiplicative inverse

5. Explain in your own words why 0 does not have a reciprocal.
Sample: The product of reciprocals is 1, but 0 times any number is zero.

In 6–11, give the reciprocal and check your answer.

6. 10 $\frac{1}{10}$; $10 \cdot \frac{1}{10} = 1$ 7. $\frac{1}{9}$ 9; $\frac{1}{9} \cdot 9 = 1$ 8. $\frac{6}{7}$ $\frac{7}{6}$; $\frac{6}{7} \cdot \frac{7}{6} = 1$

9. $\frac{13}{12}$ $\frac{12}{13}$; $\frac{13}{12} \cdot \frac{12}{13} = 1$ 10. 2.5 0.4; $2.5 \cdot 0.4 = 1$ 11. y $\frac{1}{y}$; $y \cdot \frac{1}{y} = 1$

In 12 and 13, find the area of each rectangle.

12.

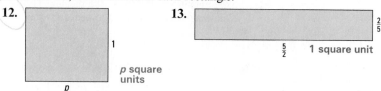

p square units

13.

$\frac{2}{5}$

$\frac{5}{2}$ 1 square unit

14. **a.** A rectangle has length $\frac{1}{3}$ unit and width 3 units. What is its area?
b. Draw a picture to justify your answer. See left.

15. Explain how the word *millimeter* is related to the idea of reciprocal. See left.

16. Evaluate $(x + 1)(x + 2)(x + 3)(x + 4)$ when **a.** $x = -3$, **b.** $x = 3$.
a) 0; b) 840

Applying the Mathematics

In 17 and 18, *multiple choice*.

17. Which does *not* equal 1? (c)
(a) $\frac{0.8}{0.8}$ (b) $0.8 \cdot \frac{5}{4}$
(c) $4.1 - 4.1$ (d) $0.9 + 0.1$

18. For which value of n is the expression $(n - 2)(n - 1)(n + 1)(n + 2)$ *not* equal to 0? (b)
(a) 1   (b) 0
(c) -1   (d) -2

In 19–22, there is a pair of numbers. **a.** Tell whether the numbers are or are not reciprocals. **b.** Justify your answer.

19. 200 and 0.005 a) reciprocals; b) $200 \cdot 0.005 = 1$

20. $\frac{1}{4}$ and 0.25 a) not reciprocals; b) $\frac{1}{4} \cdot 0.25 = 0.0625 \neq 1$

21. 1.5 and $\frac{2}{3}$ a) reciprocals; b) $1.5 = \frac{3}{2}; \frac{3}{2} \cdot \frac{2}{3} = 1$

22. $\frac{3}{5}$ and $-\frac{3}{5}$ a) not reciprocals; b) $\frac{3}{5} \cdot \frac{-3}{5} = \frac{-9}{25} \neq 1$

23. If an indoor track has length $\frac{1}{4}$ mile, you must run around it 4 times to run a mile. How many times must you run around a track of length $\frac{2}{5}$ mile in order to run a mile? $\frac{5}{2}$, or $2\frac{1}{2}$, times

Adapting to Individual Needs

Challenge
Explain to students that an "8-hour clock" has only 8 numbers—1 through 8—whereas a 12-hour clock has 12 numbers. Have them draw an 8-hour clock face, and use it to find sums and products. For addition, give students problems such as: $8 + 4 =$ [4], $7 + 2 =$ [1], and $6 + 6 =$ [4]. Then have them determine which clock number acts as a zero. [8]

For multiplication, suggest that they find the products by using repeated addition: $2 \times 6 = [6 + 6 = 4]$ and $4 \times 5 = [5 + 5 + 5 + 5 = 4]$. Finally, have students determine which numbers on the clock have multiplicative inverses. $[1 \times 1 = 1, 3 \times 3 = 1, 5 \times 5 = 1$, and $7 \times 7 = 1.]$

Students might also notice that both addition and multiplication on the clock are commutative and associative.

24. Suppose $D = (w + 2)(w - 3)(w + 6)$. For what three values of w will D have a value of 0? -2, 3, -6

25. Compute in your head: $9875 \cdot (1676 - 1675 - 1)$ 0

In 26 and 27, give the reciprocal. Assume that x, p, and $q \neq 0$.

26. $\frac{x}{4}$ $\frac{4}{x}$ **27.** $\frac{p}{q}$ $\frac{q}{p}$

28. To attract people to a grocery store, the manager decided to sell milk at the same price he paid for it, thus making a 0¢ profit for each gallon sold. How much profit is made when b gallons of milk are sold? 0¢

Review

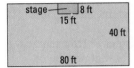

29. An auditorium has dimensions 40 ft by 80 ft. It contains a stage that is 8 ft by 15 ft. *(Lesson 2-1)* a) 3080 ft^2
  a. What is the area of the floor space not covered by the stage?
  b. If each audience member needs 6 square feet of floor space, how many people will the auditorium hold? 513 people

30. Find the area of a tablecloth with width 80 cm and length 1.5 m. *(Lesson 2-1)* 12,000 cm^2 or 1.2 m^2

31. a. What is the volume of the rectangular box pictured at the left? 10 s^3
  b. How many cubes with edge of length s can be packed in this box? 10
  c. Draw a picture and write a sentence or two explaining why your answer is correct. *(Lesson 2-1)* See left. Sample: The rectangle is two cubes deep and 5 cubes high, for a total of 10 cubes.

32. The 1-inch square at the right has been split into eight congruent rectangular regions. *(Previous course)*
  a. What is the area of the shaded region? $\frac{3}{8}$ in^2
  b. The picture shows $\frac{1}{2} \cdot \frac{3}{4} = \underline{\ ?\ }$. $\frac{3}{8}$

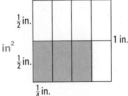

Exploration

33. The expression *numero uno* is Spanish for "number one." Translate *one* into three other languages. Sample: In French, one is "un." In Latin, one is "unus." In German, one is "ein." They seem to have a common origin.

34. Find 3 positive numbers a, b, and c such that $a^b \cdot c^a = abca$, where *abca* stands for a 4-digit number. Sample: $a = 2$, $b = 5$, $c = 9$

Follow-up 2-2 for Lesson

Practice
For more questions on SPUR Objectives, use **Lesson Master 2-2A** (shown on page 81) or **Lesson Master 2-2B** (shown on pages 82–83).

Assessment
Oral Communication Have students raise their right hands if they think the sentence is true and their left hands if they think it is false.
1. A number times its reciprocal is equal to one. [True]
2. Every number has a reciprocal. [False]
3. Another name for reciprocal is additive inverse. [False]
4. The reciprocal of a number less than one and greater than zero is greater than one. [True]
[Prompt students to discuss each sentence until they reach agreement on the correct response.]

Extension
✏ **Writing** You might ask students to describe methods for finding the reciprocal of different types of numbers—whole numbers, fractions, and decimals.

Setting Up Lesson 2-3
Materials Students will need colored pens or pencils and rulers or **Geometry Templates** for the *In-class Activity* on page 84.

The idea presented in **Question 32** of Lesson 2-2 leads directly into the *In-class Activity* and the first two paragraphs of Lesson 2-3.

From the *Teacher's Resource File*
- Answer Master 2-3

Additional Resources
- Colored pens or pencils
- Rulers or **Geometry Templates**

Have students **work with partners or in small groups.** Each student should do the activity and participate in the discussions.

This activity shows students how areas of rectangles can be used to picture multiplication of fractions. This is *not* an easy concept for many students, even if they are familiar with multiplication of fractions. It should be done before students read Lesson 2-3. Do not spend more than 15 minutes on this activity.

Multiplying Algebraic Fractions

IN-CLASS ACTIVITY

You will need paper, colored pens or pencils, and a ruler to do this activity. Work with a partner or in a small group.

1
a. Draw a square or use a square piece of paper. Assume each side of the square is 1 unit. Divide the square vertically into fourths as shown. Use one color to shade $\frac{3}{4}$ of it.

b. Divide the same square horizontally into eighths. Shade $\frac{1}{8}$ in a second color.

c. How many little rectangles are there in the square? How many are shaded in both colors? Write a fraction for that portion of the square that is shaded in both colors. **32; 3; $\frac{3}{32}$**

d. Multiply $\frac{1}{8} \cdot \frac{3}{4}$. Discuss among yourselves how the work you did in steps **a** and **b** pictures the product $\frac{1}{8} \cdot \frac{3}{4}$. **$\frac{3}{32}$**

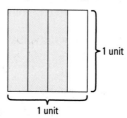

2 Use a square to picture each product. Then compute the product.
a. $\frac{3}{8} \cdot \frac{3}{4}$ See below.   b. $\frac{2}{3} \cdot \frac{5}{6}$ See below.

3 *Draw conclusions.*   Discuss in your group a rule for multiplying fractions. Write a few sentences about how the models you made in Questions 1–3 illustrate this rule. Answers may vary. Sample: Multiply the two numerators. Then multiply the two denominators.

4 In Question 1, suppose the length of each side of the square is *s* units. What product does the double shaded region represent? $\frac{3}{32}s^2$

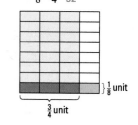

2a) $\frac{9}{32}$

2b) $\frac{10}{18}$

84

Optional Activities

Materials: Dot paper or **Teaching Aid 17**

There is a discrete analog to the continuous model in the activity. Instead of shading regions, block them off. Show students that the discrete array at the right pictures the product of $\frac{6}{8}$ and $\frac{5}{9}$ in the lower left corner. It has $\frac{6}{8}$ of the columns and $\frac{5}{9}$ of the rows, and $\frac{30}{72}$ of the dots. Have students use arrays to demonstrate other products of fractions.

A half of this, a third of that . . . *Jeff Smith is known to millions for his TV program, "The Frugal Gourmet." Operations with fractions are often necessary when using recipes.*

Multiplying Fractions

Every fraction between 0 and 1 can be considered to be part of some whole. In the previous activity, you saw three instances of how multiplying two such fractions is related to area.

Here is another example. To picture the product of the fractions $\frac{2}{7}$ and $\frac{4}{5}$, first draw a unit square. Then find $\frac{2}{7}$ of one side and $\frac{4}{5}$ of an adjacent side. The rectangle that has dimensions $\frac{2}{7}$ and $\frac{4}{5}$ is shaded. Notice that its area is $\frac{8}{35}$ of the total. This is because there are $2 \cdot 4$ shaded small rectangles out of the total of $7 \cdot 5$, or 35. Since the total area is 1 square unit, the area of the shaded region is $\frac{8}{35}$ square unit.

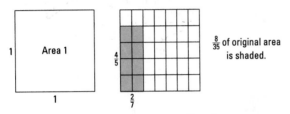

The pattern can be generalized. To multiply $\frac{a}{b}$ by $\frac{c}{d}$, you could shade ac rectangles out of bd small rectangles in the unit area. So the area would be $\frac{ac}{bd}$. This pictures the common rule for multiplying fractions.

Lesson **2-3**

Objectives
A Multiply and simplify algebraic fractions.
J Use rectangles to picture multiplication.

Resources
From the Teacher's Resource File
- Lesson Master 2-3A or 2-3B
- Answer Master 2-3
- Assessment Sourcebook: Quiz for Lessons 2-1 through 2-3
- Teaching Aid 13: Warm-up

Additional Resources
- Visual for Teaching Aid 13

Teaching Lesson 2-3

Warm-up
All of the edges of Box A are 12 centimeters long. Box B has half the length, half the width, and one third the height of Box A.
1. What is the volume of Box B? **144 cm³**
2. How do the volumes of the two boxes compare? **The volume of Box B is $\frac{1}{12}$ that of Box A.**

Notes on Reading
Pacing This is a long lesson, but it is followed by a short lesson so that the lesson-a-day pace can be maintained.

Lesson 2-3 Overview

Broad Goals In this lesson, we want the student to understand the algebraic rendering of two fundamental properties that deal with fractions—the rule for multiplying fractions (here called the Multiplying Fractions Property) and the Equal Fractions Property. Understanding these properties means being able to apply them in skill exercises and in applications, to represent them, and to see how the second of these properties follows from the first one.

Perspective Decimals and fractions are not comparable ways of representing numbers. Decimals are a *notation*, whereas fractions represent an *operation*, namely the operation of division. For this reason, patterns for operating on decimals do not have easy algebraic descriptions. However, patterns for operating on fractions do have easy algebraic descriptions; in fact, they are indispensable to an understanding of algebra.

There is always a question regarding how much to assume the students know. Here, we assume that students know how to multiply simple fractions and how to simplify fractions. The general patterns are given by the two properties that are discussed in this lesson.

Reading Mathematics Because of its length and the number of ideas presented, this is a good lesson to go through carefully with the students. Ask for instances of each property, and ask students why they think each example is presented.

❶ The Multiplying Fractions Property is applied in **Example 1** to show an important property of area; it is applied in **Example 2** to show that expressions that look quite different are, in fact, equal. It is also used to derive the Equal Fractions Property.

Error Alert It is critical that students understand the Multiplying Fractions Property. To check their understanding, you might ask students to generate examples like **Example 1**. If students have trouble, you may wish to see the suggestions in *Extra Help* in *Adapting to Individual Needs* on page 87.

❷ **Example 2** deals explicitly with the many different ways in which the same fraction can be written. That they are equivalent is not necessarily obvious to students.

❸ When discussing the Equal Fractions Property, you may want to start with a specific example. For instance, ask for fractions equal to $\frac{24}{60}$. Then ask students to justify why the fractions are equal. Some students will apply the property $\frac{a}{b} = \frac{ka}{kb}$ and multiply the numerator and denominator by the same number to find an equal fraction.

❶ | **Multiplying Fractions Property**
For all real numbers a, b, c, and d, with b and d not zero,
$$\frac{a}{b} \cdot \frac{c}{d} = \frac{ac}{bd}.$$

Whenever variables represent real numbers you may apply this property to **algebraic fractions,** that is, to fractions that have variables in the numerator or denominator.

Example 1

Multiply $\frac{b}{3} \cdot \frac{h}{2}$.

Solution

Use the Multiplying Fractions Property.
$$\frac{b}{3} \cdot \frac{h}{2} = \frac{bh}{6}$$

Check 1

Substitute values for b and h, say $b = 6$ and $h = 10$.
Does $\frac{6}{3} \cdot \frac{10}{2} = 6 \cdot \frac{10}{6}$? Yes, it does, because of the Multiplying Fractions Property.

Check 2

Use an area model. First draw a rectangle with base b and height h. Then find $\frac{b}{3}$ or $\frac{1}{3}b$ of one side and $\frac{h}{2}$ or $\frac{1}{2}h$ of the other side.

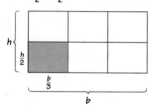

Notice that the area of the shaded rectangle is $\frac{1}{6}$ the area of the original rectangle, or $\frac{bh}{6}$.

Notice that in Example 1, $\frac{bh}{6}$ is another way of writing $\frac{1}{6}bh$. Example 2 shows how the Multiplying Fractions Property can be used to explain why many different expressions are equal to each other.

Optional Activities

Cooperative Learning As an alternate approach, you might wish to have students **work in groups** and draw a general representation of the Multiplying Fractions Property using parts of a unit square. Here are the steps they should follow:

1. Divide one side of a unit square into b parts and an adjacent side into d parts. Thus each small part of the first side has length $\frac{1}{b}$, each small part of the adjacent side has length $\frac{1}{d}$. These small parts form tiny rectangles, each $\frac{1}{bd}$ of the whole.

2. Draw the rectangle whose dimensions are $\frac{a}{b}$ and $\frac{c}{d}$, that is, the rectangle that has one side with a of the small parts of the $\frac{1}{b}$ side and c of the small parts of the $\frac{1}{d}$ side.

3. The area of the smaller rectangle is the product of $\frac{a}{b}$ and $\frac{c}{d}$. It also has ac of the tiny rectangles.

Example 2

Show that each of the following expressions equals $\frac{2h}{3}$.

a. $\frac{2}{3}h$ **b.** $\frac{1}{3} \cdot 2h$ **c.** $2 \cdot \frac{h}{3}$

Solution

Notice how each line below uses the Multiplying Fractions Property and the property that $x = \frac{x}{1}$.

a. $\frac{2}{3}h = \frac{2}{3} \cdot \frac{h}{1} = \frac{2h}{3}$

b. $\frac{1}{3} \cdot 2h = \frac{1}{3} \cdot \frac{2h}{1} = \frac{2h}{3}$

c. $2 \cdot \frac{h}{3} = \frac{2}{1} \cdot \frac{h}{3} = \frac{2h}{3}$

We have shown that $\frac{2h}{3}, \frac{2}{3}h, \frac{1}{3} \cdot 2h$, and $2 \cdot \frac{h}{3}$ are all equal to each other.

Simplifying Fractions

You should be familiar with simplifying numerical fractions. For instance, $\frac{30}{50} = \frac{3}{5}$. This is an instance of the *Equal Fractions Property*.

Equal Fractions Property

If $b \neq 0$ and $k \neq 0$, then

$$\frac{ak}{bk} = \frac{a}{b}.$$

The Equal Fractions Property holds for all fractions $\frac{a}{b}$ as long as the denominator is not 0. If there are common factors in the numerator and denominator of an algebraic fraction, you can use the Equal Fractions Property to simplify it.

Example 3

Simplify $\frac{36cd}{3d}$.

Solution 1

Look for common factors in the numerator and denominator. Notice that $3d$ is a factor of each. The solution below applies the Associative Property of Multiplication in the numerator and the Multiplicative Identity Property of 1 in the denominator.

$$\frac{36cd}{3d} = \frac{12c \cdot 3d}{1 \cdot 3d}$$
$$= \frac{12c}{1} \qquad \text{Equal Fractions Property}$$
$$= 12c$$

Lesson 2-3 *Multiplying Algebraic Fractions* **87**

Adapting to Individual Needs

Extra Help

Some students might have trouble understanding that $\frac{bh}{6} = \frac{1}{6}bh$, as stated before **Example 2**. Point out that $\frac{bh}{6} = \frac{1}{6} \cdot \frac{bh}{1}$ by the Multiplying Fractions Property and that $\frac{1}{6} \cdot \frac{bh}{1} = \frac{1}{6}bh$ because $\frac{bh}{1} = bh$. Also point out that the area of the rectangle in **Example 1** has been divided by six, which results

in six equal parts. The area of each of those parts is $\frac{1}{6}$ of the original area. So the result of dividing a quantity by 6 is the same as the result of multiplying that quantity by $\frac{1}{6}$.

The Equal Fractions Property, as stated in the text, comes from reversing the sides of $\frac{a}{b} = \frac{ka}{kb}$ and using the commutative property. Students need to realize that the Equal Fractions Property can be used in two directions, either to change $\frac{a}{b}$ into $\frac{ak}{bk}$, or to simplify $\frac{ak}{bk}$ to $\frac{a}{b}$.

You might wish to go through a proof of the Equal Fractions Property. Point out that a *proof* is a formal argument that is used to justify mathematical answers and relationships. Examples are seldom sufficient to constitute a proof of a property; they only suggest the pattern. The proof shows that the pattern follows from previously established properties.

$\frac{ak}{bk} = \frac{a}{b} \cdot \frac{k}{k}$ Multiplying Fractions Property

$= \frac{a}{b} \cdot 1$ $\frac{k}{k} = 1$, if $k \neq 0$.

$= \frac{a}{b}$ Multiplicative Identity Property of 1

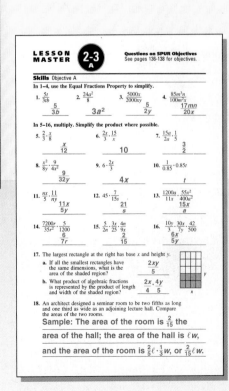

87

④ Do not expect your students to work with the laws of exponents now—they will come much later. For now, we want students to work with reducing fractions with variables and to practice with the meaning of exponents by rewriting expressions with repeated factors.

Decide how much detail students should provide when doing problems like **Example 4**. At the beginning, you may prefer that they show the steps as suggested in Solution 1; then gradually allow students to skip steps, as in Solution 2.

Additional Examples

1. Multiply $\frac{a}{4}$ by $\frac{12}{a}$. 3

2. Show that each of the following expressions equals $\frac{3ab}{4}$.

   a. $\frac{3}{4} \cdot ab$

   $$\frac{3}{4} \cdot ab = \frac{3}{4} \cdot \frac{ab}{1} = \frac{3 \cdot ab}{4 \cdot 1} = \frac{3ab}{4}$$

   b. $3a \cdot \frac{b}{4}$

   $$3a \cdot \frac{b}{4} = \frac{3a}{1} \cdot \frac{b}{4} = \frac{3a \cdot b}{1 \cdot 4} = \frac{3ab}{4}$$

   c. $3b \cdot \frac{a}{4}$

   $$3b \cdot \frac{a}{4} = \frac{3b}{1} \cdot \frac{a}{4} = \frac{3b \cdot a}{1 \cdot 4} = \frac{3ba}{4}$$
   $$= \frac{3ab}{4}$$

3. Simplify $\frac{10x}{15xy} \cdot \frac{2}{3y}$

4. Multiply and simplify. Assume $y \neq 0$ and $z \neq 0$.

   a. $\frac{6x}{3y} \cdot \frac{30y}{z} \cdot \frac{60x}{z}$

   b. $\frac{8x^3}{3y^2} \cdot \frac{5y^2}{4x^7} \cdot \frac{10}{3x^4}$

Solution 2

Experts often skip steps. They sometimes strike out the common factors with slashes.

$$\frac{\overset{12}{\cancel{36}}c\overset{1}{\cancel{d}}}{\underset{1}{\cancel{3}}\underset{1}{\cancel{d}}} = 12c$$

In Example 4, both the Multiplying Fractions Property and the Equal Fractions Property are used with algebraic fractions.

④ **Example 4**

Assume $a \neq 0$ and $m \neq 0$. Multiply $\frac{5m}{12a}$ by $\frac{3a}{10m^2}$, and simplify the result.

Solution 1

Here we show all the steps.

$$\frac{5m}{12a} \cdot \frac{3a}{10m^2} = \frac{5m \cdot 3a}{12a \cdot 10m^2}$$
$$= \frac{15ma}{120am^2}$$
$$= \frac{1 \cdot 15 \cdot m \cdot a}{8 \cdot 15 \cdot m \cdot m \cdot a}$$
$$= \frac{1}{8} \cdot \frac{15}{15} \cdot \frac{m}{m} \cdot \frac{1}{m} \cdot \frac{a}{a}$$
$$= \frac{1}{8} \cdot \frac{1}{m}$$
$$= \frac{1}{8m}$$

Solution 2

This is what others might write. They would look for common factors in the numerator and denominator.

$$\frac{5m}{12a} \cdot \frac{3a}{10m^2} = \frac{\overset{1}{\cancel{5}} \cdot \overset{1}{\cancel{m}} \cdot \overset{1}{\cancel{3}} \cdot \overset{1}{\cancel{a}}}{\underset{4}{\cancel{12}} \cdot \underset{1}{\cancel{a}} \cdot \underset{2}{\cancel{10}} \cdot \underset{1}{\cancel{m}} \cdot m} = \frac{1}{8m}$$

Ask your teacher how much detail he or she wants you to provide when multiplying or simplifying algebraic fractions.

Caution: The Equal Fractions Property is a property related to multiplication. It does not work when the same terms are *added* to the numerator and denominator.

---

1) For all real numbers a, b, c, and d with b and d not zero, $\frac{a}{b} \cdot \frac{c}{d} = \frac{ac}{bd}$.

2a)

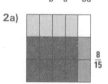

$\frac{8}{15}$

b) $\frac{2}{3} \cdot \frac{4}{5} = \frac{8}{15}$
8 of the 15 small rectangles are shaded twice.

QUESTIONS

Covering the Reading

1. State the Multiplying Fractions Property. See left.

2. **a.** Draw a picture to represent the product $\frac{2}{3} \cdot \frac{4}{5}$. a, b) See left.

   b. How does your picture illustrate the Multiplying Fractions Property?

Adapting to Individual Needs

English Language Development
As an ongoing project, have students construct a class mobile showing properties, formulas, and so on, from chapters 1 and 2. Hang the mobile in a corner of the room and add to it as you progress through the course. Have students explain the concepts on the mobile from time to time.

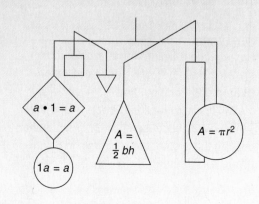

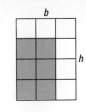

b | h (rectangle figure at top left)

3. The rectangle at the left has base b and height h.
   a. If all the small rectangles have the same dimensions, what is the area of the shaded region? $\frac{1}{2}bh$
   b. What product of algebraic fractions is represented by the shaded area? $\frac{2}{3}b \cdot \frac{3}{4}h = \frac{1}{2}bh$

In 4 and 5, multiply the fractions.

4. $\frac{a}{7} \cdot \frac{b}{2}$ $\frac{ab}{14}$

5. $\frac{x}{3} \cdot \frac{y}{z}$ $\frac{xy}{3z}$

17b) $\frac{1}{8}$

6. *True or false.* $\frac{1}{5}n = \frac{n}{5}$. **True**

7. Show that $\frac{4}{9}x$ is equal to $\frac{4x}{9}$. $\frac{4}{9}x = \frac{4}{9} \cdot \frac{x}{1} = \frac{4x}{9}$

18b) Sample: If the Chens' garden is 6 ft by 8 ft, it has an area 24 ft². The Marshalls' garden will be $\frac{2}{3} \cdot 6 = 4$ ft long and $\frac{1}{4} \cdot 4 = 1$ ft wide, so it will have area 4 ft². This is $\frac{1}{6}$ the area of the Chens' garden.

8. *Multiple choice.* Which does not equal the others? (d)
   (a) $\frac{7t}{12}$ (b) $\frac{7}{12}t$ (c) $7t \cdot \frac{1}{12}$ (d) $\frac{7}{t} \cdot 12$

In 9–12, use the Equal Fractions Property to simplify each fraction.

9. $\frac{800}{1900}$ $\frac{8}{19}$

10. $\frac{20y}{5y}$ 4

11. $\frac{3mn}{9mt}$ $\frac{n}{3t}$

12. $\frac{24gr}{18gr^2}$ $\frac{4}{3r}$

In 13–16, multiply and simplify the result.

13. $\frac{3m}{n} \cdot \frac{7m}{9}$ $\frac{7m^2}{3n}$

14. $\frac{6a}{b} \cdot \frac{b}{6a}$ 1

15. $\frac{24c}{5d} \cdot \frac{20d}{21}$ $\frac{32c}{7}$

16. $\frac{50}{9x} \cdot \frac{18x^2}{25y}$ $\frac{4x}{y}$

"Community gardening" has become popular in big cities where backyards are not available for planting. Several families may share the work and the harvest of a city-owned plot.

Applying the Mathematics

17. a. One rectangle is half as wide and one-fourth as long as another rectangle. How do the areas of the two rectangles compare?
    b. Draw a figure to illustrate your answer. **See left.**
    a) One area is 1/8 of the other.

18. The Marshall and Chen families have rectangular vegetable gardens. The length of the Marshalls' garden is $\frac{2}{3}$ the length and $\frac{1}{4}$ the width of the Chens' garden. a) The area of Marshalls' garden is $\frac{1}{6}$ the area of the
    a. How do the areas of the gardens compare? Chens' garden.
    b. Check your answer by using a specific length and width for the Chens' garden. **See left.**

19. *Skill sequence.* Compute in your head.
    a. $\frac{5}{3} \cdot 3$ 5
    b. $\frac{9}{x} \cdot x$ 9
    c. $\frac{a}{b} \cdot b$ a
    d. $n^2 \cdot \frac{a}{n^2}$ a

In 20 and 21, *multiple choice.* Find the fraction that is *not* equal to the other three.

20. (a) $\frac{9a}{11a}$ (b) $\frac{99}{121}$ (c) $\frac{90}{100}$ (d) $\frac{450}{550}$ (c)

21. (a) $\frac{100}{260}$ (b) $\frac{35t}{91t}$ (c) $\frac{38}{100}$ (d) $\frac{500x^2}{1300x^2}$ (c)

5. Suppose one box is three times as long as another but has $\frac{2}{3}$ the height and $\frac{3}{4}$ the width. How do their volumes compare? **The first box has $\frac{3}{2}$ the volume of the second.**

Notes on Questions

Question 8 Students have to realize that 7 and t must be in the numerator, and 12 must be in the denominator.

Question 18 Multicultural Connection The most famous garden in the world, Versailles in France, with its formal walkways and precisely trimmed hedges is a masterpiece of architecture as well as horticulture. Japanese gardens have their own definite image: raked sand, water, thoughtfully placed rocks, bonsai, and stone lanterns. The "floating gardens" of Xochimilco (soh chee MEEL koh), which are located near Mexico City, date back to the Aztecs who raised flowers, vegetables, and fruits on rafts made of interwoven twigs and reeds covered with mud. Over time the roots of the plants became attached to the bottom of shallow Lake Xochimilco. One of the outstanding topiary gardens in the United States is the Ladew Gardens in Maryland. Interested students may enjoy reading more about the distinctive features of the famous gardens in all parts of the world.

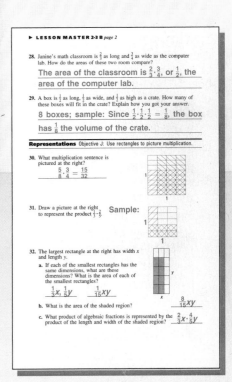

► LESSON MASTER 2-3 B *page 2*

28. Janine's math classroom is $\frac{2}{5}$ as long and $\frac{3}{4}$ as wide as the computer lab. How do the areas of these two room compare?
    The area of the classroom is $\frac{2}{5} \cdot \frac{3}{4}$, or $\frac{1}{2}$, the area of the computer lab.

29. A box is $\frac{1}{2}$ as long, $\frac{1}{2}$ as wide, and $\frac{1}{2}$ as high as a crate. How many of these boxes will fit in the crate? Explain how you got your answer.
    8 boxes; sample: Since $\frac{1}{2} \cdot \frac{1}{2} \cdot \frac{1}{2} = \frac{1}{8}$, the box has $\frac{1}{8}$ the volume of the crate.

Representations Objective J: Use rectangles to picture multiplication.

30. What multiplication sentence is pictured at the right?
    $\frac{5}{8} \cdot \frac{3}{4} = \frac{15}{32}$

31. Draw a picture at the right to represent the product $\frac{1}{3} \cdot \frac{4}{5}$. Sample:

32. The largest rectangle at the right has width x and length y.
    a. If each of the smallest rectangles has the same dimensions, what are these dimensions? What is the area of each of the smallest rectangles?
    $\frac{1}{3}x, \frac{1}{5}y$ $\frac{1}{15}xy$
    b. What is the area of the shaded region? $\frac{8}{15}xy$
    c. What product of algebraic fractions is represented by the product of the length and width of the shaded region? $\frac{2}{3}x \cdot \frac{4}{5}y$

Adapting to Individual Needs

Challenge

Have students find two fractions that have the same product and difference. [Typical answer: $\frac{1}{2}$ and $\frac{1}{3}$. Any pair of fractions of the form $\frac{1}{x}$ and $\frac{1}{y}$ will work if $y = x + 1$. More generally, if r is any fraction and $s = \frac{r}{r+1}$, then $r - s = rs$.]

Question 27 Students "undo" multiplication of fractions. Doing something both forward and backward can help students to make connections and to become more adept at finding answers. Emphasize that there are many answers.

Follow-up for Lesson 2-3

Practice

For more questions on SPUR Objectives, use **Lesson Master 2-3A** (shown on page 87) or **Lesson Master 2-3B** (shown on pages 88–89).

Assessment

Quiz A quiz covering Lessons 2-1 through 2-3 is provided in the *Assessment Sourcebook.*

Group Assessment Ask each student to write an algebraic fraction on a sheet of paper. Then have students pass the papers around the group; ask each student to write a different algebraic fraction which is equal to the fraction at the top of the paper. Have students return the papers. Tell each student to check that all of the fractions are equal to his or her original fraction. [Students demonstrate an ability to use the Multiplying Fractions and Equal Fractions Properties.]

Extension

Cooperative Learning Write the Multiplying Fractions Property on the board. Then have students **work in groups** to answer these questions.
1. What is true about the product, if $a < b$ and $c < d$? [$\frac{ac}{bd}$ is less than both $\frac{a}{b}$ and $\frac{c}{d}$; that is, the product is less than either factor.]
2. What is true about the product, if $a > b$ and $c > d$? [$\frac{ac}{bd}$ is greater than both $\frac{a}{b}$ and $\frac{c}{d}$; the product is greater than either factor.]
3. What is true about the product, if $a < b$ and $c > d$? [$\frac{ac}{bd}$ is greater than $\frac{a}{b}$ and less than $\frac{c}{d}$; the product is greater than the smaller factor and less than the greater factor.]

90

Acquiring aquariums.
When setting up a new aquarium, you should not overstock. The total length of all the fish in inches should be no greater than the number of gallons of water the tank will hold.

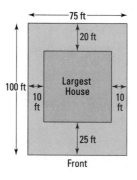

26b) If $b = 12$, the dimensions of the aquarium would be $12 \times 6 \times 4$, so the volume is 288 cubic units. Using the formula of part a, the volume is $\frac{12^3}{6} = 288$.

26c) 6; A cube with sides of length b has volume b^3. The aquarium has volume $\frac{b^3}{6}$. Six aquariums would have volume $6 \cdot \frac{b^3}{6} = b^3$.

90

In 22–25, multiply and simplify where possible.

22. $\frac{a}{b} \cdot \frac{c}{d} \cdot \frac{e}{f}$ **$\frac{ace}{bdf}$**
23. $\frac{a}{b} \cdot \frac{b}{c} \cdot \frac{c}{a}$ **1**
24. $\frac{22a^3}{7b} \cdot \frac{21b}{11a^2}$ **6a**
25. $\frac{9x^2}{10y^2} \cdot \frac{14y^3}{3x}$ **$\frac{21xy}{5}$**

26. a. Find the volume of the aquarium at the left. **$\frac{b^3}{6}$**
    b. Check your answer by letting $b = 12$. **See left.**
    c. Think of a cube with sides of length b. How many of these aquariums would fit into the cube? How can you tell? **See left.**

27. Find two *algebraic* fractions that when multiplied yield $\frac{12x^2}{5y^3}$.
    Sample: $\frac{12x}{y^2} \cdot \frac{x}{5y}$

Review

28. *Skill sequence.* Write the reciprocal of each number. *(Lesson 2-2)*
    a. $4\frac{1}{4}$
    b. $\frac{1}{9}$ **9**
    c. $\frac{4}{9}$ **$\frac{9}{4}$**

In 29 and 30, compute in your head using the Associative and Commutative Properties of Multiplication. *(Lesson 2-1)*

29. $2 \cdot 7 \cdot 4 \cdot 5$ **280**
30. $2.5 \cdot 4 \cdot 2 \cdot 9$ **180**

31. A single-story house is to be built on a lot 75 feet wide by 100 feet deep. The shorter side of the lot faces the street. The house must be set back from the street at least 25 feet. It must be 20 feet from the back lot line and 10 feet from each side lot line. What is the maximum square footage (area) the house can have? *(Lesson 2-1)* **3025 ft²**

32. *True or false.* *(Lesson 1-1)*
    a. $4x = 18$ if $x = 4.5$ **True**
    b. $-9y = 42$ if $y = -\frac{14}{3}$ **True**
    c. $\frac{4}{5}z = -96$ if $z = 120$ **False**
    d. $\frac{10}{3} = \frac{-15}{2}w$ if $w = \frac{-4}{9}$ **True**

Exploration

33. a. Calculate the following products.

    $\frac{1}{2} \cdot \frac{2}{3}$ **$\frac{1}{3}$**

    $\frac{1}{2} \cdot \frac{2}{3} \cdot \frac{3}{4}$ **$\frac{1}{4}$**

    $\frac{1}{2} \cdot \frac{2}{3} \cdot \frac{3}{4} \cdot \frac{4}{5}$ **$\frac{1}{5}$**

    b. Write a sentence or two describing the patterns you observe.
    c. Predict the following products.

    $\frac{1}{2} \cdot \frac{2}{3} \cdot \frac{3}{4} \cdot \ldots \cdot \frac{1996}{1997}$ **$\frac{1}{1997}$**

    $\frac{1}{2} \cdot \frac{2}{3} \cdot \frac{3}{4} \cdot \ldots \cdot \frac{n}{n+1}$ **$\frac{1}{n+1}$**

    b) Sample: The product is the reciprocal of the last denominator.

Setting Up Lesson 2-4

Materials Students will need newspapers for the *Warm-up* in Lesson 2-4.

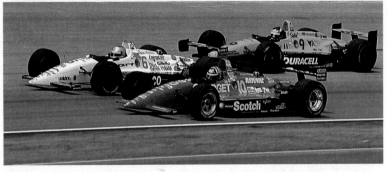

Racers, start your engines. *The Indianapolis 500 is one of the most famous races in the U.S., attracting about 300,000 people annually. Drivers reach speeds of more than 220 mph (354 km/h) as they race the 2.5-mile oval track.*

Rates appear often in everyday life. Some common rates are "55 miles per hour" or "$4.25 an hour."

Fraction forms often appear in situations involving rates. Units for rates can be expressed using a slash "/" or a horizontal bar "−". The slash and the bar are read "per" or "for each."

rate	with a slash	with a bar
99 cents per pound	99 cents/lb	$99 \frac{cents}{lb}$
88 kilometers per hour	88 km/hr	$88 \frac{km}{hr}$
W words per minute	*W* words/min	$W \frac{words}{min}$

Some rates are expressed with abbreviations. For instance, "miles per hour" is abbreviated "mph," and "miles per gallon" is abbreviated "mpg."

How to Multiply Rates

Rates can be multiplied by other quantities. The units are multiplied as if they were numerical fractions.

Example 1

At the Indianapolis Motor Speedway, the race track is 2.5 miles long. How many miles would a race car go if it went 200 times around the track?

Solution

The path around a race track is called a *lap*. The rate described is $2.5 \frac{miles}{lap}$. Multiply this rate by the number of laps. The lap units "cancel."

$$200 \text{ laps} \cdot 2.5 \frac{miles}{lap} = 500 \text{ miles}$$

The car would travel 500 miles.

This is one instance of the *Rate Factor Model for Multiplication.*

Lesson 2-4 *Multiplying Rates* **91**

Lesson 2-4

Objectives

H Apply the Rate Factor Model for Multiplication in real situations.

Resources

From the *Teacher's Resource File*
■ Lesson Master 2-4A or 2-4B
■ Answer Master 2-4
■ Teaching Aids
  14 Warm-up
  18 Additional Examples
■ Technology Sourcebook
  Computer Master 3

Additional Resources
■ Visuals for Teaching Aids 14, 18
■ Newspapers (Warm-up)

Teaching
Lesson 2-4

Warm-up

Activity
Materials: Newspapers

Work in groups. Circle all of the rates you can find in the newspaper your teacher gives you. Make a list of the different units in the rates that you have found.

Notes on Reading

Reading Mathematics You might ask students what they perceive to be the key ideas of the lesson. Our answer would be: (1) understanding the idea of rates and the Rate Factor Model for Multiplication, (2) multiplying with rates, (3) substituting one rate for another to aid in multiplication, and (4) using reciprocal rates to answer questions.

Lesson 2-4 Overview

Broad Goals This lesson discusses the Rate Factor Model for Multiplication and introduces dimensional analysis (the "arithmetic" for dealing with units) into the course.

Perspective The Rate Factor Model for Multiplication is a fundamental property, and it is applied in many future lessons. This lesson is organized around examples and problems that use *dimensional analysis*, a term students may have encoun-

tered in science class. The term comes from science and applies to all units, not merely the dimensions of geometric figures. The arithmetic of dimensional analysis is not included in many algebra books, but recent research has shown that it does help students to analyze and solve application problems. It is useful because students do not have to figure out from the setting whether to multiply or divide; they can arrange the factors so that the units cancel

properly. It also allows them to write sentences such as 7 feet = 84 inches, which would be incorrect without the units.

We encourage students to write out the dimensions when doing arithmetic, but not when solving equations, because in solving equations, dimensions can be confused with variables.

You might also ask students to name the rates in each example.
[**Example 1:** 2.5 $\frac{miles}{lap}$; **Example 2:** 540 $\frac{miles}{hour}$ or 540 mph (Point out that the unit does not have to look like a fraction to be a rate); **Example 3:** any of the numbers; **Example 4:** 3500 $\frac{calories}{pound}$, $\frac{1}{3500}$ $\frac{pound}{calories}$, and 300 $\frac{calories}{hour}$.]

We use the word *quantity* to mean a number with a unit, such as 6 oranges, 2.5 miles, or 22.3 $\frac{students}{class}$. Dimensional analysis is basically the arithmetic of quantities. Quantities help clarify the idea of reciprocal rates: the numbers in 2.5 $\frac{miles}{lap}$ and 0.4 $\frac{laps}{mile}$ are different (they are reciprocals), but the quantities describe the same situation.

Notice the use of the word *cancel* in **Example 1.** We use the word because it is the term that is commonly used with rates in science. However, as shown in Lesson 2-3, we use the Equal Fractions Property with numbers; this avoids use of the word *cancel*, which can cause confusion for some students.

❶ There is a fundamental difference between the Rate Factor and Area Models for Multiplication. In the rate factor model, each factor plays a different role, and one thinks of multiplying by a rate, rather than multiplying two numbers together. That is, instead of "multiplication of *x* and *y*," the phrase "multiplying by *x* " is used.

❷ Point out that the choice of which reciprocal rate to use is made by deciding what the unit should be in the answer and by seeing which units would cancel so as to get the correct unit. Ask students to give the units in the reciprocals of common rates such as miles per hour, dollars per hour (wages), or dollars per

❶ | **Rate Factor Model for Multiplication**
When a rate *r* is multiplied by another quantity *x,* the product is *rx.* So the unit of *rx* is the product of the units for *r* and *x.*

Here is another instance. Suppose that, when resting, your heart rate is 70 beats per minute. In 5 minutes there will be

$$70 \frac{beats}{min} \cdot 5 \ min = 350 \text{ beats.}$$

In *x* minutes, there will be

$$70 \frac{beats}{min} \cdot x \ min = 70x \text{ beats.}$$

Rates are used in many formulas. One of the most important formulas is $d = rt$, which gives the distance *d* traveled by an object moving at a constant rate *r* during a time *t*. (*r* is often called the speed.)

Example 2

If an airplane averages 540 mph for $2\frac{1}{4}$ hours, about how far does it travel?

Solution

You are given $r = 540$ mph and $t = 2\frac{1}{4}$ hr. Substitute into the formula

$$d = rt.$$
$$d = 540 \text{ mph} \cdot 2\frac{1}{4} \text{ hr}$$

Rewrite the abbreviation mph to see the units more clearly, and convert $2\frac{1}{4}$ to an improper fraction.

$$d = 540 \ \frac{miles}{hr} \cdot \frac{9}{4} \ hr$$
$$= 1215 \text{ miles}$$

The plane travels about 1200 miles.

Converting Measurement Units

Rates can be used to convert units in measurements. Since 1 hour = 60 minutes, dividing one unit by the other equals 1.

$$\frac{1 \text{ hour}}{60 \text{ min}} = \frac{60 \text{ min}}{1 \text{ hour}} = 1$$

Multiplying a quantity by one of these rates does not change its value.

Example 3

If an airplane travels at 540 mph, how far does it travel per second?

Solution

Convert miles per hour to miles per second. Multiply by a rate to change hours to minutes, and by another rate to change minutes to seconds.

$$540 \ \frac{miles}{hr} \cdot \frac{1 \ hr}{60 \ min} \cdot \frac{1 \ min}{60 \ sec} = \frac{3 \text{ miles}}{20 \text{ sec}} = \frac{3}{20} \ \text{mile per sec}$$

Optional Activities

Activity 1 After discussing **Example 4**, you might have students investigate the number of calories they burn in various activities. Then have them find how much weight they would lose if they engaged in the activity for one hour.

Activity 2 After discussing the meaning of rates, students might enjoy this game. Write "88 _____ on a _____" on the board, and ask students to fill in the blanks to give a rate.

[88 keys on a piano] Then have them **work in groups** to come up with 4 other questions of this type. Have each group select its best question to give to the other groups as a challenge. A group gets 5 points for stumping everyone with a conversion that people should know, 0 points if the conversion is so obscure that no one knows it, and 3 points for correctly answering a conversion from another group. [Some possible conversions are 64 squares on a

checkerboard, 6 sides on a die, and 12 dozen in a gross.]

Activity 3 Technology Connection
You may wish to demonstrate how to copy spreadsheet formulas. You could then assign *Technology Sourcebook, Computer Master 3.* Students use a spreadsheet program to create tables that compare dollar values to equivalent values in other currencies.

❷ Reciprocal Rates

Sometimes a rate does not help simplify the computation, but its reciprocal would. Example 3 used $\frac{1 \text{ hr}}{60 \text{ min}}$ rather than $\frac{60 \text{ min}}{1 \text{ hr}}$. These are reciprocal rates. In reciprocal rates both the numbers and units are reciprocals. For instance, $2.5 \frac{\text{miles}}{\text{lap}}$ and $\frac{1}{2.5} \frac{\text{lap}}{\text{mile}}$ are *reciprocal rates*. **Reciprocal rates** describe the same situation from different points of view. For instance, if 200 words are read in a minute, then it takes $\frac{1}{200}$ of a minute to read one word. The reciprocal rate of $200 \frac{\text{words}}{\text{min}}$ is $\frac{1}{200} \frac{\text{min}}{\text{word}}$.

Example 4 shows that you must often decide which of two reciprocal rates to use. Choose the one that cancels correctly, resulting in an answer with the appropriate units.

Example 4

People sometimes go for a walk after a big meal to "burn it off." To lose 1 pound, a person must burn 3500 calories. An average-sized person burns about 300 calories per hour by walking. If a person walks for 2 hours, how much weight will he or she lose?

Solution

The unit of the answer should be a weight, in this case pounds. The two rates $3500 \frac{\text{calories}}{\text{pound}}$ and $300 \frac{\text{calories}}{\text{hour}}$ or their reciprocals might be used. To eliminate the calorie unit we must multiply by a rate having calorie in the denominator. We also must have the pound unit left after the multiplication, so the rate used must be $\frac{\text{pound}}{\text{calories}}$. So we use the reciprocal of $3500 \frac{\text{calories}}{\text{pound}}$.

$$2 \text{ hours} \cdot \frac{1}{3500} \frac{\text{pound}}{\text{calories}} \cdot 300 \frac{\text{calories}}{\text{hour}} = \frac{2 \cdot 300}{3500} \text{ pound}$$
$$\approx .17 \text{ pound}$$

If a person walks for 2 hours, he or she will lose about $\frac{1}{6}$ pound.

Marching for the March of Dimes. *President Franklin Delano Roosevelt started the March of Dimes to combat polio in 1938. The "Dimes" in the name refers to the dimes sent to the White House during the agency's first fund-raiser.*

QUESTIONS

Covering the Reading

In 1 and 2 a rate is given. **a.** Copy the sentence and underline the rate. **b.** Write the rate unit using a slash. **c.** Write the rate unit using a fraction bar.

1. A secretary types <u>70 words per minute.</u> b) 70 words/min c) $70 \frac{\text{words}}{\text{min}}$

2. There are exactly <u>2.54 centimeters per inch.</u> b) 2.54 cm/in. c) $2.54 \frac{\text{cm}}{\text{in.}}$

3. Write the rate "6 dollars an hour" using the following symbols.
   a. a slash 6 dollars/hour   **b.** a horizontal bar $6 \frac{\text{dollars}}{\text{hour}}$

Lesson 2-4 *Multiplying Rates* **93**

---

gallon of gasoline. [hours per mile; hours per dollar; gallons per dollar.]

Additional Examples
These examples are also given on **Teaching Aid 18.**

1. It takes Felicia 25 minutes to walk one mile. At this rate, how long would it take her to walk 7 miles? **175 minutes or 2 hours and 55 minutes**

2. If a car travels 55 miles an hour, about how far will it travel in $3\frac{3}{4}$ hours? **About 206 miles**

3. If a car travels at 55 miles an hour, how far does it travel per second? **About 81 feet**

4. Refer to **Example 4** on page 93. An average-sized person burns about 500 calories per hour swimming. If a person swims for a half hour, how much weight will he or she lose? **About 0.07 pounds**

5. Suppose gasoline costs $1.20 a gallon. State the reciprocal rate and explain how it describes the same situation. $\frac{5}{6} \frac{\text{gallons}}{\text{dollar}}$; if you buy gas at $1.20 per gallon, you are getting $\frac{5}{6}$ of a gallon for every dollar you spend.

6. In 1962, Wilt Chamberlain set an NBA season scoring record, averaging 50.4 points per game. On the average, how many points did he score per minute? (There are 48 minutes in a basketball game.) $1.05 \frac{\text{points}}{\text{minute}}$

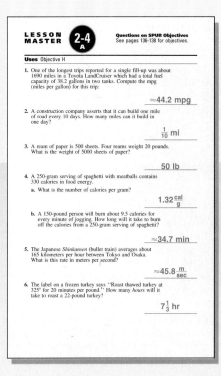

Activity 4 Sports Connection
After students answer **Question 14,** you might mention that the first Indianapolis 500 race took place in 1911. That year's winner, Ray Harroun, averaged 74.59 miles per hour. Ask students to use this speed to determine about how long it would take someone going 74.59 mph to go around the track once, and how long it would take to complete the 500-mile race. [A little more than 2 minutes; about 402 minutes or 6.7 hours]

Interested students could investigate other winning speeds at the Indianapolis 500.

Question 15 This question is important for the development of thinking with variables. The answers to **part a** and **part b** are reciprocal rates.

Question 16 You might note that $6 buys 30 shrimp. There are $\frac{30 \text{ shrimp}}{6 \text{ dollars}}$, or 5 shrimp for a dollar.

✎ **Questions 18–19 Writing** Ask students to share their answers.

Question 20 One way of thinking about 16.2 babies per 1,000 population is to treat the U.S. population as 252,000 thousand people.

Question 29 Students should multiply the answer to **part a** by 1000 to answer **part b,** and multiply that number by 1000 to answer **part c.**

History Connection As an aside for **Question 29,** you might tell students the story of Thomas Fuller who was brought as a slave to Virginia in 1724 when he was 14 years old. During his years of working in the fields, he developed a talent for calculating mentally. For example, when asked to give the number of seconds in a year and a half, it took him less than 2 minutes to answer 47,304,000 seconds.

Faster than a speeding bullet! *The world's fastest electric train is the French TGV (train à grande vitesse, or high-speed train). The TGV gets its power from an overhead wire system.*

4. While Tonisha exercises, her heart rate is 150 beats per minute. How many times will her heart beat while exercising for the following times?
   a. 10 minutes 1500 beats
   b. *m* minutes 150*m* beats

5. In the annual car race at LeMans, France, teams of drivers take turns driving for 24 hours. On the 1992 winning team, two drivers were British and one was French. They had an average speed of 123.89 mph. How many miles did the team drive during the race? 2973.36 miles

6. A small plane flies 380 miles per hour. How far will it fly in $2\frac{1}{2}$ hours? 950 miles

7. The high-speed French TGV train can go 300 km/h. Convert this rate to kilometers per second. 0.0833 km/sec

8. *Multiple choice.* What is the reciprocal rate of 40 $\frac{\text{miles}}{\text{gallon}}$? (b)
   (a) 40 $\frac{\text{gallons}}{\text{mile}}$
   (b) $\frac{1}{40} \frac{\text{gallon}}{\text{mile}}$
   (c) $\frac{1}{40} \frac{\text{mile}}{\text{gallon}}$
   (d) 40 mpg

9. Refer to Example 4. There are 16 ounces per pound. If an average person walks for 2 hours, how many ounces will he or she lose? ≈ 2.7 ounces

Applying the Mathematics

10. In the decade from 1980 to 1990, the population of West Virginia was decreasing by an average of 14,300 people per year. What was the total population loss during those 10 years? 143,000 people

11. There are 24 bottles per case. Each bottle contains 12 ounces of liquid.
    a. How many ounces are in 10 cases? 2880 ounces
    b. How many ounces are in *c* cases? 288*c* ounces

In 12 and 13, use the fact that 1 inch = 2.54 cm.

12. Elise is 60 inches tall. What is her height in centimeters? 152.4 cm

13. In his home country, Carlos wears an 80-cm belt. His friend Gloria wants to send him a belt from the United States where belts are made in 2-inch increments (28, 30, 32, and so on). What size belt should Gloria send? Explain your reasoning. Size 32; 80 cm · $\frac{1 \text{ in.}}{2.54 \text{ cm}}$ ≈ 31.5 in. The size closest to 80 cm is 32 in.

14. In 1994, Al Unser, Jr. won the Indianapolis 500 with an average speed of 160.872 mph. At this average speed, how long would it take him to go once around the $2\frac{1}{2}$-mile track? 0.0155 hr or about 55.95 sec

15. Marty can wash *k* dishes per minute. His sister Sue is twice as fast.
    a. How many dishes can Sue wash per minute? 2*k* $\frac{\text{dishes}}{\text{minute}}$
    b. How many minutes does Sue spend per dish? $\frac{1}{2k} \frac{\text{minute}}{\text{dish}}$

16. If shrimp costs $6/lb, and you get 30 shrimp/lb, how many shrimp can you buy for a dollar? Hint: Use a reciprocal rate. 5 shrimp

Adapting to Individual Needs

Extra Help
It may confuse your students that reciprocal rates describe the same situation while, in general, reciprocal numbers are not equal. Point out the use of the word *quantity* in this lesson, and explain that it stands for a number with a unit, such as $8, 55 miles, or 25 $\frac{\text{students}}{\text{class}}$. Quantities help to clarify the idea that the numbers in 2.5 $\frac{\text{miles}}{\text{lap}}$ and

0.4 $\frac{\text{laps}}{\text{mile}}$ are different, but the quantities represent the same relationship between number of laps and total distance.

17. Suppose an alpine climber begins 2400 meters from the summit of a mountain. If she climbs 48 meters per hour, and she climbs 10 hours each day, how many days will it take her to reach the summit? **5 days**

In 18 and 19, write a rate multiplication problem whose answer is the given quantity.

18. 25 miles See left.

19. $3 \frac{\text{minutes}}{\text{page}}$ See left.

20. In 1992, the birth rate in the U.S. was 16.2 babies per 1,000 people. That year the population was about 252,000,000. Use this product:

$$16.2 \frac{\text{babies}}{1,000 \text{ people}} \cdot 252,000,000 \text{ people}$$

to determine how many babies were born in 1992. **about 4,082,400**

Climb every mountain.
Most major mountains, except those in remote areas, have been climbed. The tallest peak in North America, Mt. McKinley, was first climbed in 1913. Mt. Everest, the world's highest mountain, was first scaled in 1953.

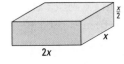

18) Sample: If you go 100 mph for 15 minutes, how far do you travel?

19) Sample: If you can read magazines at a rate of 120 minutes per magazine and each magazine has 40 pages, what is your speed in minutes per page?

Review

21. *Multiple choice.* Which is *not* equal to the others? *(Lesson 2-3)* **(d)**
(a) $\frac{42}{4} x$ (b) $\frac{42x}{4}$ (c) $\frac{7}{4} \cdot 6x$ (d) $\frac{42}{4x}$

22. Multiply and simplify $\frac{8b}{7c} \cdot \frac{21a}{2x} \cdot 5c$. *(Lesson 2-3)* $\frac{60ab}{x}$

23. Find two algebraic fractions that have a product of $\frac{8x}{15y}$. *(Lesson 2-3)*
Sample: $\frac{8}{15} \cdot \frac{x}{y} = \frac{8x}{15y}$

In 24 and 25, an expression is given. **a.** Simplify. **b.** Name the multiplication property used. *(Lessons 2-2, 2-3)*

24. $6x \cdot \frac{1}{6x}$ a) 1
b) Property of Reciprocals

25. $\frac{17t^2}{x} \cdot \frac{x^4}{901t^3} \cdot 0$ a) 0
b) Multiplication Property of Zero

26. Compute in your head $(9998 + 1) \frac{1}{9999}$. *(Lesson 2-2)* **1**

27. a. Find the volume of the box shown at the left. x^3
b. Give the dimensions of two other boxes that have the same volume. *(Lessons 2-1, 2-3)* Sample: $3x \cdot x \cdot \frac{x}{3}$; $16x \cdot \frac{x}{4} \cdot \frac{x}{4}$

Exploration

28. For what rate does the abbreviation stand, and where is it used?
a. rpm revolutions per minute; Sample: a car engine
b. psi pounds per square inch; Sample: air pressure in bicycle tires

29. Suppose that on January 1 in the year 2000, you begin counting from 1 at the rate of 1 number per second. If this counting continues around the clock, during which month and year would you reach the following numbers? Explain how you got your answer.
a. 1 million **b.** 1 billion **c.** 1 trillion

a) January, 2000; it will take 11.574 days to count to one million at this rate. b) It will take 11,574.1 days = 11,574.1 days $\cdot \frac{1 \text{ yr}}{365 \text{ days}}$ = 31.71 yrs = 31 years and 259.3 days to count to 1 billion. You would reach 1 billion in September, 2031. c) It will take approximately 31,689 years to reach 1 trillion. You would not reach this number in your lifetime.

Practice
For more questions on SPUR Objectives, use **Lesson Master 2-4A** (shown on page 93) or **Lesson Master 2-4B** (shown on pages 94–95).

Assessment
Written Communication Have each student determine how long it takes him or her to perform a task such as traveling to school, swimming one lap, or washing the dishes, and then use this rate to calculate what he or she might accomplish in one hour. [Students use rates correctly and demonstrate their use in a real-world situation.]

Extension
Project Update Project 1, *Extraterrestrial Life*, and Project 5, *Rates*, on pages 131–132, relate to the content of this lesson.

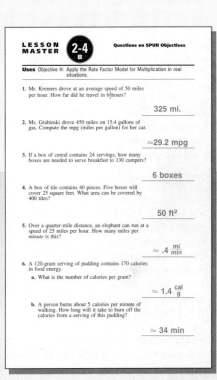

Adapting to Individual Needs

English Language Development
For this lesson, you might pair students who are learning English with competent readers of English. Have the pairs take turns reading and explaining what they have read.

Encourage students to bring a bilingual dictionary to class every day and to look up unfamiliar words.

Challenge
Have students solve the following problem:

Maria and Jan are running around an indoor track. They leave from the same point but jog in opposite directions at different constant speeds. Maria can run around the entire track in 40 seconds. She meets Jan every 15 seconds. How long does it take Jan to run around the entire track?
[24 seconds]

Objectives

B Multiply positive and negative numbers.
F Identify and apply the Multiplication Property of –1.

Resources

From the Teacher's Resource File
- Lesson Master 2-5A or 2-5B
- Answer Master 2-5
- Teaching Aid 14: Warm-up

Additional Resources
- Visual for Teaching Aid 14

Teaching Lesson 2-5

Warm-up

Diagnostic Evaluate each expression.
1. $(-1)^{100}$ 1
2. $(-1)^{99}$ –1
3. $(-3)^3$ –27
4. -3^3 –27
5. -3^2 –9
6. $(-3)^2$ 9

Notes on Reading

Reading Mathematics This is an appropriate lesson to read in class. You might call on students, in turn, to read paragraphs.

The first paragraphs of this lesson should be covered in detail so that students gain a picture of a common use of multiplication of negative numbers. They will again encounter negative rate factors in the discussions of slope.

LESSON 2-5

Products and Powers with Negative Numbers

A clear-cut problem. *This photo shows the clear-cutting of a part of the rain forest of Belize, Central America. With 50 million acres of rain forests worldwide being destroyed yearly, many species of animals and plants may become extinct.*

Multiplication with Negative Numbers

The rate factor model can be applied to both positive and negative rates. For example, recently in Brazil, an average of about 13,800 square kilometers of rain forest has been destroyed each year. Expressed as a rate, the change in the area of Brazil's rain forest has been $-13,800 \frac{km^2}{year}$. If this rate continues unchanged for 20 years, multiplying gives the total amount destroyed.

$$20 \text{ years} \cdot -13,800 \frac{km^2}{year} = -276,000 \text{ km}^2$$

The final answer is negative, which means that 276,000 square kilometers (about 107,000 square miles) of forest would be *lost* during those twenty years. This example shows that *the product of a positive and a negative number is negative.*

To multiply two negatives, again consider the decrease in Brazil's forested land. One year ago, there were 13,800 square kilometers more forest than there are now. Going back in time is represented by a negative number. Expressed as a product using rates:

1 year ago at a loss of 13,800 km² per year = 13,800 km² more than now.

$$\text{So, } -1 \text{ year} \cdot -13,800 \frac{km^2}{year} = 13,800 \text{ km}^2.$$

The positive answer indicates there was *more* forest last year than now.

Lesson 2-5 Overview

Broad Goals We assume that students can multiply positive and negative numbers. This lesson reviews the multiplication of positive or negative numbers and discusses the positive integer powers of negative numbers. Students review both the oral and written language of exponents and powers.

Perspective Often students are given three rules for multiplying positive and negative numbers: the product of a negative and a positive is a negative; the product of a positive and a negative is a negative; and the product of two negatives is a positive. Sometimes the product of two positives is included as one of the rules. But all these can be boiled down to a single algorithm: multiplying by a negative number reverses the sign. That is, if you begin with a positive number and multiply it by a negative number, the result is negative. If you begin with a negative number and multiply it by a negative number, the result is positive.

This single algorithm carries with it the essence of negative numbers; that is, a negative number involves a reversal of direction (from north to south, from gain to loss, and so on). Although the algorithm is simple, it is not always understood.

The numbers -13,800 and 13,800 are **opposites.** The last instance illustrates that multiplication by -1 changes a number to its opposite.

---

❷ Multiplication Property of -1
For any real number a, $a \cdot -1 = -1 \cdot a = -a$.

What happens when the opposite of one number is multiplied by the opposite of another number?

Since $-x = -1x$, and $-y = -1y$, then
$$-x \cdot -y = -1x \cdot -1y$$
$$= (-1 \cdot -1)xy \quad \text{Commutative Property of Multiplication}$$
$$= 1xy \quad \text{Multiplication Property of -1}$$
$$= xy.$$

The work above shows that the product of the opposites of two numbers is the same as the product of the two original numbers. When x and y are positive, $-x$ and $-y$ are negative. Thus, *the product of two negative numbers is positive.*

Rules for Multiplying Positive and Negative Numbers
If two numbers have the same sign, their product is positive.
If two numbers have different signs, their product is negative.

The rules for multiplying positive and negative numbers also apply to numerical and algebraic expressions.

Example 1

Multiply and simplify where possible.
a. $-4x \cdot -3y$
b. $-15n \cdot \frac{2}{n}$
c. $-\frac{3}{7} \cdot -\frac{7}{3}$

Solution
a. $-4x \cdot -3y = 4 \cdot 3 \cdot x \cdot y = 12xy$
b. $-15n \cdot \frac{2}{n} = -30$
c. $-\frac{3}{7} \cdot -\frac{7}{3} = \frac{3}{7} \cdot \frac{7}{3} = 1$

In part **c,** because $-\frac{3}{7} \cdot -\frac{7}{3} = 1$, the reciprocal of $-\frac{3}{7}$ is $-\frac{7}{3}$. In general, if neither a nor b is zero, the reciprocal of $-\frac{a}{b}$ is $-\frac{b}{a}$.

---

❶ Note that the quantity $-13,800 \; \frac{km^2}{yr}$ is read "negative 13 thousand 8 hundred square kilometers per year."

Geography Connection You might mention that the tropical rain forests of Brazil contain more than 40,000 varieties of plants and more species of trees than any other area of the world. Over 3,000 kinds of trees have been found in one square mile of the rain forest. These trees include the giant Brazil-nut trees, mahogany trees, rosewood trees, and rubber trees. The forests yield fruits, latex, nuts, and timber. You might have students compare the amount of rain forest that is destroyed each year and the project-ed amount that will be destroyed in 20 years with the area of your state. [13,800 km² (5,327 mi²) is greater than the area of Connecticut. 276,000 km² (107,000 mi²) is larger than the area of Wyoming.]

❷ Point out that $-x$ is read "the opposite of x." Discourage the use of "negative x" (the quantity may be positive) and "minus x" (there is no subtraction). But do not be pedantic about it; many mathematicians use the "negative" or "minus" language.

Note that justifications are given to the right of several steps. It is not necessary for students to write the reasons for the steps. However, you may occasionally ask them to do so on their homework so that you know what they were thinking.

Optional Activities

✎ **Writing** After completing the lesson, have each student write a letter to convince a younger person that a negative number times a negative number is a positive number. Or have each student write a letter to convince someone that even powers of a negative number are positive, and odd powers of a negative number are negative.

❸ Remind students that zero is neither positive nor negative, and that
−0 = 0.

The signs of powers of negative
numbers follow from the definition of
positive integer exponents: $x^1 = x$,
$x^2 = x \cdot x$; $x^3 = x \cdot x \cdot x$; and so on.
Thus, the number of factors to be
multiplied is the same as the exponent. If x is negative, each multiplication by x changes the sign; so the
first power is negative, the second
power is positive, the third power is
negative, and so on. It is exactly like
turning a light bulb on and off. (See
Question 32.)

The words *power* and *exponent* are
often confused. In the expression
$(-1)^6$, −1 is the *base*, 6 is the *exponent*, and $(-1)^6$ is the *power*. That
is, the word *power* stands for the
answer to an arithmetic problem
that involves exponentiation, just as
product stands for the answer to a
multiplication problem. Specifically,
the expression $(-1)^6$ is read as "negative 1 to the 6th," or "negative 1 to
the 6th power," or "the 6th power of
negative 1."

Example 2

Evaluate $y = ax^2 + bx + c$ when $a = -2$, $b = 3$, $c = 4$, and $x = -5$.

Solution

Substitute the values for the appropriate variables in the formula.

$$y = -2(-5)^2 + 3(-5) + 4$$

Follow the order of operations given in Lesson 1-4. Square first; then multiply; then add.

$$y = -2(25) + -15 + 4$$
$$= -50 + -15 + 4$$
$$= -61$$

The integer powers of negative numbers follow a simple pattern. Examine these powers of -2.

$$(-2)^1 = -2$$
$$(-2)^2 = -2 \cdot -2 = 4$$
$$(-2)^3 = -2 \cdot -2 \cdot -2 = -8$$
$$(-2)^4 = -2 \cdot -2 \cdot -2 \cdot -2 = 16$$
$$(-2)^5 = -2 \cdot -2 \cdot -2 \cdot -2 \cdot -2 = -32$$

Notice the pattern. Odd powers of -2 are negative. Even powers of -2 are positive. There is a more general property.

> **Properties of Multiplication of Positive and Negative Numbers**
> 1. The product of an odd number of negative numbers is negative.
> 2. The product of an even number of negative numbers is positive.

❸ **Example 3**

Without computing, determine whether the number is positive, negative, or zero.
a. $(-3)^6$ **b.** $5 \cdot 3 \cdot 1 \cdot -1 \cdot -3 \cdot -5$ **c.** $3 \cdot 2 \cdot 1 \cdot 0 \cdot -1 \cdot -2 \cdot -3$

Solution

a. This is an even power of a negative number, so $(-3)^6$ is positive.
b. Three of the numbers multiplied are negative, so the product is negative.
c. Zero is one of the factors, so the product is 0.

Recall that parentheses are important when evaluating expressions. This is particularly true when negative numbers and powers are involved. For instance,

$$(-3)^6 = -3 \cdot -3 \cdot -3 \cdot -3 \cdot -3 \cdot -3 = 729$$

In contrast,

-3^6 means the opposite of 3^6, or $-1 \cdot 3^6$.
$$-3^6 = -1 \cdot 3^6 = -1 \cdot 3 \cdot 3 \cdot 3 \cdot 3 \cdot 3 \cdot 3 = -729$$

98

Adapting to Individual Needs

Extra Help
For students who need further help understanding the process of multiplying positive
and negative numbers, review the idea of
multiplication as repeated addition. For
example, write $3(-5) = -5 + -5 + -5$ on the
board. Remind students that the sum of
three negative addends is negative: $3(-5) =$
-15. Then write $-3(-5)$ on the board. Point

out that −3 is the opposite of 3, so the
product −3(−5) will be the opposite of 3(−5):
−3(−5) = 15.

The pattern at the
right can also be
used to develop
the rule for finding
the product of two
negative numbers.

$3 \times -5 = -15$
$2 \times -5 = -10$
$1 \times -5 = -5$
$0 \times -5 = 0$
$-1 \times -5 = 5$
$-2 \times -5 = 10$
$-3 \times -5 = 15$

Graphics calculators usually allow you to calculate powers of negative numbers. Other scientific calculators often do not. Here are key sequences that work on some calculators.

$(-3)^6$: ⌈ (−) 3 ⌉ ∧ 6 ENTER   display (-3)^6 **729**

⌈ (−) 3 ⌉ x^y 6 EXE   display (-3)x^6 **729**

-3^6: (−) 3 ∧ 6 ENTER   display (-3)^6 **-729**

(−) 3 x^y 6 EXE   display (-3)x^6 **-729**

3 x^y 6 = ±   display **-729**

Check your calculator to see whether it can evaluate powers with negative numbers.

1. Multiply and simplify where possible.
   a. $-2x \cdot -5x$ $10x^2$
   b. $x \cdot -y$ $-xy$
   c. $(-a) \cdot b \cdot (-c)$ abc
2. Evaluate $\sqrt{b^2 - 4ac}$ when $a = -3$, $b = 4$, and $c = -1$. **2**
3. Without using a calculator, determine if the number is positive or negative.
   a. -7^7 Negative
   b. $(-7)^7$ Negative
   c. -7^6 Negative
   d. $(-7)^6$ Positive
   e. $-2 \cdot -3 \cdot -4 \cdot -5 \cdot -6$
      Negative
   f. $-1 \cdot -2 \cdot -3 \cdot -4 \cdot -5 \cdot -6$
      Positive

QUESTIONS

Covering the Reading

1. a. Copy and complete this table. Assume the area of Brazil's rain forest is decreasing by the amount mentioned in the reading.

Years from present	Change in Brazil's rain forest compared to now
20	-276,000
5	-69,000
1	-13,800
-1	13,800
-5	69,000

   b. What is meant by "-5 years from now"? **5 years ago**

2. In recent years, a farm's topsoil has eroded at a rate of 0.3 inch per year.
   a. What was the total change after 4 years? **-1.2 in.**
   b. What rate factor multiplication is needed to answer the question in part a? **4 years $\cdot -0.3 \frac{in.}{year}$**
   c. How much deeper was the topsoil 5 years ago? **1.5 in.**
   d. What rate factor multiplication is needed to answer the question in part c? **-5 years $\cdot -0.3 \frac{in.}{year}$**

Soil erosion can increase when land is cleared and cultivated. Trees and plants are no longer there to hold the soil in place. Farmers reduce erosion by planting crops like alfalfa in idle fields and using methods such as contour plowing and strip cropping.

In 3–6, compute in your head.
3. a. $6 \cdot -3$ -18
   b. $6x \cdot -3y$ -18xy
4. a. $4 \cdot -9$ -36
   b. $4p \cdot -9s$ -36ps
5. a. $-7 \cdot -5$ 35
   b. $-7t \cdot -5t$ $35t^2$
6. a. $-\frac{4}{3} \cdot -\frac{3}{4}$ 1
   b. $\frac{-4}{m} \cdot \frac{m}{-4}$ 1

Lesson 2-5 *Products and Powers with Negative Numbers* **99**

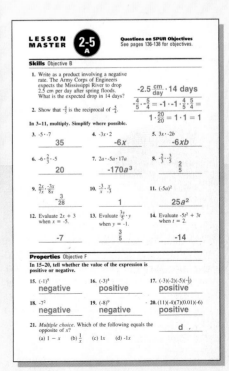

Adapting to Individual Needs

English Language Development
You might want to define the word *eroded* which is used in **Question 2**. Explain that eroded means to wear away gradually. Have students keep a list of words that appear in lessons and questions that refer to negative numbers, such as eroded, loss, decreasing, and destroyed.

Notes on Questions

✎ **Question 22 Writing** The answers students give can tell you if they understand the content of this lesson.

Question 30 Students may have trouble squaring $\sqrt{2}$. One of the most important things for students to learn about radicals in beginning algebra is that $\sqrt{n} \cdot \sqrt{n} = n$ for all nonnegative numbers n.

7. *Skill sequence.* State the reciprocal of each number.
   a. $\frac{1}{9}$ 9
   b. $-\frac{1}{9}$ -9
   c. $-\frac{11}{9}$ $-\frac{9}{11}$
   d. $-\frac{11k}{9}$ $-\frac{9}{11k}$

8. Evaluate $y = -3x^2 + 6x + 1$ when $x = -2$. -23

In 9–11, tell whether the product of the numbers is positive or negative.

9. two positive numbers and two negative numbers The product is positive.

10. one hundred negative numbers The product is positive.

11. three negative numbers and one positive number The product is negative.

In 12 and 13, evaluate without a calculator.

12. $-1 \cdot 2 \cdot -3 \cdot 4$ 24

13. $(-1)^5$ -1

14. a. Evaluate each expression.
    i. $(-3)^6$ 729   ii. $(-3)^7$ -2187   iii. $(-3)^8$ 6561   iv. $(-3)^9$ -19,683
    b. Which powers of -3 are positive? even powers
    c. Which powers of -3 are negative? odd powers

15. *True or false.* Justify your answer.
    a. $(-5)^3 = -5^3$
    b. $(-5)^4 = -5^4$
    a) True; $(-5)^3 = -125$;   b) False; since the left side is positive, but the right side is negative.

Applying the Mathematics

In 16–19, multiply and simplify.

16. $(-4a)(-a)$ $4a^2$

17. $(-3x)^2$ $9x^2$

18. $(-10n)^3$ $-1000n^3$

19. $(2a)^2 \cdot (-2a)^3$ $-32a^5$

20. Evaluate and simplify.
    a. $-\frac{1}{2} \cdot -\frac{2}{3}$ $\frac{1}{3}$
    b. $-\frac{1}{2} \cdot -\frac{2}{3} \cdot -\frac{3}{4}$ $-\frac{1}{4}$
    c. $-\frac{1}{2} \cdot -\frac{2}{3} \cdot -\frac{3}{4} \cdot -\frac{4}{5}$ $\frac{1}{5}$
    d. $-\frac{1}{2} \cdot -\frac{2}{3} \cdot -\frac{3}{4} \cdot \ldots \cdot -\frac{9}{10}$ $-\frac{1}{10}$

21. *Skill sequence.* Tell whether the number is positive, negative, or zero.
    a. $(-5)^{10}$ positive
    b. $(-1)(-5)^{10}$ negative
    c. $(-1)^{10}(-5)^{10}$ positive
    d. $(5)^{10}(-5)^{10}$ positive
    e. $(5 + -5)^{10}$ zero
    f. $(-1)^{10}(-5)$ negative

22. The number $(-3)^{500}$ cannot be evaluated on most calculators because it is too large for the memory. Describe how you can determine whether $(-3)^{500}$ is positive or negative. Since the exponent is even, the result is positive.

Adapting to Individual Needs

Challenge

Have students solve the following problem:

Two tanks in a factory each hold 160 gallons of fuel. Tank A is full, and tank B is empty. At 8 A.M., a drain is opened on tank A so that fuel is released at the rate of 3 gallons per minute. At the same time, a valve is opened to fill tank B at a rate of 5 gallons per minute. At what time will both tanks contain exactly the same amount of fuel? [After 20 minutes; 8:20 A.M.]

Bear facts. *Brown bears, known also as grizzly bears, are found mainly in Alaska and Canada. Grizzlies may grow to a height of 8 feet and weigh close to 400 pounds. They get angry quickly, but usually don't attack unless threatened.*

Review

In 23–25, tell whether the quantity is a rate. *(Lesson 2-4)*

23. 520 miles No

24. 35 $\frac{\text{miles}}{\text{gallon}}$ Yes

25. 55 mph Yes

26. An apartment rents for $600 per month. Find the rent for the given time. *(Lesson 2-4)*
  a. two years $14,400
  b. *y* years 600 · 12*y*, or $7200*y*

27. The maximum speed a grizzly bear can run is 50 km/hr. How far could a grizzly bear run in 10 seconds? *(Lesson 2-4)* ≈ .14 km

28. A contractor is planning to build a driveway. The driveway can be thought of as a rectangular solid 10 ft wide, 36 ft long, and 6 in. thick. $3\frac{1}{3}$ yards wide, 12 yards long, $\frac{1}{6}$ yd thick
  a. Convert these dimensions to yards.
  b. How many cubic yards of concrete should be ordered? (Only whole numbers of yards may be ordered.) 7 cubic yards
  c. If the concrete costs $125 per cubic yard, find the total cost of the concrete *(Lessons 2-1, 2-4)* $875

29. Multiply and simplify $\frac{3}{7} a \cdot \left(\frac{3}{7} a \cdot \frac{7}{a}\right)$. *(Lesson 2-3)* $\frac{9}{7}a$

30. A right triangle has legs of length 2 and $\sqrt{2}$. What is the length of the hypotenuse? *(Lesson 1-8)* $\sqrt{6}$

Exploration

31. The command "about-face" in the military signals a soldier to rotate 180°. Two commands of "about-face" result in the soldier facing forward again.

Number of About-faces	Facing
1	Reverse
2	Forward
3	Reverse
4	Forward
⋮	⋮

How does this relate to $(-1)^n$? *n* being odd results in $(-1)^n = -1$; *n* being even results in $(-1)^n = 1$. Similarly, the number of about-faces being odd results in the soldier facing reverse. And the number of about-faces being even results in the soldier facing forward. We know facing reverse is the opposite of facing forward just as 1 is the opposite of negative 1.

Lesson 2-5 *Products and Powers with Negative Numbers* **101**

Practice

For more questions on SPUR Objectives, use **Lesson Master 2-5A** (shown on page 99) or **Lesson Master 2-5B** (shown on pages 100–101).

Assessment

Written Communication Have students write a paragraph explaining which powers of negative numbers are positive and which powers of negative numbers are negative. Have students include several examples as part of their explanations. [Students' explanations reveal an understanding of the Multiplication Property of –1.]

Extension

As an extension of Additional Example 3, ask students to determine which numbers are odd and which are even. [a, b, c, and d are odd; e and f are even.] Then have them describe when a^n is even and when it is odd. [If *a* is even, the power will be even; if *a* is odd, the power will be odd.]

▶ **LESSON MASTER 2-5 B** *page 2*

27. Evaluate $3m + 18$ when $m = -4$. **6**

28. Evaluate $\frac{-6d}{3}$ when $d = -10$. **20**

29. Evaluate $\frac{5r}{12} \cdot r$ when $r = -6$. **15**

30. Evaluate $(-2f)^2$ when $f = 5$. **100**

31. Evaluate $-2x^2 + 7x - 1$ when $x = -3$. **-40**

Properties Objective F: Identify and apply the Multiplication Property of -1.
In 32–41, tell whether the expression is positive or negative.

32. $(-9)^3$ negative
33. $(-1)^{15}$ negative
34. $(-8)^2$ positive
35. $(-13)^4$ positive
36. $(-6)^6$ positive
37. -6^6 negative
38. $(-5)(-2)(-1)(-8)$ positive
39. $(-1)(-8)(6.4)(-1)$ negative
40. $5 \cdot 9 \cdot -3 \cdot 8 \cdot 2$ negative
41. $-(-18)$ positive

42. *Multiple choice.* Which of the following is equivalent to the opposite of the opposite of *n*? **b**
  (a) $\frac{1}{n}$ (b) $-1n$ (c) $1n$ (d) $1 - n$

Review Objective J, Lesson 1-5

43. Use the formula $V = e^3$ to find the volume *V* of a box that measures 80 cm along each edge *e*. **512,000 cm³**

44. The formula $F = \frac{9}{5}C + 32$ converts the temperature from degrees Celsius to degrees Fahrenheit. Find the Fahrenheit temperature to the nearest degree for
  a. 55°C. **131°F**
  b. 25°C. **77°F**
  c. 0°C. **32°F**
  d. -10°C. **14°F**

Setting Up Lesson 2-6

Materials Balance scale, boxes or envelopes, various weights

A demonstration of how to solve $4w = 8$ using a balance scale may help students to understand the opening situation in Lesson 2-6.

Objectives

C Solve and check equations of the form $ax = b$.

F Identify and apply the Multiplication Property of Equality.

H Apply the Rate Factor Model for Multiplication in real situations.

Resources

From the Teacher's Resource File

■ Lesson Master 2-6A or 2-6B
■ Answer Master 2-6
■ Teaching Aids:
   14 Warm-up
   19 Balance-Scale Diagrams
■ Activity Kit, Activity 3
■ Technology Sourcebook
   Computer Master 4

Additional Resources

■ Visuals for Teaching Aids 14, 19
■ Balance scale and weights
■ Boxes or envelopes

Teaching Lesson 2-6

Warm-up

For 1–5, tell which answer is the solution to the equation.

1. $13x = 52$ **c**

   a. $x = \frac{1}{4}$ **b.** $x = -4$ **c.** $x = 4$

2. $-4.5y = 36$ **b**

   a. $y = 8$ **b.** $y = -8$ **c.** $y = \frac{4}{5}$

3. $-6 = -\frac{5}{3}z$ **c**

   a. $z = -\frac{18}{5}$ **b.** $z = 3\frac{1}{5}$ **c.** $z = 3\frac{3}{5}$

4. $\frac{-5n}{8} = 1$ **c**

   a. $n = \frac{8}{5}$ **b.** $n = 8$ **c.** $n = -\frac{8}{5}$

5. $5 = -5m$ **b**

   a. $m = -\frac{1}{5}$ **b.** $m = -1$ **c.** $m = 0$

Solving $ax = b$

Pictured here is a balance scale.

Four small boxes, each of unknown weight w ounces, are on the left side of the scale. They balance the 8 one-ounce weights on the right side. This situation can be described by the equation

$$4w = 8.$$

A way to find the unknown weight is to take $\frac{1}{4}$ of each side.

This pictures the result of multiplying both sides of the equation by $\frac{1}{4}$.

$$\tfrac{1}{4}(4w) = \tfrac{1}{4} \cdot 8$$

The result can be seen in the picture. Each box weighs 2 ounces. In the language of equations,

$$w = 2.$$

In general, multiplying both sides of an equation by any nonzero number will not affect the solutions. This property is called the *Multiplication Property of Equality*.

> **Multiplication Property of Equality**
> For all real numbers a, b, and c, if $a = b$, then $ca = cb$.

This property is important in solving equations. Examples 1 and 2 show how this property and other properties you have studied are used.

Lesson 2-6 Overview

Broad Goals Array, area, and rate factor situations lead to equations of the form $ax = b$, which are solved in this lesson by multiplying both sides of the equation by $\frac{1}{a}$.

Perspective This lesson provides the foundation for the solution of more difficult and complex equations. It also illustrates how many real-life situations can be translated into algebraic sentences. Solving equations

of the form $ax = b$ will be practiced in the rest of the lessons in this chapter and in the end-of-chapter materials. This practice should enable students to be proficient by the time a chapter test is given.

Some teachers believe that the only way to practice solving $ax = b$ is to give an equation of the form and to ask students to solve it. One weakness of this approach is that there is no way to proceed if the student

does not know how to solve the equation. For this reason, we offer a variety of problems. Even if a student cannot answer a particular question, he or she still has a chance to answer the next one.

Solving Equations Using the Multiplication Property of Equality

Example 1

An auditorium can seat 40 people in each row. How many full rows will be needed if 600 people are expected to attend a lecture?

Solution

Draw a picture.

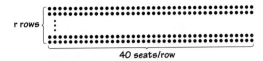

r rows {

40 seats/row

The total number of seats is $40r$. You need to solve the equation

$$40r = 600.$$

To solve this equation, multiply both sides by $\frac{1}{40}$, the reciprocal of 40.

$\frac{1}{40} \cdot 40r = \frac{1}{40} \cdot 600$	Multiplication Property of Equality
$\left(\frac{1}{40} \cdot 40\right)r = \frac{600}{40}$	Associative Property of Multiplication
$1 \cdot r = \frac{600}{40}$	Property of Reciprocals
$r = 15$	Multiplicative Identity Property of 1

So 15 rows will be needed.

Check

Are there 600 seats in 15 rows? Yes. $15 \cdot 40 = 600$.

In Example 1, both sides of the equation were multiplied by $\frac{1}{40}$ because $\frac{1}{40}$ is the reciprocal of 40. A similar thing happens in Example 2.

Example 2

Solve $\frac{7}{2} w = 4$. Check the solution.

Solution

$\frac{7}{2} w = 4$	
$\frac{2}{7} \cdot \frac{7}{2} w = \frac{2}{7} \cdot 4$	Multiplication Property of Equality
$\left(\frac{2}{7} \cdot \frac{7}{2}\right)w = \frac{2}{7} \cdot 4$	Associative Property of Multiplication
$1 \cdot w = \frac{8}{7}$	Property of Reciprocals
$w = \frac{8}{7}$	Multiplicative Identity Property of 1

Check

Substitute $w = \frac{8}{7}$ into the equation. Does $\overset{1}{\underset{}{\frac{7}{2}}} \cdot \overset{4}{\underset{}{\frac{8}{7}}} = 4$? Yes, $4 = 4$.

Notes on Reading

When discussing this lesson, you might want to represent some of the equations of the form $ax = b$ on a balance scale; that is especially true for the opening equation. If you do not have a balance scale, you can picture equations on the balance scales given on **Teaching Aid 19**, or you might use Activity 1 in *Optional Activities* below.

There is more than one way to solve an equation of the form $ax = b$ for x, but all of the ways lead to the same solution, namely, dividing b by a. We use the most general method which is to multiply both sides of the equation by $\frac{1}{a}$. This method involves the Multiplication Property of Equality, and it has been the customary method used in U.S. algebra textbooks for the past thirty years. The common representation for equations—the balance scale—is shown at the beginning of the lesson in order to lead into the use of the Multiplication Property of Equality to solve the equation.

Example 1 utilizes a situation from an array to show how such equations can arise. Because the array is discrete, the coefficient a is a whole number. **Examples 2 and 3** show solutions where a is a fraction and a negative integer. **Examples 4 and 5** give situations arising from the formula $d = rt$, while **Example 6** discusses solving this formula for one of the variables in it. An entire lesson in Chapter 5 will be devoted to this skill.

Optional Activities

Activity 1 Using Physical Models

Materials: Envelopes, paper clips

If you wish to introduce this lesson with physical models, but you do not have a balance scale, you might use this activity or *Activity Kit, Activity 3.*

1. Without showing students, put 2 paper clips in each of four envelopes. Tell students that each envelope contains n paper clips, and put the envelopes on one side of a divider, such as a pencil.

Place 8 clips on the other side of the divider. Explain that the loose clips represent the total number of clips in the envelopes.

2. Write $4n = 8$ to describe the situation.
3. Then explain that since there are 4 envelopes, they need to consider $\frac{1}{4}$ of the materials on each side of the divider. This is one envelope and two clips.
4. Then show step 3 using the Multiplication Property of Equality.

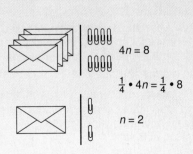

$4n = 8$

$\frac{1}{4} \cdot 4n = \frac{1}{4} \cdot 8$

$n = 2$

The examples purposely involve difficult numbers to ensure that students use algebraic techniques in solving the equations. We also want to give students practice working with decimals, fractions, and negative numbers while teaching them how to solve equations and how to write and use equations in a wide variety of settings.

If easy equations arise, do not dissuade students from solving them mentally. Solving equations mentally has the advantage of making sure that students keep track of what the answers mean. That is, students check the solutions at the same time that they are finding them.

Throughout the lesson, the solutions are given in the special writing font to emphasize what the students should be writing. Two good habits should be emphasized. First, in solving equations, equal signs should be placed below each other. Second, answers should be checked.

For an equation like $5x = 13$, some people prefer that the answer be written as $x = 2.6$. This emphasizes the idea that one finds an equation that is equivalent to the original equation. Some people just prefer to write the answer as 2.6, since this emphasizes that 2.6 is the number that works. You can use whichever method you prefer; we use both of them.

We emphasize checking the solutions to equations for several reasons. (1) It helps students catch mistakes. (2) It makes students go back to what it means to solve an equation. (3) It allows us to discuss other issues, such as using decimals for fractions.

Cincinnati. *Pictured is the Roebling Bridge over the Ohio River with Cincinnati in the background. Cincinnati is the world's leading manufacturer of soap and is the main producer of machine tools in the U.S.*

To solve $ax = b$ for x (when a is not zero), multiply both sides of the equation by the reciprocal of a.

The number a in the expression ax is the *coefficient* of the variable x. In Example 3, the coefficient of y is negative. We show the solution to the equation as you might write it, without naming the properties used.

Example 3

Solve $-6y = 117$. Check the solution.

Solution

The reciprocal of the coefficient -6 is $-\frac{1}{6}$. So, multiply both sides of the equation by $-\frac{1}{6}$.

$$-6y = 117$$
$$-\frac{1}{6} \cdot -6y = -\frac{1}{6} \cdot 117$$
$$y = -\frac{117}{6}$$
$$y = -19\frac{1}{2}$$

Check

Substitute -19.5 for y in the original equation and see if it works.

Does $-6(-19.5) = 117$? Yes, so it checks.

Since -19.5 makes the equation true, -19.5 is the solution.

Equations and Formulas

You are familiar with the formula $d = rt$, which states that if you are moving at a constant speed, the distance d you travel is equal to your rate r multiplied by the time t you travel.

Example 4

How long will it take to drive from Detroit to Cincinnati, a distance of about 270 miles, if you travel at 55 mph?

Solution 1

Use the formula $d = rt$. Let t be the length of time, in hours.

Write: $d = r \cdot t$

Think: $270 \text{ miles} = 55 \frac{\text{miles}}{\text{hour}} \cdot t \text{ hours}$

Write: $270 = 55t$

Now solve the equation: $\frac{1}{55} \cdot 270 = \frac{1}{55} \cdot 55t$

$$\frac{270}{55} = t$$
$$4.9 \approx t$$

It will take about 5 hours.

Optional Activities

Activity 2 Ask students how long it takes to travel 100 miles. Obviously, the answer depends on the means of travel. But whatever the means, the rate r (in $\frac{\text{miles}}{\text{hour}}$) and the time t (in hours) must satisfy $rt = 100$. Have students graph pairs of numbers that satisfy this equation for the following rates:

   walking at 2 mph
   running at 5 mph
   horseback riding at 8 mph
   bicycling at 10 mph
   riding in a car at 55 mph
   flying in a propeller plane at 180 mph
   flying in a jet plane at 550 mph

[(2, 50), (5, 20), (8, 12.5), (10, 10), (55, 1.8), (180, .56), and (550, .18)]

Students who have had *Transition Mathematics* should have little difficulty graphing this equation. The points lie on a hyperbola. Students can make up their own means of

transportation and add it to their graph. Since the purpose of this activity is to give students practice in solving equations, make certain that the equation is written for each point.

▶ **Solution 2**

Use a reciprocal rate. $270 \text{ mi} \cdot \frac{1}{55} \frac{\text{hr}}{\text{mi}} \approx 4.9 \text{ hours}$

Check

If you travel at 55 mph for 4.9 hours, will you travel about 270 miles? Yes, because
$$55 \tfrac{\text{mi}}{\text{hr}} \cdot 4.9 \text{ hr} = 269.5 \text{ mi} \approx 270 \text{ mi}.$$

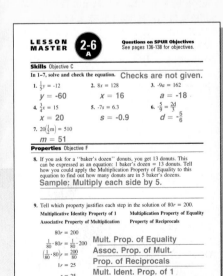

The Coming and Going of the Pony Express, *painted by Frederick Remington (1861-1909)*

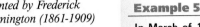

WANTED
YOUNG SKINNY WIRY FELLOWS not over eighteen. Must be expert riders willing to risk death daily. Orphans preferred. WAGES $25 per week. Apply, Central Overland Express, Alta Bldg., Montgomery St.

Example 5

In March of 1861, the Pony Express made its fastest mail delivery. That month, the riders covered the 1,966 miles from St. Joseph, Missouri, to Sacramento, California, at a rate of about 255 miles per day. How long did it take the riders to make the delivery?

Solution

Use the same strategy as in Example 4.
$$d = rt$$
$$1966 = 255t$$

Now multiply each side by the reciprocal of 255.
$$\tfrac{1}{255} \cdot 1966 = \tfrac{1}{255} \cdot 255t$$

It took the riders about 7.7 days.

If you have to do many calculations like those in Examples 4 and 5, it may be easier to rearrange the formula $d = rt$ so that the variable t is alone on one side.

Example 6

Solve $d = rt$ for t.

Solution

This problem is similar to solving $270 = 55t$ in Example 4. There the coefficient of t was 55; both sides were multiplied by $\frac{1}{55}$. In $d = rt$, the coefficient of t is r, so in order to isolate t we multiply by $\frac{1}{r}$. Write:
$$d = rt.$$
$$\tfrac{1}{r} \cdot d = \tfrac{1}{r} \cdot rt$$
$$\tfrac{d}{r} = t$$

Notice the pattern. To solve $270 = 55t$ in Example 4, we multiplied each side by $\frac{1}{55}$, the reciprocal of 55. To solve $1966 = 255t$ in Example 5, we multiplied by $\frac{1}{255}$. In both cases, the time of travel is calculated by dividing the distance by the rate of travel. This is the same calculation described in general by the formula $t = \frac{d}{r}$.

Lesson 2-6 *Solving ax = b* **105**

Activity 3 Technology Connection
In *Technology Sourcebook, Computer Master 4*, students create a spreadsheet that solves $ax = b$ automatically. Students then use their spreadsheet to solve equations.

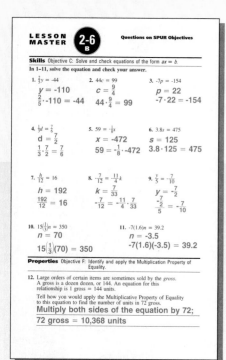

An art deco auditorium.
Art deco was a decorative style of the 1920s and 1930s that utilized vivid colors and geometric patterns. This style is visible in the decor of the Pickwick Theatre pictured above.

106

When you solve equations, we strongly recommend that you arrange your work so that the equal signs of each line are directly below each other (as the examples show). This arrangement helps avoid confusion.

QUESTIONS

Covering the Reading

1. Each box on the left side of the balance scale has the same weight.
   a. Use an equation to describe the situation pictured below.
   b. How much does each box weigh? $\frac{8}{5}$ oz $10w = 16$ oz

2. a. If $a = b$, then $6a = \underline{\ ?\ }$. $6b$
   b. What property is used to answer part **a**? **Multiplication Property of Equality**

3. In your own words, explain why multiplying each side of the equation by the reciprocal "works." **Sample: It changes the coefficient of the variable to 1.**

4. An auditorium has rows with 28 seats in each row. It is desired to rope off 500 seats for a lecture. How many rows need to be roped off? **18 rows**

In 5–10, an equation is given. **a.** What is the coefficient of the variable? **b.** By what number can you multiply both sides to solve the equation? **c.** Solve the equation.

5. $5n = 61$ a) 5; b) $\frac{1}{5}$; c) $12\frac{1}{5}$

6. $-32x = 416$ a) -32; b) $-\frac{1}{32}$; c) -13

7. $-12 = \frac{1}{4}p$ a) $\frac{1}{4}$; b) 4; c) -48

8. $\frac{3}{32}A = \frac{3}{4}$ a) $\frac{3}{32}$; b) $\frac{32}{3}$; c) 8

9. $-210 = -4.2y$ a) -4.2; b) $-\frac{1}{4.2}$ c) 50

10. $36.3 = -16.5r$ a) -16.5; b) $-\frac{1}{16.5}$ c) -2.2

11. To solve $ax = b$ for x, multiply both sides of the equation by $\underline{\ ?\ }$. $\frac{1}{a}$

12. Julie thinks $\frac{1}{4}$ is the solution to the equation $\frac{1}{3} \cdot m = \frac{4}{3}$. Is she correct? Why or why not? **No;** $\frac{1}{3} \cdot \frac{1}{4} \neq \frac{4}{3}$

13. Refer to Example 4. If you average 60 mph traveling from Detroit to Cincinnati instead of 55 mph, about how much time would you save? **≈ .4 hours or about 24 minutes**

14. Refer to Example 5. On its slowest runs, the Pony Express mail delivery took 10 full days. Then how many miles per day did the riders travel? **196.6 miles**

15. Solve $d = rt$ for r. $r = \frac{d}{t}$

Applying the Mathematics

Bike to better health.
The President's Council on Physical Fitness recommends that everyone exercise daily for 30 minutes to increase endurance and strength.

16. Solve each equation.
   a. $\frac{5x}{3} = 60$ **x = 36**   b. $60 = \frac{-5y}{3}$ **y = -36**

17. a. 1 inch = 2.54 cm, so 12 inches = __?__. **a) 30.48 cm**
   b. Explain how the Multiplication Property of Equality can be applied to get the answer to part **a.**
   b) Multiply both sides by 12 to get 12 · 1 in. = 12 · 2.54 cm.

18. Consider the equation $1.5(8x) = 300$.
   a. Simplify the left side of the equation. **12 x**
   b. Solve. **x = 25**
   c. Check your solution. **1.5(8 · 25) = 300;   1.5(200) = 300; 300 = 300**

19. Solve and check $6.5 = 5(10x)$. **x = 0.13;   6.5 = 5(1.3);   6.5 = 6.5**

20. Bicycling at a moderate speed burns about 660 calories per hour for an average-sized person. How many hours would a person need to bicycle to burn 3500 calories (about 1 pound of fat)? **≈ 5.3 hr**

21. The volume of a box needs to be 500 cubic centimeters. If the base of the box has dimensions 12.5 cm and 5 cm, how high must the box be? **8 cm**

22. Recall that the circumference C of a circle is given by the formula $C = \pi d$, where d is the diameter.
   a. Find d to the nearest hundredth, when $C = 39$ cm. **12.41 cm**
   b. Solve the formula $C = \pi d$ for d. $d = \frac{C}{\pi}$

23. The formula $F = ma$ (force = mass · acceleration) is used in physics. Solve this formula for a. $a = \frac{F}{m}$

24. According to the Museum of Natural History, a cheetah has a top speed of about 70 mph, while a greyhound has a top speed of about 39 mph. If these speeds could be maintained for one minute, how much farther would the cheetah travel? **.52 mile**

Fast cat. *The cheetah, a large cat found mainly in Africa, is the world's fastest animal when running short distances.*

1861, most of the transcontinental telegraph line was completed. The Pony Express service made a total of 308 complete runs, covering a distance of about 616,000 miles.

Question 21 You might have to remind some students to begin with the formula $V = \ell wh$.

Question 22 The answer given is based on computation with the π key on the calculator. Students who approximate π with 3.14 will answer 12.42, about .01 off the answer that is given.

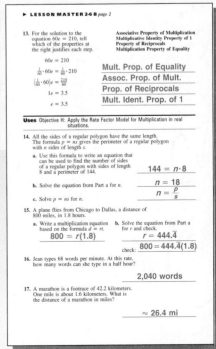

▶ **LESSON MASTER 2-6 B** *page 2*

13. For the solution to the equation $60e = 210$, tell which of the properties at the right justifies each step.

Associative Property of Multiplication
Multiplicative Identity Property of 1
Property of Reciprocals
Multiplication Property of Equality

$60e = 210$

$\frac{1}{60} \cdot 60e = \frac{1}{60} \cdot 210$ **Mult. Prop. of Equality**

$\left(\frac{1}{60} \cdot 60\right)e = \frac{210}{60}$ **Assoc. Prop. of Mult.**

$1e = 3.5$ **Prop. of Reciprocals**

$e = 3.5$ **Mult. Ident. Prop. of 1**

Uses Objective H: Apply the Rate Factor Model for Multiplication in real situations.

14. All the sides of a regular polygon have the same length. The formula $p = ns$ gives the perimeter of a regular polygon with n sides of length s.
   a. Use this formula to write an equation that can be used to find the number of sides of a regular polygon with sides of length 8 and a perimeter of 144. **144 = n·8**
   b. Solve the equation from Part a for n. **n = 18**
   c. Solve $p = ns$ for n. $n = \frac{p}{s}$

15. A plane flies from Chicago to Dallas, a distance of 800 miles, in 1.8 hours.
   a. Write a multiplication equation based on the formula $d = rt$. **800 = r(1.8)**
   b. Solve the equation from Part a for r and check. **r = 444.4̄**
   check: **800 = 444.4̄(1.8)**

16. Jean types 68 words per minute. At this rate, how many words can she type in a half hour? **2,040 words**

17. A marathon is a footrace of 42.2 kilometers. One mile is about 1.6 kilometers. What is the distance of a marathon in miles? **≈ 26.4 mi**

---

3. How much has Ryan saved? [$192]

4. What equation represents the fact that $\frac{2}{3}$ of the total amount is $192? $[\frac{2}{3}t = 192]$

5. Should the answer be more or less than $192? [More than $192]

31b) Sample: 14 · 6 + 24 · 10 + 14 · 24 = 660; and 32 · 30 − 14 · 8 − 8 · 10 − 18 · 6 = 660 square feet.

Review

25. Suppose $y = x^3$. Tell whether y is positive, negative, or zero:
   a. when $x > 0$.   **b.** when $x < 0$.   **c.** when $x = 0$.   *(Lesson 2-5)*
   a) positive   b) negative   c) zero

26. *Skill sequence.* Evaluate. *(Lesson 2-5)*
   a. 2^8 256   **b.** -2^8 -256   **c.** $(-2)^8$ 256
   d. -2^9 -512   **e.** $(-2)^9$ -512

27. Use two rates to change 4.5 yards to centimeters. *(Lesson 2-4)*
   See below.

28. If Irma dribbles a basketball twice a second and moves 4.5 ft per second, how many dribbles will she make moving 60 ft downcourt? *(Lesson 2-4)* ≈ 26 dribbles

29. A magician performs at birthday parties. If the magician charges D dollars per party, how much will be earned from P parties? *(Lesson 2-4)* DP

30. Simplify $-x \cdot \frac{2}{15x} \cdot \frac{5}{7x}$. *(Lesson 2-3)* $-\frac{2}{21x}$

31. The sketch at the right is a floor plan or map of a house. All angles are right angles.
   a. Find the area of the floor plan. 660 ft²
   b. Check your work by finding the area in another way. See left.
   c. If the house has two stories, what is the total area of the living space? 1320 ft²
   d. Another house with the same area has only one story, and has a square floor plan. What are the dimensions of its floor plan? about 25.7 ft × 25.7 ft
   (Lessons 1-6, 2-1)

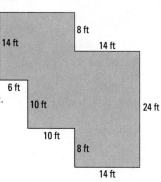

32. Tell whether the number is or is not a solution to $3x \leq 20$.
   (Lesson 1-2)
   a. 6 Yes   **b.** 6.5 Yes   **c.** 7 No
   27) 4.5 yd · 36 $\frac{in.}{yd}$ · 2.54 $\frac{cm}{in.}$ = 411.48 cm

Exploration

33. A number of well-known formulas involve only multiplication. Three of them are listed below. Tell what the variables represent in each formula.
   a. $A = \frac{1}{2}bh$ **b.** $C = 2\pi r$ **c.** $I = prt$
   a) *A* is the area of a triangle, *b* is a side of that triangle, and *h* is the altitude to that side.   b) *C* is the circumference of a circle with radius *r*.
   c) *I* is the simple interest earned on a principal of *p* dollars at an interest rate *r* for the time *t*.

Special Numbers in Equations

Zero in on this. *Some stores have sales that offer 0% interest if you pay the balance due on your purchase before a set period of time. Of course, you should always read the fine print. Equations involving zero also require careful attention.*

In the last lesson, you learned that all equations of the form $ax = b$ where $a \neq 0$ have exactly one solution. This solution is found by multiplying each side of the equation by $\frac{1}{a}$. Because the numbers 0 and -1 sometimes cause students trouble, in this lesson we examine what happens when these numbers are used as coefficients in equations.

Equations with 0

Example 1

Solve $0x = 4$.

Solution

By the Multiplication Property of 0, for any value of x, $0x = 0$. So $0x$ cannot equal 4. There is no solution.
Write: **There is no solution.**

Example 2

Solve $0x = 0$.

Solution

This is the Multiplication Property of 0. It is true no matter what value is assigned to x.
Write: **All real numbers are solutions.**

Notice that in Examples 1 and 2, you cannot multiply both sides by the reciprocal of 0. Why?—because 0 has no reciprocal! Be careful when 0 is the coefficient of the unknown. Zero is the only number that causes such problems.

Lesson 2-7 *Special Numbers in Equations* **109**

Lesson 2-7

Objectives

C Solve and check equations of the form $ax = b$ when a or b is zero or -1.

F Identify and apply the following properties: Multiplication Property of -1; Multiplication Property of Zero; Multiplication Property of Equality.

Resources

From the ***Teacher's Resource File***
- Lesson Master 2-7A or 2-7B
- Answer Master 2-7
- Assessment Sourcebook: Quiz for Lessons 2-4 through 2-7
- Teaching Aid 14: Warm-up

Additional Resources
- Visual for Teaching Aid 14

Teaching 2-7
Lesson

Warm-up

Have students fill in the blanks.

1. The reciprocal of -8 is ___. $-\frac{1}{8}$
2. The product of 0 and any number is ___. 0
3. The only number without a reciprocal is ___. 0
4. There are two numbers that equal their own reciprocal. They are ___ and ___. 1, -1

Notes on Reading

Because 0 does not have a reciprocal, equations of the form $0x = b$ cannot be solved like other multiplication equations. Two possibilities are given in **Examples 1 and 2.** In

---

Lesson 2-7 Overview

Broad Goals This lesson provides more time to discuss solving equations of the form $ax = b$. Now special cases are considered: when a or b is 0 or when a is -1.

Perspective The general mathematical principle given in this lesson pertains to groups. A group is a set S and an operation $*$ that is closed in S, that is associative, that has an identity element, and for which every element has an inverse. The set of *nonzero*

real numbers forms a group with multiplication, which means that every equation of the form $a \cdot x = b$ has a unique solution. But the set of *all* real numbers does not form a group with multiplication since 0 does not have a multiplicative inverse. This is one reason why working with 0 is complicated.

What makes -1 special is that -1 times a number is the opposite of the number. But solving an equation of the form $-1 \cdot x = b$ is

no different from solving $ax = b$ when $a \neq 0$. There is a unique solution; it is $-b$.

Students will continue to see some situations which have no solution and others (identities) which are true for all real numbers. Later, in our discussion of systems of equations involving parallel lines, students will encounter situations which either always happen or never happen.

Example 1, $b \neq 0$, and there is no solution. In **Example 2,** $b = 0$, and there are infinitely many possible solutions. **Example 3** involves zero, but this equation has a unique solution since the coefficient has a reciprocal. Similarly, in **Example 4,** the coefficient of the unknown has a reciprocal. Thus, the equations in these examples are solved in the same way we solved the equations in the preceding lesson.

❶ Either students can write complete sentences to describe these situations, or they can identify the solution set as explained here. Writing the solutions to **Examples 1–3** helps to clarify the difference between having no solution and having a solution of zero.

Continue to stress that the solutions to equations should be checked. One benefit of checking is that the solutions for the special situations that appear in **Examples 1–4** should make intuitive sense.

❷ **Reading Mathematics** This computer program is powerful—it will solve *all* equations of the form $ax = b$. Since this is the first time that students will use the IF-THEN statement in a program, it would be beneficial to go through the program, line-by-line, with your class. As you are doing this, discuss the reason for each step.

Additional Examples
In 1–4, solve the equation.
1. $3.6 = 0m$ **There is no solution.**
2. $0 = 0a$ **All real numbers are solutions.**
3. $0 = 7.2y$ $y = 0$
4. $-x = -\frac{7}{8}$ $x = \frac{7}{8}$

(Notes on Questions begin on page 112.)

Consider the equation $ax = b$, where $a \neq 0$, but $b = 0$. Then there is exactly one solution. This is because the coefficient a has a reciprocal.

Example 3

Solve $13x = 0$.

Solution 1

$$13x = 0$$

Multiply both sides by $\frac{1}{13}$, the reciprocal of 13.

$$\frac{1}{13} \cdot 13x = \frac{1}{13} \cdot 0$$
$$x = 0$$

Solution 2

Do it in your head. The only number that 13 can be multiplied by to get 0 is 0 itself. So $x = 0$. Write: The solution is 0.

❶ To avoid writing sentences as explanations of unusual solutions like these, solution sets can be written. For Examples 1, 2, and 3, the solution sets are as follows.

Equation	Sentence	Solution set
$0x = 4$	There is no solution.	{ } or ∅
$0x = 0$	All real numbers are solutions.	set of real numbers
$13x = 0$	The solution is 0.	{0}

Notice that {0} and { } are different. The set { }, or ∅, has no elements and indicates that no number works in $0x = 4$. The set {0} contains the element 0 and indicates that 0 works in $13x = 0$.

Equations with -1

When -1 appears as a coefficient, some people find it helpful to use the Multiplication Property of -1 to write $-x$ as $-1 \cdot x$.

Example 4

Solve $-x = 3.824$.

Solution 1

Rewrite $-x$ as $-1 \cdot x$. So,

$$-1 \cdot x = 3.824.$$

Multiply both sides by -1, the reciprocal of -1.

$$-1 \cdot -1 \cdot x = -1 \cdot 3.824$$
$$x = -3.824$$

Solution 2

Translate the equation into words and find the solution in your head. The opposite of what number is 3.824? Answer: -3.824.

Optional Activities
After completing this lesson, you might have students answer the following questions.
1. When does an equation of the form $ax = b$ have exactly one solution? [When $a \neq 0$.]
2. When does an equation of the form $ax = b$ have more than one solution? [When $a = 0$ and $b = 0$.]
3. When does an equation of the form $ax = b$ have no solution? [When $a = 0$ and $b \neq 0$.]

The following computer program will solve equations of the form $ax = b$ when the user enters values for a and b. The program finds the solution by computing $\frac{b}{a}$ except when $a = 0$. If a computer is instructed to divide by zero, the program will stop running and an error message will appear on the screen. To avoid this situation, an IF-THEN command instructs the computer to make a decision. When the sentence between the words IF and THEN is true, the computer executes the instruction following the THEN. When the sentence is false, the instruction following the THEN is completely ignored by the computer which proceeds to the next line. Lines 60, 70, and 80 use IF-THEN statements to deal with the different situations that arise when a or b is equal to zero. Notice that the BASIC symbol for "$\neq$" is <>. Therefore, A <> 0 means that $a \neq 0$.

```
10 PRINT "SOLVE AX = B"
20 PRINT "ENTER A"
30 INPUT A
40 PRINT "ENTER B"
50 INPUT B
60 IF A <> 0 THEN PRINT "SOLUTION IS"; B/A
70 IF A = 0 AND B = 0 THEN PRINT "ALL REAL NUMBERS ARE SOLUTIONS"
80 IF A = 0 AND B <> 0 THEN PRINT "NO SOLUTION"
90 END
```

What will happen if this program is used to solve the equations in this lesson? Let's begin with the last example. To solve $-x = 3.824$, you enter -1 (the coefficient of x) for A and 3.824 for B. At line 60 the computer checks to see if A differs from zero. Since $-1 \neq 0$ (A is not zero), it will then print SOLUTION IS -3.824 (the result of 3.824/-1). The "then" parts of lines 70 and 80 are only carried out if A = 0, so the computer ignores these parts. The program would act much the same to solve $13t = 0$, the equation in Example 3.

In Example 2 however, 0 will be entered for both A and B. At line 60, the computer checks to see if A is different from 0. Since it is not, the rest of line 60 is skipped. At line 70, since both A = 0 and B = 0 are true, the computer prints ALL REAL NUMBERS ARE SOLUTIONS.

In solving $0x = 4$ from Example 1, A is 0, but B is 4. So line 80 is the one that fits this equation. The computer will print NO SOLUTION.

QUESTIONS

Covering the Reading

2a) The solution is 0.
b) {0}

3a) There is no solution.
b) { } or ø

4a) All real numbers are solutions.
b) the set of all real numbers

1. Why can't both sides of $3 = 0x$ be multiplied by the reciprocal of 0?
   Zero does not have a reciprocal.
   In 2–4, describe the solutions **a.** with a sentence; **b.** with the solution set.
   See left.

2. $7y = 0$ 3. $0 \cdot w = 14$ 4. $0 = a \cdot 0$

Lesson 2-7 *Special Numbers in Equations* **111**

Follow-up for Lesson 2-7

Practice
For more questions on SPUR Objectives, use **Lesson Master 2-7A** (shown on page 111) or **Lesson Master 2-7B** (shown on pages 112–113).

Assessment
Quiz A quiz covering Lessons 2-4 through 2-7 is provided in the *Assessment Sourcebook*.

Oral Communication Have students select one property that they studied in this chapter. Ask them how they would explain that property to another student. [Students use their own words to correctly explain properties of multiplication.]

Extension
In **Question 32,** students find that as the coefficient of x decreases, the solution increases. Have students investigate what happens as the coefficient of x increases. For instance, have them consider $x = 10$, $2x = 10$, $3x = 10$, and so on to $nx = 10$. [As the coefficient of x increases, the solution decreases.]

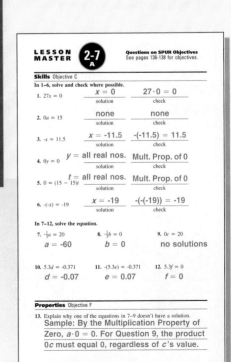

Adapting to Individual Needs

Extra Help
Some students might have difficulty understanding that some equations have no solutions and that, for some equations, all real numbers are solutions. Help students see that this happens as a result of the special nature of zero. As the Multiplication Property of Zero states, the product of two or more factors is always zero when one of the factors is zero. Therefore, there is no possible correct replacement for x when $0x = 4$.

Also, because of the same property, any real number you choose for x would make $0x = 0$ true.

Notes on Questions

Question 5 Some students may not distinguish between { } and {ø}. Explain that {ø} cannot be the empty set because it has an element in it. The key here is that a *set* is an entity—that is, it is an object. Even {{}} has an element in it, namely the empty set.

Question 20 Error Alert Students often solve equations like this one mentally, but they get the wrong answer because either they multiply by the coefficient rather than by its reciprocal, or they multiply by the reciprocal of the constant term. Stress the need to check answers to help avoid this mistake.

Question 26 Consumer Connection Insurance is a means of providing protection against financial loss. Insurance works on the principle of sharing losses. People who wish to be insured against particular types of losses or expenses agree to make regular payments, called premiums, to an insurance company. In return, the company promises to pay a certain sum of money for the types of losses or services described in the policy. The insurance company uses the premiums to invest in stocks, bonds, mortgages, government securities, and other income-producing enterprises. The company pays benefits from the premiums it collects and from the investment income the premiums earn. Insurance works because policy holders are willing to trade the

5. *Multiple choice.* Which set is the same as ø? (d)
   (a) {ø}   (b) {0}   (c) 0   (d) {}

6. What is the reciprocal of -1? -1

In 7–9, solve.

7. $-1 \cdot x = 40$ -40   8. $-y = -3$ 3   9. $-z = 0$ 0

In 10–12, suppose you want to solve the given equation using the computer program at the end of the lesson. **See left.**
a. Give the input for A and B.
b. Tell which of lines 60, 70, and 80 will cause the computer to print.
c. Write the output of the program.

10. $0x = 1.8$ 11. $24 = -x$ 12. $0x = 0$

10a) 0, 1.8
  b) 80
  c) NO SOLUTION

11a) -1, 24
  b) 60
  c) SOLUTION IS -24

12a) 0, 0
  b) 70
  c) ALL REAL NUMBERS

Applying the Mathematics

13. Refer to the formula $N = T \cdot P \cdot E \cdot L \cdot I \cdot C \cdot A$ on page 71. Some people believe that, other than Earth, the value of $L = 0$. What effect does this have on the value of N?
    N would be 0.

14. Consider the following impossible situation: The car was parked for t hours. During this time it traveled 70 miles. a) $70 = 0t$
    a. Write an equation of the form $d = rt$ to describe this situation.
    b. Explain why your equation does not have a solution.
    b) 0 times t must be 0, not 70.

15. Example 3 concerns the equation $13x = 0$. Describe a real-world situation that can be modeled by this equation. **Sample: You are traveling 13 mph. How long does it take you to go 0 miles?**

16. Solve the equation.
    a. $-(-x) = 18.5$ 18.5   b. $-(-(-x)) = 18.5$ -18.5

17. Solve and check: $15 = (6 - 7)x$. $x = -15$; $(6 - 7)(-15) = (-1)(-15) = 15$

18. Write an equation not given in this lesson with more than one solution. **Sample: $x^2 = 36$**

A lot of baloney. *The butcher is holding bologna in his right hand and other sausages in his left.*

Review

19. Solve and check. *(Lesson 2-6)*
    a. $-4p = 12$ -3; $-4(-3) = 12$ b. $12p = -4$ $-\frac{1}{3}$; $12\left(-\frac{1}{3}\right) = -\frac{12}{3} = -4$

In 20–23, solve. *(Lesson 2-6)*

20. $\frac{7}{9}q = 140$ 180   21. $\frac{3n}{5} = 2$ $\frac{10}{3}$

22. $-20 = -0.04m$ 500   23. $\frac{1}{3} = 4x$ $\frac{1}{12}$

24. A crate contains 12 cases. Each case holds 24 boxes. Each box holds 60 packages of batteries. Each package holds 2 batteries. How many crates will it take to ship 100,000 batteries? *(Lessons 2-4, 2-6)* 3 crates

25. Suppose eight ounces of sausage cost c cents. If x = cost per ounce, write a multiplication equation relating 8, c, and x. *(Lesson 2-6)*
    Sample: $8x = c$

112

Adapting to Individual Needs

English Language Development
You might want to discuss everyday situations in which *if-then* is used. Note that the word "then" is often implied: If it's sunny, (then) we will go to the game; If the team wins, (then) we will celebrate; If I can earn the money, (then) I will buy the stereo. When the statement following *if* is true, the instruction following *then* is done.

In 26 and 27, solve an equation of the form $ax = b$ to answer the question. *(Lesson 2-6)*

26. Three fourths of the company's employees are covered by dental insurance. If 165 employees are covered, how many employees does the company have? **220 employees**

27. The manager of a manufacturing company knows that the company's workers can produce 340 parts per hour. A customer has ordered 5,100 parts. How many hours will it take to fill the order?
15 hr

Sports of the Mayas.
Mayan ball courts can be found throughout Mexico. This one is near Oaxaca.

28. a. Evaluate $-1 \cdot -1 \cdot -1 \cdot -1 \cdot -1 \cdot -1 \cdot -1 \cdot -1$ **b.** Evaluate $(-1)^{25}$.
c. Give a general rule for answering questions about powers of -1.
(Lesson 2-5) a) 1;   b) -1;   c) If the exponent of -1 is odd, the result is -1. If the exponent is even, the result is 1.

29. From about 200 B.C. to 900 A.D., the Mayas of Central America and Mexico played a ball game called *pok-ta-pok*. Playing fields for pok-ta-pok varied in size and shape. One playing field had the shape shown below. All angles are right angles. What is its area?
(Lesson 2-1) **7608 m²**

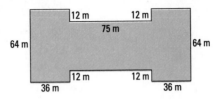

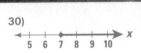

30)

30. Graph the solution set to $x \geq 7$. Use the set of real numbers as the domain. *(Lesson 1-2)* **See left.**

31. Consider the inequality $-2x < 10$. Tell whether the number is or is not a solution to the sentence. *(Lesson 1-1)*
a. 4 **Yes**   **b.** -4 **Yes**   **c.** 5 **Yes**   **d.** -5 **No**

Exploration

32. Consider the pattern at the right.
a. What will be written in row n? $\frac{1}{n}x = 10$
b. What is the solution to the equation in row n? $x = 10n$
c. What will be written in row 100?
d. What is the solution to the equation in row 100? **1000**
e. As n gets larger, to what equation are the equations getting closer and closer? What is happening to the solutions? **0x = 10; The solutions are increasing without bound.**
c) $\frac{1}{100}x = 10$

row 1	$x = 10$
row 2	$\frac{1}{2}x = 10$
row 3	$\frac{1}{3}x = 10$
row 4	$\frac{1}{4}x = 10$
row 100	? $x = $?
row n	? $x = $?

---

premiums they pay for the guarantee that they will be paid when they incur a loss or require medical or dental care.

Question 29 Multicultural Connection Archeologists are uncertain how the Mayan game of *pok-ta-pok* (also called the sacred ball game) was played. They think the game involved two teams, each defending their wall of a game court. Hitting the opponent's wall with a rubber ball seemed to be a part of the game. Players retained possession of the ball as long as they could keep it in the air. However, they could not use their hands; instead, they hit the ball with their elbows and hips. The game was played from the Amazon region of South America all the way north to the deserts of Arizona. The Mayas could have named the game *pok-ta-pok* because of the sounds the ball made when it bounced off the walls of the court.

Question 32 This question helps students to see that there is some pattern in solutions to equations: the smaller the coefficient of x, the larger the solution. It also provides an example of limits of sequences, an idea that is seen in all future UCSMP courses and an idea that is critical for calculus. You might want to use the *Extension* on page 111 along with this Exploration.

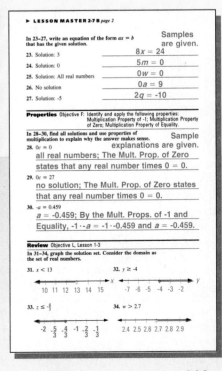

Adapting to Individual Needs

Challenge
Have students solve the following problem: A train travels at 30 miles per hour for the first half of a 60-mile trip. How fast must it travel during the second half of the trip to average 60 miles per hour for the entire trip? [Since the train averaged 30 miles per hour for the first half of the trip, this part of the trip took one hour. But, in order for the train to average 60 miles per hour for the entire trip, the entire trip could only take one

hour. So the train cannot average 60 mph for the entire trip.]

Objectives

D Solve and check inequalities of the form $ax < b$.
F Identify and apply the Multiplication Property of Inequality.
G Apply the Area Model for Multiplication in real situations.
H Apply the Rate Factor Model for Multiplication in real situations.

Resources

From the Teacher's Resource File
■ Lesson Master 2-8A or 2-8B
■ Answer Master 2-8
■ Teaching Aids
  5 Number Lines
  15 Warm-up

Additional Resources
■ Visuals for Teaching Aids 5, 15

Teaching **2-8**
Lesson

Warm-up

Give three numbers that make each sentence true.
1. $x > -3 + 6$ **any number > 3**
2. $y \geq 0.5 \times 0$ **any number ≥ 0**
3. $z \leq -3 \times -7$ **any number ≤ 21**
4. $m > -4^2$ **any number > -16**
5. $-3 > r > -18$ **any number between -18 and -3**
6. $6 < n < 25$ **any number between 6 and 25**

Notes on Reading

As you discuss the reading, emphasize two ways in which solving inequalities differs from solving

---

*Solving
$ax < b$*

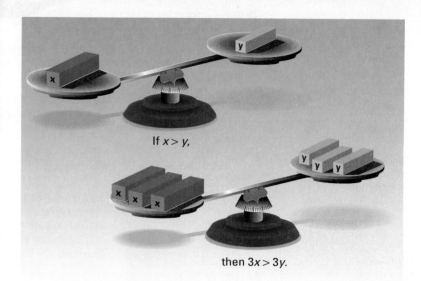

If $x > y$,

then $3x > 3y$.

The Multiplication Property of Inequality

Here are some numbers in increasing order. Because the numbers are in order, you can put the inequality sign $<$ between any two of them.

$$-10 \; < \; -6 \; < \; 5 \; < \; 30 \; < \; 30.32 \; < \; 870$$

Now multiply these numbers by some fixed *positive* number, say 10. Here are the products.

$$-100 \quad -60 \quad 50 \quad 300 \quad 303.2 \quad 8700$$

The order stays the same. You could still put a $<$ sign between any two of the numbers. This illustrates that if $x < y$, then $10x < 10y$. In general, multiplication by a *positive* number maintains the order of a pair or list of numbers.

> **Multiplication Property of Inequality (Part 1)**
> If $x < y$ and a is positive, then $ax < ay$.

The signs $>$, $\leq$, and $\geq$ between numbers or expressions also indicate order. The Multiplication Property of Inequality works with any of those signs. For instance, if $x > y$, then $3x > 3y$. This is pictured on the scales above.

Solving Inequalities with Positive Coefficients

To solve an inequality of the form $ax < b$ where a is positive, use the Multiplication Property of Inequality to multiply each side by $\frac{1}{a}$.

Lesson 2-8 Overview

Broad Goals In this lesson, students continue to multiply both sides of a sentence by the same number, but, instead of working with equations, they solve inequalities of the form $ax < b$. In solving inequalities, students must be aware of whether the number they multiply both sides of the inequality by is positive or negative, and they must understand that the check has two steps.

Perspective We use the term "inequality" to include sentences with any of the four signs $<$, $\leq$, $>$, or $\geq$. It is also possible to consider the signs $\approx$ or $\neq$ as indicating inequality, but they are not associated with the solving of inequalities. Even though the goal of isolating a variable is the same for an inequality as for an equation, some students don't know how to proceed. Also, the idea of solving and then graphing is a new concept.

Optional Activities

Materials: **Teaching Aid 5**

Use this activity as an alternate way to justify the Multiplication Property of Inequality. Mapping from one number line to another shows the change of the sense of an inequality under multiplication by a negative number. Have students graph -1 and 2 on every other number line on **Teaching Aid 5** and write a corresponding inequality. For the first line,

Example 1

a. Solve $4x \leq 20$.
b. List three elements of the solution set.
c. Graph the solution set.

Solution

a. Multiply both sides by $\frac{1}{4}$. Since $\frac{1}{4}$ is positive, the Multiplication Property of Inequality tells you that

$$\frac{1}{4} \cdot 4x \leq \frac{1}{4} \cdot 20.$$
$$x \leq 5$$

b. Pick any three real numbers less than or equal to 5. *Some elements of the solution set are -10, 3, and 5.*
c. The graph pictures all real numbers less than or equal to 5.

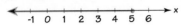

Check

Since inequalities often have infinitely many solutions, you cannot check the answer by substituting a single number. You must do two things.

Step 1: Check the boundary point by substituting it into the original inequality. It should make both sides of the inequality *equal*. The boundary point in $x \leq 5$ is 5.

$$\text{Does } 4 \cdot 5 = 20? \text{ Yes.}$$

Step 2: Check whether the sense of the inequality is correct. Pick some number that works in $x < 5$. This number should also work in the original inequality. Check the number 3. Is $4 \cdot 3 < 20$? Yes, $12 < 20$. Since both steps worked, $x \leq 5$ is the solution to $4x \leq 20$.

Example 2

The length of a rectangle is 50 cm. Its area is greater than 175 cm². Find the width of the rectangle.

Solution

It may help to draw a picture. You know that $A = \ell w$, and $\ell = 50$ cm. So the area of the rectangle is $50w$ cm².

$$\text{Thus,} \qquad 50w > 175.$$
$$\frac{1}{50} \cdot 50w > \frac{1}{50} \cdot 175 \qquad \text{Multiply both sides by } \tfrac{1}{50}.$$
$$w > 3.5$$

The width is greater than 3.5 cm.

Check

Step 1: Does $50 \cdot 3.5 = 175$? Yes.
Step 2: Pick some value that works in $w > 3.5$. We pick 10. Is $50 \cdot 10 > 175$? Yes.

50 cm

w cm

Lesson 2-8 *Solving ax < b* **115**

---

equations. First, the solutions to inequalities usually cannot be listed. Thus, either a graph or an equivalent simple sentence must be given. Both ways are shown in **Example 1.** Second, a two-step check is needed for inequalities, as shown in the examples. Students should check to see if the boundary point is correct. Then they should check if the sense of the inequality is correct. The check is very important in helping students grasp the essential elements of the problem. If a student cannot check a problem, we believe that he or she does not really know how to answer it.

As you discuss each example, ask for one solution—a number that works. Ask for another solution and then another. If all of the students are giving positive solutions, ask if there are any negative solutions. If students are giving only integers, ask for solutions that are not integers. Point out that because we want *all* values that work, naming value after value will not be enough. Then ask students how they can describe all of the numbers that work.

After learning a property for sentence-solving that does not distinguish between positive and negative numbers, the two parts of the Multiplication Property of Inequality often surprise students. In particular, the second part of the Multiplication Property of Inequality is difficult for those students who lack good intuition of what happens to an inequality under multiplication by a negative

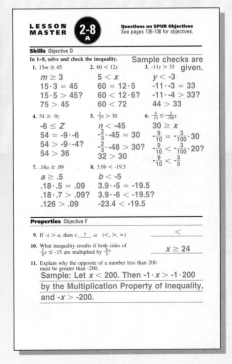

---

have students multiply both numbers by 2 and draw arrows to the products on the second number line. This is a *mapping* under multiplication by 2. Have students write an inequality for the products. Point out that under this mapping the sense of the new inequality has the same sense as the original inequality. Then have students do mappings under multiplication by –1 and $-\frac{1}{2}$. These mappings show that the sense of an inequality changes under multiplication by a negative number.

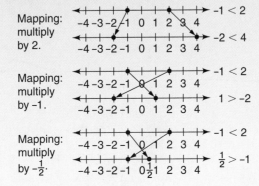

115

number. As a result, the algorithm is often memorized. The approach in this lesson, with numbers given in order as if they were on a number line, leads to enough understanding that memorization is not needed.

Additional Examples

1. Solve $\frac{5}{3}x > 30$, and graph the solution set. $x > 18$.

    16 17 18 19 20 21

2. The length of a rectangle is 80 in. Its area is less than 220 in². Find the width of the rectangle.
   Between 0 and 2.75 in.

3. Solve and check:
   a. $-4m < 50$ $m > -\frac{25}{2}$; Check:
   Does $-4(-\frac{25}{2}) = 50$? Yes
   Try -10. Is $-4(-10) < 50$? Yes
   b. $-\frac{2}{3} \le -\frac{3}{2}x$ $x \le \frac{4}{9}$; Check:
   Try $\frac{4}{9}$. Does $-\frac{2}{3} = -\frac{3}{2}(\frac{4}{9})$? Yes
   Try $\frac{1}{3}$. Is $-\frac{2}{3} \le -\frac{3}{2}(\frac{1}{3})$? Yes

4. Meg is hiking at a rate of 2.5 miles per hour. She knows that it is at least 13.5 miles to Bear Lake. How long will it take Meg to hike there? Write an inequality to find the length of time and solve your inequality.
   $2.5t \ge 13.5$; at least 5.4 hours

116

Solving Inequalities with Negative Coefficients

Here are the numbers from the beginning of this lesson.

$$-10 \;<\; -6 \;<\; 5 \;<\; 30 \;<\; 30.32 \;<\; 870$$

Multiplying these numbers by -10 yields the products below.

$$100 \qquad 60 \qquad -50 \qquad -300 \qquad -303.2 \qquad -8700$$

Notice that the numbers in the first row are in *increasing* order, while the numbers in the second row are in *decreasing* order. The order has been reversed. If you multiply both sides of an inequality by a *negative* number, you must *change the direction of the inequality*.

For instance, $-6 < 5$, but $-10 \cdot -6 > -10 \cdot 5$. This idea can be generalized:

> **Multiplication Property of Inequality (Part 2)**
> If $x < y$ and a is negative, then $ax > ay$.

As in Part 1 of the Multiplication Property of Inequality, Part 2 of the property also holds for the signs $>$, $\le$, and $\ge$. To solve an inequality of the form $ax < b$ where a is negative, multiply each side by $\frac{1}{a}$ and change the direction of the inequality sign.

> **Example 3**
>
> Solve $126 \le -7x$ and check.
>
> **Solution**
>
> Multiply both sides by $-\frac{1}{7}$, the reciprocal of -7. Since $-\frac{1}{7}$ is a negative number, Part 2 of the Multiplication Property of Inequality tells you to *change the inequality sign* from $\le$ to $\ge$.
>
> $$-\frac{1}{7} \cdot 126 \ge -\frac{1}{7} \cdot -7x$$
>
> Now simplify. $-\frac{126}{7} \ge x$
>
> $-18 \ge x$
>
> **Check**
>
> Step 1: Try -18. Does $-7 \cdot -18 = 126$? Yes.
>
> Step 2: Try a number that works in $x \le -18$. We use -20.
>   Is $-7 \cdot -20 \ge 126$? Yes, $140 \ge 126$.

Changing from $<$ to $>$, or from $\le$ to $\ge$, or vice-versa, is called **changing the sense** of the inequality. This is the same as changing the direction of the inequality sign. The only time you have to change the sense of an inequality is when you are multiplying both sides by a negative number. Otherwise, solving $ax < b$ is similar to solving $ax = b$.

You can see why the two-step check of an inequality is important. The first step checks the boundary point in the solution. The second step checks the sense of the inequality.

QUESTIONS

Covering the Reading

In 1–3, consider the inequality $20 < 30$. What inequality results if you multiply both sides of the inequality by the given number?

1. 6 $120 < 180$

2. $\frac{2}{5}$ $8 < 12$

3. -4 $-80 > -120$

4. Consider the inequality $8x \leq 42$.
   a. Solve the inequality. $x \leq 5.25$
   b. List three elements of the solution set. Sample: {5.25, 4, 0}
   c. Graph the solution set.

   number line: arrow left ← closed/open at 5.25 → x, marks 3 4 5 6 7 8, 5.25 labeled

5. Consider the inequality $-9x < -18$.
   a. Tell whether or not the number is a solution.
   i. 2   **ii.** -2   **iii.** 3   **iv.** -3   **v.** -1   **vi.** 0
   Of the choices given, only iii (3) is a solution.
   b. Graph all solutions.
   See left.

6. In what way does Part 2 of the Multiplication Property of Inequality differ from Part 1? Part 2 involves multiplying by a negative number which requires changing the direction of the inequality.

In 7 and 8, change the sense of each inequality.

7. $<$ $>$

8. $\geq$ $\leq$

In 9–14, solve and check each sentence. See left.

9. $5x \geq 10$

10. $-3y < 300$

11. $-4A < -124$

12. $13 > 2z$

13. $-2 \leq 5a$

14. $0.09 > -9c$

15. The length of a rectangle is 20 cm. Its area is less than 154 cm². Find the width of the rectangle. The width is less than 7.7 cm.

Applying the Mathematics

16. The area of the foundation of a rectangular building is not to exceed 20,000 square feet. The width of the foundation is to be 125 feet. How long can the foundation be? less than or equal to 160 feet

17. An auditorium has more than 1500 seats. There are 48 seats in each row. How many rows does the auditorium have? more than 31, or at least 32 rows

18. Parents of the bride have budgeted $2500 for the dinner after the wedding. Each person's dinner will cost $27.50. At most how many people can attend the dinner? 90 people

A wedding scene in Seoul. *Western clothing styles are popular in Korea. However, for special occasions, Koreans wear traditional, colorful clothing made of satin or cotton.*

In 19–22, solve the inequality.

19. $-m < 8$ $m > -8$

20. $-2 \geq -n$ $2 \leq n$

21. $\frac{1}{4}x \geq 96$ $x \geq 384$

22. $\frac{2}{3}p \leq \frac{1}{4}$ $p \leq \frac{3}{8}$

Lesson 2-8 *Solving* $ax < b$ **117**

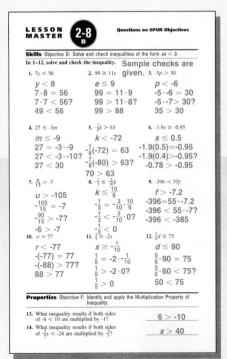

117

Follow-up
for Lesson 2-8

Practice

For more questions on SPUR Objectives, use **Lesson Master 2-8A** (shown on pages 115–116) or **Lesson Master 2-8B** (shown on pages 117–118).

Assessment

Written Communication Have students write a real-world problem that requires the use of the Multiplication Property of Inequality in its solution. [Students demonstrate an understanding of the Multiplication Property of Inequality.]

Extension

Have students find the solution sets to the following sentences.
1. $3a \neq 6$ [$a \neq 2$; any real number except 2]
2. $2n \not< 8$ [$n \not< 4$; any real number greater than or equal to 4]
3. $-6y \not> 12$ [$y \geq -2$; any real number greater than or equal to -2]

---

23. Three-fourths of a number is less than two hundred four. What are the possible values of the number? $x < 272$

24. Use the clues to find x. 4
    Clue 1: x is an integer.
    Clue 2: $2x < 10$
    Clue 3: $-3x < -9$

Review

25. *Skill sequence.* Solve the equation. *(Lesson 2-7)*
    a. $1n = 4$ b. $0n = 3$ c. $-1n = 2$ d. $-2n = 1$
    $n = 4$ no solution $n = -2$ $n = -\frac{1}{2}$
    In 26 and 27, solve. *(Lesson 2-6)*

26. $30\pi = \pi d$ 30   27. $200 = -4(5x)$ -10

28. A trill is a musical term for alternating very quickly between two notes a step or half-step apart. In Johann Sebastian Bach's *Two-Part Invention #4*, the harpsichordist or pianist is required to trill a note with the left hand for five measures. If a trill has four notes per beat, and there are three beats in each measure, how many notes are played? *(Lesson 2-4)* 60 notes

29. Multiply and simplify $\frac{1}{6}x^3 \cdot \frac{2}{5x}$. *(Lesson 2-3)* $\frac{x^2}{15}$

30. A box is made by folding the pattern at right along the dotted lines and taping the edges. What is the volume of the box?
    (Lesson 2-1)
    57 in³

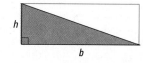

31. The formula $A = \frac{1}{2}bh$ for the area of a triangle is true for a right triangle because the area of a right triangle with legs b and h is half the area of a rectangle with sides b and h. Write a formula for the area of a triangle whose area is half the area of a square with sides of length s. *(Lesson 1-5)* $A = \frac{1}{2}s^2$

32. Write using exponents: $3 \cdot 3 \cdot x \cdot x \cdot x \cdot y \cdot y \cdot y \cdot y \cdot y$. *(Previous course)*
    $3^2 x^3 y^5$

Exploration

33. Find a number $x < 0$ such that $0.05 < x^2 < 0.06$. (A calculator may help.) Sample: -0.23

Adapting to Individual Needs

English Language Development

Have students add Part 1 and Part 2 of the Multiplication Property of Inequality to their index-card file. You might suggest that they work with classmates and review some of the terms and properties that they feel unsure about. Because the next lesson has many word problems, again suggest that students bring their bilingual dictionaries to class.

Challenge

Ask students to describe how they might answer **Question 33** given numbers other than 0.05 and 0.06. [Sample: for $a < x^2 < b$, one solution is $\sqrt{\frac{a+b}{2}}$. That is, find the mean of a and b, and then take the square root.]

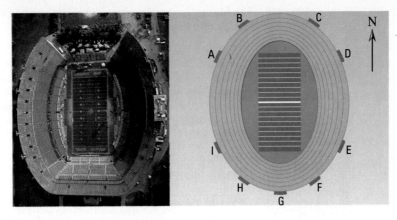

In mathematics, a procedure is said to be *elegant* if it is both clever and simple. For instance, it may surprise you that multiplication can be cleverly used to solve many types of counting problems. If you can organize the items being counted into rectangular arrays, the area model of multiplication allows you to multiply to get the counts.

Example 1

Suppose a stadium has 9 gates as in the drawing above. Gates *A, B, C,* and *D* are on the north side. Gates *E, F, G, H,* and *I* are on the south side. In how many ways can you enter the stadium through a north gate and leave through a south gate?

Solution

Create a rectangular array in which each entry is an ordered pair. The first letter represents a gate you enter; the second stands for an exit gate.

		Exit Gate (South)				
		E	F	G	H	I
	A	(A,E)	(A,F)	(A,G)	(A,H)	(A,I)
Entry	B	(B,E)	(B,F)	(B,G)	(B,H)	(B,I)
Gate	C	(C,E)	(C,F)	(C,G)	(C,H)	(C,I)
(North)	D	(D,E)	(D,F)	(D,G)	(D,H)	(D,I)

Notice that the array has 4 rows and 5 columns, so there are $4 \cdot 5 = 20$ pairs in the table. There are 20 ways of entering through a north gate and leaving through a south gate.

This elegant use of multiplication occurs often enough that we give it a special name, the *Multiplication Counting Principle*.

Multiplication Counting Principle
If one choice can be made in *m* ways and a second choice can be made in *n* ways, then there are *mn* ways of making the first choice followed by the second choice.

Lesson 2-9 Overview

Broad Goals The first goal of this lesson is to apply the Multiplication Counting Principle to both counting situations and the corresponding probability problems. A second goal is to present algebraic problems involving this principle.

Perspective The Multiplication Counting Principle is sometimes called the "Fundamental Counting Principle." The name reflects its role as a powerful tool in count-

ing problems. Until a few years ago, discussion of this principle was delayed until the 11th or 12th grade when it was taught in connection with permutations and combinations. However, the Multiplication Counting Principle is important to mathematics and its applications. It is not a difficult concept and its computation with calculators is easy. Therefore, discussion of the principle is no longer delayed.

In this lesson, the Multiplication Counting Principle is applied to situations in which the number of ways available to make a particular choice is unrelated to the number of ways available for a previous choice. In the next lesson, a special case of the Multiplication Counting Principle is considered; there the number of ways available for a particular choice is one less than the number of ways available for the preceding choice.

Lesson 2-9

Objectives
I Apply the Multiplication Counting Principle.

Resources
From the *Teacher's Resource File*
- Lesson Master 2-9A or 2-9B
- Answer Master 2-9
- Teaching Aids
  15 Warm-up
  20 Additional Examples 2–5
- Activity Kit, Activity 4
- Technology Sourcebook
  Computer Master 5

Additional Resources
- Visuals for Teaching Aids 15, 20

Teaching Lesson 2-9

Warm-up

Diagnostic Answer *true* or *false* for 1–4. You may have to guess.
1. The unit of money in Mauritius is the rupee. **True**
2. The Prime Minister of Canada in 1900 was Laurier. **True**
3. Stan Jok played baseball for the Boston Red Sox. **False; he played for the Chicago White Sox.**
4. Hannah Van Buren's maiden name was Hoes. **True**
5. List all the possible ways to answer the four questions. How many possibilities are there?
   TTTT, TTTF, TTFT, TFTT, FTTT, TTFF, TFTF, TFFT, FTTF, FTFT, FFTT, TFFF, FTFF, FFTF, FFFT, FFFF; 16 possibilities

Example 1 involves only two decisions. Since the number of choices is small, it is possible to list all of the outcomes. The array helps to organize the list. It also shows that the Multiplication Counting Principle is a special case of the discrete (array) form of the Area Model for Multiplication.

There are three very different visual images given in **Example 2**. The first image uses blanks that are to be filled in. The second lists all of the possible schedules. The same items are imbedded in the third visual image, the tree diagram, which offers another shortcut. Stress the relationship between the items on the list and the pathways on the tree. Often students think that we are interested in the number of final nodes rather than in the number of paths.

When the number of choices is small, answers can be found by counting. **Example 3**, however, involves too many choices for easy listing, so the Multiplication Counting Principle has to be applied. Students who have studied probability should have no problem understanding **part b** of **Example 3**. Since probability will be formally covered in a later chapter, a brief explanation is all that is necessary for students who have not been introduced to it. Give students the following definition: If a situation has *n* possible outcomes, and one of them is a success, then the probability of that happening is $\frac{1}{n}$.

The Multiplication Counting Principle can be extended to situations where more than two choices must be made.

Example 2

A high-school student wants to take a foreign-language class, a music course, and an art course. The language classes available are French, Spanish, and German. The music classes available are chorus and band. The art classes available are drawing and painting. In how many different ways can the student choose the three classes?

Solution

Draw a blank for each decision to be made.

$$\underline{\hspace{4cm}} \cdot \underline{\hspace{4cm}} \cdot \underline{\hspace{4cm}}$$
ways to choose language · ways to choose music · ways to choose art

Now fill in the blanks with the number of ways each subject can be chosen. There are 3 choices in foreign language, 2 choices in music, and 2 choices in art. Use the Multiplication Counting Principle.

$$\underline{\hspace{2cm}3\hspace{2cm}} \cdot \underline{\hspace{2cm}2\hspace{2cm}} \cdot \underline{\hspace{2cm}2\hspace{2cm}}$$
ways to choose language · ways to choose music · ways to choose art

There are 3 · 2 · 2 = 12 choices.

In Example 2, the Multiplication Counting Principle quickly told *how many* ways a student can choose his courses, but it did not tell *what* the choices are. One way to see all of them is to make an organized list.

French-chorus-drawing	Spanish-chorus-drawing	German-chorus-drawing
French-chorus-painting	Spanish-chorus-painting	German-chorus-painting
French-band-drawing	Spanish-band-drawing	German-band-drawing
French-band-painting	Spanish-band-painting	German-band-painting

A second way is to use a *tree diagram,* which requires less writing.

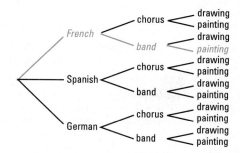

Each choice can be found by following a path from the left to the right in the diagram. One possible choice is shown in blue: *French–band–painting.*

You can count 12 paths. That is, twelve different choices are possible.

Optional Activities

Activity 1
You might want to use *Activity Kit, Activity 4,* to introduce the lesson. Students find different arrangements of four cards to generate a list of different 4-digit numerals.

Activity 2 Technology Connection
You may wish to assign *Technology Sourcebook, Computer Master 5.* This activity uses FOR...NEXT loops to demonstrate the Multiplication Counting Principle.

Activity 3
Materials: School-cafeteria menu or luncheon menu from a restaurant

Cooperative Learning This activity can be used to introduced or to conclude the lesson. Have students **work in groups**. Give each group a copy of a menu. Ask students to find the number of possible ways they can place an order—for instance, select a sandwich, a beverage, and a dessert.

Example 3

Mr. Lorio is giving his algebra class a quiz with five questions. Since Angie has not done her homework, she has to guess. The quiz has two multiple-choice questions with choices A, B, C, and D, and three true-false questions.
a. How many possible ways are there for Angie to answer all five questions?
b. What is the probability that Angie will get all the questions correct?

Solution

a. There are 4 choices for each multiple-choice question and 2 choices for each true-false question. Use the Multiplication Counting Principle.

$$\underbrace{4}_{\substack{\text{choices for}\\ \text{question \#1}}} \cdot \underbrace{4}_{\substack{\text{choices for}\\ \text{question \#2}}} \cdot \underbrace{2}_{\substack{\text{choices for}\\ \text{question \#3}}} \cdot \underbrace{2}_{\substack{\text{choices for}\\ \text{question \#4}}} \cdot \underbrace{2}_{\substack{\text{choices for}\\ \text{question \#5}}}$$

There are $4 \cdot 4 \cdot 2 \cdot 2 \cdot 2 = 128$ different ways of answering the five questions.

b. Only one of the 128 possible outcomes has the correct answer for each question. With random guessing, Angie has only 1 chance out of 128 of getting all the questions correct. The probability that she will get all the answers correct is $\frac{1}{128}$.

When the number of choices is not precisely known, variables may appear in counting problems.

Example 4

Ms. Alvarez has written a chapter test. It has three multiple-choice questions each with m possible answers, two multiple-choice questions each with n possible answers, and 5 true-false questions. How many ways are there to answer the questions?

Solution

Make a blank for each of the 10 questions. Fill each blank with the number of possible answers for that question.

Question Number   1 2 3 4 5 6 7 8 9 10
Choices m m m n n 2 2 2 2 2

Apply the Multiplication Counting Principle to get

$m \cdot m \cdot m \cdot n \cdot n \cdot 2 \cdot 2 \cdot 2 \cdot 2 \cdot 2$ sets of answers.

With exponents, this product can be expressed as $m^3 n^2 2^5$ or $32 m^3 n^2$ sets of answers.

Lesson 2-9 *The Multiplication Counting Principle* **121**

Adapting to Individual Needs

Extra Help

Help students to see that the order in which numbers of choices are multiplied will not affect the total, since multiplication is commutative. Also point out that changing the number of choices in one category might affect the total in a different way than changing the number in another category. For instance, in **Example 2,** if the number of language choices were increased by 1, the total would be $4 \times 2 \times 2$, or 16. However, if the number of art choices were increased by 1, the total would be $3 \times 2 \times 3$, or 18.

Additional Examples

Examples 2–5 are also on **Teaching Aid 20.**

1. For a math contest, schools can enter a pair of contestants consisting of a student and a teacher. The Central School math team has five student members (Alice, Bert, Carl, Denise, and Ellen) and two teacher members (Mr. Price and Ms. Quill).
   a. How many pairs can be formed? **10**
   b. List them. **(A, P), (A, Q), (B, P), (B, Q), (C, P), (C, Q), (D, P), (D, Q), (E, P), (E, Q)**

2. A restaurant offers a special breakfast of eggs, meat, and juice. The eggs can be cooked in one of three different ways (scrambled, fried, poached); there are two choices for the meat (bacon, sausage) and three choices for the juice (orange, grapefruit, tomato). How many different breakfasts can be ordered? **18**

3. While Kari was at summer camp, it was sunny for 7 days, and then it rained for 3 days. Each day Kari could do one special activity. On sunny days she had her choice of five different outside activities, and on rainy days she had her choice of two different inside activities. In how many ways could she choose her special activities? $5^7 \cdot 2^3 = 625,000$

(Additional Examples continue on page 122.)

▶ **LESSON MASTER 2-9 A** *page 2*

5. Some license plates contain three letters followed by three numbers, such as MOM104 or WIN085.
   a. How many different plates are possible?

   17,576,000 plates

   b. How many are there if you can't have letters repeat as the M does in MOM104?

   15,600,000 plates

6. Write a problem using the Multiplication Counting Principle that has as its answer $3 \cdot 5 \cdot 2$. **Sample: How many combinations are possible if a talk show chooses one child from each family? The Chins have 3 children, the Garcias have 5, and the Andersons have 2.**

7. A quiz has three multiple-choice questions, each with four options A, B, C, and D. The quiz also has five true-false questions.
   a. How many different ways are there for a student to answer the questions on the quiz?

   2,048 ways

   b. How many different ways would there be for a student to answer a quiz if there were x multiple-choice questions followed by y true-false questions?

   $4^x \cdot 2^y$

8. a. How many batting lineups can a 10-member softball team have?

   3,628,800 lineups

   b. How many lineups are there if the pitcher must bat last and the best batter (who is not the pitcher) must bat fourth?

   40,320 lineups

121

4. a. A test has 10 true-false items and 15 multiple-choice items with 4 choices each. How many different answer sheets are possible? $2^{10} \cdot 4^{15} \approx 1.1$ trillion possible sheets

b. A test has T true-false items and M multiple-choice items with 4 choices each. How many different answer sheets are possible? $2^T \cdot 4^M$

5. Suppose Mrs. Smith writes a chapter test that has 12 questions. It has four multiple-choice questions, each with r possible answers, three multiple-choice questions, each with p possible answers, and five true-false questions. How many ways are there to answer the questions? $r^4 \cdot p^3 \cdot 2^5 = 32p^3r^4$

Additional Answers
6b, c.

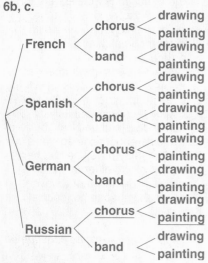

2)

	E	F	I
A	(A,E)	(A,F)	(A,I)
B	(B,E)	(B,F)	(B,I)
C	(C,E)	(C,F)	(C,I)

4) If one choice can be made in m ways and a second choice can be made in n ways, then there are mn ways of making the first choice followed by the second choice.

WBEZ. *This woman is the news director of Chicago's public radio station WBEZ. Public radio stations feature in-depth coverage of national and local issues, talk shows, and interviews.*

122

QUESTIONS

Covering the Reading

In 1–3, refer to Example 1.

1. In how many ways can a person enter through a north gate and leave through gate G? **4**

2. Using an array, list the ways to enter the stadium through a north gate and leave through a south gate if gates D, G, and H are closed. **See left.**

3. a. Suppose in Example 1 that a person could enter through any gate and leave through any gate. In how many ways can this be done?
b. Suppose in Example 1 that a person could enter through any gate and leave through any *other* gate. In how many ways can this be done? **a) 81; b) 72**

4. State the Multiplication Counting Principle. **See left.**

5. In mathematics, when is a procedure said to be *elegant?* **when it is simple and clever**

6. Suppose the school in Example 2 offered Russian as a fourth language choice.
a. Now how many ways could a student choose a schedule? **16**
b. Draw a tree diagram showing all the possible choices of schedules.
c. Noah is taking Russian, chorus, and painting. Underline his schedule. **b, c) See margin.**

7. Each of 20 questions on a quiz can be answered *true* or *false*. Suppose a student guesses randomly.
a. How many ways are there of answering the test? **1,048,576**
b. What are the chances of getting all of the answers correct? $\frac{1}{1{,}048{,}576}$

8. Suppose Ms. McCullagh gives a quiz that has two questions with x choices and three true-false questions. Give the number of ways to answer the items on the test with an expression:
a. not using exponents; **b.** using exponents.
$x \cdot x \cdot 2 \cdot 2 \cdot 2$ $x^2 \cdot 2^3$

9. If a test has five multiple-choice questions each with q possible answers and five true-false questions, how many different ways would there be to answer the test? $32q^5$

Applying the Mathematics

10. Radio station call letters, such as WNEW, must start with W or K.
a. How many choices are there for the first letter? **2**
b. How many choices are there for the second letter? **26**
c. How many different 4-letter station names are possible? **35,152**

11. Vince is buying a new suit. He must decide if he wants wide or narrow lapels. He must also choose among four colors—blue, gray, tan, and brown. Draw a tree diagram showing all the possible choices he has. **See margin.**

Adapting to Individual Needs

English Language Development
Students have encountered a number of properties in this chapter. You might have students match their index-card files of these new ideas with those listed in the Vocabulary on page 133. Suggest that they make cards for any properties they may have omitted. Then have students **work in pairs** and use their index cards to quiz each other.

Additional Answers, continued
11.

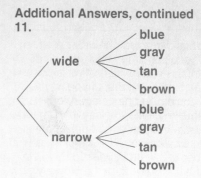

12. At the Fulton High School cafeteria, students had a choice of chicken or fish. The vegetable choices were carrots or beans. There were three dessert choices: an apple, pudding, or yogurt. **a) See margin.**
    a. Organize the possible meals consisting of one main dish, one vegetable, and one dessert using either a tree diagram or a list.
    b. How many different such meals are possible? **12**

13a) AJ, AK, AL, BJ, BK, BL, CJ, CK, CL, DJ, DK, DL

13. Aram, Brad, Carl, and Dave are candidates for Winter Carnival King. Janice, Kara, and Leshawn are the nominees for Winter Carnival Queen.
    a. Using initials, write the names of all the possible "Royal Couples."
    b. If the king and queen are chosen at random, what is the probability that the Royal Couple will be Aram and Kara? $\frac{1}{12}$
    a) See left.

14. Telephone area codes consist of 3 digits. Prior to 1989, they fit the following rule: The first digit must be chosen from 2 through 9, the second digit must be 0 or 1, and the third digit cannot be 0. In 1989, this policy changed so that the first and third digits could be any digit 0 through 9. (The second digit still must be 0 or 1.)
    a. How many area codes were possible before 1989? **144**
    b. How many area codes were possible after 1989? **200**
    c. How many area code possibilities were added by the policy change? **56**

15. Write a Multiplication Counting Principle problem whose answer is $2 \cdot 3 \cdot 5$. **Sample: A girl can choose from 2 jackets, 3 skirts, and 5 blouses. How many 3-piece outfits are possible?**

16. The Cayuga Indians played a game called Dish using a wooden bowl and six pits from peaches. The pits were blackened on one side and uncolored on the other. When pits were tossed, they landed on the black and uncolored sides with about the same frequency. A player scored five points if the six pits were tossed and six black or six uncolored sides landed up.
    a. Use the Multiplication Counting Principle to determine how many possible ways the six pits could land. **64**
    b. What is the probability that a player would score 5 points with one toss? $\frac{1}{32}$

17. How many sets of answers are possible if a true-false quiz has
    a. one question? **2**   **b.** two questions? **4**
    c. three questions? **8**   **d.** ten questions? **1024**
    e. n questions? 2^n

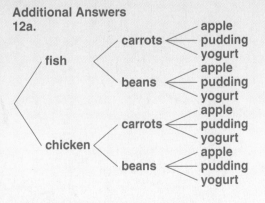

Dishing out peach pits.
Dish, also known as the bowl game, was played by nearly every Indian tribe in the U.S. Each player on a team took turns tossing and catching peach pits in a bowl. In some tribes, each player on the winning side would be given a pony by members of the losing side.

Review

In 18–21, solve. *(Lessons 2-6, 2-8)*

18. $4j < 13$ $j < \frac{13}{4}$

19. $-20k = \frac{4}{5}$ $k = -\frac{1}{25}$

20. $\frac{1}{3} > -6m$ $m > -\frac{1}{18}$

21. $-96 = -0.08n$ $n = 1200$

Additional Answers
12a.

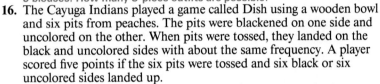

```
        carrots <  apple
               \  pudding
  fish <          yogurt
        beans <  apple
               \  pudding
                  yogurt

        carrots <  apple
               \  pudding
chicken <         yogurt
        beans <  apple
               \  pudding
                  yogurt
```

123

Notes on Questions

Question 30 This question can be illustrated using the Area Model for Multiplication. $\frac{3}{8} \cdot \frac{1}{4} = \frac{3}{32}$

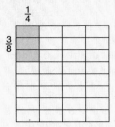

Question 31 The main reason for this question is to lay the groundwork for **Question 32.** Do not assign one question without the other.

Follow-up 2-9
for Lesson

Practice

For more questions on SPUR Objectives, use **Lesson Master 2-9A** (shown on pages 120–121) or **Lesson Master 2-9B** (shown on pages 122–123).

Assessment

Written Communication Have students describe a situation for which they could use the Multiplication Counting Principle. Then have them write a question about the situation and provide an answer. [Students describe an appropriate situation and use the Multiplication Counting Principle correctly.]

Extension

Tell your students that you are going to test their ability to read minds. You will think of 2 multiple-choice questions with 4 choices and 3 true-false questions; the students must answer without seeing the questions. Determine the answer key by tossing a coin or by using a random number generator on a calculator. (Let an odd digit stand for false and an even digit stand for true.) About $\frac{1}{128}$ of your students should have perfect papers.

Project Update Project 7, *Telephone Numbers,* on page 132, relates to the content of this lesson.

---

22. Last year a family paid $12,750, more than one third of their earned income, in income taxes. *(Lesson 2-8)*
    a. Let I = the family's earned income last year. Write a sentence that describes the situation above. **$12,750 > $\frac{1}{3}I$**
    b. Solve the sentence. **$I < $38,250$**

23. *Skill sequence.* Solve the sentence. *(Lessons 2-7, 2-8)*
    a. $0x = 5$ **No solution**
    b. $5x = 0$ **0**
    c. $5x < 0$ **$x < 0$**
    d. $-5x < 0$ **$x > 0$**

24. a. Multiply: $\frac{2}{5}x \cdot 20$. **8x**
    b. Solve: $\frac{2}{5}x = 20$. **50**
    c. Explain in your own words how the questions in parts **a** and **b** are different. *(Lessons 2-3, 2-6)* **Sample: Part a asks for the answer to a multiplication question. Part b asks for the solution to an equation.**

25. Solve $\frac{-x}{6} = 17$. *(Lesson 2-6)* **$x = -102$**

26. If a farmer harvests 40 bales of hay per acre, how many acres will produce a harvest of 224 bales? *(Lessons 2-4, 2-6)* **5.6 acres**

27. All angles in this figure are right angles. Write an expression for the area of the figure. *(Lesson 2-1)* **2x + 48**

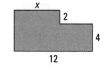

28. Evaluate $6(3xy)$ when $x = -\frac{7}{3}$ and $y = -\frac{32}{5}$. Write your answer as a fraction. *(Lessons 1-4, 2-3)* **$\frac{1344}{5}$**

29. Evaluate when $d = -\frac{1}{2}$. *(Lessons 1-4, 2-5)*
    a. d^3 **$-\frac{1}{8}$**
    b. $3d + 4$ **$\frac{5}{2}$**
    c. $-8d^4$ **$-\frac{1}{2}$**

30. At Harwood High, $\frac{3}{8}$ of the students take French, and $\frac{1}{4}$ of the French students are in Ms. Walker's French class. What fraction of Harwood High students are in Ms. Walker's French class? *(Lesson 2-3)* **$\frac{3}{32}$**

Exploration

In 30 and 31, use the fact that an *acronym* is a name made from first letters of words or parts of words.

31. Here are some famous acronyms. Tell what the letters stand for. **See below.**
    a. NASA
    b. UNICEF
    c. CIA
    d. IBM
    e. ICBM
    f. AFL-CIO
    g. NFL
    h. NATO
    i. UNESCO

32. Is it true that over a half million 4-letter acronyms are possible in English? Explain your answer using the Multiplication Counting Principle. **No, there are 26^4 = 456,976 ways, which is under a half million.**
    31a) National Aeronautics and Space Administration;
    b) United Nations International Children's Emergency Fund;
    c) Central Intelligence Agency;   d) International Business Machines;
    e) intercontinental ballistic missile;   f) American Federation of Labor-Congress of Industrial Organizations;   g) National Football League;
    h) North Atlantic Treaty Organization;   i) United Nations Educational, Scientific, and Cultural Organization

124

Setting Up Lesson 2-10

Materials Tell students they will need calculators as they read Lesson 1-10. Be sure to discuss **Question 3b** which previews Lesson 10-2.

124

Mount Rushmore. *The construction of Mount Rushmore began in 1927 and took over 14 years to complete. The four busts were cut out of the granite cliff with dynamite and drills.*

The Factorial Symbol

A special case of the Multiplication Counting Principle occurs when a list of things is to be ranked or ordered.

On Mount Rushmore in South Dakota, the sculptor Gutzon Borglum carved busts of four presidents of the United States. From left to right they are George Washington, Thomas Jefferson, Theodore Roosevelt, and Abraham Lincoln. Some students were asked to rank these men in order of greatness. Here are three possible rankings.

1st place	2nd place	3rd place	4th place
Washington	Lincoln	Roosevelt	Jefferson
Jefferson	Lincoln	Washington	Roosevelt
Lincoln	Washington	Jefferson	Roosevelt

How many rankings are possible? This question can be answered using the Multiplication Counting Principle. There are 4 people who could be ranked first. After choosing someone for first place, there are only 3 people left who could be second. Then, after 1st and 2nd places have been chosen, there are only 2 people left who could be third, and the remaining person will be last.

$$\underbrace{\frac{4}{}}_{\substack{\text{ways to choose} \\ \text{1st place}}} \cdot \underbrace{\frac{3}{}}_{\substack{\text{ways to choose} \\ \text{2nd place}}} \cdot \underbrace{\frac{2}{}}_{\substack{\text{ways to choose} \\ \text{3rd place}}} \cdot \underbrace{\frac{1}{}}_{\substack{\text{ways to choose} \\ \text{4th place}}}$$

The answer is $4 \cdot 3 \cdot 2 \cdot 1 = 24$.

A shortcut way to write $4 \cdot 3 \cdot 2 \cdot 1$ is 4!. This is read "four *factorial*."

Lesson 2-10 *Factorials and Permutations* **125**

Lesson 2-10

Objectives
E Evaluate expressions containing a factorial symbol.
I Apply the Permutation Theorem.

Resources
From the **Teacher's Resource File**
■ Lesson Master 2-10A or 2-10B
■ Answer Master 2-10
■ Teaching Aid 15: Warm-up

Additional Resources
■ Visual for Teaching Aid 15

Teaching 2-10
Lesson

Warm-up
Do as many of the following computations as you can without a calculator. Then use a calculator to find the rest of the values.
1. $1 \cdot 2 \cdot 3 \cdot 4$ 24
2. $1 \cdot 2 \cdot 3 \cdot 4 \cdot 5$ 120
3. $1 \cdot 2 \cdot 3 \cdot 4 \cdot 5 \cdot 6$ 720
4. $1 \cdot 2 \cdot 3 \cdot 4 \cdot 5 \cdot 6 \cdot 7$ 5040
5. $1 \cdot 2 \cdot 3 \cdot 4 \cdot 5 \cdot 6 \cdot 7 \cdot 8$ 40,320
6. $1 \cdot 2 \cdot 3 \cdot 4 \cdot 5 \cdot 6 \cdot 7 \cdot 8 \cdot 9$ 362,880
7. $1 \cdot 2 \cdot 3 \cdot 4 \cdot 5 \cdot 6 \cdot 7 \cdot 8 \cdot 9 \cdot 10$ 3,628,800
8. $\dfrac{1 \cdot 2 \cdot 3 \cdot 4 \cdot 5 \cdot 6 \cdot 7 \cdot 8 \cdot 9}{1 \cdot 2 \cdot 3 \cdot 4 \cdot 5 \cdot 6 \cdot 7}$ 72

Lesson 2-10 Overview

Broad Goals This lesson applies the Multiplication Counting Principle to the counting of arrangements of *n* different items; in these situations the factorial symbol (!) is convenient for describing answers. Students should be able to work with this symbol, both with and without calculators, as appropriate.

Perspective The Permutation Theorem is a special case of the Multiplication Counting Principle. The idea is to begin by asking how many arrangements can be made of *m* different items. The first place in the arrangement is any one of *m* choices; then there are *m* – 1 choices for the second place, *m* – 2 choices for the third place, and so on, until there is only one choice remaining for the last place.

For calculations of factorials, as given in the *Warm-up* and **Examples 1 and 2,** students should know what is being calculated and how to carry out the calculation by straight multiplication or with a factorial key on their calculator. Most good students will ultimately memorize the values of *n*! for *n* = 1, 2, 3, 4, 5, and 6.

We have found that many students do not have systematic ways of doing the counting. Therefore, they do not see the patterns in the numbers of arrangements of various types. After students have worked for awhile, you might want to help students start a systematic list. Have them list all rankings with Washington first (there are six). Then, it follows that there should be just as many patterns when each of the other presidents are first. This means that there would be $6 \cdot 4$ rankings altogether.

Multicultural Connection You might want to have students compare the measures of some famous statues to the height of George Washington's head on Mount Rushmore. His head measures 60 feet, which is about the height of a five-story building. The Great Buddha at Kamakura, Japan, is 42 feet high. The statues on Easter Island measure from 12 to 25 feet in height. The head of the Sphinx in Egypt is about half the size of Washington's head. Crazy Horse Memorial, which is near Mount Rushmore, will be a gigantic sculpture of Crazy Horse, the great Oglala Sioux Indian chief, seated on his horse. The memorial is being carved from an entire 600-foot mountain. Some students might like to do further research on these and other monuments and on their designers and sculptors.

Presidential facelift. *These workers are restoring the sculpture to its original beauty.*

Definition: When n is a positive integer, the symbol $n!$ (read n factorial) means the product of the integers from n to 1.

❶ Example 1

Evaluate 5!.

Solution

$$5! = 5 \cdot 4 \cdot 3 \cdot 2 \cdot 1 = 120$$

Scientific calculators usually have a factorial key [x!]. To evaluate 5! on such calculators, key in 5 [x!]. On some calculators you may have to use a second function key, [2nd] or [INV]. Then key in 5 [INV] [x!]. On graphics calculators there is often no factorial key visible. However, these machines usually have a [MATH] key. When you press the [MATH] key you will see a menu that includes a way to calculate factorials. Check your calculator now by using it to evaluate 5!. You should get 120.

Permutations

An ordered arrangement of letters, names, or objects is called a **permutation.** In the discussion of Mount Rushmore, we calculated that there are 4! permutations of four names. In general, when you are making arrangements of all n items in a set, the following theorem applies.

Permutation Theorem
There are $n!$ possible permutations of n different items when each item is used exactly once.

Example 2

A baseball manager is setting a batting order for the 9 starting players. How many batting orders are possible?

Solution

The batting order is an arrangement of the starting players. Each player is used only once so the Permutation Theorem applies.
There are 9 starting players to be ordered. So, **There are 9! possible batting orders.** With a calculator, evaluate 9!.
$$9! = 362,880$$

❷ Businesses are often interested in a type of problem that involves permutations. One type of permutation problem is called a "traveling salesman problem." It involves finding the shortest path between locations. For instance, if a salesman needs to visit 12 cities there are 12!, or 479,001,600 different orders in which he could make his stops. If there are 532 cities, there are 532! possible routes.

126

✎ **Writing** After students complete the lesson, you might have them **work in groups** to write two stories which contain problems to solve; one story should require the use of the Multiplication Counting Principle and the other the Permutation Theorem. Then have the groups read their problems to the class. Have the class tell how to solve them and then find the answers.

126

Problems of this type need not involve just salespeople. Deciding in what order to connect telephone lines is another example of a "traveling salesman problem." In 1986, a computer was used to find the shortest route connecting the 532 cities with central office switching systems of local telephone companies. The solution is shown below.

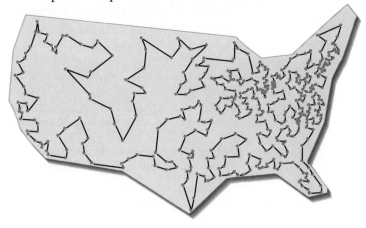

Shortcuts for Evaluating Expressions with Factorials

Problems involving $n!$ often become so difficult that even with computers, cleverness is needed to simplify expressions. Some calculations with factorials can be done more quickly with pencil and paper than with a calculator. This is often the case when factorials are divided.

❸ **Example 3**

Evaluate $\frac{12!}{10!}$.

Solution 1

Express the factorials as products and use the Equal Fractions Property to simplify.

$$\frac{12!}{10!} = \frac{12 \cdot 11 \cdot \cancel{10} \cdot \cancel{9} \cdot \cancel{8} \cdot \cancel{7} \cdot \cancel{6} \cdot \cancel{5} \cdot \cancel{4} \cdot \cancel{3} \cdot \cancel{2} \cdot \cancel{1}}{\cancel{10} \cdot \cancel{9} \cdot \cancel{8} \cdot \cancel{7} \cdot \cancel{6} \cdot \cancel{5} \cdot \cancel{4} \cdot \cancel{3} \cdot \cancel{2} \cdot \cancel{1}}$$
$$= 12 \cdot 11$$
$$= 132$$

Solution 2

Write out only as many of the factors of the factorials as necessary.

$$\frac{12!}{10!} = \frac{12 \cdot 11 \cdot \cancel{10!}}{\cancel{10!}}$$
$$= 12 \cdot 11$$
$$= 132$$

▶

Lesson 2-10 *Factorials and Permutations* **127**

❶ Make certain that students can evaluate factorials with paper and pencil if they are small, with a calculator if there are many multiplications, or with a calculator factorial key if there are a great number of multiplications. Tell students that, in order of operations, factorials take precedence over multiplication: $3 \cdot 5! = 3 \cdot 120$.

❷ Problems like the traveling salesman problem are extremely difficult to solve, even with a computer. To solve the problem for 100 cities in a straightforward way would take so long that even if every electron in the universe were actually in a computer that could do one billion calculations per second, it would take all of them 10^{11} years to do the job. Obviously, to solve the problem for 2392 cities (the largest number of cities computed so far) required much cleverness and many shortcuts. There was an article on this subject, "Math Problem, Long Baffling, Slowly Yields," by Gina Kolata, in the March 12, 1991, *New York Times*.

❸ A different type of calculation, which is very common in permutation questions, is shown in **Example 3**. Even for a factorial as small as 12!, scientific notation is needed on some calculators. In the check, even though 12! is approximated, when the division is carried out, the answer is exact because the rounding compensates for the approximation.

Adapting to Individual Needs

Extra Help
It might be helpful to have students act out a permutation situation. Present the following situation: Suppose you were Gutzon Borglum deciding the order of the 4 presidents from left to right. Have 4 volunteers come to the front of the room, and have each of them hold a card with the initial of one of the presidents, W, L, R, or J. Then ask students how many choices there are for first place [4]. Have one student stand in the first

position, and ask how many choices there are for 2nd place. [3] Have one student stand in that position, and ask how many choices there are for 3rd place. [2] Students will see that there is only 1 choice for 4th place. Thus, if they have understood the Multiplication Counting Principle, they will see that the number of possible choices for order is 4 × 3 × 2 × 1, or 24.

127

The evaluation in **Example 3** is motivated by the need to simplify expressions such as 99!/95!. You cannot enter either of the two factorials on most calculators, but the reduced form, $99 \cdot 98 \cdot 97 \cdot 96$, is computable.

Students may wonder if 0! has any meaning. [Yes, 0! = 1.] They may also wonder if n! has any meaning when n is not an integer. [Yes and no. The gamma function, which is defined using calculus ideas (integrals), generalizes the factorial function, but it is not called a factorial function.]

Additional Examples

1. Evaluate 7!. **5040**
2. In how many different orders can the four members of a track relay team run? **24**
3. Evaluate.

   a. $\frac{9!}{6!3!}$ **84**

   b. $\frac{100!}{102!}$ $\frac{1}{10302}$

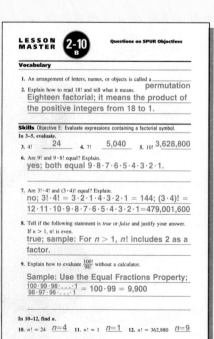

128

Check

Use a calculator to evaluate the factorials. Key in 12 ⌊x!⌋ ÷ 10 ⌊x!⌋ =

$$\frac{12!}{10!} \approx \frac{4.79 \cdot 10^8}{3,628,000} \approx 132$$

(Notice that 12! is so large that many calculators must express it in scientific notation.)

QUESTIONS

Covering the Reading

1. Make a list of all possible rankings in a poll with the three presidents Washington, Jefferson, and Lincoln.
   WJL, WLJ, JWL, JLW, LWJ, LJW

2. Gutzon Borglum did not have to put the presidents in the order from left to right as he did. How many other orders are possible? **23**

3. What is a short way to write $6 \cdot 5 \cdot 4 \cdot 3 \cdot 2 \cdot 1$? **6!**

4. What does the symbol n! mean?
   the product of the integers from n down to 1

5. Evaluate n! when n equals each of the following.
   a. 1 1 **b.** 2 2 **c.** 3 6
   d. 4 24 **e.** 5 120 **f.** 6 720

In 6 and 7, evaluate with a calculator.

6. $15! \approx 1.3077 \cdot 10^{12}$ 7. $30! \approx 2.6525 \cdot 10^{32}$

8. What is a permutation? **an arrangement of objects in order**

9) Any of the 5 singers can sing first. Then any of the 4 left can sing second, any of the 3 left can sing third, any of the 2 left can sing fourth, and then the last person left sings.

9. Five singers show up to audition for a job. Explain why there are 5! possible orders in which they can be asked to sing. **See left.**

10. In how many ways can a saleswoman arrange a trip to visit 18 cities? **In 18! or about $6.402 \cdot 10^{15} \approx 6,402,000,000,000,000$ ways**

11. How many permutations of n different objects are possible when each object is used exactly once? **$n!$**

12a) $\frac{11!}{9!} = \frac{11 \cdot 10 \cdot 9!}{9!} = 11 \cdot 10 = 110$

12. **a.** Explain how to evaluate $\frac{11!}{9!}$ without using a calculator. **See left.**

    b. Check by using a calculator. **Sample: Key in 11 ⌊x!⌋ ÷ 9 ⌊x!⌋ =**

In 13 and 14, evaluate.

13. $\frac{6!}{3!}$ **120** 14. $\frac{25!}{24!}$ **25**

128

Adapting to Individual Needs

English Language Development
Two new words in this lesson are *factorial* and *permutation*. To help students relate the word factorial to multiplication, remind them that in multiplication, the numbers that are multiplied are called *factors*.

Explain that the word permute means to rearrange. In mathematics, a permutation is a way that the objects in a set can be rearranged.

Have three students come to the front of the classroom and ask them to line up in as many different orders as they can find. Have other students list and count the arrangements. Then ask how many people can be chosen for first place [3], and have a student stand in first place. Ask how many students remain for second place? [2] Continue questioning and lead students to see that the number of permutations is $3 \cdot 2 \cdot 1$, or 6.

Many art museums employ docents who serve as tour guides and art lecturers for small groups. This group is at the Mint Museum of Art in Charlotte, North Carolina.

Applying the Mathematics

15. The curator of a museum must arrange twenty pictures in a line on a wall. In how many ways can the pictures be arranged? 20! or about $2.4 \cdot 10^{18}$

16. Suppose eight horses are in a race.
   a. In how many ways can first and second places be won? 56
   b. In how many different orders can all eight horses finish? 40,320

17. a. *True or false.* $8! = 8 \cdot 7!$ True
   b. *True or false.* $11! = 11 \cdot 10!$ True
   c. Use one variable to write a generalization of the pattern in parts **a** and **b**. $n! = n \cdot (n-1)!$

18. a. Evaluate $\frac{n!}{(n-1)!}$ when $n = 10$. 10
   b. Give another instance of $\frac{n!}{(n-1)!}$. Sample: $\frac{11!}{10!} = 11$
   c. Generalize parts **a** and **b**. $\frac{n!}{(n-1)!} = n$

19. Because of their limited memories, most calculators cannot evaluate 100! or 100^{100}. Explain how to determine which of 100! or 100^{100} is larger. Sample: $100^{100} = 100 \cdot 100 \cdot 100 \cdot \ldots \cdot 100$ whereas $100! = 100 \cdot 99 \cdot 98 \cdot \ldots \cdot 1$, so you get a bigger product from 100^{100}.

Review

20. Suppose you have just won a new car. You have your choice of body style (2-door, 4-door, or station wagon), transmission (automatic or standard), and color (white, black, red, silver, or green). *(Lesson 2-9)*
   a. How many different ways can you make your choices? 30
   b. If another color choice of yellow is given to you, how many more choices do you have? 6

21. A multiple-choice test has five questions. The first three questions have four choices each. Questions 4 and 5 have five choices each. If Mary guesses on all the questions, what are the chances that Mary will get them all correct? *(Lesson 2-9)* $\frac{1}{1600}$

22. *Skill sequence.* Solve each sentence. *(Lessons 2-6, 2-8)*
   a. $-2a = 7$ $a = -\frac{7}{2}$
   b. $7a = -2$ $a = -\frac{2}{7}$
   c. $7a \geq -2$ $a \geq -\frac{2}{7}$
   d. $-7a \geq 2$ $a \leq -\frac{2}{7}$

In 23 and 24, a sentence is given. **a.** Make up a question about a real situation that can be answered by solving the equation or inequality. **b.** Solve the sentence and answer your question. *(Lesson 2-6)* 23a and 24a, See left.

23. $10x = 723$
   b) $72.30
24. $130 > 2.5x$ b) at most 52

In 25 and 26, solve. *(Lessons 2-6, 2-8)*

25. $\frac{3}{8}y < \frac{5}{4}$ $y < \frac{10}{3}$
26. $(2-3)t \leq 8$ $t \geq -8$

27. Which property of multiplication is used to conclude from $\frac{2}{3}x = 18$, that $\frac{3}{2}\left(\frac{2}{3}x\right) = \frac{3}{2} \cdot 18$? *(Lesson 2-6)* Multiplication Property of Equality

23a) Sample: Adam's total earnings for 10 weeks was $723. How much did he earn each week?

24a) Sample: If you can read $2\frac{1}{2}$ pages a minute and the chapter is at most 130 pages long, how many minutes will it take to read the chapter?

Lesson 2-10 *Factorials and Permutations* **129**

Adapting to Individual Needs

Challenge
Have students solve the following problems.
1. Suppose you have four letters, A, B, C, and D. How many 4-letter arrangements are possible? [24]
2. Suppose two of the letters are the same, for instance A, A, B, and C. How many distinct arrangements are possible? [12]
3. Suppose three of the four letters are the same. How many distinct arrangements are possible for A, A, A, B? [4]
4. Finally, suppose all four letters are the same. How many distinct arrangements are possible? [1]
5. Make a generalization for determining the number of arrangements of *n* items if *r* items are not distinct. [Divide *n*! by *r*!]

129

Notes on Questions

Question 34 After students answer this question, you might ask for the largest *n* for which *n*! is displayed as a number in standard form on a calculator (as opposed to a display in scientific notation). [On a calculator with an 8-digit display, 11! = 39,916,800; 12! has more than 8 digits and is given in scientific notation—4.79 × 10⁸.]

Follow-up for Lesson 2-10

Practice

For more questions on SPUR Objectives, use **Lesson Master 2-10A** (shown on page 127) or **Lesson Master 2-10B** (shown on pages 128–129).

Assessment

Written Communication Have each student write a problem that applies the Permutation Theorem and then give the answer and explain how to get it. [Sentences demonstrate an understanding of permutations and factorials.]

Extension

Language Arts Connection Have students **work in groups.** Tell each group to select four letters, and then write all possible arrangements of the letters. Have them identify the arrangements that form actual English words.

Project Update Project 7, *Telephone Numbers,* on page 132, relates to the content of this lesson.

---

28. Lamar earns $7.28 per hour. Last week he earned $101.92. How many hours did he work? *(Lessons 2-4, 2-6)* **14 hours**

29. There are about 16,000 grains of sand per cubic inch, and 1728 cubic inches per cubic foot. About how many grains of sand are in a 25-cubic foot sandbox? *(Lesson 2-4)* **6.912 · 10⁸ or 691,200,000**

30. Write the reciprocal of $\frac{50n^3}{233m^5}$. *(Lesson 2-2)* $\frac{233m^5}{50n^3}$

31. Give an instance of the Commutative Property of Multiplication. *(Lesson 2-1)* **Sample: 3 · 4 = 4 · 3**

32. One rectangular solid is half as long, $\frac{2}{3}$ as wide, and $\frac{3}{4}$ as high as another. How do the volumes of the two solids compare? *(Lessons 2-1, 2-3)* **The first has $\frac{1}{4}$ the volume of the second.**

33. Consider the statement $a + b > a$. *(Lesson 1-7)*
    a. Give an instance of the statement. **Sample: 2 + 5 > 2**
    b. Give a counterexample to the statement. **Sample: 2 + -1 > 2 is not true.**
    c. For what values of *b* is the statement true? **positive numbers**

Exploration

34. What is the largest value of *n* for which your calculator can calculate or estimate *n*!? **Answers will vary.**

35. What is the smallest value of *n* for which *n*! is divisible by 100? **10**

36. Key in 2.5 |x! | on a calculator. Explain what happens. **Most calculators will give an error message. *n* must be an integer.**

37. Some puzzles involve permutations of letters.
    a. Unscramble these letters to spell four mathematical terms.

    L U Q A E **EQUAL**   E S H P R E **SPHERE**
    I R I D A **RADII**   R I N G I O **ORIGIN**

    b. Unscramble the last letters of the words you found to spell another mathematical term. **LINE**

A project presents an opportunity for you to extend your knowledge of a topic related to the material of this chapter. You should allow more time for a project than you do for typical homework questions.

1 Extraterrestrial Life

Interview a number of people about their views of life on other planets in our galaxy. What values do they give for *T, P, E, L, I, C,* and *A* on page 71? Calculate *N* for their values. Does the calculated value agree with their views?

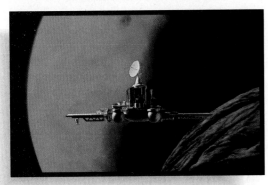

2 Properties of Operations

Multiplication and addition are both commutative and associative.
a. Are subtraction and division commutative and associative? How do you know?
b. Consider the operation # in which, for all *x* and *y*, *x* # *y* = *xy* + 2. For example,

$$1 \# 2 = 4$$
$$2 \# 2 = 6$$
$$3 \# 1 = 5$$
$$5 \# 2 = 12.$$

c. Is # a commutative operation? Is # an associative operation? Explain your reasoning. Design your own operation. Give a rule and several examples. Is your operation associative? Is it commutative?

3 Making a Box

How large a box can you make by cutting out square corners from a rectangular piece of paper?

a. Begin with an $8\frac{1}{2}''$ by 11″ sheet of paper. Cut a 1″ square from each corner. Fold and tape to make an open box.
b. What is the volume of the box you have made?
c. By cutting different-sized corners, you can create boxes of different volumes. Experiment to see how large a volume you can create using this method. Organize your data in a table and write a brief report describing your methods and results.

4 The King's Gold Coins

A king has eight gold coins. One of the coins is counterfeit and weighs less than the others. The king has only a balance scale. How can the king find the counterfeit coin using the *least* number of weighings?

▶

Chapter 2 Projects

The projects relate chiefly to the content of the lessons of this chapter as follows:

Project	Lesson(s)
1	2-1, 2-4
2	2-1
3	2-1
4	2-6
5	2-4
6	2-1
7	2-9, 2-10

1 Extraterrestrial Life Students will need to explain the definitions given for each variable on page 81 before they begin their interviews. Recommend that students prepare tables or charts so that they can record people's responses accurately.

2 Properties of Operations Suggest that students begin this project by writing an explanation of the # operation. Students may select several different values for *a* and *b* to check if the operation is commutative or associative. Remind students that one counterexample is all that is needed to determine that a property is not true. Because this is a relatively easy project, you might ask students to examine other properties, such as the existence of an identity and an inverse.

3 Making a Box In **part b,** some students may subtract only one inch, rather than 2 inches, from the length and width of the paper to find the length and width of the box. Check that students use the correct dimensions for the box [$6\frac{1}{2} \times 9 \times 1$] before they continue with the rest of the project. If students decide to increase the height by fractional increments, they should realize that it is easier to work things out arithmetically than to construct a new box each time.

4 The King's Gold Coins Some students will benefit by using a balance scale and eight weights. Other students will find drawing a scale and trying and checking several weighings helpful. Stress that the key to this project is finding the least number of weighings. You might challenge students to consider the case where it is not known whether the unknown coin weighs more or less that the other coins.

Possible Responses
1. Responses will vary.
2. **a.** No. Sample counterexamples:
   $6 - 4 \neq 4 - 6$; $6 \div 4 \neq 4 \div 6$
   c. The operation # is commutative, but it is not associative. Some students may explain their reasoning by giving examples or a counterexample. Other students may take the following algebraic approach: # is commutative because $ab + 2 = ba + 2$. It is not associative because $(a\#b)\#c =$ $abc + 2c + 2$ and $a\#(b\#c) = abc + 2a + 2$; $abc + 2c + 2 \neq abc + 2a + 2$ unless $a = c$.
   Students' operations will vary.

(Responses continue on page 132.)

5 Rates Once students have decided which situation they are going to write about, suggest that they make a list of rates that pertain to the situation. For example, if students decide to write about taking a trip, they could list miles per hour, gasoline price per gallon, hotel rate per day, campground rate per day, and miles driven per day. The list will then serve as an outline for the story. Students should try to include rates that involve different units.

6 Window Washer Students may need the help of a research librarian to find the number of windows in the skyscraper they choose. Students should realize that they have to know such things as: the number of windows, the size of the windows, the speed with which a window washer can wash a window, and if the windows are washed on both sides. Students should also consider preparation time as they make their estimates. Window washers on older skyscrapers, such as the Empire State Building, strap themselves to the outside of windows with belts in order to wash windows. Newer skyscrapers often have a permanent scaffolding system that the window washers use. A few skyscrapers, such as the Sears Tower, have automated window-washing systems.

7 Telephone Numbers Students will have to call their telephone companies to find out if there are any restrictions on the prefixes and the last four digits. For example, in Chicago there are 165 possible prefixes. This means that if there were no restrictions on the last four digits, there would be 165 · 10 · 10 · 10 · 10 = 1,650,000 possible telephone numbers.

PROJECTS 2 *(continued)*

5 Rates

As you have seen in this chapter, rates have many uses. Choose a situation that interests you, such as playing a favorite sport, taking a trip, and so on. Make up a short story about that situation. Use at least ten different rate factor multiplications.

7 Telephone Numbers

How many different telephone numbers would be possible for a given area code if there were no restrictions? In all areas, however, there are restrictions. For example, in most places, no 7-digit telephone number can begin with 911. Find out what restrictions exist for your area code. Considering the restrictions, how many telephone numbers are possible for your area code?

6 Window Washer

How long would it take one window washer to wash all the windows in the Sears Tower or in some other famous skyscraper? What information do you need and how are you going to get it? If each of the windows is to be washed at least twice a year, how many window washers need to work at once to keep the windows clean? Explain your reasoning, estimates, and answers.

132

Additional responses, page 131

3. b. 58.5 in³
   c. Sample response:

ℓ(in.)	w(in.)	h(in.)	V(in.³)
9	6.5	1	58.5
8	5.5	1.5	66
7	4.5	2	63
6	3.5	2.5	52.5
5	2.5	3	37.5
4	1.5	3.5	21
3	0.5	4	6

A box with a height between 1.5 in. and 1.6 in. will have the greatest volume. The table below shows that when h is 1.59 in., the volume is greater than for h = 1.6 in. or for h = 1.58 in.

ℓ(in.)	w(in.)	h(in.)	V(in.³)
7.8	5.3	1.6	66.144
7.82	5.32	1.59	66.1478
7.84	5.34	1.58	66.1476

4. The counterfeit coin can be found in two weighings. Divide the coins into three groups of 3, 3, and 2. Weigh the two groups of 3 coins. If they balance, the counterfeit coin is not in either of these groups. Weigh the two remaining coins to see which is lighter. If the two groups of 3 coins do not balance, the counterfeit coin is on the lighter side. Weigh two of the 3 coins in this group. If they balance, the third coin

SUMMARY

Multiplication has many uses. The product xy may stand for any one of the following.

Area Model: xy is the area of a rectangle with length x and width y.

Area Model (discrete version): xy is the number of elements in a rectangular array with x rows and y columns.

Rate Factor Model: xy is the result of multiplying a rate x by a quantity y.

Multiplication Counting Principle: xy is the number of ways of making a first choice followed by a second choice, if the first choice can be made in x ways and the second can be made in y ways.

The product of three numbers xyz may be the volume of a box with dimensions, x, y, and z. The product of an odd number of negative numbers is negative; the product of an even number of negative numbers is positive. The product of the integers from 1 to n, written $n!$, is the number of ways of arranging n objects. The commutative and associative properties allow you to rearrange multiplication expressions.

The numbers 0, 1, and -1 are special in multiplication. Multiplying any number by zero gives the same result: 0. For this reason, equations of the form $0x = b$ are either true for all real numbers or for none of them. Multiplying any number by 1 yields that number. A conversion factor is the number 1 written using different units, so multiplying by it does not change the value of a quantity. Multiplying any number by -1 changes it to its opposite.

Because of the many uses of multiplication, equations of the form $ax = b$ and inequalities of the form $ax < b$ are quite common. When $a \neq 0$, such sentences can be solved by multiplying both sides by the number $\frac{1}{a}$, the reciprocal of a. Remember to change the sense of the inequality if a is negative.

VOCABULARY

Below are the most important terms and phrases for this chapter. You should be able to give a general description and a specific example of each.

Lesson 2-1
model
Area Model for Multiplication
Commutative Property of
    Multiplication
discrete set
rectangular array, dimension
rectangular solid, box
volume
Associative Property of
    Multiplication

Lesson 2-2
Multiplicative Identity
    Property of 1
reciprocals, multiplicative
    inverses
Property of Reciprocals
Reciprocal of a Fraction Property
Multiplication Property of Zero

Lesson 2-3
Multiplying Fractions Property
algebraic fractions
Equal Fractions Property

Lesson 2-4
Rate Factor Model for
    Multiplication
reciprocal rates

Lesson 2-5
opposites
Multiplication Property of -1
Properties of Multiplication of
    Positive and Negative
    Numbers

Lesson 2-6
Multiplication Property of
    Equality

Lesson 2-7
IF-THEN

Lesson 2-8
Multiplication Property of
    Inequality
direction of an inequality sign
sense of an inequality

Lesson 2-9
Multiplication Counting
    Principle
tree diagram

Lesson 2-10
n factorial, $n!$
permutation
Permutation Theorem

Chapter 2 *Summary and Vocabulary* **133**

---

is counterfeit. If they do not balance, the lighter coin is counterfeit.
5. **Responses will vary.**
6. **Sample response:** If the Sears Tower did not have an automated window washing system, it would take one window washer 40 weeks to wash all the windows in the Sears Tower; two window washers would be needed to wash all the windows twice a year. This assumes a forty-hour week.

These estimates are based on information that the Sears Tower has about 16,000 windows, and that It takes a professional window washer approximately 6 minutes, including preparation time, to wash the inside and outside of a window.
7. If there were no restrictions, the total number of different telephone numbers would be 10^7 or 10,000,000. Because local restrictions vary, students' responses will vary.

Progress Self-Test

For the development of mathematical competence, feedback and correction, along with the opportunity to practice, are necessary. The Progress Self-Test provides the opportunity for feedback and correction; the Chapter Review provides additional opportunities and practice. We cannot overemphasize the importance of these end-of-chapter materials. It is at this point that the material "gels" for many students, allowing them to solidify skills and understanding. In general, student performance should be markedly improved after these pages.

Assign the Progress Self-Test as a one-night assignment. Worked-out *solutions* for all questions are in the Selected Answers section of the student book. Encourage students to take the Progress Self-Test honestly, grade themselves, and then be prepared to discuss the test in class.

PROGRESS SELF-TEST

Take this test as you would take a test in class. You will need graph paper. Then check your work with the solutions in the Selected Answers section in the back of the book.

1. Evaluate $\frac{22!}{20!}$. **462**

2. *True or false.* $(-5)^{10} = -5^{10}$. **False** Explain your reasoning.
$(-5)^{10} = 9,765,625 \neq -9,765,625 = -5^{10}$

In 3–5, multiply and simplify the result.

3. $\frac{20x}{3y} \cdot \frac{5}{4x}$ **$\frac{25}{3y}$**

4. $\frac{4}{x^2} \cdot \frac{11}{2x}$ **$\frac{22}{x^3}$**

5. $-5a \cdot \frac{a}{5}$ **$-a^2$**

6. Give an instance of the Commutative Property of Multiplication.
Sample: $7 \cdot 5 = 5 \cdot 7 = 35$

In 7–10, solve.

7. $50x = 10$ **$x = \frac{1}{5}$**

8. $\frac{1}{4}k = -24$ **$k = -96$**

9. $15 \le 3m$ **$5 \le m$**

10. $-y \le -2$ **$y \ge 2$**

11. **a.** Solve $-2n < 18$. **b.** Graph the result on a number line.
a) $n > -9$
b) ← + + ⊕ + + + + + → n
   -10 -9 -8 -7 -6 -5 -4

12. Solve $-48 = -\frac{4}{3}n$, and show how to check your answer. **$n = 36$;   Does $-48 = -\frac{4}{3} \cdot 36$? Yes, $-48 = -4 \cdot 12$.**

In 13 and 14, give the reciprocal.

13. $-\frac{3}{n}$ **$-\frac{n}{3}$**

14. 3.2 **$\frac{1}{3.2}$ or 0.3125 or $\frac{5}{16}$**

15. Write using symbols: The product of a number and the opposite of its reciprocal is -1. **$a \cdot -\frac{1}{a} = -1$**

16. How many centimeters are there in 8 inches? Use 1 in. = 2.54 cm. **20.32 cm**

17. A town is planning a new tax on cars owned by its citizens. The town planners want to charge $15 per car. In the U.S. there is an average of 0.57 car per person. If the population of the town is 24,000, about how much tax should the planners expect to collect? **$205,200**

18. What is the volume of a box with dimensions 4n, 8n, and 1.5n? **$48n^3$**

19. How long will it take to drive from Chicago to St. Louis, a distance of about 300 miles, if you travel at 55 mph? **5.45 hr or 5 hr, 27 min**

The Gateway Arch in St. Louis, Missouri

PROGRESS SELF-TEST

20. A cement contractor has been hired to pave this courtyard. It is in the shape of a square that is 80 ft on a side. In the center is a fountain that will not be paved. The fountain is also square, with sides 15 ft long. How many square feet will be paved? **6175 ft²**

80 ft   15 ft

In 21 and 22, a number is given.

a. Tell if the number is positive or negative.

b. Explain how you know.

21. $(-528,500)(-3,000,000)(4,150,000)$ See below.

22. $(-287)^{51}$ a) negative; b) odd power of negative number

23. Refer to the shaded rectangle below.

a. What are its length and width? $\frac{5}{6}x$, $\frac{3}{4}y$

b. What is its area? $\frac{5}{8}xy$

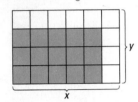

y

x

24. a. Give an example of an equation that has no real solution.   See below.

b. Explain why your equation has no real solution.   See below.

25. Mr. and Mrs. Williams bought a load of 600 used bricks to build a garden wall. They measured and found that they would need 40 bricks in each row.

a. Let r = the number of rows in the wall. Write an equation to describe this situation. $40r = 600$

b. How many rows high can they make their wall?   **15 rows**

21a) positive;   b) negative × negative = positive

24a) Sample: $0 \cdot x = 48$;   b) Sample: For any value of x, $0 \cdot x = 0$. So $0 \cdot x$ cannot equal 48.

26. At the Central Park Day Camp, a child must choose a sport (7 choices), a craft activity (5 choices), and a nature activity (3 choices). How many different programs can be designed?   **105 programs**

27. In how many ways could you arrange five musicians in a row for a photo?   **120**

28. How many different sets of answers are possible on a 25-question true-false test? $2^{25} = 33,554,432$

After taking and correcting the Self-Test, you may want to make a list of the problems you got wrong. Then write down what you need to study most. If you can, try to explain your most frequent or common mistakes. Use what you write to help you study and review the chapter.

Chapter 2 Review

Resources

From the *Teacher's Resource File*
- Answer Master for Chapter 2 Review
- Assessment Sourcebook:
  Chapter 2 Test, Forms A–D
  Chapter 2 Test, Cumulative Form

Additional Resources
- Quiz and Test Writer

The main objectives for the chapter are organized in the Chapter Review under the four types of understanding this book promotes—Skills, Properties, Uses, and Representations.

Whereas end-of chapter material may be considered optional in some texts, in *UCSMP Algebra* we have selected these objectives and questions with the expectation that they will be covered. Students should be able to answer these questions with about 85% accuracy after studying the chapter.

You may assign these questions over a single night to help students prepare for a test the next day, or you may assign the questions over a two-day period. If you work the questions over two days, then we recommend assigning the *evens* for homework the first night so that students get feedback in class the next day, then assigning the *odds* the night before the test, because answers are provided to the odd-numbered questions.

It is effective to ask students which questions they still do not understand and use the day or days as a total class discussion of the material which the class finds most difficult.

CHAPTER REVIEW

Questions on SPUR Objectives

SPUR stands for **S**kills, **P**roperties, **U**ses, and **R**epresentations. The Chapter Review questions are grouped according to the SPUR Objectives for this chapter.

SKILLS DEAL WITH THE PROCEDURES USED TO GET ANSWERS

See students' work for checks.

Objective A: *Multiply and simplify algebraic fractions.* (Lesson 2-3)

In 1–6, multiply the fractions. Simplify if possible.

1. $\frac{9x}{10} \cdot \frac{3}{4x}$ $\frac{27}{40}$
2. $\frac{3}{5} \cdot \frac{n}{2}$ $\frac{3n}{10}$
3. $\frac{7x}{2} \cdot \frac{2}{7y}$ $\frac{x}{y}$
4. $\frac{ax}{3} \cdot \frac{6x}{a}$ $2x^2$
5. $\frac{3n}{4} \cdot 4$ $3n$
6. $y \cdot \frac{5y}{3z} \cdot z^2$ $\frac{5y^2z}{3}$

In 7 and 8, simplify the fraction.

7. $\frac{13pqr}{39pq}$ $\frac{r}{3}$
8. $-\frac{48xy^2}{32x^3y^2}$ $-\frac{3}{2x^2}$

Objective B: *Multiply positive and negative numbers.* (Lesson 2-5)

In 9–12, evaluate.

9. $-6 \cdot 15 \cdot -3$ 270
10. $-24 \cdot -\frac{1}{2} \cdot -2$ -24
11. $(-2)^3$ -8
12. $(-5)^4$ 625

In 13 and 14, tell if the expression is positive or negative. 13) negative; 14) positive

13. $-3(6.2)(-872)(-6)$
14. $(-395)^{10}$

15. Evaluate. a) 36; b) -36; c) -216; d) -216
   a. $(-6)^2$ **b.** -6^2 **c.** $(-6)^3$ **d.** -6^3

16. *True or false.* $(-9)^6 = -9^6$. Explain your reasoning. False; $(-9)^6 = 531,441 \neq -531,441 = -9^6$

17. If $a = -8$, is $-3a$ positive or negative? positive

18. Describe the property that is used to determine if the product of two numbers is positive or negative. If two numbers are both positive or negative, then the product is positive. Otherwise, the product is negative.

Objective C: *Solve and check equations of the form $ax = b$.* (Lessons 2-6, 2-7)

In 19–24, solve and check.

19. $2.4m = 360$ $m = 150$
20. $-\frac{1}{2}k = -10$ $k = 20$
21. $-2 = 0.4h$ $h = -5$
22. $12 = 36m$ $m = \frac{1}{3}$
23. $\frac{5}{3}n = -45$ $n = -27$
24. $4(5x) = 0$ $x = 0$
25. Solve $d = cg$ for g. $g = \frac{d}{c}$
26. Solve $ky = 2z$ for y. $y = \frac{2z}{k}$

In 27 and 28, give an example of an equation of the form $ax = b$ that has:

27. no solution.   Sample: $0 \cdot h = 13$
28. all real numbers as solutions.   Sample: $0 \cdot t = 0$

Objective D: *Solve and check inequalities of the form $ax < b$.* (Lesson 2-8)

In 29–32, solve and check.

29. $8m \leq 16$ $m \leq 2$
30. $-250 < 5y$ $y > -50$
31. $-6u > 12$ $u < -2$
32. $-x \geq -1$ $x \leq 1$

In 33 and 34, a sentence is given. **a.** Solve. **b.** Graph the solution set on a number line.

33. $-\frac{1}{2}g \geq 5$
34. $3.6h < 720$
33, 34) See margin.

Objective E: *Evaluate expressions containing a factorial symbol.* (Lesson 2-10)

In 35 and 36, evaluate without using a calculator.

35. $4! + 3!$ 30
36. $\frac{16!}{14!}$ 240

In 37 and 38, use a calculator to evaluate.

37. $15! \approx 1.3077 \cdot 10^{12}$
38. $24! \approx 6.2045 \cdot 10^{23}$

In 39 and 40, **a.** true or false? **b.** Justify your answer. See below for 39b and 40b.

39. $\frac{10!}{10} = 1!$ a) False
40. $18! = 18 \cdot 17!$ a) True
41. Simplify $\frac{102!}{99!}$.   1,030,200

39b) $\frac{10!}{10} = \frac{10 \cdot 9!}{10} = 9! \neq 1 = 1!$
40b) $18! = 18 \cdot 17 \cdot 16 \cdot 15 \cdot \ldots \cdot 3 \cdot 2 \cdot 1 = 18 \cdot 17!$

136

Additional Answers

33a. $g \leq -10$

b.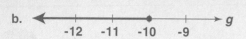

34a. $h < 200$

b.

PROPERTIES DEAL WITH THE PRINCIPLES BEHIND THE MATHEMATICS.

Objective F: *Identify and apply the following properties of multiplication.* *(Lessons 2-1, 2-2, 2-5, 2-6, 2-7, 2-8)*

Commutative Property of Multiplication
Associative Property of Multiplication
Multiplicative Identity Property of 1
Property of Reciprocals
Multiplication Property of Zero
Multiplication Property of Equality
Multiplication Property of Inequality
Multiplication Property of -1

42. Give an instance of the Associative Property of Multiplication. **Sample: $2 \cdot (3 \cdot 7) = (2 \cdot 3) \cdot 7$**

43. a. Simplify in your head: $4 \cdot x \cdot 25 \cdot 22$

  b. What properties can aid you in the simplification? **a) 2200x; b) Commutative and Associative Properties of Multiplication**

Commutative Property of Multiplication
44. $3 \cdot a = a \cdot 3$ is an instance of what property?

In 45–47, write the reciprocal of the given number.

45. -2 $-\frac{1}{2}$ **46.** 0.6 $\frac{5}{3}$ **47.** $\frac{3}{4}x$ $\frac{4}{3x}$

48. Write in symbols: The product of a number and its reciprocal is the multiplicative identity. $a \cdot \frac{1}{a} = 1$

49. Of what property is this an instance? If $m = n$, then $12m = 12n$. **See below.**

50. If $-12x < 4$, what inequality results from multiplying both sides by $-\frac{1}{12}$? $x > -\frac{1}{3}$

51. Multiplication by -1 changes a number to its __?__. **opposite**

49) Multiplication Property of Equality

USES DEAL WITH APPLICATIONS OF MATHEMATICS IN REAL SITUATIONS.

Objective G: *Apply the Area Model for Multiplication in real situations.* *(Lessons 2-1, 2-8)*

52. Consider the sketch of the $9' \times 12'$ area rug below. What is the area of the shaded part? **48 ft²**

53. The Cohens have a rectangular flower garden with length ℓ and width w. The Banerjils' vegetable garden is half as long and two thirds as wide.

  a. What are the dimensions of the Banerjils' garden? $\frac{1}{2}\ell$ **by** $\frac{2}{3}w$

  b. How do the areas of the two gardens compare? **See below.**

54. A box of grass seed will cover about 5000 square feet. The median strip on a boulevard is 60 ft wide. How long a strip can be seeded with one box? $83\frac{1}{3}$ **ft**

55. The volume of a storage bin needs to be 100,000 cubic feet. The base of the bin is a rectangle with dimensions 40 feet and 80 feet. What should the height be? **31.25 ft**

53b) The Banjerils' garden is $\frac{1}{3}$ the size of the Cohens' garden.

56. What is the volume of a box that is 12 cm long, 15 cm high, and 8 cm wide? **1440 cm³**

57. How many cubes of sugar with sides of length s can fit in a rectangular solid with dimensions $10s$ by $12s$ by $6s$? Explain how you get your answer. **720;** The volume of the solid is $720s^3$ and the volume of the cube is s^3. So $720s^3/s^3 = 720$.

Objective H: *Apply the Rate Factor Model for Multiplication to real situations.* *(Lessons 2-4, 2-6, 2-8)*

58. Express the rent for k months on an apartment that rents for $450 per month. **450 k dollars**

59. At 30 miles per gallon and $1.00 per gallon of gas, what is the cost per mile? **$0.033 or $3\frac{1}{3}$¢**

60. There are 43,560 sq ft/acre. How many square feet are there in 24 acres? **1,045,440 ft²**

61. A hairdresser charges 15 dollars per cut. How much will he earn in 5 hours if he does 3 cuts per hour? **$225**

62. On the average, B books fit on 1 foot of shelf space. If one bookcase has 24 feet of shelf space, how many books can fit on C such bookcases? **24BC**

63. How long does it take to drive from Baton Rouge to Tallahassee, a distance of 446 miles, if a person can average 50 mph? **8.92 hours or 8 hr 55 min**

Chapter 2 *Chapter Review* **137**

64. Daniel budgeted $550 for accommodations. The hotel costs $45 a day. At most how many days can he stay at the hotel? **12 days**

65. a. What is the reciprocal rate of the rate in italics below? $\frac{1}{2}$ **second per revolution**
A ballet dancer makes *2 revolutions per second* while pirouetting. **b) See below.**

   b. Explain the meaning of the result in part **a.**

66. Use the rates below to find the price per box.
$$24 \frac{\text{boxes}}{\text{carton}} \text{ and } 75.30 \frac{\text{dollars}}{\text{carton}} \approx \$3.14/\text{box}$$

65b) It takes a pirouetting ballet dancer $\frac{1}{2}$ second to make one revolution.

Objective I: *Apply the Multiplication Counting Principle and the Permutation Theorem.*
(Lessons 2-9, 2-10)

ΑΒΓΔΕΖΗΘΙΚΛΜΝΞΟΠΣΤΥΦΧΨΩ

67. The Greek alphabet has the 24 letters shown above. How many 3-letter monograms are possible if you may use a letter more than once? (3-letter monograms often are used to name fraternities and sororities.)
$24^3 = 13,824$

68. All 10 questions on a quiz are multiple choice, each with 5 possible choices. How many different sets of answers are possible on the test? **9,765,625**   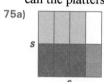 $18! \approx 6.4 \cdot 10^{15}$

69. A parade is going to contain 18 different groups (bands, dancers, and so on). In how many different orders can they march?

70. A class of 30 students is lined up to go into the school after recess. In how many ways can they be arranged? $30! \approx 2.65 \cdot 10^{32}$

71. A restaurant serves enchiladas. The customer has a choice of f fillings and s sauces. How many different types of enchiladas are possible? fs

72. A catering service is setting up a buffet table with p platters of food. In how many ways can the platters be arranged in a line? $p!$

75a)
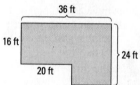

REPRESENTATIONS DEAL WITH PICTURES, GRAPHS, OR OBJECTS THAT ILLUSTRATE CONCEPTS.

Objective J: *Use rectangles, rectangular solids, or rectangular arrays to picture multiplication.*
(Lessons 2-1, 2-3)

73. Below are two rectangles with $A_1 = A_2$. What property of multiplication is illustrated?
Commutative Property of Multiplication

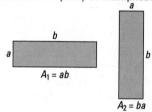

$A_1 = ab$

$A_2 = ba$

74. The square below has side of length 1. What multiplication of fractions does the drawing represent? $\frac{2}{3} \cdot \frac{1}{2}$

75a) See above.

75. Draw a square with side of length s.

   a. Shade or color the diagram to show $\frac{s}{2} \cdot \frac{3s}{4}$.

   $\frac{3}{8}s^2$ **b.** What is the result of the multiplication?

76. All angles in the L-shaped floor plan of a house illustrated below are right angles. What is the area of the base of the house?
704 ft^2

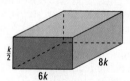

36 ft

16 ft

24 ft

20 ft

77. Find the volume of the rectangular solid pictured below. $24k^3$

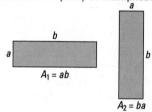

$\frac{k}{2}$

6k

8k

78. What is the volume of a box with dimensions 0.3 meter, 0.45 meter, and 4 meters? **0.54 m³**

79. A spreadsheet has rows numbered 1 to 100 and columns labeled A through Z. How many cells are in the spreadsheet? **2600**

80. How many dots are in the array at right? **736 dots**

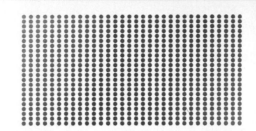

REFRESHER

Refresher

There are two ways you could use this Refresher. If you know that your students have a particularly weak background in addition as it relates to algebra, you may wish to assign this refresher to better prepare them for Chapter 3. If you do not know what your students' backgrounds are, you can use these pages as both a diagnostic tool and as remediation.

Have students do the odd-numbered questions as a part of the first assignment for the chapter, and check their answers with those given in the back of their books. If they missed more than a few questions, they should see you for help with the even-numbered questions.

Parts A and B of the Refresher cover content in Lesson 3-2, Part C covers content reviewed in Lesson 3-3, and Part D covers the simplest equations of the form seen in Lesson 3-5.

Chapter 3, which discusses addition in algebra, assumes that you have mastered certain objectives in your previous mathematics courses. Use these questions to check your mastery.

A. Add positive numbers or quantities.
In 1–14, find the sum.

1. $3.5 + 4.3$ **7.8**   **2.** $122.4 + 11 + .16$ **133.56**

3. $3.024 + 7.9999$ **11.0239**   **4.** $1\frac{1}{2} + 2\frac{1}{4}$ **3$\frac{3}{4}$**

5. $\frac{2}{3} + 8\frac{1}{3}$ **9**   **6.** $\frac{2}{5} + \frac{1}{6} + \frac{3}{7}$ **$\frac{209}{210}$**

7. $6\% + 12\%$ **18%**   **8.** $20\% + 11.2\%$ **31.2%**

9. $11 \text{ cm} + .03 \text{ cm}$ **10.** $0.4 \text{ km} + 1.9 \text{ km}$ **2.3 km**

11. $2'3'' + 9''$ **3'**   **12.** $6' + 11'' + 4''$ **7'3''**

13. $30 \text{ oz} + 8 \text{ lb}$ **158 oz or 9 lb 14 oz**

14. $4 \text{ lb } 13 \text{ oz} + 2 \text{ lb } 12 \text{ oz}$ **7 lb 9 oz**

9) 11.03 cm

B. Add positive and negative integers.
In 15–20, find the sum.

15. $30 + \text{-}6$ **24**   **16.** $\text{-}11 + \text{-}4$ **-15**

17. $\text{-}1 + \text{-}1 + 3$ **1**   **18.** $\text{-}99 + 112$ **13**

19. $\text{-}2 + 4 + \text{-}6$ **-4**   **20.** $8 + \text{-}8 + \text{-}8 + \text{-}8$ **-16**

In 21 and 22, what addition problem is pictured on the number line?

21.

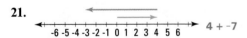

4 + -7

22.

-3 + -4

C. Graph ordered pairs on the coordinate plane. In 23–31, draw a set of axes as shown below. Plot and label each point.

23. $A = (4, 3)$ **24.** $B = (5, \text{-}2)$

25. $C = (\text{-}2, 4)$ **26.** $D = (\text{-}3, \text{-}1)$

27. $E = (0, 4)$ **28.** $F = (0, 2)$

29. $G = (\text{-}3, 0)$ **30.** $H = (3, 0)$

31. $I = (0, 0)$

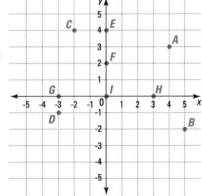

D. Solve equations of the form $x + a = b$, where a and b are positive integers. In 32–37, solve the equation.

32. $x + 3 = 11$ **x = 8**

33. $9 + z = 40$ **z = 31**

34. $665 + w = 1072$ **w = 407**

35. $7 = m + 2$ **m = 5**

36. $2000 = n + 1461$ **n = 539**

37. $472 = 173 + s$ **s = 299**

38. The sum of a number and 75 is 2000. What is the number? **1925**

Chapter 2   *Chapter Review*   **139**

Setting Up Lesson 3-1

We strongly recommend that you assign Lesson 3-1, both reading and some questions, for homework the evening of the test. It gives students work to do after they have completed the test and keeps the class moving.

Adapting to Individual Needs

The student text is written for the vast majority of students. The chart at the right suggests two pacing plans to accommodate the needs of your students. Students in the Full Course should complete the entire text by the end of the year. Students in the Minimal Course will spend more time when there are quizzes and more time on the Chapter Review. Therefore, these students may not complete all of the chapters in the text.

Options are also presented to meet the needs of a variety of teaching and learning styles. For each lesson, the Teacher's Edition provides sections entitled: *Video* which describes video segments and related questions that can be used for motivation or extension; *Optional Activities* which suggests activities that employ materials, physical models, technology, and cooperative learning; and, *Adapting to Individual Needs* which regularly includes **Challenge** problems, **English Language Development** suggestions, and suggestions for providing **Extra Help.** The Teacher's Edition also frequently includes an **Error Alert,** an **Extension,** and an **Assessment** alternative. The options available in Chapter 3 are summarized in the chart below.

Chapter 3 Pacing Chart

Day	Full Course	Minimal Course
1	3-1	3-1
2	3-2	3-2
3	3-3	3-3
4	Quiz*; 3-4	Quiz*; begin 3-4.
5	3-5	Finish 3-4.
6	3-6	3-5
7	3-7	3-6
8	Quiz*; 3-8	3-7
9	3-9	Quiz*; begin 3-8.
10	3-10	Finish 3-8.
11	Self-Test	3-9
12	Review	3-10
13	Test*	Self-Test
14	Comprehensive	Review
15	Test*	Review
16		Test*
17		Comprehensive
18		Test*

*in the Teacher's Resource File

In the Teacher's Edition...

Lesson	Optional Activities	Extra Help	Challenge	English Language Development	Error Alert	Extension	Cooperative Learning	Ongoing Assessment
3-1	●	●	●	●	●	●	●	Written
3-2	●	●	●	●	●	●	●	Written
3-3	●	●	●	●		●	●	Group
3-4	●	●	●	●	●	●	●	Written
3-5	●	●	●	●	●	●		Oral
3-6	●	●	●	●		●	●	Oral
3-7	●	●	●	●	●	●	●	Group
3-8	●	●	●	●		●	●	Oral
3-9	●	●	●	●	●	●	●	Group
3-10	●	●	●		●	●		Written

In the Additional Resources...

Lesson	In the Teacher's Resource File								
	Lesson Masters, A and B	Teaching Aids*	Activity Kit*	Answer Masters	Technology Sourcebook	Assessment Sourcebook	Visual Aids**	Technology	Video Segments
3-1	3-1	21, 24	5	3-1			21, 24, AM		
3-2	3-2	21, 25		3-2			21, 25, AM		
3-3	3-3	21, 26, 27		3-3	Comp 6		21, 26, 27, AM	GraphExplorer	
3-4	3-4	22, 28–30		3-4	Comp 7	Quiz	22, 28–30, AM	GeoExplorer	
3-5	3-5	19, 22	6	3-5			19, 22, AM		
In-class Activity		31		3-6			31, AM		
3-6	3-6	22, 26		3-6			22, 26, AM		
3-7	3-7	22	7	3-7		Quiz	22, AM		
3-8	3-8	23, 32		3-8	Comp 8		23, 32, AM	Spreadsheet	
3-9	3-9	23		3-9			23, AM		
3-10	3-10	5, 23		3-10	Comp 9		5, 23, AM	Spreadsheet	
End of chapter				Review		Tests			

*Teaching Aids are pictured on pages 140C and 140D. The activities in the Activity Kit are pictured on page 140C. Teaching Aid 31 which accompanies the In-class Activity preceding Lesson 3-6 is pictured with the lesson notes on page 176.

**Visual Aids provide transparencies for all Teaching Aids and all Answer Masters.

Also available is the Study Skills Handbook which includes study-skill tips related to reading, note-taking, and comprehension.

Integrating Strands and Applications

	3-1	3-2	3-3	3-4	3-5	3-6	3-7	3-8	3-9	3-10
Mathematical Connections										
Algebra	●	●	●	●	●	●	●	●	●	●
Geometry	●	●			●	●	●	●	●	
Measurement	●				●	●	●	●	●	
Patterns and Functions	●	●	●	●	●	●	●	●	●	●
Discrete Mathematics			●				●			
Interdisciplinary and Other Connections										
Music		●						●		
Literature				●						
Science	●	●	●	●	●	●		●	●	●
Social Studies	●	●	●	●	●	●		●	●	●
Multicultural	●		●	●		●		●		
Technology					●			●		
Career							●		●	
Consumer	●	●	●	●	●	●	●	●	●	●
Sports	●	●								
Art								●		

Teaching and Assessing the Chapter Objectives

Chapter 3 Objectives (Organized into the SPUR categories—Skills, Properties, Uses, and Representations)	Lessons	Progress Self-Test Questions	Chapter Review Questions	Chapter Test, Forms A and B	Chapter Test, Forms C	Chapter Test, Forms D
Skills						
A: Use the Distributive Property and the properties of addition to simplify expressions.	3-1, 3-2, 3-6, 3-7, 3-9	1–4	1–6	1–4, 13	2	
B: Solve and check equations of the form $x + a = b$ and $ax + b = c$.	3-2, 3-5, 3-6, 3-7	8–11	7–18	7–10	1	✓
C: Add algebraic fractions.	3-9	6, 7	19–24	5, 6	3	
D: Solve and check inequalities of the form $ax + b < c$.	3-10	12, 15	25–30	12	4	
Properties						
E: Identify and apply properties of addition or the Distributive Property.	3-1, 3-2, 3-6, 3-7, 3-9	5, 13, 14	31–38	11	2	
F: Use the Distributive Property to perform calculations in your head.	3-7	17	39–42	24	2	
Uses						
G: Apply models of addition to write linear expressions or to solve sentences of the forms $x + a = b$, $ax + b = c$, $ax + b < c$.	3-1, 3-2, 3-5, 3-6, 3-10	18, 19	43–49	14, 15	1	✓
H: Write expressions and solve problems involving linear patterns with two variables	3-8	16	50–53	16		
Representations						
I: Draw and interpret two-dimensional graphs.	3-3	23, 24	54–60	20–22	6	✓
J: Draw and interpret two-dimensional slides on a coordinate graph.	3-4	21, 22	61–65	18, 19	5	
K: Use balance scales or area models to represent expressions or sentences.	3-5, 3-6, 3-7, 3-10	20	66–70	17		
L: Graph solutions to inequalities of the form $ax + b < c$ on a number line.	3-10	12	71–74	23	4	

In the Assessment Sourcebook

Multidimensional Assessment
Quiz for Lessons 3-1 through 3-3
Quiz for Lessons 3-4 through 3-7

Chapter 3 Test, Forms A–D
Chapter 3 Test, Cumulative Form

Comprehensive Test, Chapters 1–3

Quiz and Test Writer
Multiple forms of chapter tests and quizzes; Challenges

Activity Kit

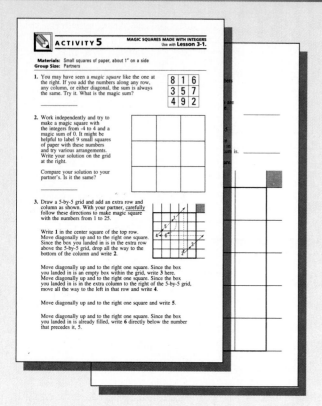

ACTIVITY 5
MAGIC SQUARES MADE WITH INTEGERS
Use with **Lesson 3-1.**

Materials: Small squares of paper, about 1" on a side
Group Size: Partners

1. You may have seen a *magic square* like the one at the right. If you add the numbers along any row, any column, or either diagonal, the sum is always the same. Try it. What is the magic sum?

8	1	6
3	5	7
4	9	2

2. Work independently and try to make a magic square with the integers from -4 to 4 and a magic sum of 0. It might be helpful to label 9 small squares of paper with these numbers and try various arrangements. Write your solution on the grid at the right.

   Compare your solution to your partner's. Is it the same?

3. Draw a 5-by-5 grid and add an extra row and column as shown. With your partner, carefully follow these directions to make magic square with the numbers from 1 to 25.

   Write **1** in the center square of the top row. Move diagonally up and to the right one square. Since the box you landed in is in the extra row above the 5-by-5 grid, drop all the way to the bottom of the column and write **2**.

   Move diagonally up and to the right one square. Since the box you landed in is an empty box within the grid, write **3** here. Move diagonally up and to the right one square. Since the box you landed in is in the extra column to the right of the 5-by-5 grid, move all the way to the left in that row and write **4**.

   Move diagonally up and to the right one square and write **5**.

   Move diagonally up and to the right one square. Since the box you landed in is already filled, write **6** directly below the number that precedes it, 5.

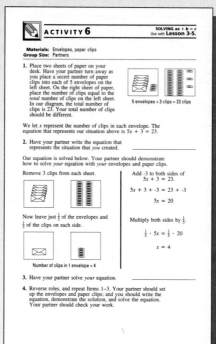

ACTIVITY 6
SOLVING $ax + b = c$
Use with **Lesson 3-5.**

Materials: Envelopes, paper clips
Group Size: Partners

1. Place two sheets of paper on your desk. Have your partner turn away as you place a secret number of paper clips into each of 5 envelopes on the left sheet. On the right sheet of paper, place the number of clips equal to the *total* number of clips on the left sheet. In our diagram, the total number of clips is 23. Your total number of clips should be different.

   5 envelopes + 3 clips = 23 clips

   We let x represent the number of clips in each envelope. The equation that represents our situation above is $5x + 3 = 23$.

2. Have your partner write the equation that represents the situation that *you* created.

   Our equation is solved below. Your partner should demonstrate how to solve *your* equation with *your* envelopes and paper clips.

   Remove 3 clips from each sheet.

   | Add -3 to both sides of $5x + 3 = 23$.
   $5x + 3 + -3 = 23 + -3$
   $5x = 20$

   Now leave just $\frac{1}{5}$ of the envelopes and $\frac{1}{5}$ of the clips on each side.

   | Multiply both sides by $\frac{1}{5}$.
   $\frac{1}{5} \cdot 5x = \frac{1}{5} \cdot 20$
   $x = 4$

   Number of clips in 1 envelope = 4

3. Have your partner solve *your* equation.

4. Reverse roles, and repeat Items 1–3. Your partner should set up the envelopes and paper clips; and you should write the equation, demonstrate the solution, and solve the equation. Your partner should check your work.

ACTIVITY 7
THE DISTRIBUTIVE PROPERTY: REMOVING PARENTHESES
Use with **Lesson 3-7.**

Materials: Algebra tiles
Group Size: Partners

1. You may already have used algebra tiles for demonstrating a number of algebraic properties. On your desk, place the algebra tiles pictured. Explain why the areas of the three different tiles are 1, x, and x^2.

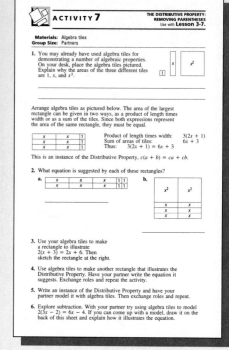

Arrange algebra tiles as pictured below. The area of the largest rectangle can be given in two ways, as a product of length times width or as a sum of the areas of the tiles. Since both expressions represent the area of the same rectangle, they must be equal.

Product of length times width: $3(2x + 1)$
Sum of areas of tiles: $6x + 3$
Thus: $3(2x + 1) = 6x + 3$

This is an instance of the Distributive Property, $c(a + b) = ca + cb$.

2. What equation is suggested by each of these rectangles?

   a.   b.

3. Use your algebra tiles to make a rectangle to illustrate $2(x + 3) = 2x + 6$. Then sketch the rectangle at the right.

4. Use algebra tiles to make another rectangle that illustrates the Distributive Property. Have your partner write the equation it suggests. Exchange roles and repeat the activity.

5. Write an instance of the Distributive Property and have your partner model it with algebra tiles. Then exchange roles and repeat.

6. Explore subtraction. With your partner try using algebra tiles to model $2(3x - 2) = 6x - 4$. If you can come up with a model, draw it on the back of this sheet and explain how it illustrates the equation.

Teaching Aids

Teaching Aid 5, Number Lines, (shown on page 4D) can be used with **Lesson 3-10.**
Teaching Aid 19, Balance Scales, (shown on page 70D) can be used with **Lesson 3-5.**

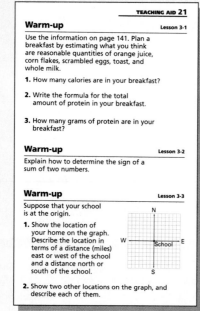

TEACHING AID 21

Warm-up   Lesson 3-1

Use the information on page 141. Plan a breakfast by estimating what you think are reasonable quantities of orange juice, corn flakes, scrambled eggs, toast, and whole milk.

1. How many calories are in your breakfast?

2. Write the formula for the total amount of protein in your breakfast.

3. How many grams of protein are in your breakfast?

Warm-up   Lesson 3-2

Explain how to determine the sign of a sum of two numbers.

Warm-up   Lesson 3-3

Suppose that your school is at the origin.

1. Show the location of your home on the graph. Describe the location in terms of a distance (miles) east or west of the school and a distance north or south of the school.

2. Show two other locations on the graph, and describe each of them.

TEACHING AID 22

Warm-up   Lesson 3-4

Name four points that are 1 unit away from (98, 32).

Warm-up   Lesson 3-5

Write the opposite and the reciprocal of each number.

1. -9   2. $\frac{2}{3}$ 3. 12   4. 1.5   5. -20
6. $\frac{1}{8}$ 7. -4   8. 16   9. $-2\frac{1}{2}$ 10. 3.65

Warm-up   Lesson 3-6

A pack of NBA basketball cards costs $2.19. Ellen bought four packs of cards last week, three packs yesterday, and two packs today.

1. How much did she spend on basketball cards, excluding tax?

2. Explain two ways in which you can find the answer.

Warm-up   Lesson 3-7

Simplify each expression.

1. $2x^2 + x^2 + 5$ 2. $y^2 + y + 4y + 2$
3. $6 + z^2 + -z^2 + 1$ 4. $4a + -3a + 8a$
5. $b^2 + 7b + 2 + 6b + -2$ 6. $-6 + 7 + 4 + -2 + 3 + 2$

TEACHING AID 23

Warm-up   Lesson 3-8

Students collected food for a food drive and displayed canned goods in a pyramid. The top three rows of the pyramid are shown at the right.

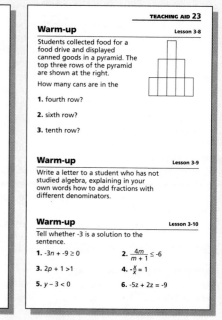

How many cans are in the

1. fourth row?

2. sixth row?

3. tenth row?

Warm-up   Lesson 3-9

Write a letter to a student who has not studied algebra, explaining in your own words how to add fractions with different denominators.

Warm-up   Lesson 3-10

Tell whether -3 is a solution to the sentence.

1. $-3n + -9 \geq 0$ 2. $\frac{4m}{m + 1} \leq -6$
3. $2p + 1 > 1$ 4. $-\frac{x}{x} = 1$
5. $y - 3 < 0$ 6. $-5z + 2z = -9$

140C

Additional Examples

1. Paula baby-sat on three days last week: 2 hours on Monday, w hours on Wednesday, and $3\frac{1}{2}$ hours on Saturday. Altogether, she baby-sat for 8 hours. Write an equation relating w and the other quantities.

2. During a drought, the level of Cottonwood Creek dropped 18 inches. After a storm, it rose 2 inches. Later, the level dropped 4 inches.
  a. Find the net change.
  b. As a check, picture this situation on a number line.

3. Ms. Worth was driving at 40 miles per hour. She sped up 15 miles an hour and then slowed down 20 miles an hour. Write an addition problem to represent these changes, and find her resulting speed.

4. Simplify $(-6 + j) + (15 + k)$.

5. Mr. Carlson is making a set of shelves. He started with a board t feet long. He cut off 3 shelves, each of which is 2 feet long, and he has a piece e feet long left over. Write a formula for t in terms of e.

Addition and Multiplication Properties

	Addition	Multiplication
Identity Property	$a + 0 = a$	$a \cdot 1 = a$
Inverse Property	$a + -a = 0$	For $a \neq 0$, $a \cdot \frac{1}{a} = 1$
Commutative Property	$a + b = b + a$	$a \cdot b = b \cdot a$
Associative Property	$a + (b + c) = (a + b) + c$	$a \cdot (b \cdot c) = (a \cdot b) \cdot c$

Challenge

The operation ✤ is defined below over the set $S = \{a, b, c, t\}$.

✤	a	b	c	t
a	b	t	a	t
b	t	c	b	a
c	a	b	c	t
t	t	a	t	b

1. Does this operation have an identity element? If so, what is it?
2. Is this operation commutative? If no, give a counterexample.
3. Is this operation associative? If no, give a counterexample.

Graph Paper

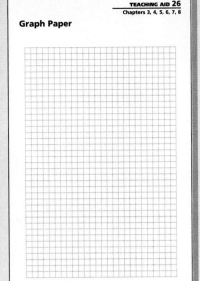

Additional Examples 2, 4 and 5

2. The average normal monthly temperatures (Fahrenheit) in Barrow, Alaska, are:

Jan. -14° Feb. -20° Mar. -16° Apr. -2°
May 19°   June 33°   July 39°   Aug. 38°
Sept. 31° Oct. 14°   Nov. -1°   Dec. -13°

  a. Graph the temperatures.
  b. When is the average temperature above freezing?
  c. Describe the temperature changes.

4. The graph shows the number of people who were in a classroom over a period of time. Write a story that explains the graph.

5. A graph can be made purposely misleading. The two graphs show the same data. Which graph is misleading and why?

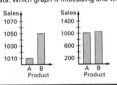

Four-Quadrant Graph Paper

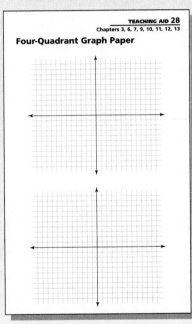

Examples 1 and 2

Example 1

Example 2

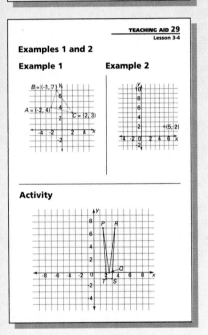

Activity

Additional Examples

1. a. Plot $\triangle RTX$, where $R = (-4, -1)$, $T = (3, 1)$ and $X = (0, -4)$.
  b. Draw the image $R'T'X'$ after sliding left 3 units and up 7 units. Find the coordinates of R', T', and X'.

2. Give the coordinates of the image of (x, y) under a slide 4 units to the left.

3. The ears of a rabbit are shown in the Activity on page 165. On the graph below, Figure $STUVW$ shows the head of the rabbit. Use the rule that the image of (x, y) is $(x + -5, y + 2)$, and draw the image of this figure. Label the image $S'T'U'V'W'$.

4. Find the images of points $P = (7, 2)$ and $Q = (-8, 1)$ under a slide of 6 units to the right and 5 units down.

Additional Examples 1–4

Use the pattern below for 1–3.

1st   2nd   3rd

1. Suppose each succeeding design is made by adding 7 stars to the previous design. How many stars will the 4th design in the pattern contain?

2. How many stars are needed for the
  a. 8th design? **b.** nth design?

3. If a design is made with 80 stars, what design number in the sequence is it?

4. If it costs $1.50 for the first hour and $0.60 for each additional hour to park in a large city, what does it cost to park for n hours?

Challenge

Find the perimeter of diagrams that have 1, 2, 3, 4 and 5 pentagons. Then write an expression for the perimeter of a diagram with n pentagons.

140D

Chapter Opener

CHAPTER 3

Pacing

We recommend spending 13 to 16 days on this chapter, including 1 day to review the Progress Self-Test, 1 to 2 days for the Chapter Review, and 1 day for a test. You may wish to spend a day on projects, and possibly a day is needed for quizzes. A test covering Chapters 1–3 is provided in the *Assessment Sourcebook*. This Comprehensive Test can be used as a quarter exam.

Using Pages 140–141

Health Connection The calculation of many kinds of totals involves both multiplication and addition. When food items are bought in a grocery store, the weight or the number of packages of each item is multiplied by its unit price; these products are added to determine the amount of money to be paid. In the situation shown here, the number of servings of each item is multiplied by the number of calories (or amount of protein, vitamin A, fat, or cholesterol), and then these products are added to find the total number of calories. The formula on the bottom of page 141 is an example of a linear combination. A linear combination is one kind of linear expression. The other kind involves constants, like the 5 in the linear expression $3x + 6y + 5$.

140

Chapter 3 Overview

This chapter has three distinguishable parts. The first part should take about a week and includes Lessons 3-1 to 3-4. These lessons cover the basic properties of addition in algebra and a review of graphing in the coordinate plane. The graphing is placed here because addition of positive and negative numbers is wonderfully pictured by two-dimensional slides on the coordinate plane. The second part of the chapter connects addition with multiplica-tion. Because multiplication has already been discussed, we are able to immediately consider equations of the form $ax + b = c$ and to examine the Distributive Property in some detail. This is done in Lessons 3-5 to 3-7. The third part of the chapter, comprising Lessons 3-8 to 3-10, continues the discussion of linear sentences. These are perhaps the most important sentences in elementary algebra, and, again, we are interested in the skills, properties, uses, and representations involving them.

The sentences that are solved in this chapter are equivalent to those of the form $ax + b = c$ or $ax + b > c$. When $a = 1$, they become the simpler sentences of the form $x + b = c$ and $x + b > c$. We do not solve $ax - b = c$ or $ax - b > c$ here; those sentences are covered in Chapter 4.

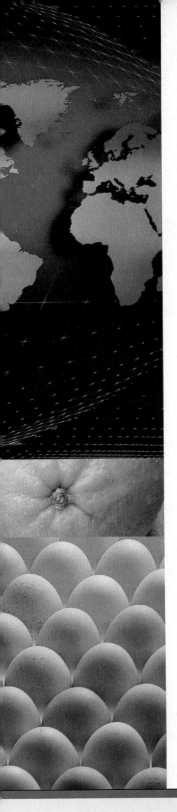

ADDITION IN ALGEBRA

There is an old saying, "You are what you eat." It is a shortened version of, "Tell me what you eat, and I will tell you what you are," written by the Frenchman Anthelme Brillat-Savarin in 1825, in a book entitled *The Physiology of Taste*.

Savarin was speaking about the tendency of different types of people to eat different foods. Today we know that foods affect not only personality but also health. For this reason, many people keep track of various ingredients in the foods they eat.

Suppose for breakfast today you ate the foods listed in the table below. The data are taken from the U.S. government document *Home and Garden Bulletin No. 72* and from information supplied by the American Heart Association.

Food	Protein	Energy	Vitamin A	Fat	Cholesterol
serving	*grams*	*calories*	*I.U.*	*grams*	*milligrams*
Orange juice (1 cup)	2	120	540	0.6	0
Corn flakes (1 cup)	2	95	1180	0.1	0
Eggs (1)	6	95	310	7.1	248
White toast (1 slice)	2	70	0	0.9	0
Whole milk (1 cup)	8	150	310	8	33

To determine the total number of calories you consumed or the amount of cholesterol in your breakfast, multiply the entries in each row by the number of portions you ate.

Suppose you had j cups of orange juice, c cups of corn flakes, e eggs, b pieces of toast, and m cups of milk. Then you would have consumed approximately

$$120j + 95c + 95e + 70b + 150m \text{ calories.}$$

This pattern involves multiplying variables by real numbers and adding the products. It is an example of a *linear expression*. Related ideas are studied in the next few chapters.

141

Photo Connections
The photo collage makes real-world connections to the content of the chapter: addition in algebra.

Fiber Optics: Fiber optic technology gives the communication industry the ability to transmit large volumes of information. Thousands of miles of optical fiber cable laid in the United States carry long-distance telephone communications faster and farther than conventional copper-wire lines and coaxial cables. The cost for telephone calls can be determined by using a form of the Distributive Property which is introduced in this chapter.

World Map: Locating a place on a globe usually requires that you know its latitude and longitude. Locations on a map can be identified by a pair of numbers called coordinates. The coordinate plane is covered in Lesson 3-3.

Oranges: To find a total number of items such as oranges, it is helpful to know properties of addition.

Bar Graph: Computers generate bar graphs to compare data such as the increase or decrease in profits. A stacked bar graph illustrates the Putting-Together Model for Addition.

Eggs: Eggs which are delivered in cartons to grocery stores are packaged in discrete arrays. The Distributive Property can be used to find the number of eggs.

Chapter 3 Projects
At this time you might want to have students look over the projects on pages 205–206.

Three forms of the Distributive Property are found in this chapter.
1. Adding or Subtracting Like Terms (Lesson 3-6):
   $$ax + bx = (a + b)x$$
   $$ax - bx = (a - b)x$$
2. Removing Parentheses (Lesson 3-7):
   $$c(a + b) = ca + cb$$
   $$c(a - b) = ca - cb$$
3. Adding Fractions (Lesson 3-9):
   $$\frac{a}{c} + \frac{b}{c} = \frac{a+b}{c}$$
   Although all these properties are derivable from the first form, they look different to students, and they need to be discussed individually.

Some people call the Adding Fractions Form the Distributive Property of Division over Addition. The two parts of Adding or Subtracting Like Terms and Removing Parentheses are sometimes called the Distributive Property of Multiplication over Addition and the Distributive Property of Multiplication over Subtraction. We believe our names are more descriptive.

Objectives

A Use properties of addition to simplify expressions.

E Identify the Commutative and Associative Properties of Addition.

G Apply the Putting-Together and Slide Models for Addition to write linear expressions and equations involving addition.

Resources

From the *Teacher's Resource File*
- Lesson Master 3-1A or 3-1B
- Answer Master 3-1
- Teaching Aids
  21 Warm-up
  24 Additional Examples
- Activity Kit, Activity 5

Additional Resources
- Visuals for Teaching Aids 21, 24

Teaching **3-1**
Lesson

Warm-up

Use the information on page 141. Plan a breakfast by estimating what you think are reasonable quantities of orange juice, corn flakes, scrambled eggs, toast, and whole milk.

1. How many calories are in your breakfast? **Responses will vary.**

2. Write the formula for the total amount of protein in your breakfast. **Grams of protein = $2g + 2c + 6e + 2b + 8m$**

3. How many grams of protein are in your breakfast? **Responses will vary.**

3-1

Models and Properties of Addition

Window shopping. *One South Wacker Drive is both the name and address of this office building. The skyscraper was designed with a step-like facade of reflective glass, allowing scenic views of downtown Chicago.*

The Putting-Together Model for Addition

Morgan Windows, Inc. (a fictitious company) has two plants, one in New York and one in New Orleans. The *bar graph* with separate bars for the two plants on the left below shows the profit made by each plant each year from 1990 to 1994. What patterns do you notice in this display?

❶ **Morgan Windows, Inc. 1990–1994 Annual Profits**

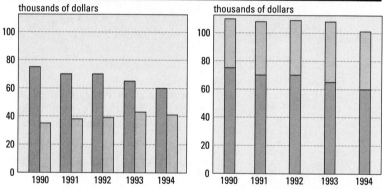

Refer to the graph on the left. Note how the bars representing profits in the New York plant get shorter as you read from left to right. This means that the profits in New York went down over the five-year period. In contrast, the profits for the New Orleans plant increased until 1993 and then decreased in 1994.

142

Lesson 3-1 Overview

Broad Goals This lesson reviews the basic applications and properties of addition, and it introduces the stacked bar graph as one representation of addition.

Perspective In this lesson we introduce students to models for addition. As with multiplication, you can think of models for addition as application postulates that connect addition to the real world. The Putting-Together Model involves the most funda-

mental use of addition. Children first learn to add by combining two groups and counting the number of items in the resulting group. Many uses of addition involve this idea, and some of them can be quite complicated. The Slide Model is the model we customarily use when we think of addition of positive and negative numbers.

Most students know when to add, so the contribution of models to students' choices

among operations may become more relevant in later chapters. However, models can also be used to verify properties. For example, in this lesson the profits from New York and New Orleans for Morgan Windows can be added in either order without changing the sum. In this way, the Putting-Together Model verifies the Commutative Property.

Are total profits for the two plants increasing or decreasing? To determine this, the data in the first bar graph can be rearranged into the *stacked bar graph* at the right. Each bar for the profit made in New Orleans is placed above the bar representing the profit made in New York for the same year. You can see that profits for the company were nearly constant until 1994.

To make this stacked bar graph, the two profits for each year shown in the left graph are added. For instance, in 1994, the New York plant had a profit of $60,000 and the New Orleans plant had a profit of $41,000. In total, they had a profit of $101,000. So the bar for 1994 is drawn to the 101 mark.

The stacked bar graph illustrates an important model for addition.

On the road again. *The cost of most business trips is covered by the company for whom the employee works.*

❷ **Putting-Together Model for Addition**
If a quantity x is put together with a quantity y *with the same units*, and there is no overlap, then the result is the quantity $x + y$.

Example 1

Ms. Kumar is given a daily allowance of $200 by her company for her travel expenses on a business trip. She spends $109.95 for her hotel room. She estimates that she will spend about $20.00 for gas and $7.50 for parking. Let E be the amount still available for other expenses. Write an equation to show how E is related to the other quantities.

Solution

The different expenses do not overlap, so the Putting-Together Model applies. The total allowance is $200.00. So
$$109.95 + 20.00 + 7.50 + E = 200.$$
This can be rewritten as
$$137.45 + E = 200.$$

The Slide Model for Addition

A second important model for addition is the *Slide Model*. In the Slide Model for Addition, positive numbers are shifts, or slides, in one direction. Negative numbers are slides in the opposite direction. The + sign means "followed by." The sum indicates the net result of the two slides.

❸ **Slide Model for Addition**
If a slide x is followed by a slide y, the result is the slide $x + y$.

The description of the Associative Property as the property that enables us to change the "order of additions" is different from the usual "change the grouping" description. We prefer the former description because grouping is a more difficult concept for students. But you should use the one that you prefer.

In **Example 4,** the result is given as $y + -12$ instead of $y - 12$ because the definition of subtraction has not yet been covered. If your students want to write $y - 12$, that is acceptable.

Additional Examples

These examples are also given on **Teaching Aid 24.**

1. Paula baby-sat on three days last week: 2 hours on Monday, w hours on Wednesday, and $3\frac{1}{2}$ hours on Saturday. Altogether, she baby-sat for 8 hours. Write an equation relating w and the other quantities. $2 + w + 3\frac{1}{2} = 8$, or $w + 5\frac{1}{2} = 8$

2. During a drought, the level of Cottonwood Creek dropped 18 inches. After a storm, it rose 2 inches. Later, the level dropped 4 inches.
   a. Find the net change. 20 in.
   b. As a check, picture this situation on a number line.

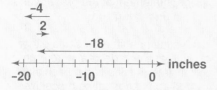

3. Ms. Worth was driving at 40 miles per hour. She sped up 15 miles an hour and then slowed down 20 miles an hour. Write an addition problem to represent these changes, and find her resulting speed. $40 + 15 + -20$; resulting speed is 35 mph

144

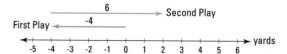

Example 2

A football team lost 4 yards on the first play and gained 6 yards on the second play. What is the net result of these two plays?

Solution

Think of -4 as a slide to the left. Think of 6 as a slide to the right. The net result is a slide to the right of 2 units. This means a net gain of 2 yards.
$$-4 + 6 = 2$$

Check

The two plays can be represented on a number line where 0 is the "line of scrimmage," or starting point, for the first play.

The first arrow, starting at 0 and ending at -4, indicates a loss of 4 yards. The next arrow, from -4 to 2, represents a gain of 6 yards. Notice that the result is a net gain of 2 yards.

The Slide Model can also describe the end result of changes from any arbitrary starting value.

Example 3

The temperature at 11 A.M. is $T°$. If it rises 3° during the next hour, what will be the temperature at noon?

Solution

This, too, is a slide. You can think of the mercury sliding up or down on a thermometer. At noon the temperature will be $T° + 3°$.

The Commutative and Associative Properties of Addition

Addition, like multiplication, has many properties. The examples for the Putting-Together and Slide Models can illustrate these properties.

When two quantities are put together, either quantity may come first. If the stacked bar graph at the start of the lesson had the bars representing profit in New York above the bars representing profit in New Orleans, the total heights would still be the same. For 1994, the total profit is

$$\$41,000 + \$60,000 = \$60,000 + \$41,000.$$

In Example 3, you could have written $3° + T°$ or $T° + 3°$. These are instances of a general pattern, the *Commutative Property of Addition.*

Commutative Property of Addition
For any real numbers a and b, $a + b = b + a$.

144

Adapting to Individual Needs

Extra Help

When discussing the Slide Model for Addition, review the idea of using the number line to represent addition of positive and negative numbers. Remind students that the starting point is always zero, that a positive number is represented by a slide to the right, and that a negative number is represented by a slide to the left. Also remind students that the stopping point of the final slide is the sum. They should realize that a

slide from zero to that stopping point would accomplish the same as the combined slides of the addends. The example at the right shows that starting at zero and sliding 3 units to the left and then 4 units to the right accomplishes the same as starting at zero and sliding 1 unit to the right; so $-3 + 4 = 1$.

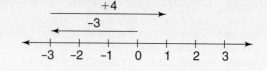

You can also regroup numbers being added without affecting the sum. For instance, the sum

$$(67 + 98) + 2$$

might be easier to calculate mentally if it is regrouped.

$$(67 + 98) + 2 = 67 + (98 + 2) = 67 + 100 = 167$$

This is an instance of the *Associative Property of Addition.*

④ Associative Property of Addition
For any real numbers *a, b,* and *c,* $(a + b) + c = a + (b + c)$.

As in multiplication, the Commutative and Associative Properties of Addition are used to evaluate or simplify expressions.

Example 4

Simplify $(-8 + y) + -4$.

Solution

First change the order, and then regroup.

$(-8 + y) + -4 = (y + -8) + -4$ Commutative Property of Addition
$ = y + (-8 + -4)$ Associative Property of Addition
$ = y + -12$

Experts often skip steps. They apply the Commutative and Associative Properties mentally. They simply write

$$(-8 + y) + -4 = y + -12, \text{ or } (-8 + y) + -4 = -12 + y.$$

Check

For any particular value of y, $(-8 + y) + -4$ must give the same value as $y + -12$. We substitute 7 for y, and then follow the order of operations.

Original: $(-8 + y) + -4 = (-8 + 7) + -4 = -1 + -4 = -5$
Answer: $y + -12 = 7 + -12 = -5$

Since both expressions have a value of -5, they are equal.

QUESTIONS

Covering the Reading

1. Refer to page 141. A person had 1 cup of orange juice, 1 cup of corn flakes, 2 slices of white bread, and $1\frac{1}{2}$ cups of milk for breakfast. How many calories did the person consume?
   580 calories
2. State the Putting-Together Model for Addition. **If a quantity x is put together with a quantity y with the same units, and there is no overlap, then the result is the quantity $x + y$.**

Lesson 3-1 *Models and Properties of Addition* **145**

4. Simplify $(-6 + j) + (15 + k)$.
   $j + k + 9$
5. Mr. Carlson is making a set of shelves. He started with a board t feet long. He cut off 3 shelves, each of which is 2 feet long, and he has a piece e feet long left over. Write a formula for t in terms of e. $t = 2 + 2 + 2 + e$ or $t = 6 + e$

Notes on Questions

Reading Mathematics Remind students that the term *simplify* has many meanings. In this set of questions, *simplify* means to "write an equal expression with fewer operation signs."

Question 1 Multicultural Connection The breakfast described here, and in the chapter opener, is a typical American breakfast. Students might be interested in "typical" breakfasts in other countries. In many European and South American countries, people eat a *continental breakfast,* which is a light meal consisting of bread or rolls with butter and jam and a beverage. In Japan, a breakfast consisting of soup, rice, grilled fish, pickles, and salad is not unusual. People in Egypt eat red beans mixed with a variety of other foods like onions, lentils or tomatoes, unleavened bread, and cheese. A Nigerian might have some soup and *gari,* the fried pulp of the cassava plant.

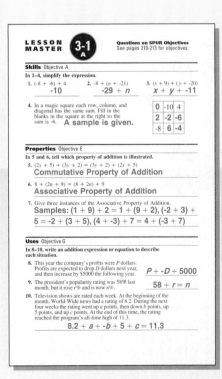

New Orleans. *Pictured is part of the French Quarter in New Orleans, Louisiana. Notice the distinctive geometric patterns on the iron grillwork.*

7a)

In 3–5, refer to the graphs of the profits for Morgan Windows, Inc.

3. In which year did both the New York and New Orleans plants show a decrease in profits? **1994**

4. Approximately what were the combined profits of both plants in 1990? **$110,000**

5. *True or false.* The total profits for Morgan Windows for the five years 1990–1994 can be found by adding the profits for each year in any order. **True**

6. A businessman spent $72.50 for a hotel room, $23.75 for food, and $20 for a cab ride. Write an equation relating these amounts and the amount E still available for other expenses from his $150 daily allowance. **72.50 + 23.75 + 20.00 + E = 150.00**

7. On the first play, a football team gained 7 yards. On the second play, the team lost 3 yards.
   a. Represent this situation on a number line. **See left.**
   b. What was the net result of the two plays? **a gain of 4 yards**

8. If the temperature is $T°$ and then it goes up 5°, what is the new temperature? **$T° + 5°$ or $5° + T°$**

In 9 and 10, simplify the expression.

9. $28 + (k + 30)$ **$k + 58$**   **10.** $(p + -139) + 639$ **$p + 500$**

In 11 and 12, *multiple choice.* Which addition property is illustrated?
(a) commutative only
(b) both commutative and associative
(c) associative only
(d) neither commutative nor associative

11. $2L + 2W = 2W + 2L$ **(a)**   **12.** $(2x + 3) + 4 = 2x + (3 + 4)$ **(c)**

Applying the Mathematics

In 13 and 14, make up your own example to illustrate the property.

13. Commutative Property of Addition **Sample: $5 + 3a = 3a + 5$**

14. Associative Property of Addition
Sample: $(a + 4) + 1 = a + (4 + 1) = a + 5$

15. Write an addition expression suggested by this situation. The temperature goes up $x°$, then falls 3°, and then rises 5°. **$x° + -3° + 5°$**

16. The symbol below at the left means $R = P + Q$. Fill in the empty squares in the large figure.

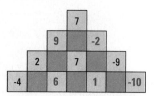

17. If Andy's age is now A, write an expression for his age at each time.
   a. 3 years from now **$A + 3$**
   b. 4 years ago **$A + -4$**

Adapting to Individual Needs

Challenge
Have students consider the operations ☆ and ✳, which are defined as $a ☆ b = 2a + b$ and $a ✳ b = 2ab$.

Have students determine several values for $a ☆ b$ and $a ✳ b$ by substituting values for a and b. Then ask if ☆ and ✳ are commutative operations and if they are associative operations. [✳ is both commutative and associative; ☆ is neither commutative nor associative.]

18. Use the bar graphs below.

Years of School Completed by Gender: 1991
(for persons 25 years old and over)

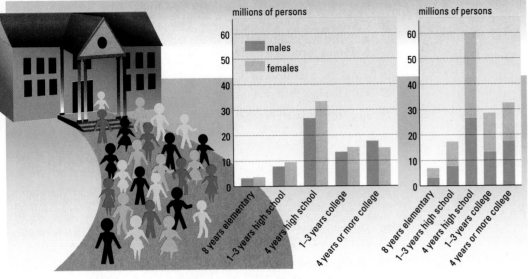

18a) about 30 million

b) about 60 million

c) Sample: More than half the number of students who completed 4 years of high school completed 4 or more years of college.

a. How many males have completed at least one year of college?

b. How many people have completed at least one year of college?

c. Write a sentence or two describing some other conclusion you can make from these data.

19. When Rita got on a scale it registered 50 kg. Then she held her baby in her arms, and the scale went up by x kg. It then read 54 kg. Write an equation using addition relating x, 50, and 54. $50 + x = 54$

20. a. Write an equation to express the area of the largest rectangle in terms of the areas of the smaller rectangles. $\text{Area} = 24 + 18 + x = 54$

b. Find x. Use trial and error if necessary. $x = 12$

c. Find the dimensions of each of the smaller rectangles. 4 in. by 6 in.; 3.6 in. by 5 in.; 2.4 in. by 5 in.

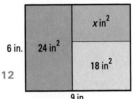

21. Write an inequality relating the three numbers mentioned in the following situation: The bill for lunch came to $10.50. Milo had M dollars. His sister Nancy had $4.25. Together they did not have enough to pay the bill. $M + 4.25 < 10.50$

In 22 and 23, simplify.

22. $(x + 4) + (5 + y)$ $x + y + 9$

23. $(a + -2) + (b + 7)$ $a + b + 5$

24. Use the associative and commutative properties to add mentally:
$$49.95 + 59.28 + 0.05 + 0.72. \quad 110$$

Lesson 3-1 *Models and Properties of Addition* **147**

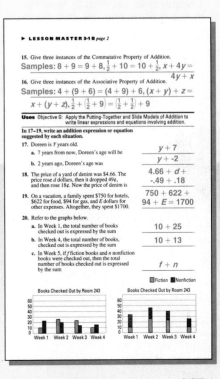

Question 28 Error Alert Some students may try to further simplify $90 + \sqrt{41}$. Because square roots are defined using multiplication, students should not expect any properties relating square roots and addition. This is the simplest form of the answer.

Question 29 This question contains specific cases of two of the properties to be discussed in Lesson 3-2.

Follow-up for Lesson 3-1

Practice

For more questions on SPUR Objectives, use **Lesson Master 3-1A** (shown on page 145) or **Lesson Master 3-1B** (shown on pages 146–147).

Assessment

Written Communication Have students each write a paragraph describing situations that could be represented by $6 + 3 + 7$. Have students decide if each situation is an example of the Slide Model for Addition or the Putting-Together Model for Addition. [Students' paragraphs reflect an understanding of the models of addition.]

Extension

Cooperative Learning Have students **work in groups** and investigate whether or not the operations of union and intersection are commutative and associative. For any sets, A, B, and C, have them tell if the following statements are true.
1. $A \cap B = B \cap A$ [Yes]
2. $A \cup B = B \cup A$ [Yes]
3. $(A \cap B) \cap C = A \cap (B \cap C)$ [Yes]
4. $(A \cup B) \cup C = A \cup (B \cup C)$ [Yes]

Project Update Project 1, *Survey Results*, on page 205, relates to the content of this lesson.

148

25b) Sample: When you multiply a number by 1, the product is the same as (or identical to) the number.

Review

25. **a.** What number is the multiplicative identity? 1
    b. Why is the name "multiplicative identity" used? *(Lesson 2-2)* See left.
26. Consider the table at the right. *(Lesson 1-9)*
    a. Write one additional row in the table.
    b. Find a formula for y in terms of x. $y = x^2$

x	y
1	1
2	4
3	9
4	16
5	25

In 27 and 28, refer to $\triangle ABD$. *(Lesson 1-8)*
27. Find the length of x. 13
28. Find the perimeter of $\triangle BCD$. $9 + \sqrt{41}$

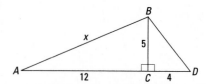

29. *Skill sequence.* Simplify without using a calculator. *(Previous course)*
    a. $12.6 + 0$ 12.6   **b.** $12.6 + \text{-}12.6$ 0   **c.** $-(\text{-}12.6 + 12.6)$ 0

30. *Skill sequence.* *(Previous course)*
    a. What is 16% of 24? 3.84
    b. What is 16% of 2400? 384
    c. Of the 24 million people aged 12–18 in the U.S., 16% like jazz. How many people is this? 3,840,000

Exploration

31. Seafood is sometimes cleaned with a saline solution. If the solution is made from $\frac{1}{4}$ cup salt and $\frac{3}{4}$ cup water, why won't there be a full cup of solution? Sample: When salt is added to water, most of the salt will dissolve in the water. Thus, there won't be a full cup of solution.

Setting Up Lesson 3-2

Be sure you have discussed students' responses to **Question 29** in Lesson 3-1. This question contains specific cases of two of the properties to be considered in Lesson 3-2.

Football for everyone. *Shown with their mascot are some members of a girl's high school football team formed for a fun, exhibition game. Addition can be used to find the total yards gained or lost by a team.*

Identity and Opposite Properties

Suppose you deposit $480 in a bank. If you make no withdrawal or deposit, you will have $480 + 0 or $480. Adding 0 to a number keeps the *identity* of that number. So 0 is called the **additive identity.**

> **Additive Identity Property**
> For any real number a, $a + 0 = 0 + a = a$.

The role of the number 0 in addition is similar to the role of the number 1 in multiplication. Recall that 1 is the multiplicative identity because
$$a \cdot 1 = 1 \cdot a = a.$$

Recall also that every number except zero has a multiplicative inverse or reciprocal. When $a \neq 0$, its multiplicative inverse is $\frac{1}{a}$. Every number, including 0, has an *additive inverse*.

Additive inverses can be illustrated by one slide followed by another of the same length, but in the opposite direction. For instance, suppose a football team were to first gain 7 yards and then lose 7 yards. After these two plays the team would be back at the original line of scrimmage. This situation shows that $7 + {-7} = 0$. Here is a picture using slides.

The numbers 7 and -7 are called *opposites,* or *additive inverses,* of each other. In general, the **opposite** of any real number a is written $-a$.

> **Property of Opposites**
> For any real number a, $a + {-a} = {-a} + a = 0$.

Lesson 3-2 *More Properties of Addition* **149**

Lesson 3-2

Objectives

A Use properties of addition to simplify expressions.
B Solve and check equations of the form $x + a = b$.
E Identify and apply the Additive Identity Property, the Property of Opposites, the Opposite of Opposites [Op-op] Property, and the Addition Property of Equality.
G Apply models for addition to write and solve equations of the form $x + a = b$.

Resources

From the *Teacher's Resource File*
■ Lesson Master 3-2A or 3-2B
■ Answer Master 3-2
■ Teaching Aids
   21 Warm-up
   25 Addition and Multiplication
      Properties and Challenge

Additional Resources
■ Visuals for Teaching Aids 21, 25

Teaching Lesson 3-2

Warm-up

✏ **Writing** Explain how to determine the sign of a sum of two numbers. **Sample: The sum is positive if both numbers are positive, and it is negative if both numbers are negative. If one number is positive and one number is negative, the sum has the same sign as the number with the larger absolute value. The sum is 0 if the numbers are opposites; zero is neither positive nor negative.**

Lesson 3-2 Overview

Broad Goals This lesson reviews basic properties that relate to zero and to opposites of numbers. It also introduces the Addition Property of Equality—the fundamental property needed to solve equations involving addition.

Perspective All four SPUR dimensions in addition are found in this lesson. The number line provides a visual *representation* of opposites. The *uses* of addition (football,

age, money, and so on) help give meaning to addition. The lesson reviews three *properties* involving opposites and applies properties to solving an equation. Throughout the lesson students practice *skills;* by the end of the chapter, we want them to be skilled in all aspects of addition.

The Slide Model gives a method for visualizing the Additive Identity Property and the Property of Opposites. Then in Chapter 4, it

should seem quite natural to define subtraction as $a - b = a + {-b}$. The context preceding the Addition Property of Equality will be used in Lesson 3-10 to introduce the Addition Property of Inequality.

As you discuss the lesson, be sure students understand each property. Also, make certain that they know how to add positive and negative numbers.

You might want to use the visual organizer shown in **Teaching Aid 25**, and discuss the parallels between the properties of addition and the properties of multiplication.

❶ When you discuss the Opposite of Opposites Property, emphasize (as you will have to do many times during the course of the year) that –*a* stands for a positive number when *a* is negative. This is the reason we call –*a* the "opposite of *a*" or "the additive inverse of *a*" and not "minus *a*."

Some teachers do not like the name Op-op; they think it does not convey the idea. Use either the short or the long name, whichever you prefer.

❷ You might want to use the *Optional Activity* on page 151 to introduce solving equations of the form *x* + *a* = *b*.

Remember that when you multiply two reciprocals, the product is 1, the multiplicative identity. Similarly, when you add two opposites, the sum is 0, the additive identity.

Example 1

Evaluate the following expressions.

a. $5 \cdot 10^{32} + \text{-}(5 \cdot 10^{32})$ **b.** $\left(\frac{11}{5} + \text{-}\frac{3}{5}\right) + \frac{3}{5}$

Solution

a. The numbers are opposites. So, $5 \cdot 10^{32} + \text{-}(5 \cdot 10^{32}) = 0$.

b. Here we write all the steps and the properties that justify them.

$$\left(\frac{11}{5} + \text{-}\frac{3}{5}\right) + \frac{3}{5} = \frac{11}{5} + \left(\text{-}\frac{3}{5} + \frac{3}{5}\right) \quad \text{Associative Property of Addition}$$

$$= \frac{11}{5} + 0 \quad \text{Property of Opposites}$$

$$= \frac{11}{5} \quad \text{Additive Identity}$$

Experts often skip steps or do them in their head. They can often see immediately that $\left(\frac{11}{5} + \text{-}\frac{3}{5}\right) + \frac{3}{5} = \frac{11}{5}$.

Every number has only one opposite. For instance, 10 is the only opposite of -10. But notice that the opposite of -10 can also be written as -(-10), read "the opposite of the opposite of 10." So, -(-10) must equal 10.

In general, the numbers *a* and -*a* are additive inverses, as are -*a* and -(-*a*). A number has only one additive inverse, so -(-*a*) = *a*. We call this the *Opposite of Opposites Property*, or the *Op-op Property*, for short.

❶ | **Opposite of Opposites (Op-op) Property**
For any real number *a*,   -(-*a*) = *a*.

Caution: The expression -*a* does not always represent a negative number. If *a* = 60, then -*a* is its opposite; so -*a* = -60. But if *a* = -60, then -*a* is the opposite of -60, so -*a* = 60. *When a is negative, -a is positive.*

The Addition Property of Equality

Suppose Tina's age is *T* years and Robert's age is *R* years. If Tina and Robert are the same age, then $T = R.$

Eight years from now, Tina's age will be *T* + 8 years and Robert's age will be *R* + 8 years. They will still be the same age, so

$$T + 8 = R + 8.$$

Similarly, Tina's age three years ago was *T* + -3 and Robert's age was *R* + -3. Since they would have been the same age then as well,

$$T + \text{-}3 = R + \text{-}3.$$

150

Visual Organizer

Teaching Aid 25 contains the visual organizer shown at the right. You might want to use the chart to show students the parallel structures between properties of addition and multiplication. In later chapters, you could add additional rows for the algebraic definitions of subtraction and division.

	Addition	Multiplication
Identity Property	$a + 0 = a$	$a \cdot 1 = a$
Inverse Property	$a + \text{-}a = 0$	For $a \neq 0$, $a \cdot \frac{1}{a} = 1$
Commutative Property	$a + b = b + a$	$a \cdot b = b \cdot a$
Associative Property	$a + (b + c) = (a + b) + c$	$a \cdot (b \cdot c) = (a \cdot b) \cdot c$

The equations relating Tina's and Robert's ages are instances of the general property known as the Addition Property of Equality.

> **Addition Property of Equality**
> For all real numbers a, b, and c, if $a = b$, then $a + c = b + c$.

The Addition Property of Equality is useful for solving equations. This property indicates that you can add any number c to both sides of the equation without changing its solutions. It is very much like the Multiplication Property of Equality that you studied in Lesson 2-6. Notice how the Addition Property of Equality is used in the first step of Solution 1 in Example 2.

Example 2

Solve $x + -26 = 83$, and check the answer.

Solution 1

We want the left side to simplify to just x. So we add 26 to both sides since 26 is the opposite of -26. Beginners put in all the steps.

$(x + -26) + 26 = 83 + 26$	Addition Property of Equality
$x + (-26 + 26) = 109$	Associative Property of Addition
$x + 0 = 109$	Property of Opposites
$x = 109$	Additive Identity Property

Solution 2

Experts do some work mentally and may write out fewer steps.

$x + -26 = 83$	
$x = 83 + 26$	Addition Property of Equality
$x = 109$	

Check

Substitute 109 for x in the original equation. Does $109 + -26 = 83$? Yes. So 109 is the solution.

All the steps were shown in Solution 1 to Example 2 to illustrate the properties that justify this process. Like the expert, you may not always need to include all steps in solving an equation. Directions in the problem and your teacher's instructions will guide you in choosing what steps to include.

The key to solving equations is knowing what should be done to both sides. For equations of the $x + a = b$ type, there is only one step to remember.

> To solve an equation of the form $x + a = b$, add $-a$ to both sides and simplify.

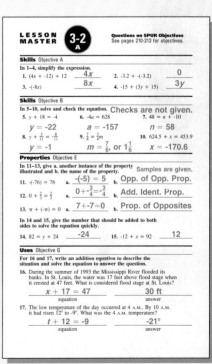

Example 3

Emily is saving money for a $179.95 compact-disc (CD) player. She has $75.50 so far. How much more money does Emily need?

Solution

Use an equation. Let x = the amount of money Emily still needs.

$$75.50 + x = 179.95$$

Add the opposite of 75.50 to each side of the equation.

$$x = 179.95 + \text{-}75.50$$

Simplify.

$$x = 104.45$$

She needs another $104.45 to buy the CD player.

Check

Does $75.50 + 104.45 = 179.95$? Yes, so the solution checks.

QUESTIONS

Covering the Reading

The CD boom. *In 1983, compact-disc players and recordings were introduced in the U.S. By 1986, Americans had purchased more CD players than turntables, making records almost obsolete.*

1. **a.** $0 + \text{-}10 = \underline{\ ?\ }$. -10   b) Adding zero to a number does not change
   b. Why is zero called the additive identity?   that number's value.
   c. What number is the multiplicative identity? 1

2. What is another name for an additive inverse? opposite

In 3–6, simplify.

3. $-\frac{9}{4} + \frac{9}{4}$ 0

4. $(x + \text{-}93.2) + 93.2$ x

5. $-(\text{-}7)$ 7

6. $-41 + \text{-}(\text{-}41)$ 0

7. **a.** What is the additive inverse of $-x$? $-(\text{-}x)$ or x
   b. Give a value of n for which $-n$ is positive.
      any negative value such as -6

In 8 and 9, an instance of what property is given?

8. $\sqrt{2} + \text{-}\sqrt{2} = 0$ **Property of Opposites**

9. $-y = 0 + \text{-}y$ Additive Identity Property

10) Four years from now you will still be the same age as your friend.

In 10 and 11, suppose your age is A, a friend's age is B, and $A = B$. What does each sentence mean?

10. $A + 4 = B + 4$ See left.

11. $A + \text{-}5 = B + \text{-}5$ Five years ago you were the same age as your friend.

12. State the Addition Property of Equality.
    For all real numbers a, b, and c, if $a = b$, then $a + c = b + c$.

13. You wish to solve $m + 42 = 87$.
    a. What number should be added to each side? -42
    b. Solve and check. $m = 45$; $45 + 42 = 87$

In 14 and 15, solve and check.

14. $-12 + y = -241$ $y = -229$
    $-12 + \text{-}229 = -241$

15. $z + 14 = 60$ $z = 46$
    $46 + 14 = 60$

152

Adapting to Individual Needs

Extra Help Help students to see that the Addition Property of Equality can be used to change a given equation to a simpler, equivalent equation. Begin by writing an equation such as $x + 5 = 12$ on the board. Illustrate that you can add any number to both sides to get an equation with the same solution. For example, adding 6 to both sides gives $x + 11 = 18$, adding –4 to both sides gives $x + 1 = 8$, and so on. However, adding –5 to both sides gives $x = 7$.

English Language Development To help reinforce the word *opposite*, have students name several opposites involving numbers [losing $5, finding $5; gaining 4 pounds, losing 4 pounds; 10-degree rise in the temperature, 10-degree fall in the temperature]. In each case, note that when taken together, the result is no change. Then point out that the Property of Opposites shows that the sum of two numbers is 0.

In 16 and 17, consider these steps used to solve $-173 + x = 209$.

Step 1: $\quad\quad\quad -173 + x = 209$
Step 2: $\quad 173 + -173 + x = 173 + 209$
Step 3: $\quad\quad\quad\quad 0 + x = 382$
Step 4: $\quad\quad\quad\quad\quad x = 382$

16. What property was used to get from step 1 to step 2?
    Addition Property of Equality
17. What property was used to get from step 3 to step 4?
    Additive Identity Property
18. Hank has $35.00. A graphics calculator costs $72.95. Let n equal the amount of money he needs.
    a. What addition equation can be solved to find out how much more money he needs? $35 + n = \$72.95$
    b. Solve this equation. $n = \$37.95$

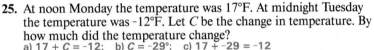

Applying the Mathematics

19. A right triangle has hypotenuse of length 17 cm and one leg of length 15 cm. Find the length of the other leg. 8 cm

20. Describe a real situation not involving football that leads to $-9 + 9 = 0$. See left.

21. Display the number 3.14 on your calculator. Press the +/– key twice.
    a. What number appears in the display? 3.14
    b. What property has been checked?
       Opposite of Opposites Property or the Op-op Property
22. If $p = -8$ and $q = -10$, then $-(p + q) = \underline{\quad?\quad}$. 18

In 23 and 24, solve and check.
23. $15.2 = f + 2.15$ $f = 13.05$
    $15.2 = 13.05 + 2.15$
24. $C + -8 + -5 = -15$ $C = -2$
    $-2 + -8 + -5 = -15$

In 25 and 26, a question is asked. a. Write an equation whose solution answers the question. b. Solve your equation. c. Check your answer.

25. At noon Monday the temperature was 17°F. At midnight Tuesday the temperature was -12°F. Let C be the change in temperature. By how much did the temperature change?
    a) $17 + C = -12$; b) $C = -29°$; c) $17 + -29 = -12$
26. A trail begins at an altitude of 562 meters and ends at 1321 meters. If a hiker climbs from the beginning to the end of the trail, what is the net change in altitude? Let A be the change in altitude.
    a) $562 + A = 1321$ b) $A = 759$ m   c) $562 + 759 = 1321$

Review

27. Mary collects and trades old records. She now has 40 Elvis Presley records. If she sells n of them and buys twice as many as she sells, how many Elvis records will she have? *(Lesson 3-1)*
    $40 - n + 2n$ records

Lesson 3-2 *More Properties of Addition* **153**

20) Sample: If you spend $9, then earn $9, you will have the same amount of money that you started with.

The king of rock 'n roll. *Shown is a commemorative U.S. stamp honoring Elvis Presley. Elvis recorded over 170 hit singles from 1955–1977.*

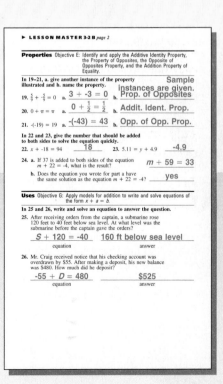

Notes on Questions
✎ **Question 20 Writing** This question is intended to encourage students to write about mathematical ideas and to express themselves clearly. It is different from the more common question which sets forth a situation and asks students to give the equation.

Question 27 Music Connection
During his career, Elvis Presley released 45 records that sold more than a million copies each. He sold about 500 million records during his lifetime, and eight million additional records were sold in the five days following his death in 1977.

Adapting to Individual Needs

Challenge
The following questions are also given on **Teaching Aid 25.** The operation ✤ is defined below over the set $S = \{a, b, c, t\}$.

✤	a	b	c	t
a	b	t	a	t
b	t	c	b	a
c	a	b	c	t
t	t	a	t	b

1. Does this operation have an identity element? If so, what is it? [Yes; c]
2. Is this operation commutative? If no, give a counter example. [Yes]
3. Is this operation associative? If no, give a counter example. [No; for example, $a ✤ (t ✤ t) = t$, but $(a ✤ t) ✤ t = b$.]

Notes on Questions

Question 29 Point out that this question is essentially asking when parentheses do not change the order of operations.

Questions 31–33 These questions help set up Lesson 3-3.

Question 34 When discussing this question, ask students for examples of negative numbers they might have seen on TV. [Samples: In football, negative numbers mean yards lost; temperatures below 0 are negative.]

Follow-up for Lesson 3-2

Practice

For more questions on SPUR Objectives, use **Lesson Master 3-2A** (shown on page 151) or **Lesson Master 3-2B** (shown on pages 152–153).

Assessment

Written Communication Have students explain in their own words the properties of addition that are introduced in this lesson and in the previous lesson. Have them include examples of each property in their explanations. [Explanations indicate students' levels of understanding and selection of appropriate examples.]

Extension

Cooperative Learning Have students **work in groups.** Ask them to experiment to see if another operation on their calculators has the property that is described in **Question 21,** that is, a key which, when pressed twice, returns to the original number. [The reciprocal key] Then ask students to find a pair of keys that can be pressed, one after the other, to return to the original value. [The keys students can understand at this time are the x^2 key and the $\sqrt{x}$ key. Other pairs of keys include e^x and ln, logarithms and antilogarithms, and trigonometric functions and inverse trigonometric functions. Some of these operations may also require pressing 2nd or INV keys on the calculator.]

154

30)

```
33
32
31
30
29
28
```

34a) Sample: a fall in the price for a share of stock; a rise in the price for a share of stock
b) Sample: the number of seconds before a rocket is launched; the number of seconds after a rocket is launched
c) Sample: three under par in a tournament; three over par in a tournament
d) Sample: amount of national debt; amount of national profit

28. a. Write a simplified expression for the area of the figure shown.
  b. What model for addition is being applied? *(Lesson 3-1)*
  a) $87 + k$ cm^2;   b) Putting-Together Model

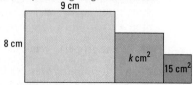

29. *Multiple choice.* In which expression would the answer be the same if the parentheses were deleted? *(Lessons 1-4, 2-5)* (b)
  (a) $(8 + 3) \cdot \text{-}5$ (b) $7 - (2 \cdot 2)$
  (c) $(2 + 6) \cdot 8 + 5$ (d) $1 + 6 \div (2 \cdot 3)$

30. Freezing temperatures are those at or below 32° Fahrenheit.
  a. Graph all possibilities for freezing temperatures on a vertical number line. *(Lesson 1-2)* See left.
  b. Write an inequality representing all freezing temperatures in the Fahrenheit scale using x as the variable. *(Lesson 1-1)* $x \le 32$

31. What is a "horizontal line"? *(Previous course)*
  Sample: a line that neither goes up or down; it is level with the horizon.

32. What term describes the pairs of lines below? *(Previous course)*
  perpendicular

33. Give the coordinates of each point on this graph. *(Previous course)*
  $A = (1, 4);$ $B = (5, 2);$ $C = (\text{-}2, 2);$
  $D = (\text{-}5, 0);$ $E = (0, \text{-}2);$ $F = (\text{-}5, \text{-}3);$
  $G = (3, \text{-}3);$ $H = (3, 0)$

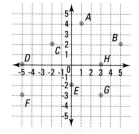

Exploration

34. Negative numbers and their opposites appear in many situations. What real situation might each number represent? What would the opposite represent? See left.
  a. $\text{-}5\frac{5}{8}$ in stock market values   **b.** -9 in rocket launches
  c. -3 in golf   **d.** -399 billion in the Federal budget

Setting Up Lesson 3-3

Materials Students will need graph paper or **Teaching Aid 26** for Lesson 3-3.

Be sure you discuss **Questions 31–33** in Lesson 3-2. Students' responses will help you assess the extent to which Lesson 3-3 is review.

You may also wish to discuss the graph for **Questions 17–20** in Lesson 3-3, so that students know how to interpret it.

LESSON 3-3

The Coordinate Plane

Watch your watching. *Several studies have linked watching a lot of TV with poor academic grades. One study found that 22% of 13-year-old students in the U.S. watch 5 or more hours of TV daily.*

A **plane** is a flat surface that stretches forever in all directions. Graphs on a plane can display a great deal of information and show trends in a small space as illustrated by the following example.

Mrs. Hernandez asked her class to keep track of the time spent at home studying and the time spent watching TV. The table below shows what her students reported the next day.

Time Spent on TV and Homework (minutes)					
Student	TV	Homework	Student	TV	Homework
Alex	60	30	Jim	120	75
Beth	0	60	Kerry	30	45
Carol	120	30	Lawanda	120	45
David	75	90	Meg	150	60
Evan	210	0	Nancy	180	15
Frank	150	30	Paula	90	75
Gary	0	90	Quincy	60	45
Harper	90	60	Ria	60	120
Irene	120	0			

To explore the relation between the time students spent watching television and the time spent studying, Mrs. Hernandez used a two-dimensional *coordinate graph*. A two-dimensional coordinate graph is needed for this data since each response involves two numbers. She drew two perpendicular number lines called **axes.** She used the horizontal axis for the time spent watching TV and the vertical axis for the time spent on homework. The axes intersect at the point labeled 0 on each number line. This point is called the **origin.**

Lesson 3-3 *The Coordinate Plane* **155**

Objectives
I Draw and interpret two-dimensional graphs.

Resources
From the *Teacher's Resource File*
- Lesson Master 3-3A or 3-3B
- Answer Master 3-3
- Teaching Aids
  21 Warm-up
  26 Graph Paper
  27 Additional Examples 2, 4, 5
- Technology Sourcebook
  Computer Master 6

Additional Resources
- Visuals for Teaching Aids 21, 26, 27

Teaching Lesson 3-3

Warm-up

Diagnostic Suppose that your school is at the origin.
1. Show the location of your home on the graph. Describe the location in terms of a distance (miles) east or west of the school and a distance north or south of the school. **Responses will vary.**
2. Show two other locations on the graph, and describe each of them. **Responses will vary.**

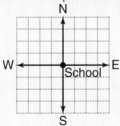

Lesson 3-3 Overview

Broad Goals The first goal of this lesson is to review plotting of points in the coordinate plane. The second is to show how graphs can tell a story.

Perspective We assume that students have plotted points before. Each example in this lesson has a specific purpose. In **Example 1,** students are asked to examine a graph to determine if there is a relation-

ship between two variables. In **Example 2,** they encounter a graph in which the axes do not intersect at (0, 0). Instead, the scales are picked so that the data can be conveniently displayed. We could have employed negative numbers in this example by picking a year and calling it year 0. Then any year before that year would be identified with a negative number. In **Example 3,** either coordinate may be positive or negative. In **Example 4,** a continuous

graph is shown, and students are asked to interpret it.

Teaching Aid 26 is graph paper. Students will need graph paper for this and many other lessons throughout the year. Since review problems with graphs are scattered throughout the text, students should always have graph paper on hand.

Reading Mathematics Point out to students that when they read a novel, they read down the page. But in reading this lesson, their eyes should move from text to graph or chart and back to text. You might have students read the lesson aloud in class. As they read, point out when they should pause to look at a graph or a chart.

Stress the connections between the graphs and the tables. You might give students **Teaching Aid 26,** and have them plot the points as they read.

In the first edition of this book we used the word "scattergram," but in this edition we use the word "scatterplot." Each term is correct; the latter has become more popular in recent years.

❶ In this example, students are asked to notice a relationship between the time spent on homework and the time spent watching TV. This is done in a very informal way, but it is a precursor of a later lesson where students will begin with a scatterplot, and draw a line to fit the data. Underlying this relationship is the idea of correlation, which is used to determine if two characteristics are dependent on each other and to measure the amount of dependence. Notice that when two variables are related, the relationship does not have to be one of cause and effect. Correlation is not covered in this book, but it is a topic in the later UCSMP book *Functions, Statistics, and Trigonometry.*

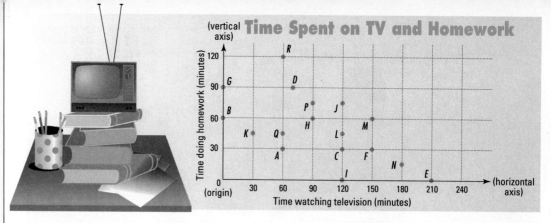

Time Spent on TV and Homework

Vertical axis: Time doing homework (minutes)
Horizontal axis: Time watching television (minutes)

Mrs. Hernandez then located a point for each student's data, plotted it on the graph, and coded it with the student's initial. For instance, Paula spent 90 minutes watching TV and 75 minutes on homework; so Paula's data point is 90 units to the right and 75 units up from the origin. This point can be expressed as the ordered pair (90, 75) and is labeled as point *P* on the graph. Notice that David's data point is (75, 90) and is labeled as point *D* on the graph.

A graph like this, in which individual points are plotted, is called a **scatterplot.** Every point in the plane of the graph can be identified with a pair of numbers called its **coordinates.** Such a plane is a **coordinate plane.**

❶ **Example 1**

Refer to the scatterplot above.
a. How many student responses are shown on the scatterplot?
b. How many students reported doing homework for exactly 90 minutes?
c. How many students watched at least 120 minutes of television?
d. Who is represented by the ordered pair (60, 120)?

Solution

a. There are 17 student responses because there are 17 data points on the scatterplot.
b. Homework time is shown by the distance above the horizontal axis. Two students, Gary and David, did exactly 90 minutes of homework. They are shown by the two data points on the horizontal line for 90.
c. "At least 120" means 120 or more. Television time is shown by distance to the right of the origin. Points showing 120 minutes of TV time are in a vertical line in the middle of the graph. Look for points on this line or to the right of it. There are 8 such points, *J, L, C, I, M, F, N,* and *E*. So 8 students watched at least 120 minutes of TV.
d. The point 60 right and 120 up is named R. It represents Ria.

From the pattern of dots, Mrs. Hernandez's class decided the headline was generally true. As students watched more TV, they did less homework.

Optional Activities

Activity 1
You can use this activity after students have read **Example 3.** Have students **work in pairs.** The first person picks any point on the coordinate plane and gives information about the point such as, "If I walk 5 blocks east and 2 blocks south, I will be at (7, –2). Where am I starting from?" [(2, 0)] The partner must identify the starting point. Then have students switch roles.

Activity 2 Technology Connection
You may wish to demonstrate how to use *GraphExplorer* or similar software to make a scatterplot. Then you could assign *Technology Sourcebook, Computer Master 6.* Students make a scatterplot then answer questions about the graph.

Activity 3 Writing
Materials: Graphs from newspapers or magazines

After completing the lesson, have students select a graph from a newspaper or magazine. Have them write a paragraph explaining what information the graph conveys. Some students may want to share their information with the class.

Recall that coordinates of points may be positive, negative, or zero. When the first coordinate of a point is negative, the point lies to the left of the vertical axis. When the second coordinate of a point is negative, the point lies below the horizontal axis.

U.S. exports. *The United States is one of the largest car producers in the world, but it exports only a small portion of its production. Pictured above is a shipment of U.S. cars being loaded for export.*

Example 2

The table below shows net *exports* of the United States in billions of dollars from 1975 through 1992. The *net exports* for a given year represents the difference of value between goods and services exported *to* other countries and goods and services imported *from* other countries. A positive net-export value represents money flowing into the United States. A negative value indicates money leaving the USA.

Year	1975	1976	1977	1978	1979	1980	1981	1982	1983
Amount	9	-8	-29	-31	-28	-24	-27	-32	-58

Year	1984	1985	1986	1987	1988	1989	1990	1991	1992
Amount	-108	-132	-153	-152	-119	-110	-102	-65	-84

a. Graph the information in this table.
b. In which year was the value of net exports the highest? the lowest?
c. Give a general description of changes in net exports between 1975 and 1980.
d. Give a general description of changes in net exports after 1980.

Solution

a. Time is usually graphed on the horizontal axis. Begin at 1975, where the table starts, and mark the horizontal axis off in years. The vertical axis will show the net-export amount. Look at the table to see the size of the numbers that must fit on the graph. The largest is 9 and the smallest is -153, so the vertical axis needs to be marked off in equal intervals that span this range. Units of 25 work well. Now plot a point for each ordered pair in the table. A graph is drawn below.

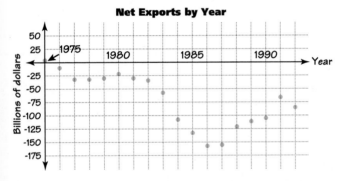

b. Look at the points that are graphed and pick out the highest and lowest ones. Net *exports were highest in 1975 and lowest in 1986.* You could also find this information in the table of values.

❷ Even students who have studied coordinate graphs in previous courses may be unaccustomed to graphs in which the axes do not intersect at (0, 0). In applications, the axes seldom intersect at (0, 0). Also, students may not know the meaning of positive and negative net exports—a negative value means the U.S. imported more than it exported. In **part b,** the intention is that comparisons should be made simply by looking at the graph.

In both **Examples 1 and 2,** the questions can be answered by looking at the chart. Ask where the answers appear in the chart, and point out that most people find it easier to gather this same information from the graph. The graph has an advantage, because it is easier to add more data points. In the next chapter, we discuss a third way of describing data involving two variables—with equations.

Adapting to Individual Needs

Activity 4
After students have completed the lesson, you might have them find data which relate directly to them. For example, they might survey classmates to find data on the time spent on TV and homework; they might find and graph population changes in their school for the past 10 years; they might graph locations with their school or homes as the origin; they might draw graphs describing car trips they have taken.

Extra Help
Review the meaning of ordered pairs with students and discuss why the order of the coordinates is important in graphing. In **Example 1,** point out that the coordinates for Point *D* are (75, 90), and the coordinates for Point *P* are (90, 75). Be sure students understand that even though the same numbers are involved, the two number pairs represent different points because the order of the numbers is

reversed. Also, be sure students recognize that the first number in an ordered pair represents a move along the horizontal axis, and the second number represents a move along the vertical axis.

❸ A detailed story about Harold's trip might be as follows: It took Harold $\frac{1}{2}$ minute to accelerate from 0 mph to 30 mph. He traveled at a constant speed of 30 mph until, at $2\frac{1}{2}$ minutes into the trip, he saw a stop sign and reduced his speed. He stopped at 3 minutes, but immediately started up again. At 4 minutes, he reached 30 mph and continued at that speed. At $5\frac{1}{2}$ minutes, he saw a stop light, came to a stop at 6 minutes, and waited at the light for $\frac{1}{2}$ minute. Between $6\frac{1}{2}$ minutes and 7 minutes, he accelerated to 30 mph and traveled at this speed for 3 minutes. Then the speed limit changed, and he accelerated to 50 mph and drove at 50 mph for 4 minutes. At $14\frac{1}{2}$ minutes he started to slow down. He stopped at 16 minutes, having reached his destination.

Additional Examples

Examples 2, 4, and 5 are also given on **Teaching Aid 27.** Students will need graph paper or **Teaching Aid 26.**

1. Use the scatterplot on page 156.
   a. How many students reported spending 60 minutes or more doing homework? **8**
   b. How many students watched television for exactly 60 minutes? **3**
   c. Did anyone spend the same amount of time on both activities? **No**
   d. Who is represented by the ordered pair (150, 30)? **Frank**

2. The average normal monthly temperatures (Fahrenheit) in Barrow, Alaska, are:

   Jan. –14° Feb. –20° Mar. –16°
   Apr. –2° May 19° June 33°
   July 39° Aug. 38° Sept. 31°
   Oct. 14° Nov. –1° Dec. –13°

   a. Graph the temperatures.

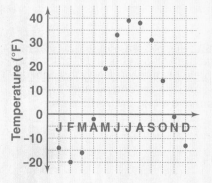

c. Find 1980 on the horizontal axis and look to the left. The points are fairly close to the horizontal axis. You might write: *Between 1975 and 1978, net exports declined. Between 1978 and 1980 they rose slightly.*
d. Look to the right of 1980. The points drop sharply until 1986 when they start to rise. *From 1981 to 1986 the value of net exports was negative and decreased each year. From 1987 to 1991 the value of net exports was still negative, but increasing. In 1992, the value decreased again.*

The coordinate plane is a natural way to represent locations on a small part of Earth. As with most maps, east is usually at the right and north at the top. They become the positive directions of the horizontal and vertical axes. Their opposites, west and south, respectively, represent the negative directions.

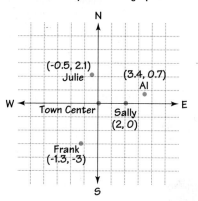

Example 3

A city or town often has a central point from which street addresses are numbered north, south, east, and west. Julie lives 0.5 mile west and 2.1 miles north of the Town Center. Frank lives 1.3 miles west and 3 miles south of the Town Center. Sally lives 2 miles due east of the Town Center. Al lives 3.4 miles east and 0.7 mile north of the Town Center. Graph these locations on a coordinate plane with the Town Center as its origin.

Solution

The first coordinate is the distance east or west. The second coordinate is the distance north or south. The points are graphed.

Notice that the points on the graphs in Examples 1 to 3 are not connected. Such a graph is called *discrete.* The graph in Example 4 is **continuous;** all points are connected.

Adapting to Individual Needs

English Language Development
Students with limited English might benefit from doing this lesson with an English-speaking partner. Remind students to use their bilingual dictionaries.

You might want to define the word *discrete.* Display a book and a pencil. Explain that the objects are distinct and not connected. In a discrete graph, the points stand alone; the points are not connected.

Example 4

Here is a graph indicating the speed Harold Hooper traveled as he drove from home to work. Write a story that explains the graph.

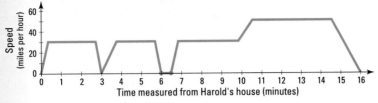

Solution

Here is one possible story: Harold began on a road driving at the 30-mph speed limit. After 3 minutes, he stopped for a stop sign. He stopped at a stoplight for about $\frac{1}{2}$ minute beginning at the six-minute mark. Harold then resumed driving at 30 mph for about $3\frac{1}{2}$ minutes. Then the road widened and the speed limit increased to 50 mph. He drove at 50 mph for about 5 minutes, until he neared work and slowed down.

QUESTIONS

Covering the Reading

1. What are the number lines used in a coordinate graph called? **axes**

In 2–4, refer to Example 1.

2. Which ordered pair describes Alex's responses? **(60, 30)**

3. **a.** According to the graph, how many students did not watch TV? **2**
   b. How much time did each of these students spend on homework?
   60 minutes and 90 minutes

4. What is the trend in this graph? **The more time students spent watching television, the less time they spent doing homework.**

In 5–7, refer to Example 2.

5. Why are the numbers on the vertical axis given in billions of dollars?
   to simplify the labeling of the intervals along the vertical axis of the graph

6. When were the net exports the greatest? **1975**

7. How much less were the net exports in 1985 than in 1975?
   $141 billion

In 8 and 9, refer to Example 3.

8a) **(-3, 1)**

8. A bowling alley is 3 miles west and 1 mile north of the Town Center.
   a. What are the coordinates of the location of the bowling alley?
   b. Which of the four people lives closest to the bowling alley? **Julie**

9. Bill lives at (1.4, -2.9) on the graph. Describe his location from the Town Center using the words north, south, east, and west.
   Bill lives 1.4 miles east and 2.9 miles south of the Town Center.

10. In Example 4, how long did it take Harold to drive to work?
    16 minutes

Lesson 3-3 *The Coordinate Plane* **159**

b. When is the average temperature above freezing? **June, July, August**

c. Describe the temperature changes. **Sample: It is coldest in February, and it is warmest in July.**

3. Jodie lives 3.2 miles west and 1.1 miles south of the school. Felipe lives 0.5 mile east and 1.5 miles north of the school.
   a. Graph these points on a coordinate plane. Use the school as the origin.

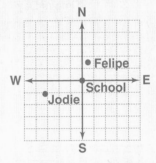

b. If Jodie walked on grid lines, how far would she have to walk to get from her home to Felipe's home? **6.3 miles**

(Additional Examples continue on page 160.)

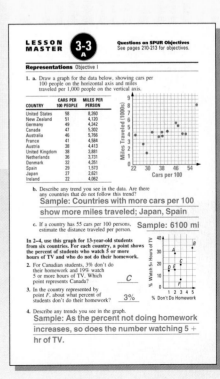

Adapting to Individual Needs

Challenge

Materials: Newspapers and magazines that contain graphs

✎ **Writing** Have students select graphs that they think are misleading from newspapers or magazines. Then have each student display a graph and write a paragraph explaining why it is misleading. The student might also draw another graph using the same data but giving a truer representation of the data.

4. The graph shows the number of people who were in a classroom over a period of time. Write a story that explains the graph.

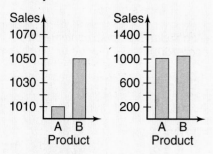

Sample: The teacher was in the room at 7:30. By 8:00 a few students arrived. At 8:15, class started. At 8:45, two students left. At 9:00 there was a passing period, leaving a few students in the room. By 9:15, a new class started.

5. A graph can be made purposely misleading. The two graphs below show the same data. Which graph is misleading and why?

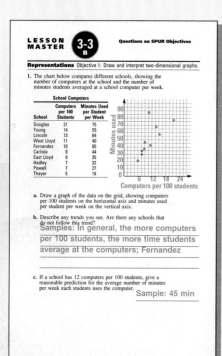

Sample: The first graph exaggerates the difference between the

11c) American; The point for the average American student falls in the middle of the scatterplot.

12a)

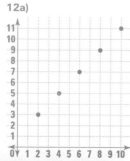

A chilling experience.
The wind chill index gives an estimated calm-air temperature based upon a combination of wind speed and actual temperature. The faster the wind blows, the faster a person loses body heat. The feeling of cold increases as the wind speed increases.

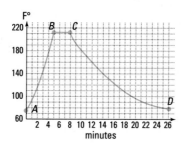

160

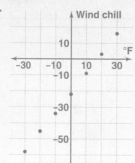

Applying the Mathematics

11. A 1990 study examined the way American and Japanese high school students spend their time. It found that the average American student spends 122 minutes per day watching TV and 46 minutes doing homework. Japanese students average 152 minutes per day watching TV and 163 minutes doing homework.
  a. If a point representing the average American student were plotted on the graph at the beginning of this lesson, which of the points already plotted on the graph would be closest to it? *L*
  b. If the point for a typical Japanese student were plotted, which point would be closest to it? *J*
  c. Would you judge Mrs. Hernandez's class to be more typical of American students or of Japanese students? Explain your answer. See left.

12. a. Make a coordinate graph showing the following set of points:
    $\{(2, 3), (4, 5), (6, 7), (8, 9), (10, 11)\}$. See left.
  b. If the pattern continues, what is the missing coordinate in $(100, \underline{\ ?\ })$? **101**
  c. If the pattern continues, what is the missing coordinate in $(m, \underline{\ ?\ })$? $m + 1$

13. a. The table at the right shows the wind chill index for various temperatures when there is a 10 mph wind. Make a graph of this data. Show the actual temperature on the horizontal axis and the wind chill on the vertical axis. See margin.
  b. Describe some pattern you observe in the scatterplot. Sample: For every 10° drop in temperature, the wind chill drops about 12°.

actual temp °F	wind chill
30°	16
20°	3
10°	-9
0°	-22
-10°	-34
-20°	-46
-30°	-58

In 14 and 15, *multiple choice.* Which of the following situations is represented by the graph?
  (a) the distance traveled in *h* hours at 50 mph
  (b) the distance traveled in *h* hours at 75 mph
  (c) the distance you are from home if you started 150 miles from home and traveled toward home at 50 mph

14. 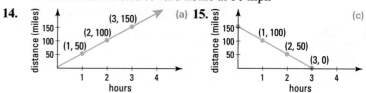 (a) **15.** (c)

16. The graph at the left shows the temperature of water in a pot on a stove. Write a story that explains the graph. Be sure to mention times and temperatures of important points on the graph.
Sample: The water has temperature of 70° when the pot is placed on the stove. After 5 minutes, it begins to boil and continues boiling for 3 minutes. When the pot is taken off the stove, the water cools to room temperature after another 18 minutes.

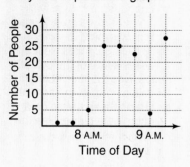

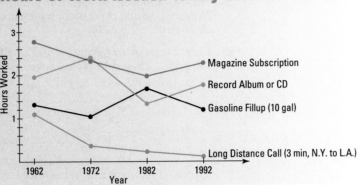

In 17–20, use the graph below. It shows how long the average American had to work to earn enough money, before taxes, to purchase the goods and services listed.

Hours of Work Needed to Buy Selected Items

(Graph: Hours Worked vs. Year, 1962–1992)
- Magazine Subscription
- Record Album or CD
- Gasoline Fillup (10 gal)
- Long Distance Call (3 min, N.Y. to L.A.)

Source: Consumer Reports, 1992

17. On the average, how many hours did a worker have to work in 1982 to earn enough to fill up a car with gasoline? about $1\frac{3}{4}$ hours

18) record album; In 1972, the average American worked about 2.4 hours to buy an album, while in 1982 about 1.3 hours of work bought an album. This is a change of 1.1 hours. No other item had a greater decrease.

18. Between 1972 and 1982, which item showed the greatest drop in hours needed? Justify your answer. See left.

19. *Multiple choice.* In hours of work required, the cost of the items in 1992 as compared with 1962 is (b)
(a) always more.
(b) always less.
(c) sometimes more, sometimes less.

20b) Sample: In 1972, the cost was about 24 minutes of work; in 1982, about 12 minutes of work; and in 1992, about 6 minutes of work. So in 2002, the cost may be about 3 minutes of work.

20. a. Describe the trend in the cost of a long-distance call between 1962 and 1972. Sample: Long distance rates decreased significantly.
b. Make a prediction about the cost of a long-distance call in 2002, and explain how you arrived at your prediction. See left.

Review

21. Suppose $h_1 + h_2 = 0$ and $h_1 = 17.3$.
a. What is the value of h_2? -17.3
b. What property is illustrated? *(Lesson 3-2)* Property of Opposites

22b) Sample: You have a $10.8 million contract to play baseball over a three-year period. How much money remains on your contract if you already received $3.5 million?

22. a. Solve the equation $x + 3.5 = 10.8$. $x = 7.3$
b. Make up a question that can be answered by solving the equation in part **a.** *(Lesson 3-2)* See left.

23. *Skill sequence.* Solve the equation. *(Lessons 2-6, 3-2)*
a. $n + 10 = 19$ $n = 9$
b. $n + -10 = 19$ $n = 29$
c. $-10 = n + 19$ $n = -29$
d. $-10 = 19n$ $n = \frac{-10}{19}$

Lesson 3-3 *The Coordinate Plane* **161**

two companies' sales by not beginning the vertical axis at 0 and by using smaller increments on the vertical axis.

Notes on Questions
Question 11 Multicultural Connection You might also mention these facts about Japanese schools: Students attend classes $5\frac{1}{2}$ days each week; in junior high school, students study mathematics, music, science, social studies, and English or another foreign language.

Question 12 This question previews patterning in Lesson 3-8 and later work with equations of lines.

Questions 14–15 These questions, which also preview equations of lines, are the type that are often found on college entrance exams.

Question 16 Writing Have some students read their answers aloud to the class so that students hear a variety of possible answers.

Questions 17–20 Consumer Connection The graph in these questions depicts the number of hours the average worker had to work to earn enough money to buy the given item. It is a good example of the complexity that is found in real-world graphs. You may want to talk about the graph before you assign the questions.

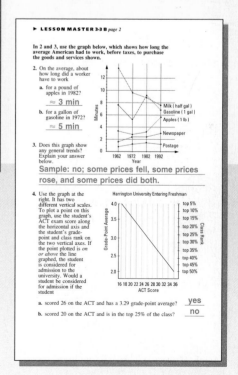

Notes on Questions

Question 26 You may want to use the notation $m\angle PQR$ for the measure of the angle PQR. This question should be easy for students who have studied *Transition Mathematics*.

Question 30 Students are asked to survey some of their friends. The same people will undoubtedly contribute data to more than one student, so the answers will not be independent; the results of the survey are apt to be more alike than if everyone had asked different friends.

Follow-up for Lesson **3-3**

Practice

For more questions on SPUR Objectives, use **Lesson Master 3-3A** (shown on page 159) or **Lesson Master 3-3B** (shown on pages 160–161).

Assessment

Group Assessment Have each student draw a continuous graph, and explain what it represents. Then have each student exchange his or her paper with another student and write a story that explains the other student's graph. [Students' stories are creative and describe a possible situation shown by the graph.]

Extension

As an extension of Additional Example 3, ask students to find the straight-line distance ("as the crow flies") from Jodie's house to Felipe's house. [Students can draw a right triangle with sides of 3.7 miles and 2.6 miles. They can use the Pythagorean Theorem to find the distance: $\sqrt{20.45} \approx 4.5$ miles.]

Project Update Project 3, *Graphs of Everyday Quantities*, on page 205, relates to the content of this lesson.

---

24. The value of Wurthmore stock went down $2\frac{3}{8}$ points on July 30. On July 31 and August 1 it went up $\frac{3}{8}$ of a point each day. Find the net change in Wurthmore stock over this three-day period. $-1\frac{5}{8}$ *(Lesson 3-1)*

25. The river dropped two feet, rose p feet, and then dropped q feet. Write an addition expression, representing the change in the height of the river. *(Lesson 3-1)* $-2 + p + -q$

26. The measure of $\angle PQR$ equals 140°. Write an equation that relates 140 and y. *(Lesson 3-1, previous course)* $95 + y = 140$

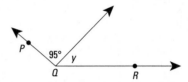

27. Suppose a submarine dives from sea level at a rate of 25 meters per minute. Then its final depth d after t minutes is given by
$$d = -25t.$$
How many minutes does it take to reach a depth of -225 meters? *(Lesson 2-6)* **9 minutes**

28. To estimate the number N of bricks needed in a wall some bricklayers use the formula $N = 7LH$, where L and H are the length and height of the wall in feet. About how many bricks would a bricklayer need for a wall 8.5 feet high and 24.5 feet long? *(Lesson 1-5)* **1458 bricks**

29. Evaluate mentally given $t = -4$. *(Lesson 1-4)*
    a. $t + -9$ -13 b. $-3t$ 12 c. $-2t^2$ -32

Exploration

30. a. Survey at least 10 of your friends. Ask them how much time they spent watching TV and doing homework yesterday.
    b. Plot your results on a scatterplot.
    c. Do your data agree with the newspaper headline in this lesson? **Answers will vary for 30 a-c.**

162

Setting Up Lesson 3-4

Materials Students will need graph paper or **Teaching Aid 28** for Lesson 3-4. They will need a map of the United States for **Question 31.**

LESSON
3-4

Two-Dimensional Slides

The invasion of video games. *Soon after the 1979 introduction of a video game called Space Invaders, video games became the toy industry's hottest items.*

You probably have played video games in which a figure moves across a video screen. Programmers of games move the figures by first imagining them on a coordinate plane. Diagram 1 below shows how you might see a screen. Diagram 2 shows how a programmer might see the screen.

1. How you see the screen

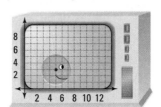

2. How the programmer sees the screen

Some of the customary language for describing graphs is shown at the right. The horizontal axis is the **x-axis;** the vertical axis is the **y-axis.** A general point is often labeled (x, y). The first coordinate of any point is called the **x-coordinate;** the second coordinate is the **y-coordinate.** The axes separate the coordinate plane into four **quadrants** identified by I, II, III, and IV as shown. The diagrams above show only part of the first quadrant of a coordinate plane.

```
         y-axis
    II  │  I
        │
●(x,y)  │ origin   x-axis
        │
    III │  IV
```

The signs of the coordinates of points in the quadrants are as follows:

quadrant	x-coordinate	y-coordinate
I	positive	positive
II	negative	positive
III	negative	negative
IV	positive	negative

Objectives

J Draw and interpret two-dimensional slides on a coordinate graph.

Resources

From the **Teacher's Resource File**
- Lesson Master 3-4A or 3-4B
- Answer Master 3-4
- Assessment Sourcebook: Quiz for Lessons 3-1 through 3-4
- Teaching Aids
  22 Warm-up
  28 Four-Quadrant Graph Paper
  29 Examples 1 and 2, and Activity
  30 Additional Examples
- Technology Sourcebook Computer Master 7

Additional Resources
- Visuals for Teaching Aids 22, 28–30
- Map of the United States (Question 31)

Teaching
Lesson 3-4

Warm-up

Name four points that are 1 unit away from (98, 32). **Sample answers: (98, 33), (98, 31), (97, 32), (99, 32)**

Lesson 3-4 Overview

Broad Goals This lesson shows students how sliding up, down, right, and left is related to changes in the coordinates of points.

Perspective The words *slide* and *translation* are synonyms, but *slide* conveys a physical meaning and is often used with younger students. We study slides in the coordinate plane (that is, two-dimensional slides) for several reasons: first, they are an obvious application of the slide model for

addition. Second, they give students the chance to practice important graphing concepts introduced in the previous lesson. Third, they give the students practice in adding integers. Fourth, translations are important transformations, both in geometry (where they relate congruent figures) and in algebra (where they relate graphs of functions and relations). Slides are important in algebra; for example, the parabola with

equation $y = x^2 + 5$ is a translation image of the parabola with equation $y = x^2$.

This content is not easy for some students. Most of them learned to graph by starting at (0, 0), and they understand the relationship of points to the origin. But they do not understand the relationships of points to each other, given relationships among their coordinates. This lesson provides an important tool for that understanding.

Reading Mathematics It may be advantageous to read this lesson in class. After each paragraph, stop to ensure that students understand the material that was presented. You might use **Teaching Aid 29** when discussing **Examples 1 and 2** and the *Activity*.

Note that two circles are used to graph the character on the screen on page 163. The point (5, 3) is the center of the larger circle that forms the outer boundary of the character. In this drawing, the character is represented by the entire circle.

❶ Some students who can graph ordered pairs cannot answer questions similar to **Example 1.** Oral questioning in class will demonstrate how quickly other students can find the coordinates of points on the image. This will make the task seem accessible for those who have trouble at first.

To slide the entire triangle (which has infinitely many points), it is sufficient to find images of key points. The vertices of a triangle are obvious choices for key points. Use the opportunity to review the word *vertex* and its plural, *vertices.* Some students think the singular of vertices is "vertice."

Emphasize that to go left or down, we add a negative number. In the next chapter, going left or down will be done by subtraction, and it will provide a nice example of the Algebraic Definition of Subtraction, which is $a - b = a + -b$.

One basic movement of a figure is a **two-dimensional slide,** or **translation.** The movement from the original position, or **preimage,** to the final position, or **image,** is shown in Diagram 3. The arrow shows the path a center point of the figure takes. The programmer could describe this movement as a horizontal slide followed by a vertical slide, as shown in Diagram 4.

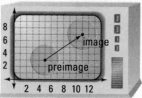

3. A slide of the figure

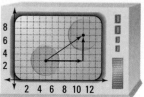

4. One way of describing the slide

In Diagrams 3 and 4, the slide is 6 units to the right and 4 units up. To slide a point 6 units to the right, you must add 6 to the first coordinate of the point. To slide 4 units up, add 4 to the second coordinate. For instance, the figure on the video screen is based on a circle. The center of the figure was originally (5, 3). The new center is (5 + 6, 3 + 4), which is (11, 7). The pattern is as follows:

> If a *preimage point* is (x, y), then the *image point* after a slide 6 units to the right and 4 units up is $(x + 6, y + 4)$.

Adding a negative number to the x-coordinate results in a slide left, and adding a negative number to the y-coordinate results in a slide down.

Example 1 illustrates the translation of a figure with more than one point. The more points the figure has, the easier it may be to see the slide. Here we adopt the common practice of placing a prime after the letters naming the points of the image. If a preimage is point P, then its image is labeled P', read "P prime."

Example 1

a. Plot $\triangle ABC$, where $A = (-2, 4)$, $B = (-1, 7)$, and $C = (2, 3)$.
b. Draw the image of $\triangle ABC$ after a slide of 1 unit to the right and 6 units down.

❶ **Solution**

a. $\triangle ABC$ is drawn at the right.
b. To find the vertices of the image after the slide, add 1 to each x-coordinate and -6 to each y-coordinate:
$A' = (-2 + 1, 4 + -6) = (-1, -2)$
$B' = (-1 + 1, 7 + -6) = (0, 1)$
$C' = (2 + 1, 3 + -6) = (3, -3)$
Graph these points, connect them, and call the image $\triangle A'B'C'$.

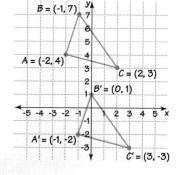

164

Materials: United States maps, almanacs, social studies books

Social Studies Connection To extend **Question 31,** have students **work in groups** and do one of these activities.

Activity 1 Explain why the population center is moving southwest. [The westward movement and, to some extent, the southerly movement are consistent with the historical development of the United States.

Originally, the states were in the eastern and northeastern part of the country. The population center moved west and south as territories were added, and people moved into them. The southern component of the movement has recently increased with the movement of industry into the once largely rural Sunbelt.]

Activity 2 Consider that in 1980, the population center was in DeSoto, Missouri, and,

in 1990, it was 9.7 miles northwest of Steelville, Missouri. Use a map to see how far the center moved between 1980 and 1990.

Does the movement agree with the numbers given in **Question 31**? [58 feet west and 29 feet south per day is about 40 miles west and 20 miles south in 10 years; the center moved about as far west as indicated but not as far south.]

Check

△*ABC* looks as if it has been slid 1 unit to the right and 6 units down to get △*A'B'C'*. (That's why this use of addition is called a two-dimensional slide.)

The rule for the slide in Example 1 can be written algebraically as "the image of (x, y) is $(x + 1, y + -6)$." When you have a rule for a slide, you can use it to compute the images of complex figures. Since a slide doesn't change the size or shape of a figure, you can compute the images of a few special points, like vertices, and then use a ruler or other tools to complete the image figure.

Activity

A graphics artist is working on a cartoon involving a rabbit. Figure *PQRST* shows a small part of the design. Using the rule that the image of (x, y) is $(x + -5, y + 2)$, draw the image of this figure. Label the image *P'Q'R'S'T'*.

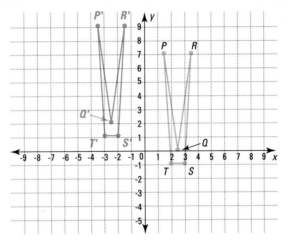

You have done the activity correctly if you slid the rabbit's ears 5 units to the left and 2 units up.

Example 2

If the point (x, y) is slid 8 units up, what is its image?

Solution

There is no move left or right, so 0 is added to the first coordinate. To move 8 units up, add 8 to the second coordinate.
The image of $(x, y) = (x + 0, y + 8) = (x, y + 8)$.

Check

Substitute values for x and y and graph. If $x = 5$ and $y = 2$, the preimage (x, y) is $(5, 2)$. The image is $(5, 2 + 8) = (5, 10)$. Is $(5, 10)$ eight units above $(5, 2)$? The graph at the left shows this, so it checks.

Lesson 3-4 *Two-Dimensional Slides* **165**

Additional Examples

These examples are given on Teaching Aid 30. Students will need graph paper or Teaching Aid 28.

1. **a.** Plot $\triangle RTX$, where $R = (-4, -1)$, $T = (3, 1)$, and $X = (0, -4)$.
   b. Draw the image $R'T'X'$ after sliding left 3 units and up 7 units. Find the coordinates of R', T', and X'.

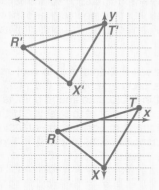

$R' = (-7, 6)$, $T' = (0, 8)$, and $X' = (-3, 3)$.

2. Give the coordinates of the image of (x, y) under a slide 4 units to the left. **The image of (x, y) is $(x + -4, y + 0) = (x + -4, y)$.**

3. The ears of a rabbit are shown in the Activity on page 165. On the graph below, Figure $STUVW$ shows the head of the rabbit. Use the rule that the image of (x, y) is $(x + -5, y + 2)$, and draw the image of this figure. Label the image $S'T'U'V'W'$.

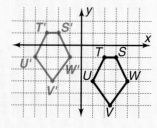

1. **a.** The first coordinate of a point is also called its __?__-coordinate. **x**
   b. The second coordinate is also called its __?__-coordinate. **y**

2. If the x-coordinate of a point is negative and the y-coordinate is positive, in which quadrant is the point? **II**

3. Which two quadrants are located to the left of the y-axis? **II, III**

4. **a.** When you slide a figure, what is the resulting figure called? **image**
   b. What is the original figure called? **preimage**

5. Find the image of $(-2, -1)$ after a slide 0.5 units to the left and 6 units up. **$(-2.5, 5)$**

6. Find the image of $(0, 0)$ after a slide 45 units up. **$(0, 45)$**

7. Draw a coordinate plane and graph the point $P = (3, 5)$ and its image after a slide of 2 units to the right and 2 units down. **See left.**

8. A preimage is $(-3, 1.5)$.
   a. Graph the preimage and its image after a slide 0.5 unit to the left and 4 units up. **See left.**
   b. In what quadrant is the image? **II**

9. **a.** Copy the graph of $\triangle PQR$ with $P = (-5, -2)$, $Q = (-7, -5)$, and $R = (-3, -8)$. **See below.**
   b. On the same axes, graph the image of this figure after a slide of 3 units to the right and 4 units up. **See below.**

7)

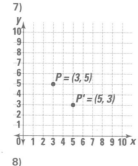

8)

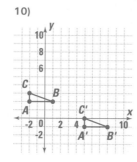

10)

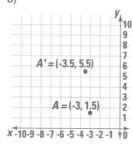

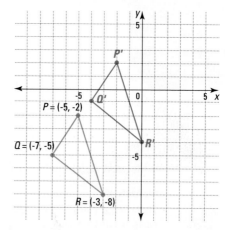

10. **a.** Draw $\triangle ABC$ with $A = (-2, 2)$, $B = (1, 2)$, and $C = (-2, 3)$. **See left.**
   b. Suppose the image of each point (x, y) on $\triangle ABC$ is $(x + 7, y + -3)$. Draw the image $\triangle A'B'C'$. **See left.**

166

Adapting to Individual Needs

Extra Help

Materials: Graph paper or **Teaching Aid 28**, cutout of a geometric shape

Use a coordinate grid (**Teaching Aid 28**) on the overhead projector to demonstrate slides. Trace a cutout of a geometric shape on the grid, and note the coordinates of the vertices. Slide the cutout straight up or down and again note the coordinates. Point out that only the y-coordinate changed.

Students should notice that the y-coordinate increases when the figure is moved up and decreases when it is moved down. Then return the figure to its original position, and move it to the right and then to the left. Students should see that only the x-coordinate changes, increasing for a move to the right and decreasing for a move to the left.

11b)

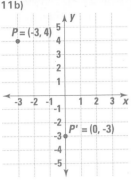

In 11 and 12, let point $P = (x, y)$. **a.** Write the image of P after the slide.
b. Check your answer to part **a** by picking values for x and y and graphing.

11. 3 units right, 7 units down $(x + 3, y + {}^-7)$ See left for graph.

12. 3 units left, 1 unit down $(x + {}^-3, y + {}^-1)$ See left for graph.

Applying the Mathematics

13. Copy the figure drawn below. Slide the figure using the rule that the image of (x, y) is $(x + 5, y + {}^-3)$.
  a. What are the coordinates of Q'? $({}^-1, {}^-9)$
  b. Graph the image of the figure. See below.

12b)

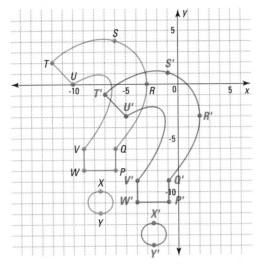

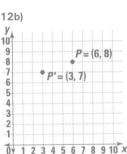

Incan pottery. *Shown is a sample of the excellent-quality pottery created by the Incas. The Incan empire prospered during the 15th century in what today is Peru and other South American countries.*

14. a. What is the image of the point (x, y) after a slide 9 units to the left? $(x + {}^-9, y)$
  b. Explain how your answer to part **a** is related to the Additive Identity Property. Sample: The identity of the second coordinate stays the same. The second coordinate of the image is $y + 0$, which is y.

15. A point is $(7, 2)$ and its image is $(15, {}^-4)$. Describe the slide: __?__ units to the (left or right) and __?__ units (up or down).
8 right   6 down

16. In the Incan empire, artists often painted simple strip patterns on pottery. Refer to the Incan strip pattern shown. Take each repetition of the pattern to be 1 unit wide. Pick one part of the design as a preimage. Give a rule for a slide that causes the image to look exactly like the preimage. Sample: The image of $(x, y) = (x + 1, y + 0)$.

⊢— 1 unit —⊣

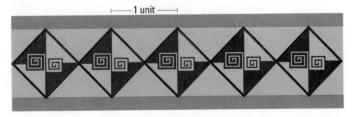

Lesson 3-4 *Two-Dimensional Slides* **167**

---

4. Find the images of points $P = (7, 2)$ and $Q = ({}^-8, 1)$ under a slide of 6 units to the right and 5 units down. **The image of P is $(13, {}^-3)$. The image of Q is $({}^-2, {}^-4)$.**

Notes on Questions

Question 16 Multicultural Connection Translations can be found in the arts and crafts of many cultures. For example, the Ashanti people of central Ghana translate a design when they make Kente cloth. Translations can be found in American Indian weaving, pottery, and beadwork; in rugs of the Middle East and Far East; and in American quilt patterns.

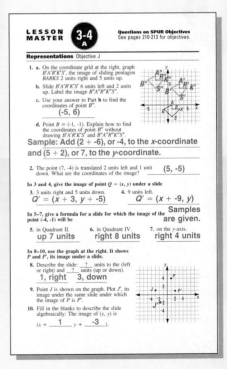

Adapting to Individual Needs

English Language Development
To help students understand two-dimensional slides, you might want to use colored chalk for points and labels in the preimages and corresponding images. For instance, draw $\triangle ABC$ using a red A, a blue B, and a yellow C. Then slide the triangle and label the image points A', B', and C' using the corresponding colors of the preimages, red, blue, and yellow.

Notes on Questions

Question 17 Students may not realize that they can determine the slide that the figure undergoes by examining one convenient point, for instance, the top of the head, and its image.

Questions 28–30 These questions can be used to lead into the next lesson, and they should be discussed.

Question 29 Science Connection Technically, BTU is the unit and the variable stands for the number of BTUs. However, this formula was found in a real-world source where it is common to use BTU = 12,600 rather than number of BTUs = 12,600. It provides a nice noncomputer example in which a variable is represented by a set of letters, not just by a single letter.

Question 31 Literature Connection Mark Twain, after whom the Mark Twain National Forest is named, is the pen name of Samuel Langhorne Clemens. A riverboat pilot at one time, Clemens wrote novels, travel narratives, essays, short stories, and sketches under the name Mark Twain. He became a well-known humorist in American literature and was a major author of American fiction. The term "mark twain" is a riverboat term meaning *two fathoms* (a depth of 12 feet).

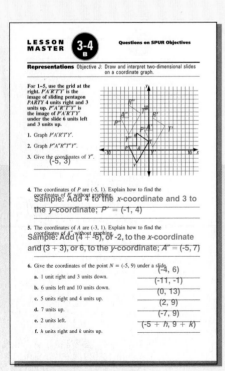

17. Examine the two-dimensional slide below.
    a. Under this slide, the image of any point is __?__ units right and __?__ units above the preimage. 9; 8
    b. Under this slide, the image of (x, y) is $(x + $__?__$, y + $__?__$)$. 9; 8

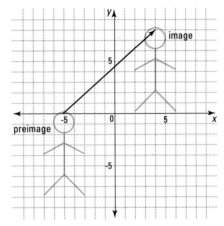

18) Sample: 4 blocks east and 4 blocks north; 1 block east, 3 blocks north, 3 blocks east, and 1 block north; 4 blocks north and 4 blocks east

18. Use the diagram at the left. One route Tony can take to get to school is by going 2 blocks east, 4 blocks north, and another 2 blocks east. Name three other routes Tony can take to get from his house to school. **See left.**

19. After a slide 3 units right and 9 units up, an image is (7, -1). What are the coordinates of its preimage? (4, -10)

Review

In 20 and 21, a person begins standing 24 ft from a sensor that measures distances to objects. The graph shows how the distance between the person and the sensor changed. *(Lesson 3-3)*

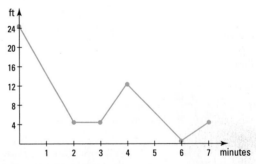

20. At what time was the person moving closer to the sensor? from 0−2 minutes and from 4-6 minutes

21. At what time was the person touching the sensor? 6 minutes

Adapting to Individual Needs

Challenge
Materials: Graph paper or **Teaching Aid 28**

Have students graph points (0, 0), (2, 4), and (8, 0), label them A, B, and C, respectively, and think of them as three vertices of a parallelogram. Ask them to find the other possible vertices of the parallelogram. [Point D = (10, 4) forms parallelogram *ABDC*; E = (6, −4) forms *ABCE*; F = (−6, 4) forms *ACBF*.]

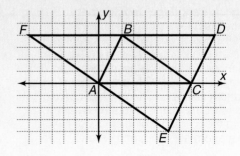

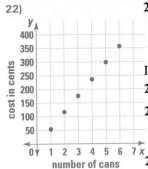

cost in cents (y-axis: 50, 100, 150, 200, 250, 300, 350, 400)
number of cans (x-axis: 1 2 3 4 5 6 7 x)

22. A can of juice sells for $.59 at the grocery store. On a coordinate graph make *cost* the unit on the vertical axis and *number of cans* the unit on the horizontal axis. Plot a graph showing the cost of 1, 2, 3, 4, 5, and 6 cans. *(Lesson 3-3)* **See left.**

In 23 and 24, simplify. *(Lessons 3-1, 3-2)*

23. $(x + 14) + {-14}$ **x**

24. $({-7} + 5x) + 7$ **5x**

25. The Ceramco Co. showed a loss of $5 million in 1983 and a profit of $3.2 million in 1984. What was the net change during this time? *(Lesson 3-1)* **-$1.8 million**

26. a. Solve $2.75x = 8.25$. **x = 3;**   b) **Multiply both sides by $\frac{1}{a}$.**
   b. What is done to solve an equation of the form $ax = b$?
   c. Solve $2.75 + x = 8.25$. **x = 5.5**
   d. What is done to solve an equation of the form $a + x = b$? *(Lessons 2-6, 3-2)* **Add -a to both sides.**

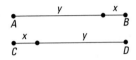

27. a. Which property tells you segments $\overline{AB}$ and $\overline{CD}$ at the left have the same length? **Commutative Property of Addition**
   b. Express that length in terms of x and y. *(Lesson 3-1)* **x + y**

28. Consider $\frac{2}{3}x = 24$,
   a. Solve this equation. **x = 36**
   b. Make up a problem which can be solved with this equation. *(Lesson 2-6)* **Sample: Crystal gave $\frac{2}{3}$ of her money, which was $24, to her sister. How much money did she have to start with?**

29. An air conditioning unit with a high energy efficient ratio (EER) gives more cooling with less electricity. To find the EER of a unit, divide the BTU (British Thermal Unit) number by the number of watts. The higher the EER, the more efficient the air conditioner.

$$EER = \frac{BTU}{watts}$$

At the center of things.
Pictured is Falling Springs Mill in Mark Twain National Forest. The forest covers an area of 608,719 acres.

   a. Find the EER to the nearest tenth for an air conditioner having BTU = 12,600 and watts = 1315. **9.6**
   b. Find the EER to the nearest tenth for an air conditioner having BTU = 5,000 and watts = 850. **5.9**
   c. Which air conditioner, in part **a** or **b**, is more efficient? Justify your answer. *(Lesson 1-5)* **a; 9.6 > 5.9**

30. Is $x = {-6}$ a solution to $4x + 15 = {-7}$? Explain how you know. *(Lesson 1-1)* **No; 4 · -6 + 15 = -9; -9 ≠ -7.**

Exploration

31. In 1990, the U.S. center of population was near Steelville, Missouri, in Mark Twain National Forest. According to American Demographics, the center of population has been moving daily about 58 feet west and 29 feet south. **See below.**
   a. At this rate, how far will it have moved by the year 2020?
   b. Where will it be? (You will need to consult a map.)
   a) 120.4 miles West;   60.2 miles South;   b) near Chesapeake, Missouri, about 20 miles west of Springfield

---

Follow-up for Lesson **3-4**

Practice

For more questions on SPUR Objectives, use **Lesson Master 3-4A** shown on page 167) or **Lesson Master 3-4B** (shown on pages 168–169).

Assessment

Quiz A quiz covering Lessons 3-1 through 3-4 is provided in the *Assessment Sourcebook.*

Written Communication Ask students to explain the meanings of slide, image, and preimage. [Students' explanations show understanding of the terms.]

Extension

Have students **work in pairs.** Give them **Teaching Aid 28.** Direct each student to first draw any triangle on the coordinate grid and then draw an image of the figure. Have students exchange graphs with their partners and determine the rule used to obtain the image.

Project Update Project 5, *Slides in Activities,* on page 206, relates to the content of this lesson.

▶ **LESSON MASTER 3-4 B** *page 2*

7. Give the coordinates of the point $Q = (x, y)$ under a slide
   a. 4 units left and 8 units up. $(x + {-4}, y + 8)$
   b. 5 units right and 4 units up. $(x + 5, y + 4)$
   c. 5 units down. $(x, y + {-5})$
   d. 9 units right. $(x + 9, y)$

8. Give a formula for a slide for which the image of the point (3, -2) is **Samples are given.**
   a. in Quadrant I. 1 unit right, 3 units up
   b. in Quadrant II. 4 units left, 3 units up
   c. in Quadrant III. 5 units left
   d. in Quadrant IV. 2 units right
   e. on the *x*-axis. 2 units up
   f. on the *y*-axis. 3 units left

In 9–12, use the graph at the right which shows *M* and its image, *M'*, after a slide.
9. Describe the slide. 3 units left, 6 units up
10. Point *H* is shown on the graph. Plot *H'*, its image under the same slide that was used to go from *M* to *M'*.
11. Fill in the blanks to describe the slide algebraically:
    The image of (x, y) is (x + **-3**, y + **6**)
12. a. Give a formula for the slide that would move *M'* onto *M*. $(x + 3, y + {-6})$
    b. Compare your answer in Part a to your answer to Question 9 and explain what you notice. Sample: They are slides in the opposite directions.

Objectives

B Solve and check equations of the form $ax + b = c$.
G Apply models of addition to write and solve equations of the form $ax + b = c$.
K Use balance scales to represent equations.

Resources

From the Teacher's Resource File
- Lesson Master 3-5A or 3-5B
- Answer Master 3-5
- Teaching Aids
  19 Balance-Scale Diagrams
  22 Warm-up
- Activity Kit, Activity 6

Additional Resources
- Visuals for Teaching Aids 19, 22
- Balance scale and weights

Teaching Lesson 3-5

Warm-up

Mental Mathematics Write the opposite and the reciprocal of each number.

1. -9 $9, -\frac{1}{9}$
2. $\frac{2}{3}$ $-\frac{2}{3}, \frac{3}{2}$
3. 12 $-12, \frac{1}{12}$
4. 1.5 $-1.5, \frac{2}{3}$ or $\frac{1}{1.5}$
5. -20 $20, -\frac{1}{20}$
6. $\frac{1}{8}$ $-\frac{1}{8}, 8$
7. -4 $4, -\frac{1}{4}$
8. 16 $-16, \frac{1}{16}$
9. $-2\frac{1}{2}$ $2\frac{1}{2}, -\frac{2}{5}$
10. 3.65 $-3.65, \frac{1}{3.65}$

LESSON 3-5

Solving $ax + b = c$

$$4W + 3 = 11$$

So far you have solved equations that involve either multiplication or addition *but not both*. Now you are ready to solve equations that involve multiplication *and* addition. One such equation is $4W + 3 = 11$.

This equation is pictured above with a balance scale. On the left side of the scale are 4 boxes, each of unknown weight W, and 3 one-ounce weights. They balance with the 11 ounces on the right.

You can find the weight W of one box in two steps. Each step keeps the scale balanced.

Step 1: Remove 3 oz from each side of the scale.

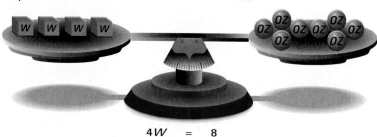

$$4W = 8$$

Step 2: Leave $\frac{1}{4}$ of the contents on each side.

$$W = 2$$

170

Lesson 3-5 Overview

Broad Goals All aspects of solving equations of the form $ax + b = c$ are discussed in this lesson: the skill (algorithm) itself; justification by the Multiplication Property of Equality and the Addition Property of Equality; the application to several problems; the representation on a balance scale.

Perspective Combining the operations of multiplication and addition in equations can present a formidable challenge to some students. It takes time for them to become accustomed to the patterns and algorithm. However, because students have already solved equations of the form $ax = b$, the most difficult aspect of solving $ax + b = c$ has already been discussed. Because we want students to begin their solutions by first adding the same number to both sides,

we try to give examples that cannot be done easily in one's head.

Even though there is substantial practice on equation solving in this chapter, students are not expected to achieve perfect mastery of all of the possible forms of linear equations of this type. By Chapter 8, where equations of lines are discussed, students should be very proficient at solving equations.

Example 1 shows the same steps without the balance scale.

❷ **Example 1**

Solve $4W + 3 = 11$.

Solution

$$4W + 3 = 11$$
$$4W + 3 + (-3) = 11 + (-3) \qquad \text{Addition Property of Equality}$$
$$4W = 8 \qquad \text{(Add -3 to each side.)}$$
$$\tfrac{1}{4}(4W) = \tfrac{1}{4}(8) \qquad \text{Multiplication Property of Equality}$$
$$W = 2 \qquad \text{(Multiply both sides by } \tfrac{1}{4}.\text{)}$$

Check

Substitute 2 for W in the original equation. Does $4 \cdot 2 + 3 = 11$? Yes.

Any equation of the form $ax + b = c$ can be solved in two steps. First add the opposite of b to both sides. Then multiply both sides by the reciprocal of a.

Example 2

Solve $\tfrac{2}{3}x + 19 = 7$, and check your answer.

Solution

This equation is of the form $ax + b = c$, with $a = \tfrac{2}{3}$, $b = 19$, and $c = 7$.

$$\tfrac{2}{3}x + 19 = 7$$
$$\tfrac{2}{3}x + 19 + -19 = 7 + -19 \qquad \text{Add -19 to each side.}$$
$$\tfrac{2}{3}x = -12 \qquad \text{Simplify.}$$
$$\tfrac{3}{2}\left(\tfrac{2}{3}x\right) = \tfrac{3}{2} \cdot -12 \qquad \text{Multiply each side by the reciprocal of } \tfrac{2}{3}.$$
$$x = -18 \qquad \text{Simplify.}$$

Check

Substitute $x = -18$ in the original equation. Do you get a true sentence?

Does $\tfrac{2}{3}(-18) + 19 = 7$?

$\tfrac{2}{3} \cdot \tfrac{-\overset{-6}{18}}{1} + 19 = 7$?

$-12 + 19 = 7$?

Yes, the sentence is true. So -18 checks.

Often equations are complicated but can be simplified into ones that you can solve. Simplifying each side is an important step in equation solving.

Notes on Reading

❶ Using Physical Models You might go through these steps with an actual balance scale. (You may have to substitute other weights for the kilogram weights shown.) If you do not have a balance scale, you could use **Teaching Aid 19** and draw the weights on the scales. Or you might use envelopes and paper clips as suggested in the *Optional Activities* below.

❷ Reading Mathematics This lesson has a long reading section; you might point out that, other than the balance-scale discussion, all of the reading is in the form of examples. The key questions to ask while reading relate to the purposes of the examples and how they differ from each other.

It is important for students to realize that there are only two major steps in solving $ax + b = c$ (as shown in **Example 1**). Other steps (as in **Example 3**) clarify the process. **Example 4** involves negative numbers. Still, the algorithm is the same.

✎ **Writing** Point out the columns of work and explanations in **Examples 1 and 2**. Note that we either name the properties that are used to justify each step or explain what was done. Discuss either format as a way for students to write what they do.

Optional Activities

Materials: Envelopes, paper clips in two colors, divider such as a ruler

If you wish to introduce this lesson with physical models, but you do not have a balance scale, you might want to use this activity or *Activity Kit, Activity 6*. Tell students that one color paper clip (for example, silver) represents 1 and the other color (for example, red) represents –1. Write $4x + 3 = 11$ on the board and in secret put

2 silver paper clips in each of 4 envelopes. Demonstrate the following steps.
1. Put the 4 envelopes and 3 silver clips on the left side of a divider. Put 11 silver clips on the right.
2. Put 3 red clips on each side of the divider. Remove pairs of silver and red clips so that 4 envelopes remain on the left and 8 silver clips remain on the right. Write $4x + 3 + -3 = 8 + -3$ and $4x = 8$.

3. One envelope is $\tfrac{1}{4}$ of the 4 envelopes and 2 clips are $\tfrac{1}{4}$ of the 8 silver clips. Show one envelope on the left and 2 silver clips on the right. Write $\tfrac{1}{4} \cdot 4x = \tfrac{1}{4} \cdot 8$ and $x = 2$. This means there are two paper clips in each envelope.

Repeat the activity for other equations of the form $ax + b = c$.

171

As students progress through the remainder of the chapter, you will have to advise them about the number of steps you want them to write down when they are solving an equation or inequality. It is best to keep in mind that the fundamental goal is getting the solution, not writing all the steps. There is research to indicate that the most capable problem solvers often skip steps; sometimes they cannot even tell you what the intermediate steps would have been. At first, most teachers ask students to show the addition and multiplication to each side of the equation. But as students' skills increase, writing down these steps can be dropped.

Some teachers use the symbol A_k to mean adding k to both sides and M_k to mean multiplying both sides by k. Then the solution to **Example 1** would be written as:

$$4W + 3 = 11$$
$$A_{-3} \qquad 4W = 8$$
$$M_{\frac{1}{4}} \qquad W = 2.$$

You may wish to apply this symbolism as you would any of the other teaching ideas that are presented here.

Leaping lemurs. *Most lemurs in the wild live in trees. The ring-tailed lemur, however, usually dwells on the ground. This ring-tailed lemur is in the Royal Zoological Gardens in Melbourne, Australia.*

Example 3

When Val works overtime at the zoo on Saturday, she earns $9.80 per hour. She is also paid $8.00 for meals and $3.00 for transportation. Last Saturday she earned $77.15. How many hours did she work?

Solution

Let h = the number of hours Val worked. In h hours she earned $9.80h$ dollars. So
$$9.80h + 8.00 + 3.00 = 77.15.$$

Solve for h.

$$9.80h + 11 = 77.15$$
$$9.80h + 11 + {-11} = 77.15 + {-11}$$
$$9.80h = 66.15$$
$$\frac{1}{9.80} \cdot 9.80h = \frac{1}{9.80} \cdot 66.15$$
$$h = 6.75$$

Val worked $6\frac{3}{4}$ hours.

Check

If she worked 6.75 hours at $9.80 per hour, she earned $6.75 \cdot 9.80$ dollars. That comes to $66.15. Now add $8 for meals and $3 for transportation. The total is $77.15, as it needs to be.

Even if the coefficient of x in $ax + b = c$ is negative, the equation is solved in the same way. If the equation is written with the variable on the right side, such as $c = ax + b$, the solution is still obtained by adding the opposite of b, and multiplying by the reciprocal of a.

Example 4

Solve $-2 = -8x + {-6}$.

Solution

First add the opposite of -6 to both sides. The opposite is 6.
$$-2 = -8x + {-6}$$
$$6 + {-2} = -8x + {-6} + 6$$
$$4 = -8x$$

Now multiply each side by $-\frac{1}{8}$, which is the reciprocal of -8.
$$-\frac{1}{8}(4) = -\frac{1}{8} \cdot {-8x}$$
$$-\frac{1}{2} = x$$

Check

Substitute $x = -\frac{1}{2}$ into the equation.
Does $-2 = -8\left(-\frac{1}{2}\right) + {-6}$?
$$-2 = 4 + {-6}?$$
Yes, since $-2 = -2$ the equation checks.

172

Covering the Reading

1. The boxes are of unknown equal weight W.
   a. What equation is pictured by this balance scale? $2W + 4 = 12$

1b) Remove 4 oz from both sides. Divide the remaining number of ounces on the right by the number of boxes on the left (2).

   b. What two steps can be done with the weights on the scale to find the weight of a single box? See left.
   c. How much does each box weigh? 4 oz.

2. a. When solving $4n + 8 = 60$, first add __?__ to both sides. Then __?__ both sides by __?__. -8; multiply; $\frac{1}{4}$
   b. Solve and check $4n + 8 = 60$. $n = 13$; $4 \cdot 13 + 8 = 60$

3. The steps used to solve $55v + 61 = 556$ are shown here.

   Given: $55v + 61 = 556$
   Step 1: $55v = 495$
   Step 2: $v = 9$

   a. What was done to arrive at Step 1? -61 was added to both sides.
   b. What was done to arrive at Step 2? Both sides were multiplied by $\frac{1}{55}$.

In 4–7, solve and check.

4. $8x + 15 = 47$
   $x = 4$; $8 \cdot 4 + 15 = 47$
5. $7y + 11 = 74$
   $y = 9$; $7 \cdot 9 + 11 = 74$
6. $-2z + 32 = 288$
   $z = -128$; $-2 \cdot -128 + 32 = 288$
7. $2 = 9x + -3$
   $x = 5/9$; $2 = 9 \cdot 5/9 + -3$

8. a. What should be the first step in solving $3.5 + 2x + 5.6 = 10$? Add 3.5 and 5.6.
   b. Solve and check this equation.
   $x = 0.45$; $3.5 + 2(.45) + 5.6 = 10$

9. Refer to Example 3. If Val's pay two Saturdays ago was $89.40, how many hours did she work that day? 8 hours

In 10–13, solve and check.

10. $\frac{3}{4}x + 12 = 27$
    $x = 20$; $\frac{3}{4} \cdot 20 + 12 = 27$
11. $5 = -4x + 15$
    $x = \frac{5}{2}$; $5 = -4 \cdot \frac{5}{2} + 15$
12. $-8n + -18 = 88$
    $x = -13.25$; $-8 \cdot -13.25 + -18 = 88$
13. $16 = \frac{2}{3}a + 20$
    $a = -6$; $16 = \frac{2}{3} \cdot -6 + 20$

Adapting to Individual Needs

English Language Development
If students have made index cards listing the properties of addition and multiplication, you might want to have them review the properties at this time.

If your students have started a mobile (See *English Language Development* on page 88), you might have students add the properties of addition and multiplication to it.

Additional Examples
In 1–2, solve and check your answers.
1. $125 = 6m + 11$ $m = 19$
   Check: Does $125 = 6 \cdot 19 + 11$? $125 = 114 + 11$? $125 = 125$? yes
2. $\frac{5}{8}m + 20 = 85$ $m = 104$
   Check: Does $\frac{5}{8} \cdot 104 + 20 = 85$? $65 + 20 = 85$? $85 = 85$? yes
3. The height of an office building is 133.5 feet, and the height of the entrance level is 15.5 feet. If the building contains 11 floors of offices, and the roof is 2.5 feet thick, what is the height of each floor of offices? (Your answer will include the thickness of the ceiling and the floor.) 10.5 feet
4. Solve $-685 = -5v + 1025$.
   $v = 342$

Notes on Questions
Questions 7, 11, and 13
Error Alert Some students have difficulty if the variable term is on the right side of the equation. Yet this is a common kind of equation to be solved when lines are given in the form $y = mx + b$. Students have to recognize that solving $c = ax + b$ involves the same processes as solving $ax + b = c$.

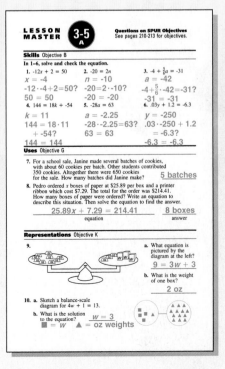

New England beauty.
Pictured is a view of Starke, New Hampshire. In the fall, tourists visit to see the changing colors of the leaves.

15b) x = $23.70; Total interest for June was $23.70.

19)

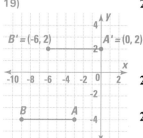

Applying the Mathematics

In 14–16, a situation is given. **a.** Write an equation to describe the situation. **b.** Solve the equation and answer the question.

14. Luisa lives in New Hampshire, where there is no sales tax. She bought three hamburgers with a $5 bill and received $0.53 change. What was the price of one hamburger? a) $5 − 3x = $0.53; b) x = $1.49; The cost of one hamburger is $1.49.

15. On June 2, Carlos's savings account showed a balance of $4347.59. During the next month he deposited a total of $752.85 and withdrew $550.00. His July 1 bank statement reported that Carlos had $4574.14 including interest. How much interest had he earned during June? a) $4347.59 + $752.85 + -$550.00 + x = $4574.14 b) See left.

16. The Kuderskis are saving for their children's education. They have 150 shares of a single stock and $1500 cash. If the total value of their savings is currently $3637.50, what is the value of one share of the stock? a) 150x + 1500 = $3637.50 b) x = $14.25; the value of one share of the stock is $14.25.

In 17 and 18, solve and check.

17. $3\frac{1}{4} + x = 10\frac{1}{2}$
$x = 7\frac{1}{4}$; $3\frac{1}{4} + 7\frac{1}{4} = 10\frac{1}{2}$

18. $\frac{2}{3}t + \frac{1}{3} = 7$
$t = 10$; $\frac{2}{3} \cdot 10 + \frac{1}{3} = 7$

Review

In 19 and 20, graph $A = (-3, -4)$ and $B = (-9, -4)$, and connect the points with a line segment.

19. If the image of (x, y) is $(x + 3, y + 6)$, draw the image of $\overline{AB}$. *(Lesson 3-4)* See left.

20. What rule would describe a slide of $\overline{AB}$ 5 units down? *(Lesson 3-4)* The image of (x, y) is $(x, y − 5)$

21. Triangle $D'E'F'$ is a slide image of triangle DEF. $D = (0, 0)$, $E = (1, 4)$, $F = (3, 6)$, and $F' = (5, 2)$. *(Lesson 3-4)*
  a. Describe the slide choosing the appropriate directions: 2 right; __?__ units (left or right) and __?__ units (up or down). 4 down
  b. What are the coordinates of D' and E'? $D' = (2, -4)$; $E' = (3,0)$

22. **a.** Evaluate $-(-39) + -(-(-39))$. 0
  b. Explain how you got your answer. *(Lesson 3-2)* Sample: The right term is the opposite of the left term, so they add to zero.

23. The numbers in the table below represent the cost c (in dollars) of n note pads. *(Lessons 1-9, 2-4)*

n	1	2	3	4
c	.50	1.00	1.50	2.00

  a. How much would you expect to pay for 6 note pads? $3.00
  b. Write a formula for the cost of n note pads. $.50n = c$

24. The rectangle at right is made from a square with sides x units long and two rectangles with sides of lengths 1 and x. Find the area of the rectangle. *(Lesson 2-1)* $x^2 + 2x$

174

Adapting to Individual Needs

Challenge
Have students solve the following problem: When asked to give her birth date, a math teacher said, "I was born in a Leap Year. If I had been born 10 days later, then $\frac{2}{3}$ of the year would have elapsed." When is the teacher's birthday? [August 21]

25. *Skill sequence.* Write as a decimal. *(Previous course)*
a. 20% .2
b. 2% .02
c. 102% 1.02
d. 120% 1.20

In 26–29, a consumer research organization evaluated the flavor and texture of popular strawberry ice creams. The rating scale had a maximum possible score of 6 (flavor and texture very good) and a minimum possible of -6 (very bad). The data are presented in the table and scatterplot. *(Lesson 3-3)*

Cost and Ratings for Popular Strawberry Ice Cream Brands

Brand	Cost per Serving	Rating
Berry N'ice	57	3
Perfect Parfait	55	5
Delicious	52	5
Merry Berry	49	-1
Sundae Special	46	3
Gourmet	43	2
Fabulous Flavors	26	1
Bon Appetit	22	2
Betty's Best	19	3
Select	18	-1
P. Good	18	1
Creamy Creations	17	-2
Mix-in Magic	17	-4
I. Scream	16	3
Ambrosia	16	-1
Tasty Treat	12	-2
Nuts and Berries	12	-1
Sweet Swirl	12	-3

26. Which point (*A, B, C, D,* or *E*) represents Gourmet? D

27. Which point represents Select? B

28. Which ice cream seems to be a poor value; that is, it costs a lot but has a low rating? Merry Berry

29. Is there a tendency for ice cream which costs more to taste better? Justify your answer. Yes, several of the higher priced ice creams have a high rating.

30. a. Make up an equation of the form $x + a = b$, where a and b are positive, and the solution is negative. Sample: x + 10 = 7
b. Solve your equation. *(Lesson 3-2)* x = -3

Exploration

31. Consider equations of the form $ax + b = c$, where $a \neq 0$.
a. Write a program for a calculator or computer that accepts values of a, b, and c as input, and gives the value of x as output.
Answers will vary.
b. Run your program with different values of a, b, and c leading to both positive and negative solutions.
The key is a step that finds $x = \frac{c - b}{a}$.

Lesson 3-5 *Solving ax + b = c* **175**

Follow-up 3-5 for Lesson

Practice
For more questions on SPUR Objectives, use **Lesson Master 3-5A** (shown on page 173) or **Lesson Master 3-5B** (shown on pages 174–175).

Assessment
Oral Communication Ask students to name and give examples of some of the possible errors that could be made when solving equations in this lesson. [Responses include multiplying by the reciprocal before adding the opposite, adding *b* to both sides instead of the opposite of *b*, and computing incorrectly.]

Extension
The formula for converting Celsius temperatures to Fahrenheit, $F = \frac{9}{5}C + 32$, is of the form $ax + b = c$. Have students solve the equation for C. $[C = \frac{5}{9}(F + -32)]$

175

In-class Activity

Resources

From the *Teacher's Resource File*
- Answer Master 3-6
- Teaching Aid 31: Algebra Tiles

Additional Resources
- Visual for Teaching Aid 31

This activity helps students in two fundamental ways. First, it gives a concrete illustration of the drawings in Lesson 3-6. Second, it points out why the sum of different powers of the same variable cannot be simplified.

Because the area model is used in Lesson 3-7 to justify the removing of parentheses and in Chapter 10 to multiply polynomials, this activity should not be neglected. If you do not have commercial algebra tiles, have students cut tiles out of cardboard. Or, have them paste the tiles from **Teaching Aid 31** on heavy paper, and cut them out. Students should keep the tiles for use with other activities thoughout this book.

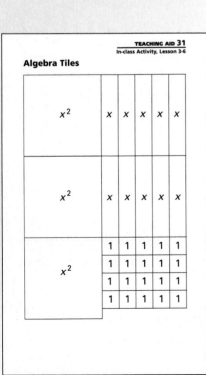

TEACHING AID 31
In-class Activity, Lesson 3-6

Algebra Tiles

Using Algebra Tiles to Add Expressions

IN·CLASS
ACTIVITY

Work on this activity in small groups. Each group will need about eight tiles of each size.

Many algebraic expressions can be illustrated by using *algebra tiles*. Algebra tiles are rectangular tiles whose areas represent 1, x, and x^2.

You can arrange tiles to represent an expression. The expressions $2x^2 + 3x$ and $2x + 3$ are shown below.

$$x^2 + x^2 + x + x + x = 2x^2 + 3x \qquad x + x + 1 + 1 + 1 = 2x + 3$$

See margin for additional answers.

In 1 and 2, use tiles to represent the expression. Draw pictures of your tiles.

1. a. $4x^2$
   b. $4x^2 + 2x$
   c. $4x^2 + 2x + 2$

2. a. $4x$
   b. $3x^2 + 4x$
   c. $3x^2 + 4x + 1$

In 3 and 4, what expression is shown?

3.
$x^2 + 4x + 5$

4.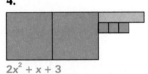
$2x^2 + x + 3$

5. To add algebraic expressions, arrange tiles representing each addend and count like tiles. Use tiles to illustrate this sum. Then copy and complete the equation.
$$(x^2 + 3x) + (2x^2 + x + 2) = \underset{3}{\underline{\,?\,}}\,x^2 + \underset{4}{\underline{\,?\,}}\,x + \underset{2}{\underline{\,?\,}}$$

In 6, use tiles to illustrate the sum, and give the sum.

6. a. $(2x^2 + 4x + 1) + (x^2 + 4)$ **b.** $(x^2 + 3) + (2x + 2)$
   c. $(x^2 + 3x) + (x^2 + x)$ **d.** $(4 + 2x + x^2) + (3x^2 + x + 1)$

Additional Answers

1. a. $4x^2$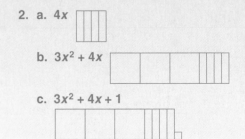

b. $4x^2 + 2x$

c. $4x^2 + 2x + 2$

2. a. $4x$

b. $3x^2 + 4x$

c. $3x^2 + 4x + 1$

(Answers continue on page 208.)

The Distributive Property and Adding Like Terms

The latest addition. *As this library obtained new editions, it found it needed a new addition. The total area of the library, after its completed addition, can be found by using the Distributive Property.*

Suppose two rectangles, each having width *c,* are placed end to end. What is the total area? You can calculate the area two ways. First, you can add the areas of the two smaller rectangles. The total area is $ac + bc$.

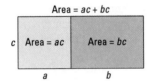

Area = $ac + bc$

Or, you can multiply the width *c* by the total length $a + b$. The total area is $(a + b)c$.

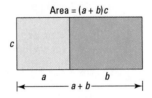

Area = $(a + b)c$

The area is the same, regardless of how you calculate it:
$ac + bc = (a + b)c$. This is an instance of the *Distributive Property*.

> **Distributive Property: Adding or Subtracting Like Terms Forms**
> For any real numbers *a, b,* and *c,*
> $$ac + bc = (a + b)c \text{ and}$$
> $$ac - bc = (a - b)c.$$

Lesson **3-6**

Objectives
A Use the Distributive Property to simplify expressions.
B Solve and check equations of the form $ax + b = c$.
E Identify and apply the Distributive Property.
G Apply models for addition to write and solve equations involving like terms.
K Use area models to represent the Distributive Property.

Resources
From the *Teacher's Resource File*
- Lesson Master 3-6A or 3-6B
- Answer Master 3-6
- Teaching Aids
  22 Warm-up
  26 Graph Paper

Additional Resources
- Visuals for Teaching Aids 22, 26

Teaching **3-6**
Lesson

Warm-up
A pack of NBA basketball cards costs $2.19. Ellen bought four packs of cards last week, three packs yesterday, and two packs today.
1. How much did she spend on basketball cards, excluding tax? **$19.71**
2. Explain two ways in which you can find the answer. **(1) Multiply the total number of packs by $2.19; (2) Multiply $2.19 by 4, by 3, and by 2; then find the sum of the products. This shows 9 · 2.19 = 4 · 2.19 + 3 · 2.19 + 2 · 2.19.**

Lesson 3-6 Overview

Broad Goals The goals of this lesson are for students to simplify expressions of the form $ax \pm bx$ and to apply this skill in solving equations of the form $ax \pm bx = c$.

Perspective Here the Distributive Property is applied in only one direction: the change from the sum $ac + bc$ to the product $(a + b)c$. The reverse direction, converting the product $a(b + c)$ into the sum $ab + ac$, is discussed in Lesson 3-7.

The Area Model for Multiplication and the Putting-Together Model for Addition combine to give the familiar area picture of the Distributive Property that begins the lesson. If you think of ac and bc as multiples of c, the Distributive Property becomes the justification for adding like terms. That is how this form of the property gets its name.

The corresponding property for subtraction, that the difference $ac - bc$ equals the

product $(a - b)c$, is also treated here. It too has a geometric picture, in this case a combination of the Area Model for Multiplication and the Take-Away Model for Subtraction. Both addition and subtraction cases will be considered further in the next chapter, so students need not master the idea here.

Reading Mathematics You can use **Questions 1–15** to review the reading. Go around the class, calling on students to read a paragraph. As you finish relevant paragraphs, refer to the questions that apply to the ideas. The questions relate to the reading as follows:

Question 1—page 176;
Questions 2–4—the Activity;
Questions 5–6—Example 1;
Questions 7–10—Example 2;
Questions 11–14—Example 3;
Question 15—Example 4.

Have students record the results of the *Activity* for use in **Question 2** on page 180.

Two pictures of the Distributive Property to combine like terms are shown below. You might want to discuss them with your students.

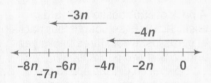

$$2a + 3a = 5a$$

$$3n^2 + 4n^2 = 7n^2$$

Additional Examples

1. Simplify $-4n + -3n$.
   a. Use the Distributive Property.
      $(-4 + -3)n = -7n$
   b. Use a number line.

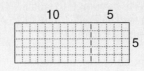

2. Simplify.
   a. $6 + a + 5b + -a + -b + 2a + 7$
      $2a + 4b + 13$
   b. $(7y)(3y) + 7(4y^2)$ $49y^2$
3. Solve.
   a. $9x - x = 144$ $x = 18$
   b. $6 + -2x + -9x = 39$ $x = -3$

Take a rectangular piece of paper of length 11 in. and any width x in. Cut off a piece of length 4 in. What is the area of the remaining piece?
$7x$ in^2

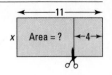

Adding Like Terms.

A **term** is either a single number or a variable, or a product of numbers and variables. The expressions $7s$ and $-2s$ are called **terms,** and the 7 and -2 are the **coefficients** of s. When the variables in the terms are the same, they are called **like terms,** and the addition can be performed by adding the coefficients. This simplification is called **adding like terms.** Adding like terms is an instance of the Distributive Property.

Example 1

Simplify $7s + -2s$.

Solution 1

Use the Distributive Property to add the like terms.

$$7s + -2s = (7 + -2)s = 5s$$

Recall the Multiplicative Identity Property of 1. For any real number n, $n = 1n$. When this property is combined with the Distributive Property, many expressions can be simplified. For instance, $k + 8k = 1k + 8k = 9k$.

Example 2

Simplify $(3s + d + 6) + (2d + s)$.

Solution 1

Use the Commutative and Associative Properties to group like terms.
$$(3s + d + 6) + (2d + s) = (3s + s) + (d + 2d) + 6 \qquad s = 1 \cdot s$$
$$= (3s + 1s) + (1d + 2d) + 6 \qquad d = 1 \cdot d$$
$$= 4s + 3d + 6 \qquad \text{Add like terms.}$$

So $(3s + d + 6) + (2d + s) = 4s + 3d + 6$.

Solution 2

Think of segments of lengths s, d, and 6. Use the Putting-Together Model of Addition.

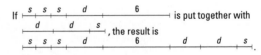

This segment has length $4s + 3d + 6$.
So $(3s + d + 6) + (2d + s) = 4s + 3d + 6$.

178

Optional Activities

Materials: **Teaching Aid 26**

After you have discussed the Distributive Property, have students copy the rectangles shown at the right on graph paper or on **Teaching Aid 26.** Then ask them to find the area of each rectangle in two ways. [Left rectangle: $5 \cdot 10 + 5 \cdot 5 = 50 + 25 = 75$; $5 \cdot 15 = 75$. Right rectangle: $10 \cdot 10 + 10 \cdot 5 + 5 \cdot 10 + 5 \cdot 5 = 100 + 50 + 50 + 25 = 225$; $15 \cdot 15 = 225$.]

Adding Like Terms in Equations

The Distributive Property can be used in solving equations.

Example 3

Solve $-3x + 5x = -12$.

Solution

Apply the Distributive Property to add like terms.

$$(-3 + 5)x = -12$$
$$2x = -12$$
$$\tfrac{1}{2} \cdot 2x = \tfrac{1}{2} \cdot -12 \qquad \text{Multiply both sides by } \tfrac{1}{2}.$$
$$x = -6$$

Check

Substitute -6 for x in the original equation.
Does $-3 \cdot -6 + 5 \cdot -6 = -12$?
$$18 + -30 = -12?$$
$$-12 = -12? \text{ Yes, } -6 \text{ checks.}$$

Example 4

A $150,000 estate is to be split among three children, a grandchild, and a charity. Each child gets the same amount, while the grandchild gets half as much. If the charity receives $10,000, how much will each child receive?

Solution

Write an equation. Let c represent each child's portion. Then $\tfrac{1}{2}c$ is the grandchild's portion.

$$c + c + c + \tfrac{1}{2}c + 10{,}000 = 150{,}000$$

$$1c + 1c + 1c + \tfrac{1}{2}c + 10{,}000 = 150{,}000 \qquad \text{Use the Multiplicative Identity Property of 1.}$$

$$3\tfrac{1}{2}c + 10{,}000 = 150{,}000 \qquad \text{Use the Distributive Property to add like terms.}$$

$$3\tfrac{1}{2}c = 150{,}000 + -10{,}000 \qquad \text{Add } -10{,}000 \text{ to each side.}$$

$$3\tfrac{1}{2}c = 140{,}000$$

$$c = 40{,}000 \qquad \text{Multiply each side by the reciprocal of } 3\tfrac{1}{2}, \text{ or by } \tfrac{2}{7}.$$

Each child should receive $40,000.

Check

The grandchild receives half as much as each child does, and so gets $20,000. Does $40{,}000 + 40{,}000 + 40{,}000 + 20{,}000 + 10{,}000 = 150{,}000$? Yes.

Lesson 3-6 The Distributive Property and Adding Like Terms **179**

Estate Sale. *Sometimes a home is included in a person's estate. This two-story frame house would sell for about $150,000 in some sections of the U.S.*

---

4. Last week, Waverly Hardware had a sale on varnish. At the beginning of the week, there were 16 cans on the shelf. Those cans were sold, along with three additional cases containing cans of varnish. If a total of 112 cans was sold, how many cans of varnish did each case hold? Write an equation and give the answer. **$16 + n + n + n = 112$, or $16 + 3n = 112$; 32 cans**

5. Sheila has to read two short stories for her English class. One of the stories is $2\tfrac{1}{2}$ times as long as the other. If she wants to read both stories in an hour, about how much time should she allow for the first story? **About 17 minutes**

6. A $225,000 estate is to be split among four children and two nieces. The children will each receive the same amounts of money, and each niece will receive one-quarter as much. How much money should each child receive? **$50,000**

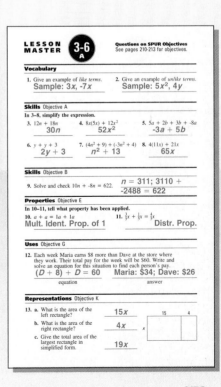

Adapting to Individual Needs

Extra Help

Give students the following saying and ask them what they think it means: *It's like trying to add apples and oranges.* [Sample: You cannot add unlike quantities.] Point out that terms with variables such as $3x$ and $5x$ are like the phrases 3 apples and 5 apples. As quantities, 3 apples and 5 apples can be added to get 8 apples because $3 + 5 = 8$ and *apples* is a common label. Likewise, $3x$ and $5x$ can be added to get $8x$ because x is

a common factor. On the other hand, the phrases 3 apples and 5 oranges do not have a common label. Likewise, $5x$ and $3y$ do not have a common factor, so they cannot be added. Be sure students understand that the purpose of adding like terms is to simplify an expression or equation so there are fewer terms to work with.

Question 15 Point out that this kind of situation is not uncommon in wills. A person who writes a will never knows exactly what the value of the estate will be at the time of his or her death. Often, wills refer to parts of an estate in terms of percents of the total estate or in terms of multiples, like those given in this question.

Question 20 Like the division of the estate in **Question 15,** this is not an unusual way to split a purse.

(Notes on Questions continue on page 182.)

Note: The arithmetic in Example 4 could have been made easier by thinking of all amounts "in thousands." Then the equation $3\frac{1}{2}c + 10 = 150$ would describe the situation. It would still be solved using the same steps as in the example.

QUESTIONS

Covering the Reading

1. State the Distributive Property. For any real numbers *a, b,* and *c,* $ac + bc = (a + b)c$ and $ac - bc = (a - b)c$.

2. What answer did you get for the Activity in the lesson? $7x$ in^2

3. What instance of the Distributive Property is pictured below? $21n + 8n = (21 + 8)n$

4)

3   7

y

5b) Mark the number line in units of *s.* Start at 0*s* and draw an arrow 5 units to the left followed by an arrow 8 units to the right. The slide ends at 3*s.*

4. Draw rectangles to picture the addition $3y + 7y = 10y$. See left.

5. **a.** Simplify $-5s + 8s$. 3*s*
   b. Explain how to check your answer by using a number line. See left.

6. Refer to the figure below. Find the length of each segment.
   a. AB $2x + y$ **b.** BC $2y + x$ **c.** AC $3x + 3y$

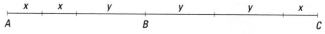

In 7–10, simplify the expression.

7. $9x + -3x$ 6*x*

8. $5z + z$ 6*z*

9. $(3a + b) + (2a + 3b)$ $5a + 4b$

10. $(12p + 2q + 8) + (-4p + 5q)$ $8p + 7q + 8$

In 11–14, simplify one side of the equation, and then solve.

11. $3h + 2h = 40$ $5h = 40$; $h = 8$

12. $x + 3x = -20$ $4x = -20$; $x = -5$

13. $67.9 = r + r$ $67.9 = 2r$; $r = 33.95$

14. $321 = a + 2a + 3a$ $321 = 6a$; $a = 53.5$

15. **a.** $90,000 is to be divided among three heirs. Two of the heirs receive equal amounts. The third heir receives one-fourth that amount. Write an equation and find how much money each heir will receive.
    b. Suppose that $10,000 is given to charity before the heirs get any money. Write an equation and solve it to determine how much each heir will receive.

a) $r + r + \frac{1}{4}r = 90,000$; two heirs receive $40,000; the third heir receives $10,000.

b) $r + r + \frac{1}{4}r + 10,000 = 90,000$; 2 heirs receive $35,555.56; the third heir receives $8,888.89.

Adapting to Individual Needs

English Language Development
Help students understand the ideas given in the title of this lesson, *The Distributive Property and Adding Like Terms.* You might explain the word *distribute* by giving a book to each of several students, and telling them that you are "distributing" the books among them. Have students add the Distributive Property to their index-card list of properties.

Then you might show students what is meant by *adding like terms.* Ask two students how many notebooks and pencils they each have. Ask the class how many of each item they have altogether. [Sample answer: 1 notebook + 2 pencils + 2 notebooks + 3 pencils = 3 notebooks and 5 pencils] Explain that they added like terms to get 5 pencils. Similarly, 1 notebook and 2 notebooks can be added because they are like terms.

Universal hobby. *Stamp collecting has been called "the hobby of kings and the king of hobbies." Collectors value stamps for different reasons. Some stamps are valuable because they are rare.*

Applying the Mathematics

16. Ramon and Ramona collect stamps. Ramon has s stamps, and Ramona has 5 times as many stamps as Ramon. How many stamps do they have together? **$6s$ stamps**

17. Some taxicab companies allow their drivers to keep $\frac{3}{10}$ of all fares collected. The rest goes to the company. If a driver receives F dollars from fares, write an expression for the company's share.
$F - .3F$ or $.7F$

In 18 and 19, simplify.

18. $(x + {^-}6) + (2x + 4) + (3x + {^-}3)$ $6x + {^-}5$

19. $5f + (4f - 6) + (6 + {^-}9f)$ **0**

20. In a boxing match, the money divided between the fighters is called the purse. If the loser receives one-fifth of what the winner will get and the total purse is $500,000, how much will each boxer receive?
Winner gets $416,666.67;   loser gets $83,333.33

21. Around 800 A.D., the Islamic law of inheritance stated that when a woman died her husband received one-fourth of the estate and the rest was the children's share with a son receiving twice as much as a daughter. How many camels would a daughter inherit if the estate had 60 camels and her father and two brothers were still living?
9 camels

22. Solve and check $-n + 2n + {^-}5n + 7 = {^-}9$.
$n = 4$; $-4 + 2 \cdot 4 + {^-}5 \cdot 4 + 7 = {^-}9$

Review

23. The scale below is balanced. Each box has the same weight. The other weights are 1 ounce each.
    a. What equation is pictured? $3w + 2 = 8$
    b. How much does each box weigh?   *(Lesson 3-5)*

    $w = 2$ oz

24. Solve and check $93 = \frac{2}{3}x + 17$.   *(Lesson 3-5)* $x = 114$; $93 = \frac{2}{3}(114) + 17$

25. Explain how to solve any equation of the form $ax + b = c$, in which $a \neq 0$. Make up your own equation(s) to illustrate your explanation.
(Lesson 3-5) Sample: First add $-b$ to both sides; then multiply both sides by $\frac{1}{a}$. To solve $3x + 5 = 11$, add -5 to both sides to get $3x = 6$; then multiply both sides by $\frac{1}{3}$ to get $x = 2$.

Lesson 3-6   *The Distributive Property and Adding Like Terms*   **181**

Follow-up for Lesson 3-6

Practice
For more questions on SPUR Objectives, use **Lesson Master 3-6A** (shown on page 179), or **Lesson Master 3-6B** (shown on pages 180–181).

Assessment
Oral Communication Ask students to define and give examples of each of the following words or phrases: variable, term, coefficient, like terms, and adding like terms. Have the class decide if it agrees that the definitions and examples given are accurate. [Students can distinguish between variables and coefficients, recognize like terms, and use the Distributive Property to add like terms.]

Extension
Cooperative Learning The quantities *ax, bx,* and *cx* are said to be in the *extended ratio a:b:c*. Extended ratios can be simplified just as fractions are simplified. For instance, the extended ratio 6:8:10 simplifies to 3:4:5. Have students **work in pairs** to answer these questions.
1. Any triangle with sides in the extended ratio 3:4:5 is a right

(Extension continues on page 182.)

▶ **LESSON MASTER 3-6B** *page 2*

Skills Objective B: Solve and check equations of the form $ax + b = c$.

In 21 and 22, solve and check the equation.
21. $10q + {^-}4q = {^-}72$ 22. $21d + 16 + 13d = 67$

$q = {^-}12$ $d = 1.5$
$10 \cdot {^-}12 + {^-}4 \cdot {^-}12 = {^-}72?$ $21 \cdot 1.5 + 16 +$
${^-}72 = {^-}72$ $13 \cdot 1.5 = 67?$
                                       $67 = 67$

Properties Objective E: Identify and apply the Distributive Property.

In 23–25, tell whether or not the Distributive Property is involved. Write *yes* or *no*.
23. ${^-}({^-}9) = 9$ 24. ${^-}9a + 3a = {^-}6a$ 25. $\frac{2}{3}b + \frac{1}{3}b = b$
    no   yes   yes

Uses Objective G: Apply models for addition to write and solve equations involving like terms.

In 26 and 27, write an equation to describe the situation, solve the equation, and answer the question.
26. Helen bought a blouse, jeans, and a pair of shoes for $72. The blouse and jeans cost the same amount, and the shoes cost $6 more than the blouse. How much did the jeans cost?

$c + c + (c + 6) = 72$ $c = 22$ 22
   equation   solution   answer

27. The area of Ms. Whitecloud's property is 7,800 square feet. Her house occupies one fourth the area of land as the rest of the property. How many square feet of land does the house cover?

$\frac{1}{4}x + x = 7,800$ $x = 6,240$ $1,560$ ft²
   equation   solution   answer

Representations Objective K: Use area models to represent the Distributive Property.

28. a. What is the area of the top rectangle? $13x$
    b. What is the area of the bottom rectangle? $5x$
    c. What is the area of the largest rectangle? Give your answer in simplified form. $18x$

triangle, and it is called a 3-4-5 triangle. Find a 3-4-5 right triangle whose perimeter is 60 centimeters. [The lengths of the sides are 15 cm, 20 cm, and 25 cm.]

2. A professional tennis tournament pays the top four winners in the extended ratio 10:5:2:1. If the total purse is $200,000, how much will each of the top four winners receive? [$111,111.11, $55,555.56, $22,222.22, $11,111.11]

Notes on Questions

Question 33 There is always the danger that students will remember an incorrect form as being the correct one, so do not spend much time on this question. Concentrate on the process of substituting for x to help determine whether the property is true. Emphasize that such substitutions cannot determine certain truth, but they can determine falsity.

26c)
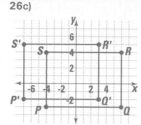

Sizzling temperatures.
The highest temperature ever recorded in the U.S. was in Death Valley. The temperature soared to 134°F (57°C) on July 10, 1913. The valley's warm winter and geological attractions have made it a popular winter resort area.

26. On a coordinate graph, plot and connect in order points P, Q, R, and S. $P = (-4, -3)$, $Q = (6, -3)$, $R = (6, 4)$, $S = (-4, 4)$.
   a. What geometric figure is $PQRS$? rectangle
   b. What is the area of $PQRS$? 70 square units
   c. Draw $P'Q'R'S'$, the image of $PQRS$ under the slide in which the image of (x, y) is $(x + -3, y + 1)$. See left.
   d. How is the area of $P'Q'R'S'$ related to the area of $PQRS$? *(Lessons 2-1, 3-4)* The areas are equal.

In 27 and 28, a number is given. **a.** State its opposite. **b.** State its reciprocal. *(Lessons 2-2, 3-2)*

27. 17 a) -17; b) $\frac{1}{17}$ 28. $-\frac{39}{2}$ a) $\frac{39}{2}$; b) $\frac{-2}{39}$

29. The elevation of Death Valley, California, is listed as -282 feet. What does the minus sign mean in this situation? *(Lesson 3-1)*
   The minus sign indicates the Death Valley area is 282 ft below sea level.

30. *Skill sequence.* Add. *(Previous course)*
   a. $\frac{3}{10} + \frac{1}{10}$ $\frac{4}{10} = \frac{2}{5}$ b. $\frac{3}{10} + \frac{1}{5}$ $\frac{5}{10} = \frac{1}{2}$ c. $\frac{3}{10} + \frac{2}{15}$ $\frac{13}{30}$

31. Suppose a laser printer prints 8 pages per minute. How long will it take to print 2400 documents with 3 pages per document?
   (Lesson 2-4) 900 minutes or 15 hours

32. The average mass of air molecules is $30 \cdot 1.66 \cdot 10^{-24}$ grams. Write this number in scientific notation. *(Previous course)* 4.98×10^{-23}

Exploration

33. Some people overgeneralize the Distributive Property. They think that because $6x + 2x = 8x$, all of the following should be true.
   (a) $6x \cdot 2x = 12x$ False; $6 \cdot 3 \cdot 2 \cdot 3 \neq 12 \cdot 3$
   (b) $\frac{6x}{2x} = 3x$ False; $\frac{6 \cdot 8}{2 \cdot 8} \neq 3 \cdot 8$
   (c) $6^x + 2^x = 8^x$ False; $6^3 + 2^3 \neq 8^3$
   (d) $6^x \cdot 2^x = 12^x$ True
   (e) $6\sqrt{x} + 2\sqrt{x} = 8\sqrt{x}$ True

   Only two of the above statements are true for all positive values of x. Which two are true? Give a counterexample for each of the others to show that they are false.

LESSON

3-7

The
Distributive
Property and
Removing
Parentheses

Removing parentheses. *The display shows that the three expressions have the same result. Some people prefer the third expression because it has no parentheses.*

You have used the Distributive Property to add like terms. Another form of the Distributive Property results when properties of addition and multiplication are applied.

$ac + bc = (a + b)c$	Add like terms.
$(a + b)c = ac + bc$	Switch sides of the equation.
$c(a + b) = ca + cb$	Use the Commutative Property of Multiplication.

We call this the **Removing Parentheses** form of the Distributive Property.

The Distributive Property: Removing Parentheses
For all real numbers *a, b,* and *c,*
$$c(a + b) = ca + cb \text{ and}$$
$$c(a - b) = ca - cb.$$

This form of the Distributive Property can be used to multiply a sum by a single term. It shows that *c* times the quantity $a + b$ is the same as the sum of *c* times each of its terms. The *c* is "distributed" over each term.

Lesson **3-7**

Objectives
A Use the Distributive Property to simplify expressions.
B Solve and check equations of the form $ax + b = c$.
E Identify and apply the Distributive Property.
F Use the Distributive Property to perform calculations mentally.
K Use area models to represent the Distributive Property.

Resources
From the *Teacher's Resource File*
■ Lesson Master 3-7A or 3-7B
■ Answer Master 3-7
■ Assessment Sourcebook: Quiz for Lessons 3-5 through 3-7
■ Teaching Aid 22: Warm-up
■ Activity Kit, Activity 7

Additional Resources
■ Visual for Teaching Aid 22

Teaching **3-7**
Lesson

Warm-up
Simplify each expression.
1. $2x^2 + x^2 + 5$ $3x^2 + 5$
2. $y^2 + y + 4y + 2$ $y^2 + 5y + 2$
3. $6 + z^2 + -z^2 + 1$ 7
4. $4a + -3a + 8a$ $9a$
5. $b^2 + 7b + 2 + 6b + -2$ $b^2 + 13b$
6. $-6 + 7 + 4 + -2 + 3 + 2$ 8

Lesson 3-7 Overview

Broad Goals Students apply the product form of the Distributive Property $c(a + b) = ca + cb$ to problems like the ones encountered in previous lessons; they simplify expressions, solve equations, and describe patterns. They also use this property to justify some mental computations.

Perspective The Distributive Property is used in this lesson to multiply a polynomial by a monomial (terms we do not introduce

until a later chapter). Three settings are given in the lesson. The first is the simplification of expressions, the second is mental arithmetic, and the third is solving equations.

The Area Model shows that the rewriting of $c(a + b)$ as $ca + cb$ (in this lesson) and the rewriting of $ac + bc$ as $(a + b)c$ (in Lesson 3-6) involves the same property. But the feel of the two procedures is quite different,

and we give them different colloquial names: *adding like terms* for the form found in Lesson 3-6 and *removing parentheses* for the form found in this lesson.

Just like pencil-and-paper skills, mental calculations, as used in **Examples 2 and 3,** take practice.

Questions 1–20 in *Covering the Reading* follow the lesson as shown below. So you can either go through the reading and connect the questions to it, or go through the questions and connect them to the reading.

Questions 1–6: the reading through **Example 1**
Questions 7–8: Example 2
Questions 9–11: Example 3
Questions 12–17: Example 4
Questions 18–20: Example 5

Career Connection The hourly wage in **Example 3** is more than double the federal minimum wage. The minimum wage—the smallest amount of money per hour that an employer can legally pay a worker—went from 25 cents per hour in 1938 to $4.25 per hour in 1991.

Note that in **Example 5**, on page 186, the cost for n minutes is $.40 + .13(n − 3)$, but this expression can be simplified to $.01 + .13n$. Either form shows that the increase is $.13n$ for every increase of 1 in n. This idea will be used later in the discussion of slope. The expression with the parentheses, $.40 + .13(n − 3)$, has the advantage that each number in it is part of the given information in the situation: .40 is the initial cost; $n − 3$ relates to the cost after the first three minutes, and .13 is the unit increase.

Answer for caption: $8.66 each

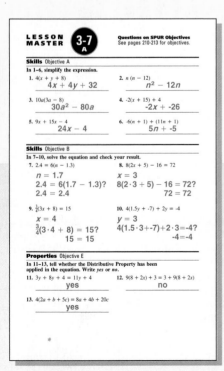

How much would one CD cost?

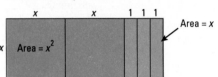

Example 1

Multiply the following.
a. $2(2x + 3)$ **b.** $x(2x + 3)$

Solution
a. Each term of $2x + 3$ is multiplied by 2.
$$2(2x + 3) = 2 \cdot 2x + 2 \cdot 3$$
$$= 4x + 6$$
b. Each term of $2x + 3$ is multiplied by x.
$$x(2x + 3) = x \cdot 2x + x \cdot 3$$
$$= 2x^2 + 3x$$

Check

Use algebra tiles.
a. Consider a rectangle with length $2x + 3$ and width 2.

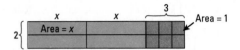

Its area is $2(2x + 3)$. This equals the sum of the area of the four rectangles and six squares. So the area equals $4x + 6$.

b. Draw a rectangle with length $2x + 3$ and width x.

Its area is $x(2x + 3)$. You can also think of the area as being made up of the 5 individual parts: two squares of area x^2, and 3 rectangles, each with area $1 \cdot x = x$. So the area equals $2x^2 + 3x$.

The Distributive Property and Mental Arithmetic

The Distributive Property can be used to help you perform some calculations mentally.

Example 2

Calculate mentally how much 5 tapes cost if they sell for $8.97 each.

Solution
Think of $8.97 as $9.00 − 3¢.
So $5 \cdot \$8.97 = 5(\$9 − 3¢)$
$$= 5 \cdot \$9 − 5 \cdot 3¢ \quad \text{Do all this in your head.}$$
$$= \$45 − 15¢$$
$$= \$44.85$$

Check
Use pencil and paper or calculator to show that $5(8.97) = 44.85$.

Optional Activities

Activity 1 Consumer Connection
You can use this activity after students have completed the lesson. Give students the following problems, and have them **work in groups** to develop ways to calculate, or approximate, the amounts mentally. After they have worked on each problem, discuss their responses.

1. Often, a restaurant patron will leave a 15% tip. How can you calculate 15% of a bill mentally? [Sample: 15% = 10% +

$\frac{1}{2} \cdot$ 10%; it is easy to calculate 10% of a number mentally by moving the decimal point one place to the left; 15% of $25 = $2.50 + $\frac{1}{2}$ of $2.50 = $2.50 + $1.25 = $3.75]

2. It is common to see stores advertise, "Sale: 25% off." How might you calculate 25% of a number mentally? [Samples: (1) 25% = $\frac{1}{4}$, so take $\frac{1}{4}$ of the number;

Working overtime.
Many workers, including certain airline employees, earn overtime pay when they work more than a certain number of hours per day or per week.

Example 3

Monica's hourly wage is $12.00. If she receives time and a half for overtime, what is her overtime hourly wage?

Solution

Time and a half means $1\frac{1}{2}$ times the regular hourly wage. Since $1\frac{1}{2} = 1 + \frac{1}{2}$, use the Distributive Property to calculate the wage mentally.

$$12 \cdot 1\frac{1}{2} = 12 \cdot (1 + \frac{1}{2})$$
$$= 12 \cdot 1 + 12 \cdot \frac{1}{2}$$
$$= 12 + 6$$
$$= 18$$

Monica receives $18 an hour for overtime.

Check

$18 is halfway between her hourly wage ($12) and twice that amount ($24).

The Distributive Property and Solving Equations

Examples 4 and 5 show how the Distributive Property is used to remove parentheses and to add like terms in the same problem.

Example 4

Solve $-5(x + 2) + 3x = 8$.

Solution 1

$-5 \cdot x + -5 \cdot 2 + 3x = 8$	Distributive Property: Removing Parentheses
$-5x + -10 + 3x = 8$	
$-5x + 3x + -10 = 8$	Commutative Property of Addition
$-2x + -10 = 8$	Distributive Property: Adding Like Terms
$-2x + -10 + 10 = 8 + 10$	Addition Property of Equality
$-2x = 18$	Property of Opposites
$x = -9$	Multiplication Property of Equality

Solution 2

Experts do some work mentally and may write down only a few steps.
$$-5x - 10 + 3x = 8$$
$$-2x - 10 = 8$$
$$-2x = 18$$
$$x = -9$$

Check

Substitute -9 for x in the original sentence. Follow the order of operations. Does $-5(-9 + 2) + 3 \cdot -9 = 8$?
$$-5 \cdot -7 + 3 \cdot -9 = 8?$$
$$35 + -27 = 8? \text{ Yes.}$$

Lesson 3-7 The Distributive Property and Removing Parentheses **185**

185

25% of $16.50 = \frac{1}{4} \cdot $16.50 = 4.13.
(2) 25% is $\frac{1}{2}$ of 50% and 50% is $\frac{1}{2}$ of the 100%, so take $\frac{1}{2}$ of the number and then take $\frac{1}{2}$ of that number; 25% of $16.50 = \frac{1}{2} \cdot $16.60 = $8.25, \frac{1}{2}$ of $8.25 = $4.13.]

Activity 2 You might want to use *Activity Kit, Activity 7,* as an alternate approach to **Example 1** on page 183, or as a follow-up to the lesson. In this activity, students use algebra tiles to illustrate the Distributive Property, Removing Parentheses Form.

Additional Examples

1. Rewrite each expression without parentheses.
   a. $-4(5n + 2)$ $-20n - 8$
   b. $15(\frac{2}{3}x - \frac{4}{5}y)$ $10x - 12y$
   c. $2x(x - 11y + 8)$
      $2x^2 - 22xy + 16x$

In 2–3, calculate mentally.

2. If stereo components sell for $199 each, how much would three components cost?
   Sample thought process:
   $3 \cdot $199 = 3 \cdot ($200 - $1) =$
   $3 \cdot $200 - 3 \cdot $1 = $600 - $3 =$
   $597

3. One lap of the Indianapolis Speedway is $2\frac{1}{2}$ miles. If a driver completed 32 laps before having a flat tire, how far had the driver traveled? **Sample thought process:** $2\frac{1}{2}$ miles $\cdot 32 =$
   2 miles $\cdot 32 + \frac{1}{2}$ mile $\cdot 32 =$
   64 miles + 16 miles = 80 miles

4. Solve $-4y + 7(y + 2) = 31$.
   $y = \frac{17}{3}$

5. Suppose the cost C of mailing a letter is 29¢ for the first ounce and 23¢ for each additional ounce or fraction of an ounce. An equation that gives C in terms of n, the whole number of ounces, is $C = .29 + .23(n - 1)$. How much does a letter weigh if it costs $1.21 to mail it? **5 ounces**

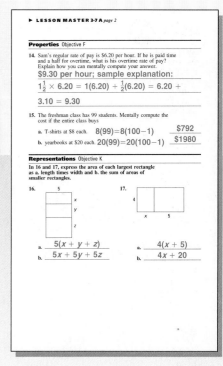

Notes on Questions

✏️ **Question 7 Writing** Having students write out the processes that they use helps them to analyze their thinking more closely. However, even though some students will know how to do the mental arithmetic, they will not be able to write down the process.

Question 23 Error Alert
Subscripts can be confusing for some students because they want to use the numbers in their calculations. This question might be easier for these students if b_1 and b_2 are replaced by x and y.

Example 5

Suppose the cost of a phone call is 40¢ for the first 3 minutes and 13¢ for each additional minute. An equation that gives the cost C in terms of the whole number n of minutes you talk is $C = .40 + .13(n - 3)$. (Here $n \geq 3$, and n is a whole number.) How long can you talk for $5.00?

Solution
The cost is to equal $5. So substitute $C = 5.00$ and solve.
$$.40 + .13 \cdot (n - 3) = 5.00$$

Apply the Distributive Property to remove parentheses.
$$.40 + .13n - .13 \cdot 3 = 5.00$$
$$.40 + .13n - .39 = 5.00$$
$$.13n + .01 = 5.00$$
$$.13n = 4.99$$
$$n \approx 38.385$$

You can talk for 38 minutes for $5.00.

2) x 1 1

3) x 1 1

12) $x = 1.8$;
$2(1.8 + 3.1) =$
$2 \cdot 4.9 = 9.8$

13) $m = \frac{8}{3}$;
$6(\frac{8}{3} + \text{-}1) = 6 \cdot \frac{5}{3} = 10$

14) $u = 3$;
$7(3 + \text{-}3) = 7 \cdot 0 = 0$

15) $x = \frac{3}{4}$;
$9 = 2(2 \cdot \frac{3}{4} + 2) + 2 =$
$2(\frac{3}{2} + 2) + 2 =$
$2 \cdot \frac{7}{2} + 2 = 7 + 2$

16) $v = \text{-}3$;
$2 + 3(\text{-}3 + 4) =$
$2 + 3 \cdot 1 = 2 + 3 = 5$

17) $t = \text{-}9$;
$\text{-}5(\text{-}9 + 2) + 3(\text{-}9) =$
$\text{-}5 \cdot \text{-}7 + 3 \cdot \text{-}9 =$
$35 + \text{-}27 = 8$

186

QUESTIONS

Covering the Reading

1. State the Removing-Parentheses form of the Distributive Property.
For all real numbers a, b, and c, $c(a + b) = ca + cb$ and $c(a - b) = ca - cb$.
In 2 and 3, multiply. Check your answer by drawing rectangles.

2. $5x(x + 2)$ $5x^2 + 10x$;
See left for diagram.

3. $5(x + 2)$ $5x + 10$;
See left for diagram.

In 4–6, use the Removing-Parentheses form of the Distributive Property to eliminate parentheses.

4. $4(n + 6)$
$4n + 24$

5. $12(k - 5)$
$12k - 60$

6. $10b(b + c)$
$10b^2 + 10bc$

7. Show how the Distributive Property can help you mentally compute the price of 5 CDs if each CD costs $9.96.
$5 \cdot \$9.96 = 5 \cdot (\$10 - 4¢) = \$50 - 20¢ = \$49.80$

8. Mentally compute the total cost of four gallons of milk at $2.07 each.
$8.28

In Questions 9 and 10, mentally compute the overtime hourly wage (at time and a half for overtime) if the normal hourly wage is the given amount.

9. $14.00 **$21**
10. $6.50 **$9.75**
11. $9.99
$14.98 or $14.99

In 12–17, solve and check. **See left.**

12. $2(x + 3.1) = 9.8$
13. $6(m + \text{-}1) = 10$
14. $7(u + \text{-}3) = 0$
15. $9 = 2(2x + 2) + 2$
16. $2 + 3(v + 4) = 5$
17. $\text{-}5(t + 2) + 3t = 8$

In 18 and 19, refer to Example 5.

18. Why was the answer not stated as 38.39 minutes?
The number of minutes must be a whole number.

19. At these prices how long could you talk for $2.00? **15 minutes**

Adapting to Individual Needs

Extra Help
Be sure students understand that the two forms of the Distributive Property discussed in this lesson and the preceding lesson are useful for different purposes. When like terms are to be added, it is helpful to put in parentheses such as: $8x + 9x = (8 + 9)x$. When computing mentally, as in $9 \cdot 3.5$, it is helpful to think of the problem as $9(3 + .5) = 9 \cdot 3 + 9 \cdot .5$.

English Language Development
Review the meaning of the word *distributive*. Involve students by asking them to give real-world examples, such as distributing advertising leaflets to every home or apartment in an area.

20. Suppose the cost of a phone call is 49¢ for the first 3 minutes and 16¢ for each additional minute.
   a. What will it cost to talk for an hour? **$9.61**
   b. How long can you talk for less than $6.00? **37 minutes or less**

Applying the Mathematics

21. Mentally compute 6 times 999,999. **5,999,994**

22. For each hour of television, there is an average of $8\frac{1}{2}$ minutes of commercials. If you watch 6 hours of television in a week, compute mentally how many minutes of commercials you will see.
   51 minutes

23. The area A of a trapezoid with parallel bases b_1 and b_2 and height h is given by the formula $A = \frac{1}{2}h(b_1 + b_2)$. A trapezoid has base $b_1 = 5$ cm, height 6 cm, and area 60 cm². $60 = \frac{1}{2} \cdot 6(5 + b_2)$
   a. Substitute these values into the area formula above.
   b. Solve to find b_2, the length of the other base. $b_2 = 15$ cm

In 24 and 25, the daily charge at a car rental company is $19.95 with the first 100 miles free. The charge for each mile after that is $.25.

24. How much would you pay to rent a car for a day if you drove the indicated distances?
   a. 76 mi **$19.95**   b. 100 mi **$19.95**   c. 150 mi **$32.45**

25. A formula for the cost C of renting a car from this company and driving m miles, where $m \geq 100$, is $C = 19.95 + .25(m - 100)$. A sales representative was charged $25.70 to rent a car. How many miles did the sales representative drive that day? **123 miles**

29a) $m < 12$;
$5 \cdot 12 + 2 \cdot 12 = 84$
and $5 \cdot 10 + 2 \cdot 10 < 84$

Talking turkey. *Your call to a distant city could be to Istanbul, Turkey. Istanbul is unique in that it is in two continents—Asia and Europe. The waterway shown, the Bosporus, divides the city into its Asian and European parts.*

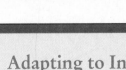

Review

In 26–28, add and simplify. *(Lesson 3-6)*

26. $(x^2 + 3x + 1) + (2x^2 + x + 8)$ $3x^2 + 4x + 9$

27. $(3a + 2b + c) + (-a + 4b + -3c)$ $2a + 6b + -2c$ 28. $n + .04n + .15n$ $1.19n$

29. a. Solve and check $5m + 2m < 84$. *(Lessons 2-8, 3-6)* **See left.**
   b. Is -5 a solution of $5m + 2m < 84$? How can you tell? *(Lesson 1-1)*
   Yes; -5 is less than 12.

In 30 and 31, multiply in your head. *(Lessons 1-4, 2-5)*

30. $(-1)(-2)(-3)(4)$ **-24**   31. $(\sqrt{3} \cdot \sqrt{3})(\sqrt{4} \cdot \sqrt{4})$ **12**

Exploration

32. Investigate phone rates to a distant city you'd like to call. How do the rates compare to those given in Example 5? **Answers will vary.**

Lesson 3-7 *The Distributive Property and Removing Parentheses* **187**

Practice
For more questions on SPUR Objectives, use **Lesson Master 3-7A** (shown on pages 184–185) or **Lesson Master 3-7B** (shown on pages 186–187).

Assessment

Quiz A quiz covering Lessons 3-5 through 3-7 is provided in the *Assessment Sourcebook.*

Group Assessment Have students **work in groups.** Ask each group to write five problems that are similar to those in **Examples 2 and 3** and that can be solved mentally using the Distributive Property. Then have groups exchange problems and solve them. [Each group can explain how the Distributive Property was used to solve the problem.]

Extension

Cooperative Learning Students often enjoy doing problems like the one in **Question 21** after they realize that some seemingly difficult problems can be calculated mentally. Have students **work in groups** and write computation problems that can be done mentally. Have students in other groups do the calculations and give the properties they used.

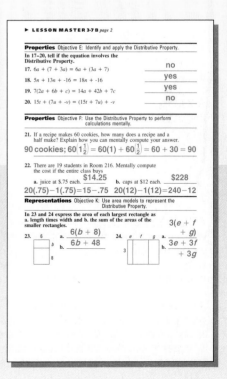

Adapting to Individual Needs

Challenge
The rectangle at the right is divided into four smaller rectangles with sides of integer length and areas of 45, 25, 15, and x square units. Find x. Then give the dimensions of the large rectangle.
$[x = 27; 14$ by $8]$

45	25
x	15

Objectives

H Write expressions and solve problems involving linear patterns with two variables.

Resources

From the *Teacher's Resource File*
- Lesson Master 3-8A or 3-8B
- Answer Master 3-8
- Teaching Aids
  23 Warm-up
  32 Additional Examples 1–4 and Challenge
- Technology Sourcebook
  Computer Master 8

Additional Resources
- Visuals for Teaching Aids 23, 32

Teaching Lesson 3-8

Warm-up

Students collected food for a food drive and displayed canned goods in a pyramid. The top three rows of the pyramid are shown below.

How many cans are in the
1. fourth row? **7 cans**
2. sixth row? **11 cans**
3. tenth row? **19 cans**

Students find the number of cans in the nth row in *Optional Activities* on page 189.

3-8

Writing Linear Expressions

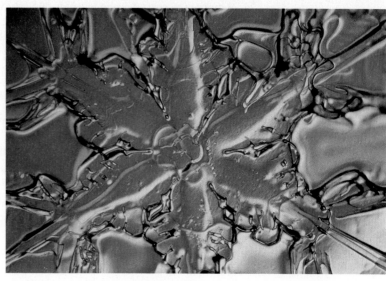

Facts about flakes. *Snowflakes are made up of masses of tiny ice crystals. Although they differ in shape, all ice crystals have six sides. The crystals collide and adhere to each other to produce snowflakes.*

Patterns of the form $ax + b$ or equations of the form $ax + b = c$ often arise from situations of repeated addition. For instance, Suzie made a *sequence* of designs, which she called snowflake designs, using circular chips. She began each design by placing one chip and surrounding it with six other chips. Here are the first three designs. What patterns do you see as Suzie continues to make designs?

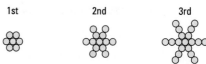

Suzie noticed the following pattern. Each snowflake design can be thought of as having six "spokes." Here is the sketch she drew to illustrate the spokes for a friend.

She then noticed in each case that the number of chips in each spoke equals the design's place in the sequence. For instance, the 2nd design has 2 chips per spoke, and the 3rd design has 3 chips per spoke.

Lesson 3-8 Overview

Broad Goals The goal of this lesson is to write an algebraic relationship between two variables found in tables, made by computer programs or by hand, given that the relationship is one of constant increase.

Perspective This lesson applies the problem strategy often called *making a table;* it repeats an idea that students saw in Chapter 1, but now there is a particular pattern in mind. Here, tables are used to help find patterns and formulas for applications that involve repeated addition. Similar problems with arithmetic sequences are then considered.

The emphasis is on the linear expression that results from each situation. That expression is of the form $a + bx$ where a is the zeroth term, and b is the constant difference. In a later chapter, this same idea appears again with the graphing of lines using the slope-intercept form. The zeroth term eliminates some of the problems that students have in seeing patterns. It is best to avoid writing the formulas in the form $a + (n - 1)d$, as this tends to confuse students. Note that in a real situation, the expression for the zeroth term may be artificial. For instance, in **Example 4,** you would not pay $2.75 to park for 0 hours. The zeroth term is just an aid in establishing the pattern.

Example 1

Suppose that Suzie makes a 4th snowflake design by adding 6 more chips to the 3rd snowflake. How many chips will she need in all?

Solution 1

Draw or make the 4th snowflake.

Count the number of chips needed. There are 25 in the fourth snowflake.

Solution 2

Generalize Suzie's observation. There will be one chip in the center, and 6 spokes with 4 chips each. So there will be $1 + 6 \cdot 4$ or 25 chips.

Each solution can be used to determine how many chips Suzie will need to make such a snowflake of any size. However, the first solution strategy might be tedious for a very large snowflake.

Example 2

a. How many chips will Suzie need to make the 10th such snowflake design?

b. If Suzie makes the *d*th design, how many chips will she need?

Solution

a. Generalize the pattern used in Solution 2 of Example 1.

Design Number	Number of chips/spoke	Total number of chips
1	1	$1 + 6 \cdot 1 = 7$
2	2	$1 + 6 \cdot 2 = 13$
3	3	$1 + 6 \cdot 3 = 19$
4	4	$1 + 6 \cdot 4 = 25$
⋮	⋮	⋮

In the 10th design there will be 1 center chip and 6 spokes with 10 chips each. So there will be $1 + 6 \cdot 10$ or 61 chips.

b. There will be 1 chip in the center and 6 spokes with *d* chips each. So there will be $1 + 6d$ chips. If you let $c =$ the number of chips, then you can write $c = 1 + 6d$.

Once you have found an algebraic expression or formula for the number of chips, you can use it to work backward.

Notes on Reading

There are two contexts discussed in this lesson, and they illustrate the two most common ways that people picture situations when they want to find a pattern.

❶ The first context is that of a sequence. Here the variable stands for the number of the term in the sequence. The basic question to ask is, "What is the number in the *n*th term of the sequence?" Once that question has been answered (as it is in **Example 2b,** where *d* is the variable), then many other similar questions can also be answered. One such question is in **Example 3.** Others are in **Questions 1–4.**

Although the main topic of this chapter is *equations,* expressions are also involved. You may have to help students distinguish between these two ideas. We look for an *expression* for the *n*th term; then we often use it to write an *equation* to answer a question.

Optional Activities

Activity 1
After considering **Examples 1 and 2,** you might refer students back to the pattern described in the *Warm-up.* Have them determine the number of cans in the *n*th row. [2*n* – 1] Then ask students how many rows they could make with 100 cans. [10]

As an additional activity, suggest that they look for a pattern, and then write a formula for the total number of cans in *n* rows.

[Total number of cans: in 1 row = 1 can, in 2 rows = 4 cans, in 3 rows = 9 cans, in 4 rows = 16 cans, and so on. The total number of cans in *n* rows = n^2.]

Activity 2 Technology Connection You may wish to assign *Technology Source-book, Computer Master 8.* Students write a linear expression for car cost, and then use a spreadsheet program to create a table of values based on the expression.

❷ The second context discussed involves a table in which there is a constant increase from one line to the next. The variable stands for the row number, and the basic question to ask is, "How are the numbers in the line related?" Specifically, in **Example 4,** *h* stands for the number of hours and the question becomes, "What is the cost of parking for *h* hours?" This question is answered by going through the inductive process below the example. **Questions 5–8** also relate to this situation.

Going around in spirals.
Marina City Towers provided the first high-rise spiral parking in the U.S. Built in Chicago in 1962, the towers include 19 levels of parking that can accommodate 503 cars.

PARKING CHARGES

up to 1 HOUR $2.75

2 HOURS 4.00

3 HOURS 5.25

4 HOURS 6.50

5 HOURS 7.75

Each add'l hr $1.25

Example 3

Suzie has made a big snowflake design with 97 chips. What design number in the sequence is it?

Solution

Use the formula in part **b** of Example 2. You are given that $c = 97$. Substitute into the formula and solve for *d*.

$$c = 1 + 6d$$
$$97 = 1 + 6d$$
$$96 = 6d$$
$$16 = d$$

97 chips are in the 16th snowflake pattern.

The expression $1 + 6d$ is a *linear expression* in one variable. In **linear expressions,** all variables are to the first power. If there are two or more variables, they are either added or subtracted. Numbers may have any position. The equations $c = 1 + 6d$ and $97 = 1 + 6d$ are called *linear equations* because each side is either an arithmetic expression or a linear expression.

Real situations in which there is some initial amount followed by a constant amount repeatedly added or subtracted can often be modeled by linear expressions.

❷ ### Example 4

As shown in the sign at the left, a parking garage charges $2.75 for parking up to 1 hour and $1.25 for each additional hour or fraction thereof. If the car is left for *h* hours, what is the parking charge?

Solution 1

Make a table and look for a pattern. Notice that each entry in the sign is $1.25 more than the previous one. This suggests that it may be helpful to rewrite each of the costs after the first using multiples of $1.25.

Hours	Charges	Cost Pattern
1	2.75	2.75
2	4.00	2.75 + 1.25 · 1
3	5.25	2.75 + 1.25 · 2
4	6.50	2.75 + 1.25 · 3
5	7.75	2.75 + 1.25 · 4

Notice how the hours and cost pattern are related. The number on the far right is one less than the number of hours. This suggests the following: The cost *c* for parking *h* hours is
$$c = 2.75 + 1.25(h - 1).$$
This could also be written using the Distributive Property as
$$c = 2.75 + 1.25h - 1.25$$
$$= 1.25h + 1.50.$$

190

Adapting to Individual Needs

Extra Help

Materials: Paper clips, box

Some students might have difficulty translating information from a real situation into a mathematical expression. The following activity may be helpful. Have a student put an unknown number of paper clips (about a handful) into a box. Tell students that *p* represents the number of paper clips in the box. Then have another student put 5 more

paper clips into the box. Ask how many are in the box now. [$p + 5$] Next, ask how many clips would be required to have 2 boxes with that same number of clips. [$2(p + 5)$] Then ask how many clips would be in the box

1. if half of them were removed? [$\frac{p+5}{2}$]
2. if 10 were removed? [$(p + 5) - 10$ or $p - 5$]

3. if 25 more clips were added? [$(p + 5) + 25$ or $p + 30$]

Solution 2

Translate the given information directly into an equation. Let h = the number of hours parked and c = the cost for h hours. Then h − 1 = the number of hours over 1. Each of these hours costs $1.25. Therefore, the cost of parking h − 1 hours is 1.25(h − 1). The total cost is c = 2.75 + 1.25(h − 1).

The examples in this lesson involve patterns in which a constant amount is repeatedly added. Computers are very useful when jobs require speed or a lot of repetition. The following computer program will make a list of the first 200 terms of the sequence in Examples 1 to 3. The program uses a FOR/NEXT loop. The FOR statement tells the computer the number of times to execute the loop. The first time through the loop, the variable D is 1. Each time through, the NEXT statement increases D by one, and sends the computer back to the FOR statement.

❸

```
10  PRINT "NUMBER OF CHIPS IN SNOWFLAKE DESIGN"
20  FOR D = 1 TO 200     The loop will be executed 200 times.
30  LET C = 1 + 6 * D    The formula from Example 2 is evaluated.
40  PRINT D, C           Print the value of the term.
50  NEXT D               Go back to line 20 with a new value for D.
60  END
```

When the program is run, the computer will print 200 terms. The first three terms printed are:

The last three terms are:

NUMBER OF CHIPS IN SNOWFLAKE DESIGN	
1	7
2	13
3	19
⋮	⋮
198	1189
199	1195
200	1201

QUESTIONS

Covering the Reading

In 1–4, consider the snowflake designs described in the first part of the lesson.

1. **a.** How many chips will Suzie need to make the 5th design? 31
   b. Draw the 5th design. See left.

1b)

2. Refer to the formula c = 1 + 6d.
   a. What does the variable *d* represent? the number of the design
   b. What does *c* represent? the number of chips in the design

3. How many chips does Suzie need for the 13th design? 79

Lesson 3-8 *Writing Linear Expressions* **191**

❸ The computer program shows how to generate terms of the snowflake sequence. **Question 9** relates to this program.

Computers can easily generate sequences. Not only does the FOR-NEXT loop introduce one of the most important concepts in computer programming, but it also gives us opportunities to use variables that truly vary and that take on many values in succession. In the program in this lesson, the values of *N* and *T* change with every pass through the loop. This is a different use of a variable than the ones that students have seen before in equations or formulas.

You (or your students) may notice that line 20 in the program could include a STEP command. For example, if the line is 20 FOR N = 1 TO 200 STEP 6, then the loop would be executed only for N = 1, 7, 13, 19,. . ., 199, computing only the first term of the sequence and every sixth term thereafter. We do not use STEP, so we can focus on determining the formula for the *n*th term of the sequence. With the STEP command, there would be no need for line 30.

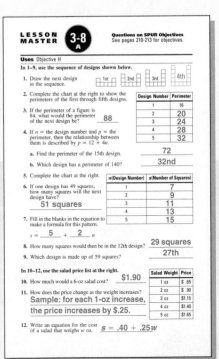

Additional Examples

Examples 1–4 are given on **Teaching Aid 32.**

Use this pattern for 1–3.

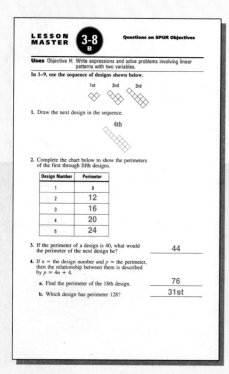

1st   2nd   3rd

1. Suppose each succeeding design is made by adding 7 stars to the previous design. How many stars will the 4th design in the pattern contain? **31 stars**

2. a. How many stars are needed for the 8th design? **59**
   b. How many stars are needed for the *n*th design?
      $10 + 7(n - 1)$ or $3 + 7n$

3. If a design is made with 80 stars, what design number in the sequence is it? **11th**

4. If it costs $1.50 for the first hour and $0.60 for each additional hour to park in a large city, what does it cost to park for *n* hours?
   $1.50 + 0.60(n - 1)$ or $0.90 + 0.60n$

5. Al opened a savings account with $45. Then he deposited $4 in the account each week.
   a. Write an expression for the amount Al has in the account after *w* weeks. $45 + 4w$
   b. How long will it take Al to save the $425 he needs for a new racing bike? **95 weeks**

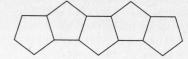

---

4. Suzie made a snowflake design with 103 chips. Which design in the sequence was it? **the 17th design**

In 5–8, use the parking lot formula $c = 1.50 + 1.25h$.

5. a. What does the *h* in the formula represent? **the number of hours**
   b. What does the 1.25 in the formula represent?
      b) the additional charge for each hour
   c. What would it cost to park 24 hours in this garage? **$31.50**

6. a. Does the formula work for parking one hour? **Yes**
   b. Does it work for $2\frac{1}{2}$ hours? **No, but you would round up to 3 hours anyway.**
   c. What is the domain for *h* in the formula? **the set of positive integers**

7. Your aunt parked in this garage for 10 hours. How much did she pay for parking? **$14**

8. Your uncle was charged $17.75 for parking in this garage. How many hours did he park? **13 hours**

9. Refer to the computer program in this lesson. Suppose line 20 reads FOR D = 1 TO 999.
   a. How many times would the loop be executed? **999 times**
   b. What would be the first term printed? **7**
   c. What would be the last term printed? **5995**
   d. Find the value of C in line 30 when D = 86. **517**

Applying the Mathematics

10. *Multiple choice.* Which of these graphs pictures the parking rate data from Example 4? **(a)**

(a) 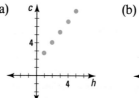 (b) 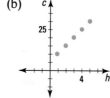 (c)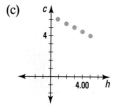

In 11–13, refer to the sequence of designs made from toothpicks shown below.

Let *n* = the number of triangles, and *t* = the number of toothpicks used.

11. Copy and complete the table below.

n	1	2	3	4
t	?	?	?	?
	3	5	7	9

192

Adapting to Individual Needs

Challenge

Show students the diagram at the right or give them **Teaching Aid 32,** and have them find the perimeter of diagrams that have 1, 2, 3, 4, and 5 pentagons. Then have them write an expression for the perimeter of a diagram with *n* pentagons. [The perimeters of the diagrams are 5, 8, 11, 14, and 17, respectively; the expression for the perimeter of a diagram with *n* pentagons is $3n + 2$.]

12b)

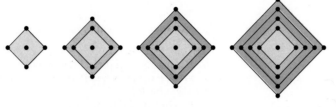

Mexican Art. *These colorful, woven yarn designs are known as "Eyes of God" or Ojos de dios. Mexicans sometimes use them as decorations during their Green Squash Festival.*

15a)

Minutes	Cost
100	65.95
200	65.95
300	86.95
400	107.95
500	128.95

16a)

days	gallons
1	7500
2	15000
3	22500
4	30000
5	37500
6	45000

17) Sample:
```
10 PRINT "GALLONS OF
   GASOLINE CONSUMED"
20 FOR N = 1 TO 20
30 LET G = 7500*N
40 PRINT N, G
50 NEXT N
60 END
```

12. a. If the toothpick designs are continued, how many toothpicks will be needed to form 7 triangles? **15**
b. Justify your answer by making or drawing such a design. **See left.**

13. a. How many toothpicks are needed to make a design with n triangles?
b. How many triangles are formed by a design with 23 toothpicks?
a) $t = 1 + 2n$; b) 11

14. The Huichol Indians of Mexico often stretch strands of yarn onto bamboo sticks to form squares having patterns like those shown below. Each new set of dots represents the vertices of a different colored square.

a. How many dots are needed for a pattern with 10 colors? **41**
b. Let c = the number of colors and d = the number of dots. Find a formula for d in terms of c. Explain how you got this formula.
$d = 4c + 1$; We begin with one dot. Each new color requires four new dots.

15. A cellular phone company charges $65.95 for up to 200 minutes of phone calls per month, and 21¢ per minute thereafter.
a. Make a table showing the cost of using this phone for 100, 200, 300, 400, and 500 minutes during the month. **See left.**
b. Write a formula for the cost c in terms of the number m of minutes the phone is used. $c = 65.95 + .21(m - 200)$
c. To what values of m does your formula apply? $m \geq 200$

In 16 and 17, suppose a school uses 7500 gallons of gas per day for buses.

16. a. Make a table showing gas consumption for 1, 2, 3, 4, 5, and 6 days. **See left.**
b. Find a formula for gas consumed in n days. $g = 7500n$
c. Calculate the number of gallons of gas consumed in 20 days.
d. If 7.5 million gallons of gas were used, how many days passed?
c) 150,000 gal; d) 1000 days

17. Write a computer program that will print a list of the gallons of gas consumed for 1 through 20 days. **See left.**

Review

In 18 and 19, explain how to use the Distributive Property to calculate the cost mentally. *(Lesson 3-7)* Sample answers are given.

18. the cost of four T-shirts at $9.95 each
$4 \cdot \$9.95 = 4(\$10 - 5¢) = 4 \cdot \$10 - 4 \cdot 5¢ = \$40 - 20¢ = \$39.80$

19. the cost of 25 notebooks at $1.99 each
$25(\$1.99) = 25(\$2 - 1¢) = 25 \cdot \$2 - 25 \cdot 1¢ = \$50 - 25¢ = \$49.75$

Lesson 3-8 *Writing Linear Expressions* **193**

6. The owner of a frozen yogurt shop calculates that she pays $120 in wages and utilities for each day the store is open. On the average, for every serving of frozen yogurt that is sold, the profit is $0.48. Write an expression for the owner's profit if x servings of frozen yogurt are sold in one day. $0.48x + -120$

Notes on Questions

Question 10 This question previews the graphing of lines which is presented in Chapter 4.

Question 14 Art Connection
The Huichol Indians live in western Mexico. Their arts and crafts include simple pottery, embroidery, and cord making. The Huichol also weave sashes, carrying bags, and wool blankets.

Questions 16–17 The zeroth term is zero. Running the buses no days means that no gas is used.

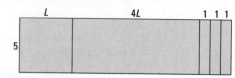

Follow-up 3-8
for Lesson

Practice
For more questions on SPUR Objectives, use **Lesson Master 3-8A** (shown on page 191) or **Lesson Master 3-8B** (shown on pages 192–193).

Assessment
Oral Communication Ask students to explain how they can tell if a situation can be described by using a linear expression. [Responses include recognizing a pattern and finding a constant amount that is either added or subtracted.]

Extension
Cooperative Learning Have students **work with a partner** and write an equation to describe the cost for renting computer time for m minutes and for p pages based on the following information.

A computer-information service charges $4 for the first five minutes of computer time and 50¢ per minute thereafter. There is a 30¢ charge per page for printing.
$[C = 4 + .50(m - 5) + .30p$, or $C = 1.50 + .50m + .30p]$

Project Update Project 2, *Patterns in Expanding Letters,* and Project 4, *Staircase Patterns,* on pages 205–206, relate to the content of this lesson.

---

20. Find the area. *(Lessons 2-1, 3-7)* $25L + 15$

In 21–24, solve. *(Lessons 3-5, 3-6, 3-7)*

21. $3x + -5x + 12 + -15 = -4$ **22.** $t - 0.1t = 1.8$ $t = 2$
     $x = \frac{1}{2}$

23. $\frac{5}{2}x + 1 = 26$ $x = 10$ **24.** $-3 = -6n + 1 + 2(n + 1)$
     $n = \frac{3}{2}$

25. In which quadrant is the x-coordinate negative and the y-coordinate positive? *(Lesson 3-3)* Quadrant II

26. Refer to the graph below. Douglas, Arizona, is typical of a monsoon area in which a wind system causes yearly rain to be concentrated in a few months.
  a. During which months is the average rainfall in Douglas less than 1 inch? *(Lesson 3-3)* Jan., Feb., Mar., Apr., May, June, Oct., Nov.
  b. Which months have the highest average rainfall? July, August
  c. Give the average rainfall for April in Douglas. 0 inches
  d. Between which two consecutive months is there the greatest change in rainfall? between June and July

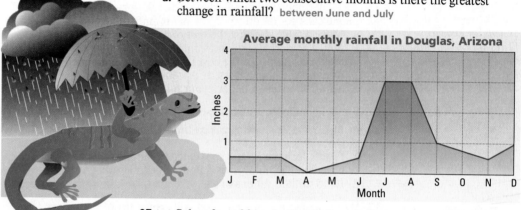

Average monthly rainfall in Douglas, Arizona

27. a. Solve: $3z < 231$.   **b.** Graph the solution set on a number line.
     (Lessons 2-8, 1-2) $z < 77$;

28. Roberto averaged 53 mph for $2\frac{1}{2}$ hours. About how many miles did he travel? *(Lesson 2-4)* 132.5 miles

---

Exploration

29. Make up or find a situation in which a pattern leads to a linear expression. Describe your situation to a friend. Ask your friend to write a formula to describe the pattern. Answers will vary.
Sample: Susie opens a savings account with a $100 deposit. She then deposits $5 per week into her account. What is her bank balance after w weeks, assuming the account earns no interest? Total $= 100 + 5(w - 1)$

Adding Algebraic Fractions

A note on fractions. *Composers need to add fractions. In this piece, there are 3 counts per measure. The quarter notes get 1 count each, the eighth notes get one-half count each, and the sixteenth notes get one-fourth count each.*

The slide model for addition can help you picture addition of fractions. For instance, the slide model confirms that $\frac{1}{4} + \frac{3}{4} = 1$.

To add fractions with the same denominator, add the numerators and keep the same denominator, called the **common denominator.** This is the Adding Fractions form of the Distributive Property.

> **Distributive Property: Adding Fractions**
> For all real numbers *a, b,* and *c,* with $c \neq 0$, $\frac{a}{c} + \frac{b}{c} = \frac{a+b}{c}$.

Notice the similarity with adding like terms. The statement
$$a \cdot \frac{1}{c} + b \cdot \frac{1}{c} = (a + b) \cdot \frac{1}{c}$$
is the same as $ax + bx = (a + b)x$, when $\frac{1}{c}$ is substituted for *x.*

Example 1

Simplify $\frac{x}{3} + \frac{2y}{3}$.

Solution

By the Adding-Fractions form of the Distributive Property,
$$\frac{x}{3} + \frac{2y}{3} = \frac{x + 2y}{3}.$$
Because *x* and *y* are unlike terms, $\frac{x + 2y}{3}$ cannot be simplified further.

Lesson 3-9 *Adding Algebraic Fractions* **195**

Lesson **3-9**

Objectives
C Add algebraic fractions.
E Identify and apply the Distributive Property.

Resources
From the *Teacher's Resource File*
■ Lesson Master 3-9A or 3-9B
■ Answer Master 3-9
■ Teaching Aid 23: Warm-up

Additional Resources
■ Visual for Teaching Aid 23

Teaching 3-9
Lesson

Warm-up

✎ **Writing** Write a letter to a student who has not studied algebra, explaining in your own words how to add fractions with different denominators. **Responses will vary. Letters should explain how to find a common denominator and write each fraction with this denominator and how to add fractions with common denominators. Some students may also include how to rewrite the sum, if necessary, in lowest terms.**

Notes on Reading

Pacing You may be tempted to stay on this topic for more than one day. However, we recommend that you not linger here. There is a review of addition of fractions in the Chapter Review and throughout the rest of the book.

Lesson 3-9 Overview

Broad Goals In this lesson, we apply the Distributive Property to the adding of fractions with like or unlike denominators.

Perspective Many (if not most) algebra students still need practice in adding fractions. This lesson provides assistance in several ways. First, it uses the slide model to illustrate the idea. Second, it applies the Distributive Property to the addition of fractions with the same denominator. Third, a

method is shown for adding positive and negative fractions. Fourth, algebraic fractions with unlike denominators are considered.

Our treatment emphasizes commonly used fractions (for example, thirds, fourths, eighths, tenths). However, this lesson is intended to develop algebraic skills, so many of the fractions involve variables.

There are a number of inexpensive calculators which can compute with fractions, but these calculators do not accept algebraic fractions. Some computer software, however, can perform operations with algebraic fractions.

Ask students to summarize the main ideas of the lesson. We would respond as follows: Fractions with the same denominator can be collected together by using the Distributive Property because the denominators can be viewed as like terms. If the denominators are different, then the Equal Fractions Property (not mentioned, but used in **Example 4**) can be applied to obtain fractions with the same denominator, after which the fractions can be added. Whether the fractions to be added are positive or negative has no impact on the methods that are used to add the fractions.

One of the difficulties that students have with fractions is determining when they are really finished with the addition. We would usually simplify an expression like $\frac{5}{2} + x + -\frac{3}{4}$ to $x + \frac{7}{4}$. However, when the x is part of a numerator or denominator, to simplify usually means to write as one fraction. For example, $\frac{5}{2} + \frac{x}{4}$ is simplified to $\frac{10+x}{4}$.

Emphasize that what is simple in one situation may not be so simple in another, and that the context of the problem has to be used in order to determine the form in which an answer is desired. In all of the questions in this lesson, the simplification means to rewrite the expression as a single fraction.

Consumer Connection As you discuss **Example 3,** you might mention that the Ford Motor Company has 75 assembly and manufacturing plants in the United States, making it one of the largest companies in the country. Henry Ford organized the company in 1903, and it was controlled by his family for 53 years. In 1956, the Ford Foundation sold 10,200,000 shares of company stock to the public. At the time, it was the largest single stock issue ever

A classic car. In 1994, President Clinton joined thousands of other people for the 30th birthday of the Ford Mustang car. President Clinton drove his 1967 Mustang at the Charlotte Motor Speedway, where the celebration took place.

Check

Substitute values for x and y. We let $x = 5$ and $y = 6$.

Then in the original expression, $\frac{x}{3} + \frac{2y}{3} = \frac{5}{3} + 2 \cdot \frac{6}{3} = \frac{5}{3} + \frac{12}{3} = \frac{17}{3}$.

In the answer, $\frac{x + 2y}{3} = \frac{5 + 2 \cdot 6}{3} = \frac{17}{3}$ also.

Example 2

Simplify $\frac{-9 + 3b}{b} + \frac{9}{b}$.

Solution

Since the denominators are the same, the Adding-Fractions form of the Distributive Property can be applied.

$$\frac{-9 + 3b}{b} + \frac{9}{b} = \frac{-9 + 3b + 9}{b}$$

$$= \frac{3b}{b} \qquad \text{Adding like terms; Additive Identity Property}$$

$$= 3 \qquad \text{Equal Fractions Property}$$

The expression equals 3, regardless of the value of b, provided $b \neq 0$.

Check

Pick a value for b. We substitute 2 for b in the original expression and follow the order of operations

$\frac{-9 + 3 \cdot 2}{2} + \frac{9}{2} = \frac{-9 + 6}{2} + \frac{9}{2} = \frac{-3}{2} + \frac{9}{2} = \frac{6}{2} = 3$. It checks.

The procedure for adding fractions is more complicated when the denominators are different. The next example uses negative numbers in fraction form.

Example 3

On Monday, Ford Motor Co. stock fell $\frac{3}{4}$ of a point; on Tuesday it rose $1\frac{1}{8}$. What was the net change?

Solution

A loss of $\frac{3}{4}$ is a change of $-\frac{3}{4}$. The answer can be found by computing $-\frac{3}{4} + 1\frac{1}{8}$. A common denominator of 8 can be used.

$$-\frac{3}{4} + 1\frac{1}{8} = -\frac{6}{8} + 1\frac{1}{8}$$

$$= \frac{-6}{8} + \frac{9}{8}$$

$$= \frac{-6 + 9}{8}$$

$$= \frac{3}{8}$$

The stock rose $\frac{3}{8}$ of a point for a net change of $\frac{3}{8}$.

Optional Activities

After discussing the Distributive Property: Adding Fractions, you might want to use this activity. Explain that the sum of any two fractions can be written as $\frac{a}{b} + \frac{c}{d}$. To add them, we can find the common denominator bd. Using the Equal Fractions Property and then applying the Distributive Property, we get $\frac{a}{b} + \frac{c}{d} = \frac{ad}{bd} + \frac{bc}{bd} = \frac{ad+bc}{bd}$. Have students select numbers for a, b, c, and d

($b \neq 0$ and $d \neq 0$), and demonstrate how the formula works.

This formula can be used as an alternative to the traditional method of least common denominators. Some students prefer the formula and use it with good results. (Note that the formula does not always give the most efficient denominator, and it does not work well when more than two fractions are being added.)

Example 4

Write $\frac{3x}{4} + \frac{x}{3}$ as a single fraction.

Solution 1

Use a common multiple of 3 and 4. The least common multiple is 12. Rewrite each fraction with denominator equal to 12.

$$\frac{3x}{4} + \frac{x}{3} = \frac{3x}{4} \cdot \frac{3}{3} + \frac{x}{3} \cdot \frac{4}{4}$$

$$= \frac{9x}{12} + \frac{4x}{12}$$

$$= \frac{13x}{12}$$

Solution 2

Show the use of the Distributive Property.

$$\frac{3x}{4} + \frac{x}{3} = \frac{3}{4} \cdot x + \frac{1}{3} \cdot x$$

$$= \left(\frac{3}{4} + \frac{1}{3}\right)x$$

$$= \left(\frac{9}{12} + \frac{4}{12}\right)x$$

$$= \frac{13}{12}x$$

Check

Substitute a number for x. We use $x = 2$.

Then $\frac{3x}{4} + \frac{x}{3} = \frac{6}{4} + \frac{2}{3} = 1.5 + .\overline{6} = 2.1\overline{6}$ and $\frac{13x}{12} = \frac{26}{12} = 2.1\overline{6}$.

It checks.

An engineering feat.
Engineers build reservoirs by constructing a dam across a valley or by digging a basin in a level tract of land. Man-made reservoirs can be used to supply water, to generate power, or to provide a place for recreation.

QUESTIONS

Covering the Reading

1. To add two fractions by adding the numerators, what must be true of the denominators? **They must be equal.**

2. One day the water level in a reservoir rose $\frac{3}{10}$ inch. The next day it fell $\frac{2}{5}$ inch. What was the total change in water level in the two days? $-\frac{1}{10}$ in.

In 3–8, perform the additions.

3. $\frac{2}{5} + -\frac{1}{5} + 3\frac{4}{5}$ **4**

4. $-\frac{11}{3} + -\frac{2}{3} + -\frac{8}{3}$ **-7**

5. $\frac{2a}{3} + \frac{28a}{3}$ **10a**

6. $\frac{6y + 11}{2y} + -\frac{11}{2y}$ **3**

7. $\frac{x}{5} + \frac{x}{5} + \frac{2x}{5}$ $\frac{4x}{5}$

8. $\frac{a}{6} + \frac{2a}{6}$ $\frac{a}{2}$

9. Consider the sum of $\frac{x}{5}$ and $\frac{3x}{4}$.
   a. What common denominator will help you add?   **20**
   b. Add and simplify. $\frac{19x}{20}$

Lesson 3-9 *Adding Algebraic Fractions* **197**

offered to the public. As a result of the sale, Ford Motor Company became a publicly owned company with about 285,000 stockholders.

Additional Examples

1. Simplify $\frac{5x+2}{x} + \frac{3x+2}{x}$. $\frac{8x+4}{x}$

2. Find the perimeter of this rectangle. $14\frac{1}{3}$

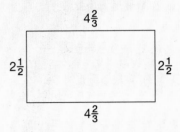

4$\frac{2}{3}$

2$\frac{1}{2}$ 2$\frac{1}{2}$

4$\frac{2}{3}$

3. The value of a share of International Consolidated Stock dropped $1\frac{1}{8}$ dollars one day and rose $\frac{1}{2}$ dollar the next day. What was the net change?   **The price dropped $\frac{5}{8}$ dollar.**

4. Write $\frac{5}{n} + \frac{11}{x}$ as a single fraction.

   $\frac{5x + 11n}{nx}$

5. Simplify $\frac{3m}{8} + \frac{-2y}{4}$. $\frac{3m + -4y}{8}$

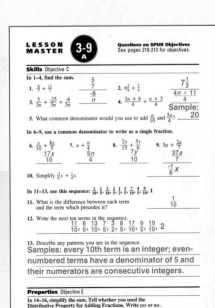

Adapting to Individual Needs

Extra Help

Some students might not understand the use of the Distributive Property for adding fractions as it was explained on the first page of this lesson. To help them see how the equation $\frac{a}{c} + \frac{b}{c} = \frac{a+b}{c}$ is obtained, you might use a numerical instance. Note the use of the Distributive Property.

$$\frac{3}{8} + \frac{4}{8} = 3 \cdot \frac{1}{8} + 4 \cdot \frac{1}{8}$$

$$= (3 + 4) \cdot \frac{1}{8}$$

$$= \frac{3 + 4}{8}$$

$$= \frac{7}{8}$$

Notes on Questions

Question 18 Error Alert The most common error in adding fractions is to add the numerators and add the denominators. This question is here to emphasize that this procedure is incorrect.

Question 20 Students can check their answers by converting the fractions of feet to inches.

Follow-up for Lesson 3-9

Practice

For more questions on SPUR Objectives, use **Lesson Master 3-9A** (shown on page 197) or **Lesson Master 3-9B** (shown on pages 198–199).

Assessment

Group Assessment Have students **work in pairs.** Ask each student to write two algebraic fractions, and then have the partner find the sum. Students should verify that the answers are correct. [Students should agree that a sum is correct and be able to explain how the sum was found.]

---

18) Sample: Let $a = 1$, $b = 2$, $c = 3$, and $d = 4$; $\frac{1}{2} + \frac{3}{4} = \frac{5}{4}$, $\frac{1+3}{2+4} = \frac{4}{6} = \frac{2}{3}$, $\frac{5}{4} \neq \frac{2}{3}$

In 10–17, simplify each sum.

10. $\frac{a}{6} + \frac{a}{3}$ $\frac{a}{2}$

11. $\frac{2d}{7} + \frac{3d}{4}$ $\frac{29d}{28}$

12. $C + \frac{C}{3} + \frac{C}{3}$ $\frac{5C}{3}$

13. $B + -\frac{B}{2}$ $\frac{B}{2}$

The timeless tug-of-war. *Tug-of-war games were common as far back as the Middle Ages. Knights and squires engaged in this contest while training for combat.*

Applying the Mathematics

14. $\frac{k}{2} + \frac{2k}{3} + \frac{k}{4}$ $\frac{17k}{12}$

15. $\frac{5}{x} + \frac{3}{x} - \frac{9}{x}$ $-\frac{1}{x}$

16. $\frac{2n}{3} + 4 \cdot \frac{n}{3} + 5\left(\frac{1}{3}n\right)$ $\frac{11n}{3}$

17. $-\frac{2}{x} + \frac{3}{2x} - \frac{1}{x}$ $-\frac{3}{2x}$

18. Find values of a, b, c, and d so that $\frac{a}{b} + \frac{c}{d} = \frac{a+c}{b+d}$ is false. **See above left.**

19. Rectangle *ABCD* has length L and width W. Rectangle *BEFG* has half the length and half the width of *ABCD*.
    a. In terms of L and W, what is the perimeter of *ABCD*? $2W + 2L$
    b. What is the perimeter of *BEFG*? $L + W$

20. In a tug-of-war game, team A pulled the rope $3\frac{1}{2}$ ft toward its side, and then team B pulled it $1\frac{2}{3}$ ft toward its side. After another minute, team B pulled the rope $4\frac{5}{6}$ ft more in its direction. Describe where the middle of the rope is now. **3 feet on the side of team B**

Review

21. A photo shop has the following charges for making prints from slides.

number of prints	cost
1	$0.75
2	$1.25
3	$1.75
4	$2.25
5	$2.75

a) Sample: After the first slide at 75¢, the cost is 50¢ per slide. The cost is always divisible by 25¢.

    a. Describe some patterns you notice in the data.
    b. Find the cost of making 8 prints of one slide. Describe how you found your answer.
    c. A proud grandmother paid $7.75 for some copies of a slide of her new grandson. How many copies did she order? *(Lesson 3-8)* 15
    b) $4.25;   75 + 50(n − 1) = c;   75 + 50(8 − 1) = 425¢

22. Refer to the figure at the right.
    a. How many rectangles are pictured? 3
    b. Find the area of the largest rectangle in two different ways.
    c. What property is illustrated here?
    (Lessons 3-6, 3-7) Distributive Property
    b) 5(3 + 8) = 5 · 11 = 55 or 5 · 3 + 5 · 8 = 15 + 40 = 55

198

Adapting to Individual Needs

English Language Development
You might want to review the terms *numerator* and *denominator* with students. Also emphasize that *common* means "shared by two or more things," and fractions with *common denominators* have the same denominators.

23. Investigate patterns in designs made from toothpicks placed as shown below.

Let n = the number of squares and t = the number of toothpicks used. **b) Sample:** t increases by 3 for every increase of one in n.
   a. Make a table showing values for n and t. **See left.**
   b. Describe patterns you find in the numbers in your table.
   c. How many toothpicks would you need to make a design with 60 squares? **181 toothpicks**
   d. Suppose t = 301. Find n, and write a question about squares and toothpicks that has the answer you just found.   *(Lesson 3-8)*
       See left.

In 24 and 25, solve and check.   *(Lessons 3-6, 3-7)*

24. $x + 2x + 3x + 4x = 5$ $x = .5$ **25.** $8 = 2(n + 3) + 4(5n + 6)$
      See left for check. $n = -1$;   **See left for check.**

26. *Multiple choice.*   Which of the following *must* be negative?
   (Lesson 3-2) **(c)**

   (a) $-x$ (b) $-(-3)$ (c) $-\left(-\left(-\frac{1}{3}\right)\right)$ (d) $-(-a)$

In 27 and 28, write an expression to describe the total change in each situation.   *(Lesson 3-1)*

27. Marie climbed u meters up the hill and then d meters back down.
   $u + -d$

28. Stanley earned $7e$ dollars and then paid back $5e$ dollars to one friend while collecting c dollars from another. $2e + c$

29. Without a factorial key ⌧, how can you calculate 11! on a calculator?   *(Lesson 2-10)* $11 \cdot 10 \cdot 9 \cdot 8 \cdot 7 \cdot 6 \cdot 5 \cdot 4 \cdot 3 \cdot 2 \cdot 1$

30. a. Solve $-2n > 10$. $n < -5$ **b.** Graph the solution set.   *(Lesson 2-8)*
                                        See left.

31. Jamie earns $14.40 per hour as a critical-care nurse. How many hours must she work in a week in order to earn more than $400?   *(Lessons 2-4, 2-8)* **more than $27\frac{7}{9}$ hours**

32. Write about a situation that could be represented by the number line graph at the right.   *(Lesson 1-2)* **Sample: The temperature on a winter day ranged from a high of 4° to a low of -3°.**

33. In the nine-year period from January 1, 1984, through January 1, 1993, the movie *The Return of the Jedi* grossed approximately $169,000,000. What was the average gross per year?   *(Previous course)*
   $18,777,777.78 per year

A box-office hit. *Released in 1983,* Return of the Jedi *was the third of the Star Wars spectacles. It was also the final chapter of the Luke Skywalker trilogy. Pictured above are Princess Leia, the robot C-3PO, and Chewbacca.*

Exploration

34. a. *Skill sequence.*   Compute each sum.
   (i) $\frac{1}{2} + \frac{1}{4} + \frac{1}{8}$ $\frac{7}{8}$ (ii) $\frac{1}{2} + \frac{1}{4} + \frac{1}{8} + \frac{1}{16}$ $\frac{15}{16}$
   (iii) $\frac{1}{2} + \frac{1}{4} + \frac{1}{8} + \frac{1}{16} + \frac{1}{32}$ $\frac{31}{32}$
   b. If you could do an infinite addition problem, what sum would you predict for $\frac{1}{2} + \frac{1}{4} + \frac{1}{8} + \frac{1}{16} + \frac{1}{32} + \frac{1}{64} + \ldots$? **1**

Lesson 3-9 *Adding Algebraic Fractions* **199**

Extension

Explain that a fraction that has a numerator of 1 is a unit fraction, and that any unit fraction can be written as the sum of two unit fractions. For instance, two ways to write $\frac{1}{2}$ as the sum of two unit fractions are $\frac{1}{4} + \frac{1}{4}$ and $\frac{1}{3} + \frac{1}{6}$. Then have students write other unit fractions as the sum of two different unit fractions. Ask them if they see a pattern when the two unit fractions are different. [The first denominator is one larger than the given one and the second denominator is the product of the other two denominators. For instance, $\frac{1}{3} = \frac{1}{4} + \frac{1}{12}, \frac{1}{4} = \frac{1}{5} + \frac{1}{20}, \frac{1}{5} = \frac{1}{6} + \frac{1}{30}$, and, in general, $\frac{1}{n} = \frac{1}{n+1} + \frac{1}{n(n+1)}$.]

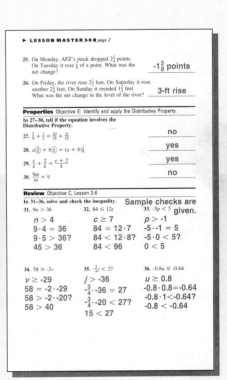

Adapting to Individual Needs

Challenge
Question 34 suggests the idea of a finite sum of an infinite series. Encourage students to look up Zeno's paradoxes and to find out more about the *dichotomy paradox.* [The paradox is that a moving object can never get anywhere, because, to get somewhere, it first has to get halfway. But to get halfway, it has to get a quarter of the way, and to get a quarter of the way, it has to get an eighth of the way, and so on.] Will the

sum in **Question 34b** ever get to the number 1? [The answer is that no finite number of its terms adds to 1 but that *all* of them together add to 1.] The sum of the infinite number of terms is called the *limit* of the finite sums. We think of the sum of the infinite number of terms every time we write the fraction equivalent to an infinite decimal. For example, $\frac{1}{7} = \frac{1}{10} + \frac{4}{100} + \frac{2}{1000} + \frac{8}{10000}$ $+ \ldots = .142857142857142857 \ldots$]

Objectives

D Solve and check inequalities of the form $ax + b < c$.

G Apply models for addition to write and solve inequalities of the form $ax + b < c$.

K Use balance scales to represent sentences.

L Graph solutions to inequalities of the form $ax + b < c$ on a number line.

Resources

From the *Teacher's Resource File*

■ Lesson Master 3-10A or 3-10B
■ Answer Master 3-10
■ Teaching Aids
   5 Number Lines
   23 Warm-up
■ Technology Sourcebook
   Computer Master 9

Additional Resources

■ Visuals for Teaching Aids 5, 23

Teaching
Lesson **3-10**

Warm-up

Tell whether –3 is a solution to the sentence.

1. $-3n + -9 \geq 0$ **True**

2. $\frac{4m}{m+1} \leq -6$ **False**

3. $2p + 1 > 1$ **False**

4. $-\frac{x}{x} = 1$ **False**

5. $y - 3 < 0$ **True**

6. $-5z + 2z = -9$ **False**

Solving
$ax + b < c$

I will always be younger than you. *These photos were taken several years apart. The boy is younger than his sister. In algebra, as in real life, if one quantity is less than another, it will always be less if the same amount is added to both.*

If you are x years old and an *older* friend's age is y, then
$$x < y.$$
Five years from now you will still be younger than your friend. In other words,
$$x + 5 < y + 5.$$

In general, J years from now you will still be younger than your friend. This can be written
$$x + J < y + J.$$

These examples illustrate the *Addition Property of Inequality*.

Addition Property of Inequality
For all real numbers a, b, and c,

if $a < b$,
then $a + c < b + c$.

The Addition Property of Inequality can be pictured with a balance scale. Suppose a and b represent the weights of two packages and $a < b$.

Lesson 3-10 Overview

Broad Goals Students should be able to solve sentences of the form $ax + b < c$ and to recognize situations that lead to such sentences.

Perspective Emphasize that the steps used in solving $ax + b < c$ correspond to those used in solving $ax + b = c$. Note that the age context which was used to explain the Addition Property of Equality explains the Addition Property of Inequality just as

well. So this lesson provides an opportunity to review the solving of equations of the form $ax + b = c$.

Remind students, however, that inequalities differ from equations in significant ways. For inequalities, there are often an infinite number of solutions, and they cannot be listed. So the answer has to be given either as an equivalent inequality, or it has to be graphed. Because students know they must

reverse the sense of the inequality when they multiply both sides by a negative number, they may think that they should also do this when adding a negative number to both sides. Emphasize that adding a number to both sides does *not* change the sense of the inequality.

If the same weight c is added to each side of the scale, then $a + c < b + c$.

So, if $a < b$, then $a + c < b + c$. The same idea works for $>$, $\leq$, and $\geq$.

Thus, sentences with $=$, $<$, $>$, $\leq$, or $\geq$ can all be solved in the same way.

> You may add the same number to both sides of an equation or inequality without affecting the solutions.

Solving Inequalities with Positive Coefficients

Example 1

A crate weighs 6 kg when empty. A lemon weighs about 0.2 kg. For shipping, the crate and lemons must weigh at least 50 kg. How many lemons should be put in the crate?

Solution

Let n be the number of lemons. Then the weight of n lemons is $0.2n$. The weight of the crate with n lemons is $0.2n + 6$, so the question can be answered by solving the inequality

$$0.2n + 6 \geq 50.$$

This inequality is of the form $ax + b \geq c$ and is solved the same way you solve $ax + b = c$.

$0.2n + 6 + \text{-}6 \geq 50 + \text{-}6$ First, add -6 to both sides and simplify.

$0.2n \geq 44$

$\dfrac{0.2n}{0.2} \geq \dfrac{44}{0.2}$ Multiply both sides by $\frac{1}{0.2}$, and simplify.

$n \geq 220$

At least 220 lemons should be put in the crate.

Check

Part 1: Does $0.2(220) + 6 = 50$? $44 + 6 = 50$? Yes.

Part 2: Pick some value that works for $n > 220$. We choose 250.
Is $0.2(250) + 6 > 50$? $50 + 6 > 50$? Yes, so $n \geq 220$ checks.

Where do lemons grow?
Four-fifths of the nation's lemons are harvested in California. About half of the lemon crop is processed into juice and oil. The other half is sold as fresh fruit.

Optional Activities

Activity 1 Using Physical Models
Materials: Balance scale and weights

You might use this activity to introduce the lesson. Place weights on the scale so that the pans balance. Note that if the weight on each pan is increased or decreased by the same amount, the balance is maintained. Repeat the activity, but now put more weight on one pan. If the weight on each pan is increased or decreased by the same amount, the same imbalance is maintained.

Activity 2 Technology Connection
In *Technology Sourcebook, Computer Master 9,* students use a spreadsheet program to solve equations and inequalities.

$$\xleftarrow{\hspace{1cm}} \underset{-4\ -3\ -2\ -1\ \ 0\ \ 1\ \ 2\ \ 3}{\bullet} \xrightarrow{\hspace{1cm}} n$$

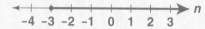
Solving Inequalities with Negative Coefficients

Recall that when you multiply each side of an inequality by a negative number, you must reverse the direction of the inequality. Otherwise, these sentences are solved just as in Example 1.

❷ 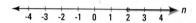 **Example 2**

a. Solve $-4n + 9 \le 1$.
b. Graph the solution set.

Solution

a. Add the opposite of 9 to each side of the inequality.

$$-4n + 9 \le 1$$
$$-4n + 9 + -9 \le 1 + -9$$
$$-4n \le -8$$

Multiply each side by the reciprocal of -4. Remember to switch the sign of the inequality.

$$-\frac{1}{4}(-4n) \ge -\frac{1}{4}(-8)$$
$$n \ge 2$$

b. A graph of the solution set is below.

$$\xleftarrow{\hspace{1cm}} \underset{-4\ -3\ -2\ -1\ \ 0\ \ 1\ \ 2\ \ 3\ \ 4}{\bullet} \xrightarrow{\hspace{1cm}} n$$

Check

Again, you should check two numbers: the boundary point 2 and a number larger than 2. Substitute $n = 2$ in the original inequality. You should get equality.
For n = 2, $-4(2) + 9 = -8 + 9 = 1$. It checks.
Try n = 3. $-4(3) + 9 = -12 + 9 = -3$. It checks because $-3 \le 1$.

QUESTIONS

Covering the Reading

1. Use the symbol $>$ to state the Addition Property of Inequality.
   For all real numbers a, b, and c, if $a > b$ then $a + c > b + c$.
2. **a.** What inequality is suggested below?
   b. What is the solution to the inequality?
   a) $4w + 3 > 11$;   b) $w > 2$

Adapting to Individual Needs

Extra Help
If students seem confused about when to reverse the direction of an inequality, illustrate the idea by using numerical instances, such as those shown below.

$6 < 8$	$9 > 5$	$4 < 12$	$5 > 2$
$6 + 2 ? 8 + 2$	$9 + -3 ? 5 + -3$	$3(4) ? 3(12)$	$-1(5) ? -1(2)$
$[8 < 10]$	$[6 > 2]$	$[12 < 36]$	$[-5 < -2]$

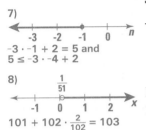

5)
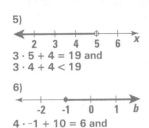
$3 \cdot 5 + 4 = 19$ and
$3 \cdot 4 + 4 < 19$

6)

$4 \cdot -1 + 10 = 6$ and
$6 < 4 \cdot 0 + 10$

7)

$-3 \cdot -1 + 2 = 5$ and
$5 \le -3 \cdot -4 + 2$

8) $\frac{1}{51}$

$101 + 102 \cdot \frac{2}{102} = 103$
and $101 + 102 \cdot 1 > 103$

Support the
Student C
Buy a T-Sh

3. Refer to Example 1. If a loaded crate of lemons can weigh no more than 200 kg, at most how many lemons can be put in the crate?
   at most 970 lemons

4. An empty crate weighs 10 kg. A grapefruit weighs about 0.5 kg. How many grapefruit can be packed in the crate and still keep the total weight under 50 kg? **79 grapefruit**

In 5–8, solve, graph, and check. **See left for graphs and checks.**

5. $3x + 4 < 19$ $x < 5$

6. $6 \le 4b + 10$ $-1 \le b$

7. $5 \le -3n + 2$ $n \le -1$

8. $101 + 102x > 103$
   $x > \frac{2}{102}$ or $x > \frac{1}{51}$

Applying the Mathematics

9. Three consecutive integers can be expressed as n, $n + 1$, and $n + 2$. Write an inequality and use it to find the three smallest consecutive integers whose sum is greater than 79.
   $n + n + 1 + n + 2 > 79$; **26, 27, 28**

In 10–13, solve.

10. $3(x + 4) < 12$ $x < 0$

11. $-.02y + \frac{1}{2} \ge 0.48$ $y \le 1$

12. $15 \ge 12 + \frac{1}{3}y$ $y \le 9$

13. $\frac{-5x}{6} + 30 < 120$ $x > -108$

14. Find a negative number which is a solution to $-4x + 7(x + -2) > -18$.
    Sample: Since $x > \frac{-4}{3}$, x could be -1.

In 15 and 16, use the formula $C = \frac{5}{9}(F - 32)$ relating Celsius and Fahrenheit temperatures.

15. What Celsius temperatures are greater than the normal body temperature of 98.6°F? **Celsius temperatures greater than 37°C**

16. What Celsius temperatures are below 68°F?
    temperatures less than 20°C

17. A student council must order at least 350 T-shirts to get the school seal printed on them in 4 colors. The students are advised that the number of shirts they can expect to sell is given by $N = -90P + 1200$, where N is the number of shirts and P is the selling price.
    a. What price should they charge if they estimate 350 shirts will be sold? **$9.45**
    b. What price might they charge if the council is willing to sell as few as 300 shirts? **$10**

18. a. Solve for x in the sentence: $ax + b < c$ when $a > 0$. $x < \frac{c - b}{a}$
    b. How does the result from part **a** change if $a < 0$?
       The direction of the inequality would change: $x > \frac{c - b}{a}$.

Lesson 3-10 *Solving $ax + b < c$* **203**

Adapting to Individual Needs

Challenge
Have students solve the following problem:
A swim-team member has promised her coach that she will swim at least 100 laps per week. She has also promised that she will increase by one lap the number of laps she swims each day. She will swim 6 days this week. What is the least number of laps she must swim on the first day? [15 laps]

203

Written Communication Have each student write about one important idea presented in the chapter. Then have students share these ideas with others, either in small groups or with the entire class. [Students demonstrate that they understand the ideas they have chosen by explaining them to the group. Ideas students are likely to select include the Distributive Property, coordinate graphing, and solving equations and inequalities.]

Extension

Have students find three inequalities equivalent to those shown below. Tell them that the inequalities they write should be of the form $ax + b > c$, $ax + b \geq c$, $ax + b < c$, or $ax + b \leq c$. [Sample responses are given.]
1. $n > -2$ [$n + -4 > -6$, $2n + 6 > 2$, $-3n + 2 < 8$]
2. $x < 4$ [$2x + 1 < 9$, $5x + -12 < 8$, $3 + -x > -1$]
3. $y \geq 3$ [$y + 6 \geq 9$, $3y + -2 \geq 7$, $-2y + 5 \leq -1$]

Project Update Project 6, *BASIC Solution of Inequalities,* on page 206, relates to the content of this lesson.

24) Does $(4 \cdot -2 + 3) + 2 \cdot -2 = 9$?; $-5 + -4 = -9$; Yes, it checks.

25) Does $6(4 \cdot 4 + -1) -2 \cdot 4 = 82$? $6 \cdot 15 - 8 = 90 - 8 = 82$. Yes, it checks.

x	y
1	10
2	14
3	18
4	22
5	26

Pictured above is a banner from Indiana University in Bloomington. Their athletic teams are known as the Indiana Hoosiers.

In 19–21, add and simplify.   *(Lesson 3-9)*

19. $\frac{3a}{5} + \frac{7a}{5}$ $2a$

20. $\frac{3}{x} + \frac{-2}{x} + \frac{4}{x}$ $\frac{5}{x}$

21. $\frac{x}{3} + \frac{-2x}{5}$ $\frac{-x}{15}$

22. Consider the table at the left.   *(Lesson 3-8)*
   a. Describe the pattern. Sample: As x increases by one, y increases by 4.
   b. Find y when $x = 8$. $y = 38$
   c. Find x when $y = 96$. y is never 96.

23. The three L-shaped figures begin a pattern. How many cubes are needed to make each figure?   *(Lesson 3-8)*
   a. the 1st 4
   b. the 4th 10
   c. the *n*th $2(n + 1)$ or $2n + 2$

In 24 and 25, solve and check.   *(Lessons 3-5, 3-6, 3-7)* See left for checks.

24. $(4x + 3) + 2x = -9$ $x = -2$

25. $6(4y + -1) + -2y = 82$ $y = 4$

26. Darrell was asked to simplify $-3(x + 2y + -6)$. His answer was $-3x + -6y + -6$. Write a note to Darrell telling him what he did wrong.   *(Lesson 3-7)* Sample: Darrell, you forgot to multiply $-3 \cdot -6$.

27. If you work 40 hours a week for $5.25 an hour and h additional hours earning time and a half for overtime, how long must you work to earn $250 in one week?   *(Lessons 3-5, 3-6, 3-7)* about 45 hours

28. The Booster Club ordered a bolt of cloth 100 yd long. They will use 2 yds for a table cloth, and the rest for banners showing the school mascot. If each banner takes $\frac{2}{3}$ yd of cloth, how many banners can they make?   *(Lesson 3-5)* 147 banners

29. a. Which number is larger, $75!$ or 75^{75}? 75^{75}
   b. Explain your reason for your answer to part **a.**   *(Lesson 2-10)* See below.

30. Use the clues to find x.   *(Lessons 1-1, 1-4, 2-8)* $x = 10$
   Clue 1: x is greater than the average of 5, 11, and 2.
   Clue 2: $-3x > -33$.
   Clue 3: $x \neq \sqrt{64}$.
   Clue 4: x is an integer.
   Clue 5: x is not an odd number.
   29b) Sample: Each factor in $75!$ is less than or equal to 75, but $75^{75} = 75 \cdot 75 \cdot 75 \ldots \cdot 75$. So $75^{75} > 75!$

31. Make up five inequalities of the form $ax + b < c$ whose solutions are $x < 24$. Samples: $-2x + 5 > -43$; $x + 1 < 25$; $3x + 4 < 76$; $-x > -24$; $100x + 100 < 2500$

A project presents an opportunity for you to extend your knowledge of a topic related to the material of this chapter. You should allow more time for a project than you do for typical homework questions.

1 Survey Results

Design a short survey on a topic of interest to you or your class, such as favorite lunch food, type of pet, time spent on homework, or favorite radio station. Design a short survey of the question you chose. Ask 20 students in your class or grade and 20 students in a different class or grade (or 20 adults) to respond to your survey. Design a stacked bar graph, like that in Lesson 3-1 that compares the responses of your class to the other class. Write a paragraph to explain your graph and the results of your survey.

2 Patterns in Expanding Letters

The diagram below shows a sequence of letter As, each one larger than the previous one. Find a formula for the number of squares that make up the *n*th letter A. Choose several letters of the alphabet (perhaps your initials). For each one, design a way to make the letter out of squares. Make a sequence of enlarged versions of that letter, and then find a formula for the number of squares that make up the *n*th term in the sequence.

3 Graphs of Everyday Quantities

In Lesson 3-3, a graph shows changes in Harold Hooper's speed while driving. Choose several other quantities that vary during the course of a person's day. For each one, write a paragraph describing how the quantity changes and draw a graph. Some suggestions for topics are:

- The outside air temperature in town during the day
- The amount of gasoline in the tank of a car during the day

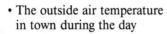

Possible responses
1. Responses will vary.
2. To find the *n*th letter A:
   $6n + 4$ or $6(n - 1) + 10$
3. Responses will vary.

Chapter 3 Projects

Chapter 3 projects relate to the content of the lessons as follows.

Project	Lesson
1	3-1
2	3-8
3	3-3
4	3-8
5	3-4
6	3-10

1 Survey Results Suggest that students design their survey questions so that there is a limited number of possible answers. If, however, the questions have many possible answers, students may decide to write five or six possible answers from which to choose. If a question requires a numeric answer, suggest that students use a range of numbers for responses if it is appropriate for the question. Have students discuss whether the responses to their survey would be different if they were asked at a different school, in a different state or country, or at a different time of year. The graphs should be neat and titled appropriately.

2 Patterns in Expanding Letters Students may have to draw a few more As in the sequence before they are able to write a formula. Have students check their formulas by making sure that they are true for the first As in the sequence. Then have them use their formulas to find the number of squares needed for the 100th and 1,000th term. [604, 6004] Students' designs for the letters they choose should be accurate. Have students compare their formulas, and decide if more than one letter sequence can be described with the same formula.

3 Graphs of Everyday Quantities Some students will draw very detailed graphs. This is not necessary, but it should not be discouraged. Temperatures, recorded on an hourly basis for a 24-hour period, can often be found on the weather page of the local newspaper. Radio and television stations, as well as some computer on-line programs, also offer the same information. Some other suggestions for this topic are: the amount of money in your pocket or wallet during the day or the speed of the school bus on the way to school.

4 Staircase Patterns

Cuisenaire® rods are sets of colored rods which can be used to study mathematics at many different levels. There are 10 different lengths, each of a different color as follows:

Length/Color	Length/Color
1 tan	6 dark green
2 red	7 black
3 light green	8 brown
4 purple	9 violet
5 yellow	10 orange

A review of volume and surface area may be necessary for some students. Suggest that students use tables to organize the data they find as they build their staircases. Students should recognize and be able to formulate the pattern for the volume of the staircase without difficulty. Some students will be able to recognize and describe a pattern for the surface area of the staircase, but they will not be able to write linear expressions describing the pattern.

5 Slides in Activities

Students who have experience playing basketball or football or performing in a marching band or dance ensemble will appreciate this application of mathematics. Remind students that if the entire group moves in the same manner, one slide can describe the movement. To graph an entire routine would be far too much work. Expect students to show a few basic slides of a large number of participants. Students may want or need to describe rotations both of participants moving from one point to the next and of a participant standing still and changing the direction in which he or she is facing. This is far more difficult and beyond the level of this course.

6 BASIC Solution of Inequalities

This project includes much of what is needed to write a BASIC program. Stress that students should read it carefully and refer to it as they write their programs. Remind students that they have to test their programs for negative and positive values for A to make sure that their programs are correct.

PROJECTS 3 *(continued)*

4 Staircase Patterns

Consider the following situation: a staircase is made from Cuisenaire® rods of a single color. Each time a rod is added to the staircase, it is offset by the space of a white (one unit) rod. For instance, shown below is a staircase made from three purple rods (each is 4 units in length).

a. Pick any color rod other than the unit cube. Record its volume and surface area.

b. Build staircases of different sizes with that color rod. Each time you build a staircase, record the number of rods used, the volume of the staircase, and the surface area of the staircase.

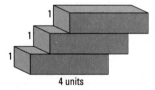

4 units

c. What patterns do you find in your data? What do you predict will be the volume and surface area of the staircase that has 10 rods? 25 rods? *n* rods?

d. How do the patterns change if you build a staircase from rods of a different length and different color?

5 Slides in Activities

In activities such as marching band, football, basketball, dance ensembles, and show choirs, participants need to move in a manner very similar to a slide. Use a coordinate plane and graph paper to design a move in a performance or an offensive play in a sport. Using a drawing and a written explanation, show how each person or group must move.

6 BASIC Solution of Inequalities

Write a BASIC program that will solve inequalities of the form $ax + b > c$. Your program should ask the user for the values of *a*, *b*, and *c*, and then print an appropriate solution. You will probably need to use an IF-THEN statement in your program. This statement allows the computer to make a choice, depending on what values of *a*, *b*, and *c* are given. You may also need to determine how to use the INPUT statement and the PRINT statement on your computer. Test your program to make sure it works for all values of *a*, *b*, and *c*.

Possible responses, page 206

4. a. Responses will vary.
   b. Responses will vary.
   c. Sample response: The volume of the staircase is equal to the volume of the color rod times the number of steps. If the staircase is made with rods that are four units in length, the volume of a 10-rod staircase is 40 cu units, and the surface area is 126 sq units; the volume of a 25-rod staircase is 100 cu units, and the surface is 306 sq units; and the volume of a staircase that has *n* rods is 4*n* cu units, and the surface area is 12*n* + 6 sq units.

SUMMARY

In algebra as in arithmetic, addition is a basic operation. The most frequent applications of addition occur in situations which can be represented by putting together or a slide. Putting together occurs when quantities that do not overlap are combined. A slide occurs when you start with a quantity and go higher or lower by a given amount. Slides can help picture addition of integers, fractions, and like terms.

The properties of addition can be verified through their uses. For example, putting together quantities in a different order yields the same sum, so addition is commutative.

Graphing provides a picture that can help clarify solutions to a problem or trends in data. If two quantities are being considered, a coordinate graph in a plane can show both values. A two-dimensional slide can be represented as a combination of a horizontal and vertical slide on a coordinate graph.

Sentences of the forms $ax + b = c$ or $ax + b < c$ (in which $a \neq 0$) combine multiplication and addition. To solve this type of sentence, first add $-b$ to both sides, and then multiply both sides by $\frac{1}{a}$. Sometimes it is necessary to simplify expressions on either side of the inequality first.

When addition and multiplication occur in the same expression, the Distributive Property may provide a link between the operations. It tells how to change between a form where the multiplication is done first, $ac + bc$, and one where the addition is done first, $(a + b)c$. Forms of the Distributive Property are used to add fractions, to add like terms, and to remove parentheses from expressions.

VOCABULARY

Below are the most important terms and phrases for this chapter. You should be able to give a general description and specific examples of each.

Lesson 3-1
bar graph, stacked bar graph
Putting-Together Model for
 Addition
Slide model for Addition
Commutative Property of
 Addition
Associative Property of
 Addition

Lesson 3-2
additive identity
Additive Identity Property
opposite, additive inverse
Property of Opposites
Opposite of Opposites (Op-op)
 Property
Addition Property of Equality

Lesson 3-3
plane
coordinate graph, axes, origin
scatterplot
coordinates, coordinate plane
continuous

Lesson 3-4
x-axis, y-axis
x-coordinate, y-coordinate
quadrant
two-dimensional slide,
 translation
preimage, image

Lesson 3-6
Distributive Property: Like
 Terms
term, coefficient
like terms, adding like terms

Lesson 3-7
Distributive Property:
 Removing Parentheses

Lesson 3-8
sequence
linear expression
linear equation
FOR-NEXT loop

Lesson 3-9
common denominator
Distributive Property: Adding
 Fractions

Lesson 3-10
Addition Property of
 Inequality

4. d. Let n = number of rods

Length (units)	Volume (cu units)	Surface Area (sq units)		Length (units)	Volume (cu units)	Surface Area (sq units)
1	1n	6n		7	7n	18n + 12
2	2n	8n + 2		8	8n	20n + 14
3	3n	10n + 4		9	9n	22n + 16
4	4n	12n + 6		10	10n	24n + 18
5	5n	14n + 8		5. Responses will vary.		
6	6n	16n + 10				

6. Sample response:

```
10 PRINT "SOLVING AX + B > C"
20 INPUT "A", A, "B", B, "C", C
30 PRINT "A=", A, "B=", B,
   "C=", C
40 X = (C – B)/A
50 IF A > 0 THEN GO TO 70
60 IF A < 0 THEN GO TO 90
70 PRINT "X IS GREATER THAN", X
80 GO TO 100
90 PRINT "X IS LESS THAN", X
100 END
```

207

Progress Self-Test

For the development of mathematical competence, feedback and correction, along with the opportunity to practice, are necessary. The Progress Self-Test provides the opportunity for feedback and correction; the Chapter Review provides additional opportunities and practice. We cannot overemphasize the importance of these end-of-chapter materials. It is at this point that the material "gels" for many students, allowing them to solidify skills and understanding. In general, student performance should be markedly improved after these pages.

Assign the Progress Self-Test as a one-night assignment. Worked-out *solutions* for all questions are in the Selected Answers section of the student book. Encourage students to take the Progress Self-Test honestly, grade themselves, and then be prepared to discuss the test in class.

PROGRESS SELF-TEST

Take this test as you would take a test in class. Then check your work with the solutions in the Selected Answers section in the back of the book.

In 1–7, simplify.

1. $m + 3m$ 4m

2. $\frac{5}{2}(4v + 100 + w)$ $10v + 250 + \frac{5w}{2}$

3. $-9k + 3(k + 3)$ $-6k + 9$

4. $(x + 5 + x) + (-8 + -x)$ $x + -3$

5. $-(-(-p))$ $-p$

6. $\frac{2}{n} + \frac{5}{n} + \frac{-3}{n}$ $\frac{4}{n}$

7. $\frac{3x}{2} + \frac{5x}{3}$ $\frac{19x}{6}$

In 8–11, solve.

8. $8r + 14 = 74$ $r = 7.5$

9. $-4q + 3 + 9q = -12$ $q = -3$

10. $3(x + 2) + 100 = 54$ $x = -\frac{52}{3} = -17\frac{1}{3}$

11. $85 = x + 2(3x + 4)$ $x = 11$

12. Solve and graph the solutions to $30v + -18 > 15$. $v > \frac{11}{10}$

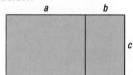

In 13 and 14, name the property that is illustrated. 13–15) See below.

13. If $y + 11 = 3$, then $y + 15 = 7$.

14. $8x + -15x = -7x$

15. Explain why -100 is or is not an element of the solution set of $15 \le x + 87$.

16. You have $137.25 in your savings account, and you add $2.50 each week. Disregarding interest, how much will be in the account after w weeks? $137.25 + 2.50w$

17. Irving bought 6 pairs of socks at $2.99 per pair. Show how Irving could use the Distributive Property to calculate mentally the total cost of the socks. See right.

18. If $F = \frac{9}{5}C + 32$, find the Celsius equivalent of a Fahrenheit temperature of 50°. 10°C

13) Addition Property of Equality
14) Adding Like Terms form of the Distributive Property
15) It is not an element because $-100 + 87 = -13$ and $15 > -13$.

208

19. Juana and Jill had a lemonade stand. Juana worked twice as long as Jill, so Juana received twice as much of the profits as Jill. If the total profits were $58.50, how much should Jill receive? $19.50

20. **a.** Write two expressions to describe the total area of the figure below. $(a + b)c$; $ac + bc$
    b. Explain how your expressions represent the Distributive Property. See below.

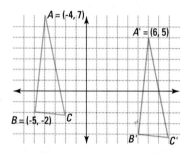

21. Find the image of $(5, -2)$ after a slide of 4 units to the left and 5 units up. $(1, 3)$

22. $\triangle A'B'C'$ is the image of $\triangle ABC$ under a slide. Find the coordinates of B'. $(5, -4)$

17) $6 \cdot $2.99 = 6($3 - 1¢) = 6 \cdot $3 - 6 \cdot 1¢ = $18 - 6¢ = 17.94

20b) The total area is also the sum of the areas of the two smaller rectangles ($ac + bc$). So $(a + b)c = ac + bc$.

Additional Answers, page 176

5. $3x^2 + 4x + 2$

6. a. $3x^2 + 4x + 5$

    b. $x^2 + 2x + 5$

c. $2x^2 + 4x$

d. $4x^2 + 3x + 5$

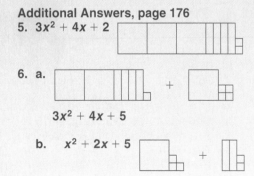

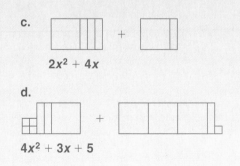

PROGRESS SELF-TEST

23. The graph below shows the tornado death rate per 100,000 population since 1917.

  a. What conclusion can you draw from the graph?

  b. Give some possible reasons for your conclusion.

a) Although deaths do not decrease every year, the likelihood of being killed by a tornado has generally decreased during the last 70 years.
b) Sample: Better health care makes it possible for more victims of natural disasters to survive.

U.S. Tornado Death Rates, 1917-1990

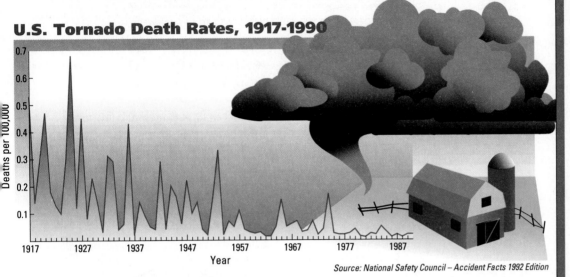

Source: National Safety Council – Accident Facts 1992 Edition

24. The following chart shows total public secondary-school enrollment in the United States. Draw a scatterplot of the data. Plot years on the horizontal axis.

Year	Number of Students
1955	8,521,000
1965	15,504,000
1975	19,151,000
1985	15,219,000
1995 (estimate)	16,431,000

24)

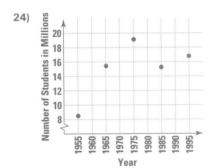

After taking and correcting the Self-Test, you may want to make a list of the problems you got wrong. Then write down what you need to study most. If you can, try to explain your most frequent or common mistakes. Use what you write to help you study and review the chapter.

Chapter 3 Review

Resources

From the *Teacher's Resource File*
- Answer Master for
  Chapter 3 Review
- Assessment Sourcebook:
  Chapter 3 Test, Forms A–D
  Chapter 3 Test, Cumulative Form
  Comprehensive Test,
  Chapters 1–3

Additional Resources
- Quiz and Test Writer

The main objectives for the chapter are organized in the Chapter Review under the four types of understanding this book promotes—Skills, Properties, Uses, and Representations.

Whereas end-of chapter material may be considered optional in some texts, in *UCSMP Algebra* we have selected these objectives and questions with the expectation that they will be covered. Students should be able to answer these questions with about 85% accuracy after studying the chapter.

You may assign these questions over a single night to help students prepare for a test the next day, or you may assign the questions over a two-day period. If you work the questions over two days, then we recommend assigning the *evens* for homework the first night so that students get feedback in class the next day, then assigning the *odds* the night before the test, because answers are provided to the odd-numbered questions.

It is effective to ask students which questions they still do not understand and use the day or days as a total class discussion of the material which the class finds most difficult.

Additional Answers
39. 7($3.00 + 4¢) = $21.00 + 28¢ = $21.28
40. 35(100 + 1) = 3500 + 35 = 3535
41. 3(100 − 5) = 300 − 15 = 285
42. 9($20 − 1¢) = $180 − 9¢ = $179.91

210

CHAPTER REVIEW

Questions on SPUR Objectives

SPUR stands for **S**kills, **P**roperties, **U**ses, and **R**epresentations. The Chapter Review questions are grouped according to the SPUR Objectives for this chapter.

SKILLS DEAL WITH THE PROCEDURES USED TO GET ANSWERS.

Objective A: *Use the Distributive Property and the properties of addition to simplify expressions.* *(Lessons 3-1, 3-2, 3-6, 3-7)*

In 1–6, simplify.
1. $8x + -3x + 10x$ 15x
2. $-3m + 4m + -m$ 0
3. $c + \frac{1}{2}c$ $\frac{3}{2}c$
4. $-\frac{2}{3}(6 + -9v + 4v)$ $-4 + \frac{10v}{3}$
5. $11(3x + 2) + 4(5x + 6)$ 53x + 46
6. $3w + 4 + 5(4w + 6)$ 23w + 34

Objective B: *Solve and check equations of the form $x + a = b$ and $ax + b = c$.* *(Lessons 3-2, 3-5, 3-6, 3-7)* 7) t = -0.6

In 7–18, solve and check. See students' papers for checks.
7. $2.5 = t + 3.1$
8. $x + -11 = 12$ x = 23
9. $(3 + n) + -11 = -5 + 4$ n = 7
10. $\left(2\frac{1}{2} + 1\frac{1}{4}\right) + -\frac{3}{4} = (a + 6) + -2$ a = -1
11. $4n + 3 = 15$ n = 3
12. $-470 + 2n = 1100$ n = 785
13. $\frac{2}{3}x + 14 = 15$ x = $\frac{3}{2}$
14. $5m + -3m + 6 = 12$ m = 3

32) Associative Property of Addition
33) Opposite of the Opposite Prop.

15. $17r + 12 + 9r = 1312$ r = 50
16. $5(x + 3) = 95$ x = 16
17. $2x + 3(1 + x) = 18$ x = 3
18. $16 = \frac{3}{4}b + 22$ b = -8

Objective C: *Add algebraic fractions.* *(Lesson 3-9)*

In 19–24, simplify each sum.
19. $\frac{x}{3} + \frac{y}{3}$ $\frac{x + y}{3}$
20. $\frac{30}{a} + \frac{10}{a} + \frac{20}{a}$ $\frac{60}{a}$
21. $\frac{2}{3}x + \frac{1}{3}x$ x
22. $\frac{x}{3} + \frac{x}{4}$ $\frac{7x}{12}$
23. $\frac{x}{5} + -\frac{3x}{2}$ $\frac{-13x}{10}$
24. $\frac{2x}{5} + \frac{3y}{5} + \frac{-3x}{5}$ $\frac{-x + 3y}{5}$

Objective D: *Solve and check inequalities of the form $ax + b < c$.* *(Lesson 3-10)* See students' papers for checks.

In 25–30, solve and check.
25. $2x + 11 < 201$ x < 95
26. $\frac{3}{4}t + 21 > 12$ t > -12
27. $-2 + (5 + x) > 4$ x > 1
28. $-28 ≤ 17 + (y + 5)$ y ≥ -50
29. $4 < -16g + 7g + 5$ g < $\frac{1}{9}$
30. $p + 2p + 3p + 4p ≤ 85$ p ≤ 8.5

34) Adding Fractions form of the Distributive Property
35) Adding Like Terms form of the Distributive Prop.

PROPERTIES DEAL WITH THE PRINCIPLES BEHIND THE MATHEMATICS.

Objective E: *Identify and apply properties of addition or the Distributive Property.* *(Lessons 3-1, 3-2, 3-6, 3-7, 3-9)* 32) 35) See above.

In 31–36, what property has been applied?
31. $2(L + W) = 2(W + L)$ Commutative Prop. of Addition
32. $(28 + -16) + -23 = 28 + (-16 + -23)$
33. $-(-31) = 31$
34. $\frac{x}{31} + \frac{y}{31} = \frac{x + y}{31}$
35. $8x + -13x = -5x$
36. If $t + 18 < -3$, then $t + 18 + -18 < -3 + -18$. Addition Property of Inequality

37. Hillary adds -14 to both sides of $x + -7 = 14$. What sentence results? x + -21 = 0
38. If x is a negative integer, what is $-x$? positive integer

39–42) See margin.

Objective F: *Use the Distributive Property to perform calculations in your head.* *(Lesson 3-7)*

In 39–42, explain how the Distributive Property can be used to do the calculations mentally.
39. $7 \cdot \$3.04$
40. $101 \cdot 35$
41. $3 \cdot 95$
42. the cost of 9 shirts if each one costs $19.99

210

USES DEAL WITH APPLICATIONS OF MATHEMATICS IN REAL SITUATIONS.

Objective G: *Apply models for addition to write linear expressions or to solve sentences of the form $x + a = b$, $ax + b = c$, or $ax + b < c$.* (Lessons 3-1, 3-2, 3-5, 3-6, 3-10) 44) $T_1 + C > T_2$

43. If the temperature is -11°C, by how much must it increase to become 13°C? **24°**

44. The temperature was T_1 degrees. It changed by C degrees. Now it is more than T_2 degrees. Give a sentence relating T_1, C, and T_2.

45. If Wisconsin produced w billion pounds of milk and California produced c billion pounds, how much milk did the two states produce together? **$w + c$ billion pounds**

46. Mark has $5.40 and would like to buy a pair of jeans for $26. He earns d dollars babysitting and $7.50 for mowing the lawn, but still does not have enough money. What sentence relates $5.40, $26, $7.50, and d?

47. Eli needs $5 more for a concert ticket. How much must he earn to go to the concert and have at least $4 for bus fare and food?

48. Katy earns $7.80 per hour at the zoo. She also receives a $25.00 meal allowance, $15.00 for transportation, and $7.50 for dry cleaning. Last week she was paid a total of $320.50. How many hours did she work?

49. A $67,500 estate is to be split among four children and a grandchild. Each child gets the same amount and the grandchild gets half that amount. How much will each receive?
children—$15,000;   grandchild—$7,500
46) $5.40 + d + $7.50 < $26
47) at least $9
48) 35 hours

Objective H: *Write expressions and solve problems involving linear patterns with two variables.* (Lesson 3-8)

50. Anna opened a savings account with $45. She plans to deposit $6 each week.

  a. Disregarding interest, how much will be in the account after w weeks? **45 + 6w**

  b. When will she have saved $195? **25 wks**

51. Refer to the table.

x	y
1	10
2	13
3	16
4	19
5	22

  a. What is the next row in the table? **6, 25**

  b. Find a formula that relates x and y.
  $y = 3x + 7$

52. In 1993 the cost of mailing a letter was 29¢ for one ounce or less and 23¢ for each additional ounce, rounded up. The table shows different mailing costs. **See below.**

Weight (oz)	Charges	Cost Pattern
1	.29	.29 + .23 · 0
2	.29 + .23	.29 + .23 · 1
3	.29 + .23 + .23	.29 + .23 · 2
4	.29 + .23 + .23 + .23	.29 + .23 · 3

  a. Write the next row of the table.

  b. Write an expression for the cost of mailing a letter that weighs n ounces.

53. A business with a 900 exchange charges callers $2.95 for a 3-minute call and $.75 for each additional minute. Find the cost of calling for each of the times.

  a. 4 minutes **b.** 10 minutes **c.** n minutes
  $3.70   **$8.20**
c) $2.95 + .75($n$ − 3) when n > 3

REPRESENTATIONS DEAL WITH PICTURES, GRAPHS, OR OBJECTS THAT ILLUSTRATE CONCEPTS.

Objective I: *Draw and interpret two-dimensional graphs.* (Lesson 3-3)

54. The table shown, from *Places Rated Almanac of 1989*, lists some of the metropolitan areas expecting new jobs between 1989 and 1995.

  a. What do the negative signs mean? **jobs lost**

  b. Draw a graph using number of blue-collar jobs created as the horizontal axis. Plot and label the points given in the table.
  See margin.

Jobs to be Created 1989–95		
Metro area	Blue Collar	White Collar
Akron, OH	-5,540	13,800
Bellingham, WA	180	3,320
Casper, WY	-1540	-120
Danbury, CT	1110	13,490
Elkhart-Goshen, IN	5,540	2,880
Fort Smith, AR	4,190	4,650

52a) 5; .29 + .23 + .23 + .23 + .23; .29 + .23 · 4
b) .29 + .23(n − 1)

Chapter 3   *Chapter Review*   **211**

Evaluation The *Assessment Sourcebook* provides five forms of the Chapter 3 Test. Forms A and B present parallel versions in a short-answer format. Forms C and D offer performance assessment. The fifth test is Chapter 3 Test, Cumulative Form. About 50% of this test covers Chapter 3; 25% of it covers Chapter 2, and 25% of it covers Chapter 1. In addition to these tests, Comprehensive Test Chapters 1–3 gives roughly equal attention to all chapters covered thus far.

For information on grading see *General Teaching Suggestions: Grading* in the *Professional Sourcebook* which begins on page T20 in Part 1 of the Teacher's Edition.

Feedback After students have taken the test for Chapter 3 and you have scored the results, return the tests to students for discussion. Class discussion on the questions that caused trouble for most students can be very effective in identifying and clarifying misunderstandings. You might want to have students write down the items they missed and work either in groups or at home to correct them. It is important for students to receive feedback on every chapter test and we recommend that students see and correct their mistakes before proceeding too far into the next chapter.

Additional Answers
54b.

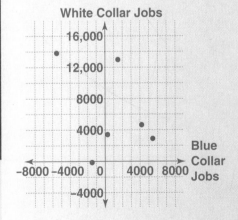

White Collar Jobs

60.

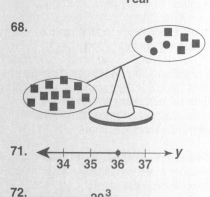

68.

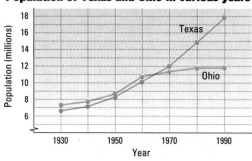

71.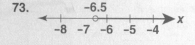

72. $-20\frac{3}{5}$

73. -6.5

74.

In 55 and 56, the graph below shows the height of a boy's head from the ground as he rides in a Ferris wheel.

55. Where is the boy (top, bottom, or halfway up) after 40 seconds on the ride? **halfway up**

56. After everyone is on, how many times does the Ferris wheel go around before it begins to let people off? **4**

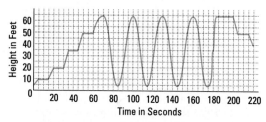

In 57–59, use the graph below.

57. Which state had more people in 1930, Texas or Ohio? **Ohio**

58. In which decade were the populations of Ohio and Texas the same? **1960–1970**

59. In which decade did Ohio have its greatest increase in population? **1950–1960**

Population of Texas and Ohio in various years

60. Draw a graph to illustrate these data (year, the U.S. population per square mile): (1800, 6.1), (1850, 7.9), (1900, 50.7), (1980, 62.6). Label the axes. **See margin.**

Objective J: *Draw and interpret two-dimensional slides on a coordinate graph.* *(Lesson 3-4)*

61. Find the image of (2, -4) after a slide of 40 units to the left and 60 units up. **(-38, 56)**

62. Find the image of (x, y) after a slide of 4 units to the right and 10 units down. $(x + 4, y - 10)$

63. The image of the point (4, 9) after a slide is (3, 17). Describe the slide with a rule or words. **The image of (x, y) is $(x - 1, y + 8)$**

64. If $R = (-3, 2)$, use the rule $(x, y) \rightarrow (x + 3, y)$ to find R'. **(0, 2)**

65. After a slide, the image of C is $C' = (6, 4)$. Graph the image of $\triangle ABC$ shown at the right by finding the image of each vertex.

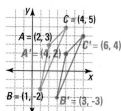

Objective K: *Use balance scales or area models to represent expressions or sentences.* *(Lessons 3-5, 3-6, 3-7, 3-10)*

66. Use the picture of a balance below. All the boxes weigh the same.

   a. Write an equation describing the situation with b representing the weight of one box. $3b + 2 = 8$

   b. What does one box weigh? **2 kg**

67. Use the picture below.

   a. Write an equation to describe this situation with W representing the weight of one box. $13 = 5W + 8$

   b. What is the weight of one box? **1 kg**

212

68. Draw a picture to illustrate the inequality $3w + 4 < 11$. See margin.

In 69–70, write two different expressions to describe the total area of each large rectangle.

69.

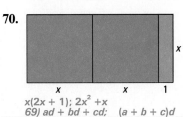

70.

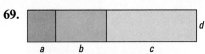

$x(2x + 1); 2x^2 + x$
69) $ad + bd + cd$; $(a + b + c)d$

Objective L: *On a number line graph solutions to inequalities of the form $ax + b < c$.*
(Lesson 3-10)

In 71–74, graph all solutions. See margin.

71. $12 + y \leq 48$ **72.** $\frac{-3}{5} > z + 20$

73. $-2x + 4 < 17$ **74.** $5(2 + 3x) + 6 \geq 106$

R E F R E S H E R

Chapter 4, which discusses subtraction in algebra, assumes that you have mastered certain objectives in your previous studies of mathematics. Use these questions to check your mastery.

A. Subtract positive numbers or quantities. In 1–6, find the difference.

1. $8\frac{2}{3} - 3\frac{1}{3}$ $5\frac{1}{3}$ **2.** $13.96 - 4.89$ 9.07
3. $12.5 - 6.85$ 5.65   **4.** $18\frac{1}{2} - 10\frac{3}{4}$ $7\frac{3}{4}$
5. $100\% - 4\%$ 96%   **6.** $100\% - 8.5\%$ 91.5%

B. Subtract positive and negative integers. In 7–12, find the difference. 7) -160 10) -1

7. $40 - 200$ **8.** $76 - 79$ -3 **9.** $-2 - 6$ -8
10. $-12 - -11$ **11.** $111 - -88$ **12.** $-2 - -3$ 1
                         199

C. Solve simple equations of the form $x - a = b$ when a and b are integers. In 13–16, solve the equation.

13. $x - 40 = 11$ $x = 51$
14. $878 = y - 31$ $y = 909$
15. $w - 64 = 49$ $w = 113$
16. $-100 = z - 402$ $z = 302$

D. Measure angles.

17. *Multiple choice.* Without using a protractor, tell whether the measure of angle V below is:
(a) between 0° and 45°,
(b) between 45° and 90°, (b)
(c) greater than 90°.

18. *Multiple choice.* Without using a protractor, tell whether the measure of angle W below is:
(a) between 0° and 45°,
(b) between 45° and 90°,
(c) greater than 90°. (c)

19. Measure $\angle V$ to the nearest degree. 74°
20. Measure $\angle W$ to the nearest degree. 120°
21. Draw an angle whose measure is 110°.
22. Draw an angle whose measure is 11°.
21-22) See margin.

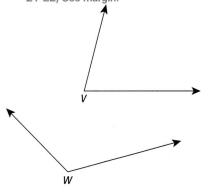

Refresher

There are two ways you might use this refresher. If you know that your students have a particularly weak background in subtraction as it relates to algebra, you may wish to assign this Refresher to better prepare them for Chapter 4. If you do not know what your students' backgrounds are, you can use these questions as both a diagnostic tool and as remediation.

Have students do the odd-numbered questions as part of the first assignment for the chapter and then have them check their answers with those given in the back of their books. If they missed more than a few questions, they should see you for help with the even-numbered questions.

Parts A and B cover content seen in Lesson 3-2, Part C covers content reviewed in Lesson 3-3, and Part D covers the simplest equations of the form seen in Lesson 3-5.

Additional Answers
21.

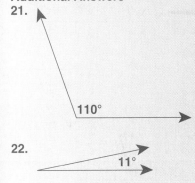

Setting Up Lesson 4-1
We strongly recommend that you assign Lesson 4-1, both reading and some questions, for homework the evening of the test. It gives students work to do after they have completed the test and keeps the class moving. If you do not do this consistently after tests, you may cover one less chapter over the course of the year.

Chapter 4 Pacing Chart

Day	Full Course	Minimal Course
1	4-1	4-1
2	4-2	4-2
3	4-3	4-3
4	4-4	4-4
5	Quiz*; 4-5	Quiz*; begin 4-5.
6	4-6	Finish 4-5.
7	4-7	4-6
8	Quiz*; 4-8	4-7
9	4-9	Quiz*; begin 4-8.
10	Self-Test	Finish 4-8.
11	Review	4-9
12	Test*	Self-Test
13		Review
14		Review
15		Test*

*in the Teacher's Resource File

Adapting to Individual Needs

The student text is written for the vast majority of students. The chart at the right suggests two pacing plans to accommodate the needs of your students. Students in the Full Course should complete the entire text by the end of the year. Students in the Minimal Course will spend more time when there are quizzes and more time on the Chapter Review. Therefore, these students may not complete all of the chapters in the text.

Options are also presented to meet the needs of a variety of teaching and learning styles. For each lesson, the Teacher's Edition provides sections entitled: *Video* which describes video segments and related questions that can be used for motivation or extension; *Optional Activities* which suggests activities that employ materials, physical models, technology, and cooperative learning; and, *Adapting to Individual Needs* which regularly includes **Challenge** problems, **English Language Development** suggestions, and suggestions for providing **Extra Help.** The Teacher's Edition also frequently includes an **Error Alert,** an **Extension,** and an **Assessment** alternative. The options available in Chapter 4 are summarized in the chart below.

In the Teacher's Edition...

Lesson	Optional Activities	Extra Help	Challenge	English Language Development	Error Alert	Extension	Cooperative Learning	Ongoing Assessment
4-1	●	●	●	●	●	●	●	Written
4-2	●	●	●	●	●	●		Oral
4-3	●	●	●	●	●	●	●	Group
4-4	●	●	●	●		●	●	Oral
4-5	●	●	●	●	●	●	●	Written
4-6	●	●	●	●		●	●	Oral
4-7	●	●	●	●		●	●	Group
4-8	●	●	●	●		●	●	Written
4-9	●	●	●	●	●	●	●	Oral

In the Additional Resources...

Lesson	In the Teacher's Resource File								
	Lesson Masters, A and B	Teaching Aids*	Activity Kit*	Answer Masters	Technology Sourcebook	Assessment Sourcebook	Visual Aids**	Technology	Video Segments
4-1	4-1	26, 33		4-1			26, 33, AM		
4-2	4-2	33		4-2	Calc 2		33, AM		
4-3	4-3	34		4-3			34, AM		
4-4	4-4	34, 37, 38		4-4	Comp 10	Quiz	34, 37, 38, AM	Spreadsheet	
4-5	4-5	35	8	4-5			35, AM		
4-6	4-6	35, 39, 40	9	4-6	Comp 11		35, 39, 40, AM	GraphExplorer	
4-7	4-7	35, 41		4-7		Quiz	35, 41, AM		
In-class Activity		42		4-8			42, AM		
4-8	4-8	36, 43–45		4-8			36, 43–45, AM		
4-9	4-9	26, 36, 39, 46		4-9	Comp 12		26, 36, 39, 46, AM	GraphExplorer	
End of chapter				Review		Tests			

*Teaching Aids are pictured on pages 214C and 214D. The activities in the Activity Kit are pictured on page 214C. Teaching Aid 42 which accompanies the In-class Activity preceding Lesson 4-8 is pictured with the lesson notes on page 259.

**Visual Aids provide transparencies for all Teaching Aids and all Answer Masters.

Also available is the Study Skills Handbook which includes study-skill tips related to reading, note-taking, and comprehension.

Integrating Strands and Applications

	4-1	4-2	4-3	4-4	4-5	4-6	4-7	4-8	4-9
Mathematical Connections									
Number Sense	●							●	●
Algebra	●	●	●	●	●	●	●	●	●
Geometry		●		●	●	●	●	●	●
Measurement		●		●				●	●
Logic and Reasoning				●					
Patterns and Functions	●	●		●	●	●	●		●
Interdisciplinary and Other Connections									
Science	●	●	●			●	●	●	●
Social Studies	●	●	●		●	●		●	●
Multicultural	●	●				●			●
Technology	●			●	●				●
Career		●		●	●				
Consumer	●	●	●	●	●	●	●	●	●
Sports			●		●	●	●		●

Teaching and Assessing the Chapter Objectives

Chapter 4 Objectives (Organized into the SPUR categories—Skills, Properties, Uses, and Representations)	Lessons	Progress Self-Test Questions	Chapter Review Questions	Chapter Test, Forms A and B	In the Assessment Sourcebook Chapter Test, Forms	
					C	D
Skills						
A: Simplify expressions involving subtraction.	4-1	3, 4, 7	1–8	2, 3	1	
B: Solve and check linear equations involving subtraction.	4-3	9, 11	9–18	6, 7, 9	3	✓
C: Solve and check linear inequalities involving subtraction.	4-3	10	19–22	8, 10	2	
D: Use the Opposite of a Sum or Difference to simplify expressions and solve sentences.	4-5	5, 6, 12	23, 24	4, 5	3	
Properties						
E: Apply the algebraic definition of subtraction.	4-1	1, 2	35–38	1	1	
F: Use the definitions of supplements and complements, and the Triangle Sum Theorem.	4-7	18, 20	39–46	15, 17	4	
G: Use Triangle Inequality to determine possible lengths of sides of triangles.	4-8	21	47–52	18		
Uses						
H: Use models of subtraction to write expressions and sentences involving subtraction.	4-2	8	53–60	11	2	
I: Solve problems using linear sentences involving subtraction.	4-3	13, 14	61–64	16	2	✓
J: Apply the Triangle Inequality in real situtations.	4-8	17	65, 66	19	4	
Representations						
K: Use a spreadsheet to show patterns and make tables from formulas.	4-4	22	67–70	20	5	
L: Graph equations of the forms $x \pm y = k$, or $y = ax \pm b$ by making a table of values.	4-6, 4-9	15, 16, 19	71–77	12–14		✓

Assessment Sourcebook
Quiz for Lessons 4-1 through 4-4   Chapter 4 Test, Forms A–D
Quiz for Lessons 4-5 through 4-7   Chapter 4 Test, Cumulative Form

Quiz and Test Writer
Multiple forms of chapter tests and quizzes; Challenges

Activity Kit

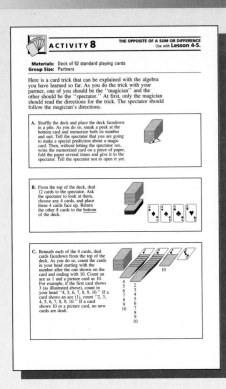

ACTIVITY 8 THE OPPOSITE OF A SUM OR DIFFERENCE
Use with **Lesson 4-5.**

Materials: Deck of 52 standard playing cards
Group Size: Partners

Here is a card trick that can be explained with the algebra you have learned so far. As you do the trick with your partner, one of you should be the "magician" and the other should be the "spectator." At first, only the magician should read the directions for the trick. The spectator should follow the magician's directions.

A. Shuffle the deck and place the deck facedown in a pile. As you do so, sneak a peek at the bottom card and memorize both its number and suit. Tell the spectator that you are going to make a special prediction about a magic card. Then, without letting the spectator see, write the memorized card on a piece of paper, fold the paper several times and give it to the spectator. Tell the spectator not to open it yet.

B. From the top of the deck, deal 12 cards to the spectator. Ask the spectator to look at them, choose any 4 cards, and place these 4 cards face up. Return the other 8 cards to the bottom of the deck.

C. Beneath each of the 4 cards, deal cards facedown from the top of the deck. As you do so, count the cards in your head starting with the number after the one shown on the card and ending with 10. Count an ace as 1 and a picture card as 10. For example, if the first card shows 3 (as illustrated above), count in your head "4, 5, 6, 7, 8, 9, 10." If a card shows an ace (1), count "2, 3, 4, 5, 6, 7, 8, 9, 10." If a card shows 10 or a picture card, no new cards are dealt.

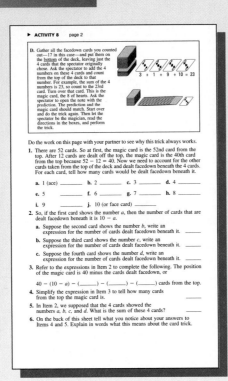

ACTIVITY 8 page 2

D. Gather all the facedown cards you counted out—17 in this case—and put them on the bottom of the deck, leaving just the 4 cards that the spectator originally chose. Ask the spectator to add the 4 numbers on these 4 cards and count from the top of the deck to that number. For example, the sum of the 4 numbers is 23, so count to the 23rd card. Turn over that card. This is the magic card, the 8 of hearts. Ask the spectator to open the note with the prediction. The prediction and the magic card should match. Start over and do the trick again. Then let the spectator be the magician, read the directions in the boxes, and perform the trick.

3 + 1 + 9 + 10 = 23

Do the work on this page with your partner to see why this trick always works.

1. There are 52 cards. So at first, the magic card is the 52nd card from the top. After 12 cards are dealt off the top, the magic card is the 40th card from the top because 52 − 12 = 40. Now we need to account for the other cards taken from the top of the deck and dealt facedown beneath the 4 cards. For each card, tell how many cards would be dealt facedown beneath it.

   a. 1 (ace) _____ **b.** 2 _____ **c.** 3 _____ **d.** 4 _____

   e. 5 _____ **f.** 6 _____ **g.** 7 _____ **h.** 8 _____

   i. 9 _____ **j.** 10 (or face card) _____

2. So, if the first card shows the number a, then the number of cards that are dealt facedown beneath it is $10 − a$.

   a. Suppose the second card shows the number b, write an expression for the number of cards dealt facedown beneath it. _____

   b. Suppose the third card shows the number c, write an expression for the number of cards dealt facedown beneath it. _____

   c. Suppose the fourth card shows the number d, write an expression for the number of cards dealt facedown beneath it. _____

3. Refer to the expressions in Item 2 to complete the following. The position of the magic card is 40 minus the cards dealt facedown, or

   $40 − (10 − a) − ($_____$) − ($_____$) − ($_____$)$ cards from the top.

4. Simplify the expression in Item 3 to tell how many cards from the top the magic card is.

5. In Item 2, we supposed that the 4 cards showed the numbers a, b, c, and d. What is the sum of these 4 cards?

6. On the back of this sheet tell what you notice about your answers to Items 4 and 5. Explain in words what this means about the card trick.

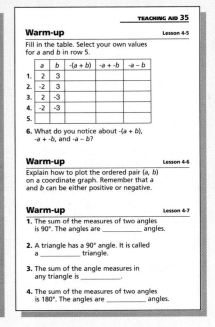

ACTIVITY 9 GRAPHING x + y = k AND x − y = k
Use with **Lesson 4-6.**

Materials: 15 pennies, small box, grid paper
Group Size: Small groups

1. Place 10 pennies in a box and shake the box. Spill the pennies on a desk or table. Record how many pennies landed heads up and how many landed tails up. Write the results as an ordered pair (heads, tails).

Example:

Results: _3_ heads, _7_ tails;
ordered pair: (_3, 7_)

2. On your grid paper set up a coordinate graph in Quadrant I. Label the axes from 0 to 10. Then graph the ordered pair.

3. Repeat the procedure above twenty times. Record the ordered pairs below. Graph all of the ordered pairs on the same graph you used in Item 2. (For duplicate ordered pairs, the point is shown just once.)

   (__,__); (__,__); (__,__); (__,__); (__,__);

   (__,__); (__,__); (__,__); (__,__); (__,__);

   (__,__); (__,__); (__,__); (__,__); (__,__);

   (__,__); (__,__); (__,__); (__,__); (__,__);

4. Look at your ordered pairs. What is the sum of the two numbers in each case? _____

5. Look at your graph. What do you notice about the points? _____

6. Did any of your results show no heads? _____

7. If there are no heads in a result, where is the point for that result on the graph? _____

8. Suppose you used 15 pennies instead of 10. On a new grid, sketch what you think the results would look like. If you need help, actually do the experiment.

Given h and t are the numbers of heads and tails.
Circle the equation that best describes the experiment.

9. In Items 1–7. (a) $h − t = 10$ (b) $h + t = 10$ (c) $t − h = 10$

10. In Item 8. (a) $h − t = 15$ (b) $h + t = 15$ (c) $t − h = 15$

Teaching Aids

Teaching Aid 26, Graph Paper, (shown on page 140D) can be used with **Lessons 4-1 and 4-9.**

TEACHING AID 33

Warm-up Lesson 4-1

Simplify.

1. $r − 2s + 5r + -2s$

2. $\frac{1}{2}m + \frac{3}{4}n − \frac{2}{3}m − 2\frac{3}{4}n$

3. $.3p − q − p − 3q$

Evaluate both the original expression and your simplified answer to Questions 1, 2, and 3 when

4. $r = 2$ and $s = 3$.

5. $m = 12$ and $n = 4$.

6. $p = 5$ and $q = 2$.

Warm-up Lesson 4-2

Use the figure to answer the questions. $ABCD$ and $ARST$ are both squares.

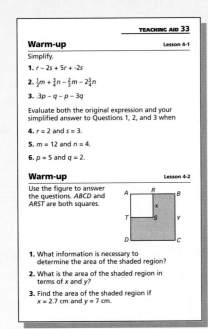

1. What information is necessary to determine the area of the shaded region?

2. What is the area of the shaded region in terms of x and y?

3. Find the area of the shaded region if $x = 2.7$ cm and $y = 7$ cm.

TEACHING AID 34

Warm-up Lesson 4-3

Find the difference between the record high and low temperatures for each of these states.

1. Alaska: High: 100°F (June 27, 1915)
   Low: -80°F (January 23, 1971)

2. Florida: High: 109°F (June 29, 1931)
   Low: -2°F (February 13, 1899)

3. Pennsylvania: High: 111°F (July 10, 1936)
   Low: -42°F (January 5, 1904)

4. Nevada: High: 122°F (June 26, 1990)
   Low: -50°F (January 8, 1937)

5. California: High: 134°F (July 10, 1913)
   Low: -45°F (January 20, 1937)

Warm-up Lesson 4-4

The following students took three quizzes and received these scores.

Rosa: 83, 88, 84
Al: 83, 86, 92
Sam: 80, 78, 88
Liz: 76, 85, 91

1. Compute each student's average (mean) score.

2. Organize the data from Question 1 in a table. Label the columns "Name," "Q 1," "Q 2," "Q 3," and "Avg." Label the rows under "Name" with students' names. Save your table for later use.

TEACHING AID 35

Warm-up Lesson 4-5

Fill in the table. Select your own values for a and b in row 5.

	a	b	-(a + b)	-a + -b	-a − b
1.	2	3			
2.	-2	3			
3.	2	-3			
4.	-2	-3			
5.					

6. What do you notice about $-(a + b)$, $-a + -b$, and $-a − b$?

Warm-up Lesson 4-6

Explain how to plot the ordered pair (a, b) on a coordinate graph. Remember that a and b can be either positive or negative.

Warm-up Lesson 4-7

1. The sum of the measures of two angles is 90°. The angles are _____ angles.

2. A triangle has a 90° angle. It is called a _____ triangle.

3. The sum of the angle measures in any triangle is _____.

4. The sum of the measures of two angles is 180°. The angles are _____ angles.

Warm-up
Lesson 4-8

Mr. Smith is going to the hardware store and then to the grocery store. After shopping for groceries, he is going home. He lives 6 miles from the hardware store and 5 miles from the grocery store. Sketch the location of Mr. Smith's home and the two stores for each case.

Case 1: Mr. Smith's trip is as short as possible.
Case 2: Mr. Smith's trip is as long as possible.
Case 3: Mr. Smith's trip is somewhere between the shortest and longest trip.

Warm-up
Lesson 4-9

For 1–3, tell if the line shows a constant-increase pattern, a constant-decrease pattern, or no increase or decrease.

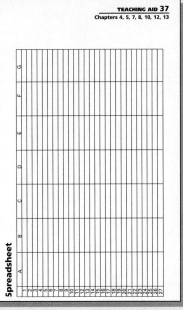

1. Line c

2. Line d

3. Line e

For 4–6, describe the line in words or draw an example of the line on the same grid as lines c, d, and e.

4. Line r showing no increase or decrease

5. Line s showing a constant decrease

6. Line t showing a constant increase

Spreadsheet

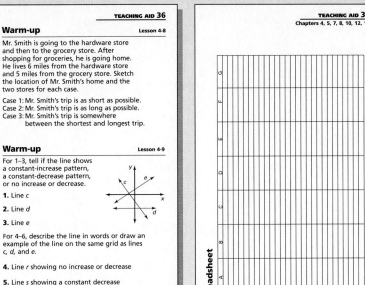

Additional Examples 1 and 2

1. The spreadsheet below shows the number of tickets sold and the revenue from ticket sales for a 3-game soccer tournament.

	A	B	C	D
1	Game		Sales	$$$
2	9 A.M.		280	700
3	2 P.M.		174	435
4	7 P.M.		321	
5				
6	Total			

a. Which cell contains the word "Total"?
b. What is in cell C2?
c. Which cell contains the number 174?
d. Cell C6 is computed by typing "=C2+C3+C4". What number will appear in C6?
e. What is in cell D5?
f. If the number in C4 is changed to 327, what other entry will change? What will it become?

2. Make a spreadsheet to give examples of two ways to find the perimeter of a rectangle: $\ell + w + \ell + w = 2\ell + 2w$.

a. Label the columns and rows of your spreadsheet. Fill in row 1.
b. Pick values for ℓ and w. Where will you write them?
c. What formula will you write in C2? What will cell C2 show?
d. What formula will you write in D2? What will cell D2 show?

Graphing Equations

Equation: _____

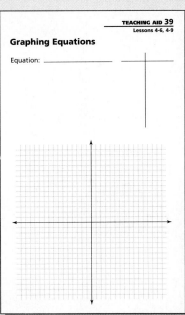

Question 27

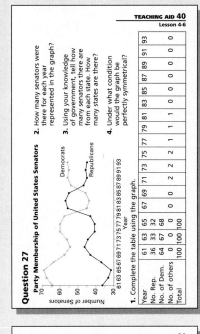

2. How many senators were there for each year represented in the graph?

3. Using your knowledge of government, tell how many senators there are from each state. How many states are there?

4. Under what condition would the graph be perfectly symmetrical?

1. Complete the table using the graph.

Activity

a. Measure all the angles in each triangle below, and find the sum of the angle measures.
b. Draw another triangle of a different size and shape. Measure its angles and find the sum of its angle measures.
c. What patterns do you notice?

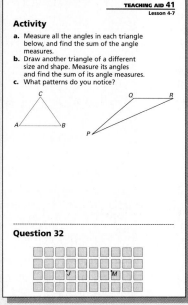

Question 32

Example 1

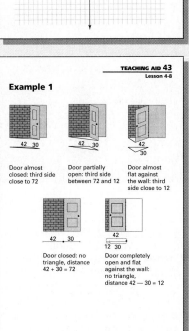

Door almost closed: third side close to 72

Door partially open: third side between 72 and 12

Door almost flat against the wall: third side close to 12

Door closed: no triangle, distance 42 + 30 = 72

Door completely open and flat against the wall: no triangle, distance 42 — 30 = 12

Additional Examples

1. If two sides of a triangle have lengths 3 and 19, write an interval to describe the possible lengths of the third side.

2. Two sides of a triangle each have length 5 cm. What are the possible lengths of the third side?

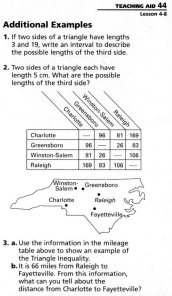

	Charlotte	Greensboro	Winston-Salem	Raleigh
Charlotte	----	96	81	169
Greensboro	96	----	26	83
Winston-Salem	81	26	----	106
Raleigh	169	83	106	----

3. a. Use the information in the mileage table above to show an example of the Triangle Inequality.
b. It is 66 miles from Raleigh to Fayetteville. From this information, what can you tell about the distance from Charlotte to Fayetteville?

Question 24

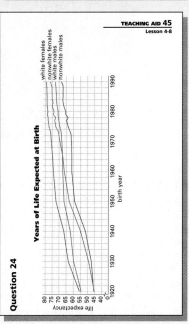

214D

Chapter Opener

Pacing

All of the lessons in this chapter are designed to be covered in one day. At the end of the chapter, you should plan to spend 1 day to review the Progress Self-Test, 1 to 2 days for the Chapter Review, and 1 day for a test. You may wish to spend a day on projects, and perhaps a day is needed for quizzes. Therefore, this chapter should take 12 to 15 days. We strongly advise that you not spend more than 17 days on this chapter; there is ample opportunity to review the ideas in later chapters.

Using Pages 214–215

These pages should be used as a preview of the chapter. The questions on page 215 will be formally solved elsewhere in the chapter—the first problem is Example 3 in Lesson 4-3, the second problem is Question 10 in Lesson 4-3, and the graph is of the type found in Lesson 4-8. By showing the equation $500 - 30x = 1000$, we try to demonstrate that the methods of this chapter will prepare students to solve a wide variety of equations that are not easily solved mentally or by trial and error. At the same time, the problems are easy to follow, so students can understand what they will be studying in the chapter.

Chapter 4 Overview

This chapter has three themes. The first, subtraction, parallels the theme of addition in Chapter 3. Lessons 4-1 and 4-2 deal with the definition of subtraction in terms of addition and with models for the operation. Lesson 4-3 addresses linear equations of the forms $ax - b = c$ and $a - bx = c$. The former can be solved by rewriting the subtraction as an addition; the latter can be solved by doing the same and multiplying both sides by a negative number. With the

subtraction of quantities, which is covered in Lesson 4-5, students will have covered all of the simpler linear equations in which the variable is on one side of the equation.

The second theme consists of applications to geometry. This theme begins in Lesson 4-2 where certain of the applications are geometric. It is more evident in Lessons 4-7 and 4-8, where complementary and supplementary angles, the Triangle-Sum Theorem,

and the Triangle Inequality are discussed. Two lessons are devoted to the third theme, graphing. Lesson 4-6 covers the basic idea of plotting points whose coordinates satisfy a sentence. Lesson 4-9 extends the idea of Lesson 4-6 to any linear sentence. At this point, we do not analyze the graphs using properties such as slope; they are covered in Chapter 7.

SUBTRACTION IN ALGEBRA

Many situations lead to linear sentences involving subtraction. For instance, answers to the questions below can be found by solving the equation

$$5000 - 30x = 1000.$$

1. You want to go to Kenya to see lions and elephants in their native habitats. The trip will cost $5000. Your parents tell you that if you can save all but $1000, they will provide that amount. You think that you can get a job and save $30 a week. How many weeks will it take for you to save the necessary amount?

2. The area of rectangle *ABCD* is 5000 square units, and the area of rectangle *AEFD* is 1000 square units. What is the length of $\overline{FC}$?

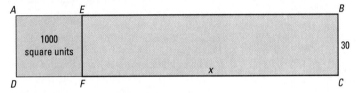

In this chapter, you will learn that you can use variations on techniques that you learned in Chapter 3 to solve the equation $5000 - 30x = 1000$. You will also learn to make and use graphs, such as the one at the right, to solve equations.

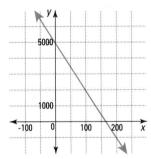

The photo collage makes real-world connections to the content of the chapter: subtraction in algebra.

Fabric: If a customer needs two pieces of material cut from the same fabric bolt, the clerk can either cut each piece separately or cut one large piece which represents the sum of the two pieces. This situation is an example of the Opposite of a Sum Property.

Antarctica: The Algebraic Definition of Subtraction—subtracting a number is the same as adding its opposite—can be used to determine the temperature in Antarctica after a temperature drop.

Bicyclist: A smart shopper compares prices on items such as bicycles and uses both the Comparison and Take-Away Models for Subtraction to determine how much money can be saved.

River: Sometimes the changes in the water level of a river can be described using either a constant-increase or a constant-decrease pattern. For instance, a flooded river 20 inches above its normal level and dropping 2 inches per hour can be expressed as a linear equation and graphed.

African Elephants: Elephants are just one of the many animals that can be photographed by tourists who go on camera safaris in Kenya.

Chapter 4 Projects

At this time you might want to have students look over the projects on pages 274–275.

Lesson 4-4 introduces spreadsheets. It should be done, if possible, with computers. However, if computers are not available, you can still use the lesson, having students record data in the blank spreadsheet on **Teaching Aid 37.** If computers are available, but you have not yet used them in your classroom, you may want to read *General Teaching Suggestions: Technology* in the *Professional Sourcebook* which begins on page T20 of this Teacher's Edition.

Objectives

A Simplify expressions involving subtraction.
E Apply the Algebraic Definition of Subtraction.

Resources

From the *Teacher's Resource File*
■ Lesson Master 4-1A or 4-1B
■ Answer Master 4-1
■ Teaching Aids
  26 Graph Paper
  33 Warm-up

Additional Resources
■ Visuals for Teaching Aids 26, 33

Teaching Lesson **4-1**

Warm-up

Diagnostic Simplify.
1. $r - 2s + 5r + -2s$ $6r - 4s$
2. $\frac{1}{2}m + \frac{3}{4}n - \frac{2}{3}m - 2\frac{3}{4}n$ $-\frac{1}{6}m - 2n$
3. $.3p - q - p - 3q$ $-.7p - 4q$
Evaluate both the original expression and your simplified answer to Questions 1, 2, and 3 when
4. $r = 2$ and $s = 3$. 0
5. $m = 12$ and $n = 4$. -10
6. $p = 5$ and $q = 2$. -11.5

You might ask students if they changed any of their answers to Questions 1–3 based upon their substitutions for Questions 4–6.

Subtraction of Real Numbers

Sub-zero subtraction. *Plants like the mosses and lichen pictured can survive in the frigid climate of Antarctica. Subtraction of negative numbers is required to find Antarctica's daily temperature range.*

Defining Subtraction in Terms of Addition

Many situations can be thought of either as addition or as subtraction. Consider the following situation.

Example 1

The coldest temperatures recorded in the world have been in Antarctica. Suppose a temperature of -50°C is recorded there. If the temperature then falls 30°, what is the new temperature?

① **Solution 1**

Begin with -50. Subtract 30.
$$-50 - 30 = -80$$
The new temperature is -80°C.

Solution 2

Begin with -50. Add -30.
$$-50 + -30 = -80$$
The new temperature is -80°C.

Notice that, in this instance, subtracting a number is the same as adding its opposite. This pattern is true for all real numbers. It is known as the *Algebraic Definition of Subtraction*.

> **Algebraic Definition of Subtraction**
> For all real numbers a and b,
> $$a - b = a + -b.$$

216

Lesson 4-1 Overview

Broad Goals The goal of this lesson is to be able to apply the Algebraic Definition of Subtraction in a variety of situations.

Perspective The Algebraic Definition of Subtraction, $a - b = a + -b$, allows for any subtraction to be converted to addition. This definition is particularly helpful because students already know how to add positive and negative numbers. Also, the commutative and associative properties apply to addition

but not to subtraction. Converting to addition prevents errors in the order of operations when there are more than two numbers involved.

In first grade, students learn that subtraction means "take away." This meaning could be considered a definition of subtraction in terms of real-world situations; however, we prefer to call it a model, and it will be referred to as the Take-Away Model for

Subtraction in Lesson 4-2. The problem with this early model is that it does not apply well to negative numbers. The situation that is described in **Example 1** of Lesson 4-2 uses a variant of the Slide Model for Addition where, instead of adding a negative, we subtract. The Slide Model for Subtraction will be familiar to students who have studied *Transition Mathematics*. In this book, we do not formally mention that model.

Evaluating Expressions Using the Algebraic Definition of Subtraction

You should be able to subtract any two real numbers using this definition.

Example 2

Evaluate $x - y$ when $x = 7.31$ and $y = -5.62$.

Solution

Substitute the values for x and y.

$$x - y = 7.31 - -5.62$$

The opposite of -5.62 is 5.62, so by the definition of subtraction,

$$x - y = 7.31 + 5.62$$
$$= 12.93.$$

Check

Use a calculator.

7.31 [−] 5.62 [±] [=] or 7.31 [−] [(−)] 5.62 [ENTER]

You should see 12.93 displayed.

Caution: Subtraction is *not* associative. For example, in $3 - 9 - 1$ you will get one answer if you do $3 - 9$ first and another answer if you do $9 - 1$ first. You must follow the order of operations and subtract from left to right. (Do $3 - 9$ first.) However, since *addition* is associative, you can gain flexibility by changing the subtractions to adding the opposites.

$$3 - 9 - 1 = 3 + -9 + -1.$$

In $3 + -9 + -1$, either addition can be done first, and the answer is -7.

Simplifying Expressions Using the Definition of Subtraction

You should also be able to use the definition of subtraction and other properties of real numbers to simplify expressions.

---

❷ Example 3

Simplify $-10 - (-y)$.

Solution

$-10 - (-y) = -10 + y$	Algebraic Definition of Subtraction
$= y + -10$	Commutative Property of Addition
$= y - 10$	Algebraic Definition of Subtraction

Check

The original and final values of the expression should be the same for any value of y. We let $y = 25$. Then $-10 - (-y) = -10 - (-25) = -10 + 25 = 15$. Also, $y - 10 = 25 - 10 = 15$. It checks.

Lesson 4-1 *Subtraction of Real Numbers* **217**

Optional Activities

Materials: Daily stock quotations for a one-week period, graph paper or **Teaching Aid 26**

Cooperative Learning After students answer **Question 18,** you might have them **work in groups** for this activity. Tell each group to select two or more stocks and keep track of the changes in the values of the stocks during a one-week period. Then

have them find the net change for the week. Students might also graph the daily changes.

Notes on Reading

❶ Emphasize that two approaches for subtracting positive and negative numbers are shown. Solution 1 involves thinking of a use of subtraction: −50 − 30 is viewed as the result when a temperature of −50° goes down 30°. No formal definition is needed for this approach. Solution 2 uses the Algebraic Definition of Subtraction, which reduces the problem to one of addition: −50 − 30 becomes −50 + −30.

❷ In **Example 3,** one could argue that −10 + y, which is found in the first step of the solution, is an acceptable answer. We usually write y − 10 based on a preference for positive numbers over negative numbers whenever possible and on an avoidance of using two signs (whether operation or opposite) between numbers in answers. Thus students should not leave the answer as y + −10. However, you might allow an answer of −10 + y.

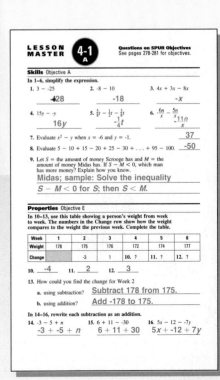

Additional Examples

1. Suppose that prospectors in Death Valley enter a mine on the valley floor (elevation –86 ft), and go down the shaft 30 feet.
   a. Show the answer using subtraction.
      $-86 - 30 = -116$; –116 feet
   b. Show the answer using addition.
      $-86 + -30 = -116$; –116 feet
2. Evaluate $x - y$ when $x = -16.8$ and $y = 21.4$. **–38.2**
3. Simplify $-a - (-b)$.
   $b - a$ or $-a + b$
4. Simplify $4j - 7j + 5x + j$.
   $5x - 2j$ or $-2j + 5x$
5. A hospital patient's temperature is 101.2° at 8 P.M. Over the next two days it undergoes the following changes.

   Day 1 8 A.M. up .3°
          8 P.M. down 1.1°
   Day 2 8 A.M. down .4°
          8 P.M. up .8°

   What is the patient's temperature at 8 P.M. of Day 2? **100.8°**

2a) $-2 + -7$
 b) -9

3a) $28 + 63$
 b) 91

4a) $\frac{3}{5} + \frac{7}{10}$
 b) $1\frac{3}{10}$

5a) $-3.5 + -0.9$
 b) -4.4

7a) Sample: $73\ \boxed{\pm}\ \boxed{-}$
    $91\ \boxed{\pm}\ \boxed{=}$
 b) Sample: $73\ \boxed{\pm}\ \boxed{+}$
    $91\ \boxed{=}$

The answer $-10 + y$ is also correct in Example 3, but the form $y - 10$ uses fewer symbols. So, many people think $y - 10$ is easier to read and check than is $-10 + y$.

③ Example 4

Simplify $5x + 3y - 2 - x$.

Solution

First, think of x as $1x$.

$5x + 3y - 2 - 1x = 5x + 3y - 2 + -1x$	Algebraic Definition of Subtraction
$= 5x + -1x + 3y - 2$	Commutative and Associative Properties of Addition
$= 4x + 3y - 2$	Combining Like Terms form of Distributive Property

QUESTIONS

Covering the Reading

1. State the Algebraic Definition of Subtraction.
   For all real numbers a and b, $a - b = a + -b$.
   In 2–5, **a.** apply the Algebraic Definition of Subtraction to rewrite the subtraction as an addition; **b.** evaluate the expression. **See left.**

2. $-2 - 7$ 3. $28 - -63$ 4. $\frac{3}{5} - -\frac{7}{10}$ 5. $-3.5 - 0.9$

6. The temperature is 12°F. It falls 15°. a) $12 + -15 = -3°F$
   a. Write an addition expression and find the new temperature.
   b. Write a subtraction expression and find the new temperature.
      $12 - 15 = -3°F$
7. Write the key sequence to do $-73 - -91$ on your calculator. **See left.**
   a. Use the $\boxed{-}$ key.   b. Use the $\boxed{+}$ key.

8. a. *True or false.* $(3 - 9) - 1 = 3 - (9 - 1)$ **False**
   b. What property is or is not verified in part **a?**
      Associative Property of Subtraction is not verified.
   In 9 and 10, calculate.

9. $20 - 4 - 3$ **13**   10. $-7 - 30 - 20$ **–57**

In 11–14, simplify.

11. $x - (-d)$ $x + d$ 12. $-y - (-5)$ $5 - y$

13. $10p - 2q + 4 + 8q$ 14. $-2a - 3a + 4b - b$
    $10p + 6q + 4$ $-5a + 3b$ or $3b - 5a$

Applying the Mathematics

In 15–17, evaluate the expression using the given value(s).

15. $3 - x^2$, when $x = 5$ **–22**   16. $-x - y$, when $x = -12$ and $y = 2$ **10**

17. $a - y - b$, when $a = -1$, $b = 2$, and $y = -3$ **0**

218

Adapting to Individual Needs

Extra Help
In **Example 4,** some students might have trouble understanding that $5x - x$ simplifies to $4x$; they may want to write 5. There are several ways you can help these students.
1. Use a number line to show combining terms.

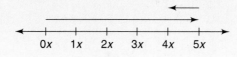

2. Use units for x, such as 5 inches – 1 inch = 4 inches.
3. Use order of operations—explain that the multiplication in $5x$ is done before the subtraction.
4. Substitute a number for x in the original and final expressions.

18. During a six-week period, the value of a stock in dollars per share changed as follows.

Week 1	Week 2	Week 3	Week 4	Week 5	Week 6
down $4\frac{7}{8}$	up $1\frac{3}{4}$	down $1\frac{3}{4}$	up $1\frac{1}{4}$	up $2\frac{1}{8}$	down $\frac{5}{8}$

Find the net change of the stock over the six weeks. $-2\frac{1}{8}$

19. Mr. Whittaker's doctor advised him to exercise more. The changes in Mr. Whittaker's weight were:

First Week	Second Week	Third Week	Fourth Week
lost 4 lb	lost 3 lb	lost 3 lb	gained 5 lb

a) $-4 + -3 + -3 + 5$ b) $-4 - 3 - 3 + 5$
  a. Write an expression for the net change using addition.
  b. Write an expression for the net change using subtraction.
  c. What was the net change for the four weeks? -5 lb

20. Let t be Toni's age. Let f be Fred's age. Suppose $t - f = 35$.
  a. Find a value for t and a value for f such that $t - f = 35$.
  b. Who is older, Toni or Fred? Toni
  c. Find the value of $f - t$. -35
    a) Sample: Let $t = 40$ and $f = 5$
21. Find all possible values for x using the clues. $x = 1$
  Choices for x: $-7, -4, -3, -2, 1, 3, 4, 7$

  Clue 1: $x > 0 - 2$
  Clue 2: $x < 4 - -1$
  Clue 3: $x \neq 2 - -1$
  Clue 4: $-x \neq -4$

22. In parts **a–d** evaluate $p - q$ and $q - p$ when:
  a. $p = 5$ and $q = -1$; 6, -6
  b. $p = 1$ and $q = 3$; -2, 2
  c. $p = -2$ and $q = 0$; -2, 2
  d. $p = -3$ and $q = -6$. 3, -3
  e. Based upon parts **a** to **d**, does subtraction seem to be commutative? Why or why not? No, switching p and q when $p \neq q$ gives different answers.
  f. Describe the relationship between $p - q$ and $q - p$.
    $p - q$ is the opposite of $q - p$.

Review

23. Simplify $n + .2(n + 15)$. *(Lessons 3-6, 3-7)* $1.2n + 3$

In 24 and 25, solve. *(Lessons 3-2, 3-5)*

24. $-3 = x + (-7)$ $x = 4$ **25.** $2.7 + 7y = 3.4$ $y = 0.1$

26. How many four-digit numerals do not contain zeros and have no repeated digits? *(Lesson 2-9)* 3024

27. Find 30% of 74.95. *(Previous course)* 22.485

Lesson 4-1 *Subtraction of Real Numbers* **219**

Take stock in this.
Shown is the trading floor of the New York Stock Exchange. Stockbrokers act as agents for the public in buying and selling shares of stock of various companies.

Notes on Questions
Question 6 This question parallels **Example 1.** Carefully review this question to insure that students have a concrete basis for the Algebraic Definition of Subtraction.

Question 7a Remind students that $\boxed{-}$ represents the subtraction key, not the opposite key.

Question 18 Make sure students understand that the answer represents a change in the value of one share. It is not a loss or a profit until the stock is sold and the selling price is compared to the purchase price.

Question 19 Health Connection
Point out that the healthy way to lose weight not only requires exercise, but also eating nutritious, low fat meals and snacks. Whenever a person wants to lose large amounts of weight, both diet and exercise should be under the supervision of a doctor.

Question 21 This question reinforces the general problem-solving strategy of eliminating possibilities. Point out that the mathematical phrase *domain of x* could have been used in place of *choices for x.*

Question 22 These questions establish a handy pattern: $(a - b) = -(b - a)$. This property is discussed in Lesson 4.5.

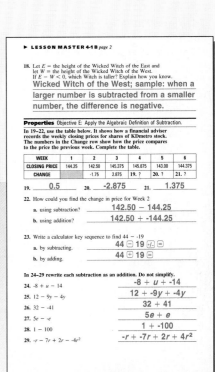

Adapting to Individual Needs
Challenge
Have students tell how each false equation can be turned into a true equation by moving one toothpick.

1. $||+\square=|$

2. $|-|||=||$

[1. Sample answers: Put one toothpick from 11 under + to get $1 \pm 0 = 1$, or put the vertical toothpick from + next to the 1 to get $11 - 0 = 11$ or preceeding 0 to get $11 -10 = 1$. **2.** Put one toothpick from = under − to get $1 = 3 - 2$.]

Question 29 Ask students which of the four Roman numeral examples involve the subtraction of values. [All but the first]

History Connection Benjamin Banneker was also a well known surveyor. In 1791, Thomas Jefferson recommended that he assist with the job of laying out the boundaries for the District of Columbia. Some students might be interested in learning more about Benjamin Banneker.

Follow-up 4-1
for Lesson

Practice

For more questions on SPUR Objectives, use **Lesson Master 4-1A** (shown on page 217) or **Lesson Master 4-1B** (shown on pages 218–219).

Assessment

Written Communication Ask students to write a paragraph explaining how they would convince someone who has not taken algebra that the Algebraic Definition of Subtraction is true. [Students' explanations demonstrate understanding of the relationship between addition and subtraction.]

Extension

To extend **Question 29,** first have students apply the definition of subtraction to rewrite each expression below. Then have them simplify the expressions, writing the answers as Roman numerals.
1. XXXIV – –LXXXIII – XLVII
[XXXIV + LXXXIII + –XLVII =
LXX (34 + 83 + –47 = 70)]
2. MDXLVI – DLXXXVII
[MDXLVI + –DLXXXVII = CMLIX
(1546 + –587 = 959)]
3. CCCLXVII – CDXXXII – MCCV
[CCCLXVII + –CDXXXII +
–MCCV = –MCCLXX
(367 + –432 + –1205 = –1270)]

Project Update Project 1, *Patterns in Fraction Products,* on page 274, relates to the content of this lesson.

28. Tell which sentence best describes each graph. *(Lesson 3-3)*
   a. The number of people in a restaurant from 6 A.M. to 6 P.M.
   b. The number of people in a school from 6 A.M. to 6 P.M.
   c. The number of people in a hospital from 6 A.M. to 6 P.M.

Number of **b**
People

6 A.M.   12 noon   6 P.M.   time

Number of **a**
People

6 A.M.   12 noon   6 P.M.   time

Number of **c**
People

6 A.M.   12 noon   6 P.M.   time

Exploration

29. Roman numerals were the most common way of writing numbers in Western Europe from about 100 B.C. to 1700 A.D. Even in this century, they have often been used to give dates on buildings and to name the hours on timepieces. Here are the values of the individual letters in a Roman numeral.

I	V	X	L	C	D	M
1	5	10	50	100	500	1000

When a letter appears to the left of a letter with a higher value, the value of the first letter is subtracted. So IV = 5 − 1 = 4, and CM = 1000 − 100 = 900. Match each year with its corresponding Roman numeral.

   1731 (i)
   a. the year Benjamin Banneker, one of the first African-American mathematicians, was born   (i) MDCCXXXI
   b. the year Christopher Columbus first sailed for the New World 1492 (ii)   (ii) MCDXCII
      (iii) MCMXXVIII
   c. the year Jeannette Rankin, the first woman to serve in the U.S. Congress, was elected to the House of Representatives 1917 (iv)   (iv) MCMXVII
   d. the year the character "Mickey Mouse" first appeared in a cartoon 1928 (iii)

A man of many talents.
Benjamin Banneker was an astronomer, farmer, and mathematician.

Mickey Mouse's debut.
Mickey Mouse debuted in Walt Disney's cartoon, Steamboat Willie. *It was the first cartoon to use synchronized sound. Disney himself provided the high-pitched voice for Mickey in this classic cartoon.*

© The Walt Disney Company

220

Adapting to Individual Needs

English Language Development
Spend some time listening to non-English-speaking students when they read and interpret expressions like 6 – (–2) and –6 – 2. Have them read the expressions aloud to clear up any misconceptions they might have about the words *minus* and *negative.*

Setting Up Lesson 4-2

Materials Students will need sale advertisements from newspapers for the *Optional Activities* in Lesson 4-2.

Strong storms. *Beaches along a coastline are often eroded by hurricanes. Subtraction can be used to find the amount of beach area left after the storm passes.*

The Take-Away Model for Subtraction

An island had an area of 27.8 square miles. During a hurricane, 1.6 square miles of beach were washed away. The area of the island left was $27.8 - 1.6$, or 26.2, square miles. This situation illustrates an important model for subtraction.

> **Take-Away Model for Subtraction**
> If a quantity y is taken away from an original quantity x, the quantity left is $x - y$.

The take-away model leads to algebraic expressions involving subtraction.

Example 1

Suppose a giant submarine sandwich has length L inches. You eat 6 inches of it. How much is left?

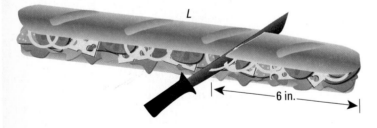

L

|← 6 in. →|

Solution
Take 6 inches away from L inches. There are $L - 6$ inches left.

Lesson 4-2 *Models for Subtraction* **221**

Lesson 4-2

Objectives

H Use the Take-Away and Comparison Models for Subtraction to write expressions and equations involving subtraction.

Resources

From the *Teacher's Resource File*
- Lesson Master 4-2A or 4-2B
- Answer Master 4-2
- Teaching Aid 33: Warm-up
- Technology Sourcebook Calculator Master 2

Additional Resources
- Visual for Teaching Aid 33

Teaching
Lesson 4-2

Warm-up

Use the figure below to answer the questions. *ABCD* and *ARST* are both squares.

1. What information is necessary to determine the area of the shaded region? **The lengths of the sides of the squares**
2. What is the area of the shaded region in terms of x and y? $y^2 - x^2$ **square units**
3. Find the area of the shaded region if $x = 2.7$ cm and $y = 7$ cm. **41.71 cm²**

Lesson 4-2 Overview

Broad Goals The two major connections between subtraction and the real world—take away and comparison—are presented in algebraic and geometric settings.

Perspective The two models for subtraction discussed in this lesson have been familiar to students since first or second grade. Consequently, the key ideas are not with the arithmetic of positive numbers, but rather with extending what students know

about applying subtraction to negative numbers, to geometric settings, to discounts, and to utilizing the language of algebra.

The Take-Away Model for Subtraction can be viewed as the counterpart to the Putting-Together Model for Addition. The Take-Away Model is the one most often encountered in school texts, and the situations are usually those in which the numbers are counts of discrete objects.

The comparison model is appropriate for negative numbers. For instance, suppose we want to compare –15 and –19. On a number line, these numbers are 4 units apart. The answer to –15 – –19 is 4, because the smaller number is being subtracted from the larger one. Subtracting in the other direction, the answer to –19 – –15 is –4.

Notes on Reading

This lesson consists mainly of examples. You might begin by asking students to identify the examples that are instances of the Take-Away Model [**Examples 1–3**] and to tell which examples are instances of the Comparison Model [**Examples 5 and 6**].

❶ Consumer Connection In **Examples 3 and 4,** the Subtracting Like Terms and Adding Like Terms forms of the Distributive Property are used. Each example demonstrates a very important quality of discounts and markups (or taxes); the final result can be found by multiplying the original price by a single number so no subtraction or addition is needed. Specifically, in **Example 3,** the sale price, after a 15% discount, can be found by multiplying the original price by .85. The sale price is 85% of the original price. In **Example 4,** the total cost can be found by multiplying the purchase price by 1.065. The total cost is 106.5% of the purchase price.

❷ Students might want to write this answer as $x^2 - y^2$ because x^2 is the area of the higher floor. Technically, this answer is not wrong. However, it gives you a chance to emphasize that, unless stated otherwise, the smaller number should be subtracted from the larger number.

In general, unless directed to do otherwise, we compare in the direction which gives a positive answer for the result. That is, we subtract the smaller number from the larger one, and we use the context to decide whether the answer is positive or negative. The exception is when a quantity changes over a period of time. In this case, we subtract the earlier amount from the later one. The sign of the result shows whether the quantity increased or decreased over that period.

Discounts are a very important use of the take-away model.

Example 2

Josie bought a new bicycle. The *list price* was $225. The store gave a 30% discount. What was the *sale price?*

Solution 1

Take away the discount from the list price.

$$\text{Sale price} = \text{list price} - \text{discount}$$
$$= 225 - (30\% \text{ of } 225)$$
$$= 225 - .30(225)$$
$$= 225 - 67.50$$
$$= 157.50$$

The sale price was $157.50.

Solution 2

Compute the percent left after the discount. If an item is on sale for 30% off, you pay 100% − 30%, or 70%, of the original price.

$$70\% \text{ of } 225 = .70(225) = 157.50$$

The sale price was $157.50.

If an item is discounted x%, you pay $(100 - x)$% of the original price.

❶ Example 3

A microwave oven is on sale for 15% off the regular price. If the regular price is P, what is the sale price?

Solution

The discount is 15% of the regular price or $.15P$.

$$\text{sale price} = \text{regular price} - \text{discount}$$
$$= P - .15P$$
$$= 1P - .15P \quad \text{Multiplicative Identity Property of 1}$$
$$= .85P \quad \text{Subtract like terms.}$$

The sale price is $.85P$ or $.85$ of the regular price.

If the original price of an item is increased by a given percent, a *markup* results. Taxes and profits often involve markups.

Example 4

The Alvarez family is buying a new van. The purchase price is D dollars. They must also pay a 6.5% sales tax. What is the total cost of the van?

Solution

The sales tax is 6.5% of D, or $.065D$.

$$\text{total cost} = \text{purchase price} + \text{sales tax}$$
$$= D + .065D$$
$$= 1D + .065D$$
$$= 1.065D$$

The total cost is $1.065D$ dollars.

Optional Activities

Activity 1
Materials: Newspaper advertisements

After discussing **Example 2,** have students use newspapers to find several examples of discounts. For each example, have them give the original price, the sale price, and the percent of discount.

Activity 2
You might want to ask students to generalize **Question 29** by asking them the following question: Suppose a person was born within the past thousand years in year B and died in year D. How old was that person at the time of death? [Either $D - B$ or $D - B - 1$.] Give examples of each possibility. [Sample: Consider the years 1993 and 1923: $1993 - 1923 = 70$ and $1993 - 1923 - 1 = 69$. A person born in December, 1923,

would be a little over 69 years old in the beginning of 1993 and 70 years old at the end of 1993.

Activity 3 Technology Connection
In *Technology Sourcebook, Calculator Master 2,* students explore patterns involving subtraction.

The ideas illustrated in Examples 2 to 4 are summarized below.

> If an item is discounted x%, you pay $(100 - x)$% of the original or listed price. If an item is marked up or taxed x%, you pay $(100 + x)$% of the original or listed price.

The Comparison Model for Subtraction

In Example 2, Josie paid $157.50 for the bicycle. Another store advertised the same item for $170. To find out how much money Josie saved, you subtract.

$$\$170 - \$157.50 = \$12.50$$

This is an instance of a second model for subtraction.

> **Comparison Model for Subtraction**
> The quantity $x - y$ tells how much the quantity x differs from the quantity y.

❷ Example 5

The Transamerica Building in San Francisco is shaped like a pyramid. Each floor is approximately square. Let x be the side of one floor and let y be the side of a lower floor. How much greater is the area of the lower floor than the area of the upper floor?

Area x^2

Area y^2

Solution

The two floors have areas x^2 and y^2. Since y^2 is the greater area, the difference in area is $y^2 - x^2$.

What Is the Range of a Set of Numbers?

An important application of the comparison model is the calculation of the *range* of a set of numbers. The **range** of a set is the difference obtained when the set's **minimum** (least) value is subtracted from its **maximum** (greatest) value.

❸ Example 6

The greatest recorded difference in temperature during a single day occurred in Browning, Montana, in January of 1916. During one 24-hour period, the low temperature was -56°F and the high temperature was 44°F. What was the range of the temperatures?

Solution

Compare the numbers by subtracting.

$$\text{range} = \text{maximum} - \text{minimum}$$
$$= 44 - (-56)$$
$$= 44 + 56 = 100$$

The range of the temperatures was 100°F.

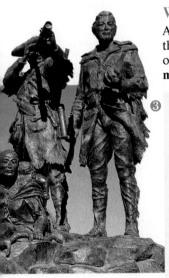

A statue of Lewis, Clark, and Sacagawea stands at Ft. Benton, Montana. Sacagawea, a Shoshone woman, acted as an interpreter for the explorers Lewis and Clark.

Adapting to Individual Needs

Extra Help

A number line illustration might help students understand **Example 6.** Draw the number line shown at the right on the board or overhead. Point out that the distance from -56 to zero is 56 units or, in this case, 56 degrees. Then the distance from zero to 44 is 44 units, or 44 degrees. So, it is easy to see that the minimum temperature of -56° differs from the maximum temperature of 44° by 100 degrees.

-60 | -40 -20 0 20 40 | 60

-56   44

A person can always compare in two ways and arrive at the opposites $a - b$ or $b - a$. This is analogous to forming ratios in division, either $\frac{a}{b}$ or $\frac{b}{a}$, to compare numbers. In the subtraction case, the differences are opposites. In the divisions, the ratios are reciprocals. These analogies between subtraction and division are akin to the analogies between addition and multiplication. Pointing this out helps students to realize that mathematics is not simply a collection of facts; mathematics also has a wonderful structure.

With powers, the conversion from subtracting to adding the opposite can be troublesome. Note that $x^2 - y^2$ equals $x^2 + -y^2$ but that $x^2 + -y^2$ is not the same as $x^2 + (-y)^2$. In the order of operations, taking the opposite is treated like multiplication; it occurs after powering but before adding or subtracting. In $x^2 + (-y)^2$, the parentheses cause the opposite to occur before the powering. You might use numerical values to clarify this for students:

$$5^2 - 3^2 = 25 - 9 = 16$$
$$5^2 + -3^2 = 25 + -9 = 16$$
$$5^2 + (-3)^2 \quad 25 + 9 = 34$$

❸ *Change*, such as the change in temperature, is a special application of comparison; it is very important in mathematics. In Chapter 7, when we speak of rate of change, we will do subtractions to find the change.

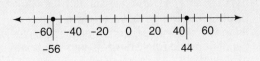

223

Additional Examples

1. Sal's Sandwich Shop began the day with P pounds of pastrami. After two people each bought $\frac{1}{2}$ pound and one person bought $2\frac{1}{2}$ pounds, how much pastrami was left?
$P - 3\frac{1}{2}$ pounds

2. A skirt that normally costs $29.95 is on sale at 20% off. What is the sale price? **$23.96**

3. A pair of slacks that normally costs N dollars is on sale for 20% off. What is the sale price? **.80N, or .80 of the regular price**

4. A blouse costs M dollars plus 4% sales tax. What is the total cost of the blouse?
1.04M dollars

5. A cube with edge e is inside a cube with edge f. What is the volume of the space between the two cubes? **$f^3 - e^3$**

6. Yesterday, the high temperature was 22°F, and the low temperature was –12°F. What was the range of temperatures?
34°F

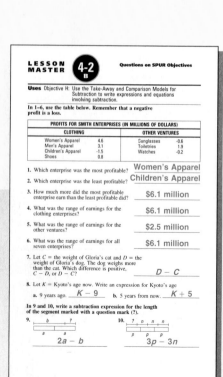
224

ARCHIE'S APPLIANCES
ALWAYS 20% OFF

Refrigerator (list) $800
Discount – $160
Your Price $640

A modern pyramid.
The Transamerica Building is one of San Francisco's landmarks. Built in 1972, this skyscraper towers 853 feet (260 m).

Covering the Reading

1. A carpenter has a board that is x feet long. He cuts a 3-foot piece from it. Write an expression for the length of the remaining piece. **($x - 3$) feet**

2. Refer to the sales tag at the left.
   a. What is the amount of the discount? **$160**
   b. What is the percent of discount? **20%**
   c. What is the sale price? **$640**

3. Suppose a coat originally cost C dollars, but it is on sale now for 25% off.
   a. What is the amount (in dollars) of the discount? **.25 C dollars**
   b. What is the sale price of the coat? **.75 C dollars**

4. Suppose a pair of jeans is on sale for 40% off. If the regular price of the jeans is J dollars, what is the sale price of the jeans? **.60 J dollars**

5. The price of an item is P dollars, and there is a 4% sales tax.
   a. Express the tax paid in terms of P. **.04 P dollars**
   b. What is the total amount paid for the item? **1.04 P dollars**
   c. If P = $65, what is the total amount paid? **$67.60**

6. Refer to Example 5. Suppose one side of a floor in the Transamerica Building has length 40 meters. Let b meters be the length of a side of a higher floor. Write an expression for the positive difference in the areas of the two floors. **$1600 - b^2$**

7. An unusual temperature change was recorded in Spearfish, South Dakota, on January 22, 1943. Over a period of just two minutes, the temperature rose from -4°F to 45°F. By how much did the temperature change during this time? **49°**

8. As of the summer of 1993, the highest temperature ever recorded in the United States occurred on July 10, 1913, at Greenland Ranch, California, where the temperature reached 134°F. The lowest temperature ever recorded occurred on January 23, 1971, in Prospect Creek, Alaska, where the temperature fell to -80°F. What is the range of the temperatures in the U.S.? **214°F**

Applying the Mathematics

9. What is the difference in area between the two rectangles at the left? **$4x$**

10. A company bought a piece of property which has an area of 14,000 square feet. On it the company built a store with area S square feet and a parking lot with area 2580 square feet. Write an expression for the area left for the lawn. **($14{,}000 - S - 2580$) ft^2**

224

Adapting to Individual Needs

English Language Development
A language conversion chart might help students translate English words into algebraic expressions.

+	−	×	=
plus	minus	times	equal
markup	discount	of	is
gain	loss		
deposit	withdraw		

In 11 and 12, Bernie's age is B, John's age is $B - 3$, and Robin's age is $B - 7$.

11. **a.** Who is older, Robin or Bernie? **b.** How much older? **7 years**
    Bernie
12. **a.** Who is older, John or Robin? **b.** How much older? **4 years**
    John
13. Sam's Super Saver Store is offering 20% off on all merchandise sold this week. An item with a regular price R is purchased.
    a. Give the sale price of the item in terms of R. **.80 R**
    b. Freda receives an additional 10% employee discount off the customer price. Express the cost of this item to Freda in terms of R.
    c. If the state sales tax is 3%, what is the total cost of the item to Freda?
    b) $.80 R - .10(.80 R) = .72 R$; c) $.72R + .03(.72 R) = .7416 R$
14. The thermometers below show a hospital patient's temperature at three times on the same day.
    a. What was the change from 3 P.M. to 6 P.M.? **0.5°**
    b. What was the change from 3 P.M. to 9 P.M.? **-1.5°**

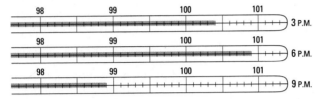

15. **a.** In New York City, the sun's rays make a $72\frac{1}{2}°$ angle with the ground at noon on the first day of summer (about June 21). On the first day of winter (about December 21), the angle is $25\frac{1}{2}°$. By how much do the angles differ? **47°**
    b. If in another city the angles the sun's rays make with the ground are a and b, what are the possible values of the difference in angle measure? $a - b$ or $b - a$

16. Some students took a chapter pretest and posttest.
    Suppose $Change = Posttest - Pretest$. **a.** Complete the table.
    b. Which student's test scores showed most imporvement? **L. Chui**

Student	Pretest	Posttest	Change
Chui, L.	57	65	8
Fields, S.	43	41	? -2
Ivan, J.	63	? 70	7
Washington, C.	? 54	51	-3

A glimpse of NYC. *New York City is often called America's melting pot. The five largest ethnic groups in the city are African-American, Irish, Italian, Jewish, and Puerto Rican. These groups constitute 80% of the population.*

Review

In 17–20, simplify. *(Lesson 4-1)*

17. $-3 - (-3)$ **0**

18. $-8.7 - 16.03$ **-24.73**

19. $-p - (-q)$ $-p + q$

20. $-7ab + 2a - 5b - 6ab - 4a + b$
    $-13ab - 2a - 4b$

Lesson 4-2 *Models for Subtraction* **225**

Notes on Questions

Question 9 This diagram gives a pictorial representation of the Take-Away Model for Subtraction.

Questions 11–12 Error Alert
Some students may have difficulty comparing terms with variables. Encourage these students to use specific values for B. For instance, if Bernie is 16 years old, how old are John and Robin? [13 and 9]

Questions 14 and 16 Students should subtract the first value from the second value. The direction of the change (positive or negative) is important.

▶ **LESSON MASTER 4-2 B** *page 2*

11. At the right are the attendance figures for Crestville's Pioneer Festival.

1991	3,043
1992	2,945
1993	2,760
1994	3,178

a. What was the change from 1992 to 1993?
   -185; decrease of 185 people
b. What was the change from 1993 to 1994?
   418; increase of 418 people

12. Each spring, Lurvelle's discounts all winter merchandise 40%.
a. If a winter coat was originally priced at $256, what is the amount of discount? **$102.40**
b. What is the sale price of the coat in Part a? **$153.60**
c. If a winter jacket was originally priced at J dollars, what is the sale price of the jacket? **J − .4J, or .6J**

13. Let M = Meg's age. Sam's age is M − 8, and Lill's age is M + 2.
a. Arrange the three ages in order from least to greatest.
   M − 8, M, M + 2; Sam, Meg, Lill
b. How much older is the oldest person than the youngest person? Explain how you determined the answer.
   10 years; subtracted; (M + 2) − (M − 8) = 10

14. Point M is x units to the right of -16. N is 8 units to the left of 10.
a. Write an expression for the coordinate of M. **-16 + x**
b. Find the coordinate of N. **10 − 8 = 2**

15. At the right are the weights of four of Dr. Norton's weight-loss patients.
a. Complete the table.
b. Which patient lost the most weight? **Morgan, S.**

Patient	Jan.	Oct.	Change
Morgan, S.	192	166	-26
Rojas, F.	214	195	-19
Ozu, D.	166	155	-11
Lake, M.	183	189	6

Adapting to Individual Needs

Challenge
Show students the following directions for a number puzzle, and have them try it for numbers they select. [A sample is given.]
1. Think of a whole number between 0 and 10. **[8]**
2. Multiply it by 2. **[16]**
3. Add 3. **[19]**
4. Multiply the answer by 5. **[95]**
5. Add another whole number that is between 0 and 10. **[95 + 3 = 98]**

6. Subtract 15. **[83]**
Ask students how the result shows the two numbers they selected. [The digit in the tens place is the first number selected, and the digit in the units place is the second number selected.]

Now have students use algebraic expressions to explain how the puzzle works.
[a; $2a$; $2a + 3$; $(2a + 3)5$; $(2a + 3)5 + b$; $(2a + 3)5 + b - 15 = 10a + b$]

Notes on Questions

Question 21 Remind students to think of moving to the right on a horizontal number line (or up on a vertical number line) as adding a positive number, and to think of moving to the left (or down) either as adding a negative number or as subtracting a positive number.

Questions 22–25 These questions lead into the next lesson. You might, ask students to give ideas on how they might solve a related sentence with subtraction, such as $7t - 6 > 41$, $3x - 8 = 5$, or $16 - x > 0$.

Follow-up Lesson 4-2

Practice

For more questions on SPUR Objectives, use **Lesson Master 4-2A** (shown on page 223) or **Lesson Master 4-2B** (shown on pages 224–225).

Assessment

Oral Communication Ask students to explain how the Comparison Model for Subtraction is different from the Take-Away Model for Subtraction. [Students distinguish between comparing two quantities and finding the amount of a remaining quantity.]

Extension

As an extension of **Question 27,** ask students to show that the difference in the areas in **Example 5,** $y^2 - x^2$, could be written as $(y + x)(y - x)$. [Move the striped section shown below. Then the difference in the areas is represented by a rectangle $y + x$ units long and $y - x$ units wide.]

Shaded area: $y^2 - x^2$

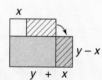

Shaded area: $(y + x)(y - x)$

---

21. E is 4 units to the left of A. F is n units to the right of A. *(Lesson 4-1)*
    a. What is the coordinate of E? **-10**
    b. Write an expression for the coordinate of F. **-6 + n (n > 0)**
    c. Why do you think point F was not included on the number line below?
    Sample: Point F could be located anywhere to the right of A.

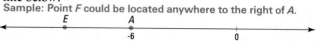

In 22–25, solve. *(Lessons 3-5, 3-10)*

22. $7t + 6 > 41$ **t > 5**

23. $3x + 8 = 5$ **x = -1**

24. $16 + x = 0$ **x = -16**

25. $-28.3 > -x + 17.5$ **x > 45.8**

26. The image of (x, y) is $(7, -1)$. It results from a slide four units to the right and two units down. Find x and y. *(Lesson 3-4)* **x = 3, y = 1**

27. Three instances of a pattern are given below.
$$9^2 - 4^2 = (9 + 4)(9 - 4)$$
$$31^2 - 29^2 = (31 + 29)(31 - 29)$$
$$3.5^2 - 2.5^2 = (3.5 + 2.5)(3.5 - 2.5)$$
    a. Do a mental check or use a calculator to verify that the sentences are true. **81 − 16 = 13 · 5; 961 − 841 = 60 · 2; 12.25 − 6.25 = 6 · 1**
    b. Describe the general pattern using two variables. $a^2 - b^2 = (a + b)(a - b)$
    c. Write another instance of this pattern. Is your instance true?
    (Lesson 1-7) Sample: $3^2 - 2^2 = (3 + 2)(3 - 2)$; **True**

28. Find the area of each triangle. *(Lesson 1-5)*

a.

b.

c.

Exploration

29. The number of years between two historical events can be calculated by subtracting the years in which the events occurred. You will be within a year of the number of years between them.
    a. Nicholas and Nicole were born in two consecutive years. What is the least and greatest number of days between their birthdays?
    b. Maria Gaetana Agnesi, an Italian mathematician after whom a special mathematical curve is named, was born in 1718 and died in 1799. How old was she when she died? **80 or 81**
    c. How many years apart are the Declaration of Independence and the end of the Civil War? **89 years**
    d. How many years are between the death of Archimedes in 212 B.C. and the death of the Roman emperor Nero in 68 A.D.? (Be careful! There was no year 0.) **279 years**
    29a) smallest number is 1 day; largest number is 1 day less than 2 years or 729 days

Important inkstand.
This silver inkstand was used to sign both the Declaration of Independence in 1776 and the U.S. Constitution in 1787. It is displayed in Independence Hall in Philadelphia, PA.

Setting Up Lesson 4-3

Materials Students will need almanacs for Activity 2 in *Optional Activities* in Lesson 4-3.

Questions 22–25 in this lesson can be used as a lead-in to Lesson 4-3.

LESSON 4-3

Solving Sentences Involving Subtraction

Venus Volcano. *Shown is Maat Mons, an active volcano on Venus, discovered in 1991 by the U.S. space probe* Magellan.

Solving $ax - b = c$

In Chapter 3, you solved sentences of the form $ax + b = c$ by adding the same number to both sides. Sentences of the form $ax - b = c$ are solved in much the same way.

For instance, scientists have found that the range of temperatures recorded on the planets of our solar system is about 695°C. The minimum temperature of -220°C was recorded on Pluto. The maximum was recorded on Venus. To find the maximum recorded temperature, you can use a subtraction equation.

Let T = the maximum temperature recorded. Substitute into the formula for range.

$$\text{range} = \text{maximum} - \text{minimum}$$
$$695 = T - (\text{-}220)$$
$$695 = T + 220$$

Notice that you can change the subtraction to addition. Now solve as you would an addition equation. Add -220 to each side.

$$695 + \text{-}220 = T + 220 + \text{-}220$$
$$475 = T$$

The maximum recorded temperature is about 475°C.

The subtraction equation above was changed to one involving addition by using the Algebraic Definition of Subtraction. You can do this with *any* sentence involving subtraction. Then you can apply anything you already know about solving sentences.

Objectives

B Solve and check linear equations involving subtraction.

C Solve and check linear inequalities involving subtraction.

H Use models for subtraction to write sentences involving subtraction.

I Solve problems using linear sentences involving subtraction.

Resources

From the *Teacher's Resource File*
■ Lesson Master 4-3A or 4-3B
■ Answer Master 4-3
■ Teaching Aid 34: Warm-up

Additional Resources
■ Visual for Teaching Aid 34

Teaching Lesson **4-3**

Warm-up

Find the difference between the record high and low temperatures for each of these states.

1. Alaska
High: 100°F (June 27, 1915)
Low: -80°F (Jan. 23, 1971) **180°**

2. Florida
High: 109°F (June 29, 1931)
Low: -2°F (Feb. 13, 1899) **111°**

3. Pennsylvania
High: 111°F (July 10, 1936)
Low: -42°F (Jan. 5, 1904) **153°**

4. Nevada
High: 122°F (June 26, 1990)
Low: -50°F (Jan. 8, 1937) **172°**

5. California
High: 134 °F (July 10, 1913)
Low: -45°F (Jan. 20, 1937) **179°**

Lesson 4-3 Overview

Broad Goals The goal of this lesson is for students to be able to solve sentences of the form $ax - b = c$, $ax - b < c$, $b - ax = c$, and $b - ax < c$. In all cases, the suggested strategy is to change the subtraction to adding the opposite, and then to use the ideas from Chapter 3 to solve the resulting sentence.

Perspective This lesson combines ideas from Chapter 3 and the first two lessons of this chapter. Students are expected to use the models for subtraction to find sentences to solve. Then they can solve these sentences using the procedures described.

Two general ideas are typically involved in the solving of linear sentences. The first idea is simplifying one side of the equation or inequality. To simplify, we may use the Distributive Property or any of the other properties of operations. The second idea involves doing something to both sides of the sentence in order to obtain a simpler equation or inequality. To do this, we use the Addition or Multiplication Properties of Equality or Inequality.

227

For an alternate approach to teaching this lesson, see *Optional Activities* below.

❶ Notice that our suggested solution of equations of the form $ax - b = c$ uses both the idea of simplifying one side of the equation and the idea of doing something to both sides of the equation; the result is a simpler equation. The first step, obtaining $ax + -b = c$, employs the Algebraic Definition of Subtraction and involves only one side of the equation. The second and third steps apply to both sides; first b is added to obtain $ax = b + c$, and then both sides are multiplied by $\frac{1}{a}$ to obtain the solution. Some students are able to combine the first and second steps into one step and add b to both sides from the start.

❷ One advantage of the three-step process is that the same three steps can be used in solving $b - ax = c$. First, change the subtraction to addition: $b + -ax = c$. Then add $-b$ to each side: $-ax = c + -b$. Lastly, multiply both sides by $-\frac{1}{a}$ to obtain the solution.

When solving $b - ax = c$, some students may use a different procedure. First they add ax to each side to get $b = c + ax$, then they add $-c$ to both sides to get $-c + b = ax$, and the last step is to multiply by $\frac{1}{a}$. We prefer to delay the adding of expressions with the variable to both sides until the next chapter, so we do not mention this alternate algorithm. Feel free to use this strategy if your students suggest it.

❶ **Example 1**

Solve $14x - 21 = -133$.

Solution

Change the subtraction to addition of the opposite.
$$14x + -21 = -133$$
This is now an equation of the same type you solved in the last chapter.
$$14x + -21 + 21 = -133 + 21 \quad \text{Add 21 to each side.}$$
$$14x = -112 \quad \text{Simplify.}$$
$$x = -8 \quad \text{Multiply both sides by } \tfrac{1}{14} \text{ and simplify.}$$

Check

Substitute -8 for x in the original equation. Does $14 \cdot -8 - 21 = -133$?
$14 \cdot -8 - 21 = -133$, so the solution is -8.

Solving Equations When the Unknown Is Subtracted

In Example 1, you probably noticed that changing subtraction to addition was not essential. However, in the next example you will see how this technique can be helpful.

Example 2

A metal bar was 1.2 cm too long. It was shortened and found to be 0.03 cm too short. How much was cut off?

❷ **Solution**

Let the amount cut off be c. "Too short" means -0.03. Use the Take-Away Model for Subtraction. The answer is the solution to
$$1.2 - c = -0.03.$$
$$1.2 + -c = -0.03 \quad \text{Definition of Subtraction}$$
$$-1.2 + 1.2 + -c = -1.2 + -0.03 \quad \text{Addition Property of Equality}$$
$$-c = -1.23$$
$$c = 1.23 \quad \text{Multiplication Property of Equality}$$
The amount cut off was 1.23 cm.

Check

If 1.23 cm is cut off from a bar 1.2 cm too long, will it be 0.03 cm too short? Yes, it will.

Solving Inequalities When the Unknown Is Subtracted

The questions from page 215 can be answered using the same idea as used in Example 2.

Example 3

You want to go to Kenya to see lions and elephants in their native habitats. The trip will cost $5000. Your parents say that if you save all but $1000, they will provide that amount. You think you can get a job and save $30 per week. How many weeks will it take to save the necessary amount? ▶

228

Solution

Let x = the number of weeks you must save until the balance is $1000 or less. Solve $5000 - 30x \leq 1000$.

Change the subtraction to addition of the opposite.
$$5000 + {-}30x \leq 1000$$

Now add -5000 to each side. This isolates the expression with the variable.
$$-5000 + 5000 + {-}30x \leq -5000 + 1000$$
$$-30x \leq -4000$$

Multiply both sides by $-\frac{1}{30}$ and simplify. This changes the sense of the inequality.

$$-\frac{1}{30} \cdot ({-}30x) \geq -\frac{1}{30} \cdot {-}4000$$
$$x \geq \frac{400}{3}$$
$$x \geq 133.\overline{3}$$

Because your savings occur only once a week, you will need to save for at least 134 weeks (a little over $2\frac{1}{2}$ years) in order for the balance to be $1000 or less.

Caution: The most common student error in solving sentences like those in Examples 2 and 3 is ignoring the subtraction sign. You can lessen your chances of making this error by changing the subtraction to an addition *on paper* (not just in your head) and by checking the answer you get.

QUESTIONS

Covering the Reading

1. The range of temperatures recorded on Mercury one day was $573°C$. The minimum temperature recorded that day was $-154°C$.
   a. Using the formula for range, write an equation to find Mercury's maximum recorded temperature that day. $x - {-}154 = 573$
   b. Solve to find the maximum temperature. $x = 419$

2. In each example in this lesson, the first step in solving the equation is the same. What is done in that step?
   Change the subtraction to adding the opposite.

In 3–6, solve and check.

3. $12y - 9 = -3$ $y = \frac{1}{2}$

4. $\frac{1}{2}x - 7 = 8$ $x = 30$

5. $5z - 3.4 = 2.9$ $z = 1.26$

6. $-9A - 1 = 0$ $A = -\frac{1}{9}$

A safari sight. *African elephants are the largest animals that live on land.*

7. A bar was 3.01 mm too long. It was shortened by c and still found to be 0.54 mm too long. Solve an equation to find c.
   $3.01 - c = 0.54$; $c = 2.47$ mm

In 8 and 9 solve.

8. $-3 - t = -1$ $t = -2$

9. $-10 = 400 - A$ $A = 410$

Lesson 4-3 *Solving Sentences Involving Subtraction* **229**

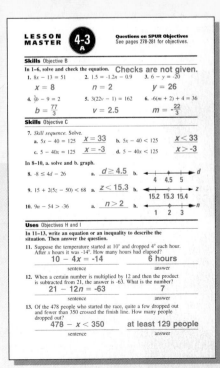
229

Question 10 The context of the problem determines if and how the answer should be rounded.

Question 11 Error Alert Using the answers for **parts a and b** to determine the answers for **parts c and d** cannot be done easily. It might be helpful to put solutions to the sentences side-by-side on the board; then you can compare and contrast the steps.

Question 12 To locate the error, substitute $\frac{1}{3}$ for x in each line of Ali's solution. Ask when it works and when it does not work.

Question 32 Additional questions you might ask are: Where would you place a point to represent the distance that is traveled in 2.5 hours? [Midway between (2, 60) and (3, 90)] When will you have traveled 120 miles? [After 4 hours]

Follow-up for Lesson 4-3

Practice

For more questions on SPUR Objectives, use **Lesson Master 4-3A** (shown on page 229) or **Lesson Master 4-3B** (shown on pages 230–231).

LESSON MASTER 4-3 B — Questions on SPUR Objectives

Skills Objective B: Solve and check linear equations involving subtraction.

In 1–9, solve and check each equation.

1. $5m - 12 = 38$
$m = 10$
$5 \cdot 10 - 12 = 38$?
$38 = 38$

2. $-8g - 13 = 43$
$g = -7$
$-8 \cdot -7 - 13 = 43$?
$43 = 43$

3. $-50 = 6e - 44$
$e = -1$
$-50 = 6 \cdot -1 - 44$?
$-50 = -50$

4. $84 - x = 27$
$x = 57$
$84 - 57 = 27$?
$27 = 27$

5. $-18.4 = -0.3y - -3.4$
$y = 50$
$-18.4 = -0.3 \cdot 50 - 3.4$?
$-3.4 = -3.4$

6. $\frac{5}{6}u - -17 = 102$
$u = 102$
$\frac{5}{6} \cdot 102 - -17 = 102$?
$102 = 102$

7. $7(19h - 3) = 112$
$h = 1$
$7(19 \cdot 1 - 3) = 112$?
$112 = 112$

8. $-3(a + 20) - 2a = 25$
$a = -17$
$-3(-17 + 20) - 2(-17) = 25$?
$25 = 25$

9. $102 - 7d = 11$
$d = 13$
$102 - 7 \cdot 13 = 11$?
$11 = 11$

Skills Objective C: Solve and check linear inequalities involving subtraction.

10. *Skill sequence.* Solve.
a. $8x - 40 = 360$ $x = 50$
b. $8x - 40 < 360$ $x < 50$
c. $8 - 40x = 360$ $x = -8.8$
d. $8 - 40x < 360$ $x > -8.8$

---

10. Use Example 3 of this lesson to answer Question 2 on page 215. ≈ 133.4 units

11. *Skill sequence.* Solve.
a. $2x - 16 = 20$ $x = 18$
b. $2x - 16 \geq 20$ $x \geq 18$
c. $16 - 2x = 20$ $x = -2$
d. $16 - 2x \geq 20$ $x \leq -2$

Applying the Mathematics

12. Here is Ali's work to solve $4 - 3x = 5$. Answer his last question.
$$4 - 3x = 5$$
$$4 + -3x = 5$$
$$-4 + 4 + -3x = -4 + 5$$
$$3x = 1$$
$$x = \frac{1}{3}$$
Check. Substitute $\frac{1}{3}$ for x in the original equation.
$$\text{Does } 4 - 3 \cdot \frac{1}{3} = 5?$$
$$4 - 1 = 5?$$
No. It doesn't check.
Where did I go wrong? When Ali simplified $-4 + 4 + -3x = -4 + 5$, Ali forgot about the negative sign attached to the 3x.

13. Three less than 10 times a number is 84.
a. Write an equation which represents this situation. Let $n =$ the unknown number. $10n - 3 = 84$
b. What is the number? 8.7

14. Hometown Bank and Trust requires a minimum balance of $1500 for free checking. If Mr. Archer can withdraw $3276 and still have free checking, how much is in his account? at least $4,776

15. A small town's population was 11,200 in 1990. Each year since 1990, about 60 people moved away. If this trend continues, in what year will the town's population reach 8,000? (Hint: Make a table to help determine the equation.) 2044

16. At the 1994 Winter Olympics, Bonnie Blair won her third consecutive gold medal in the women's 500-meter speed skating event with a time of 39.25 seconds. This was 0.15 second slower than when she won for the first time, in 1988. What was her 1988 Olympic time? 39.10 seconds

In 17–20, solve.

17. $-12.2 - p = -0.56$ $p = -11.64$
18. $-1 \leq -1 - y$ $y \leq 0$
19. $\frac{3}{4}t - 11 > 7$ $t > 24$
20. $-3(2n + 1) - 4 = -11$ $n = \frac{2}{3}$

Bonnie's bounty. *U.S. speedskater Bonnie Blair is shown after winning the 1,000-meter race at the 1994 Winter Olympics. Bonnie has won five Olympic gold medals, more than any woman in U.S. history.*

Review

21. The Dolans celebrated their 50th (golden) wedding anniversary in year y. In what year were they married? *(Lesson 4-2)* $y - 50$

Adapting to Individual Needs

Extra Help
For equations like those in **Example 2**, some students might want to stop with the equation $-c = -1.23$. Remind students that $-c$ is read "the opposite of c" and that the equation isn't solved until it is in the form $c =$ some number. Also remind them that $-c$ is the same as $-1c$, so the equation can be solved by multiplying both sides by the reciprocal of -1, which is -1.

Challenge
Have students solve the following problem. When rounded to the nearest thousand, x is 3000. When rounded to the nearest thousand, y is 7000. What is the range of values for $x + y$? [If 5 is to the right of the digit in the place to be rounded, the digit may be rounded up or down depending on the instance. Since x and y were rounded to the nearest thousand, $2500 \leq x \leq 3500$ and $6500 \leq y \leq 7500$; $9000 \leq x + y \leq 11,000$.]

22. The Valases will celebrate their *n*th wedding anniversary in 2000. In what year were they married? *(Lesson 4-2)* **2000 − n**

23. Susan currently earns $20.00 per hour. **$22.00**
    a. Suppose she receives a 10% raise. What is her new hourly wage?
    b. After receiving the raise in part **a**, her employer's profits decrease, so her wages are cut 10%. What is her hourly wage at this point?
    c. Explain why the result in part **b** is not $20.00. *(Lesson 4-2)* **$19.80**
       See left.

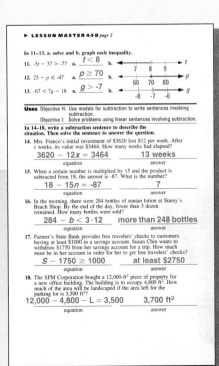

23c) The amount subtracted from 22, 10% of 22, is larger than the amount added to 20, 10% of 20. So the net result is less than 20.

24. A stock was valued at $120\frac{1}{4}$ one day. The next day its value fell $9\frac{3}{8}$. What was its value at that point? *(Lessons 3-9, 4-2)* $110\frac{7}{8}$

In 25–27, *multiple choice.* Suppose that *x* is negative and *y* is positive. Tell whether the value of the expression is (a) always negative, (b) always zero, (c) always positive, or (d) none of these. *(Lessons 2-5, 3-2, 4-1)*

25. $x \cdot y$ (a)   26. $x + y$ (d)   27. $x - y$ (a)

In 28 and 29, simplify. *(Lessons 1-4, 4-1)*

28. $5 - (4 - (3 - (2 - 1)))$ **3**   29. $1 - (2 - (3 - (4 - 5)))$ **3**

30. Simplify $\frac{4a}{5} + \frac{a}{3}$. *(Lesson 3-9)* $\frac{17a}{15}$

31. Use the Distributive Property to simplify $-1(3x + -5)$. *(Lesson 3-7)*
    −3x + 5

32. *Multiple choice.* Which of the following real-world situations is represented by the graph below? Write a brief explanation to justify your answer(s). *(Lesson 3-3)* **(a) In an hour, the traveler has traveled 30 miles.**
    (a) the distance traveled in *h* hours at 30 mph
    (b) the distance traveled in *h* hours at 50 mph
    (c) the distance you are from home if you started 90 miles from home and traveled home at 30 mph

Exploration

33. During gym class, the students formed a circle and counted off. (The first student counted "1," the second student counted "2," and so on.)
    a. Student number 7 was directly across the circle from student number 28. How many students are in the class? **42 students**
    b. Suppose student number 7 was directly across from student number *n*. Then how many students are in this class? $(n - 7) \cdot 2$

Group Assessment Have each student **work with a partner.** Ask each student to write and solve two subtraction equations. Tell students to include an error in the solution of one of the equations. Have partners exchange papers, check solutions, and find the error that was made. [Students understand how to check a solution and can recognize and correct errors.]

Extension

You can extend **Questions 28 and 29** by asking students to generalize these patterns. They could use the problem-solving strategies of trying a simpler case or making a table. [Note that in the equations below, all but one of the right-hand parentheses are omitted.]

Question 28 generalization:
$n - (n - 1 - (n - 2 - \ldots 2 - 1)$
$= \frac{n}{2}$ if *n* is even.
$= \frac{n+1}{2}$ if *n* is odd.

Question 29 generalization:
$1 - (2 - (3 - \ldots n)$
$= -\frac{n}{2}$ if *n* is even.
$= \frac{n+1}{2}$ if *n* is odd.]

Project Update Project 2, *Credit-Card Balances,* and Project 4, *Situations Leading to 300 − 5x > 40,* on pages 274–275, relate to the content of this lesson.

Setting Up Lesson 4-4

Materials Computers and spreadsheet software or blank spreadsheets (**Teaching Aid 37**)

The next lesson is about spreadsheets. Before assigning the lesson, you might ask how many students have used a spreadsheet before, either in school or at home. Ask how many students have computers at home, and if they do, whether they have spreadsheet software for that computer.

Those students who have used spreadsheets may be of assistance to you. The presence of such software in homes also indicates the relevance of the topic.

If computers are not available, you can still do the lesson by having students make the spreadsheets using **Teaching Aid 37**.

K Use a spreadsheet to show patterns and make tables from formulas.

Resources

From the *Teacher's Resource File*
- Lesson Master 4-4A or 4-4B
- Answer Master 4-4
- Assessment Sourcebook: Quiz for Lessons 4-1 through 4-4
- Teaching Aids
  34 Warm-up
  37 Spreadsheet
  38 Additional Examples 1 and 2
- Technology Sourcebook
  Computer Master 10

Additional Resources
- Visuals for Teaching Aids 34, 37, 38
- Computer and spreadsheet software

Teaching Lesson 4-4

Warm-up

The following students took three quizzes and received these scores.
Rosa: 83, 88, 84
Al: 83, 86, 92
Sam: 80, 78, 88
Liz: 76, 85, 91
1. Compute each student's average (mean) score. Rosa: 85; Al: 87; Sam: 82; Liz: 84

Then and now. *This house was custom-built in Chicago in 1946 for a cost of $31,500. This is equivalent to a cost of over $300,000 today.*

Construction Statement									
			Total Contract		Amount Paid		Balance Due		
Excavating	340	00							
Work Order #1	15	30	355	30	225	00	130	30	
Foundation			1731	00	1150	00	581	00	
Brickwork	4385	00							
Work Order #1	10	00	4395	00	3750	00	645	00	
Ornamental Iron			230	00			230	00	
Structural Iron			142	00	142	00			
Metal Windows & Damper			49	00	49	00			
Carpenter	6560	00							
Work Order #1	375	00	6935	00	700	00	6235	00	
Insulation			110	00			110	00	
Roofing	195	00							
Work Order #1	25	00	220	00			220	00	
Heating	1220	00							
Work Order #1	245	00							
Credit Order #1	(53	00)	1412	00			1412	00	

❶

What Is a Spreadsheet?

Shown above is a copy of part of a bill sent in 1946 by a builder of a home to the family that was having the home built. It is an example of a *spreadsheet*. In many situations, very large pages or pages taped together were used for records like these. These pages were sometimes folded for storage and then spread out for examination. That is how "spreadsheets" got their name.

Notice that some numbers are added or subtracted to yield other numbers in the spreadsheet. Consequently, maintaining a spreadsheet used to be quite difficult. If one entry was changed, many other numbers would need to be changed as a result. By the mid 1970s, large companies were using computers for this purpose, but the process was still tedious.

Lesson 4-4 Overview

Broad Goals The purpose of this lesson is to introduce students to spreadsheets and to the use of formulas in spreadsheets.

Perspective The teachers who field tested this book reported that having their students actually use spreadsheets "made the difference." However, even teachers who did not have access to spreadsheets thought that the lesson was worthwhile.

There are many references to spreadsheets in later chapters, so even if you don't have access to a spreadsheet, we suggest you teach this lesson.

After a historical introduction, this lesson introduces the language of spreadsheets in **Example 1. Examples 2 and 3** use expressions and formulas in spreadsheets. The lesson ends with a discussion of the use

of spreadsheets to construct a table through the process of replication. On some spreadsheets, this process is initiated by the command "Copy," just as text is copied when using word-processing software.

The language used in this lesson is that found with Microsoft® Excel. There may be slight differences with other software.

In 1978, Dan Bricklin and Bob Frankston, graduate students at the Harvard University School of Business, recognized that desktop computers could save them a great deal of work. They prepared a computer spreadsheet program that would recompute their work as they tried new values for costs or prices. Their program, *VisiCalc,* was a major advance in computer applications because it had the power to hold formulas. Each formula indicates how a number in a particular place in the chart is computed from other numbers on the spreadsheet. When one number is changed, the computer uses the formulas to change the corresponding numbers.

Computer spreadsheets were an immediate success. Nowadays they are used to organize data, experiment with complicated computations, determine patterns, and test properties. Many people use spreadsheets to keep personal or household financial records.

Cells in Spreadsheets

A typical computer spreadsheet has *rows* identified by numbers and *columns* identified with letters. The locations or boxes formed by the intersection of rows and columns are called **cells.** A spreadsheet can have hundreds of columns and thousands of rows. How many depends on the software and on the amount of memory in the computer.

Typically the location of a cell is named by the column letter first and the row number second.

The spreadsheet below shows the number of coupon books sold by students to raise money for their school. This spreadsheet tells you that Susan sold 50 books. Her name is in cell A2, and the number 50 is in cell C2. You can think of a cell name as a variable because the number or other entry in the cell can change.

	A	B	C	D
1	Student		Books	Sales
2	Susan		50	
3	Sam		25	
4	Rashana		33	
5				
6	Total		108	

The number 108 in C6 is the result of adding 50 + 25 + 33. It is an instance of the formula C6 = C2 + C3 + C4. To enter this formula in C6 on many spreadsheets you can type the phrase = C2 + C3 + C4 in cell C6. The "=" symbol tells the computer to calculate the value of the expression and to display the result, not the formula. (Some spreadsheets allow the use of other symbols, such as a + or − sign instead of an equal sign.)

2. Organize the data from Question 1 in a table. Label the columns "Name," "Q 1," "Q 2," "Q 3," and "Avg." Label the rows under "Name" with students' names. Save your table for later use.

Name	Q 1	Q 2	Q 3	Avg.
Rosa	83	88	84	85
Al	83	86	92	87
Sam	80	78	88	82
Liz	76	85	91	84

Notes on Reading

❶ The spreadsheet that introduces this lesson is part of an actual bill; it was given to the parents of one of the authors when they were building the home in which the author grew up.

Although this lesson can be done without computers, it is desirable for students to have the experience of working with a spreadsheet on a computer. Students can use **Teaching Aid 37** if computers are not available.

Technology Connection Prior to 1978, large companies used computer spreadsheets to keep accounting records, but each company had to hire programmers to design special software for its use. The invention of *VisiCalc* was a breakthrough in software development. A spreadsheet of its power and size required more than 16K of storage, so *VisiCalc* was first used on large machines.

The first computer designed for desktop use, the Apple computer with the then very large (for personal use) internal storage of 16K (16,384 bytes), was introduced in 1977. Today machines with at least 512K are the norm rather than the exception, and spreadsheet programs abound.

The key difference between the use of variables in spreadsheet formulas and their use in other applications is that the variable stands for a particular cell in the spreadsheet. Because a spreadsheet is two-dimensional, the variable is named with two symbols, typically a letter and a number. Here, letters stand for columns and the numbers stand for rows. The variable has the same name as the cell. That is, C5 is the name of the cell in the third column and the fifth row, and it is also the name of the entry in that cell. Putting an entry into that cell is equivalent to substituting a value for the variable. The domain of the variable is consequently the set of allowable values that can be substituted for the variable.

If your students have done the *Warm-up* for this lesson, explain that their tables are simple spreadsheets. Have them add a column to the left of their table and number the rows 1 through 5. Then have them add a row at the top of their tables and label the columns A through E, beginning with the "Name" column. Note that there is no label in the upper left corner of the resulting spreadsheet.

	A	B	C	D	E
1	Name	Q 1	Q 2	Q 3	Avg.
2	Rosa	83	88	84	85
3	Al	83	86	92	87
4	Sam	80	78	88	82
5	Liz	76	85	91	84

Ask students what formula they would use to find the average score for Rosa. [=(B2 + C2 + D2)/3]

Example 1

Use the spreadsheet pictured on the previous page.
a. Which cell contains the number 33?
b. What is in cell A3?
c. What cell contains the word "Books"?
d. Suppose D6 is computed by typing = C2 + C4. What number would appear in D6?
e. What is in cell B6?
f. Suppose Rashana sells one more coupon book, so the number in C4 changes from 33 to 34. What other entry will change?

Solution

a. The number 33 is in C4. b. The word "Sam" is in A3.
c. C1   d. 83
e. Nothing; it is empty.   f. C6 will change to 109.

❷ Expressions and Formulas in Spreadsheets

The language of expressions and formulas in most spreadsheets is similar to that in many computer languages. The arithmetic symbols are + for addition, − for subtraction, * for multiplication, / for division, ^ for powering, and ( ) for grouping. SQRT( ) is usually used for square root. Typically, every operation must be shown by a symbol. So to multiply the value in C7 by 5 you would type = C7 * 5.

Spreadsheets can quickly give instances of properties.

Example 2

Use a spreadsheet to give examples of the Distributive Property, $a(b - c) = ab - ac$.

Solution

The examples will involve different values of *a*, *b*, and *c*, so make columns for these numbers. Then make a column for $a(b - c)$ and a column for $ab - ac$. The columns are named in row 1. Since = signs do not precede these expressions, the spreadsheet program does no calculations in this row.

	A	B	C	D	E
1	a	b	c	a(b − c)	ab − ac
2					
3					

▶

234

Adapting to Individual Needs

Challenge
Materials: Computer and spreadsheet program or **Teaching Aid 37**

Have students make a spreadsheet of at least four rows to illustrate the following statement: When you multiply any four consecutive integers and add 1, the result is a perfect square. [The spreadsheet showing formulas is shown at the right. The display is shown on page 237.]

Spreadsheet with formulas:

	A	B	C	D	E	F
1	1	=A1+1	=B1+1	=C1+1	=A1*B1*C1*D1+1	=SQRT(E1)
2	7	=A2+1	=B2+1	=C2+1	=A2*B2*C2*D2+1	=SQRT(E2)
3	50	=A3+1	=B3+1	=C3+1	=A3*B3*C3*D3+1	=SQRT(E3)
4	-3	=A4+1	=B4+1	=C4+1	=A4*B4*C4*D4+1	=SQRT(E4)

Now pick some values for *a, b,* and *c.* We pick 10, 15, and -3.
Type these in cells A2, B2, and C2. In cell D2, type the formula
= A2*(B2 − C2). In cell E2, type the formula = A2*B2 − A2*C2.
When these formulas are entered, the spreadsheet will look like this.

	A	B	C	D	E
1	a	b	c	a(b − c)	ab − ac
2	10	5	-3	80	80
3					

You can put any real numbers you wish in cells A3, B3, and C3. Now in
cell D3, enter the formula = A3*(B3 − C3). In cell E3, enter the formula
= A3*B3 − A3*C3. Because the property $a(b − c) = ab − ac$ holds
for all real numbers, you should see the same numbers in cells D3 and E3.

Replicating Formulas

It is tedious to type in each formula needed in Example 2, and it is easy
to make a mistake. Fortunately, all spreadsheets have a feature that
enables you to copy formulas from one cell to another in a way that
changes the cell names in the formula to agree with the column and row
position of the new cell. Consider again the formulas needed in column
D of the spreadsheet of Example 2.

Cell	Formula
D2	= A2*(B2 − C2)
D3	= A3*(B3 − C3)
D4	= A4*(A4 − C4)

The formulas follow a pattern as you go down the column. The formulas
that are to be entered in column D are the same except for the cell
names used in the formula. Each formula refers to cells in the same
positions relative to the cell containing the formula. When this occurs,
you can type the first formula (in cell D2), and then command the
program to copy the formula to the cells below D2. The references to the
cells in columns A, B, and C will automatically change as it does the
copying. This way of copying is called **replication.** The formulas are
replicated from the first cell to reflect the changes in cell references.

Different spreadsheets have different commands for replicating
formulas. If you have access to a spreadsheet program, you should
determine how you can replicate a formula in it.

Many different kinds of formulas can be used in spreadsheets.

Display:

	A	B	C	D	E	F
1	1	2	3	4	25	5
2	7	8	9	10	5041	71
3	50	51	52	53	7,027,801	2651
4	-3	-2	-1	0	1	1

Additional Examples

Examples 1 and 2 are given on **Teaching Aid 38.**

1. The spreadsheet shows the number of tickets sold and the revenue from ticket sales for a 3-game soccer tournament.

	· A	B	C	D
1	Game		Sales	$$$
2	9 A.M.		280	700
3	2 P.M.		174	435
4	7 P.M.		321	
5				
6	Total			

a. Which cell contains the word "Total"? **A6**
b. What is in cell C2? **280**
c. Which cell contains the number 174? **C3**
d. Cell C6 is computed by typing "=C2+C3+C4". What number will appear in C6? **775**
e. What is in cell D5? **It is empty.**
f. If the number in C4 is changed to 327, what other entry will change? What will it become? **C6; 781**

2. Make a spreadsheet to give examples of two ways to find the perimeter of a rectangle: $\ell + w + \ell + w = 2\ell + 2w$.
a. Label the columns and rows of your spreadsheet. Fill in row 1. **See sample following Question 2d.**
b. Pick values for ℓ and w. Where will you write them? **A2 and B2**

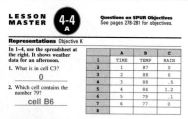

Example 3

Alex Ploor is learning about the Pythagorean Theorem. Alex wants to see how increasing the length of one leg in a right triangle affects the length of the hypotenuse. So Alex created the following spreadsheet. Row 1 contains the names of the columns. Row 2 lists the variables assigned to the column names.

	A	B	C	D	E
1	Leg 1	Leg 2		Hypotenuse	
2	a	b	c^2	c	
3	1	1			
4	1	2			
5	1	3			
6	1	4			

a. What formula should be put in cell C3?
b. What formula should be put in cell D3?
c. What number will appear in cell D3?
d. What formulas should be put in each of cells C4 through C6 and D4 through D6 to complete the spreadsheet?
e. What will the completed spreadsheet show on the screen?

Solution

a. By the Pythagorean Theorem, $c^2 = a^2 + b^2$. Thus C3 should contain the sum of the squares of the numbers in A3 and B3. So in cell C3, Alex should type the following:

$$= A3\wedge2 + B3\wedge2$$

b. The number c is the positive square root of c^2. So in cell D3, Alex should type the following:

$$= SQRT(C3)$$

c. Since $1^2 + 1^2 = 2$, the number 2 will appear in C3, and 1.414213 . . . (the decimal for $\sqrt{2}$) will appear in D3.
d. The formula for cell C4 would be = A4^2 + B4^2. The formula for cell C5 would be = A5^2 + B5^2, and for C6 it would be = A6^2 + B6^2. Alex can replicate the formula in cell C3 in cells C4 to C6 to avoid all this typing. Similarly, he can replicate the formula in cell D3 to cells D4 to D6.

Adapting to Individual Needs

Extra Help

Explain that a cell name is used as a variable so that when a formula is entered into a cell and executed, the computer substitutes the appropriate values and computes. Write the following formula on the board: (A2+B2)/2. The computer will add the values from cells A2 and B2, and divide the sum by 2. Point out the operation symbols that must be used when writing formulas. Write the following formulas on the board,

and ask students to explain what values will be used and what operation(s) will be performed.

1. C2 − B2 [Subtract the value in cell B2 from the value in cell C2.]
2. A2∧2 [Square the value in cell A2.]
3. 3*D2 [Multiply the value in cell D2 by 3.]
4. (A2+B2)∧2 [Square the sum of the values in cell A2 and cell B2.]
5. SQRT(A2) [Find the square root of the value in cell A2.]

e. Columns A and B will stay as shown. In cells C3 through C6 and D3 through D6 the formulas given in parts *a, b,* and *d* will be evaluated. The spreadsheet will show the following:

	A	B	C	D	E
1	Leg 1	Leg 2		Hypotenuse	
2	a	b	c^2	c	
3	1	1	2	1.414	
4	1	2	5	2.236	
5	1	3	10	3.162	
6	1	4	17	4.123	

QUESTIONS

Covering the Reading

1. Refer to the spreadsheet that begins this lesson. Suppose the cost of excavating were $350 instead of $340. What other numbers would change? **Total Contract, $355.30 changes to $365.30; Balance Due, $130.30 changes to $140.30; Total Balance Due, $1412 changes to $1422.**

2. Who designed the first electronic spreadsheet software, and when? **Dan Bricklin and Bob Frankston in 1978**

3. What is the term for the places in a spreadsheet into which you can type words, numbers, or formulas? **cells**

4. Suppose cell A5 in a spreadsheet contains the number 18 and B5 contains the number -3. If C5 contains the formula $= A5 + B5 \wedge 2$, what number will appear in cell C5? **27**

In 5 and 6, refer to Example 2.

5. If .6 is typed in cell A3, 4 in B3, and 5 in C3, what numbers will appear in cells D3 and E3? **D3 = -0.6; E3 = -0.6**

6. **a.** What formula should be typed in cell D4? **= A4*(B4 − C4)**
   b. What formula should be typed in cell E4? **= A4*B4 − A4*C4**
   c. Why will these formulas yield the same values? **See left.**

6c) because the property $a(b − c) = ab − ac$ holds true for all real numbers

7. What is the term for copying formulas in a way that allows the spreadsheet to change cell references? **replication**

8. Refer to Example 3. Suppose the table is extended so A7 contains the number 1 and B7 contains the number 5.
   a. What formula should be typed in cell C7? **= A7 $\wedge$ 2 + B7 $\wedge$ 2**
   b. What will appear in C7? **26**
   c. What formula should be typed in cell D7? **= SQRT(C7)**
   d. What will appear there? **5.0990195. . . ≈ 5.099**

c. What formula will you write in C2? What will cell C2 show? **=A2+B2+A2+B2; display will depend on the numbers in A2 and B2.**

d. What formula will you write in D2? What will cell D2 show? **=2*A2+2*B2; the display will depend on numbers in A2 and B2, but it should agree with the display in C2.**

	A	B	C	D
1	ℓ	w	$\ell + w + \ell + w$	$2\ell + 2w$
2	8	6	28	28

3. Refer to **Example 3** on page 236. Suppose Alex also wants to calculate the area of each triangle and store it in the appropriate cell in column E.
   a. What do you suggest that Alex type in each of the cells E1 to E6? **See "Cell Entry" column below.**
   b. What will the completed spread sheet show on the screen for cells E1 to E6? **See "Display" column below.**

Cell	Cell Entry	Display
E1	Area	Area
E2	*ab*/2	*ab*/2
E3	=A3*B3/2	.5
E4	=A4*B4/2	1
E5	=A5*B5/2	1.5
E6	=A6*B6/2	2

Adapting to Individual Needs

English Language Development

Students with limited English proficiency may have used spreadsheets before. They might understand how spreadsheets work, but they may have difficulty with the terminology. As these students read the lesson, give special attention to terms relating to spreadsheets, such as *cells, active cells, rows,* and *columns.*

Question 16 The use of spreadsheets makes it possible for this table to be easily extended both horizontally and vertically to give many more entries.

Question 17 On some spreadsheets, a symbol for multiplication must precede the parentheses.

Applying the Mathematics

In 9–12, use the spreadsheet below. It shows a listing of students who took two tests. The mean is computed from their test scores.

9. What is the entry in cell B4? **86**

10. What cell shows the number 75? **D3**

11. What does the 80 in D5 represent? **Marcel's mean**

12. The mean of John's scores is computed in cell D2 by the formula = (B2 + C2) / 2.
    a. Write the formula for Marcel's mean. **= (B5 + C5) / 2**
    b. What cell contains this formula? **D5**

	A	B	C	D
1	Name	Test 1	Test 2	Mean
2	John	90	95	92.5
3	Gordon	70	80	75
4	Anne	86	86	86
5	Marcel	64	96	80

13. Write a formula for the mean of the values in cells J5, K5, J6, and K6.
    = (J5 + K5 + J6 + K6) / 4
14. Suppose that cell F6 contains the number x and cell F7 contains y. Write the expression in x and y represented by the formula = (F6 − F7) / (2 * F6 + F7 ^ 3). **$(x - y) / (2x + y^3)$**

15. Cell T5 contains the number 16, and cell T6 contains the number 25. Cell T7 shows the number 9. Could the formula in T7 be = SQRT(T5 + T6)? Why or why not?
    No, because $\sqrt{16 + 25} = \sqrt{41}$, which does not equal 9.
16. A student wants to make a table of powers of numbers. He types in names of columns as shown here.

	A	B	C	D	E
1	x	square	cube	4th power	5th power
2					

He wants to be able to enter a number in cell A2 and have the program automatically calculate the values in B2, C2, D2, and E2. What formulas should he enter in those cells?
$= A2^2$; $= A2^3$; $= A2^4$; $= A2^5$

17. A local newspaper charges by the word for classified ads. Refer to the ad at the left. A formula to compute the cost of an ad containing 25 or more words is $C = 5.00 + .50(W - 25)$.
  a. How much does the newspaper charge for an ad with 39 words?   **a) $12.00**
  b. Suppose you wanted to calculate the cost for any ad from 25 to 100 words long. Explain how you can get a spreadsheet to build a table of costs with the number of words in column A and the cost for the ad in column B. **See left.**

Practice
For more questions on SPUR Objectives, use **Lesson Master 4-4A** (shown on pages 236–237) or **Lesson Master 4-4B** (shown on pages 238–239).

Assessment
Quiz A quiz covering Lessons 4-1 through 4-4 is provided in the *Assessment Sourcebook*.

Oral Assessment Have students summarize what they have learned about spreadsheets. You might help students to get started by asking them to explain what a spreadsheet is. [Students understand what a spreadsheet is and can explain how to use a typical computer spreadsheet program. Students understand appropriate uses of spreadsheets.]

Extension
Career Connection Ask students if they know someone who uses spreadsheets in his or her work. Students might interview that person, or invite him or her to talk to the class. Students should ask how spreadsheets are used and how a similar job might have been accomplished without the use of spreadsheets.

Review

17b) Sample: In cell A1 enter the label "Number of words." In cell B1 enter the label "Cost of ad." In cell A2 enter 25, and in cell A3 enter the formula = A2 + 1. Replicate this formula in cells A4 through A77. Enter the formula = 5.00 + .50*(A2 – 25) in cell B2. Finally replicate the formula from cell B2 in cells B3 through B77.

In 18–21, solve. *(Lesson 4-3)*

18. $9x - 18 = 432$ $x = 50$

19. $9(x - 18) = 432$ $x = 66$

20. $\frac{y}{2} - 7 = -6$ $y = 2$

21. $-4 < 8z - 4$ $z > 0$

22. *Multiple choice.* Below is a table produced by one of the four formulas listed. Which formula is it? *(Lesson 1-9)* **(d)**

(a) $y = 3x$
(b) $y = x + 3$
(c) $y = 3x + 1$
(d) $y = 3x + 3$

x	y
0	3
1	6
2	9
3	12
4	15

23. One ski lift at the Alpine Ski Resort in East Troy, Wisconsin, is represented by the diagram. How far is it from *A* to *B*? *(Lesson 1-8)*
2499.8 ft ≈ 2500 ft

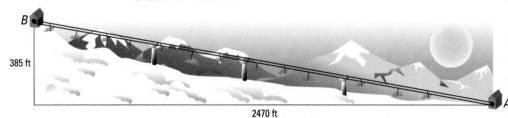

385 ft

2470 ft

24. Without using a calculator, find two consecutive whole numbers *a* and *b* so that $a < \sqrt{53} < b$. Explain how you found your answer.
(Lesson 1-6) **7 and 8; 53 is between the perfect squares 49 and 64, so $\sqrt{49} < \sqrt{53} < \sqrt{64}$.**

Exploration

25. Find an actual spreadsheet program and try it out. What is the name of the cell in the bottom right-hand corner of this spreadsheet? How many rows and columns does this spreadsheet have? How many cells does it have? What would be the answers to Example 2 on this spreadsheet? **Answers will vary.**

Lesson 4-4 *Spreadsheets* **239**

239

Objectives

D Use the Opposite of a Sum or Difference Property to simplify expressions and solve sentences.

Resources

From the Teacher's Resource File
■ Lesson Master 4-5A and 4-5B
■ Answer Master 4-5
■ Teaching Aid 35: Warm-up
■ Activity Kit, Activity 8

Additional Resources
■ Visual for Teaching Aid 35

Teaching Lesson 4-5

Warm-up

Fill in the table. Select your own values for *a* and *b* in row 5. **Sample numbers are given in row 5.**

	a	b	-(a + b)	-a + -b	-a - b
1.	2	3	-5	-5	-5
2.	-2	3	-1	-1	-1
3.	2	-3	1	1	1
4.	-2	-3	5	5	5
5.	9	-6	-3	-3	-3

6. What do you notice about -(a + b), -a + -b, and -a - b? **They are equal.**

The Opposite of a Sum or Difference

Could you bank on them? *Shown is a re-creation of an 1850s town. Some banks in those days failed, and depositors often lost their savings. Today, most deposits up to $100,000 are insured by a branch of the U.S. government.*

❶ An Example of the Opposite of a Sum

Suppose Anton has $500 in his savings account. He withdraws *a* dollars from his account. Deciding that this is not enough, he makes another withdrawal of *b* dollars. Notice that the amount of money left in his savings account can be expressed in several different ways.

Anton can subtract one amount from 500 and then subtract the other from the difference. This can be written

$$500 - a - b, \text{ or } 500 + {-a} + {-b}.$$

Anton could also add the two withdrawals and then subtract the total from 500. This is written as

$$500 - (a + b), \text{ or } 500 + {-(a + b)}.$$

The fact that $-(a + b)$ is the same as $-a - b$ is related to the Distributive Property. To see how, start with $-(a + b)$. Recall that the Multiplication Property of -1 states that for any real number n, $-n = -1n$. So,

$-(a + b) = -1(a + b)$	Multiplication Property of -1
$= -1a + -1b$	Distributive Property
$= -a + -b$	Multiplication Property of -1
$= -a - b.$	Definition of Subtraction

Opposite of a Sum Property
For all real numbers *a* and *b*,
$$-(a + b) = -a + -b = -a - b.$$

The first part of this property, $-(a + b) = -a + -b$, says that *the opposite of a sum is the sum of the opposites of its terms.*

Lesson 4-5 Overview

Broad Goals Two topics are discussed in this lesson. The first is the property that the opposite of a sum is the sum of the opposites of the terms. This allows us to express the opposites of quantities simply. This property is then used in the second topic, which is subtracting quantities. The goal of the lesson is to provide students with the tools needed to deal with expressions that contain opposites.

Perspective The more ways that students have to check what they are doing and to relate what they are doing to something else, the more likely they are to deal with a concept accurately. Here we apply this approach to subtracting quantities, which is a troublesome topic for some students.

The Opposite of a Sum Property, $-(a + b) = -a + -b$, is the special case of the Distributive Property $c(a + b) = ca + cb$ when $c = -1$.

However, another approach avoids multiplication. You can think of $-(a + b)$ as the number which, when added to $a + b$, gives a sum of 0. Since $(a + b) + (-a + -b) = 0$, the opposite of the quantity $(a + b)$ is $-a + -b$. A third approach, in which you think of the opposite sign as being distributed over the terms of the quantity, comes closest to the idea of changing the signs of the terms that are being subtracted.

Example 1

Simplify $-(2k + 14)$.

Solution

Apply the Opposite of a Sum Property.
$$-(2k + 14) = -2k - 14$$

The Opposite of a Difference

Suppose the expression in parentheses involves subtraction rather than addition. How can you rewrite its opposite? Again, the Distributive Property can be used.

$$
\begin{aligned}
-(a - b) &= -(a + -b) && \text{Algebraic Definition of Subtraction} \\
&= -a + -(-b) && \text{Opposite of a Sum} \\
&= -a + b && \text{Op-op Property}
\end{aligned}
$$

Now we can rewrite the opposite of a difference.

Opposite of a Difference Property
For all real numbers a and b,
$$-(a - b) = -a + b.$$

Example 2

Simplify $-(4a - 7)$.

Solution

$$-(4a - 7) = -4a + 7$$

When a difference is subtracted from another number or expression, the Opposite of a Difference Property can be used. First use the Algebraic Definition of Subtraction to change the subtraction of the difference to the addition of its opposite.

❷ Example 3

Simplify $(10a + 6) - (4a - 7)$.

Solution 1

Change the subtracting of $(4a - 7)$ to addition.
$$x \quad - \quad y \quad = \quad x \quad + \quad -y$$

$$
\begin{aligned}
(10a + 6) - (4a - 7) &= (10a + 6) + -(4a - 7) && \text{Algebraic Definition of} \\
& && \text{Subtraction} \\
&= 10a + 6 + -4a + 7 && \text{Opposite of a Difference} \\
&= 6a + 13 && \text{Add like terms.}
\end{aligned}
$$

▶

Notes on Reading

The skills in this lesson are tricky. We recommend that you go through each example in detail.

❶ The lesson begins with a justification for the subtraction of a sum. For some students, this explanation is quite illustrative. It leads to the basic property of the lesson, which is immediately applied in **Example 1**. A variant of the property is derived and then applied in **Example 2**.

Error Alert Obtaining correct signs when parentheses are removed will remain a problem for many students. Often, much practice is needed before mastery, and constant reminders are needed after mastery has been achieved. Thus, this is a skill that we review throughout this chapter and again in later chapters. Still, we encourage you to begin skipping steps as soon as is reasonable, because students often make errors in rewriting from one step to the next.

❷ Knowledge of chunking—thinking of an expression as a single object—is necessary to fully understand **Example 3.** (Specific information on chunking is presented at the end of Chapter 5.) Students must view $(10a + 6) - (4a - 7)$ as the subtraction of two numbers, and then rewrite it as the first number plus the opposite of the second number. Students might benefit from the explanation given in *Extra Help* in *Adapting to Individual Needs* on page 242.

Optional Activities

Activity 1 After students do **Questions 22 and 23,** you might ask them to measure their own feet at home and to check and see how accurately these formulas predict their shoe sizes.

Activity 2 You can use *Activity Kit, Activity 8,* as a follow-up to the lesson. In the activity, students learn a card trick that uses the Opposite of a Difference Property.

Activity 3 After completing the lesson, students might enjoy adding these numbers:
$b =$ the year in which they were born
$e =$ the year of another event in their life
$a =$ their age at the end of this year
$d =$ the positive difference between this year and the year of the other event

Ask students to compare their answers. They might be surprised to learn that they are all the same—twice the current year c.

Ask them to explain why this is true. [The year they were born plus their age at the end of the year equals the current year. The year of the other event, plus the result of subtracting that year from the current year, equals the current year, so the sum is twice the current year. Algebraically, $b + a = c$ and $e + d = c$. Thus $b + a + e + d = 2c$.

Additional Examples

In 1–3, simplify each expression.
1. $-(k + 23)$ $-k - 23$
2. $-(6c - 5)$ $-6c + 5$
3. $(3y + 8) - (2y - 7)$ $y + 15$
4. Solve: $47z - (9 + 23z) = 3$.
   $z = \frac{1}{2}$
5. Simplify $\frac{3x}{2} - \frac{x+6}{4}$. $\frac{5x - 6}{4}$
6. Carrie had 27 almonds in a bag. On the way to school, she ate x almonds. Then she gave 15 almonds to her friend. Express in two different ways the number of almonds she had left.
   $27 - x - 15$; $27 - (x + 15)$

▶ **Solution 2**

An expert might write the following:
$$(10a + 6) - (4a - 7) = 10a + 6 - 4a + 7$$
$$= 6a + 13$$

Opposites of Expressions in Equations

In the next example, the left side of the equation may seem complicated. It shows that first $2 + 4x$ is multiplied by 3, and then the result is subtracted from $13x$. Again we begin work by using the Algebraic Definition of Subtraction.

Example 4

Solve $13x - 3(2 + 4x) = 25$.

❸ **Solution 1**

Change the subtraction to an addition.

$13x - 3(2 + 4x) = 25$	
$13x + -3(2 + 4x) = 25$	Algebraic Definition of Subtraction
$13x + -6 + -12x = 25$	Distributive Property (Remove Parentheses.)
$x + -6 = 25$	Distributive Property (Add like terms.)
$x = 31$	Addition Property of Equality

Solution 2

Experts sometimes apply the Algebraic Definition of Subtraction, the Distributive Property, and the Opposite of a Sum Property in one step. They might write the following:

$$13x - 3(2 + 4x) = 25$$
$$13x - 6 - 12x = 25$$
$$x - 6 = 25$$
$$x = 31$$

Check

Does $13 \cdot 31 - 3(2 + 4 \cdot 31) = 25$?
Does $403 - 3(126) = 25$? Yes, so it checks.

Opposites of Expressions in Fractions

To subtract fractions, you must have a common denominator. When numerators involve sums of differences, you must be careful with the signs.

242

Adapting to Individual Needs

Extra Help

In **Example 3**, some students might have trouble seeing that $(10a + 6) - (4a - 7)$ is the same situation as $x - y$. The following demonstration might help. Write $\square - \bigcirc$. Ask students how they could rewrite this expression using the Algebraic Definition of Subtraction. Write $\square + -\bigcirc$. Tell students to imagine that the square represents $(10a + 6)$ and write this expression in the square. Then write $(4a - 7)$ in the circle. Finally, simplify the expression.

Students must view $(10a + 6) - (4a - 7)$ as the subtraction of two numbers and rewrite it as the first number plus the opposite of the second. Students might also benefit from the following explanation:

$(10a + 6)$ minus $(4a - 7)$
$= (10a + 6)$ plus the opposite of $(4a - 7)$
$= (10a + 6) + (-4a + 7)$

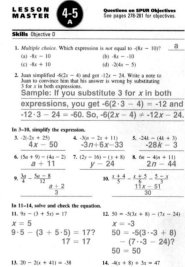

④ **Example 5**

Simplify $\frac{4x}{5} - \frac{2x+1}{10}$.

Solution

A common denominator is 10.

$$\frac{4x}{5} - \frac{2x+1}{10} = \frac{8x}{10} - \frac{2x+1}{10}$$

$$= \frac{8x - (2x+1)}{10}$$

$$= \frac{8x - 2x - 1}{10}$$

$$= \frac{6x - 1}{10}$$

Check

Substitute a value for x in the given and the answer.

$$\frac{4 \cdot 2}{5} - \frac{2 \cdot 2 + 1}{10} = \frac{8}{5} - \frac{5}{10} = \frac{16}{10} - \frac{5}{10} = \frac{11}{10}$$

$$\frac{6 \cdot 2 - 1}{10} = \frac{11}{10}. \text{ It checks.}$$

QUESTIONS

Covering the Reading

1. A clerk has a 20-yard bolt of cloth. She first cuts r yards of cloth from the bolt and then cuts t yards from the same bolt.
   a. Express the amount of cloth left in two different ways.
   b. Let $r = 3$ yards and $t = 7$ yards to check that the two expressions in part **a** are equal. 10; 10; Yes, they are equal.
   a) $20 - r - t$ or $20 - (r + t)$

2. You begin the day with D dollars. You spend L dollars for lunch and \$10 for a book. Write two expressions for the amount of money you have left. $D - L - 10$ or $D - (L + 10)$

In 3 and 4, *multiple choice*.

3. Which of the following equals $-(x + 4)$? (c)
   (a) $-x + 4$　　　　(b) $x + -4$　　　　(c) $-x + -4$

4. Which expression does not equal $-(x - y)$? (b)
   (a) $-x + y$　　　　(b) $-1x + -1y$　　　　(c) $-x - (-y)$

In 5–10, simplify.

5. $-(x + 15)$　$-x - 15$

6. $-(4n - 3m)$　$-4n + 3m$

7. $x - (x + 2)$　-2

8. $3y - 5(y + 1)$　$-2y - 5$

9. $(3k + 4) - (7k - 9)$　$-4k + 13$

10. $-(5 + k) + (k - 18)$　-23

In 11–14, solve and check.

11. $-(A - 9) = 11$　$A = -2$

12. $2 - (x + 3) = 4$　$x = -5$

13. $12 - (2y - 4) = 18$　$y = -1$

14. $5x - 3(5 - 2x) = -15$　$x = 0$

Lesson 4-5 *The Opposite of a Sum or Difference* **243**

Notes on Questions

Question 19 Expect both 90 − (4f + p) and 90 − 4f − p as answers; they are equivalent because of the properties in this lesson. You might note that in baseball the amount of territory a fielder can cover is called the *range;* that usage is related to its statistical use in Lesson 4-2. Of course, if a ball is hit more slowly, then fielders can cover more of an angle. Point out that the angles that are not part of the triangles must have measures that add to 32°.

Questions 23–24 Social Studies Connection Students might be interested to know that shoe sizes are based on the length of barleycorns. An inch is equal to three barleycorns. Centuries ago, an average large foot measured exactly 39 barleycorns or 13 inches. This became the length of a size 13 men's shoe. A size 12 men's shoe was 38 barleycorns in length, a size 11 shoe was 37 barleycorns in length and so on. Women's shoe sizes also are linear with a size 11 women's shoe equal to 11 inches in length.

Question 27 Cooperative Learning This is a good question for encouraging dialogue among students. Have students **work in small groups** to share the patterns that they notice. This question leads directly into the next lesson.

Question 30 This question, and several in Lesson 4-6, review concepts of angle measure in preparation for Lesson 4-7.

In 15 and 16, simplify.

15. $\dfrac{8x}{3} - \dfrac{3x+2}{6}$ $\dfrac{13x-2}{6}$

16. $\dfrac{n+1}{2} - \dfrac{n-1}{3}$ $\dfrac{n+5}{6}$

Applying the Mathematics

17. Rewrite without parentheses: $-(a + 2b − c)$. $-a - 2b + c$

18. Using A_1 and A_2 write an expression for the area of the shaded part of the rectangle at the left. $270 − (A_1 + A_2)$ or $270 − A_1 − A_2$

19. In baseball, the batter hits into a playing field. The foul lines form a 90° angle. Suppose that each of the four infielders can cover an angle of about $f°$. The pitcher can cover about $p°$. How much of the infield is left for the hitter to hit through? $(90 − 4f − p)°$ or $(90 − (4f + p))°$

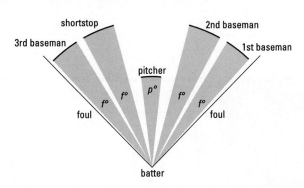

In 20 and 21, solve and check.

20. $3x − 2(x + 6.5) < 25.5$
$x < 38.5$

21. $3(t + 9) − (9 + t) + 6(t + 9) = 80$
$t = 1$

22. Create a spreadsheet with the following entries.

	A	B	C	D	E
1	Month	Income	Expenses	Profit 1	Profit 2
2		I	E	I − E	I + -E
3	January	10,312	9,080	1232	1232
4	February	11,557	12,364	-807	-807

a. Fill in cells D3, D4, E3, and E4 using the formulas in cells D2 and E2.   a) See above.   b) The results are the same.
b. Compare what you get in column D to what you get in column E.
c. Explain your results for columns D and E.
Sample: The results are the same because I − E = I + -E. Subtracting a number is the same as adding its opposite.

244

244

Adapting to Individual Needs

Challenge
Have students **work in pairs** to simplify each expression.
1. $-(4x − (5x − (2x − 5)))$ $[-x + 5$ or $5 − x]$
2. $-(x − (x − (x − (x − y))))$ $[-y]$

Then have each student write and simplify an expression that has several pairs of "nested" parentheses (similar to those above). Students can exchange expressions with their partners, and check that they have been simplified correctly.

In 23 and 24, use these formulas relating shoe sizes and approximate foot length L in inches. *(Lessons 1-5, 4-3)*

for men: $S = 3L - 26$
for women: $S = 3L - 22$

23. If a man wears a size 10 shoe, about how long are his feet? **12 inches**

24. If a woman wears a size $6\frac{1}{2}$ shoe, about how long are her feet?
9.5 inches

25. A person buys dinner for D dollars and has a 6% tax and a 15% tip (on the dinner only) added to the bill. Express the amount paid in terms of D. *(Lessons 3-1, 4-2)* **1.21 D dollars**

26. A peanut vendor at Bulldog baseball games is paid $15 a game plus $.10 for each bag sold. How many bags must be sold to earn at least $25? *(Lessons 3-8, 3-10)* **at least 100 bags**

27. **a.** Plot the points $A = (-3, 1)$, $B = (0, 4)$, $C = (2, 6)$, and $D = (3, 7)$.
   b. What pattern(s) do you notice in the graph?
   c. What patterns do you see in the coordinates of the points?
   (Lessons 3-3, 3-8) $y = x + 4$
   a) See margin.   b) The points lie along the same line.

28. If the dots continue on a line in the graph at the left, how much would you pay for 20 tapes? Explain how you got your answer.
   (Lesson 3-3) **100 dollars;   Total cost = 5 · number of tapes.**

29. Make a table showing what will be printed when this program is run. *(Lesson 3-3)*

```
10  PRINT "TABLE OF (X, Y) VALUES"
20  PRINT "X VALUE", "Y VALUE"
30  FOR X = 0 TO 5
40  LET Y = 12 - X
50  PRINT X, Y
60  NEXT X
70  END
```

TABLE OF (X, Y) VALUES

X VALUE	Y VALUE
0	12
1	11
2	10
3	9
4	8
5	7

30. *Multiple choice.* What is the measure of the angle drawn at the left? *(Previous course)* **(b)**
   (a) 15°   (b) 45°   (c) 75°   (d) 90°

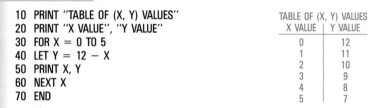

31. The difference of two numbers is subtracted from their sum. What can be said about the answer? Write a short paragraph to explain how you explored this problem. **See left.**

32. A Japanese mathematics textbook for eighth-grade students has the following problem. Try to solve it. $x < \frac{5}{2}$
$$\frac{x - 1}{3} - \frac{2x + 5}{4} > -2$$

Lesson 4-5 *The Opposite of a Sum or Difference* **245**

A baseball tradition.
This peanut vendor is working in Kauffman Stadium, home of the Kansas City Royals.

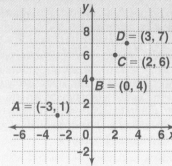

31) Sample: The answer is equal to twice the second number. If x and y are the numbers, then the quantity we want is $x + y - (x - y)$. By the properties of this lesson, that quantity is $x + y - x + y$, or $2y$.

Additional Answers
27a.

$D = (3, 7)$
$C = (2, 6)$
$B = (0, 4)$
$A = (-3, 1)$

Setting Up Lesson 4-6

Materials Students will need graph paper or **Teaching Aid 26** for Lesson 4-6 and for each of the remaining lessons in this chapter.

Be sure you discuss **Questions 28 and 29** because they lead into Lesson 4-6.

Practice

For more questions on SPUR Objectives, use **Lesson Master 4-5A** (shown on page 243) or **Lesson Master 4-5B** (shown on pages 244–245).

Assessment

Written Communication Have each student write a paragraph summarizing what he or she has learned in this lesson. Ask students to tell about two or three skills, properties, or mathematical ideas that they learned previously and which were used in this lesson. [Summaries show an understanding of subtracting quantities and students recognize skills, properties, and ideas presented previously.]

Extension

Have students answer each of the following questions.
1. If a board is cut by making c cuts, how many pieces are there? [$c + 1$ pieces]
2. If x through y are consecutive days in one month, what expression names the number of elapsed days? [$y - x + 1$]

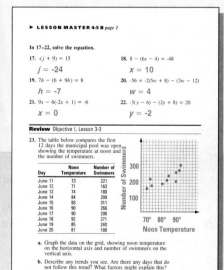

▶ **LESSON MASTER 4-5 B** *page 2*

In 17–22, solve the equation.

17. $-(j + 9) = 15$ 18. $8 - (6x - 4) = -48$
   $j = -24$ $x = 10$

19. $7h - (6 + 9h) = 8$ 20. $-56 = -2(5w + 8) - (3w - 12)$
   $h = -7$ $w = 4$

21. $9x - 6(-2x + 1) = -6$ 22. $-3(y - 6) - (2y + 8) = 20$
   $x = 0$ $y = -2$

Review Objective I, Lesson 3-3

23. The table below compares the first 12 days the municipal pool was open, showing the temperature at noon and the number of swimmers.

Day	Noon Temperature	Number of Swimmers
June 11	73	221
June 12	71	163
June 13	74	180
June 14	84	209
June 15	93	311
June 16	90	266
June 17	90	206
June 18	92	271
June 19	85	240
June 20	81	188

a. Graph the data on the grid, showing noon temperature on the horizontal axis and number of swimmers on the vertical axis.

b. Describe any trends you see. Are there any days that do not follow this trend? What factors might explain this?
Sample: The warmer the temperature, the more swimmers there are; June 11 is an exception; perhaps June 11 was opening day.

Objectives

L Graph equations of the forms $x + y = k$ and $x - y = k$ by making a table of values.

Resources

From the **Teacher's Resource File**
- Lesson Master 4-6A or 4-6B
- Answer Master 4-6
- Teaching Aids
  35 Warm-up
  39 Graphing Equations
  40 Question 27
- Activity Kit, Activity 9
- Teachnology Sourcebook
  Computer Master 11

Additional Resources
- Visuals for Teaching Aids 35, 39, 40

Teaching Lesson 4-6

Warm-up

✎ **Writing** Explain how to plot the ordered pair (a, b) on a coordinate graph. Remember that a and b can be either positive or negative. Students' explanations will vary.

Notes on Reading

Students will need graph paper for this and for many later lessons.
Teaching Aid 39 provides a blank table and coordinate grid. If students use their own graph paper, we suggest that they do the entire assignment on the graph paper. Not only does this ensure that there will be a

LESSON 4-6

Graphing $x + y = k$ and $x - y = k$

No time to loaf. *Bakery inspectors check to ensure that goods meet production standards. If you want to buy five loaves of bread from the bakery—wheat or rye—you can show all of the possibilities by graphing.*

Graphing Constant-Sum Situations

Tim was asked to buy a dozen muffins. He was told to buy only raisin or bran muffins.

At the left below is a table of all the ways he can purchase a dozen muffins. Notice that there are 13 ordered pairs. For example he may buy 0 raisin and 12 bran, or 1 raisin and 11 bran.

The patterns in the table can be described with two variables. If Tim buys R raisin muffins and B bran muffins, then Tim's choices can be described by the equation $R + B = 12$. You could solve for B and write $B = 12 - R$. You could also solve for R and write $R = 12 - B$.

Because the solutions to the equation $R + B = 12$ are ordered pairs, they can be graphed. Below at the right is a graph of Tim's possible choices for a dozen muffins.

❶

R Raisin	B Bran	(R, B) Ordered Pairs
0	12	(0, 12)
1	11	(1, 11)
2	10	(2, 10)
3	9	(3, 9)
4	8	(4, 8)
5	7	(5, 7)
6	6	(6, 6)
7	5	(7, 5)
8	4	(8, 4)
9	3	(9, 3)
10	2	(10, 2)
11	1	(11, 1)
12	0	(12, 0)

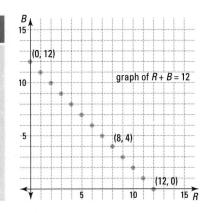

graph of $R + B = 12$

246

Lesson 4-6 Overview

Broad Goals In this lesson, the first on graphing solutions to sentences with two variables, the goal is for students to see how an equation and its graph are related and how points on a graph are determined from an equation. It will be a review for many students.

Perspective *Making a table* is an important problem-solving strategy. Here, it is combined with the strategy of *drawing a graph.*

Both ideas help students find patterns and make generalizations. By the end of the book, students will have seen a variety of tables and graphs that represent important linear and curvilinear patterns. Using mathematics to describe the relationship between two variables is a fundamental component of scientific and statistical methods. This lesson is especially important if students have never graphed lines. The investigation of how the equation of a line

relates to its graph is one of the major topics covered in this book.

In this lesson, we graph only equations of the form $x \pm y = k$. In Lesson 4-9, more linear equations are graphed. Because we first want to have students focus on the basic idea of the graph of an equation, we intentionally delay any discussion of slope and intercepts until Chapter 7.

The points are all on the same line. There are 13 points on the graph because there are 13 combinations of muffins Tim can buy. He cannot buy a fraction of a muffin and he certainly can't have a negative number of muffins.

Suppose you wanted to graph *all the pairs* of numbers x and y whose sum is 12. Then you are graphing $x + y = 12$, where x and y can be any real numbers. The graph includes $(15, -3)$, $(4.5, 7.5)$, and infinitely many other pairs whose sum is 12. The points still all lie in a straight line. The graph of $x + y = 12$ is continuous and is the line through the points $(0, 12)$ and $(12, 0)$.

❷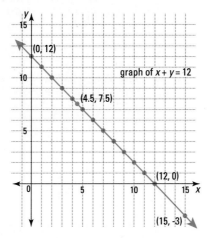

The situations leading to sentences such as $R + B = 12$ or $x + y = 12$ are called *constant-sum* situations. The pairs of numbers change, but the sum is always 12. The graph of any constant-sum situation will look much like the graph above and on page 246.

Graphing Constant-Difference Situations

There are situations in which the difference between two expressions is a constant number. The graph of a *constant-difference* situation is also a line.

Example

Graph all ordered pairs of temperatures which would produce a daily range of 20°.

Solution

Let x equal the maximum daily temperature, and let y equal the minimum daily temperature. Then the range equals x – y.
So x – y = 20.

▶

---

handy place to draw a graph, but it also encourages students to draw neat tables.

Demonstrating how to draw coordinate planes and graphs can use valuable class time. You can use the visual for **Teaching Aid 26** (Graph Paper) or **Teaching Aid 28** (Four-Quadrant Graph Paper) to show students the process. Or, you might want to make your graphs on transparencies in advance. If an automatic grapher with a projection device is available, you may find it more efficient for generating the graphs that you want to show to the class.

❶ This chart describes thirteen ordered pairs. Students may expect there to be twelve ordered pairs, not thirteen. In a counting problem, it is easy to miss one case. For instance, many people would say that there are 30 numbers in the set {60, 61, 62, . . . 90}, but 31 is the correct number. Careful counting and numbering are also important when plotting a display on a computer or a calculator screen. Some computers divide the screen into 40 columns, but they number the columns 0–39.

❷ **Reading Mathematics** Since the relationship between the equation of a line and its graph is so important, encourage students to use the appropriate language associated with them. A solution to a sentence with two variables is an *ordered pair*. The graph of that ordered pair is a *point*. The graph of the set of all solutions is thus a *set of points*, and, in all cases in this lesson, that set of points is a line. We often informally call the graph of all solutions to a sentence the "graph of the sentence." So we say "the graph of $x + y = 12$ is a line," when, specifically, we mean "the graph of the set of all solutions to $x + y = 12$ is a line."

Optional Activities

Activity 1 You can use *Activity Kit, Activity 9,* as an alternate approach to the first situation in Lesson 4-6. This activity explores graphs of the form $x + y = k$.

Activity 2 Technology Connection You may wish to demonstrate how to graph equations using *GraphExplorer* or similar software. You could then assign *Technology Sourcebook, Computer Master 11.* Students enter and graph linear equations, and use

the program's trace feature to locate points on the lines.

Activity 3
Materials: Four-Quadrant Graph Paper or **Teaching Aid 28**

After students have read the lesson, you might have them **work in groups.** Give each group one copy of **Teaching Aid 28.** Then have students write equations of the

form $x + y = k$ and take turns graphing them on the first coordinate plane. For each group, students should select different values of k. Have students describe the lines. [Sample answers: The lines are parallel. All the lines slant downward from left to right. The lines cross the y-axis at different points which correspond to k.] Repeat the process for equations of the form $x - y = k$ using the second coordinate plane.

❸ Students may not realize how many numbers they can choose to be a value of x. To test understanding of this idea, you might ask if x and y must be multiples of 5. [No] Give examples where they are not multiples of 5, such as (47, 27) and (72.5, 52.5) Ask if these points will also be on the graph of the line. [Yes]

Additional Examples

Students might use **Teaching Aid 39** which contains a blank table and coordinate grid.

1. Paula went shopping with x dollars. She spent y dollars, and returned home with $1. Graph all possible pairs (x, y).

Sample ordered pairs and graph for x – y = 1.

x	y
7	6
6	5
4	3
3	2
2	1
1	0

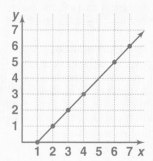

Prepare a table with various values of x and y. You can find some ordered pairs in your head. Think of two numbers whose difference is 20, say 50 and 30. So $x = 50$ and $y = 30$ is one solution. You can find other solutions by choosing a value of x, substituting it into $x - y = 20$, and solving for y. For example, if $x = -30$, then $-30 - y = 20$, and $y = -50$. The ordered pair is (-30, -50). The table below shows six possible ordered pairs.

❸

x	y	(x, y)
50	30	(50, 30)
40	20	(40, 20)
30	10	(30, 10)
10	-10	(10, -10)
-30	-50	(-30, -50)
-5	-25	(-5, -25)

Now plot the ordered pairs as shown in the graph below. Since x and y can be any real number, the graph should include points whose coordinates are fractions and negative numbers. Connect the points to form a line. This line has equation $x - y = 20$.

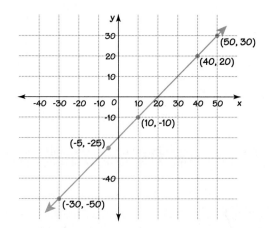

Check

Try a value of x that is not listed in the table. Let $x = 15°$. The corresponding y value on the line appears to be -5°. Do these values satisfy the equation?

$$x - y = 15 - -5 = 20.$$ So, the solution checks.

When the scales on the axes are the same, the lines in constant-sum and constant-difference situations form a 45° angle with the y-axis. Later in this chapter you will study equations for other lines.

Adapting to Individual Needs

Extra Help

Help students think of real-life examples that qualify as constant-sum situations. For example, on a 50-mile trip, the distance traveled plus the distance left to travel always equals 50. Since x and y can be any positive real numbers, the graph is a segment—the part of the line $x + y = 50$ that lies in the first quadrant. Help students to also think of real-life examples of constant-difference situations. For example, a brother and sister were born on the same date, 3 years apart. The difference in their ages will always be 3 years. Here the ages must be positive real numbers.

Covering the Reading

In 1–3, consider the muffin example in this lesson.

1. If Tim buys 10 raisin muffins, how many bran muffins must he buy?
2 bran muffins

2. *True or false.*   The pair (0, 12) is a solution to $R + B = 12$.   **True**

3. a. How many solutions does the equation $R + B = 12$ have?   **13**
   b. How is each solution represented on the graph?   **as a point**

4. Describe the graph of all pairs of real numbers whose sum is 12.
   The graph is a line.

5. The sum of two numbers is 7. $x + y = 7$
   a. Using x and y, write an equation that describes this relationship.
   b. Copy and complete this table to show ordered pairs that satisfy your equation.

x	y	(x, y)
4	3	(4, 3)
3	4	(3, 4)
2	5	(2, 5)
1	6	(1, 6)
0	7	(0, 7)
-1	8	(-1, 8)

   c. Graph all ordered pairs of real numbers whose sum is 7.
   See left.

5c)
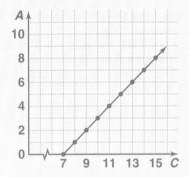

6. Suppose in the Example of this lesson that x has the values as indicated in the table below.

x	y	(x, y)
4	-16	(4, -16)
5	-15	(5, -15)
6	-14	(6, -14)
7.5	-12.5	(7.5, -12.5)

   a. Find the corresponding values of y and (x, y).   **See above.**
   b. Are these points on the line graphed in the Example?   **Yes**

7. Xandra and Yvonne each have earned medals in track-and-field events. Yvonne has 5 more medals than Xandra. Let x = the number of medals Xandra has, and y = the number of medals Yvonne has.
   a. Which equation, $y - x = 5$ or $x + y = 5$, describes this situation?   **$y - x = 5$**
   b. Copy and complete the chart to show some possible numbers of medals for the girls.
   c. Graph the ordered pairs from the chart.   **See margin.**
   d. In this situation does it make sense to connect the points on the graph? Why or why not?   **No.**
   Sample: because they cannot earn a fraction of a medal

x	y	(x, y)
1	6	(1, 6)
2	7	(2, 7)
3	8	(3, 8)
4	9	(4, 9)
5	10	(5, 10)
6	11	(6, 11)

The triple jump. *This athlete is competing in the triple jump. After a hop and a step, the athlete jumps and lands on both feet in a sandpit. The total distance covered is then measured.*

Lesson 4-6   *Graphing $x + y = k$ and $x - y = k$*   **249**

---

2. Carlos is 7 years older than his sister Alicia. Neither one is yet old enough to drive a car. Assuming the minimum driving age is 16, what are all the possible ages for Carlos and Alicia?
   a. Make a table of values for (C, A).

C	7	8	9	10	11	12	13	14	15
A	0	1	2	3	4	5	6	7	8

   b. Graph all the possible pairs (C, A).

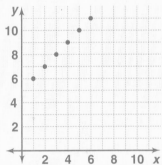

Additional Answers
7c.

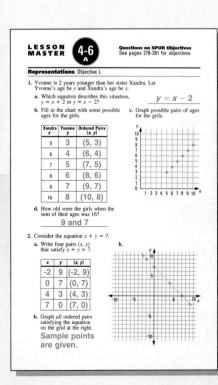

Adapting to Individual Needs

English Language Development

Be certain students understand the meaning of the word *constant* as something that does not change. For example, the total number of people on a 12-person jury is a constant, but the number of men m and women w on a jury varies or changes from trial to trial. For instance, one jury may have 7 men and 5 women, while another has 8 women and 4 men. The equation $m + w = 12$, where 12 is the constant term and m and w are variables, describes all instances. Then have students **work in groups** and direct each group to list other examples where the sum is *constant* and the pair of addends can change.

Questions 8 and 9b These questions are intended to lay the groundwork for some ideas that will be used in Chapter 11 with systems of equations. Note that there are many ordered pairs which satisfy the first condition but that including the second condition narrows the possibilities down to one pair. Or, one could begin with the second condition, and narrow it down with the first one. Mention the connection with intersection of sets.

Questions 11–12 To answer these questions, students must work backward. That is, students should read coordinates of points on the graph, and then check that they satisfy the equation.

Additional Answers

9a.

Sal	Al
1	7
2	6
3	5
4	4
5	3
6	2
7	1

Red-eyes. *This tropical fish is known as the red-spotted cardinal. It can be found in the warm waters of the Indian Ocean.*

10b)

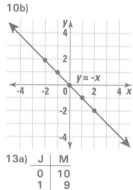

$y = -x$

13a)

J	M
0	10
1	9
2	8
3	7
4	6
5	5
6	4
7	3
8	2
9	1
10	0

13b)

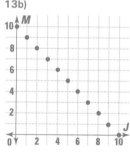

250

---

8. In the muffin example, suppose Tim buys twice as many bran muffins as raisin muffins. Which ordered pair fits this situation? (4, 8)

9. Sal and Al each have tropical fish. Together they have eight fish.
   a. Make a table listing all possible number pairs of fish Sal and Al may have. See margin.
   b. If Sal has two more fish than Al, how many fish does Al have? 3

10. a. Copy and complete the chart below to show ordered pairs (x, y) in which the y-coordinate is the opposite of the x-coordinate.

x	y	(x, y)
-2	2	(-2, 2)
-1	1	(-1, 1)
0	0	(0, 0)
1	-1	(1, -1)
2	-2	(2, -2)

   b. On a coordinate plane, graph all ordered pairs of real numbers for which $y = -x$. See left.
   c. Write an equation which shows that this is a constant-sum situation. $x + y = 0$

In 11 and 12, identify all listed equations that describe the points graphed.

11. 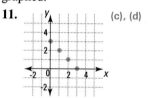 (c), (d)

   (a) $y = 3x$
   (b) $y = x + 3$
   (c) $y = 3 - x$
   (d) $3 = x + y$

12. 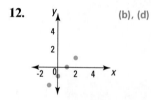 (b), (d)

   (a) $x + y = 1$
   (b) $x - y = 1$
   (c) $y - x = 1$
   (d) $y = x - 1$

13. Calvin is giving 10 cassettes to Jorge and Maria. See left.
   a. Make a table showing the possible ways to divide the cassettes.
   b. Graph the possibilities with the number of Jorge's cassettes on the horizontal axis and the number of Maria's cassettes on the vertical axis.

14. Make up a situation that leads to an equation of the form $x + y = 20$ in which x and y may be fractions. Sample: Jack spent x dollars the same day that Joyce spent y dollars. Together they spent 20 dollars.

Adapting to Individual Needs

Challenge
Some calendars list number pairs alongside each calendar date. For example, 33/332 is listed alongside February 2 in one such calendar. Have students explain the meaning of these number pairs, and then write a general equation connecting the numbers in each pair. [The first number is the number of days that have elapsed in the year, and the second number is the number of days remaining in the year. If the number pair is denoted as x/y, then $x + y = 365$.] Then have students write a similar equation for a leap year calendar. [$x + y = 366$] Finally, ask students how the graphs for the two equations would differ. [The graphs would be parallel lines, but for each value of x, the corresponding y value for the second line is always one more than for the first.]

In 15 and 16, simplify. *(Lesson 4-5)*

15. $12a - 3(5a + 4)$ $-3a - 12$

16. $\frac{11n + 1}{5} - \frac{3n + 4}{5}$ $\frac{8n - 3}{5}$

17. Distances after various times when traveling at 55 mph are shown on the spreadsheet at the right. *(Lessons 1-5, 2-4, 4-4)*
   a. Complete the table.
   b. What formula could have been used to get the value in cell B6? $= A6 * 55$

	A	B
1	Time (hrs)	Distance (mi)
2	1.0	55
3	1.5	82.5
4	2.0	110
5	2.5	137.5
6	3.0	165
7	3.5	192.5

In 18 and 19, solve. *(Lessons 4-3, 4-5)*

18. $16 - 5x = 21$ $x = -1$

19. $y - (7 - 4y) = 11$ $y = \frac{18}{5}$

20. The table below gives the maximum and minimum temperatures on four continents. *(Lesson 4-2)*

continent	maximum temp.	minimum temp.
Africa	58°C; El Azizia, Libya	-24°C; Ifrane, Morocco
Australia	53°C; Cloncurry, Queensland	-22°C; Charlottes Pass, N.S.W.
North America	57°C; Death Valley, CA, U.S.A.	-63°C; Snag, Yukon, Canada
South America	49°C; Rivadavia, Argentina	-33°C; Sarmiento, Argentina

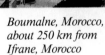

Boumalne, Morocco, about 250 km from Ifrane, Morocco

   a. Which of these continents has the smallest range of temperatures?
   b. Which of these continents has the largest range of temperatures?
   a) Australia; b) North America

In 21 and 22, use the following information. A factory packs mixed 5-pound packages of peanuts and cashews. If c pounds of cashews are in a package, the price p of the package can be found using the formula

$$p = 2.39c + 1.69(5 - c).$$

21. If a package contains 1.5 pounds of cashews, find its price. *(Lesson 1-5)* $9.50

22. If a package costs $9.95, how many pounds of cashews does it contain? *(Lesson 3-7)* about 2.14 pounds

23. *Skill sequence.* Evaluate in your head when $x = 10$. *(Lesson 1-4)*
   a. x^3 1000
   b. $2x^3$ 2000
   c. $\left(\frac{1}{2}x\right)^3$ 125

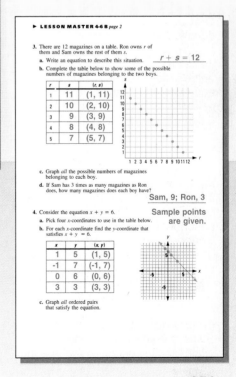

Question 25 Supplementary angles are used in Lesson 4-7.

Question 26 Multicultural Connection Technically, the Jewish and Gregorian calendar year numbers (*J, G*) do not lie exactly on a line because the years start on different days, and the Jewish year is not always 365 or 366 days long. But they are never more than 1 unit off of a line, and the question still has meaning.

Cooperative Learning For **part c,** you might have students **work in groups** with each group investigating another kind of calendar. Then have each group report their findings to the class.

✎ **Question 27 Writing** You might use **Teaching Aid 40** which provides some guidelines for answering this question. [See below for answers to the teaching aid.]

<table>
<tr><td>**Follow-up**
for Lesson</td><td>**4-6**</td></tr>
</table>

Practice

For more questions on SPUR Objectives, use **Lesson Master 4-6A** (shown on page 249) or **Lesson Master 4-6B** (shown on pages 250–251).

Assessment

Oral Communication Write the equation $x + y = 15$ on the board. Ask students to describe situations that lead to this equation, and to name ordered pairs that satisfy the equation. [Students name ordered pairs that are appropriate for the situations they describe.]

Extension

Show students a graph in which all the points lie on a horizontal line. Then ask them if either $x + y = k$ or $x - y = k$ can be used to describe the graph. [No; no] Ask what equation could be used. [$y = k$] Then ask the same questions for a graph in which all the points lie on a vertical line. [The equation is of the form $x = k$.]

Project Update Project 6, *Angle Sums in Polygons,* on page 275, relates to the content of this lesson.

---

24. At 3:00, what is the measure of the angle between the hands of a clock? *(Previous course)* **90°**

25. The top of a portable computer swings up 120° from the keyboard. What is the angle *b* between the top and the back of the case? *(Previous course)* **60°**

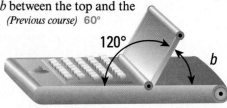

120° ... *b*

Exploration

26a) Subtract: 5755 – 1995 = 3760. Add 3760 to obtain the Jewish year. 1066 + 3760 = 4826 in the Jewish calendar.

26. **a.** The year 1995 roughly corresponds to the year 5755 in the Jewish calendar. The Norman conquest of England occurred in 1066. What year is 1066 in the Jewish calendar? See left.
   b. If you graph ordered pairs (*J, G*), where *J* is the year in the Jewish calendar and *G* the year in the Gregorian calendar (the official one in the United States), the graph is a line. Does the line slant up or down as you go to the right? up
   c. Look in an almanac or other reference book. What other calendars are there? Sample: Islamic, Chinese, Julian

27. This graph for the number of Democrats and Republicans in the U.S. Senate is almost perfectly symmetric; that is, the graphs are nearly reflection images of each other. Write an explanation for what causes this. The sum of the Democrats and Republicans in the U.S. Senate is usually 100.

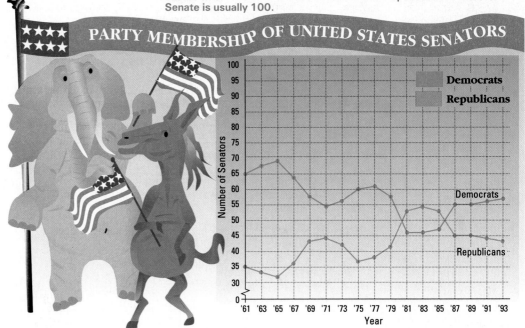

252

Airport angles. *The sum of the measures x and y of the angles in the above runway is 180°.*

Two Angles Whose Sum Is 180°

Constant sums occur in many places in geometry. In each picture below, the pendulum makes two angles with the crossbar of the clock. As the pendulum swings, the measures x and y of the angles between the pendulum and the horizontal frame vary. But the sum of the measures of the angles is always 180°. That is, $x + y = 180$.

Often it is useful to solve the equation for y.

$$x + y = 180$$
$$-x + x + y = 180 + -x$$
$$0 + y = 180 + -x$$
$$y = 180 - x$$

So if x is known, y can be found by subtracting x from 180.

Lesson 4-7 *Sums and Differences in Geometry* **253**

Lesson 4-7

Objectives

F Use the definitions of supplements and complements, and the Triangle Sum Theorem.

Resources

From the *Teacher's Resource File*

- Lesson Master 4-7A or 4-7B
- Answer Master 4-7
- Assessment Sourcebook: Quiz for Lessons 4-5 through 4-7
- Teaching Aids
  35 Warm-up
  41 Activity and Question 32

Additional Resources

- Visuals for Teaching Aids 35, 41
- Protractors or **Geometry Templates**

Teaching
Lesson 4-7

Warm-up

Diagnostic Fill in the blanks.
1. The sum of the measures of two angles is 90°. The angles are _____ angles.
   complementary
2. A triangle has a 90° angle. It is called a _____ triangle. **right**
3. The sum of the angle measures in any triangle is _____. **180°**
4. The sum of the measures of two angles is 180°. The angles are _____ angles.
   supplementary

The answers for *Warm-up* are terms used in Lesson 4-7. Accept other answers, such as *acute* for Question 1 and *right* for Question 4, if students explain their reasoning.

Lesson 4-7 Overview

Broad Goals Four important geometric concepts are covered in this lesson—the definitions of *supplementary angles* and *complementary angles,* the Triangle Sum Property, and the convention for marking right angles. Most students have studied these concepts before; they should master them now.

Perspective Supplementary angles, complementary angles, and the Triangle Sum

Property are rich sources of algebra questions because they are instances of the constant-sum model:
    $a + b$ = constant.
As the development at the beginning of the lesson shows, solving for b gives
    b = constant $- a$.
The definition in this book for *supplementary angles* does not explicitly state that 0° and 180° could be the measures of supplementary angles. The graph in the lesson

does not include the points (180, 0) and (0, 180). However, some books define angles with measure 180° and 0° and would, therefore, permit these two points.

Both the words *complement* and *supplement* mean to fill out something: a complement fills out a right angle; a supplement fills out a straight angle. But neither complementary angles nor supplementary angles have to be located next to each other.

Students will need protractors or **Geometry Templates** for this lesson.

Reading Mathematics Go over the vocabulary carefully. To help students distinguish between complementary and supplementary, note that the terms are presented in alphabetical order, and that 90 and 180 are in increasing order.

❶ Take advantage of the two scales on protractors to show measures of linear pairs (adjacent supplementary angles). When the protractor is in position, the measure of one angle can be read from one scale and its linear pair from the other scale. A clear plastic protractor can be used directly on an overhead projector.

❷ You might use the suggestions in *Optional Activities* below in place of, or in addition to, this activity.

Activity Students can use **Teaching Aid 41** which contains the triangles given in the activity and space for drawing other triangles.

❸ **Error Alert** Some students may think that the *three* angles in a triangle are supplementary because the sum of the three measures is 180°. Emphasize that being supplementary (or being complementary) is a property of exactly *two* angles.

a) m∠A = 53°,
m∠B = 53°,
m∠C = 74°;
m∠P = 17°,
m∠Q = 140°,
m∠R = 23°.
53 + 53 + 74 = 180;
17 + 140 + 23 = 180.

b) Triangles will vary.
The sum of the angle measures should be 180°.

Example 1

Using the angles shown on page 253, find *y* if *x* is 128°.

Solution 1

$$y = 180 - x$$
$$= 180 - 128$$
$$= 52$$

❶ **Solution 2**

$$x + y = 180$$
$$128 + y = 180 \quad \text{Substitute 128 for } x.$$
$$y = 52 \quad \text{Solve for } y.$$

Two angles whose sum is 180° are quite common, so they are given a name: **supplementary angles** or simply **supplements.**

Below is a table of measures of some supplementary angles. If the pairs of possible measures of supplementary angles are graphed, they lie on the part of the line $x + y = 180$ that is in the first quadrant. Below on the right is a graph of these pairs. The points from the table are identified. Because the measure of an angle is always positive, neither (0, 180) nor (180, 0) is on the graph.

x	y
40	140
90	90
128	52
⋮	⋮

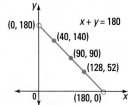

The Sum of Angle Measures in a Triangle

Another constant-sum situation involves triangles.

Activity

a. Measure all the angles in each triangle below, and find the sum of the angle measures.

❷ b. Draw another triangle of a different size and shape. Measure its angles and find the sum of its angle measures.

c. What patterns do you notice? The sum of the measures of the angles of any triangle seems to be 180°.

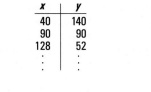

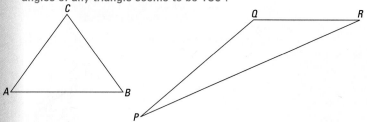

254

Optional Activities

Using Physical Models
Materials: Scissors, protractors or **Geometry Templates**

You can use this activity in place of, or in addition to, the activity on page 254 of the lesson. Have each student draw a large triangle on a piece of paper and then cut the triangle out. Then have them measure the angles of the triangle to confirm the Triangle Sum Property. Ask if any student has found

a sum that is not 180°. Check that student's measuring techniques.

To show the Triangle Sum Property in another way, have students label the measures of the angles $a°$, $b°$, and $c°$. Then have them tear the triangle into three parts and reassemble it to form a straight angle, which has a measure of 180°.

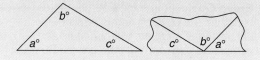

In a triangle, regardless of its shape or size, the sum of the measures of the three angles is 180. This gives a constant sum with three variables.

③ Triangle Sum Theorem
In any triangle with angle measures *a*, *b*, and *c* in degrees,
$$a + b + c = 180.$$

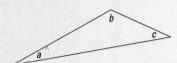

Using this theorem, if you know the measures of two angles of a triangle, you can find the measure of the third angle.

Example 2

Find the measure of the third angle in a triangle whose other angles measure 51° and 19°.

Solution
Use the Triangle Sum Theorem.
$$51 + 19 + x = 180$$
$$70 + x = 180$$
$$x = 110$$

Because the numbers in Example 2 are easy to add, some people solve it without paper or pencil. In Example 3, the relation between the angles is more complicated.

To save space, the following symbols are often used.

△	triangle
∠	angle
m∠	measure of angle

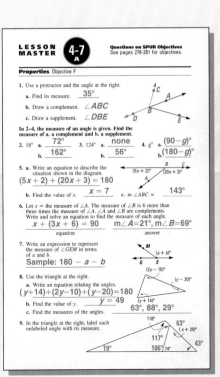

Adapting to Individual Needs

Extra Help
Students should understand that if the sum of two angle measures is 90° and one of them is x°, then the other is 90° − x°. Some students may not understand how subtraction arises from a constant-sum situation. To help them, call on one student to pick an angle measure between 0° and 90°. Then ask another student to give the measure of its complement. Do this four or five times so that students can see that subtracting from 90° results in the answer. Next, do the same activity for supplements. Finally, ask for the generalization: If the sum of two numbers is S and if one of the numbers is a, what is the other number? [S − a] How do we know this? [a + (S − a) = S]

④ Students need to understand that if two numbers add to 90, and one of them is *x*, then the other is 90 − *x*. If students have trouble with this idea, see *Extra Help* in *Adapting to Individual Needs* on page 255.

Additional Examples

1. If $x + y = 180$ and $x = 83.7$, find *y*. **96.3**
2. Find the measure of the third angle in a triangle if the other two angles measure 32° and 123°, respectively. **25°**
3. The measures of the angles of a triangle are *c*, 2*c*, and 3*c*. Find the measure of each angle. **30°, 60°, and 90°**
4. If the measures of complementary angles are *x* and *y*, write an equation relating *x* and *y*. **$x + y = 90$**
5. What is the measure of a supplement of a right angle? **90°**

Notes on Questions

Questions 9–11 Some students will be able to answer these questions without having to write and solve equations. Remind these students that they could have done the problems using algebra.

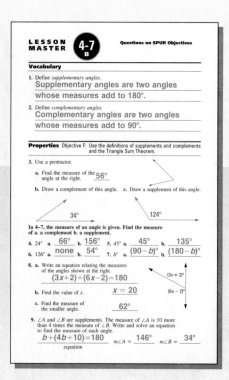

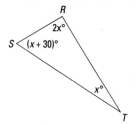

Example 3

In △*RST* at the left, the angles have measures as shown. Find the measure of each angle.

Solution

By the Triangle Sum Theorem, we have the following:
$$x + 2x + (x + 30) = 180$$
$$4x + 30 = 180$$
$$4x = 150$$
$$\tfrac{1}{4}(4x) = \tfrac{1}{4}(150)$$
$$x = 37.5$$

So, $m\angle T = 37.5°$,
$m\angle R = 2x° = 2(37.5°) = 75°$,
$m\angle S = (x + 30)° = (37.5 + 30)° = 67.5°$.

Two Angles Whose Sum Is 90°

Recall that in a right triangle one of the angles measures 90°. In drawings, a 90° angle is often marked with the symbol ⌐.

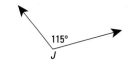

x ④

Example 4

Write a formula for *y* in terms of *x* in the triangle at the left.

Solution

Triangle Sum Theorem $y + x + 90 = 180$
Solve for *y* and simplify. $y = 180 + -90 + -x$
    $y = 90 - x$

Two angles are **complementary angles,** or **complements,** if the sum of their measures is 90°. In Example 4, the angles with measures *y* and *x* are complements.

QUESTIONS

Covering the Reading

6a) $m\angle A = 53°$, $m\angle B = 53°$, $m\angle C = 74°$; $m\angle P = 17°$, $m\angle Q = 140°$, $m\angle R = 23°$

In 1–3, use the drawing at the right.
1. Write an equation that relates *y* and *x*. $x + y = 180$
2. If $x = 42°$, what is *y*? **138°**   3. Find *x* if *y* is 137.5°. $x = 42.5°$
4. If $m\angle F = 58°$ and $m\angle G = 132°$, are $\angle F$ and $\angle G$ supplementary? Explain your reasoning. No, because 58° + 132° ≠ 180°
5. Find the measure of a supplement of $\angle J$, shown at the left. **65°**
6. **a.** What are the measures of each angle in the triangles in the Activity?
   b. Describe how your results are related to the Triangle Sum Theorem.
   b) They are instances of the Triangle Sum Theorem.

256

Adapting to Individual Needs

English Language Development
To help students understand the meanings of *complementary* and *supplementary,* write various angle measures between 0° and 180° on index cards. Then write these sentences on the board:

The supplement of _____ is _____ because the sum of these measures is _____.

The complement of _____ is _____ because the sum of these measures is _____.

Have students take turns picking a card, showing it to the class, and filling in the appropriate blanks. Then have them read the sentence or sentences aloud. Note that for angles with measures less than 90°, students can give both a complementary- and a supplementary-angle measure. For angles with measures greater than or equal to 90°, they can give a supplementary-angle measure.

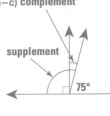
A leap of faith. *After sliding down a steep track, Olympic ski jumpers leap more than 90 meters in the air. Jumpers such as the one shown are scored on their style as well as on the distance of the leap.*

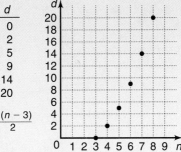

7. Find the measure of the third angle in a triangle whose other angles measure 114° and 46°. **20°**

8. Two angles of a triangle have measures of 37° and 53°.
   a. Find the measure of the third angle. **90°**
   b. What kind of triangle is this triangle? **right triangle**

In 9–11, find the value of the variable.

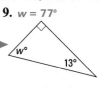
9. $w = 77°$

10. $x = 72°$

11. $d = 24°$

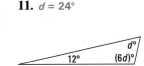

12. *True or false.* 65° and 25° are measures of complementary angles. **True**
13. If $m\angle Q$ is 29°, what is the measure of a complement? **61°**

Applying the Mathematics

14. a. Give the measures of five pairs of complementary angles.
   b. Graph your pairs on the coordinate plane.
   c. Show the possible measures of all pairs of complementary angles on your graph. **a) See left. b–c) See margin.**
   d. Find an equation to describe the graph in part **c.** $x + y = 90$

15. Angles *A* and *B* are complementary. If $m\angle A = x$, write an expression to represent the measure of $\angle B$. $m\angle B = 90 - x$

16. a. Use a protractor to draw a 75° angle. **a–c) See left.**
   b. Draw a complement of the angle in part **a.**
   c. Draw a supplement of the angle in part **a.**
   d. How much greater is the measure of the supplement than the measure of the complement? **90° more**

17. To achieve a long jump, a ski jumper needs to lean forward quite a bit, as shown in the photo. The angle formed by the jumper's legs and the front part of the skis measures 15°. Describe and find the measure of another angle in this situation. **Sample: The angle formed by the jumper's legs and the back part of the skis measures 165°.**

18. When a light ray strikes a smooth surface, the light ray is reflected so that the measure of the angle of incidence (*i*) equals the measure of the angle of reflection (*r*). Refer to the diagram at the left. If $i = 32°$, find the angle measures *x* and *y*. $x = 58°;\quad y = 58°$

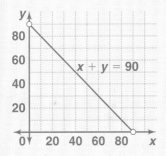
mirror

19. Two angles in a triangle have equal measure; the third measure is 12° less than either of the others. Find the measure of each angle.
64°, 64°, 52°

20. a. What is the measure of $\angle BIG$ at the left?
   b. What is the measure of $\angle ZIG$ at the left?
   a) 98.5° b) 81.5°

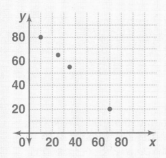

21. Refer to the triangle at the right. Write a formula to determine $m\angle C$ in terms of $m\angle A$ and $m\angle B$.
$m\angle C = 180 - m\angle A - m\angle B$

Adapting to Individual Needs

Challenge
Explain that a *diagonal* of a polygon is a segment that joins one vertex to another, but it is not a side of the polygon. Then give students the following problems.
1. Find the number of diagonals that can be drawn from one vertex of a polygon with *n* sides. [$n - 3$]
2. Graph (*n*, *d*) where n is the number of sides of a polygon and *d* is the total number of diagonals of the polygon.

n	d
3	0
4	2
5	5
6	9
7	14
8	20

$d = \dfrac{n(n-3)}{2}$

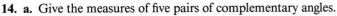

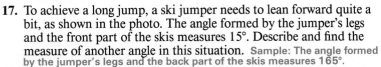
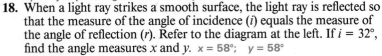
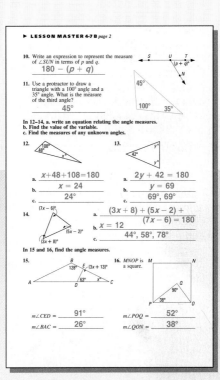
257

Notes on Questions

Question 32 Teaching Aid 41 provides the diagram for this question. While each of the four corners at an intersection could count as a different location for the theater, we do not count the additional distance one would have to travel to cross the street. Most students are surprised to learn that if J and M were points in a field and there were no streets, the points where the sum of the distances to J and M is 6 lie on an ellipse. You might want to give students similar problems by changing the distance or the locations of J and M.

Follow-up for Lesson 4-7

Practice

For more questions on SPUR Objectives, use **Lesson Master 4-7A** (shown on page 255) or **Lesson Master 4-7B** (shown on pages 256–257).

Assessment

Quiz A quiz covering Lessons 4-5 through 4-7 is provided in the *Assessment Sourcebook*.

Group Assessment Have students **work in small groups**. Ask one student in each group to give the measures of two angles of a triangle, another student to write an equation to find the measure of the third angle, another student to solve the equation, and another student to check that the solution is correct. Repeat the activity several times with students changing roles. [Angle choices and work with equations show understanding of the Triangle Sum Theorem and its algebraic applications.]

Extension

Have each student draw a circle with diameter $\overline{AB}$. Then have students pick one other point P on the circle, and measure angles A, B, and P. Have them repeat the process several times and then make a generalization. $[m\angle A + m\angle B = m\angle P = 90]$

258

22a) Sample:

savings	checking
2	23
5	20
8	17
21	4
22	3

22c)

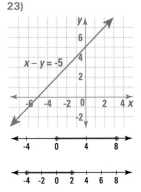

23)

29a)

time	charge
$\frac{1}{2}$ hr	$70
1 hr	$90
$1\frac{1}{2}$ hr	$110
2 hr	$130
$2\frac{1}{2}$ hr	$150
3 hr	$170

30)

$-4 \le x \le 8$

31)

$0 \le x \le 2$

258

Review

22. Gordon puts $25 in the bank each week. He puts some of the money in his savings account and some in his checking account.
   a. Make a table showing 5 possibilities of his savings and checking deposits. **See left.**
   b. Write this situation as a constant-sum equation. Let $x =$ amount in savings, and $y =$ amount in checking. $x + y = 25$
   c. Graph the possibilities. *(Lesson 4-6)* **See left.**

23. Graph all solutions to $x - y = -5$. *(Lesson 4-6)* **See left.**

In 24 and 25, solve. *(Lessons 3-10, 4-5)*

24. $50 + x > 30$ $x > -20$

25. $12n + 5 - (2n + 20) = -20$ $n = -\frac{1}{2}$

26. *Multiple choice.* Which is not equal to $w + -k$? *(Lesson 4-1)* (b)
   (a) $w - k$ (b) $k - w$ (c) $-k + w$

In 27 and 28, simplify. *(Lessons 3-9, 4-1)*

27. $\frac{1}{2}x - \frac{1}{3}x - \frac{3}{4}x$ $-\frac{7}{12}x$

28. $\frac{y}{2} - \frac{y}{3} - \frac{3y}{4}$ $-\frac{7}{12}y$

29. Suppose the cost to repair a refrigerator is $50 for the service call plus $20 for each half hour of labor.
   a. Make a table showing total charges for repairs which take $\frac{1}{2}$, 1, $1\frac{1}{2}$, 2, $2\frac{1}{2}$, and 3 hours. **See left.**
   b. Write a formula which gives the total cost c in terms of the number n of half-hour periods. *(Lesson 3-8)* $c = 50 + 20n$

In 30 and 31, consider the two segments pictured at the left. *(Lesson 1-3)*

30. Draw their union, and describe it with an inequality. **See left.**

31. Draw their intersection and describe it with an inequality. **See left.**

Exploration

32. Below is a map of Centerville. John lives at the corner marked J. His friend Mary lives by the corner marked M. John and Mary each walk to the theater. The sum of the distances they walk is 6 blocks. Copy the diagram and show all possible locations of the theater. The theater could be on any corner of any of the intersections marked in red on the diagram.

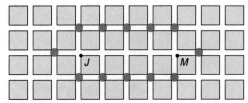

Setting Up Lesson 4-8

Materials If you plan to use the activity in *Extra Help* on page 262, you will need a yardstick and a 12-inch ruler. Students doing Activity 2 in *Optional Activities* on page 261 will need a road atlas of the United States.

The Triangle Inequality

IN-CLASS
ACTIVITY

In-class Activity
Resources
From the *Teacher's Resource File*
- Answer Master 4-8
- Teaching Aid 42: The Triangle Inequality

Additional Resources
- Visual for Teaching Aid 42
- Rulers or **Geometry Templates**, straws

The purpose of this activity is to help students see the Triangle Inequality in a concrete way. The key new concept is the notion that a formula with an inequality symbol can have some meaning.

Work in small groups. Cut straws into the following lengths:
1 in., 2 in., 2 in., 3 in., 3 in., 4 in., 5 in., 6 in.
Then make a table like the one shown below.

1 Place the three straws listed in each of parts **a–h** on your desk. With the straws touching only at the ends, try to make a triangle. In the second column of the table below, indicate whether you could make a triangle.

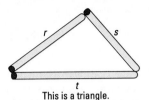

This is a triangle.   This is not a triangle.

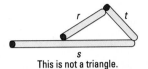

	Length of Straws			Triangle? (Yes or No)	Compare, Use <, >, or = $r+s \overset{?}{\_} t$	$s+t \overset{?}{\_} r$	$r+t \overset{?}{\_} s$
	r	*s*	*t*				
a.	1 in.	2 in.	2 in.	Yes	>	>	>
b.	3 in.	3 in.	6 in.	No	=	>	>
c.	3 in.	6 in.	1 in.	No	>	>	<
d.	2 in.	3 in.	4 in.	Yes	>	>	>
e.	2 in.	2 in.	3 in.	Yes	>	>	>
f.	5 in.	2 in.	3 in.	No	>	=	>
g.	3 in.	4 in.	5 in.	Yes	>	>	>
h.	1 in.	2 in.	5 in.	No	<	>	>

Now complete the last three columns of the table in which the sum of the lengths of two sides is compared to the length of the third side. Discuss the results with your group.

2 *Draw conclusions.* Complete the following statement using one of the following:
less than, greater than, or *the same as.*
The sum of the lengths of two sides of any triangle must be _?_ the length of the third side. **greater than**

259

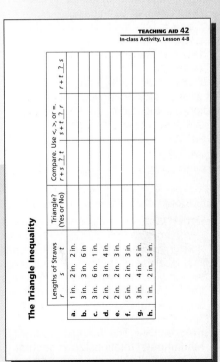

Objectives

G Use the Triangle Inequality to determine possible lengths of sides of triangles.

J Apply the Triangle Inequality in real situations.

Resources

From the *Teacher's Resource File*
- Lesson Master 4-8A or 4-8B
- Answer Master 4-8
- Teaching Aids
  36 Warm-up
  43 Example 1
  44 Additional Examples
  45 Question 24

Additional Resources
- Visual for Teaching Aids 36, 43–45

Teaching Lesson 4-8

Warm-up

Mr. Smith is going to the hardware store and then to the grocery store. After shopping for groceries, he is going home. He lives 6 miles from the hardware store and 5 miles from the grocery store. Sketch the location of Mr. Smith's home and the two stores for each case.

Case 1: Mr. Smith's trip is as short as possible.

Case 2: Mr. Smith's trip is as long as possible.

Case 3: Mr. Smith's trip is somewhere between the shortest and longest trip. **Sample sketches are given on page 261.**

4-8

The Triangle Inequality

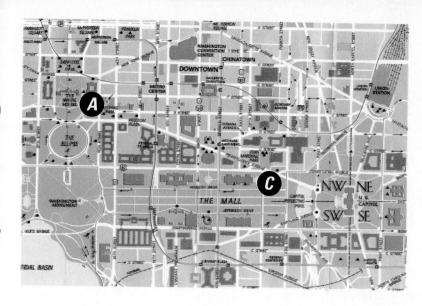

Some students are visiting Washington, D.C. They have just toured the White House, and are standing where point A is located on the map. Their next tour is at the U.S. Capitol building. They agree to split into small groups and to meet in an hour at the Mall on the corner of Pennsylvania Avenue and 4th Street, point C on the map. Notice that the students have their choice of many paths from A to C.

❶ What Is the Triangle Inequality?

A fundamental property of distance is that the shortest path from A to C is along the line segment connecting points A and C. We denote that segment as $\overline{AC}$ and its length as the number AC. On the map $\overline{AC}$ corresponds to the direct route from A to C along Pennsylvania Avenue.

Suppose each group decides to stop for lunch at some point B. Now compare the distance AC with the length of a path from point A to a selected point B and then to point C, where B is any point other than A or C. There are two possibilities, as shown.

(1) B is on $\overline{AC}$.

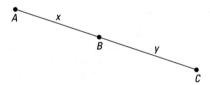

Then $AB + BC = AC$
$x + y = AC$

Lesson 4-8 Overview

Broad Goals This lesson continues to present formulas that involve addition (and, by solving for one of the variables, formulas that involve subtraction). The goal of this lesson is to familiarize students with a most important inequality from geometry—the Triangle Inequality.

Perspective The Triangle Inequality is a fundamental relationship in geometry and in advanced mathematics. At the same time, it

is the algebraic description of the popular adage "The shortest distance between two points is a straight line." The two parts of the inequality presented on page 261 represent the case where the three points are allowed to lie on the same line (Part 1), and the case where the three points are not on the same line (Part 2).

Despite the obviousness of the adage, the problems do not at first strike students as

trivial. Therefore, they view the solving of the inequality as a true help and not merely as a difficult way of doing something that they could solve in their heads. However, once the inequalities have been solved once or twice, most students quickly see the pattern that is represented in the Third Side Property. This illustrates the use of algebra—in this case the solving of a system of inequalities—to *find* patterns, not just to *describe* them.

(2) *B* is not on $\overline{AC}$.

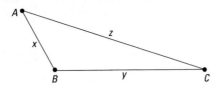

Then $AB + BC > AC$

$\qquad x + y > z$

That is, if you stop for lunch at any point *B* that is not between *A* and *C* on Pennsylvania Avenue, you will be going out of your way.

These ideas are summarized in the following general properties, known together as the *Triangle Inequality*.

> **Triangle Inequality**
> **Part 1:** If *A, B,* and *C* are any three points, then $AB + BC \geq AC$.
>
> **Part 2:** If *A, B,* and *C* are vertices of a triangle, then $AB + BC > AC$.

Part 2 of the Triangle Inequality can be stated as follows: the sum of the lengths of two sides of any triangle is greater than the length of the third side. This is the relation you found in the Activity on page 259.

In $\triangle ABC$ as drawn above with sides of length *x, y,* and *z,* the following three inequalities are true:

$$x + y > z \qquad \text{and} \qquad x + z > y \qquad \text{and} \qquad y + z > x.$$

How Is the Triangle Inequality Used?

A surprising application of the Triangle Inequality is that you can calculate the possible lengths of the third side of a triangle if you know the lengths of the other two sides.

Example 1

Suppose two sides of a triangle have lengths 42 and 30. What are the possible lengths of the third side?

Solution 1

Draw a picture, naming the sides *x, y,* and *z*.

By the Triangle Inequality, the following are true:

$$x + y > z \qquad \text{and} \qquad x + z > y \qquad \text{and} \qquad y + z > x.$$

▶

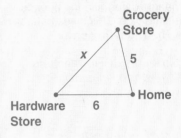

Pennsylvania Avenue.
Shown is a view of the Capitol Building as seen from the White House along Pennsylvania Avenue.

Case 1:

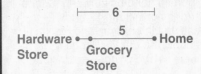

Case 2:

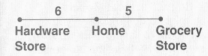

Case 3:

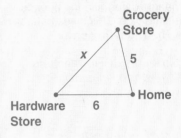

$0 < x < 11$

Notes on Reading

❶ History Connection In 1792, when the federal government wanted a design for the U.S. Capitol building, it held a contest. William Thornton, a doctor who was also an amateur architect, submitted the winning entry. The cornerstone for the building Thornton designed was laid in 1793. Congress met in the Capitol for the first time in 1800.

261

❷ Make sure students realize that the phrase "lengths between 12 and 72" does not include 12 and 72. Recall that in general, and also in this book, the phrase "lengths between *a* and *b*" does not include either *a* or *b*. To include 12 and 72, we say "from 12 to 72."

❸ **Using Physical Models**
You might use the door of your classroom to illustrate **Example 1,** Solution 2. By this time, students may already know that the sum and difference of the lengths of two sides of a triangle determine the bounds on the third side. This leads naturally to the Third Side Property.

You might want to use **Teaching Aid 43** which contains *Solution 2*.

Now substitute 42 for *x* and 30 for *y*, and solve the three inequalities.

$$42 + 30 > z \quad \text{and} \quad 42 + z > 30 \quad \text{and} \quad 30 + z > 42$$
$$z < 72 \quad \text{and} \quad z > \text{-}12 \quad \text{and} \quad z > 12$$

The solution to the problem is the intersection of these three inequalities.

❷

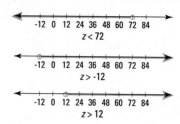

This indicates that *z* is between 12 and 72. The third side can have lengths between 12 and 72.

Solution 2
Imagine that the side of length 42 is a wall and the side of length 30 is a door. The segment that connects their ends along the floor is the third side of a triangle. Imagine how that length changes as the door swings.

❸

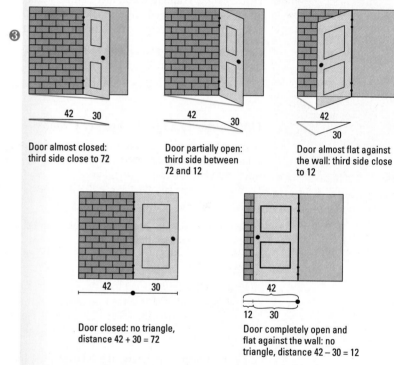

Door almost closed: third side close to 72

Door partially open: third side between 72 and 12

Door almost flat against the wall: third side close to 12

Door closed: no triangle, distance 42 + 30 = 72

Door completely open and flat against the wall: no triangle, distance 42 − 30 = 12

So when a triangle is formed, the length of the third side is between 12 and 72.

262

Adapting to Individual Needs

Extra Help
Materials: Yardstick and 12-inch ruler

The Triangle Inequality can be demonstrated using a 12-inch ruler and a yardstick. Hold the yardstick so that one end is resting on a desk or table. Hold one end of the ruler against the top end of the yardstick. Tell students you want to find how far apart the other ends could be. Rotate the ruler up so that it forms a straight line with the yard

stick. Help students see that the distance between the ends is 36 in. + 12 in. = 48 in. Then rotate the ruler around so that the free end points down. Ask how far apart the ends are. [36 in. − 12 in. = 24 in.] Point out that neither of these positions forms two sides of a triangle. Rotate the ruler to several positions in which the ruler and the yardstick could be two sides of a triangle.

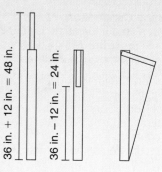

Notice in Example 1 that 42 + 30 = 72 and 42 − 30 = 12. That is, the possible lengths of the third side of the triangle are between the *sum* and the *difference* of the two given sides. We can use algebra to prove that this is *always* the case. Consider a triangle with two sides x and y. We want to describe all possible lengths z of the third side.

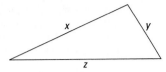

(For convenience, we assume that if x and y differ, x is the longer side.) The Triangle Inequality tells us that the sum of two sides is greater than the third. So

$$y + z > x \qquad \text{and} \qquad x + y > z \qquad \text{and} \qquad z + x > y.$$

Now solve these inequalities for z.

$$z > x - y \qquad \text{and} \qquad z < x + y \qquad \text{and} \qquad z > y - x$$

The third inequality, $z > y - x$, yields no new information because if x is the longest side, $y - x$ is negative. We summarize the relation as follows.

Third Side Property
If x and y are the lengths of two sides of a triangle, and $x > y$, then the length z of the third side must satisfy the inequality

$$x - y < z < x + y.$$

Example 2

Two sides of a triangle are 4 cm and 6 cm. How long is the third side?

Solution

Use the Third Side Property. Let $x = 6$ and $y = 4$. (Remember that x is the longer side.) The third side has a length z that satisfies

$$6 - 4 < z < 6 + 4.$$

That is, $2 < z < 10.$

The third side can be any length between 2 cm and 10 cm.

The Third Side Property enables you to obtain information involving unknown distances. In some situations you must deal with three points, and you do not know if they form a triangle or if they all lie on a line.

Adapting to Individual Needs

English Language Development
Several new properties are introduced in this lesson. Have students update their index cards by matching them with the vocabulary list on page 276. Suggest that they make cards for any properties that they have missed.

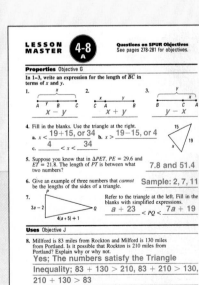

When answers for real-world situations are inequalities, some students are concerned because an exact value is not known. What good is it, they may ask, to know only that the third side is between two numbers? Tell them that a little information can sometimes be quite important. For instance, in the situation of **Example 3**, suppose that bus service is only available to students who live more than 1.5 miles from school. Then you know that Larry cannot use the bus service.

Additional Examples

These examples are also given on **Teaching Aid 44.**

1. If two sides of a triangle have lengths 3 and 19, write an interval to describe the possible lengths of the third side.
   $16 < x < 22$

2. Two sides of a triangle each have length 5 cm. What are the possible lengths of the third side?
   Between 0 and 10 cm

3. a. Use the information in the mileage table below to show an example of the Triangle Inequality.

	Charlotte	Greensboro	Winston-Salem	Raleigh
Charlotte	----	96	81	169
Greensboro	96	----	26	83
Winston-Salem	81	26	----	106
Raleigh	169	83	106	----

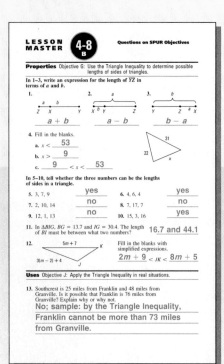

LESSON MASTER **4-8** B   Questions on SPUR Objectives

Properties Objective G: Use the Triangle Inequality to determine possible lengths of sides of triangles.

In 1–3, write an expression for the length of $\overline{YZ}$ in terms of a and b.
1. $a + b$ 2. $a - b$ 3. $b - a$

4. Fill in the blanks.
   a. $x < $ **53**
   b. $x > $ **9**
   c. **9** $< x < $ **53**

In 5–10, tell whether the three numbers can be the lengths of sides in a triangle.
5. 3, 7, 9 **yes**   6. 4, 6, 4 **yes**
7. 2, 10, 14 **no**   8. 7, 17, 7 **no**
9. 12, 1, 13 **no**   10. 15, 3, 16 **yes**

11. In $\triangle BIG$, $BG = 13.7$ and $IG = 30.4$. The length of BI must be between what two numbers? **16.7 and 44.1**

12. Fill in the blanks with simplified expressions.
    $2m + 9 < JK < 8m + 5$

Uses Objective J: Apply the Triangle Inequality in real situations.

13. Southcrest is 25 miles from Franklin and 48 miles from Granville. Is it possible that Franklin is 76 miles from Granville? Explain why or why not.
    No; sample: by the Triangle Inequality, Franklin cannot be more than 73 miles from Granville.

Example 3

May lives one mile from school and 0.4 mile from Larry. How far does Larry live from school?

Solution

Let d be the distance from Larry's house to school. Think of the extreme cases first. If the houses and the school lie on a line, the distance from Larry's house to school can be as large as $1.0 + 0.4 = 1.4$ miles or as small as $1.0 - 0.4 = 0.6$ mile.

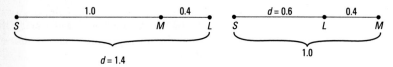

If the houses and school do not lie on a line, they form a triangle, and by the Third Side Property, $0.6 < d < 1.4$.

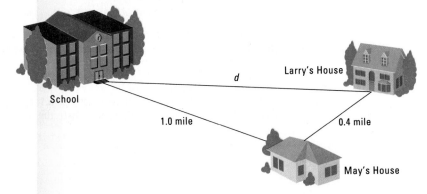

So $0.6 \leq d \leq 1.4$. Larry lives from 0.6 to 1.4 miles from school.

QUESTIONS

Covering the Reading

1. In the drawing below, A is on $\overline{BC}$. How long is $\overline{BC}$? **$10 + d$**

2. If M is between P and Q on a line, $PM = 5$, and $PQ = 7$, what is MQ?
   2

3. State the Triangle Inequality. **If A, B, and C are any three points, then $AB + BC \geq AC$. If A, B, and C are vertices of a triangle, then $AB + BC > AC$.**

4. Refer to the triangle at the left. Copy and complete.
   a. $k + n > \underline{\ ?\ }$ **m**
   b. $n + m > \underline{\ ?\ }$ **k**
   c. $\underline{\ ?\ } + \underline{\ ?\ } > n$ **$k + m > n$**

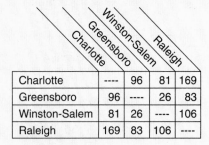

Adapting to Individual Needs

Challenge

Have students find the missing numbers in the mileage chart if A, B, C, and D are collinear. [All of the numbers but AB can be found by using the symmetry of the chart: $AD = 32$, $BC = 12$, $CA = 60$, $DB = 16$, and $DC = 28$. The distance from A to B is 48, which can be determined by adding AD and DB.]

	A	B	C	D
A	----	?	60	?
B	?	----	?	16
C	?	12	----	28
D	32	?	?	----

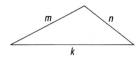

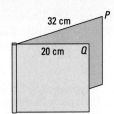

32 cm
20 cm

5. Two metal plates are joined by a hinge as in the drawing at the left.
  a. PQ can be no shorter than __?__ cm. **12**
  b. PQ can be no longer than __?__ cm. **52**

6. Refer to the triangle at the right.
  a. x must be less than __?__. **9**
  b. x must be greater than __?__. **1**
  c. __?__ $< x <$ __?__. **1, 9**

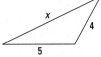

7. If two sides of a triangle are 6.5 cm and 8.2 cm, what inequality must the length of the third side satisfy? **1.7 < x < 14.7**

8. Suppose Larry lives 1.3 km from school and 0.8 km from May. The distance May lives from school must be greater than or equal to __?__ but less than or equal to __?__. **.5 km, 2.1 km**

Applying the Mathematics

9. In an *isosceles triangle*, at least two sides are the same length. If the congruent sides are each 3 in. long, how long can the third side be?
between 0 in. and 6 in.

10. If two sides of a triangle have lengths $100x^2$ and $75x^2$, the third side can have any length between __?__ and __?__. $25x^2, 175x^2$

11. Why is there no triangle with sides of lengths 1 cm, 2 cm, and 4 cm?
because 1 + 2 is not greater than 4

A $8x + 1$
    B
223    $13x + 12$
     C

12. a. Refer to the triangle at the left. Use the Triangle Inequality to write a sentence using x that compares the sum of AB and BC with AC.
  b. Solve the inequality for x. $x > 10$
  a) $(8x + 1) + (13x + 12) > 223$

13. Sirius, the brightest star in the nighttime sky, is 8.7 light-years from Earth. Procyon, a bright star near Sirius, is 11.3 light-years from Earth. Let m be the distance between Sirius and Procyon. Knowing only this information, what are the smallest and largest values that m can have?
2.6 light-years $\leq m \leq$ 20 light-years

14. Betty can walk to school in 25 minutes. She can walk to her boyfriend's house in 10 minutes. Let t be the length of time for her boyfriend to walk to school. If they walk at the same rate, what are the largest and smallest possible values of t? **15 $\leq t \leq$ 35**

15. A road atlas states that the driving mileage from Boston to Los Angeles is 3028 miles. Do you think that the flying distance is greater or less than the driving distance? Explain why. **Sample: The flying distance will be less because you can fly in a straight line from one city to another; while on land the Triangle Inequality may be applied many times between the cities.**

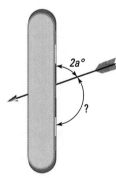

$2a°$
?

Review

16. An arrow enters a target at an angle of $2a°$. What is the measure of the supplementary angle as shown at the left? *(Lesson 4-7)* $(180 - 2a)°$

17. One angle in a triangle is twice the measure of the smallest angle. The third angle is four times the measure of the smallest angle. What are the measures of the three angles? *(Lesson 4-7)*
$25\frac{5}{7}°, 51\frac{3}{7}°, 102\frac{6}{7}°$

Sample: G to R = 83, R to W = 106, G to W = 26; G to R + G to W > R to W (83 + 26 > 106)

b. It is 66 miles from Raleigh to Fayetteville. From this information, what can you tell about the distance from Charlotte to Fayetteville? **It is between 103 and 235 miles.**

Notes on Questions

Since many of the questions deal with geometry, encourage students to draw pictures of the situations as a first step in their solutions.

Question 6 Some students may use the Third Side Property and answer Triangle Inequality questions without solving inequalities. Nonetheless, they should go through the algebra to verify their work.

Question 9 You might demonstrate how to get the answer with a pair of scissors. Using the point where the scissors are joined as a vertex of a triangle, explain that scissors have two "sides" of equal length and show how the length of the "third side" can vary from zero (closed scissors) to the sum of the lengths of the two "sides" of the scissors.

Question 12 To find the entire restriction on x, at the very least, $223 + (8x + 1) > 13x + 12$ must also be considered.

✐ **Question 15 Writing** Ask students for their explanations.

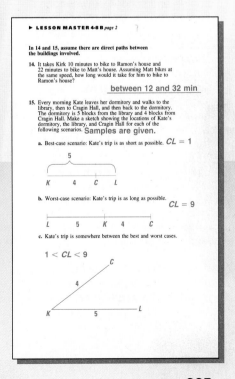

▶ **LESSON MASTER 4-8 B** *page 2*

In 14 and 15, assume there are direct paths between the buildings involved.

14. It takes Kirk 10 minutes to bike to Ramon's house and 22 minutes to bike to Matt's house. Assuming Matt bikes at the same speed, how long would it take for him to bike to Ramon's house?
between 12 and 32 min

15. Every morning Kate leaves her dormitory and walks to the library, then to Cragin Hall, and then back to the dormitory. The dormitory is 5 blocks from the library and 4 blocks from Cragin Hall. Make a sketch showing the locations of Kate's dormitory, the library, and Cragin Hall for each of the following scenarios. **Samples are given.**

a. Best-case scenario: Kate's trip is as short as possible. $CL = 1$

b. Worst-case scenario: Kate's trip is as long as possible. $CL = 9$

c. Kate's trip is somewhere between the best and worst cases.

$1 < CL < 9$

Follow-up
for Lesson **4-8**

Practice

For more questions on SPUR Objectives, use **Lesson Master 4-8A** (shown on page 263) or **Lesson Master 4-8B** (shown on pages 264–265).

Assessment

Written Communication Have each student write a note to his or her parents that explains what was learned from this lesson. [Notes include the fact that the sum of the lengths of two sides of any triangle is greater than the length of the third side, and given the lengths of two sides of a triangle, a range can be found for the length of the third side.]

Extension

You might want to give students one of the following situations.

✎ **Writing** Have students use distances they travel frequently (such as the distance between their homes and school, between their homes and the location of a nearby shopping center, etc.) to make up and solve a problem utilizing the Triangle Inequality.

Activity Tell each student to draw a segment 5 cm long on a piece of paper and label the endpoints A and B. Then have them use AB as one side of several different triangles ABC in which AC is 8 cm long. Finally, have them **work in groups** to generalize about possible locations for point C. [Point C is anywhere on a circle with A as the center and with a radius of 8 cm; it cannot be on $\overleftrightarrow{AB}$.]

Project Update Project 5, *Triangles with Integer Sides,* on page 275, relates to the content of this lesson.

266

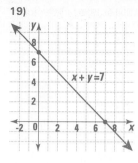
19)

18. In a right triangle, one of the acute angles measures $5b°$. The other measures $4b°$. What are the numerical measures of these two angles? *(Lesson 4-7)* 50°, 40°

19. Plot the line $x + y = 7$. *(Lesson 4-6)* See left.

20. Suppose two girls start a lawn-mowing business by spending $200 for a mower and then earn $15 per lawn cut. How many lawns do they need to mow if they wish to earn a profit of at least $350? *(Lesson 3-10)* 37 or more lawns

21. Simplify $4x + -3(u + 2x + v^2) + 2x$. *(Lessons 3-6, 3-7)* $-3u + -3v^2$

22. *Skill sequence.* Simplify. *(Lessons 2-1, 3-6)*
    a. $p + p + p$ $3p$
    b. $p \cdot p \cdot p$ p^3

23. Find the image of the point $P = (3, 6)$ after a slide of 4 units to the right and 6 units up. *(Lesson 3-4)* (7, 12)

24. The graph below gives the life expectancy at birth for four groups of Americans with years of birth from 1920 to 1990. *(Lesson 3-3)*

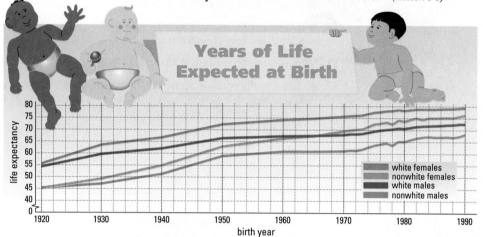

Source: *The World Almanac and Book of Facts, 1994*

a. Which group has had the greatest increase in life expectancy since 1920? nonwhite females
   b) Answers will vary.
b. In your year of birth, how long could a newborn be expected to live?
c. Identify three or more conclusions that you can make from studying the graph. Sample: Females live longer than males; people are living longer; white females live longer than nonwhite females.

Exploration

25. The perimeter of a triangle is 15. The sides all have different integer lengths. How many different combinations of side lengths are possible? (Hint: The answer may be fewer than you think. Use trial and error and the Triangle Inequality.)
    There are 3 combinations: 2, 6, 7; 3, 5, 7; and 4, 5, 6.

266

Setting Up Lesson 4-9

On page 270 in Lesson 4-9, students are shown a computer program that will print a table of values for **Example 3.** If possible, have a computer available so that you or a student can run the program or show the spreadsheet in class. Some calculators also can be programmed to do this.

Profitable practice. *Shown is Beth making her weekly deposit of $5 into a savings account. By saving money at a constant rate and by using a table or making a graph, Beth can accurately predict her bank balance at any given time.*

Graphing a Constant-Increase Pattern

Suppose Beth begins with $10 in the bank and adds $5 to her account each week. After w weeks she will have $10 + 5w$ dollars. Let t be the total amount in her account at the end of w weeks. Beth's bank balance can be described in three different ways.

with an equation	with a table	with a graph

$t = 10 + 5w$

w	t
0	10
1	15
2	20
3	25
4	30
⋮	⋮

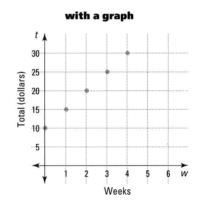

The table lists the ordered pairs (0, 10), (1, 15), (2, 20), (3, 25), and (4, 30). All these pairs make the equation $t = 10 + 5w$ true. The equation $t = 10 + 5w$ is called a **linear equation** because all the points of its graph lie on the same line. Because Beth puts money into her account at specific whole-number intervals, the domain of w is the set of whole numbers. It does not make sense to connect the points, because numbers such as $2\frac{1}{2}$ are not in the domain of w.

Lesson **4-9**

Objectives

L Graph equations of the forms $y = ax + b$ and $y = ax - b$ by making a table of values.

Resources

From the *Teacher's Resource File*
- Lesson Master 4-9A or 4-9B
- Answer Master 4-9
- Teaching Aids
  26 Graph Paper
  36 Warm-up
  39 Graphing Equations
  46 Graphing Constant
     Increase and Decrease
- Technology Sourcebook
  Computer Master 12

Additional Resources
- Visuals for Teaching Aids 26, 36, 39, 46
- Computer and spreadsheet software

Teaching 4-9
Lesson

Warm-up

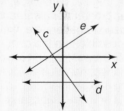

For 1–3, tell if the line shows a constant-increase pattern, a constant-decrease pattern, or no increase or decrease.
1. Line c **Constant decrease**
(Warm-up continues on page 268.)

Lesson 4-9 Overview

Broad Goals This lesson extends Lesson 4-5 to graphing and interpreting graphs of linear equations. The goals of the lesson are for students to be able to generate a table of values from an equation, and be able to graph a line from the table of values. They should also be able to answer questions about a situation from the graph, table, or equation.

Perspective Students have to know how to graph lines by plotting points before they analyze the graphs. In Chapter 7, we will examine slope and rate of change, so by that time students must be convinced that an equation and the points of its graph are related. It is therefore important that you resist the temptation to speak about slope; though you certainly might talk about the intercepts when looking at a graph, do not

connect them with an equation at this time unless your students raise the issue.

In some situations it is useful to get coordinates in sequence: first *x*, then *y*. At other times, for instance, when graphing $x + y = 4$, it is best to get both coordinates at the same time. Be sure that students see both of these ideas.

2. Line *d* No increase or decrease
3. Line *e* Constant increase

For 4–6, describe the line in words or draw an example of the line on the same grid as lines *c*, *d*, and *e*.

4. Line *r* showing no increase or decrease **Any line parallel to the x-axis or to the y-axis.**

5. Line *s* showing a constant decrease **From left to right, any line that slants downward**

6. Line *t* showing a constant increase **From left to right, any line that slants upward.**

Notes on Reading

Reading Mathematics You might want to use **Teaching Aid 46** as you go through *Graphing a Constant-Increase Pattern* and **Examples 1 and 2**. We suggest that you go over the reading paragraph by paragraph.

❶ The flood situation might be simpler than the bank example on page 267 because the flood waters recede continuously and the line is continuous. You might have to explain that the points highlighted by dots on a continuous graph are identified for convenience. They do not mean that a portion of the graph is partly discrete. You may want to ask students what the points on the graph in the 4th quadrant represent. [The water level is below normal.]

❷ Here students make a table by hand. On page 270 they see how a computer program or a spreadsheet can be used to generate a similar table. If possible, run the computer program in class. You can have students change the values in line 40 so they can experiment with different equations and see that changing the coefficients and/or the constant terms changes the graph. They can gain insight that will be helpful later when slope and intercept are formally studied.

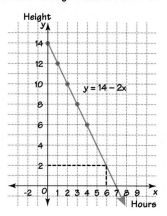

Flash flood. *Heavy rains can produce flash floods if small rivers or streams rise suddenly and overflow. Shown is a flooded road in Zulia State, Venezuela.*

Graphing a Constant-Decrease Pattern

Other situations lead to equations whose variables may take on any real numbers as values. Their graphs are straight lines.

Example 1

A flooded stream is now 14 inches above its normal level. The water level is dropping 2 inches per hour. Its height y in inches above normal after x hours is given by the equation $y = 14 - 2x$. Graph this relationship.

❶ **Solution**

Find the height at various times and make a table. Below is a table for 0, 1, 2, 3, and 4 hours.

hour (x)	height (y = 14 – 2x)	ordered pair (x, y)
0	14 – 2 · 0 = 14	(0, 14)
1	14 – 2 · 1 = 12	(1, 12)
2	14 – 2 · 2 = 10	(2, 10)
3	14 – 2 · 3 = 8	(3, 8)
4	14 – 2 · 4 = 6	(4, 6)

Plot the ordered pairs in the table and look for patterns. You should see that the five points lie on the same line. Now think about the domain of x. Time in hours can be any nonnegative real number, such as $1\frac{3}{4}$ or $3\frac{1}{2}$.

This means that other points lie between the ones you have already plotted. So, draw the line through them for $x \geq 0$.

Once the graph of an equation has been drawn, you can use it to answer questions about its points.

Optional Activities

Activity 1 Cooperative Learning
Use **Question 29** to stimulate discussion. You may wish to have students **work in small groups** while analyzing the question. Allow any answer for which a student can provide an adequate rationale. However, the answers must fit the labels "Time" and "Speed" on the axes.

Activity 2
Materials: Graph paper or **Teaching Aid 26**

After students have graphed some equations, you might have them graph the equation $x + y = 8$. Then ask them to name at least two different equations that have the same graph. [Sample equations: $y = 8 - x$, $x = 8 - y$, and $2x + 2y = 16$.]

Activity 3 Technology Connection
In *Technology Sourcebook, Computer Master 12*, students use *GraphExplorer* or similar software to graph linear patterns. Then they use the program's trace feature to answer questions about particular values.

Example 2

In Example 1, how many hours will it take for the water level to fall to 2 inches above normal?

Solution 1

Look at the graph on page 268. The height of the water above normal level is given by y. Find the point for 2 inches on the y-axis, and then look across to find the point on the graph that has this height. The x-coordinate of this point is 6. This is shown by the dashed path on the graph. The water will be 2 inches above normal after 6 hours.

Solution 2

Use the equation $y = 14 - 2x$. The height "2 inches above normal" means that $y = 2$. So solve $2 = 14 - 2x$.

$$2 = 14 - 2x$$
$$-12 = -2x \qquad \text{Add } -14 \text{ to each side.}$$
$$6 = x \qquad \text{Multiply both sides by } -\tfrac{1}{2}.$$

Graphing a Linear Equation

If you are not told the domain of a variable in a linear pattern, you should assume that any real number may be substituted for x. The graph will then be a straight line.

Example 3

Draw the graph of $y = -2x + 1$.

② Solution

You can choose *any* values for x. We choose -1, 0, 1, 2, 3, and 4. Make a table of solutions. Plot the points. Because there are no restrictions on the values of x and y, they may be any real numbers. Draw a line through the points.

x	-2x + 1 = y
-1	$-2 \cdot -1 + 1 = 3$
0	$-2 \cdot 0 + 1 = 1$
1	$-2 \cdot 1 + 1 = -1$
2	$-2 \cdot 2 + 1 = -3$
3	$-2 \cdot 3 + 1 = -5$
4	$-2 \cdot 4 + 1 = -7$

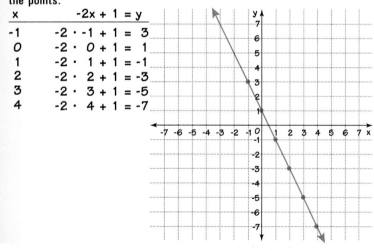

Additional Examples

1. A frostbite victim's temperature was 7° below normal, but it increased by 2° per hour. If t is the amount that the temperature is below normal after h hours, then $t = -7 + 2h$. Graph this relationship.

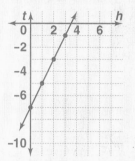

2. How does the graph show the number of hours it will take for the person's temperature to return to normal? **The person's temperature is normal when $t = 0$. The graph crosses the h-axis when $t = 0$. The h-coordinate of that point is between 3 and 4. So the number of hours is between 3 and 4. That can be verified by solving $-7 + 2t = 0$.**

3. Make a table of values for the equation $y = 3x - 4$. Then graph the equation.

x	0	1	2
y	-4	-1	2

(2, 2)
(1, -1)
(0, -4)

(Additional Examples continue on page 270.)

Adapting to Individual Needs

Extra Help
Materials: **Teaching Aid 46**

To help students understand constant-increase and constant-decrease patterns, put the graphs given on pages 267–268 on an overhead projector. **Teaching Aid 46** contains these graphs. Relate *increase* to "going up" from left to right on the first graph, and relate *decrease* to "going down" from left to right on the second graph. To

explain *constant increase,* point out that for each one-week interval, Beth saves $5. If she saved different amounts each week, there would not be a constant increase. Illustrate this by using an overlay on the graph on page 267, and graph these ordered pairs:

Week	0	1	2	3	4	5
Total	10	15	19	26	32	37

Note that for a constant increase, the points fall on a line; when the increase is not constant, the points do not fall on a line. If necessary, explain *constant decrease* using water levels and the second graph.

4. Suppose you wish to print a table of values for $y = 3x - 4$ for $x = 0$, 1, 2, 3, and 4. Do either part a or part b.

a. Write a computer program that will print the table.

```
10   PRINT "TABLE OF (X,Y)
     VALUES"
20   PRINT "X VALUE", "Y
     VALUE"
30   FOR X = 0 TO 4
40   LET Y = 3 * X - 4
50   PRINT X, Y
60   NEXT X
70   END
```

b. Explain how to get the table of values with a spreadsheet. In cell A1, enter X. In cell B1, enter Y. In cell A2, enter 0. Enter =A2+1 in cell A3, and copy this in cells A4, A5, and A6. Enter = 3∗A2− 4 in cell B2. Copy this in cells B3 to B6.]

You have seen that a computer can be used to make tables. The following program will print a table of values similar to the one calculated on page 269. Lines 30–60 use a FOR/NEXT loop in which the first time through the loop, *x* is -1.

```
10 PRINT "TABLE OF (X,Y) VALUES"
20 PRINT "X VALUE", "Y VALUE"
30 FOR X = -1 TO 4
40 LET Y = -2 * X + 1
50 PRINT X,Y
60 NEXT X
70 END
```

When the program is run the computer will print the following.

```
TABLE OF (X, Y) VALUES
X VALUE        Y VALUE
   -1             3
    0             1
    1            -1
    2            -3
    3            -5
    4            -7
```

You can change line 30 to specify a different set of *x* values for your table. You can change line 40 to specify a different equation.

A spreadsheet can also be used to make a table of values for an equation. Many spreadsheet programs will automatically make a scatterplot for any identified set of ordered pairs, as well. Here is how one spreadsheet can be started.

	A	B
1	x	y
2	-1	= -2∗A2+1
3	=A2+1	
4		
5		
6		

To fill in the columns, copy A3 down the A column as far as you want. Then copy B2 down the B column. The result should be the same as found with the computer program.

270

270

Adapting to Individual Needs

English Language Development
Students who are just learning English should take some time to review the terms and phrases from this chapter. Have these students **work in pairs** and quiz one another using their index cards.

Challenge
Materials: Graph paper or **Teaching Aid 26**

Have students use the following data to draw a graph for renting the same kind of car at each agency for one day. Have them make the graphs on the same coordinate grid, and use them to answer **Questions 1–3.**

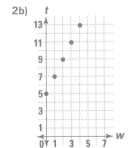

Covering the Reading

1. Consider Beth's savings plan described in the lesson.
   a. How much money will she have in her account after 3 weeks? **$25**
   b. How much money will she have in her account after 6 weeks? **$40**

2. Suppose Miguel begins with $5 in an account and adds $2 per week.
   a. Copy and complete the chart below, showing t, the total amount Miguel will have at the end of w weeks.

weeks (w)	total (t)
0	5
1	7
2	9
3	11
4	13

   b. Graph the ordered pairs (w, t). That is, plot w along the horizontal axis, and t along the vertical axis. **See left.**
   c. Write an equation that represents t in terms of w. $t = 5 + 2w$
   d. What is the domain of w? **the set of whole numbers**

In 3–6, refer to Examples 1 and 2.

3. After how many hours will the stream be 10 inches above normal?
   2 hours
4. How high above normal will the stream be after 4 hours?
   6 inches above normal
5. After how many hours will the stream level be back to normal?
   (Hint: y will be equal to zero.) **7 hours**

6. What do the points in Quadrant IV on the graph represent?
   the times and heights when the river is below its normal level

In 7 and 8, refer to Example 3.

7. a. When $x = \frac{1}{2}$, what is y? $y = 0$
   b. Will this point lie on the line that is graphed? **Yes**

8. Find the x-coordinate of the point on the graph which has a y-coordinate of -2. $\frac{3}{2}$

9. Refer to the computer program after Example 3.
   a. Rewrite line 30 so that ordered pairs are printed for $x = 0, 1, 2, 3, 4, 5, 6,$ and 7 when the program is run. **30 FOR X = 0 TO 7**
   b. Rewrite the program to print a table of values for $y = 8x - 3$ from $x = -5$ to $x = 5$. **See left.**

10. Refer to the spreadsheet in the lesson.
    a. Describe how you would modify the spreadsheet to show values for $x = 0, 2, 4, 6, 8,$ and 10. **See left.**
    b. What would change if you wanted a table of values for $y = 3x + 40$?
    Change the formula in cell B2 to = 3*A2 + 40.

Lesson 4-9 *Graphing Linear Patterns* **271**

2b)

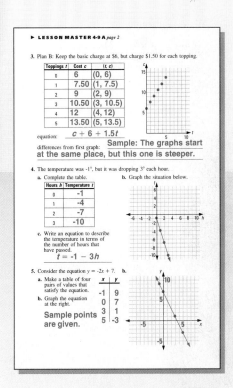

9b)

```
10 PRINT "TABLE OF (X, Y) VALUES"
20 PRINT "X VALUE", "Y VALUE"
30 FOR X = -5 TO 5
40 LET Y = 8 * X - 3
50 PRINT X, Y
60 NEXT X
70 END
```

10a) Change cell A2 to 0, change the formula in cell A3 to =A2 + 2, and copy A3 into A4 through A7.

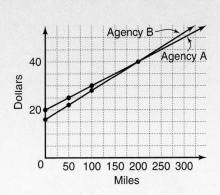

Agency A: $20 a day plus $0.10 a mile
Agency B: $16 a day plus $0.12 a mile

1. If you plan to drive only 50 miles, which agency offers the better deal?
   [Agency B]
2. If you plan to drive 300 miles, which agency offers the better deal?
   [Agency A]
3. For what number of miles would both agencies charge the same amount?
   [200 miles]

271

Notes on Questions

Question 15 Some students may notice the "up 3, over 1" or "down 3, over 1" patterns. If they do, point out that these patterns determine a measure of steepness of the line, which they will study in detail in Chapter 7.

Question 29 Activity 1 in *Optional Activities*, on page 268, relates to this question.

Follow-up for Lesson 4-9

Practice

For more questions on SPUR Objectives, use **Lesson Master 3-8A** (shown on pages 270–271) or **Lesson Master 3-8B** (shown on pages 272–273).

Assessment

Oral Communication Ask students to name three ways that a constant-increase pattern can be described. Then have them describe situations in which they would use a particular method to describe a pattern. [Students understand that an equation, a table, or a graph can describe a constant-increase pattern.]

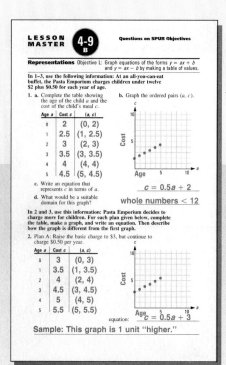

World's tallest trees.
The redwood tree stump shown below is in Myers Flat, California. You can tell how fast this tree grew by examining the width of its rings. Redwoods often grow 200 to 275 feet high and have trunks that are 8 to 12 feet in diameter.

11a)

w	b
0	30
1	25
2	20
3	15
4	10

11c)

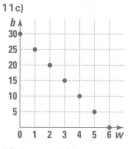

13a) Sample:

x	y
0	10
1	10.5
2	11
3	11.5
4	12

13c)
$y = 0.5x + 10$

272

Applying the Mathematics

11. Oprah begins with $30 in the bank and withdraws $5 per week. Let b = the balance after w weeks.   See left.
    a. Describe her bank balance with a chart using $w = 0, 1, 2, 3, 4$.
    b. Describe her bank balance with an equation using variables b and w for balance and number of weeks respectively. $b = 30 - 5w$
    c. Make a graph of all solutions to the equation in part **b**. See left.
    d. In what week will Oprah withdraw her last dollar? week 6

12. a. Make a table of values which satisfy $y = 4x - 2$.
    b. Graph the equation.
       a,b) See margin.

13. A tree now has a trunk with a 10 cm radius. The radius is increasing by 0.5 cm per year. Its radius y after x years is described by $y = 10 + 0.5x$.
    a. Make a table of values for this relationship. See left.
    b. What is the domain of x? the set of nonnegative real numbers
    c. Draw a graph of this situation. See left.
    d. After how many years will the radius equal 20 cm? 20 years

14. Use the graph below to complete the table.

x	y
-2	-75
-1	-25
0	25
1	75

15a,b)

$y = -3x$ $y = 3x$

15. a. Draw the graph of $y = 3x$. Choose your own values for x.
    b. On the same grid that you used in part **a,** draw the graph of $y = -3x$. See above right.
    c. At what point(s) do the graphs of parts **a** and **b** intersect? (0, 0)
    d. Describe any patterns you observe in these graphs. Sample: The lines are reflection images of each other over the y-axis.

16. The *St. Louis Post-Dispatch* reported that the level of the Mississippi River in St. Louis County on August 16, 1993, was 39.1 feet. It was expected to drop 0.6 feet by the next day. Let x equal the number of days since August 16 and y equal the level of the Mississippi River (in feet).
    a. Suppose the river continued to drop at the same speed. Write an equation for y in terms of x. $y = 39.1 - 0.6x$
    b. Graph your equation from part **a**. See margin.
    c. Use your graph from part **b** to estimate when the Mississippi River was expected to drop to the lowest "flood stage level," of 30 feet, in St. Louis County. Sample: in about 16 days (Sept. 1, 1993)

17. What is the minimum number of points needed to graph a straight line? 2 points

Additional Answers

12a, b. Sample:

x	y
0	-2
1	2
2	6

$y = 4x - 2$

16b.

$y = 39.1 - 0.6x$

Level of Mississippi River (feet)

Days after August 16, 1993

Japanese fishermen in Tokyo Bay Harbor unload the day's catch.

18. What do all the graphs you saw or made in this lesson have in common? How are they different? **Samples: They are all straight lines or parts of straight lines. They pass through different points on the x-axis and y-axis. Some slant to the right and some slant to the left.**

Review

19. A triangle has sides of length 20 and 27. What are the possible lengths of the third side? *(Lesson 4-8)* **7 < length < 47**

20. Osami lives 2 km from Tokyo Bay and 1.4 km from Toshiki's house. How far does Toshiki live from Tokyo Bay? *(Lesson 4-8)*
0.6 km ≤ distance from Tokyo Bay ≤ 3.4 km

21. The angles in a triangle have measures $x - 10$, $x + 10$, and $x + 30$. What are the measures of these three angles? *(Lesson 4-7)* **40°, 60°, 80°**

22. The measure of an angle is $x°$.
  a. What is the measure of its supplement? **$(180 - x)°$**
  b. What is the measure of its complement? **$(90 - x)°$**
  c. What is the difference between the measures of the supplement and complement? *(Lesson 4-7)* **90°**

23. *Multiple choice.* The graph of which equation is pictured at the left? *(Lesson 4-6)* **(d)**
  (a) $x + y = 5$ (b) $x + y = -5$ (c) $x - y = 5$ (d) $x - y = -5$

24. Solve $3(w - 4) = 48$. *(Lessons 3-7, 4-3)* **$w = 20$**

25. Simplify $\frac{x}{7} - \frac{2x}{5}$. *(Lessons 3-9, 4-1)* **$-\frac{9x}{35}$**

26. Write $\frac{12!}{3!\,4!}$ in scientific notation. *(Lesson 2-10, Appendix B)* **$3.3264 \cdot 10^6$**

27. *Skill sequence.* Write as a decimal. *(Previous course)*
  a. 1 divided by 4 **0.25**   **b.** 1 divided by .4 **2.5**
  c. 1 divided by .04 **25**   **d.** 1 divided by .000004 **250,000**

28. Find the area of $\triangle RST$ at the left. *(Lesson 1-5)* **46.2 in²**

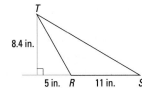

Exploration

29. Which activity listed below could produce a graph like this? Explain what is happening during the activity over the time period shown and how this relates to the graph. **See margin.**

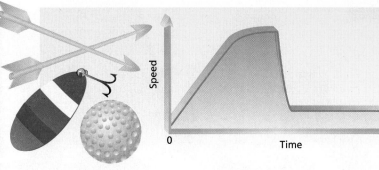

Fishing
Skydiving
Drag Racing
Pole Vaulting
Golf
Javelin Throwing
100-Meter sprint
Archery

Lesson 4-9 *Graphing Linear Patterns* **273**

Additional Answers
29. Sample: A skydiver initially picks up speed while falling and then reaches a terminal velocity. When the chute opens, velocity drops sharply; then the diver floats at a relatively constant rate.

Extension

You might extend the problem involving Beth's bank account on page 267. Explain that we can allow the domain of w to contain the real numbers. Then the graph would consist of half-open segments as shown below. It could be described by the equation $t = 5\lfloor 2 + w \rfloor$ where $\lfloor 2 + w \rfloor$ is the greatest integer less than or equal to $2 + w$. For example, if $w = 1\frac{1}{4}$, then $t = 5\lfloor 2 + 1\frac{1}{4} \rfloor = 5\lfloor 3\frac{1}{4} \rfloor = 5 \cdot 3 = 15$, because 3 is the greatest integer less than $3\frac{1}{4}$.

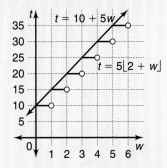

The equation $t = 10 + 5w$ gives points on the line that contain the left-hand endpoints of these segments.

Project Update Project 3, *Prices Versus Sales of CDs*, on page 275, relates to the content of this lesson.

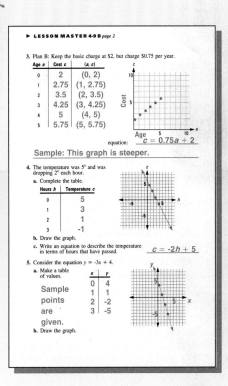

Chapter 4 Projects

The projects relate to the content of the lessons of this chapter as follows.

Project	Lesson
1	4-1
2	4-3
3	4-9
4	4-3
5	4-8
6	4-6

1 Patterns in Fraction Products
If students have to find additional products before they are sure of the pattern, have them find products when $(1 - \frac{1}{7})$, $(1 - \frac{1}{8})$, and $(1 - \frac{1}{9})$ are the last terms. Tell students that they are not expected to multiply 99 terms to find the product of $(1 - \frac{1}{2})$ ... $(1 - \frac{1}{100})$. Stress that they are to use the pattern they discovered in **parts a–c** and apply it to this question. Because this project involves only a single pattern, tell students to write their answers in detail—as if they were presenting them to the class. To extend this project, have students find the product of the terms when the fractions are added to one instead of subtracted from one. Then have them describe the patterns they find. They should find that the product is $\frac{n}{2}$ where n is the denominator of the last fraction.

2 Credit-Card Balances The key to this project is setting up the formulas for the spreadsheets. Students must realize that the amount owed before each month's payment is found by multiplying the interest charge times the amount owed after the last monthly payment. Once students have set up their spreadsheets and compared the purchase price and actual cost, ask them to explain why they would, or would not, make a purchase under the terms described in this project.

3 Price versus Sales of CDs
Students are asked to determine a selling price for the CD that would make the greatest profit. This project should lead students to understand that charging more for an item may not necessarily increase the overall profit earned on that item. The key to pricing is to determine the highest price most people are willing to spend for an item. Point out that if a CD is overpriced, fewer people will

274

A project presents an opportunity for you to extend your knowledge of a topic related to the material of this chapter. You should allow more time for a project than you do for typical homework questions.

1 Patterns in Fraction Products
Find each product.

a. $\left(1 - \frac{1}{2}\right)\left(1 - \frac{1}{3}\right)\left(1 - \frac{1}{4}\right)$

b. $\left(1 - \frac{1}{2}\right)\left(1 - \frac{1}{3}\right)\left(1 - \frac{1}{4}\right)\left(1 - \frac{1}{5}\right)$

c. $\left(1 - \frac{1}{2}\right)\left(1 - \frac{1}{3}\right)\left(1 - \frac{1}{4}\right)\left(1 - \frac{1}{5}\right)\left(1 - \frac{1}{6}\right)$

Write your answers as fractions. Do you see any patterns? Find this product. (There are 99 terms in the product.)

d. $\left(1 - \frac{1}{2}\right)\left(1 - \frac{1}{3}\right)\left(1 - \frac{1}{4}\right) \cdots \left(1 - \frac{1}{99}\right)\left(1 - \frac{1}{100}\right)$
Can you predict what this product will be?

e. $\left(1 - \frac{1}{2}\right)\left(1 - \frac{1}{3}\right)\left(1 - \frac{1}{4}\right) \cdots \left(1 - \frac{1}{n-1}\right)\left(1 - \frac{1}{n}\right)$
Write about the patterns you see in these products.

274

---

2 Credit-Card Balances
Mr. Spendalot bought a $5,000 computer and charged it to his Gotta-Have-It Credit Card which had no previous balance. The Gotta-Have-It Credit Card charges 1.5% interest per month, based on the unpaid balance. So if Mr. Spendalot makes a partial payment of only $200, there will be a finance charge added to next month's bill.

Use a spreadsheet to show the month-to-month changes in Mr. Spendalot's account. Assume he will pay $200 a month toward his debt and will not charge any more purchases. How long will it take him to pay off the $5,000? How much money will he end up paying for the computer? Compare the purchase price to the actual cost.

Possible responses

1. **a.** $\frac{1}{4}$ **b.** $\frac{1}{5}$ **c.** $\frac{1}{6}$

   d. The product of 99 terms is $\frac{1}{100}$.

   e. When n is the denominator of the last fraction subtracted, the product is $\frac{1}{n}$.

2. It will take 31 months to pay off $5,000. Mr. Spendalot will pay a total of $6,195.05 for the computer. The purchase price is $1,195.05 more than the actual cost.

A sample spreadsheet is given on pages 275–276. In C2 is the formula =B2 − 200. In B3 is the formula =C2*1.015. These are copied down the B and C columns.

3 Price versus Sales of CDs

Choose a popular CD title, and ask 20 of your classmates whether or not they would buy the CD if the price were \$1, \$2, \$3, . . . up to \$18. Make a graph of the price versus the number of people who would buy the CD. Explain the graph. If you knew that the CD cost the store \$4, what price would you recommend that the store charge for the CD, and why?

4 Situations Leading to $300 - 5x > 40$

On page 215 you read about two situations leading to the equation $5000 - 30x = 1000$. Write four different questions that could be answered by the linear sentence $300 - 5x > 40$. Make sure that one of the questions leads to meaningful negative values for x.

5 Triangles with Integer Sides

Consider triangles with sides of integer lengths and with no two sides having the same length. Explain why there are only three such triangles with all sides of length 5 or less. Then find all such triangles with all sides of length 10 or less.

6 Angle Sums in Polygons

The sum of the measures of the three angles of a triangle always equals 180°. The sum of the measures of the angles of a quadrilateral equals 360°. Consider polygons with more than four sides. Do you think that the sum of the measures of the angles of a pentagon is always a particular number? Draw several different pentagons and measure all five angles with a protractor. From one vertex, draw segments that connect with each of the other vertices. What is formed? Use what you know about triangles to explain the sum of the angle measures in a pentagon. Repeat this experiment with some hexagons (six sides) and heptagons (seven sides). Do all polygons with the same number of sides have angles whose measures yield a constant sum? Why or why not?

---

be willing to buy it, and the overall profit may not be as high it could be. Students might try more than one CD title to see how tastes in music and the amounts of money people are willing to spend differ.

4 Situations Leading to $300 - 5x > 40$

This project is more difficult than it first appears. Suggest that students reread the problems on page 228 to familiarize themselves with a variety of situations that lead to the same equation. Students may find it helpful to solve $300 - 5x > 40$ for x before writing their problems. Tell students to use familiar situations, such as school activities, hobbies, and sports as settings for their situations.

5 Triangles with Integer Sides

Students might apply the Multiplication Counting Principle to determine the number of ways they can order three different integers from 1 through 10. This number, 720, in itself can be discouraging to some students. Students may overlook the Triangle Inequality as a means of limiting the number of choices. If they have trouble progressing beyond this point, suggest that they create an organized list of all number sequences in which $x + y > z$, $x + z > y$, and $y + z > x$. The complete list should be examined to eliminate any duplicate number patterns.

6 Angle Sums in Polygons

Have each student display his or her data on polygons in a table. The table should include the name of the polygon, the number of sides of the polygon, the number of triangles formed, and the sum of measures of all the angles. Have students look for patterns in their tables. They should recognize that as the number of sides of a polygon increases by one, the sum of the measures of the angles of the polygon increases by 180°. Ask each student to write a formula to find the measure of all the angles of an n-sided polygon. $[180(n - 2)]$

Month	Owed before payment	Owed after payment
1	5000.00	4800.00
2	4872.00	4672.00
3	4742.08	4542.08
4	4610.21	4410.21
5	4476.36	4276.36
6	4340.51	4140.51
6	4340.51	4140.51
7	4202.62	4002.62

8	4062.66	3862.66
9	3920.60	3720.60
10	3776.41	3576.41
11	3630.05	3430.05
12	3481.50	3281.50
13	3330.72	3130.72
14	3177.69	2977.69
15	3022.35	2822.35
16	2864.69	2664.69

(Spreadsheet continues on page 276)

Progress Self-Test, page 277
Additional Answers
14. Solve the sentence:
$$1100 - 6x > 350$$
$$-6x > -750$$
$$x < 125 \text{ minutes}$$

15.

Yes	No
9	0
8	1
7	2
6	3
5	4
4	5
3	6
2	7
1	8
0	9

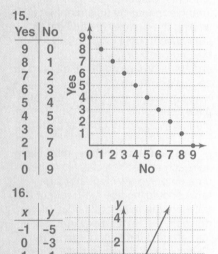

16.

x	y
-1	-5
0	-3
1	-1

$y = 2x - 3$

SUMMARY

You can think of this chapter as having three major topics. The first topic includes the algebraic definition and uses of subtraction and solving subtraction sentences. The second topic is graphs of lines. Properties of geometric figures that relate to addition and subtraction are the third topic.

The Algebraic Definition of Subtraction is in terms of addition: $a - b = a + {-b}$. This definition enables you to solve subtraction sentences of the form $ax - b = c$ or $ax - b < c$ by converting them to addition. Such sentences arise from the uses of subtraction. The two major models for subtraction are take-away and comparison. Discounts apply the take-away model. Finding the range of a data set is an application of the comparison model.

When an equation has two variables, its solutions may be graphed by making a table of values and plotting the resulting points on a coordinate plane.

Several important geometry properties involve sums and differences. The Triangle Inequality leads to the fact that if two sides of a triangle have lengths x and y, where $y > x$, the length of the third side is between $y - x$ and $y + x$. Two angles whose measures add to 180° are supplementary; two angles whose measures add to 90° are complementary. The three angle measures of a triangle must total 180°.

Any of the properties in this and previous chapters can be illustrated on a spreadsheet. Formulas relating the cells of a spreadsheet make spreadsheets powerful tools for storing and obtaining information.

VOCABULARY

Below are the most important terms and phrases for this chapter. You should be able to give a general description and a specific example of each.

Lesson 4-1
Algebraic Definition of Subtraction

Lesson 4-2
Take-Away Model for Subtraction
Comparison Model for Subtraction
range of a set, maximum, minimum

Lesson 4-4
spreadsheet
row, column, cell

Lesson 4-5
Opposite of a Sum Property
Opposite of a Difference Property

Lesson 4-6
constant sum
constant difference

Lesson 4-7
supplementary angles, supplements
Triangle Sum Theorem
⌐ symbol for 90° angle
complementary angles, complements

Lesson 4-8
Triangle Inequality
Third Side Property

Lesson 4-9
linear equation

276

17	2704.66	2504.66
18	2542.23	2342.23
19	2377.36	2177.36
20	2210.02	2010.02
21	2040.17	1840.17
22	1867.77	1667.77
23	1692.79	1492.79
24	1515.18	1315.18

25	1334.91	1134.91
26	1151.93	951.93
27	966.21	766.21
28	777.71	577.71
29	586.37	386.37
30	392.17	192.17
31	195.05	-4.95

3. Responses will vary.

PROGRESS SELF-TEST

See margin for answers to 14–16, 19, and 21.
Take this test as you would take a test in class.
You will need graph paper. Then check your
work with the solutions in the Selected Answers
section in the back of the book.

1. According to the Algebraic Definition of
Subtraction, adding -7 to a number is the
same as doing what else? **subtracting 7**

2. Yesterday it was 53°. Today it is warmer,
and the temperature is D degrees. How much
warmer is it today than it was yesterday?
$D - 53$

In 3–7, simplify.

3. $9p - 7q - (-14z)$ **4.** $n - 16 - 2n - (-12)$

5. $-8x - (2x - x)$ **-9x** **6.** $-(2b - 6)$ **-2b + 6**

7. $\frac{1}{2}m - \frac{7m}{2}$ **-3m**   3) $9p + -7q + 14z$; 4) $-n - 4$

8. A set of skis costing S dollars is on sale for
20% off. Write an expression for the sale
price of the skis. **.80S**

In 9–12, solve.

9. $5n - 6 = 54$ **$n = 12$** **10.** $8 < 6 - 3p$ **$p < -\frac{2}{3}$**

11. $\frac{3}{4} - \frac{1}{4}m = 12$ **$m = -45$**   **12.** $201 = 15f - 2(3 + 6f)$ **$f = 69$**

13. If $C = \frac{5}{9}(F - 32)$, find the Fahrenheit
equivalent of 50°C. **122°F**

14. Each minute a computer printer prints
6 sheets of paper. Suppose the printer starts
with 1100 sheets of paper and prints
continuously. For how long will there be
more than 350 sheets left? Explain how you
got your solution.

15. The 9 members of the U.S. Supreme Court
each vote "yes" or "no" on an issue. Graph
all possible ordered pairs representing the
number of possible yes votes and no votes.

16. a. Make a table of values of x and y that
satisfy the equation $y = 2x - 3$, using
$x = -1, 0, 1, 2,$ and 3.

b. Graph all solutions to $y = 2x - 3$.

17. The distance from Los Angeles to El Paso is
786 miles and from El Paso to San Antonio
is 582 miles. What is the greatest possible
distance from Los Angeles to San Antonio?
1368 miles

18. An angle has measure 18°. **162°**
a. What is the measure of its supplement?
b. What is the measure of its complement?
72°

19. Graph the set of ordered pairs that
represent the possible measures of all pairs
of complementary angles.

20. Find the measure of
$\angle L$. Show your work.
$n + 2n + 2n - 4 = 180$
$5n - 4 = 180$
$5n = 184$
$n = 36.8$
$m\angle L = 2 \cdot 36.8° = 73.6°.$

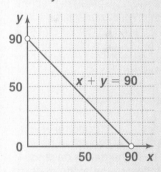

21. Find the possible values of p.
Explain how you got your
answer.

22. Use the spreadsheet below, which is similar
to that used in many businesses. It has
columns for base pay, federal tax, state tax,
and take-home pay. **c) 143.02**

a. What is in cell B2? **428.75**
b. Which cell contains the name Wojak, D.?
A4
c. The formula in cell C3 is = .3565 · B3.
What number will be printed in cell C3?
d. An employee's take-home pay is found
by subtracting federal and state taxes
from the base pay. Write the formula that
should be used in cell E2. **= B2 – C2 – D2**

	A	B	C	D	E
1	NAME	BASE PAY	FED TAX	STATE TAX	TAKE-HOME
2	Chavez, M.	428.75	152.85	38.21	
3	Lee, S.	401.18		35.76	
4	Wojak, D.	410.34	146.29		

Progress Self-Test

For the development of mathematical competence, feedback and correction, along with the opportunity to
practice, are necessary. The
Progress Self-Test provides the
opportunity for feedback and correction; the Chapter Review provides
additional opportunities and practice.
We cannot overemphasize the
importance of these end-of-chapter
materials. It is at this point that the
material "gels" for many students,
allowing them to solidify skills and
understanding. In general, student
performance should be markedly
improved after these pages.

Assign the Progress Self-Test as a
one-night assignment. Worked-out
solutions for all questions are in the
Selected Answers section of the student book. Encourage students to
take the Progress Self-Test honestly,
grade themselves, and then be prepared to discuss the test in class.

Advise students to pay special
attention to those Chapter Review
questions (pages 278–281) which
correspond to the questions that
they missed on the Progress
Self-Test.

Additional Answers (continued)
19. $x + y = 90$

[graph showing line $x + y = 90$ from (0, 90) to (90, 0)]

21. Use the Triangle Inequality.
Since $p + 3 > 7$ and $3 + 7 > p$,
$p > 4$ and $10 > p$; $4 < p < 10$.

4. Sample responses:
(a) Tom planned a 5-day vacation. He
has saved $300, but he must keep
more than $40 in his savings account.
How much can he spend on each day
of his vacation?
(b) The area of a rectangular dog kennel is 300 square meters. The width is
5 meters. The dog house is 5 meters
wide and must contain more than 40
square meters. What is the possible
length of the kennel outside of the
house area?
(c) When five times a number is subtracted from 300, the difference is
greater than 40. What are the possible
values of the number?
(d) The Booster Club ordered
300 shirts to sell at five games. If they
had more than 40 shirts left after the
sale, could they have sold an average
of 55 shirts at each game?

(Responses continue on page 278.)

Chapter 4 Review

The main objectives for the chapter are organized in the Chapter Review under the four types of understanding this book promotes— Skills, Properties, Uses, and Representations.

Whereas end-of chapter material may be considered optional in some texts, in *UCSMP Algebra* we have selected these objectives and questions with the expectation that they will be covered. Students should be able to answer these questions with about 85% accuracy after studying the chapter.

You may assign these questions over a single night to help students prepare for a test the next day, or you may assign the questions over a two-day period. If you work the questions over two days, then we recommend assigning the *evens* for homework the first night so that students get feedback in class the next day, then assigning the *odds* the night before the test because answers are provided to the odd-numbered questions.

It is effective to ask students which questions they still do not understand and use the day or days as a total class discussion of the material which the class finds most difficult.

CHAPTER REVIEW

Questions on SPUR Objectives

SPUR stands for **S**kills, **P**roperties, **U**ses, and **R**epresentations. The Chapter Review questions are grouped according to the SPUR Objectives for this chapter.

SKILLS DEAL WITH THE PROCEDURES USED TO GET ANSWERS.

Objective A: *Simplify expressions involving subtraction.* *(Lesson 4-1)*

In 1–8, simplify.

1. $3x - 4x + 5x$ 4x
2. $-\frac{2}{3} - \frac{4}{5}$ $-\frac{22}{15}$
3. $\frac{3a}{2} - \frac{9a}{2}$ -3a
4. $\frac{1}{3}x - \frac{5x}{3}$ $-\frac{4}{3}x$
5. $c - \frac{c}{3} - 2c$ $-\frac{4c}{3} - 2$
6. $3x + y - 4x - 7y$ $-x - 6y$
7. $z^3 - 7 + 8 - 4z^3$ $-3z^3 + 1$
8. $3(x - 6) - 5x$ $-2x - 18$

Objective B: *Solve and check linear equations involving subtraction.* *(Lesson 4-3)*

9. $x - 47 = -2$ x = 45
10. $2.5 = t - 3.34$ t = 5.84
11. $\frac{3}{2} + y - \frac{1}{4} = \frac{3}{4}$ y = $-\frac{1}{2}$
12. $8 = \frac{3}{4}a - 10$ a = 24
13. $4n - 3 = 17$ n = 5
14. $470 - 2n = 1100$ n = -315
15. $m - 3m = 10$ m = -5
16. $46n - 71n - 6 = 144$ n = -6
17. $0 = 4a - 6$ a = $\frac{3}{2}$
18. $18(2x - 4) - 6 = -168$ x = -2.5

Objective C: *Solve and check linear inequalities involving subtraction.* *(Lesson 4-3)*

19. $2x - 11 < 201$ x < 106
20. $-8y + 4 \le 12$ y ≥ -1
21. $32 - y > 45$ y < -13
22. $0.9(90n - 14) - 3n \ge 455.4$ n ≥ 6

Objective D: *Use the Opposite of a Sum or Difference Property to simplify expressions and solve sentences.* *(Lesson 4-5)*

In 23–28, simplify.

23. $-(4a + 7)$ -4a - 7
24. $-(3f - 4g + 6)$ -3f + 4g - 6
25. $1 - (z - 1)$ 2 - z
26. $3x - (2x - 9)$ x + 9
27. $2(a - 3) - 5(a + 2)$ -3a - 16
28. $-3(n + 6) - 6(n - 3)$ -9n

In 29–34, solve.

29. $-(p - 6) = 14$ p = -8
30. $-(r + 3) > 9$ r < -12
31. $5 - 2(x - 3) < -9$ x > 10
32. $1\frac{1}{2} - \left(\frac{3}{4} - y\right) = 7$ y = $\frac{25}{4}$
33. $(5x - 8) - (3x + 1) = 36$ x = $\frac{45}{2}$
34. $75 = 4e - 5(3 + 2e)$ e = -15

PROPERTIES DEAL WITH THE PRINCIPLES BEHIND THE MATHEMATICS.

Objective E: *Apply the Algebraic Definition of Subtraction.* *(Lesson 4-1)*

In 35 and 36, rewrite each subtraction as an addition.

35. $x - y + z$ x + -y + z
36. $-8 - v = 42$ -8 + -v = 42
37. *True or false.* The sum of $m - k$ and $k - m$ is zero. True
38. *Multiple choice.* Which does not equal the others? (d)
    (a) $a - b$
    (b) $a + -b$
    (c) $-b + a$
    (d) $b + -a$

Objective F: *Use the definitions of supplements and complements, and the Triangle Sum Theorem.* *(Lesson 4-7)*   a) 73°;   b) 163°

39. If $m\angle Q = 17°$, find the measure of
    a. its complement.   **b.** its supplement.
40. $\angle R$ and $\angle S$ are complements. If $m\angle R = x°$ and $m\angle S = z°$, write an equation relating x and z.   x + z = 90
41. *True or false.* The measure of the supplement of any angle is always greater than the measure of its complement. Justify your answer. True. The supplement of an angle with measure x° is 180 − x. The complement is 90 − x. 180 − x is greater than 90 − x.

278

Additional responses, page 275

5. There are 50 possible triangles. The lengths of the sides are:

2, 3, 4	3, 4, 5	3, 8, 10	4, 5, 6	4, 8, 10	5, 6, 7	6, 7, 8	7, 8, 9	8, 9, 10
2, 4, 5	3, 4, 6	3, 9, 10	4, 5, 7	4, 9, 10	5, 6, 8	6, 7, 9	7, 8, 10
2, 5, 6	3, 5, 6		4, 5, 8		5, 6, 9	6, 7, 10	7, 9, 10
2, 6, 7	3, 5, 7		4, 6, 7		5, 6, 10	6, 8, 9
2, 7, 8	3, 6, 7		4, 6, 8		5, 7, 8	6, 8, 10
2, 8, 9	3, 6, 8		4, 6, 9		5, 7, 9	6, 9, 10
2, 9, 10	3, 7, 8		4, 7, 8		5, 7, 10
	3, 7, 9		4, 7, 9		5, 8, 9
	3, 8, 9		4, 7, 10		5, 8, 10
			4, 8, 9		5, 9, 10

42. Find the measure of each angle in the figure below. Explain how you found your answers.

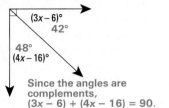

(3x − 6)°
42°

48°
(4x − 16)°

Since the angles are complements,
(3x − 6) + (4x − 16) = 90.

43. Two angles of a triangle measure 75° and 32°. What is the measure of the third angle? **73°**

44. In a triangle, the largest angle has measure 10 times the smallest; the other angle has measure 10° more than the smallest. Find the measure of each. **$14\frac{1}{6}°$, $24\frac{1}{6}°$, $141\frac{2}{3}°$**

45. A triangle has a 40° angle. Two of the angles of the triangle have equal measures. Find all possible measures of the other two angles.

46. Find the measure of each angle in △MAC. **$m\angle C = 43\frac{2}{3}°$, $m\angle A = 53\frac{2}{3}°$, $m\angle M = 82\frac{2}{3}°$**

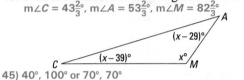

(x − 29)°

(x − 39)°   x°
C   M

45) 40°, 100° or 70°, 70°

Objective G: *Use the Triangle Inequality to determine possible lengths of sides of triangles.* *(Lesson 4-8)*

In 47 and 48, tell whether the three numbers can be the lengths of sides of a triangle. If they cannot be, justify your answer.

47. 16, 3, 5 **No; 3 + 5 < 16**   **48.** 16, 8, 10 **Yes**

In 49 and 50, use the Triangle Inequality to write the three inequalities which must be satisfied by lengths of sides in the triangle.

49.   **50.**

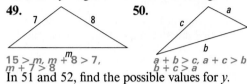

7   8   c
                                          b
            m   a

15 > m, m + 8 > 7,   a + b > c, a + c > b
m + 7 > 8   b + c > a

In 51 and 52, find the possible values for y.

51.   **52.**

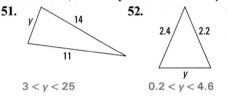

y   14   2.4   2.2

      11   y

3 < y < 25   0.2 < y < 4.6

USES DEAL WITH APPLICATIONS OF MATHEMATICS IN REAL SITUATIONS.

Objective H: *Use models for subtraction to write expressions and sentences involving subtraction.* *(Lessons 4-2, 4-3)*

53. Last week Carla earned E dollars, saved S dollars, and spent P dollars. Relate E, S, and P in a subtraction sentence. **S = E − P**

54. An elevator won't run if it holds more than L kilograms. A person weighing 80 kg gets on a crowded elevator and an "overload" light goes on. How much did the other passengers weigh? **more than L − 80 kg**

55. The total floor area of a three-story house is advertised as 3500 sq ft. If the first floor's area is F sq ft and the third floor's area is 1000 sq ft, what is the area of the second floor? **2500 − F**

56. After spending $40, Mort has less than $3 left. If he started with S dollars, write an inequality to describe the possible values of S. **S − 40 < 3 or S < 43**

58) 31,500 ft

57. Donna is 5 years older than Eileen. If Donna's age is D, how old is Eileen? **D − 5**

58. A plane 30,000 feet above sea level is radioing a submarine 1500 feet below sea level. What is the difference in their altitudes?

59. A video game is regularly priced at V dollars. Save-a-Buck is selling the game for 30% off.

   a. Write an expression for the amount of the discount you get at Save-a-Buck. **.3V**

   b. Write an expression for the sale price of the game. **.7V**

60. A family went out for dinner. The total cost of the food was F dollars. The restaurant automatically adds 15% as the standard tip for service.

   a. Write an expression for the cost of the food and tip. **(1 + 15%)F = 1.15F dollars**

   b. The family has a coupon worth $5 off the cost of the food. How much does the dinner, including tip, actually cost them? **1.15(F − 5) dollars**

6. Segments drawn from one vertex to each of the other vertices of a pentagon separate the polygon into three triangles. The sum of the measures of all angles of any pentagon is 3 · 180° or 540°; of any hexagon is 4 · 180° or 720°; of any heptagon is 5 · 180° or 900°. The sum of the measures of all polygons with the same number of sides is the same.

Additional Answers

71.

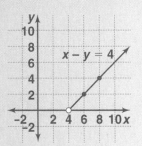

72.

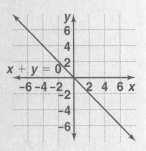

73.

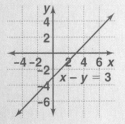

74.

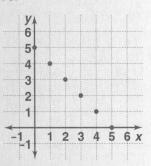

Objective I: *Solve problems using linear sentences involving subtraction.* *(Lesson 4-3)*

61. Liz saves $15 per week. She has $750 in the bank and needs $1500 in the bank before she can afford to go on vacation. For how many weeks must she save before she has more than the required amount? Explain how you got the answer. 51 wks; Solve $750 + 15w > 1500$.

62. If $F = \frac{9}{5}C + 32$, find the Celsius equivalent of 100°F. ≈ 37.8°C

63. Radio station WARM has a trivia contest. The first day that a question is asked, the prize for a correct answer is $200. If no one wins the money, the prize increases by $92 per day until a correct answer is received. If the program director budgets $1400 for the contest, for how many days will the potential prize remain within the budget? 13 days

64. Each minute, a computer printer prints 8 sheets of paper. Suppose the printer starts with 1500 sheets of paper and prints continuously. a) $1500 - 8m$

   a. Write an expression that represents the number of sheets left after m minutes.

   b. After how many minutes will 200 sheets be left? 162.5 minutes

Objective J: *Apply the Triangle Inequality in real situations.* *(Lesson 4-8)*

65. It is 346 miles from El Paso to Phoenix and 887 miles from Dallas to Phoenix. Based on this information, what is the greatest possible distance from Dallas to El Paso? 1233 mi

66. Malinda lives 20 minutes by train from Roger and 30 minutes by train from Charles. By train, how long would it take her to get from Roger's place to Charles's place? (Assume all trains go at the same rate.) 10 min ≤ train time ≤ 50 min

---

REPRESENTATIONS DEAL WITH PICTURES, GRAPHS, OR OBJECTS THAT ILLUSTRATE CONCEPTS

Objective K: *Use a spreadsheet to show patterns and make tables from formulas.* *(Lesson 4-4)*

67. Use the spreadsheet below.

   a. The formula in cell B1 is = A1^2 + A1. This was replicated down the column. What is the formula for B6? = A6^2 + A6

   b. Find the value that belongs in cell B7. 6

   c. Describe what would happen if you changed the value in cell A6 to -20. B6 would change to 380.

	A	B
1	3	12
2	2	
3	1	2
4	0	
5	−1	0
6	−2	2
7	−3	

68. This spreadsheet shows the evaluation of the formula $d = 180n - 360$.

   a. What formula gives the values in cell B2? = A2 * 180 − 360

   b. What formula gives the values in cell B6? = A6 * 180 − 360

   c. Complete the table.

	A	B
1	n	d
2	2	0
3	3	180
4	4	360
5	5	540
6	6	720
7	7	900

75.

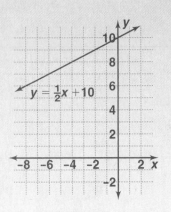

76.

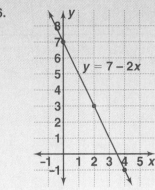

77.

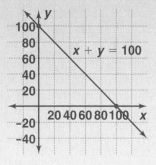

69. The spreadsheet below calculates the total ticket income for a movie theater on a series of days. Adult tickets cost $6.00 each. Children's tickets cost $4.00 each.

   a. Complete the totals in column D.

   b. Write a formula for computing the value of cell D4 from cells B4 and C4. **= B4 * 6 + C4 * 4**

   c. What day recorded the most income? **Aug. 30**

	A	B	C	D
1	Day	Adult	Children	Total
2	August 26	100	20	680
3	August 27	110	20	740
4	August 28	91	10	586
5	August 29	145	62	1118
6	August 30	170	40	1180
7	August 31	60	40	520

70. The spreadsheet below gives the scoring for a team of basketball players. Column B gives the number of free throws they completed (each worth one point). Column C gives the number of 2-point field goals for each player. Column D gives the number of 3-pointers scored by each player. Column E gives the total number of points scored by the player in the game. Ken scored 16 points, since $5 \cdot 1 + 4 \cdot 2 + 1 \cdot 3 = 16$.

   a. Complete column E in the score sheet.

   b. What cell contains the number 8? **C5**

   c. What formula is in cell E5?

   d. Write a formula for cell C8 that would total the number of 2-point field goals.
   = C2 + C3 + C4 + C5 + C6 + C7

c) **= B5 * 1 + C5 * 2 + D5 * 3**

	A	B	C	D	E
1	Player	Free Throws	Field Goals	3-pointers	POINTS
2	Jose	2	6	1	17
3	Djin	1	4	0	9
4	Ken	5	4	1	16
5	Arunas	1	8	2	23
6	Bill	2	2	0	6
7	Mike	0	1	1	5
8					

Objective L: *Graph equations of the forms $x \pm y = k$ or $y = ax \pm b$ by making a table of values.* *(Lessons 4-6, 4-9)* See margin for 71–77.

71. Xavier is four years older than his sister Yvonne. Graph all possible ordered pairs that represent their ages. Let x represent Xavier's age and y represent Yvonne's age.

72. The sum of two numbers is 0. Graph all possible pairs of numbers.

73. Mary and Peter have a total of 5 pets. Graph all possible ways the pets may be divided between them.

In 74–77, graph all ordered pairs (x, y) that satisfy the equation.

74. $x - y = 3$

75. $y = \frac{1}{2}x + 10$

76. $y = 7 - 2x$

77. $x + y = 100$

Assessment

Evaluation The *Assessment Sourcebook* provides five forms of the Chapter 4 Test. Forms A and B present parallel versions in a short-answer format. Forms C and D offer performance assessment. The fifth test is Chapter 4 Test, Cumulative Form. About 50% of this test covers Chapter 4; 25% covers Chapter 3, and 25% covers earlier chapters.

For information on grading see *General Teaching Suggestions; Grading* in the *Professional Sourcebook* which begins on page T20 in Part 1 of the Teacher's Edition.

Feedback After students have taken the test for Chapter 4 and you have scored the results, return the tests to students for discussion. Class discussion on the questions that caused trouble for most students can be very effective in identifying and clarifying misunderstandings. You might want to have them write down the items they missed and work either in groups or at home to correct them. It is important for students to receive feedback on every chapter test, and we recommend that students see and correct their mistakes before proceeding too far into the next chapter.

Setting Up Lesson 5-1

We recommend that you assign Lesson 5-1, both reading and some questions, for homework the evening of the test. It gives students work to do after they have completed the test and keeps the class moving.

Adapting to Individual Needs

The student text is written for the vast majority of students. The chart at the right suggests two pacing plans to accommodate the needs of your students. Students in the Full Course should complete the entire text by the end of the year. Students in the Minimal Course will spend more time when there are quizzes and more time on the Chapter Review. Therefore, these students may not complete all of the chapters in the text.

Options are also presented to meet the needs of a variety of teaching and learning styles. For each lesson, the Teacher's Edition provides sections entitled: *Video* which describes video segments and related questions that can be used for motivation or extension; *Optional Activities* which suggests activities that employ materials, physical models, technology, and cooperative learning; and, *Adapting to Individual Needs* which regularly includes **Challenge** problems, **English Language Development** suggestions, and suggestions for providing **Extra Help.** The Teacher's Edition also frequently includes an **Error Alert,** an **Extension,** and an **Assessment** alternative. The options available in Chapter 5 are summarized in the chart below.

Chapter 5 Pacing Chart

Day	Full Course	Minimal Course
1	5-1	5-1
2	5-2	5-2
3	5-3	5-3
4	Quiz*; 5-4	Quiz*; begin 5-4.
5	5-5	Finish 5-4.
6	5-6	5-5
7	Quiz*; 5-7	5-6
8	5-8	Quiz*; begin 5-7.
9	5-9	Finish 5-7.
10	Self-Test	5-8
11	Review	5-9
12	Test*	Self-Test
13		Review
14		Review
15		Test*

*in the Teacher's Resource File

In the Teacher's Edition...

Lesson	Optional Activities	Extra Help	Challenge	English Language Development	Error Alert	Extension	Cooperative Learning	Ongoing Assessment
5-1	●	●	●	●	●	●	●	Written
5-2	●	●	●	●		●	●	Oral
5-3	●	●	●	●	●	●	●	Group
5-4	●	●	●			●	●	Oral
5-5	●	●	●	●		●	●	Group
5-6	●	●	●	●		●	●	Oral/Written
5-7	●	●	●	●	●	●	●	Oral
5-8	●	●	●	●		●	●	Written
5-9	●	●	●	●		●	●	Group

In the Additional Resources...

Lesson	In the Teacher's Resource File									
	Lesson Masters, A and B	Teaching Aids*	Activity Kit*	Answer Masters	Technology Sourcebook	Assessment Sourcebook	Visual Aids**	Technology	Video Segments
5-1	5-1	28, 47, 50, 51	10	5-1			28, 47, 50, 51, AM		
5-2	5-2	37, 47, 52		5-2	Comp 13		37, 47, 52, AM	Spreadsheet	
5-3	5-3	19, 47, 53	11	5-3		Quiz	19, 47, 53, AM		
5-4	5-4	39, 48, 54		5-4			39, 48, 54, AM		
5-5	5-5	26, 28, 48, 55		5-5	Comp 14, Calc 3		26, 28, 48, 55, AM	GraphExplorer	
5-6	5-6	39, 48, 55, 56		5-6	Comp 15	Quiz	39, 48, 55, 56, AM	GraphExplorer	
5-7	5-7	39, 49, 55		5-7			39, 49, 55, AM		
5-8	5-8	49		5-8			49, AM		
5-9	5-9	49	12	5-9			49, AM		
End of chapter				Review		Tests			

*Teaching Aids are pictured on pages 282C and 282D. The activities in the Activity Kit are pictured on page 282C.

**Visual Aids provide transparencies for all Teaching Aids and all Answer Masters.

Also available is the Study Skills Handbook which includes study-skill tips related to reading, note-taking, and comprehension.

Integrating Strands and Applications

	5-1	5-2	5-3	5-4	5-5	5-6	5-7	5-8	5-9
Mathematical Connections									
Number Sense								●	●
Algebra	●	●	●	●	●	●	●	●	●
Geometry		●	●	●	●		●		●
Measurement		●	●				●		●
Logic and Reasoning								●	●
Patterns and Functions	●			●	●	●	●		
Interdisciplinary and Other Connections									
Literature				●					
Science	●					●	●		●
Social Studies	●	●	●	●		●	●	●	
Multicultural	●			●				●	
Technology		●		●	●	●	●		
Career		●		●					
Consumer	●	●		●	●	●	●	●	●
Sports	●		●					●	

Teaching and Assessing the Chapter Objectives

Chapter 5 Objectives (Organized into the SPUR categories—Skills, Properties, Uses, and Representations)	Lessons	Progress Self-Test Questions	Chapter Review Questions	Chapter Test, Forms A and B	Chapter Test, Forms C	Chapter Test, Forms D
Skills						
A: Solve linear equations of the form $ax + b = cx + d$.	5-3, 5-8	3, 4, 6, 8, 9	1–12	4, 5, 8	1	
B: Solve linear inequalities of the form $ax + b < cx + d$.	5-6, 5-8	5, 7	13–22	6, 7, 9	3	
C: Use chunking to simplify or evaluate expressions or to solve equations.	5-9	10–13	23–32	3, 11	1	
D: Find equivalent forms of formulas and equations.	5-7	14, 15	33–40	12, 13	2	
Properties						
E: Apply and recognize properties associated with linear sentences.	5-3, 5-6, 5-7, 5-8	1, 2	41–48	1, 2	3	
Uses						
F: Use linear equations and inequalities of the form $ax + b = cx + d$ or $ax + b < cx + d$ to solve real-world problems.	5-3, 5-6, 5-8	17, 18	49–56	14, 16		✓
G: Use tables or spreadsheets to solve real-world problems involving linear situations.	5-2	19, 20	57–59	15, 19		
Representations						
H: Graph horizontal and vertical lines.	5-1	16	60–65	10	4	
I: Use graphs to solve problems involving linear expressions.	5-1, 5-4	18, 21	66–67	17, 18	4	✓
J: Given an equation, be able to use an automatic grapher to draw and interpret a graph.	5-5	22	68–75	20, 21		✓

In the Assessment Sourcebook

Multidimensional Assessment
Quiz for Lessons 5-1 through 5-3
Quiz for Lessons 5-4 through 5-6

Chapter 5 Test, Forms A–D
Chapter 5 Test, Cumulative Form

Quiz and Test Writer
Multiple forms of chapter tests and quizzes; Challenges

Activity Kit

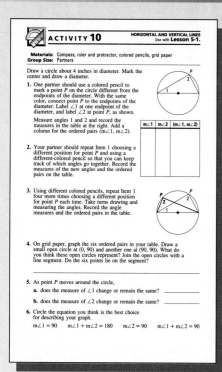

ACTIVITY 10 — HORIZONTAL AND VERTICAL LINES — Use with **Lesson 5-1.**

Materials: Compass, ruler and protractor, colored pencils, grid paper
Group Size: Partners

Draw a circle about 4 inches in diameter. Mark the center and draw a diameter.

1. One partner should use a colored pencil to mark a point P on the circle different from the endpoints of the diameter. With the same color, connect point P to the endpoints of the diameter. Label $\angle 1$ at one endpoint of the diameter, and label $\angle 2$ at point P, as shown.

   Measure angles 1 and 2 and record the measures in the table at the right. Add a column for the ordered pairs $(m\angle 1, m\angle 2)$.

$m\angle 1$	$m\angle 2$	$(m\angle 1, m\angle 2)$

2. Your partner should repeat Item 1 choosing a different position for point P and using a different-colored pencil so that you can keep track of which angles go together. Record the measures of the new angles and the ordered pairs on the table.

3. Using different colored pencils, repeat Item 1 four more times choosing a different position for point P each time. Take turns drawing and measuring the angles. Record the angle measures and the ordered pairs in the table.

4. On grid paper, graph the six ordered pairs in your table. Draw a small open circle at (0, 90) and another one at (90, 90). What do you think these open circles represent? Join the open circles with a line segment. Do the six points lie on the segment?

5. As point P moves around the circle,
   a. does the measure of $\angle 1$ change or remain the same? _____
   b. does the measure of $\angle 2$ change or remain the same? _____

6. Circle the equation you think is the best choice for describing your graph.

   $m\angle 1 = 90$ $m\angle 1 + m\angle 2 = 180$ $m\angle 2 = 90$ $m\angle 1 + m\angle 2 = 90$

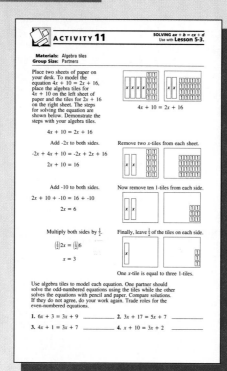

ACTIVITY 11 — SOLVING $ax + b = cx + d$ — Use with **Lesson 5-3.**

Materials: Algebra tiles
Group Size: Partners

Place two sheets of paper on your desk. To model the equation $4x + 10 = 2x + 16$, place the algebra tiles for $4x + 10$ on the left sheet of paper and the tiles for $2x + 16$ on the right sheet. The steps for solving the equation are shown below. Demonstrate the steps with your algebra tiles.

$4x + 10 = 2x + 16$

$4x + 10 = 2x + 16$

Add $-2x$ to both sides.   Remove two x-tiles from each sheet.

$-2x + 4x + 10 = -2x + 2x + 16$

$2x + 10 = 16$

Add -10 to both sides.   Now remove ten 1-tiles from each side.

$2x + 10 + -10 = 16 + -10$

$2x = 6$

Multiply both sides by $\frac{1}{2}$.   Finally, leave $\frac{1}{2}$ of the tiles on each side.

$\left(\frac{1}{2}\right)2x = \left(\frac{1}{2}\right)6$

$x = 3$

One x-tile is equal to three 1-tiles.

Use algebra tiles to model each equation. One partner should solve the odd-numbered equations using the tiles while the other solves the equations with pencil and paper. Compare solutions. If they do not agree, do your work again. Trade roles for the even-numbered equations.

1. $6x + 3 = 3x + 9$ _____   2. $3x + 17 = 5x + 7$ _____

3. $4x + 1 = 3x + 7$ _____   4. $x + 10 = 3x + 2$ _____

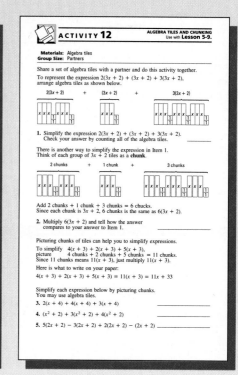

ACTIVITY 12 — ALGEBRA TILES AND CHUNKING — Use with **Lesson 5-9.**

Materials: Algebra tiles
Group Size: Partners

Share a set of algebra tiles with a partner and do this activity together.

To represent the expression $2(3x + 2) + (3x + 2) + 3(3x + 2)$, arrange algebra tiles as shown below.

$2(3x + 2)$ $+$ $(3x + 2)$ $+$ $3(3x + 2)$

1. Simplify the expression $2(3x + 2) + (3x + 2) + 3(3x + 2)$. Check your answer by counting all of the algebra tiles. _____

There is another way to simplify the expression in Item 1. Think of each group of $3x + 2$ tiles as a **chunk**.

2 chunks $+$ 1 chunk $+$ 3 chunks

Add 2 chunks + 1 chunk + 3 chunks = 6 chunks.
Since each chunk is $3x + 2$, 6 chunks is the same as $6(3x + 2)$.

2. Multiply $6(3x + 2)$ and tell how the answer compares to your answer to Item 1. _____

Picturing chunks of tiles can help you to simplify expressions.

To simplify $4(x + 3) + 2(x + 3) + 5(x + 3)$, picture 4 chunks + 2 chunks + 5 chunks = 11 chunks. Since 11 chunks means $11(x + 3)$, just multiply $11(x + 3)$.
Here is what to write on your paper:
$4(x + 3) + 2(x + 3) + 5(x + 3) = 11(x + 3) = 11x + 33$

Simplify each expression below by picturing chunks. You may use algebra tiles.

3. $2(x + 4) + 4(x + 4) + 3(x + 4)$ _____

4. $(x^2 + 2) + 3(x^2 + 2) + 4(x^2 + 2)$ _____

5. $5(2x + 2) - 3(2x + 2) + 2(2x + 2) - (2x + 2)$ _____

Teaching Aids

Teaching Aid 19, **Balance Scales,** (shown on page 70D) can be used with **Lesson 5-3.**
Teaching Aid 26, **Graph Paper,** (shown on page 140D) can be used with **Lesson 5-5.**
Teaching Aid 28, **Four-Quadrant Graph Paper,** (shown on page 140D) can be used with **Lessons 5-1 and 5-5.** Teaching Aid 37, **Spreadsheet,** (shown on page 214D) can be used with **Lesson 5-2.** Teaching Aid 39, **Graphing Equations,** (shown on page 214D) can be used with **Lessons 5-4, 5-6, and 5-7.**

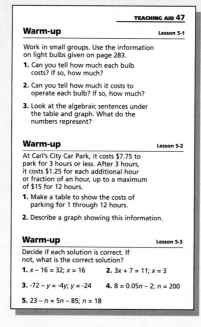

TEACHING AID 47

Warm-up — Lesson 5-1

Work in small groups. Use the information on light bulbs given on page 283.

1. Can you tell how much each bulb costs? If so, how much?

2. Can you tell how much it costs to operate each bulb? If so, how much?

3. Look at the algebraic sentences under the table and graph. What do the numbers represent?

Warm-up — Lesson 5-2

At Carl's City Car Park, it costs $7.75 to park for 3 hours or less. After 3 hours, it costs $1.25 for each additional hour or fraction of an hour, up to a maximum of $15 for 12 hours.

1. Make a table to show the costs of parking for 1 through 12 hours.

2. Describe a graph showing this information.

Warm-up — Lesson 5-3

Decide if each solution is correct. If not, what is the correct solution?

1. $x - 16 = 32$; $x = 16$ 2. $3x + 7 = 11$; $x = 3$

3. $-72 - y = -4y$; $y = -24$ 4. $8 = 0.05n - 2$; $n = 200$

5. $23 - n = 5n - 85$; $n = 18$

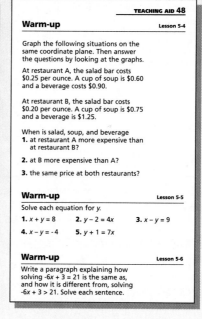

TEACHING AID 48

Warm-up — Lesson 5-4

Graph the following situations on the same coordinate plane. Then answer the questions by looking at the graphs.

At restaurant A, the salad bar costs $0.25 per ounce. A cup of soup is $0.60 and a beverage costs $0.90.

At restaurant B, the salad bar costs $0.20 per ounce. A cup of soup is $0.75 and a beverage is $1.25.

When is salad, soup, and beverage
1. at restaurant A more expensive than at restaurant B?

2. at B more expensive than A?

3. the same price at both restaurants?

Warm-up — Lesson 5-5

Solve each equation for y.

1. $x + y = 8$ 2. $y - 2 = 4x$ 3. $x - y = 9$
4. $x - y = -4$ 5. $y + 1 = 7x$

Warm-up — Lesson 5-6

Write a paragraph explaining how solving $-6x + 3 = 21$ is the same as, and how it is different from, solving $-6x + 3 > 21$. Solve each sentence.

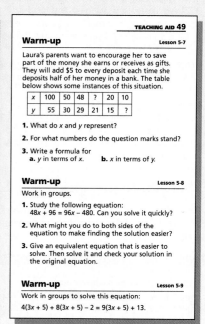

TEACHING AID 49

Warm-up — Lesson 5-7

Laura's parents want to encourage her to save part of the money she earns or receives as gifts. They will add $5 to every deposit each time she deposits half of her money in a bank. The table below shows some instances of this situation.

x	100	50	48	?	20	10
y	55	30	29	21	15	?

1. What do x and y represent?

2. For what numbers do the question marks stand?

3. Write a formula for
   a. y in terms of x.   b. x in terms of y.

Warm-up — Lesson 5-8

Work in groups.

1. Study the following equation: $48x + 96 = 96x - 480$. Can you solve it quickly?

2. What might you do to both sides of the equation to make finding the solution easier?

3. Give an equivalent equation that is easier to solve. Then solve it and check your solution in the original equation.

Warm-up — Lesson 5-9

Work in groups to solve this equation:
$4(3x + 5) + 8(3x + 5) - 2 = 9(3x + 5) + 13$.

Additional Examples

1. Charles received $8 allowance for each of the first five weeks of the year. Imagine that the points (1, 8), (2, 8), (3, 8), (4, 8), and (5, 8) are graphed to represent this situation.

   a. What kind of line contains these points, a horizontal line or a vertical line?

   b. What is an equation for the line?

2. Graph $y = -4$
   a. on a number line.   b. on a coordinate plane.

3. Use the situation described in Example 3 on page 287. Suppose that Mac does not have to pay a service fee when his account is under $300. Explain how to use a graph to find the time at which Mac will have a balance of $100 in his account.

4. a. Write an equation for the line containing $(-\frac{1}{2}, 6)$ and $(-\frac{1}{2}, -6)$.

   b. Tell whether the line is horizontal, vertical, or neither.

5. Give a sentence describing all points on the boundary of the shaded region.

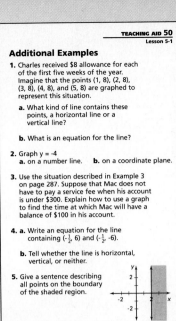

Question 22

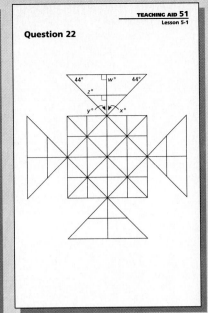

Example 2

Number of Copies n	Acme's Charges $250 + 0.01n$	Best's Charges $70 + 0.03n$
0	250	70
2,000	270	130
4,000	290	190
6,000		
8,000		
10,000		
12,000		
14,000		
16,000		
18,000		
20,000		

Question 30

Example 2

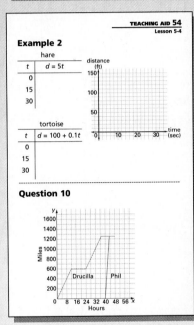

hare

t	$d = 5t$
0	
15	
30	

tortoise

t	$d = 100 + 0.1t$
0	
15	
30	

Question 10

Automatic Grapher Grids

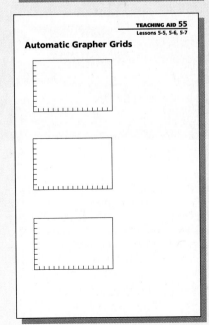

Example 2

t number of years	height h in ft maple	beech
0		
2		
4		
6		
8		
10		
12		

Questions 5 and 6

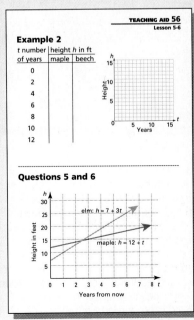

elm: $h = 7 + 3t$

maple: $h = 12 + t$

282D

Chapter Opener

Pacing

All lessons in this chapter are designed to be covered in one day. At the end of the chapter, you should plan to spend 1 day to review the Progress Self-Test, 1 to 2 days for the Chapter Review, and 1 day for a test. You may wish to spend a day on projects, and possibly a day is needed for quizzes. Therefore this chapter should take 12 to 15 days. We strongly advise that you not spend more than 16 days on this chapter; there is ample opportunity to review the ideas in later chapters. Chapter 6 will continue the sentence solving, and Chapter 7 will solidify the study of graphing techniques.

Using Pages 282–283

Page 283 provides students with an advance organizer for the content of the chapter. Students are told that the information on the page helps to determine which of two types of light bulbs costs less to use. Point out that they will learn three methods for solving situations that lead to linear sentences: using tables, using graphs, and operating on both sides of a sentence. Using tables is an arithmetic method. However, it is not very efficient. For solving linear sentences, most people would say that operating on both sides of a sentence is the best method. However, there are some sentences where that method does not work (for instance, $2^x = 3 + x$), and then graphing can be the most convenient method.

History Connection Thomas Edison, known as the Wizard of Menlo Park, played a key role in introducing the modern age of electricity. His

282

Chapter 5 Overview

This chapter concludes the discussion of the solving of linear sentences that was begun in Chapter 1. These are perhaps the most important sentences in elementary algebra, and again we are interested in the skills, properties, uses, and representations involving them.

The chapter presents graphical representations first. In Lesson 5-1, horizontal and vertical lines are graphed so that the student

can solve $ax + b = c$ by looking for the point of intersection of the lines $y = ax + b$ and $y = c$. Later, in Lesson 5-4, the same idea is applied for solving $ax + b = cx + d$. That is, the lines $y = ax + b$ and $y = cx + d$ are graphed and the pcint of intersection examined. The skills begin in Lesson 5-2 where students use tables to solve equations of the form $ax + b = cx + d$; skills continue in Lesson 5-3 with the standard technique of operating on both sides of the equation. The

corresponding inequalities are considered in Lesson 5-6. The next two lessons cover more complicated forms of linear equations: those involving formulas that are sometimes called "literal equations" (Lesson 5-7) and those with fractions (Lesson 5-8). The chapter concludes with the powerful, more general technique of chunking.

LINEAR SENTENCES

A light-bulb manufacturer produces two kinds of bulbs—regular bulbs and new energy-efficient (EE) bulbs. The EE bulbs use less electricity, but they cost more. Does the money you save in electricity make up for the higher initial cost of the bulb?

This question and other related questions can be answered by using tables or spreadsheets, graphs, and algebraic sentences, as shown below.

1. In a table:

	A	B	C
1	Hours	EE	Regular
2	0	$0.92	$0.70
3	100	$1.34	$1.18
4	200	$1.76	$1.66
5	300	$2.18	$2.14
6	400	$2.60	$2.62
7	500	$3.02	$3.10
8	600	$3.44	$3.58
9	700	$3.86	$4.06
10	800	$4.28	$4.54
11	900	$4.70	$5.02
12	1000	$5.12	$5.50

2. With a graph:

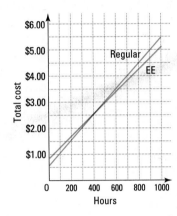

3. By algebraic sentences:

	Total cost with EE	Total cost with regular
When is the regular bulb cheaper?	$.92 + .0042h > 70 + .0048h$	
When is the EE bulb cheaper?	$.92 + .0042h < 70 + .0048h$	
When are the costs the same?	$.92 + .0042h = 70 + .0048h$	

In this chapter, you will study all three of these ways to solve linear sentences and learn how they are related to each other.

patents for the phonograph (1877) and the incandescent lamp (1879) are but a few of the world-record 1,093 patents that he held either singly or with others. Interested students might look up other data on this famous American inventor and tell the class about them.

Photo Connections
The photo collage makes real-world connections to the content of the chapter: linear sentences.

Swimmer: Linear sentences can be used to determine future winning times for freestyle swimming events given certain assumptions.

Light Bulb: The striking picture of an ordinary light bulb directs attention to the situation on page 283 and to the ways which represent it.

Child: This child represents the 31.3% of Alaska's population which was under 18 years of age in 1990. In Chapter 5 many real-world applications of solving linear sentences involve population changes in cities and states.

Oil Drums: Crude oil is shipped from its point of origin by tanker or pipeline. After processing, some petroleum products are stored in drums. Lesson 5-8 applies an advanced solving technique to questions about world oil reserves.

Cars: In Lesson 5-2, students use tables to compare charges at two garages. You might want students to consider the cost of parking the cars pictured here.

Chapter 5 Projects
At this time you might want to have students look over the projects on pages 338–339.

In Lesson 5-5, students learn to use an automatic grapher—using either a graphing calculator or a computer program—which automatically draws a graph when an equation is given. This technology allows students to see examples of linear and nonlinear graphs. Graphs made with a graphing calculator or with one of the many computer graphing programs are far more accurate and are, therefore, far more instructive than those made by hand.

While automatic graphers are not required, we encourage their use. If such technology is not available, students can still read the problems for which automatic graphers are suggested and sketch the graphs on graph paper. If classroom sets of graphing calculators are available, but students cannot take them home, you might adjust your assignments so that students can do the examples and questions that require their use in class.

Many of the applications in this chapter involve the constant-increase or constant-decrease situations which were used in Chapters 3 and 4. Such situations naturally lead to graphs and also are background for Chapter 7.

LESSON 5-1

Horizontal and Vertical Lines

This music's a gas. *In 1973, lines at gas stations were so long that in some places entertainers performed to keep customers from becoming angry.*

Equations for Horizontal Lines

Before 1974, there was no national speed limit in the United States. Each state set its own limit, and some states had none. But in 1973, oil became scarce and its price jumped. Long lines appeared at many gas stations because gasoline (a by-product of oil) was in short supply. To reduce gasoline usage, the U.S. Congress passed a law that set a national highway speed limit of 55 $\frac{\text{miles}}{\text{hr}}$, beginning in 1974. Even though the oil crisis passed, a benefit of this law was that at reduced speeds there were fewer highway deaths. Congress increased the national highway speed limit to 65 $\frac{\text{miles}}{\text{hr}}$ on July 1, 1987.

The preceding paragraph has described in *writing*, or *prose*, what have been the national speed limits since 1974. Here are three other ways.

❶   In a table:

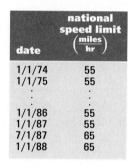

date	national speed limit ($\frac{\text{miles}}{\text{hr}}$)
1/1/74	55
1/1/75	55
⋮	⋮
1/1/86	55
1/1/87	55
7/1/87	65
1/1/88	65

With a graph:

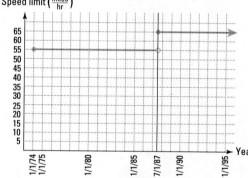

284

By algebraic sentences:

Let x = the date and y = the national speed limit $\left(\text{in } \frac{\text{miles}}{\text{hr}}\right)$.

When $1974 \le x < 1987.5$, $y = 55$.

When $1987.5 \le x$, $y = 65$.

Each description has its advantages. The description by algebraic sentences is brief and precise.

② The graph shows that all the points from 1/1/74 to 7/1/87, not including 7/1/87, have the same *y-coordinate*. For all of these points, the *y*-coordinate equals 55. Therefore, an equation for the line is $y = 55$. Beginning halfway through 1987, the value of y is 65, so these points lie on a second horizontal line, with equation $y = 65$. Every *horizontal line* has an equation of this type.

> Every **horizontal line** has an equation of the form $y = k$, where k is a fixed real number.

Example 1

Give an equation describing all points on line m graphed below.

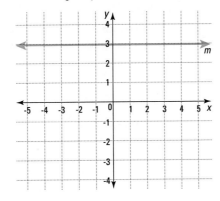

Solution

The points are on a horizontal line that crosses the y-axis at 3. An *equation for line m is* $y = 3$.

Check

Two of the points on line m have coordinates (0, 3) and (5, 3). These numbers satisfy the equation $y = 3$.

Police occasionally set up radar to inform motorists of their speeds.

Example 1 goes from graph to equation; **Example 2** goes from equation to graph. Such reversibility is emphasized in the work with graphing in the rest of the text.
Example 3 shows the importance of horizontal and vertical lines in locating coordinates of points.

Reading Mathematics The reading in this lesson may present difficulties for some of your students. Reading it aloud in class may be helpful. After the first two paragraphs are read, discuss the table and the graph.

① To determine whether or not students understand this table and graph, ask why the date 7/1/87 is given. [That is the date on which the speed limit was changed.] Then ask why there is an open circle on the graph. [Until 7/1/87, the speed limit was 55 miles per hour.]

If any students in your class come from other countries, they may think that 7/1/87 stands for January 7th, not July 1st. In most countries other than the United States, the "day/month/year" shorthand is used.

② Be sure students understand that $y = k$ means that the y-coordinate is always k. The equation $y = 55$ is short for "y-coordinate equals 55." Note that the lack of any statement about x means that x could have any value. This explanation should help to minimize difficulties students might have interpreting the equation. Point out that $y = 55$ is equivalent to $0 \cdot x + y = 55$ and ask for pairs of values (x, y) that are solutions to this equation. The graph of all pairs of values is a horizontal line.

Optional Activities

Activity 1
You can use *Activity Kit, Activity 10,* as an introduction to lesson 5-1. In this activity students collect data from geometric figures to produce a graph that is a horizontal line.

Activity 2
✎ **Writing** After students study the solutions to **Example 3,** ask them to explain in writing which solution they prefer and why. A discussion of what they wrote may be quite interesting.

③ Any equation of the form $x = h$ can be rewritten with two variables as $x + 0 \cdot y = h$. This emphasizes that y can have any value but x can only be h. The graph of all pairs of values (x, y) is a vertical line.

④ The description of a graph using two different sentences with two domains is called a *piecewise description*. Each sentence describes a piece of the graph. Do not expect students to understand this example the first time they read it. It often takes a while for students to put all of the elements together.

Equations for Vertical Lines

A *vertical line* is drawn at the right. Notice that each point on the line has the same *x-coordinate*, 2.5. Thus an equation for the line is $x = 2.5$. This means x is fixed at 2.5, but y can be any number.

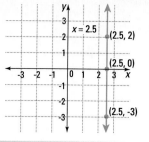

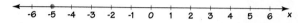

③ Every **vertical line** has an equation of the form $x = h$, where h is a fixed real number.

An equation with only one variable, such as $x = -5$ or $y = 8$, can be graphed on a number line (in which case its graph is a point), or on a coordinate plane (in which case its graph is a line). The directions or the context of the problem will usually tell you which type of graph to make.

Example 2

a. Graph $x = -5$ on a number line.
b. Graph $x = -5$ on a coordinate plane.

Solution

a. Draw a number line. Mark the point with coordinate equal to -5.

The graph of $x = -5$ on a number line is the single point with coordinate -5.

b. Draw x- and y-axes. Plot points whose x-coordinate is -5. Some points are (-5, 2), (-5, 0), and (-5, -3). Draw the line through these points.

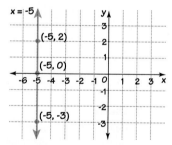

The graph of $x = -5$ in a coordinate plane is the vertical line that crosses the x-axis at -5.

286

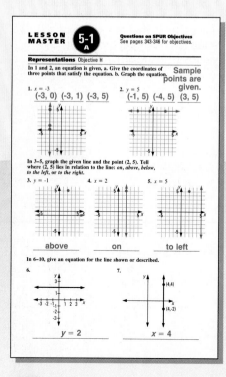
Adapting to Individual Needs

Extra Help

Some students might not understand why the graph of an equation of the form $y = k$ is a horizontal line. Show them a graph of the equation $y = 3$. Have students locate and label as many points as necessary until everyone realizes that any point with a y-coordinate of 3 satisfies this equation. Since $y = 3$ for every value of x, the graph will be parallel to the x-axis. A similar example and explanation can be used to show that the graph of an equation of the form $x = k$ is a vertical line.

Using Horizontal and Vertical Lines

Horizontal and vertical lines can be used to solve equations or inequalities.

④ Example 3

At the beginning of the year, Mac had $580 in his savings account. As long as he has at least $300 in the account, he does not have to pay a service fee. For how long can he withdraw $20 per week without paying a service fee?

Solution 1

Let y equal Mac's bank balance, and x equal the number of weeks after the start of school. Then, y = 580 – 20x.
This line is graphed using a table of (x, y) values. Also graphed is the horizontal line y = 300 to represent the minimum balance that he must keep to avoid service charges.

x	y
0	580
5	480
10	380
15	280

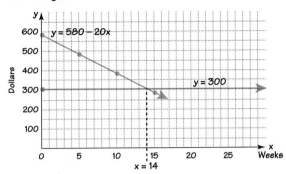

As long as Mac's balance is at or above the line y = 300, he does not have to pay a service fee. The lines appear to cross at about x = 14. For x ≤ 14 weeks, Mac's balance is high enough that he does not have to pay a service charge.

Solution 2

Translate "Mac's balance is at least $300" into an inequality.
Let x = the number of weeks after the start of school.

Solve 580 – 20x ≥ 300.

580 – 20x – 580 ≥ 300 – 580   Subtract 580 from each side.
            -20x ≥ -280

$-\frac{1}{20} \cdot -20x \leq -\frac{1}{20} \cdot -280$ Multiply each side by $-\frac{1}{20}$, and change the sense of the inequality.

            x ≤ 14

For the first 14 weeks Mac does not pay a service fee.

In Solution 2, we began solving 580 − 20x ≥ 300 by subtracting 580 from each side. This is equivalent to adding -580 to each side. We use both techniques in this book. You or your teacher may prefer one method over the other.

Lesson 5-1 *Horizontal and Vertical Lines* **287**

Additional Examples

These examples are given on **Teaching Aid 50.** Students will need graph paper or **Teaching Aid 28.**

1. Charles received $8 allowance for each of the first five weeks of the year. Imagine that the points (1, 8), (2, 8), (3, 8), (4, 8), and (5, 8) are graphed to represent this situation.
   a. What kind of line contains these points, a horizontal line or a vertical line?
      Horizontal line
   b. What is an equation for the line? **y = 8**

2. Graph y = −4
   a. on a number line.

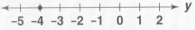

   b. on a coordinate plane.

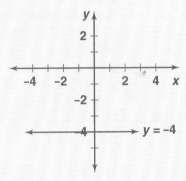

(Additional Examples continue on page 288.)

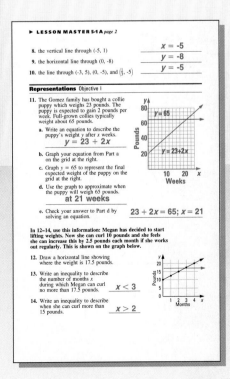

Adapting to Individual Needs

English Language Development
Materials: Graph paper or **Teaching Aid 28**

The English words *horizontal* and *vertical* may be new to some students. Use the image of the horizon line to remind students of horizontal. The term *vertigo*, which means fear of heights, is less familiar, but it has a tie-in to the word vertical. You might want to show students physical examples of

the terms by holding a pencil vertically and holding a ruler horizontally.

Then you might have students graph y = 5 and x = 5 on a coordinate grid. Ask which line is vertical [x = 5] and which line is horizontal [y = 5].

287

3. Use the situation described in **Example 3** on page 287. Suppose that Mac does not have to pay a service fee when his account is under $300. Explain how to use a graph to find the time at which Mac will have a balance of $100 in his account.
Draw the line $y = 100$. At the point where this line intersects the graph of $y = 580 - 20x$, draw a vertical line down to the x-axis. The x-coordinate of the point of intersection of the vertical line with the x-axis is the solution.

4. a. Write an equation for the line containing $(-\frac{1}{2}, 6)$ and $(-\frac{1}{2}, -6)$.
$x = -\frac{1}{2}$
b. Tell whether the line is horizontal, vertical, or neither.
Vertical

5. Give a sentence describing all points on the boundary of the shaded region. $x = 2$

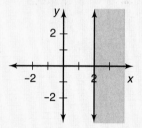

9b)

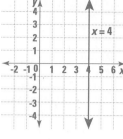

10b)

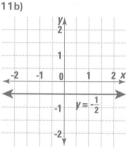

11b)

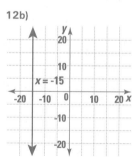

12b)

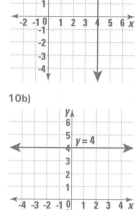

288

QUESTIONS

Covering the Reading

In 1 and 2, what was the national speed limit at the indicated time?
1. before 1/1/74
   There was none.
2. on July 1, 1987 65 $\frac{miles}{hour}$

In 3 and 4, let y = the national speed limit. Describe y during the indicated time period.
3. between 1975 and 1977
   $y = 55$ mph
4. between 1989 and 1991
   $y = 65$ mph
5. All points on a horizontal line have the same __?__ -coordinate. y
6. All points on a vertical line have the same __?__ -coordinate. x

In 7 and 8, write an equation for each graph.

7.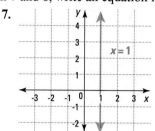

8.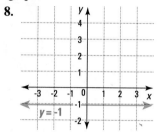

In 9–12, an equation is given.
  a. Graph the points on a number line which satisfy the equation.
  b. Graph the points in the coordinate plane which satisfy the equation. **See left.**

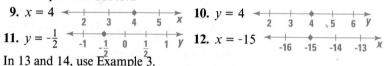

9. $x = 4$

10. $y = 4$

11. $y = -\frac{1}{2}$

12. $x = -15$

In 13 and 14, use Example 3.

13. Suppose the bank raised the minimum balance required for avoiding a service fee from $300 to $400.
  a. Use the graph to estimate the number of weeks that Mac would not have to pay the service fee. **9 weeks**
  b. Use an inequality to find the number of weeks Mac would not have to pay the service fee. $580 - 20x \geq 400$; $x \leq 9$; Mac would not have a service fee for 9 weeks.

14. Suppose Mac started the school year with $680. Draw a coordinate graph to show the amount of money that he will have each week after making a $20 withdrawal. **See page 289.**

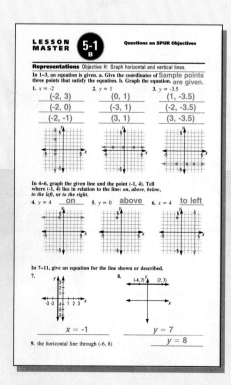
Adapting to Individual Needs

Challenge
Materials: Graph paper or **Teaching Aid 28**

Have students draw the following segments on a coordinate grid:
$y = -1$ for $3 \leq x \leq 6$
$y = -6$ for $3 \leq x \leq 6$
$x = 3$ for $-1 \leq y \leq -11$
$x = 6$ for $-1 \leq y \leq -11$
Ask what capital letter this might be. [A]

Then have students **work in pairs** to draw other capital letters using only horizontal and vertical segments. The letters can be any size and they can be drawn anywhere on the coordinate grid. [Answers will vary.]

Then you might have each student draw a letter in secret and write the equations that form the letter. Have students exchange equations with their partners and find their partners' letters.

14)

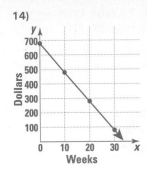

15a)

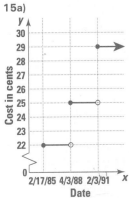

18)

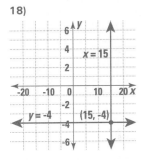

21b,c)

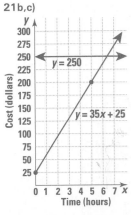

Applying the Mathematics

15. In recent years, the cost of mailing a first-class letter weighing 1 ounce or less has been as follows:

from 2/17/85 to 4/2/88	22¢
from 4/3/88 to 2/2/91	25¢
from 2/3/91 on	29¢.

a. Graph the relationship between date and cost. **See left.**
b. With algebraic sentences, describe the graph that you drew in part **a.** **Let x = the date and y = the cost in cents. From 2/17/85 to 4/2/88, y = 22. From 4/3/88 to 2/2/91, y = 25. From 2/3/91 on, y = 29.**

In 16 and 17, write an equation for the line containing the points given.

16. $(-9, 12)$, $(4, 12)$, $(0.3, 12)$ **17.** $(-6, -3)$, $(-6, 0)$, $(-6, 200)$
$y = 12$ $x = -6$
18. Graph the lines $y = -4$ and $x = 15$. Find the coordinates of the point of intersection. **See left.**

19. a. Write an equation of the horizontal line through $(7, -13)$. $y = -13$
   b. Write an equation of the vertical line through $(7, -13)$. $x = 7$

20. Horizontal lines are parallel to the __?__ axis and perpendicular to the __?__ axis. x; y

21. Ron's Refrigerator Repair Service charges $25 for travel time plus $35 per hour to repair coolers. Sasha's Steak House has a cooler that needs repairs. Sasha is willing to spend no more than $250 on repairs. a) $y = 35x + 25$; b,c) **See left**
   a. Write an equation to relate the repair cost y to the time spent x.
   b. Draw a graph of the equation that you wrote in part **a.**
   c. Use the same coordinate axes as part **b.** Draw the line $y = 250$ to represent the money that Sasha is willing to spend on repairs.
   d. Use your graph to determine the maximum whole number of hours that Ron could work and still keep Sasha's bill under $250.
   e. Check your answer to part **d** by solving an inequality. **6 hr**
   $35x + 25 \leq 250$; $x \leq 6.43$; Ron could work for 6 whole hours.

Review

22. The geometric board shown at right is used in the game called Cows and Leopards. The game is popular in southern Asia. Find the angle measures w, x, y, and z.
(Lesson 4-7)
$w = 90°$, $x = 46°$,
$y = 46°$, $z = 136°$

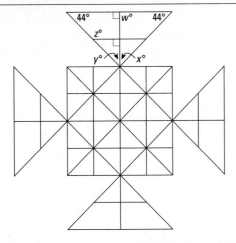

Lesson 5-1 *Horizontal and Vertical Lines* **289**

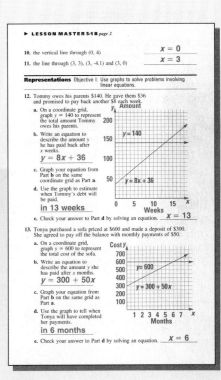
Notes on Questions

Question 18 This question suggests that when one writes $y = -4$ and $x = 15$ as the solution to some system of equations, one can think of that graphically as the intersection of a horizontal and a vertical line.

Question 19 Error Alert Many students are stymied by this question. Suggest that they identify several other points on the line, and then write the pattern as an equation.

Question 22 The game board is given on **Teaching Aid 51.** Students might check their answers by measuring the angles. They can use their protractors or **Geometry Templates.**

289

Notes on Questions

Question 24 Science Connection
Glaciers form high up in mountains where snow collects. The snow, pressed down by its own weight, turns to ice. The great thickness of the ice causes it to move. The ice layers, acting like sheets of paper on a slant, slide past each other. Glaciers have a unique topography that is carved by the elements and heaved and twisted by the stresses in the advancing ice. The fastest moving glacier, the Quarayaq Glacier in Greenland, moves at a speed of about 24 meters a day. The continent of Antarctica is covered by an ice sheet that moves over the ground as one giant glacier. It measures 14 million square kilometers and has an average thickness of 2,150 meters. It contains 99 percent of the ice on Earth.

Question 28 Suggest that students use the problem-solving strategy of drawing a picture.

Follow-up for Lesson 5-1

Practice
For more questions on SPUR Objectives, use **Lesson Master 5-1A** (shown on pages 286–287) or **Lesson Master 5-1B** (shown on pages 288–289).

Assessment
Written Communication Have students **work in pairs**. Each student should draw on a coordinate plane a line that is parallel to either the *x*-axis or the *y*-axis. Then students should exchange papers with their partners and describe the graphs in writing. The description should include the equation of the line. [Explanations reflect an understanding of the graphs of horizontal and vertical lines.]

Extension
Show students a square or rectangle that is drawn on a coordinate grid and that has sides parallel to the axes. Have them determine the equations for the lines of which each side is a part.

Project Update Project 5, *Light Bulbs*, on page 339, relates to the content of this lesson.

23. The regular price of a compact-disc player is *d* dollars. What is the sale price if a discount of 20% is offered? *(Lesson 4-2)* .80*d*

24. A glacier has already moved 25 inches and is moving at a rate of 2 inches per week. Let *t* be the total number of inches the glacier has moved after *w* additional weeks. Write a formula for *t* in terms of *w*. *(Lesson 3-8)* $t = 25 + 2w$

25. Show two ways to find the total area of the rectangles below. *(Lesson 3-6)* 9.8(25) + 14.2(25) or (9.8 + 14.2)25

In 26 and 27, simplify. *(Lessons 2-2, 2-3, 2-5)*

26. $(-a \cdot b) \cdot -a$ a^2b

27. $-\frac{3}{2} \cdot \left(-\frac{2}{3}a\right)$ a

Al and Scott are in separate automobiles traveling in the same direction at 232 mph. If Al reaches his destination 0.043 seconds before Scott, how far ahead of Scott does Al reach his destination?"

28. Shown at the left is part of an ad that appeared in the June 19, 1992, edition of *USA Today*.

"Al and Scott" refer to Al Unser, Jr., and Scott Goodyear, who finished first and second in the 1992 Indianapolis 500 motor race. The margin of victory was the closest in the history of the race, with only 0.043 second separating Al and Scott. In a follow-up article in *USA Today*, on June 25, 1992, it was reported that the answer given in the original ad, 6 feet, was incorrect. Over 200 readers of the newspaper had called or written the company to report the error. To the nearest tenth of a foot, how far ahead of Scott did Al reach his destination? *(Lesson 2-4)* 14.6 feet

Split-second service. *Pit stops are important in racing events such as the Indianapolis 500. Pit crews are expected to refuel a car and change the tires during the race, usually within about 20 seconds.*

29. a. In your own words, state the Multiplicative Identity Property of 1.
   b. Give an instance of this property. *(Lesson 2-2)*
a) Any real number multiplied by one equals the same real number.
b) Sample: 1 · 5 = 5

Exploration

30. What is the maximum speed limit on highways in your state? Answers may vary.

Setting Up Lesson 5-2

Materials Computer or calculator with spreadsheet capability

If possible, show students **Example 2** in Lesson 5-2 using an actual spreadsheet (from a calculator or computer) on an overhead projector.

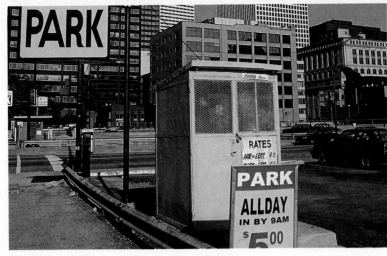

Using Tables to Compare Linear Expressions

No free parking. *In many cities, parking spaces are scarce and costly. Motorists are wise to compare the rates of different parking facilities.*

Tables are often useful for comparing values from two or more situations.

Example 1

The table below gives the charges for parking a car at two different garages.
a. When does it cost less to park at Gil's Garage?
b. When does it cost less to park at Patsy's Parking?

Number of hours	Parking Charge	
	Gil's Garage	Patsy's Parking
1	$1.50	$1.80
2	2.30	2.55
3	3.10	3.30
4	3.90	4.05
5	4.70	4.80
6	5.50	5.55
7	6.30	6.30
8	7.10	7.05
9	7.90	7.80
10	8.70	8.55
each add'l hr	$0.80	$0.75

Solution
Read down the columns for charges at Gil's and Patsy's.
Let h = the number of hours parked.
a. When h ≤ 6 it costs less to park at Gil's.
b. When h ≥ 8 it costs less to park at Patsy's.

If a table is not given, it is often helpful to make one.

Lesson 5-2 *Using Tables to Compare Linear Expressions* **291**

Objectives

G Use tables or spreadsheets to solve real-world problems involving linear situations.

Resources

From the ***Teacher's Resource File***
■ Lesson Master 5-2A or 5-2B
■ Answer Master 5-2
■ Teaching Aids
    37 Spreadsheet
    47 Warm-up
    52 Example 2
■ Technology Sourcebook
    Computer Master 13

Additional Resources
■ Visuals for Teaching Aids 37, 47, 52
■ Computer and spreadsheet software

Teaching 5-2
Lesson

Warm-up

At Carl's City Car Park, it costs $7.75 to park for 3 hours or less. After 3 hours, it costs $1.25 for each additional hour or fraction of an hour, up to a maximum of $15 for 12 hours.
1. Make a table to show the costs of parking for 1 through 12 hours.

Hr	Cost	Hr	Cost
1	$7.75	7	$12.75
2	$7.75	8	$14.00
3	$7.75	9	$15.00
4	$9.00	10	$15.00
5	$10.25	11	$15.00
6	$11.50	12	$15.00

2. Describe a graph showing this information. **Sample response: The graph starts with an open circle at (0, 7.75) and is horizontal to (3, 7.75); then it slants up to (9, 15) and is horizontal again to (12, 15).**

Lesson 5-2 Overview

Broad Goals Many students solve equations of the form $ax + b = cx + d$ (and the related inequalities) mechanically, but do not realize that their solutions are related to the values of the two linear expressions $ax + b$ and $cx + d$. This lesson uses tables to focus on the values of the linear expressions and to solve such sentences.

Perspective In this chapter three approaches are described for solving linear

sentences. The traditional algebraic approach—to operate on both sides of a sentence—is found in Lessons 5-3 and 5-6. A graphical method, which might be thought of as a geometric approach, is found in Lesson 5-4. In this lesson, we begin with the most concrete of the approaches— an arithmetic approach that uses tables or spreadsheets.

Notes on Reading

Teaching Aid 52 contains the table in **Example 2**.

Example 1 provides practice in reading a table and writing a solution based on it. **Example 2** shows how a table can be made for a particular pair of linear expressions. Then the table is expanded using a spreadsheet. Emphasize that creating tables like the one on page 291 provides a way to solve many problems. If all the rows increase or decrease by constant amounts, as do the rows in most of the tables in the lesson, then the general pattern relating the columns is linear. Note that once *h* is used to stand for the number of hours, students can use algebraic language to answer the questions. In **Example 1**, the general pattern is not given.

In **Example 2**, linear expressions are given for each column; however, it is not necessary to use these expressions to draw conclusions about the data.

Solving a sentence like $250 + 0.01n = 70 + 0.03n$ involves comparing the values of the two expressions $250 + 0.01n$ and $70 + 0.03n$ to determine when they are equal. Thus, the most basic way to attempt to solve the sentence is to substitute values for *n*, calculate the values of the two expressions, and change the substituted value until the solution is found. The equation $250 + 0.01n = 70 + 0.03n$ is solved using the traditional algebraic means in **Example 2** of Lesson 5-3.

You may wish to demonstrate **Example 2** using an actual spreadsheet (from a calculator or computer) on an overhead projector. Point out how the table allows you to determine when the costs at the two companies are equal and when one cost exceeds the other.

Is "Best" the better buy? *Many businesses rent photocopy machines rather than buy them. Office managers need to determine which rental company offers the best rate.*

Example 2

You are the manager of an office. Your company needs another copy machine. After contacting several office supply firms, you have obtained the following rental rates.

Acme Copiers offers a copier for $250 per month and an additional charge of 1 cent ($.01) per copy.

Best Printers offers the same machine for $70 per month and a per-copy charge of 3 cents ($.03).

Records show that your office made as few as 482 copies during a holiday month and as many as 17,386 copies during inventory month. Make a table showing the costs for 0, 2000, 4000, 6000, . . . , 20,000 copies per month. Use the table to draw conclusions about which company charges less for making copies.

Solution

Let n = the number of copies made per month.
Cost from Acme Copiers: $250 + 0.01n$
Cost from Best Printers: $70 + 0.03n$

Substitute the values 0, 2000, 4000, 6000, . . . , 20,000 for *n* into each of the expressions and record the results in a table.

Number of Copies n	Acme's Charges 250 + 0.01n	Best's Charges 70 + 0.03n
0	250	70
2,000	270	130
4,000	290	190
6,000	310	250
8,000	330	310
10,000	350	370
12,000	370	430
14,000	390	490
16,000	410	550
18,000	430	610
20,000	450	670

Best's price is lower than Acme's for 8,000 or fewer copies. Acme's price is lower for 10,000 or more copies. From this table you cannot be sure which company charges less if the number of copies made per month is between 8,000 and 10,000.

To determine the "break-even" point for the two rental companies, you can evaluate the expressions $250 + 0.01n$ and $70 + 0.03n$ for values of *n* between 8,000 and 10,000. This is easily done with a computer program that prints tables, or with a spreadsheet.

Optional Activities

Activity 1 Technology Connection
You may wish to assign *Technology Sourcebook, Computer Master 13*. Students use a spreadsheet to compare cost expressions for two brands of computers.

Activity 2 Writing
After students have discussed the tables in the lesson, you might have them write more complex questions that can be answered by including more entries in the table. For example, for the table on page 292, they might write "When is Acme's charge more than twice that of Best?" [For less than 2200 copies] or "When are Best's charges more than twice Acme's charges?" [For more than 43,000 copies]

Activity 3
After discussing page 293, ask students to find formulas for a spreadsheet that would produce the data in **Example 1**. To do this, students must recognize linear patterns like those in Lesson 3-8. At Gil's garage, the linear pattern is $.70 + .80h$ dollars for *h* hours of parking. At Patsy's Parking, the pattern is $1.05 + .75h$ dollars for *h* hours of parking. It costs less to park at Gil's Garage when $.70 + .80h < 1.05 + .75h$.

You can set up the spreadsheet with column A representing the number of copies. Start at 8000. Continue down the column in increments of 200. In cell B3 put the Acme charge formula = 250+.01*A3. In cell C3 put the Best charge formula =70+.03*A3. Replicate the formulas in B3 and C3 down to B13 and C13, respectively. In the spreadsheet shown, you can see that 9000 copies (row 8) produces the same charge for both companies. If you make fewer than 9000 copies, Best is cheaper. If you make more than 9000 copies, Acme offers the better deal.

	A	B	C
1	# OF COPIES	ACME COST	BEST COST
2	N	250+.01*N	70+.03*N
3	8000	330	310
4	8200	332	316
5	8400	334	322
6	8600	336	328
7	8800	338	334
8	9000	340	340
9	9200	342	346
10	9400	344	352
11	9600	346	358
12	9800	348	364
13	10000	350	370

Copy cats. *Today's copy centers offer a variety of services such as typesetting résumés, creating colorful brochures, and printing business forms.*

To answer the question "When is renting from Acme cheaper or the same as renting from Best?" in algebraic terms, solve the inequality:

$$250 + 0.01n \le 70 + 0.03n.$$

As shown in the spreadsheet above, there are many solutions to this inequality. The spreadsheet shows the solutions 9000, 9200, . . . , 10,000 copies. In the next three lessons you will learn other methods for solving linear sentences like this one.

Lesson 5-2   *Using Tables to Compare Linear Expressions*   **293**

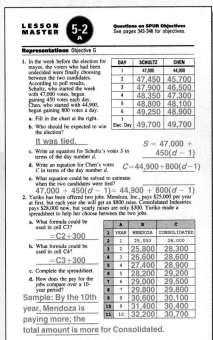

293

Notes on Questions

Students can use **Teaching Aid 37** with these questions.

Question 1 Ask students why there is no linear expression to describe the cost of *n* copies at Phil's Photos. [The differences between successive rows is not constant; it costs $.50 for the second copy but $.75 for all others.]

Questions 7–8 Solutions to these questions can be demonstrated with a spreadsheet on an overhead projector.

Question 9 Students may need guidance for **parts a and b.** Each equation should be for the amount saved in terms of *w*.

Covering the Reading

1. The table below gives the charges for copies of photos at two different shops.

Number of copies	Charges at Phil's Photos	Charges at Peggy's Prints
1	.75	.80
2	1.25	1.40
3	2.00	2.00
4	2.75	2.60
5	3.50	3.20

   a. For how many copies does it cost less at Phil's? **less than 3 copies**
   b. For how many copies does it cost less at Peggy's? **more than 3 copies**

In 2 and 3, refer to Example 2.

2. What would it cost to rent a copier from Best Printers for a month and use it to print 4,292 copies? **$198.76**

3. If your office averaged about 4,500 copies per month, which company should you select? Why? **Best Printers;   Best is cheaper if fewer than 9,000 copies are needed per month.**

In 4–6, refer to the spreadsheet on page 293.

4. Write the formula for cell B10. **= 250 + .01*A10**

5. Write the formula for cell C11. **= 70 + .03*A11**

6. a. Use the spreadsheet to tell which company provides the better deal for 9100 copies a month. **Acme Copiers**
   b. Compute the price each company charges for 9100 copies per month. **Acme's cost is $341. Best's cost is $343.**

7. Suppose that Best Printers wishes to get more customers by reducing their charge per copy to 2 cents while keeping the basic monthly charge of $70. In response, Acme drops their charge per month to $200 plus 1¢ per copy.
   a. Copy and complete the table below. **b) for 13,000 copies**
   b. When will the charges be the same for both companies?

Number of Copies	Cost with Acme	Cost with Best
10,000	300	270
11,000	310	290
12,000	320	310
13,000	330	330
14,000	340	350
15,000	350	370

Adapting to Individual Needs

English Language Development
Because this lesson has a great deal of reading, students with limited English proficiency might find it helpful to work with English-speaking partners. Have the partners take turns reading questions and explaining how the questions relate to the tables. Encourage students to use bilingual dictionaries.

LESSON MASTER 5-2 B   Questions on SPUR Objectives

Representations Objective G: Use tables or spreadsheets to solve real-world problems involving linear situations.

1. At the Children's Museum, children can watch chicks and ducks hatch. Today there are 40 baby chicks and 25 ducks. Each day, 4 chicks and 7 ducks are expected to hatch.
   a. Complete the table below.

DAY	CHICKS	DUCKS
0	40	25
1	44	32
2	48	39
3	52	46
4	56	53
5	60	60
6	64	67

   b. At the end of 6 days, will there be more chicks or ducks? **ducks**
   c. Write an equation for the number of chicks *C* in terms of the day *d*. **$C = 40 + 4d$**
   d. Write an equation for the number of ducks *D* in terms of the day *d*. **$D = 25 + 7d$**
   e. What equation could be used to find when there will be an equal number of chicks and ducks? **$40 + 4d = 25 + 7d$**

2. Marta uses a spreadsheet (shown on the next page) to compare the salaries between two companies that have offered her a job. The O'Connell Company offers $29,000 the first year with annual raises of $900. Tri-Tech, Inc. pays $27,800 the first year and gives annual raises of $1,200. The cells of the spreadsheet contain yearly salaries.
   a. What formula could be used in cell B3? **=B2+900**
   b. What formula could be used in cell C3? **=C2+1200**
   c. Complete the spreadsheet.

Applying the Mathematics

8. Suppose price changes in Question 7 expired at the end of the month, and the original prices were reinstated. At that point, Best Printers realized that they were not competitive in offices that copied in high volume. To be more competitive with these customers, Best advertised "Maximum Rental Charge: $600 per month." How many copies could be copied for $600 at Acme?
35,000 copies

9. Kim starts with $20 and is *saving* at a rate of $6 per week. Jenny starts with $150 and is *spending* at a rate of $4 per week. **a,b) See left.**
   a. Write an expression for the amount Kim has after w weeks.
   b. Write an expression for the amount Jenny has after w weeks.
   c. Make a table. Use it to determine when Kim and Jenny would have the same amount. **See left for table. After 13 weeks, Kim and Jenny will have the same amount of money.**

10. Rufus is offered two sales positions. With Company A he would earn $800 per month plus 5% commission on sales. With Company B he would earn $600 per month plus 6% commission on sales.
   a. If Rufus expects sales of about $10,000, which company would pay him more? **Company A**
   b. Complete this table and determine how much he must sell to be paid more at Company B than at Company A.
   He must have sales of more than $20,000.

9a) $m = 20 + 6w$
b) $m = 150 - 4w$
c)

Week	Kim	Jenny
1	26	146
2	32	142
3	38	138
4	44	134
5	50	130
6	56	126
7	62	122
8	68	118
9	74	114
10	80	110
11	86	106
12	92	102
13	98	98

Sales	Earnings at Company A	Earnings at Company B
12,000	1400	1320
14,000	1500	1440
16,000	1600	1560
18,000	1700	1680
20,000	1800	1800
22,000	1900	1920
24,000	2000	2040
26,000	2100	2160
28,000	2200	2280
30,000	2300	2400

Review

11. Give the coordinates of three points on the line $y = -6$. *(Lesson 5-1)*
   Sample: $(-3, -6)$; $(0, -6)$; $(17, -6)$

12. Write an equation for the line k graphed at the left. *(Lesson 5-1)*
   $x = 6$

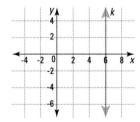

Additional Answers

13a.

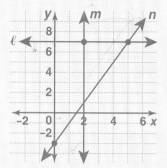

15a.

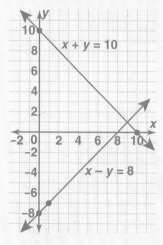

19. $x + y - 3(z + w) = x + y - 3z - 3w$. Sample: multiplication by –3 was not distributed over the w term.

26. Sample:

```
10    PRINT "Week", "Kim",
      "Jenny"
20    FOR W = 1 TO 20
30    LET X = 20 + 9 * W
40    Let Y = 150 – 4 * W
50    PRINT W, X, Y
60    IF X = Y THEN GO
      TO 80
70    NEXT W
80    PRINT "Weeks = "; W
90    END
```

The program will print

Week	Kim	Jenny
1	29	146
2	38	142
3	47	138
4	56	134
5	65	130
6	74	126
7	83	122
8	92	118
9	101	114
10	110	110

Weeks = 10

13. **a.** On one coordinate grid, graph the following three lines.
    line ℓ: $y = 7$ See margin.
    line m: $x = 2$
    line n: $y = 2x - 3$
    b. At what point do lines ℓ and m intersect? (2, 7)
    c. At what point do lines ℓ and n intersect? (5, 7)
    d. Find the area of the triangle formed by the three lines.
    (Lessons 4-9, 5-1, Previous course) **9 square units**

14. By air, it is 1061 miles from Miami to St. Louis and 1724 miles from St. Louis to Seattle. Based on this information and the Triangle Inequality, what is the longest possible air distance from Miami to Seattle? *(Lesson 4-8)* **2785 miles**

15. **a.** On the same coordinate plane, graph all solutions to $x + y = 10$ and $x - y = 8$. See margin.
    b. At what point do the graphs intersect? *(Lesson 4-6)* (9, 1)

In 16 and 17, solve. *(Lessons 3-10, 4-3, 4-5)*

16. $1 = 9 - (c - 2)$ $c = 10$ 17. $42(m - 4) + 210 < 252$ $m < 5$

18. A farm worker picking grapes earns $5.40 per hour plus $.28 per box. If the worker picks grapes 8 hours, how many boxes would he or she have to pick to earn at least $50.00 for the day? *(Lessons 3-5, 3-10)* **25 boxes**

19. The equation below is incorrect. Correct it by changing the right side of the equation. Explain the error that was made. *(Lesson 3-2)* See margin.
$$x + y - 3(z + w) = x + y - 3z + w$$

20. After school Alonzo needs to practice the piano, visit a friend in the hospital, and do homework for algebra, biology, and Spanish.
    a. In how many different orders can he do these things? **120**
    b. If he visits his friend first, in how many orders can he do the other things? *(Lesson 2-10)* **24**

In 21 and 22, simplify. *(Lessons 1-4, 1-6)*

21. $(\sqrt{37})^2$ **37**   22. $(8c)^2$ $64c^2$

23. In 1991, the national debt was about 3.46 trillion dollars. Write 3.46 trillion in scientific notation. *(Previous course, Appendix)*
    $3.46 \cdot 10^{12}$

In 24 and 25, estimate mentally to the nearest whole number. *(Previous course)*

24. $12 \cdot 9.95$ **120**   25. $\frac{5}{6} + \frac{7}{8} + \frac{13}{12}$ **3**

Exploration

26. Computer programs in BASIC can be used to create tables like the one that is asked for in Question 9. Suppose Kim is saving $9 per week. Write and run a BASIC program to find out when Kim and Jenny will have the same amount of money. See margin.

Setting Up Lesson 5-3

Materials If you want to demonstrate solving equations using balance scales, see Activity 1 in *Optional Activities* on page 298. Students who do the *Extension* on page 302 will need almanacs.

Diagnostic If you have time, find out how much your students know about solving equations of the form $ax + b = cx + d$, which is the subject matter of the next lesson. Ask if any of them can solve the equation $20 + 6w = 150 - 4w$, an equation that can be used to find the answer to **Question 9** on page 295. Explain that this type of equation, just like others they have studied, is solved by working with both sides. Then have students begin reading Lesson 5-3.

A delicate balance. *In balancing equations, as in balancing on a high-wire, you need to keep equal amounts on both sides of the middle.*

Representing $ax + b = cx + d$

This balance scale is similar to the one pictured in Lesson 3-5. Each ball represents 1 ounce, and all boxes have equal weight w. If the two sides of the scale are balanced, what is the weight of one box? The answer can be found algebraically. If w is the weight of one box, then the situation is described by the equation

$$5w + 1 = 2w + 13.$$

The difference between this equation and ones that you have solved before is that the variable w is on each side of the equation.

To solve this equation pictorially, remove 2 boxes from each pan.

$$3w + 1 = 13$$

This equation is of the form $ax + b = c$, so remove 1 oz from each pan.

Lesson 5-3

Objectives
A Solve linear equations of the form $ax + b = cx + d$.
E Apply and recognize properties associated with linear equations.
F Use linear equations to solve real-world problems.

Resources
From the *Teacher's Resource File*
■ Lesson Master 5-3A or 5-3B
■ Answer Master 5-3
■ Assessment Sourcebook: Quiz for Lessons 5-1 through 5-3
■ Teaching Aids
  19 Balance-Scale Diagrams
  47 Warm-up
  53 Question 30
■ Activity Kit, Activity 11

Additional Resources
■ Visuals for Teaching Aids 19, 47, 53
■ Balance scales, weights, small objects to weigh (Optional Activities)
■ Almanacs (Extension)

Teaching Lesson 5-3

Warm-up

Diagnostic Decide if each solution is correct. If not, what is the correct solution?
1. $x - 16 = 32$; $x = 16$
   Incorrect, $x = 48$
2. $3x + 7 = 11$; $x = 3$
   Incorrect, $x = \frac{4}{3}$

(Warm-up continues on page 298.)

Lesson 5-3 Overview

Broad Goals In this lesson, students set up equations of the form $ax + b = cx + d$ and solve them algebraically. All of the situations presented are constant-increase or constant-decrease situations, the type found in the preceding lesson.

Perspective At this time, we deal with linear equations that have variable terms on both sides of the equal sign. The corresponding inequalities are treated in

Lesson 5-6. Once students master solving these sentences, additional work with equations will involve learning to simplify expressions on either side of the equal sign.

There is a significant difference in the equation-solving process that occurs when the variable appears on both sides and the one that occurs when the variable is on only one side. Now equations cannot be solved by merely undoing the operations. Also, it is

possible to have a single variable on the left side but still not have the solution, as in $x = 2x - 3$. These new situations carry the potential for errors by students.

The equation $ax + b = cx + d$ is important because a category of applications—the constant-increase and constant-decrease applications—leads to equations of this form.

3. $-72 - y = -4y$; $y = -24$
Incorrect, $y = 24$
4. $8 = 0.05n - 2$; $n = 200$ **Correct**
5. $23 - n = 5n - 85$; $n = 18$
Correct

Notes on Reading

We suggest that the reading be reviewed simultaneously with the *Questions Covering the Reading*. The relationship is given below.

Introduction: **Question 1**
Example 1: **Question 2**
Example 2: **Question 3**
Example 3: **Question 4**
Example 4: **Question 13**

Since the algorithm for solving $ax + b = cx + d$ has just one more step than that for solving $ax + b = c$, it is appropriate to talk about the famous Polya problem-solving strategy—*If you cannot solve a problem, try to reduce it to one that you can solve.* The balance-scale representation is useful for reducing an equation to one that can be solved; in one step, the equation $5w + 1 = 2w + 13$ is reduced to $3w + 1 = 13$, an equation of the form students have already studied.

Cooperative Learning You may want to have students solve some equations by using a balance scale or by drawing the balance-scale steps on **Teaching Aid 19.** See *Optional Activities* below for specific suggestions. When solving these equations, students may collect the variable terms on either side. However, it is convenient to avoid having a negative coefficient for the variable. You may want to have your students follow the rule of eliminating the variable term that has the smaller coefficient.

$$3w = 12$$

Then leave one-third of the contents of each pan.

$$w = 4$$

One box weighs 4 ounces.

Solving $ax + b = cx + d$ Algebraically

Example 1 shows this process algebraically. There are three major steps.

❶ **Example 1**

Solve $5w + 1 = 2w + 13$.

Solution 1

$-2w + 5w + 1 = -2w + 2w + 13$	Addition Property of Equality, (Add $-2w$ to each side.)
$3w + 1 = 13$	
$3w + 1 + -1 = 13 + -1$	Addition Property of Equality,
$3w = 12$	(Add -1 to each side.)
$\frac{1}{3}(3w) = \frac{1}{3}(12)$	Multiplication Property of Equality,
$w = 4$	(Multiply each side by $\frac{1}{3}$.)

Solution 2

Some people do the additions and multiplications in their heads.

$$5w + 1 = 2w + 13$$
$$3w + 1 = 13$$
$$3w = 12$$
$$w = 4$$

Check

Substitute 4 for w in the original equation.
Does $5 \cdot 4 + 1 = 2 \cdot 4 + 13$?
Does $20 + 1 = 8 + 13$? Yes.

Optional Activities

Activity 1 Using Physical Models
Materials: Balance scale, weights, small objects to weigh, or **Teaching Aid 19**

There is no substitute for at least one hands-on demonstration of equation solving with the balance scale. If you have enough scales, have students **work in groups.** Begin with the scales balanced with known weights (such as grams or ounces and

unknown weights of something like hard candy, pennies or washers. Experiment before class to find combinations that balance on a scale. Then have students subtract equal known weights (which are the constants in the equations) or equal unknown weights (the variable expressions) from each side, and divide to find the solution (the unknown weight of a single object).

If you do not have balance scales, students can use **Teaching Aid 19** and draw weights on the scales.

The equation in Example 1 has the unknown variable on each side. It is of the form

$$ax + b = cx + d$$

and is called the **general linear equation.** To solve equations of this type, you can add either $-cx$ or $-ax$ to both sides. Or, subtract either cx or ax from both sides. This step removes the variable from one side and leaves an equation of the kind you have solved in previous lessons.

Applying $ax + b = cx + d$

Let us return to the copier example of Lesson 5-2. There we compared costs of Acme Copiers and Best Printers. Acme's charge for n copies was given by $C = 250 + 0.01n$ and Best's was $C = 70 + 0.03n$. By solving an equation, we can determine precisely when the charges are equal.

Example 2

Solve $250 + 0.01n = 70 + 0.03n$. Check your answer.

Solution

Either $0.01n$ or $0.03n$ can be subtracted from both sides. We choose to subtract $0.01n$.

$250 + 0.01n - 0.01n = 70 + 0.03n - 0.01n$

$250 = 70 + 0.02n$ Combine like terms.

$250 - 70 = 70 + 0.02n - 70$ Subtract 70 from each side.

$180 = 0.02n$

$\frac{1}{0.02} \cdot 180 = 0.02n \cdot \frac{1}{0.02}$ Multiply both sides by $\frac{1}{0.02}$ (or 50).

$9000 = n$

Check

This is the same solution we found in Lesson 5-2 by using a table. Substitute 9000 for n wherever n appears in the original equation.

Does $250 + 0.01 \cdot 9000 = 70 + 0.03 \cdot 9000$?

$250 + 90 = 70 + 270$

$340 = 340$ Yes, it checks.

So when 9000 copies are made in a month, the charges of Acme and Best are equal.

Solving Linear Equations with Subtraction

In Example 2, subtracting $0.03n$ from both sides would have introduced a negative coefficient. Still, the solution would have been the same, and it would have taken the same number of steps. Sometimes the choice of what term to add to both sides of an equation can lead to a shorter solution, as shown in Example 3.

Error Alert Some students may think that all equations are solved by the process of collecting the variable terms on one side and collecting the numerical terms on the other side. A word of caution should be given. This process will be contradicted when solving quadratic equations. When using the Quadratic Formula, students will want to get all non-zero terms on the same side.

❶ Discuss the two solutions to **Example 1.** In particular, tell students what you expect to see when you read their solutions to sentences like this one. When can they skip steps? When should they include all steps? Do you want to see the justifications? Our recommendation is that students include the steps that they feel they need to have. Then they can gradually reduce the number of steps, but not to the point that they introduce errors.

Activity 2
You can use *Activity Kit, Activity 11,* before you cover the lesson. In this activity students model equations of the form $ax + b = cx + d$ and demonstrate how to solve the equations using algebra tiles.

Activity 3 Writing
You might have students do **Question 21** in class. Tell them to follow **Example 4** when writing their explanations.

❷ Both **Example 4** and **Question**
13 can be simplified by thinking of the populations in thousands. Then the equations become $515 + 9n = 628 - 0.8n$ and $550 + 15n = 666 + 7n$, respectively. The equivalent to thinking of the population in thousands involves beginning with the natural equation and then dividing both sides by 1000. This technique is formalized in Lesson 5-9.

Students are expected to obtain the expressions in **Example 4** by using patterns that are discussed in Lesson 3-8 and reinforced in Lesson 4-3. Still, they will need practice, and it is possible that this concept will not be mastered until the discussion of slope in Chapter 7.

Additional Examples

In 1–3, solve and check.
1. $14k + 20 = 21k - 43$ $k = 9$
   Does $14 \cdot 9 + 20 = 21 \cdot 9 - 43$?
   $126 + 20 = 189 - 43$? $146 = 146$?
   Yes
2. $x + 1.05x = 2x - 1000$
   $x = -20,000$
   Does $-20,000 + 1.05 \cdot -20,000 = 2 \cdot -20,000 - 1000$?
   $-20,000 + -21,000 = -40,000 - 1000$? $-41,000 = -41,000$? Yes
3. $-a + 11 = -6a$ $a = -\frac{11}{5}$
   Does $\frac{11}{5} + 11 = 6 \cdot \frac{11}{5}$?
   $13\frac{1}{5} = 13\frac{1}{5}$? Yes
4. In a tall office building, one elevator leaves the third floor and ascends at a speed of 2 floors per second. Another elevator leaves the 59th floor at exactly the same moment and descends at a speed of 2 floors per second.
   a. If the two elevators do not stop, how long will it take them to pass each other?
      Let t be the elapsed time in seconds. Solving $3 + 2t = 59 - 2t$ gives $t = 14$ seconds.
   b. At what floor will the elevators pass each other? 31st

300

Example 3

Solve $-7y - 55 = 4y$.

Solution 1

Add $7y$ to both sides. The equation can now be solved in two additional steps.
$$7y + -7y - 55 = 7y + 4y$$
$$-55 = 11y \qquad \text{Add like terms.}$$
$$-5 = y \qquad \text{Multiply by } \tfrac{1}{11}.$$

Solution 2

Add $-4y$ to both sides. The solution takes three additional steps.
$$-4y + -7y - 55 = 4y + -4y$$
$$-11y - 55 = 0 \qquad \text{Add like terms.}$$
$$-11y = 55 \qquad \text{Add 55 to each side.}$$
$$y = -5 \qquad \text{Multiply each side by } -\tfrac{1}{11}.$$

Check

Does $\quad -7(-5) - 55 = 4(-5)$?
$\qquad 35 - 55 = -20$? Yes, it checks.

In general, solving equations of the form $ax = bx + c$, or $bx + c = ax$, by adding $-bx$ to both sides of the equation requires fewer steps than adding $-ax$ to both sides.

Example 4 shows another real application of solving a linear equation.

El Paso, Texas

Example 4

The 1990 population of El Paso, Texas, was 515,000. In the 1980s, its population increased at an average rate of 9000 people per year. In 1990, the population of Milwaukee, Wisconsin, was 628,000. In the 1980s, its population decreased at the rate of 800 people a year. If these rates continue, in what year will the populations of the cities be the same?

Solution

Find expressions for the populations in years after 1990. In El Paso, n years after 1990 the population will be $515,000 + 9000n$. In Milwaukee, n years after 1990 the population will be $628,000 - 800n$. The populations will be the same when the two expressions are equal. Solve this equation for n.

$$515,000 + 9000n = 628,000 - 800n$$

Add $800n$ to each side.

$$515,000 + 9000n + 800n = 628,000 - 800n + 800n$$
$$515,000 + 9800n = 628,000$$

Add $-515,000$ to both sides.

$$-515,000 + 515,000 + 9800n = -515,000 + 628,000$$
$$9800n = 113,000$$
$$n \approx 11.53 \quad \text{Multiply by } \tfrac{1}{9800}.$$

At these rates, about 11.53 years after 1990, that is, in 2001 or 2002, the populations would be the same. ▶

Adapting to Individual Needs

English Language Development
Students who are not proficient in English might have difficulty translating situations into algebraic equations. To help them with **Examples 2 and 4,** have them write the equation with words and then use the numbers from the problem.

Example 2:

Starting point	+	rate · number of copies	=	starting point	+	rate · number of copies
250	+	$0.01n$	=	70	+	$0.03n$

Example 4:

Starting point	+	rate · time	=	starting point	–	rate · time
515,000	+	$9000n$	=	628,000	–	$800n$

Check

In 11.53 years after 1990, the population of El Paso will be $515{,}000 + 11.53 \cdot 9000$, or 618,770. The population of Milwaukee will be $628{,}000 - 11.53 \cdot 800$, or 618,776. These figures are close enough, given the accuracy of the information.

Because there are many situations that lead to linear equations, solving linear equations is considered by many people to be the most important skill in beginning algebra.

QUESTIONS

Covering the Reading

1. The boxes are of equal weight. Each ball represents 1 ounce.
   a. What equation is pictured by this balance scale? $5W + 6 = 3W + 10$

   b. Describe the steps you could use to find the weight of a box using a scale. **See left.**
   c. What is the weight of one box? **2 oz**

2. a. To solve $8x + 7 = 2x + 9$, what could you add to both sides so x is on only one side of the equation? **-2x or -8x**
   b. Solve the equation in part **a**. $x = \frac{1}{3}$

3. Solve the equation of Example 2 by subtracting $0.03n$ from both sides. $250 - 0.02n = 70$; $-0.02n = -180$; $n = 9{,}000$

4. In solving Example 3, what advantage does adding $7y$ to both sides of the equation have over adding $-4y$?
   Sample: Adding 7y saves one step in the solution.

In 5–12, solve and check. **5–12) See left for checks.**

5. $2p + 38 = 5p + 5$ $p = 11$

6. $4n = -2n + 3$ $n = \frac{1}{2}$

7. $12x + 1 = 3x - 8$ $x = -1\frac{?}{4}$

8. $43 - 8w = 25 + w$ $w = 2$

9. $7y = 5y - 3$ $y = \frac{-3}{2}$

10. $2 - z = 3 - 4z$ $z = \frac{1}{3}$

11. $12 + 0.6f = 1.2f$ $f = 20$

12. $2.85p - 3.95 = 9.7p + 9.75$
    $p = -2$

13. Alaska's population, which had been increasing at a rate of 15,000 people a year, reached 550,000 in 1990. Delaware's population, which had been increasing at a rate of 7,000 people a year reached 666,000 in 1990. If the rates of increase do not change, when will the populations be equal? **in 2004 or 2005**

Lesson 5-3   *Solving $ax + b = cx + d$*   **301**

Adapting to Individual Needs

Extra Help
Students who are having difficulty solving equations of the form $ax + b = cx + d$ first need to use the Algebraic Definition of Subtraction correctly (if it applies), and then they need to look at the resulting equation carefully to identify like terms. Ask students to double underscore the variable terms or use a colored pencil to underline them. Until these students become better skilled at solving equations of this type, have them

identify the lesser variable term and add the opposite of it to both sides of the equation. Then point out that the resulting equation is in the form $ax + b = c$ or $c = ax + b$, which they already know how to solve. Be sure students check their answers.

Notes on Questions
Questions 2–4 The purpose of these questions is to show that the variable terms can be collected on either side of an equation and to encourage discussion of alternate solution strategies. At this point, it is more important for the student to use a strategy correctly than to use a more efficient strategy incorrectly.

(Notes on Questions continue on page 303.)

Follow-up for Lesson 5-3

Practice
For more questions on SPUR Objectives, use **Lesson Master 5-3A** (shown on page 301) or **Lesson Master 5-3B** (shown on pages 302–303).

Assessment

Quiz A quiz covering Lessons 5-1 through 5-3 is provided in the *Assessment Sourcebook*.

Group Assessment Have students **work in pairs.** Ask each student to draw balance scales or to use **Teaching Aid 19** to show each step of the solution of an equation. Tell students not to write the equation or the steps on their drawings. Then have partners exchange papers and supply the equation as well as the

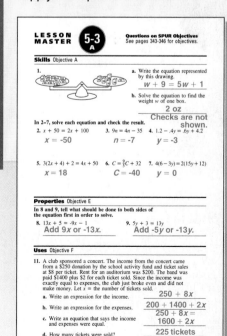

301

Extension

Materials: Almanacs
Have students refer to an almanac to
find two different cities, one where
the population has increased and
one where the population has
decreased. Then have them make
up a problem similar to the situation
in **Example 4.**

14. Refer to Example 4. The 1990 population of Jacksonville, Florida, was 673,000. It had been increasing at a rate of 13,200 people each year. Assuming the rates had not changed, when *were* the populations of El Paso and Jacksonville the same? **in 1952 or 1953**

15. An equation is solved below. Fill in the blanks to explain the steps of the solution.

$$x - 1 = -2x - 3 \qquad \text{Add } \underline{\text{ a. }} \text{ to each side. } 2x$$
$$3x - 1 = -3 \qquad \underline{\text{ b. }} \text{ to each side. Add 1}$$
$$3x = -2 \qquad \underline{\text{ c. }} \text{ each side by } \underline{\text{ d. }}$$
$$x = -\frac{2}{3} \qquad \text{Multiply} \qquad \frac{1}{3}$$

Applying the Mathematics

In 16–19, solve.

16. $1.5c + 17 = 0.8c - 32$ *c* = -70
17. $3d + 4d + 5 = 6d + 7d + 8$ $d = -\frac{1}{2}$
18. $3(x - 4) = 4(x - 3)$ *x* = 0
19. $7(3y - 6) = 14y$ *y* = 6

20. Five more than twice a number is three more than four times the number. What is the number? **1**

21. In 1992, the women's Olympic winning time for the 100-meter freestyle in swimming was 54.64 seconds. The winning time had been decreasing at an average rate of 0.33 second per year. The men's winning time was 49.36 seconds and had been decreasing by an average of 0.18 second a year. Assume that these rates continue.
   a. What will the women's 100-meter winning time be *x* years after 1992? **a) 54.64 − 0.33*x*;   b) 49.36 − 0.18*x***
   b. What will the men's 100-meter winning time be *x* years after 1992?
   c. After how many years will the winning times be the same? **after about 35 years, at the Olympics in the year 2028**

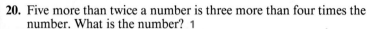

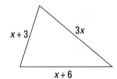

Swimming for the gold.
In 1988, U.S. Olympic swimmer Janet Evans won 3 gold medals and set an Olympic record in the 800-meter freestyle with a time of 8:20.20 minutes.

22. Refer to the figures below. The perimeter of the triangle is equal to the perimeter of the square. Find the length of a side of the square. **6**

23a)

hour	Lamont's distance	Chris's distance
0	24	0
1	33	13
2	42	26
3	51	39
4	60	52
5	69	65
6	78	78

Review

23. Lake Mills is 24 miles by road north of Columbus. Lamont bicycles north from Lake Mills at a rate of 9 mph. Chris leaves Columbus at the same time, also traveling north but at a rate of 13 mph. *(Lesson 5-2)*
   a. Make a table showing how far each bicyclist is from Columbus after hours 0 through 6. **See left.**
   b. How long does it take Chris to catch up to Lamont? **6 hours**

24. Write an equation for the line containing the points (4, *n*), (0, *n*), and (-2, *n*). *(Lesson 5-1)* **y = n**

Adapting to Individual Needs

Challenge
Give students the following situation:
On Monday, Eddie bought two old clocks at an antique store. He set both clocks to the correct time. The first clock gained one minute every hour, and the second clock lost two minutes every hour. The next morning, the first clock showed 7:00 and the second showed 6:00. What is the correct time? [6:40 A.M.] At what time on Monday did he set the clocks? [10:40 A.M.]

25. Graph $y = 4x - 6$. *(Lesson 4-8)* **See left.**

26. Refer to the triangle at the left.
   a. What are the possible values of x? **2 < x < 14**
   b. If $\angle A$ is a right angle, what is the value of x? **x = 10**
   c. Redraw the picture making $\angle B$ a right angle and find x.
   (Lessons 1-8, 4-7) **See left.**

27. Rewrite $3(x + 2)$ using the stated property.
   a. Commutative Property of Addition **3(2 + x)**
   b. Commutative Property of Multiplication **(x + 2)3**
   c. Distributive Property *(Lessons 2-1, 3-1, 3-6)* **3x + 6**

28. The opposite of 4 is added to the reciprocal of 4. What is the result?
(Lessons 2-2, 3-2) $\frac{-15}{4}$ or $-3\frac{3}{4}$

29. Tell whether the number is a solution to $3x \leq 2x + 6$. *(Lesson 1-1)*
   a. 6 **Yes**   **b.** 10 **No**   **c.** $\sqrt{31}$ **Yes**

Exploration

30. This puzzle is from the book *Cyclopedia of Puzzles,* written by Sam Loyd in 1914. If a bottle and a glass balance with a pitcher, a bottle balances with a glass and a plate, and two pitchers balance with three plates, how many glasses will balance with a bottle?
5 glasses

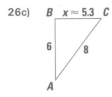

25)

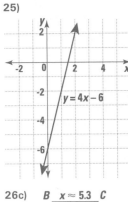

26c) B $x \approx 5.3$ C

Lesson 5-3   *Solving ax + b = cx + d*   **303**

Questions 17–19 Point out that simplifying the equation is the appropriate first step.

Question 21 Explain that in this situation, we are assuming the rates of change will remain constant, which will probably not happen. This allows us to make some predictions, but the quality of the predictions is only as good as the quality of the assumption. The assumption that the winning times might become the same is not far-fetched; at longer distances women have sometimes held the overall world record. For instance, the record for swimming the English Channel has at times been held by a woman.

Sports Connection Zhuang Yong of China won the women's 100-meter freestyle swimming event at the 1992 Summer Olympic Games in Barcelona, Spain. Chinese women also won the 50-meter freestyle, 100-meter butterfly, and 200-meter medley swimming events, and the platform and springboard diving events.

Question 30 A diagram for this puzzle is given on **Teaching Aid 53.** Students may enjoy working other puzzles by Sam Loyd. His books are still being sold, and they may be available in your library. Many of his puzzles first appeared in newspapers and his books include discussions of readers' solutions.

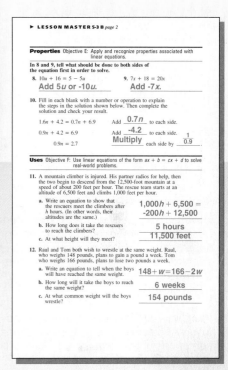

Setting Up Lesson 5-4

Materials Students will need graph paper or **Teaching Aid 39** for Lesson 5-4.

The setting for **Example 2** in the next lesson is an Aesop's fable, "The Tortoise and the Hare." You might want to have a copy of the fable in class when discussing the example.

Objectives

I Use graphs to solve problems involving linear expressions.

Resources

From the Teacher's Resource File
- Lesson Master 5-4A or 5-4B
- Answer Master 5-4
- Teaching Aids
  39 Graphing Equations
  48 Warm-up
  54 Example 2 and Question 10

Additional Resources
- Visuals for Teaching Aids 39, 48, 54
- Aesop's Fable, "The Tortoise and the Hare"

Teaching Lesson 5-4

Warm-up

Graph the following situations on the same coordinate plane. Then answer the questions by looking at the graphs.

At restaurant A, the salad bar costs $0.25 per ounce. A cup of soup is $0.60 and a beverage costs $0.90.

At restaurant B, the salad bar costs $0.20 per ounce. A cup of soup is $0.75 and a beverage is $1.25.

When is salad, soup, and beverage
1. at restaurant A more expensive than at restaurant B? **Whenever a customer takes more than 10 ounces from the salad bar**

The Tortoise and the Hare. *This detail from a picture of Aesop's famous fable was drawn by Arthur Rackham in 1912. See Example 2.*

In Lesson 5-2, situations leading to linear expressions were described with tables. In Lesson 5-3, equations were used. Here, we use graphs.

Consider again the costs of renting copiers from Acme Copiers and Best Printers. Recall that Acme charges $250 per month plus $.01 per copy, and Best charges $70 per month plus $.03 per copy. The table below is from Lesson 5-2. The graph is of the cost equations $y = 250 + 0.01x$ for Acme and $y = 70 + 0.03x$ for Best.

Number of Copies x	Acme's Charges $y = 250 + 0.01x$	Best's Charges $y = 70 + 0.03x$
0	250	70
2,000	270	130
4,000	290	190
6,000	310	250
8,000	330	310
10,000	350	370
12,000	370	430
14,000	390	490

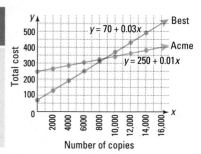

Notice that the graph of each equation is a line. The line for the cost of renting a copier from Best starts lower on the graph. Look on the y-axis for the cost when 0 copies are made; Best's price is $70. The basic fee for an Acme copier is higher; when $x = 0$, the price is $250.

Now look to the right of the y-axis. Notice that as the number of copies goes up, the price charged by each plan goes up. The cost increases faster for a Best copier, because its "per-copy" charge is greater.

Lesson 5-4 Overview

Broad Goals In previous lessons students used tables and equations to answer questions about constant-increase and constant-decrease situations. In this lesson, the same kinds of questions are examined using graphs.

Perspective This lesson provides the following geometric way of solving linear sentences of the form $ax + b = cx + d$:

(1) Graph $y = ax + b$.
(2) Graph $y = cx + d$ on the same grid.
(3) Examine the point of intersection—the x-coordinate of that point is the solution.

A key issue in working with the ideas in this lesson is to determine a scale for the graph. There is no automatic rule that you can give students; judgment is necessary and developing this judgment may take time. Suggest that students mentally, or on paper, calcu-

late the coordinates of a few points on the graph before determining a scale.

Example 1

Use the graph to estimate the answer to each question.
a. For how many copies per month are the costs of Acme and Best equal?
b. For how many copies per month is Best more expensive than Acme?
c. For how many copies per month is Best less expensive than Acme?

Solution

a. Find the point where the two lines intersect. The x-coordinate of this point is the "break-even" value. The two lines cross at about $x \approx 9000$. So the costs are equal when $x \approx 9000$.
b. Best is more expensive than Acme when Best's line is higher. That is about when $x > 9000$.
c. Best is less expensive than Acme when Best's line is lower. That is about when $x < 9000$.

Check

The equation $250 + 0.01x = 70 + 0.03x$ tells when the costs are equal. This was solved as Example 2 in the last lesson. The solution is $x = 9000$.

Graphs, tables, and algebraic sentences each have advantages in describing information. Graphs can picture a great deal of information, and they are very useful for comparing values. Graphs may be time-consuming to make, but automatic graphers draw them quickly. Tables can include important specific values. Long tables might be time-consuming to make, but computer programs such as spreadsheets can make them easily. Solving sentences is often preferred because it is the most efficient tool, and the result is a precise answer.

For the next example, recall Aesop's fable about the tortoise and the hare. Their race can be pictured with a graph.

Example 2

The tortoise and the hare decide to have a race. To be generous, the hare decides to give the tortoise a 100-ft head start. The hare runs at 5 ft/sec, and the tortoise's speed is 0.1 ft/sec.
a. Write equations to show the distance d each animal is from the starting point after t seconds.
b. Graph the equations over the interval $0 \leq t \leq 30$ seconds.
c. Use the graph to tell when the hare reaches the tortoise.
d. Use an equation to tell when the hare reaches the tortoise.

Solution

a. Let t = the number of seconds an animal runs, and let d = the number of feet the animal is from the starting point. The hare's distance at t sec is given by d = 5t. Due to the head start, when the race begins the tortoise is already 100 ft from the starting point. After t seconds, the tortoise has gone 100 + 0.1t ft. The tortoise's distance is given by d = 100 + 0.1t.

▶

2. at B more expensive than A?
   Whenever a customer takes less than 10 ounces
3. the same price at both restaurants? Whenever a customer takes 10 ounces

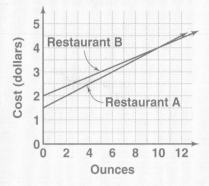

Notes on Reading

Students can work through **Example 2** using **Teaching Aid 54**.

Cooperative Learning The entire lesson is based on two examples which should be carefully reviewed. You might want to read the lesson with your students. If you do, stop at each paragraph to make sure that students understand the ideas. After discussing **Example 1,** have students answer **Question 1** if they have not already done so.

You might summarize the procedure for solving a linear equation of the form $ax + b = cx + d$ by graphing:
1. Graph $y = ax + b$.
2. Graph $y = cx + d$ on the same grid.
3. Identify the x-coordinate of the point of intersection; this will be the solution to $ax + b = cx + d$.

Students will need graph paper or **Teaching Aid 39** for the *Additional Examples* and the *Questions*.

Optional Activities

This activity provides an alternate approach to **Questions 8–10.** Have students **work in groups** with different students in each group assigned to make the tables, draw the graphs, solve the equations, and write the answers to questions based on the graphs.

You could select two groups to put their graphs on transparencies, and have a whole-class discussion about **Questions 8 and 9.** In each case, the domain is discrete,

but, because of the size of the numbers, it is appropriate to draw a continuous graph.

Additional Examples

Given the complexity of the Additional Examples, you may want to have students **work with partners.**

1. Consider the situation in **Example 4** on page 300 of Lesson 5-3.
   a. Use an interval of 100,000 on the y-axis. Graph $y = 515{,}000 + 9000n$ and $y = 628{,}000 - 800n$ on the same coordinate grid.

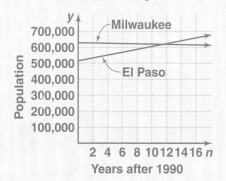

b. From the graph, estimate when El Paso will have a population greater than that of Milwaukee. **Sample: between 2000 and 2002**

2. Car M, traveling at 25 mph, is 3 miles ahead of Car N when Car N passes the checkpoint traveling at 30 mph.
   a. Graph the distance d that Car M has traveled from the checkpoint t minutes after Car N passes the checkpoint. **See graph under part b on page 307.**

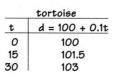

b. To graph each equation over the interval $0 \le t \le 30$, make a table with $t = 0$ and $t = 30$. You should also choose a third point (here, we use $t = 15$) to check that the other two points and the line you draw between them are correct. Plot the points and draw the two lines.

hare

t	d = 5t
0	0
15	75
30	150

tortoise

t	d = 100 + 0.1t
0	100
15	101.5
30	103

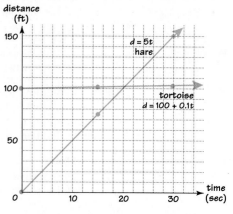

c. Look to see where the lines cross. This happens at a point whose first coordinate is between 20 and 22 seconds. **The hare passes the tortoise after about 21 seconds.**

d. When the hare reaches the tortoise, their distances will be equal.

$$\text{tortoise's distance} = \text{hare's distance}$$
$$100 + 0.1t = 5t$$

Now solve the equation.

$$100 + 0.1t - 0.1t = 5t - 0.1t$$
$$100 = 4.9t$$
$$\frac{1}{4.9} \cdot 100 = \frac{1}{4.9} \cdot 4.9t$$
$$20.4 \approx t$$

The hare reaches the tortoise after about **20.4 seconds.** This result verifies the answer found in part **c** and is more accurate.

QUESTIONS

Covering the Reading

In 1–5, use Example 2.

1. Find the distance each animal is from the starting point after 12 seconds. **The hare is 60 ft from the starting point; the tortoise is 101.2 ft away.**

2. Find the distance each animal is from the starting point after 60 seconds. **The hare is 300 ft away; the tortoise is 106 ft away.**

3. When the hare reaches the tortoise, about how far are they from the starting point? **102 feet**

306

Adapting to Individual Needs

Extra Help

As you discuss **Example 1,** be sure students realize that each line on the graph represents the rental charges of one of the office-supply firms. Also be sure students understand that the point where the two lines intersect represents the "break-even point," that is, the point where the cost (y) will be the same for the same number of copies (x). Emphasize that the x-value at this point gives the information needed to make a decision about which company to patronize.

306

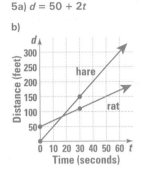

5a) $d = 50 + 2t$

b)

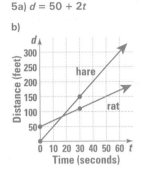

Distance (feet) vs Time (seconds) graph showing "hare" and "rat" lines.

8a) American: $y = 70 + 0.10x$
Coast-to-Coast: $y = 50 + 0.13x$

8c)

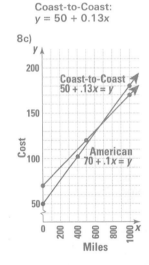

Cost vs Miles graph showing "Coast-to-Coast $50 + .13x = y$" and "American $70 + .1x = y$"

4. Suppose the race course is 110 ft long.
  a. Who will win the race? **b.** How long will it take?
  the hare   22 seconds
5. The hare had another race, one with a rat that ran 2 ft/sec. The rat had a 50-foot head start. **a, b) See left.**
  a. Write an equation to describe the rat's distance d after t seconds.
  b. Draw a graph showing the hare's and rat's distances over the interval $0 \le t \le 60$ seconds.
  c. Use your graph to find out when the hare reaches the rat.
  after about 17 seconds

In 6 and 7, use the graph at the right. It shows the graph from the beginning of this lesson with another line added to show the prices for renting from Carlson's Copy Machines. Carlson's charges a \$10-per-month basic fee and 5¢ a copy. So for Carlson's, $y = 10 + 0.05x$.

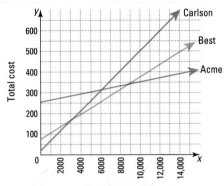

Total cost vs Number of copies graph showing lines labeled Carlson, Best, Acme.

6. a. For about how many copies per month is Carlson's price the same as Best's price? ≈ 3,000 copies
  b. About how much will it cost for the number of copies in part **a**? ≈ $160
  c. Solve an equation to verify your answer to part **a**.
  $10 + 0.05x = 70 + 0.03x$; $0.02x = 60$; $x = 3,000$
7. a. For how many copies do Carlson's and Acme charge the same price?
  b. About how much will it cost for the number of copies in part **a**?
  c. Solve an equation to verify your answer to part **a**.
  $10 + 0.05x = 250 + 0.01x$; $0.04x = 240$; $x = 6,000$
  a) 6,000 copies; b) ≈ $310

Applying the Mathematics

8. Julio needs to rent a car for a week. For comparable cars, American Rental charges \$70 per week plus 10¢ per mile, and Coast-to-Coast Rent-a-Car charges \$50 per week plus 13¢ per mile. **a) See left.**
  a. Write equations to describe the cost of the rental car at each agency. Let x = the number of miles driven, and y = the cost in dollars.
  b. How much would it cost to rent a car from American for 1 week if you drove 600 miles? $130
  c. Draw a graph showing the cost of renting from each company for trips up to 1000 miles during the week. **See left.**
  d. According to your graph, for what mileage will the two rental agencies cost the same amount? ≈ 700 miles
  e. Use an equation to tell when the two rental agencies will cost the same amount. $50 + 0.13x = 70 + 0.10x$; $x \approx 667$ miles
  f. Julio expects to drive between 700 and 1000 miles during the week. What advice would you give him? Rent a car from American Rental, because their cost is less when you drive more than 667 miles.

Lesson 5-4 *Using Graphs to Compare Linear Expressions* **307**

b. Graph the distance Car N is from the checkpoint x minutes after it passes the checkpoint.

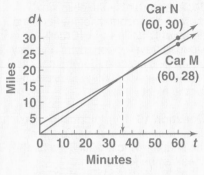

Miles vs Minutes graph showing Car N (60, 30) and Car M (60, 28).

c. According to the graph, when will Car N overtake Car M?
  Sample: between 35 and 40 minutes
d. If t = time in hours, the cars will meet when $30t = 25t + 3$. Solve this equation to find the answer. $t = \frac{3}{5}$ hour, or 36 minutes

Notes on Questions
An alternate way to approach **Questions 8–10** is given in *Optional Activities* on page 305.

Question 8 This is a good question to use as a basis for a discussion on how a scale might be selected.

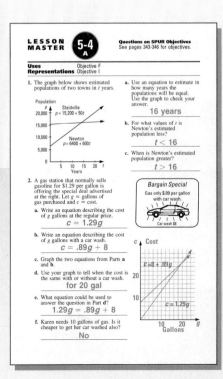

Adapting to Individual Needs

English Language Development
You might use colored chalk to visually show students how information is translated from a table to a graph. For instance, in **Example 1** the table heading "Acme's Charges $y = 250 + 0.01x$" and the column of charges under it should be written in the same color as the line used to represent this information on the graph.

307

Question 10 The graph for this question is given on **Teaching Aid 54**. Ask students to explain why there is a horizontal segment on the graph of Drucilla's trip. [Drucilla stopped traveling for any of a variety of reasons including having her car repaired, eating a meal, or sleeping for the night.]

Question 16 This information was first given on the opening page of the chapter, where equations for the lines can be found.

Follow-up for Lesson 5-4

Practice

For more questions on SPUR Objectives, use **Lesson Master 5-4A** (shown on page 307) or **Lesson Master 5-4B** (shown on pages 308–309).

Assessment

Oral Communication Have students give the three ways to describe situations. [graph, tables, algebraic sentences] Then have them give an advantage for each. [Graphs picture the information and are useful for comparing data. Tables include specific values. Solving sentences is efficient and gives a precise answer.]

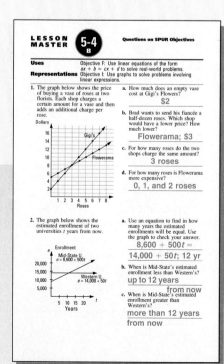

9a)
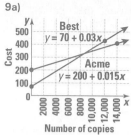

At about 9,000 copies costs are equal.

b) $200 + 0.015x = 70 + 0.03x$;
$x \approx 8667$; Costs are equal for about 8,667 copies

This is a modern Chinese algebra book. The title (written vertically far right) is Junior High School Algebra I.

10a) Drucilla; the graph shows she reached 1250 miles in about 36 hours and Phil arrived about 8 hours later.

308

---

9. Refer to the data at the start of the lesson. Acme Copiers decides to change prices. Their copy machines will now cost $200 plus $1\frac{1}{2}$ cents per copy. Best Printers will keep their prices the same.
   a. Use a graph to determine what number of copies will cost the same for both companies. **See left.**
   b. Use an equation to find out when the costs will be equal.

10. Drucilla and Phil traveled from Omaha, Nebraska, to Boise, Idaho, a distance of about 1250 miles. Drucilla drove, while Phil left later and flew. The graph shows the distance y each had traveled x hours after Drucilla began her trip.
   a. Who arrived in Boise first? How can you tell? **See left.**
   b. How long did Phil's trip take? **about 4 hours**

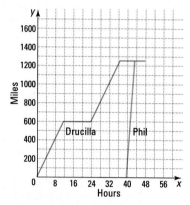

11. "Pursuit" problems, as in the story of the tortoise and the hare in Example 2, have been around for a long time. The following problem appeared in an ancient Chinese textbook around the first century A.D.

    A hare runs 50 pu (paces) ahead of a dog. The dog pursues the hare for 125 pu but the hare is still 30 pu ahead. How many pu will the dog have traveled altogether when he overtakes the hare? Solve the problem, and explain how you solved it.
    See below.

Review

In 12–15, solve. *(Lesson 5-3)*

12. $3p - 5 = 2p + 12$ $p = 17$ 13. $-7r + 54 = 2r - 36$ $r = 10$

14. $6(x + 3) + 4(3x - 75) = 258$ $x = 30$ 15. $6m = 2m + 2$ $m = \frac{1}{2}$

11) Using a table, you get 312.5 pu.

$x =$ distance dog travels	$y =$ distance hare is ahead
0	50
125	30
250	10
312.5	0

Using a graph, you may approximate the answer. Graph the line from (0, 50) through (125,30). When the distance (y) the hare is ahead reaches zero, the x-value tells the total distance traveled by the dog.

Adapting to Individual Needs

Challenge

Many stores have copiers that make copies at 5 cents apiece. Recently, however, the prices of copy machines have dropped considerably. Have students research the costs of home copiers, including the cost of toner cartridges, the expected number of copies from each cartridge, the cost of copier paper, and so on. Then have them determine approximately how many copies they could make at 5 cents each before it would be less expensive to buy a home copier.

16. GE sells a type of light bulb called Energy Choice™ that uses less electricity than its regular Soft White bulbs. However, the initial cost of the bulb is more than that of the regular Soft White brand. The table below shows the cost of using a 60-watt bulb of each type in one part of the country. *(Lesson 5-2)*

hours	Energy Choice	Soft White
0	$0.75	$0.59
100	$1.17	$1.07
200	$1.59	$1.55
300	$2.01	$2.03
400	$2.43	$2.51
500	$2.85	$2.99
600	$3.27	$3.47
700	$3.69	$3.95
800	$4.11	$4.43
900	$4.53	$4.91
1000	$4.95	$5.39

A bright idea. *This is a replica of the first light bulb invented by Thomas Edison in 1879. Edison's first bulb burned brightly for only two days.*

a. How much does a new Soft White 60-watt bulb cost? **$0.59**
b. How much more expensive is an Energy Choice bulb? **$0.16**
c. After approximately how many hours of use are the total costs of the two bulbs the same? **after 300 hours of use**
d. If a bulb lasts for 1000 hours of use (the average life according to GE), how much money would you save by buying an Energy Choice bulb? **$0.44**

17. a. On one coordinate grid graph $y = -3$ and $x = 4$. **See left.**
    b. Give the coordinates of the point the two lines have in common. *(Lesson 5-1)* **(4, -3)**

18. *Multiple choice.* Which of the following does *not* equal $\frac{x}{6}$? *(Lesson 2-3)*

(a) $\frac{1}{6}x$ (b) $\frac{2}{12}x$ (c) $\frac{3x}{18}$ (d) $\frac{4x}{10}$ **(d)**

19. What will be printed when this BASIC program is run? *(Lessons 1-4, 1-6)*

```
10 PRINT "SQUARE ROOTS AND SQUARES"
20 FOR A = 1 TO 6
30 PRINT SQR(A), A, A^2
40 NEXT A
50 END
```

SQUARE ROOTS AND SQUARES		
1	1	1
1.41421356	2	4
1.73205081	3	9
2	4	16
2.23606789	5	25
2.44948974	6	36

17a)

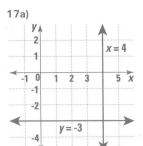

Exploration

20. Find examples of two similar situations that lead to linear expressions, as in Example 1 of this lesson. You may want to look in newspapers or magazines or visit a store. Draw a graph to compare the values of these expressions. What conclusions can you make based on your graph? **Answers will vary.**

Lesson 5-4 *Using Graphs to Compare Linear Expressions* **309**

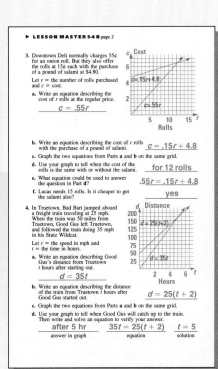

Setting Up Lesson 5-5

Materials Automatic graphers

Lesson 5-5 assumes that students have access to automatic graphers. If such graphers are not available, do not assign **Questions 2 and 7–16.** Instead, you may want to discuss these questions in class.

Homework You need to tell students how you want them to transfer graphs from a computer or calculator screen to their papers.

At the very least, they should show the following:
(1) a scale on each axis or an indication of the bounds of the window;
(2) the equation or inequality that is graphed;
(3) a sketch that looks similar to the graph;
(4) a few key points on the graph.

You might want to have students transfer their graphs to **Teaching Aid 55.**

Objectives

J Given an equation, be able to use an automatic grapher to draw and interpret a graph.

Resources

From the Teacher's Resource File
- Lesson Master 5-5A or 5-5B
- Answer Master 5-5
- Teaching Aids
  26 Graph Paper
  28 Four-Quadrant Graph Paper
  48 Warm-up
  55 Automatic Grapher Grids
- Technology Sourcebook
  Computer Master 14
  Calculator Master 3

Additional Resources
- Visuals for Teaching Aids 26, 28, 48, 55
- Automatic graphers

Teaching Lesson 5-5

Warm-up

Solve each equation for *y*.
1. $x + y = 8$ $y = -x + 8$
2. $y - 2 = 4x$ $y = 4x + 2$
3. $x - y = 9$ $y = x - 9$
4. $x - y = -4$ $y = x + 4$
5. $y + 1 = 7x$ $y = 7x - 1$

Notes on Reading

This lesson is best done when students are able to work with the technology for the entire lesson. If your students do not have automatic graphers to take home, have them do the activities and examples on pages 310–313 in class. Then

---

LESSON

5-5

Using an Automatic Grapher

Graph it your way. *This student is displaying the same graph on both the computer screen and the graphics calculator. Both tools allow you to display multiple graphs at one time and find points of intersection using a zoom feature.*

What Is an Automatic Grapher?

Graphs of equations are so helpful in solving problems that there are now several makes of calculators that will automatically display part of a graph. Also, there are programs for every personal computer that will display graphs. Because computer screens are larger than calculator screens, they can show a greater part of a graph, but graphing calculators are less expensive and easier to carry around.

Graphing calculators and computer graphing programs work in much the same way. As such we call them **automatic graphers** and do not distinguish between them. Of course, no grapher is completely automatic. For each you must learn particular keys to press. Here we discuss some of the general features of automatic graphers.

Instructions

The part of the coordinate grid that is shown is called a **window.** The screen below displays a window in which

$$-2 \le x \le 12$$
$$\text{and } -3 \le y \le 7.$$

Lesson 5-5 Overview

Broad Goals In this lesson, we deal with automatic graphers; that is, students learn how to use computer software or a graphing calculator which can graph an equation that has been properly entered into the machine.

Perspective Graphing calculators and computer programs make it quick and easy to graph several functions and to compare them. They help students to see relationships between equations and their graphs.

Automatic graphers also make it as easy to graph functions with "messy" coefficients as those with "nice" numbers, so they are a great convenience when dealing with applications. The extraordinary growth in the use of these graphers within the past few years is evidence of their value. Any function plotter that displays multiple graphs is appropriate.

The equipment that you have available (in the classroom or in a computer lab) will

affect how you approach this lesson and how you use automatic graphers in the lessons that follow. Regardless of whether students work mostly in a computer lab or in the classroom with graphics calculators, we recommend that you introduce the technology with a teacher demonstration and class discussion. It is helpful for students to see how the technology works and for you to relate the text illustrations to what they will see.

Most graphers have a **default window,** set by the manufacturer. In this lesson we use -15 ≤ x ≤ 15 and -10 ≤ y ≤ 10 as the default window. If your graph does not appear on the default window, you will need to determine a new window to use.

You usually enter the instructions for the window first, and then enter the equation to be graphed. On almost all graphers, the equation to be graphed must be a formula for y in terms of x.

$$y = 4x - 5 \quad \text{can be handled.}$$
$$x + y = 180 \quad \text{cannot be handled.}$$

On calculator screens, the intervals for x and y are often left unmarked.

Graphing a Linear Equation on an Automatic Grapher

Example 1

Draw the graph of $y = 4x - 5$ using an automatic grapher's default window.

Solution

Notice that y is given in terms of x, so the equation may be entered directly. Enter the equation. Here is a key sequence for one calculator.

$$\boxed{y=} \; 4 \; \boxed{\times} \; \boxed{X, T, \theta} \; \boxed{-} \; 5 \; \boxed{ENTER}$$

Press $\boxed{GRAPH}$ to display the graph.

Here is the graph as it appears on our default screen.

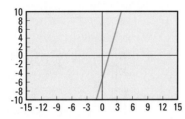

You need to clear each equation before you graph the next one unless you wish both graphs to appear.

Activity 1)

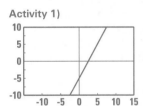

Activity 1

Draw the graph of $y = 2x - 5$ on your default window. Copy it on paper. Describe one thing your graph has in common with the graph in Example 1. See left for graph. Samples: Both graphs intersect the y-axis at -5. Both graphs slant in the same direction.

have them do **Question 2** and **Questions 7–16** in class. Students can transfer their graphs to graph paper (**Teaching Aid 26**) or to automatic grapher grids (**Teaching Aid 55**).

Many automatic graphers require that equations be solved for y before they can be graphed. These graphers will graph horizontal lines, because they are of the form y = k. Some graphers do not graph vertical lines, so the equation for x = h cannot be graphed.

If your graphers require equations in the form "f(x) = __" you may wish to explain the f(x) notation or to simply tell students to think of f(x) as y. If you explain the notation, note that f(x) means "function of x," and that it means the coordinate f(x) depends on the value of x. This use of function notation is more difficult than the abbreviations N(S) or P(E), which is why we do not introduce it at this time.

The window that is used most often in this book is
$$-15 \le x \le 15$$
$$-10 \le y \le 10.$$
On some machines you can get this window by pressing $\boxed{zoom}$ Standard, then $\boxed{zoom}$ Square. On other machines, you may want to use a square window or to experiment to find a window that works well for your screen. Check other calculators for their default windows. Note that numerical labels are provided on the windows for clarity. They do not appear on the screens of all automatic graphers

Some software programs do not have a TRACE feature. If you are using such software, students will have to estimate the coordinates of the desired points visually. Using a $\boxed{zoom}$ feature or resetting the window will help.

Optional Activities

Activity 1
You might give students equations that have interesting graphs to graph on their automatic graphers. Have them write descriptions of the shapes of the graphs, where they cross the x-axis, and where they are increasing or decreasing. Some possible graphs to present are:

1. $y = \sqrt{100 - x^2}$ [Semicircle; points at (–10, 0), (0, 10), and (10, 0)]

2. $y = x^2 + 8$ [Parabola; in the first and second quadrants, symmetric with respect to the y-axis, minimum point at (0, 8)]

3. $y = x^3$ [Curve containing point (0, 0); increasing in the first quadrant and decreasing in the third quadrant]

4. $y = \sin x$ with suggested window $-400 \le x \le 410, -2 \le y \le 2$, where x is in degrees [Sine wave]

5. The equations $y = 3x - 5$, $y = 3x + 2$, and $y = 3x + 6$ [Parallel lines increasing from left to right, crossing the y-axis at (0, –5), (0, 2) and (0, 6), respectively]

Additional Examples

1. Show the graph of $y + 2x = 5$ on your default window. Note that numerical labels are provided for clarity. They do not appear on the screens of all automatic graphers.
Possible display:

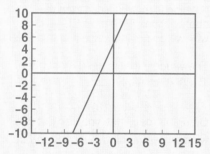

2. a. Choose an appropriate window and show the graph of $x + y = 50$.
Possible display:

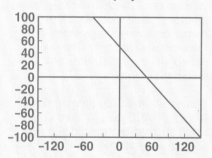

b. Use the trace option to find the point on the graph that is closest to (29, 23). **(28, 22)**

Example 2

Draw a graph of $x + y = 180$.

Solution

To graph this equation on most automatic graphers you must first solve for y. That is, you must enter $y = -x + 180$ or $y = 180 - x$. Enter one of these equations on your grapher, and graph it on the default window. You should not see any of the graph—all the points on the graph are off the screen. So on most graphers, you must change the window. You need to pick the x values for each end of the window. These are sometimes called x-min (for minimum x value) and x-max (for maximum x value). Some graphers automatically pick the y values after you have chosen the x values so all the key features of the graph can be seen. On other graphers, you must also enter y-min and y-max. If your grapher shows **tick marks** (marks on the x- and y-axes), you may change the intervals for the tick marks too.

Below are graphs of $y = 180 - x$ on four different windows.

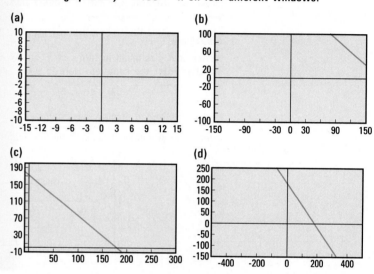

Notice how changing the window can change the appearance of the graph. In (d) the graph appears steep; in (b) and (c) it appears less steep. On (b) you see points in only the first quadrant; on others you see points in quadrants I, II, and IV. The mathematical properties of the graph, however, do *not* change when you change the window. For instance, each graph contains the points (0, 180) and (60, 120) even though they may not appear on the screen.

Most automatic graphers have a **trace** option. This allows you to move a **cursor,** often an arrow or blinking pixel, along the graph. As the cursor moves, it tells you one or both coordinates of the point it is on.

Optional Activities

Activity 2 Technology Connection
You may wish to demonstrate how to use *GraphExplorer* or similar software to find the intersection of two graphs. Then you could assign *Technology Sourcebook, Computer Master 14.* Students graph $y = x$ and $y = \frac{5}{9}(x - 320)$. By finding the coordinates of the point of intersection, they determine the Celsius temperature that equals its Fahrenheit equivalent.

Activity 3 Technology Connection
With *Technology Sourcebook, Calculator Master 3,* students use a graphics calculator to solve linear equations.

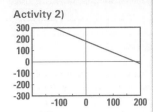

Activity 2

Clear the equation from Activity 1. Draw a graph of $x + y = 180$ on a window different from those in Example 2. Trace along the line on the screen. Sketch the graph on paper. You should see that, as the cursor moves to the right along the graph of $y = 180 - x$, the x-coordinate increases, and the y-coordinate decreases. You should also verify that the sum of the x- and y-coordinates is always 180. Write the coordinates of three points that are on your graph. **See left for graph. Sample coordinates: (0, 180); (60, 120); (90, 90)**

Graphing Two Equations at a Time

Automatic graphers can graph more than one equation at a time. They also can easily graph complicated equations. This enables them to help you solve problems like those in the previous lesson.

Example 3

❶ The cost per month y of renting a copier and making x copies from Acme Copiers is given by $y = 250 + 0.01x$. The cost from Best Printers is given by $y = 70 + 0.03x$. For what number of copies is Acme cheaper?

Solution

With an automatic grapher, first enter the equation $y = 250 + 0.01x$ to be graphed. (You may need to enter the multiplication symbol between 0.01 and x.) Then enter the second equation $y = 70 + 0.03x$. The window $0 \le x \le 16{,}000$, $0 \le y \le 550$ will give a graph like the one on page 304.

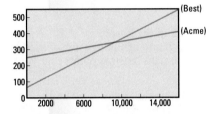
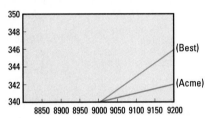

Now use the trace option to move the tracer near the point of intersection of the two lines. Our grapher indicates a point of intersection near (9095, 343). To be more accurate, either **zoom in** on the point of intersection or create a new window. We created a new window, $8800 \le x \le 9200$ and $340 \le y \le 350$. It is shown at the right above. This window indicates that the intersection is very near (9000, 340). Check these values in the equations to confirm that this is the point of intersection. Thus, the line for Acme is below the line for Best when $x > 9000$. This means that Acme is cheaper when the number of copies is greater than 9000.

Many automatic graphers will print a **hard copy**, which is a paper copy of the graph from the screen. When copying or printing graphs, be sure to identify the limits of the window, as we have done.

Lesson 5-5   *Using an Automatic Grapher*   **313**

3. Use the information in **Question 8** on page 307. On an automatic grapher, draw a graph showing the cost of renting from each company. According to your graph, what point is near the intersection? Answers will vary; about (667, 137) Possible display:

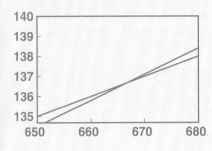

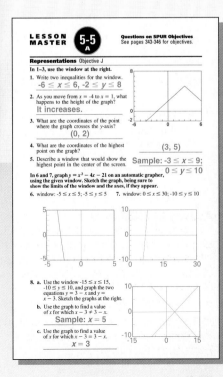

Adapting to Individual Needs

Extra Help

Have students **work in groups.** Make sure at least one student in each group knows how to use an automatic grapher. Have each group graph simple equations. Students should focus on putting the equation in "$y = $ ___" form, entering the equation into the grapher, and then viewing it—which might involve changing the window.

7) Sample:

8) Sample:

9) Sample:

10a) Answers may vary.
Sample:
($-200 < x < 200$;
$-300 < y < 300$)

11a) Answers will vary.
Sample graph:

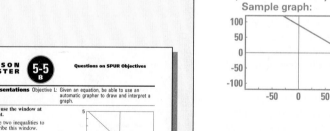

314

QUESTIONS

Covering the Reading

1. On an automatic grapher,
   a. what is a window? the part of the coordinate grid shown on the screen
   b. What is a default window? the window that appears automatically when you turn on the grapher

2. What are the dimensions of the default window on your automatic grapher? Answers will vary.

3. Use two inequalities to describe the window shown below.
   $-15 < x < 15$; $-10 < y < 10$

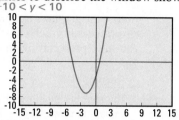

In 4–6, tell whether the equation is in a form with which it can be entered into your grapher.

4. $y = 4 + 3x^2$ Yes
5. $y = 2.7x$ Yes
6. $x - y = 7$ No

7. Write your answer to Activity 1 in the lesson. See left for graph. Both lines pass through the point (0, -5)

In 8 and 9, use an automatic grapher to graph the equation on your default window. See left for 8 and 9.

8. $y = -2x + 1$
9. $x - y = -5$

10. Refer to Activity 2 in the lesson.
    a. Sketch the graph and label the window used. See left.
    b. Give the coordinates of three points that your cursor shows are on this graph. Samples: (0, 180); (60, 120); (90, 90)

11. a. Graph the solutions to $x + y = 90$ on three different windows.
    b. *True or false.* The point (5, 85) is on each graph you drew in part **a.** a) See left. b) True
    c. Trace along the graph from left to right with a cursor. Describe what happens to the *x*- and *y*-coordinates. As the x-coordinate increases, the y-coordinate decreases.

12. Refer to Example 3.
    a. Sketch the two graphs on an appropriate default window.
    b. What point on the grid is closest to the point where the two lines intersect? Answers will vary but should be close to (9000, 340).

314

Adapting to Individual Needs

English Language Development

For this lesson, you might pair non-English-speaking students with English-speaking students. Have each pair of students go through the lesson together. Make sure the non-English-speaking students know what the bold terms, *window, default window, tick marks, trace,* and *cursor,* mean.

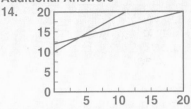

14.

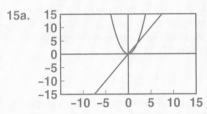

15a.

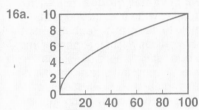

16a.

It's a tossup. *Some pizza chefs toss the dough to stretch it to the correct thickness. Other chefs say flipping the dough isn't essential for good pizza.*

13. Set the window of your grapher to $-10 \le x \le 10$, $-15 \le y \le 15$.
   a. Graph $y = x$, $y = 2x$, $y = 3x$, and $y = 4x$ on the same screen. See left.
   b. Describe the graphs. How are they similar? How are they different? See left.
   c. Predict what the graph of $y = 5x$ will look like. Check by graphing. See left.

14. Battaglia's Pizza Parlor charges $10 for a large cheese pizza plus $0.90 for each additional topping. Tonelli's charges $12 for the same pizza but only $0.40 for each additional topping. Graph the equations $y = 10 + .90x$ and $y = 12 + .40x$ to find the number of toppings for which Tonelli's is cheaper than Battaglia's. See margin for graph. Tonelli's price is cheaper for pizza with more than 4 toppings.

15. a. Use the window $-15 \le x \le 15$, $-10 \le y \le 10$ to graph $y = 2x$ and $y = x^2$. Copy the graphs. See margin.
   b. Use the graphs to explain why $x + x$ is or is not equal to x^2. Sample: The graphs are not equal. One is a line and one is a curve.

16. a. Graph $y = \sqrt{x}$ when $0 \le x \le 100$ and $0 \le y \le 10$. See margin.
   b. Use your cursor to find the coordinates of five points on the graph. Samples: (1, 1); (2, 1.41); (3, 1.73); (4, 2); (5, 2.24)

Review

17. Solve $7(d + 5) = 11(2d - 20)$. *(Lessons 3-7, 5-3)* $d = 17$

18. Answer Question 14 by making a table. *(Lesson 5-2)* See below.

19. *Multiple choice.* Which equation describes the ordered pairs? *(Lesson 4-6)* (c)

   a. $y = 5x$
   b. $y = x + 5$
   c. $y = x - 5$
   d. $y = \frac{x}{5}$

x	y
0	-5
1	-4
2	-3
3	-2

20. Simplify $(17a + 12) - (a - 4)$. *(Lesson 4-5)* $16a + 16$

21. Solve $(4x - 1) - 3(x + 2) = 2$. *(Lesson 4-5)* $x = 9$

22. *Skill sequence.* Solve. *(Lesson 4-3)*
   a. $2W - 7 < 1$ $W < 4$
   b. $7 - 2x < 1$ $x > 3$
   c. $2y - 7 < -1$ $y < 3$
   d. $7 - 2z < -1$ $z > 4$

13a)

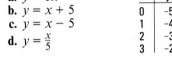

b) Sample: All lines pass through (0, 0). Some lines are steeper than others. The higher the coefficient of x, the steeper the graph is.

c) Sample: It will pass through the origin and be steeper than the other graphs.

18)
Number of Extra Items x	Battaglia's Charges $y = 10 + .9x$	Tonelli's Charges $y = 12 + .4x$
0	$10.00	$12.00
1	$10.90	$12.40
2	$11.80	$12.80
3	$12.70	$13.20
4	$13.60	$13.60
5	$14.50	$14.00
6	$15.40	$14.40
7	$16.30	$14.80

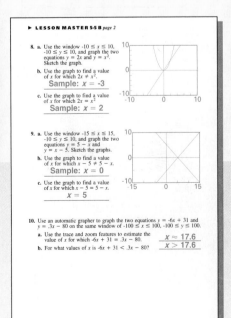

▶ LESSON MASTER 5-5 B *page 2*

8. a. Use the window $-10 \le x \le 10$, $-10 \le y \le 10$, and graph the two equations $y = 2x$ and $y = x^2$. Sketch the graph.
   b. Use the graph to find a value of x for which $2x \ne x^2$. Sample: $x = -3$
   c. Use the graph to find a value of x for which $2x = x^2$. Sample: $x = 2$

9. a. Use the window $-15 \le x \le 15$, $-10 \le y \le 10$, and graph the two equations $y = 5 - x$ and $y = x - 5$. Sketch the graphs.
   b. Use the graph to find a value of x for which $x - 5 \ne 5 - x$. Sample: $x = 0$
   c. Use the graph to find a value of x for which $x - 5 = 5 - x$. $x = 5$

10. Use an automatic grapher to graph the two equations $y = -6x + 31$ and $y = .3x - 80$ on the same window of $-100 \le x \le 100$, $-100 \le y \le 100$.
   a. Use the trace and zoom features to estimate the value of x for which $-6x + 31 = .3x - 80$. $x \approx 17.6$
   b. For what values of x is $-6x + 31 < .3x - 80$? $x > 17.6$

Adapting to Individual Needs

Challenge
Have students use an automatic grapher to graph $y = x^2$, $y = x^3$, $y = x^4$, and $y = x^5$. Suggest that they use windows that are approximately the same size. Then have them answer the following questions:

1. For even powers of x, how are the graphs similar? [The values of y are always positive, and the graphs occur in the first and second quadrants.]

2. For even powers of x, how are the graphs different? [The higher the power, the steeper the graphs]

3. For odd powers of x, how are the graphs similar? [The graphs occur in the first and third quadrants.]

4. For odd powers of x, how are the graphs different? [The higher the power, the steeper the graphs]

315

Practice

For more questions on SPUR Objectives, use **Lesson Master 5-5A** (shown on page 313) or **Lesson Master 5-5B** (shown on pages 314–315).

Assessment

Group Assessment Have students **work in small groups.** Ask each group to write five questions that apply to automatic graphers. Then have groups exchange papers and answer each other's questions. Allow time for checking questions and discussing answers. [Questions reflect understanding of graphing with an automatic grapher.]

Extension

As an extension of **Question 16a**, have students use automatic graphers to graph $y = \sqrt{x} - 3$. [See the graph below.] Ask students how this graph compares to the graph in Question 16a. [This graph is a translation image, 3 units lower]. Then ask for an equation whose graph is a translation image of the original figure, 3 units higher. [$y = \sqrt{x} + 3$]

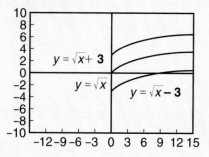

In 23 and 24, a cook has x slices of pastrami for sandwiches. The cook needs s slices for a small sandwich and m slices for a medium sandwich. Write an expression for the amount of pastrami left in each situation. *(Lessons 3-8, 4-2)*

23. **a.** The cook takes meat first for one small sandwich, then for two medium ones. $x - s - 2m$
    b. The cook takes enough at one time for one small and two medium sandwiches. (Use parentheses.) $x - (s + 2m)$

24. **a.** The cook takes enough for 3 smalls and a medium, then later takes enough for 1 small and 2 mediums. $x - (3s + m) - (s + 2m)$
    b. Simplify your answer to part **a.** $x - 4s - 3m$

25. *Multiple choice.* Suppose $j < n$. What is true about $j - n$? (b)
    (a) It is always positive.
    (b) It is always negative.
    (c) It can be either positive or negative. *(Lesson 4-1)*

26. A tortoise is walking at a rate of $3 \frac{\text{feet}}{\text{minute}}$. Assume this rate continues.
    a. How long will it take the tortoise to travel 20 feet? ≈ 6.7 minutes
    b. How long will it take the tortoise to travel f feet? *(Lesson 2-4)* $\frac{f}{3}$ min

27. *Skill sequence.* Solve in your head. *(Lesson 1-4)*
    a. $x + \sqrt{9} = \sqrt{25}$ $x = 2$
    b. $\sqrt{y} + \sqrt{9} = \sqrt{25}$ $y = 4$
    c. $\sqrt{z} + \sqrt{z} = \sqrt{64}$ $z = 16$

29a) magnifies the graph around the cursor; Press the ZOOM key for access.
b) displays a greater portion of the graph that is centered around the cursor location; To access, select ZOOM OUT from the ZOOM menu.
c) draws each data point as a coordinate on the display; To access press [2nd] [STAT] ← to display the STAT DATA menu. Select <Edit>. Enter the value for x and press ENTER. Enter the value for y and press ENTER. When finished entering all data values, press [2nd] [STAT] → to display the STAT DRAW menu. Select <scatter>. Press ENTER, then the scatter plot is displayed on the screen.

Exploration

28. Find four equations whose graphs are lines that form a square, as shown below. Sample: $y = 7 - x$; $y = 7 + x$; $y = -7 - x$; $y = -7 + x$

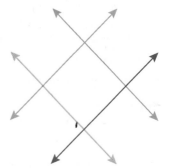

29. Determine whether or not your automatic grapher has the following features. If so, describe what the feature does and how to access it.
    a. zoom in Answers may vary. See left for sample.
    b. zoom out
    c. scatterplot of individual points

Arbor Day. *These students are observing Arbor Day by planting trees on the school grounds. Arbor Day is observed at different times throughout the U.S.*

The Addition and Multiplication Properties of Inequality from Chapters 2 and 3 can be used to solve linear inequalities of the form $ax + b < cx + d$.

Consider the following situation. When they are young, many species of trees grow at rates that are nearly constant. Some years ago the Lee family planted two trees, a beech tree that was 8 feet tall and a maple tree that was only 3 feet tall. Maple trees grow at a rate of about $1 \frac{ft}{year}$.

Beech trees grow more slowly, at about $\frac{1}{2} \frac{ft}{year}$. So t years after planting, the height of the beech tree is $8 + 0.5t$ feet and the height of the maple tree is $3 + t$ feet.

Example 1

Mr. Lee looked at an old photograph of the two trees. In it, the beech tree was taller than the maple tree. He wondered when the photo was taken.

Solution 1

The beech was taller than the maple, so the heights satisfy the inequality

$$8 + 0.5t > 3 + t.$$

Solve this inequality as you would an equation with a variable on both sides.

$8 + 0.5t + -0.5t > 3 + t + -0.5t$	Add $-0.5t$ to both sides.
$8 > 3 + 0.5t$	Add like terms.
$8 + -3 > 3 + -3 + 0.5t$	Add -3 to both sides.
$5 > 0.5t$	Add like terms
$\frac{1}{0.5} \cdot 5 > \frac{1}{0.5} \cdot 0.5t$	Multiply both sides by $\frac{1}{0.5}$.
$10 > t$	

So $t < 10$. The photo was taken less than 10 years after the Lees planted the trees.   ▶

Lesson 5-6

Objectives

B Solve linear inequalities of the form $ax + b < cx + d$.

E Apply and recognize properties associated with linear inequalities.

F Use linear inequalities to solve real-world problems.

Resources

From the **Teacher's Resource File**
■ Lesson Master 5-6A or 5-6B
■ Answer Master 5-6
■ Assessment Sourcebook: Quiz for lesson 5-4 through 5-6
■ Teaching Aids
  39 Graphing Equations
  48 Warm-up
  55 Automatic Grapher Grids
  56 Example 2 and
     Questions 5–6
■ Technology Sourcebook
  Computer Master 15

Additional Resources
■ Visuals for Teaching Aids 39, 48, 55, 56
■ Automatic graphers

Teaching 5-6
Lesson

Warm-up

✎ **Writing** Write a paragraph explaining how solving $-6x + 3 = 21$ is the same as, and how it is different from, solving $-6x + 3 > 21$. Solve each equation. **The solution steps for both are the same; the sense of the inequality is reversed;** $x = -3$; $x < -3$.

Lesson 5-6 Overview

Broad Goals This lesson covers the symbolic and graphical solutions of linear inequalities; it also gives students more experience in writing sentences to describe real situations.

Perspective Students have already encountered the Multiplication Property of Inequality, and there are no new properties needed for solving these inequalities. Because students have already solved

equations of the form $ax + b = cx + d$, no additional steps are needed. And because they have already set up sentences from linear expressions, that too is not a new skill. Thus, this lesson combines many previously encountered concepts, and it provides the opportunity to review them.

Solving linear inequalities is almost like solving equations, but that in itself presents a problem—students can forget to reverse

the sense of the inequality when multiplying both sides by a negative number. Therefore, it is advantageous to solve $ax + b < cx + d$ by arranging to have the coefficient of the variable be positive. In fact, the issue of multiplying by a negative can always be avoided by maneuvering the terms so that the variable term is on the side which makes the coefficient positive, even if there is only one term with a variable.

To determine if students understand **Example 1**, review **Questions 1–6**. To determine if **Example 2** is understood, cover **Question 7**, including the two-step check. Then skip to **Question 12** and review the idea in **Example 3**.

Science Connection Most trees in temperate regions grow a layer of wood each year. After a tree is cut down, the layers in a cross-section of the tree can be counted to approximate its age. A stand of Bristle-cone pines in the Inyo National Forest in California is estimated to be 4,600 years old; the pines are believed to be the oldest living things on earth. Interested students might want to investigate other large or old trees and share their findings with the class.

❶ A numerical check for **Example 1** is not given because one solution checks the other. Ask students if they did numerical checks as they read. Applaud any students who did so, and ask volunteers to explain what they did. If no one checked, ask students what they would do to make such a check. [First check to see that $t = 10$ makes each side of the original sentence a true equality; then check to see that a number less than 10 satisfies the original inequality.]

Throughout this lesson, emphasize the two-step checking method. The more complicated the problem, the more likely it is that there will be an error, so it is especially important to do a careful check.

❷ You might mention to students that it is always possible to keep the coefficient of the variable positive, as shown in Solution 1. This, however, requires the flexibility of solving sentences with the variable on the right side.

❸ Students often find sentences like $3n < 2n$ harder to solve than the more complicated ones like $3n + 4 = 2n + 5$. They think that adding $-2n$ to both sides of $3n < 2n$ results in "nothing left" on the right side—they are forgetting about zero. Remind students that zero is a perfectly legitimate number and the answer to many calculations. The fact that zero causes difficulties is not strange; throughout history people have been so uncomfortable with zero that they have avoided using it.

Trees and their leaves.
Beech trees have thin papery leaves that turn gold-colored in the fall. Maple leaves are known for their broad, flat shape with three to seven lobes that resemble fingers. Their dark-green leaves turn red, orange, or yellow in autumn.

Solution 2

Graph the two equations giving the heights of the two trees after t years, $h = 8 + 0.5t$ and $h = 3 + t$. Then compare the graphs.

t number of years	height h in ft maple	height h in ft beech
0	3	8
2	5	9
4	7	10
6	9	11
8	11	12
10	13	13
12	15	14

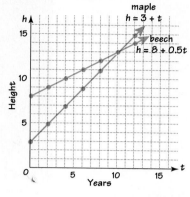

The lines cross at the point where $t = 10$. So ten years after they were planted, the trees were the same height. We are looking for the times when the beech was taller than the maple. So look for values of t where the beech's line is *above* that for the maple. These times lie to the left of the intersection point (10, 13). This is where $t < 10$. The photo was taken less than 10 years after the trees were planted.

The Addition and Multiplication Properties of Inequality can be used to solve any inequality of the form $ax + b < cx + d$, where $a \neq 0$ and $c \neq 0$. In Example 2, two algebraic solutions are given. Solution 2 involves multiplying the inequality by a negative number. Recall that multiplying an inequality by a negative number reverses the sense of the inequality.

Example 2

a. Solve $6 - 9x \leq 5x - 1$.
b. Check your answer.

Solution 1

a. It is reasonable to add either $9x$ or $-5x$ to each side of the sentence.

$6 - 9x + 9x \leq 5x - 1 + 9x$	Begin by adding $9x$ to each side.
$6 \leq 14x - 1$	Add like terms.
$7 \leq 14x$	Add 1 to both sides.
$\frac{1}{14} \cdot 7 \leq 14x \cdot \frac{1}{14}$	Multiply both sides by $\frac{1}{14}$.
$\frac{1}{2} \leq x$	Simplify.

Thus $x \geq \frac{1}{2}$.

Optional Activities

Activity 1
Materials: **Teaching Aid 39**

After discussing the lesson, have students **work in groups** and graph $y = \frac{1}{x^2}$ using $\{-3, -2.5, -2, \ldots 3\}$ as the domain. Suggest that they use the square and reciprocal keys on their calculators and that they use intervals of at least .2 on the vertical axis. After completing the graph, have students discuss any patterns that they notice.

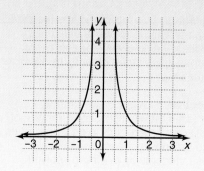

Solution 2

a.
$$6 - 9x + -5x \leq 5x - 1 + -5x \qquad \text{Add } -5x \text{ to each side.}$$
$$6 - 14x \leq -1 \qquad \text{Add like terms.}$$
$$6 - 14x + -6 \leq -1 + -6 \qquad \text{Add } -6 \text{ to both sides.}$$
$$-14x \leq -7 \qquad \text{Add like terms.}$$
$$-\frac{1}{14}(-14x) \geq -7\left(-\frac{1}{14}\right) \qquad \text{Multiply each side by } -\frac{1}{14},$$
$$\text{so reverse the inequality sign.}$$
$$x \geq \frac{1}{2} \qquad \text{Simplify.}$$

b. Recall that checking an inequality requires two steps.

Step 1: Check that $x = \frac{1}{2}$ makes each side of the original sentence true as an equality.

Does $6 - 9 \cdot \frac{1}{2} = 5 \cdot \frac{1}{2} - 1$?

$$6 - 4\frac{1}{2} = 2\frac{1}{2} - 1?$$

Yes, each side equals $1\frac{1}{2}$.

Step 2: Try a number that satisfies $x > \frac{1}{2}$. Does this number satisfy the original inequality? Try $x = 1$.

Is $6 - 9 \cdot 1 \leq 5 \cdot 1 - 1$?

$$-3 \leq 4? \text{ Yes.}$$

Example 3

Three times a number is less than two times the same number. Find the number.

Solution

It may seem that there is no such number. But work it out to see. Let n be such a number. Then n must be a solution to

$$3n < 2n.$$

③ Solve this as you would any other linear inequality. Add $-2n$ to each side.

$$3n + -2n < 2n + -2n$$
$$n < 0$$

So n can be any negative number.

Check

Step 1: If $n = 0$, $3 \cdot 0 = 2 \cdot 0$, and $0 = 0$.
Step 2: Pick a value of n that is less than 0. We let $n = -5$.
Is $3 \cdot -5 < 2 \cdot -5$? $-15 < -10$? Yes, it checks.
So if n is any negative number, 3 times n will be less than 2 times n.

Adapting to Individual Needs

Activity 2 Technology Connection
You may wish to assign *Technology Source-book, Computer Master 15.* Students use *GraphExplorer* or similar software to compare a linear expression for red meat consumption to a linear expression for poultry and fish consumption

English Language Development
Be sure students remember what is meant by "changing the sense" of an inequality when multiplying by a negative number. You might want to go through a few simple examples to be sure that students understand the meaning of the phrase.

Additional Examples

1. Printer A charges $10 to set up a job and $2.00 for each 100 copies. Printer B charges $15 to set up and $1.75 for each 100 copies. For how many sets of 100 copies is Printer B less expensive than Printer A?

   a. Let $n =$ the number of sets of 100 copies. Write an inequality and solve it.
   $$10 + 2n > 15 + 1.75n$$
   For more than 20 sets, printer B charges less.

   b. Find the answer by graphing.
   The lines cross when $n = 20$. To find when Printer B is cheaper, look at values of B below the line for A.

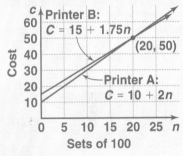

2. Solve $-2n - 16 \leq 9n + 17$ and check the answer. $n \geq -3$
   Check: Does $-2(-3) - 16 = 9(-3) + 17$? $-10 = -10$? Yes. Try a number which satisfies $n \geq -3$. We try 0. Is $-2(0) - 16 \leq 9(0) + 17$? $-16 \leq 17$? Yes

3. Nine times a number is less than the sum of 5 times that number and 13. What is the number?
   Any number less than $3\frac{1}{4}$

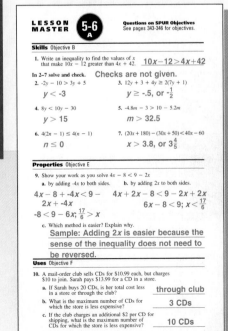

319

Notes on Questions

Question 7 By working out both solutions, students see that the processes give the same result. Some students may prefer having a positive coefficient of k before the last step; other students may prefer having the variable on the left side.

Question 24 Ask students what is true about the numbers in this problem that make this question easier than it might be. [The average speed is 60 $\frac{mi}{hr}$, which is 1 mile per minute. This rate makes it possible to calculate the time mentally.]

Question 25 If multiplication took precedence over factorial in order of operations, these would be equal. However, since it does not, you might want to ask how many times greater 12! is than $2 \cdot 6!$ [$11 \cdot 10 \cdot 9 \cdot 8 \cdot 7 \cdot 6$, or 332,640].

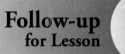

Follow-up for Lesson 5-6

Practice

For more questions on SPUR Objectives, use **Lesson Master 5-6A** (shown on page 319) or **Lesson Master 5-6B** (shown on pages 320–321).

320

QUESTIONS

Covering the Reading

In 1–4, refer to Example 1.

1. Which tree was taller when they were planted? beech tree

2. Which tree was taller 7 years after they were planted? beech tree

3. Which tree will be taller 20 years after they were planted? maple tree

4. **a.** Solve $8 + 0.5t < 3 + t$. $t > 10$
   b. What does the answer indicate? Sample: More than 10 years after they were planted, the maple tree was taller than the beech tree.

In 5 and 6, use the graph at the left showing the growth habits of two trees.

Height in feet

$h = 7 + 3t$ elm
maple $h = 12 + t$

Years from now

5. Which tree will be taller 4 years from now? How much taller will it be? the elm tree; 3 ft taller

6. When is the maple tree taller than the elm? during the first $2\frac{1}{2}$ years

7. **a.** Solve $4k + 3 > 9k + 18$ by first adding $-4k$ to each side. See left.
   b. Solve $4k + 3 > 9k + 18$ by first adding $-9k$ to each side. See left.
   c. Should you get the same answer for parts **a** and **b**? Yes
   d. Describe how the steps in the solutions to parts **a** and **b** are different. See left.

7a) $3 > 5k + 18;$
$-15 > 5k;$ $-3 > k$

b) $-5k + 3 > 18;$
$-5k > 15;$ $k < -3$

d) Sample: In part a, the sense of the inequality does not change; in part b, the sense of the inequality is reversed.

In 8–11, **a.** solve, and **b.** check. See left for checks.

8. $5n + 7 \geq 2n + 19$ $n \geq 4$
9. $-48 + 10a \leq -8 + 20a$ $a \geq -4$
10. $4x + 12 < -2x - 6$ $x < -3$
11. $12 - 3y > 27 + 7y$ $y < -\frac{3}{2}$

12. Five times a number is less than three times the same number. Find such a number. $x < 0$; Any negative number is part of the solution set.

8) Try $x = 10$.
Is $5 \cdot 10 + 7 > 2 \cdot 10 + 19$?
$57 > 39$; yes, it checks.

9) Try $x = 0$. Is $-48 + 10 \cdot 0 < -8 + 20 \cdot 0$?
$-48 < -8$; yes, it checks.

10) Try $x = -5$. Is $4 \cdot -5 + 12 < -2 \cdot -5 - 6$?
$-8 < 4$; yes, it checks.

11) Try $x = -2$. Is $12 - 3 \cdot -2 > 27 + 7 \cdot -2$?
$18 > 13$; yes, it checks.

Applying the Mathematics

In 13 and 14, solve.

13. $5 - 3(x + 2) < 10x$ $x > -\frac{1}{13}$
14. $-3t \geq -t + 3 + 9t$ $t \leq -\frac{3}{11}$

15. The Smith family is planning to advertise their used car for sale. The *Gazette* charges $2.00 plus 8¢ per word. The *Herald* charges $1.50 plus 10¢ per word. For what length are the *Gazette's* ad rates cheaper? Justify your answer. ads more than 25 words; Sample: $2 + 0.08x < 1.50 + 0.10x;$ $0.5 < 0.02x;$ $x > 25$

16. Sending a package by Fast Fellows shipping service costs $3.50 plus 25 cents per ounce. Speedy Service charges $4.75 plus 10 cents per ounce.
   a. If your package weighs 1 lb 4 oz, which service is cheaper? Justify your answer.
   b. What advice would you give someone who needs to use one of these services? Packages 8 oz or less are cheaper at Fast Fellows; packages 9 oz or more are cheaper at Speedy Service.
   a) Speedy Service is cheaper. It charges $6.75, while Fast Fellows charges $8.50.

320

Adapting to Individual Needs

Extra Help

If students have difficulty remembering to reverse the sense of an inequality when multiplying by a negative number, tell them to arrange their work so that the coefficient of the variable is positive. To help them understand what you mean, write the following sentences on the board and have students discuss what needs to be done so that all of the x's are on one side of the equation, and the coefficient of x is positive.

If students have difficulty working with the variable on the right side of the equation, show them how they can reverse the sides.

1. $-6x + 5 = 2x - 3$ [Add $6x$ to both sides to get $5 = 8x - 3$; rewrite as $8x - 3 = 5$.]
2. $2a - 8 \geq 5a - 4$ [Add $-2a$ to both sides to get $-8 \geq 3a - 4$; rewrite as $3a - 4 \leq -8$.]
3. $-4n + 3 < 8$ [Add $4n$ to both sides to get $3 < 8 + 4n$; rewrite as $8 + 4n > 3$.]

The River Walk (Paseo del Rio) is a popular dining and shopping area that stretches along the San Antonio River in San Antonio, Texas.

Review

17. a. Graph $y = 10 + x$ and $y = 2 + 3x$ on the same set of axes.   **See left.**
b. According to the graph, for what value(s) of x is $10 + x = 2 + 3x$? *(Lesson 5-4)*   **x = 4**

In 18–21, solve.   *(Lesson 5-3)*

18. $4x + 12 = -2(x + 3)$ **x = -3**

19. $60t - 1 = 48t$ $t = \frac{1}{12}$

20. $109 - m = 18m - 5$ **m = 6**

21. $3n - n + 5 = 4n - n + 20$
   n = -15

22. a. Use an automatic grapher to find the intersection of the lines $y = 8$ and $y = 4 + 0.75x$.   **The intersection point is about (5, 8). See left for graph.**
b. Solve $8 = 4 + 0.75x$.   *(Lessons 3-5, 5-1, 5-5)*
   $x = \frac{16}{3} \approx 5.33$

23. Simplify $\frac{t}{4} + \frac{t}{3}$.   *(Lesson 3-9)* $\frac{7t}{12}$

24. The distance from Los Angeles to New Orleans, along Interstate 10 as shown, is 1946 miles. At an average speed of $60\frac{\text{miles}}{\text{hour}}$, estimate the driving time from San Antonio to Houston.   *(Lessons 2-6, 3-1)*
   3 hours 21 minutes

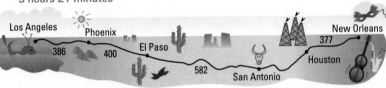

25. Are 12! and $2 \cdot 6!$ equal? Explain your answer.   *(Lesson 2-10)*   **No; Sample: because** $12! = (12 \cdot 11 \cdot 10 \cdot 9 \cdot 8 \cdot 7) \cdot 6! \neq 2 \cdot 6!$

26. *Multiple choice.*   Which of the following does not equal $\frac{4x}{3}$?   *(Lesson 2-3)* **(d)**

(a) $\frac{4}{3}x$ (b) $4\left(\frac{x}{3}\right)$ (c) $4\left(\frac{1}{3}x\right)$ (d) $4\left(\frac{1}{3x}\right)$

27. *Skill sequence.*   Multiply.   *(Lesson 2-3)*

a. $30 \cdot \frac{1}{6}$ **b.** $30 \cdot \frac{5}{6}$ **c.** $30 \cdot \frac{x}{6}$ **d.** $30 \cdot \frac{5}{6}x$
   5   **25**   **5x**   **25x**

28. Four instances of a general pattern are given below.   *(Lesson 1-7)*
$$-(7 - 4) = 4 - 7$$
$$-\left(\frac{8}{3} - \frac{5}{6}\right) = \frac{5}{6} - \frac{8}{3}$$
$$-(1.2 - 2.1) = 2.1 - 1.2$$
$$-(v - 9) = 9 - v$$

a. Write the pattern using the variables a and b. $-(a - b) = b - a$
b. Is the pattern true for all real number values of a and b? Justify your answer.
   Yes; $-(a - b) = -1 \cdot (a - b) = -1 \cdot a + -1 \cdot -b = -a + b = b - a$

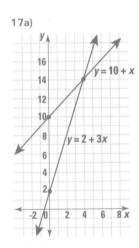

17a)

22a)

Exploration

29. The square of a number is less than the product of one less than the number and two greater than the number.
a. Find one such number.   **3**   **b.** Find all such numbers.
   any number x such that x > 2

Lesson 5-6 *Solving $ax + b < cx + d$*   **321**

Assessment

Quiz A quiz covering Lessons 5-4 through 5-6 is provided in the *Assessment Sourcebook.*

Oral/Written Communication Have students **work with partners.** Have each student write an inequality of the form $ax + b < cx + d$ on a sheet of paper. Remind students that they can use any of the inequality symbols. Collect all the papers, and give each pair of students two inequalities to solve. Call on different pairs to explain their work to the class. [Students display the ability to write and solve inequalities.]

Extension

If students did the *Extension* on page 296 in Lesson 5-2, have them use the data to graph the costs of renting the same kind of automobile from two different rental agencies. Then have them use the graph to explain when renting from one dealer is less expensive than renting from another dealer.

Project Update Project 2, *Tree Growth*, on page 338, relates to the content of this lesson.

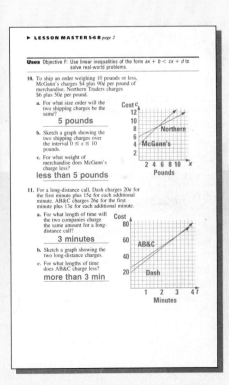

▶ **LESSON MASTER 5-6 B** *page 2*

Uses Objective F: Use linear inequalities of the form $ax + b < cx + d$ to solve real-world problems.

10. To ship an order weighing 10 pounds or less, McGann's charges $4 plus 90¢ per pound of merchandise. Northern Traders charges $6 plus 50¢ per pound.
a. For what size order will the two shipping charges be the same?   **5 pounds**
b. Sketch a graph showing the two shipping charges over the interval $0 \leq x \leq 10$ pounds.
c. For what weight of merchandise does McGann's charge less?   **less than 5 pounds**

11. For a long-distance call, Dash charges 20¢ for the first minute plus 15¢ for each additional minute. AB&C charges 26¢ for the first minute plus 13¢ for each additional minute.
a. For what length of time will the two companies charge the same amount for a long-distance call?   **3 minutes**
b. Sketch a graph showing the two long-distance charges.
c. For what lengths of time does AB&C charge less?   **more than 3 min**

Adapting to Individual Needs

Challenge
The relation "is greater than" has the following property: If $a > b$ and $b > c$, then $a > c$. This property is called the transitive property and it does not hold true for all relations. For example, consider the relation "is a parent of." The property would be written: "If a is a parent of b and b is a parent of c, then a is a parent of c." Of course, the preceding statement is false, so the transitive property does not hold true for this relation.

Have students determine if the transitive property holds true for each relation listed below. Then have them find other examples of relations that are transitive.

1. Is taller than [Yes]
2. Is the child of [No]
3. Is the next-door neighbor of [No]
4. Is younger than [Yes]
5. Is in the same math class as [Yes]
6. Is a first cousin of [No]

Objectives

D Find equivalent forms of formulas and equations.
E Apply and recognize properties associated with linear sentences.

Resources

From the **Teacher's Resource File**
- Lesson Master 5-7A or 5-7B
- Answer Master 5-7
- Teaching Aids
  39 Graphing Equations
  49 Warm-up
  55 Automatic Grapher Grids

Additional Resources
- Visuals for Teaching Aids 39, 49, 55
- Automatic graphers

Teaching
Lesson **5-7**

Warm-up

Laura's parents want to encourage her to save part of the money she earns or receives as gifts. They will add $5 to every deposit each time she deposits half of her money in the bank. The table below shows some instances of this situation.

x	100	50	48	?	20	10
y	55	30	29	21	15	?

1. What do x and y represent?
   x is Laura's earnings; y is Laura's deposit.
2. For what numbers do the question marks stand? **$x = 32$; $y = 10$**
3. Write a formula for
   a. y in terms of x. **$y = \frac{1}{2}x + 5$**
   b. x in terms of y. **$x = 2y - 10$**

Notes on Reading

You may want to go through the steps of each example with the class. If automatic graphers are available, students can use them with **Example 2**, Additional Example 2, and **Question 16**.

A drive-in volcano. *Kilauea is an active volcano in Hawaii. A nearby road allows visitors to view the lava flow. The stick this tourist is holding ignites as it touches the hot lava that is about 2000°F (about 1100°C).*

❶ Two different temperature scales are in common use throughout the world. The scale used wherever people use the metric system is the **Celsius scale.** That scale is also called the **centigrade scale** because of the 100-degree interval between the freezing point of water, 0°C (read "0 degrees Celsius" or "0 degrees centigrade"), and the boiling point 100°C. (The Latin word for 100 is "centum.") The other scale is the **Fahrenheit scale,** which is now used only in the United States and a few other countries. The freezing and boiling points of water are 32°F (read "32 degrees Fahrenheit") and 212°F, respectively.

A person who visits the United States from most other countries may wish to translate Fahrenheit temperatures into the Celsius temperatures more familiar to himself or herself. One formula for C in terms of F is

$$C = \tfrac{5}{9}(F - 32).$$

But if you visit another country, you may wish to convert in the other direction, from Celsius to Fahrenheit. This can be done by solving the above formula for F.

Lesson 5-7 Overview

Broad Goals This lesson discusses solving a formula for one of the variables.

Perspective In this lesson we extend the concept of solving a linear equation in one variable to solving a formula for a particular variable. The ability to find an equivalent rendering of a formula is a very important skill in algebra. Although the process is like equation solving, the variety of techniques that is available for solving equations with numerical coefficients is usually not available with formulas: tables do not help arrive at solutions and making graphs is not always possible. Consequently, this kind of solving tends to be more abstract, more mechanical, and, for some students, more difficult than other kinds of solving. Thus, although these equations seldom have the unknown on both sides, we have delayed discussion until this point.

Example 1

Solve $C = \frac{5}{9}(F - 32)$ for F.

Solution

Start with the given equation.

$$C = \frac{5}{9}(F - 32)$$

② One way to solve for F is to "undo" the multiplication by $\frac{5}{9}$.

$$\frac{9}{5}C = \frac{9}{5} \cdot \frac{5}{9}(F - 32) \qquad \text{Multiply each side by } \frac{9}{5}.$$

$$\frac{9}{5}C = F - 32$$

$$\frac{9}{5}C + 32 = F \qquad \text{Add 32 to each side.}$$

The desired formula is $F = \frac{9}{5}C + 32$.

Although the formulas $C = \frac{5}{9}(F - 32)$ and $F = \frac{9}{5}C + 32$ look different, they are **equivalent formulas** because every pair of values of F and C that works in one formula also works in the other. One important use of equivalent formulas arises when using most automatic graphers, where formulas to be entered must give y in terms of x.

❸ Example 2

Use an automatic grapher to graph $5x - 2y = 100$.

Solution

It is often necessary to solve for y. Do this as if you were solving any other linear equation for y.

$$5x - 2y = 100$$
$$-5x + 5x - 2y = -5x + 100 \qquad \text{Add } -5x \text{ to both sides.}$$
$$-2y = -5x + 100 \qquad \text{Add like terms.}$$
$$\left(-\frac{1}{2}\right)(-2y) = -\frac{1}{2}(-5x + 100) \qquad \text{Multiply both sides by } -\frac{1}{2}.$$
$$y = -\frac{1}{2}(-5x + 100) \qquad \text{Use the Property of Reciprocals.}$$
$$y = 2.5x - 50 \qquad \text{Use the Distributive Property.}$$

Now enter the equation $y = 2.5x - 50$ into the grapher, and instruct it to graph. The graph is a line. A window of $-20 \le x \le 30$ and $-60 \le y \le 60$ is shown here.

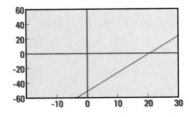

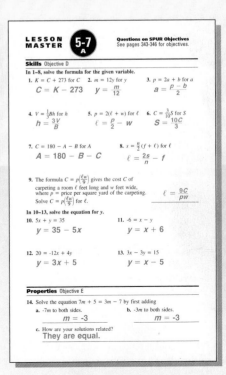

Optional Activities

Activity 1 Science Connection

Three temperature scales are mentioned in the lesson: Fahrenheit, Celsius, and Kelvin. After completing the lesson, students might investigate how and when these scales were developed. [The Fahrenheit scale was developed by the German physicist Gabriel Fahrenheit in 1714 when he constructed the first mercury thermometer. The Celsius scale was developed by the Swedish astronomer Anders Celsius in 1742 as a scale in which the difference between the freezing and boiling points of water was 100. The Kelvin scale was developed by William Thomson (Baron Kelvin of Largs) in 1848. Using this scale, absolute zero is defined as the theoretical temperature at which substances would have no heat whatever and all molecules would stop moving. It is -273.16 degrees Celsius, -459.69 degrees Fahrenheit, and 0 degrees Kelvin.]

For some students, part of the difficulty in solving a formula for a particular variable is that the variable is on the right-hand side of the equation. (This is one reason why we have included so many equations with variables on the right side in previous lessons.) Explain that it is always possible to switch sides of the equation so that the variable is on the left side.

Additional Examples

Students will need graph paper (**Teaching Aid 39**) or automatic grapher grids (**Teaching Aid 55**) for showing their graphs.

1. The formula $P = 100 + \frac{a}{2}$ relates normal blood pressure P in millimeters and age a in years. Solve the formula for a.
$2P - 200 = a$

2. Use an automatic grapher to graph $3x + 2y = 18$.
   a. What equation will you need to enter? **On many graphers,**
   $y = -\frac{3}{2}x + 9$
   b. Graph the equation.
      Possible display:

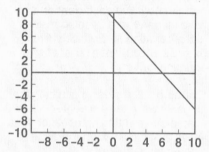

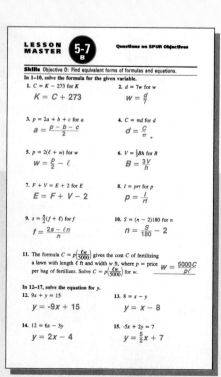

324

▶ **Check 1**

Use the trace feature to read the coordinates of some points on the line. Check that these satisfy the original equation. For instance, our trace showed the point with $x \approx 10.5$, $y \approx -23.7$ on the graph.

Does $\quad\quad 5(10.5) - 2(-23.7) = 100$?
Is $\quad\quad\quad\quad\quad\quad 99.9 \approx 100$? Yes. It checks.
The point $(10.5, -23.7)$ is very close to the graph of $5x - 2y = 100$.

Check 2

Compute the coordinates of a point on the line. For instance,
when $x = 0$, $\quad\quad 5(0) - 2y = 100$.
$\quad\quad\quad\quad\quad\quad -2y = 100$
$\quad\quad\quad\quad\quad\quad\quad y = -50$
The trace on our grapher shows that the point $(0, -50)$ is on the line.

Examples 1 and 2 each have two variables. Some important formulas have more than two variables. These can also be rewritten in equivalent forms.

Example 3

The formula $A = p + pr$ gives the amount A (in dollars) after one year in a bank account which started with p dollars and which has an annual yield of r. Solve this formula for r. (This gives you the rate if you know what you started with and what you ended up with.)

Solution

④ To solve the formula $A = p + pr$ for r, you must isolate the variable r.
$$A = p + pr$$
$$A - p = pr$$
Now multiply each side by $\frac{1}{p}$.
$$\frac{1}{p}(A - p) = \frac{1}{p} \cdot pr$$
$$\frac{A - p}{p} = r$$
So an equivalent formula is $r = \frac{A - p}{p}$.

Check

Pick values for all variables that work in the original formula. They should work in the equivalent formula. For instance, if $p = \$100$ and $r = 5\%$, then in the original equation $A = 100 + 100 \cdot 0.05 = 105$. Now substitute these values in $r = \frac{A - p}{p}$. Does $5\% = \frac{105 - 100}{100}$? Yes, it checks.

324

Optional Activities

Activity 2
As students encounter formulas in this and future lessons, you may want to have them keep a list of equivalent formulas. Stress that being able to solve equations means that one needs only one formula of each type.

Anchorage, Alaska. *With a population of about 226,000, Anchorage is Alaska's largest city.*

QUESTIONS

Covering the Reading

1. As of 1994, the highest recorded temperature in both Alaska and Hawaii was 100°F. Change this record temperature to degrees Celsius. **37.8°C**

2. Change 200°C to degrees Fahrenheit. **392°F**

In 3 and 4, solve for y.

3. $5x + y = 6$ **$y = -5x + 6$**

4. $3x - 6y = 12$ **$y = \frac{1}{2}x - 2$**

5. Name a use for solving equations for y such as those in Questions 3 and 4. **Sample: To use automatic graphers, you need to enter equations that give y in terms of x.**

6. What formula can be used to find the amount of money after one year in a bank account? **$A = p + pr$**

7. Below the formula in Example 3 is solved for p. Fill in the blanks to explain the steps used.

$A = p + p \cdot r$
$A = p \cdot 1 + p \cdot r$ Use the __a.__ Property of 1.
$A = p(1 + r)$ Use the __b.__ Property.
$\frac{1}{1+r} \cdot A = p(1+r) \cdot \frac{1}{1+r}$ Multiply each side by __c.__
$\frac{A}{1+r} = p$ Simplify. c) $\frac{1}{1+r}$

a) Multiplicative Identity
b) Distributive

In 8 and 9, solve the formula for the indicated variable.

8. $t = \frac{d}{r}$; d **$d = rt$**

9. $P = 2(L + W)$; L **$L = \frac{1}{2}P - W$**

10. $F = m \cdot a$; a **$a = \frac{F}{m}$**

11. $A = \frac{1}{2}(b_1 + b_2)h$; h **$h = \frac{2A}{b_1 + b_2}$**

Applying the Mathematics

12. The formula $C = K + 273$ converts temperatures from the Kelvin scale to the Celsius scale. Solve this formula for K. **$K = C + 273$**

13. A formula for the circumference of a circle is $C = \pi d$.
    a. Solve this formula for π. **$\pi = C/d$**
    b. How could you use the formula to find a value of π? **See left.**
    c. Use your answer to part b to estimate π from the measurements of some circular object you have. **Answers may vary.**

14. The formula $V = 2\pi r^2 + 2\pi rh$ gives the total surface area of a cylindrical solid with radius r and height h. Solve this formula for h. **$h = (V/2\pi r) - r$**

15. Many calculators will convert angle measures from degrees D to grads G, using the formula $G = \frac{10}{9}D$.
    a. Solve the formula for D. **$D = \frac{9}{10}G$**
    b. Convert 100 grads to degrees. **90°**

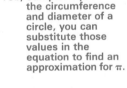

13b) Sample: If you know the circumference and diameter of a circle, you can substitute those values in the equation to find an approximation for π.

3. If a coin is tossed and H heads and T tails appear, the relative frequency r of heads is expressed by the formula $r = \frac{H}{H+T}$.
    a. Solve this formula for T.
    $T = \frac{H - rH}{r}$
    b. Check your work. Sample: If $H = 60$ and $T = 40$, from the original formula, $r = 0.6$. Substituting these values for r and H in the final formula,
    $T = \frac{60 - 0.6(60)}{.06} = \frac{24}{0.6} = 40$,
    which checks.

4. In a particular college there are six times as many students as professors. Let S be the number of students and P be the number of professors. How are S and P related? **$S = 6P$. (Many people answer $P = 6S$. Point out that these are not equivalent formulas. Make a table of values to check any formulas that are suggested by students.)**

Notes on Questions

Question 13 Students are recovering the formula that is often used to define π. Point out that even though π is not a variable, we can still solve for it. This is not as unusual as students might think; in future work they might solve an equation like $x = 2y$ for 2 and get $\frac{x}{y} = 2$, which is a ratio of the two quantities x and y.

Lesson 5-7 *Equivalent Formulas* **325**

Adapting to Individual Needs

Extra Help
Some students might be frustrated by the fact that solving $C = \frac{5}{9}(F - 32)$ does not lead to a strictly numerical answer. Rather, it defines F in terms of C. Emphasize that *solving a formula* for a particular variable simply means rewriting the formula so that one variable is expressed in terms of the other. The variable being solved for is alone on one side of the equation.

English Language Development
Materials: Customary and metric rulers

Have students measure the length of their Algebra book in inches and in centimeters, and write the results on the board. Ask if these are equivalent measurements. Then explain that measuring temperatures is a similar process. The formulas $C = \frac{5}{9}(F - 32)$ and $F = \frac{9}{5}C + 32$ are equivalent.

Follow-up for Lesson 5-7

Practice

For more questions on SPUR Objectives, use **Lesson Master 5-7A** (shown on page 323) or **Lesson Master 5-7B** (shown on pages 324–325).

Assessment

Oral Communication Give students the formula $P = 2\ell + 2w$. Remind them that ℓ and w are the length and width of a rectangle and P stands for the perimeter. Then have students describe situations in which an equivalent form of this equation could be used, and state the equivalent formula they would use. [Responses indicate an understanding of equivalent formulas and their uses.]

Extension

As a preview of work in Lesson 7-9, ask students to solve $Ax + By = C$ for y. $\left[y = \frac{C - Ax}{B}\right]$

Project Update Project 4, *Equivalent Formulas*, on page 339, relates to the content of this lesson.

Rush hour in Lagos.
With a population of 1,149,200, Lagos is the largest city in Nigeria.

16. Use an automatic grapher to graph the equations $4x + 3y = 12$ and $4x + 3y = 24$. What seems to be true about these graphs? **They are parallel.**

17. Some banks have "time and temperature" displays that often alternately display temperature in degrees Fahrenheit and Celsius.
    a. What temperature gives the same reading on both the Fahrenheit and Celsius scales? **-40°**
    b. Explain how you obtained your answer to part **a.** **Solve $C = \frac{9}{5}C + 32$ for C, or solve $F = \frac{5}{9}(F - 32)$ for F.**

Review

In 18 and 19, solve. *(Lesson 5-6)* $x \le \frac{6}{5}$

18. $-3z - 4 > 2z - 24$ $z < 4$ 19. $7(x - 2) + 5(2 - x) \ge 4(3x - 4)$

20. a. Make up a question about a real situation that can be answered by solving the equation $150 + 2x = 100 + 5x$. **See margin.**
    b. Solve the equation. $x = \frac{50}{3} \approx 16.67$
    c. Answer the question in part **a.** *(Lesson 5-3)* **Sample: They will have the same amount of money after about 17 weeks.**

21. Graph $x = 1$ in the coordinate plane. *(Lesson 5-1)* **See margin.**

22. Give an equation for the line. *(Lesson 5-1)*
    a. the x-axis   b. the y-axis $x = 0$
    $y = 0$

23. In 1990 the population of Lagos, Nigeria, was 7,602,000 and growing at a rate of about 395,000 people per year. In 1990 the population of metropolitan London, England was 9,170,000 and declining at a rate of about 55,000 per year. If these rates continue, in what year will the population of Lagos first exceed the population of London? Explain how you got your answer. *(Lessons 5-2, 5-4, 5-6)*
    1993; Solve $7{,}602{,}000 + 395{,}000x > 9{,}170{,}000 - 55{,}000x$; $x > 3.48$ years

24. *Skill sequence.* Simplify. *(Lesson 3-9)*
    a. $\frac{2}{3} + \frac{1}{8}$ $\frac{19}{24}$ b. $\frac{2}{3}a + \frac{1}{8}a$ $\frac{19}{24}a$ c. $\frac{2a}{3} + \frac{a}{8}$ $\frac{19a}{24}$

25.

Figure 1   Figure 2   Figure 3

These figures are made from dots. Suppose the pattern continues.
    a. How many dots would make up Figure 10? **40 dots**
    b. How many dots would make up Figure n? *(Lessons 1-7, 3-8)*
    $4n$ dots

26. Mentally compute 6 times 999,999. *(Lesson 3-7)* **5,999,994**

Exploration

27. Find an example of a formula different from those in this lesson. Explain what the variables represent. Solve the formula for one of its other variables. **Answers will vary. Sample: The formula to find the volume of a pyramid is $V = \frac{1}{3}Bh$, where B is the area of the base and h is the altitude. Solve for h; $h = \frac{3V}{B}$.**

326

Adapting to Individual Needs

Challenge
Have students discuss the following problem: Mr. Smith, an eccentric who travels all over the world, told his travel agent, "I want to go on a vacation where the daily high temperature in Fahrenheit degrees is exactly twice as much as the corresponding Celsius temperature." Can the travel agent recommend such a place? [No. The only such temperature is 320°F which is 160°C.]

Additional Answers
20a. Sample: Jack opened a bank account with a deposit of $150. Every week he deposited $2 to his account. At the same time, Mary opened an account with a deposit of $100. Every week she added $5 to her account. After how many weeks will they have the same amount of money in the bank (ignoring interest)?

21.
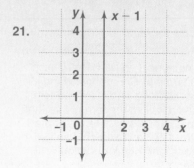

Multiplying through in baseball. *In 1993, Andres Galarraga led the National League with a batting average of .370. Batting averages are read as if the reader had multiplied through by 1000. So .370 is read, "three seventy."*

Clearing Fractions

With the techniques you have learned you can solve any linear equation. However, when you want to solve an equation with several fractions, for instance,

$$\tfrac{1}{4}t = 21 - \tfrac{1}{3}t,$$

you may want to *clear the fractions* before you do anything else. A technique called *multiplying through* can then help. The idea is to multiply both sides of the equation by a common multiple of the denominators. The result is an equation in which all the coefficients are integers.

Example 1

Solve $\tfrac{1}{4}t = 21 - \tfrac{1}{3}t$.

Solution 1

Multiply each side of the equation by a number that will produce an equation that has only *integer* coefficients. What number should be used? Use 12, the same number that would be the least common denominator if the fractions were added.

$12 \cdot \tfrac{1}{4}t = 12(21 - \tfrac{1}{3}t)$	Multiply both sides by 12.
$3t = 12 \cdot 21 - 12 \cdot \tfrac{1}{3}t$	Apply the Distributive Property.
$3t = 252 - 4t$	Simplify.

Notice—now there are no fractions!

$7t = 252$	Add $4t$ to both sides.
$t = 36$	Multiply both sides by $\tfrac{1}{7}$.

▶

Lesson 5-8 *Advanced Solving Technique I: Multiplying Through* **327**

Lesson **5-8**

Objectives

A Clear fractions or multiply through by a fraction to solve linear equations of the form $ax + b = cx + d$.
B Clear fractions or multiply through by a fraction to solve linear inequalities of the form $ax + b < cx + d$.
E Apply and recognize properties associated with linear sentences.
F Use linear equations and inequalities to solve real-world problems.

Resources

From the *Teacher's Resource File*
■ Lesson Master 5-8A or 5-8B
■ Answer Master 5-8
■ Teaching Aid 49: Warm-up

Additional Resources
■ Visual for Teaching Aid 49

Teaching 5-8
Lesson

Warm-up

Work in groups.
1. Study the following equation:
   $48x + 96 = 96x - 480$.
   Can you solve it quickly?
   Answers will vary.
2. What might you do to both sides of the equation to make finding the solution easier? Sample:
   multiply both sides by $\tfrac{1}{48}$.

(Warm-up continues on page 328.)

Lesson 5-8 Overview

Broad Goals A specific goal of this lesson is the application of the Multiplication Property of Equality (and the Multiplication Property of Inequality) as a first step to simplify the numbers in an equation. The broader goal is for students to realize that advance planning and a judicious first step can help simplify solving equations. Throughout the lesson, another goal is achieved—to give more practice in solving linear equations and inequalities.

Perspective We have noted before that a process used once is called a *trick,* but when that process is used twice, it is a *technique.* The technique of multiplying both sides of a sentence by a number, in order to simplify the numbers in the equation, is so useful that we devote an entire lesson to it.

The general idea of the lesson is to use common sense. If the constants and coefficients on both sides of the equation

are fractions, then multiply both sides by a number large enough to get rid of the fractions. This is done in **Examples 1–3.** If the coefficients on both sides of the equation are decimals, as in **Example 4,** then multiply by the power of 10 that is the number of decimal places. If the constants and coefficients on both sides of the equation are multiples of the same number, then divide by that number. This is done in **Example 5.**

3. Give an equivalent equation that is easier to solve. Then solve it and check your solution in the original equation. **Sample:**
$x + 2 = 2x - 10$; $x = 12$
Check: Does $48 \cdot 12 + 96 = 96 \cdot 12 - 480$? $576 + 96 = 1152 - 480$? $672 = 672$?
Yes, it checks.

Notes on Reading

The execution of multiplying both sides of an equation by a number to get a simpler equation takes practice, and students are often unsure about what to do. There are no hard and fast rules regarding the number by which both sides should be multiplied. Emphasize that one can multiply both sides by any number other than zero, and there is little risk when multiplying to see what happens. With experience, students learn what is helpful and what is not. In general, multiplying through by a common multiple clears the fractions; multiplying through by the least common multiple simplifies the arithmetic.

If you write the solutions to the examples on the board or on the overhead, you might write the number by which both sides are multiplied in a second color. Review why each number was chosen, and then ask students to summarize this information. **Examples 1 and 2** use a common denominator to clear fractions in an equation, **Example 3** does the same for an inequality. **Questions 1–7, 9, 10, 13, and 14**

A vacation in Acapulco.
This is the atrium inside a large hotel in Acapulco, Mexico.

328

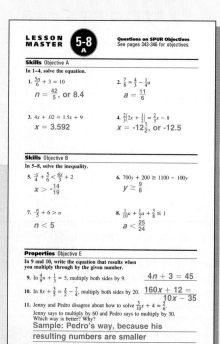

328

▶ **Solution 2**
Use the techniques of Lesson 5-3.

$\frac{1}{4}t = 21 - \frac{1}{3}t$

$\frac{1}{4}t + \frac{1}{3}t = 21$ Add $\frac{1}{3}t$ to each side.

$\frac{7}{12}t = 21$ Add like terms. $\left(\frac{1}{4}t + \frac{1}{3}t = \frac{7}{12}t\right)$

$\frac{12}{7} \cdot \frac{7}{12}t = \frac{12}{7} \cdot 21$ Multiply both sides by $\frac{12}{7}$.

$t = 36$ Simplify.

In Solution 1, we say that the fractions were cleared by multiplying each side of the equation by 12.

To clear fractions in a linear sentence:
1. Choose a common multiple of each of the denominators in the sentence.
2. Multiply each side of the sentence by that number.

Example 2

The DeVries family took a vacation. They spent $\frac{1}{3}$ of the vacation cost on transportation, $\frac{2}{5}$ on hotels, and $\frac{1}{5}$ on food. They spent \$350 on other things. What was the total amount they spent for their trip?

Solution
Let t = total dollar amount spent on vacation. Notice that
$$\text{transportation} + \text{hotel} + \text{food} + \text{other} = \text{total}$$
$$\frac{1}{3}t + \frac{2}{5}t + \frac{1}{5}t + 350 = t$$
Multiply each side of the equation by a common multiple of 3 and 5. We use 15.
$$15\left(\frac{1}{3}t + \frac{2}{5}t + \frac{1}{5}t + 350\right) = 15 \cdot t$$
Apply the Distributive Property.
$$15 \cdot \frac{t}{3} + 15 \cdot \frac{2t}{5} + 15 \cdot \frac{t}{5} + 15 \cdot 350 = 15 \cdot t$$
$$5t + 6t + 3t + 5250 = 15t$$
$$14t + 5250 = 15t$$
$$5250 = t$$
The family spent \$5250 for the vacation.

Check
If the DeVries spent \$5250 in all, then they spent:
$\frac{1}{3} \cdot \$5250 = \$1750$ for transportation;
$\frac{2}{5} \cdot \$5250 = \$2100$ for hotels;
$\frac{1}{5} \cdot \$5250 = \$1050$ for food; and had \$350 left over.
Does $1750 + 2100 + 1050 + 350 = 5250$? Yes, it checks.

Optional Activities

✏️ **Activity 1 Writing** As students read each example, you might ask them to write the number by which both sides are multiplied and why. [**Examples 1–3:** common multiples of the denominators (12, 15, and 20 respectively) eliminate the denominators. **Example 4:** 100 eliminates decimals in hundredths and tenths. **Example 5:** $\frac{1}{100}$ because each number is a number of hundreds.]

Activity 2 Cooperative Learning
After students complete the lesson, you might use this activity. Write three linear sentences: one with fractional coefficients, one with decimal coefficients, and one with large whole-number coefficients. Have students **work in small groups** to see how many different strategies they can use to solve each problem. Encourage students to use algebraic solutions, as well as tables or graphs.

The techniques described in this lesson for solving equations with fractions may also be used to solve inequalities with fractions.

Example 3

Solve $\frac{n}{4} + \frac{3n}{10} + 7 < 3n$.

Solution

The two denominators in the sentence are 4 and 10. Their least common multiple is 20. So multiply each side of the inequality by 20.

$$20\left(\frac{n}{4} + \frac{3n}{10} + 7\right) < 20 \cdot 3n$$

$$20 \cdot \frac{n}{4} + 20 \cdot \frac{3n}{10} + 20 \cdot 7 < 60n$$

$$5n + \quad 6n + \quad 140 < 60n$$

$$11n + \quad 140 < 60n$$

$$140 < 49n$$

$$\frac{140}{49} < n$$

$$\text{or } n > \frac{20}{7}$$

Clearing Decimals

Like fractions, decimals can be cleared from an equation to give a simpler equation with integer coefficients. A decimal can be thought of as a fraction whose denominator is given by 10 to the power that is the number of decimal places. For instance, the "denominator" of 0.8 is 10, because $0.8 = \frac{8}{10}$. Similarly, the "denominators" of 38.15 and -2.001 are 100 and 1000, respectively.

Example 4

Solve $0.92m + 2 = m - 0.4$.

Solution

The equation involves two decimal fractions, 0.92 and 0.4. Their "hidden denominators" are 100 and 10. Since 100 is divisible by both 100 and 10, multiply each side of the equation by 100.

$$100(0.92m + 2) = 100(m - 0.4)$$

$$100 \cdot 0.92m + 100 \cdot 2 = 100 \cdot m - 100 \cdot 0.4$$

$$92m + 200 = 100m - 40$$

Now that the coefficients are integers, the equation can be solved easily without a calculator.

$$240 = 8m$$

$$30 = m$$

Lesson 5-8 *Advanced Solving Technique I: Multiplying Through* **329**

also involve fractions. **Example 4** and **Question 11** involve the clearing of decimals. **Example 5** and **Question 12** illustrate multiplying both sides of an equation by a fraction to get an equivalent equation with smaller coefficients.

Be sure students note that **Example 5** repeats **Example 4** on page 300. You might have them contrast the two solutions.

Activity 3 Multicultural Connection

As you teach this lesson, you might mention that the ancient Babylonians (1900–1650 B.C.) solved algebraic equations in much the same way as we do today, but without our symbols. In 1949, excavations in the Mesopotamia area unearthed some mathematical textbooks. A problem from one of these books was translated as follows:

"If you are asked: Multiply two-thirds of [your share] by two-thirds [of mine] plus a hundred *qa* [a unit of measure] of barley to get my total share, what is [my] share?"

You might ask students to write and solve an equation to answer the question.

$[\frac{2}{3} \cdot \frac{2}{3}x + 100 = x; x = 180; 180 \text{ qa}]$

1. Solve $\frac{2}{5}x + 11 = \frac{3}{4}x$. $x = \frac{220}{7}$

2. A comptroller figured that his state's revenue would increase $150 million if the state income tax increased from 3% to 3.25%. On how much total income was this revenue calculated? Write an equation and solve it. **.03R + 150,000,000 = .0325R; R = 60,000,000,000; The revenue was calculated on 60 billion dollars.**

3. Solve each sentence.
   a. $\frac{5}{12} - \frac{7d}{24} \geq \frac{d}{2} + \frac{1}{3}$. $d \leq \frac{2}{19}$
   b. $\frac{5}{12} - \frac{7d}{24} = \frac{d}{2} + \frac{1}{3}$. $d = \frac{2}{19}$

4. .48(y + 5) = .6y $y = 12$

5. The following problem is **Question 13** in Lesson 5-3. Alaska's population, which had been increasing at a rate of 15,000 people a year, reached 550,000 in 1990. Delaware's population, which had been increasing at a rate of 7,000 people a year, reached 666,000 in 1990. If the rates of increase do not change, when will the populations be equal?
   a. What equation did you solve when you did this problem in Lesson 5-3?
   Sample: 550,000 + 15,000x = 666,000 + 7000x
   b. Simplify the equation and solve it. **Sample: 550 + 15x = 666 + 7x; x = 14.5**

6. Solve 490(y + 12) = 980 + 980y. $y = 10$

Summer fun. *The "City of Festivals" parade, which takes place each summer in Milwaukee, Wisconsin, features multiethnic costumes and food.*

2a) 3a = 240 – 2a; a = 48

b) 6a = 480 – 4a; a = 48

c) Sample: Fractions in an equation can be cleared by multiplying by any common multiple of the denominators in the equation.

Clearing Large Numbers

Sometimes the numbers that appear in a sentence are quite large. Then it is wise to consider multiplying through by a fraction or a decimal to get an equivalent equation with smaller coefficients. Compare the solution to Example 5 with the solution to Example 4 of Lesson 5-3, where this technique was not used.

Example 5

The 1990 population of El Paso, Texas, was 515,000. In the 1980s its population had been increasing at an average rate of 9000 people per year. In 1990, the population of Milwaukee, Wisconsin, was 628,000. In the 1980s, its population was decreasing at the rate of 800 people a year. If these rates continue, in what year will the population of El Paso and Milwaukee be the same?

Solution

Let n be the number of years after 1990. The populations are the same when

$$515,000 + 9000n = 628,000 - 800n.$$

Each number is a multiple of 100, so multiply both sides by $\frac{1}{100}$.

$$\frac{1}{100}(515,000 + 9000n) = \frac{1}{100}(628,000 - 800n)$$

Again apply the Distributive Property. We do the arithmetic mentally.

$$5150 + 90n = 6280 - 8n$$

You might now notice that each number is divisible by 2. This suggests multiplying both sides by $\frac{1}{2}$. But that does not reduce the amount of work. The rest of the solution is left up to you.

Multiplying through is simply a special use of the Multiplication Properties of Equality and Inequality. So this technique can be applied to solving all sentences, not just the linear sentences of this lesson.

QUESTIONS

Covering the Reading

1. Suppose $\frac{1}{3}x + 5 = \frac{5}{12}x$.
   a. Multiply each side of the equation by 12. 4x + 60 = 5x
   b. Solve the resulting equation. $x = 60$
   c. Check your answer. Does $\frac{1}{3} \cdot 60 + 5 = \frac{5}{12} \cdot 60$? 25 = 25; Yes, it checks.

2. Consider the equation $\frac{a}{4} = 20 - \frac{a}{6}$.
   a. Multiply each side by 12 and solve the resulting equation.
   b. Multiply each side by 24 and solve the resulting equation.
   c. What conclusions can you make from your work in parts **a** and **b**?

3. Check the solution to Example 1. Does $\frac{1}{4} \cdot 36 = 21 - \frac{1}{3} \cdot 36$? Does 9 = 21 – 12? 9 = 9; Yes, it checks.

Adapting to Individual Needs

Extra Help
Be sure students understand that clearing fractions is not a necessary step in solving an equation that has fractions. Point out that it does not necessarily reduce the number of steps in the solution, but it is used to make the computation easier. In fact, sometimes the computation can be done mentally, as in **Examples 2 and 4.** Point out that clearing fractions before solving can help to

reduce errors that are caused by adding or subtracting fractions incorrectly.

---

4. On what property does the "multiplying through" technique rely?
Multiplication Properties of Equality and Inequality

5. The first $\frac{1}{5}$ of Toni's drive to work is on I-90. The next leg, about $\frac{1}{2}$ of the trip, is on Elm Street. The last leg takes 18 minutes. How long does the whole commute take?
   a. Write an equation to describe this situation. $\frac{1}{5}t + \frac{1}{2}t + 18 = t$
   b. Solve by first clearing the fractions.
   $2t + 5t + 180 = 10t$; $t = 60$ minutes

In 6 and 7, a sentence and a number are given. **a.** Write the sentence that results if both sides of the given sentence are multiplied by the given number. **b.** Solve the sentence.

6. $\frac{8a}{15} - 2 = \frac{a}{5}$; multiply by 15. a) $8a - 30 = 3a$; b) $a = 6$

7. $\frac{x}{2} + \frac{x}{6} + 10 < \frac{5}{9}x$; multiply by 18. a) $9x + 3x + 180 < 10x$; b) $x < {-90}$

8. Finish the solution to Example 5. $98n = 1130$; $n = \frac{1130}{98} \approx 11.53$

In 9–14, solve and check. **See left for checks.**

9. $\frac{5}{6}x + \frac{1}{2} = \frac{2}{3}$ $x = \frac{1}{5}$

10. $\frac{a}{5} - 1 = \frac{a}{30}$ $a = 6$

11. $0.03y - 1.5 = 0.09y - 0.48$ $y = {-17}$

12. $6000n + 9000 = 11000 - 2000n$ $n = 1/4$

13. $\frac{3x}{5} - \frac{x}{10} < 5$ $x < 10$

14. $\frac{n}{2} - 1 \geq \frac{4}{5} + \frac{3n}{10}$ $n \geq 9$

Applying the Mathematics

15. Mr. Bigbear owns $\frac{3}{8}$ of the stock in Amalgamated Industries and Mrs. Bigbear owns $\frac{1}{4}$ of it. This means that they receive, respectively, $\frac{3}{8}$ and $\frac{1}{4}$ of the dividends paid to stockholders.
    a. Last year, the Bigbears together earned $25,400 from this stock. What was the total amount of dividends paid to stockholders?
    b. How much did stockholders other than Mr. and Mrs. Bigbear receive in dividends? a) $40,640 b) $15,240

16. Saudi Arabia is reported to have about $\frac{1}{4}$ of the world's crude-oil reserves, while the rest of the Middle East has about 40%, or $\frac{2}{5}$, of the world's reserves. Altogether the Middle East's crude-oil reserves amount to 660 billion barrels. How many barrels are estimated to be in the world's total crude-oil reserves? about 1015.4 billion

Due to the wealth from its oil exports, Saudi Arabia has become a leading economic power in the Middle East. Shown is an oil-pumping station located in the eastern part of the country.

17. In solving $x - 2000 = 4000x$, a student first multiplies both sides by $\frac{1}{1000}$. Is this a good idea? Why or why not? No; the term $\frac{1}{1000}x$ would appear in the equation, which would not simplify the solution.

In 18–21, solve the sentence.

18. $\frac{n}{3} - 5 = \frac{n}{4} - 2n$ $n = \frac{12}{5}$

19. $\frac{1}{4}(x + 6) + \frac{1}{8}x = \frac{1}{2}(x + 1)$ $x = 8$

20. $\frac{a + 3}{3} = \frac{2a - 3}{6} + \frac{a + 2}{4}$ $a = 4$

21. $\frac{y - 2}{6} - \frac{1}{15} < \frac{2y + 1}{10}$ $y > {-15}$

Notes on Questions

Questions 9–10 Some students may multiply by a number that is too large. Emphasize that any non-zero number is legal, but the best number to use is one which will clear fractions and result in the smallest (in absolute value) integers.

▶ **LESSON MASTER 5-8 B** *page 2*

15. Consider the equation $\frac{x}{3} + \frac{5}{6} = \frac{5}{2}$.

   a. Multiplying through by 6 is an application of which property?
   Multiplication Property of Equality

   b. Give two other numbers by which you could multiply through.
   Sample: 12   **Sample: 18**

16. Tell what to multiply each side by to solve more easily. **Samples are given.**
   a. $12,000e + 16,000 = 19,000e - 3,000$ $\frac{1}{1,000}$
   b. $1.6 - .5u \leq 2.2$ **10**
   c. $\frac{1}{5}(12y + 7) > \frac{3y}{4}$ **20**

Uses Objective F: Use linear equations of the form $ax + b = cx + d$ and linear inequalities of the form $ax + b < cx + d$ to solve real-world problems.

17. For an upcoming election, $\frac{1}{4}$ of the registered voters support Candidate A, $\frac{2}{5}$ support Candidate B, and the rest, 7,700, are undecided.
   a. Write an equation to find the number of registered voters. $\frac{1}{4}v + \frac{2}{5}v + 7,700 = v$
   b. How many registered voters are there? **22,000 reg. vot.**
   c. Check your answer to Part b by finding the number of registered voters who support each candidate. **5,500 for A; 8,800 for B**

18. In Adeline County, 22% of the elementary-school children attend Jackson School, 18% attend Traynor School, and 240 students attend Claridge School. The students at these three schools make up more than 50% of the county's elementary-school children. $.22c + .18c + 240 > .5c$
   a. Write an inequality to describe this situation.
   b. How many elementary-school children live in Adeline County? **fewer than 2400**
   c. How many children attend the other schools in Adeline County? **fewer than 1200**

Adapting to Individual Needs

English Language Development

You might want to spend some time explaining what "multiplying through" means. Tell students that when both sides of an equation are multiplied by the same number, each term is multiplied by that number; so we say we have *multiplied through* the equation. Then use the following example to illustrate this idea.

$$\frac{1}{3}x + 4 = \frac{2}{5}x - 2$$

Multiplying through by 15 gives the following.

$$15\left(\frac{1}{3}x + 4\right) = 15\left(\frac{2}{5}x - 2\right)$$
$$15\left(\frac{1}{3}x\right) + 15(4) = 15\left(\frac{2}{5}x\right) - 15(2)$$
$$5x + 60 = 6x - 30$$
$$90 = x$$

Note how the multiplication affects each term of the equation and the fact that the resulting equation can be solved rather easily.

Follow-up
for Lesson **5-8**

Practice

For more questions on SPUR Objectives, use **Lesson Master 5-8A** (shown on pages 328–329) or **Lesson Master 5-8B** (shown on pages 330–331).

Assessment

Written Communication Have each student write a short paragraph explaining what he or she is able to do as a result of what was learned in this lesson. [Students understand that numbers in an equation or inequality can be simplified, and they realize that solving an equivalent, simpler equation or inequality takes less time and reduces the possibility of computation errors.]

Extension

Point out that for any two numbers a and b, the product of a and b is equal to the greatest common factor of a and b multiplied by the least common multiple of a and b. Then have students use this information to find the greatest common factor and least common multiple for each pair of numbers.
1. $a = 40$, $b = 50$ [10 and 200]
2. $a = 72$, $b = 48$ [24 and 144]
3. $a = 75$, $b = 100$ [25 and 300]
4. $a = 144$, $b = 168$ [24 and 1008]

Auto advice. *Before buying a new or used car, consult with a car-buying guide. These magazines rate features such as safety, repair frequency, and resale value.*

24b)

4.5

2 3 4 5 6 7 X

27a)

Years from now	Town A pop.	Town B pop.
0	25000	35500
1	26200	35200
2	27400	34900
3	28600	34600
4	29800	34300
5	31000	34000
6	32200	33700
7	33400	33400
8	34600	33100

332

Review

In 22 and 23, solve for *v*.   *(Lesson 5-6)*

22. $x = \frac{2uv}{g}$ $v = \frac{gx}{2u}$

23. $d = \frac{1}{2}gt - vt$ $v = \frac{1}{2}g - \frac{d}{t}$

24. a. Solve for *x*: $3(x - 9) < 9(3 - x)$. $x < 4.5$
   b. Graph the solutions on a number line.   *(Lessons 1-2, 2-8, 5-6)*
   See left.

In 25 and 26, the values of two cars, *A* and *B*, are compared.   *(Lesson 5-5)*

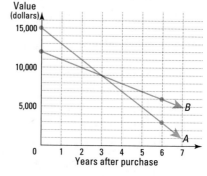

25. a. Which car is depreciating in value faster?   *A*
   b. About how much does the value of that car change each year? $2,000
26. a. After about how many years are the cars the same in value?
   b. If you are trading the car in after 4 years, for which car will you get more money, and about how much more will you get?
   a) about 3 yr;   b) car *B*, about $1,000
27. Town *A* has a population of 25,000 and is growing at a rate of 1200 people per year. Town *B* has 35,500 people and is declining at a rate of 300 people per year.
   a. Make a table showing the population of each town for 0, 1, 2, 3, . . . , 8 years from now.   See left.
   b. In how many years will the populations of the towns be equal?   *(Lessons 3-8, 5-2, 5-3)*   about 7 years from now

28. Simplify $\sqrt{9} \cdot x + 3! \cdot x - 50\% \cdot x$.   *(Lessons 1-6, 2-10, 3-2)*   8.5x

29. Solve for *p*: $p^2 = 10000$.   *(Lesson 1-1)* $p = 100$ or $p = -100$

Exploration

30. Recall that Diophantus was the first known person to use letters to stand for unknown numbers. Very little is known about the life of Diophantus. Over 800 years ago someone wrote this problem in his honor:

   Diophantus passed one sixth of his life in childhood, one twelfth in youth, and one seventh more as a bachelor. Five years after his marriage his son was born, who died four years before his father, at half his father's final age. How long did Diophantus live?   84 years

---

LESSON 5-9

Advanced Solving Technique II: Chunking

Word puzzles. *In solving word puzzles, letter tiles are arranged to form words. Forming words from letters can be thought of as a type of "chunking."*

What Is Chunking?

When an expression involves repeated occurrences of the same expression, you can often simplify it in more than one way.

Example 1

Simplify $8(x + 4) - 3(x + 4)$.

Solution 1

Use the Distributive Property. Then add like terms.
$$8(x + 4) - 3(x + 4) = (8x + 32) + -3(x + 4)$$
$$= 8x + 32 - 3x - 12$$
$$= 5x + 20$$

Solution 2

The expression has the form $8n - 3n$ where $n = x + 4$. Just as you can subtract the like terms $8n - 3n$ to get $5n$, you can simplify the given expression in one step.
$$8(x + 4) - 3(x + 4) = 5(x + 4)$$
$$= 5x + 20$$

The idea used in Example 1 is called *chunking*. **Chunking** is a term psychologists use to describe the process of grouping some small bits of information into a single piece of information. For instance, when reading the word "store," you don't think "s, t, o, r, e." You group the five letters into one word. In algebra, chunking can be done by viewing an entire algebraic expression as one variable. Example 2 shows how chunking can be used to simplify fractions.

Lesson 5-9 *Advanced Solving Technique II: Chunking* **333**

Lesson 5-9

Objectives

C Use chunking to simplify or evaluate expressions or to solve equations.

Resources

From the **Teacher's Resource File**
- Lesson Master 5-9A or 5-9B
- Answer Master 5-9
- Teaching Aid 49: Warm-up
- Activity Kit, Activity 12

Additional Resources
- Visual for Teaching Aid 49

Teaching 5-9
Lesson

Warm-up

Work in groups to solve this equation:
$4(3x + 5) + 8(3x + 5) - 2 = 9(3x + 5) + 13.$ $x = 0$

After students solve the equation, discuss the different solution strategies. Ask if anyone solved the equation by letting $y = 3x + 5$ and then solved $4y + 8y - 2 = 9y + 13$. This is an example of thinking of $3x + 5$ as a chunk.

Lesson 5-9 Overview

Broad Goals This lesson is designed to get students to think about an entire expression as single entity—a fundamental idea in all of mathematics. Consequently, the equations and expressions that are given here are both linear and non-linear.

"Chunking" is the treatment of a group (the "chunk") of symbols as a single symbol. Like *drawing a picture*, it is a fundamental problem-solving skill that does not have a

specific mathematical definition but that does have many mathematical applications. The term *chunking* comes from studies of psychology and information processing. Sometimes chunking is viewed as a type of substituting. However, substitution usually involves putting numbers into expressions, whereas chunking involves treating expressions as single numbers or entities.

The significance of chunking in algebra is that if a property holds for all values of a variable, then it also holds for expressions which have those values. For example, just as $2a + 3a = 5a$ is an instance of the Distributive Property, so $2(x + y) + 3(x + y) = 5(x + y)$ is also an instance.

333

Notes on Reading

Reading Mathematics This is a lesson of examples; the common thread is that there is a "chunk" in each one. To help students understand chunking, you might call on different students to read aloud. As students read the examples, have the class listen carefully for repeated quantities. Then ask students to name each chunk. [**Example 1,** $x + 4$; **Example 2,** $3x + 1$; **Example 3,** $3x + 5$; **Example 4,** $3y$; **Example 5,** $k + 6$] The *Covering the Reading* questions parallel the examples, so you can use them to reinforce the ideas.

Some examples of chunking that students have already seen are: 3.5×10^6 as representing a single number; $\frac{2}{3}$ as representing a single number (when thought of as $2 \div 3$, the chunk is broken); (x, y) as being a single point; operating on a side of an equation rather than on an individual term.

❶ One way to help students use chunking effectively is to focus their attention on the last operation to be performed in an expression rather than on the first operation. For example, to simplify $4(3x + 5) + 8(3x + 5)$, you could perform the multiplications and then add like terms. However, if you focus on the last operation—addition—you can perceive the problem as adding like expressions, the sum of which is $12(3x + 5)$. Then the final simplification is easier.

Example 2

Simplify $\dfrac{4}{3x + 1} + \dfrac{3}{3x + 1}$.

Solution

Think of $(3x + 1)$ as a single chunk c. Then the addition looks like $\dfrac{4}{c} + \dfrac{3}{c}$ and its sum is $\dfrac{7}{c}$.

$$\frac{4}{3x + 1} + \frac{3}{3x + 1} = \frac{7}{3x + 1}$$

Check

Substitute a number for x. We use $x = 5$.

Does $\dfrac{4}{3 \cdot 5 + 1} + \dfrac{3}{3 \cdot 5 + 1} = \dfrac{7}{3 \cdot 5 + 1}$?

Does $\dfrac{4}{16} + \dfrac{3}{16} = \dfrac{7}{16}$? Yes, it checks.

In Example 2, since $3x + 1$ is in the denominator it cannot be 0. Your teacher may want you to include $3x + 1 \neq 0$ in your solution.

Using Chunking in Linear Equations

Example 3

❶ Use chunking to solve $4(3x + 5) + 8(3x + 5) + 1 = 6(3x + 5) + 13$.

Solution

Notice that $3x + 5$ occurs in three places in the equation. Think of $3x + 5$ as one variable.

$12(3x + 5) + 1 = 6(3x + 5) + 13$	Add like chunks.
$6(3x + 5) + 1 = 13$	Add -6 chunks to each side.
$6(3x + 5) = 12$	Add -1 to each side.
$3x + 5 = 2$	Multiply each side by $\frac{1}{6}$.
$3x = -3$	Simplify.
$x = -1$	Multiply each side by $\frac{1}{3}$.

If the value of an algebraic expression is known, it can be substituted as a chunk into other expressions.

Example 4

If $3y = 8.5$, find $6y + 5$.

Solution

This can be done without solving for y. Think of $3y$ as a chunk. Since you know the value of $3y$, you can double it to get $6y$. Then add 5.

$$3y = 8.5$$
$$6y = 2 \cdot 8.5 = 17$$
$$6y + 5 = 17 + 5 = 22$$

▶

Optional Activities

Activity 1 You can use *Activity Kit, Activity 12,* to introduce Lesson 5-9. In this activity students use the technique of chunking by modeling expressions with algebra tiles.

Activity 2 After discussing chunking in mathematics, explain that chunking is also a tool that many people use to memorize such things as the "Pledge of Allegiance" or telephone numbers. Have students **work in groups** to find examples of situations where they have used chunking to help them remember something.

Check

If $3y = 8.5$, then $y = \frac{1}{3}(8.5) \approx 2.83$. So $6y + 5 \approx 6 \cdot 2.83 + 5 = 21.98$.

Using Chunking to Solve Other Equations

You know that the solutions to $x^2 = 81$ are $x = 9$ and $x = -9$. Using this fact, you can solve any equation of the form $(\text{chunk})^2 = 81$. Example 5 shows how.

Example 5

Solve $(k + 6)^2 = 81$.

Solution

The two numbers which give 81 when squared are 9 and -9. So the expression $k + 6$ must equal 9 or -9.

$$(k + 6)^2 = 81$$

$$k + 6 = 9 \qquad \text{or} \qquad k + 6 = -9$$
$$k = 3 \qquad \text{or} \qquad k = -15$$

There are two solutions, 3 and -15.

Check

Each solution must be checked.

Check 3.   Does $(3 + 6)^2 = 81$?
                               $9^2 = 81$?   Yes, it checks.
Check -15.   Does $(-15 + 6)^2 = 81$?
                              $(-9)^2 = 81$?   Yes, it checks.

❷ The technique used in Example 5 generalizes so you can solve many other equations of the form: $(\text{linear expression})^2 = \text{a constant}$.

QUESTIONS

Covering the Reading

1. What is chunking? the process of grouping small bits of information into a single piece of information

In 2 and 3, use chunking to simplify the expression.

2. $8(12t - 7) - 3(12t - 7)$
   $5(12t - 7) = 60t - 35$

3. $12(10 - a) - 4(10 - a)$
   $8(10 - a) = 80 - 8a$

4. a. When adding $\frac{11}{2y - 6} + \frac{4}{2y - 6}$, what should you think of as a chunk?
   b. Perform the addition.
   c. What value can $2y - 6$ not have?
   a) $2y - 6$;   b) $\frac{15}{2y - 6}$;   c) 0

---

❷ Emphasize the last operation by first leaving the inside of the parentheses blank.
$(\quad)^2 = 81$
$(\quad) = 9$ or $(\quad) = -9$
$(k + 6) = 9$ or $(k + 6) = -9$

Additional Examples

1. Simplify $9\sqrt{2} - 7\sqrt{2} - \sqrt{2}$. $\sqrt{2}$
2. Simplify $\frac{x+5}{x-3} + \frac{x-11}{x-3}$.
   2, except when $x = 3$
3. Use chunking to solve:
   $3(4x - 3) - 6(4x - 3) - 15 = 2(4x - 3) - 4(4x - 3)$ $x = -3$
4. If $8y - 7 = 22$, what does $8y + 7$ equal?   36
5. Solve $(2n - 1)^2 = 49$.
   $n = 4$ or $n = -3$
6. If $7n + 5y = 19$, find $70n + 50y + 3$.   193

Notes on Questions

Questions 2–3 Students can check their work by using the Distributive Property and adding like terms.

Adapting to Individual Needs

Extra Help

Remind students that a term is often the product of a number and a variable. When the variable in two or more terms is the same, the terms are called *like terms,* and addition can be performed by adding the coefficients. For example, $3x + -5x = -2x$ because both terms have the variable x and $3 + -5 = -2$. Then, for **Example 1,** write $8y - 3y$ on the board and have students simplify the expression to $5y$. Then

substitute $x + 4$ for y to show that $8(x + 4) - 3(x + 4) = 5(x + 4)$.

Questions 9–11 These questions show the strategy which motivates completing the square to solve quadratic equations.

Questions 12–13 Many students see $\sqrt{5}$ as being two symbols, the radical sign meaning "take the square root of," and then the numeral 5. When we think of $\sqrt{5}$ as a single number ("thesquarerootof5," which we say quickly), we are chunking.

Question 30 Science Connection Sir Isaac Newton was an English physicist and mathematician who had a long and varied career. Among his many achievements as a scientist, he studied the mechanics of planetary motion and derived the inverse square law which later became crucial to his theory of universal gravitation. As a mathematician, he established the foundation for calculus.

Question 36 The world record for memorizing digits of pi (set in 1987) is held by a Japanese man, who memorized the first 40,000 digits. Over 2 billion decimal places of π have been calculated using a supercomputer.

6a) $3(2a + 3) = 39$;
$2a + 3 = 13$;
$2a = 10$;
$a = 5$

b) $20a + 30 - 14a - 21 = 39$; $6a + 9 = 39$; $6a = 30$; $a = 5$

5. **a.** Simplify $\frac{x}{x+8} - \frac{5}{x+8}$. $\frac{x-5}{x+8}$
   b. What value(s) can x *not* have? -8

6. **a.** Solve the equation $10(2a + 3) - 7(2a + 3) = 39$ using chunking.
   b. Solve the equation in part **a** another way. See left for 6a, b.
   c. Which method do you prefer? Answers may vary.

7. If $3x = 8.5$, find $6x - 1$. 16

8. If $18a = 12$, find $9a + 7$. 13

9. Follow Example 5 to solve these equations.
   a. $(x + 1)^2 = 81$ **b.** $(4x + 1)^2 = 81$ $x = 2$ or $x = \frac{-5}{2}$
   $x = 8$ or $x = -10$

10. **a.** If $(m - 11)^2 = 64$, what two values can $m - 11$ have? -8, 8
    b. Find two solutions to $(m - 11)^2 = 64$. $m = 19$ or $m = 3$

11. Find all solutions to $(p + 3)^2 = 225$. $p = 12$ or $p = -18$

Applying the Mathematics

In 12–17, simplify.

12. $3\sqrt{5} + 6\sqrt{5} - 2\sqrt{5}$ $7\sqrt{5}$ 13. $5\sqrt{a} - 7\sqrt{a}$ $-2\sqrt{a}$

14. $7(x^2 - 9) - 4(x^2 - 9)$ $3x^2 - 27$ 15. $3(x^2 - 2y) + 6(x^2 - 2y) - 4(x^2 - 2y)$ $5x^2 - 10y$

16. $\frac{8(x+7)}{5a} \cdot \frac{3a}{2(x+7)}$ $\frac{12}{5}$ 17. $\frac{x+10}{x+5} + \frac{2x+5}{x+5}$ 3

18. Approximate the solutions of $(d + 11)^2 = 57$ to two decimal places.
    -3.45; -18.55

19. If $5y = 7$, find the value of $(5y)^2 + 3$. 52

20. If $a + 7 = 91$, what is the value of $2a + 14$? 182

21. If $18y - 12t = 25$, find $9y - 6t$. 12.5

22. If $5x + 4y = 32$ and $2y = 1$, give the value of each expression.
    a. $5x$ 30   **b.** x 6

In 23 and 24, find all real-number solutions.

23. $(3p + 5)^2 = 625$ 24. $(x^2)^2 = 256$.
    $p = \frac{20}{3}$ or $p = -10$ $x = 4$ or $x = -4$

Review

25. State a property that can be used to transform $\frac{a+3}{4} = \frac{1}{2}$ to $a + 3 = 2$.
    (Lesson 5-8) Multiplication Property of Equality

In 26 and 27, solve. *(Lesson 5-8)*

26. $\frac{3w}{4} - 2 \leq \frac{1}{2}$ 27. $\frac{x}{2} + \frac{x}{3} - \frac{1}{4} = \frac{1}{6}$
    $w \leq \frac{10}{3}$ $x = \frac{1}{2}$

Adapting to Individual Needs

English Language Development
You might want to define *chunk* as a piece of something. Then give examples, such as a chunk of chalk or a chunk of cheese. When writing examples on the board, use different colored chalk to show chunking. For instance, in **Example 1,** write each $(x + 4)$ using the same colored chalk while telling students to view $(x + 4)$ as one variable or *chunk*.

28. The Koenigs bought a farm. They did not know the capacity of the heating-oil storage tank. At one point, the tank was $\frac{1}{8}$ full. After a delivery of 450 gallons, the tank's gauge showed that it was $\frac{7}{8}$ full. How many gallons of oil does the tank hold? *(Lesson 5-8)*
600 gallons

29. Bertrand spends half his monthly income on housing and food, and budgets the other half as follows: $\frac{1}{4}$ of the half on clothes, $\frac{1}{3}$ on entertainment, $\frac{1}{4}$ on transportation, and the remaining $40 in savings. What are his monthly earnings? *(Lesson 5-8)* **$480**

30. Newton's laws of motion state that the velocity v of an object moving in a circular path is related to its acceleration a and the radius of the path r by the formula $v^2 = ar$. Solve this formula for r. *(Lesson 5-7)* $r = v^2/a$

31. a. Solve for y: $2x + 5y = 10$. $y = -\frac{2}{5}x + 2$
b. Graph the line. *(Lessons 4-9, 5-7)* **See left.**

32. a. Make up a question about a real situation that can be answered by solving the equation $200 - 3x = 240 - 5x$. **See left.**
b. Solve the equation. *(Lessons 3-8, 5-3)* $x = 20$

33. Give an instance of the Commutative Property of Addition. *(Lesson 3-1)* **Sample: $44 + 31 = 31 + 44$**

34. A catalog company that sells travel bags sews customers' 3-letter monograms onto the bags. However, some bags are returned. As a promotion, the company advertises that if you could find your monogram on a bag among those they have on hand, the bag is free. How many different 3-letter monograms are possible? *(Lesson 2-9)*
$26^3 = 17{,}576$

35. Refer to the figures below. The triangle and rectangle have equal perimeters. What is the length of a side of the triangle? *(Lesson 5-3)*
6 units

$x + 4$ $x + 4$ x

$x + 4$ $x + 5$

Exploration

36. Often people use chunking as a help in memorization. Here are the first twenty decimal places of π.

$$3.14159265358979323846$$

Try memorizing these 20 digits by memorizing the following four chunks of five digits each.

14159   26535   89793   23846

Lesson 5-9 *Advanced Solving Technique II: Chunking* **337**

31b)

$y = -\frac{2}{5}x + 2$

32a) Sample: One balloonist is 200 ft above the ground and is descending at a rate of 3 ft per second. Another is at 240 ft and is descending 5 ft per second. When will they be at the same altitude?

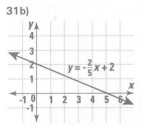

Adapting to Individual Needs
Challenge
Have students simplify the following expression. $[\frac{4}{5}]$

$$\cfrac{1}{2 - \cfrac{1}{2 - \cfrac{1}{2 - \cfrac{1}{2 - \frac{1}{2}}}}}$$

Follow-up 5-9
for Lesson

Practice
For more questions on SPUR Objectives, use **Lesson Master 5-9A** (shown on page 335) or **Lesson Master 5-9B** (shown on pages 336–337).

Assessment
Group Assessment Have students **work in small groups.** Have each group start with an algebraic expression for which the value is known, such as $4t = 9$ or $5t + 3 = 10.5$. Ask each student in the group to write an expression that uses $4t$ or $5t + 3$ as a chunk, such as $(4t)^2 + 4t$ or $8(5t + 3) - 5(5t + 3)$. Have students exchange papers, and find the values of each others' expressions. [Students demonstrate an ability to use chunking to find the value of an expression.]

Extension
Have students solve each equation.
1. $\sqrt{k + 3} = 10$ [The chunk $k + 3$ equals 100, so $k = 97$.]
2. $2^{3t-1} = 2^{11}$. [The chunk $3t - 1$ equals 11, so $t = 4$.]

Project Update Project 1, *Chunking*, on page 338, relates to the content of this lesson.

▶ **LESSON MASTER 5-9 B** *page 2*

In 21–28, solve the equation.
21. $2(4a + 6) + 6(4a + 6) = 80$ **22.** $(2a + 3)^2 = 49$
$a = 1$ $a = 2$ or $a = -5$

23. $(x + 3)^2 = 36$ **24.** $(m - 8)^2 = 121$
$x = 3$ or $x = -9$ $m = 19$ or $m = -3$

25. $(u^2)^2 = 625$ **26.** $3(x^2 + 1) - 4(x^2 + 1) = -26$
$u = 5$ or $u = -5$ $x = 5$ or $x = -5$

27. $10(w + 1) - 5(w + 1) + (w + 1) = -42$
$w = -8$

28. $12(2w^2 + 4) - 5(2w^2 + 4) - (2w^2 + 4) = 24$
$w = 0$

29. If $\sqrt{x + 3} = 81$, what is the value of $x + 3$?   **6,561**
30. If $\sqrt{x + 3} = 81$, what is the value of x?   **6,558**
31. If $\sqrt{x + 3} = 81$, what is the value of $3\sqrt{x + 3}$?   **243**
32. If $14y + 21 = 17$, what is the value of $2y + 3$? $\frac{17}{7}$

337

Chapter 5 Projects

The projects relate to the content of the lessons of this chapter as follows.

Project	Lesson(s)
1	5-9
2	5-6
3	5-2, 5-4
4	5-7
5	5-1, 5-4
6	5-4

1 Chunking After students have solved this equation using chunking, have them check their solutions using the multiplying through technique. You may want to compile the equations that the students write, and use them as a worksheet or quiz.

2 Tree Growth Suggest that students talk to a science teacher to determine the best resources available in your school library. Students should graph the growth of each tree on the same graph. You may want to have students write an equation and a table describing the growth. Tell students that the maximum height of a beech tree is about 120 feet, and the maximum height of many species of maple trees is 125 feet. Ask them to find the maximum height of each species of tree that they select.

3 Lifetime Cost of an Appliance Energy guides are posted on all major appliances sold in the United States. Energy guides use interval graphs to show the range of operating costs for appliances of equal size. Suggest that students describe these closed intervals using an inequality. Have students tell some reasons why they might purchase an appliance that is not the best value over a period of years. Their reasons might include the initial affordability of the appliance, the availability of the appliance, or the style and features of the appliance.

A project presents an opportunity for you to extend your knowledge of a topic related to the material of this chapter. You should allow more time for a project than you do for typical homework questions.

1 Chunking
Explain how the following equation can be solved by repeated applications of chunking:

$$\frac{\frac{x+3}{4} + 5}{2} + 6 = 7.$$

Then make up a few similar equations and solve them.

2 Tree growth
Do trees really grow as described in Lesson 5-6? Find a book that explains the growth of various species of trees. For at least three species, graph the height of a typical tree as it grows to its mature size.

3 Lifetime Cost of an Appliance
Visit a store where appliances are sold, or check your phone book for such a store. New major appliances, like refrigerators, are tested for their expected energy consumption per year. That information is available to consumers to aid them in their decisions. Pick a range of sizes of refrigerators (for instance 16 to 21 cu ft), and find the price and expected yearly energy cost for at least four different models. For each model develop an equation that describes its total cost over its life span. Graph these equations. Is the least expensive model always the most economical? Which model is the best value over 10 years?

338

Possible responses

1. First chunk the entire large fraction. It must equal 1 because $1 + 6 = 7$. Since the fraction equals 1 and its denominator is 2, the numerator $\frac{x+3}{4} + 5$ must equal 2. Now $\frac{x+3}{4}$ must equal -3, since $-3 + 5 = 2$. Thus $\frac{x+3}{4} = -3$. The numerator of this fraction must equal -12, since $\frac{-12}{4} = -3$.

Thus $x + 3 = -12$, and $x = -15$. Students' examples will vary.

2. Rates of growth of trees are approximate. Under normal conditions trees will grow as described in the lesson, and each tree will reach a maximum height. Students' graphs will vary.

338

4 Equivalent formulas

Below are formulas for the areas of various common figures studied in geometry. For each formula, draw a figure and indicate on the figure what each variable represents. Solve every formula for each of the other variables in it.

a. triangle $A = \frac{1}{2}hb$

b. parallelogram $A = bh$

c. kite $A = \frac{1}{2}d_1 d_2$

d. trapezoid $A = \frac{1}{2}h(b_1 + b_2)$

e. ellipse $A = \pi ab$

5 Light Bulbs

On the opening page of this chapter, a table of prices of two kinds of light bulbs is given. Visit a store and find the costs of these or other similar bulbs in your area. Also find the cost of electricity, perhaps by calling your local electric company. Organize the information you collect in a table and a graph, and based upon your information, answer the questions.

a. How much does a regular light bulb cost?

b. How much does an energy-efficient bulb cost?

c. After approximately how many hours of use will the total costs (purchase price of bulb plus cost of electricity) of the two bulbs be the same?

d. If the average life of a bulb is 1000 hours, how much money would you save by buying and using an energy-efficient bulb?

6 Long-distance Telephone Rates

Find out the rates for telephone calls from where you live to a city or town that has a different area code. Compare the rates from two long-distance companies for calls of various lengths. You may have to consider different times of the day and week. Do not make the calls to determine their costs!

4 Equivalent Formulas

This is a straightforward project that will help future geometry students. As an extension of this project, ask students to write several questions that can be answered using one of the equivalent formulas they have written.

5 Light Bulbs

Explain to students that electrical costs are usually calculated from the rate per kilowatt hour. One kilowatt-hour is a unit of electrical energy equal to the work of 1000 watts of electricity being used for 1 hour. Make sure that students are comparing bulbs that have the same amount of wattage. Energy-efficient bulbs (EE) use less wattage than a regular light bulb and are therefore less costly to operate. A 100-watt energy-efficient light bulb uses 90 watts of electricity, a 75-watt EE bulb uses 67 watts of electricity, and a 60-watt EE bulb uses 52 watts of electricity. Students will need this information to determine costs.

6 Long-distance Telephone Rates

Students can begin this project by selecting a town or city in which they have friends or relatives, or a town or city they would like to visit. Suggest that students put the information they gather into several tables listing location, long-distance company used, time of day, and length of call. Some students may be surprised by the range of costs of calls to the same location. Ask them to explain why they think such differences in cost exist.

---

3. Sample: ranges of operating costs for standard-size refrigerators:

Size (cu ft)	Lowest cost	Highest cost
16.8	$47	$86
18.1	$47	$86
18.6	$57	$106
19.9	$57	$106
20.6	$60	$108
21.6	$60	$108

Equations for the total cost of operating an appliance over its life span:
Total Cost = Cost of appliance + (yearly operating cost times the life span in years). Data may show that the least expensive model is not always the most economical over the life of the appliance.

(Responses continue on page 340.)

SUMMARY

The chapter begins by examining two special forms of equations: $x = h$ and $y = k$. If an equation of the form $x = h$ is graphed in the coordinate plane, its graph is a vertical line. If $y = k$ is graphed in the coordinate plane, its graph is a horizontal line.

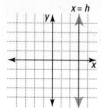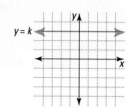

The next five lessons of the chapter deal with ways to compare two quantities described by linear expressions such as $ax + b$ and $cx + d$. One way to compare them is to make a table that shows the value of each expression for different values of x. This can be done with paper and pencil or with a spreadsheet. Questions can then be answered by examining the numbers that appear in the chart.

A second method of comparison is to write an equation to describe each pattern, in the form $y = ax + b$ and $y = cx + d$. Graph the two equations, and examine where the two graphs cross or where one is below the other. Graphing can be done with paper and pencil or with an automatic grapher.

The third technique discussed is to solve an equation or inequality. To find when the two quantities are equal, solve $ax + b = cx + d$. To find when the first is less than the second, solve $ax + b < cx + d$. Solving sentences has the advantage of yielding exact solutions.

The last lessons discuss special techniques involved in solving sentences. Many formulas or equations that contain more than one variable can be "solved" for any of the variables in them. The process is similar to that for equations with just one variable. To solve a sentence containing fractions, find the least common multiple of the denominators, and then multiply each term by it. If numbers in a sentence are all large, then multiply both sides by a small fraction.

Chunking is a problem-solving technique by which an expression is considered as a single number. Many complicated expressions and equations can be handled by recognizing their similarities with simpler patterns.

VOCABULARY

Below are the most important terms and phrases for this chapter. You should be able to give a general description and a specific example of each.

Lesson 5-1
horizontal line, $y = k$
vertical line, $x = h$

Lesson 5-3
general linear equation

Lesson 5-5
automatic grapher
window, default window
tick marks
trace, cursor
hard copy

Lesson 5-7
Fahrenheit, Celsius, Centigrade
    temperature scales
equivalent formulas

Lesson 5-8
clearing fractions
multiplying through

Lesson 5-9
chunking

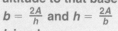

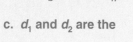
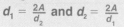
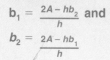

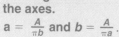

PROGRESS SELF-TEST

Take this test as you would take a test in class. Use graph paper, a ruler, and a calculator. Then check your work with the solutions in the Selected Answers section in the back of the book.

1. a. To solve the equation $5y - 9 = 12 - 3y$ an effective first step is to add __?__ to each side of the equation. **3y or -5y**

   b. What property is being applied in part **a**?

2. For the equation $\frac{3}{5}x - \frac{2}{3} = \frac{1}{5}x + 7$, by what number can each side of the equation be multiplied to clear the fractions? **15**

1b) Addition Property of Equality

In 3–9, solve. Show your work.

3. $4x - 3 = 3x + 14$ **x = 17**

4. $3.9z - 56.9 = 6.1 - 4.7z$ **z ≈ 7.33**

5. $5n \geq 2n + 12$ **n ≥ 4**

6. $5(10 - y) = 6(y + 1)$ **y = 4**

7. $-5a + 6 < -11a + 24$ **a < 3**

8. $\frac{1}{2}m - \frac{3}{4} = \frac{2}{3}$ **m = $\frac{17}{6}$**

9. $5000 - 4000v = 11000v + 680{,}000$ **v = -45**

10. If $4y = 2.6$, find the value of $20y + 3$. **16**

In 11 and 12, simplify.

11. $\frac{4}{t+7} + \frac{5}{t+7}$ **$\frac{9}{t+7}$**

12. $8(x^2 - 5) + 3(x^2 - 5)$ **11x² − 55**

13. Find all solutions to $(n + 3)^2 = 49$. **4, -10**

14. Solve the sentence $3x + 5y = 15$ for y. **See below.**

15. Solve the formula $C = np$ for p. **p = $\frac{C}{n}$**

16. Graph the points in the coordinate plane satisfying the equation $x = 3$. **See margin.**

17. Suppose the perimeter of the triangle is equal to the perimeter of the square. Then find the lengths of the sides of the triangle and the length of a side of the square. **Triangle sides are 24, 36, and 48. All sides of the square are 27.**

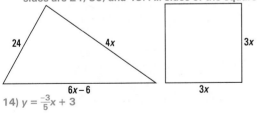

14) y = $\frac{-3}{5}$x + 3

18. Two children in a family want to see who can save more money. The younger child has saved \$1200 and is saving \$50 per month. The older child has saved \$1500 and is saving \$25 per month. After how many months will the younger child have more money saved than the older child?

   a. Make a graph to represent this situation. Explain how the graph can be used to answer the question. **See margin.**

   b. Answer the question by solving an inequality. **m > 12**

19. Jolisa is considering two different sales positions. Sun Fashions pays a total salary of \$400 per month plus 12% of her sales. Her second option is to work at Today's Outerwear, where she would receive \$750 per month plus 10% of her sales.

   a. Complete the table.

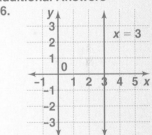

Monthly Sales	Sun Fashions Total Salary	Today's Outerwear Total Salary
\$ 0	\$ 400	750
\$5000	1000	1250
\$10000	1600	\$1750
\$15000	2200	2250
\$20000	2800	2750
\$25000	\$3400	3250

   b. Use the table to find amounts of sales for which Sun Fashions will pay Jolisa a greater total salary. **sales ≥ \$20,000**

   c. Jolisa thinks she can sell \$12,000 of merchandise each month. Explain which job you think she should take and why. **Today's Outerwear would pay more for sales less than or equal to \$15,000.**

Progress Self-Test

For the development of mathematical competence, feedback and correction, along with the opportunity to practice, are necessary. The Progress Self-Test provides the opportunity for feedback and correction; the Chapter Review provides additional opportunities and practice. We cannot overemphasize the importance of these end-of-chapter materials. It is at this point that the material "gels" for many students, allowing them to solidify skills and understanding. In general, student performance should be markedly improved after these pages.

Assign the Progress Self-Test as a one-night assignment. Worked-out *solutions* for all questions are in the Selected Answers section of the student book. Encourage students to take the Progress Self-Test honestly, grade themselves, and then be prepared to discuss the test in class.

Advise students to pay special attention to those Chapter Review questions (pages 343–347) which correspond to the questions that they missed on the Progress Self-Test.

Additional Answers

16.

(graph showing vertical line x = 3)

18a. After 12 months, the graph of the younger child is higher than the graph of the older child.

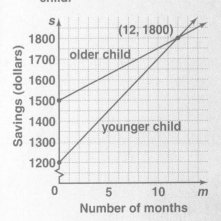

PROGRESS SELF-TEST

20. This year, the Green family bought a new home and a new car. They anticipate that their $80,000 home will increase in value by $3500 per year, but their $14,000 car will decrease in value by $1800 per year.

a. Copy and complete the spreadsheet below to show the values of their home and auto over the next six years.

b. Give a formula for the value of their home t years from now.
$v = 80,000 + 3500t$

	A	B	C
1	years from now	House value	Car value
2	0	80,000	14,000
3	1	83,500	12,200
4	2	87,000	10,400
5	3	90,500	8,600
6	4	94,000	6,800
7	5	97,500	5,000
8	6	101,000	3,200

21b) for fewer than 7 pictures

21. The graph below shows the cost of having film developed at two different stores.

a. For how many photos is it cheaper to go to Picture Perfect? **for more than 7 pictures**

b. For how many photos is it more expensive to go to Picture Perfect?

c. For how many photos do the two stores charge the same price?
for exactly 7 pictures

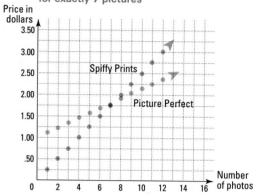

22. Use an automatic grapher. The graph of $y = 0.5x + 7$ passes through three quadrants. **a) See below.**

a. Find a window that shows the graph in all three quadrants. Sketch the graph on that window and label the window used.

b. Use the trace key to estimate the x-coordinate when $y = 0$. $x = -14$

c. Describe what happens to the y-coordinate when the x-coordinate increases. **The y-coordinate increases.**

22a)

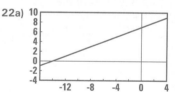

CHAPTER REVIEW

Questions on SPUR Objectives

SPUR stands for **S**kills, **P**roperties, **U**ses, and **R**epresentations. The Chapter Review questions are grouped according to the SPUR Objectives for this chapter.

SKILLS DEAL WITH THE PROCEDURES USED TO GET ANSWERS.

Objective A: *Solve linear equations of the form* $ax + b = cx + d$. *(Lessons 5-3, 5-8)*

In 1–12, solve. **5–8) See below.** $\frac{63}{5}$ or 12.6

1. $A + 5 = 9A - 11$ 2. $-12k + 144 = 3k - 45$
3. $2a - 6 = -2a$ $\frac{3}{2}$ 4. $3n = 2n + 4 + 5n$ -1
5. $4x - 11.7 = -0.3x$ 6. $10e = 4e - 5(3 + 2e)$
7. $3(x + 10) = -2(2x - 1)$ 8. $5(4 - y) = 2(y + 10)$
9. $\frac{n}{2} + \frac{3}{2} = 3$ 3   10. $\frac{1}{4}a - 1 = -2a$ $\frac{4}{9}$
11. $\frac{x}{3} + \frac{x}{5} + 21 = x$ 45 12. $193.4x + 193.4 = 1934$
$\qquad\qquad\qquad\qquad\qquad\qquad\qquad x = 9$

Objective B: *Solve linear inequalities of the form* $ax + b < cx + d$. *(Lessons 5-6, 5-8)*

In 13–16, solve.   **15, 16) See below.**
13. $11h + 71 \geq 13h - 219$ $h \leq 145$
14. $4x - 1 < 2x + 1$ $x < 1$
15. $5(5 + z) < 3(2 + 2z)$ 16. $-3x + 7 \geq -9x + 25$

In 17 and 18, **a.** solve; and **b.** graph all solutions on a number line. **17, 18) See margin.**
17. $9(x + 3) + 2 \leq 4 - x$ 18. $4x + 3 < 6x$

In 19–22, solve. $n < \frac{-7}{2}$ $x < 22$
19. $\frac{3}{10}n + \frac{3}{5} < -\frac{1}{2}n - \frac{11}{5}$ 20. $\frac{x}{2} + \frac{5}{3} > \frac{2x}{3} - 2$
21. $5000x - 9000 > 3500x - 15,000$ $x > -4$
22. $0.12x + 4 \leq 0.2x - 0.32$ $x \geq 54$
5) $x = \frac{117}{43} \approx 2.72$ 6) $e = \frac{-15}{16}$ 7) $x = -4$ 8) 0
15) $z > 19$
16) $x \geq 3$

Objective C: *Use chunking to simplify or evaluate expressions or to solve equations.* *(Lesson 5-9)*

23. If $7y = 21.2$, find $21y + 4$. 67.6
24. If $11x + 5 = 29.5$, find $22x + 10$. 59
In 25–28, simplify the expression.
25. $13(x - 7) - 10(x - 7)$ $3x - 21$
26. $99(12a + 19) - 98(12a + 19)$ $12a + 19$
27. $\frac{-8(x + y)}{z} + \frac{9(x + y)}{z}$ 28. $\frac{4(n + 3)}{n - 7} \cdot \frac{n - 7}{n + 3}$ 4
In 29–32, find all solutions. **32) See below.**
29. $(m + 2)^2 = 64$ 6, -10 30. $(z - 4)^2 = 144$ 16, -8
31. $(2x)^2 = 400$ 10, -10 32. $(3x + 7)^2 = 676$
$\qquad\qquad\qquad\qquad\qquad\qquad -11, \frac{19}{3}$
27) $\frac{x + y}{z}$

Objective D: *Find equivalent forms of formulas and equations.* *(Lesson 5-7)*

In 33–36, solve for the stated variable.
33. $A = \frac{1}{2}bh$ for b $b = \frac{2A}{h}$ 34. $V = \ell wh$ for h $h = \frac{V}{\ell w}$
35. $P = 2(\ell + w)$ for w 36. $S = 2\pi r^2 + 2\pi rh$ for h
37. Solve $y = \frac{x}{z}$ for x. $x = yz$ $h = \frac{s - 2\pi r^2}{2\pi r}$
38. Solve $T = a + (n - 1)d$ for n. $n = \frac{T - a}{d} + 1$
In 39 and 40, solve for y.
39. $10x + 8y = 40$ 40. $6y - 5x = 12$
35) $w = \frac{1}{2}P - \ell$ 39) $y = -\frac{5}{4}x + 5$ 40) $y = \frac{5}{6}x + 2$

PROPERTIES DEAL WITH THE PRINCIPLES BEHIND THE MATHEMATICS.

Objective E: *Apply and recognize properties associated with linear sentences.*
(Lessons 5-3, 5-6, 5-7, 5-8)

41. Consider the equation $6x + 3 = 8x + 5$.

a. Solve the equation by first adding $-6x$ to each side. $x = -1$
b. Solve by first adding $-8x$ to each side. $x = -1$
c. Compare your answers to parts **a** and **b**. They are equal.

Chapter 5 Review

Resources
From the *Teacher's Resource File*
■ Answer Master for Chapter 5 Review
■ *Assessment Sourcebook:* Chapter 5 Test, Forms A–D Chapter 5 Test, Cumulative Form

Additional Resources
■ Quiz and Test Writer

The main objectives for the chapter are organized in the Chapter Review under the four types of understanding this book promotes—Skills, Properties, Uses, and Representations.

Whereas end-of chapter material may be considered optional in some texts, in *UCSMP Algebra* we have selected these objectives and questions with the expectation that they will be covered. Students should be able to answer these questions with about 85% accuracy after studying the chapter.

You may assign these questions over a single night to help students prepare for a test the next day, or you may assign the questions over a two-day period. If you work the questions over two days, then we recommend assigning the *evens* for homework the first night so that students get feedback in class the next day, then assigning the *odds* the night before the test because answers are provided to the odd-numbered questions.

It is effective to ask students which questions they still do not understand and use the day or days as a total class discussion of the material which the class finds most difficult.

Additional Answers
17a. $x \leq -\frac{5}{2}$

b.

18a. $x > \frac{3}{2}$

b.

Assessment

Evaluation The *Assessment Sourcebook* provides five forms of the Chapter 5 Test. Forms A and B present parallel versions in a short-answer format. Forms C and D offer performance assessment. The fifth test is Chapter 5 Test, Cumulative Form. About 50% of this test covers Chapter 5; 25% covers Chapter 4, and 25% covers earlier chapters. Comprehensive Test Chapters 1–5 gives roughly equal attention to all chapters covered thus far.

For information on grading see *General Teaching Suggestions; Grading* in the *Professional Sourcebook* which begins on page T20 in Part 1 of the Teacher's Edition.

Feedback After students have taken the test for Chapter 5 and you have scored the results, return the tests to students for discussion. Class discussion on the questions that caused trouble for most students can be very effective in identifying and clarifying misunderstandings. You might want to have them write down the items they missed and work either in groups or at home to correct them. It is important for students to receive feedback on every chapter test, and we recommend that students see and correct their mistakes before proceeding too far into the next chapter.

344

42a) $a > -1$; b) $a > -1$

42. Consider the inequality $a + 2 < 3a + 4$.
  a. Solve it by first adding $-a$ to each side.
  b. Solve it by first adding $-3a$ to each side.
  c. How are your answers to parts **a** and **b** related? They are equal.

In 43 and 44, a sentence is solved. Write the steps in the solution replacing the blanks with a number, operation, or property.

43. $\frac{3}{4}x - 5 = \frac{1}{8}x + 10$
$16\left(\frac{3}{4}x - 5\right) = 16\left(\frac{1}{8}x + 10\right)$
$16 \cdot \frac{3}{4}x - 16 \cdot 5 = 16 \cdot \frac{1}{8}x + 16 \cdot 10$

$12x - 80 = 2x + 160$
$10x - 80 = 160$
$10x = 240$
$x = 24$

a) Multiply;   b) 16
 a each side by **b** .
c) distributive
Apply the **c** property.
Simplify.
 d to each side.
 e to each side.
d) Add $-2x$
e) Add 80

44. $3y + 8 \geq -5y - 2$
$8y + 8 \geq -2$
$8y \geq -10$
$y \geq -\frac{10}{8}$

44a) 5y;   b) Add -8
c) Multiply   d) $\frac{1}{8}$
Add **a** to each side.
 b to each side.
 c each side by **d** .

In 45 and 46, multiply each side by a number to result in an equation in which all numbers are integers. (You need not solve the equation.)

45. $\frac{1}{4} - 2x = \frac{5}{6}x + 9$ **46.** $3.6y = 0.15 - 0.04y$

In 47 and 48, multiply each side by a number to result in an equation in which all numbers are smaller integers. (You need not solve the equation.)

47. $4800t - 120,000 = 3600t$ by $\frac{1}{100}$; $48 - 1200 = 36t$
48. $35w + 21 = 105(w + 2)$ by $\frac{1}{7}$; $5w + 3 = 15(w + 2)$
45) Sample: Multiply by 12; $3 - 24x = 10x + 108$.
46) Sample: Multiply by 100; $360y = 15 - 4y$.

USES DEAL WITH APPLICATIONS OF MATHEMATICS IN REAL SITUATIONS.

Objective F: *Use linear equations and inequalities of the form $ax + b = cx + d$ or $ax + b < cx + d$ to solve real-world problems.*
(Lessons 5-3, 5-6, 5-8)

49. Kate has $1500 in an account and adds $45 each month. Melissa has $2000 and adds $20 a month.
  a. How much will each girl have in her account after n months? See below.
  b. After how many months will they have the same amount of money in their accounts? 20

50. Len has $25 and is saving at the rate of $9 a week. Basil has $100 and is spending $5 a week. a) $25 + 9x > 100 - 5x$
  a. Let x = the number of weeks that have passed. Write a linear inequality which can be used to find out when Len will have more money than Basil.
  b. Solve the sentence in part **a.** $x > \frac{75}{14} \approx 5\frac{5}{14}$

51. Willow trees grow quickly, about 3 feet per year, while American elms grow about 1.5 feet per year. If a landscaping company plants an 8-foot willow tree and a 12-foot elm tree, after how many years will the willow tree be taller than the elm? $2\frac{2}{3}$ years

49a) Kate will have $1500 + 45n$. Melissa will have $2000 + 20n$.

52. For what number of miles driven will the cost of renting a car for $100 per week and $.15 per mile equal the cost of renting a car with fees of $150 and $.12 per mile? ≈ 1666.7 mi

53. The new Newton Bakery can produce 550 loaves of bread per day. The old bakery has produced 109,000 loaves over the years and still makes 200 loaves per day. When will the new bakery have made more loaves of bread than the old one? after 312 days

54. Angie is racing her younger sister, so she gives her sister a 50-m head start. If Angie can run at $5 \frac{m}{sec}$ and her sister runs at $3 \frac{m}{sec}$, how long will it take Angie to catch up with her sister? 25 seconds

55. An automobile gas tank was about $\frac{1}{8}$ full. 10.4 gallons of gas were needed to fill the tank. What is the capacity of the tank, rounded to the nearest gallon? 12 gallons

56. A couple budgets their after-tax income as follows: 25% for housing; 15% for food; 12% for savings; and 10% each for transportation, health care, clothing, and education. If next year the couple wants to have at least $3000 left for entertainment and other expenses, what must their after-tax income be? at least $37,500

Objective G: *Use tables or spreadsheets to solve real-world problems involving linear situations.* (Lesson 5-2)

57. Two mail-order CD clubs offer discount prices. The first one has a $15 membership fee and charges $9 per CD. The second club charges $11 to join, plus $9.50 for each CD.

a. Copy and complete the chart below.

Number of CDs	Charges	
	First club	Second club
2	$33	$30
4	$51	$49
6	$69	$68
8	$87	$87
10	$105	$106

57c) more than 8 CDs   d) less than 8 CDs

b. How many CDs must you buy for the two clubs' charges to be equal? 8

c. When is the first club's price better?

d. When is the second club's price better?

58. Alicia is considering two different sales positions. Appliance World would pay a total salary of $1000 per month plus a commission of 4% of sales. Better Kitchens would pay a total salary of $600 plus a commission of 6% of sales.

a. Complete the table.

Sales	Appliance World Total Salary	Better Kitchens Total Salary
$ 0	$1,000	$600
5,000	$1,200	$900
10,000	$1,400	$1,200
15,000	$1,600	$1,500
20,000	$1,800	$1,800
25,000	$2,000	$2,100
30,000	$2,200	$2,400

b. For what amounts of sales will Better Kitchens pay a greater total salary?
more than $20,000 in sales

59. A farmer plans to increase his crop production over the next 10 years by adding acreage and improving farming techniques. This year he harvested 10,200 bushels of corn. He feels he can increase this by 100 bushels each year. Similarly, this year he harvested 6750 bushels of soybeans and plans to increase the output by 500 bushels per year.

a. Complete a spreadsheet like the one below to show the farmer's production over the next ten years. (The abbreviation for bushels is bu.)

	A	B	C
	yrs from now	bu. corn	bu. soybeans
1			
2	0	10200	6750
3	1	10300	7250
4	2	10400	7750
5	3	10500	8250
6	4	10600	8750
7	5	10700	9250
8	6	10800	9720
9	7	10900	10250
10	8	11000	10750
11	9	11100	11250
12	10	11200	11750

b. What formulas are used in cells B5 and C5? See margin.

c. In what year will the number of bushels of soybeans produced exceed the number of bushels of corn? See margin.

d. Assume that the farmer can sell his corn for $2.60 per bushel and his soybeans for $7.70 per bushel. Add a column showing the dollar value of the farmer's corn crop for each of the years and a column for the value of the soybean crop. See margin.

e. Write a short paragraph describing the values of the two crops over this 10-year period. See margin.

Additional Answers

59b. In B5: = 10200 + A5 * 100
In C5: = 6750 + A5 * 500

59c. in the 9th year

59d. See below

59e. This year the soybean crop is worth about twice the corn crop's value. Ten years from now, it will be worth about three times as much.

Additional Answers, continued

59d.

	A	B	C	D	E
1	yrs from now	bu. corn	bu. soybeans	corn value	soybean value
2	0	10200	6750	[$26520]	[$51975]
3	1	10300	7250	[$26780]	[$55825]
4	2	10400	7750	[$27040]	[$59675]
5	3	10500	8250	[$27300]	[$63525]
6	4	10600	8750	[$27560]	[$67375]
7	5	10700	9250	[$27820]	[$71225]
8	6	10800	9750	[$28080]	[$75075]
9	7	10900	10250	[$28340]	[$78925]
10	8	11000	10750	[$28600]	[$82775]
11	9	11100	11250	[$28860]	[$86625]
12	10	11200	11750	[$29120]	[$90475]

Additional Answers

60.
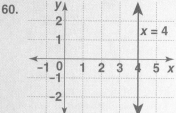

61.
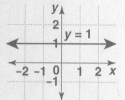

66b.
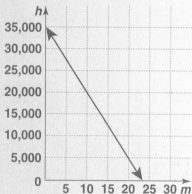

67.
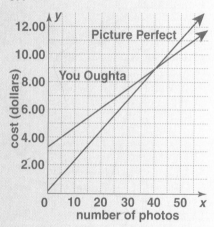

68a.
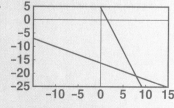

69.
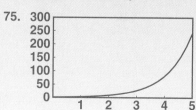

346

REPRESENTATIONS DEAL WITH PICTURES, GRAPHS, OR OBJECTS THAT ILLUSTRATE CONCEPTS.

Objective H: *Graph horizontal and vertical lines.* *(Lesson 5-1)*

In 60 and 61, graph the points in the coordinate plane satisfying each equation. **See margin.**

60. $x = 4$ **61.** $y = 1$

In 62 and 63, *true* or *false*.

62. The graph of all points in the plane satisfying $x = -0.4$ is a vertical line. **True**

63. The graph of all points in the plane satisfying $y = 73$ is a horizontal line. **True**

64. Write a sentence describing the line in the graph below. **See below.**

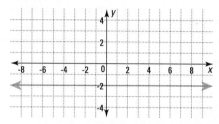

65. Write an equation for the line containing the points (5, 11), (5, 4), and (5, -7). $x = 5$

64) Sample: The graph contains all the solutions to $y = -2$.

Objective I: *Use graphs to solve problems involving linear expressions.* *(Lessons 5-1, 5-4)*

66. A plane is cruising at 35,000 feet when it begins its descent into the airport at 1500 feet per minute. a) $h = 35,000 - 1500m$

  a. Write an equation that relates the plane's height h and the time m since starting to descend. b) **See margin.**

  b. Graph your equation from part **a.**

  c. Use the graph to determine how many minutes it will take to land. ≈23 minutes

67. Picture Perfect will develop a roll of film for 22¢ a photo with no developing charge. You Oughta Be in Pictures charges 14¢ a photo plus a $3.20 developing charge. Make a graph to determine what number of photos would cost the same at both developers. **See margin.**

346

Objective J: *Given an equation, be able to use an automatic grapher to draw and interpret a graph.* *(Lesson 5-5)*

68. a. On an automatic grapher, graph the line $18x + 6y = 90$ using the window $-5 \le x \le 5$ and $-10 \le y \le 20$. **See margin.**

  b. For what values of x is $y > 0$? $x < 5$

69. On an automatic grapher draw the graphs of $y = -0.7x - 16.8$ and $y = -3.2x + 4.4$. Use the trace feature to determine what values of x make the following sentences true.

  a. $-0.7x - 16.8 = -3.2x + 4.4$ $x = 8.48$

  b. $-0.7x - 16.8 < -3.2x + 4.4$ $x < 8.48$

  c. $-0.7x - 16.8 > -3.2x + 4.4$ $x > 8.48$
    See margin for graph.   70) See below.

70. What is a *window* on an automatic grapher?

71. Use two inequalities to describe the window pictured below. $-5 \le x \le 15;\ -8 \le y \le 12$

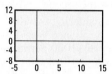

72. What does the trace command on an automatic grapher do? **See margin.**

In 73–75, use an automatic grapher. **See margin.**

73. Graph $y = x + 4$ on the window $-5 \le x \le 10$, $-10 \le y \le 15$. Trace to find the value of x for which $y = 0$. $x = -4$ when $y = 0$

74. a. Graph $y = x - 30$ on two different windows. **Answers may vary.**

  b. Describe what happened when you changed your window. **See margin.**

75. Graph $y = 3^x$ on the window $0 \le x \le 5$, $0 \le y \le 300$. Then use the trace key to solve the equation $3^x = 81$. $x = 4$

70) the visible portion of the coordinate grid

72. It moves the cursor along the graph and identifies the coordinates of the point it is on.

73.
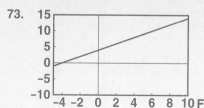

74b. Sample: A different part of the line may become visible, and the line may be less steep.

75.
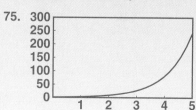

REFRESHER

Chapter 6, which discusses division in algebra, assumes that you have mastered certain objectives in your previous mathematics work. Use these questions to check your mastery. Do not use a calculator when it is easy to do the question without it. **See below for 1–4.**

A. Identify the **a.** divisor; **b.** dividend; and **c.** quotient in a division situation.

1. $21 \div 3 = 7$ **2.** $0.2 = 20 \div 100$

3. $\frac{56}{7} = 8$ **4.** $9\overline{)11.7}^{\,1.3}$

B. Divide positive numbers.

5. a. $40 \div 100$ 0.4   **b.** $100 \div 40$ 2.5

6. a. Divide 30 by $\frac{1}{2}$. 60   **b.** Divide $\frac{1}{2}$ by 30. $\frac{1}{60}$

7. a. What is $\frac{1}{4}$ divided by $\frac{1}{5}$? 1.25 or $\frac{5}{4}$

    b. What is $\frac{1}{5}$ divided by $\frac{1}{4}$? 0.8 or $\frac{4}{5}$

In 8–19, divide without using a calculator.

8. $7.2 \div 3$ 2.4   **9.** $80 \div 0.05$ 1600

10. $\frac{0.06}{0.3}$ 0.2   **11.** $\frac{6.8}{34}$ 0.2

12. $\frac{12}{7} \div \frac{2}{7}$ 6   **13.** $\frac{3}{5} \div \frac{3}{4}$ $\frac{4}{5}$

14. $\frac{2}{9} \div \frac{1}{3}$ $\frac{2}{3}$ **15.** $\frac{3}{2} \div \frac{4}{5}$ $1\frac{7}{8}$

16. 6 ft $\div$ 2 3 ft   **17.** 10 m $\div$ 4 2.5m

18. 100 kg $\div$ 7 $14\frac{2}{7}$ kg **19.** 6 lb $\div$ 25 0.24 lb

C. Divide positive and negative integers.

In 20–25, divide without using a calculator.

20. $-8 \div -4$ 2   **21.** $-40 \div 5$ -8

22. $60 \div -120$ $-\frac{1}{2}$ **23.** $2 \div -80$ -0.025

24. $\frac{-3}{-6}$ $\frac{1}{2}$ **25.** $\frac{400}{-4}$ -100

D. Convert any simple fraction to a decimal and percent.

In 26–28, give the decimal and percent equivalents.

26. $\frac{3}{4}$ **27.** $\frac{1}{40}$ **28.** $\frac{73}{100}$

0.75; 75%   0.025; 2.5%   0.73; 73%

1a) 3   b) 21   c) 7   2a) 100   b)20   c)0.2
3a) 7   b) 56   c) 8   4a) 9   b)11.7   c)1.3

In 29–31, write as a decimal. Round to the nearest hundredth.

29. $\frac{1}{7}$ 0.14   **30.** $\frac{20}{3}$ 6.67   **31.** $\frac{110}{17}$ 6.47

In 32–34, write as a percent. Round to the nearest whole percent.

32. $\frac{11}{5}$ 220%   **33.** $\frac{27}{100}$ 27%   **34.** $\frac{8}{9}$ 89%

E. Convert a percent to **a.** a decimal and **b.** a fraction. **See below for 35b–40b.**

35. 30% 0.3   **36.** 1% .01   **37.** 300% 3

38. 2.46%   **39.** .03%   **40.** $\frac{1}{4}$%
    0.0246   0.0003   0.0025

F. Find a percent of a number or quantity.

41. 32% of 750 240

42. 94% of 72 questions 68 questions

43. 7.3% of 40,296 voters 2942 voters

44. 100% of 12,000 square miles 12,000 mi^2

45. 0% of 60 0

46. 150% of $10,000 $15,000

G. Find the mean of a set of numbers.

47. 14, 9, 47, 17 21.75

48. 3, 3.1, -6, 0, 14, 5.5 3.267

H. Find the area of a circle.

49. What is the area of the circle shown? ≈ 78.54 cm^2

5 cm

50. Find the area of a circle with diameter 8 inches. ≈ 50.27 in^2

35b) $\frac{3}{10}$ 36b) $\frac{1}{100}$ 37b) $\frac{300}{100}$ 38b) $\frac{123}{5000}$
39b) $\frac{3}{10,000}$ 40b) $\frac{25}{10,000}$

Setting Up Lesson 6-1

We recommend that you assign Lesson 6-1, both reading and some questions, for homework the evening of the test. It gives students work to do after they have completed the test and keeps the class moving. If you do not do this consistently after tests, you may cover one less chapter over the course of the year.

Refresher

The Chapter 6 Refresher covers skills which have been previously taught to students. There are two ways you could use this Refresher. If you know that your students have a particularly weak background in division as it relates to algebra, you may want to assign these questions to better prepare them for Chapter 6. If you do not know what your students' backgrounds are, you can use this page as both a diagnostic tool and as remediation.

Have students do the odd-numbered questions as a part of the first assignment for the chapter, and check their answers with those given in the back of their books. If they missed more than a few questions, they should see you for help with the even-numbered questions.

Part A of the Refresher covers the language students are expected to know. Parts B and C involve ideas that will be reviewed in Lessons 6-1 and 6-2. Parts D, E, and F involve ideas that are used in Lessons 6-3 through 6-5. Part G involves division. Part H is applied in Lesson 6-6.

If you discuss the questions, find out how many students used a calculator and how many did the questions with paper and pencil. Point out that when an answer can be found mentally, students should try to do the computation without a calculator. Discuss Part A first because it presents language you can use when discussing the other questions. Remind students of the Equal Fractions Property (from Lesson 2-3), which implies that both the divisor and the dividend can be multiplied by the same number without affecting the quotient. **Questions 5–6:** Note that the answers to the two parts are reciprocals. **Questions 8–11:** Multiplying both the divisor and dividend by 10 or 100 makes it easy to find the answer mentally. **Question 12:** Multiply divisor and dividend by 7. **Questions 26–30:** No calculator is needed. **Questions 35–40:** No calculator is needed.

347

Chapter 6 Planner

Chapter 6 Pacing Chart

Day	Full Course	Minimal Course
1	6-1	6-1
2	6-2	6-2
3	6-3	6-3
4	6-4	6-4
5	Quiz*; 6-5	Quiz*; begin 6-5.
6	6-6	Finish 6-5.
7	6-7	6-6
8	Quiz*; 6-8	6-7
9	6-9	Quiz*; begin 6-8.
10	Self-Test	Finish 6-8.
11	Review	6-9
12	Test*	Self-Test
13	Comprehensive Test*	Review
14		Review
15		Test*
16		Comprehensive Test*

*in the Teacher's Resource File

Adapting to Individual Needs

The student text is written for the vast majority of students. The chart at the right suggests two pacing plans to accommodate the needs of your students. Students in the Full Course should complete the entire text by the end of the year. Students in the Minimal Course will spend more time when there are quizzes and more time on the Chapter Review. Therefore, these students may not complete all of the chapters in the text.

Options are also presented to meet the needs of a variety of teaching and learning styles. For each lesson, the Teacher's Edition provides sections entitled: *Video* which describes video segments and related questions that can be used for motivation or extension; *Optional Activities* which suggests activities that employ materials, physical models, technology, and cooperative learning; and, *Adapting to Individual Needs* which regularly includes **Challenge** problems, **English Language Development** suggestions, and suggestions for providing **Extra Help.** The Teacher's Edition also frequently includes an **Error Alert,** an **Extension,** and an **Assessment** alternative. The options available in Chapter 6 are summarized in the chart below.

In the Teacher's Edition...

Lesson	Optional Activities	Extra Help	Challenge	English Language Development	Error Alert	Extension	Cooperative Learning	Ongoing Assessment
6-1	●	●	●	●		●	●	Written
6-2	●	●	●	●		●	●	Written
6-3	●	●	●	●		●	●	Written/Oral
6-4	●	●	●	●		●	●	Written
6-5	●		●	●	●		●	Group
6-6	●	●		●	●	●	●	Oral/Written
6-7	●		●	●	●	●	●	Group
6-8	●	●	●	●	●	●	●	Group
6-9	●	●	●	●	●	●	●	Written

In the Additional Resources...

Lesson	In the Teacher's Resource File						Visual Aids**	Technology	Video Segments
	Lesson Masters, A and B	Teaching Aids*	Activity Kit*	Answer Masters	Technology Sourcebook	Assessment Sourcebook			
6-1	6-1	26, 57, 60		6-1	Calc 4		26, 57, 60, AM		
6-2	6-2	57		6-2			57, AM		
6-3	6-3	57	13	6-3			57, AM		
In-class Activity		61		6-4			61, AM		
6-4	6-4	58, 62		6-4	Comp 16	Quiz	58, 62, AM	StatExplorer	
6-5	6-5	58		6-5	Comp 17		58, AM	Spreadsheet	
6-6	6-6	58, 63–66	14	6-6			58, 63–66, AM		
6-7	6-7	28, 59, 67	15	6-7	Comp 18	Quiz	26, 59, 67, AM	GeoExplorer	
6-8	6-8	59		6-8			59, AM		
In-class Activity		26, 68		6-9			26, 68, AM		
6-9	6-9	59, 69, 70		6-9	Comp 19		59, 69, 70, AM	GeoExplorer	
End of chapter				Review		Tests			

*Teaching Aids are pictured on pages 350C and 350D. The activities in the Activity Kit are pictured on page 350C. Teaching Aid 61 which accompanies the In-class Activity preceding Lesson 6-4 is pictured with the lesson notes on page 368. Teaching Aid 68 which accompanies the In-class Activity preceding Lesson 6-9 is pictured with the lesson notes on page 401.

**Visual Aids provide transparencies for all Teaching Aids and all Answer Masters.

Also available is the Study Skills Handbook which includes study-skill tips related to reading, note-taking, and comprehension.

Integrating Strands and Applications

	6-1	6-2	6-3	6-4	6-5	6-6	6-7	6-8	6-9
Mathematical Connections									
Algebra	•	•	•		•		•	•	•
Geometry	•		•	•	•	•	•	•	•
Measurement	•	•			•	•		•	•
Logic and Reasoning								•	
Probability				•		•			•
Patterns and Functions		•	•	•			•		
Interdisciplinary and Other Connections									
Literature								•	
Science			•	•	•			•	•
Social Studies	•	•	•	•	•	•	•	•	
Multicultural	•							•	
Technology	•	•		•	•	•			•
Career			•	•	•	•	•		•
Consumer		•	•	•	•	•	•	•	•
Sports		•	•	•		•	•	•	

Teaching and Assessing the Chapter Objectives

Chapter 2 Objectives (Organized into the SPUR categories—Skills, Properties, Uses, and Representations)	Lessons	Progress Self-Test Questions	Chapter Review Questions	**In the Teacher's Resource File**		
				Chapter Test, Forms A and B	Chapter Test, Forms C	Chapter Test, Forms D
Skills						
A: Divide real numbers and algebraic fractions.	6-1	1–3, 10	1–10	1–3, 7	1	
B: Solve percent problems.	6-5	7, 8	11–16	14, 15	3	
C: Solve proportions.	6-8	4–6	17–22	4–6	2	
Properties						
D: Use the language of proportions and the Means-Extremes Property.	6-8	11	23–26	13	2	
Uses						
E: Use the Rate Model for Division.	6-2	16	27–34	8, 17		
F: Use ratios to compare two quantities.	6-3	13	35–40	9		
G: Calculate relative frequencies or probabilities in situations with a finite number of equally likely outcomes.	6-4	9, 17	41–50	11, 12	4	✓
H: Solve percent problems in real situations.	6-3, 6-5, 6-7	12, 15	51–58	16	3	✓
I: Solve problems involving proportions in real situations.	6-8, 6-9	19	59–64	21		✓
Representations						
J: Find probabilities involving geometric regions.	6-6	18, 23	65–69	10	4	
K: Apply the Size Change Model for Multiplication.	6-7	20, 21	70–76	20		
L: Find lengths and ratios of similitude in similar figures.	6-9	14, 22	77–83	18, 19	5	✓

Multidimensional Assessment
Quiz for Lessons 6-1 through 6-4
Quiz for Lessons 6-5 through 6-7

Chapter 6 Test, Forms A–D
Chapter 6 Test, Cumulative Form

Comprehensive Test, Chapters 1-6

Quiz and Test Writer
Multiple forms of chapter tests and quizzes; Challenges

Activity Kit

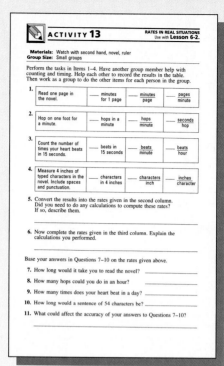

ACTIVITY 13
RATES IN REAL SITUATIONS
Use with **Lesson 6-2.**

Materials: Watch with second hand, novel, ruler
Group Size: Small groups

Perform the tasks in Items 1–4. Have another group member help with counting and timing. Help each other to record the results in the table. Then work as a group to do the other items for each person in the group.

1. Read one page in the novel.	____ minutes for 1 page	____ minutes page	____ pages minute
2. Hop on one foot for a minute.	____ hops in a minute	____ hops minute	____ seconds hop
3. Count the number of times your heart beats in 15 seconds.	____ beats in 15 seconds	____ beats minute	____ beats hour
4. Measure 4 inches of typed characters in the novel. Include spaces and punctuation.	____ characters in 4 inches	____ characters inch	____ inches character

5. Convert the results into the rates given in the second column. Did you need to do any calculations to compute these rates? If so, describe them. _____

6. Now complete the rates given in the third column. Explain the calculations you performed. _____

Base your answers in Questions 7–10 on the rates given above.

7. How long would it take you to read the novel? _____
8. How many hops could you do in an hour? _____
9. How many times does your heart beat in a day? _____
10. How long would a sentence of 54 characters be? _____
11. What could affect the accuracy of your answers to Questions 7–10? _____

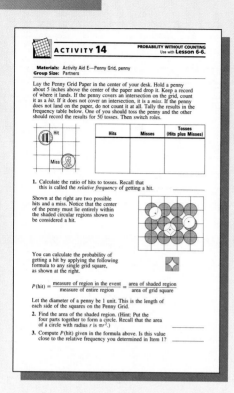

ACTIVITY 14
PROBABILITY WITHOUT COUNTING
Use with **Lesson 6-6.**

Materials: Activity Aid E—Penny Grid, penny
Group Size: Partners

Lay the Penny Grid Paper in the center of your desk. Hold a penny about 5 inches above the center of the paper and drop it. Keep a record of where it lands. If the penny covers an intersection on the grid, count it as a *hit*. If it does not cover an intersection, it is a *miss*. If the penny does not land on the paper, do not count it at all. Tally the results in the frequency table below. One of you should toss the penny and the other should record the results for 50 tosses. Then switch roles.

	Hits	Misses	Tosses (Hits plus Misses)

1. Calculate the ratio of hits to tosses. Recall that this is called the *relative frequency* of getting a hit. _____

Shown at the right are two possible hits and a miss. Notice that the center of the penny must lie entirely within the shaded circular regions shown to be considered a hit.

You can calculate the probability of getting a hit by applying the following formula to any single grid square, as shown at the right.

$$P(\text{hit}) = \frac{\text{measure of region in the event}}{\text{measure of entire region}} = \frac{\text{area of shaded region}}{\text{area of grid square}}$$

Let the diameter of a penny be 1 unit. This is the length of each side of the squares on the Penny Grid.

2. Find the area of the shaded region. (Hint: Put the four parts together to form a circle. Recall that the area of a circle with radius r is πr^2.)

3. Compute $P(\text{hit})$ given in the formula above. Is this value close to the relative frequency you determined in Item 1?

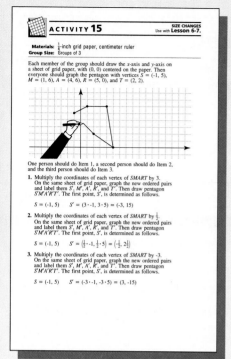

ACTIVITY 15
SIZE CHANGES
Use with **Lesson 6-7.**

Materials: $\frac{1}{4}$-inch grid paper, centimeter ruler
Group Size: Groups of 3

Each member of the group should draw the x-axis and y-axis on a sheet of grid paper, with (0, 0) centered on the paper. Then everyone should graph the pentagon with vertices $S = (-1, 5)$, $M = (1, 6)$, $A = (4, 6)$, $R = (5, 0)$, and $T = (2, 2)$.

One person should do Item 1, a second person should do Item 2, and the third person should do Item 3.

1. Multiply the coordinates of each vertex of *SMART* by 3. On the same sheet of grid paper, graph the new ordered pairs and label them S', M', A', R', and T'. Then draw pentagon $S'M'A'R'T'$. The first point, S', is determined as follows.

$S = (-1, 5)$ $S' = (3 \cdot -1, 3 \cdot 5) = (-3, 15)$

2. Multiply the coordinates of each vertex of *SMART* by $\frac{1}{2}$. On the same sheet of grid paper, graph the new ordered pairs and label them S', M', A', R', and T'. Then draw pentagon $S'M'A'R'T'$. The first point, S', is determined as follows.

$S = (-1, 5)$ $S' = \left(\frac{1}{2} \cdot -1, \frac{1}{2} \cdot 5\right) = \left(-\frac{1}{2}, 2\frac{1}{2}\right)$

3. Multiply the coordinates of each vertex of *SMART* by -3. On the same sheet of grid paper, graph the new ordered pairs and label them S', M', A', R', and T'. Then draw pentagon $S'M'A'R'T'$. The first point, S', is determined as follows.

$S = (-1, 5)$ $S' = (-3 \cdot -1, -3 \cdot 5) = (3, -15)$

Teaching Aids

Teaching Aid 26, Graph Paper, (shown on page 140D) can be used with **Lesson 6-1** and the In-class Activity preceding **Lesson 6-9**. Teaching Aid 28, Four-Quadrant Graph Paper, (shown on page 140D) can be used with **Lesson 6-7.**

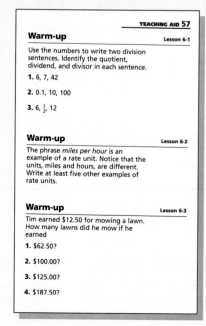

TEACHING AID 57

Warm-up Lesson 6-1

Use the numbers to write two division sentences. Identify the quotient, dividend, and divisor in each sentence.

1. 6, 7, 42
2. 0.1, 10, 100
3. 6, $\frac{1}{2}$, 12

Warm-up Lesson 6-2

The phrase *miles per hour* is an example of a rate unit. Notice that the units, miles and hours, are different. Write at least five other examples of rate units.

Warm-up Lesson 6-3

Tim earned $12.50 for mowing a lawn. How many lawns did he mow if he earned

1. $62.50?
2. $100.00?
3. $125.00?
4. $187.50?

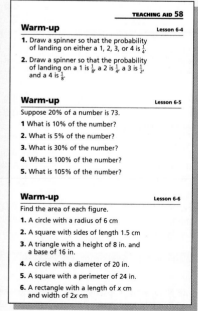

TEACHING AID 58

Warm-up Lesson 6-4

1. Draw a spinner so that the probability of landing on either a 1, 2, 3, or 4 is $\frac{1}{4}$.
2. Draw a spinner so that the probability of landing on a 1 is $\frac{1}{8}$, a 2 is $\frac{1}{4}$, a 3 is $\frac{1}{2}$, and a 4 is $\frac{1}{8}$.

Warm-up Lesson 6-5

Suppose 20% of a number is 73.

1 What is 10% of the number?
2. What is 5% of the number?
3. What is 30% of the number?
4. What is 100% of the number?
5. What is 105% of the number?

Warm-up Lesson 6-6

Find the area of each figure.

1. A circle with a radius of 6 cm
2. A square with sides of length 1.5 cm
3. A triangle with a height of 8 in. and a base of 16 in.
4. A circle with a diameter of 20 in.
5. A square with a perimeter of 24 in.
6. A rectangle with a length of x cm and width of $2x$ cm

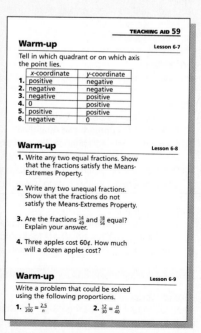

TEACHING AID 59

Warm-up Lesson 6-7

Tell in which quadrant or on which axis the point lies.

	x-coordinate	y-coordinate
1.	positive	negative
2.	negative	negative
3.	negative	positive
4.	0	positive
5.	positive	positive
6.	negative	0

Warm-up Lesson 6-8

1. Write any two equal fractions. Show that the fractions satisfy the Means-Extremes Property.
2. Write any two unequal fractions. Show that the fractions do not satisfy the Means-Extremes Property.
3. Are the fractions $\frac{14}{49}$ and $\frac{18}{56}$ equal? Explain your answer.
4. Three apples cost 60¢. How much will a dozen apples cost?

Warm-up Lesson 6-9

Write a problem that could be solved using the following proportions.

1. $\frac{1}{200} = \frac{2.5}{n}$ **2.** $\frac{12}{30} = \frac{n}{40}$

Question 34

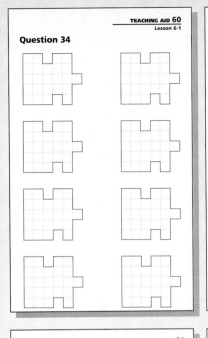

Relative Frequency and Probability

Relative Frequency	Probability
1. calculated from an experiment	1. deduced from assumptions (like randomness) or assumed to be close to some relative frequency
2. the ratio of the number of times an event has occurred to the number of times it could occur	2. if outcomes are equally likely, the ratio of the number of outcomes in an event to the total number of possible outcomes
3. 0 means that an event did not occur. 1 means the event occurred every time it could.	3. 0 means that an event is impossible. 1 means that an event is sure to happen.
4. The more often an event occurred relative to the number of times it could occur, the closer its relative frequency is to 1.	4. The more likely an event is, the closer its probability is to 1.
5. If the relative frequency of an event is r, then the relative frequency of its complement is 1 − r.	5. If the probability of an event is p, then the probability of its complement is 1 − p.

Examples 1–4

Example 1

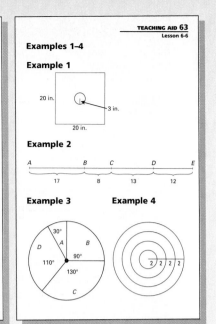

20 in.

3 in.

20 in.

Example 2

A   B   C   D   E

17   8   13   12

Example 3   **Example 4**

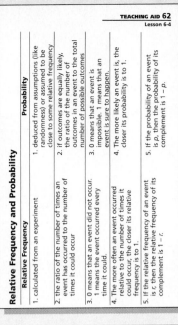

30°
D   A   B
90°
110°
130°
C

2 2 2 2

Additional Examples

1. A round dart board has a large bull's-eye of radius 5. The board has a radius of 15. If a dart lands randomly on any point of the board, what is the probability that it will land on the bull's eye?

2. The Roadrunner runs down a mile-long stretch of highway. He stops once at random. If the Roadrunner stops on the 100-foot section patrolled by the Coyote, the Coyote will chase him. What is the probability that this will happen?

3. A spinner is equally likely to land at any position on a dial. In the diagram at the right, what is the probability that it lands in region B? in region C or D?

30°
A / 40°
B
240°   C 50°
D

4. In the square at the right, everything outside the triangle has been shaded. If a point is chosen at random, what is the probability that it will lie in the shaded portion? (Remember that the area of a triangle = $\frac{1}{2}$ • base • height.)

9"

2.5"   4"   2.5"

Questions 11, 13 and 14

11.

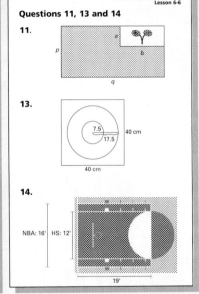

p

q

13.

7.5
17.5   40 cm

40 cm

14.

NBA: 16'   HS: 12'

19'

Challenge

Solve the following problem. A kidney-shaped swimming pool is located in a rectangular back yard. The sides of the pool consist of four connecting semicircles. A parachutist is hired to land in the back yard during a party. Assuming the parachutist lands somewhere in the back yard, what is the probability he or she will land on dry land?

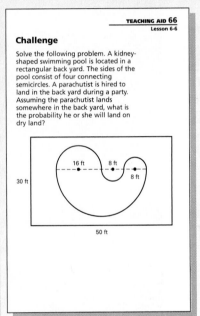

16 ft   8 ft
30 ft   8 ft

50 ft

Example 2

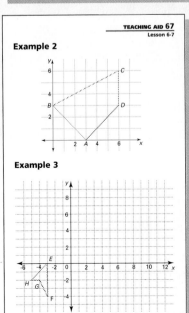
y
6   C
4
B   D
2

2 A 4   6   x

Example 3

y
8
6
4
2
-6 -4 -2 0   2   4   6   8 10 12 x
E
-2
H G
-4
F

Additional Examples

1. The quadrilaterals are similar with corresponding sides parallel.
   a. Find x and y.
   b. What are the two possible ratios of similitude for the figures?

D
x   G   J
6   7   M
4
E   15   F   K   y   L

2. A vase is sold in two sizes. The small vase is similar to the large vase. Find the height of the small vase.

11.7

5.2   4

Questions 8, 12 and 13

8.

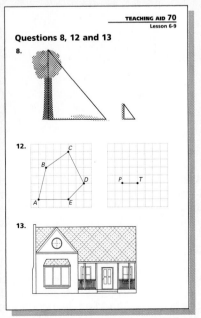

12.

C
B
D
A   E

P   T

13.

348D

Chapter Opener

Pacing

All of the lessons in this chapter are designed to be covered in one day. At the end of the chapter, you should plan to spend 1 day to review the Progress Self-Test, 1 to 2 days for the Chapter Review, and 1 day for a test. You may wish to spend a day on projects, and possibly a day is needed for quizzes. This chapter should therefore take 12 to 15 days. We strongly advise that you not spend more than 16 days on this chapter; there is ample opportunity to review ideas in later chapters.

Using Pages 348–349

After reading the introductory example on page 349, some students might jump to the conclusion that a rectangle whose area is divisible by 4 can be split into the T-shaped regions. You might consider the two rectangles below. The area of each is 48, and $\frac{48}{4} = 12$. The first rectangle can be split into 12 T-shaped regions as shown. The second rectangle cannot be split up in this manner. Students explore this idea in more detail in the *Extension* for Lesson 6-1 on page 355.

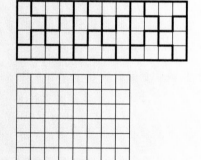

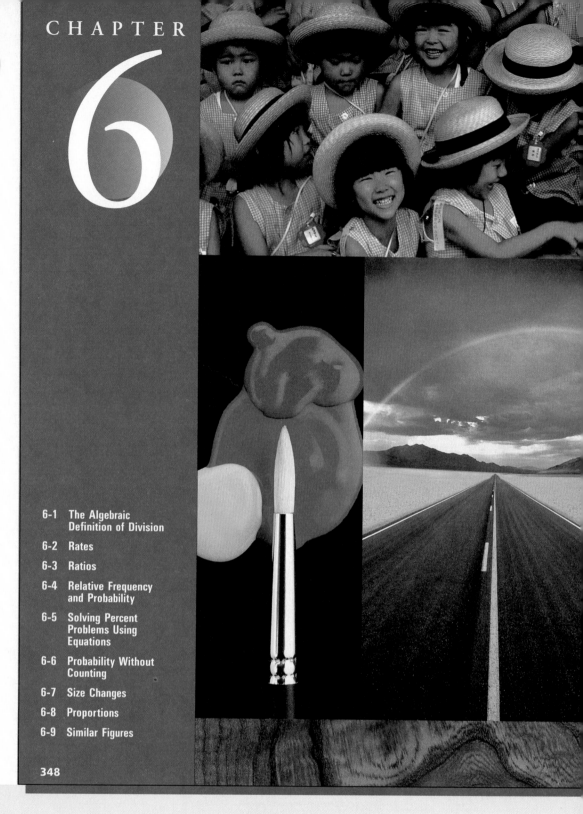

348

Chapter 6 Overview

This chapter uses properties, applications, and geometric representations, as well as skill development, to cover a broad range of mathematics that is centered on the algebra of division. It also concludes the study of the four fundamental operations of arithmetic.

The chapter starts by relating division to multiplication. This conceptualization of division from the standpoint of properties is followed by two models for division: rate and ratio. The rate model helps to explain the division of positive and negative numbers. The ratio model finds immediate applications to probability, relative frequency, and percent.

The last three lessons of the chapter have direct connections to geometry. The Size Change Model for Multiplication, when pictured on the coordinate plane, gives rise to proportions and to similar figures.

Proportions may involve either the equality of rates or the equality of ratios, thus uniting the end of the chapter with the topics at the beginning of the chapter.

The introductory example on page 349 illustrates what is sometimes called the Splitting Up Model of Division. This idea is used when an item, or set of items, is divided into parts of equal size. Determining how many T-shaped pieces are needed in the example

DIVISION IN ALGEBRA

When manufacturers cut sheets of metal or wood or paper, they try to minimize the waste and cost of leftover material. Mathematicians are also concerned about minimizing waste. Consider this problem.

Can the 6-by-7 rectangle on the left below be split into little regions of the T shape shown with no squares left over?

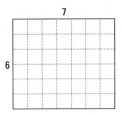

You could try to solve this problem by using trial and error. Shown below is a start that leads to a situation which does *not* work. But maybe the start was wrong.

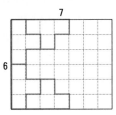

There is another way to examine the problem. The area of the rectangle is 42 square units. The area of the T-shaped region is 4 square units. If the rectangle can be cut into these T-shapes, there will be $\frac{42}{4}$, or $10\frac{1}{2}$ T-shaped regions. Since the number of regions must be a whole number, no attempt at splitting the rectangle will work.

When you first studied division you answered questions about splitting objects into equal parts with no "leftovers." In this chapter, you will extend this idea of division to other uses, including applications to rates, ratios, percents, probability, and similarity.

Photo Connections
The photo collage makes real-world connections to the content of the chapter: extending the idea of partitive division to applications such as rates, ratios, proportions, and probability.

Japanese Children: In 1992, the population of Japan was estimated at 124,460,000 people. The area of Japan is 145,856 square miles. The Rate Model for Division can be used to calculate the population density which is about 850 people per square mile.

Paints: Manufacturers, hardware-store employees, and artists use the Ratio Model for Division to mix the colors of paints.

Highway: When using a map, you can determine the distance between cities by using proportions.

Dart Board: The probability of a dart landing in the given section of a regulation dart board can be calculated using the Probability Formula for Geometric Regions.

Wood: As an industry, lumber and wood products accounted for 25.6 billion dollars worth of business in the United States in 1989. It is easy to see why manufacturers are concerned about minimizing waste and maximizing usage.

Chapter 6 Projects
At this time you might want to have students look over the projects on pages 408–409.

349

requires splitting an area of 42 square units into pieces that are each 4 square units. This is an instance of the Ratio Model for Division:

$$\frac{42 \text{ square units}}{4 \text{ square units}} = 10\frac{1}{2}$$

Utilizing the Rate Factor Model of Multiplication is another possible interpretation of this problem.

Since $10\frac{1}{2}$ pieces $\cdot$ $4 \frac{\text{square units}}{\text{piece}} = 42$ square units, it is also the case that

$$\frac{42 \text{ square units}}{4 \frac{\text{square units}}{\text{piece}}} = 10\frac{1}{2} \text{ pieces.}$$

Some researchers call this interpretation the *Measurement Model for Division* because the $10\frac{1}{2}$ tells how many times the 4 fits into 42.

Lesson 6-1

Objectives
A Divide real numbers and algebraic fractions.

Resources

From the Teacher's Resource File
■ Lesson Master 6-1A or 6-1B
■ Answer Master 6-1
■ Teaching Aids
  26 Graph Paper
  57 Warm-up
  60 Question 34
■ Technology Sourcebook
  Calculator Master 4

Additional Resources
■ Visuals for Teaching Aids 26, 57, 60

Teaching Lesson 6-1

Warm-up

Use the numbers to write two division sentences. Identify the quotient, dividend, and divisor in each sentence.

1. 6, 7, 42
  $42 \div 6 = 7$; quotient: 7; dividend: 42; divisor: 6;
  $42 \div 7 = 6$; quotient: 6; dividend: 42; divisor: 7

2. 0.1, 10, 100
  $10 \div 0.1 = 100$; quotient: 100; dividend: 10; divisor: 0.1;
  $10 \div 100 = 0.1$; quotient: 0.1; dividend: 10; divisor: 100

LESSON 6-1

The Algebraic Definition of Division

Appealing fruit. *Shown is an orange grove in Australia. New South Wales and South Australia produce most of the country's oranges. Although Australia is not a leading producer of oranges, citrus fruit is grown there.*

The Relation Between Division and Multiplication

Abe divided a quart of orange juice equally among his five children.
❶ How many ounces of orange juice did each child receive?

This question can be answered by either division or multiplication. Either way, you must change 1 quart to 32 ounces. You can view Abe's problem as dividing 32 ounces among 5 children,

$$32 \div 5 = 6.4,$$

or as giving each child $\frac{1}{5}$ of the orange juice,

$$32 \cdot \frac{1}{5} = 6.4.$$

Both ways the answer is the same, 6.4 ounces. Dividing by 5 is the same as multiplying by $\frac{1}{5}$. In general, dividing by b is the same as multiplying by its reciprocal $\frac{1}{b}$.

Algebraic Definition of Division
For any real numbers a and b, $b \neq 0$,

$$a \div b = a \cdot \frac{1}{b}.$$

Recall that $a \div b$ can also be written as $\frac{a}{b}$ or a/b. So if $b \neq 0$,

$$a \div b = \frac{a}{b} = a/b = a \cdot \frac{1}{b}.$$

The Algebraic Definition of Division allows any division situation to be converted to multiplication. For instance, consider the division of fractions $\frac{a}{b} \div \frac{c}{d}$. According to the Algebraic Definition of Division, dividing by $\frac{c}{d}$ is the same as multiplying by its reciprocal $\frac{d}{c}$.

$$\frac{a}{b} \div \frac{c}{d} = \frac{a}{b} \cdot \frac{d}{c}.$$

For example, $\frac{5}{2} \div \frac{9}{7} = \frac{5}{2} \cdot \frac{7}{9} = \frac{35}{18}$. This is sometimes called the "invert and multiply" rule. Algebraic fractions are divided in the same way.

350

Lesson 6-1 Overview

Broad Goals The broad goal of this lesson is for students to see the algebraic definition of division used in three contexts: division of fractions, division of positive and negative numbers, and division of both sides of an equation by the same number.

Perspective The structure of Lesson 6-1, which relates multiplication and division, parallels that of Lesson 4-1, which relates addition and subtraction. In Lesson 4-1, the algebraic definition of subtraction was given as adding the opposite. This definition gave us a method for subtracting integers. The algebraic definition of division—multiplication by the reciprocal—provides the rationale for division of fractions and also for division of positive and negative numbers.

Stress that every division can be converted to a multiplication. However, just as with subtraction and addition, not every property of multiplication is a property of division. For instance, division is not commutative.

The discussion on page 350 shows that a division can be interpreted as a multiplication. The uses are instances of the Rate Model for Division and the Size Change Model for Multiplication.

Dividing Algebraic Fractions

Example 1

Simplify $\frac{x}{5} \div \frac{3}{4}$.

Solution

Dividing by $\frac{3}{4}$ is the same as multiplying by $\frac{4}{3}$.

$$\frac{x}{5} \div \frac{3}{4} = \frac{x}{5} \cdot \frac{4}{3} = \frac{4x}{15}$$

Check

Substitute some value for x. Use this number to evaluate the original expression and your answer. Suppose $x = 2$. Does $\frac{2}{5} \div \frac{3}{4} = \frac{4 \cdot 2}{15}$? To determine this, change each fraction to a decimal. Does $0.4 \div 0.75 = \frac{8}{15}$? Yes, each side equals $0.5\overline{3}$.

Dividing Complex Fractions

Recall that a fraction bar also indicates division. In the next example, there are three fractions. One is the numerator and the second is the denominator of a third "bigger" fraction. Fractions of the form $\frac{\frac{a}{b}}{\frac{c}{d}}$ are called **complex fractions.** To simplify a complex fraction, first rewrite the complex fraction as an expression using division.

Example 2

Simplify $\dfrac{\frac{7\pi}{3}}{-\frac{\pi}{21}}$ and check your answer.

Solution

Rewrite the fraction using division. Then use the Algebraic Definition of Division to rewrite using multiplication.

$$\frac{7\pi}{3} \div -\frac{\pi}{21} = \frac{7\pi}{3} \cdot -\frac{21}{\pi}$$

Now, use the Multiplying Fractions Property.

$$= \frac{7\overset{1}{\cancel{\pi}}}{\underset{1}{\cancel{3}}} \cdot -\frac{\overset{7}{\cancel{21}}}{\underset{1}{\cancel{\pi}}}$$

$$= -49$$

❷ For the check, use a calculator. Notice how we are careful to use parentheses to group the numerator and denominator separately.

$\underbrace{(\ 7\ \times\ \pi\ \div\ 3\ )}_{\text{numerator}} \div \underbrace{(\ \pi\ \pm\ \div\ 21\ )}_{\text{denominator}} =$

---

3. $6, \frac{1}{2}, 12$

$6 \div \frac{1}{2} = 12$; quotient: 12;
dividend: 6; divisor: $\frac{1}{2}$;
$6 \div 12 = \frac{1}{2}$: quotient: $\frac{1}{2}$;
dividend: 6; divisor: 12

In general, students see that if $a \div b = c$, then $a = bc$ and $a \div c = b$.

Notes on Reading

❶ The introductory example shows that a division can be interpreted as a multiplication. This is more easily seen when the units are attached to the numbers: $32 \div 5$ is the rate $\frac{32 \text{ ounces}}{5 \text{ children}} = 6.4 \frac{\text{ounces}}{\text{child}}$. The product $32 \cdot \frac{1}{5}$ is the quantity 32 ounces multiplied by the size change factor $\frac{1}{5}$ and $\frac{1}{5} \cdot 32$ ounces $= 6.4$ ounces.

❷ Students can check **Example 2** by using the Equal Fractions

Property: $\dfrac{\frac{7\pi}{3}}{-\frac{\pi}{21}} \cdot \frac{21}{21} = \frac{49\pi}{-\pi} = -49.$

In general, $\dfrac{\frac{a}{b}}{\frac{c}{d}} = \dfrac{\frac{a}{b}}{\frac{c}{d}} \cdot \frac{bd}{bd} = \frac{ad}{bc}.$

Examples 1 and 2 should look similar to problems that students have seen in earlier work with arithmetic, except that each example has an algebraic twist. **Example 1** uses variables, while **Example 2** has a negative number and the number π, which looks like a variable for many students.

Example 3 uses division to solve an equation and contrasts the multiplication approach with the division approach. From now on, we will use either method. (With fractions, multiplication is usually easier; with non-integer decimals, division is usually easier; with integers, either method works.) We do not consider solving equations by using division to be a key objective of the lesson; it is simply an alternate method that many people use.

Additional Examples

1. Simplify $\frac{2n}{5} \div \frac{10n}{7}$. $\frac{7}{25}$
2. Simplify each complex fraction.

   a. $\frac{\frac{x}{6}}{\frac{5}{x}}$ $\frac{x^2}{30}$ **b.** $\frac{\frac{4xy}{11}}{22x}$ $\frac{2y}{121}$

3. Solve and check: $2.3w = 18.4$.
   $w = 8$ Check: Does $2.3 \cdot 8 = 18.4$? $18.4 = 18.4$? Yes. It checks.

In Example 2, a positive number is divided by a negative number. The divisor is replaced by its reciprocal when converting the division into a multiplication. Since a number and its reciprocal have the same sign, the signs of answers to division problems follow the same rules as those for multiplication. This is why the answer to Example 2 is negative.

If two numbers have the same + or − sign, their quotient is positive. If two numbers have different signs, their quotient is negative.

Notice that in Example 2, the negative sign is written in front of the fraction, $-\frac{\pi}{21}$. The rules of division tell us that the negative sign could also have been in the numerator or in the denominator without altering the value. This means that

$$-\frac{\pi}{21} = \frac{-\pi}{21} = \frac{\pi}{-21}.$$

In general, for all a and b, $b \neq 0$,

$$-\frac{a}{b} = \frac{-a}{b} = \frac{a}{-b}.$$

Solving Equations Using Division

The Algebraic Definition of Division leads to another method for solving equations of the form $ax = b$. In the first solution of Example 3, both sides of the equation are multiplied by $-\frac{1}{31}$. This is the same as dividing by -31, as shown in the second solution.

Example 3

Solve $-31m = 527$.

Solution 1

$$-31m = 527$$
$$-\frac{1}{31} \cdot -31m = -\frac{1}{31} \cdot 527 \quad \text{Multiply both sides by } -\frac{1}{31}.$$
$$m = -\frac{527}{31}$$
$$m = -17$$

Solution 2

$$-31m = 527$$
$$\frac{-31m}{-31} = \frac{527}{-31} \quad \text{Divide both sides by -31.}$$
$$m = -17$$

Check

Substitute -17 for m. Does $-31(-17) = 527$? Yes. It checks.

Both methods of Example 3 are acceptable.

Optional Activities

Activity 3 Technology Connection
Explain the difference between *integer division* and *real number division*. The division studied throughout this book is *real number division*. Suppose $a = 32$ and $b = 5$. In real number division, $a \div b$ is a single number (6.4). In early grades, students encounter integer division in which $a \div b$ is a pair of integers; one is called the quotient and the other is called the remainder (32 ÷ 5 has quotient 6 and remainder 2).

If you have students who are familiar with the INT function in BASIC, you can ask them to write a program that accepts the dividend and divisor of a division problem as input and prints the quotient (under integer division) with the remainder. For instance, the computer should print "25/7 = 3 WITH REMAINDER 4." A program that accomplishes this is shown at the right.

```
10 PRINT "THIS PROGRAM WILL DO THE
   INTEGER DIVISION A/B WHEN A AND
   B ARE POSITIVE."
20 INPUT "ENTER THE VALUE OF A.";A
30 INPUT "ENTER THE VALUE OF B.";B
40 PRINT
50 PRINT A; "/";B;"=";INT(A/B);"WITH
   REMAINDER";A – INT(A/B)*B
```

Covering the Reading

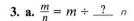

The United States produces about 18% of the world's annual orange harvest, or about 15.5 billion pounds of oranges.

1. Suppose Abe had divided a quart of orange juice equally among his five children *and himself.* Show two ways to determine how many ounces of orange juice each person received.
$32 \div 6 = 5.\overline{3}$; $\quad 32 \cdot (1/6) = 5.\overline{3}$ ounces

2. State the Algebraic Definition of Division.
For any real numbers a and b, $b \neq 0$, $a \div b = a \cdot \frac{1}{b}$.

In 3 and 4, fill in the blanks.

3. **a.** $\frac{m}{n} = m \div \underline{\ ?\ }$ $\quad n$ **b.** $\frac{m}{n} = m \cdot \underline{\ ?\ }$ $\quad \frac{1}{n}$

4. **a.** $\frac{\frac{p}{q}}{\frac{r}{s}} = \frac{p}{q} \div \underline{\ ?\ }$ $\quad \frac{r}{s}$ **b.** $\frac{p}{q} \div \frac{r}{s} = \frac{p}{q} \cdot \underline{\ ?\ }$ $\quad \frac{s}{r}$

In 5–10, simplify.

5. $\frac{\frac{3}{4}}{-\frac{4}{5}}$ $\quad -\frac{15}{16}$ 6. $\frac{\frac{x}{4}}{-\frac{4}{y}}$ $\quad -\frac{xy}{16}$

7. $\frac{5}{6} \div \frac{n}{10}$ $\quad \frac{25}{3n}$ 8. $-\frac{12\pi}{5} \div \frac{\pi}{4}$ $\quad -\frac{48}{5}$

9. $1\frac{2}{3} \div 3\frac{1}{3}$ $\quad \frac{1}{2}$ 10. $\frac{\frac{3\pi}{5}}{\frac{6}{\pi}}$ $\quad \frac{\pi^2}{10}$

11. Suppose you are asked to solve $-3j = -48$ in one major step.
a. By what could you multiply both sides? $-\frac{1}{3}$
b. By what could you divide both sides? -3

12. *Multiple choice.* Which of these expressions is *not* equivalent to the others? c
(a) $\frac{-7}{2}$ (b) $-\frac{7}{2}$ (c) $\frac{-7}{-2}$ (d) $\frac{7}{-2}$

13. Round to the nearest thousandth.
a. $\frac{-3}{11}$ $\;-0.273$ **b.** $\frac{3}{-11}$ $\;-0.273$ **c.** $-\frac{3}{11}$ $\;-0.273$

14. Generalize the idea of Questions 12 and 13 using two variables.
$\frac{-a}{b} = -\frac{a}{b} = \frac{a}{-b}$

In 15–20, solve.

15. $-143 = 13x$ $\;-11$ 16. $-1.5q = -75$ $\;50$

17. $2.5k = -0.7$ $\;-0.28$ 18. $-1900 = -0.2n$ $\;9500$

19. $\frac{2}{3}t = \frac{5}{6}$ $\;\frac{5}{4}$ 20. $3x = -\frac{5}{3}$ $\;-\frac{5}{9}$

Run the program using the following pairs: A = 25, B = 7; A = 32, B = 5; A = 32, B = 2; A = 10, B = 10. In each case, ask the students to predict the output before running the program. Then ask them what they predict the output to be when A = 10, B = 20 are input. [The real number division $\frac{10}{20} = \frac{1}{2}$. The integer division should be 0 with remainder 10.]

At least one calculator on the market does this kind of integer division.

Notes on Questions

Questions 5–6 These are examples of complex fractions that might look intimidating. This in itself increases the difficulty of the questions. However, rewriting the division using the ÷ sign results in an expression that will be familiar to students. Explain that the ability to write a fraction as a division (and vice versa) gives a second way to think about division; thus, it is quite beneficial.

Question 9 If students need a hint, tell them that the first step is to convert the mixed numbers to fractions.

Question 13 Once students have done **part a**, **parts b and c** should require no additional computation except, perhaps, to check what a calculator might do.

Question 15 Ask students to give two ways to solve the equation. Note the equivalence of multiplying by $\frac{1}{13}$ and dividing by 13. Also note that each method is equally easy.

Questions 16–17 For these questions, students might prefer dividing both sides of the equation by the same number rather than multiplying by the reciprocal of the coefficient of the unknown.

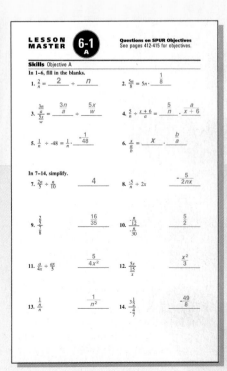

Notes on Questions

Question 23 This question should be interpreted as $\frac{1}{2} \div 3$ and then converted to the multiplication $\frac{1}{2} \cdot \frac{1}{3}$. Students might draw a picture to verify that $\frac{1}{6}$ is the correct answer.

Question 30 At some point, students might divide both sides by 1.06.

Question 31 Note that students will have to use trial and error to find n.

Question 32 Geography Connection Lake Tanganyika is the longest freshwater lake in the world. It is 410 miles long and varies in width from 10 to 45 miles.

Question 33 Be sure that students understand how to do this question; problems involving areas of circles will appear throughout the chapter.

Question 34 Cooperative Learning This question is appropriate for **small group work**. The diagram is shown on **Teaching Aid 60**. Students should first count to determine the area of the region (24 square units). Then they should divide the 24 square units by 6 to determine the area of each congruent piece. Finally, students have to think about the possible shapes that can have an area of 4 square units.

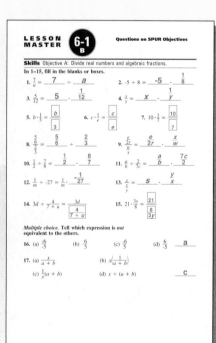

354

Applying the Mathematics

21. Le Parfum Company produces perfume in 200-ounce batches and bottles it in quarter-ounce bottles. Suppose you want to know how many bottles will be filled by a batch.
    a. Write a division problem that will tell you. $200 \div \frac{1}{4}$
    b. Find the answer. **800**

22. A gallon of milk was divided equally among x people. How many ounces did each person receive? $\frac{128}{x}$

23. Half of a pizza was divided equally among 3 people. How much of the original pizza did each person receive? $\frac{1}{6}$

In 24 and 25, simplify.

24. $b \div \frac{1}{b}$ b^2

25. $\frac{xy}{21} \div \frac{x}{4y}$ $\frac{4y^2}{21}$

26. a. Evaluate $x \div y$ and $y \div x$ for each of the following.
    i. $x = 12$ and $y = 2$ $6; \ \frac{1}{6}$
    ii. $x = 20$ and $y = -5$ $-4; \ -\frac{1}{4}$
    iii. $x = \frac{2}{3}$ and $y = \frac{4}{5}$ $\frac{5}{6}; \ \frac{6}{5}$
    b. Does your answer to part **a** indicate that division is commutative? Explain. **No, the answers are different.**
    c. Describe how $x \div y$ and $y \div x$ are related in general. $x \div y = \frac{1}{y \div x}$

27. In 1577, Guillaume Gosselin published a book titled *De Arte Magna*. It contained some of the first work on positive and negative numbers. It was written in Latin. Here are some rules Gosselin wrote. Translate these rules into English. **See left.**
    a. P in P diviso quotus est P.   b. M in M diviso quotus est P.
    c. M in P diviso quotus est M.   d. P in M diviso quotus est M.

Scents for cents. *The cost of one ounce of perfume can range from $150 to over $300. The cost of one ounce of cologne can range from $25 to over $40.*

27a) A positive number divided by a positive number is positive.
b) A negative number divided by a negative number is positive.
c) A negative number divided by a positive number is negative.
d) A positive number divided by a negative number is negative.

Review

28. A $100 investment grows at 7% interest annually for 5 years. The interest is added to the investment each year. The value of the investment at the end of each year is shown in the table below. *(Lesson 4-2)*

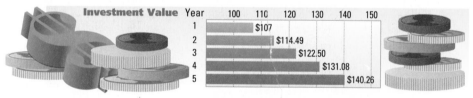

Investment Value

Year	Value
1	$107
2	$114.49
3	$122.50
4	$131.08
5	$140.26

    a. How much did the investment grow in value between years 2 and 3? **$8.01**
    b. In what year is the growth in the investment the largest? **year 5**

Adapting to Individual Needs

Extra Help
If some students consistently find quotients that are the opposite of the correct quotient, they might be mixing the ideas of reciprocals and opposites. Review the meaning of *reciprocal*. Note that the product of any number and its reciprocal must be positive 1; two numbers must have the same sign in order to have a positive product.

English Language Development
Discuss the words *simple* and *complex* by giving illustrations of easy and hard tasks. Explain that the numerator and denominator of simple fractions are integers—easy numbers with which to work; the numerator and denominator of complex fractions are fractions—harder numbers with which to work. Have students add *complex fractions*, *the algebraic definition of division*, *reciprocal*, and *quotient* to their card files.

29. Use the picture of a balance scale below. The cylinders are equal in weight and the balls are one-kilogram weights. *(Lesson 3-5)*

a. Write an equation describing the situation with B representing the weight of one cylinder. **$3B + 2 = 10$**
b. What is the weight of one cylinder? **$2\frac{2}{3}$ kg**

30. Solve $V + 0.06V + 100 = 14,289.16$. *(Lessons 3-5, 3-6)* **13,386**

31. If $100 < n! < 200$, find n. *(Lesson 2-10)* **5**

32. Let $y =$ the depth of a point in Lake Tanganyika in Africa, the second deepest lake in the world.
a. Give a reasonable domain for y. **$y \le 0$**
b. It is known that the deepest point in Lake Tanganyika is 1470 meters below the surface of the lake. What inequality does y satisfy? **$-1470 \le y \le 0$**
c. Graph the solution set to part **b.** *(Lesson 1-2)* **See left.**

32c)

-1470

-1500 500 0 500

33. A circle has a radius of 1.2 m. Find its area to the nearest tenth of a square meter. *(Previous course)* **4.5 m²**

Longest lake, too. *These fishermen prepare their net for fishing on Lake Tanganyika. With a length of 680 km, it is the longest freshwater lake in the world.*

Exploration

34. Congruent figures are figures with the same size and shape. Split this region into 6 congruent pieces.

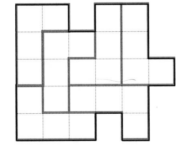

Lesson 6-1 *The Algebraic Definition of Division* **355**

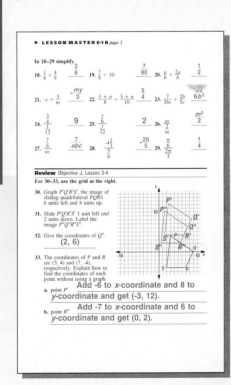

Adapting to Individual Needs

Challenge
Have students simplify.

1. $\dfrac{\frac{1}{2}}{\frac{1}{3}} \quad \dfrac{1}{\frac{1}{4}} \quad \dfrac{1}{5}$ $\left[\frac{6}{5}\right]$

2. $\dfrac{\frac{5}{8}}{\frac{11}{16}} \quad \dfrac{2}{\frac{11}{5}} \quad \dfrac{5}{8}$ $\left[\frac{25}{8}\right]$

3. $\dfrac{\frac{a}{b}}{\frac{c}{d}} \quad \dfrac{e}{\frac{f}{g}} \quad \dfrac{g}{h}$ $\left[\frac{adfg}{bceh}\right]$

Setting Up Lesson 6-2

Materials If you use the *Assessment* on page 361, students will need food packages that show the number of servings and the price. Students doing *Activity 1* in *Optional Activities* on page 357 will need almanacs. *Activity 2* on page 358 requires newspapers or supermarket ads that can be used to compare costs. You will need a stopwatch or a watch with a second hand for *Extra Help* on page 359.

355

Objectives

E Use the Rate Model for Division.

Resources

From the Teacher's Resource File
- Lesson Master 6-2A or 6-2B
- Answer Master 6-2
- Teaching Aid 57: Warm-up
- Activity Kit, Activity 13

Additional Resources
- Visual for Teaching Aid 57
- Food packages, each showing the number of servings and the cost

Teaching Lesson 6-2

Warm-up

The phrase *miles per hour* is an example of a rate unit. Notice that the units, miles and hours, are different. Write at least five other examples of rate units. **Samples: miles per gallon, price per pound, cards per box, students per class, bushels per acre**

LESSON

6-2

Rates

Southwest is Key West. *Shown is part of the Old Town section of Key West, a popular resort town about 100 miles southwest of the Florida mainland.*

Situations involving splitting up can lead to rates. If 100 tickets are split up evenly among 4 people, then there are

$$\frac{100 \text{ tickets}}{4 \text{ people}} = \frac{25 \text{ tickets}}{\text{person}}.$$

The result is a *rate,* like the ones you multiplied in Lesson 2-4.

The situation above is an instance of the *Rate Model for Division.*

❶ Rate Model for Division
If a and b are quantities with different units, then $\frac{a}{b}$ is the amount of quantity a per quantity b.

The rate model says that if you are not given a rate, you can calculate one using division.

Using Division to Calculate Rates

Example 1

Ivan and Katya drove from Key West to Tampa, Florida, a trip of 400 miles. The trip took 8 hours. What was their average rate?

Solution 1

❷ Divide the distance in miles by the time in hours.

$$\frac{400 \text{ miles}}{8 \text{ hours}}$$

Separate the measurement units from the numerical parts.

$$\frac{400 \text{ miles}}{8 \text{ hours}} = \frac{400}{8} \frac{\text{miles}}{\text{hours}}$$
$$= 50 \text{ miles per hour}$$

Their average rate was 50 miles per hour.

Lesson 6-2 Overview

Broad Goals The goal of this lesson is to introduce, or to review (for students who have had *Transition Mathematics*), how positive and negative rates are calculated.

Perspective The Rate Model for Division summarizes an exceedingly important application of this operation. From the early splitting-up problems of grade school through calculus and beyond, rate is a fundamental idea. **Examples 1–4** show

only a few of the many arithmetic situations to which this idea applies. The rate model is applied repeatedly in this book. For instance, in the next chapter the rate model is utilized to become rate of change, which is slope. Students have already been *using* rates in problems that involve rate-factor multiplication, but then the rates were given. Here the emphasis is on *finding* the rate. Because rates are meaningless without units, insist that the students show them.

The rate model is used in the paragraph between **Example 4** and **Example 5** to explain why dividing by zero is impossible. This confirms the results that were found using properties of multiplication in Lesson 2-2. The rate model can also explain why $\frac{0}{b} = 0$ when $b \neq 0$: if you drive zero miles in b hours, then your rate is zero miles per hour.

Is the marker correct?
Yes. Hawaii is farther south than Key West, but Hawaii is not part of the continental U.S.A.

▶ **Solution 2**

You could also divide the time by the distance.

$$\frac{8 \text{ hours}}{400 \text{ miles}} = \frac{8}{400} \frac{\text{hours}}{\text{miles}}$$

$$= \frac{1}{50} \text{ hour per mile}$$

This means that, on the average, it took them $\frac{1}{50}$ of an hour to travel each mile.

The first solution gives the rate in *miles per hour*. You are familiar with the meaning of this rate from speed limit signs or from the speedometer in a car. The second solution gives the rate in *hours per mile,* or how long it takes to travel one mile. Notice that $\frac{1}{50}$ of an hour is $\frac{1}{50} \cdot 60$ minutes, or 1.2 minutes. In other words, it takes a little over a minute to go one mile. Either rate is correct. The one to use depends on the situation in which you use it.

Averages can also be thought of as rates.

Example 2

In 1991, total medical costs in the United States were about $728,600,000,000. That year the population was about 252,700,000. What was the average cost per person for medical care?

Solution

This situation should prompt you to find dollars per person. To get this rate, divide the total spent by the number of people.

$$\frac{728,600,000,000 \text{ dollars}}{252,700,000 \text{ people}} = \frac{728,600,000,000}{252,700,000} \frac{\text{dollars}}{\text{people}}$$

$$\approx 2883 \text{ dollars/person}$$

In 1991 the average cost per person for medical care was about $2883.

In dividing by a rate, the arithmetic of units follows the Algebraic Definition of Division.

Example 3

Alice reads $12 \frac{\text{pages}}{\text{day}}$. At this rate how long will it take her to read a book that is 190 pages long?

Solution

Think of splitting up the 190 pages into chunks of $12 \frac{\text{pages}}{\text{day}}$.

$$\frac{190 \text{ pages}}{12 \frac{\text{pages}}{\text{day}}} = 190 \text{ pages} \cdot \frac{1}{12} \frac{\text{day}}{\text{page}} = \frac{190}{12} \text{ days} = 15.8\overline{3} \text{ days}$$

It will take her about 16 days.

Lesson 6-2 *Rates* **357**

Notes on Reading

❶ Emphasize that if one quantity is divided by another, and the units are different, the quotient is a rate. Rates may be positive or negative (or zero).

❷ Ivan and Katya's rate could be found by using the formula $d = rt$ and solving an equation, but the emphasis here is purposely on the Rate Model for Division.

❸ For many students, rate means speed; so **Example 1** seems to be naturally named. Students may not recognize **Examples 2–4** as rates. Explain that the word *per* can be used whenever there is a rate.

Optional Activities

Activity 1 Sports Connection
Materials: Almanacs

An almanac is a good source of sports statistics, many of which lend themselves to comparing rates. After completing the lesson, have students **work in groups,** and ask them to find the speeds (in km/hr) of the Olympic record-holders in the following events. Have them tell which record-holder was faster. (The answers given are

as of the 1992 Olympics.)
1. The men's 100-meter run and the men's 10,000-meter run [36.4 km/hr; 21.7 km/hr; the 100-meter runner was faster.]
2. The men's 100-meter run and the men's 100-meter freestyle swimming [36.4 km/hr; 7.4 km/hr; the runner was faster.]
3. The women's 1500-meter run and the women's 1500-meter speed skating [23.1 km/hr; 43.8 km/hr; the speed skater was faster.]

If you have access to data on teams in your school, you might ask comparable questions for groups to answer. You could also ask students to determine how many times as fast the Olympic record holders are than the holders of the comparable school records. This also leads naturally into a discussion of ratios, which are studied in the following lesson.

❹ This paragraph uses the rate model to explain that "you can't divide by zero." The *Extension* on page 361 uses an indirect proof to explain the same idea.

Additional Examples

1. As of 1992, the Olympic record for the 26.2-mile marathon is held by Carlos Lopez of Portugal. He ran the race in about 2.16 hours. What was his average speed in miles per hour? **≈12.1 miles per hour**

2. Ramon worked $7\frac{1}{2}$ hours last week and earned $53.55. What did he earn per hour? **$7.14/hr**

3. If a glacier is receding at a rate of 3 cm per year, how long will it take to recede 20 meters?
   $$\frac{-20 \ meters}{-.03 \ \frac{meters}{year}} \approx 667 \ years$$

4. From 1989 to 1994, the enrollment at Middlewood School dropped by 62 students. How fast was the enrollment changing during this period?
   $$\frac{-62 \ students}{5 \ years} = -12.4 \ \frac{students}{years}$$

5. What value can *n not* have in $\frac{n+3}{10-2n}$? **5**

Rates and Negative Numbers

Rates can be negative quantities.

Example 4

If the temperature goes down 12 degrees in 5 hours, what is the rate of temperature change in degrees per hour?

Solution

To find the rate, divide the number of degrees changed by the number of hours.

$$\text{rate of temperature change} = \frac{\text{drop of 12 degrees}}{5 \text{ hours}}$$
$$= \text{drop of 2.4 degrees per hour}$$

This can be written as

$$\frac{-12 \text{ degrees}}{5 \text{ hours}} = -2.4 \text{ degrees per hour.}$$

The temperature drops at a rate of 2.4 degrees per hour.

Division by Zero and Rates

❹ Consider a rate such as $\frac{0 \text{ meters}}{10 \text{ seconds}}$, which has 0 in the numerator. This means that you did not travel at all in 10 seconds. So your rate is 0 m/sec. Thus, $\frac{0}{10} = 0$. In contrast, consider a rate such as $\frac{10 \text{ meters}}{0 \text{ seconds}}$, which has 0 in the denominator. It would mean you are traveling 10 meters in 0 seconds. To be true, you would have to be in two places at the same time! Since that is impossible, this model illustrates that it is meaningless to think of $\frac{10}{0}$. *Division by zero is impossible.* Thus, the denominator of a fraction cannot be zero.

When variables appear in expressions involving division, you must make sure that you don't attempt to divide by zero.

Example 5

What value(s) can *k not* have in $\frac{k-7}{k-5}$?

Solution

Solve $k - 5 = 0$ to find out when the denominator is 0.

If $k - 5 = 0$, then $k = 5$. Thus k *cannot* be 5.

Check

If $k = 5$, then $\frac{k-7}{k-5} = \frac{5-7}{5-5} = \frac{-2}{0}$, which is impossible.

Optional Activities

Activity 2 Consumer Connection
Materials: Newspapers

After completing the lesson, you might have students look in local newspapers, or go to the supermarket, and get information on the prices of various sizes of common household items, such as laundry detergent or spaghetti sauce. Then have them **work in groups** to decide which brands and which sizes are the best buys based on unit cost.

Ask them to also determine some factors other than unit cost that should be considered when determining which product is the best buy. [Sample: the size of the package needed—a large package might be cheaper per unit, but the extra contents might go to waste; brand preference; location of stores with "best" buys—they may not be convenient.]

Activity 3
You can use *Activity Kit, Activity 13,* to introduce or to conclude Lesson 6-2. In this activity, students generate their own set of rates. They practice expressing these rates in different ways and use the rates to solve problems.

If a calculator or computer is instructed to divide by zero, it won't do it! Instead it will display an error message. When we tried to evaluate the expression $\frac{5-7}{5-5}$ with a calculator, we keyed in

$$(\; 5 \; - \; 7 \;) \; \div \; (\; 5 \; - \; 5 \;) \; = .$$

One calculator showed $\boxed{E \qquad 0}$.
Another showed $\boxed{\text{Error} \quad 02 \quad \text{Math}}$.

Caution: Note in Example 5 that it is possible to have a numerator equal to 0. When $k = 7$, the value of $\frac{k-7}{k-5}$ is $\frac{7-7}{7-5} = \frac{0}{2} = 0$.

QUESTIONS

Covering the Reading

1. Suppose Carmen and Ricardo traveled 300 miles and it took them 8 hours.
   a. What was their average speed in miles per hour? **37.5 mph**
   b. On the average, how long did it take them to travel a mile?
      2/75 or ≈ 0.027 hour
2. State the Rate Model for Division. **If *a* and *b* are quantities with different units, then *a/b* is the amount of quantity *a* per quantity *b*.**
3. Give a rate suggested by each situation.
   a. A family drove 24 miles in $\frac{2}{3}$ hour. **36 mph**
   b. A family drove *m* miles in $\frac{2}{3}$ hour. **1.5 *m* mph**
   c. A family drove 24 miles in *h* hours. $\frac{24}{h}$ **mph**
   d. A family drove *m* miles in *h* hours. $\frac{m}{h}$ **mph**

In 4–6, calculate a rate suggested by each situation.

4. In 9 days Julian earned $495. **$55 per day**

5. You buy *c* cans of natural lemonade for $2.10. $\frac{2.10}{c}$ **dollars per can**

6. You use 7.8 gallons of gasoline in traveling 270 miles.
   ≈ 34.6 miles per gallon
7. In the 1992–93 school year, Harvard University had 6,799 undergraduate students and 931 faculty members. What was the average number of undergraduate students per faculty member?
   7.3 students per faculty member

In 8–10, calculate the rate of temperature change for each of the following situations.

8. The temperature drops 11 degrees in 5 hours. **-2.2° per hour**

9. The temperature rose 6 degrees in 12 hours. **0.5° per hour**

10. The temperature stayed the same for 4 hours. **0° per hour**

11. What happens on your calculator when you divide by 0?
    An error message (E) appears.

Oldest U.S. college.
Founded in 1636, Harvard University is located in Cambridge, MA. These Harvard sculling teams are practicing on the nearby Charles River.

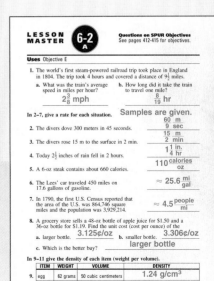

Questions 12–13 Students should be able to see what value of the variable makes the denominator zero. Point out that whenever the answer is not obvious, students should set the denominator equal to zero and solve the resulting equation.

Question 17 Consumer Connection Consumer decisions are often based on "cost (in pennies) per ounce." Ask students if comparing ounces per penny would serve the purpose as well. Ask them how they would judge the better buy using "ounces per penny." [The better buy gives more ounces per penny.]

Question 18 Social Studies Connection Bangladesh has one of the highest population densities of any nation in the world. Its population is about 45% that of the United States, and its area is only slightly larger than the state of Wisconsin.

Question 32 Technology Connection You might have a student, or a group of students, run this program for the rest of the class.

In 12–14, what value can the variable *not* have in each expression?

12. $\frac{18}{k-4}$ 4

13. $\frac{x-6}{x+1}$ –1

14. $\frac{w+1}{3}$
w can have any value.

Applying the Mathematics

In 15 and 16, divide by the rate to obtain a new piece of information.

15. The family needed $120 a week for food and had only $300 on hand. They had enough money for $2\frac{1}{2}$ weeks.

16. Willie can type 35 words a minute. He needs to type a 500-word essay. He needs 14.3 minutes to type the essay.

17. In one store a 20-ounce can of pineapple cost $1.78 and a 6-ounce can of the same kind of pineapple cost $.78. The unit cost is calculated as the rate *cost per ounce*.
    a. Calculate the unit cost of the 20-ounce can. 8.9¢
    b. Calculate the unit cost of the 6-ounce can. 13¢
    c. Based on the unit cost, which is the better buy? 20-ounce can

18. a. For each place, find the number of people per square mile. (This is the **population density**.)
    Bangladesh: 1993 population 122,255,000 (estimated);
    area 55,813 sq mi ≈ 2190 people per square mile
    Greenland: 1993 population 57,000 (estimated);
    area 840,000 sq mi ≈ 0.068 people per square mile
    b. The population density of Bangladesh is how many times the population density of Greenland? ≈32,206 (using the answers given for part a)

19. A very fast runner can run a half mile in 2 minutes. Express the average rate in each of these units.
    a. miles per minute $\frac{1}{4}$ mile per minute
    b. miles per hour 15 mph

20. *Multiple choice.* In *t* minutes, a copy machine made *n* copies. At this rate, how many copies per hour can be made? b
    (a) $\frac{60t}{n}$ (b) $\frac{60n}{t}$ (c) $\frac{n}{60t}$ (d) $\frac{t}{60n}$

21. In baseball, batting averages are computed by dividing the number of hits by the official number of at bats and rounding to three decimal places. In the 1993 regular season, Chicago White Sox first baseman Frank Thomas had 174 hits in 549 at bats, and Toronto Blue Jays first baseman John Olerud had 200 hits in 551 at bats. Which player had the better batting average? John Olerud

22. Give the domain of the variable in each expression. See left.
    a. $\frac{5}{2n+3}$ b. $\frac{5n+1}{7}$ c. $\frac{5n+1}{7(2n+3)}$

23. Suppose a spreadsheet program is opened, 100 is typed in cell A1, and 0 is typed in cell B1. See left.
    a. If = A1/B1 is typed in cell C1, what is printed in cell C1, and why?
    b. If = B1/A1 is typed in cell D1, what is printed in cell D1, and why?

Traffic tangles.
Pedestrians and pedicabs in the cities of Bangladesh often create traffic jams. With the eighth largest population, Bangladesh is one of the world's most densely populated countries.

22a) the set of all real numbers, *n* such that $n \neq \frac{-3}{2}$
b) the set of all real numbers
c) the set of all real numbers, *n* such that $n \neq \frac{-3}{2}$

23a) an error message because division by 0 is undefined
b) 0, because $\frac{0}{100} = 0$

Adapting to Individual Needs

English Language Development
Have students add the definition of *rate* to their index cards. In their examples, be sure they include the units.

Challenge
Have students solve the following problem: On a 150-mile trip, a car averaged 40 miles per hour for the first part of a trip. For the second part, the car traveled twice as far, and the car averaged 50 miles per hour. What was the average speed for the entire trip? [$46\frac{2}{13}$ miles per hour]

Review

In 24–27, simplify. *(Lesson 6-1)*

24. $\dfrac{\frac{5}{2}}{3}$ 7.5

25. $\dfrac{-3}{4} \div \dfrac{-3}{2}$ $\dfrac{1}{2}$

26. $\dfrac{x}{2y} \div \dfrac{11y}{3}$ $\dfrac{3x}{22y^2}$

27. $6x \div \dfrac{x}{2}$ 12

28. A cook has x pounds of ground beef. If it takes $\frac{1}{4}$ lb of ground beef to make one hamburger, how many hamburgers can the cook make? *(Lesson 6-1)* 4x

29. Let a be the measure of an angle.
  a. Write an expression for the supplement of the angle. $180 - a$
  b. Can the supplement of the angle ever equal the complement of the angle? Explain. See left.
  c. Can the supplement of an angle ever be 4 times the complement of the angle? Explain. *(Lessons 4-7, 5-3)* Yes. When an angle is 60° its complement is 30° and its supplement is 120°.

29b) No. If a supplement were less than 90°, then the angle would be obtuse and not have a complement.

30. Use the equation $5x - 4y = 40$. *(Lessons 4-3, 4-6)*
  a. If $x = 10$, find the value of y. 2.5
  b. What point on the graph of $5x - 4y = 40$ have you found in part **a**? (10, 2.5)

31. *Skill sequence.* Solve. *(Lessons 2-8, 3-10, 5-6)*
  a. $-x > 8$ $x < -8$
  b. $-2x > 8$ $x < -4$
  c. $-3x + 4 > 8$ $x < -\frac{4}{3}$
  d. $-5x + 6 > 8 - 7x$ $x > 1$

Exploration

32. Refer to the BASIC program below or use an equivalent calculator program. See left.

```
10 PRINT "EVALUATE 7/(K − 5)"
20 PRINT "ENTER VALUE OF K"
30 INPUT K
40 PRINT "VALUE OF 7/(K − 5)"
50 IF K = 5 THEN PRINT "DIVISION BY ZERO IS IMPOSSIBLE"
60 IF K <> 5 THEN PRINT 7/(K − 5)
70 END
```

  a. Run the program and input the values 8, 7.5, 7, 6.5, 6, 5.5, and 5. Record your results in a table.
  b. Input the values 4.5, 4, 3.5, 3, 2.5, and 2, and record the results.
  c. Describe some patterns you find in the data you collect.

32a)
K	Value of 7/(K − 5)
8	2.3̄
7.5	2.8
7	3.5
6.5	4.6̄
6	7
5.5	14
5	NONE

b)
K	Value of 7/(K − 5)
4.5	−14
4	−7
3.5	−4.6̄
3	−3.5
2.5	−2.8
2	−2.3̄

c) Sample: Values for K that are the same distance from 5 give values for $\frac{7}{K-5}$ that are opposites.

33. Use an almanac or some other source to find the national debt. Find the U.S. population. Then calculate the average debt per capita. (The phrase *per capita* means "per person.") Answers will vary. Sample: In 1992, the debt per capita was about $15,900.

34. See Question 18. Find the population density of the community or place where you live. Answers will vary.

Lesson 6-2 *Rates* **361**

Follow-up for Lesson 6-2

Practice
For more questions on SPUR Objectives, use **Lesson Master 6-2A** (shown on page 359) or **Lesson Master 6-2B** (shown on pages 360–361).

Assessment
Written Communication Have labels from various packages of food that show the number of servings and the cost of the package. Have students use this information to prepare a table that shows the cost of a single serving for several kinds of foods. [Students calculate rates correctly and use units correctly to identify rates.]

Extension
You might want to show students an indirect proof of why division by zero is impossible:

Assume a is not zero and that $\frac{a}{0}$ gives a number b. Then $\frac{a}{0} = b$. Multiply both sides by 0: $a = 0 \cdot b$. Therefore, a has to be zero. But we assumed that a is not zero. This leads to a contradiction, and the original supposition that $\frac{a}{0}$ gives a number b can't be true.

▶ **LESSON MASTER 6-2 B** *page 2*

12. In 1990, the population of Alaska was 550,403 and its area was 656,424 square miles. Give two rates suggested by this information. .84 per./mi², 1.19 mi²/per.

13. Mr. Santos stuffed 4200 envelopes in 3 hours. Give two rates, one using hours and one using minutes. 1400 env./hr, 23.3̄ env./min

14. For each situation, give a rate.
  a. The committee made 144 bean bags in 6 hours. 24 b.b./hr
  b. The committee made 200 bean bags in h hours. $\frac{200}{h}$ b.b./hr
  c. The committee made b bean bags in $\frac{1}{2}$ hour. 2b bb./hr

15. A 20-oz jar of lotion costs $4.09 and a 12-oz jar costs $2.49.
  a. Find the unit cost (cost per ounce) for 20 ounces. $.2045/oz
  b. Find the unit cost of the smaller bottle. $.2075/oz
  c. Which is the better buy? 20-oz jar

16. If it takes 7 minutes to call the names of 100 graduates, how long will it take to call the names of 448 graduates? ≈31 min

In 17–19, give the density (weight per volume) of each item.

	WEIGHT	VOLUME	DENSITY
17. aluminum	8,097 grams	3,000 cubic centimeters	2.699 g/cm³
18. copper	4,928 grams	550 cubic centimeters	8.96 g/cm³
19. gold	4,338 grams	225 cubic centimeters	19.28 g/cm³

20. Which is faster, typing $5p$ pages in $4h$ hours or $4p$ pages in $3h$ hours? Explain your answer. $\frac{5p}{4h} = 1.25\frac{p}{h}$ and $\frac{4p}{3h} = 1.33\frac{p}{h}$; 1.33 > 1.25; so $4p$ pages in $3h$ hr is faster.

21. Which is less expensive, 6c cases of juice for $10 or 4c cases of juice for $6? Explain your answer. $4c$ cases for $6; $\frac{\$10}{6c} = 1.66\frac{\$}{c}$ and $\frac{\$6}{4c} = 1.50\frac{\$}{c}$; 1.5 < 1.66; so $4c$ cases for $6 is less expensive.

Setting Up Lesson 6-3
Materials Students doing the *Optional Activities* on page 363 will need newspaper advertisements and cookbooks.

Example 1 on page 362 discusses the ratio of waist measurement to hip measurement. You might ask students to find their hip and waist measurements at home and answer the problem using their own data.

361

Objectives

F Use ratios to compare two quantities.
H Solve percent problems in real situations.

Resources

From the **Teacher's Resource File**
■ Lesson Master 6-3A or 6-3B
■ Answer Master 6-3
■ Teaching Aid 57: Warm-up

Additional Resources
■ Visual for Teaching Aid 57
■ Tape measures, or cord and a yardstick

Teaching Lesson 6-3

Warm-up

Diagnostic Tim earned $12.50 for mowing a lawn. How many lawns did he mow if he earned

1. $62.50? **5 lawns**
2. $100.00? **8 lawns**
3. $125.00? **10 lawns**
4. $187.50? **15 lawns**

LESSON 6-3

Ratios

Steps in the right direction. *Many people join aerobics classes to increase endurance and energy and to help maintain proper weight. Regular aerobic exercise may also help lessen the risk of heart disease.*

What Is a Ratio?

Being overweight increases the probability that a person will suffer from heart disease. The chart below shows a way to test whether an adult has an increased risk. Dividing the waist measure by the hip measure results in a *ratio* which can be used to compare them.

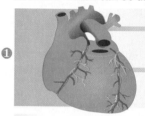

❶
1. Measure waist and hips. Call these w and h.

2. For women; risk of heart disease increases if $\frac{w}{h} > 0.8$.

3. For men; risk of heart disease increases if $\frac{w}{h} > 1.0$.

Example 1

Ms. Mott's waist measure is 26 in. Her hip measure is 35 in. According to the chart above, does she run an increased risk of heart disease?

Solution

$$\frac{\text{waist measure}}{\text{hip measure}} = \frac{26''}{35''} \approx 0.74.$$

Since $0.74 < 0.8$, her risk (according to this test) is not increased.

The direction of the comparison is important. If Ms. Mott compared her hip measure to her waist measure, the result would be $\frac{35''}{26''} \approx 1.35$, which is greater than 0.8. She would be using the wrong number and would misinterpret the test.

362

Lesson 6-3 Overview

Broad Goals This lesson reviews the Ratio Model for Division and its applications to "parts of" and certain percent problems.

Perspective Ratios are comparisons that are made with division when the units are the same. If $a < b$, the ratio $\frac{a}{b}$ represents what fraction a is of b. If $a > b$, $\frac{a}{b}$ tells how many times as large as b that a is.

In this lesson, both subtraction and division are used to compare two quantities. However, students may not distinguish between these two methods. They may be surprised to realize that if numbers have a constant difference, they will not have a constant ratio. For instance, suppose a parent is 30 years old, and the child is 2 years old. The parent's age is 15 times the child's age. However, this ratio will change. In just 2 years the parent's age will be only 8 times

the child's age. Nevertheless, the difference in their ages will always remain the same. Analogously, if pairs of numbers have a constant ratio (unless the ratio is 1:1), the differences will vary. If, in an election, the ratio between the number of votes cast for the winner to the number cast for the loser is 3 to 2. You can not be sure of the margin of victory; 300 votes to 200 votes gives a difference of 100 votes, but 6000 votes to 4000 votes gives a difference of 2000 votes.

As you know, subtraction provides one way to compare quantities. Division is another way.

> **Ratio Model for Division**
> Let a and b be quantities with the same units.
> Then the **ratio** $\frac{a}{b}$ compares a to b.

Similarly, the ratio $\frac{b}{a}$ compares b to a.

Notice the difference between a rate and a ratio. In the rate a per b, the units for a and b are different. In a ratio, the units are the same.

$$\frac{40 \text{ km}}{2 \text{ hr}} = 20 \frac{\text{km}}{\text{hr}} \text{ is a rate.} \qquad \frac{40 \text{ km}}{2 \text{ km}} = 20 \text{ is a ratio.}$$

Example 2

It takes Mr. Garcia $\frac{3}{4}$ hour to go to work and it takes Ms. Wang 10 minutes to go to work. Find a ratio comparing Ms. Wang's time to Mr. Garcia's time.

Solution

The units of measure for 10 minutes and $\frac{3}{4}$ hour are not the same. So we change hours to minutes. Since Ms. Wang's time is to be compared to Mr. Garcia's, her time is the numerator.

$$\frac{\text{Ms. Wang's time}}{\text{Mr. Garcia's time}} = \frac{10 \text{ minutes}}{\frac{3}{4} \text{ hour}} = \frac{10 \text{ minutes}}{\frac{3}{4} \cdot 60 \text{ minutes}} = \frac{10 \text{ minutes}}{45 \text{ minutes}} = \frac{2}{9}$$

This means that, on the average, Ms. Wang travels 2 minutes for every 9 minutes that Mr. Garcia travels. It takes Ms. Wang $\frac{2}{9}$ of the time it takes Mr. Garcia to go to work.

Ratios and Percents

Ratios often are written as percents. In Example 2, $\frac{2}{9} = .\overline{22} \approx 22\%$, so you could say that it takes Ms. Wang about 22% of the time it takes Mr. Garcia to go to work. A percent can always be interpreted as a ratio, in this case about $\frac{22}{100}$.

In problems involving discounts, the **percent of discount** is the ratio of the discount to the original price. The **percent of tax** is the ratio of the tax to the selling price.

Remind students that they used percents of discount and tax in Lesson 3-3, but now they are learning how to calculate these percents. Notice that each percent in **Example 3** has to be rounded.

Reading Mathematics For most students, the newest idea in this lesson is the one that is found in **Example 4** (and **Questions 11, 17, and 18**). It is a good idea to read this example with students and discuss it in detail. Ask students to give some possible numbers of gallons of water to gallons of concentrate. [Samples: 3 to 1, 4.5 to 1.5, 60 to 20] Then ask what all of these answers have in common. [They are of the form 3x gallons of water to x gallons of concentrate.)

Additional Examples

1. Bob's height is 5 ft 10 inches. His daughter is 40 inches tall. What is the ratio of their heights? $\frac{7}{4}$ or $\frac{4}{7}$

2. A park is an eighth of a mile long and 300 feet wide. Find a ratio comparing length to width. $\frac{11}{5}$

3. A pair of shoes that originally sold for $40 is on sale for $8 less.
   a. What is the percent of discount on the shoes? 20%
   b. If there is $1.92 tax on the sale price, what is the tax rate? 6%

4. A recipe for fresh lemonade calls for 5 parts water for each part fresh lemon juice. How much of each ingredient is needed to make 2 quarts of lemonade? $1\frac{2}{3}$ quarts of water; $\frac{1}{3}$ quart of fresh lemon juice

5. For many years the Empire State building (1250 feet tall) was the world's tallest building. However, in 1974, the Sears Tower (1454 feet tall) became the tallest building. The height of the Empire

The first U.S. jeans.
In 1850, a miner asked Levi Strauss, a canvas peddler, for a pair of durable canvas pants. Before long, Strauss was making pants from a tough, cotton fabric now known as denim. In 1879, Levi's denim jeans with rivet-reinforced pockets sold for $1.46 a pair.

364

Example 3

A pair of jeans originally cost $29.95. They were reduced to $23.95. The tax on the reduced price is $1.20.
a. What is the percent of discount?
b. What is the percent of tax?

Solution

a. Percent of discount $= \frac{\text{amount of discount}}{\text{original price}} = \frac{29.95 - 23.95}{29.95}$

$$= \frac{6.00}{29.95}$$

$$\approx 0.2003 \approx 20\%$$

b. Calculate the ratio between the amount of tax and the reduced price.

Percent of tax $= \frac{1.20}{23.95} \approx 0.0501 \approx 5\%$

Using Ratios to Set Up Equations

Suppose in Example 2 you knew only that Ms. Wang travels 2 minutes for every 9 minutes that Mr. Garcia travels. Then, whatever times W and G they travel, the ratio of W to G equals $\frac{2}{9}$.

$$\frac{W}{G} = \frac{2 \text{ minutes}}{9 \text{ minutes}} = \frac{2}{9}$$

But you also know that for all nonzero values of x, $\frac{2x}{9x} = \frac{2}{9}$.

So there is a value of x with $W = 2x$ and $G = 9x$. This idea is very useful in many problems, because directions for mixing foods or chemicals are frequently given as ratios. You can use equations to determine actual quantities from the ratios.

Example 4

Instructions for preparing a lemonade drink call for 3 parts of water for each part of lemonade concentrate. How much of each ingredient is needed to make 10 gallons of lemonade?

Solution

Because the water and concentrate are in the ratio of 3 to 1, let $3x$ be the number of gallons of water and $1x$ be the number of gallons of concentrate. The total needed is 10 gallons, so

$$3x + 1x = 10.$$
$$4x = 10$$
$$x = \frac{10}{4} = 2.5$$

So $3x = 3 \cdot 2.5 = 7.5$.
You need 2.5 gallons of lemonade concentrate and 7.5 gallons of water.

Check

$\frac{7.5 \text{ gal}}{2.5 \text{ gal}} = \frac{3}{1}$ and 7.5 gal + 2.5 gal = 10 gal. It checks.

Adapting to Individual Needs

Extra Help
Materials: Counters of two different colors

To help visual learners, display a quantity of counters (or other objects) of two different colors (have more of one color than the other). Have students name the ratio of, for example, red counters to white counters, then the ratio of white counters to red counters. Then ask for the ratio of white counters to the total number of counters.

Covering the Reading

In 1–3, refer to the method for testing heart disease risk.

1. Does a woman run an increased risk of heart disease if her waist and hip measurements are 32 in. and 37 in., respectively? **Yes**

2. If w is a man's waist measure and h is his hip measure, write a sentence describing when a man's risk of heart disease increases. $\frac{w}{h} > 1$

3. Does a man run an increased risk of heart disease if his waist is 34 in. and his hips are 36 in.? **No**

4. Let x and y be two quantities with the same units. Write two ratios comparing x and y. $\frac{x}{y}; \frac{y}{x}$

5. What is the difference between a rate and a ratio? **See left.**

> 5) A rate is a comparison of quantities with different units. A ratio is a comparison of quantities with the same units.

6. *Multiple choice.* Which is not a ratio? **b**
   (a) $\frac{14 \text{ seconds}}{23 \text{ seconds}}$ (b) $\frac{150 \text{ miles}}{3 \text{ hours}}$ (c) $\frac{27 \text{ cookies}}{13 \text{ cookies}}$

7. Suppose it takes Ms. Lopez 25 minutes to complete a particular job and it takes Mr. Sampson half an hour to complete the same job. Write a ratio which:
   a. compares Ms. Lopez's time to Mr. Sampson's time; $\frac{5}{6}$
   b. compares Mr. Sampson's time to Ms. Lopez's time. $\frac{6}{5}$

8. An item is on sale for $15. It originally cost $21.
   a. What is the discount (in dollars)? **$6**
   b. What is the percent of discount? **about 29%**

9. You pay 64¢ tax on a $16.00 purchase.
   a. Write a ratio of tax to purchase price. $\frac{.64}{16} = \frac{1}{25}$
   b. What is the percent of tax? **4%**

10. Tell whether the fraction equals the ratio of 4 to 3.
    a. $\frac{4}{3}$ **Yes**   b. $\frac{3}{4}$ **No**   c. $\frac{8}{6}$ **Yes**
    d. $\frac{6}{5}$ **No**   e. $\frac{4x}{3x}$ **Yes**   f. $\frac{3x}{4x}$ **No**

11. In Example 4, determine the amounts of lemonade concentrate and water you would use to make 2 quarts of lemonade drink. $\frac{1}{2}$ **quart lemonade, 1.5 quarts water**

Applying the Mathematics

12. Banner High School has won 36 of its last 40 football games.
    a. Write a ratio of games won to games played. $\frac{36}{40} = \frac{9}{10}$
    b. What percent of these 40 games has it won? **90%**
    c. Winning percentages are often written as three-place decimals. Write the answer from part **a** as a three-place decimal. **0.900**

Lesson 6-3 *Ratios* **365**

State building is what percent of the height of the Sears Tower? ≈ **86%**

6. When the first U.S. census was taken in 1790, the area of the country was 891,364 square miles. In the 1990 census, it was 3,618,770 square miles. How many times as large is the United States now than it was in 1790? ≈ **4.1**

Notes on Questions

Question 2 The most common answer given to this ratio problem is $\frac{w}{h} > 1$. However, this inequality can be transformed into $w > h$ by multiplying both sides by h (since $h > 0$). This is an opportunity to apply the Multiplication Property of Inequality, since $w > h$ gives a more meaningful description of a person's measurements.

Question 10 Note that while there are three correct answers in this question, there are infinitely many ways to write the ratio of 4 to 3.

Adapting to Individual Needs

English Language Development
Have students add the definition of *ratio* to their index-card files. Be sure they include the units in their examples. You may note that with rates, the units will be different; with ratios, they will be the same.

Question 19 These problems give the students some experience in working with ratios in similar figures. Students should determine the ratio from the formulas that are given in the question. The formula for the area of a circle is used in Lesson 6-6.

Question 25 Point out that there are two possible solution strategies: (1) use chunking, and then evaluate the expression, or (2) evaluate each expression first, and then simplify. Point out how chunking simplifies the problem.

Follow-up 6-3
for Lesson

Practice
For more questions on SPUR Objectives, use **Lesson Master 6-3A** (shown on page 365) or **Lesson Master 6-3B** (shown on pages 366–367).

Assessment
Written/Oral Communication Have students **work in groups** and write several different ratio situations. Then call on each group to give one situation. List the different situations on the board. [Students understand the meaning of ratio.]

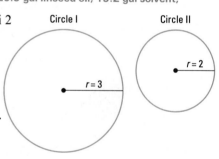

13. According to a teacher group, the average teacher salary for 1991–92 was $34,413. In 1870 it was $189. The 1991–92 salary is about how many times the 1870 salary? **182**

In a class by itself. The *Country School*, a painting by Winslow Homer, shows a one-room school that was common in rural U.S. during the 1800s. Most had one teacher who taught all grade levels.

14. Frieda owns x sweaters while her twin brother Fred owns y sweaters.
    a. Fred owns __?__ times as many sweaters as Frieda does. $\frac{y}{x}$
    b. Is the answer to part **a** a rate or a ratio? **ratio**

15. The ratio of x to y is the __?__ of the ratio of y to x. **reciprocal**

16. The ratio of adults to children at a concert is expected to be 4 to 1. If 200 people attend, how many are expected to be children? **40**

17. If two quantities are in the ratio a to b and the first is ax, then what is the second? **bx**

18. A paint mixture calls for 7 parts of linseed oil, 5 parts of solvent, and one part of pigment. How much of each ingredient is needed to make 50 gallons of paint? **26.9 gal linseed oil, 19.2 gal solvent, and 3.8 gal pigment**

19. The circles below have radii 2 and 3.
    a. Find the ratio of the diameter of Circle I to the diameter of Circle II.
    b. Give the ratio of the area of Circle I to the area of Circle II, in lowest terms.
    c. Write the ratio in part **b** as a decimal.
    a) $\frac{6}{4} = \frac{3}{2}$; b) $\frac{9}{4}$; c) **2.25**

Circle I — $r = 3$ Circle II — $r = 2$

Review

20. In the five years from 1987 to 1992, the U.S. federal debt increased by about $1,500,000,000,000.
    a. Write this amount in words. **one trillion five hundred billion dollars**
    b. Estimate the amount of increase per year. *(Lesson 6-2, previous course)* **300 billion dollars**

Adapting to Individual Needs
Challenge
Have the students solve the following problem: Arturo bought a television at a 20% discount and a video recorder at a 30% discount. The original prices of the television and video recorder were $300 and $200, respectively. What is the single percent of discount for the entire purchase? [24%]

Martin Lopez-Zubero

21. In the 200-meter backstroke competition at the 1992 Olympics, Martin Lopez-Zubero of Spain set an Olympic record by completing the race in 118.47 seconds. What was his average rate in meters per second? *(Lesson 6-2)* **1.69 meters per second**

22. For what values of x is $\frac{5-2x}{5+2x}$ undefined? *(Lesson 6-2)* $\frac{-5}{2}$

23. Simplify $\frac{3x}{4} \div \frac{x}{2}$. *(Lesson 6-1)* $\frac{3}{2}$

24. *Multiple choice.* Which of the following is *not* equal to $-\frac{a}{b}$? *(Lesson 6-1)* **c**

(a) $\frac{a}{-b}$ (b) $\frac{-a}{b}$ (c) $\frac{-a}{-b}$ (d) $-\frac{-a}{-b}$

25. If $5a = 36$, find the value of $\sqrt{5a} + 7\sqrt{5a}$. *(Lessons 3-6, 5-9)* **48**

26. *Skill sequence.* Solve for x. *(Lessons 2-6, 3-5)*
 a. $5x = 19$ **3.8**
 b. $0.05x = 19$ **380**
 c. $x + 0.05x = 19$ **18.1**

27. A student has earned the following scores on algebra tests this term: 75, 90, 86, 78, 80. What is the student's test average? *(Previous course)* **81.8**

Exploration

28. Consider this right triangle with an angle of about 37°. The three sides can form six different ratios.

 a. Write the values of all six of these ratios. $\frac{5}{4}, \frac{5}{3}, \frac{4}{3}, \frac{4}{5}, \frac{3}{4}, \frac{3}{5}$
 b. Some of these ratios have special names. One of these is called the *sine*. For the triangle above it is written sin 37°. Find the value of sin 37° on your calculator using the key sequence 37 [sin] or [sin] 37 (depending on your calculator), and determine which of the six ratios in part **a** is the sine. **0.601815; 3/5**
 c. Another special ratio is called *cosine*. Find the value of cos 37° on your calculator and determine which of the six ratios in part **a** is the cosine. **0.798636; 4/5**
 d. A third special ratio is called the *tangent*. Find the value of tan 37° on your calculator and determine which of the six ratios in part **a** is the tangent. **0.753554; 3/4**

Lesson 6-3 *Ratios* **367**

Setting Up Lesson 6-4
Materials Each group of 2 or 3 students will need two dice to do the *In-class Activity* for Lesson 6-4.

Resources

This activity introduces Lesson 6-4 and should be done before the questions for that lesson are assigned as homework. The purpose of the activity is to give an example of the difference between relative frequencies (ratios which result from repeated trials of an experiment) and probability (numbers that are assumed or calculated from assumptions about a situation).

Some students may be familiar with the probabilities of obtaining sums from 2 to 12 when two dice are tossed. This activity is commonly used at the upper elementary or middle-school level. Still, because frequencies are different virtually every time this activity is done, students can participate as if the idea were new to them. The experience could well enhance their skills in making better predictions.

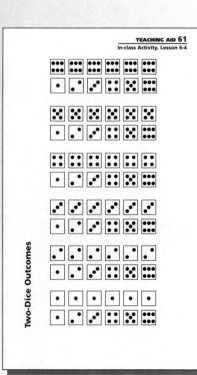

**Introducing
Lesson 6-4**

Relative Frequencies and Probabilities

IN-CLASS
ACTIVITY

Work in groups of 2 or 3 students.
Materials: Two dice per group

1 When two dice are tossed and the numbers on top are added, the sum can be any whole number from 2 to 12. Which sum do you think is most likely to occur? Why did you pick this number?
Sample: 7, since there are more ways to get 7;   1, 6;   2, 5;   3, 4

2 Toss the dice 50 times. Each time, record the result in the column labeled frequency in a table like the one below. The table shows the sums of the first 10 tosses of one group. Tables will vary.

Sum	Frequency	Relative Frequency		Probability
		fraction	**decimal**	
2				$1/36 \approx 0.028$
3	I			$2/36 \approx 0.056$
4	I			$3/36 \approx 0.083$
5	II			$4/36 \approx 0.111$
6	I			$5/36 \approx 0.139$
7	III			$6/36 \approx 0.167$
8				$5/36 \approx 0.139$
9				$4/36 \approx 0.111$
10				$3/36 \approx 0.083$
11	I			$2/36 \approx 0.056$
12	I			$1/36 \approx 0.028$

3 After you have tossed the dice 50 times, calculate the relative frequency of getting each sum. For instance, the relative frequency of getting a 2 is the ratio between the number of 2s you got and 50. If you got three 2s in 50 tosses of the dice, the relative frequency of getting a sum of 2 is $\frac{3}{50}$ = .06. Write each relative frequency as both a fraction and a decimal.
Answers will vary.

4 ***Draw a conclusion.*** Based on your table, how, if at all, would you revise your prediction in part 1?
Answers will vary.

368

5 The diagram below shows the 36 possible outcomes when two dice are tossed.

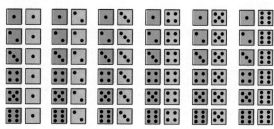

Notice that there is only 1 way to get a sum of 2. We say that the *probability* of getting a sum of 2 is $\frac{1}{36} \approx .028$. In contrast, there are 3 ways of getting a sum of 10 (▦▦, ▦▦, ▦▦), so the probability of getting a sum of 10 is $\frac{3}{36} \approx .083$.

5a) **See table on page 368.**

a. Calculate the probability of getting each of the other sums from 2 to 12, and record these numbers in the last column of the table.

b. How close are your group's relative frequencies to the probabilities? Answers will vary.

6 **a.** Combine the results of all the groups in your class. Calculate the relative frequency for each sum from 2 to 12 for the entire class. Make a new column labeled class relative frequency and record the results from the whole class. Answers will vary.

b. Which set of relative frequencies— those from your small group, or those from the whole class—are closer to the probabilities? Answers will vary.

369

Objectives

G Calculate relative frequencies or probabilities in situations with a finite number of equally likely outcomes.

Resources

From the **Teacher's Resource File**
- Lesson Master 6-4A or 6-4B
- Answer Master 6-4
- Assessment Sourcebook: Quiz for Lessons 6-1 through 6-4
- Teaching Aids
  58 Warm-up
  62 Relative Frequency and Probability
- Technology Sourcebook
  Computer Master 16

Additional Resources
- Visuals for Teaching Aids 58, 62
- Compasses, protractors, and/or **Geometry Templates**
- Deck of playing cards, dice, coins

Teaching
Lesson **6-4**

Warm-up

Diagnostic Students can use compasses, protractors, and/or **Geometry Templates** to draw the spinners in Questions 1–2.

1. Draw a spinner so that the probability of landing on either a 1, 2, 3, or 4 is $\frac{1}{4}$. **Any spinner that is equally divided into $4n$ sections with each number appearing in n sections**

Relative Frequency and Probability

Frequencies and Relative Frequency

The **frequency** of an event is simply the number of times the event occurs. For instance, in 1990 there were 2,129,000 boys born in the United States, so the frequency of male births that year was 2,129,000. The *relative frequency* of an event compares the frequency with the total number of times the event could have occurred. In 1990, there were 4,158,000 children born in the United States. The relative frequency of boys to births is found by dividing the number of boys born by the total number of births.

$$\frac{\text{relative}}{\text{frequency}} = \frac{\text{number of boys born}}{\text{total number of births}} = \frac{2,129,000}{4,158,000} \approx 0.512 = 51.2\%$$

Relative Frequency of an Event

Suppose a particular event has occurred with a frequency of F times in a total of T opportunities for it to happen. Then the relative frequency of the event is $\frac{F}{T}$.

Like other ratios, relative frequencies may be written as fractions, decimals, or percents.

Example 1

The Illinois Department of Public Health reported that for the years 1980 to 1990, 3840 skunks were examined for rabies. Of that number, 1446 actually had rabies. From 1980 to 1990 what was the relative frequency of skunks with rabies among those tested?

Solution

Here the event is "having rabies." You are asked to compare the skunks with rabies to the entire group of skunks.

$$\frac{F}{T} = \frac{1446 \text{ skunks with rabies}}{3840 \text{ skunks in all}} = \frac{1446}{3840} \approx 0.377 = 37.7\%$$

The relative frequency of skunks with rabies was about 38%.

370

Lesson 6-4 Overview

Broad Goals Probabilities and relative frequencies are both measures of the likelihood of an event. We assume that students have seen the basic definition of probability before. The goal of this lesson is to compare *probability*, which is a theoretical value, with *relative frequency*, which is a ratio that is calculated from actual data.

Perspective In this lesson we determine probabilities only in situations that involve

equally likely outcomes. We use the term *random* and give a rule for defining the probability of an event. We use the term *relative frequency* rather than the older term *experimental probability*. Notice the difference between relative frequencies and probabilities. Probabilities are assumed, or they are deduced from assumptions. Relative frequencies arise from data. Although the probability of a *fair* coin coming up heads is $\frac{1}{2}$, the relative frequency from an

experiment in which a coin thought to be fair is tossed 100 times will not always be $\frac{1}{2}$. However, if the same coin is repeatedly tossed 100 times, the distribution of the relative frequencies of heads should center around $\frac{1}{2}$. Statisticians often hypothesize a probability. Then they run an experiment to see if a relative frequency agrees with that probability.

In Example 1, the relative frequency could have been as low as $\frac{0}{3840}$ or 0, if no skunks had rabies. It could have been as high as $\frac{3840}{3840}$, or 1, if all the skunks tested had rabies. In the table you made for the dice activity, all the relative frequencies you calculated should also be between 0 and 1.

Probability

You have already calculated probabilities. Now we examine this idea in more detail. The *probability* of an event measures how likely it is that the event happens. Like relative frequency, a probability is a number between 0 and 1. Sometimes a relative frequency is used to estimate a probability. For instance, for many years the relative frequency of male births has been about 0.51, so we say that the probability of a newborn being a boy is about 0.51.

At other times, the probability of an event is determined by some theoretical assumptions. When a coin is tossed, we think that heads and tails are equally likely. Then the probability of getting a head is $\frac{1}{2}$ and the probability of getting a tail is $\frac{1}{2}$.

A possible result of an experiment is an **outcome.** For instance, suppose slips of paper with the integers from 1 to 25 are put into a hat. If one slip is drawn, the set S of outcomes is $\{1, 2, 3, \ldots, 25\}$, and the number of elements in set S, written $N(S)$, equals 25. An **event** is a set of outcomes chosen from S. The event "picking a number greater than 18" is the set $\{19, 20, 21, 22, 23, 24, 25\}$. If all 25 outcomes are assumed to be equally likely, then the probability of this event is $\frac{7}{25}$. This is the ratio of the number of outcomes in the event to the total number of possible outcomes.

Whirling probabilities.
This NASA photo of Hurricane Elena was taken from the space shuttle Discovery *in 1985. The probability of a hurricane reaching a specific area is partially based on past records of such storms reaching that area.*

Probability of an Event

Let S be the set of all outcomes of an experiment and let E be an event. If the outcomes are equally likely, then the **probability of the event E, $P(E)$,** is $\frac{N(E)}{N(S)}$.

Example 2

Hurricanes happen often enough in some states that public officials must have evacuation plans ready. If hurricanes are equally likely to occur on any day of the week, what is the probability that one occurs on Saturday or Sunday, times when there are the fewest people in schools and offices?

Solution

There are seven possible outcomes, which are the days of the week. Thus here $N(S) = 7$. The event that we are interested in is $E = \{$Saturday, Sunday$\}$. So $N(E) = 2$. If a hurricane occurs, the probability that it hits on Saturday or Sunday = P(Saturday or Sunday) = $\frac{N(E)}{N(S)} = \frac{2}{7}$.

---

2. Draw a spinner so that the probability of landing on a 1 is $\frac{1}{8}$, a 2 is $\frac{1}{4}$, a 3 is $\frac{1}{2}$, and a 4 is $\frac{1}{8}$.

Any spinner that is equally divided into $8n$ sections with 1 and 4 appearing in n sections, 2 appearing in $2n$ sections, and 3 appearing in $4n$ sections

Notes on Reading

Cooperative Learning Many of the ideas in this lesson may be new to students. You might want to have them read the material as a class.

Relative frequencies and probabilities may be expressed as fractions, decimals, or percents. It is reasonable to accept answers in any one of these forms. Students should be guided by the type of information that is given in a problem. For example, if the given information is in percent form, the answer should be a percent. In many cases, fractions are the most appropriate way of writing and computing with probabilities. However, in some probability problems, fractions in lowest terms may not be helpful. For instance, when comparing whether it is more likely that the sum will be 5 or 6 when tossing two dice, most people agree that it is easier to compare $\frac{4}{36}$ and $\frac{5}{36}$ than it is to compare $\frac{1}{9}$ and $\frac{5}{36}$.

Science Connection Hurricane winds swirl counterclockwise in the Northern Hemisphere and clockwise in the Southern Hemisphere. The center, or eye, of a hurricane is calm. Winds in the wall cloud area that surrounds the eye may blow at speeds of 130 to 150 miles per hour while the eye of the hurricane travels 10 to 15 miles per hour.

Optional Activities

Activity 1 Probability Experiment
Materials: Coins

After students have read the lesson, you might have them conduct this experiment **with partners.** One student should toss a coin 40 times while the other student records heads or tails. Summarize the activity by noting the difference between the probability of heads—a number that tells what part of the time we think the toss will come up heads—and the relative frequency of heads—a number that changes with every toss and may or may not be close to what we think is the probability.

Activity 2 Probability Experiment
Materials: Coins, dice, or cards

This activity can also be done after students have read the lesson. Have **groups of students** make up simple probability questions about coins, dice, or cards, and calculate the (theoretical) probability to answer the questions. Then have them conduct experiments to calculate the relative frequencies of the events. Explain that, in theory, if the trials for the outcome are indeed randomly generated, the more times the experiment is carried out, the closer the relative frequency should be to the theoretical probability. Have students double the number of trials to see if this holds true for their events.

When were playing cards invented? *Playing cards may have originated in China around 800 A.D. The four suits originated in France in the 1500s.* ❶

Forecasting the future. *Shown is TV meteorologist Spencer Christian. Meteorologists use computers to help analyze weather data gathered from satellites and observation stations.*

When all outcomes in an experiment have the same probability of occurring, then they are said to occur **at random** or **randomly**.

Example 3

A standard deck of playing cards has 52 cards. There are four suits: clubs ♣, diamonds ♦, hearts ♥, and spades ♠. Each suit has 13 cards: ace, 2, 3, 4, 5, 6, 7, 8, 9, 10, jack, queen, king. Suppose you shuffle the cards well and pull one card at random. Find:
a. P(ace of hearts)
b. P(queen)

Solution

a. There are 52 possible outcomes, the number of cards in the deck. So $N(S) = 52$. Only one outcome is in the event: the ace of hearts. So $N(E) = 1$.

$$P(\text{ace of hearts}) = \frac{N(E)}{N(S)} = \frac{1}{52}$$

b. The event "getting a queen" has 4 outcomes: Q♣, Q♦, Q♥, and Q♠.

$$P(\text{getting a queen}) = \frac{4}{52} = \frac{1}{13}$$

Probability and Complementary Events

If the probability of a hurricane occurring on a week*end* is $\frac{2}{7}$, then the probability of a hurricane occurring on a week*day* is $\frac{5}{7}$. The events "occurring on a weekend" and "occurring on a weekday" are called *complements* of each other. Two events are **complements** if their intersection is the empty set and their union is the set of all possible outcomes.

The sum of the probability of an event and the probability of its complement is 1. The same is true for relative frequencies. Thus the probability or relative frequency of the complement of an event is found by subtracting the probability or relative frequency of the original event from 1.

$$P(E) + P(\text{complement of } E) = 1$$
$$P(\text{complement of } E) = 1 - P(E)$$

Example 4

A weather forecaster reports that the probability of rain tomorrow is 70%. What is the probability that it does not rain?

Solution

The events "rain tomorrow" and "no rain tomorrow" are complements. So the probability of no rain is 100% – 70% = 30%.

372

The table below summarizes some of the important similarities and differences between relative frequencies and probabilities.

Relative frequency	Probability
1. calculated from an experiment	1. deduced from assumptions (like randomness) or assumed to be close to some relative frequency
2. the ratio of the number of times an event has occurred to the number of times it could occur	2. if outcomes are equally likely, the ratio of the number of outcomes in an event to the total number of possible outcomes
3. 0 means that an event did not occur. 1 means the event occurred every time it could.	3. 0 means that an event is impossible. 1 means that an event is sure to happen.
4. The more often an event occurred relative to the number of times it could occur, the closer its relative frequency is to 1.	4. The more likely an event is, the closer its probability is to 1.
5. If the relative frequency of an event is r, then the relative frequency of its complement is $1-r$.	5. If the probability of an event is p, then the probability of its complement is $1-p$.

QUESTIONS

Covering the Reading

1. a. How many girls were born in 1990? 2,029,000
   b. What was the relative frequency of female births in 1990? 0.488

2. The Illinois Department of Health reported that for the years 1971 to 1991, of 474 horses tested for rabies only 22 actually had the disease.
   a. What percent of horses tested had rabies? 4.6%
   b. What percent did not have rabies? 95.4%

3. What is the meaning of a relative frequency of 0?
   The event did not occur.
4. What is the meaning of a relative frequency of 1?
   The event occurred every time it could.
5. There were 93 million households in the U.S. with televisions in 1992. Of these homes, 67 million also had a VCR.
   a. Find the relative frequency of households with a television that also have a VCR. 72%
   b. Find the relative frequency of households with a television that have no VCR. 28%

6. *Multiple choice.* A student flipped a coin 100 times and counted 47 heads. Which phrase best describes the ratio $\frac{47}{100}$? b
   (a) the probability of a toss coming up heads
   (b) the relative frequency of a toss coming up heads

Lesson 6-4 *Relative Frequency and Probability* **373**

d. P(tossing a number greater than 7). $\frac{5}{12}$

4. Suppose that you have a fair die with a number on each side. If the probability of throwing an even number is $\frac{1}{2}$, what is the probability of throwing an odd number? $\frac{1}{2}$

5. If a number is randomly picked from {11, 12, 13, 14, 15, 16, 17}, what is the probability that it is divisible by 3? $\frac{2}{7}$

6. A commercial reports that 3 out of 10 people use Sparkleclean detergent. Give some possible number for the persons surveyed and for those using Sparkleclean. Sample: out of 1000 people, 300 use Sparkleclean; out of 110 people, 33 use Sparkleclean.

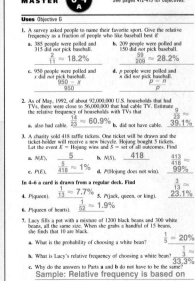

This will reseed (restart) the random number generator each time the program is run.

If you have only one computer, demonstrate the program by running it five times. If students have computers, have them **work in pairs**, run the program five times, and count the times that each number appears. Have students write a paragraph about what they did and whether they obtained the results they were expecting.

Activity 4 Technology Connection You may wish to demonstrate how to simulate random events using *StatExplorer*. You could then assign *Technology Sourcebook, Computer Master 16*. Students use *StatExplorer* or similar software to simulate the activity that precedes this lesson.

7. Suppose a multiple-choice question has 4 choices, A, B, C, and D, and you guess randomly.
   a. What is the probability that you will get the question correct? $\frac{1}{4}$
   b. If choice C is the correct answer, identify the event E, $N(E)$, the set of all outcomes S, $N(S)$, and $P(E)$ for the situation in part **a.**
   c. What is the probability that you will miss the question? $\frac{3}{4}$
   d. What are the events in parts **a** and **c** called? complements
   b) $E = \{C\}$; $N(E) = 1$; $S = \{A, B, C, D\}$; $N(S) = 4$; $P(E) = 1/4$

8. Suppose that slips containing the numbers from 1 to 50 are put in a hat. A number x is drawn. Determine each probability.
   a. $P(x > 32)$ $\frac{18}{50} = \frac{9}{25}$ b. $P(x < 32)$ $\frac{31}{50}$ c. $P(x = 32)$ $\frac{1}{50}$

In 9–11, a card is drawn randomly from a standard deck of cards. Find:

9. P(selecting the 7 of clubs) $\frac{1}{52}$

10. P(selecting a king) $\frac{1}{13}$

11. P(selecting a diamond) $\frac{1}{4}$

12. What is the meaning when a probability equals 0?
    An event is impossible.

13. What is the meaning when a probability equals 1?
    An event is sure to happen.

14. If p is the probability of an event, and q is the probability of its complement, what is the value of $p + q$? 1

Applying the Mathematics

15. A letter is picked randomly from the English alphabet. Calculate P(A, E, I, O, or U), the probability of picking a vowel. $\frac{5}{26}$

16. A student mails an entry to a magazine sweepstakes. The student says, "The probability of winning is $\frac{1}{2}$, since either I will win or I won't." What is wrong with this argument? The event is winning; the number of possible outcomes is the number of people who enter.

17. Suppose X, Y, and Z are events, $P(X) = \frac{3}{4}$, $P(Y) = \frac{1}{2}$, and $P(Z) = \frac{2}{3}$.
    a. If you could find actual relative frequencies of these events, which event would you expect to have the largest relative frequency? Explain. X, because it has the largest probability
    b. Event Y has the smallest probability. Must it have the smallest relative frequency? Explain.
    No; relative frequency can vary from experiment to experiment.

Mileage until worn out	Number of tires
10,000–14,999	1
15,000–19,999	3
20,000–24,999	6
25,000–29,999	15
30,000–34,999	14
35,000–39,999	7
40,000 or more	4

In 18 and 19, consider the following. A tire company tested 50 tires to see how long they last under typical road conditions. The results they obtained are given in the table at the left.

18. What is the relative frequency that a tire lasted less than 25,000 miles? (Write as a fraction.) $\frac{1}{5}$

19. What is the relative frequency that a tire lasted at least 10,000 miles? $\frac{50}{50} = 1$

374

Adapting to Individual Needs

Extra Help
Some students may not understand why probabilities and relative frequencies are always between zero and one. Write the letters a, a, b, b, b, and c on separate slips of paper. Put the slips of paper in a box, and then draw one out without looking. Ask how many slips of paper have letters on them and how many slips there are altogether [6, 6]. Explain that the definition of the probability of an event shows that the probability of drawing a letter is $\frac{6}{6}$, or 1. Note that it would be impossible to draw more than 6 letters and have a fraction greater than 1. Then ask how many slips have the letter f and the probability of drawing a slip with an f. [0; $\frac{0}{6}$, or 0]. Finally, ask for the probability of drawing an a [$\frac{2}{6}$, or $\frac{1}{3}$], b [$\frac{3}{6}$, or $\frac{1}{2}$], or c [$\frac{1}{6}$]. Point out that these probabilities are all numbers between zero and one.

In 20 and 21, *multiple choice.*

20. An event occurred c times out of t possible occurrences. The relative frequency of the event was 30%. Which is true? **a**

(a) $\frac{c}{t} = 0.3$ (b) $\frac{t}{c} = 0.3$ (c) $ct = 0.3$ (d) $t - c = 0.3$

21. Of the people surveyed, $\frac{4}{9}$ thought the American League team would win the World Series. If $36n$ people were surveyed, how many thought the American League team would win? **d**

(a) $\frac{4}{9}n$ (b) $4n$ (c) $9n$ (d) $16n$

Review

22. a. Sneakers were originally $79.95 and now are on sale for $59.95. Give the percent of discount. **25%**
    b. Sneakers were originally F dollars and now are on sale for S dollars. Give the percent of discount. $\frac{F - S}{F}$
    c. If in part **a** you must pay $3.30 tax, what is the tax rate? *(Lesson 6-3)* **5.5%**

23. An orange punch is made by mixing two parts orange juice with three parts ginger ale. Six gallons of punch are needed. How many quarts of orange juice and how many quarts of ginger ale will it take? *(Lesson 6-3)* **9.6 quarts orange juice, 14.4 quarts ginger ale**

24. What is the domain of t in the expression $t + \frac{t - 1}{t}$? *(Lesson 6-2)*
the set of all real numbers, t, such that $t \neq 0$

25. Refer to the figure at the left. If the area of square S is 9 and the *perimeter* of square T is 20, find the area of square R. *(Lesson 1-5)*
64

26. *Skill sequence.* Suppose a and b are not zero. Simplify the expression. *(Lessons 2-3, 3-9, 4-1, 6-1)*

a. $\frac{2a}{5} + \frac{a}{b}$ $\frac{2ab + 5a}{5b}$ **b.** $\frac{2a}{5} - \frac{a}{b}$ $\frac{2ab - 5a}{5b}$ **c.** $\frac{2a}{5} \cdot \frac{a}{b}$ $\frac{2a^2}{5b}$ **d.** $\frac{2a}{5} \div \frac{a}{b}$ $\frac{2b}{5}$

In 27 and 28, solve. *(Lessons 2-6, 4-3)*

27. $\frac{5}{8}m = \frac{10}{3}$ $\frac{16}{3}$ **28.** $P - 0.06P - 14 = 98.8$ **120**

29. The list price of a bicycle is b dollars. Find the selling price according to the following conditions.
    a. You get a 25% discount, and there is no tax. $b - .25b = .75b$
    b. You pay 4% sales tax and get no discount. $b + .04b = 1.04b$
    c. You get a 25% discount and pay a 4% sales tax. *(Lesson 4-2)*
      $.75b + .04(.75b) = .78b$

Exploration

30. a. Make a paper airplane. After flying it 5 times, guess the probability that when it is flown, it will land right side up.
    b. Fly the plane a large number of times and calculate the relative frequency that it landed right side up.
    c. Having done the experiment, decide whether or not you should change the probability you guessed. Explain your decision.
    a, b, c) Answers will vary.

Paper airplanes can take many forms.

Adapting to Individual Needs

English Language Development
The following terms may be new to students: *event, complement, at random, relative frequency, probability.* You might perform an actual experiment, and emphasize the terminology as you proceed.

Challenge
Have the students solve the following problem: The letters A, H, M, and T are written on four identical cards and put into a hat. If the cards are then drawn one at a time until all four have been selected, what is the probability that they will be drawn in the order MATH? $[\frac{1}{4} \cdot \frac{1}{3} \cdot \frac{1}{2} \cdot \frac{1}{1}, \text{ or } \frac{1}{24}.]$

Practice
For more questions on SPUR Objectives, use **Lesson Master 6-4A** (shown on page 373) or **Lesson Master 6-4B** (shown on pages 374–375).

Assessment
Quiz A quiz covering Lessons 6-1 through 6-4 is provided in the *Assessment Sourcebook.*

Written Communication Ask each student to write a sentence or two about anything in this lesson that was not understood. Explain that you will be the only person who will see the papers. [Students' papers are specific and reveal concepts that need to be reviewed.]

Extension
Ask students what the information in Additional Example 4 tells them about the die. [Sample: The die has an even number of sides; $\frac{1}{2}$ of the numbers on the die are even.]

Project Update Project 5, *Lotteries,* on page 409, relates to the content of this lesson.

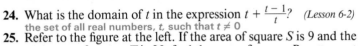
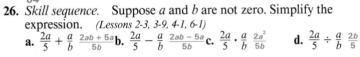

▶ **LESSON MASTER 6-4 B** *page 2*

5. A teacher filled a box with 700 yellow and 400 green centimeter cubes. A student randomly grabbed a handful of 22 cubes and found that 16 were yellow.
   a. Give the probability of randomly selecting a yellow cube. $\frac{7}{11}$
   b. Give the student's relative frequency of randomly selecting a yellow cube. $\frac{8}{11}$

6. Describe the complement of each event.
   a. Toss a number cube and get a number greater than 4.
   Toss a number cube and get a number less than or equal to 4.
   b. The lake is frozen.
   The lake is not frozen.
   c. The name of a state begins with a vowel.
   The name of a state begins with a consonant.

7. Music Boosters sold 814 raffle tickets. One ticket will be drawn at random, and the winner will receive tickets to a concert. Rose bought 12 tickets. Let the event E = Rose wins and S = set of outcomes. Find each of the following.
   a. $N(E)$ 12
   b. $N(S)$ 814
   c. $P(E)$ $\frac{6}{407}$
   d. P(Rose does not win.) $\frac{401}{407}$

8. A card is drawn at random from a regular deck. Find each of the following.
   a. P(four) $\frac{1}{13}$
   b. P(four of diamonds) $\frac{1}{52}$
   c. P(four, five, six, seven, or eight) $\frac{5}{13}$
   d. P(spade) $\frac{1}{4}$

9. Consider tossing a die. Give an example of an event.
   a. with probability 0.   Sample: tossing a 7
   b. with probability 1.   Sample: tossing a number less than 7

375

Objectives

B Solve percent problems.
H Solve percent problems in real situations.

Resources

From the *Teacher's Resource File*
- Lesson Master 6-5A or 6-5B
- Answer Master 6-5
- Teaching Aid 58: Warm-up
- Technology Sourcebook Computer Master 17

Additional Resources
- Visual for Teaching Aid 58

Teaching Lesson 6-5

Warm-up

Suppose 20% of a number is 73.
1. What is 10% of the number?
   36.5
2. What is 5% of the number?
   18.25
3. What is 30% of the number?
   109.5
4. What is 100% of the number?
   365
5. What is 105% of the number?
   383.25

Encourage students to use the fact that 10% is $\frac{1}{2}$ of 20%, and calculate $\frac{1}{2}$ of 73. In each case, using a relation about multiples or sums makes it easier to find the answer. For instance, 105% of 73 is 100% of 73 plus 5% of 73.

LESSON

6-5

Solving Percent Problems Using Equations

Women in uniform. *In 1991, 35,000 U.S. women participated in the Persian Gulf War. They represented 6% of the U.S. troops who served there. See Example 3.*

The word **percent** (often written as the two words **per cent**) comes from the Latin words "per centum," meaning "per 100." So 7% literally means 7 per 100, or the ratio $\frac{7}{100}$, or 0.07. The symbol % for percent is only about 100 years old.

Recall that to find a percent p of a given quantity q you can multiply q by the decimal or fraction form of p.

To find 50% of 120,000 calculate $0.5 \cdot 120{,}000 = 60{,}000$.
To find $5\frac{1}{4}$% of \$3000 calculate $0.0525 \cdot 3000 = \$157.50$.

This gives a straightforward method for solving many percent problems. Just translate the words into an equation of the form $pq = r$.

Example 1

a. 112% of 650 is what number?
b. 7% of what number is 31.5?
c. What percent of 3.5 is 0.84?

Solution

a. 112% of 650 is what number?

$$
\begin{array}{ccccc}
\downarrow & \downarrow & \downarrow & \downarrow & \downarrow \\
p & \cdot & q & = & r \\
1.12 & \cdot & 650 & = & r \\
& & 728 & = & r
\end{array}
\qquad \text{Change 112\% to 1.12.}
$$

112% of 650 is 728.

Check

$\frac{728}{650} = 1.12 = 112\%.$

▶

Lesson 6-5 Overview

Broad Goals In this lesson, students learn a method by which all three types of percent problems can be solved—translating the percent problems into equations.

Perspective In previous courses, some students may have learned about the three different problems involving percent that are illustrated in **Example 1,** and they may have been taught three different ways of finding the answers. This lesson shows the strength of algebra—it gives students one way to set up all three problems. Then, after equations are set up, students can apply the properties of algebra to find the solutions.

We include work with percents that are greater than 100% because this will be important in working with exponential growth in Chapter 8. At that time, students must be comfortable using percents greater than 100%, and they must be able to convert the percent form to a decimal.

The numbers used in real percent problems are often quite large, and the use of a calculator is most appropriate. But as noted on page 378, the percent key is often programmed in special ways. That is why we ask students to explore the percent key (if they have it) on their calculators to see how the key works.

Solution

b. 7% of what number is 31.5?

$$\begin{array}{ccc} \downarrow \downarrow & \downarrow & \downarrow \downarrow \\ p \cdot & q & = r \end{array}$$

$0.07 \cdot \quad q \quad = 31.5$ 7% is 0.07.

$\dfrac{0.07q}{0.07} = \dfrac{31.5}{0.07}$ Divide both sides by 0.07.

$q \quad = 450$

31.5 is 7% of 450.

Check
7% of 450 = 0.07 · 450 = 31.5

Solution

c. What % of 3.5 is 0.84?

$$\begin{array}{ccc} \downarrow & \downarrow \downarrow \downarrow & \downarrow \\ p & \cdot \ q \ = & r \end{array}$$

$p \cdot 3.5 = 0.84$

$\dfrac{p \cdot 3.5}{3.5} = \dfrac{0.84}{3.5}$ Divide both sides by 3.5.

$p = 0.24$ This is the solution to the equation.

$p = 24\%$ Rewrite the solution as a percent.

Check
24% · 3.5 = 0.24 · 3.5 = 0.84

Example 2

It was reported that in 1991 about 59% of the 52.5 million married couples in the United States had two incomes. Approximately how many couples had two incomes in 1991?

Solution

Let c be the number of millions of couples with two incomes.

$$0.59 \cdot 52.5 = c$$
$$30.975 = c$$

In 1991, approximately 31 million couples had two incomes.

Example 3

In 1992, there were 207,828 women serving in the Armed Forces of the United States, accounting for about 11.5% of total military personnel. In all, how many persons were serving in the Armed Forces in 1992?

Solution

Let x be the number of persons in the Armed Forces.

$$11.5\% \cdot x = 207,828$$
$$0.115 \cdot x = 207,828$$
$$x = \frac{207,828}{0.115}$$
$$x = 1,807,200$$

About 1,807,200 persons served in the Armed Forces in 1992.

Lesson 6-5 *Solving Percent Problems Using Equations* **377**

In 1960, about 32% of married women were in the labor force. By 1980, that figure had jumped to about 50%.

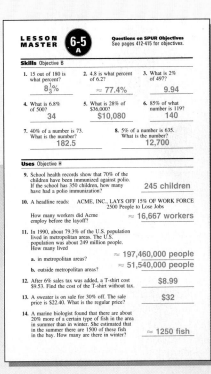
Optional Activities

Activity 1 Consumer Connection
Materials: Newspapers or magazines

After students read the lesson, they might make up an advertisement announcing the sale of items. They can decide what to sell and give its real price and its sale price. Then they can compute the amount of discount.

As a variation of the activity, students might cut out an advertisement about a sale from a newspaper or magazine and write two questions based on the advertisement. You can use their questions as a review on subsequent days. Or you could have students **work with partners** and then have the partners exchange questions, solve them, and discuss the solutions.

Many problems related to business involve percents. If the problems involve discounts (or markups), you often must use subtraction (or addition) as well as multiplication and division to solve them.

Example 4

The total cost of a video game was $51.89. This included the 6% sales tax. What was the price of the game without the tax?

Solution

Let V be the price of the video game.

$$\text{total cost} = \text{price} + 6\% \text{ sales tax}$$
$$51.89 = V + .06V$$

Remember, $V = 1V$ $51.89 = (1 + .06)V$
$$51.89 = 1.06V$$
$$\frac{51.89}{1.06} = \frac{1.06V}{1.06}$$
$$48.95 \approx V$$

The price without sales tax was $48.95.

Check

$48.95 + 0.06(48.95) = 51.887 \approx 51.89$.

Percent problems are so common that many calculators have a $\boxed{\%}$ key. If you press 5 $\boxed{\%}$ on such a calculator you will see 0.05, which equals 5%. On many calculators when the $\boxed{\%}$ key is used after an addition or subtraction sign, it will calculate discounts or markups without having to enter the original amount again.

Activity

If your calculator has a $\boxed{\%}$ key, enter the following key sequence.

$$48.95 \; \boxed{+} \; 6 \; \boxed{\%} \; \boxed{=}$$

What does your calculator display? If it shows 51.887, it is interpreting the "$\boxed{+}$ 6 $\boxed{\%}$" to mean "plus 6% of the previous amount"; the calculator evaluates $48.95 + 6\% \cdot 48.95$. If it displays 49.01, your calculator has evaluated $48.95 + 0.06$.

QUESTIONS

Covering the Reading

1. 123% of 780 is what number? 959.4

2. 40% of what number is 440? 1100

3. What percent of 4.7 is 0.94? 20%

4. What number is 62% of 980? 607.6

378

5. a. In 1991, how many married couples were there in the United States? **52.5 million**
b. Of these, how many did not have two incomes? **21.5 million**

6. a. In 1992, what percent of U.S. military personnel were men? **88.5%**
b. How many men were in the U.S. Armed Forces in 1992? **1,599,372**

7. About 67,000 or 13.1% of U.S. Navy personnel are officers.
a. Write an equation that you can use to determine how many Navy personnel there are in all. **0.131 N = 67,000**
b. Solve the equation. **511,450**

8. In Example 4, if the price with sales tax was $42.39, find the price without sales tax. **$39.99**

9. The total cost of a camera including an 8.5% sales tax is $59. How much tax was paid in this purchase? **$4.62**

10. The Richardsons bought a new car. The total amount they paid was $14,064.75, including the 5% sales tax. What was the price before the sales tax was added? **$13,395**

Applying the Mathematics

11. On a mathematics test there were 8 As, 12 Bs, 10 Cs, 2 Ds and 0 Fs. What percent of the students earned As? **25%**

12. Clearwater High School expects a 14% increase in enrollment next year. There are 1850 students enrolled this year.
a. How many students will the school gain? **259**
b. What is the expected enrollment next year? **2109**

13. In the decade of the 1980s the U.S. Congress passed many bills designating commemorative days, weeks, months, and so on. These included National Prune Day, Tap Dance Day, and Dairy Goat Awareness Week. This type of law amounted to about 250 bills per session or 38% of all laws passed. What was the total number of laws passed per session? **658**

In 14 and 15, use this information. Sucrose, or common table sugar, is composed of carbon, hydrogen, and oxygen. Suppose an experiment calls for 68.4 grams of sucrose.

14. If 4.2% of the weight of sucrose is carbon, how much carbon is in the 68.4 grams? (Round your answer to the nearest tenth of a gram.) **2.9 grams**

15. If 35.2 of the 68.4 grams is oxygen, what percent of the weight of sucrose is oxygen? (Round your answer to the nearest whole number percent.) **51%**

16. Pat bought some new clothes at a "30% off" sale. She spent $73.50. What was the price of the clothes before the discount? **$105**

17. A TV originally cost $320. It is on sale for $208. What is the percent of discount? **35%**

Goat awareness.
These goats are grazing on the roof of a Swedish restaurant in Wisconsin. In Sweden, many homes in small villages are designed so that goats may graze on the roofs.

Lesson 6-5 *Solving Percent Problems Using Equations* **379**

6. Here is an actual newspaper quote in which the arithmetic is incorrect: The 400-page report says that "the average citizen had a better than 18 percent chance of falling victim to a serious crime, with an average of 5,480 offenses per 100,000 Americans." Where is the error? **It appears that the reciprocal $\frac{100,000}{5480}$ was used instead of the correct ratio $\frac{5480}{100,000}$. The correct percent can be estimated as follows: $\frac{5480}{100,000} \approx 5.5\%$.**

Notes on Questions

Question 5b Error Alert Some students may answer this question by saying 52% because they do not see the difference between finding the number of couples and finding the percent of couples. Have them reread the question. Then ask whether the word *many* indicates that they should find a number or a percent.

Question 12 There are two ways to solve the problem. The first way is to multiply .14 · 1850 to find the increase in enrollment and then to add that number to 1850. The second method includes realizing that if enrollment is up 14%, then it will be 114% of its present number; so you would calculate 1.14 · 1850. The second method is more efficient and relates to the way we will do exponential growth problems.

Adapting to Individual Needs

English Language Development
To help students translate from English statements of percent problems to algebraic expressions, write the three sentences in **Example 1** on the board. Then, under each sentence, write the algebraic expression. Emphasize that "of" means "times" and "is" means "equals." Tell students to use the symbol · for multiplication and the symbol = for equals. Words like "what number" and "what percent" refer to the unknown and are written with a variable.

Notes on Questions

Question 27 Relate this question to the lesson. Since $\frac{2}{3} = 66\frac{2}{3}\%$, this problem could have been restated as a percent problem.

Question 28 Like the previous question, this question could be seen as a percent problem. What percent of a complete turn is 45°? $[\frac{45}{360} = 12.5\%]$ Students will have to use the fact that a complete turn is 360° in Lesson 6-6.

Question 30 The solution can employ the ideas of percent increase and percent decrease that students will use in Chapter 8. To increase by 30%, multiply by 130% or 1.30. To decrease by 30%, multiply by 70% or .70. If you begin with x, the result is $x \cdot 1.3 \cdot .70 = .91x$ or 91% of the beginning amount.

Follow-up
for Lesson 6-5

Practice
For more questions on SPUR Objectives, use **Lesson Master 6-5A** (shown on page 377) or **Lesson Master 6-5B** (shown on pages 378–379).

Assessment
Group Assessment Tell one student in each group to write a percent problem using 15%, and have the rest of the group members solve it. Then have another student in each group write a percent problem that contains the answer from the first problem, and have the other group members solve it. Continue until each student has written a problem. [Students write and solve a variety of percent problems.]

Extension
If your state has a sales tax, you might have students answer **Questions 9 –10** using that tax rate. If the rate is the combination of rates from more than one taxing body, you could also have students find the amount of the tax that is allotted to each body. For example, in 1994, Chicago's sales tax was 8.75%, the sum of the state's portion of 6.25% and the city's portion of 2.5%.

380

18. Refer to the figure at the left. The area of the circle is what percent of the area of the square? **78.5%**

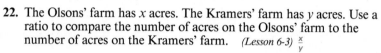

Review

19. In Seattle, Washington, it rained or snowed an average of 156 days per year in the 30 years from 1961 through 1990. What was the relative frequency of a day without rain or snow? *(Lesson 6-4)* **0.57**

20. A fair die is tossed once.
  a. Which event is more likely, "the number showing is divisible by three" or "the number showing is even"? **even**
  b. Explain your answer to part **a.** *(Lesson 6-4)* **See left.**

20b) The probability of the number being divisible by 3 is $\frac{1}{3}$. The probability of the number being even is $\frac{1}{2}$.

21. Stanley took $1\frac{1}{4}$ hours to do his homework; Jenile took 35 minutes.
  a. What is the ratio of Jenile's homework time to Stanley's? $\frac{7}{15}$
  b. What is the ratio of Stanley's homework time to Jenile's? $\frac{15}{7}$ *(Lesson 6-3)*

22. The Olsons' farm has x acres. The Kramers' farm has y acres. Use a ratio to compare the number of acres on the Olsons' farm to the number of acres on the Kramers' farm. *(Lesson 6-3)* $\frac{x}{y}$

23. The Nguyen family earned $19,600 last year on their 80-acre farm.
  a. What is the income per acre? **$245**
  b. Is the income per acre a ratio or a rate? *(Lessons 6-2, 6-3)* **rate**

24. When the expression $\frac{4}{b-7}$ is written, what is assumed about the value of b? *(Lesson 6-2)* $b \neq 7$

25. Solve $(m-6)^2 = 100$. *(Lesson 5-9)* **16; −4**

26. **a.** Solve for y: $-4x + 3y = 10$. $y = \frac{4}{3}x + \frac{10}{3}$
  b. Graph the equation on the coordinate plane. *(Lesson 5-7)*
  See left.

27. Two thirds of a number is 87. Find the number. *(Lesson 2-6)* **130.5**

28. What fraction of a complete turn is a turn of 45°? *(Previous course)* $\frac{1}{8}$

29. Convert 0.325823224 to the nearest percent. *(Previous course)* **33%**

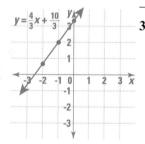

This farm is located in northwestern Connecticut.

26b)

$y = \frac{4}{3}x + \frac{10}{3}$

Exploration

30. a. Pick a number and increase it by 30%. Decrease this result by 30%. Did you end up with the number you started with? **No**
  b. Repeat part **a** three times using a different number to start with each time. **Answers will vary.**
  c. Explain how the final result is related to the original number.
  Sample: The final result will be 0.91 times the original: $x + .30x = 1.30x$ **and** $1.30x − .30(1.30x) = 0.91x.$

Adapting to Individual Needs

Challenge
Have students solve the following problem: There are 49 red jelly beans and one green jelly bean in a jar. How many red jelly beans would have to be added to the jar to change the percent of red jelly beans from 98% to 99%? [50]

Setting Up Lesson 6-6

Materials You will need a spinner for the overhead projector to simulate **Example 3** on page 382. You can use **Teaching Aid 63** and a paper clip for the arrow (holding it in place with a pencil point).

Students doing Activity 2 in *Optional Activities* on page 382 will need toothpicks.

6-6

Probability Without Counting

On target. *Archery is enjoyed both as an amateur and as a professional sport. Through practice, the probability of hitting the target should increase.*

When a situation has equally likely outcomes, the probability of an event is the ratio of the number of outcomes in the event to the total number of outcomes. But sometimes the number of outcomes is infinite. In such cases, if you can set up a geometric model, you can still use division to find probabilities.

Example 1

Suppose a dart is thrown at a 20-inch square board containing a circle of radius 3 inches. Assuming that the dart hits the board, and that it is equally likely to land on any point on the board, what is the probability that the dart lands in the circle?

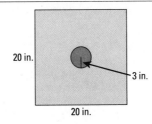

20 in.

3 in.

20 in.

Solution

Recall that the area of a circle with radius r is πr^2. Compare the area of the circle to the area of the square.

$$P(\text{dart lands in circle}) = \frac{\text{area of circle}}{\text{area of square}}$$

$$= \frac{(\pi \cdot 3^2) \text{ sq in}}{(20 \cdot 20) \text{ sq in}}$$

$$= \frac{9\pi}{400}$$

$$\approx 0.071 \text{ or about 7\%}$$

So, the probability that the dart lands in the circle is about 7%.

Example 1 illustrates the *Probability Formula for Geometric Regions.*

Lesson 6-6 *Probability Without Counting* **381**

Lesson 6-6

Objectives

J Find probabilities involving geometric regions.

Resources

From the **Teacher's Resource File**
- Lesson Master 6-6A or 6-6B
- Answer Master 6-6
- Teaching Aids
  58 Warm-up
  63 Examples 1-4
  64 Additional Examples
  65 Questions 11, 13, 14
  66 Challenge
- Activity Kit, Activity 14

Additional Resources
- Visuals for Teaching Aids 58, 63–66
- Globe (Question 10)

Teaching 6-6
Lesson

Warm-up

Find the area of each figure.
1. A circle with a radius of 6 cm ≈ **113.04 cm²**
2. A square with sides of length 1.5 cm **2.25 cm²**
3. A triangle with a height of 8 in. and a base of 16 in. **64 in²**
4. A circle with a diameter of 20 in. ≈ **314 in²**
5. A square with a perimeter of 24 in. **36 in²**
6. A rectangle with a length of x cm and width of $2x$ cm **2x^2 cm²**

Lesson 6-6 Overview

Broad Goals In Lesson 6-4, students learned that probabilities are often calculated by taking ratios of the numbers of elements in sets. The goal of this lesson is to show that probabilities can also be calculated by determining ratios of measures, such as lengths or areas.

Perspective The geometric representation of probability gives students a model that facilitates the understanding of the probability of an event. Geometric probabilities may be ratios of lengths, angle measures, areas, or volumes.

Geometric interpretations of probability are quite important in statistics. The normal curve used in standardized tests exhibits this idea. Areas of sections under the curve are related to the probabilities that students will achieve certain scores.

Optional Activities

Activity 1 You might want to use *Activity Kit, Activity 14,* to introduce or to follow up Lesson 6-6. In this activity, students run an experiment to approximate a probability, and then they determine the probability by calculating areas.

Teaching Aid 63 contains the diagrams for **Examples 1–4.**

Geometry Connection There are two key ideas to emphasize in this lesson. The first is that probabilities can be ratios of lengths, angle measures, areas, or volumes; in this lesson, examples of the first three are given. Ask students which type of measure is used in each example. [**Examples 1 and 4** involve areas; **Example 2** involves lengths; **Example 3** involves angle measures.]

The second key idea to emphasize is that the probability is the ratio of measures of regions but only if the outcomes are random throughout the region.

Cooperative Learning Students usually enjoy seeing **Example 3** demonstrated on an overhead projector. Use **Teaching Aid 63.** Hold a paper clip (arrow) in place with a pencil point. Spin the spinner several times, counting the number of times the spinner stops in region A. Note that, if the spinner is fair, spinning it more and more will result in the relative frequency coming closer and closer to the probability predicted by the geometric ratio.

Ask students to estimate when the relative frequency would convince them that the spinner is biased. Direct their attention to the spinner in **Example 3**, and note that $P(B) = \frac{1}{4}$. Ask them to imagine spinning the pointer 100 times and to tell which of the following would be reasonable for a fair spinner: 10 Bs, 24 Bs, 30 Bs, or 55 Bs. [24 Bs] This kind of question is formalized in statistics courses. It is acceptable to ask the question informally at this point in order to emphasize the difference between a relative frequency and a probability.

> **Probability Formula for Geometric Regions**
> Suppose points are selected at random in a region, and part of that region's points represent an event E. The probability $P(E)$ of the event is given by
> $$P(E) = \frac{\text{measure of region in the event}}{\text{measure of entire region}}.$$

In Example 1, the probability is the ratio of two areas. In Example 2, the probability is the ratio of two lengths.

Example 2

Points A, B, C, D, and E below represent exits on an interstate highway.

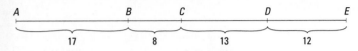

The distances between the exits are measured in miles. If accidents occur at random along the highway between points A and E, what is the probability that an accident occurs between B and C?

Solution

Use the Putting-Together Model for Addition to find the length of AE.
$AE = 17 + 8 + 13 + 12 = 50.$

$$P(\text{the accident is in } \overline{BC}) = \frac{BC}{AE}$$
$$= \frac{8 \text{ miles}}{50 \text{ miles}}$$
$$= 0.16 \text{ or } 16\%$$

The probability that an accident occurs between B and C is about 16%.

Traffic-safety engineers might compare the probabilities in Example 2 with the actual relative frequency of accidents. If the relative frequency along one stretch of the highway is too large, then that part of the highway might be a candidate for repair or new safety features.

Probabilities can also be determined by finding ratios of angle measures.

Example 3

At the left is a picture of a spinner like that used in many games. Suppose the spinner is equally likely to point in any direction. What is the probability that it stops in region A?

Solution

The sum of the measures of all the angles around the center of the circle is 360°. $P(\text{spinner stops in A}) = \frac{30°}{360°} = \frac{1}{12}$.

Optional Activities

Activity 2
Materials: Toothpicks

Question 28 illustrates an activity you might want to use with **small groups of students.** Instead of needles, students can use toothpicks. To minimize experimental error and to save time, we suggest you provide each group with worksheets on which you have drawn lines that are the correct distance apart. Have students follow the directions,

and calculate the ratio given in **Question 28.** When they have finished, have each group write its data in a table on the chalkboard. Then calculate the following ratio using the data from the entire class:

$$\frac{\text{number of toothpicks touching line}}{\text{number of times toothpick is dropped}}$$

As you discuss the data, four things are worth noting in your discussion:

1. The final $\frac{A}{B}$ for the whole class is a *weighted average* of the data from each group. Unless each group drops the toothpicks the same number of times, the final average *cannot* be determined by averaging the individual group ratios.
2. When students do the experiment, the ratios determined by individual groups are not likely to be very close to $\frac{2}{\pi}$. However, the value calculated by aggregating

Sometimes to compute a probability you must add or subtract first.

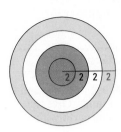

Example 4

A target consists of four evenly spaced concentric circles as shown at the left. The smallest circle (called the "bull's-eye") has radius equal to 2 inches. If a point is selected at random from inside the target, what is the probability that it lies in the blue region?

Solution

Probability that a point lies in blue region $= \dfrac{\text{area of blue region}}{\text{area of largest circle}}$.

The area of the blue region equals the difference in the areas of the circles with radii 4 and 2.

$$\text{Area of blue region} = \pi(4)^2 - \pi(2)^2$$
$$= 16\pi - 4\pi$$
$$= 12\pi$$

$$\text{Area of largest circle} = \pi(8)^2 = 64\pi$$

Thus the probability of choosing a point in the blue region is $\dfrac{12\pi}{64\pi}$, or $\dfrac{3}{16}$.

QUESTIONS

Covering the Reading

1. Consider the square archery target board at the left.
   a. What is the area of the bull's-eye? **$16\pi = 50.3$ in^2**
   b. What is the area of the entire target board? **625 in^2**
   c. What is the probability that an arrow hitting the board at random will land in the bull's-eye? **0.08**
   d. What is the probability that the arrow will land on the target outside the circle? **0.92**

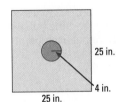

25 in.

4 in.

25 in.

In 2 and 3, refer to Example 2. What is the probability that an accident occurring between exits A and E occurs between the given exits?

2. B and E **$\frac{33}{50}$ or 66%**

3. C and E **$\frac{1}{2}$ or 50%**

In 4–6, refer to Example 3.

4. What is the probability that the spinner will land in region B? **$\frac{1}{4}$**

5. What is the probability that the spinner will land in region C? **$\frac{13}{36}$**

6. What is the probability that the spinner will not land in region C? **$\frac{23}{36}$**

7. In general, what is the probability of an event involving a geometric region? **the measure of the region in the event divided by the measure of the entire region**

Lesson 6-6 *Probability Without Counting* **383**

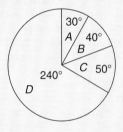
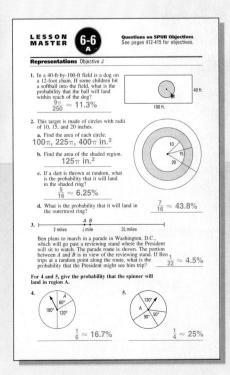
each group's data is likely to be closer to the true value of $\frac{2}{\pi}$. Still, it will not be too close because huge numbers of trials are needed to get accuracy to two decimal places.

3. Buffon's needle experiment is sometimes used to estimate the value of π. You might ask your class to estimate π based on the class data. [For instance, if your class found a ratio of .66, then

$.66 = \frac{2}{\pi}$. Solving for π gives $\pi = \frac{2}{.66} \approx 3$.]

4. You might also ask students what rational numbers are close to $\frac{2}{\pi}$. [One method of finding them is to think first of rational approximations to π, then to $\frac{\pi}{2}$, and then to take the reciprocal. In this way, the estimate $\frac{22}{7}$ to π becomes the estimate $\frac{7}{11}$ to $\frac{2}{\pi}$.]

4. In the square below, everything outside the triangle has been shaded. If a point is chosen at random, what is the probability that it will lie in the shaded portion? (Remember that the area of a triangle = $\frac{1}{2} \cdot$ base $\cdot$ height.) $\frac{7}{9}$

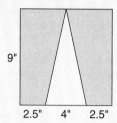

9"

2.5"   4"   2.5"

Notes on Questions

The diagrams for **Questions 11, 13, and 14** are given on **Teaching Aid 65.**

Question 10 Notice that surface area is used in this question. Use a globe to illustrate that the earth's surface has much more water than land. You can review ratio ideas by asking for the ratio of water to land on the earth. [140 million square miles to 58 million miles is about 2.4 to 1.]

Question 12 This question can be solved by thinking of the circle as being divided into twelfths or by realizing that the arc is 30° for each hour.

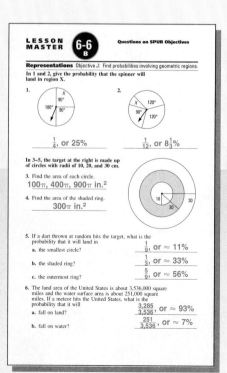

In 8 and 9, refer to Example 4. Suppose a point on the circular target is chosen at random.

8. What is the probability that it lies inside the bull's-eye? $\frac{1}{16}$

9. What is the probability that it lies in the outermost ring? $\frac{7}{16}$

Applying the Mathematics

10. The land area of the earth is about 57,510,000 square miles and the water surface area is about 139,440,000 square miles. Give the probability that a meteor hitting the surface of the earth will:
a. fall on land. 0.29   **b.** fall on water. 0.71

11. In a rectangular yard of dimensions q by p is a rectangular garden of dimensions b by a. If a newspaper is thrown randomly into the yard, what is the probability that it lands on a point in the garden? $\frac{ab}{pq}$

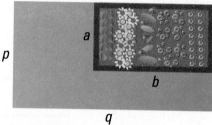

12. An electric clock was stopped by a power failure. What is the probability that the minute hand stopped between the following two numerals on the face of the clock?
a. 12 and 3 $\frac{1}{4}$ **b.** 1 and 5 $\frac{1}{3}$ **c.** 11 and 1 $\frac{1}{6}$

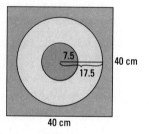

13. Suppose a 40-cm square dart board has two concentric circles, as shown below. The larger has a radius of 17.5 cm, and the bull's-eye has radius 7.5 cm. Suppose a dart is thrown and that each point on the board is equally likely to be hit.

7.5   40 cm
17.5

40 cm

a. What is the probability that the dart lands inside the larger circle? 0.60
b. What is the probability that the dart lands inside the larger circle but outside the bull's-eye? 0.49
c. What is the probability that the dart lands outside both circles? 0.40

Optional Activities

Activity 3 Technology Connection
The program at the right will simulate spinning the spinner in **Example 3** twenty times, and that number can be increased by changing line 20. Students can run this program to determine relative frequencies, and compare them with the probabilities. The variable (Z$) is a string variable; it will print out its succeeding values in a string (such as ACDAB . . .).

```
10 PRINT "ON SPIN", "THE SPINNER
   LANDED ON"
20 FOR X = 1 TO 20
30 LET Y = INT(RND(1)*360)
40 IF Y ≤ 30 THEN LET Z$ = "A"
50 IF Y > 30 AND Y ≤ 120 THEN LET
   Z$ = "B"
60 IF Y > 120 AND Y ≤ 250 THEN LET
   Z$ = "C"
70 IF Y > 250 THEN LET Z$ = "D"
```

The rebounding Rocket. *Nigerian-born Hakeem Olajuwon of the Houston Rockets did not start playing basketball until age 15. He was named NBA's Most Valuable Player in 1994.*

15)
Grade Level Groups

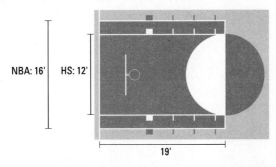

Angle sizes: 9th is 30°; 10th is 90°; 11th is 102°; 12th is 138°.

14. The basketball court used in the NBA (National Basketball Association) has a wider free-throw lane than that used in high schools and colleges. The dimensions of the NBA lane are 16′ by 19′. For high schools they are 12′ by 19′. Assuming that rebounds are equally likely to land anywhere in the NBA lane, what is the probability that a rebound which lands in the NBA lane would also land in the high school lane? **0.75**

NBA: 16′   HS: 12′

19′

15. The table at the right gives the membership in a high school club. Design a spinner that can be used to select a representative group from the club. **See left.**

Grade	Enrollment
9	5
10	15
11	17
12	23

Review

16. Compute in your head. *(Lesson 6-5)*
   a. What is 25% of 60? **15**
   b. 50% of what number is 13? **26**
   c. 8 is what percent of 24? **$33\frac{1}{3}$%**

17. A television station has scheduled n hours of news, c hours of comedy, d hours of drama, s hours of sports, and x hours of other programs during the week.
   a. What is the ratio of hours of comedy to hours of sports? $\frac{c}{s}$
   b. What is the ratio of hours of drama to total number of hours of programs during the week? $\frac{d}{n+c+d+s+x}$
   c. If you turn on this station at some randomly chosen time, and a show is on the air, what is the probability that it is a news program? *(Lessons 6-4, 6-3)* $\frac{n}{n+c+d+s+x}$

18. A 10-foot-long board is cut so that the two pieces formed have lengths in a ratio of $\frac{5}{3}$. How long is each piece? *(Lesson 6-3)*
   6.25 ft;   3.75 ft

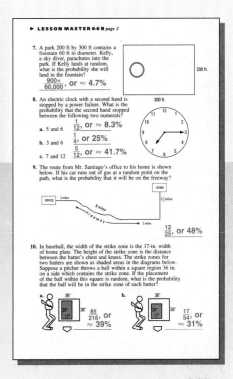

Adapting to Individual Needs

```
80 PRINT X, Z$
90 NEXT X
100 END
```

The random-number function on your calculator or computer may have different requirements. You may have to type RANDOMIZE or use the random-number generator. Consult the manual for information on how to do this.

Extra Help
Some students might need to review the area formulas. Draw a rectangle, a square, a triangle, and a circle on the board, and label the appropriate dimensions of each figure. Then ask volunteers to explain how to find the area of each shape. For the circle, be sure to review the meaning of *radius* and the approximate value of π. Also point out that it is sometimes unnecessary to substitute an approximation of π (as in **Example 4**).

385

In 1777, Buffon proved the property which bears his name by using calculus. It was realized some time later that this property could be used to obtain an approximation to π. In 1901, Marió Lazzarini reported doing an experiment in which he threw 3408 needles down and 1808 of them touched a line. Lazzarini's relative frequency gives an approximation close to π. Students extend this idea in Activity 2 in *Optional Activities* on pages 382–383. (For more information, see "Lazzarini's Lucky Approximation of π" by Lee Badger in the April, 1994, issue of *Mathematics Magazine*.)

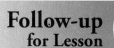

Follow-up **6-6**
for Lesson

Practice

For more questions on SPUR Objectives, use **Lesson Master 6-6A** (shown on page 383) or **Lesson Master 6-6B** (shown on pages 384–385).

Assessment

Oral/Written Communication Ask students to name and give an example of each type of probability. [Students recognize the difference between finding probabilities by counting and by using geometric regions.]

Extension

Have students **work in groups** to design a four-region circular spinner (Regions *A, B, C,* and *D*) for which the probability of the spinner landing in Region *A* is $\frac{3}{8}$, in Region *B* is $\frac{1}{3}$, and in Region *C* is $\frac{1}{4}$. [The regions will have central angles of 135°, 120°, 90°, and 15°. Note that the probability of landing in region *D* is not given; it is $\frac{1}{24}$.]

Project Update Project 4, *Archery*, on page 409, relates to the content of this lesson.

A marathon winner. *In 1994, Jean Driscoll of Champaign, Illinois, won her fifth straight women's wheelchair title in the Boston Marathon with a record time of 1:34.21. This is an average rate of about 7.46 meters per second!*

19a) 10.152 for the 100 m; 10.142 for the 200m

25)

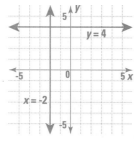

19. In July of 1994, a new world record in the 100-meter dash was set by American Leroy Burrell with a time of 9.85 seconds. The world record in the 200-meter dash, set by Italian Pietro Mennea in 1979, was 19.72 seconds.
    a. Find the average number of meters per second in each record run. See below left.
    b. By this measure, which runner is faster? Explain your answer. *(Lesson 6-2)*
       Burrell is about 0.01 m/sec faster.

In 20–22, perform the operation and simplify. *(Lessons 3-9, 6-1)*

20. $1\frac{5}{9} \div 2\frac{1}{7}$ $\frac{98}{135}$ 21. $\frac{2x}{s} \div \frac{x}{10}$ $\frac{20}{s}$ 22. $\frac{q}{2} + \frac{q}{3}$ $\frac{5q}{6}$

23. Solve $\frac{x}{2} - 4 = \frac{3x}{4}$. *(Lesson 5-8)* -16

24. Solve for *y*: $x + 10y = 15$. *(Lesson 5-7)* $y = -\frac{1}{10}x + \frac{3}{2}$

25. Graph $y = 4$ and $x = -2$ in the coordinate plane. *(Lesson 5-1)* See below left.

26. The volume of a box is to be more than 1700 cm³. The base has dimensions 8 cm by 15 cm. What are the possible heights of the box? *(Lessons 2-1, 2-8)* greater than 14.16 cm

27. In the U.S. Army a *squad* is usually 10 enlisted soldiers. A *platoon* is 4 squads. A *company* is 4 platoons. A *battalion* is 4 companies. A *brigade* is 3 battalions. A *division* is 3 brigades. A *corps* is 2 divisions. A *field army* is 2 corps. How many enlisted personnel are there in a field army? *(Lesson 2-4)* 23,040

Exploration

28. In 1760, the French mathematician Buffon performed an experiment and discovered an amazing property. He drew four parallel lines as close to exactly ℓ units apart as possible, where ℓ was the length of a needle. He dropped the needle onto the lines and counted how often it touched a line and how often it did not. Buffon discovered that if the needle is dropped randomly onto the lines, then the probability the needle touches a line is $\frac{2}{\pi}$.

    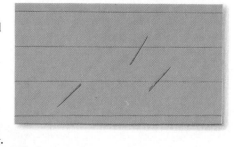

    That is, $\dfrac{\text{number of times needle touches line}}{\text{number of times needle is dropped}} = \dfrac{2}{\pi}$.
    Try Buffon's experiment, drawing the lines and then dropping the needle at least 100 times. How close do you get to $\frac{2}{\pi}$?
    Answers will vary.

Adapting to Individual Needs

Challenge Have students solve the following problem, which is also given on **Teaching Aid 66**: A kidney-shaped swimming pool is located in a rectangular back yard. The sides of the pool consist of four connecting semicircles. A parachutist is hired to land in the back yard during a party. Assuming the parachutist lands somewhere in the back yard, what is the probability he or she will land on dry land? [≈ 0.67]

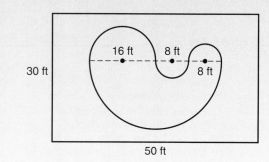

LESSON 6-7

Size Changes

Honey of a size change. *This scene from a Disney film,* Honey, I Shrunk the Kids, *shows what happened to the kids when their father accidentally shrunk them with a gadget that had a size change factor of about 1%.*

Size Changes and Multiplication

Some photocopy machines can reduce or enlarge a preimage to a given percentage of its original size. The percent of reduction or enlargement is called a *size change factor*.

For instance, the figure below was reduced to 75% of its original size to form image *A*. It was reduced to 64% of its original size to form image *B*. It was enlarged to 120% of its original size to form image *C*. Notice that the lengths and widths of the original figure are multiplied by each size change factor.

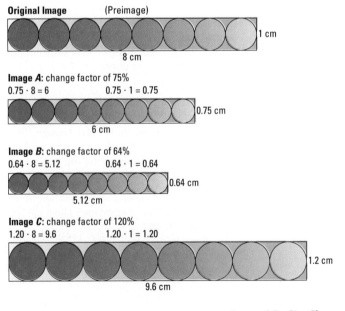

Original Image (Preimage)

1 cm
8 cm

Image *A*: change factor of 75%
0.75 · 8 = 6   0.75 · 1 = 0.75

0.75 cm
6 cm

Image *B*: change factor of 64%
0.64 · 8 = 5.12   0.64 · 1 = 0.64

0.64 cm
5.12 cm

Image *C*: change factor of 120%
1.20 · 8 = 9.6   1.20 · 1 = 1.20

1.2 cm
9.6 cm

Lesson 6-7 *Size Changes* **387**

Lesson 6-7

Objectives

H Solve percent problems in real situations.
K Apply the Size Change Model for Multiplication.

Resources

From the *Teacher's Resource File*
- Lesson Master 6-7A or 6-7B
- Answer Master 6-7
- Assessment Sourcebook: Quiz for Lessons 6-5 through 6-7
- Teaching Aids
  28 Four-Quadrant Graph Paper
  59 Warm-up
  67 Examples 2 and 3
- Activity Kit, Activity 15
- Technology Sourcebook
  Computer Master 18

Additional Resources
- Visuals for Teaching Aids 28, 59, 67

Teaching Lesson 6-7

Warm-up

Tell in which quadrant or on which axis the point lies.

	x-coordinate	*y*-coordinate
1.	positive	negative
2.	negative	negative
3.	negative	positive
4.	0	positive
5.	positive	positive
6.	negative	0

1. Quadrant IV; 2. Quadrant III;
3. Quadrant II; 4. *y*-axis;
5. Quadrant I; 6. *x*-axis

Lesson 6-7 Overview

Broad Goals This lesson discusses the Size Change Model for Multiplication—*kx* can be interpreted as the result of applying a size change of magnitude *k* to the quantity *x*. Both this lesson and the next one on proportions set up the discussion of similar figures that is found in Lesson 6-9.

Perspective The Size Change Model for Multiplication is in this chapter on division because the size change factor can always

be thought of as a result of ratio division. In the geometric sense, the ratio of corresponding sides of a size change image and its preimage is the magnitude of the size change. This lesson covers the multiplication resulting in size change. Lessons 6-8 and 6-9 include the results of size changes in discussing proportions and similar figures.

A multiplication is usually of the size change type when one factor has no unit—that is,

when one factor is a *scalar*. This occurs in "times as many" and "part of" situations, in all percent applications, and with probability and relative frequencies. All of these illustrate one-dimensional size changes.

Seeing a size change in two-dimensions is easier and gives twice the practice with the multiplications. Consequently, the example that opens the lesson and the coordinate diagrams in this lesson are two-dimensional.

This lesson is a review for students who have studied the corresponding material in *Transition Mathematics*. The preimages for **Examples 2 and 3** are given on **Teaching Aid 67**. You might demonstrate the size changes or have students draw them as you discuss the examples.

❶ When considering size changes in the coordinate plane (as in **Example 2**), you may want to first show the image of (x, y) as $k(x, y)$ and then as (kx, ky). This idea is used with vectors in more advanced courses where the operation is called *scalar multiplication*.

Absolute value is not presented in this text until Chapter 9. But if your students have already studied absolute value, the definitions of expansion and contraction can be rewritten. Let k be the magnitude of a size change. If $|k| > 1$, then the size change is an expansion. If $|k| < 1$, then the size change is a contraction. Ask students what would happen if k were allowed to be zero. [The figure would shrink to a single point which has no length or width. That is why we disallow 0 as a magnitude.]

The word *similar* is not introduced until Lesson 6-9, but you may want to use it here to describe the relationship between the figures in **Examples 2 and 3** and, more generally, between a figure and its size-change image.

These are instances of the *Size Change Model for Multiplication*.

> **Size Change Model for Multiplication**
> Let k be a nonzero number without a unit. Then kx is the result of applying a size change of magnitude k to the quantity x.

If you know the size of an image, by working backwards you can find the size of the preimage.

Example 1

After a size change of 75% has been applied, an image is 10 cm long. What is the length of the original figure?

Solution

An equation describing this situation is 75% · original length = 10 cm. Let L be the original length. Change 75% to 0.75. The equation becomes:

$$0.75L = 10$$
$$\frac{0.75L}{0.75} = \frac{10}{0.75} \quad \text{Divide both sides by 0.75.}$$
$$L = 13.\overline{3}$$

The original length was $13\frac{1}{3}$ cm.

Check

75% of 13.3 is just about 10. So the solution checks.

Types of Size Changes

When the size change factor k is greater than 1 or less than -1, the size change is called an **expansion.** Since 120% = 1.2, image C on page 387 illustrates an expansion. An expansion always produces an image larger than the preimage figure. If k is between -1 and 1, the size change is a **contraction.** Since 75% = 0.75 and 64% = 0.64, images A and B picture contractions. A contraction always produces an image smaller than the preimage. If the size change factor is 1 or -1, the image is the same size as the preimage.

Expansions and contractions can be done easily when figures are graphed in a coordinate plane. In geometric situations, the size change factor is called the **magnitude of the size change.** To find the image of a figure in the coordinate plane under a size change, just multiply the coordinates of each point on the figure by the magnitude of the size change.

❶ **Example 2**

A quadrilateral in a coordinate plane has vertices $A = (3, 0)$, $B = (0, 3)$, $C = (6, 6)$, and $D = (6, 3)$.
a. Draw its image under a size change of magnitude $\frac{1}{3}$.
b. Is the image an expansion, a contraction, or neither?

Optional Activities

Activity 1 You may want to use *Activity Kit, Activity 15*, before covering the lesson or as an alternate approach to **Examples 2 and 3**. In this activity, students study size changes by exploring what happens to a figure when the coordinates of its vertices are multiplied by various numbers.

Activity 2 As an extension of the discussion at the beginning of the lesson, tell students to imagine that a copy machine can be adjusted to make size changes for values of k from 50% to 200%. Then ask these questions.

1. How could you make an enlargement that is 4 times as large as the original? [Sample: Enlarge the original by 200%; then enlarge the enlargement by 200%.]
2. How could you make an enlargement that is 3 times as large as the original?

[Sample: enlarge it 150%, and then enlarge the enlargement 200%.]

3. How could you reduce the original to $\frac{1}{8}$ the original size? [Sample: reduce it 50%, reduce that reduction 50%, and reduce that reduction 50%.]

Students might test their answers using an actual copy machine.

Solution

a. Multiply the coordinates of each vertex of *ABCD* by $\frac{1}{3}$ to find the new image points *A'*, *B'*, *C'*, and *D'*.

Preimage Point	Image point
A = (3, 0)	$A' = \left(\frac{1}{3} \cdot 3, \frac{1}{3} \cdot 0\right) = (1, 0)$
B = (0, 3)	$B' = \left(\frac{1}{3} \cdot 0, \frac{1}{3} \cdot 3\right) = (0, 1)$
C = (6, 6)	$C' = \left(\frac{1}{3} \cdot 6, \frac{1}{3} \cdot 6\right) = (2, 2)$
D = (6, 3)	$D' = \left(\frac{1}{3} \cdot 6, \frac{1}{3} \cdot 3\right) = (2, 1)$

Draw *A'B'C'D'*. Below we show both the preimage and image.

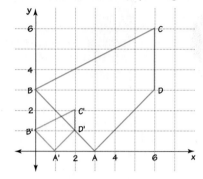

b. The size change factor $k = \frac{1}{3}$ is less than 1 but greater than -1, so the size change is a **contraction**. You can check this by looking at the graph.

In Example 2, notice that under a size change of magnitude $\frac{1}{3}$, the image of the point (x, y) is $\left(\frac{1}{3}x, \frac{1}{3}y\right)$. The general pattern is quite simple.

> Multiplying the coordinates of all points of a figure by a nonzero number performs a size change of magnitude k. The image of (x, y) under a size change of magnitude k is (kx, ky).

In Example 3 a size change with a negative size change factor is shown. That is, the coordinates of the points are multiplied by a negative number.

② Example 3

A quadrilateral has vertices $E = (-3, 0)$, $F = (-3, -4)$, $G = (-4, -2)$, and $H = (-5, -2)$.
a. Find its image under a size change of magnitude -2.
b. Describe the size and location of the image in relation to the original figure.

---

② Explain that in **Example 3**, the preimage is rotated 180° about the origin to form the image; this is the result of multiplying by a negative value of *k*. The size change can be broken down into two steps to illustrate this point—first, multiply by 2, and then multiply by –1. (Note that the operation is commutative.) Students may be surprised that it works even if the preimage figure contains points with negative coordinates, as in Additional Example 3 on page 390.

Activity 3
Materials: Four-Quadrant Graph Paper or **Teaching Aid 28**

After students work with **Examples 2 and 3**, you might have them consider situations in which the dimensions are multiplied by different numbers. These are the transformations known as scale changes, which, in two dimensions, have the formula that the image of (x, y) is (ax, by). Have students start with a square and apply the transformation that maps (x, y) to $(2x, 3y)$. Then have students describe the result. Next, have them apply this same transformation to a figure of their choice and describe the result. [The transformation multiplies the lengths of all horizontal segments by 2 and the lengths of all vertical segments by 3; the image usually has a different shape than the preimage; the area of the image is 6 times the area of the preimage. For instance, the image of a square is a rectangle with 6 times the area of the square.]

Activity 4 Technology Connection You may wish to assign *Technology Sourcebook, Computer Master 18*. Students use *GeoExplorer* or similar software to apply size changes to polygons. Students then compare the side lengths, angle measures, and area of the image with those of the original figure.

1. From 1970 to 1992, the cost of consumer goods, as measured by the Consumer Price Index, was multiplied (on the average) by a factor of 362%. If an item cost $100 in 1992, about how much would it have cost in 1970? **$27.62**

2. Graph the triangle with vertices $A = (0, 8)$, $B = (8, 10)$, and $C = (2, 4)$ and its image under a size change of magnitude $\frac{3}{4}$.

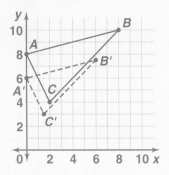

3. Graph the rectangle with vertices $P = (2, -1)$, $Q = (3, -1)$, $R = (3, 4)$, and $S = (2, 4)$. Draw its image under a size change of magnitude -4.

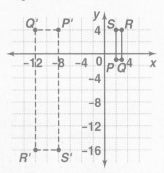

4. If a plumber receives $52.50 per hour of overtime at time and a half, what does he or she receive as normal pay per hour? **$35**

Solution

a. Multiply the coordinates of each vertex of *EFGH* by -2. Label the new figure $E'F'G'H'$.

Preimage	Image
$E = (-3, 0)$	$E' = (6, 0)$
$F = (-3, -4)$	$F' = (6, 8)$
$G = (-4, -2)$	$G' = (8, 4)$
$H = (-5, -2)$	$H' = (10, 4)$

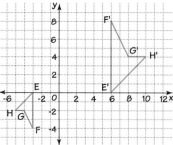

b. The size change is an expansion. Each side of E'F'G'H' is twice as long as the corresponding side of EFGH. The image seems to be rotated a half turn from the position of the original figure.

In general, if the magnitude is negative, the original figure is rotated 180° to obtain the image. Turn the book upside down to see that the image in Example 3 looks like the original, only larger.

Size Changes Not Involving Figures

Size changes can involve quantities other than lengths or geometric figures.

Example 4

A tool and die maker receives time and a half for overtime. In February of 1993, the average overtime wage for this occupation in St. Louis, Missouri, was $28.28 per hour. What was a tool and die maker's normal hourly wage?

Solution

Time and a half means that the overtime wage is $1\frac{1}{2}$ times the normal wage.
Let W be the normal hourly wage.

$$1\frac{1}{2} \cdot W = \$28.28$$
$$1.5W = 28.28$$
$$W = \frac{28.28}{1.5} \quad \text{Divide both sides by 1.5.}$$
$$W = 18.85\overline{3}$$

The normal hourly wage is about $18.85.

Check

Half of $18.85 is about $9.43, and that added to $18.85 equals $28.28.

The tools of the trade.
This tool and die maker is using a metal lathe to produce a die. A die is a precision tool used to shape or cut metals.

Adapting to Individual Needs

Extra Help

For size changes not involving figures, some students might benefit from practice in thinking through *times as many* and *fraction of* situations. Write the following situations and size changes on the board, and ask students to tell whether the change is an expansion or a contraction and to give the result.

1. Vacation of 14 days
   a. Twice as long [Expansion; 28 days]
   b. Half as long [Contraction; 7 days]
   c. 3 times as long [Expansion; 42 days]
2. Rental fee of $6 per hour
   a. $\frac{1}{3}$ the amount [Contraction; $2/hr]
   b. $1\frac{1}{2}$ times as much [Expansion, $9/hr]
   c. $\frac{1}{4}$ the amount [Contraction; $1.50/hr]

Covering the Reading

1. In the photocopy machine discussed at the beginning of this lesson, what are the magnitudes of the size change factors mentioned? **75%, 64%, 120%**

In 2–4, tell if a size change of the given magnitude produces an image larger than, smaller than, or the same size as the original figure.

2. 1.5 **larger**   3. 100% **same**   4. $\frac{1}{2}$ **smaller**

5. A picture with dimensions 10 inches by 15 inches is reduced on a photocopy machine by a factor of 64%. What are the dimensions of the image? **6.4 in. by 9.6 in.**

6. The photo at the left is 5.5 cm tall. It is to be enlarged on a photocopy machine by a factor of 120%. How tall will the image be? **6.6 cm**

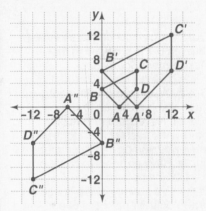

7. After a size change of 120%, the image of a figure is 18 cm long.
   a. Write an equation using L for the length of the original figure.
   b. What is the length of the original figure? **a) 1.20 L = 18; b) 15 cm**

8. What is the image of (3, -9) under a size change of magnitude -7? **(-21, 63)**

9. What is the image of (x, y) under a size change of magnitude 8? **(8x, 8y)**

10. a. Graph the quadrilateral $ABCD$ in Example 2. **a–c) See margin.**
    b. Graph its image under a size change of magnitude 2.
    c. Graph its image under a size change of magnitude -2.
    d. Are the size change images in parts **b** and **c** expansions, contractions, or neither? **expansions**

11. a. Draw $\triangle ABC$ with $A = (-8, 2)$, $B = (-4, -2)$, and $C = (-4, -10)$.
    b. Draw $\triangle A'B'C'$, the image of $\triangle ABC$ under a size change of magnitude $\frac{1}{4}$. **a, b) See left.**
    c. Draw $\triangle A^*B^*C^*$, the image of $\triangle ABC$ under a size change of magnitude $-\frac{1}{4}$. **See left.**
    d. Describe in your own words the relationships among the three triangles. **See left.**

12. The magnitude k of a size change is given. Tell whether the size change is an expansion, a contraction, or neither.
    a. $-1 < k < 1$ **contraction**
    b. $k > 1$ **expansion**
    c. $k < -1$ **expansion**
    d. $k = -1$ **neither**

13. $J'K'L'M'N'$ is the image of pentagon $JKLMN$ under a size change with rule that the image of (x, y) is $\left(\frac{3}{2}x, \frac{3}{2}y\right)$.
    a. Find the coordinates of J', K', L', M' and N'.
    b. Graph pentagon $J'K'L'M'N'$.

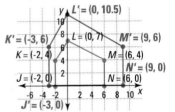

Lesson 6-7 *Size Changes* **391**

11a,b,c)

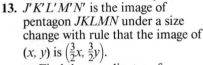

d) Samples: The triangles in **b** and **c** are contractions of **a**. The triangle in **c** seems to be rotated a half turn from the triangle in **b**.

Notes on Questions

Question 5 Error Alert Students might also want to apply the reduction factor to the area. Note that the reduction factor applies to the length; the area is multiplied by the square of the size change factor.

Question 10 These questions show the difference between multiplying by a size change factor and multiplying by its opposite. Mention the general property: the size change images are congruent, but one is the image of the other under a rotation of 180°.

Question 11 Whereas **Question 10** dealt with expansions, this question discusses contractions whose magnitudes are opposites.

Additional Answers
10a, b, c

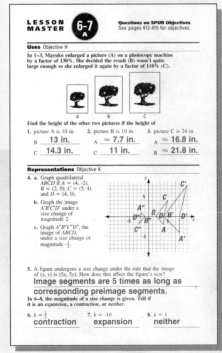

Adapting to Individual Needs

English Language Development

You might want to define *expansion* (to make bigger) and *contraction* (to make smaller) by showing students how a rubber band *expands* when you pull it and *contracts* when you release it.

Notes on Questions

Question 20 This is a critical objective in students' later study of geometry. Here we examine a single instance in which the ratio of the perimeters is *k* to 1, but the ratio of the areas is k^2 to 1. Do not expect students to generalize from this one case.

Follow-up for Lesson 6-7

Practice

For more questions on SPUR Objectives, use **Lesson Master 6-7A** (shown on page 391) or **Lesson Master 6-7B** (shown on pages 392–393).

Assessment

Quiz A quiz covering Lessons 6-5 through 6-7 is provided in the *Assessment Sourcebook.*

Group Assessment Students will need graph paper or **Teaching Aid 28.** Have students **work in pairs.** Ask each student to draw a preimage and an image on graph paper. Have partners exchange papers and determine the magnitude of the size change of the image drawn on their partner's paper. [Students display ability to determine size changes in the coordinate plane.]

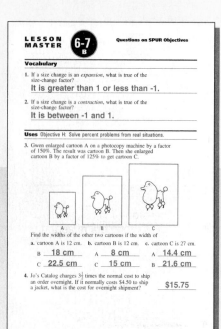

14. Maintenance electricians were averaging $30.98 per overtime hour in San Jose, California, in August of 1992. If an electrician receives time and a half for overtime, what was the normal hourly wage? **$20.65**

Applying the Mathematics

15. Lorenzo is one year old and weighs 10 kg. This is $3\frac{1}{2}$ times his birth weight. How much did he weigh at birth? **2.86 kg**

16. A human hair is 0.1 mm thick. Suppose that under a certain microscope it appears 15 mm thick. By how many times has it been magnified? **150**

17. Under a size change of magnitude 6, the image *P'* of a point *P* is (9, -42). What are the coordinates of *P*? **(1.5, -7)**

18. a. Describe the graph of the image of the quadrilateral at the left under a size change of magnitude 1. **same as given**
    b. What property of multiplication does this size change represent? **Multiplicative Identity Property of 1**

19. Refer to the four figures at the start of this lesson.
    a. Find the area of each rectangle. **8 cm²; 4.5 cm²; 11.52 cm²; 3.2768 cm²;**
    b. *True or false.* If a figure undergoes a size change of magnitude *k*, the area of the image is *k* times the area of the preimage. Justify your answer. **False; The area of the image is k^2 times the area of the preimage.**

20. a. Draw the rectangle with vertices *A* = (1, -1), *B* = (3, -1), *C* = (3, 2), and *D* = (1, 2). **a, b) See left.**
    b. Draw its image *A'B'C'D'* under a size change of magnitude 3.
    c. Find the ratio of the perimeter of the larger figure to the perimeter of the smaller. **$\frac{3}{1}$**
    d. Find the ratio of the area of the larger figure to the area of the smaller. **$\frac{9}{1}$**

Review

21. A farmer is thinking of installing an irrigation system on his farm. The system consists of a 100-ft-long pipe that rotates around a fixed point. The farm's crops are planted in rows in a 200-ft by 200-ft square as shown at the left.
    a. What percent of the crops planted in the square would be irrigated by this system? **78.5%**
    b. If a wind-blown seed falls randomly into the square, what is the probability that it will fall in the irrigated region? *(Lessons 6-5, 6-6)* **0.785**

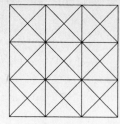

Adapting to Individual Needs

Challenge
Have students solve the following problem: How many different-sized squares can you find in the figure at the right? [5] How many squares are in the figure? [31]

22. A football field has the measurements given below. The vertical lines are equally spaced. If a balloon floats down to a random spot on the field, what is the probability it will land in the darker area of play? *(Lesson 6-6)* $\approx 0.135 = 13.5\%$

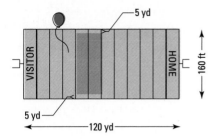

23. The Environmental Protection Agency calculated that in 1990, of 195.7 million tons of solid waste generated in the U.S., 73.3 million tons consisted of paper. What percent of the total waste is paper? *(Lesson 6-5)* **37.5%**

24. A scarf normally sells for $23.95. It is on sale for 30% off.
  a. What percent of the price does the customer pay? **70%**
  b. Write an equation to find the sale price. $c = .70(23.95)$
  c. How much does the scarf cost on sale? *(Lesson 6-5)* **$16.77**

25. About one in 86 pregnancies in the United States results in twins.
  a. What is the relative frequency of having twins? $\frac{1}{86} \approx 0.012$
  b. What is an estimate of the probability that a pregnancy results in twins? *(Lessons 6-3, 6-4)* $\frac{1}{86}$

26. In a standard deck of cards, the probability that a fourteen of hearts will be drawn is $\frac{0}{52} = 0$. What does a probability of 0 mean?
(Lesson 6-4) **The event is impossible.**

27. Give an example of an event with a probability of 1. *(Lesson 6-4)*
Answers will vary.

28. *Skill sequence.* Simplify. *(Lessons 2-3, 3-9, 4-1, 6-1)*
  a. $\frac{x}{2} + \frac{x}{3}$ $\frac{5x}{6}$ **b.** $\frac{x}{2} - \frac{x}{3}$ $\frac{x}{6}$ **c.** $\frac{x}{2} \cdot \frac{x}{3}$ $\frac{x^2}{6}$ **d.** $\frac{x}{2} \div \frac{x}{3}$ $\frac{3}{2}$

Exploration

29. a. Using grid paper, draw a rectangle with dimensions 24 units by 36 units. Draw a rectangle whose sides are $\frac{1}{4}$ the lengths of sides of the first rectangle. How many of the small rectangles can fit in the large rectangle? **16**
  b. Repeat part **a**, except make the sides of the small rectangle $\frac{1}{6}$ of the sides of the first rectangle. **36**
  c. Draw a rectangle with dimensions 15 by 36. Draw a rectangle whose sides are $\frac{1}{3}$ the lengths of the sides of the first rectangle. How many of the small rectangles can fit in the large rectangle? **9**
  d. What pattern(s) do you see from parts **a, b,** and **c?** Test your pattern(s) with another rectangle and another fraction.
Sample: The number of rectangles $= \left(\frac{1}{\text{magnitude}}\right)^2$

Lesson 6-7 *Size Changes* **393**

Twins Tia and Tamera Mowry star in the TV comedy series, Sister, Sister.

Setting Up Lesson 6-8
Materials Students will need a stopwatch or a watch with a second hand for the *Group Assessment* on page 400. Students using the *Extension* on page 400 will need maps showing distances between locations and rulers or **Geometry Templates.**

Extension
Students will need graph paper or **Teaching Aid 28**. Have them draw the image of each parallelogram under a size change of magnitude –1.

1. *ABCD* with $A = (0, 0)$, $B = (5, 0)$, $C = (7, 3)$, and $D = (2, 3)$
[The vertices of the image are: $A' = (0, 0)$, $B' = (-5, 0)$, $C' = (-7, -3)$, and $D' = (-2, -3)$.]

2. *EFGH* with $E = (0, 2)$, $F = (-1, 4)$, $G = (-4, -2)$, and $H = (-3, -4)$
[The vertices of the image are: $E' = (0, -2)$, $F' = (1, -4)$, $G' = (4, 2)$, and $H' = (3, 4)$.]

3. *PQRS* with $P = (2, 2)$, $Q = (1, 4)$, $R = (-2, -2)$, and $S = (-1, -4)$
[The figures are the same, but the vertices are not their own images. $P' = (-2, -2)$, $Q' = (-1, -4)$, $R' = (2, 2)$, and $S' = (1, 4)$.]

Ask what special relationship the image and preimage have in Question 3. [They are identical.] Then have students **work in small groups** to find other figures whose preimage and image are identical under a size change of magnitude –1. Ask them to make conjectures about the characteristics of these figures. [They have rotation symmetry about the origin; that is, when rotated a half-turn around the origin, the figure maps onto itself.]

Project Update Project 3, *Area, Perimeter, and Size Changes,* on page 408, relates to the content of this lesson.

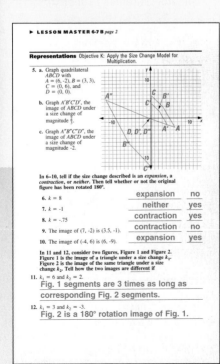

393

Objectives

C Solve proportions.
D Use the language of proportions and the Means-Extremes Property.
I Solve problems involving proportions in real situations.

Resources

From the *Teacher's Resource File*
■ Lesson Master 6-8A or 6-8B
■ Answer Master 6-8
■ Teaching Aid 59: Warm-up

Additional Resources
■ Visual for Teaching Aid 59
■ Stopwatch or watch with a second hand (Assessment)
■ Rulers or **Geometry Templates**
■ Maps showing distances between locations (Extension)

Teaching **6-8**
Lesson

Warm-up

Diagnostic Have students answer the following questions. You might have students **work in groups.**

1. Write any two equal fractions. Show that the fractions satisfy the Means-Extremes Property. **Answers will vary.**

2. Write any two unequal fractions. Show that the fractions do not satisfy the Means-Extremes Property. **Answers will vary.**

3. Are the fractions $\frac{14}{49}$ and $\frac{18}{56}$ equal? Explain your answer. **The product of the means is $49 \cdot 18 = 882$; the product of**

Scale: 1 in. = 800 miles

Map scales. *A map scale is a ratio of the map distance to the actual distance. From a map, a proportion can be used to find actual distance, as in Example 2.*

A **proportion** is a statement that two fractions are equal. Thus any equation of the form

$$\frac{a}{b} = \frac{c}{d}$$

is a proportion. This equation is sometimes written $a:b = c:d$, and is read "*a* is to *b* as *c* is to *d*." Because of the order of reading the proportion, the numbers *b* and *c* are called the **means** of the proportion; the numbers *a* and *d* are called the **extremes.** For example, in the proportion $\frac{30}{x} = \frac{6}{7}$, the means are *x* and 6. The extremes are 30 and 7. The equation $\frac{x}{2} + \frac{5}{4} = \frac{1}{2}$ is not a proportion because the left side of the equation is not a single fraction.

The Means-Extremes Property

Suppose two fractions are equal. What is true about the means and extremes of the proportion? Below we show a specific case on the left and the general case on the right.

$$\frac{9}{12} = \frac{30}{40} \qquad\qquad \frac{a}{b} = \frac{c}{d}$$

To clear the fractions, multiply both sides by the product of the denominators: $12 \cdot 40 = 480$, and $b \cdot d = bd$.

$$480 \cdot \frac{9}{12} = 480 \cdot \frac{30}{40} \qquad\qquad bd \cdot \frac{a}{b} = bd \cdot \frac{c}{d}$$

Simplify the equation.

$$\overset{40}{\cancel{480}} \cdot \frac{9}{\cancel{12}} = \overset{12}{\cancel{480}} \cdot \frac{30}{\cancel{40}} \qquad\qquad \cancel{b}d \cdot \frac{a}{\cancel{b}} = b\cancel{d} \cdot \frac{c}{\cancel{d}}$$
$$40 \cdot 9 = 12 \cdot 30 \qquad\qquad ad = bc$$

The general pattern is that the product of the means equals the product of the extremes.

Lesson 6-8 Overview

Broad Goals The goals of this lesson are the justification and use of the Means-Extremes Property in solving proportions.

Perspective Proportions arise from equal rates and from equal ratios; they are important because they appear so often in applications. As **Examples 1 and 2** indicate, it is quite easy to find everyday problems that can be solved by using proportions.

The standard method of solving a proportion, using the Means-Extremes Property, is unique to this type of equation. But its application is so simple that some students will want to use it for other questions. Consequently, it must be emphasized that the Means-Extremes Property is a property of equal fractions.

The Means-Extremes Property is a theorem—a statement which can be deduced

from other properties. The steps in the deduction are given in the paragraph preceding the statement of the property. You could call this property the Means-Extremes Theorem.

Means-Extremes Property

For all real numbers *a, b, c,* and *d* (with *b* and *d* not zero),

$$\text{if } \frac{a}{b} = \frac{c}{d}, \text{ then } ad = bc.$$

Many questions can be answered by writing a proportion from two equal ratios or two equal rates, and then using the Means-Extremes Property to solve the proportion.

Using the Means-Extremes Property to Solve Proportions

Example 1

A motorist traveled 283.5 miles on 9.0 gallons of gas. With the same driving conditions, how far could the car go on 14 gallons of gas?

Solution

Let x be the number of miles traveled on 14 gallons. Since conditions are the same, the rate $\frac{283.5 \text{ mi}}{9 \text{ gal}}$ should equal the rate $\frac{x \text{ mi}}{14 \text{ gal}}$.

$$\frac{283.5 \text{ miles}}{9 \text{ gallons}} = \frac{x \text{ miles}}{14 \text{ gallons}}$$

$$\frac{283.5}{9} = \frac{x}{14}$$

Use the Means-Extremes property to solve for x.

$$283.5 \cdot 14 = 9x$$
$$3969 = 9x$$
$$441 = x$$

The car could travel about 441 miles on 14 gallons.

Example 1 was set up by equating two *rates*. Proportions can also be set up using equal *ratios*. In Example 2 below, Solution 1 uses rates. Solution 2 uses ratios.

Example 2

In the map on page 394, 1 inch represents 800 miles. If New York and Miami are $1\frac{5}{8}$ inches apart on the map, how many miles apart are they?

Solution 1

Let x be the actual distance between the cities. Set up a proportion using equal rates in inches per mile.

$$\frac{1 \text{ inch}}{800 \text{ miles}} = \frac{1\frac{5}{8} \text{ inches}}{x \text{ miles}}$$

Use the Means-Extremes Property.

$$1 \cdot x = 800 \cdot 1\frac{5}{8}$$

$$x = 1300$$

The cities are about 1300 miles apart.

▶

Lesson 6-8 *Proportions* **395**

Notes on Reading

Emphasize that if there is one proportion in a situation, then there are many other correct proportions in a given situation. This is an advantage, but it may also confuse students. If $\frac{a}{b} = \frac{c}{d}$, then $\frac{b}{a} = \frac{d}{c}$ (reciprocals of equals are equal), and $\frac{a}{c} = \frac{b}{d}$ (means can be switched), and $\frac{d}{b} = \frac{c}{a}$ (extremes can be switched). The switching of the means or the extremes often changes equal rates to equal ratios and vice versa. In general, we have found that students prefer setting up rates on each side of the equal sign rather than setting up ratios. That is, in **Example 2**, most students seem to prefer Solution 1 to Solution 2.

Solution 2

Let x be the actual *distance between the cities*. Set up a proportion using equal ratios. One ratio compares inches; the other compares miles.

$$\frac{1 \text{ inch}}{1\frac{5}{8} \text{ inches}} = \frac{800 \text{ miles}}{x \text{ miles}}$$

$$1 \cdot x = 800 \cdot 1\frac{5}{8}$$

$$x = 1300$$

The cities are about 1300 miles apart.

Often several correct proportions can be used to solve a problem. Here are two other proportions which could have been used to find the distance from New York to Miami.

$$\frac{800 \text{ miles}}{1 \text{ inch}} = \frac{x \text{ miles}}{1\frac{5}{8} \text{ inches}} \quad \text{or} \quad \frac{1\frac{5}{8} \text{ inches}}{1 \text{ inch}} = \frac{x \text{ miles}}{800 \text{ miles}}$$

Each gives the same final answer.

Activity

Measure the distance on the map between Chicago and San Francisco. About how far apart are the cities in miles? about 2100 miles

If the numerators or denominators in a proportion are expressions with variables, you can treat them as chunks. You can solve the resulting equations using techniques you have seen in earlier chapters.

Example 3

Solve $\frac{3g + 4}{5} = \frac{4g - 8}{4}$.

Solution 1

Use the Means-Extremes Property.

$4(3g + 4) = 5(4g - 8)$	
$12g + 16 = 20g - 40$	Apply the Distributive Property.
$16 = 8g - 40$	Add $-12g$ to both sides.
$56 = 8g$	Add 40 to each side.
$7 = g$	Divide each side by 8.

Solution 2

Clear the fractions by multiplying each side of the equation by the least common multiple of the denominators.

$$\overset{4}{\cancel{20}} \cdot \frac{3g + 4}{\underset{1}{\cancel{5}}} = \overset{5}{\cancel{20}} \cdot \frac{4g - 8}{\underset{1}{\cancel{4}}}$$

$$4(3g + 4) = 5(4g - 8)$$

Now apply the Distributive Property and find the value of g as in Solution 1.

Check

Substitute. Does $\frac{3 \cdot 7 + 4}{5} = \frac{4 \cdot 7 - 8}{4}$?

$$\frac{25}{5} = \frac{20}{4}?$$

$$5 = 5? \text{ Yes.}$$

Some proportions have more than one solution.

Example 4

Solve $\frac{p}{2} = \frac{32}{p}$.

Solution

Apply the Means-Extremes Property.

$p^2 = 64$

There are two solutions.

$p = 8$ or $p = -8$

Check

Check each solution by substitution.

Is $\frac{8}{2} = \frac{32}{8}$? Yes, $4 = 4$.

Is $\frac{-8}{2} = \frac{32}{-8}$? Yes, $-4 = -4$.

QUESTIONS

Covering the Reading

1. What is a *proportion?* a statement that two fractions are equal

2. *Multiple choice.* Which of the following is a proportion? b
   (a) $2 + \frac{x}{3} = \frac{1}{5}$ (b) $\frac{a}{b} = \frac{b}{x}$ (c) $\frac{a}{b} \cdot \frac{c}{d}$

3. According to the Means-Extremes Property, if $\frac{x}{y} = \frac{z}{w}$, then ___?___.
   $xw = yz$

In 4 and 5, a proportion is given. **a.** Use the Means-Extremes Property to solve the proportion. **b.** Check your work.

4. $\frac{x}{12} = \frac{3}{18}$ 2; $\frac{2}{12} = \frac{3}{18}$? Yes   5. $\frac{-15}{12} = \frac{x}{-20}$ 25; $\frac{-15}{12} = \frac{25}{-20}$? Yes

6. A motorist keeps records of his car's gas mileage. The last time he filled the tank, he had gone 216 miles on 13.8 gallons of gas. At this rate, how far can the car go on a full tank of 21 gallons?
   ≈ 328.7 miles

7. In parts **a–c,** write the equation that results from using the Means-Extremes Property.
   a. $\frac{3}{5} = \frac{n}{7}$ $5n = 21$ **b.** $\frac{3}{7} = \frac{n}{5}$ $7n = 15$ **c.** $\frac{7}{5} = \frac{n}{3}$ $5n = 21$
   d. Which of the proportions in parts **a–c** has a different solution from that of the other two? b

Lesson 6-8 *Proportions* **397**

Notes on Questions

Question 2 Reading Mathematics
Recognizing proportions requires paying careful attention to the symbolic patterns when reading. Have students explain why the equation in **part b** is a proportion and why the equation in **part a** and the expression in **part c** are not proportions. Stress that a proportion is the only type of equation that is solved by the Means-Extremes Property.

Question 7 Proportions with the same solution (as in **parts a and c**) have the same numbers positioned diagonally. The same situation occurs in **Question 8c.**

LESSON MASTER 6-8 A

Questions on SPUR Objectives
See pages 412-415 for objectives.

Skills Objective C

In 1–6, use the Means-Extremes Property to solve.

1. $\frac{7}{8} = \frac{x}{4}$ 2. $\frac{5a}{3} = \frac{15}{2}$ 3. $\frac{18}{w+8} = \frac{2}{3}$

   $x = \frac{7}{2}$, or 3.5 $a = \frac{9}{2}$, or 4.5 $w = 19$

4. $\frac{2x+1}{3} = \frac{5x-5}{6}$ 5. $\frac{v+5}{v+7} = -8$ 6. $\frac{2}{w} = \frac{w}{18}$

   $x = 7$ $v = -\frac{61}{9}$, or -6.8 $w = 6$ or $w = -6$

In 7 and 8, a. give the exact solutions, and b. give the solutions rounded to the nearest hundredth.

7. $\frac{x}{3} = \frac{1}{x}$ 8. $\frac{5}{2y} = \frac{y}{6}$
   a. $x = \sqrt{3}$ or $-\sqrt{3}$ a. $y = \sqrt{15}$ or $-\sqrt{15}$
   b. $x = 1.73$ or -1.73   b. $x = 3.87$ or -3.87

Properties Objective D

9. Explain how you can use the Means-Extremes Property to determine if the fractions $\frac{3}{5}$ and $\frac{7.5}{12.5}$ are equal.
   Sample: Find the product of means (5·7.5) and extremes (3·12.5). If the products are equal, the fractions are equal.

Uses Objective I

10. In 1990, 39.5 million foreigners visited the U.S. Of these, 17.3 million were from Canada. If the total number of visitors increases to 50 million in the year 2000, how many can be expected to be from Canada? ≈ 22.1 million

11. Carlo figures that when he is driving at highway speed his car's engine turns at a rate of 3000 revolutions per minute. He has also found that when the engine turns 7 times, the wheels turn 2 times. If Carlo drives for 1 hour,
    a. how many times does the engine turn?   180,000 times
    b. how many times does a wheel turn? $\approx 51,400$ times

12. On the 10 o'clock news, the sportscaster can cover 10 sports stories in 3 minutes 45 seconds. If his time slot is increased to 5 minutes, how many stories can he cover? ≈ 13 stories

Adapting to Individual Needs

Challenge

Have students make scale drawings of a room or a rectangular object such as a carpet, a picture frame, or a window. They will have to choose an appropriate scale, measure the object, and then make the drawing. Then have them exchange their drawings with another student, and show the appropriate scale on the drawing. Each student should then use the scale drawing to determine the dimensions of the original room or object.

Snow in Sapporo. *Long winters and heavy snowfalls make Sapporo, Japan, an ideal spot for winter sports. Shown is a child enjoying the snow slide during the annual Winter Festival in Sapporo.*

In 8 and 9, refer to the map on page 394.

8. On the map the distance between Seattle and Houston is $2\frac{7}{8}$ in.
   a. Write a proportion that can be used to estimate the distance between the two cities. $\frac{1 \text{ in.}}{800 \text{ mi}} = \frac{2\frac{7}{8} \text{ in.}}{x \text{ mi}}$
   b. Use your proportion in part **a** to estimate the distance between Seattle and Houston. **about 2300 miles**
   c. Write another proportion that can be used to estimate the distance between Seattle and Houston. c) Sample: $\frac{1}{2\frac{7}{8}} = \frac{800}{x}$
   d. Solve the proportion in part **c**. **about 2300 miles**

9. About how far apart in miles are Chicago and San Francisco? **about 2100 miles**

In 10–15, solve using the Means-Extremes Property.

10. $\frac{2}{a} = \frac{-14}{15}$ $-\frac{15}{7} = -2.14$ 11. $\frac{15}{2a} = \frac{3}{10}$ 25   12. $\frac{g+3}{4} = \frac{g-2}{2}$ 7

13. $\frac{3x}{4} = \frac{3x+1}{6}$ $\frac{2}{3} = 0.\overline{6}$ 14. $\frac{x}{4} = \frac{9}{x}$ 6; −6   15. $\frac{98}{x} = \frac{x}{8}$ 28; −28

Applying the Mathematics

16. A basketball team scores 17 points in the first 6 minutes of play. At this rate, how many points will the team score in a 32-minute game? **91**

17. One of the heaviest snowfalls in recent history occurred in Bessans, France, on April 5–6, 1969, when about 173 cm of snow fell in 19 hours. At this rate, how many centimeters of snow would fall in 24 hours? **218.5 cm**

18. The fastest scheduled passenger train in the United States in 1992 traveled from Wilmington, Delaware, to Baltimore, Maryland, a distance of 68.4 miles, in 42 minutes. At this rate, what distance could this train cover in an hour? **97.7 miles**

19. Helen of Troy was described as having "a face that could launch a thousand ships." If a face could launch a thousand ships, what would it take to launch five ships? **0.005 face**

20. a. Multiply $\frac{10}{16} \cdot \frac{15}{x}$. $\frac{75}{8x}$ b. Solve $\frac{10}{16} = \frac{15}{x}$. **24**

21. Consider the equation $\frac{2}{d} = \frac{d}{11}$. Express the solution(s)
    a. exactly; $\pm\sqrt{22}$ b. as decimals rounded to the nearest hundredth. **4.69; −4.69**

22. For each gear setting on a bicycle, there is a ratio of the number of turns of the pedals to the number of turns of the rear wheel.

Gear	Number of pedal turns	Number of rear-wheel turns
1st	9	14
2nd	4	7
3rd	1	2
4th	3	7
5th	5	14

While in 2nd gear, Bonnie turned the pedals 15 times. How many times did the rear wheel turn? $26\frac{1}{4}$ **times**

398

398

In 23–25, use the Means-Extremes Property to determine whether the given fractions are equal.

23. $\frac{1}{3}, \frac{33}{100}$ No

24. $\frac{4.5}{-5}, \frac{-153}{170}$ Yes

25. $\frac{388,162}{171,958}, \frac{430,262}{190,603}$ No

26. Solve $\frac{13x - 78}{x} = \frac{0}{7953}$. 6

27. Is there a fraction equal to $\frac{3}{4}$ whose numerator is five more than its denominator? If there is, find the fraction. If there is not, explain why such a number cannot exist. Yes; $\frac{-15}{-20}$

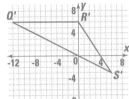
28a,b)

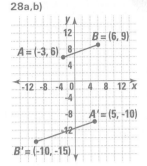

A = (-3, 6)
B = (6, 9)
A' = (5, -10)
B' = (-10, -15)

29a)

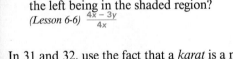

Q'
R'
S'

Review

28. a. Plot $A = (-3, 6)$ and $B = (6, 9)$, and draw $\overline{AB}$. a, b) See left.
   b. Find the image of $\overline{AB}$ under a size change of magnitude $-\frac{5}{3}$.
   c. Is the size change an expansion or a contraction? *(Lesson 6-7)*
   expansion

29. a. Copy the figure below. Draw the image of $\triangle QRS$ using the rule that the image of (x, y) is $(3x, 3y)$. Call the image $Q'R'S'$.
   b. What is QR? 4
   c. What is $Q'R'$? 12
   d. Describe how the image and preimage are related.
   (Lessons 1-7, 6-7)
   The perimeter of the image is three times as large as the perimeter of the preimage.

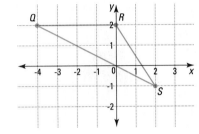

30. What is the probability of a randomly picked point inside rectangle $ABCD$ at the left being in the shaded region?
(Lesson 6-6) $\frac{4x - 3y}{4x}$

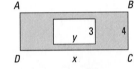

In 31 and 32, use the fact that a *karat* is a measure of fineness used for gold and other precious materials. Pure gold is 24 karats. Gold of 18-karat fineness is 18 parts pure gold and 6 parts other metals giving 24 parts altogether. *(Lessons 6-3, 6-5)*

31. A bracelet is 18-karat gold. What percent gold is this? 75%

32. A necklace weighing 5 ounces is 10-karat gold. How many ounces of pure gold is in the necklace? 2.1 oz

33. What value(s) can m *not* have in the expression $\frac{m - 7}{m + 5}$? *(Lesson 6-2)*
-5

Golden treasures. *In 1989, an archeological dig in Nimrud, Iraq, uncovered this gold jewelry that dates back to the Assyrians. The Assyrian empire began in the 800s B.C. and declined after 612 B.C.*

Lesson 6-8 *Proportions* **399**

Practice

For more questions on SPUR Objectives, use **Lesson Master 6-8A** (shown on page 397) or **Lesson Master 6-8B** (shown on pages 398–399).

Assessment

Group Assessment Students will need stopwatches or watches with a second hand. Have students time one another performing a simple task, such as tying their shoes or writing their name and address. Then have them write and solve proportions to determine how long it would take them to complete the task one million times. [Students work together to write and solve proportions.]

Extension

Students will need rulers or **Geometry Templates.** Give students maps in which distances between locations are shown, but the scales are not shown. Have students estimate the scale. Then have them check their estimates with the actual scale.

Project Update Project 3, *Area, Perimeter, and Size Change*, on page 408, relates to the content of this lesson.

34a) New Mexico (85.9 cars per 100 people);   New Hampshire (85.3); New Jersey (73.1); New York (56.7)

b) Answers will vary. Sample: New York and New Jersey are states with large cities where public transportation is frequently used.

34. Below are some data from the 1990 census about the states whose names begin with "new." See left.

State	Population	Number of Motor Vehicles Registered
New Hampshire	1,109,252	945,743
New Jersey	7,730,188	5,652,382
New Mexico	1,515,069	1,301,261
New York	17,990,455	10,196,153

a. Rank these states from greatest to lowest in the number of motor vehicles registered per 100 people.
b. What reasons do you think account for the differences in motor vehicle registration rates you found in part **a**? *(Lesson 6-2)*

35. a. The statement "driver is to car as pilot is to airplane" is called an *analogy*. This analogy corresponds to the proportion $\frac{a}{b} = \frac{c}{d}$, where a = driver, b = car, c = pilot, and d = airplane. Find the missing word in each of the following analogies.
  i. Soup is to bowl as water is to __?__. glass
  ii. Inch is to centimeter as __?__ is to kilogram. pound
  iii. __?__ is to Earth as Earth is to sun. moon
  iv. Cow is to __?__ as hen is to chick. calf
  v. Hoop is to __?__ as net is to soccer. basketball
  vi. Author is to novel as __?__ is to symphony. conductor or composer
  vii. __?__ is to Maryland as Sacramento is to California. Annapolis
  viii. Motorist is to car as __?__ is to bicycle. bicyclist
b. Make up two analogies similar to those in part **a**.
Samples: Japan is to Asia as France is to Europe. Shoes are to feet as hat is to head.

Setting Up Lesson 6-9

Materials Students will need rulers and protractors or **Geometry Templates** for Lesson 6-9.

In preparation for Lesson 6-9, discuss **Question 29**. Take the ratio of image sides to the corresponding preimage sides, for example $\frac{Q'R'}{QR}$. Note that this is the same ratio as the ratio of any other image side to preimage side. Note that the corresponding angles are congruent.

*Similar
Figures*

IN-CLASS
ACTIVITY

Work in a small group.
Materials: graph paper, ruler, protractor

See margin for answers to 1a, b, e, h, i, and 2a, b, c, e.

1 **a.** Draw a set of axes about in the middle of the graph paper.
Draw $\triangle ABC$ with $A = (0, -2)$, $B = (4, 2)$, and $C = (7, 0)$.

b. Draw the image of $\triangle ABC$ under a size change of magnitude 2.

c. Measure the sides and angles of each triangle and record your
results in a table like the one below. Side lengths vary depending
upon size of graph paper.

$\triangle ABC$						$\triangle A'B'C'$					
AB	BC	AC	m∠A	m∠B	m∠C	A'B'	B'C'	A'C'	m∠A'	m∠B'	m∠C'

See below.

d. Calculate the ratios $\frac{A'B'}{AB}$, $\frac{B'C'}{BC}$, and $\frac{A'C'}{AC}$. What conclusions can you
draw? All ratios are equal: $\frac{2}{1}$.

e. What is true about the angle measures in $\triangle ABC$ and $\triangle A'B'C'$?

f. Pick a scale factor k other than 1 or 2. For instance, use $k = \frac{1}{2}$ or
$k = 3$. (Each person should use a different scale factor.) Draw
$\triangle A''B''C''$, the image of $\triangle ABC$ under the size change with your scale
factor k. Check students' graphs.

g. Calculate the ratios $\frac{A''B''}{AB}$, $\frac{B''C''}{BC}$, and $\frac{A''C''}{AC}$ for your figures. How are
these ratios related? All ratios are equal to k.

h. Measure $\angle A''$, $\angle B''$, and $\angle C''$. How are these angle measures related
to the measures of angles A, B, and C?

i. *Draw conclusions.* Compare your results with those of the others
in your group. Write several sentences to summarize what you found.

2 **a.** Use the other side of the graph paper. Draw a set of axes in the
middle of the paper. Draw quadrilateral $WXYZ$ with $W = (-3, 2)$,
$X = (-3, -3)$, $Y = (9, -4)$, and $Z = (2, 7)$.

b. Pick a scale factor k other than 1. (Each person in the group should
pick a different value.) Describe how you think the image of $WXYZ$
will be related to $WXYZ$ under a size change of magnitude k.

c. Draw the image of $WXYZ$ under the size change of magnitude k.
Label it $W'X'Y'Z'$. Graphs will vary. See margin for sample.

d. Measure the sides and angles of each quadrilateral. Calculate ratios
of lengths of corresponding sides. Answers will vary.

e. Discuss your work in parts **a** to **d** with the other members of your
group. Write several sentences summarizing what you found.

1c) $AB = 3.5$ cm, $BC = 2.3$ cm, $AC = 4.2$ cm,
m $\angle A = 30°$, m $\angle B = 100°$, m $\angle C = 50°$

$A'B' = 7$ cm, $B'C' = 4.6$ cm, $A'C' = 8.4$ cm,
m $\angle A' = 30°$, m $\angle B' = 100°$, m $\angle C' = 50°$

401

In-class Activity

Resources

From the *Teacher's Resource File*
■ Answer Master 6-9
■ Teaching Aids
  26 Graph Paper
  68 Similar Figures

Additional Resources
■ Visuals for Teaching Aids 26, 68
■ Rulers and protractors or
  Geometry Templates

This activity should be done before
students read page 402.

Additional Answers
1a, b

1e, h The measures of the corresponding sides are equal.

1i. Sample: Under every size
change, ratios of the sides
of the image to the sides
of the preimage are equal
to each other and are equal
to k. The corresponding
angles of the image and
preimage have equal
measures.

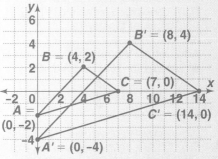

TEACHING AID 68
In-class Activity, Lesson 6-9

Similar Figures

$\triangle ABC$	$\triangle A'B'C'$	Ratios	$\triangle A''B''C''$	Ratios
AB	A'B'		A"B"	
BC	B'C'		B"C"	
AC	A'C'		A"C"	
m∠A	m∠A'		m∠A"	
m∠B	m∠B'		m∠B"	
m∠C	m∠C'		m∠C"	

Quadrilateral WXYZ	Quadrilateral W'X'Y'Z'	Ratios
WX	W'X'	
XY	X'Y'	
YZ	Y'Z'	
WZ	W'Z'	
m∠W	m∠W'	
m∠X	m∠X'	
m∠Y	m∠Y'	
m∠Z	m∠Z'	

Additional Answers, continued
2a, c

2b. Adapt the answer for 2e given
below for a magnitude of $\frac{1}{2}$.

2e. Sample: Under every size change,
the ratios of the sides of the image
to the sides of the preimage are
equal to each other and they are
equal to k. The corresponding
angles of the images and preimage
have equal measures.

Objectives

I Solve problems involving proportions in real situations.
L Find lengths and ratios of similitude in similar figures.

Resources

From the Teacher's Resource File
■ Lesson Master 6-9A or 6-9B
■ Answer Master 6-9
■ Teaching Aids
  59 Warm-up
  69 Additional Examples
  70 Questions 8, 12, and 13
■ Technology Sourcebook
  Computer Master 19

Additional Resources
■ Visuals for Teaching Aids 59, 69, 70
■ Rulers or **Geometry Templates**

Teaching **6-9**
Lesson

Warm-up

✎ **Writing** Write a problem that could be solved using the following proportions.

1. $\frac{1}{200} = \frac{2.5}{n}$ Sample: On a map, 1 inch represents 200 miles. How many miles do 2.5 inches represent?

2. $\frac{12}{30} = \frac{n}{40}$ Sample: Ribbon is sold for $.30 per foot. Robin spent $.40, before tax, on ribbon. How much ribbon did she buy?

Similar stacking dolls. *Russian stacking dolls, painted to look like peasants, are hollowed and fit inside one another. Woodcarvers make these dolls, called* matreshka, *in sets of 4 or more.*

What Are Similar Figures?

❶ The image of a figure under a size change has the same shape as the preimage. Such figures are called **similar figures.** All the triangles you drew in Question 1 of the In-class Activity are similar to each other. All the quadrilaterals in Question 2 are similar.

Two fundamental properties of similar figures are given below.

> **Fundamental Properties of Similar Figures**
> If two figures are similar, then
> (1) corresponding angles have the same measure.
> (2) ratios of lengths of corresponding sides are equal.

You saw several instances of these properties in the In-class Activity.

Not only are the ratios of corresponding sides equal, but they equal the size change factor. This ratio is called a **ratio of similitude.** In Question **1d** of the In-class Activity you should have found that

$$\frac{A'B'}{AB} = \frac{B'C'}{BC} = \frac{A'C'}{AC} = 2.$$

If $\triangle ABC$ were considered to be the image of $\triangle A'B'C'$, then the reciprocals of these ratios would be taken. The ratio of similitude would then be $\frac{1}{2}$.

Finding Lengths in Similar Figures

When two figures are similar, a true proportion can be written using corresponding sides. If three of the four lengths in the proportion are known, the fourth can be found by solving an equation.

Lesson 6-9 Overview

Broad Goals This lesson uses proportions to find the lengths of the sides of similar figures. The proportions come from ratios of the lengths of corresponding sides.

Perspective The importance of proportional thinking and of similar figures (in all of mathematics) makes this lesson an important one, even though you might be surprised to see it in a text that is more devoted to algebra. Usually, this lesson is not difficult

for students, and it will help them greatly when they study geometry.

In this book, similar figures almost always have parallel corresponding sides, as in the pictures in this lesson. Using colored chalk or pens to indicate corresponding sides can help students to see the pairing, a task that increases in difficulty with the number of sides in the polygons. The emphasis in algebra is on writing and solving proportion;

it is not on recognizing when two figures are similar.

Example 1

2 The two quadrilaterals below are similar, with corresponding sides parallel. Find *x*, the length of $\overline{CD}$.

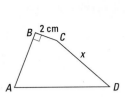
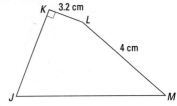

Solution

The side corresponding to $\overline{CD}$ is $\overline{LM}$. Now find a pair of corresponding sides whose lengths are known. These are $\overline{BC}$ and $\overline{KL}$. Since the figures are similar, the ratios of lengths of these corresponding sides are equal.

$$\frac{CD}{LM} = \frac{BC}{KL}$$

Substitute the known lengths.

$$\frac{x}{4} = \frac{2}{3.2}$$

Use the Means-Extremes Property to solve for *x*.

$$3.2 \cdot x = 2 \cdot 4$$
$$3.2\,x = 8$$
$$x = \frac{8}{3.2} = 2.5$$

Check

Find the ratio of similitude first using *BC* and *KL*, then using *CD* and *LM*.
$\frac{BC}{KL} = \frac{2}{3.2} = \frac{20}{32} = \frac{5}{8}$ and $\frac{CD}{LM} = \frac{2.5}{4} = \frac{25}{40} = \frac{5}{8}$. They are equal.

Using Similar Figures to Find Lengths Without Measuring

3 Similar figures have many uses. For instance, you can use similar triangles to find the height of an object you cannot measure easily.

Suppose you want to find the height *h* of the flagpole in front of your school. Here is how you can do it. Hold a yardstick parallel to the flagpole and measure the length of its shadow. Then measure the length of the shadow of the flagpole. The following picture illustrates one possible set of measurements.

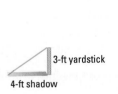
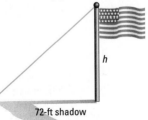

Lesson 6-9 *Similar Figures* **403**

Notes on Reading

1 Reading Mathematics You might want to have students read this introductory paragraph in class. Relate the discussion to the In-class Activity on page 401.

2 You may want to stress that in similar figures, corresponding sides do not have to be parallel. That is why, in **Example 1**, we must state that the corresponding sides are parallel. However, if the figures are size change images of each other, then the corresponding sides are parallel.

3 We assume students will accept that the triangles are similar. Students will be given additional information on this topic when they study geometry.

Optional Activities

Activity 1 Writing Use this activity after completing the lesson. Have students **work in groups**. On a sunny day, send them outside to use the method that is described on page 403 to determine the height of a tree, your school building, the flagpole, or some other tall object as in **Question 29**.

Have each group prepare a brief oral or written report about the procedures that were used and the results that were obtained.

Activity 2 Technology Connection
With *Technology Sourcebook, Computer Master 19,* students use *GeoExplorer* to discover conditions that guarantee similarity in triangles and quadrilaterals.

These examples are also given on
Teaching Aid 69.

1.

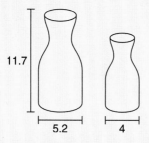

The quadrilaterals are similar
with corresponding sides parallel.
a. Find x and y. 10.5, 10
b. What are the two possible
ratios of similitude for the
figures? $\frac{2}{3}, \frac{3}{2}$

2.

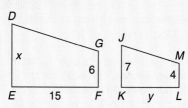

A vase is sold in two sizes. The
small vase is similar to the large
vase. Find the height of the small
vase. **9 units**

Example 2

Use the measurements on page 403 to find the height h of the flagpole.

Solution

Two similar right triangles are formed. Now, use ratios of corresponding
sides.

$$\frac{3}{h} = \frac{4}{72}$$
$$4h = 72 \cdot 3$$
$$4h = 216$$
$$h = 54.$$

The flagpole is 54 feet tall.

QUESTIONS

Covering the Reading

1. In similar figures, what is true about lengths of corresponding line
segments? Their ratios are equal.

In 2–5, the two triangles below are similar. Corresponding sides are
parallel.

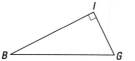

2. Which side of $\triangle BIG$ corresponds to the given side of $\triangle ACT$?
a. $\overline{AT}$ $_{BG}$ **b.** $\overline{CT}$ $_{IG}$ **c.** $\overline{AC}$ $_{BI}$

3. Find two ratios equal to $\frac{AC}{BI}$. $\frac{CT}{IG}, \frac{AT}{BG}$

4. Suppose $AC = 15$, $CT = 8$, $AT = 17$, and $BI = 30$. Find
a. IG. 16   **b.** BG. 34

5. Suppose $\triangle BIG$ is the image of $\triangle ACT$ under a size change of
magnitude 3 and $BG = 12$. What other lengths can be found? $_{AT = 4}$

6. The rectangles below are similar.

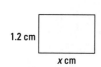

a. Write a proportion that could be used to find x. Sample: $\frac{2}{1.2} = \frac{3}{x}$
b. Solve the proportion you wrote in part **a.** 1.8
c. What are the two possible ratios of similitude? $\frac{2}{1.2} = \frac{5}{3}; \frac{1.2}{2} = \frac{3}{5}$

404

---

7. $\triangle ABC$ is similar to $\triangle A'B'C'$.

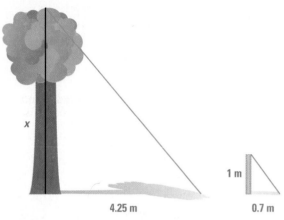

a) Sample: $\frac{16}{20} = \frac{AB}{16}$

a. Write a proportion that could be used to find the length of $\overline{AB}$.

b. Find AB. 12.8

8. A tree casts a shadow that is 4.25 m long. A meter stick casts a shadow that is 0.7 m long.

a. Copy this diagram and label the given lengths.

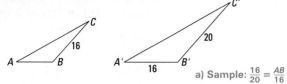

1 m

x

4.25 m   0.7 m

b. Write a proportion that can be used to find the height of the tree.

c. How tall is the tree? 6.1 m

b) Sample: $\frac{x}{4.25} = \frac{1}{0.7}$

Applying the Mathematics

9. The two quadrilaterals below are similar. Corresponding sides are parallel.

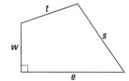

a. Write another ratio which must equal $\frac{s}{a}$. Samples: $\frac{t}{p}$; $\frac{w}{k}$; $\frac{e}{r}$

b. Write three ratios which must equal $\frac{p}{t}$. $\frac{k}{w}$; $\frac{r}{e}$; $\frac{a}{s}$

10. The two rectangles at the right are similar. Find the length and width of the larger rectangle.

$x = 15$; $x + 9 = 24$

x

x + 9

10

16

Lesson 6-9 *Similar Figures* **405**

Question 7a There are many correct proportions. You may want to make a list of all the correct statements that students have found. When incorrect statements are made, point out the errors.

Question 8b As in **Question 7a,** there is more than one correct answer; however, each of them leads to the same solution in **part c.**

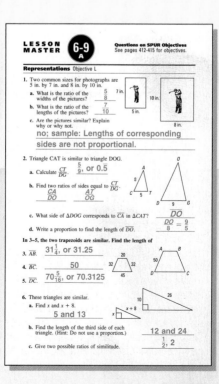

Adapting to Individual Needs

English Language Development

Show students objects that are similar, such as a drawing and a reduced copy of it. Note that while they are *similar*, they are not entirely alike. Draw several triangles on the board, two of which are similar. Explain that in geometry, figures that are the same shape are *similar*. Use your illustrations to point out that all triangles do not necessarily have the same shape but that when they do, they are similar.

As you discuss similar figures, use colored chalk to show the relationship between pairs of corresponding sides.

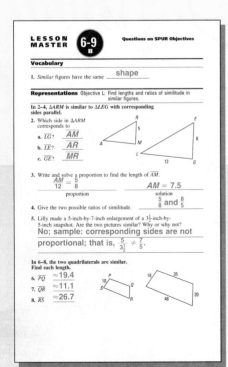

11. At a certain time on a sunny day Jim, who is 6 feet tall, casts a shadow that is 10 feet long. A nearby building, which is *t* feet tall, casts a shadow that is 25 feet long.
    a. Draw a diagram of this situation. Write in the lengths. **Drawings will vary.**
    b. Write a proportion that describes this situation.
    c. How tall is the building? **15 ft** b) Sample: $\frac{6}{t} = \frac{10}{25}$

12. Copy the second drawing and draw the complete pentagon $PQRST$ which is similar to $ABCDE$, given that $\overline{PT}$ corresponds to $\overline{AE}$.

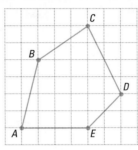
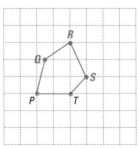

13. For this question, you need to use a ruler and properties of similar figures. A scale drawing of a house is shown below. The actual width (across the front) of the house is 9 m.

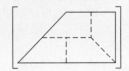
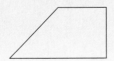

    a. Write a ratio comparing the width of the house in the drawing to the actual width of the house. $\frac{8.7 \text{ cm}}{9 \text{ m}}$
    b. Write a proportion you could use to find the actual distance from the ground to the peak of the roof. Sample: $\frac{8.7}{9} = \frac{5.5}{x}$
    c. Solve the proportion in part **b**. **5.7 m**

14. Triangles ABC and DEF at the left are similar. Corresponding sides are parallel.
    a. *Multiple choice.* Which proportion could you use to find *x*? **c**
       (a) $\frac{24}{30} = \frac{1.5x}{y}$
       (b) $\frac{x}{y} = \frac{1.5x}{40}$
       (c) $\frac{24}{30} = \frac{x}{40}$
    b. Solve the equation you choose for *x*. **32**
    c. Use your solution to part **a** to find *y*. **60**
    d. Based on your answers, what is the ratio of the *perimeter* of $\triangle ABC$ to the *perimeter* of $\triangle DEF$? $\frac{4}{5}$

406

Adapting to Individual Needs

Challenge
Have student divide the following figure into four congruent parts that are similar to the original figure.

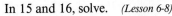

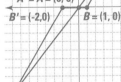

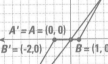

Mayberry

In 15 and 16, solve. *(Lesson 6-8)*

15. $\frac{48}{2x} = \frac{9}{5}$ $\frac{40}{3}$

16. $\frac{1}{x-1} = \frac{3}{x-2}$ $\frac{1}{2}$

17. Be careful! Some students confuse these two types of problems.
(Lessons 2-3, 6-8)
  a. Multiply $\frac{9}{n} \cdot \frac{n}{25}$. $\frac{9}{25}$
  b. Solve $\frac{9}{n} = \frac{n}{25}$.   15; -15

18. a. Draw $\triangle ABC$ with $A = (0, 0)$, $B = (1, 0)$, and $C = (4, 5)$.
  b. Draw the image of $\triangle ABC$ under a size change of magnitude -2.
  (Lesson 6-7) a, b) See left.

19. Pixley is 38 kilometers by road from Mayberry. A bicycle shop is
somewhere between 5 and 10 km from Pixley. If a bicyclist has a flat
tire at some point between the two towns, what is the probability of
its occurring within $\frac{1}{2}$ km of the shop?   *(Lesson 6-6)* $\frac{1}{38}$

20. The dinner bill at some restaurants includes the tip. If a $38.81 bill
included a 15% tip, what was the amount of the original bill before
the tip was added?   *(Lesson 6-5)* $33.75

21. On sale, a sweater costs $17. It originally cost $21. What is the
percent of discount?   *(Lesson 6-5)*   19%

22. A letter is chosen randomly from the English alphabet. What is the
probability that it is a letter in the word MATH?   *(Lesson 6-4)*
$\frac{4}{26} \approx 0.15$

23. How many times as large as $\frac{1}{2}x$ is $3x$?   *(Lesson 6-3)*   6

24. Simplify $\frac{3\pi}{y^2} \div \frac{\pi}{5}$.   *(Lesson 6-1)* $\frac{15}{y^2}$

In 25 and 26, use the expression $\frac{c-d}{a-b}$.   *(Lessons 1-5, 6-1)*

25. Evaluate the expression when $a = 3$, $b = 4$, $c = 5$, and $d = 2$.   -3

26. If $a = 7$, and $d = 8$, for what values is the expression not defined?
not defined for $b = 7$

27. *Skill sequence.*   Solve.   *(Lessons 2-6, 3-5, 4-3)*
  a. $p + 8 = 23$ **b.** $8p = 23$ $\frac{23}{8}$ **c.** $8 - p = 23$ **d.** $\frac{1}{8}p = 23$ 184
  15   -15

28. Light travels at the incredibly rapid rate of about 186,000 miles per
second. About how many miles does light travel in one hour?
(Lesson 2-4)   669,600,000 miles

Time to retire.
*Bicycle mechanics
perform a variety of repair
jobs, such as fixing flat
tires, replacing worn or
broken parts, and
reconditioning bikes.*

18a,b)

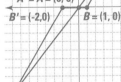

Exploration

29. Find the highest point of a tree, or a building, or some other object,
using the shadow method described in this lesson. Draw a diagram
to illustrate your method.   Answers will vary.

Practice

For more questions on SPUR Objectives, use **Lesson Master 6-9A**
(shown on page 405) or **Lesson Master 6-9B** (shown on pages 406–407).

Assessment

Written Communication Ask students to write three proportions that could be used for **Question 8b**. [Students show that more than one proportion can be used to solve a problem.]

Extension

Students will need rulers, or **Geometry Templates.** Have them draw the following: any $\triangle ABC$; any point P not on the triangle; rays PA, PB, and PC; $\triangle A'B'C'$ so that segment PA' is three times as long as PA, PB' is three times as long as PB, and PC' is three times as long as PC. Then have them show that $\triangle ABC$ and $\triangle A'B'C'$ are similar, and give a ratio of similitude. [Drawings will vary; ratios of lengths of corresponding sides should be equal; the ratio of similitude is 3 or $\frac{1}{3}$.]

Project Update Project 2, *Indirect Measurement*, on page 408, relates to the content of this lesson.

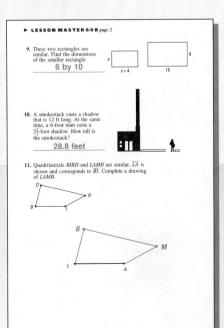

▶ **LESSON MASTER 6-9 B** *page 2*

9. These two rectangles are similar. Find the dimensions of the smaller rectangle.
6 by 10

10. A smokestack casts a shadow that is 12 ft long. At the same time, a 6-foot man casts a $2\frac{1}{2}$-foot shadow. How tall is the smokestack?
28.8 feet

11. Quadrilaterals *BIRD* and *LAMB* are similar. $\overline{IA}$ is shown and corresponds to $\overline{BI}$. Complete a drawing of *LAMB*.

407

Chapter 6 Projects

The projects relate to the content of the lessons of this chapter as follows:

Project	Lesson(s)
1	6-3
2	6-9
3	6-7, 6-8
4	6-6
5	6-4
6	6-3

1 Population Densities Explain to students that population densities in the U.S. are given in terms of population per square mile, using land area only. Population information can be found in a variety of sources. It is important that students include their source in their projects. A good source of information is the *Encyclopedia Britannica World Data Annual*. The densities of the four largest metropolitan areas of the U.S. were estimated in 1991 as follows: New York: 11,480 people per square mile; Los Angeles: 9,126 people per square mile; Chicago: 8,566 people per square mile; Philadelphia: 8,499 people per square mile.

2 Indirect Measurement Have students compare the methods and the advantages and disadvantages of the methods they described with other students.

3 Area, Perimeter, and Size Changes This project leads students to discover the Fundamental Theorem of Similarity: If two figures are similar with ratio of similitude *k*, then the ratio of corresponding lengths (and thus corresponding perimeters) is *k*, and the ratio of corresponding areas is k^2. Point out to students that they must be capable of finding the area and perimeter of the figure they draw. Suggest that students draw polygonal figures that

A project presents an opportunity for you to extend your knowledge of a topic related to the material of this chapter. You should allow more time for a project than you do for typical homework questions.

PROJECTS 6 CHAPTER SIX

1 Population Densities
A *population density* is a rate, defined as the number of people living in a region divided by the area of that region.
a. Find the population and area of your town or city, your state, the United States, and the world. Calculate the population densities in people per square mile. On the basis of population density, rank these four places from least crowded to most crowded.
b. Which states in the United States have the highest population densities? Which have the lowest?
c. Name some countries that have much higher population densities than that of the United States; name some countries that have much lower population densities.

2 Indirect Measurement
In Lesson 6-9, we described how similar triangles can be used to find the height of an object indirectly, that is, without measuring the object's height. There are many other ways to measure heights indirectly. Find at least four ways to determine the height of your school building or some other tall object in your neighborhood. Describe the methods you used, and discuss the advantages and disadvantages of using each.

3 Area, Perimeter, and Size Changes
a. Draw an interesting figure on a coordinate grid. Find its perimeter and area.
b. Draw its image under size changes of magnitude 2, 3, 4, and $\frac{1}{2}$. Find the perimeter and area of each image.
c. Describe the patterns you find in your data. How are the perimeter and the area of the image related to the perimeter and the area of its preimage?

408

Possible responses
1. The following answers have the unit "people per square mile."
   a. Responses will vary. The population density of the United States is 70 and the population density of the world is 94.
   b. Highest: New Jersey: 1,042.0; Rhode Island: 960; Massachusetts: 767.6; Connecticut: 678.4
   Lowest: Alaska: 1.0;

   Wyoming: 4.7; Montana: 5.5; South Dakota: 9.2
   c. Sample response: High densities: Monaco: 49,520; Singapore: 12,464; Malta: 2,901; Bangladesh: 2,132; Bahrain: 2,055
   Low densities: Namibia: 4; Australia: 5.9; Iceland: 6; Canada: 7; Chad: 10
2. Sample responses:
   a. Compare the known height of a

   nearby object with the height of the building or object. Advantage—no calculation needed; disadvantage—might be difficult to find a building or nearby object for which the height is known.
   b. Use blueprints of the building to find the actual height. Advantage—accurate measurements can be found; disadvantage—blueprints might be hard to obtain.

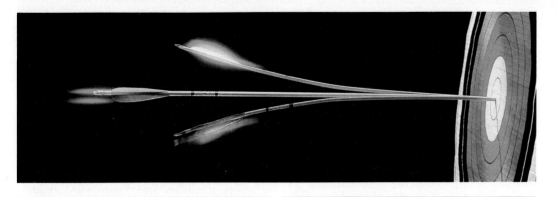

Archery

4 A sport that often uses targets with concentric circles like those used in Lesson 6-6 is archery. Find out the sizes of the targets, the sizes of the different regions of the targets, and how scores are calculated in this sport. What is the relationship between the sizes of the regions and the points for a "hit" in each region? Make up some mathematics questions based on archery and probability.

Lotteries

5 Many states have lotteries to raise money for education, public works, or other needs. If your state has a lottery, find out how it works. Include information about how winners are determined, how prize

money is calculated, and how the chances of winning are determined. How are the concepts of relative frequency and probability applied in your state's lottery?

Density and Floating

6 In science the *density* of an object is determined by dividing the mass (weight in grams) of the object by its volume (in cubic centimeters). For instance, the density of cool tap water is one gram per cubic centimeter.

a. Find some blocks of different types of wood, such as pine, oak, maple, and cedar. Calculate the density of each block.
b. Fill a tub with enough tap water to see if the blocks of wood will float. Which blocks of wood float?
c. Write up your methods and conclusions. How does density appear to be related to an object's ability to float?

they can divide into simple regions. Have students organize all the data they collect in a table.

4 **Archery** Tell students to assume that outcomes are random throughout the target when they write their mathematical questions. Point out, however, that good archers do not hit the targets at random and that they achieve bull's eyes almost all of the time. Students will need to find the area of each of the concentric rings to use the Probability Formula for Geometric Regions.

5 **Lotteries** By the end of 1993, 37 states had lotteries. If the state in which you live has a lottery, students can contact the agency that regulates the lottery for specific information. Students may be interested in finding out how lottery earnings are allocated.

6 **Density and Floating** The density of liquids or solids is measured in grams per milliliter, grams per cubic centimeter, or pounds per cubic foot. Density of liquids can be found by measuring the mass needed to fill a container of a known volume. Density of solids can be found by measuring the object's mass and dividing by its volume. The volume of a solid can be found either by measuring the object and applying the appropriate volume formula or by finding how much water it displaces. Expect variations in students' results. Explain to students that the density of wood varies depending on the percent of moisture content in the wood, and the density of vegetable oil varies with the type of oil used. Students may need to use the following conversion factors to complete this project: 1 cup ≈ 240 milliliters, 1 fl. oz ≈ 29.573 grams, 1 pound ≈ 453 grams, and 1 cubic foot ≈ 29791 cubic centimeters.

---

c. Use shadows to set up a proportion to find the height of the building or object. Advantage—easy to measure; disadvantage—must have adequate sunlight.
d. Have someone take a photograph of you standing next to the object and set up a proportion that compares your height to the height of the object. Advantage—easy measurements to make; disadvan-

tage—must have a camera and wait for photograph to be developed.
3. a. Responses will vary.
b. Responses will vary.
c. The perimeter of the images will be 2, 3, 4, and $\frac{1}{2}$ times the perimeter of the preimage. The area of the images will be 4, 9, 16, and $\frac{1}{4}$ times the area of the preimage.

In general, the perimeter of an image is found by multiplying the perimeter of the preimage by the magnitude of the size change. The area of an image is found by multiplying the area of the preimage by the square of the magnitude of the size change.

(*Responses continue on page 410.*)

Summary

The Summary gives an overview of the entire chapter and provides an opportunity for students to consider the material as a whole. Thus, the Summary can be used to help students relate and unify the concepts presented in the chapter.

Vocabulary

Terms, symbols, and properties are listed by lesson to provide a checklist of concepts that students must know. Emphasize that students should read the vocabulary list carefully before starting the Progress Self-Test. If students do not understand the meaning of a term, they should refer back to the indicated lesson.

SUMMARY

Division is closely related to multiplication. The definition of division states that to divide by a number is the same as to multiply by its reciprocal. This definition is applied directly to divide fractions. Because zero has no reciprocal, division by zero is impossible.

Rates and ratios are models for division. A rate compares quantities with different units; ratios compare quantities with the same units. A statement that two fractions are equal is called a proportion. The Means-Extremes Property can be used to find missing values in a proportion. One important place proportions appear is in similar figures.

Percent, relative frequency, probability in geometry, and size changes are applications involving rates and ratios. It is possible to translate most percent problems to equations of the form $ab = c$. Solving the equation then gives an answer to the problem. Since it is impossible to count the infinite number of points in a geometric region, a ratio of lengths or areas is used to compute probabilities in geometric situations. Size changes yield similar figures. If the magnitude is k and $k > 1$ or $k < -1$, then the size change is an expansion. If $-1 < k < 1$, the size change is a contraction.

VOCABULARY

Below are the most important terms and phrases for this chapter. You should be able to give a general description and a specific example of each.

Lesson 6-1
Algebraic Definition
    of Division
complex fraction

Lesson 6-2
rate
Rate Model for Division
population density

Lesson 6-3
ratio
Ratio Model for Division
percent of discount
percent of tax

Lesson 6-4
frequency
relative frequency
probability
outcome, event
at random, randomly
complement

Lesson 6-5
percent

Lesson 6-6
Probability Formula for
    Geometric Regions

Lesson 6-7
size change factor
Size Change Model for
    Multiplication
expansion, contraction
magnitude of a size change

Lesson 6-8
proportion
means, extremes
Means-Extremes Property

Lesson 6-9
similar figures
Fundamental Properties of
    Similar Figures
ratio of similitude

410

Additional responses, page 409

4. The following information is a sample of what students might include in their reports. There are two standard-sized targets used in archery. Each target is made up of 10 concentric scoring zones. The bull's eye has a value of ten points and the nine rings around the bull's eye are assigned values from nine points through one point, with one point being the value of the outermost ring. The value of hitting a ring increases as its area decreases. The chart shows point value, area, and probability for a target with 10 rings of equal width and a diameter of 48 inches. Sample questions will vary.

Ring Number and Points	Area (sq. in.)	Probability
10	18.1	0.01
9	54.3	0.03
8	90.5	0.05
7	126.7	0.07
6	162.9	0.09
5	199.1	0.11
4	235.2	0.13
3	271.4	0.15
2	307.6	0.17
1	343.8	0.19

PROGRESS SELF-TEST

Take this test as you would take a test in class. You will need a calculator and graph paper. Then check your work with the solutions in the Selected Answers section in the back of the book.

In 1–3, simplify.

1. $15 \div -\frac{3}{2}$ **-10**
2. $\frac{x}{9} \div \frac{2}{3} \cdot \frac{x}{6}$
3. $\frac{\frac{2b}{3}}{\frac{b}{3}}$ **2**

In 4–6, solve. Show your work.

4. $\frac{y}{11} = \frac{2}{23}$ **$\frac{22}{23}$**
5. $\frac{b}{49} = \frac{25}{b}$ **35; -35**
6. $\frac{4g-3}{26} = \frac{g}{8}$ **4**

7. If 14% of a number is 60, what is the number? **about 428.6**

8. $\frac{1}{2}$ is what percent of $\frac{4}{5}$? **62.5%**

9. When rolling a single die, what is the probability that at least a 5 will result? **$\frac{1}{3}$**

10. What value can v not have in the expression $\frac{10v}{v+1}$? Why can it not have this value? **-1; fraction is undefined.**

11. In the proportion $\frac{2}{3} = \frac{x}{10}$, which numbers are the means? **3; x**

12. Horatio spent 36 minutes on his English homework. Mary Ellen spent a half hour on her English homework.

    a. Horatio's time is what percent of Mary Ellen's time? **120%**

    b. Horatio studied __?__ percent longer than Mary Ellen. **20**

13. A kennel has c cats and d dogs, but no other animals. What is the ratio of the number of dogs to the number of animals? **$\frac{d}{c+d}$**

14. The two triangles below are similar with corresponding sides parallel.

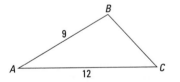

    a. What are the two possible ratios of similitude in this situation? **$\frac{9}{4}$; $\frac{4}{9}$**

    b. Find z. **5.$\overline{3}$**

16) p pages in $7y$ min; The same number of pages are read in less time.

17) 0.09; $\frac{36}{400} = \frac{\text{no. with Alzheimer's}}{\text{no. surveyed}}$; **9%**

15. A television cost $236 after a 20% discount. What was the original price? **$295**

16. Which is faster, reading p pages in $7y$ minutes or p pages in $8y$ minutes? Justify your answer. **See below left.**

17. In a survey of 400 people over the age of 70, 36 were found to have Alzheimer's disease. What is the relative frequency of Alzheimer's disease in this group of people? Explain how you found your answer. Write your answer as a percent. **See below left.**

18. If the electricity goes out and a clock stops, what is the probability that the second hand stops between 2 and 3? **$\frac{1}{12}$**

19. If a car travels 280 miles on 12 gallons of gas, about how far (to the nearest mile) can the car travel on 14 gallons of gas? **327 miles**

20. a. Graph the triangle with vertices $A = (2, 3)$, $B = (-1, -3)$, and $C = (3, 1)$.

    b. Graph the image of $\triangle ABC$ under a size change of -2. **a, b) See margin.**

21. a. What is the image of (-6, 4) under the size change with the rule that the image of (x, y) is $\left(\frac{2}{3}x, \frac{2}{3}y\right)$? **$\left(-4, \frac{8}{3}\right)$**

    b. Is the size change an expansion, a contraction, or neither? **contraction**

22. The rectangles below are similar. Find the length and width of the smaller rectangle. Show your work. **length = $6\frac{2}{3}$; width = $4\frac{2}{3}$**

23. In a certain video game, if villains appear in the shaded area of the screen you will not be able to destroy them. Suppose the villains are equally likely to be in any part of the screen. What is the probability that you will not be able to destroy the villains? **$\frac{3}{14} \approx 0.21$**

For the development of mathematical competence, feedback and correction, along with the opportunity to practice, are necessary. The Progress Self-Test provides the opportunity for feedback and correction; the Chapter Review provides additional opportunities and practice. We cannot overemphasize the importance of these end-of-chapter materials. It is at this point that the material "gels" for many students, allowing them to solidify skills and understanding. In general, student performance should be markedly improved after these pages.

Assign the Progress Self-Test as a one-night assignment. Worked-out solutions for all questions are in the Selected Answers section of the student book. Encourage students to take the Progress Self-Test honestly, grade themselves, and then be prepared to discuss the test in class.

Advise students to pay special attention to those Chapter Review questions (pages 412–415) which correspond to the questions that they missed on the Progress Self-Test.

Additional Answers
20a, b

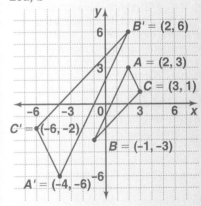

5. Responses will vary. The amount of prize money distributed is determined by the number of tickets sold and the actual prize amount awarded to a winner is determined by the total number of winners. The probability of winning is determined by dividing the number of winning combinations by the possible combinations that can arise. This amount is usually very small, but never zero. The relative frequency of winning is determined by dividing the number of times a person has won by the number of tickets a person has purchased. The relative frequency is often zero.

6. a. Sample responses:
   Pine: 0.38 to 0.46 g/cc
   Oak: 0.64 to 0.71 g/cc
   Maple 0.59 to 0.68 g/cc
   Cedar: 0.32 to 0.41 g/cc
   b. Responses will vary.
   c. Responses will vary. If an object is less dense than water, it will float.

Chapter 6 Review

Resources

From the *Teacher's Resource File*
- Answer Master for
  Chapter 6 Review
- Assessment Sourcebook:
  Chapter 6 Test, Forms A–D
  Chapter 6 Test, Cumulative Form
  Comprehensive Test,
  Chapters 1–6

Additional Resources
- Quiz and Test Writer

The main objectives for the chapter are organized in the Chapter Review under the four types of understanding this book promotes – Skills, Properties, Uses, and Representations.

Whereas end-of-chapter material may be considered optional in some texts, in *UCSMP Algebra* we have selected these objectives and questions with the expectation that they will be covered. Students should be able to answer these questions with about 85% accuracy after studying the chapter.

You may assign these questions over a single night to help students prepare for a test the next day, or you may assign the questions over a two-day period. If you work the questions over two days, then we recommend assigning the *evens* for homework the first night so that students get feedback in class the next day, then assigning the *odds* the night before the test because answers are provided to the odd-numbered questions.

It is effective to ask students which questions they still do not understand and use the day or days as a total class discussion of the material which the class finds most difficult.

CHAPTER REVIEW

Questions on SPUR Objectives

SPUR stands for **S**kills, **P**roperties, **U**ses, and **R**epresentations. The Chapter Review questions are grouped according to the SPUR Objectives for this chapter.

SKILLS DEAL WITH PROCEDURES USED TO GET ANSWERS.

Objective A: *Divide real numbers and algebraic fractions.* *(Lesson 6-1)*

In 1–8, simplify.   1) -125

1. $-25 \div \frac{1}{5}$ 2. $\frac{a}{14} \div \frac{7}{2}$ $\frac{a}{49}$ 3. $\frac{2\pi}{9} \div \frac{\pi}{6}$ $\frac{4}{3}$ 4. $\frac{x}{z} \div \frac{x}{y}$ $\frac{y}{z}$

5. $\frac{\frac{3x}{2}}{\frac{15x}{16}}$ $\frac{-8}{5}$ 6. $\frac{\frac{a}{b}}{\frac{c}{d}}$ $\frac{ad}{bc}$ 7. $\frac{60}{\frac{1}{4}}$ 240   8. $\frac{x}{-\frac{x}{4}}$ -4

In 9 and 10, what value(s) can the variable not have?

9. $\frac{x+1}{x+4}$ -4

10. $\frac{15x}{x-0.2}$ 0.2

Objective B: *Solve percent problems.* *(Lesson 6-5)*

11. What is 75% of 32?   24

12. What is 20% of 18?   3.6

13. 10 is what percent of 5?   200%

14. 1.2 is what percent of 0.8?   150%

15. 85% of what number is 170?   200

16. 30% of a number is $\frac{3}{4}$. What is the number?   2.5

Objective C: *Solve proportions.* *(Lesson 6-8)*

In 17–22, solve.

17. $\frac{x}{130} = \frac{6}{5}$ 18. $\frac{6}{25} = -\frac{10}{m}$ 19. $\frac{4}{x} = \frac{x}{225}$

20. $\frac{y}{7} = \frac{10}{y}$ 21. $\frac{2m-1}{21} = \frac{m-5}{24}$

22. $\frac{5+r}{3} = \frac{r+2}{2}$ 4

17) 156;   18) $-\frac{125}{3}$;   19) 30;   -30
20) $\pm\sqrt{70}$;   21) -3

PROPERTIES DEAL WITH THE PRINCIPLES BEHIND THE MATHEMATICS.

Objective D: *Use the language of proportions and the Means-Extremes Property.* *(Lesson 6-8)*

23. In the proportion $\frac{5}{8} = \frac{15}{24}$,
    a. which numbers are the means?   8 and 15
    b. which numbers are the extremes?   5 and 24

24. If $\frac{m}{n} = \frac{p}{q}$, then by the Means-Extremes Property $\underline{\ ?\ } = \underline{\ ?\ }$. $mq = pn$

25. If $\frac{2}{3} = \frac{x}{5}$, what does $\frac{5}{x}$ equal? $\frac{3}{2}$

26. If $\frac{a}{b} = \frac{c}{d}$, then $\frac{c}{a} = \underline{\ ?\ }$. $\frac{d}{b}$

USES DEAL WITH APPLICATIONS OF MATHEMATICS IN REAL SITUATIONS.

Objective E: *Use the Rate Model for Division.* *(Lesson 6-2)*

27. Assume a 22-mile bike trip took 2 hours.
    a. What was the rate in miles per hour?
    b. What was the rate in hours per mile?
    a) 11 mph;   b) $\frac{1}{11}$ hour per mile

28. A train travels from Newark to Trenton, a distance of 48.1 miles, in 30 minutes. At what average speed, in miles per hour, does the train travel?   96.2 miles per hour.

29. Marlene worked $3\frac{1}{2}$ hours and earned $21. How long does it take her to earn a dollar? $\frac{1}{6}$ of an hour, or 10 minutes

In 30–32, make up a question based on the given information and calculate a rate to answer the question. **See margin for 30–32, 33a.**

30. The Johnsons drove 30 miles in $\frac{3}{4}$ hours.

31. In d days Tony spent $400.

32. 4 weeks ago the puppy weighed 3 kilograms less than it does today.

33. In one store a 46-ounce can of tomato juice costs $1.77, and a 6-ounce can costs 28 cents.

  a. Calculate the cost per ounce for each size.

  b. Based on the cost per ounce, which is the better buy? **46-ounce can**

34. Which is faster, reading w words in m minutes or $6w$ words in $2m$ minutes? How can you tell?
  $6w$ in $2m$; $\frac{3w}{m}$ is larger than $\frac{w}{m}$.

Objective F: *Use ratios to compare two quantities.* *(Lesson 6-3)*

35. In an algebra class of 27 students, there are 10 girls. The number of boys is how many times the number of girls? **1.7**

36. Life expectancy increased from an estimated 18 years in 3000 B.C. to about 76 years in 1990. Compare the life expectancy in 1990 to life expectancy in 3000 B.C. a) $\frac{76}{18}$ b) **422%**

  a. using a ratio.   **b.** using a percent.

37. An item selling for $36 is reduced by $6. What is the percent of discount? **16.7%**

38. The profit on an item selling for $20 is $8. What percent of the item's selling price is profit? **40%**

39. Carl has x CDs and Carla has y CDs. Express the ratio of the number of Carl's CDs to the total number of CDs. $\frac{x}{x+y}$

40. What is the ratio of the total number of heads to the total number of feet among m cows and n chickens? $\frac{m+n}{4m+2n}$

Objective G: *Calculate relative frequencies or probabilities in situations with a finite number of equally likely outcomes.* *(Lesson 6-4)*

41. A number is selected randomly from the integers $\{-5, -4, -3, \ldots, 5\}$. What is the probability that the number is less than 4? $\frac{9}{11}$

42. A fair die is thrown once. Find the probability of getting an odd number. $\frac{3}{6} = \frac{1}{2}$

In 43 and 44, one card is drawn at random from a standard deck of playing cards. $\frac{13}{52} = \frac{1}{4}$

43. What is the probability of drawing a club?

44. What is the probability of drawing a jack or a king? $\frac{8}{52} = \frac{2}{13}$

45. If the probability of winning a prize in a lottery is $\frac{1}{1,000,000}$, what is the probability of not winning? $\frac{999,999}{1,000,000}$

46. Event A has a probability of 0.3. Event B has a probability of $\frac{4}{9}$. Event C has a probability of 33%. Which event is

  a. most likely to happen? **B**

  b. least likely to happen? **A**

47. In one community, 116 of 200 people surveyed had at least one pet. What is the relative frequency of pet owners in this survey? $\frac{29}{50} = 0.58 = 58\%$

48. If the relative frequency of adults who smoke in one town is 14.2%, what is the relative frequency of adults who don't smoke? **85.8%**

In 49 and 50, consider the following. A company with forty salespeople keeps records of how many sales calls are made each week. The results from one week are given in the table.

Number of sales calls	Number of salespersons
10–14	1
15–19	2
20–24	5
25–29	11
30–34	12
35–39	6
40 or more	3

49. What is the relative frequency of a salesperson making fewer than 25 sales calls? (Write as a fraction.) $\frac{1}{5}$

50. What is the relative frequency of a salesperson making 10 or more sales calls? **100%**

Objective H: *Solve percent problems in real situations.* *(Lessons 6-3, 6-5, 6-7)*

51. A sofa is on sale for $450. It originally cost $562.52. What percent of the original price is the sale price? **80%**

Additional Answers
Answers will vary. Samples are given for 30–32.
30. What was the average speed? [40 mph]
31. How much did Tony spend per day? [$\frac{400}{d}$]
32. How much did the puppy gain per week? [$\frac{3}{4}$ kg]
33a. 46-oz can $\approx$ 3.8¢
    6-oz can $\approx$ 4.6¢

Assessment

Evaluation The *Assessment Sourcebook* provides six forms of the Chapter 6 Test. Forms A and B present parallel versions in a short-answer format. Forms C and D offer performance assessment. The fifth test is Chapter 6 Test, Cumulative Form. About 50% of this test covers Chapter 6; 25% covers Chapter 5, and 25% covers earlier chapters. In addition to these tests, Comprehensive Test Chapters 1–6 gives roughly equal attention to all chapters covered thus far.

For information on grading see *General Teaching Suggestions; Grading* in the *Professional Sourcebook* which begins on page T20 in Part 1 of the Teacher's Edition.

Feedback After students have taken the test for Chapter 6 and you have scored the results, return the tests to students for discussion. Class discussion on the questions that caused trouble for most students can be very effective in identifying and clarifying misunderstandings. You might want to have them write down the items they missed and work either in groups or at home to correct them. It is important for students to receive feedback on every chapter test, and we recommend that students see and correct their mistakes before proceeding too far into the next chapter.

52. A $15.99 tape is on sale for $11.99. To the nearest percent, what is the percent of discount? **25%**

53. In August of 1992, *Popular Mechanics* reported that the magnesium valve covers of a BMW automobile weighed 3.7 pounds each and were 37% lighter than the prior year's aluminum covers. How much did the prior year's aluminum valve covers weigh? **5.9 lb**

54. In 1992, 48% of all accidental deaths occurred in motor vehicle accidents. If 86,000 people died accidentally that year, how many were killed in motor-vehicle accidents? **41,280**

55. After a 30% discount and a 5% tax, you paid $7.30 for a shirt. What was the price of the shirt before the discount? **$9.93**

56. Model trains of HO gauge are $\frac{1}{87}$ actual size (no fooling!). If a model locomotive is 30 cm long, how long is the real locomotive? **2610 cm**

57. In 1991, accounting clerks in Boston were earning an average of $437 per week, an increase of 5.4% from 1990. What was their average salary in 1990? **$414.61**

58. Between September 1991 and August 1992 Super Nintendo© dropped in price by 55.3% to $89. What was the September 1991 price? **$199.11**

Objective I: *Solve problems involving proportions in real situations.* *(Lessons 6-8, 6-9)*

59. Anne was saving for a class trip. For every $35 that Anne earned her mother added an extra $15. If Anne earned $245, how much would her mother add? **$105**

60. If $\frac{3}{4}$ cup of sugar equals 12 tablespoons of sugar, how many tablespoons are there in 3 cups of sugar? **48**

61. In the first seven days of November, one family made 45 calls. At this rate, about how many calls will they make during the month? **193**

62. In 1993 for every dollar, you could get 1.60 deutschemarks (the currency in Germany). If a crystal vase cost 120 deutschemarks in 1993, what would its cost be in dollars? **$75**

In 63 and 64, *multiple choice.*

63. Suppose *s* sweaters cost *d* dollars. At this rate, how many sweaters can be bought for $75? **b**
   (a) $\frac{s}{75d}$ (b) $\frac{75s}{d}$ (c) $\frac{75d}{s}$ (d) $\frac{d}{75s}$

64. People planning a party estimate they will need one 2-liter bottle of soda pop for 5 people. How many liters of soda pop will they need for *n* people? **c**
   (a) $\frac{n}{5}$ (b) $\frac{5}{n}$ (c) $\frac{2n}{5}$ (d) $\frac{2}{5n}$

REPRESENTATIONS DEAL WITH PICTURES, GRAPHS, OR OBJECTS THAT ILLUSTRATE CONCEPTS.

Objective J: *Find probabilities involving geometric regions.* *(Lesson 6-6)*

65. A 3-cm square inside a 4-cm square is shown at the right. If a point is selected at random from the figure, what is the probability that it lies in the shaded region? $\frac{7}{16}$

66. The map below shows the roads from town *A* to town *B*. Accidents occur randomly on these roads. What is the probability that an accident on these roads occurs on the 8 km stretch of road drawn in blue? $\frac{1}{2} = 0.5$

67. A target consists of a set of 4 concentric circles with radii of 3″, 6″, 9″, and 12″. The largest circle is inscribed in a square. A sharpshooter shoots blindly so that all points inside the square are equally likely to be hit. A bullet hits somewhere inside the square.

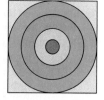

   a. What is the probability that it hits the bull's eye? **0.049**

   b. What is the probability that it hits within one of the two outer rings (but not within the innermost rings)? **0.589**

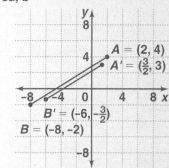

68. At the right is a picture of a spinner. Suppose all positions of the spinner are equally likely. What is the probability that the spinner lands in region A or B? $\frac{K+40}{360}$

69. In a storm, the electricity sometimes goes out and clocks stop. What is the probability that a clock's second hand will stop between the 5 and the 7? $\frac{1}{6} = 0.167$

Objective K: *Apply the Size Change Model for Multiplication.* *(Lesson 6-7)*

70. A drawing of height 6 cm undergoes an expansion of 120%. What is the height of the image? 7.2 cm

71. Give the image of (2, 4) under a size change of magnitude 3. (6, 12)

72. Give the image of (-8, -12) under a size change of magnitude $-\frac{1}{4}$. (2, 3)

73. a. Draw $\overline{AB}$, where $A = (2, 4)$ and $B = (-8, -2)$.
   b. Draw the image of $\overline{AB}$ under the size change in which the image of (x, y) is $\left(\frac{3}{4}x, \frac{3}{4}y\right)$. a, b) See margin.
   c. Is this size change an expansion or a contraction? contraction

In 74 and 75, copy quadrilateral $ABCD$. Then draw its image under the size change with the given magnitude. **See margin.**

74. $\frac{1}{2}$ **75.** -3

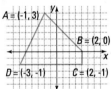

$A = (-1, 3)$
$B = (2, 0)$
$D = (-3, -1)$ $C = (2, -1)$

76. If a size change has magnitude -1, what is its effect on the preimage? Justify your answer. **Sample: Same size as original; coordinates of preimage are opposites.**

82b) $\frac{6}{15} = \frac{x}{140}$; $x = 56$ 83b) $\frac{x}{9} = \frac{3}{n}$; $x = \frac{27}{n}$

Objective L: *Find lengths and ratios of similitude in similar figures.* *(Lesson 6-9)*

In 77 and 78, refer to the similar rectangles below. Corresponding sides are parallel.

77. *Multiple choice.* Which proportion is incorrect? c
   (a) $\frac{d}{h} = \frac{c}{g}$ (b) $\frac{e}{a} = \frac{f}{b}$ (c) $\frac{g}{c} = \frac{a}{e}$ (d) $\frac{h}{d} = \frac{f}{b}$

78. If $a = 12$, $b = 15$, and $e = 10$, what is f? 12.5

79. One rectangle has dimensions 6 cm by 10 cm; another rectangle has dimensions 5 cm by 9 cm. Are the rectangles similar? Explain your reasoning. **No; Ratios of sides are not equal.**

80. Refer to the similar triangles below. Corresponding sides are drawn in the same color. a) $\frac{1}{5}$; $\frac{5}{1}$
   a. Give the two possible ratios of similitude.
   b. Find the length of $\overline{AB}$. 19
   c. Find the length of $\overline{DF}$. 200

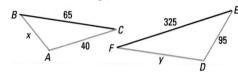

81. The quadrilaterals below are similar. Corresponding sides are parallel.

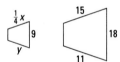

   a. Solve for y. 5.5 **b.** Solve for x. 30

In 82 and 83 **a.** draw a sketch of the situation; **b.** show how a proportion can be used to solve the problem. **Sketches will vary. See left for part b.**

82. A man 6 feet tall casts a shadow 15 feet long. At the same time, the shadow of a tree is 140 feet long. How tall is the tree? 56 ft

83. A tree casts a shadow that is 9 feet long. A yardstick casts a shadow n feet long. How tall is the tree? $\frac{27}{n}$

74.

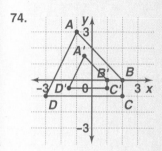

75.

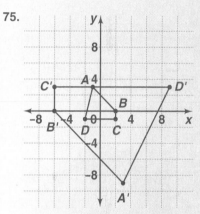

Setting Up Lesson 7-1

We recommend that you assign Lesson 7-1, both reading and some questions, for homework the evening of the test. It gives students work to do after they have completed the test and keeps the class moving.

Table of Contents

The Reasons for UCSMP

Recommendations for Change

The mathematics curriculum has undergone changes in every country of the world throughout this century, as a result of an increasing number of students staying in school longer, the need for a greater number of technically competent workers and citizens, and major advances in mathematics itself. In the last twenty years, these developments have accelerated due to the widespread appearance of computers with their unprecedented abilities to handle and display information.

In the last 100 years, national groups have examined the curriculum periodically in light of these changes in society. A study of reports before 1970 can be found in *A History of Mathematics Education in the United States and Canada,* the 30th Yearbook of the National Council of Teachers of Mathematics, 1970. A summary of reports from 1970 to 1984 can be found in Z. Usiskin, "We Need Another Revolution in Secondary School Mathematics," in *The Secondary School Mathematics Curriculum,* the 1985 Yearbook of NCTM.

The most recent era of reports can be said to have begun in the years 1975–1980, with the publication of reports by various national mathematics organizations calling attention to serious problems in the education of our youth. These reports from inside mathematics education were joined by governmental and private reports through the 1980s decrying the state of American education and providing broad recommendations for school practice. Two of the most notable of these reports for their specific remarks about mathematics education appeared in the year that UCSMP began.

1983: National Commission on Excellence in Education. *A Nation At Risk.*

> The teaching of mathematics in high school should equip graduates to: (a) understand geometric and algebraic concepts; (b) understand elementary probability and statistics; (c) apply mathematics in everyday situations; and (d) estimate, approximate, measure, and test the accuracy of their calculations.

In addition to the traditional sequence of studies available for college-bound students, new, equally demanding mathematics curricula need to be developed for those who do not plan to continue their formal education immediately. (p. 25)

1983: College Board (Project EQuality). *Academic Preparation for College: What Students Need to Know and Be Able to Do.*

> All students (college-bound or not) should have:
>
> The ability to apply mathematical techniques in the solution of real-life problems and to recognize when to apply those techniques.
>
> Familiarity with the language, notation, and deductive nature of mathematics and the ability to express quantitative ideas with precision.
>
> The ability to use computers and calculators.
>
> Familiarity with the basic concepts of statistics and statistical reasoning.
>
> Knowledge in considerable depth and detail of algebra, geometry, and functions. (p. 20)

The specific remarks about school mathematics in these documents for the most part mirror what appeared in the earlier reports. Thus, given what seemed to be a broad consensus on the problems and desirable changes in pre-college mathematics instruction, it was decided, at the outset of UCSMP, that UCSMP would not attempt to form its own set of recommendations, but undertake the task of translating the existing recommendations into the reality of classrooms and schools. It was also decided that UCSMP would look at the best that other countries had to offer, and so in 1983 UCSMP began to translate materials from Japan and some countries of Eastern Europe known for excellence in mathematics education.

Universities for many years have recognized that mathematics encompasses far more than algebra, geometry, and analysis. The term *mathematical sciences* is an umbrella designation which includes traditional mathematics as well as a number of other disciplines. The largest of these other disciplines today are statistics, computer science, and applied mathematics, not coincidentally the areas in which recent reports have recommended greater emphasis. In 1983, the Conference Board of the Mathematical Sciences produced a report, *The Mathematical Sciences Curriculum: What Is Still Fundamental and What Is Not.* The UCSMP Grades 7–12 curriculum is the first mathematical sciences curriculum for average students in the United States.

In the middle 1980s, as the first edition of UCSMP secondary textbooks were being developed and tested, studies comparing the achievement of secondary school students in the U.S. with the achievement of students in other countries verified our conception that we were quite a bit behind those countries in performance.

The Second International Mathematics Study (SIMS) was conducted in 1981–1982 and involved 23 populations in 21 countries. At the eighth-grade level, virtually all students attend school in all those countries, and our students scored at or below the international average on all five subtests: arithmetic, measurement, algebra, geometry, and statistics. We are far below the top: Japan looked at the test and decided it was too easy for their 8th-graders, and so they gave it at 7th grade. Still, the median Japanese 7th-grader performed at the 95th percentile of the United States 8th-graders. SIMS recommended steps to renew school mathematics in the United States.

At the 12th-grade level in 1981–82, about 13% of our population was enrolled in precalculus or calculus; the mean among developed countries is about 16%. Thus, the U.S. no longer kept more students in mathematics than other developed countries, yet our advanced placement students did not perform well when compared to their peers in other countries. SIMS found:

1987: Second International Mathematics Study (SIMS). *The Underachieving Curriculum.*

> In the U.S., the achievement of the Calculus classes, the nation's best mathematics students, was at or near the average achievement of the advanced secondary school mathematics students in other countries. (In most countries, all advanced mathematics students take calculus. In the U.S., only about one-fifth do.)

> The achievement of the U.S. Precalculus students (the majority of twelfth grade college-preparatory students) was substantially below the international average. In some cases the U.S. ranked with the lower one-fourth of all countries in the Study, and was the lowest of the advanced industrialized countries. (*The Underachieving Curriculum*, p. vii)

The situation has been even worse for those who do not take precalculus mathematics in high school. Such students either have performed poorly in their last mathematics course, a situation which has caused them not to go on in mathematics, or they were performing poorly in junior high school and had to take remedial mathematics as 9th-graders. If these students go to college, they invariably take remedial mathematics, which is taught at a faster pace than in high school, and the failure rates in such courses often exceed 40%. If they do not go to college but join the job market, they lack the mathematics needed to understand today's technology. It is no understatement to say that **UCSMP has received its funding from business and industry because those who leave schooling to join the work force are woefully weak in the mathematics they will need.**

SIMS recommended:

> A fundamental revision of the U.S. school mathematics curriculum, in both form and substance, is needed. This activity should begin at the early grades of the elementary school.

> With respect to form, the excessive repetition of topics from year to year should be eliminated. A more focused organization of the subject matter, with a more intense treatment of topics, should be considered.

> Concerning substance, the continued dominating role of arithmetic in the junior high school curriculum results in students entering high school with very limited mathematical backgrounds. The curriculum for all students should be broadened and enriched by the inclusion of appropriate topics in geometry, probability and statistics, as well as algebra. (*The Underachieving Curriculum*, p. xii)

These SIMS results have been confirmed in other studies comparing students at the eighth-grade levels.

In a study conducted by the Educational Testing Service in 1988–89, U.S. eighth-grade students were last in average mathematics proficiency compared with students in Ireland, South Korea, Spain, the United Kingdom, and Canada (Center for the Assessment of Educational Progress, *A World of Differences,* 1989).

Why do we perform so poorly? National Assessment results have shown that emphasizing algebra and geometry leads to higher test scores for eighth graders (U.S. Department of Education, National Center for Education Statistics, *The State of Mathematics Achievement: NAEP's 1990 Assessment of the Nation and the Trial Assessment of the States,* 1992). Historically, schools in the United States have delayed concentrated study of algebra and geometry longer than schools in other countries of the world.

The UCSMP secondary curriculum implements the curriculum recommendations of the Second International Mathematics Study.

In 1986, the National Council of Teachers of Mathematics began an ambitious effort to detail the curriculum it would like to see in schools. The "NCTM Standards," as they have come to be called, involve both content and methodology. The long *Curriculum and Evaluation Standards* document is divided into four sections, K–4, 5–8, 9–12, and Evaluation. Space limits our discussion here to just a few quotes from the 9–12 standards.

1989: National Council of Teachers of Mathematics. *Curriculum and Evaluation of Standards for School Mathematics.*

> The standards for grades 9–12 are based on the following assumptions:
>
> Students entering grade 9 will have experienced mathematics in the context of the broad, rich curriculum outlined in the K–8 standards.
>
> The level of computational proficiency suggested in the K–8 standards will be expected of all students; however, no student will be denied access to the study of mathematics in grades 9–12 because of a lack of computational facility.
>
> Although arithmetic computation will not be a direct object of study in grades 9–12, conceptual and procedural understandings of number, numeration,

and operations, and the ability to make estimations and approximations and to judge the reasonableness of results will be strengthened in the context of applications and problem solving, including those situations dealing with issues of scientific computation.

> Scientific calculators with graphing capabilities will be available to all students at all times.
>
> A computer will be available at all times in every classroom for demonstration purposes, and all students will have access to computers for individual and group work.
>
> At least three years of mathematical study will be required of all secondary school students.
>
> These three years of mathematical study will revolve around a core curriculum differentiated by the depth and breadth of the treatment of topics and by the nature of applications.
>
> Four years of mathematical study will be required of all college-intending students.
>
> These four years of mathematical study will revolve around a broadened curriculum that includes extensions of the core topics and for which calculus is no longer viewed as the capstone experience.
>
> All students will study appropriate mathematics during their senior year. (pp. 124–125)

In 1991, NCTM came out with a second Standards document, concerned with the development of teachers and classroom teaching processes. Space limits our discussion to just a few quotes from the Standards for Teaching Mathematics section of this document.

1991: National Council of Teachers of Mathematics. *Professional Standards for Teaching Mathematics.*

> The standards for teaching are based on four assumptions about the practice of mathematics teaching:
>
> 1. The goal of teaching mathematics is to help all students develop mathematical power . . .
>
> 2. What students learn is fundamentally connected with *How* they learn.
>
> 3. All students can learn to think mathematically.
>
> 4. Teaching is a complex practice and hence not reducible to recipes or prescriptions. (pp. 21–22)
>
> The teacher of mathematics should pose tasks that are

based on—

   sound and significant mathematics;

   knowledge of students' understandings, interests, and experiences;

   knowledge of the range of ways that diverse students learn mathematics;

and that

   engage students' intellect;

   develop students' mathematical understandings and skills;

   stimulate students to make connections and develop a coherent framework for mathematical ideas;

   call for problem formulation, problem solving, and mathematical reasoning;

   promote communication about mathematics;

   represent mathematics as an ongoing human activity;

   display sensitivity to, and draw on, students' diverse background experiences and dispositions;

   promote the development of all students' dispositions to do mathematics. (p. 25)

The UCSMP secondary curriculum is the first full mathematics curriculum that is consistent with the recommendations of the NCTM standards.

In 1989, the Mathematical Sciences Education Board (MSEB), a committee of the National Research Council that coordinates efforts for improvement of mathematics education in the United States, came out with the report *Everybody Counts,* emphasizing the need for the mathematics curriculum to be appropriate for as many students as possible. This thrust reflects the UCSMP position that as many students as possible be accommodated with the curriculum taken by those who go to college. It represents a change in thinking from the two-tiered system recommended in *A Nation at Risk.*

Following up and elaborating on the NCTM Evaluation Standards, many national reports have dealt with issues related to assessment. Among these are three MSEB reports: *For Good Measure* (1991),

Measuring Up (1993), and *Measuring What Counts* (1993). A Working draft of *Assessment Standards for School Mathematics* has also been distributed. The themes of these reports are that we need to change assessment instruments to be aligned with new curricula, to incorporate a variety of ways in which students can demonstrate their knowledge of mathematics, and to ensure that assessments are used in positive ways to enhance learning and teaching rather than in negative ways to keep students from having future opportunities to learn. (For further discussion of assessment, see pages T51–T54.

Some changes have already occurred in assessment. The SAT, Mathematics Achievement, and Advanced Placement calculus exams of the Educational Testing Service now allow any calculator without a QWERTY keyboard. Some states have altered their testing to focus on applying mathematics and higher-order thinking rather than on skills out of context.

Many of the ideas of recent reports are summarized in a 1991 MSEB report, *Reshaping School Mathematics: A Philosophy and Framework for Curriculum.* Six changes are identified there as affecting the context of mathematics education:

■ Changes in the need for mathematics.

■ Changes in mathematics and how it is used.

■ Changes in the role of technology.

■ Changes in American society.

■ Changes in understanding of how students learn.

■ Changes in international competitiveness.

In the UCSMP secondary curriculum we have attempted to respond to each of these changes.

Accomplishing the Goals

Three general problems in mathematics education in the United States lead to three major goals of the UCSMP secondary mathematics curriculum.

General Problem 1: Students do not learn enough mathematics by the time they leave school.

Specifically:

(A) Many students lack the mathematics background necessary to succeed in college, on the job, or in daily affairs.

(B) Even those students who possess mathematical skills are not introduced to enough applications of the mathematics they know.

(C) Students do not get enough experience with problems and questions that require some thought before answering.

(D) Many students terminate their study of mathematics too soon, not realizing the importance mathematics has in later schooling and in the marketplace.

(E) Students do not read mathematics books and, as a result, do not learn to become independent learners capable of acquiring mathematics outside of school when the need arises.

Goal 1: Upgrade students' achievement.

General Problem 2: The school mathematics curriculum has not kept up with changes in mathematics and the ways in which mathematics is used.

Specifically:

(A) Many mathematics curricula have not taken into account today's calculator and computer technology.

(B) Students who do succeed in secondary school mathematics generally are prepared for calculus, but generally are not equipped for the other mathematics they will encounter in college.

(C) Statistical ideas are found everywhere, from newspapers to research studies, but are not found in most secondary school mathematics curricula.

(D) The emergence of computer science has increased the importance of a background in discrete mathematics.

(E) Mathematics is not applied to areas outside the realm of the physical sciences, as much as within the field itself, but these applications are rarely taught and even more rarely tested.

(F) Estimation and approximation techniques are important in all of mathematics, from arithmetic on.

Goal 2: Update the mathematics curriculum.

General Problem 3: Too many students have been sorted out of the mathematics needed for employment and further schooling.

Specifically:

(A) Tracks make it easy to go down levels but almost impossible to go up.

(B) Remedial programs tend to put students further behind instead of catching them up.

(C) Enrichment classes often cover many topics, such as probability, statistics, discrete mathematics, and applications, and with activities of broader scope that are appropriate and important for all students.

(D) Courses for better students are often taught following the belief that the difficulty of a course is more important than its content, and with the view that if all survive, then the course was not a good one.

(E) Relative standards and preset numbers of students who go into special classes are incorrectly used as absolute indicators of ability to perform.

Goal 3: Increase the number of students who take mathematics beyond algebra and geometry.

We at UCSMP believe that these goals can be accomplished, because they already have been realized in some school districts. But substantial reworking of the curriculum has to be involved.

It is not enough simply to insert applications, a bit of statistics, and take students a few times a year to a computer. Currently the greatest amount of time in arithmetic is spent on calculation, in algebra on manipulating polynomials and rational expressions, in geometry on proof, in advanced algebra and later courses on functions. These topics are the most affected by technology.

It is also not enough to raise graduation requirements, although that is the simplest action to take. Increases in requirements often lead to one of two situations. If the courses are kept the same, the result is typically a greater number of failures and an even greater number of dropouts. If the courses are eased, the result is lower performance for many students as they are brought through a weakened curriculum.

The fundamental problem, as SIMS noted, is the curriculum, and the fundamental problem in the curriculum is *time*. There is not enough time in the current 4-year algebra-geometry-algebra-precalculus curriculum to prepare students for calculus. The data reported by Bert Waits and Frank Demana in the *Mathematics Teacher* (January, 1988) are typical. Of students entering Ohio State University with exactly four years of college preparatory high-school mathematics, only 8% placed into calculus on the Ohio State mathematics placement test. The majority placed into pre-calculus, with 31% requiring one semester and 42% requiring two semesters of work. The remaining 19% placed into remedial courses below precalculus. Thus, even with the current curriculum, four years are not enough to take a typical student from algebra to calculus.

Today even most students who take four years of college preparatory mathematics successfully in high schools do not begin college with calculus. Given that the latest recommendations ask for students to learn more mathematics, *we believe five years of college preparatory mathematics beginning with algebra are necessary to provide the time for students to learn the mathematics they need for college in the 1990s.* Thus we do not believe the current NCTM Curriculum Standards for grades 9–12 can be accomplished in four years.

The time can be found by starting reform in grades 6–8. Examining textbooks of the early 1980s, James Flanders found that over half the pages in grades 6–8 are totally review ("How Much of the Content in Mathematics Textbook is New?" *Arithmetic Teacher,* September, 1987). This amount of review, coupled with the magnitude of review in previous years, effectively decelerates students at least 1–2 years compared to students in other countries. It explains why almost all industrialized countries of the world, except the U.S. and Canada (and some French-speaking countries who do geometry before algebra), can begin concentrated study of algebra and geometry in the 7th or 8th grade.

In stark contrast to the review in grades 6–8, Flanders found that almost 90% of the pages of first-year algebra texts have content new to the student. This finding indicates why so many students in the U.S. have difficulty in first-year algebra. The student, having sat for years in mathematics classes where little was new, is overwhelmed. Some people interpret the overwhelming as the student "not being ready" for algebra, but we interpret it as the student being swamped by the pace. When you have been in a classroom in which at most only 1 of 3 days is devoted to anything new, you are not ready for a new idea every day. Thus we believe that algebra should be taught one year earlier to most students than is currently the case (Z. Usiskin, "Why Elementary Algebra Can, Should, and Must Be an Eighth-Grade Course for Average Students," *Mathematics Teacher,* September 1987).

Some school districts are attempting to do away with tracking by placing all students in the same classes, and with very similar expectations. We believe this is too simplistic a solution. Almost all of the many schools that have implemented the UCSMP secondary curriculum with all their students *at the same time* have found that student differences in interests, cultural background, and learning style can be handled by their teachers who take advantage of the richness of the UCSMP textbooks and the wealth of teaching suggestions and ancillary materials that accompany them. Even so, they have almost all had to create slower-paced sections for students who enter with the least knowledge or who are unwilling to do homework. And they almost all realize that many students could have begun the curriculum a year earlier than the other students.

The most successful school districts realize that complex problems seldom have simple solutions. We believe strongly that the UCSMP curriculum is appropriate for virtually all students, but not at the same time. No student should be deprived of the opportunity to be successful in any of the courses, but no child who is ready should have to wait a year or two to begin the curriculum. Our evidence is strong that the national percentiles that we show on page T29 are good predictors of readiness for UCSMP courses. We recommend that school districts follow these percentiles by strongly recommending that students who fit them take our courses. Additionally, students who miss these percentiles by small amounts or who very much wish to take our courses should be allowed to take them. We strongly urge school districts to emphasize the importance of entering knowledge by strengthening their curricula in the preceding years, and stress that students must do homework *every day* when studying from UCSMP materials.

Finally, because UCSMP materials are not like traditional materials, we urge that school districts provide sufficient in-service training on the newer ideas incorporated in them. Teachers differ in ability, entering knowledge, preferred teaching style, and cultural background almost as much as students differ. Some love cooperative learning; others have never used it. Some are computer experts; others are neophytes. Some enjoy using manipulative materials; others avoid them. Some have had courses in statistics and discrete mathematics; others have not. Some are already trying writing and alternate assessment in their classrooms; others have not heard of these things. No single in-service can handle such variety. We encourage school districts to send teachers to professional conferences where teachers have choices

on what to attend. In particular, districts should take advantage of in-service opportunities offered by UCSMP and ScottForesman. It is also beneficial to hold periodic meetings on site to discuss local issues.

The UCSMP Secondary Curriculum

The Six UCSMP Courses

Each UCSMP course is designed for the equivalent of a school year of at least 170 days in which mathematics is taught for at least 45 minutes (preferably 50 minutes or more) each day. All of the courses have the following general features: wider scope of content; continual emphasis on applications to the real world and to problem solving; up-to-date use of calculators and computers; a multi-dimensional (SPUR) approach to understanding; and review and mastery strategies for enhancing performance. These are described below and on pages *iv-v* of the Student Edition.

Transition Mathematics (TM) weaves three themes—applied arithmetic, pre-algebra and pre-geometry—by focusing on arithmetic operations in mathematics and the real world. Variables are used as pattern generalizers, abbreviations in formulas, and unknowns in problems, and are represented on the number line and graphed in the coordinate plane. Basic arithmetic and algebraic skills are connected to corresponding geometry topics.

Algebra has a scope far wider than most other algebra texts. Applications motivate all topics. Exponential growth and compound interest are covered. Statistics and geometry are settings for work with linear expressions and sentences. Probability provides a context for algebraic fractions, functions, and set ideas. Technology for graphing is assumed to be available.

Geometry integrates coordinates and transformations throughout, and gives strong attention to measurement formulas and three-dimensional figures in the first two-thirds of the book. Work with proof-writing follows a carefully sequenced development of the logical and conceptual precursors to proof. Geometry drawing technology is highly recommended.

Advanced Algebra emphasizes facility with algebraic expressions and forms, especially linear and quadratic forms, powers and roots, and functions based on these concepts. Students study logarithmic, trigonometric, polynomial, and other special functions both for their abstract properties and as tools for modeling real-world situations. A geometry course or its equivalent is a prerequisite, for geometric ideas are utilized throughout. Technology for graphing functions and making spreadsheets is assumed to be available.

Functions, Statistics, and Trigonometry (FST) integrates statistical and algebraic concepts, and previews calculus in work with functions and intuitive notions of limits. Technology is assumed available for student use in plotting functions, analyzing data, and simulating experiments. Enough trigonometry is available to constitute a standard precalculus course in trigonometry and circular functions.

Precalculus and Discrete Mathematics (PDM) integrates the background students must have to be successful in calculus (advanced work with functions and trigonometry, an introduction to limits and other calculus ideas), with the discrete mathematics (number systems, combinatorics, recursion, graphs) helpful in computer science. Mathematical thinking, including specific attention to formal logic and proof, is a theme throughout. Automatic graphing technology is assumed available for students.

Target Populations

We believe that all high-school graduates should take courses through *Advanced Algebra*, that all students planning to go to college should take courses through *Functions, Statistics, and Trigonometry*, and that students planning majors in technical areas should take all six UCSMP courses.

The critical juncture is when first-year algebra is completed. All qualified students should be afforded the possibility of taking *Transition Mathematics* in 6th grade so as to maximize the potential for them to complete *Algebra* in 7th grade and thus take calculus in high school without any acceleration.

The fundamental principle in placing students into courses is that entry should not be based on age, but on mathematical knowledge. Our studies indicate that with a standard curriculum, about 10% of students nationally are ready for *Transition Mathematics* at 6th grade, about another 40% at 7th grade, another 20% at 8th grade, and another 10–15% at 9th grade. We caution that these percentages are national, not local percentages, and the variability in our nation is enormous. We have tested the materials in school districts where few students are at grade level, where *Transition Mathematics* is appropriate for no more than the upper half of 8th-graders. We have tested also in school districts where as many as 90% of the students have successfully used *Transition Mathematics* in 7th grade. School districts have increased the percentages at the 6th and 7th grade by strengthening the mathematics curriculum in grades K–5 or K–6.

We also caution that the percentages are not automatic. Students who do not reach 7th-grade competence until the 9th-grade level often do not possess the study habits necessary for successful completion of these courses. At the 9th-grade level, *Transition Mathematics* has been substituted successfully either for a traditional pre-algebra course or for the first year of an algebra course spread out over two years. It often does not work as a substitute for a general mathematics course in which there is no expectation that students will take algebra the following year.

On page T29 is a chart identifying the courses and the populations for which they are intended. The percentiles are national percentiles on a 7th-grade standardized mathematics test using 7th-grade norms, and apply to potential *Transition Mathematics* students. Page T29 also provides advice for starting in the middle of the series.

Left column: These students are often more interested in school, and they should be offered the Challenges suggested in the Teacher's Edition. Teachers may also wish to enrich courses for these students further with problems from mathematics contests.

2nd column: These students should be expected to take mathematics at least through the 11th grade, by which time they will have the mathematics needed for all college majors except those in the hard sciences and engineering. For that they will have the opportunity to take 12th-grade mathematics.

3rd column: Students in the 30th–70th percentile can complete *Advanced Algebra* by taking three years of high school mathematics. Currently over half of these students go to college. By completing *FST,* they will have studied the kind of mathematics needed for all majors.

The top 10% of students are ready for *Transition Mathematics* in 6th grade. These students can proceed through the entire curriculum by the 11th grade and take calculus in the 12th grade.

Students in the 50th–90th percentile on a 7th-grade standardized mathematics test should be ready to take *Transition Mathematics* in 7th grade.

Students who do not reach the 7th-grade level in mathematics until the 8th grade **(in the 30th–70th percentile)** begin *Transition Mathematics* in 8th grade.

Students who do not reach the 7th-grade level in mathematics until the 9th grade **(in the 15th–50th percentile)** begin *Transition Mathematics* in 9th grade.

Grade				
6	Transition Mathematics			
7	Algebra	Transition Mathematics		
8	Geometry	Algebra	Transition Mathematics	
9	Advanced Algebra	Geometry	Algebra	Transition Mathematics
10	Functions, Statistics, and Trigonometry	Advanced Algebra	Geometry	Algebra
11	Precalculus and Discrete Mathematics	Functions, Statistics, and Trigonometry	Advanced Algebra	Geometry
12	Calculus (not available through UCSMP)	Precalculus and Discrete Mathematics	Functions, Statistics, and Trigonometry	Advanced Algebra

Right column: Students in the 15th–50th percentile should not be tracked into courses that put them further behind. Rather they should be put into this curriculum and counseled on study skills. The logic is simple: Students who are behind in mathematical knowledge need to work harder at it, not less, in order to catch up.

Starting in the Middle of the Series

Every UCSMP course has been designed so that it could be used independently of other UCSMP courses. Accordingly, about half of the testing of UCSMP courses after *Transition Mathematics* has been with students who have not had any previous UCSMP courses. We have verified that any of the UCSMP courses can be taken successfully following the typical prerequisite courses in the standard curriculum.

Starting with *UCSMP Algebra* No additional prerequisites other than those needed for success in any algebra course are needed for success in *UCSMP Algebra*.

Students who have studied *Transition Mathematics* tend to cover more of *UCSMP Algebra* than other students because they have been introduced to more of the applications of algebra.

UCSMP Algebra prepares students for any standard geometry course.

Starting with *UCSMP Geometry* No additional prerequisites other than those needed for success in any geometry course are needed for success in *UCSMP Geometry*.

UCSMP Geometry can be used with faster, average, and slower students who have these prerequisites. Prior study of *Transition Mathematics* and *UCSMP Algebra* ensures this background, but this content is also found in virtually all existing middle school or junior high school texts. Classes of students who have studied *UCSMP Algebra* tend to cover more *UCSMP Geometry* than other classes because they know more geometry and are better at the algebra used in geometry. Students who have studied *UCSMP Geometry* are ready for any second-year algebra text.

Starting with *UCSMP Advanced Algebra* *UCSMP Advanced Algebra* can be used following any standard geometry text.

Students who have had *UCSMP Geometry* before *UCSMP Advanced Algebra* tend to be better prepared in the transformations and coordinate geometry they will need in this course, and geometry courses using other books should be careful to cover this content. Students who have studied from *UCSMP Algebra* tend to be better prepared for the graphing and applications found in this course.

Students who have studied *UCSMP Advanced Algebra* are prepared for courses commonly found at the senior level, including trigonometry or precalculus courses.

Starting with *Functions, Statistics, and Trigonometry* *FST* assumes that students have completed a second-year algebra course. Students who have studied some trigonometry, like that found in *UCSMP Advanced Algebra*, will be at an advantage. No additional prerequisites other than those found in any second-year algebra text are needed for success in *FST*.

FST provides sufficient background for success in a non-proof-oriented calculus, such as is often taken by business or social studies majors in college, and for many of the reform calculus courses that emphasize applications and technology.

Starting with *Precalculus and Discrete Mathematics* *PDM* can be taken successfully by students who have had *FST*, by students who have had typical senior level courses that include study of trigonometry and functions, and by top students who have successfully completed *full* advanced algebra and trigonometry courses.

PDM provides the background necessary for any typical calculus course, either at the high school or college level, including those that place a heavy emphasis on proof, and including advanced placement calculus courses at either the AB or BC level.

Professional Sourcebook: SECTION **2** **ABOUT *UCSMP ALGEBRA***

Goals of *UCSMP ALGEBRA*

UCSMP Algebra introduces students to all the dimensions of the understanding of algebra: its skills, its properties, its uses, and its representations. For each, we want to update the curriculum and upgrade students' achievement. Specifically, we want students to be better able to apply algebra; we want them to be able to connect algebra to geometry, to statistics, and to probability; and we want them to be more successful in future years in their study of mathematics.

Additionally, we want students to learn how to study mathematics. To accomplish this goal we want students to learn to take advantage of many resources.

They should try to learn from the reading of the lesson, as well as from their teacher and from their fellow classmates.

Finally, we have another, more lofty goal. We want students to view their study of mathematics as worthwhile, as full of interesting and entertaining information, as related to almost every endeavor. We want them to realize that mathematics is still growing and is changing fast. We want them to look for and recognize mathematics in places they haven't before, to use the library, to search through newspapers or almanacs, to get excited by knowledge.

In summary, we would like to help students

develop what the NCTM Standards call *mathematical power,* that is, the ability to explore, conjecture, and reason logically; to solve non-routine problems; to communicate about and through mathematics; and to connect ideas within mathematics and between mathematics and other disciplines. We also want students to develop personal self-confidence, positive attitudes, and effective study skills in mathematics.

Who Should Take *UCSMP Algebra?*

Virtually every student who expects to graduate from high school should take algebra. The reasons for college-bound students to take algebra are obvious: algebra is required for admission to almost all colleges; algebra is found on all college-entrance examinations; algebra is necessary to understand even the basics of science, statistics, computers, and economics, and helps students to understand the social sciences and business. Without algebra, doors are open to only a few colleges — and even at those colleges a student who has no algebra has the choice of only a few college majors.

There are just as many reasons for non-college-bound students to take algebra. Technical schools, such as those for the trades, require that students be familiar with formulas and with graphs, for which algebra provides the most effective exposure. Computers abound in the workplace; algebra is the language of programs and algebraic thinking underlies the operation of spreadsheets and many other software packages. Algebra is the language of generalization; without it arithmetic is often seen merely as a collection of unrelated rules and procedures. It is no surprise that study of algebra helps competence in arithmetic.

Students who take *UCSMP Algebra* should have the following prerequisites:

(1) *Transition Mathematics* or a strong pre-algebra course the previous year, as much for getting used to the pace as for the background in algebra that such a course gives;

(2) a willingness and the maturity to learn to do homework every night;

(3) the expectation of studying geometry the next year if successful in algebra.

In addition, the teacher of *UCSMP Algebra* should believe that every student with the above prerequisites can learn algebra.

Thousands of students who have successfully completed *Transition Mathematics* in Grades 6, 7, and 8 have studied from *UCSMP Algebra* the next year. We continue to advocate the study of algebra in Grade 7 or 8 for students who have the above prerequisites (Usiskin, 1987). The evidence is that students who successfully complete *UCSMP Algebra* in these grades are well-prepared for *UCSMP Geometry* and other geometry courses in the next year.

Problems *UCSMP Algebra* Addresses

The general problems addressed by the UCSMP secondary curriculum are discussed in Section 1, on pages T21–T30. More specifically, *UCSMP Algebra* responds to eight serious problems which cannot be treated by small changes in content or approach.

Problem 1: Large numbers of students do not know why they need algebra.

Some algebra courses have been motivated almost exclusively by the needs of a minority of the population: those who will take calculus four or five years later. Other algebra courses consist entirely of dozens of problems of one type followed by dozens of another, or of one skill after another, introduced without motivation, ostensibly designed for the poorer student but actually of ultimate use to few if any students.

It is no surprise, then, that many adults—even many of the most educated of adults—wonder why they studied algebra. We believe that this is a result of the kind of algebra courses they studied, and the lack of applications in them. Algebra has many real-world applications even though school algebra has often ignored them. Most age, digit, work, and other so-called "word problems" or "story problems" do not constitute applications; problems like them are not encountered outside school.

The *UCSMP Algebra* response: Instead of holding off on applications until after skills have been developed, applications are used to motivate all concepts and skills. The ability to apply algebra is made a priority. Word problems that have little or no use are replaced by more meaningful types of problems. Algebra is continually connected with the arithmetic the student knows and the geometry the student will study. We have evidence from earlier work with an applications approach to algebra and from the first edition of *UCSMP Algebra* that we can greatly reduce and almost eliminate the "Why are we studying this?" kind of question.

Problem 2: *The mathematics curriculum has been lagging behind today's widely available and inexpensive technology.*

Calculators and computers allow students to work with realistic numbers, to practice estimation skills, to avoid tedious and repetitious calculations, and to solve problems that would not be accessible otherwise. There is unanimous sentiment in recent national reports on mathematics education in favor of the use of calculators and computers in all mathematics courses. Yet until the development of materials by UCSMP, there was no curriculum for secondary schools that made systematic use of this technology.

The *UCSMP Algebra* response: We support the recommendations of the NCTM regarding access to calculators and computers. In particular, we assume that scientific calculators are available to students at all times, and they are used starting in the first chapter of *Algebra*. We strongly recommend that automatic graphers be available as tools for generating or analyzing tables of value or for making and analyzing graphs.

Many connections with computers are given in this course. We introduce the notation of the BASIC computer language, give templates for programs, and introduce spreadsheets. But the influence of computers ranges further than this. Certain content has been included because of its importance in a computer age, including discrete and continuous domains, iteration, interpretation of algorithms, and a great deal of interpretation of graphs. However, we note that many of the functions performed only by computers as recently as a few years ago are now available on hand-held graphics calculators, and we encourage the use of such powerful calculators.

Problem 3: *Too many students fail algebra.*

National surveys indicate that approximately 25% of the students who study algebra fail or drop out from the course. In some schools the failure rate is as high as 50%. In particular, students who have not had prior experience with algebra rarely master all the concepts of first-year algebra in a single year.

The *UCSMP Algebra* response: We smooth out the development of algebraic ideas, introducing some traditional first-year algebra ideas in *Transition Mathematics,* and delaying others until later in the UCSMP series. Thus *Transition Mathematics* students work not only on the transition into algebra, but also on some important concepts of algebra such as the uses of variables as unknowns and as pattern generalizers. *UCSMP Algebra* extends work with these ideas and builds understanding of linear, quadratic, and exponential functions. Some work with polynomial and rational expressions is done, but concentrated work on polynomial and rational functions is delayed until *Functions, Statistics, and Trigonometry* and *Precalculus and Discrete Mathematics,* because not all students need to have an acquaintance with these ideas.

The evidence from our studies is that students using *Transition Mathematics* know much more algebra at the end of the school year than students in comparison classes. Thus, although we expect students to do well in *UCSMP Algebra* even if they have not had *Transition Mathematics,* we expect much better performance from those who have had that kind of rich experience.

Problem 4: *Even students who succeed in algebra often do poorly in geometry.*

The evidence is that the knowledge of geometry among American secondary school students is atrocious. In the Second International Mathematics Study the mean score of 8th graders in the United States on the geometry subtest ranked at the 25th percentile of the distribution of means for participating countries. The best predictor of success with proof in geometry is a student's geometry knowledge at the beginning of a course. Yet in a study conducted at the University of Chicago in the early 1980s, more than half of the students entering high school geometry had so little knowledge of geometry that they were unable to identify simple polygons or describe their properties.

The *UCSMP Algebra* response: As with algebra, it is too much to expect students to learn all of geometry in a single year in high school. *UCSMP Algebra* continues the strong emphasis on geometry that is found in *Transition Mathematics,* with particular attention paid to the numerical relationships involving lines, angles, and polygons, and an algebraic view of geometric transformations.

The evidence from our studies of the First Editions of *Algebra* and *Transition Mathematics* validates the UCSMP integration of geometry into these courses. In the *Transition Mathematics* first edition summative evaluation, students in comparison classes showed no increase in geometry knowledge from September to June. However, students using *Transition Mathematics* knew almost as much at the end of the year as typical students entering a geometry class. The results of the first edition summative evaluation study of *Algebra* showed that UCSMP students did better than the comparison students on *every* geometry question on the final examinations.

Problem 5: *High school students know very little statistics and probability.*

It is often assumed that students learn the most basic of statistics and probability before high school; such content has been in schoolbooks for some time. Our evidence is that such learning is meager at best. In the Second International Mathematics Study the mean score of 8th graders in the United States on the statistics subtest ranked at the 25th percentile of the distribution of means for participating countries. In the first edition summative evaluation of *UCSMP Algebra,* students were asked to find the median of a set of nine numbers given in increasing order. Whereas 75% of *UCSMP Algebra* students correctly responded, only 36% of comparison students could do so. On an item to calculate a probability from the results of a poll, the percentages were 61% for *UCSMP Algebra* students and 37% for comparison students.

Customarily, the only time probability is discussed in high schools has been together with the study of permutations and combinations in second-year algebra. Statistics usually is not discussed at all. The result is that most high school students never encounter either of these subject areas.

The UCSMP response to this problem is to give strong attention to statistics and probability in three places: in *Transition Mathematics,* in *Algebra,* and in *Functions, Statistics, and Trigonometry.*

In *Algebra,* we assume students have displayed data in various ways, calculated averages (means), and have encountered the basic definition of probability. Intuitions and fundamental properties of probability are discussed early and then applied throughout the course. Since statistics starts with data, we use data throughout this book so that students become accustomed to it. We ask students to graph, organize, and interpret data. These are easy things for students to do, but they are often ignored. Then, as algebra topics relate to statistical ideas, we do the statistics.

Problem 6: *Students are not skillful enough, regardless of what they are taught.*

The evidence is that students are rather skillful at routine problems but not with problems involving complicated numbers, different wordings, or new contexts. It is obvious that in order to obtain such skill, students must see problems with all sorts of numbers, in a variety of wordings, and in many different contexts. We also ask that students do certain problems mentally, which expands the level of competence expected of algebra students.

The *UCSMP Algebra* response: Encountering such problems is not enough. **UCSMP Algebra employs a four-stage approach to develop skill.**

Stage 1: involves a concentrated introduction to the ideas surrounding the skill: why it is done, how it is done, and the kinds of problems that can be solved with it. Most books are organized to have this stage, because teachers recognize that explanations of an idea require time. At the end of this stage, typically only the best students have the skill. But in *UCSMP Algebra* this is only the beginning.

Stage 2: occupies the following lessons in the chapter and consists of questions designed to establish some competence in the skill. These are found in the Review questions. By the end of the lessons of the chapter, most students should have some competence in the skills, but some may not have enough.

Stage 3: involves mastery learning. At the end of each chapter is a Progress Self-Test for students to take and judge how they are doing. Worked-out solutions are included to provide feedback and help to the student. This is followed by a Chapter Review, organized by objectives, to enable students to acquire those skills they didn't have when taking the Progress Self-Test. Teachers are expected to spend 1–3 days on these sections to give students time to reach mastery. By the end of this stage, most students should have gained mastery at least at the level of typical students covering the content.

Stage 4: continues the review through daily Review questions in subsequent chapters. Vital algebra skills, such as solving linear equations, receive consistent emphasis throughout the book. Included also are skill sequences consisting of 3 or 4 questions that provide practice on related problems. The evidence is that this four-stage process enables students to gain competence over a wider range of content than comparable students normally possess. (See pages T54–T59 on research.)

Problem 7: Students don't read mathematics.

Students using traditional texts tell us they don't read because (1) the text is uninteresting, and (2) they don't have to read because the teacher explains it for them. But students must learn to read for future success in mathematics.

The *UCSMP Algebra* response to (1) above: We have paid careful attention to the explanations, examples, and questions in each lesson. So every lesson of this book contains reading and questions covering the reading. *UCSMP Algebra* is more than a resource for questions; it is a resource for information, for examples of how to do problems, for the history of major ideas, for applications of the ideas, for connections between ideas in one place in the book and in another, and for motivation.

Our response to (2) above is to encourage teachers not to explain everything in advance to students. Because students can read and understand the *UCSMP Algebra* text, the teacher has the freedom to teach in a variety of ways, and it is not necessary to explain every day what the textbook says. The teacher can concentrate on helping students with difficult new symbols and vocabulary, or on developing further examples, explanations, and investigations tailored to his or her class. More detailed information about reading can be found on pages T47–T48.

In our First Edition studies, teachers of *UCSMP Algebra* who had not taught *Transition Mathematics* were skeptical at first about the amount of reading in the book. As the year progressed, they joined those who had taught *Transition Mathematics* in viewing the reading as one of the strongest features of this series. Some teachers felt that UCSMP was teaching reading comprehension; they all felt that the requirement to read helped develop thinkers who were more critical and aware. Now the UCSMP approach to reading is being adopted by many other textbooks.

Student comments confirm these beliefs. In 1986–87 one group of eighth-grade students used *UCSMP Algebra* in their home school. They simultaneously studied algebra from a standard text at a nearby high school. Their comments comparing the two texts:

> ". . . the UCSMP book allows me to figure out things for myself. I feel it makes me more independent in terms of doing my homework."

> "UCSMP is easier to understand."

> "The UCSMP homework is much easier to do at home. Applying the Reading (the former name to the section of problems now called 'Applying the Mathematics') makes you think."

Comments from students and teachers of the First Edition published by ScottForesman continue to support the positive features of the reading.

Problem 8: *Students are not very good at communicating mathematics in writing.*

Students write mathematics every time they "show work," but they typically do not realize that they are engaged in a task to communicate an argument. Rather, they see their writing as somehow proving that they did the work that was required, and writing becomes simply showing a more detailed answer. Geometry students have great difficulty writing even the simplest of proofs. In general, students at the level of *UCSMP Algebra* are quite poor at putting together any sort of logical argument. We think this is because they are seldom given writing tasks that require such arguments.

There are many reasons to put some emphasis on writing. Writing can organize and clarify thinking, thus making it a route for exploring a subject and gaining ownership of it. This makes it a valuable learning tool. Writing stimulates communication among individuals; students can express frustrations and other difficulties with a concept at hand. Some who might not otherwise ask questions may use writing as their means to communicate with a teacher. Thus writing can also be a valuable teaching tool.

There is also a strong link between problem solving and writing. Both require critical decision-making and involve the development of strategies. Both provide the learner with many possible avenues to follow, demonstrating that there are many ways to approach a problem.

The *UCSMP Algebra* response: Writing is developed from the beginning of the year. Lesson questions ask students to explain their methods, describe representations and procedures, and compare algorithms. Writing questions are found on Progress Self-Tests and in the Chapter Review questions. The notes in the Teacher's Edition also provide suggestions for incorporating writing.

What's New in the Second Edition

The publication of the complete six-year UCSMP series has given another perspective on each text and its role in the long-term development of mathematical concepts and competence. National reports that have been issued since the publication of the first version of *UCSMP Algebra* in 1985 have stressed the importance of many of the innovations present in UCSMP texts. Widespread availability of graphics calculators and computer spreadsheets indicates that algebra courses can incorporate technology beyond the scientific calculator. The Second Edition of *UCSMP Algebra* has also benefited from user reports, focus group discussions, and ScottForesman surveys of users from all regions throughout the United States.

A person familiar with the First Edition of *UCSMP Algebra* will note the following changes:

■ There has been a reordering of the content of the first seven chapters. The first equation to be solved with an algorithm is $ax = b$, which allows multi-step linear equations to be studied in Chapter 3, and the general linear equation $ax + b = cx + d$ to be studied in Chapter 5.

■ The use of spreadsheets and automatic graphers has been incorporated throughout the text, with a lesson on using a spreadsheet in Chapter 4 and a lesson on using an automatic grapher in Chapter 5.

■ The study of quadratic equations begins in Chapter 1.

■ There is a greater emphasis on generalizing from patterns to expressions and properties involving variables.

■ A chapter is devoted to factoring.

■ Colored headers appear in the lessons to help outline the reading.

- Full-page In-class Activities and shorter Activities (within lessons) are included to provide students with more hands-on experiences. Many of the In-class Activities are especially suitable for small-group work.

- Each chapter includes a set of Projects to provide students opportunities to explore concepts in a more in-depth way. Students may find it beneficial to work on the Projects in small groups. (See pages T42–T43.)

- Solutions to Examples are printed in a special font to help model what students should write when they do the Questions.

- A global, multicultural view of mathematics is enhanced with new photos from around the world. Informative captions are now included.

- Graphic displays are drawn with a contemporary look to emphasize that the data in the text are like that found in newspapers, magazines, and other sources outside the classroom.

- An enhanced Teacher's Edition now provides daily suggestions for adapting to individual needs, optional activities, and assessment alternatives.

- An augmented ancillary package offers two sets of Lesson Masters, performance tests and forms for authentic assessment, and an expanded Technology Sourcebook.

- Interactive multimedia components, emphasizing real-world applications, are designed to further enhance instruction and provide motivation.

Professional Sourcebook: SECTION

3

GENERAL TEACHING SUGGESTIONS FOR *UCSMP ALGEBRA*

UCSMP Algebra is the core of a mathematics course. It is not meant to stand alone without a teacher or without other materials. Nor does it attempt to prescribe a single way of teaching mathematics. We have seen the First Edition of this text used effectively with a variety of models of teaching—from direct instruction through cooperative learning, and we expect the Second Edition to be at least as flexible.

We feel a need to restate one of the assumptions of the *Professional Standards for Teaching Mathematics* (NCTM, 1991), that "teaching is a complex practice and hence not reducible to recipes or prescriptions." The suggestions which follow should not be construed as rigid: students, teachers, classes, and schools vary greatly. But the suggestions should not be ignored. They come from extensive discussions with teachers of earlier versions of these materials, written comments from experienced users of the First Edition, and from test results. We encourage you to read them, and to try as many of them as you can in your classroom.

Planning

It hardly needs to be said that good teaching begins with careful planning. In this section we concentrate on features that may be different from other books from which you have taught.

First Steps

1. Find out more about these materials. If you have not already done so, skim Section 1 and read Section 2 of this Professional Sourcebook. These sections will inform you if your students are among the typical *UCSMP Algebra* students, and they give the motivation for many of the features you will find. Also read pages *iv-v* of the Student Edition for additional information on UCSMP and *UCSMP Algebra*.

2. Make certain that you have all the materials you need. A list of components that are available with the Second Edition of *UCSMP Algebra* is on page T19 of this book. If you do not have all the materials, contact your local ScottForesman representative or call ScottForesman at 1-800-554-4411.

Before the school year starts you should assemble some resources for your teaching. Some materials you will want to have in your classroom throughout the year are: a dictionary, an atlas, an almanac, and either a globe or a large world map for the wall.

3. Check that your students will have all the materials they need. In addition to pencils and paper, all students are expected to have a scientific calculator, a ruler calibrated in centimeters and inches, and a protractor. A list of specifications is given in the "To the Student" section on pages 1–3. Be certain to cover this section with your students.

4. Familiarize yourself with the general layout of the two-part Teacher's Edition (this part and one other). Part 1 of the Teacher's Edition contains Chapters 1–6. Part 2 contains Chapters 7–13. At the beginning of each chapter are four extra pages (tinted) that display pacing schedules, objectives, available materials, and overall notes for the chapter. Following Chapter 6 in Part 1 are the Selected Answers (for Chapters 1–6) and the Glossary and Index to the entire Student Edition. In Part 2, Chapter 13 is followed by the Selected Answers (for Chapters 7–13), and again the Glossary and Index.

5. Familiarize yourself with the features of the Student Edition. There are 13 chapters, with 7–10 lessons each. Each chapter begins with a 2-page chapter opener that serves as an introduction and is meant to be read. Then come the lessons, each with reading followed by four types of questions: Covering the Reading, Applying the Mathematics, Review, and Exploration. Following the lessons are Projects. (See pages T42–T43.) Each chapter ends with a Summary and list of new Vocabulary for the chapter, a Progress Self-Test, and a Chapter Review. The Progress Self-Test and Chapter Review are not optional; they are designed to focus students' attention to the important material and objectives of the chapter. (See page T40.) The Selected Answers section, beginning on page 838 in the student edition, provides answers to odd-numbered Applying the Mathematics and Review Questions.

6. Consider sending information about *UCSMP Algebra* home with your students. A letter or flyer to parents conveys your and your school district's concern for each child and at the same time can let parents know your expectations regarding materials and homework. Suggestions concerning what form a letter or flyer can take, and what to put in it are provided below. These suggestions come from mailings sent to us by UCSMP users.

Sample Letter to Parents

Because the adoption of books is generally done by a school or school district, it may be best if the letter comes from the mathematics department, the mathematics department chair or supervisor, or the principal. The letter should be on school or school district stationery. Here are the kinds of information schools have conveyed:

UCSMP beliefs/philosophy Mathematics is valuable to the average citizen. All students can learn a significant amount of mathematics. We can learn from other countries. A major cause of our problems lies in the curriculum. The mathematics curriculum can make better use of time by spending less time on review (from previous years) and outmoded content and skills. Calculators and computers render some content obsolete, make other content more important, and change the ways we should view still other content. The scope of mathematics should expand at all levels. The classroom should draw examples from the real world. To make significant changes in any school, teachers, administrators, and parents must work together.

Features of UCSMP texts that parents will notice Students are expected to read. They are expected to use calculators. There are a variety of problems in each question set rather than a single type of problem repeated a large number of times. *It is best if each feature is followed by a sentence or two with a rationale for that feature. Such information may be found throughout this Sourcebook.*

Materials students need This can be similar to the list found in the "To The Student" section of the student book (pages 1–3). This should include a list of the features of the calculators students should have, and information on how students can obtain such calculators (whether from the school or from a local store). If possible, include prices.

How parents can help It is wise to include statements that describe the roles of parents in their child's education, particularly because at this level, parents are sometimes given the feeling that they no longer are integral. Here are some suggestions: Encourage your child to read the textbook. Check with your children to see that they have the supplies they need. See that your children are doing homework every night. Encourage determination and perseverance; if your child is having a problem, ask your child to tell you what he or she knows about the idea. Monitor your child's absences (perhaps include the school's absence policy). Contact the teacher as soon as a problem arises; do not wait. Encourage your child to seek help whenever necessary (give places to get help).

With this letter, some school districts include their mathematics course sequence. Some indicate their grading policies. Whatever you include, you should expect responses from parents who seek clarification. *Welcome* each response as a sign of an interested parent and because the responses will help you in drafting what you send next year.

Planning for Teaching

Planning for teaching with *UCSMP Algebra* is similar to the planning you might do for any mathematics class. *Global planning can be done by looking over the Table of Contents and setting goals for each grading period.* The chapters in this book are meant to be covered in order, at a pace of about one lesson per day, and we suggest that first-time users adhere to this pattern. This means that most teachers should plan to cover about 12 chapters. This amounts to approximately two chapters each marking period if you give grades every six weeks, or three chapters per marking period if you give grades every nine or ten weeks. Teachers of very well-prepared students in schools which do not lose much instructional time to other matters are likely to be able to cover more, and those who are teaching underprepared students in classes with numerous interruptions may cover less.

To get an overview of the content in each chapter, read the Chapter Overview on the tinted pages in this Teacher's Edition; read the lesson titles; and scan the Summary and Vocabulary, Progress Self-Test, and Chapter Review at the end of the chapter. Collectively these will give you a good idea of what the chapter is about, and how much of the content will be new to you or your students. Make a tentative schedule for working through the chapter. Be sure to leave 2 or 3 days for review before the chapter test (See *Strategies for Mastery* on page T40.)

Read each lesson in the Student Edition. Then read the Overview, the Notes on Reading, the Notes on the Questions, and other side and bottom notes in the Teacher's Edition. They indicate the Resources you may need for the lesson. They also provide ideas for various ways of approaching the lesson. They will help you decide what instructional modes (whole-class discussion, small-group work, demonstration, lecture, etc.) you might use, how you might go over the assignment from the previous day, how you could sequence the class activities from opening to closing, and what assignment you can make for the next class.

Do all of the Questions before assigning them. Note any questions with directions which might need clarification to your students, or any questions which you think are particularly important or exceptionally difficult.

Pace

There is a natural tendency, when using a new book, to go more slowly, to play it safe should you forget something. Teachers using these materials for the first time have almost invariably said that they would move more quickly the next year. Do not be afraid to move quickly. As in all UCSMP texts, virtually all lessons in *UCSMP Algebra* are intended to be read and discussed in one day.

Students adjust to the pace set by the teacher. It is especially important that Chapter 1 be taught at a one-day-per-lesson pace. At the end of the chapter, spend a few days on the Progress Self-Test and Chapter Review to cinch the major skills. We know from our studies that this pace produces the highest performance levels. Students need to be exposed to content in order to learn it.

Some classes in our studies of this book went very slowly; their teachers seemed reluctant to move to any new content. Where this happens, the students get into a rut. Better students are bored because they know the material. Slower students are frustrated because they are being asked to spend more time on the stuff they don't know. They all get discouraged and perform far lower than any other comparable students at the end of the year. We can state this rather strongly: If you want to guarantee poor performance, go slowly through a book.

There are times when it will be difficult to maintain this pace. But be advised: a slow pace can make it too easy to lose perspective and difficult to relate ideas. You need to get to later content to realize why you were asked to learn earlier content! If you spend too much time in the lessons, you may find that your slowest students may have learned more by having gone through content slowly, but all the other students will have learned less. The wise teacher strikes a balance, goes quickly enough to keep things interesting but slowly enough to have time for explanations. David R. Johnson's booklets *Every Minute Counts* and *Making Minutes Count Even More* give excellent practical suggestions on making use of class time.

Average students should be able to complete 12 chapters of *UCSMP Algebra*. Classes with better-than-average students have usually been able to complete the entire text. If you find in spring that you have been going through the chapters more slowly than recommended, rather than omitting entire chapters, we suggest omitting certain lessons. However, please be aware that these lessons are reviewed later. You will need to adjust your homework assignments accordingly.

Assignments

We recommend that a typical homework assignment be one of the following:

1. read Lesson n; write answers to all Questions in Lesson n; or

2. read Lesson n; write answers to Questions Covering the Reading in Lesson n, and Applying the Mathematics, Review, and Exploration in Lesson $n - 1$.

Thus virtually every day students should be expected to do the equivalent of a complete set of questions from a lesson. At times you will want to preview the reading, but for typical classes this should not be a regular part of the plan. (See *Using the Reading*, pages T47–T48.)

The Questions in each lesson have been designed to cover the key skills, properties, uses, and representations in the lesson. Questions were not written with an odd-even assignment plan in mind. Skipping questions may lead to gaps in student understanding. The Exploration questions may be assigned for all to do, or left as optional work for extra credit.

We also recommend that assignments be given on the days following chapter tests. If this is not done, then there will be up to 13 days without homework, the equivalent of a complete chapter's work.

Taking Review Into Account

Every lesson includes a set of Review questions. These questions serve a variety of purposes. First, they develop competence in a topic. Because we do not expect students to master a topic on the day they are introduced to it, these questions, coming on the days after introduction, help to solidify the ideas. Second, they maintain competence from preceding chapters. This review is particularly effective with topics that have not been studied for some time.

At times, we are able to give harder questions in reviews than we could expect students to be able to do on the day they were introduced to the topic. Thus the reviews sometimes serve as questions which integrate ideas from previous lessons.

Finally, we occasionally review an idea that has not been discussed for some time, just before it is to surface again in a lesson. The notes on the Questions usually alert you to this circumstance.

Teachers of classes that perform the best assign all the Review questions, give students the answers each day, and discuss them when needed. Those who do not assign all reviews tend to get poorer performance; their students never get enough practice to solidify and master the ideas and, even when mastered, the ideas are forgotten. *The Review questions must be assigned to ensure optimum performance.*

Strategies for Mastery

Some students master the content of one lesson in one day; but many do not. Why then do we suggest that you spend only one day per lesson? We do so because the combination of Review questions in each lesson and the end-of-chapter material has proved to be a powerful vehicle for achieving mastery, while allowing teachers and students to cover a substantial amount of material.

The mastery strategy used at the end of each chapter of *UCSMP Algebra* is one that has been validated by a great deal of research. Its components are a Progress Self-Test (the "formative test" in the parlance of some mastery learning literature), solutions to that test in the student's textbook (the "feedback"), review questions tied to the same objectives used to make up the self-test (the "correctives"), and finally a chapter test covering the same objectives.

Following the strategy means assigning the Progress Self-Test as a homework assignment to be done *under simulated test conditions*. The next day should be devoted to answering student questions about the problems and doing some problems from the Chapter Review.

For most classes, as a second night's assignment, we suggest the even-numbered questions from the Chapter Review. Neither solutions nor answers to the even-numbered questions are in the student text, so students will have to work on their own without these aids. The next day, discuss these questions in class.

Give the test on the third day. The odd-numbered Chapter Review questions, for which answers are given in the student text, can be useful for studying for that test. In some classes, a third day before the test may be needed. If so, either the odd-numbered Chapter Review questions, selected Lesson Masters, or questions generated by the *Quiz and Test Writer* software can be used as sources of problems.

We strongly recommend that, except for classes of exceptionally talented students (where less review may be needed), teachers follow this strategy. The evidence is substantial that it promotes higher levels of performance.

Using Technology

We use calculators and computers in UCSMP because they are tools important to most users of mathematics today, whether on the job or in one's personal life. The popularity of their use is because they make important mathematical ideas accessible to students at an early age and to people who might otherwise find mathematics difficult; they relieve the drudgery of calculation, particularly with numbers and equations encountered in realistic contexts; and they facilitate exploration and open-ended problem solving by making multiple instances easy to examine. Furthermore, as indicated in Section 4 (Research and Development), our use of technology has resulted in no loss of paper-and-pencil skill in arithmetic, and has freed up time in the curriculum to spend on other topics that lead to overall better performance by UCSMP students.

Calculators Hand-held calculators first appeared in 1971. Not until 1976 did the price for a four-function calculator come below $50 (equivalent to well over $100 today). Still, in 1975, a national commission recommended that hand calculators be used on all mathematics tests starting in eighth grade, and in 1980 the National Council of Teachers of Mathematics recommended that calculators be used in all grades of school from kindergarten on. The SATs, Achievement, and Advanced Placement tests of the College Board already allow all standard scientific and graphing calculators. Several standardized test batteries are being developed with calculators. And slowly but surely calculators are being expected on more and more licensing exams outside of school.

The business and mathematics education communities generally believe that paper-and-pencil algorithms are becoming obsolete. Do not be surprised. The long division algorithm we use was born only in the late 1400s; it can have a death as well.

It is wonderful to live in the age when calculators have been developed that quickly and efficiently do arithmetic. This frees us to use arithmetic more and, as teachers, to spend more time on mental arithmetic, estimation, and problem solving. It is inevitable that calculators will be considered as natural as pencils for doing mathematics. A century from now people will be amazed when they learn that some students as recently as the 1990s went to schools where calculators were not used. Students of the future will no doubt consider it cruel and unusual punishment.

UCSMP Algebra assumes the student has a *scientific* calculator, one that can display numbers in scientific notation. This is required for the large and small numbers found throughout the book. There is also need for the π, square root, power, and parentheses keys found on such calculators. The order of operations on a scientific calculator is the same as in algebra, so this kind of calculator motivates and reinforces algebra skills. CAUTION: Some calculators that do fractions are *not* scientific calculators.

Students will overuse calculators. Part of learning to use any machine is to make mistakes: using it when you shouldn't, not using it when you should. Anyone who has a word processor has used it for short memos that could much more easily have been handwritten. Anyone who has a microwave has used it for food that could have been cooked either in a conventional oven or on top of the stove.

The overuse dies down, but it takes some months. In the meantime, stress this important idea. There are three ways to get answers to arithmetic problems: by paper and pencil, mentally, or by using some automatic means (a table, a calculator, a trusty friend, etc.). Some problems require more than one of

these means, but the wise applier of arithmetic knows when to use each of these ways.

Generally this means that good arithmeticians do a lot of calculations mentally, either because they are basic facts (e.g., 3×5) or because they follow simple rules (e.g., $2/3 \times 4/5$ or 100×4.72). They may not use a calculator on these because the likelihood of making an error entering or reading is greater than the likelihood of making a mental error. As a rule, we seldom say, "Do not use calculators here." We want students to learn for themselves when calculator use is appropriate and when it is not. However, you may feel the need to prod some students to avoid the calculator. An answer of 2.9999999 to $\sqrt{9}$ should be strongly discouraged.

Many lessons include questions to be done "in your head." These are designed to develop skill in mental arithmetic and show students situations in which mental calculation is an appropriate approach to calculation. You may wish to give quizzes on these kinds of problems and have a "no calculator" rule for these problems.

Further information about the UCSMP approach to calculators is found in an article by Dan Hirschhorn and Sharon Senk in the 1992 NCTM Yearbook.

Graphics calculators Even at this level, we strongly recommend that students have graphics calculators like the TI-81, TI-82, Casio fx-7700G, or Sharp EL 9300C. A good graphics calculator should display as many as four graphs simultaneously, allow the window to be changed with ease, and in general be easy to use. These calculators can perform all the operations we expect in a scientific calculator. Though their order of operations is often different from that found in scientific calculators, and key sequences for scientific calculators will often not work with them, their key sequences more closely parallel what is written on a page.

Some questions ask students to use an *automatic grapher*. By this we mean a graphics calculator or a computer with a function grapher. If students do not have access to a computer or graphics calculator, exercise caution in your assigning of such questions and, if assigned, do not have high expectations of student success. It takes time to do a good graph, and many of these questions require comparing two or more graphs.

The reasons for a graphics calculator go beyond the fact that they can display the graph of any function students will encounter in this course. They have the advantage of displaying numbers in computations, allowing students to more easily see patterns and detect errors in their work. Many of them have the ability to perform statistical operations such as finding a line of best fit. Recent models can generate tables, which enables them to simulate spreadsheet operations.

Computers The computer is a powerful tool for you to use in your classroom to demonstrate the relationships, patterns, properties, and algorithms of arithmetic. From the very first chapter of this book, computer exercises appear. Do not ignore the computer questions even if you do not have computers available. The goal is not to teach computer programming, but to use the computer as a tool. Students are not surprised that the computer can do difficult tasks, but many students are surprised that a computer can do easy things, for instance, act as a calculator.

Some questions ask students to use a computer. If students do not have access to a computer, exercise caution in your assigning of such questions. As mathematical tools, a desirable computer has the ability to deal with a good amount of data and to display graphs with accuracy and precision. *GraphExplorer, StatExplorer,* and *GeoExplorer* software, published by ScottForesman for IBM (or IBM compatibles) and Macintosh computers, is designed for this course.

The BASIC computer language was selected for use in this book because it is available for the computers which are most popular in American schools and because it is easy to understand and translate into other languages. The programs have been kept short so that students can type them relatively quickly. It is not necessary for every student to type and run a program. Most programs can be used as classroom demonstrations.

Computer educators have recommended that students be required to provide a block structure to programs; document their programs with abundant remarks; and declare variables. Since this is a mathematics course, not a programming course, you should emphasize the *computational* steps of a program. Can the students follow the steps of a program and tell what the output will be? Can the student modify a given program to solve an exercise with different values?

Whether you are a novice or expert in BASIC, we encourage you to try the programs we provide on your own system. Each version of BASIC and each computer has slightly different characteristics, and our generic programs may need to be modified slightly for your system. The BASIC programs can also be modified to run on graphics calculators.

Projects

Based on very positive responses from teachers and students of both *Functions, Statistics, and Trigonometry* and *Precalculus and Discrete Mathematics* to the projects in those books, and numerous requests from teachers for some similar activities for this course, we have developed projects for each chapter of the Second Edition of *UCSMP Algebra*. Each project is an extended activity, often open-ended, meant to take the student several hours to complete. Some provide an opportunity to engage in library research; others require that students draw or build something; some require the student to collect data through surveys or measurements; others involve independent work with computers. The projects are designed for the wide range of interests and abilities one might find in a class of average students.

The projects serve many purposes.

(a) Students experience using real data in a mode comparable to that actually used by people in business, science, and many other careers.

(b) Students understand that a higher level of persistence than normal is expected. Too often in mathematics the greatest demand we make of students is to apply 5–10 minutes of effort on a single task. Longer-term projects demand more persistence and stretch a student's personal level of expectation.

(c) Projects, with some allowances for student choice, provide a sense of ownership of a task.

(d) Projects provide a chance for students to share their learning publicly in a visual or oral presentation.

(e) Projects provide an opportunity for students to apply graphic, writing, and oral talents in mathematical situations.

(f) Projects provide an alternative way to assess students' achievement.

The Projects appear immediately after the last lesson in the chapter, but we do not recommend that they be done immediately after the last lesson has been completed. Typically this would interrupt the flow of the chapter. You can schedule work on them in a number of ways. Here are two suggestions: (1) Assign one project when you reach the middle of a chapter, due in the middle of the next chapter. (2) Assign one project per grading period from any of the chapters covered in that period. Some teachers are more comfortable limiting the students' choice of projects at the beginning (e.g., do any one of Projects 2 or 5); other teachers want to give students free choice at all times. Do whatever makes sense for you and your class.

All students need guidance on projects, even if they have done projects in *Transition Mathematics* the year before. Be very specific and clear on what you expect (e.g. length of paper, format of poster, number of minutes of oral presentation, etc.). If possible, show sample student work. Tell students how you will grade their work. You may want to use the first project as a trial run, with somewhat relaxed grading standards. Then you can show (without mentioning names) work you consider exemplary, and work which is good but not exemplary, in preparation for the second project. English, social studies or art teachers, or the school librarian can often assist with advice on how to structure assigning or grading projects.

Here are two suggested ways to grade projects: (1) Give a certain number of points for various parts of the project, e.g., 20 points for completing all required work, 20 points for the mathematical content, 5 points for neatness and organization, and 5 points for mechanics of the paper (spelling, grammar, etc.); then convert the total number of points (in the previous case as a percent of 50) to the grading scale you use on other assignments. Teachers using this type of grading scheme often give a small number of bonus points for creativity. (2) Use a holistic approach. Develop a set of general criteria (often called a rubric), and sort the papers into categories based on your criteria. This is the way many English and social studies teachers grade papers. See Stenmark (1989, 1991) for descriptions of rubrics with four and seven categories developed in California for use in a new state mathematics assessment program.

We recommend that however you use the projects, please do not avoid them. They often have impact far beyond the mathematics classroom. Teachers from one school remarked that by the end of the year graphs like those that had been made for projects were appearing in the school yearbook! In fact, you may find students to be encouraged if they are given time to put together a first-rate presentation to be displayed on a bulletin board or a school display case, or to be entered in a mathematics fair.

Teaching

Teaching Models and Strategies

Traditionally teachers have relied heavily on lecture, supervised practice, and recitation of answers as their dominant modes of instruction. When these dominate instruction, the mathematics studied is often limited to simple algorithms which can be easily mimicked, and students learn to depend almost exclusively on the teacher as the sole source of their information.

In recent years the importance of communication skills in all school subjects has been noted. To achieve these skills students must read, write, and speak *to each other* in class. These skills are in line with the broader curricular and process goals of *UCSMP Algebra* and are more easily developed in classrooms which are dominated less by the teacher, that is, in classrooms in which students are actively engaged throughout the period.

Thus, in effective UCSMP classrooms, one sees smaller amounts of lecture, recitation, and individual seatwork than in comparison classes, and more discussions in small groups or with the whole class, individual or group work with calculators, computers, or other physical materials, and opportunities for students to do extended projects outside of class. Also, students read more of the book outside of class because they realize that this reading enables more to go on inside class.

The notes with each lesson in this Teacher's Edition provide a variety of teaching ideas, grouped under the following categories: Warm-up, Notes on Reading, Additional Examples, Optional Activities, Notes on Questions, Adapting to Individual Needs, Assessment, and Extension. All lessons contain more ideas than can be used in one period. None of the lists is exhaustive; there are, no doubt, many other ways to teach the lesson.

You should use your professional judgment to select and sequence the activities you think are appropriate for the length of your class period and your students' needs. This selection needs to be made before you enter class. We note that teachers who have never used group work, manipulatives, or technology often assume that they are very time-consuming. Our experience is that when well-planned ahead of time, many such activities can be done in relatively short periods of time, and we encourage you to try them. Also, you should understand that when a particular type of activity is done for the first time, it always takes longer because students need more guidance. The second time to the computer lab, or using group work, or presenting projects, or bringing out some manipulatives should go more easily than the first.

A variety of teaching models and strategies have been effectively used in the classroom by UCSMP teachers. Some teachers have students read each lesson and do all the questions before class. Then the teacher and students (sometimes in small groups, sometimes as the entire class) discuss the lesson and engage in various activities related to it during the next period. Some teachers preview the next day's lesson with some guidance as to the key points they think their students will need in reading or doing the questions. Some teachers begin the reading of the next lesson in class.

With less-prepared students, teachers need to adjust strategies. Most teachers do more reading out loud in class, and engage in more manipulative activities and use more Lesson Masters. Group work is often more important in these classes.

To give you a better picture of the variety of instructional techniques employed in classes using UCSMP materials, we have included reprints of the articles, "A 'Typical Day' in a UCSMP Classroom," and "Using Cooperative Reading Strategies," both written by experienced UCSMP teachers.

A "TYPICAL DAY" IN A UCSMP CLASSROOM

by Sharon Mallo, Lake Park High School, Roselle, IL

No matter how much our textbooks may or may not change over the years, one fact remains: students have different learning styles, and teachers need to address each of them. Therefore, there's really no "typical day" in the classroom. In my classroom, means of presentation vary from lesson to lesson, with common threads woven in for continuity and class management. The threads that tie my teaching strategies together are those that reinforce good mathematics study skills and those that help students "learn how to learn."

The UCSMP program gives me an easy-to-use, flexible tool through which to accomplish these goals. I'd like to show you some of the ways I use the supplementary materials and options in the program for presenting lessons—particularly the UCSMP Lesson Masters, Technology Masters, Teaching Aids, and Activity Sourcebook. Each class begins with a warm-up activity, followed by coverage of the previous day's homework. These two activities take up no more than half of the class period. Next, there is an introduction to the new lesson, followed by a related activity.

Warm-up Activity

The warm-up activity usually consists of the Lesson Master from the previous day's lesson being handed out as students arrive. I ask students to work out some or all of the questions, depending on the length of the master. This allows me to identify students who are having difficulty. I give individual help, reteach, and/or ask students to help each other as I circulate. For example, on the day I will be teaching Lesson 4-2 of *Transition Mathematics,* I will use Lesson Master 4-1 as the warm-up. This Lesson Master on order of operations allows me to say "No calculators" and check for understanding.

The warm-up can also be cooperative, such as with Lesson 5-4 on turns. I'll have each student use a protractor to draw with ten equally spaced spokes, and label each spoke with a different letter like on the Ferris wheel in questions 22–24 from the homework. Each student writes three problems about his/her diagram. Then students exchange papers and solve the problems.

The warm-up can also be a lead-in for today's lesson

or a problem-solving activity that will later tie into today's lesson.

Going Over Homework

One of my most import requirements is that students correct each answer on their homework and write out the steps for answers they've gotten wrong. Using the answers found at the back of the book to correct their work is part of the assignment. Students have already marked problems they need help with before coming to class. After we've done the warm-up activity, I'll put answers on the overhead projector. Then we discuss problems I've chosen as the most important or students have identified as stumbling blocks. Three or four times during the chapter, I have students discuss their questions within their cooperative groups, (Groups have one high, two middle, and one low student, and they change after every two chapter tests.)

Students need a reason to be concerned about whether or not their homework answers are correct and, more importantly, how to get the correct answer. I give an unannounced Homework Quiz once or twice a week. Students use their own notebooks of homework assignments and a clean sheet of paper—no textbook. They divide their papers into four or six sections. I do the same on a transparency to show them which questions I want. Students are to copy the correct answer for each question from their notebooks. If they've made the corrections in their notebooks, each student should have a perfect paper. It takes five to ten minutes to correct a set of these quizzes. Scores are low at the beginning but they steadily get better.

Lesson 5-6	Lesson 5-7
#14	#18
Lesson 5-8	**Lesson 5-8**
#14	#30
Lesson 5-9	**Lesson 5-9**
#18	#24

Lesson 4-2	
#8	#12
#18	#22

Presenting a Lesson

The method I choose to present a lesson depends on the difficulty of the content and the applications. For instance, Lesson 4-2 is one that the class usually reads together. I stop students at each Example. Using Teaching Aid 42 and different-colored overhead pens, we choose a variable and fill in the blanks of the patterns. Then we reverse the problem where I write the pattern on the overhead and we identify the variable. Students take turns making up instances.

If the students are able to read a lesson on their own, either in school or at home, I focus their reading. Vocabulary words (not their definitions) are pointed out. Sometimes I write an Additional Example from the margin of the Teacher's Edition and tell students that they should have an idea of how to solve it once they've read the lesson. Now they have a purpose for reading.

When students have read a difficult lesson in class, I put one of the Additional Examples on the overhead. (Some are already on transparencies in the Teaching Aids.) Then I ask students to find the parallel Example in the reading. This is one of the hardest things for them to do when they get stuck on a problem at home, so we practice it in class.

I do lectures and give notes on a lesson about 10–15 percent of the time. This is usually after students have read the lesson and done the Covering the Reading questions. The most common assignment I give is to complete the Applying the Mathematics, Review, and Exploration questions of a given lesson and then to read or re-read the following lesson and do Covering the Reading. Occasionally, they read a lesson and do all the questions, and once in a while I develop an assignment from outside the book.

As you can see, there is no "typical day" in my classroom. With UCSMP, my students have much stronger number sense by the end of the year. They are working with all types of numbers: fractions, decimals, integers, and percents—*every day* in practice problems, literal examples, and applications. They're not afraid to tackle problems, and they're learning how to learn.

Sharon Mallo has been teaching UCSMP Courses in the Chicago area since 1984.
She is an author on the Second Edition of Transition Mathematics.

USING COOPERATIVE READING STRATEGIES:
Students helping each other understand their textbook
by Tom Stone, Sheldon High School, Eugene, OR

There are many ways in which cooperative learning strategies can be used effectively in the mathematics classroom. Because of the important role reading plays in determining students' success in the UCSMP program, I would like to focus on this application of these strategies and to share some ways that the use of cooperative learning groups can help students learn good reading habits.

First, let me briefly explain my classroom organization. My students are familiar with two seating arrangements: 1) individual seating in six rows of desks, and 2) group seating with each set of four desks formed into a tight square. Each student in the group is assigned a number, 1 through 4. I do this for management purposes which should become clear later. The following scenarios illustrate how I use small-group instruction to help my students with their reading. (All section references are to *UCSMP Geometry.*)

Scenario 1 (Key Ideas)

Students are seated individually. After identifying a few vocabulary words they will encounter, I assign the reading of Section 1-3 in the textbook. Students read the material individually and take notes as they go along. When they have had time to finish, they move into their groups. Using his/her notes, Student 1 in each group selects a major idea from the reading and shares it with the group. After several minutes, Student 2 in each group discusses another idea found in the reading. This is continued until all four students in each group have had an opportunity to share. In this way, students receive important practice identifying the key ideas from a given section of their book.

Scenario 2 (Share the Pain)

Say the reading of Section 7-5 is to be done outside of class as part of the homework assignment. It includes two examples that I expect will be difficult for my students to read. Therefore, I have them encounter the challenging part of the reading in class in teams before they try to handle it on their own outside of class. I assign the reading of the first example to Students 1 and 2 in each group and the second example to Students 3 and 4. After students have completed the reading, they move into their groups. Students 1 and 2 discuss their understanding of the first example while Students 3 and 4 do the same with the second example. Now all students should be able to comprehend the reading of the section on their own.

Scenario 3 (Experts)

Section 9-7 breaks down into four main ideas. Student 1 is assigned to read the first ideas, Student 2 the second, and so on. Upon finishing the reading, students move into their groups and each student takes a turn presenting to the rest of the group. Then students begin working on the problem set for the section. Each student acts as the "expert" for questions related to the idea for which he/she was responsible.

Scenario 4 (The Set-up)

Let's suppose my geometry class is going to learn about traversability of networks (as in the Königsberg Bridge problem) tomorrow. Today, I have students move into their groups and I give each team a worksheet with five figures. After determining which figures are traversable and which are not, teams list the number of even and odd vertices for each figure. Finally, each group writes out and tests a conjecture for the connection between traversability and the number of even and/or odd vertices in a figure. Tomorrow, the students will be well prepared to read about the applications of traversability in networks.

The above scenarios are only a few examples of how small-group instruction and cooperative-learning strategies can be used to help students develop the skill needed for reading mathematics. Equally important, they provide variety in lesson structure. I hope that the ideas presented here are helpful and can serve as catalysts for generating more ideas that can be put to effective use in the classroom.

Tom Stone taught UCSMP courses in the Oregon area for many years. He was chosen as the 1991 Oregon Secondary Mathematics Teacher of the Year by the American Electronic Association.

Using the Reading

In order to become an independent learner of mathematics, a student must learn to learn mathematics from reading. You should expect students to read all lessons. At the beginning of the course, this may require time in class. Do not expect overnight changes in behavior from students who have never read their math book before.

A student in *UCSMP Algebra* who has studied from *Transition Mathematics* will generally be accustomed to reading mathematics. But students new to UCSMP texts may require some period of adjustment to a new style of text and to new types of questions. Such students may never have been asked to read mathematics. As a result, it is common for students to ask why they have to read.

We tell them: You must read because you must learn to read for success in all future courses that use mathematics, not just in mathematics; because you must learn to read for success in life outside of school and on any job; because the reading will help you understand the uses of mathematics; because the reading contains interesting information; because the reading tells you how the material from one lesson is related to other material in the book; because there is not enough time in class to spend doing something that you can do in a study period or at home.

Students often do not know how to read a mathematics text. They read too quickly and they gloss over little words ("if," "but,","not," and so on) that may be very important to the meaning of a statement. They may not realize that text and graphics are often related and they should move back and forth from one to the other. Students may not be able to read 2^5 (2 to the 5th power) or $x + 5 = 9$ (x plus 5 is equal to 9), for they may have no vocabulary for symbols such as $+$, $-$, $\times$, $\div$, $=$, or $<$. (Many of us have trouble reading Greek letters such as ψ or μ, because we have never had to give their names out loud.) For many students the same is true for common mathematical symbols. Thus it is important to have students read out loud as well as to give them assignments that involve silent reading.

To teach students how to read mathematics, we suggest that at the beginning of the school year some class time be spent each day reading the lesson in class. Some days you can have students read out loud, and provide feedback on their ability to read technical words and symbols correctly. (In general, it is not a good idea to call on students in any particular obvious order. That just gets some students nervous that their turn is coming up, and encourages others not to pay attention, because they are likely not to be called on.) Be sure to point out how the colored headers in the lessons help outline the important concepts and provide an overview (advance organizer) of what they are about to read.

You might have students answer the Covering the Reading questions orally, and point out how these questions are meant to test comprehension of the material in the text. The answers for these questions can be found literally in the reading or by mimicking worked examples. The questions can be used as oral exercises during or after oral reading of the text, or as part of a written assignment. Once students are comfortable with the format of the lessons, we suggest you begin to expect that reading be done outside of class on a regular basis.

Some days you may want to ask some questions that set up the reading of the lesson. Other days you might give a brief summary of the key ideas in the reading, have students read silently in class, and then ask them to identify where in the exposition those main ideas are covered. Once students have become somewhat comfortable with reading on their own, you

can rely more and more on them to summarize or probe key ideas without your assistance.

To help stress the importance of reading as a tool for learning mathematics, some teachers give brief (2–5 minute) "reading quizzes" at the beginning of class. These may consist of a request for a summary of the key ideas in the text, or the answers to several even-numbered questions from the homework. Doing so for 3 or 4 consecutive days early in the year lets students know you are serious about their attempts to do the reading and to answer the questions. Allowing students to use their notes, but not their book, encourages students to take good notes, and to organize their solutions to homework problems.

Although we believe that reading their text is an important strategy by which students learn mathematics, we know that it is not the only way they learn. In particular, if you want to give a brief overview of the new lesson before students read it, please do. We do, however, wish to discourage the practice of *always* explaining how to do questions before the students have had the opportunity to learn on their own. Particularly counterproductive is to tell students that certain problems do not have to be tried "because we have not yet done them in class." This only teaches students that they cannot learn on their own and to be dependent on you.

Students learn enormous amounts from discussing alternate strategies to problems with you and their classmates, from engaging in well-constructed activities, and from doing open-ended explorations and projects. By teaching students to read outside of class, you are free to use class time more creatively and effectively than if you were compelled to develop all major ideas yourself in class.

Going Over Homework Questions

Feedback to student work is very important, and to reinforce the positive aspects of doing homework it is important to go over questions. We are frequently asked how we want the teacher to go over the questions. Our response is that there are multiple ways to do so. We recommend that each teacher use a couple of methods regularly so students can get used to a routine, and a couple of others occasionally for variety.

Below are some of the more commonly used techniques which we support:

1. Show answers (using the Answer Masters provided) on an overhead projector at beginning of period; have students correct their own papers (you can use time to take roll); have whole class discussion on questions that were particularly troublesome.

2. Same as (1) above; but after students have checked their own papers, have them form groups of 2 to 4 to discuss what they missed; after a few minutes have a whole class discussion only on questions the groups could not resolve.

3. Have students form small groups; provide one copy of answers on paper to each group; have groups discuss what they missed; after a few minutes have a whole class discussion only on questions the groups could not resolve.

4. Read all answers out loud; have students correct their own papers; when done reading answers, have whole class discussion to explain questions that were particularly troublesome.

5. Have students write the numbers of the questions they could not answer on the board as they come into class; have them put tick marks after numbers to indicate how many students want to discuss that one; have student volunteers do those problems on the board, and explain their work; explain how to do the ones no student could solve.

6. Preselect questions which you feel are particularly important or may be particularly troublesome; have a whole class discussion about those.

It is important to remember that "going over the homework" should be more than providing correct answers. It is a wonderful opportunity to consider alternate solution strategies, to address any misconceptions that are uncovered, to relate ideas in one question to ideas in another, and to extend ideas in the questions via "what if" questions. In short, it is an opportunity to have the kind of rich classroom discourse described in the NCTM's Professional Teaching Standards. Many ideas are given in the Notes on Questions for each lesson.

Writing in Mathematics

The NCTM *Curriculum and Evaluation Standards* stress the importance of students' ability to communicate mathematics. Through writing, communication opens up in the classroom on a variety of levels. As they write, students apply concepts to their own experience; construct meaning for mathematical symbols, procedures, and concepts; and internalize meaning as they explore and examine mathematical ideas in words.

At times, writing may consist simply of the steps in answering a question, but to be most effective it should be more than that. It can include comments about what was being done, why a particular strategy was chosen, and how the student felt about the question. The careful examination of thought that writing requires may lead students to see the process of thinking as more important than the ability to quote rules; consequently, mathematics becomes a richer pastime. Furthermore, students will be developing a skill that many of them will need throughout their lives, the ability to explain what they are thinking to others.

In *UCSMP Algebra* we begin the multi-year process of asking students on occasion to write explanations of what they are doing. Do not be surprised if at first students' explanations are vague, imprecise, or too brief. Writing good explanations takes time, experience, and guidance, and students may have never been asked to write in their previous mathematics classes. You can encourage greater thoroughness and effectiveness by discussing good explanations in the text with your students. The solutions of the examples in each lesson are excellent models. The portions of the solutions that you may expect students to write are printed in a special font.

To be considered important by students, writing must be discussed in class. Reading good student efforts aloud in class can encourage good writing. Having students read their own efforts in small groups or to the entire class can inform them about whether others understood what they wrote.

There are different forms which writing may take. *Chatter* refers to writing explanations of procedures a student used to solve a problem. It can communicate a student's thought process, and can therefore alert you (and the student!) to hidden misconceptions and incomplete understandings as well as to wonderful insights. Arthur Powell of Rutgers University suggests that chatter be written in a separate column of the page from the actual solution of the problem.

Journal writing is believed by some people to be one of the most effective methods of writing to learn mathematics; however, *informal explorative writing* in class and on homework (not necessarily in a bound or spiral notebook) achieves similar results. Journals and informal explorative writing allow students to put concepts in their own words, to speculate on extensions to problems, and to relate material they are learning to what they already know. This kind of writing allows students to write freely without worrying excessively over mechanics. It also can focus students' minds. Writing at the beginning of a period can interest and involve students in a topic; writing at the end of a period can help them to summarize and organize what happened that day.

Here is some general advice: If you use journals with 7th or 8th graders, you may wish to keep the journals in the classroom; asking young students to re-member yet another item to bring to class may prove difficult for them and frustrating to you. For this rea-son, informal explorative writing on ideas and on homework may prove to be a better option.

In general, undirected journal writing does not provoke as much focus or response from students as carefully and thoughtfully worded questions, some-times called *prompts*. The more concise the prompt, the better. Longer, more complex prompts that are in-tended to yield more writing often do not.

Collect journals regularly to communicate to students that they are important. You do not have to collect all journals at the same time. (Reading students' writing is often not as time-consuming as you might think, and it can be very interesting.) Give credit for journals, but don't grade them. When giving credit, look for frequency and length of entries and for self-initiated topics. Give feedback on the writing to students; comments indicate that you care. Do not emphasize mechanics or grammar. Above all, be patient and flexible.

Do not penalize students when they don't write. When students have difficulty writing, claiming they do not know what to say, you might try *freewriting*, an activity where the goal is simply to empty thoughts on the page without censoring. Write yourself and share what you wrote with your students.

It is appropriate to keep examples of student writing of mathematics in a portfolio along with other examples of student work.

Dealing with Individual Differences

Every student differs from all others in many ways. Differences in ability, entering knowledge, willingness to work, interest, learning style, and cultural back-ground are the most commonly referred by teachers and researchers.

In Section 1 of this Professional Sourcebook, we pointed out that not enough is known about individ-ual differences in ability to make judgments based on them. Individual differences in entering knowledge are far better predictors. These differences are great enough to warrant differences in what is offered to students at a particular grade level, and based on them we suggest that students take *UCSMP Algebra* at different ages. However, a wide range of entering knowledge exists within every class and needs to be considered when teaching.

For all students, we have included an enormous variety of activities, questions, and contexts to bring out the brilliance, surprise, applicability, and structure of mathematics, and to appeal to students with the panoply of cultural backgrounds found in the United States. Note the many cultural activities in this Teacher's Edition as well. You should take these into account, because familiar contexts are critical to the understanding of mathematics, the contributions of various cultures are important in conveying the universality of mathematical ideas, and because it helps students to develop a sense of ownership of these ideas. Differences in interest can be handled by giving students choice of the end-of-chapter Projects, by asking students to elaborate on questions and or ideas they particularly liked, and by other optional activities.

For better-prepared students, or students with more willingness to work, you may wish to offer, assign, and discuss:

- ■ Challenge and Extension problems and activities contained in the Teacher's Notes;

- ■ Technology activities from the *Technology Sourcebook;*

- ■ Contest problems from such sources as Math-Counts or the American Junior High School Mathematics Examination (AJHSME)

For students needing more preparation or with limited language development, consider using:

- ■ Suggestions for additional practice contained in these Teacher's Notes;

- ■ Manipulative activities from the *Activity Sourcebook;*

- ■ English Language Development and Extra Help activities provided in these Teacher's Notes.

We must stress that *many of these ideas should be used with all your students.* In particular, manipulative, technology, and other activities are appropriate for all students, and all students need some practice in order to develop high levels of competence.

Assessment

The Evaluation Standards provide some sensible guidelines for student assessment. The first is Alignment. Simply put, this standard suggests that you assess what you teach. In particular, because the *UCSMP Algebra*

course has much broader goals than most other courses at this level, many tests, quizzes, final exams, and other forms of assessment you have used in the past will not be appropriate for this course.

The second Evaluation Standard is Multiple Forms of Assessment. This standard reminds us that no single instrument is perfect. Each test, quiz, or homework assignment provides a small picture of what each student knows. A teacher who wants to develop mathematical power must use instruments which reflect the broad range of goals of the curriculum. In particular, using the Projects to assess understanding will give you insights into student thinking that you cannot get from tests and quizzes.

The third Evaluation Standard is Purposes of Assessment. This standard reminds the reader that instruments developed for one purpose usually are not appropriate for another purpose. Specifically, traditional standardized tests are usually not appropriate for evaluating students at the end of any single mathematics course because they are usually not well-aligned with the objectives of the course. The best measure of success of a student is the extent to which the student has accomplished the goals and objectives of the individual course.

Assessment Options

To help you accomplish the above goals, the *Assessment Sourcebook* (in the Teacher's Resource File) provides a wide variety of assessment instruments. These include Quizzes, Chapter Tests, Cumulative Tests (by chapter), Comprehensive Tests, and several types of alternative assessment. The Chapter Tests include parallel traditional Forms A and B, in which most questions are short-answer, and Forms C and D, which provide more open-ended performance assessment. The *Quiz and Test Writer* software enables you to produce a virtually unlimited number of versions for a quiz or chapter test. The notes in the Teacher's Edition provide additional assessment suggestions for every lesson.

Tests, quizzes, or homework assignments provide only a small picture of what each student knows.

In order to help you develop your students' abilities to do open-ended questions or longer more elaborate tasks, you should consider the Exploration questions at the end of each lesson and the Projects at the end of each chapter as part of your assessment tool kit. (The grading of Projects is discussed on page T43.)

Understanding — The SPUR Approach

"Understanding" is an easy goal to have, for who can be against it? Yet understanding means different things to different people. In UCSMP texts an approach to the development of mathematical power is taken that we call the SPUR approach. The SPUR approach involves four different aspects, or dimensions, of understanding.

Skills: For many people, understanding mathematics means simply knowing *how* to get an answer to a problem with no help from any outside source. But in classrooms, when we speak of understanding how to use a calculator or a computer, we mean using a computer to do something for us. In UCSMP texts, these are both aspects of the same kind of understanding, the understanding of algorithms (procedures) for getting answers. This is the S of SPUR, the Skills dimension, and it ranges from the rote memorization of basic facts to the development of new algorithms for solving problems. These include doing things "in your head," with paper and pencil, or with technology.

Properties: During the 1960s, understanding *why* became at least as important as understanding *how*. Mathematicians often view this kind of understanding as the ultimate goal. For instance, mathematics courses for prospective elementary school teachers assume these college students can do arithmetic and instead teach the properties and principles behind that arithmetic. This is the P of SPUR, the Properties dimension, and it ranges from the rote identification of properties to the discovery of new proofs.

Uses: To the person who applies mathematics, neither knowing how to get an answer nor knowing the mathematical reasons behind the process is as important as being able to *use* the answer. For example, a person does not possess full understanding of linear equations until that person can apply them appropriately in real situations. This dimension ranges from the rote application of ideas (for instance, when you encounter a take-away situation, subtract) to the discovery of new applications or models for mathematical ideas. *UCSMP Algebra* is notable for its attention to this dimension of understanding.

Representations: To some people, even having all three dimensions of understanding given above does not comprise full understanding. They require that students represent a concept and deal with the concept in that representation in some way. Ability to use concrete materials and models, or graphs and other pictorial representations demonstrates this dimension of understanding. This is the R of SPUR, the Representations dimension, and it ranges from the rote manipulation of objects to the invention of new representations of concepts.

There are continual arguments among educators as to which dimension should come first and which should be emphasized. For each there are people for whom that type of understanding is preeminent, and who believe that the other types do not convey the *real* understanding of mathematics.

Each dimension has aspects that can be memorized, and each has the potential for the highest level of creative thinking. Also, each dimension has its easy aspects and its difficult ones. Some skills (for example, long division) take at least as long to learn as geometry proofs; some uses are as easy as putting together beads. Furthermore, some students prefer applications, some would rather do manipulative skills, some most want to know the theory, and still others like the models and representations best. Thus we believe that the most effective teaching allows students opportunities in all these dimensions.

For a specific example of what understanding means in these four dimensions, consider solving $100 + 5x = 50 + 10x$ and what would constitute evidence of that understanding.

Skills understanding means knowing a way to obtain a solution. (Obtain $x = 10$ by some means.)

Properties understanding means knowing properties which you can apply. (Identify or justify the steps in obtaining an answer.)

Uses understanding means knowing situations in which you could apply the solving of this equation. (Set up or interpret a solution: If one person has 100 tapes and buys 5 tapes a month, and another person has 50 tapes and buys 10 tapes a month, in how many months will they have the same number of tapes?)

Representations understanding means having a representation of the solving process or a graphical way of interpreting the solution. (Graph $y = 100 + 5x$ and $y = 50 + 10x$ and interpret the x-coordinate of the point of intersection.)

The SPUR approach is not a perfect sorter of knowledge; many ideas and many problems involve more than one dimension. Some understandings do not fit any of these dimensions. In some UCSMP texts we add a fifth dimension C—the Culture dimension—for it provides still another way of looking at knowledge. (The ninth century Arabian mathematician Al-Khowarizmi, from whose name we get the word "algorithm," was the first to solve equations like $100 + 5x = 50 + 10x$ by performing the same operations on both sides of the equation. His work, "Hisab al-jabr w'al muqabalah," was so influential in Europe that its second word became synonymous with such problems. This is the origin of our word "algebra." But not until François Vieté in the late 1500s did we have variables and the notation we use today.)

In this book, you see the SPUR categorization at the end of each chapter with the Chapter Review questions. The Progress Self-Test for each chapter and the Lesson Masters (in the Teacher's Resource File) are also keyed to these objectives. We never ask students (or teachers) to categorize tasks into the various kinds of understanding; that is not a suitable

goal. The categorization is meant only to be a convenient and efficient way to ensure that the book provides the opportunity for teachers to teach and for students to gain a broader and deeper understanding of mathematics than is normally the case.

Grading

No problem seems more difficult than the question of grading. If a teacher has students who perform so well that they all deserve *A*s and the teacher gives them *A*s as a result, the teacher will probably not be given plaudits for being successful but will be accused of being too easy. This suggests that the grading scale ought to be based on a fixed level of performance, which is what we recommend. We recommend this because the performance that gives an *A* in one school or with one teacher may only rate a *C* in another, and we think it unfair.

Seldom in this book are there ten similar questions in a row. To teach students to be flexible, questions have all sorts of wordings. The problems are varied because that's the way problems come in later courses and in life outside of school. We believe a student should be able to do each set of objectives at about the 85% mastery level. An 85% score on a test deserves no less than a high *B*, and probably an *A*. In the past, our tests have often led us to the following curve: 85–100 = *A*, 72–84 = *B*, 60–71 = *C*, 50–59 = *D*, 0–49 = *F*. Such a low curve alarms some teachers, but students in UCSMP courses generally learn more mathematics overall than students in comparison classes. We believe that the above grading policy rewards students fairly for work well done.

Some teachers have said our suggested grading scale is too easy. Maybe they have better students. They simply raise our scale. Why? Must every class have *D* students? Wouldn't it be nice if all students got *A*s?

One January a teacher of *Transition Mathematics* presented us with a problem.

She had to make out grades for the fall semester. Her quandary was as follows: "I've never had a class that learned so much, but my grades are lower." Later she said, "I have students who are failing. But I can't switch them to another class [using another book at the same level] because they know too much." Her problem is not unusual: scores on tests of higher-order thinking are generally lower than scores on tests of routine skills. To encourage students, we often make a basketball analogy. In a traditional course, all the shots students ever have are lay-ups (exercises) and an occasional free throw (easy problems). They shoot these over and over again, from the same spot ("Do the odds from 1–49."). In *UCSMP Algebra,* almost every question is a different shot (a problem)—some close in, some from middle distance, and a few from half-court. To expect percentages of correct shots to be the same is unrealistic.

We have found that a word to your students about why your grading scale is "different" is helpful. They may be so accustomed to another grading scale that they feel they are doing poorly, while you think they are doing well.

Some teachers have found that because of the way that the Review questions maintain and improve performance, cumulative tests at the end of each marking period give students an opportunity to do well. The *Assessment Sourcebook* has Cumulative Tests for each chapter beginning with Chapter 2. When you want to practice one specific shot to make it automatic, we suggest focusing in on a few topics for quizzes.

Two final points: First, let students know what they need to know in order to get good grades. All research on the subject indicates that telling students what they are supposed to learn increases the amount of material covered and tends to increase performance. Second, have confidence in your students. Do not arbitrarily consign some of them to low grades. Let them know that it is possible for all of them to get As if they learn the material. If students perform well on tests, it has a real effect on interest and motivation. As the newer evaluation documents stress, you should endeavor to use grading as a vehicle for breeding success as well as for evaluating students.

Professional Sourcebook: SECTION **4**

RESEARCH AND DEVELOPMENT OF *UCSMP ALGEBRA*

Development of the First Edition

The development of the First Edition of each UCSMP text was in four stages. First, the overall goals for each course were created by UCSMP in consultation with a national advisory board of distinguished professors, and through discussion with classroom teachers, school administrators, and district and state mathematics supervisors. At the second stage, UCSMP selected authors who wrote first drafts of the courses. Half of all UCSMP authors currently teach mathematics in secondary schools, and all authors and editors for the first five courses have secondary school teaching experience. After teaching by the authors, selected teachers, and revision by the authors and UCSMP

editors, materials entered the third stage in the text development. Classes of teachers not connected with the project used the books, and independent evaluators closely studied student achievement, attitudes, and issues related to implementation. The fourth stage consisted of a wider comparative evaluation.

The specific ideas for *Transition Mathematics* originated as a result of two previous projects directed by Zalman Usiskin at the University of Chicago. The first was an NSF-sponsored project which developed a first-year algebra text entitled *Algebra Through Applications with Probability and Statistics.* The text was distributed by the National Council of Teachers of Mathematics in a two-volume paperback version from

1979–85. Many of its ideas are found in this book and in *Transition Mathematics.* In developing that text, we found that one of the major reasons students had so much trouble applying algebra was that they did not know how to apply arithmetic beyond the arithmetic of adding and subtracting whole numbers. We also developed the precursor to the end-of-chapter mastery strategy that is a feature of all UCSMP texts.

In the years 1979–82, the Cognitive Development and Achievement in Secondary School Geometry project did much testing of senior high school geometry students. It was found in these studies that the geometry knowledge of students entering a high school geometry course was very low. Yet the best predictor of success in that course, be it with proof or with performance on a standardized test at the end of the year, was incoming geometry knowledge.

As a result of these two studies, it was felt that any algebra course should incorporate the ideas of applying arithmetic and the geometry students needed for success later. From the development of *Transition Mathematics,* the continual review strategy used in the elementary school curricula of many foreign countries was adopted in all UCSMP texts.

In the summer of 1985, a six-member team spent 8 weeks at the University of Chicago writing the first draft of *UCSMP Algebra.* This draft was edited in Chicago by UCSMP staff (all experienced mathematics teachers) and used in six schools in the year 1985–86. The teachers during that year received loose-leaf materials a chapter at a time, often only days before they had to teach from them.

In the summer of 1986, four of the authors returned to revise the materials. The revision was guided by the comments of the pilot teachers and by the algebra needed for *UCSMP Geometry,* which was then in its planning stages. The formative evaluation in 1986–87 took place in a dozen schools. (The schools in this and in the previous year's evaluations are acknowledged on page *iii* of the student text.) Teachers periodically came to the University and commented on how things were going, what they thought were strong and weak points, how long it took to cover various lessons, which questions were most interesting, which questions might be deleted, and so on. Evaluators visited classes and interviewed students, teachers, and administrators.

First Edition Summative Evaluation and Test Results

In 1987–88, a carefully controlled study involving 40 matched pairs of classes in 9 states, half using *UCSMP Algebra* and half using other algebra texts was conducted by the Evaluation Component of UCSMP. This and all other studies of UCSMP materials are designed, conducted, and controlled independently from the writing of the materials. The design chosen by the Evaluation Component did not allow any 8th-grade *UCSMP Algebra* class to be tested against a comparison group of students not taking algebra because it was felt that an algebra final exam would be totally unfair and possibly quite disturbing to the comparison students.

No teacher in this study taught both UCSMP and comparison classes. The size of the study, approximately 2400 students, was so that evaluators could eliminate classes that did not match for any reason and still be left with enough pairs to judge overall results and enough students to conduct comparative item analyses. Information on obtaining the detailed results of this study is available by writing UCSMP, 5835 S. Kimbark Avenue, Chicago, IL 60637. Herein is a summary:

Students were pretested on arithmetic, geometry, and algebra readiness. This uncovered many pairs of classes that did not match. Students were tested again in the late spring a few weeks before the end of the year. To keep the match, the fall scores of students who took the spring tests in these classes had to match. That is, those students who were left in the classes had to have been well-matched at the beginning of the year. These matching criteria eliminated 23 of the 40 pairs.

Six of the 17 remaining matched pairs of classes required some statistical equating to be matched. For the analysis, these six pairs were removed, because item analyses are not as reliable if equating is needed. The 11 remaining pairs of classes were from seven states, California, Colorado, Connecticut, Michigan,

Ohio, South Carolina, and Wisconsin, representing rural, urban, and suburban areas and including both 8th- and 9th-grade students. The statistics are based on all 226 students in the 11 *UCSMP Algebra* classes and the 190 students in the 11 comparison algebra classes who took all tests in the fall and spring.

Three tests were given. First was a standardized test, the American Testronics *High School Subjects Test: Algebra (HSST)* 40-question multiple-choice test, chosen because it is rather representative of such tests, and is new and thus less likely to be familiar to any teacher. Students in all classes were tested for two other complete periods, during which they were given 70 additional items selected to represent either the wider range of content found in *UCSMP Algebra* or topics deemed of particular importance to all classes. These tests are called *UCSMP Algebra, Pt. I* and *Pt. II.* It was felt that the first test would be biased against UCSMP students and the remaining two tests biased in favor. The results are given below.

Mean Percentages Correct for All Students in the Sample of Well-matched Pairs			
Test	UCSMP ($n = 226$)	Comparison ($n = 190$)	Difference (UCSMP minus Comparison)
HSST	51.5	50.3	+1.2
Algebra Pt. I	51.1	36.9	+14.2
Algebra Pt. II	57.6	43.1	+14.5

For the American Testronics *High School Subjects Test: Algebra (HSST),* the independent evaluators wrote: "The overall conclusion from the data presented is that there were no significant differences between UCSMP and Comparison classes on what could be considered traditional algebra concepts and skills." The item analysis for *HSST* showed, in the words of the evaluators, that "UCSMP students did better (over 10% higher) on items which asked student to:

justify a property,

identify an inequality on a number line,

select the equation for a line given two points,

find the slope of a line,

determine when an expression is undefined,

find an equation to represent a graphed line,

identify a linear expression for a word problem, and

determine when an arrow shot in the air will be at a certain height.

Items Comparison students did better [scored over 10% better] on asked them to:

multiply binomials,

reduce a rational expression with powers,

factor a simple trinomial,

subtract radicals, and

divide a trinomial by a binomial."

For the *UCSMP Algebra* tests, Part I and Part II, the 70 items were grouped into 11 subtests: Applied Geometry, Probability, Statistics, Linear Equations, Quadratics, Models for Operations, Calculators or Computers, Exponential Models, Applications, Arithmetic, and Linear Systems. The evaluators wrote: **"The most striking feature is that on no sub-test did the Comparison classes score higher . . ."**

At the item level, UCSMP students outperformed Comparison students by more than 25% correct on:

finding the third angle in a triangle,

applying a formula,

obtaining the median of a set of 9 numbers,

evaluating $\frac{102!}{100!}$,

finding the area between rectangles,

calculating a probability,

applying the multiplication counting principle,

determining the output of a BASIC program,

calculating compound interest, and

finding a length in similar triangles.

On no item on these two tests did Comparison students score more than 5% above UCSMP students.

Globally, the evaluators concluded: **These student achievement data can be interpreted as a fairly strong statement in favor of UCSMP *Algebra* . . ."**

Second Edition Studies

Over the years 1989–92, UCSMP kept notes on comments made by many users of *UCSMP Algebra*. All Second Edition authors are experienced teachers of *UCSMP Algebra* who had made presentations about the book to school districts. Thus the authors had both firsthand experience and many discussions about the materials with other teachers. Also, to help in preparation for the Second Edition, during the school year 1991–92, ScottForesman asked a small number of *UCSMP Algebra* users to evaluate each chapter of the text as they completed it. ScottForesman also mailed a series of questionnaires during the year to a larger number of users. The results from these surveys were used to help in the planning and writing of the Second Edition materials.

Writing of the first draft of the Second Edition began in the summer and continued through the fall of 1992. In the 1992–93 school year, 28 classes in 13 schools participated in a formal study of the Second Edition materials. The schools were chosen to reflect the wide range of students who are currently using *UCSMP Algebra*. Teachers completed detailed forms evaluating the materials and were invited to come to the University of Chicago twice during the year to give detailed feedback on the lessons.

Their students were tested along with students from 26 comparable classes at the same grade level in the same school. Because we felt that the First Edition studies had compared *UCSMP Algebra* with traditional textbooks, most of the comparable classes in the Second Edition studies used First Edition *UCSMP Algebra* materials. To our knowledge, the UCSMP studies comparing Second Edition with First Edition books marks the first time that a project has compared its own mathematics materials with an earlier edition of itself.

From these 54 classes, we were able to obtain 20 pairs of classes between which there were no significant differences on pretest scores of those students who took all tests. The table on page T58 provides the pretest and posttest scores of these classes. In sixteen pairs, the comparison class used the First Edition of *UCSMP Algebra*. In the other four pairs, the comparison class did not use UCSMP materials. The small number of students in some classes is due to the requirement that for a student to be included, that student had to be present for all pretests and posttests.

The *Iowa Academic Aptitude Test (IAAT)* was used as a pretest. The *High School Subjects Test: Algebra (HSST)* that was used in the First Edition formative evaluation was also used as a posttest in the present study. This test was comprised of 40 multiple-choice questions and was chosen as a representative of standardized tests. An *Algebra* posttest designed by UCSMP covered topics not tested in the HSST. Two additional tests, *Problem Solving and Understanding*, Forms A and B (*PS&U*, A and *PS&U*, B), were created to assess the problem-solving and understanding ability of the students. One test was administered to half the students and the other to the other half of each class. All students were allowed to use calculators on all tests, except on the *High School Subjects Test: Algebra*.

The results of the above study are provided on page T58.

Mean Scores of Students in Matched Pairs						
Group	N	Pretest *IAAT*	Posttest *HSST*	Posttest *Algebra*	Posttest *PS&U*, A	Posttest *PS&U*, B
UCSMP 2nd Edition	234	49 (11)	18.29 (6.36)	22.77 (6.49)	4.96 (3.62)	7.63 (3.82)
UCSMP 1st Edition	245	48 (9.6)	17.83 (5.83)	21.79 (5.95)	5.27 (3.55)	7.23 (3.27)
UCSMP 2nd Edition	75	46 (11)	18.03 (6.13)	**18.72** (5.95)	**5.53** (3.29)	**6.57** (3.39)
Other texts (non-UCSMP)	62	45 (11)	16.94 (5.48)	**14.05** (5.71)	**3.08** (2.18)	**3.15** (1.82)

The table above contains the mean scores (standard deviations in parentheses) of the students in the 20 matched pairs of classes.

Mean scores in the boldface for "UCSMP 2nd Edition" are significantly higher than the corresponding scores for non-UCSMP Students using "Other texts." The *Algebra* posttest and the *Problem Solving and Understanding,* Forms A and B means are all significantly higher for Second Edition students at the 0.001 level. No other differences are statistically significant.

Despite the widespread belief that conditions favor newer materials in such studies, there is at least as much evidence that comparison classes have an advantage. In this study, teachers of comparison classes knew they were being tested from the first day of the year; we have evidence that comparison classes tested at the beginning of the year scored higher on our spring tests than classes not tested at the beginning of the year. Some comparison teachers may have had the advantage of many years of teaching out of the books they use. In contrast, UCSMP teachers have the advantage of the excitement of using materials for the first time. However, the UCSMP teachers were using the Second Edition for the first time and did not even have the entire text at the beginning of the school year. It is possible that some UCSMP and comparison classes covered a wider range of content than normal because their teachers knew what is in the other book and wanted to make sure their students had been exposed to it.

These results confirm conclusions from the First Edition studies, namely that *UCSMP Algebra* students maintain competence on traditional standardized tests while outperforming non-UCSMP students in tests of problem solving and understanding, and tests of the wide range of content found in the UCSMP texts. They also show that students using the Second Edition perform as well as those using the First Edition in all areas.

The detailed reports from the teachers applauded the new sequence of topics at the beginning of the materials, confirmed the value of the projects, and in general favored all the major changes we had made in the materials. However, many suggestions were made for improvements in individual questions and lessons, and as a result we made numerous small changes for this ScottForesman edition. We also reorganized Chapters 10 and 12.

While there is not room here to exhibit the results from each class, these studies also confirm the vast range that exists among algebra classes in our nation. As we have found in every large study we have ever conducted, mean posttest scores in some classes are lower than mean pretest scores in other classes using the same book. There is also a vast range in the mean amount of growth that took place over the year, and that variable shows remarkable school effects. That is, comparison and Second Edition classes in the same school tended either both to show large increases or both to show small increases. This indicates how important school climate is if one wishes to improve achievement.

Continuing Research and Development

Since August of 1989, UCSMP has sponsored an in-service on its texts open to all those who will be using the materials the next school year. We encourage users to attend these conferences.

Since November of 1985, UCSMP has sponsored an annual conference at the University of Chicago at which users *and* prospective users of its materials can meet with each other and with authors. This conference also provides UCSMP authors and staff with a valuable opportunity for reports on UCSMP materials from those not involved in formal studies.

Both ScottForesman and UCSMP welcome comments on our books. Please address comments either to Mathematics Product Manager, ScottForesman, 1900 East Lake Avenue, Glenview, IL 60025, or to Zalman Usiskin, Director, UCSMP, 5835 S. Kimbark Avenue, Chicago, IL 60637.

Professional Sourcebook: SECTION 5   BIBLIOGRAPHY

References for Sections 1–4 of Professional Sourcebook

Center for the Assessment of Educational Progress. *A World of Differences*. Princeton, NJ: Educational Testing Service, 1989.

College Board. *Academic Preparation for College: What Students Need To Know and Be Able To Do*. New York: College Board, 1983.

Flanders, James. "How Much of the Content in Mathematics Textbooks Is New?" *Arithmetic Teacher*, September 1987: 18–23.

Hirschhorn, Daniel B. and Senk, Sharon L. "Calculators in the UCSMP Curriculum for Grades 7 and 8." *Calculators in Mathematics Education*, edited by James T. Fey and Christian R. Hirsch, pp. 79–90. Reston, VA: National Council of Teachers of Mathematics, 1992.

Johnson, David R. *Every Minute Counts*. Palo Alto, CA: Dale Seymour Publications, 1982.

Johnson, David R. *Making Minutes Count Even More*. Palo Alto, CA: Dale Seymour Publications, 1986.

Jones, Philip and Coxford, Arthur F. *A History of Mathematics Education in the United States and Canada*. 30th Yearbook of the National Council of Teachers of Mathematics. Reston, VA: National Council of Teachers of Mathematics, 1970.

McKnight, Curtis, et al. *The Underachieving Curriculum: Assessing U.S. School Mathematics from an International Perspective*. Champaign, IL: Stipes Publishing Company, 1987.

National Commission on Excellence in Education. *A Nation at Risk: The Imperative for Educational Reform*. Washington, DC: U.S. Department of Education, 1983.

National Council of Teachers of Mathematics. *Curriculum and Evaluation Standards for School Mathematics*. Reston, VA: National Council of Teachers of Mathematics, 1989.

National Council of Teachers of Mathematics. *Professional Standards for Teaching Mathematics*. Reston, VA: National Council of Teachers of Mathematics, 1991.

National Research Council. *Everybody Counts*. Washington, DC: National Academy Press, 1989.

National Research Council. *For Good Measure*. Washington, DC: National Academy Press, 1991.

National Research Council. *Measuring Up: Prototypes for Mathematics Assessment*. Washington, DC: National Academy Press, 1993.

National Research Council. *Measuring What Counts*. Washington, DC: National Academy Press, 1993.

National Research Council. *Reshaping School Mathematics: A Philosophy and Framework for Curriculum*. Washington, DC: National Academy Press, 1991.

Polya, George. *How To Solve It*. Princeton, NJ: Princeton University Press, 1952.

Senk, Sharon L. "How Well Do Students Write Geometry Proofs?" *Mathematics Teacher*, September 1985: 448–456.

Steen, Lynn, editor. *On the Shoulders of Giants*. Washington, DC: National Academy Press, 1991.

Stenmark, Jean Kerr. Assessment Alternatives in Mathematics. Berkeley, CA: EQUALS, 1989.

Stenmark, Jean Kerr, editor. *Mathematics Assessment: Myths, Models, Good Questions, and Practical Suggestions*. Reston, VA: National Council of Teachers of Mathematics, 1991.

Usiskin, Zalman. "Conceptions of School Algebra and Uses of Variables." *The Ideas of Algebra, K–12* edited by Arthur F. Coxford and Albert P. Shulte, pp. 8–19. Reston, VA: National Council of Teachers of Mathematics, 1988.

Usiskin, Zalman. "Why Elementary Algebra Can, Should, and Must Be an Eighth-Grade Course for Average Students." *Mathematics Teacher*, September 1987: 428–438.

Waits, Bert, and Demana, Franklin. "Is Three Years Enough?" *Mathematics Teacher*, January 1988: 11–15.

Additional General References

Fey, James T. and Hirsch, Christian R., editors. *Calculators in Mathematics Education*. Reston, VA: National Council of Teachers of Mathematics, 1992.
> This 1992 Yearbook of the NCTM contains dozens of articles about using calculators, including graphics calculators, in teaching and assessment from Grades K–12.

Hirsch, Christian R., and Laing, Robert, editors. *Activities for Active Learning and Teaching: Selections from the Mathematics Teacher*. Reston, VA: NCTM, 1993.

Hirsch, Christian R., and Zweng, Marilyn J., editors. *The Secondary School Mathematics Curriculum*. Reston, VA: NCTM, 1985.
> This forward-looking NCTM yearbook gives background for many of the ideas found in UCSMP texts.

Joseph, Goerge Gheverghese. *The Crest of the Peacock: Non-European Roots of Mathematics*. New York, NY: Penguin Books USA, 1991.
> This book contains a broad account of the history of algebra.

Katz, Victor J. *A History of Mathematics*. New York, NY: HarperCollins, 1993.
> This very fine recently published history of mathematics is notable for its scope, its mention of the original sources for our knowledge, and its inclusion of contributions from China, India, and the Islamic world.

Kieran, Carolyn, and Wagner, Sigrid, editors. *Research Issues in Learning and Teaching Algebra*. Reston, VA: NCTM, 1989.
> An overview of recent research and its implications for learning and teaching algebra. See particularly the chapters by Fey and Senk on the impact of computer technology.

Mathematics Teacher. National Council of Teachers of Mathematics. 1906 Association Drive, Reston, VA.
> This journal is an excellent source of applications and other teaching suggestions. We believe that every secondary school mathematics teacher should join the NCTM and read this journal regularly.

Mathematics Teaching in the Middle School. National Council of Teachers of Mathematics. 1906 Association Drive, Reston, VA.
> This is NCTM's new journal for grades 5–8.

Shulte, Albert and Smart, James R. *Teaching Statistics and Probability*. Reston, VA: NCTM, 1981.
> This NCTM yearbook contains many ideas for the teaching of these topics.

Silver, Edward A., Kilpatrick, Jeremy, and Schlesinger, Beth. *Thinking through Mathematics: Fostering Inquiry and Communication in Mathematics Classrooms*. New York: College Entrance Examination Board, 1990.
> This booklet contains many practical suggestions for improving communication in the classroom, techniques for reaching *all* students, not just a select few, and some suggestions for how to modify traditional tests and quizzes to make them more open-ended.

Whitmer, John C. *Spreadsheets in Mathematics and Science Teaching*. Bowling Green, OH: School, Science and Mathematics Association, 1992.
> Specific ideas on how to use spreadsheets from algebra through precalculus, chemistry and physics.

Sources for Additional Problems

Austin, Joe Dan, editor. *Applications of Secondary School Mathematics: Readings from the Mathematics Teacher*. Reston, VA: NCTM, 1991.

Burrill, Gail, et al. *Data Analysis and Statistics*. Reston, VA: National Council of Teachers of Mathematics, 1992.
> As part of the NCTM's Addenda Series for Grades 5–8, this booklet gives teachers ideas and hands-on materials to support the Data Analysis and Statistics strand of the *Curriculum and Evaluation Standards*.

Coxford, Arthur F., and Shulte, Albert P., editors. *The Ideas of Algebra, K–12*. Reston, VA: National Council of Teachers of Mathematics, 1988.
> This NCTM yearbook contains 34 articles on all aspects of the teaching of algebra, including articles by authors of *UCSMP Algebra*.

The Diagram Group. *Comparisons*. New York. St. Martin's Press, 1980.
> This is an excellent source of visual and numerical data on such quantities as distance, area and volume, and time and speed.

Eves, Howard. *An Introduction to the History of Mathematics*. 5th ed. Philadelphia. Saunders College Publishing, 1983.
> This comprehensive history includes references to recent 20th century mathematics, such as the proof of the four-color theorem. There is an outstanding collection of problems.

Hanson, Viggo P., and Zweng, Marilyn J, editors. *Computers in Mathematics Education*. Reston, VA: NCTM, 1984.
> This NCTM yearbook provides practical suggestions about some computer activities that can be added to mathematics classes. Chapter 15 is a particularly good overview of our view of how programming-related exercises can help teach mathematics.

Hoffman, Mark, editor. *The World Almanac and Book of Facts, 1995.* New York: World Almanac, 1995.

Johnson, Otto, executive ed. *The 1995 Information Please Almanac.* Boston: Houghton Mifflin Company, 1995.

Joint Committee of the Mathematical Association of America and the National Council of Teachers of Mathematics. *A Sourcebook of Applications of School Mathematics.* Reston, VA: National Council of Teachers of Mathematics, 1980.

> This comprehensive source of applied problems is organized in sections by mathematical content (advanced arithmetic through combinatorics and probability). It is a *must* for every high school mathematics teacher.

Kastner, Bernice. *Applications of Secondary School Mathematics.* Reston, VA.: National Council of Teachers of Mathematics, 1978.

> This short paperback book provides interesting applications in physics, chemistry, biology, economics, and other fields. There is a chapter on mathematical modeling.

Phillips, Elizabeth, et al. *Patterns and Functions.* Reston, VA: National Council of Teachers of Mathematics, 1991.

> As part of the NCTM's Addenda Series for Grades 5–8, this booklet gives teachers ideas and hands-on materials to support the Patterns and Functions strand of the *Curriculum and Evaluation Standards.*

Sharron, Sidney, and Reys, Robert E., editors. *Applications in School Mathematics.* Reston, VA.: NCTM, 1979.

> This NCTM yearbook is a collection of essays on applications, ways of including applications in the classroom, mathematical modeling, and other issues related to applications. There is an extensive bibliography on sources of applications.

UMAP Journal, Consortium for Mathematics and Its Applications Project, Inc. 271 Lincoln Street, Suite Number 4, Lexington, MA.

> This journal is a wonderful source of applications, although many of them are at the college level. COMAP also publishes a quarterly newsletter called *Consortium* that includes "The HiMAP Pull-Out Section." *Consortium* provides information on COMAP modules which are appropriate for high schools.

U.S. Bureau of the Census. *Statistical Abstract of the United States: 1994.* 114th ed. Washington, D.C., 1993.

> This outstanding data source, published annually since 1878, summarizes statistics on the United States and provides reference to other statistical publications.

Software

Abrams, Joshua. *GraphExplorer.* Glenview, IL: ScottForesman.

> For Macintosh or IBM/Tandy/Compatibles. A powerful user-friendly piece of software which can be used with all UCSMP courses beginning with *Algebra.* It has a feature for drawing families of functions easily.

GeoExplorer, Glenview, IL: ScottForesman.

> For Macintosh, IBM/Tandy/Compatibles, or Apple II. With this sophisticated software, students can easily draw, measure, and transform geometric figures to illustrate and explore geometric postulates, definitions, and theorems. Teachers can use *GeoExplorer* to demonstrate complex figures, theorems, and properties.

StatExplorer, Glenview, IL: ScottForesman.

> For Macintosh or IBM/Tandy/Compatibles. Students can enter data in a spreadsheet format, then build bar, circle, line, and scatter graphs, histograms, and box plots. They can perform general statistical analysis on any data set or group of data sets. Other features include mathematical modeling, simulations, and frequency tables.

*Scientific
Calculators*

You should be using a scientific calculator throughout this book, so it is important for you to know how to use one. As you read, you should use your calculator to do all the calculations described. Some of the problems are very easy. They were selected so that you can check whether your calculator does the computations in the proper order. Your scientific calculator should follow the order of operations used in algebra.

Suppose you want to use your calculator to find 3 + 4. Here is one way to do it:

	Display shows
Press 3	3
Now press +	3
Now press 4	4
Now press =	7

Pressing calculator keys is called **entering** or **keying in.** The set of instructions in the left column is called the **key sequence** for this problem. We write the key sequence for this problem using boxes for everything pressed except the numbers.

$$3 \boxed{+} 4 \boxed{=}$$

Sometimes we put what you would see in the calculator display underneath the key presses.

Key sequence: 3 $\boxed{+}$ 4 $\boxed{=}$
Display: 3   3   4   7

Some calculators do not have an equal sign, but have a key that enters the calculation $\boxed{\text{ENTER}}$ or executes it $\boxed{\text{EXE}}$. Key sequences for finding 3 + 4 on these calculators are:

$$3 \boxed{+} 4 \boxed{\text{ENTER}} \qquad 3 \boxed{+} 4 \boxed{\text{EXE}}$$

Next consider $12 + 3 \cdot 5$. In the algebraic order of operations, multiplication is performed before addition. Perform the key sequence below on your calculator. See what your calculator does.

Key sequence: 12 $\boxed{+}$ 3 $\boxed{\times}$ 5 $\boxed{=}$
Display: 12   12   3   3   5   27

Different calculators may give different answers even when the same buttons are pushed. If you have a calculator appropriate for algebra, the calculator displayed 27. If your calculator gave you the answer 75, then it has done the addition first and does not follow the algebraic order of operations. Using such a calculator with this book may be confusing.

824

Example 1

Evaluate $ay + bz$ when $a = 0.05$, $y = 2000$, $b = 0.06$ and $z = 9000$. (This is the total interest in a year if $2000 is earning 5% and $9000 is earning 6%.)

Solution

Key sequence: a [×] y [+] b [×] z [=]

Substitute in the key sequence:

Key sequence: 0.05   [×]   2000   [+]   0.06   [×]   9000   [=]

Display   [0.05] [0.05] [2000] [100] [0.06] [0.06] [9000] [640]

The total interest is $640.

Most scientific calculators have parentheses keys, [( ] and [ )]. To use them just enter the parentheses when they appear in the problem. You may need to use the [×] key every time you do a multiplication, even if × is not in the expression.

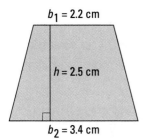

$b_1 = 2.2$ cm

$h = 2.5$ cm

$b_2 = 3.4$ cm

Example 2

Use the formula $A = 0.5h(b_1 + b_2)$ to calculate the area of the trapezoid at the left.

Solution

Remember that $0.5h(b_1 + b_2)$ means $0.5 \cdot h \cdot (b_1 + b_2)$.

Key sequence: 0.5 [×] h [×]   [( ] b_1 [+] b_2 [ )]   [=]

Substitute: 0.5 [×]   2.5   [×]   [( ]   2.2   [+]   3.4   [ )]   [=]

Display: [0.5] [0.5] [2.5] [1.25] [1.25] [2.2] [2.2] [3.4] [5.6] [7.]

The area of the trapezoid is 7 square centimeters.

Some frequently used numbers have special keys on the calculator.

4.6 miles

Example 3

Find the circumference of the circle at the left.

Solution

The circumference is the distance around the circle, and is calculated using the formula $C = 2\pi r$, where C = circumference and r = radius. Use the π key.

Key sequence: 2 [×] [π] [×] r [=]

Substitute: 2 [×] [π] [×] 4.6 [=]

Rounding to the nearest tenth, the circumference is 28.9 miles.

As a decimal, $\pi = 3.141592653\ldots$ and the decimal is unending. Since it is impossible to list all the digits, the calculator rounds the decimal. Some calculators, like the one in Example 3, round to the nearest value that can be displayed. Some calculators truncate or round down. If the calculator in the example had truncated, it would have displayed 3.1415926 instead of 3.1415927 for π.

On some calculators you must press two keys to display π. If a small π is written above a key, two keys are probably needed. Then you should press INV, 2nd, or F before pressing the key below π.

Negative numbers can be entered in your calculator. On many calculators this is done with a plus-minus key +/– or ± . Enter -19.

Key sequence: 19   +/–
Display: 19   -19

If your scientific calculator has an opposite key (–), you can enter a negative number in the same order as you write it.

Key sequence: (–)   19
Display: –   -19

You will use powers of numbers throughout this book. The scientific calculator has a key y^x (or x^y or $\wedge$) used to raise numbers to powers.

The key sequence for 3^4 is   3 y^x 4   =
You should see displayed   3   3   4   81 .
This display shows that $3^4 = 81$.

Example 4

A formula for the volume of a sphere is $V = \frac{4\pi r^3}{3}$, where r is the radius. The radius of the moon is about 1080 miles. Estimate the volume of the moon.

Solution

Key sequence:	4	×	π	×	r	y^x
Substitute:	4	×	π	×	1080	y^x
Display:	4	4	3.1415927	12.566371	1080	1080 . . .

Key sequence:	3	÷	3	=
Substitute:	3	÷	3	=
Display:	. . . 3	1.583 10	3	5.2767 09

The display shows the answer in scientific notation. If you do not understand scientific notation, read Appendix B.
The volume of the moon is about $5.28 \cdot 10^9$ cubic miles.

826

Note: You may be unable to use a negative number as a base on your calculator. Try the key sequence 2 $\boxed{\pm}$ $\boxed{y^x}$ 5 to evaluate $(-2)^5$. The answer should be -32. However, some calculators will give you an error message. You can, however, use negative *exponents* on scientific calculators.

QUESTIONS

Covering the Reading

1. What is meant by the phrase "keying in"? pressing calculator keys

2. To calculate $28.5 \cdot 32.7 + 14.8$, what key sequence can you use?
   28.5 $\boxed{\times}$ 32.7 $\boxed{+}$ 14.8 $\boxed{=}$

3. Consider the key sequence 13.4 $\boxed{-}$ 15 $\boxed{\div}$ 3 $\boxed{=}$. What arithmetic problem does this represent? $13.4 - 15 \div 3$

4. a. To evaluate $ab - c$ on a calculator, what key sequence should you use? a $\boxed{\times}$ b $\boxed{-}$ c $\boxed{=}$
   b. Evaluate $297 \cdot 493 - 74{,}212$. 72,209

5. Estimate 26π to the nearest thousandth. 81.681

6. What number does the key sequence 104 $\boxed{\pm}$ yield? -104

7. a. Write a key sequence for entering -104 divided by -8 on your calculator. 104 $\boxed{\pm}$ $\boxed{\div}$ 8 $\boxed{\pm}$ $\boxed{=}$
   b. Calculate -104 divided by -8 on your calculator. 13

8. Calculate the area of the trapezoid below. 36.08

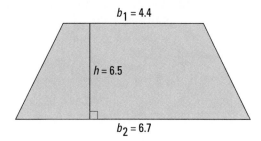

$b_1 = 4.4$

$h = 6.5$

$b_2 = 6.7$

9. Find the circumference of a circle with radius 6.7 inches. 42.10 in.

10. Which is greater, $\pi \cdot \pi$ or 10? 10

11. What expression is evaluated by 5 $\boxed{y^x}$ 2 $\boxed{=}$? 5^2

12. A softball has a radius of about 1.92 in. What is its volume? 29.65 in³

13. What kinds of numbers may not be allowed as bases when you use the $\boxed{y^x}$ key on some calculators? negative numbers

14. Use your calculator to help find the surface area $2LH + 2HW + 2LW$ of the box below. **455.3 in²**

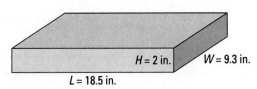

$H = 2$ in. $W = 9.3$ in.
$L = 18.5$ in.

15. Remember that $\frac{2}{3} = 2 \div 3$. **Answers will vary.**

   a. What decimal for $\frac{2}{3}$ is given by your calculator?

   b. Does your calculator *truncate* or *round to the nearest*?

16. Order $\frac{3}{5}, \frac{4}{7}$, and $\frac{5}{9}$ from smallest to largest. **$\frac{5}{9}, \frac{4}{7}, \frac{3}{5}$**

17. Use the clues to find the mystery number y.

   Clue 1: y will be on the display if you alternately press 2 and ⊠ again and again. . . .

   Clue 2: $y > 20$.

   Clue 3: $y < 40$. **32**

18. $A = \pi r^2$ is a formula for the area A of a circle with radius r. Find the area of the circle in Example 3. **66.5 mi²**

19. What is the total interest in a year if $350 is earning 5% and $2000 is earning 8%? (Hint: use Example 1.) **$177.50**

20. To multiply the sum of 2.08 and 5.76 by 2.24, what key sequence can you use? ⊏ 2.08 ⊕ 5.76 ⊐ ⊠ 2.24 ⊜

Scientific Notation

The first three columns in the chart below show three ways to represent integer powers of ten: in exponential notation, with word names, and as decimals. The fourth column describes a distance or length in meters. For example, the top row tells that Mercury is about ten billion meters from the sun.

Integer Powers of Ten

Exponential Notation	Word Name	Decimal	Something near this length in meters
10^{10}	ten billion	10,000,000,000	distance of Mercury from Sun
10^{9}	billion	1,000,000,000	radius of Sun
10^{8}	hundred million	100,000,000	diameter of Jupiter
10^{7}	ten million	10,000,000	radius of Earth
10^{6}	million	1,000,000	radius of Moon
10^{5}	hundred thousand	100,000	length of Lake Erie
10^{4}	ten thousand	10,000	average width of Grand Canyon
10^{3}	thousand	1,000	5 long city blocks
10^{2}	hundred	100	length of a football field
10^{1}	ten	10	height of shade tree
10^{0}	one	1	height of waist
10^{-1}	tenth	0.1	width of hand
10^{-2}	hundredth	0.01	diameter of pencil
10^{-3}	thousandth	0.001	thickness of window pane
10^{-4}	ten-thousandth	0.000 1	thickness of paper
10^{-5}	hundred-thousandth	0.000 01	diameter of red blood corpuscle
10^{-6}	millionth	0.000 001	mean distance between successive collisions of molecules in air
10^{-7}	ten-millionth	0.000 000 1	thickness of thinnest soap bubble with colors
10^{-8}	hundred-millionth	0.000 000 01	mean distance between molecules in a liquid
10^{-9}	billionth	0.000 000 001	size of air molecule
10^{-10}	ten-billionth	0.000 000 000 1	mean distance between molecules in a crystal

You probably know the quick way to multiply by 10, 100, 1000, and so on. Just move the decimal point as many places to the right as there are zeros.

$$84.3 \cdot 100 = 8430 \qquad 84.3 \cdot 10,000 = 843,000$$

It is just as quick to multiply by these numbers when they are written as powers.

$$489.76 \cdot 10^{2} = 48,976 \qquad 489.76 \cdot 10^{4} = 4,897,600$$

Appendix B   *Scientific Notation*   **829**

The general pattern is as follows.

> To multiply by 10 raised to a positive power, move the decimal point to the *right* as many places as indicated by the exponent.

The patterns in the chart on the previous page also help to explain powers of 10 where the exponent is negative. Each row describes a number that is $\frac{1}{10}$ of the number in the row above it. So 10^0 is $\frac{1}{10}$ of 10^1.

$$10^0 = \frac{1}{10} \cdot 10 = 1$$

To see the meaning of 10^{-1}, think: 10^{-1} is $\frac{1}{10}$ of 10^0 (which equals 1).

$$10^{-1} = \frac{1}{10} \cdot 1 = \frac{1}{10} = .1$$

Remember that to multiply a decimal by 0.1, just move the decimal point one unit to the left. Since $10^{-1} = 0.1$, to multiply by 10^{-1}, just move the decimal point one unit to the left.

$$435.86 \cdot 10^{-1} = 43.586$$

To multiply a decimal by 0.01, or $\frac{1}{100}$, move the decimal point two units to the left. Since $10^{-2} = 0.01$, the same goes for multiplying by 10^{-2}.

$$435.86 \cdot 10^{-2} = 4.3586$$

The following pattern emerges.

> To multiply by 10 raised to a negative power, move the decimal point to the *left* as many places as indicated by the exponent.

Example 1

Write $68.5 \cdot 10^{-6}$ as a decimal.

Solution
To multiply by 10^{-6}, move the decimal point six places to the left. So $68.5 \cdot 10^{-6} = 0.0000685$.

The names of the negative powers are very similar to those for the positive powers. For instance, 1 billion = 10^9 and 1 billionth = 10^{-9}.

Example 2

Write 8 billionths as a decimal.

Solution
8 billionths = $8 \cdot 10^{-9} = 0.000000008$

830

Most calculators can display only the first 8, 9, or 10 digits of a number. This presents a problem if you need to key in a large number like 455,000,000,000 or a small number like 0.00000000271. However, powers of 10 can be used to rewrite these numbers in **scientific notation.**

$$455,000,000,000 = 4.55 \cdot 10^{11}$$
$$0.00000000271 = 2.71 \cdot 10^{-9}$$

> **Definition:** In scientific notation, a number is represented as $x \cdot 10^n$, where $1 \leq x < 10$ and n is an integer.

Scientific calculators can display numbers in scientific notation. The display for $4.55 \cdot 10^{11}$ will usually look like one of these shown here.

| 4.55 E 11 | 4.55 11 | 4.55 x10 11 |

The display for $2.71 \cdot 10^{-9}$ is usually one of these

| 2.71 E -09 | 2.71 -09 | 2.71 x10 -09 |

Numbers written in scientific notation are entered into a calculator using the EXP or EE key. For instance, to enter $6.0225 \cdot 10^{23}$ (known as Avogadro's number), key in

6.0225 EE 23.

You should see this display.

| 6.0225 23 |

In general, to enter $x \cdot 10^n$, key in x EE n.

Example 3

The total number of hands possible in the card game bridge is about 635,000,000,000. Write this number in scientific notation.

Solution

Move the decimal point to get a number between 1 and 10. In this case the number is 6.35. This tells you the answer will be:

$$6.35 \cdot 10^{exponent}.$$

The exponent of 10 is the number of places you must move the decimal point in 6.35 in order to get 635,000,000,000. You must move it 11 places to the right, so *the answer is $6.35 \cdot 10^{11}$.*

Example 4

The charge of an electron is 0.00000000048 electrostatic units. Put this number in scientific notation.

Solution

Move the decimal point to get a number between 1 and 10. The result is 4.8. To find the power of 10, count the number of places you must move the decimal to change 4.8 to 0.00000000048. The move is 10 places to the left, so the charge of the electron is $4.8 \cdot 10^{-10}$ electrostatic units.

Example 5

Enter 0.00000000123 into a calculator.

Solution

Rewrite the number in scientific notation.

$0.00000000123 = 1.23 \cdot 10^{-9}$.

Key in 1.23 [EE] 9 [+/−] or 1.23 [EE] 9 [(−)].

QUESTIONS

Covering the Reading

9a) set of real numbers greater than or equal to one and less than ten

1. Write one million as a power of ten. 10^6

2. Write 1 billionth as a power of 10. 10^{-9}

In 3–5, write as a decimal.

3. 10^{-4} 0.0001   **4.** $28.5 \cdot 10^7$ **5.** 10^0 1
                       285,000,000

6. To multiply by a negative power of 10, move the decimal point to the _?_ as many places as indicated by the _?_.   left, exponent

7. Write $2.46 \cdot 10^{-8}$ as a decimal.   0.0000000246

8. Why is $38.25 \cdot 10^{-2}$ not in scientific notation?
38.25 is not between one and ten.

9. Suppose $x \cdot 10^y$ is in scientific notation.
    a. What is the domain of x?   **b.** What is the domain of y?
        See left.   set of integers

In 10–14, rewrite the number in scientific notation.

10. 5,020,000,000,000,000,000,000,000,000 tons, the mass of Sirius, the brightest star $5.02 \cdot 10^{27}$

11. 0.0009 meters, the approximate width of a human hair $9 \cdot 10^{-4}$

12. 763,000   **13.** 0.00000328   **14.** 754.9876
    $7.63 \cdot 10^5$ $3.28 \cdot 10^{-6}$ $7.549876 \cdot 10^2$

832

15. One computer can do an arithmetic problem in $2.4 \cdot 10^{-9}$ seconds. What key sequence can you use to display this number on your calculator? 2.4 (EE) 9 (+/−)

Applying the Mathematics

In 16 and 17, write in scientific notation.

16. 645 billion $6.45 \cdot 10^{11}$

17. 27.2 million $2.72 \cdot 10^7$

In 18–21, use the graph below. Write the estimated world population in the given year: **a.** as a decimal; **b.** in scientific notation. See left.

18. 10,000 B.C. **19.** 1 A.D. **20.** 1700 **21.** 1970

18a) 10,000,000;
  b) $1.0 \cdot 10^7$
19a) 300,000,000;
  b) $3.0 \cdot 10^8$
20a) 625,000,000;
  b) $6.25 \cdot 10^8$
21a) 3,575,000,000;
  b) $3.575 \cdot 10^9$

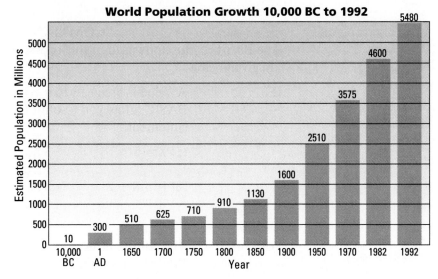

World Population Growth 10,000 BC to 1992

22. How can you enter the world population in 1992 into your calculator? 5.480 (EE) 9

23. How many digits are in $1.7 \cdot 10^{100}$? 101

In 24–26, write the number in scientific notation.

24. 0.00002 $2 \cdot 10^{-5}$

25. 0.0000000569 $5.69 \cdot 10^{-8}$

26. 400.007 $4.00007 \cdot 10^2$

In 27–29, write as a decimal.

27. $3.921 \cdot 10^5$ 392,100

28. $3.921 \cdot 10^{-5}$ 0.00003921

29. $8.6 \cdot 10^{-2}$ 0.086

Exploration

Answers may vary.

30. a. What is the largest number you can display on your calculator?
  b. What is the smallest number you can display? (Use scientific notation and consider negative numbers.) Answers may vary.
  c. Find out what key sequence you could use to enter -5×10^{-7} in your calculator. Sample: 5 (+/−) (EE) 7 (+/−)

Appendix B *Scientific Notation* **833**

BASIC

In BASIC (Beginner's All Purpose Symbolic Instruction Code), the arithmetic symbols are: + (for addition), − (for subtraction), ∗ (for multiplication), / (for division), and ∧ (for powering). In some versions of BASIC, ↑ is used for powering. The computer evaluates expressions according to the usual order of operations. Parentheses ( ) may be used. The comparison symbols =, >, < are also used in the standard way, but BASIC uses <= instead of ≤, >= instead of ≥, and <> instead of ≠.

Variables are represented by letters or letters in combination with digits. Consult the manual for your version of BASIC for restrictions on the length or other aspects of variable names. Examples of variable names allowed in most versions are N, X1, and AREA.

COMMANDS

The BASIC commands used in this course and examples of their uses are given below.

LET . . . A value is assigned to a given variable. Some versions of BASIC allow you to omit the word LET in the assignment statement.

LET X = 5	The number 5 is stored in a memory location called X.
LET N = N + 2	The value in the memory location called N is increased by 2 and the result is stored in the location N.

PRINT . . . The computer prints on the screen what follows the PRINT command. If what follows is not in quotes, it is a constant or variable, and the computer will print the value of that constant or variable. If what follows is in quotes, the computer prints exactly what is in quotes.

PRINT X	The computer prints the number stored in memory location X.
PRINT "X-VALUES"	The computer prints the phrase X-VALUES.

INPUT . . . The computer asks the user to give a value to the variable named and stores that value.

INPUT X	When the program is run, the computer will prompt you to give X a value by printing a question mark, and then will store that value in memory location X.
INPUT "HOW OLD?";AGE	The computer prints HOW OLD? and stores your response in memory location AGE. (Note: Some computers will not print the question mark.)

834

REM . . .
REM stands for *remark*. This command allows remarks to be inserted in a program. These may describe what the variables represent, what the program does, or how the program works. REM statements are often used in long complex programs or programs other people will use.

REM PYTHAGOREAN THEOREM

A statement that begins with REM has no effect when the program is run.

FOR . . .
NEXT . . .
STEP . . .
FOR and NEXT are used when a set of instructions must be performed more than once, a process which is called a *loop*. The FOR command assigns a beginning and ending value to a variable. The first time through the loop, the variable has the beginning value in the FOR command. When the computer hits the line reading NEXT, the value of the variable is increased by the amount indicated by STEP. The commands between FOR and NEXT are then repeated. When the value of the incremented variable is larger than the ending value in the FOR command, the computer leaves the loop and executes the rest of the program. If STEP is not written, the computer increases the variable by 1 each time through the loop.

10 FOR N = 3 TO 6 STEP 2
20 PRINT N
30 NEXT N
40 END

The computer assigns 3 to N and then prints the value of N. On reaching NEXT, the computer increases N by 2 (the STEP amount) and prints 5. The next N would be 7 which is too large. The computer executes the command after NEXT, ending the program.

IF . . . THEN . . .
The computer performs the consequent (the THEN part) only if the antecedent (the IF part) is true. When the antecedent is false, the computer *ignores* the consequent and goes directly to the next line of the program.

IF X > 100 THEN END
PRINT X

If the X value is less than or equal to 100, the computer ignores END, goes to the next line, and prints the value stored in X. If the X value is greater than 100, the computer stops and the value stored in X is not printed.

GOTO . . .   The computer goes to whatever line of the program is indicated. GOTO statements are generally avoided because they interrupt program flow and make programs hard to interpret.

GOTO 70   The computer goes to line 70 and executes that command.

END . . .   The computer stops running the program. No program should have more than one END statement.

FUNCTIONS

The following built-in functions and many others are available in most versions of BASIC. Each function name must be followed by a variable or a constant enclosed in parentheses.

ABS   The absolute value of the number that follows is calculated.

LET X = ABS(-10)   The computer calculates $|-10| = 10$ and assigns the value 10 to memory location X.

SQR   The square *root* of the number that follows is calculated.

C = SQR(A*A + B*B)   The computer calculates $\sqrt{A^2 + B^2}$ using the values stored in A and B and stores the result in C.

PROGRAMS

A program is a set of instructions to the computer. In most versions of BASIC, every step in the program must begin with a line number. We usually start numbering at 10 and count by ten, so intermediate steps can be added later. The computer reads and executes a BASIC program in order of the line numbers. It will not go back to a previous line unless told to do so.

To enter a new program, type NEW, and then type the lines of the program. At the end of each line press the key named RETURN or ENTER. You may enter the lines in any order. The computer will keep track of them in numerical order. If you type LIST, the program currently in the computer's memory will be printed on the screen. To change a line, retype the line number and the complete line as you now want it.

To run a new program after it has been entered, type RUN, and then press the RETURN or ENTER key.

Programs can be saved on disk. Consult your manual on how to do this for your version of BASIC. To run a program already saved on disk you must know the exact name of the program including any spaces or punctuation. To run a program called TABLE SOLVE, type RUN "TABLE SOLVE" and press the RETURN or ENTER key.

The following program illustrates many of the commands used in this course.

10 PRINT "A DIVIDING SEQUENCE"	The computer prints A DIVIDING SEQUENCE.
20 INPUT "NUMBER PLEASE?";X	The computer prints NUMBER PLEASE? and waits for you to enter a number. You must give a value to store in the location X. Suppose you use 20. X now contains 20.
30 LET Y = 2	2 is stored in location Y.
40 FOR Z = -5 TO 4	Z is given the value -5. Each time through the loop, the value of Z will be increased by 1.
50 IF Z = 0 THEN GOTO 70	When $Z = 0$ the computer goes directly to line 70. When $Z \neq 0$ the computer executes line 60.
60 PRINT X" TIMES "Y " DIVIDED BY "Z" = " (X*Y)/Z	On the first pass through the loop, the computer prints -8 because $(20 \cdot 2)/(-5) = -8$.
70 NEXT Z	The value in Z is increased by 1 to -4 and the computer goes back to line 50.
80 END	After going through the FOR . . . NEXT . . . loop with Z = 4, the computer stops.

The output of this program is:

```
A DIVIDING SEQUENCE
NUMBER PLEASE? 20
20  TIMES 2 DIVIDED BY -5 = -8
20  TIMES 2 DIVIDED BY -4 = -10
20  TIMES 2 DIVIDED BY -3 = -13.3333
20  TIMES 2 DIVIDED BY -2 = -20
20  TIMES 2 DIVIDED BY -1 = -40
20  TIMES 2 DIVIDED BY 1 = 40
20  TIMES 2 DIVIDED BY 2 = 20
20  TIMES 2 DIVIDED BY 3 = 13.3333
20  TIMES 2 DIVIDED BY 4 = 10
```

GETTING STARTED (pp. 1–3)

7. a. 3 **b.** scientific calculators, scientific notation, BASIC **9.** page 841 in the back of the book. The answers to the odd-numbered questions in the sections Applying the Mathematics and the Review are given. **11.** Skills, Properties, Uses, Representations **13.** Viète, a French lawyer of the late 16th century, invented the use of letters to describe arithmetic patterns.

LESSON 1-1 (pp. 6–10)

19. $\frac{2}{3} < \frac{7}{10} < \frac{3}{4}$ **21.** 2 and 4 **23. a.** $y < 1990$ **b.** $p > 2.1$
25. $-4 + 7 = 3$ **27.** -4 **29.** Sample: 0.3333 **31.** 3

LESSON 1-2 (pp. 11–16)

21. a. closed **b.** x is greater than or equal to zero and less than or equal to ten. **c.** $0 \le x \le 10$ **23. a.** neither open nor closed **b.** z is greater than or equal to negative ten and less than negative four.
c. $-10 \le z < -4$ **25.** {6, 9} **27.** $y > -15$ **29.** $x = 256$ **31.** -15
33. -350 **35.** $350

LESSON 1-3 (pp. 17–22)

13. a. {3, 9} **b.** {1, 3, 5, 6, 7, 9} **15. See below. 17. See below.**
19. True **21.** True **23.** 4; 8; 12; Sample pattern: $-4 \cdot n = -(4 \cdot n)$

15.   **17.**

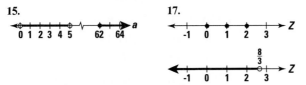

LESSON 1-4 (pp. 23–26)

17. 0 **19.** ≈ 10.9 mph **21.** {2} **23. a.** $d > 1800$ **b. See below.**
25. $1\frac{11}{16}$ yd **27. a.** 8 sq units **b.** 4 complete squares plus 8 half-squares equals 8.

23. b.

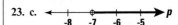

LESSON 1-5 (pp. 27–30)

9. 23 cm **11.** 87°F **13. a.** line 40: L * W; line 50: 2 * L + 2 * W
b. area = 1995; perimeter = 181 **15. a.** + **b.** / **c.** * **d.** ∧
17. $q < -36$, $q > 12$ **19. a.** 0 **b.** Sample: -1 **c.** Sample: $\frac{1}{2}$
21. $1\frac{3}{4}$ cups

LESSON 1-6 (pp. 31–36)

19. $\sqrt{25} = 5$ and $\sqrt{36} = 6$, so $5 < \sqrt{32} < 6$ **21. a.** 18 **b.** 6 **c.** 12
23. 2.5 seconds **25. a.** $A = \$1030$ **b.** $A = \$1045$ **27.** 3

CHAPTER 1 PROGRESS SELF-TEST (pp. 63–64)

1. When $a = 3$ and $b = 5$, $2(a + 3b) = 2(3 + 3 \cdot 5) = 2(18) = 36$
2. When $n = 4$, $5 \cdot 6^n = 5 \cdot 6^4 = 5 \cdot 1296 = 6480$ **3.** When $p = 5$
and $t = 2$, $\frac{p + t^2}{p - t} = \frac{5 + 2^2}{5 - 2} = \frac{9}{3} = 3$ **4.** $(\sqrt{50})^2 = \sqrt{50} \cdot \sqrt{50} = 50$
5. $10 * 3 \wedge 2 + 5 = 10 * 9 + 5 = 90 + 5 = 95$ **6.** By calculator, $3\sqrt{42} = 19.442221 \approx 19.4$ **7. a.** {2, 3, 4, 6, 8, 9, 10, 12, 14, 15, 16}
b. {6, 12} **8.** S > 25 **9.** (a) **10.** $4 \cdot 2 + 7 \ne 2 \cdot 2 + 23$;
$4 \cdot 5 + 7 \ne 2 \cdot 5 + 23$; $4 \cdot 8 + 7 = 2 \cdot 8 + 23$; so 8 is a solution.
11. Samples: 6, 7, 7.9 **12.** $C = 23(4 - 1) + 29$, $C = 98¢$

29. See below. 31. a. positive real numbers **b.** $2 \le w \le 6$
c. See below. 33. a. 2 **b.** $\frac{10}{9}$ **c.** $\frac{38}{39}$

29.   **31. c.**

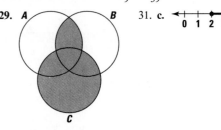

LESSON 1-7 (pp. 37–43)

13. a. L heads of lettuce and T tomatoes cost $L \cdot 89¢ + T \cdot 24¢$.
b. Sample: 10 heads of lettuce and 4 tomatoes cost $10 \cdot 89¢ + 4 \cdot 24¢$. **c.** $C = .89L + .24T$ **15. a.** Sample: $10(11 - 0) = 10 \cdot 11 - 0$, true $110 = 110$, $10(4 - 4) = 10 \cdot 4 - 4$, false $0 \ne 36$, $10(0 - 10) = 10 \cdot 0 - 10$, false $-100 \ne -10$ **b.** No; counterexamples can be found. **17. a.** $n \cdot n > n$ **b.** Sample: $-8 \cdot -8 > -8$
c. Sample: $0 \cdot 0 = 0$ **d.** Sample: $\frac{1}{2} \cdot \frac{1}{2} < \frac{1}{2}$ **19. a.** ⋮⋮⋮⋮⋮
b. Sample: The first design has 3 pennies, the second design has $3 \cdot 2$ pennies, the third design has $3 \cdot 3$ pennies, and so on.
c. $20 \cdot 3$ or 60 pennies **21.** 20 **23. a.** ≈ 54.8 feet **b.** Sample: 60 feet by 50 feet **25.** 176 pounds **27. a.** Sample: 4 **b.** Sample: 2
c. 3 **29.** $1.245 \le d \le 1.255$

LESSON 1-8 (pp. 45–51)

13. a. 6 km **b.** ≈ 4.5 km **c.** ≈ 1.5 km **15. a.** $\sqrt{12} \approx 3.5$ cm
b. See students' drawings. The hypotenuse ≈ 3.5 cm **c.** Answers will vary. Sample: Both answers are close to 3.5 cm. **17.** >
19. 41.4 meters **21.** $3\frac{1}{2}$ **23.** $\frac{5}{6}$ **25.** $\approx \$4.50$

LESSON 1-9 (pp. 53–59)

11. a.

w	1	2	3	4	5
p	2	4	6	8	10

b. The total number of panes in a design is equal to twice the number of panes in one row. **c.** $p = 2w$ **13. a.** 2 **b.** 4

n	1	2	3	4
t	2	4	8	16

c.   **d.** $t = 2^n$ **e.** 512 **15.** (b)
17. $\sqrt{45}$ **19. a.** $37.50 **b.** $5.00a + 1.50c$ **21.** ≈ 5.7 kilograms
23. a. 0 **b.** -6 **c. See below d.** No. Between any two real numbers, there are always an infinite number of real numbers.

23. c.

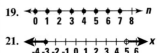

13. $A = 3.14159 \cdot 3^2 = 28.27431 \text{ m}^2 \approx 28 \text{ m}^2$ **14.** False,
$\sqrt{100} + \sqrt{36} = 10 + 6 = 16 \ne \sqrt{136}$ **15.** 13 **16.** Sample: n tickets cost $3.50 \cdot n$. **17.** Sample: $\frac{3}{5} - \frac{2}{5} = \frac{3 - 2}{5}$; $\frac{12}{5} - \frac{2}{5} = \frac{12 - 2}{5}$;
$\frac{1.9}{5} - \frac{6.13}{5} = \frac{1.9 - 6.13}{5}$ **18.** $y = 8x$ **19. See below. 20. a.** $x \ge 10$
b. Answers will vary. **21. See below. 22.** $\ell^2 = 45^2 + 10^2$,
$\ell^2 = 2025 + 100$, $\ell^2 = 2125$, $\ell \approx 46.1$ ft **23.** $\sqrt{193600} = 440$ yards
24. 25 in.

19.

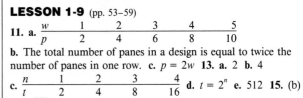

21.

The chart below keys the **Progress Self-Test** questions to the objectives in the **Chapter Review** on pages 65–68. This will enable you to locate those **Chapter Review** questions that correspond to questions missed on the **Progress Self-Test**. The lesson where the material is covered is also indicated on the chart.

Question	1	2	3	4	5	6	7	8	9	10	11	12	13	14
Objective	C	C	C	F	C	D	B	I	I	A	A	J	J	D
Lesson	1-4	1-4	1-4	1-6	1-4	1-6	1-3	1-2	1-2	1-1	1-1	1-5	1-5	1-6
Question	15	16	17	18	19	20	21	22	23	24				
Objective	E	H	G	H	L	L	L	K	K	D				
Lesson	1-2	1-7	1-7	1-9	1-2	1-2	1-2	1-8	1-8	1-6				

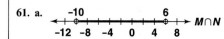

CHAPTER 1 REVIEW (pp. 65–68)

1. 4 **3.** Sample: $-5, -4.2, -3$ **5.** $3, -3$ **7. a.** {15, 25} **b.** {10, 11, 15, 19, 20, 23, 25, 30} **9. a.** $\{-1, 0, 1, 2, 3, \ldots\}$ **b.** {0, 1, 2}
11. a. $8\frac{3}{5}$ **b.** 11 **13.** 529 **15.** 576 **17.** 3 **19.** 9 **21.** 30 **23.** False; $5 + 2 \neq \sqrt{29}$ **25.** 4 and 5 **27.** 14.107 **29.** 50 **31. a.** empty or null set **b.** Sample: the set of integers between -3 and -2 **33.** 7
35. 39 **37.** Sample: $2 + 2 = 2 \cdot 2; -3 + -3 = 2 \cdot -3; 4.9 + 4.9 = 2 \cdot 4.9$ **39.** Sample: $9 = 4.5 \cdot 2; 36 = 4.5 \cdot 8$ **41.** Sample: n sheep have $n \cdot 4$ legs. **43. a.** 21,000 people **b.** $2100y$ people **45.** $y = 4^x$
47. (c) **49.** 25% **51.** 25% **53.** $399 **55.** 10 ft **57.** ≈ 1.78 ft or about 2 ft **59. See right. 61. See right. 63. See right.**
65. (b) **67. a.** $n \geq 18$ **b.** Sample: A U.S. citizen may vote when he or she is at least 18 years old.

59.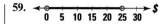

61. a. $M \cap N$

61. b. $M \cup N$

63. a. y

63. b. y

REFRESHER (p. 69)

1. 15.087 **3.** 0.00666 **5.** 20 **7.** $\frac{1}{6}$ **9.** $2\frac{21}{32}$ **11.** $180 **13.** 27,000 cartons **15.** 402 miles **17.** -6 **19.** -24 **21.** 0 **23.** 3540
25. $x = 4$ **27.** $z = \frac{1}{2}$ **29.** $a = \frac{3}{25}$ **31.** $c = \frac{1}{2}$ **33.** 180 in^2 **35.** 8 m^2
37. 96 cm^3 **39.** $\frac{1}{8}$ ft^3 or 0.125 ft^3

LESSON 2-1 (pp. 72–78)
13. a. No **b.** Yes **c.** No **d.** Sample: Washing your hair followed by drying your hair; not commutative. **15.** $240x^2$ **17. a.** kn
b. $k + k + n + n$ or $2k + 2n$ **19.** 576 m^2 **21.** 180 in^3
23. Sample: Area is a measure of the amount of 2-dimensional surface; volume is a measure of 3-dimensional space. The amount of space in a box is its volume; the size of one of its sides is an area. **25.** $2L$ **27.** $\frac{3}{10}$

LESSON 2-2 (pp. 79–83)
17. (c) **19. a.** reciprocals **b.** $200 \cdot 0.005 = 1$ **21. a.** reciprocals
b. $1.5 = \frac{3}{2}; \frac{3}{2} \cdot \frac{2}{3} = 1$ **23.** $\frac{5}{2}$ or $2\frac{1}{2}$ times **25.** 0 **27.** $\frac{q}{p}$
29. a. 3080 ft^2 **b.** 513 people **31. a.** $10s^3$ **b.** 10
c. See below.

31. c. Sample: The rectangle is two cubes deep and 5 cubes high, for a total of 10 cubes.

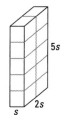

LESSON 2-3 (pp. 85–90)
17. a. One area is $\frac{1}{8}$ of the other. **b. See below. 19. a.** 5 **b.** 9
c. a **d.** a **21.** (c) **23.** 1 **25.** $\frac{21xy}{5}$ **27.** Sample: $\frac{12x}{y^2} \cdot \frac{x}{5y}$
29. 280 **31.** 3025 ft^2

17. b. $\frac{1}{8}$

LESSON 2-4 (pp. 91–95)
11. a. 2880 ounces **b.** $288c$ ounces **13.** Size 32.
80 cm $\cdot \frac{1 \text{ in.}}{2.54 \text{ cm}} \approx 31.5$ in. The size closest to 80 cm is 32 in.
15. a. $2k \frac{\text{dishes}}{\text{minute}}$ **b.** $\frac{1}{2k} \frac{\text{minutes}}{\text{dish}}$ **17.** 5 days **19.** Sample: If you can read magazines at a rate of 120 minutes per magazine and each magazine has 40 pages, what is your speed in minutes per page?
21. (d) **23.** Sample: $\frac{8}{15} \cdot \frac{x}{y} = \frac{8x}{15y}$ **25. a.** 0 **b.** Multiplication Property of Zero **27. a.** x^3 **b.** Sample $3x \cdot x \cdot \frac{x}{3}; 16x \cdot \frac{x}{4} \cdot \frac{x}{4}$

LESSON 2-5 (pp. 96–101)
17. $9x^2$ **19.** $-32a^5$ **21. a.** positive **b.** negative **c.** positive
d. positive **e.** zero **f.** negative **23.** No **25.** Yes **27.** $\approx .14$ km
29. $\frac{9}{7}a$

839

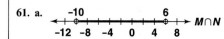

T77

LESSON 2-6 (pp. 102–108)

17. a. 30.48 cm **b.** Multiply both sides by 12 to get $12 \cdot 1$ in. = $12 \cdot 2.54$ cm. **19.** $x = 0.13$; $6.5 = 5(1.3)$; $6.5 = 6.5$ **21.** 8 cm
23. $a = \frac{F}{m}$ **25. a.** positive **b.** negative **c.** zero **27.** 4.5 yd $\cdot$
$36 \frac{\text{in.}}{\text{yd}} \cdot 2.54 \frac{\text{cm}}{\text{in.}} = 411.48$ cm **29.** DP **31. a.** 660 ft^2 **b.** Sample:
$14 \cdot 6 + 24 \cdot 10 + 14 \cdot 24 = 660$; and $32 \cdot 30 - 14 \cdot 8 - 8 \cdot 10 - 18 \cdot 6 = 660$ square feet **c.** 1320 ft^2 **d.** about 25.7 ft $\times$ 25.7 ft

LESSON 2-7 (pp. 109–113)

13. N would be 0. **15.** Sample: You are traveling 13 mph. How long does it take you to go 0 miles? **17.** $x = -15$; $(6 - 7)(-15) = (-1)(-15) = 15$ **19. a.** -3; $-4(-3) = 12$ **b.** $-\frac{1}{3}$; $12(-\frac{1}{3}) = \frac{-12}{3} = -4$
21. $\frac{10}{3}$ **23.** $\frac{1}{12}$ **25.** Sample: $8x = c$ **27.** 15 hr **29.** 7608 m^2
31. a. Yes **b.** Yes **c.** Yes **d.** No

LESSON 2-8 (pp. 114–118)

17. more than 31, or at least 32 rows **19.** $m > -8$ **21.** $x \geq 384$
23. $x < 272$ **25. a.** $n = 4$ **b.** no solution **c.** $n = -2$ **d.** $n = -\frac{1}{2}$
27. -10 **29.** $\frac{x^2}{15}$ **31.** $A = \frac{1}{2}s^2$

LESSON 2-9 (pp. 119–124)

11. See below. **13. a.** $AJ, AK, AL, BJ, BK, BL, CJ, CK, CL,$ DJ, DK, DL **b.** $\frac{1}{12}$ **15.** Sample: A girl can choose from 2 jackets, 3 skirts and 5 blouses. How many 3-piece outfits are possible?
17. a. 2 **b.** 4 **c.** 8 **d.** 1024 **e.** 2^n **19.** $k = -\frac{1}{25}$ **21.** $n = 1200$
23. a. no solution **b.** 0 **c.** $x < 0$ **d.** $x > 0$ **25.** $x = -102$
27. $2x + 48$ **29. a.** $-\frac{1}{8}$ **b.** $\frac{5}{2}$ **c.** $-\frac{1}{2}$

11.

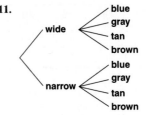

LESSON 2-10 (pp. 125–130)

15. 20! or about $2.4 \cdot 10^{18}$ **17. a.** True **b.** True **c.** $n! = n \cdot (n - 1)!$ **19.** Sample: $100^{100} = 100 \cdot 100 \cdot 100 \ldots \cdot 100$ whereas $100! = 100 \cdot 99 \cdot 98 \cdot \ldots \cdot 1$, so you get a bigger product from 100^{100}. **21.** $\frac{1}{1600}$ **23. a.** Sample: Adam's total earnings for 10 weeks was $723. How much did he earn each week? **b.** $72.30
25. $y < \frac{10}{3}$ **27.** Multiplication Property of Equality **29.** $6.912 \cdot 10^8$ or 691,200,000 **31.** Sample: $3 \cdot 4 = 4 \cdot 3$ **33. a.** Sample: $2 + 5 > 2$ **b.** Sample: $2 + -1 > 2$ is not true. **c.** positive numbers

---

CHAPTER 2 PROGRESS SELF-TEST (pp. 134–135)

1. $\frac{22!}{20!} = \frac{22 \cdot 21 \cdot 20!}{20!} = 22 \cdot 21 = 462$ **2.** False because $(-5)^{10} = 9,765,625 \neq -9,765,625 = -5^{10}$ **3.** $\frac{20x}{3y} \cdot \frac{5}{4x} = \frac{5}{3y} \cdot \frac{5}{1} = \frac{25}{3y}$
4. $\frac{4}{x^2} \cdot \frac{11}{2x} = \frac{2 \cdot 11}{x^3} = \frac{22}{x^3}$ **5.** $-5a \cdot \frac{a}{5} = -a \cdot a = -a^2$ **6.** Sample:
$7 \cdot 5 = 5 \cdot 7 = 35$ **7.** $\frac{1}{50} \cdot 50x = \frac{1}{50} \cdot 10$; $x = \frac{10}{50}$; $x = \frac{1}{5}$
8. $4 \cdot \frac{1}{4}k = 4 \cdot (-24)$; $k = -96$ **9.** $\frac{1}{3} \cdot 15 \leq \frac{1}{3} \cdot 3m$; $5 \leq m$
10. $-y \leq -2$; $y \geq 2$ **11. a.** $-\frac{1}{2} \cdot -2n > -\frac{1}{2} \cdot 18$; $n > -9$
b. See right. **12.** $-48 = -\frac{4}{3}n$; $-\frac{3}{4} \cdot -48 = -\frac{3}{4} \cdot -\frac{4}{3}n$; $36 = n$.
Check: Does $-48 = -\frac{4}{3}(36)$? Yes, $-48 = -4 \cdot 12$. **13.** $-\frac{n}{3}$ **14.** $\frac{1}{3.2}$ or
0.3125 or $\frac{5}{16}$ **15.** $a \cdot -\frac{1}{a} = -1$ **16.** 8 inches $\cdot 2.54 \frac{\text{cm}}{\text{in.}} = 20.32$ cm

17. 24000 people $\cdot 0.57 \frac{\text{car}}{\text{person}} \cdot 15 \frac{\text{dollars}}{\text{car}} = 205,200$ dollars
18. Volume $= 4n \cdot 8n \cdot 1.5n = 48n^3$ **19.** $55t = 300$; $\frac{1}{55} \cdot 55t = \frac{1}{55} \cdot 300$; $t \approx 5.45$ hours $\approx$ 5 hours, 27 minutes **20.** $80^2 - 15^2 = 6400 - 225 = 6175$ ft^2 **21. a.** positive **b.** negative $\times$ negative $=$ positive **22. a.** negative **b.** odd power of negative number
23. a. $\frac{5}{6}x, \frac{3}{4}y$ **b.** $\frac{5}{8}xy$ **24. a.** Sample: $0 \cdot x = 48$ **b.** Sample: For any value of x, $0 \cdot x = 0$. So $0 \cdot x$ cannot equal 48. **25. a.** $40r = 600$ **b.** $\frac{1}{40} \cdot 40r = \frac{1}{40} \cdot 600$; $r = 15$ 15 rows **26.** $7 \cdot 5 \cdot 3 = 105$ programs **27.** $5! = 5 \cdot 4 \cdot 3 \cdot 2 \cdot 1 = 120$ **28.** $2^{25} = 33,554,432$

11. b.
$$\xleftarrow{\hspace{0.5cm}} \overset{-10 \ -9 \ -8 \ -7 \ -6 \ -5 \ -4}{\circ\!-\!\!-\!\!-\!\!-\!\!-\!\!-\!\!-\!\!\rightarrow} \ n$$

The chart below keys the **Progress Self-Test** questions to the objectives in the **Chapter Review** on pages 136–139. This will enable you to locate those **Chapter Review** questions that correspond to questions missed on the **Progress Self-Test**. The lesson where the material is covered is also indicated on the chart.

Question	1	2	3	4	5	6	7	8	9	10	11	12
Objective	E	B	A	A	A	F	C	C	D	D	D	C
Lesson	2-10	2-5	2-3	2-3	2-3	2-1	2-6	2-6	2-8	2-8	2-8	2-7

Question	13	14	15	16	17	18	19	20	21	22	23	24
Objective	F	F	F	H	H	H	G	G	B	B	J	F
Lesson	2-2	2-2	2-2	2-4	2-6	2-4	2-1	2-1	2-5	2-5	2-1	2-7

Question	25	26	27	28
Objective	G	I	I	I
Lesson	2-8	2-9	2-10	2-9

840

CHAPTER 2 REVIEW (pp. 136–139)

1. $\frac{27}{40}$ **3.** $\frac{x}{y}$ **5.** $3n$ **7.** $\frac{r}{3}$ **9.** 270 **11.** -8 **13.** negative **15. a.** 36
b. -36 **c.** -216 **d.** -216 **17.** positive **19.** $m = 150$ **21.** $h = -5$
23. $n = -27$ **25.** $g = \frac{d}{c}$ **27.** Sample: $0 \cdot h = 13$ **29.** $m \le 2$
31. $u < -2$ **33. a.** $g \le -10$ **b.** See right. **35.** 30 **37.** $\approx 1.3077 \cdot$
10^{12} **39. a.** False **b.** $\frac{10!}{10} = \frac{10 \cdot 9!}{10} = 9! \ne 1 = 1!$ **41.** 1,030,200
43. a. $2200x$ **b.** Commutative and Associative Properties of
Multiplication **45.** $-\frac{1}{2}$ **47.** $\frac{4}{3x}$ **49.** Multiplication Property of
Equality **51.** opposite **53. a.** $\frac{1}{2} \ell$ by $\frac{2}{3} w$ **b.** The Banjerils' garden
is $\frac{1}{3}$ the size of the Cohens' garden. **55.** 31.25 feet **57.** 720;
The volume of the solid is $720s^3$ and the volume of the cube is s^3.

So $\frac{720s^3}{s^3} = 720$. **59.** \$0.033 or $3\frac{1}{3}$¢ **61.** \$225 **63.** 8.92 hours or
8 hours 55 minutes **65. a.** $\frac{1}{2}$ second per revolution **b.** It takes a
pirouetting ballet dancer $\frac{1}{2}$ second to make one revolution.
67. $24^3 = 13,824$ **69.** $18! \approx 6.4 \times 10^{15}$ **71.** fs **73.** Commutative
Property of Multiplication **75. a.** See below. **b.** $\frac{3}{8} s^2$ **77.** $24k^3$
79. 2600

33. b.

75. a.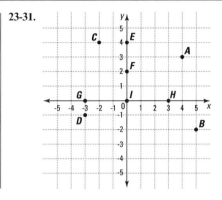

REFRESHER (p. 141)

1. 7.8 **3.** 11.0239 **5.** 9 **7.** 18% **9.** 11.03 cm **11.** $3'$
13. 158 oz or 9 lb 14 oz **15.** 24 **17.** 1 **19.** -4 **21.** $4 + {}^-7$
23-31. See right. **33.** $z = 31$ **35.** $m = 5$ **37.** $s = 299$

23-31.

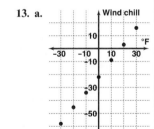

LESSON 3-1 (pp. 142–148)

13. Sample: $5 + 3a = 3a + 5$ **15.** $x° + {}^-3° + 5°$ **17. a.** $A + 3$
b. $A + {}^-4$ **19.** $50 + x = 54$ **21.** $M + 4.25 < 10.50$ **23.** $a + b + 5$
25. a. 1 **b.** Sample: When you multiply a number by 1, the
product is the same as (or identical to) the number. **27.** 13
29. a. 12.6 **b.** 0 **c.** 0

LESSON 3-2 (pp. 149–154)

19. 8 cm **21. a.** 3.14 **b.** Opposite of Opposites or the Op-Op
Property **23.** $f = 13.05$; $15.2 = 13.05 + 2.15$ **25. a.** $17 + C =$
-12 **b.** $C = -29$ **c.** $17 + {}^-29 = -12$ **27.** $40 - n + 2n$ records
29. (b) **31.** Sample: a line that neither goes up nor down; it is level
like the horizon. **33.** $A = (1, 4)$; $B = (5, 2)$; $C = (-2, 2)$;
$D = (-5, 0)$; $E = (0, -2)$; $F = (-5, -3)$; $G = (3, -3)$; $H = (3, 0)$

LESSON 3-3 (pp. 155–162)

11. a. L **b.** J **c.** American: The
point for the average American
student falls in the middle of the
scatterplot. **13. a.** See right.
b. Sample: For every 10° drop in
temperature, the wind chill drops
about 12°. **15.** (c) **17.** about $1\frac{3}{4}$ hr
19. (b) **21. a.** -17.3 **b.** Property
of Opposites **23. a.** $n = 9$
b. $n = 29$ **c.** $n = -29$ **d.** $n = \frac{-10}{19}$
25. $-2 + p + {}^-q$ **27.** 9 minutes
29. a. -13 **b.** 12 **c.** -32

13. a.

Wind chill

LESSON 3-4 (pp. 163–169)

13. a. $(-1, -9)$ **b.** See below. **15.** 8 right, 6 down **17. a.** 9, 8
b. 9, 8 **19.** $(4, -10)$ **21.** 6 minutes **23.** x **25.** $-\$1.8$ million
27. a. Commutative Property of Addition **b.** $x + y$ **29. a.** 9.6
b. 5.9 **c. a;** $9.6 > 5.9$

13. b.

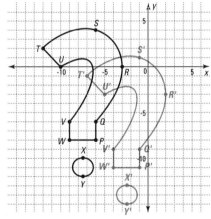

LESSON 3-5 (pp. 170–175)

15. **a.** $4347.59 + 752.85 + ^-550.00 + x = 4574.14$ **b.** $x = \$23.70$; Total interest for June was \$23.70. **17.** $x = 7\frac{1}{4}$; $3\frac{1}{4} + 7\frac{1}{4} = 10\frac{1}{2}$
19. See below. **21. a.** 2 right; 4 down **b.** $D' = (2, ^-4)$; $E' = (3, 0)$ **23. a.** \$3.00 **b.** $.50n = c$ **25. a.** .2 **b.** .02 **c.** 1.02
d. 1.20 **27.** B **29.** Yes, several of the higher priced ice creams have a high rating.

19.

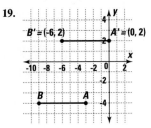

LESSON 3-6 (pp. 177–182)

17. $F - .3F$ or $.7F$ **19.** 0 **21.** 9 camels **23. a.** $3w + 2 = 8$
b. $w = 2$ oz **25.** Sample: First add ^-b to both sides; then multiply both sides by $\frac{1}{a}$. To solve $3x + 5 = 11$, add $^-5$ to both sides to get $3x = 6$; then multiply both sides by $\frac{1}{3}$ to get $x = 2$. **27. a.** $^-17$
b. $\frac{1}{17}$ **29.** The minus sign indicates the Death Valley area is 282 feet below sea level. **31.** 900 minutes or 15 hours

LESSON 3-7 (pp. 183–187)

21. 5,999,994 **23. a.** $60 = \frac{1}{2} \cdot 6(5 + b_2)$ **b.** $b_2 = 15$ cm
25. 123 miles **27.** $2a + 6b + ^-2c$ **29. a.** $m < 12$; $5 \cdot 12 + 2 \cdot 12 = 84$ and $5 \cdot 10 + 2 \cdot 10 < 84$ **b.** Yes, $^-5$ is less than 12.
31. 12

LESSON 3-8 (pp. 188–194)

11. 3; 5; 7; 9 **13. a.** $t = 1 + 2n$ **b.** 11
15. a.

Minutes	Cost
100	65.95
200	65.95
300	86.95
400	107.95
500	128.95

b. $c = 65.95 + .21(m - 200)$
c. $m \geq 200$

17. Sample:

```
10 PRINT "GALLONS OF GASOLINE CONSUMED"
20 FOR N = 1 TO 20
30 LET G = 7500*N
40 PRINT N, G
50 NEXT N
60 END
```

19. $25(\$1.99) = 25(\$2 - 1¢) = 25 \cdot \$2 - 25 \cdot 1¢ = \$50 - 25¢ = \$49.75$ **21.** $x = \frac{1}{2}$ **23.** $x = 10$ **25.** Quadrant II **27. a.** $z < 77$
b. See below.

27. b.

LESSON 3-9 (pp. 195–199)

15. $-\frac{1}{x}$ **17.** $-\frac{3}{2x}$ **19. a.** $2W + 2L$ **b.** $L + W$ **21. a.** Samples: After the first slide at 75¢, the cost is 50¢ per slide. The cost is always divisible by 25¢. **b.** \$4.25; $75 + 50(n - 1) = c$; $75 + 50(8 - 1) = 425¢$ **c.** 15

23. a.

n	1	2	3	4
t	4	7	10	13

b. Sample: t increases by 3 for every increase of 1 in n.
c. 181 toothpicks **d.** $n = 100$; Sample: How many squares are formed by 301 toothpicks arranged side by side in one row?
25. $n = ^-1$; Does $8 = 2(^-1 + 3) + 4(5 \cdot ^-1 + 6)$? Yes, it checks.
27. $u + ^-d$ **29.** $11 \cdot 10 \cdot 9 \cdot 8 \cdot 7 \cdot 6 \cdot 5 \cdot 4 \cdot 3 \cdot 2 \cdot 1$ **31.** more than $27\frac{7}{9}$ hours **33.** \$18,777,777.78 per year

LESSON 3-10 (pp. 200–204)

9. $n + n + 1 + n + 2 > 79$; 26, 27, 28 **11.** $y \leq 1$ **13.** $x > ^-108$
15. Celsius temperatures greater than 37°C **17. a.** \$9.45 **b.** \$10
19. $2a$ **21.** $\frac{^-x}{15}$ **23. a.** 4 **b.** 10 **c.** $2(n + 1)$ or $2n + 2$ **25.** $y = 4$; Does $6(4 \cdot 4 + ^-1) - 2 \cdot 4 = 82$? $6 \cdot 15 - 8 = 90 - 8 = 82$. Yes, it checks. **27.** about 45 hours **29. a.** 75^{75} **b.** Sample: each factor in 75! is less than or equal to 75, but $75^{75} = 75 \cdot 75 \cdot 75 \cdot \ldots \cdot 75$. So $75^{75} > 75!$

CHAPTER 3 PROGRESS SELF-TEST (pp. 208–209)

1. $m + 3m = 1m + 3m = (1 + 3)m = 4m$ **2.** $\frac{5}{2}(4v + 100 + 2) = \frac{5}{2} \cdot 4v + \frac{5}{2} \cdot 100 + \frac{5}{2} \cdot w = \frac{20v}{2} + \frac{500}{2} + \frac{5w}{2} = 10v + 250 + \frac{5w}{2}$
3. $^-9k + 3(k + 3) = ^-9k + 3k + 9 = (^-9 + 3)k + 9 = ^-6k + 9$
4. $(x + 5 + x) + (^-8 + ^-x) = (x + x + ^-x) + (5 + ^-8) = x + ^-3$
5. $^-(^-(^-p)) = ^-p$ **6.** $\frac{2}{n} + \frac{5}{n} + \frac{^-3}{n} = \frac{2 + 5 + ^-3}{n} = \frac{4}{n}$ **7.** $\frac{3x}{2} + \frac{5x}{3} = \frac{9x}{6} + \frac{10x}{6} = \frac{19x}{6}$ **8.** $8r = 60$; $r = \frac{60}{8} = 7.5$ **9.** $5q + 3 = ^-12$;
$5q = ^-15$; $q = \frac{^-15}{5} = ^-3$ **10.** $3x + 6 + 100 = 54$; $3x + 106 = 54$;
$3x = ^-52$; $x = \frac{^-52}{3} = ^-17\frac{1}{3}$ **11.** $85 = x + 2 \cdot 3x + 2 \cdot 4$; $85 = x + 6x + 8$; $85 = 7x + 8$; $85 + ^-8 = 7x + 8 + ^-8$; $77 = 7x$;
$11 = x$ **12.** $30v > 33$; $v > \frac{33}{30}$; $v > \frac{11}{10}$ **See right.**
13. Addition Property of Equality **14.** Adding Like Terms form of the Distributive Property **15.** It is not an element because $^-100 + 87 = ^-13$ and $15 > ^-13$ **16.** $137.25 + 2.50w$ **17.** $6 \cdot \$2.99 = 6(\$3 - 1¢) = 6 \cdot \$3.00 - 6 \cdot 1¢ = \$18 - 6¢ = \$17.94$ **18.** $50 = \frac{9}{5}C + 32$; $18 = \frac{9}{5}C$; $\frac{5}{9} \cdot 18 = C$; $10 = C$; 10°C **19.** Let X stand for Jill's share. Juana receives $2X$. $X + 2X = \$58.50$; $3X = \$58.50$;

$X = \$19.50$; Jill receives \$19.50. **20. a.** $(a + b)c$; $ac + bc$ **b.** The total area is also the sum of the areas of the two smaller rectangles $(ac + bc)$. So $(a + b)c = ac + bc$. **21.** $(5 + ^-4, ^-2 + 5) = (1, 3)$
22. $(^-4 + x, 7 + y) = (6, 5)$; $x = 10$; $y = ^-2$; So $B' = (^-5 + 10, ^-2 + ^-2) = (5, ^-4)$ **23. a.** Although deaths do not decrease every year, the likelihood of being killed by a tornado has generally decreased during the last 70 years. **b.** Sample: Better health care makes it possible for more victims of natural disaster to survive.
24. See below.

12.

0	.5	1	1.5

24.

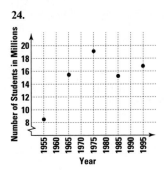

The chart below keys the **Progress Self-Test** questions to the objectives in the **Chapter Review** on pages 210–213. This will enable you to locate those **Chapter Review** questions that correspond to questions missed on the **Progress Self-Test.** The lesson where the material is covered is also indicated on the chart.

Question	1	2	3	4	5	6	7	8	9	10	11	12	13
Objective	A	A	A	A	E	C	C	B	B	B	B	D	E
Lesson	3-6	3-7	3-7	3-6	3-2	3-9	3-9	3-5	3-6	3-7	3-7	3-10	3-2

Question	14	15	16	17	18	19	20	21	22	23	24
Objective	E	D	H	F	G	G	K	J	J	I	I
Lesson	3-6	3-10	3-8	3-7	3-5	3-6	3-6	3-4	3-4	3-3	3-3

CHAPTER 3 REVIEW (pp. 210–213)

1. $15x$ **3.** $\frac{3}{2}c$ **5.** $53x + 46$ **7.** $t = -0.6$; $2.5 = -0.6 + 3.1$; $2.5 = 2.5$ **9.** $n = 7$; $(3 + 7) + -11 = -5 + 4$; $-1 = -1$ **11.** $n = 3$; $4 \cdot 3 + 3 = 15$; $15 = 15$ **13.** $x = \frac{3}{2}$; $\frac{2}{3} \cdot \frac{3}{2} + 14 = 15$; $15 = 15$ **15.** $r = 50$; $17 \cdot 50 + 12 + 9 \cdot 50 = 1312$; $1312 = 1312$ **17.** $x = 3$; $2 \cdot 3 + 3(1 + 3) = 18$; $18 = 18$ **19.** $\frac{x + y}{3}$ **21.** x **23.** $\frac{-13x}{10}$ **25.** $x < 95$; Check: $2 \cdot 95 + 11 = 190 + 11 = 201$ and $2 \cdot 10 + 11 = 20 + 11 = 31 < 201$. **27.** $x > 1$; Check: $-2 + (5 + 1) = -2 + 6 = 4$ and $-2 + (5 + 10) = -2 + 15 = 13 > 4$. **29.** $g < \frac{1}{9}$; Check: $-16 \cdot \frac{1}{9} + 7 \cdot \frac{1}{9} + 5 = -\frac{9}{9} + 5 = -1 + 5 = 4$ and $4 < -16 \cdot 0 + 7 \cdot 0 + 5$; $4 < 5$. **31.** Commutative Property of Addition **33.** Opposite of the Opposite Prop. **35.** Adding Like Terms form of the Distributive Prop. **37.** $x + -21 = 0$ **39.** $\$21.28$; $7(\$3.00 + 4¢) = \$21.00 + 28¢ = \$21.28$ **41.** 285; $3(100 - 5) = 300 - 15 = 285$ **43.** $24°$ **45.** $w + c$ billion pounds **47.** at least $\$9$ **49.** children $\$15,000$ grandchild $\$7,500$ **51. a.** 6, 25 **b.** $y = 3x + 7$ **53. a.** $\$3.70$ **b.** $\$8.20$ **c.** $\$2.95 + .75(n - 3)$ when $n > 3$ **55.** halfway up **57.** Ohio **59.** 1950–1960 **61.** $(-38, 56)$ **63.** The image of (x, y) is $(x - 1, y + 8)$. **65.** See below. **67. a.** $13 = 5W + 8$ **b.** 1 kg **69.** $ad + bd + cd$; $(a + b + c)d$ **71.** See below. **73.** See below.

65.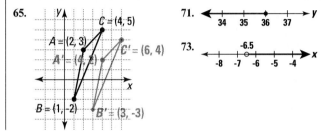

71.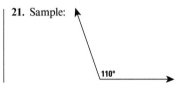

73.
A number line with point at -6.5 (open circle), marked from -8 to -4.

REFRESHER (p. 213)

1. $5\frac{1}{3}$ **3.** 5.65 **5.** 96% **7.** -160 **9.** -8 **11.** 199 **13.** $x = 51$ **15.** $w = 113$ **17.** (b) **19.** $74°$ **21.** See right.

21. Sample: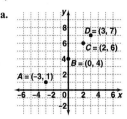
$110°$

LESSON 4-1 (pp. 216–220)

15. -22 **17.** 0 **19. a.** $-4 + -3 + -3 + 5$ **b.** $-4 - 3 - 3 + 5$ **c.** -5 lb **21.** $x = 1$ **23.** $1.2n + 3$ **25.** $y = 0.1$ **27.** 22.485

LESSON 4-2 (pp. 221–226)

9. $4x$ **11. a.** Bernie **b.** 7 years **13. a.** $.80R$ **b.** $.80R - .10(.80R) = .72R$ **c.** $.72R + .03(.72R) = .7416R$ **15. a.** $47°$ **b.** $a - b$ or $b - a$ **17.** 0 **19.** $-p + q$ **21. a.** -10 **b.** $-6 + n$ $(n > 0)$ **c.** Sample: Point F could be located anywhere to the right of A. **23.** $x = -1$ **25.** $x > 45.8$ **27. a.** $81 - 16 = 13 \cdot 5$; $961 - 841 = 60 \cdot 2$; $12.25 - 6.25 = 6 \cdot 1$ **b.** $a^2 - b^2 = (a + b)(a - b)$ **c.** Sample: $3^2 - 2^2 = (3 + 2)(3 - 2)$; True

LESSON 4-3 (pp. 227–231)

13. a. $10n - 3 = 84$ **b.** 8.7 **15.** 2044 **17.** $p = -11.64$ **19.** $t > 24$ **21.** $y - 50$ **23. a.** $\$22.00$ **b.** $\$19.80$ **c.** The amount subtracted from 22, 10% of 22, is larger than the amount added to 20, 10% of 20. So the net result is less than 20. **25.** (a) **27.** (a) **29.** 3 **31.** $-3x + 5$

LESSON 4-4 (pp. 232–239)

9. 86 **11.** Marcel's mean **13.** $= (J5 + K5 + J6 + K6)/4$ **15.** No, because $\sqrt{16 + 25} = \sqrt{41}$, which does not equal 9. **17. a.** $\$12.00$ **b.** Sample: In cell A1 enter the label "Number of words." In cell B1 enter the label "Cost of ad." In cell A2 enter 25, and in cell A3 enter the formula $= A2 + 1$. Replicate this formula in cells A4 through A77. Enter the formula $= 5.00 + .50*(A2 - 25)$ in cell B2. Finally, replicate the formula from cell B2 in cells B3 through B77. **19.** $x = 66$ **21.** $z > 0$ **23.** $2499.8 \approx 2500$ ft

LESSON 4-5 (pp. 240–245)

17. $-a - 2b + c$ **19.** $(90 - 4f - p)°$ or $(90 - (4f + p))°$ **21.** $t = 1$ **23.** 12 inches **25.** 1.21 D dollars **27. a.** See below. **b.** The points lie along the same line. **c.** $y = x + 4$ **29.** TABLE OF (X, Y) VALUES

X VALUE	Y VALUE
0	12
1	11
2	10
3	9
4	8
5	7

27. a.
A coordinate graph showing points $D = (3, 7)$, $C = (2, 6)$, $B = (0, 4)$, $A = (-3, 1)$.

843

LESSON 4-6 (pp. 246–252)

9. a.

Sal	Al
1	7
2	6
3	5
4	4
5	3
6	2
7	1

b. 3 **11.** (c), (d)

13. a.

J	M
0	10
1	9
2	8
3	7
4	6
5	5
6	4
7	3
8	2
9	1
10	0

b. See below.
15. $-3a - 12$
17. a. B2 = 55;
B3 = 82.5; B7 = 192.5
b. = A6 * 55
19. $y = \frac{18}{5}$ **21.** $9.50
23. a. 1000 **b.** 2000
c. 125 **25.** 60°

13. b.

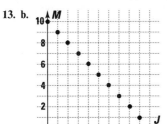

LESSON 4-7 (pp. 253–258)

15. $m\angle B = 90 - x$ **17.** Sample: The angle formed by the jumper's legs and the back part of the skis measures 165°. **19.** 64°, 64°, 52° **21.** $m\angle C = 180 - m\angle A - m\angle B$ **23.** See below.
25. $n = -\frac{1}{2}$ **27.** $-\frac{7}{12}x$

29. a.

time	charge
$\frac{1}{2}$ hr	$70
1 hr	$90
$1\frac{1}{2}$ hr	$110
2 hr	$130
$2\frac{1}{2}$ hr	$150
3 hr	$170

b. $c = 50 + 20n$ **31.** See below.

23.

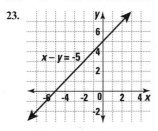

31.

$0 \leq x \leq 2$

LESSON 4-8 (pp. 260–266)

9. between 0 in. and 6 in. **11.** because 1 + 2 is not greater than 4 **13.** 2.6 light-years $\leq m \leq$ 20 light-years **15.** Sample: The flying distance will be less because you can fly on a straight line from one city to another, while on land the Triangle Inequality may be applied many times between the cities. **17.** $25\frac{5}{7}°$, $51\frac{3}{7}°$, $102\frac{6}{7}°$
19. See below. **21.** $-3u + -3v^2$ **23.** (7, 12)

19.

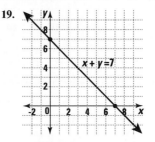

LESSON 4-9 (pp. 267–273)

11. a.

w	b
0	30
1	25
2	20
3	15
4	10

b. $b = 30 - 5w$ **c.** See below. **d.** week 6
13. a. Sample:

x	y
0	10
1	10.5
2	11
3	11.5
4	12

b. the set of nonnegative real numbers **c.** See below.
d. 20 years **15. a., b.** See below. **c.** (0, 0) **d.** Sample: The lines are reflection images of each other over the y-axis.
17. 2 points **19.** 7 < length < 47 **21.** 40°, 60°, 80° **23.** (d)
25. $-\frac{9x}{35}$ **27. a.** 0.25 **b.** 2.5 **c.** 25 **d.** 250,000

11. c.

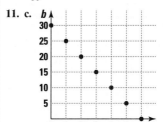

13. c.

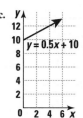

15. a., b.

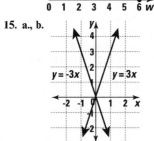

CHAPTER 4 PROGRESS SELF-TEST (p. 277)

1. subtracting 7 **2.** Apply the Comparison Model for Subtraction. $D - 53$ **3.** $9p + {}^-7q + 14z$ **4.** $-n - 16 + 12 = -n - 4$
5. $-8x - (2x - x) = -8x - 2x + x = -9x$ **6.** $-2b + 6$
7. $\frac{m}{2} - \frac{7m}{2} = \frac{-6m}{2} = -3m$ **8.** $S - .20S = (1 - .20)S = .80S$
9. $5n = 60; n = 12$ **10.** $2 < -3p; -\frac{2}{3} > p$ or $p < -\frac{2}{3}$ **11.** $\frac{3}{4} - \frac{1}{4}m =$
$12; -\frac{1}{4}m = 11\frac{1}{4}; -\frac{1}{4}m = \frac{45}{4}; -4 \cdot -\frac{1}{4}m = -4 \cdot \frac{45}{4}; m = -45$
12. $201 = 15f - 6 - 12f; 207 = 3f; f = 69$ **13.** $50 = \frac{5}{9} \cdot (F - 32);$
$50 = \frac{5}{9}F - \frac{160}{9}; \frac{450}{9} + \frac{160}{9} = \frac{5}{9}F; \frac{9}{5} \cdot \frac{610}{9} = F; F = 122°F$ **14.** Solve
the sentence: $1100 - 6x > 350; -6x > -750; x < 125$ minutes

15.
Yes	9	8	7	6	5	4	3	2	1	0
No	0	1	2	3	4	5	6	7	8	9

16. a.
x	-1	0	1	2	3
y	-5	-3	-1	1	3

b. See right.
b. See right.
17. Use the Triangle Inequality. $786 + 582 \geq$ distance from LA to SA; so greatest possible distance is 1368 miles. **18. a.** $180 - 18 = 162°$ **b.** $90 - 18 = 72°$ **19.** $x + y = 90$ See right.
20. $n + 2n + 2n - 4 = 180; 5n - 4 = 180; 5n = 184;$

$n = \frac{184}{5} = 36.8$. So m$\angle L = 2 \cdot 36.8° = 73.6°$. **21.** Use the Triangle Inequality. Since $p + 3 > 7$ and $3 + 7 > p; 10 > p;$ $4 < p < 10$. **22. a.** 428.75 **b.** A4 **c.** 143.02 **d.** $= B2 - C2 - D2$

15. b.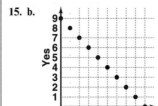

16. b.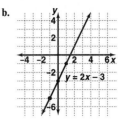
$y = 2x - 3$

19.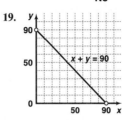
$x + y = 90$

The chart below keys the **Progress Self-Test** questions to the objectives in the **Chapter Review** on pages 278–281. This will enable you to locate those **Chapter Review** questions that correspond to questions missed on the **Progress Self-Test**. The lesson where the material is covered is also indicated on the chart.

Question	1	2	3	4	5	6	7	8	9	10
Objective	E	E	A	A	D	D	A	H	B	C
Lesson	4-1	4-2	4-1	4-1	4-5	4-5	4-1	4-2	4-3	4-3

Question	11	12	13	14	15	16	17	18	19	20
Objective	B	D	I	I	L	L	J	F	L	F
Lesson	4-3	4-5	4-3	4-3	4-6	4-6	4-8	4-7	4-9	4-7

Question	21	22
Objective	G	K
Lesson	4-8	4-4

CHAPTER 4 REVIEW (pp. 278–281)

1. $4x$ **3.** $-3a$ **5.** $-\frac{4c}{3} - 2$ **7.** $-3z^3 + 1$ **9.** $x = 45$ **11.** $y = -\frac{1}{2}$
13. $n = 5$ **15.** $m = -5$ **17.** $a = \frac{3}{2}$ **19.** $x < 106$ **21.** $y < -13$
23. $-4a - 7$ **25.** $2 - z$ **27.** $-3a - 16$ **29.** $p = -8$ **31.** $x > 10$
33. $x = \frac{45}{2}$ **35.** $x + -y + z$ **37.** True **39. a.** 73° **b.** 163°
41. True. The supplement of an angle with measure $x°$ is $180 - x$. The complement is $90 - x$. $180 - x$ is greater than $90 - x$.
43. 73° **45.** 40°, 100° or 70°, 70° **47.** No; $3 + 5 < 16$ **49.** $15 > m$, $m + 8 > 7, m + 7 > 8$ **51.** $3 < y < 25$ **53.** $S = E - P$
55. $2500 - F$ **57.** $D - 5$ **59. a.** $.3V$ **b.** $.7V$ **61.** 51 wks; Solve $750 + 15w > 1500$. **63.** 14 days **65.** 1233 mi **67. a.** $= A6^\wedge 2 + A6$
b. 6 **c.** B6 would change to 380. **69. a.** D3 = 740; D4 = 586; D5 = 1118; D6 = 1180; D7 = 520 **b.** = B4 * 6 + C4 * 4
c. Aug. 30 **71.** See right. **73.** See right. **75.** See right.
77. See right.

71.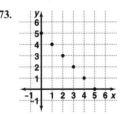
$x - y = 4$

73.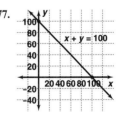

75.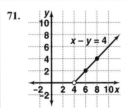
$y = \frac{1}{2}x + 10$

77.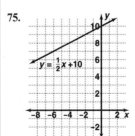
$x + y = 100$

LESSON 5-1 (pp. 284–290)

15. a. See below. **b.** Let x = the date and y = the cost (in cents). From 2/17/85 to 4/2/88, $y = 22$. From 4/3/88 to 2/2/91, $y = 25$. From 2/3/91 to the present, $y = 29$. **17.** $x = -6$ **19. a.** $y = -13$ **b.** $x = 7$ **21. a.** $y = 35x + 25$ **b., c.** See below. **d.** 6 hr **e.** $35x + 25 \leq 250$; $x \leq 6.43$; Ron could work for 6 whole hours. **23.** $.80d$ **25.** $9.8(25) + 14.2(25)$ or $(9.8 + 14.2)25$ **27.** (a) **29. a.** Any real number multiplied by 1 equals that same real number. **b.** Sample: $1 \cdot 5 = 5$

15. a.

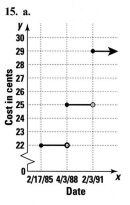

21. b, c

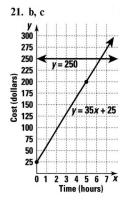

LESSON 5-2 (pp. 291–296)

9. a. $m = 20 + 6w$ **b.** $m = 150 - 4w$

c.

week	1	2	3	4	5	6	7	8	9	10	11	12	13
Kim	26	32	38	44	50	56	62	68	74	80	86	92	98
Jenny	146	142	138	134	130	126	122	118	114	110	106	102	98

After 13 weeks, Kim and Jenny will have the same amount of money. **11.** Sample: $(-3, -6)$, $(0, -6)$, $(17, -6)$ **13. a.** See below. **b.** $(2, 7)$ **c.** $(5, 7)$ **d.** 9 sq units **15. a.** See below. **b.** $(9, 1)$ **17.** $m < 5$ **19.** $x + y - 3(z + w) = x + y - 3z - 3w$. Sample: multiplication by -3 was not distributed over the w term. **21.** 37 **23.** $3.46 \cdot 10^{12}$ **25.** 3

13. a.

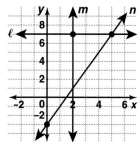

15. a.

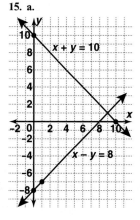

LESSON 5-3 (pp. 297–303)

17. $d = -\frac{1}{2}$ **19.** $y = 6$ **21. a.** $54.64 - 0.33x$ **b.** $49.36 - 0.18x$ **c.** after about 35 years at the Olympics in the year 2028

23. a.

hour	Lamont's distance	Chris's distance
0	24	0
1	33	13
2	42	26
3	51	39
4	60	52
5	69	65
6	78	78

b. 6 hours **25.** See below. **27. a.** $3(2 + x)$ **b.** $(x + 2)3$ **c.** $3x + 6$ **29. a.** Yes **b.** No **c.** Yes

25.

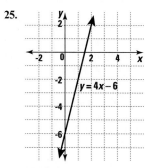

LESSON 5-4 (pp. 304–309)

9. a. See below. At about 9,000 copies costs are equal. **b.** $200 + 0.015x = 70 + 0.03x$; $x \approx 8,667$; Costs are equal for about 8,667 copies. **11.** Using a table, you get 312.5 pu.

$x =$ distance dog travels	$y =$ distance hare is ahead
0	50
125	30
250	10
312.5	0

Using a graph, you may approximate the answer. Graph the line from $(0, 50)$ through $(125, 30)$. When the distance (y) the hare is ahead reaches zero, the x-value tells the total distance traveled by the dog. **13.** $r = 10$ **15.** $m = \frac{1}{2}$ **17. a.** See below. **b.** $(4, -3)$

19. SQUARE ROOTS AND SQUARES

1	1	1
1.41421356	2	4
1.73205081	3	9
2	4	16
2.23606789	5	25
2.44948974	6	36

9. a.

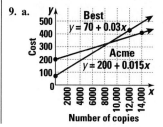

17. a.

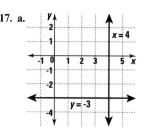

846

LESSON 5-5 (pp. 310–316)

13. a. See below. **b.** Sample: All lines passing through (0, 0). Some are steeper than others. The higher the coefficient of x, the steeper the graph is. **c.** It will pass through the origin and be steeper than the other graphs. **15. a.** See below. **b.** Sample: The graphs are not equal; one is a line and one is a curve. **17.** $d = 17$ **19.** (c) **21.** $x = 9$ **23. a.** $x - s - 2m$ **b.** $x - (s + 2m)$ **25.** (b) **27. a.** $x = 2$ **b.** $y = 4$ **c.** $z = 16$

13. a.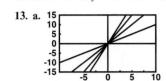

15. a.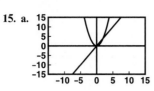

LESSON 5-6 (pp. 317–321)

13. $x > -\frac{1}{13}$ **15.** ads more than 25 words; Sample: $2.00 + 0.08x < 1.50 + 0.10x$, $0.5 < 0.02x$, $x > 25$. **17. a.** See right. **b.** $x = 4$ **19.** $t = \frac{1}{12}$ **21.** $n = -15$ **23.** $\frac{7t}{12}$ **25.** No; Sample: because $12! = (12 \cdot 11 \cdot 10 \cdot 9 \cdot 8 \cdot 7) \cdot 6! \neq 2 \cdot 6!$ **27. a.** 5 **b.** 25 **c.** $5x$ **d.** $25x$

17. a.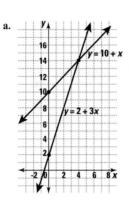

LESSON 5-7 (pp. 322–326)

13. a. $\pi = \frac{C}{d}$ **b.** Sample: If you know the circumference and diameter of a circle, you can substitute those values in the equation to find an approximation for π. **c.** Answers may vary. **15. a.** $D = \frac{9}{10}G$ **b.** 90° **17. a.** $-40°$ **b.** Solve $C = \frac{9}{5}C + 32$ for C, or solve $F = \frac{5}{9}(F - 32)$ for F. **19.** $x \leq \frac{6}{5}$ **21.** See above right. **23.** 1993; $7,602,000 + 395,000x > 9,170,000 - 55,000x$; $x > 3.48$ years **25. a.** 40 dots **b.** $4n$ dots

21.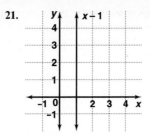

LESSON 5-8 (pp. 327–332)

15. a. \$40,640 **b.** \$15,240 **17.** No. The term $\frac{1}{1000}x$ would appear in the equation, which would not simplify the solution. **19.** $x = 8$ **21.** $y > -15$ **23.** $v = \frac{1}{2}g - \frac{d}{t}$ **25. a.** A **b.** \$2,000 **27. a.**

years from now	Town A pop.	Town B pop.
0	25000	35500
1	26200	35200
2	27400	34900
3	28600	34600
4	29800	34300
5	31000	34000
6	32200	33700
7	33400	33400
8	34600	33100

b. about 7 years from now **29.** $p = 100$ or $p = -100$

LESSON 5-9 (pp. 333–337)

13. $-2\sqrt{a}$ **15.** $5x^2 - 10y$ **17.** 3 **19.** 52 **21.** 12.5 **23.** $p = \frac{20}{3}$ or $p = -10$ **25.** Multiplication Property of Equality **27.** $x = \frac{1}{2}$ **29.** \$480 **31. a.** $y = -\frac{2}{5}x + 2$ **b.** See below. **33.** Sample: $44 + 31 = 31 + 44$ **35.** 6 units

31. b.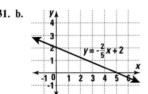

CHAPTER 5 PROGRESS SELF-TEST (pp. 341–342)

1. a. $3y$ or $-5y$; each gives an equation with a variable on only one side **b.** Addition Property of Equality **2.** 15 (or any other common multiple of 3 and 5) **3.** $4x - 3 = 3x + 14$, $x - 3 = 14$, $x = 17$ **4.** $3.9z - 56.9 = 6.1 - 4.7z$, $39z - 569 = 61 - 47z$, $86z = 630$, $z \approx 7.33$ **5.** $5n \geq 2n + 12$, $3n \geq 12$, $n \geq 4$ **6.** $5(10 - y) = 6(y + 1)$, $5 \cdot 10 - 5y = 6y + 6 \cdot 1$, $50 = 11y + 6$, $44 = 11y$, $4 = y$ **7.** $-5a + 6 < -11a + 24$, $6a + 6 < 24$, $6a < 18$, $a < 3$ **8.** $\frac{1}{2}m - \frac{3}{4} = \frac{2}{3}$, $12 \cdot \frac{1}{2}m - 12 \cdot \frac{3}{4} = 12 \cdot \frac{2}{3}$, $6m - 9 = 8$, $6m = 17$, $m = \frac{17}{6}$ **9.** $5000 - 4000v = 11000v + 680000$, $\frac{1}{1000} \cdot 5000 - \frac{1}{1000} \cdot 4000v = \frac{1}{1000} \cdot 11000v + \frac{1}{1000} \cdot 680000$, $5 - 4v = 11v + 680$, $-15v = 675$, $v = -45$ **10.** If $4y = 2.6$, then $20y = 5 \cdot 2.6$ or 13. So $20y + 3 = 13 + 3 = 16$ **11.** Use chunking. $\frac{4}{t + 7} + \frac{5}{t + 7} = \frac{4 + 5}{t + 7} = \frac{9}{t + 7}$ **12.** Use chunking. $8(x^2 - 5) + 3(x^2 - 5) = 11(x^2 - 5) = 11x^2 - 11 \cdot 5 = 11x^2 - 55$ **13.** Use chunking. $49 = 7^2$ or $(-7)^2$ so $n + 3 = 7$ or $n + 3 = -7$. Hence $n = 4$ or

$n = -10$. **14.** $3x + 5y = 15$, $5y = -3x + 15$, $\frac{1}{5} \cdot 5y = \frac{1}{5}(-3x + 15)$, $y = \frac{1}{5} \cdot -3x + \frac{1}{5} \cdot 15$, $y = -\frac{3}{5}x + 3$ **15.** $C = np$, $\frac{1}{n} \cdot C = np \cdot \frac{1}{n}$, $\frac{C}{n} = p$ **16.** See p. 848. **17.** $4x + 6x - 6 + 24 = 3x + 3x + 3x + 3x$, $10x + 18 = 12x$, $18 = 2x$, $9 = x$, Triangle sides are 24, 36, and 48. All sides of the square are 27. **18. a.** See p. 848. After 12 months, the graph of the younger child is higher than the graph of the older child. **b.** Let m = number of months, $1200 + 50m > 1500 + 25m$, $50m > 300 + 25m$, $25m > 300$, $m > 12$

19. a.

Monthly Sales	Sun Fashions Total Salary	Today's Outerwear Total Salary
$0	$400	$750
$5000	$1000	$1250
$10000	$1600	$1750
$15000	$2200	$2250
$20000	$2800	$2750
$25000	$3400	$3250

b. sales $\geq$ \$20,000 **c.** Today's Outerwear would pay more for sales less than or equal to \$15,000.

20. a. See right. b. Let v = value of home. $v = 80000 + 3500t$
21. a. for more than seven pictures **b.** for fewer than seven pictures **c.** for exactly seven pictures **22. a.** Sample: **See right.**
b. $x = -14$ **c.** The y-coordinate increases.

16.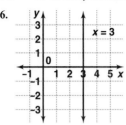

18. a.

20. a.

	A	B	C
1	yrs from now	house value	car value
2	0	80000	14000
3	1	83500	12200
4	2	87000	10400
5	3	90500	8600
6	4	94000	6800
7	5	97500	5000
8	6	101000	3200

22. a. Sample:

The chart below keys the **Progress Self-Test** questions to the objectives in the **Chapter Review** on pages 343–346. This will enable you to locate those **Chapter Review** questions that correspond to questions you missed on the **Progress Self-Test.** The lesson where the material is covered is also indicated on the chart.

Question	1	2	3	4	5	6	7	8	9	10
Objective	E	E	A	A	B	A	B	A	A	C
Lesson	5-3	5-8	5-3	5-8	5-6	5-3	5-6	5-8	5-8	5-9

Question	11	12	13	14	15	16	17	18	19	20
Objective	C	C	C	D	D	H	F	I, F	G	G
Lesson	5-9	5-9	5-9	5-7	5-7	5-1	5-3	5-4, 5-6	5-2	5-2

Question	21	22
Objective	I	J
Lesson	5-4	5-5

CHAPTER 5 REVIEW (pp. 343–346)

1. $A = 2$ **3.** $a = \frac{3}{2}$ **5.** $x = \frac{117}{43} \approx 2.72$ **7.** $x = -4$ **9.** 3 **11.** 45
13. $h \le 145$ **15.** $z > 19$ **17. a.** $x \le -\frac{5}{2}$ **b. See p. 849.**
19. $n < -\frac{7}{2}$ **21.** $x > -4$ **23.** 67.6 **25.** $3x - 21$ **27.** $\frac{x+y}{z}$
29. 6, -10 **31.** 10, -10 **33.** $b = \frac{2A}{h}$ **35.** $w = \frac{1}{2}P - \ell$ **37.** $x = yz$
39. $y = -\frac{5}{4}x + 5$ **41. a.** $x = -1$ **b.** $x = -1$ **c.** They are equal.
43. a. multiply **b.** 16 **c.** distributive **d.** Add $-2x$ **e.** Add 80
45. Sample: Multiply by 12; $3 - 24x = 10x + 108.$ **47.** by $\frac{1}{100}$;
$48t - 1200 = 36t.$ **49. a.** Kate will have $1500 + 45n.$
Melissa will have $2000 + 20n$ **b.** 20 **51.** $2\frac{2}{3}$ years
53. after 312 days **55.** 12 gallons
57. a. Charges

Number of CDs	First club	Second Club
2	$33	$30
4	$51	$49
6	$69	$68
8	$87	$87
10	$105	$106

b. 8 **c.** more than 8 CDs **d.** less than 8 CDs **59. a., d. See right.**
b. In B5; = 10200 + A5 * 100 In C5; = 6750 + A5 * 500 **c.** in the 9th year **e.** This year the soybean crop is worth about twice the corn crop's value. Ten years from now it will be worth about three times as much. **61. See page 849. 63.** True **65.** $x = 5.$
67. See page 849. 69. See page 849. a. $x = 8.48$ **b.** $x < 8.48$
c. $x > 8.48$ **71.** $-5 \le x \le 15; -8 \le y \le 12$ **73. See page 849.**
$x = -4$ when $y = 0.$ **75. a. See page 849. b.** $x = 4$

59. a., d.

	A	B	C	D	E
1	yrs from now	bu. corn	bu. soybeans	corn value	Soybean value
2	0	10200	6750	$26520	$51975
3	1	10300	7250	$26780	$55825
4	2	10400	7750	$27040	$59675
5	3	10500	8250	$27300	$63525
6	4	10600	8750	$27560	$67375
7	5	10700	9250	$27820	$71225
8	6	10800	9750	$28080	$75075
9	7	10900	10250	$28340	$78925
10	8	11000	10750	$28600	$82775
11	9	11100	11250	$28860	$86625
12	10	11200	11750	$29120	$90475

17. b.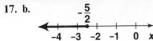
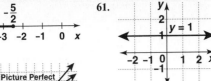

61.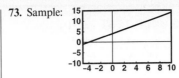

73. Sample: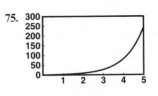

67.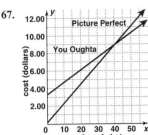

69.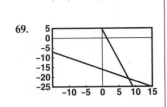

75.

REFRESHER (p. 347)

1. a. 2 **b.** 21 **c.** 7 **3. a.** 7 **b.** 56 **c.** 8 **5. a.** 0.4 **b.** 2.5
7. a. 1.25 or $\frac{5}{4}$ **b.** 0.8 or $\frac{4}{5}$ **9.** 1600 **11.** 0.2 **13.** $\frac{4}{5}$ **15.** $1\frac{7}{8}$
17. 2.5 m **19.** 0.24 lb **21.** -8 **23.** -0.025 **25.** -100 **27.** 0.025;

2.5% **29.** 0.14 **31.** 6.47 **33.** 27% **35. a.** 0.3 **b.** $\frac{3}{10}$ **37. a.** 3
b. $\frac{300}{100}$ **39. a.** 0.0003 **b.** $\frac{3}{10000}$ **41.** 240 **43.** 2942 voters
45. 0 **47.** 21.75 **49.** ≈ 78.54 cm^2

LESSON 6-1 (pp. 350–355)
21. a. $200 \div \frac{1}{4}$ **b.** 800 **23.** $\frac{1}{6}$ **25.** $\frac{4y^2}{21}$ **27. a.** A positive number divided by a positive number is positive. **b.** A negative number divided by a negative number is positive. **c.** A negative number divided by a positive number is negative. **d.** A positive number divided by a negative number is negative. **29. a.** $3B + 2 = 10$ **b.** $2\frac{2}{3}$ kg **31.** 5 **33.** 4.5 m^2

LESSON 6-2 (pp. 356–361)
15. They had enough money for $2\frac{1}{2}$ weeks. **17. a.** 8.9¢ **b.** 13¢
c. 20-ounce can **19. a.** $\frac{1}{4}$ mile per minute **b.** 15 mph
21. John Olerud **23. a.** An error message because division by 0 is undefined. **b.** 0, because $\frac{0}{100} = 0$. **25.** $\frac{1}{2}$ **27.** 12 **29. a.** $180 - a$
b. No. If a supplement were less than 90°, then the angle would be obtuse and not have a complement. **c.** Yes. When an angle is 60°, its complement is 30° and its supplement is 120°. **31. a.** $x < -8$
b. $x < -4$ **c.** $x < -\frac{4}{3}$ **d.** $x > 1$

LESSON 6-3 (pp. 362–367)
13. 182 **15.** reciprocal **17.** bx **19. a.** $\frac{6}{4} = \frac{3}{2}$ **b.** $\frac{9}{4}$ **c.** 2.25
21. 1.69 meters per second **23.** $\frac{3}{2}$ **25.** 48 **27.** 81.8

LESSON 6-4 (pp. 370–375)
15. $\frac{5}{26}$ **17. a.** $P(X)$ because it has the largest probability. **b.** No; relative frequency can vary from experiment to experiment.
19. $\frac{50}{50} = 1$ **21.** (d) **23.** 9.6 quarts orange juice, 14.4 quarts ginger ale **25.** 64 **27.** $m = \frac{16}{3}$ **29. a.** $b - .25b = .75b$
b. $b + .04b = 1.04b$ **c.** $.75b + .04(.75b) = .78b$

LESSON 6-5 (pp. 376–380)
11. 25% **13.** 658 **15.** 51% **17.** 35% **19.** 0.57 **21. a.** $\frac{7}{15}$ **b.** $\frac{15}{7}$
23. a. $245 **b.** rate **25.** 16; -4 **27.** 130.5 **29.** 33%

LESSON 6-6 (pp. 381–386)
11. $\frac{ab}{pq}$ **13. a.** 0.60 **b.** 0.49 **c.** 0.40 **15.** See below.
17. a. $\frac{c}{s}$ **b.** $\frac{d}{n+c+d+s+x}$ **c.** $\frac{n}{n+c+d+s+x}$ **19. a.** 10.152 for the 100m; 10.142 for the 200m **b.** Burrell is about 0.01 m/sec faster. **21.** $\frac{20}{s}$ **23.** -16 **25.** See below. **27.** 23,040

15. Grade Level Groups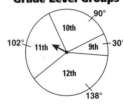

25.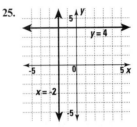

LESSON 6-7 (pp. 387–393)
15. 2.86 kg **17.** (1.5, -7) **19. a.** 8 cm^2; 4.5 cm^2; 3.2768 cm^2;
11.52 cm^2 **b.** False; The area of the image is k^2 the area of the preimage. **21. a.** 78.5% **b.** 0.785 **23.** 37.5% **25. a.** $\frac{1}{86} \approx 0.012$
b. $\frac{1}{86}$ **27.** Answers will vary.

LESSON 6-8 (pp. 394–400)
17. 218.5 cm **19.** 0.005 face
21. a. $\pm\sqrt{22}$ **b.** 4.69; -4.69
23. No **25.** No **27.** Yes; $\frac{-15}{-20}$.
29. a. See right. **b.** 4
c. 12 **d.** The perimeter of the image is three times as large as the perimeter of the preimage. **31.** 75% **33.** -5

29. a.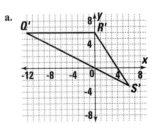

LESSON 6-9 (pp. 402–407)
9. a. $\frac{t}{p}; \frac{w}{k}; \frac{e}{r}$ **b.** $\frac{k}{w}; \frac{r}{e}; \frac{a}{s}$ **11. a.** Drawings will vary. **b.** Sample:
$\frac{6}{t} = \frac{10}{25}$ **c.** 15 ft **13. a.** $\frac{8.7 \text{ cm}}{9 \text{ m}}$ **b.** Sample: $\frac{8.7}{9} = \frac{5.5}{x}$ **c.** 5.7 m
15. $\frac{40}{3}$ **17. a.** $\frac{9}{25}$ **b.** 15; -15 **19.** $\frac{1}{38}$ **21.** 19% **23.** 6 **25.** -3
27. a. 15 **b.** $\frac{23}{8}$ **c.** -15 **d.** 184

CHAPTER 6 PROGRESS SELF-TEST (pp. 411)

1. $15 \cdot -\frac{2}{3} = -10$ **2.** $\frac{x}{9} \cdot \frac{3}{2} = \frac{3x}{18} = \frac{x}{6}$ **3.** $\frac{2b}{3} \cdot \frac{3}{b} = \frac{6b}{3b} = 2$
4. $23y = 22$, $y = \frac{22}{23}$ **5.** $b \cdot b = 25 \cdot 49$, $b^2 = 1225$, $b = 35$ or
$b = -35$ **6.** $8(4g - 3) = 26g$, $32g - 24 = 26g$, $6g = 24$, $g = 4$
7. $0.14 \cdot b = 60$, $b \approx 428.6$ **8.** $\frac{1}{2} = x \cdot \frac{4}{5}$; $x = \frac{1}{2} \cdot \frac{5}{4} = \frac{5}{8}$; $x =$
62.5% **9.** $P(5 \text{ or } 6) = \frac{2}{6} = \frac{1}{3}$ **10.** -1, because $-1 + 1 = 0$, therefore
the fraction is undefined. **11.** 3; x **12. a.** $36 = x \cdot 30$;
$x = \frac{36}{30} = 1.2 = 120\%$ **b.** 20 **13.** The number of animals is $d + c$.
So the ratio of the number of dogs to the number of animals is $\frac{d}{c + d}$.
14. a. $\frac{9}{4}, \frac{4}{9}$ **b.** $\frac{z}{12} = \frac{4}{9}$; $9z = 48$; $z = \frac{48}{9} = 5\frac{1}{3} = 5.\overline{3}$ **15.** $\$295$;
$0.8(x) = 236$, $x = 236 \div 0.8$, $x = 295$ **16.** p pages in 7y min; the
same number of pages are read in less time. **17.** 0.09;
$\frac{36}{400} = \frac{\text{no. with Alzheimer's}}{\text{no. surveyed}}$; 9% **18.** $\frac{30°}{360°} = \frac{1}{12}$ **19.** $\frac{280}{12} = \frac{x}{14}$,
$12x = 3920$; $x = 326.\overline{6}$. To the nearest mile, this is 327 miles.

20. a., b. See below. **21. a.** $\left(\frac{2}{3} \cdot -6, \frac{2}{3} \cdot 4\right) = \left(-4, \frac{8}{3}\right)$
b. contraction **22.** $\frac{x}{7} = \frac{x + 2}{10}$, $10x = 7x + 14$, $3x = 14$,
$x = \frac{14}{3} = 4\frac{2}{3} = $ width; $x + 2 = \frac{20}{3} = 6\frac{2}{3} = $ length
23. $\frac{6 \cdot 8}{14 \cdot 16} = \frac{48}{224} = \frac{3}{14} = \approx 0.21$

20. a., b.

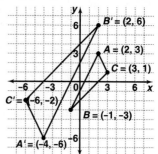

The chart below keys the **Progress Self-Test** questions to the objectives in the **Chapter Review** on pages 412–415. This will enable you to locate those **Chapter Review** questions that correspond to questions you missed on the **Progress Self-Test**. The lesson where the material is covered is also indicated on the chart.

Question	1	2	3	4	5	6	7	8	9	10
Objective	A	A	A	C	C	C	B	B	G	A
Lesson	6-1	6-1	6-1	6-8	6-8	6-8	6-5	6-5	6-4	6-1

Question	11	12	13	14	15	16	17	18	19	20
Objective	D	H	F	L	H	E	G	J	I	K
Lesson	6-8	6-5	6-3	6-9	6-5	6-2	6-4	6-6	6-8	6-7

Question	21	22	23
Objective	K	L	J
Lesson	6-7	6-9	6-6

CHAPTER 6 REVIEW (pp. 412–415)

1. -125 **3.** $\frac{4}{3}$ **5.** $-\frac{8}{5}$ **7.** 240 **9.** -4 **11.** 24 **13.** 200% **15.** 200
17. 156 **19.** $30; -30$ **21.** -3 **23. a.** 8 and 15 **b.** 5 and 24 **25.** $\frac{3}{2}$
27. a. 11 mph **b.** $\frac{1}{11}$ hour per mile **29.** $\frac{1}{6}$ of an hour or 10 min
31. Sample: How much did Tony spend per day? $\frac{400}{d}$ dollars
per day **33. a.** 46 oz: $\approx$ 3.8¢ per oz; 6 oz: $\approx$ 4.7¢ per oz
b. 46-ounce can **35.** 1.7 **37.** 16.7% **39.** $\frac{x}{x + y}$ **41.** $\frac{9}{11}$
43. $\frac{13}{52} = \frac{1}{4}$ **45.** $\frac{999,999}{1,000,000}$ **47.** $\frac{29}{50} = 0.58 = 58\%$ **49.** $\frac{1}{5}$ **51.** 80%
53. 5.9 lb **55.** $\$9.93$ **57.** $\$414.61$ **59.** $\$105$ **61.** 193 **63.** (b)
65. $\frac{7}{16}$ **67. a.** 0.049 **b.** 0.589 **69.** $\frac{1}{6} = 0.167$ **71.** (6, 12) **73. a.,
b.** See right. **c.** contraction **75.** See right. **77.** (c) **79.** No; Ratios
of sides are not equal. **81. a.** 5.5 **b.** 30 **83. a.** Sketches will vary.
b. $\frac{x}{9} = \frac{3}{n}$, $x = \frac{27}{n}$

73. a., b.

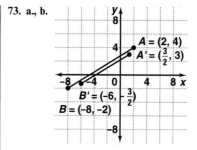

75.

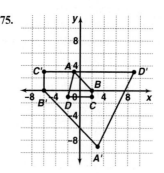

ABS(x)   A BASIC function that gives the absolute value of *x*. (784, 836)

absolute value function   A function with an equation of the form $f(x) = a|x - b| + c$. (784)

absolute value   If $n < 0$, then the absolute value of *n* equals –*n*; if $n \geq 0$, then the absolute value of *n* is *n*. The absolute value of a number is its distance on a number line from the point with coordinate 0. (593)

Absolute Value-Square Root Property   For all real numbers *x*, $\sqrt{x^2} = |x|$. (596)

acute angle   An angle with measure between 0° and 90°.

Adding Like Terms Property   See *Distributive Property: Adding or Subtracting Like Terms.*

addition method for solving a system   The method of adding the sides of two equations to yield a third equation which contains solutions to the system. (682)

Addition Property of Equality   For all real numbers *a, b,* and *c*: if $a = b$, then $a + c = b + c$. (151)

Addition Property of Inequality   For all real numbers *a, b,* and *c*: if $a < b$, then $a + c < b + c$. (200)

additive identity   The number zero. (149)

Additive Identity Property   For any real number *a*: $a + 0 = a$. (149)

additive inverse   The additive inverse of any real number *x* is –*x*. Also called *opposite*. (149)

Algebraic Definition of Division   For any real numbers *a* and *b*, $b \neq 0$: $a \div b = a \cdot \frac{1}{b}$. (350)

Algebraic Definition of Subtraction   For all real numbers *a* and *b*: $a - b = a + {-b}$. (216)

algebraic expression   An expression that includes one or more variables. (23)

algebraic fraction   A fraction which has variables in its numerator or denominator. (86)

algorithm   A finite step-by-step recipe or procedure. (640)

annual yield   The percent the money in an account earns per year. (486)

array   See *rectangular array*. (74)

Area Model for Multiplication (discrete version)   The number of elements in a rectangular array with *x* rows and *y* columns is *xy*. (74)

Area Model for Multiplication   The area of a rectangle with length ℓ and width *w* is ℓw. (72)

"as the crow flies"   The straight line distance between two points. (599)

Associative Property of Addition   For any real numbers *a, b,* and *c*: $(a + b) + c = a + (b + c)$. (145)

Associative Property of Multiplication   For any real numbers *a, b,* and *c*: $(ab)c = a(bc)$. (75)

automatic grapher   A graphing calculator or a computer graphing program that enables equations to be graphed on a coordinate plane. (310)

average   See *mean*.

axes   The perpendicular number lines in a coordinate graph from which the coordinates of points are determined. (155)

axis of symmetry   The line over which a figure coincides with its reflection image. (548)

bar graph   A way of displaying data using rectangles or bars with lengths corresponding to the data. (142)

base   The number *x* in the power x^n. (486)

BASIC   A computer language, short for Beginner's All-purpose Symbolic Instruction Code. (24, 834)

binomial   A polynomial with two terms. (617)

boundary point   A point that separates solutions from nonsolutions on a number line. (469)

box   See *rectangular solid*. (74)

cell   The location or box formed by the intersection of a row and a column in a spreadsheet. (233)

Celsius scale   The temperature scale in which 0° is the freezing point of water and 100° is the boiling point. Also called the centigrade scale. (322)

center of symmetry   A point about which a figure with rotation symmetry can be rotated 180° to coincide with itself. (801)

centigrade scale   See *Celsius scale*. (322)

changing the sense (direction) of an inequality   Changing from < to >, or from ≤ to ≥, or vice-versa. (116)

Chi-Square Statistic   A number calculated from data used to determine whether the difference in two frequency distributions is greater than that expected by chance. (652)

chunking   The process of grouping several bits of information into a single piece of information. In algebra, viewing an entire algebraic expression as one variable. (333)

clearing fractions   Multiplying each side of an equation by a constant to get an equivalent equation without fractions as coefficients. (327)

closed interval   An interval that includes its endpoints. (14)

coefficient   A number multiplied by a variable or variables. In the term –6*x*, –6 is the coefficient of *x*. (178)

coincident lines   Two lines that contain the same points. (695)

column   A vertical list in a table, rectangular array, or spreadsheet. (233)

common denominator   The same denominator for two or more fractions. (720)

common factor   A number that is a factor of two or more given numbers. (721)

Common Factor Sum Property   If *a* is a common factor of *b* and *c*, then it is a factor of $b + c$. (721)

common logarithm function   The function with equation $y = \log x$. (813)

common monomial factoring   Isolating a common factor from each term of a polynomial. (726)

Commutative Property of Addition
For any real numbers a and b:
$a + b = b + a$. (144)

Commutative Property of Multiplication   For any real numbers a and b: $ab = ba$. (73)

Comparison Model for Subtraction
The quantity $x - y$ tells how much quantity x differs from the quantity y. (223)

complementary angles   Two angles whose measures have a sum of $90°$. Also called *complements*. (256)

complementary events   Two events which have no elements in common and whose union is the set of all possible outcomes. (372)

complete factorization   A factorization into prime polynomials in which there are no common numerical factors left in the terms. (727)

complex fraction   A fraction whose numerator and/or denominator contains a fraction. (351)

composite number   A positive integer that has one or more positive integer factors other than 1 and itself. (721)

compound interest   A form of interest payment in which the interest is placed back into the account so that it too earns interest. (487)

Compound Interest Formula
$T = P(1 + i)^n$ where T is the total after n years if a principal P earns an annual yield of i. (488)

condition of the system   A sentence in a system. (666)

constant decrease   A situation in which a positive number is repeatedly subtracted. (425)

constant increase   A situation in which a positive number is repeatedly added. (498)

constant term   A term in a polynomial without a variable. (574)

constant difference   A situation in which the difference of two expressions is a constant. (247)

constant sum   A situation in which the sum of two expressions is a constant. (247)

continuous   A situation in which numbers between any two numbers have meaning. (158)

contraction   A size change in which the factor k is nonzero and between -1 and 1. (388)

coordinate graph   A graph displaying points as ordered pairs of numbers. (155)

coordinates   The numbers identified with a point in the coordinate plane. (156)

coordinate plane   A plane in which every point can be identified by two numbers. (156)

cosine function   A function defined by $y = \cos x$. (813)

cosine of an angle (cos A)   The ratio of sides in a right triangle given by $\cos A = \dfrac{\text{length of leg adjacent}}{\text{length of hypotenuse}}$. (813)

counterexample   An example for which a pattern is false. (39)

cubic unit   The basic unit of volume. (74)

cubing function   The function defined by $y = x^3$. (800)

cursor   An arrow or pixel which may be moved along a graph on an automatic grapher. (312)

default window   The window preprogrammed for use by an automatic grapher when no other window is specified. (311)

degree of a monomial   The sum of the exponents of the variables in the monomial. (616)

degree of a polynomial   The highest degree of any of its terms after the polynomial has been simplified. (617)

degrees of freedom   The number of events minus one, used in the Chi-Square Statistic. (653)

deviation   The absolute value of the difference between an expected number and an actual observed number. (652)

difference of squares   An expression of the form $x^2 - y^2$. (648)

Difference of Two Squares Pattern
$(a + b)(a - b) = a^2 - b^2$. The product of the sum and the difference of two numbers equals the difference of squares of the numbers. (648)

dimensions   The number of rows and columns of an array. The lengths of sides of a rectangle or a rectangular solid. (74)

discount   The percent by which the original price of an item is lowered. (222)

discrete   A situation in which some numbers between given numbers do not have meaning. (13)

discrete set   A set of objects that can be counted. (74)

discriminant   In the quadratic equation $ax^2 + bx + c = 0$, $b^2 - 4ac$. (582)

Discriminant Property   Suppose $ax^2 + bx + c = 0$ and a, b, and c are real numbers with $a \neq 0$. Let $D = b^2 - 4ac$. Then when $D > 0$, the equation has exactly two real solutions. When $D = 0$, the equation has exactly one real solution. When $D < 0$, the equation has no real solutions. (582)

Discriminant Theorem   When a, b, and c are integers, with $a \neq 0$, three conditions happen at exactly the same time:
1. The solutions to $ax^2 + bx + c = 0$ are rational numbers.
2. $b^2 - 4ac$ is a perfect square.
3. $ax^2 + bx + c$ is factorable over the set of polynomials with integer coefficients. (761)

Distance Formula in the Coordinate Plane   The distance AB between points $A = (x_1, y_1)$ and $B = (x_2, y_2)$ is $AB = \sqrt{(x_2 - x_1)^2 + (y_2 - y_1)^2}$. Also called *Pythagorean Distance Formula*. (601)

Distance Formula on a Number Line   If two points on a line have coordinates x_1 and x_2, the distance between them is $|x_1 - x_2|$. (595)

Distributive Property: Adding Fractions   For all real numbers a, b, and c, with $c \neq 0$, $\dfrac{a}{c} + \dfrac{b}{c} = \dfrac{a + b}{c}$. (195)

Distributive Property: Adding or Subtracting Like Terms   For all real numbers a, b, and c: $ac + bc = (a + b)c$ and $ac - bc = (a - b)c$. (177)

Distributive Property: Removing Parentheses   For all real numbers a, b, and c: $c(a + b) = ca + cb$ and $c(a - b) = ca - cb$. (183)

domain   The values which may be meaningfully substituted for a variable. (12)

domain of a function   The set of possible replacements for the first variable in a function. (789)

edge   A line in a plane that separates solutions from nonsolutions. (470)

element   An object in a set. Also called *member*. (11)

empty set   A set which has no elements in it. (19)

END   A BASIC command which stops a program. (30, 836)

endpoints   The smallest and largest numbers in an interval. The points A and B in the segment $\overline{AB}$. (14)

Equal Fractions Property   For all numbers a, b, and k, if $k \neq 0$ and $b \neq 0$, then $\frac{a}{b} = \frac{ak}{bk}$. (87)

equal sets   Two sets that have the same elements. (11)

equally likely outcomes   Outcomes in a situation where the likelihood of each outcome is assumed to be the same. (381)

equation   A sentence with an equal sign. (6)

equivalent formulas   Formulas in which every set of values that satisfies one formula also satisfies the other. (323)

equivalent systems   Systems with exactly the same solutions. (687)

evaluating an expression   Finding the numerical value of an expression. (23)

event   A set of possible outcomes. (371)

expanding a power of a polynomial   Writing the power of a polynomial as a single polynomial. (646)

expansion   A size change in which the size change factor k is greater than 1 or less than –1. (388)

expected number   The mean frequency of a given event that is predicted by probability. (651)

exponent   The number n in the power x^n. (486)

exponential decay   A situation in which the original amount is repeatedly multiplied by a growth factor between zero and one. (505)

exponential function   A function with an equation of the form $y = ab^x$. (775)

exponential growth   A situation in which the original amount is repeatedly multiplied by a growth factor greater than one. (493)

exponential curves   Graphs of equations of the form $y = b \cdot g^x$, where $b \neq 0$, $g > 0$, and $g \neq 1$. (493)

Extended Distributive Property   To multiply two sums, multiply each term in the first sum by each term in the second sum. (634)

extremes   The numbers a and d in the proportion $\frac{a}{b} = \frac{c}{d}$. (394)

f(x)   The value of the function f at x. (778)

factorial   The product of the integers from 1 to a given number. $n! = 1 \cdot 2 \cdot \ldots \cdot (n - 1) \cdot n$. (126)

factoring   The process of expressing a given number (or expression) as the product of two or more numbers (or expressions). (726)

factorization   The result of factoring a number or expression. (727)

factors   Numbers or expressions whose product is a given number or expression. If $ab = c$, then a and b are factors of c. (720)

Fahrenheit scale   A temperature scale in which $32°$ is the freezing point and $212°$ is the boiling point. (322)

fitting a line to data   Finding a line that closely describes data points which themselves may not all lie on a line. (458)

FOIL algorithm   A method for multiplying two binomials; the sum of the product of the First terms, plus the product of the Outside terms, plus the product of the Inside terms, plus the product of the Last terms: $(a + b)(c + d) = ac + ad + bc + bd$. (640)

FOR/NEXT loop   A sequence of steps in a BASIC program which enables a procedure to be repeated a certain number of times. (191, 835)

formula   A sentence in which one variable is given in terms of other variables and numbers. (27)

frequency   The number of times an event occurs. (370)

function   A set of ordered pairs in which each first coordinate appears with exactly one second coordinate. (774)

function key on a calculator   A key which produces the value of a function when a value in the domain is entered. (812)

function notation   Notation to indicate a function, such as $f(x)$, and read as "f of x". (778)

general form of a linear equation   An equation of the form $ax + b = cx + d$, where $a \neq 0$. (299)

general form of a quadratic equation   A quadratic equation in which one side is 0 and the other side is arranged in descending order of exponents: $ax^2 + bx + c = 0$, where $a \neq 0$. (573)

Generalized Addition Property of Equality   For all numbers or expressions a, b, c, and d: if $a = b$ and $c = d$, then $a + c = b + d$. (681)

GOTO   A BASIC command which tells the computer to go to the indicated program line number. (836)

greatest common factor for integers   The greatest integer that is a common factor of two or more integers. (726)

greatest common factor for monomials   The product of the greatest common factor of their coefficients and the greatest common factor of their variables. (726)

growth factor   In exponential growth or decay, the nonzero number which is repeatedly multiplied by the original amount. (493)

growth model for powering   When an amount is multiplied by g, the growth factor in each of x time periods, then after the x periods, the original amount will be multiplied by g^x. (493)

half-plane   In a plane, the region on either side of a line. (470)

hard copy   A paper copy printed by a computer or calculator of a graph or other information on a screen. (313)

horizontal line A line with an equation of the form $y = k$, where k is a fixed real number. (285)

hypotenuse The longest side of a right triangle. (45)

IF . . . THEN A BASIC command which tells the computer to perform the THEN part only if the IF part is true. (111, 835)

image The final figure resulting from a transformation. (164)

inequality A sentence with one of the following signs: "$\neq$", "$<$", "$>$", "$\leq$", or "$\geq$". (7)

INPUT A BASIC statement that makes the computer pause and wait for a value of the variable to be entered. (30, 834)

instance An example for which a pattern is true. (37)

integers The whole numbers and their opposites. (12)

interest The money a bank pays on the principal in an account. (486)

intersection of sets The set of elements in both set A and set B, written $A \cap B$. (17)

interval The set of numbers between two numbers a and b, possibly including a or b. (14)

irrational number A real number that is not rational. A number that can be written as a nonrepeating infinite decimal. (755)

latitude A measure of the distance of a place on Earth north or south
of the equator, given in degrees. (456)

leg of a right triangle One of the sides forming the right angle of a triangle. (45)

LET A BASIC command which assigns a value to a given variable. (30, 834)

like terms Two or more terms in which the variables and corresponding exponents are the same. (178)

linear equation An equation in which the variable or variables are all to the first power and none multiply each other. (267)

linear expression An expression in which all variables are to the first power. (190)

linear function A function with an equation of the form $y = mx + b$. (775)

linear inequality A linear sentence with an inequality symbol. (317, 472)

linear polynomial A polynomial of degree one. (618)

linear sentence A sentence in which the variable or variables are all to the first power and none multiply each other. (618)

linear system A system of equations, each of degree one. (665)

log (x) The common logarithm of x. (813)

loop Repetition of a set of instructions in a computer program. (191, 835)

magnitude of a size change See *size change factor*. (388)

mark-up A percent by which the original price of an item is raised. (222)

maximum The greatest value in a set of numbers; the highest point on a graph. (223, 550)

mean The sum of the numbers in a collection divided by the number of numbers in the collection. Also called *average*. (725)

means The numbers b and c in the proportion $\frac{a}{b} = \frac{c}{d}$. (394)

Means-Extremes Property For all real numbers $a, b, c,$ and d (b and d nonzero): if $\frac{a}{b} = \frac{c}{d}$, then $ad = bc$. (395)

median In a collection consisting of an odd number of numbers in numerical order, the middle number. In a collection of an even number of numbers arranged in numerical order, the average of the two middle terms. (725)

member An object in a set. Also called *element*. (11)

minimum The smallest value in a set of numbers; the lowest point on a graph. (223, 550)

mirror image The reflection image of a figure. (548)

mode The object(s) in a collection that appear(s) most often. (725)

model A general pattern for an operation that includes many of the uses of the operation. (72)

monomial A polynomial with one term. An expression that can be written as a real number, a variable, or a product of a real number and one or more variables with non-negative exponents. (616)

multiple of a number n A number that has n as a factor. (720)

Multiplication Counting Principle If one choice can be made in m ways and a second choice can be made in n ways, then there are mn ways of making the choices in order. (119)

Multiplication of Positive and Negative Numbers The product of an odd number of negative numbers is negative, and the product of an even number of negative numbers is positive. (98)

Multiplication Property of –1 For any real number a: $a \cdot -1 = -1 \cdot a = -a$. (97)

Multiplication Property of Equality For all real numbers $a, b,$ and c: if $a = b$, then $ca = cb$. (102)

Multiplication Property of Inequality If $x < y$ and a is positive, then $ax < ay$. If $x < y$ and a is negative, then $ax > ay$. (114, 116)

Multiplication Property of Zero For any real number a: $a \cdot 0 = 0 \cdot a = 0$. (81)

Multiplicative Identity Property of One For any real number a: $a \cdot 1 = 1 \cdot a = a$. (79)

multiplicative identity The number 1. (79)

multiplicative inverse The multiplicative inverse of a nonzero number n is $\frac{1}{n}$. Also called *reciprocal*. (79)

Multiplying Fractions Property For all real numbers a and c, and all nonzero b and d: $\frac{a}{b} \cdot \frac{c}{d} = \frac{ac}{bd}$. (86)

Multiplying Positive and Negative Numbers If two numbers have the same sign, their product is positive. If the two numbers have different signs, their product is negative. (97)

multiplying through The process of multiplying each side of an equation by a common multiple of the denominators to result in an equation for which all coefficients are integers. (327)

n factorial (*n*!) The product of the integers from 1 to *n*. (126)

Negative Exponent Property For all *n* and all nonzero *b*, $b^{-n} = \frac{1}{b^n}$, the reciprocal of b^n. (516)

nth power The nth power of a number *x* is the number x^n. (486)

null set A set which has no elements in it. Also called *empty set*. (19)

numerical expression An expression which includes numbers and operations and no variables. (23)

oblique line A line which is neither horizontal nor vertical. (465)

obtuse angle An angle with measure greater than 90° and less than 180°.

open interval An interval that does not include its endpoints. (14)

open sentence A sentence that contains at least one variable. (7)

Opposite of a Difference Property For all real numbers *a* and *b*, $-(a - b) = -a + b$. (241)

Opposite of a Sum Property For all real numbers *a* and *b*, $-(a + b) = -a + -b = -a - b$. (240)

Opposite of Opposites Property (Op-op Property) For any real number *a*: $-(-a) = a$. (150)

opposite The opposite of any real number *x* is -*x*. Also called *additive inverse*. (97)

order of operations The correct order of evaluating numerical expressions: first, work inside parentheses, then do powers. Then do multiplications or divisions, from left to right. Then do additions or subtractions, from left to right. (23)

origin The point (0, 0) on a coordinate plane. (155)

outcome A result of an experiment. (371)

parabola The curve that is the graph of an equation of the form $y = ax^2 + bx + c$, where $a \neq 0$. (548)

pattern A general idea for which there are many instances. (37)

P(E) The probability of event *E* or "*P* of *E*." (371)

percent (%), times $\frac{1}{100}$, or "per 100." (376)

percent of discount The ratio of the discount to the original price. (363)

percent of tax The ratio of tax to the selling price. (363)

perfect square A number which is the square of a whole number. (32)

perfect square trinomial A trinomial which is the square of a binomial. (647)

Perfect Square Patterns
$(a + b)^2 = a^2 + 2ab + b^2$ and
$(a - b)^2 = a^2 - 2ab + b^2$. (647)

permutation An arrangement of letters, names, or objects. (126)

Permutation Theorem There are *n*! possible permutations of *n* different objects, when each object is used exactly once. (126)

plus or minus symbol (±) A symbol which shows that a calculation should be done twice, once by adding and once by subtracting. (574)

polynomial An algebraic expression that is either a monomial or a sum of monomials. (617)

polynomial function A function whose range values are given by a polynomial. (800)

polynomial in the variable x An expression of the form $a_n x^n + a_{n-1} x^{n-1} + \ldots a_1 x + a_0$, where $a_0, a_1, \ldots, a_n$ are real numbers. (617)

polynomial over the integers A polynomial with integer coefficients. (727)

population density The number of people per unit of area. (360)

power An expression written in the form x^n. (486)

Power of a Power Property For all *m* and *n*, and all nonzero *b*, $(b^m)^n = b^{mn}$. (512)

Power of a Product Property For all *n*, and all nonzero *a* and *b*, $(ab)^n = a^n \cdot b^n$. (527)

Power of a Quotient Property For all *n*, and all nonzero *a* and *b*, $\left(\frac{a}{b}\right)^n = \frac{a^n}{b^n}$. (529)

preimage The original figure before a transformation takes place. (164)

prime factorization The writing of a number as a product of primes. (722)

prime number An integer greater than 1 whose only integer factors are itself and 1. (721)

prime polynomial A polynomial which cannot be factored into polynomials of a lower degree. (727)

principal Money deposited in an account. (486)

PRINT A BASIC command which tells the computer to print what follows the command. (30, 834)

Probability Formula for Geometric Regions If all points occur randomly in a region, then the probability *P* of an event is given by $P = \frac{\text{measure of region for event}}{\text{measure of entire region}}$, where the measure may be length, area, etc. (382)

probability function A function that maps a set of outcomes onto their probabilities. (795)

probability of an event A number from 0 to 1 that measures the likelihood that an event will occur. (371)

Product of Powers Property For all *m* and *n*, and all nonzero *b*, $b^m \cdot b^n = b^{m+n}$. (510)

Product of Square Roots Property For all nonnegative real numbers *a* and *b*, $\sqrt{a} \cdot \sqrt{b} = \sqrt{ab}$. (587)

projectile An object that is thrown, dropped, or shot by an external force and continues to move on its own. (567)

Property of Opposites For any real number *a*: $a + -a = 0$. (149)

Property of Reciprocals For any nonzero real number *a*: $a \cdot \frac{1}{a} = \frac{1}{a} \cdot a = 1$. (79)

proportion A statement that two fractions are equal. Any equation of the form $\frac{a}{b} = \frac{c}{d}$. (394)

Putting-Together Model for Addition If a quantity *x* is put together with a quantity *y* with the same units and if there is no overlap, then the result is the quantity *x* + *y*. (143)

Pythagorean Distance Formula See *Distance Formula in the Coordinate Plane.*

Pythagorean Theorem In a right triangle with legs *a* and *b* and hypotenuse *c*, $a^2 + b^2 = c^2$. (46)

870

quadrant   One of the four regions of the coordinate plane formed by the x-axis and y-axis. (163)

quadratic equation   An equation that can be written in the form $ax^2 + bx + c = 0$. (573)

Quadratic Formula   If $a \neq 0$ and $ax^2 + bx + c = 0$, then $x = \frac{-b \pm \sqrt{b^2 - 4ac}}{2a}$. (574)

quadratic function   A function with an equation of the form $y = ax^2 + bx + c$ or $y = \frac{k}{x}$. (775)

quadratic polynomial   A polynomial of degree two. (618)

Quotient of Powers Property   For all m and n, and all nonzero b, $\frac{b^m}{b^n} = b^{m-n}$. (521)

radical sign ($\sqrt{\ }$)   The symbol for square root. (31)

random outcomes   Outcomes in a situation where each outcome is assumed to have the same probability. (372)

range   The length of an interval. The maximum value minus the minimum value. (223)

range of a function   The set of possible values of a function. (789)

Rate Factor Model for Multiplication   When a rate is multiplied by another quantity, the unit of the product is the product of units. Units are multiplied as though they were fractions. The product has meaning when the units have meaning. (92)

Rate Model for Division   If a and b are quantities with different units, then $\frac{a}{b}$ is the amount of quantity a per quantity b. (356)

rate of change   The rate of change between points (x_1, y_1) and (x_2, y_2) is $\frac{y_2 - y_1}{x_2 - x_1}$. (419)

ratio   A quotient of quantities with the same units. (363)

Ratio Model for Division   Let a and b be quantities with the same units. Then the ratio $\frac{a}{b}$ compares a to b. (363)

ratio of similitude   The ratio of corresponding sides of two similar figures. (402)

rational number   A number that can be written as the ratio of two integers. (754)

real numbers   Numbers which can be represented as finite or infinite decimals. (12)

reciprocal   The reciprocal of a nonzero number n is $\frac{1}{n}$. Also called *multiplicative inverse*. (79)

Reciprocal of a Fraction Property   If $a \neq 0$ and $b \neq 0$ the reciprocal of $\frac{a}{b}$ is $\frac{b}{a}$. (80)

reciprocal rates   Two rates in which the quantities are compared in reverse order. (93)

rectangular array   A two-dimensional display of numbers or symbols arranged in rows and columns. (74)

rectangular solid   A 3-dimensional figure with 6 rectangular faces. (74)

reflection symmetry   The property held by a figure that coincides with its image under a reflection over a line. Also called *symmetry with respect to a line*. (548)

relation   A set of ordered pairs. (775)

relative frequency   The ratio of the number of times an event occurred to the total number of possible occurrences. (370)

Relative Frequency of an Event   Suppose a particular event has occurred with a frequency of f times in a total of T opportunities for it to happen. Then the relative frequency of the event is $\frac{f}{T}$. (370)

REM   A BASIC statement for a remark or explanation that will be ignored by the computer. (835)

Removing Parentheses Property   See *Distributive Property*. (183)

Repeated Multiplication Model for Powering   When n is a positive integer, $x^n = x \cdot x \cdot \ldots \cdot x$ where there are n factors of x. (486)

replication   The process of copying a formula in a spreadsheet in which the cell references in the original formula are adjusted for new positions in the spreadsheet. (235)

right angle   An angle with measure $90°$.

rotation symmetry   A property held by some figures where a rotation of some amount other than $360°$ results in an image which coincides with the original image. (801)

row   A horizontal list in a table, rectangular array, or spreadsheet. (233)

scatterplot   A two-dimensional coordinate graph of individual points. (156)

scientific notation   A number represented as $x \cdot 10^n$, where $1 \leq x < 10$ and n is an integer. (829–833)

sentence   Two algebraic expressions connected by "$=$", "$\neq$", "$<$", "$>$", "$\leq$", "$\geq$", or "$\approx$". (6)

sequence   A set of numbers or objects in a specific order. (188)

set   A collection of objects called elements. (11)

similar figures   Two or more figures that have the same shape. (402)

simple fraction   A numerical expression of the form $\frac{a}{b}$, where a and b are integers. (754)

simplifying radicals   Rewriting a radical with a smaller integer under the radical sign. (588)

sine function   The function defined by $y = \sin x$. (813)

sine of an angle (sin A)   In a right triangle, $\sin A = \frac{\text{length of the leg opposite}}{\text{length of the hypotenuse}}$. (813)

sinusoidal curve   The curve that is the graph of a sine or cosine function. (813)

size change   A transformation in which the image of (x,y) is (kx, ky). (387)

size change factor   The number k in the transformation in which the image of (x, y) is (kx, ky). Also called *magnitude*. (387)

Size Change Model for Multiplication   If a quantity x is multiplied by a size change factor k, $k \neq 0$, then the resulting quantity is kx. (388)

Slide Model for Addition   If a slide x is followed by a slide y, the result is the slide $x + y$. (143)

Slope and Parallel Lines Property   If two lines have the same slope, then they are parallel. (694)

slope   The rate of change between points on a line. The amount of change in the height of the line as you go 1 unit to the right. The slope of the line through (x_1, y_1) and (x_2, y_2) is $\frac{y_2 - y_1}{x_2 - x_1}$. (432)

871

slope-intercept form An equation of a line in the form $y = mx + b$, where m is the slope and b is the y-intercept. (439)

Slope-Intercept Property The line with equation $y = mx + b$ has slope m and y-intercept b. (440)

solution A replacement of the variable(s) in a sentence that makes the sentence true. (7)

solution set of an open sentence The set of numbers from the domain that are solutions. (12)

solution set to a system The intersection of the solution sets for each of the sentences in the system. (666)

spreadsheet A computer program in which data are presented in a table and calculations upon entries in the table can be made. The table itself. (232)

SQR(X) A BASIC function that gives the square root of x. (812, 836)

Square of the Square Root Property For any nonnegative number n, $\sqrt{n} \cdot \sqrt{n} = n$. (33)

square root If $A = s^2$, then s is a square root of A. (31)

square unit The basic unit for area. (72)

squaring function A function defined by $y = x^2$. (778)

stacked bar graph A display of data using rectangles or bars stacked on top of each other. (143)

standard form for an equation of a line An equation of the form $Ax + By = C$, where not both A and B are zero. (464)

standard form of a prime factorization The form of a factorization where the factors are primes in increasing order and where exponents are used if primes are repeated. (722)

standard form of a polynomial A polynomial written with the terms in descending order of the exponents of its terms, with the largest exponent first. (618)

standard form of a quadratic equation An equation written in the form $ax^2 + bx + c = 0$, where $a \neq 0$. (576)

STEP A BASIC command that tells the computer how much to add to the counter each time through a FOR/NEXT loop. (556, 835)

stopping distance The length of time for a car to slow down from the instant the brake is applied until the car is no longer moving. (554)

substitution method for solving a system A method in which one variable is written in terms of other variables, and then this expression is used in place of the original variable in subsequent equations. (672)

supplementary angles Two angles whose measures have a sum of 180°. Also called *supplements*. (254)

symmetric Having some symmetry. See *reflection symmetry* and *rotation symmetry*. (548)

symmetry with respect to a line See *reflection symmetry*.

system A set of conditions separated by the word *and*. (666)

system of equations A system in which the conditions are equations. (666)

system of inequalities A system in which the conditions are inequalities. (704)

Take-Away Model for Subtraction If a quantity y is taken away from an original quantity x, the quantity left is $x - y$. (221)

tangent function A function defined by $y = \tan x$. (807)

tangent of an angle (tan A) The ratio of sides given by
$$\tan A = \frac{\text{length of leg opposite}}{\text{length of leg adjacent}}.$$ (808)

term A number, a variable, or a product of numbers and variables. (178)

testing a special case A strategy for determining whether a pattern is true by trying out specific instances. (535)

theorem A property that has been proved to be true. (46)

Third Side Property If x and y are the lengths of two sides of a triangle, and $x > y$, then the length z of the third side must satisfy the inequality $x - y < z < x + y$. (263)

tick marks Marks on the x and y axes of a graph to show distance. (312)

tolerance The specific amount that manufactured parts are allowed to vary from an accepted standard size. (598)

trace An option on an automatic grapher that allows the user to move a cursor along the graph while displaying the coordinates of the point the cursor indicates. (312)

translation A two-dimensional slide. (164)

tree-diagram A tree-like way of organizing the possibilities of choices in a situation. (120)

Triangle Inequality The sum of the lengths of two sides of any triangle is greater than the length of the third side. (261)

Triangle-Sum Theorem In any triangle with angle measures a, b, and c: $a + b + c = 180$. (255)

trigonometry The study of the trigonometric functions sine, cosine, and tangent, and their properties. (813)

trinomial A polynomial with three terms. (617)

two dimensional slide A transformation in which the image of (x, y) is $(x + h, y + k)$. (164)

undefined slope The situation regarding the slope of a vertical line, which does not exist. (435)

union of sets The set of elements in either set A or set B, written $A \cup B$. (18)

Unique Factorization Theorem Every integer can be represented as a product of primes in exactly one way, disregarding order of the factors. (722)

Unique Factorization Theorem for Polynomials Every polynomial can be represented as a product of prime polynomials in exactly one way, disregarding order and real number multiples. (727)

value of a function The value of the second variable (often called y) in a function for a given value of the first variable. (774)

variable A letter or other symbol that can be replaced by a number (or other object). (6)

Venn diagram A diagram used to show relationships among sets. (18)

vertex The intersection of a parabola with its axis of symmetry. (548)

vertical line A line with an equation of the form $x = h$, where h is a fixed real number. (286)

volume The space contained by a three-dimensional figure. The volume of a rectangular solid is the product of its dimensions. (74)

whole numbers The set of numbers {0, 1, 2, 3, . . . }. (12)

window The part of the coordinate grid that is shown on an automatic grapher. (310)

x-axis The horizontal axis in a coordinate graph. (163)

x-coordinate The first coordinate of a point. (163)

x-intercept The x-coordinate of a point where a graph crosses the x-axis. (446)

y-axis The vertical axis in a coordinate graph. (163)

y-coordinate The second coordinate of a point. (163)

y-intercept The y-coordinate of a point where a graph crosses the y-axis. (439)

Zero Exponent Property If g is any nonzero real number, then $g^0 = 1$. (493)

Zero Product Property For any real numbers a and b, if $ab = 0$, then $a = 0$ or $b = 0$. (739)

zoom A feature on an automatic grapher that allows the user to see a graph on a window of different dimensions without having to input the dimensions. (313)

$=$	is equal to	$f(x)$	function notation "f of x"; the second coordinates of the points of a function
$\neq$	is not equal to		
$<$	is less than	(x, y)	ordered pair x, y
$\leq$	is less than or equal to	$N(E)$	the number of elements in set E
$\approx$	is approximately equal to	$P(E)$	the probability of an event E
$>$	is greater than	$P(A \text{ and } B)$	the probability that A and B occur
$\geq$	is greater than or equal to	$\tan A$	tangent of $\angle A$
$\pm$	plus or minus	$\sin A$	sine of $\angle A$
π	Greek letter pi; $= 3.141592...$ or $\approx \frac{22}{7}$	$\cos A$	cosine of $\angle A$
A'	image of point A	ABS(X)	in BASIC, the absolute value of X
$\overleftrightarrow{AB}$	line through A and B	SQR(X)	in BASIC, the square root of X
$\overrightarrow{AB}$	ray starting at A and containing B	X * X	in BASIC, X $\cdot$ X
$\overline{AB}$	segment with endpoints A and B	X ^ Y	in BASIC, X^Y
AB	length of segment from A to B	$\boxed{1/x}$	calculator reciprocal key
$\angle ABC$	angle ABC	$\boxed{y^x}$	calculator powering key
$m\angle ABC$	measure of angle ABC	$\boxed{x^2}$	calculator squaring function key
$\triangle ABC$	triangle ABC		
$\{\ldots\}$	the symbol used for a set	$\boxed{\sqrt{\ }}$	calculator square root function key
$\emptyset, \{\ \}$	the empty or null set	$\boxed{x!}$	calculator factorial function key
$A \cap B$	the intersection of sets A and B		
$A \cup B$	the union of sets A and B	$\boxed{\tan}$	calculator tangent function key
W	the set of whole numbers		
I	the set of integers	$\boxed{\sin}$	calculator sine function key
R	the set of real numbers	$\boxed{\cos}$	calculator cosine function key
$\ulcorner$	symbol for 90° angle	$\boxed{\log}$	calculator logarithm function key
$\%$	percent		
$\sqrt{\ }$	square root symbol; radical sign	$\boxed{\text{INV}}$, $\boxed{\text{2nd}}$, or $\boxed{\text{F}}$	calculator second function key
$\sqrt{n}$	positive square root of n		
$\lvert x \rvert$	absolute value of x	$\boxed{\text{EE}}$ or $\boxed{\text{EXP}}$	calculator scientific notation key
$-x$	opposite of x		
$n°$	n degrees		
$n!$	n factorial		

885

Acknowledgments

Unless otherwise acknowledged, all photographs are the property of Scott, Foresman and Company. Page abbreviations are as follows: (T) top, (C) center, (B) bottom, (L) left, (R) right.

COVER & TITLE PAGE Steven Hunt (c)1994 **vi(L)** Stephen Studd/Tony Stone Images **vi(R)** George Hall/Check Six **vii** Uniphoto **viii** Index Stock International **ix** Nadia Mackenzie/Tony Stone Images **x(R)** Pete McArthur/Tony Stone Images **x(L)** West Light **3** AP/Wide World **4-5T** Profiles West **4C** Stephen Studd/Tony Stone Images **4BL** Backgrounds/West Light **4BR** Michael Mazzeo/The Stock Market **5** Ed Manowicz/Tony Stone Images **6** Tom Ives **8** Clive Brunskill/ALLSPORT USA **9** PhotoFest **11** B.Markel/Gamma-Liaison **13** Bob Daemmrich/The Image Works **15** Louis Psihoyos/Matrix **16** Hank Ketcham **17** Clearwater Florida Fire and Police Departments of Public Safety **20** Tony Freeman/Photo Edit **21** Paul Conklin **22** Rita Boseruf **26T** Library of Congress **26C&B** Courtesy United Air Lines **27** Michael Newman/Photo Edit **28** Robinson/ANIMALS ANIMALS **29B** Zig Leszczynski/ANIMALS ANIMALS **30** California Institute of Technology **31** Sidney Harris **35** Milt & Joan Mann/Cameramann International, Ltd. **37** Lawrence Migdale **38** Dr. Duane de Temple **39** Bob Daemmrich/Tony Stone Images **41** Photo: Bill Hogan/Copyrighted, Chicago Tribune Company, all rights reserved, **45** The Vatican/Art Resource, New York **53** L.Rorke/The Image Works **55** David Spangler **59** NASA **60B** Telegraph Color Library/FPG **60T** Eddie Adams/Leo de Wys **70-71T** Tony Hallas/SPL/Photo Researchers **70C** George Hall/Check Six **70-71B** David Lawrence/Panoramic Stock Images **71C** Steven E.Sutton/Duomo Photography Inc. **72** Robert Frerck/Odyssey Productions, Chicago **74-75** Tony Stone Images **76** NASA **79** Martha Swope **82** Milt & Joan Mann/Cameramann International, Ltd. **85** AP/Wide World **89** Christopher Morris/Black Star **91** Focus On Sports **92** Milt & Joan Mann/Cameramann International, Ltd. **93** Bob Daemmrich/Stock Boston **94** John Elk III/Stock Boston **95** David Falconer/David R. Frazier Photolibrary **96** JPL/NASA **99B** Grant Heilman/Grant Heilman Photography **101** Johnny Johnson/ANIMALS ANIMALS **104** Pasley/Stock Boston **105** THE COMING AND GOING OF THE PONY EXPRESS by Remington, Thomas Gilcrease Institute of American History & Art, Tulsa **106** Don DuBroff Photo **107T** Mary Kate Denny/Photo Edit **107B** Conte/ANIMALS ANIMALS **108** Michael Newman/Photo Edit **109** Milt & Joan Mann/Cameramann International, Ltd. **112** Robert Frerck/Tony Stone Images **113** Robert Frerck/Odyssey Productions, Chicago **117** Milt & Joan Mann/Cameramann International, Ltd. **118** Scala/Art Resource, New York **119** Alex S.MacLean/Landslides **120** Bob Daemmrich **122** Milt & Joan Mann/Cameramann International, Ltd. **125** Patrick Ward/Stock Boston **126** AP/Wide World **129** Chip Henderson/Tony Stone Images **131T** Julian Baum/SPL/Photo Researchers **131B** Ken Korsh/FPG **132T** Charly Franklin/FPG **132C** Scott Spiker/The Stock Shop **132B** Donovan Reese/Tony Stone Images **134** Ron Thomas/FPG **135** Bob Daemmrich/Stock Boston **140B** Telegraph Colour Library/FPG **140-141(TR)** Imtek Imagineering/Masterfile **140TL** Pelton & Associates/West Light **140-141C** G.Biss/Masterfile **141B** Uniphoto **143** Milt & Joan Mann/Cameramann International, Ltd. **144** Mark Burnett/Photo Edit **146** William Johnson/Stock Boston **149** Kevin Syms/David R. Frazier Photolibrary **150** Robert W.Ginn/Photo Edit **155** Jeff Greenberg/dMRp/Photo Edit **156** Jeff Greenberg/dMRp/Photo Edit **157** Rick Maiman/Sygma **160** David R. Frazier Photolibrary **165** Andy Hayt 1994 **167** Lee Boltin **169** Mark Twain National Forest/U.S.Forestry Service **172** J.C.Stevenson/ANIMALS ANIMALS **174** William Johnson/Stock Boston **177** Milt & Joan Mann/Cameramann International, Ltd. **179** Milt & Joan Mann/Cameramann International, Ltd. **182** Janice Rubin/Black Star **184** Mary Kate Denny/Photo Edit **185** Milt & Joan Mann/Cameramann International, Ltd. **187** Elk/Bruce Coleman Inc. **188** Scott Camazine/Photo Researchers **190** Art Pahlke **195** FPG **196** Reuters/Bettmann **197** Milt & Joan Mann/Cameramann International, Ltd. **198** Freeman/Grishaber/Photo Edit **199** Ralph Nelson, Jr./PhotoFest **200ALL** Carol Zacny **201** Leslye Borden/Photo Edit **205C** Ken Reid/FPG **205BL** Bruce Bishop/PhotoFile **205BR** Marc Chamberlain/Tony Stone Images **206T** John Terence Turner/FPG **206B** The name Cuisenaire and the color sequences of the rods, squares, and cubes are registered trademarks of the Cuisenaire Company of America, Inc. **214-215T** Steven Curtis **214CL** Gordon Wilts/Adventure Photo **214CR** C.Moore/West Light **214-215B** Gerry Ellis Nature Photography **215C** Perry Conway/The Stock Broker **216** Jan Kanter **219** Jim Pickerell/Stock Boston **220B** Museum of Modern Art/Film Stills Archive **221** Naoki Okamoto/The Stock Market **222** Photo Edit **223** Mike Penney/David R. Frazier Photolibrary **224** James Blank/Bruce Coleman Inc. **225** Beryl Goldberg **226** Independence National Historical Park Collection **227** JPL/NASA **228-229** Don W.Fawcett/Visuals Unlimited **230** Sygma **232** Karen Usiskin **233** David Young-Wolff/Photo Edit **234** The Stock Market **240** Reproduced from the Story of the Great American West ©1977 The Readers Digest Association, Inc. Used by permission. Artist: David K.Stone **243** Milt & Joan Mann/Cameramann International, Ltd. **245** David R. Frazier Photolibrary **246** Milt & Joan Mann/Cameramann International, Ltd. **249** Tony Freeman/Photo Edit **250** Max Gibbs/Oxford Scientific Films/ANIMALS ANIMALS **251** Tony Stone Images **253** Milt & Joan Mann/Cameramann International, Ltd. **255** Sygma **257** Focus On Sports **260** Copyright, National Geographic Society **261** Stacy Pick/Stock Boston **268** Milt & Joan Mann/Cameramann International, Ltd. **272** Rhodes/Earth Scenes **273** Milt & Joan Mann/Cameramann International, Ltd. **274** Adamsmith Productions/ West Light **275L** Telegraph Color Library/FPG **282-283T** The Stock Market **282C** Charly Franklin/FPG **282BL** Ron Watts/West Light **282-283B** Jean Miele/The Stock Market **283C** Jeff Schultz/Leo de Wys **284** M.Richards/Photo Edit **285** Phil McCarten/Photo Edit **290** Focus On Sports **291** Milt & Joan Mann/Cameramann International, Ltd. **293** Milt & Joan Mann/Cameramann International, Ltd. **294** Carol Zacny **297** Jerry Wachter/Focus On Sports **300** Bob Daemmrich/Stock Boston **302** Focus On Sports **304** Arthur Rackham Illustration **309** Courtesy General Electric Corp. **315** Michael Newman/Photo Edit **317** Stephen McBrady/Photo Edit **318T** John Stern/Earth Scenes **318B** Donald Specker/Earth Scenes **321** John Neubauer/Photo Edit **322** Scott Zapel **325** Danny Daniels/AlaskaStock Images **326T** Gail McCann/Photo Researchers **326B** Jerry Cooke **327** Focus On Sports **328** Milt & Joan Mann/Cameramann International, Ltd. **330** Joanne K.Peterson **331** Nick Sapiena/Stock Boston **337** Milt & Joan Mann/Cameramann International, Ltd. **338T** C.Brewer/H. Armstrong Roberts **338C** Dave Reede/First Light **338-339B** Alan Briere/Natural Selection **339T** Chris Springman/PhotoFile **339** Charly Franklin/FPG **348-349T** R.Gage/FPG **348CL** Robert George Young/Masterfile **348CR** Charly Franklin/FPG **348-349B** Richard Fukubara/West Light **349C** Index Stock International **350** David R. Austen/Stock Boston **353** Robert Torre/Tony Stone Images **355** Yoram Lehmann/Peter Arnold, Inc. **356** Jim Schwabel/Southern Stock Photos **357** James Blank/Southern Stock Photos **359** William Johnson/Stock Boston **360** B.P.Wolff/Photo Researchers **362** Michael Newman/Photo Edit **364** Courtesy Levi Strauss & Company, San Francisco, CA. **366** City Art Museum of St.Louis **367** Focus On Sports **370** Barbara Campbell/Gamma-Liaison **371** NASA **372B** Timothy White/ABC News **376** Stephen Ferry/Gamma-Liaison **377** Michael Newman/Photo Edit **379** Ric Patzke **380** Zig Leszczynski/Earth Scenes **385** Focus On Sports **386T** AP/Wide World **387** Everett Collection **390** Milt & Joan Mann/Cameramann International, Ltd. **391** David Spangler **393** Everett Collection **398** Joseph F.Viesti/Viesti Associates **399** Barry Iverson/Woodfin Camp & Associates **407** Milt & Joan Mann/Cameramann International, Ltd. **408** Telegraph Colour Library/FPG **409T** Tony Garcia/Tony Stone Images **409BR** Tecmap/West Light **416T** Index Stock International **416C** Richard Laird/FPG **416BL** Penny Tweedie/Tony Stone Images **416BR** R.Ian Lloyd/West Light **417T** Deuter/Zefa/H. Armstrong Roberts **418** Robert E. Daemmrich/Tony Stone Images **420** Willard Luce/ANIMALS ANIMALS **422** M.A.Chappell/ANIMALS ANIMALS **423** Charles Gupton/Stock Boston **425** Mark M. Lawrence/The Stock Market **432** James Blank/Stock Boston **434** David Spangler **437** Patricia Woeber **439** Owaki/Kulla/The Stock Market **442** Tony Freeman/Photo Edit **444** Katoomba Scenic Railway, New South Wales, Australia **447** Milt & Joan Mann/Cameramann International, Ltd. **448** Fritz Prenzel/ANIMALS ANIMALS **449** Robert Frerck/Odyssey Productions, Chicago **454** Jim Merli/Visuals Unlimited **457** Imtek Imagineering-1/Masterfile **458** Boisvieux/Photo Researchers **459** Robert Frerck/Woodfin Camp & Associates **460T** Robert Frerck/Odyssey Productions, Chicago **460B** Delip Mehta/Woodfin Camp & Associates **463** Robert E. Daemmrich/The Image Works **465** Felicia Martinez/Photo Edit **469** Robert Rathe/Stock Boston **472** Robert E. Daemmrich/The Image Works **473** Focus On Sports **476T** AP/Wide World **476BL** C.Ursillo/H. Armstrong Roberts **476R** L.Powers/H. Armstrong Roberts **477C** Gregory Heisler/The Image Bank **482** Historical Pictures/Stock Montage, Inc. **483** Mike Andrews/Earth Scenes **484T** Chris Michaels/FPG **484CL** SuperStock, Inc. **484CR** Ralph Mercer/Tony Stone Images **484B** Joe Riley/Folio **485B** Mark Tomalty/Masterfile **488ALL** Scott Zapel **491** Murray Alcosser/The Image Bank **492T** Oxford Scientific Films/ANIMALS ANIMALS **492B** Leonard Lee Rue III/ANIMALS ANIMALS **493ALL** Leonard Lee Rue III/ANIMALS ANIMALS **496** Benn Mitchell/The Image Bank **498** Everett Collection **500** PhotoFest **502** Mary Kate Denny/Photo Edit **505** Carol Zacny **506** John Elk III/Stock Boston **509** Leo Touchet/Woodfin Camp & Associates **511** Dr. Kari Lounatmaa/SPL/Photo Researchers **513** The National Archives **515** Nuridsany et Perennou/Photo Researchers **519** MGM/Photo:/The Kobal Collection **522T** Smithsonian Institution **522-523** U. S. Bureau of Printing and Engraving **525** Felicia Martinez/Photo Edit **526** Martin Rogers/Stock Boston **527** NASA **528** Copyright the British Museum **530** NASA **531** Cara Moore/The Image Bank **537** D.Woo/Stock Boston **538** Mark C. Burnett/Photo Researchers **539** Imtek Imagineering/ Masterfile **540** Telegraph Colour Library/FPG **546-547T** R.Krubner/H. Armstrong Roberts **546C** Nadia Mackenzie/Tony Stone Images **546B** Tom Sanders/Adventure Photo **547C** R.Faris/West Light **547B** SuperStock, Inc. **550-551** David Young-Wolff/Photo Edit **558** Marco Corsetti/FPG **560** Robert Pearcy/ANIMALS ANIMALS **562** Jan Kanter **567** Eric Meola/The Image Bank **568** Focus On Sports **569** Focus On Sports **570** Shaun Botterill/ALLSPORT USA **571** Focus On Sports **573** Travelpix/FPG **576** Ken Cole/Earth Scenes **579** Tom Nebbia/The Stock Market **583** Richard Hutchings/Photo Edit **584T** Tony Freeman/Photo Edit **584B** Dennis MacDonald/Photo Edit **586** Brett Froomer/The Image Bank **591** NASA **593** Oliver Strewe/Tony Stone Images **598** Kaluzny/Thatcher/Tony Stone Images **605T** Mason Morfit/FPG **605B** Erich Lessing/Art Resource, New York **606L** Dennis Hallinan/FPG **606R** Tim Davis/AllStock Inc. **611** Bruno Brokken/ALLSPORT USA **613** Tom Stewart/The Stock Market **614TL** Charles O'Rear/West Light **614-615T** Steven Hunt/The Image Bank **614-615C** Telegraph Colour Library/FPG **614B** Telegraph Colour Library/FPG **615B** Arthur Tilley/FPG **619** THE STUDIO, 1977, Jacob Lawrence, Gift of Gull Industries John H. and Ann H. Hauberg, Links, Seattle and by exchange from the estate of Mark Tobey. Photo: Paul Macapia **620** Goltzer/The Stock Market **622-623** Brett Froomer/The Image Bank **625** David R. Frazier/Tony Stone Images **631** Photo: Milbert Orlando Brown/Copyrighted, Chicago Tribune Company, all rights reserved **633** COMPOSITION WITH RED, BLUE, YELLOW & BLACK, 1921 - Piet Mondrian. Collection Haags Gemeentemuseum, The Hague. **642** Myrleen Ferguson Cate/Photo Edit **644** Therese Smith **645** Mark Antman/The Image Works **650** John Running **651** Milt & Joan Mann/Cameramann International, Ltd. **654T** Courtesy The White House Collection **654C** Courtesy The White House Collection **654B** Copyright by the White House Historical Association **655** AP/Wide World **658L** Gwendolen Cates/Sygma **658CL** Aloma/Shooting Star **658C** Julie Dennis/SS/Shooting Star **658CR** Stephen Begleiter/Shooting Star **658R** Terry O'Neill/Sygma **658BG** Pelton & Associates, Inc./West Light **664T** Chuck O'Rear/West Light **664C** The Stock Shop **664B** Mike Fizer/Check Six **665C** Mark MacLaren **665B** Gary Conner/Photo Edit **666** Focus On Sports **671** Bob Thomason/Tony Stone Images **672** John Madere/The Stock Market **673** Fay Torresyap/Stock Boston **674** Paul Steel/The Stock Market **675** Mark E. Gibson/The Stock Market **676** Spunbarg/Photo Edit **679** James J. Hill. Reference Library St. Paul, MN. **680** Pechter/The Stock Market **681** Reuters/Bettmann **682** Photo by Gail Toerpe Publishers-Washington Island Observer Newspaper **685** The Museum of the City of New York **687** Tony Freeman/Photo Edit **689** Milt & Joan Mann/Cameramann International, Ltd. **691** Milt & Joan Mann/Cameramann International, Ltd. **692** Fred Whitehead/ANIMALS ANIMALS **693** Mark Greenberg/Visions **693B** Mark Greenberg/Visions **694** Photo Edit **695** Focus On Sports **698** Tony Freeman/Photo Edit **699** Walt Disney Collection/Everett Collection **701** Bob Torrez/Tony Stone Images **707** Focus On Sports **709** The Kobal Collection **710** Paul Conklin **711T** FPG **711C** McFarland/SuperStock, Inc. **712T** L.Powers/H. Armstrong Roberts **712C** D.E.Cox/Tony Stone Images **712B** Denis Scott/FPG **714** Vince Streano/Tony Stone Images **716** Tony Freeman/Photo Edit **718T** Jook Leung/FPG **718-719C** West Light **718BL** Larry Lee/West Light **718-719BR** Ralph Mercer/Tony Stone Images **719T** West Light **720** Pete Saloutos/The Stock Market **722** U.S. Department of Defense **725** Michael Yelman **730** Roy Morsch/The Stock Market **731** Argonne National Lab **738** Jan Kanter **740** Everett Collection **741** Focus On Sports **742** David Parker/SPL/Photo Researchers **743** Fred Whitehead/Earth Scenes **746** Milt & Joan Mann/Cameramann International, Ltd. **748** Susan Copen Oken/Dot **749** Bettmann Archive **753** MISS PEACH/Creators Syndicate **754** Sidney Harris **757** Carol Zacny **758** Owen Franken/Stock Boston **764** Calspan Corporation **765L** Jon Riley/Tony Stone Images **765C** Ralph Mercer/Tony Stone Images **765R** Karageorge/H. Armstrong Roberts **766T** Roxana Villa/Stock Illustration Source, Inc. **772-773T** Index Stock International **772C** Pete McArthur/Tony Stone Images **772-773B** Kazu Studio Ltd/FPG **773C** Telegraph Colour Library/FPG **775** Peter Sidebotham/Tony Stone Images **777** Tony Freeman/Photo Edit **778** Reprinted with Special permission of King Features Syndicate **780** Claudia Parks/The Stock Market **784** Judith Canty/Stock Boston **787** Mark Richards/Photo Edit **789** Woodfin Camp & Associates **790** Jean-Claude Figenwald **793** Rob Crandall/Stock Boston **797** Frank Siteman/Stock Boston **798** Gay Bumgarner/Tony Stone Images **799** Milt & Joan Mann/Cameramann International, Ltd. **800** Focus On Sports **801** Tom & Michelle Grimm/Tony Stone Images **807** John Gerlach/Earth Scenes **811** Mark Lewis/Tony Stone Images **812** David Young-Wolff/Photo Edit **814** Paul Conklin/Photo Edit **816** Culver Pictures **818TL** Elizabeth Simpson/FPG **818TR** The Wood River Gallery **818CL** D.Degnan/H. Armstrong Roberts **818CR** Stock Illustration Source, Inc. **818B** Arthur Tilley/FPG

INDEX

multiplying fractions, 86
negative exponent, 516
of multiplication of positive and negative numbers, 98
of opposites, 149
of reciprocals, 79
opposite of a difference, 241
opposite of a sum, 240
opposite of opposites (op-op), 150
power of a power, 512
power of a product, 527
power of a quotient, 529
product of powers, 510
product of square roots, 587
quotient of powers, 521
reciprocal of a fraction, 80
slopes and parallel lines, 694
slope-intercept, 439
square of square root, 33
third side, 263
zero exponent, 491, 493
zero product, 739
Properties of Multiplication of Positive and Negative Numbers, 98
Property of Opposites, 149
Property of Reciprocals, 79
proportion, 394
extremes, 394
means, 394
Putting-Together Model for Addition, 143
Pythagoras, 45, 46, 75
Pythagorean Distance Formula in the Coordinate Plane, 601
Pythagorean Theorem, 45–48, 236, 586

quadrant(s), 163
quadratic equation, 547, 573
analyzing, 579–582
discriminant, 582
graphs, 550, 555, 774
number of real solutions, 580
rational solutions, 759
standard form, 576
Quadratic Formula, 574
quadratic function, 775
graph of, 550, 555, 774
quadratic polynomial, 618
quadrilateral, 388, 391, 403, 604
Quayle, Dan, 11
quotient(s)
of powers, 521
power of a, 529
Quotient of Powers Property, 521

Rackham, Arthur, 304
radical(s)
simplifying, 575, 588, 610
radical sign ($\sqrt{\ }$), 31
randomly occurring outcomes, 372
range of a function, 789
restricted, 790
range
of a function, 789–791 of a set, 223
Rankin, Jeanette, 220
Raphael, 45
rate(s), 91–93, 356, 395
in distance formula, 104, 105

multiplying, 91–93, 96–98
of change, 418–421
reciprocal, 93
Rate Factor Model for Multiplication, 92
Rate Model for Division, 356
rate of change, 358, 418–421, 425
constant-decrease, 425
graphs, 421
ratio, 362–364, 395
of similitude, 402
percent form, 363
trigonometric, 367
Ratio Model for Division, 363
ratio of similitude, 402
rational expressions, simplifying, 243–245, 334–336, 791–792
rational number, 754
Reading Mathematics, 1, 2, 6, 12, 18, 23, 27, 32, 37, 46, 54, 73, 79, 85, 86, 91, 96, 103, 109, 110, 114, 120, 126, 143, 145, 150, 156, 164, 171, 178, 184, 189, 195, 201, 217, 222, 228, 233, 241, 246, 247, 254, 261, 268, 285, 292, 298, 305, 310, 318, 322, 328, 334, 351, 357, 363, 364, 371, 374, 377, 388, 395, 397, 403, 418, 425, 434, 440, 446, 451, 459, 464, 470, 484, 486, 493, 499, 506, 510, 516, 522, 528, 534, 549, 554, 562, 568, 574, 580, 582, 587, 588, 594, 600, 617, 622, 628, 633, 640, 647, 648, 652, 667, 673, 677, 682, 688, 695, 700, 705, 721, 727, 734, 739, 745, 749, 754, 759, 775, 779, 781, 785, 790, 796, 801, 808, 812
real numbers, 12
graphing, 462
reciprocal, 79
Reciprocal of a Fraction Property, 80
reciprocal rates, 93
rectangle, 5, 30, 392
area, 72, 177
perimeter, 30
rectangular array, 74
dimensions, 74
rectangular solid,
volume, 74
reflection symmetry, 548
Refresher, 69, 139, 213, 347
regrouping, 75
relation, 452, 775
relative frequency, 368–370, 373, 797
Remington, Frederick, 105
removing parenthesis, 183
Repeated Multiplication Model for Powering, 486
repeating decimals in fraction form, 363, 388
replication, 235
Return of the Jedi, 199
Review questions, 10, 16, 22, 26, 30, 36, 42–43, 50–51, 58–59, 78, 83, 90, 95, 101, 108, 112–113, 118, 123–124, 129–130, 148, 153–154, 161–162, 168–169, 174–175, 181–182, 187, 193–194, 198–199, 204, 219–220, 225–226, 230–231, 239, 245, 251–252, 258, 265–266, 273, 290, 295–296, 302–303, 308–309, 315–316, 321, 326, 332, 336–337, 354–355, 361, 366–367, 375, 380, 385–386, 392–393, 399, 407, 424, 431, 437–438, 444, 448–449, 455,

462, 468, 474–475, 491, 497, 503–504, 509, 514, 519–520, 525–526, 532, 537–538, 553, 560, 566, 571–572, 577–578, 584–585, 591–592, 598, 604, 620, 626, 631–632, 637, 645, 650, 656, 670–671, 675, 680, 685–686, 692–693, 697–698, 702–703, 710, 725, 730–731, 737, 742–743, 747–748, 753, 758, 764, 777, 783–783, 788, 793, 799, 805, 811, 815–816
right angle, 45, 50, 257
right triangle, 44, 45–48
and trigonometric ratios, 367
hypotenuse, 45
legs, 45
Pythagorean theorem, 46
Rivera, Diego, 460
Roosevelt, Franklin Delano, 93
Roosevelt, Theodore, 125
rotation symmetry, 180, 801
rounding numbers
decimals, 30, 34, 35, 51, 353
row, 233
Rules for Multiplying Positive and Negative Numbers, 97
Rutan, Dick, 693

Sacagawea, 223
scale factor, 622
scatterplot, 156, 270, 457, 743
Schwarzenegger, Arnold, 658
scientific notation, (Appendix B), 29
segment, 401
sense of an inequality, 116
sentence, 6–8
always true, 699
linear, 704
never true, 700
open, 7
solution, 7
sequence, 188
Servois, François, 73
set(s), 11–14
and, 17–20
discrete, 74
domain, 12
elements, 11
empty, 19
equal, 11
graphing, 12–14, 19, 20, 74
intersection of, 17–20, 262
members, 11
null, 19
or, 19
range, 223
solution, 12
symbols of, 11
union of, 18
Venn diagram of, 18–20
sides
of an equation, 102, 201
of an inequality, 114, 115, 201
of a triangle, 259, 261–263
similar figures, 389, 402, 431, 604
ratio of similitude, 402
simple fraction, 754
simplifying
expressions, 217, 218, 241
fractions, 243, 334
radicals, 575, 588, 610